DUTCH IMMIGRANT MEMOIRS
AND RELATED WRITINGS

REVISED EDITION

DUTCH IMMIGRANT MEMOIRS AND RELATED WRITINGS

Selected and Arranged for Publication by

Henry S. Lucas

REVISED EDITION

WILLIAM B. EERDMANS PUBLISHING COMPANY
GRAND RAPIDS, MICHIGAN / CAMBRIDGE, U.K.

PUBLISHER'S NOTE

This combined edition reprints the text of the original two-volume 1955 edition exactly as it appeared in that edition. Thus the pagination for the second volume begins again at page 1 midway through this volume.

Several documents in the original edition were printed only in Dutch, and they appear in that form in this edition as well. We have, however, provided translations for each of these documents in the Appendix.

Originally published 1955 in two volumes by
Koninklijke Van Gorcum & Comp. N.V.
Assen, the Netherlands
© 1955 Koninklijke Van Gorcum & Comp. N.V.

Combined edition, with additional translations,
© 1997 Wm. B. Eerdmans Publishing Co.
255 Jefferson Ave. S.E., Grand Rapids, Michigan 49503 /
P.O. Box 163, Cambridge CB3 9PU U.K.
All rights reserved

Printed in the United States of America

02 01 00 99 98 97   7 6 5 4 3 2 1

Library of Congress Cataloging-in-Publication Data

Dutch immigrant memoirs and related writings /
[compiled by] Henry S. Lucas.
p.   cm.
ISBN 0-8028-4224-0 (pbk.: alk. paper)
1. Dutch Americans — History — Sources. 2. Dutch Americans — Michigan —
History — Sources. 3. Dutch Americans — Biography. 4. Dutch Americans —
Michigan — Biography. 5. Netherlands — Emigration and immigration — History —
Sources. 6. United States — Emigration and immigration — History — Sources.
7. Immigrants' writings, Dutch. 8. Immigrants' writings, Dutch — Michigan.
I. Lucas, Henry Stephen, 1889-1961.
E184.D9D867   1997
973'.04931 — dc21   96-48104
                                                    CIP

In Memory of
My Great-grandparents

STEVEN LUCAS

BORN IN THE GRAAFSCHAP BENTHEIM MARCH 30, 1794
LIVED AT VORWOLD BENTHEIM
CONTRIBUTED TO THE FOUNDING OF THE
OLD (SECEDED) REFORMED CHURCH IN BENTHEIM
FINED AND IMPRISONED FOR HIS CONVICTIONS
EMIGRATED TO AMERICA IN THE SPRING OF 1847
HELPED FOUND GRAAFSCHAP, MICHIGAN
DIED JULY 28, 1863

and

GEERTRUIDA WALTERS

HIS WIFE

DIED IN GRAAFSCHAP, MICHIGAN, MARCH 1, 1853

God baande door de woeste baren
En breede stroomen ons een pad;
Daar rees Zijn lof op stem en snaren,
Nadat Hij ons beveiligd had.
Hij zal eeuw uit eeuw in regeeren;
Zijn oog bewaakt het Heidendom;
Hij zal d'afvalligen verneêren;
Hij keert hun trotsch' ontwerpen om.

PSALM 66:3 (FROM THE DUTCH PSALTER)

ERRATA

Vol. II: p. 12, *1.* 6, H. C. Knol *read* H. G. Knol; p. 75, *1.* 4, for Classiswege *read* Classis wege; p. 89, *1.* 38, *for* strenght *read* strength; p. 123, *1.* 11, *for* Van van *read* C. van; p. 124, *1,* 1, *for* Reimch *read* Reimich; p. 124, *1.* 7, *for* Reimchr *read* Reimich; p. 126, *1.* 40, *for* guota *read* quota; p. 133, *1.* 3, *for* Nasse *read* Masse; p. 137, *1.* 5, *for* Hallendyke *read* Hallerdyk; p. 149, *1.* 8, *for* Dennison *read* Denissen; p. 157. *1.* 19, *for* meony *read* money; p. 185, *1.* 20, *for* vaail *read* avail; p. 187, *1.* 33, *for* inudced *read* induced; p. 194, *1.* 9, *for* compications *read* complications.

CONTENTS

(A full listing of the writings in each chapter
is found with the table of contents with each volume, below)

VOLUME 1

Contents

VOLUME 2

Contents

PREFACE TO THE REVISED EDITION

THE DUTCH AMERICAN Historical Commission (DAHC), in cooperation with William B. Eerdmans Publishing Company, is pleased to be able to offer a reprinted edition of Henry Lucas's *Dutch Immigrant Memoirs and Related Writings*. The Commission is made up of representatives from Calvin College, Calvin Seminary, Hope College, Western Theological Seminary, The Joint Archives of Holland, and the A. C. Van Raalte Institute for Historical Studies.

The DAHC is committed to enhancing the historical reference materials available to those interested in Dutch American history. One of the ways in which this is done is through encouragement of archival facilities in the western Michigan area that focus on this heritage, namely, Heritage Hall at Calvin College and The Joint Archives of Holland at Hope College. The Commission also works to support and encourage republication of key monographs that are out of print and discusses and promotes ongoing scholarship as well as similar activities. The Commission meets twice per year.

Dutch Immigrant Memoirs and Related Writings was originally published in 1955 by Van Gorcum and Company in the Netherlands. It was printed in small numbers and in recent years has been increasingly difficult to obtain. By issuing this reprint it is our hope that we can continue to make these important memories available as well as encourage readers to consult the extensive primary resources at our two western Michigan archival repositories on which this volume is based. The additional translations and the new index by Dr. Robert P. Swierenga are key enhancements to this new edition.

As Dr. Swierenga's introduction indicates, Lucas's assemblage of memoirs was influenced by several Dutch-Americans, such as Dr. Henry Beets, Peter Theodore Moerdyke, and Willard Wichers. Of these three, Moerdyke and Wichers played a significant role in the actual selection of items to include, and provided reference service in the archival collection to Dr. Lucas. Willard Wichers served as director of the Netherlands Information Service as well as the Netherlands Museum for nearly half a century. P. T. Moerdyke served as "historian" of the museum and kept extensive historical files in addition to the collection itself. It was in the collections of the museum, now renamed the Holland Museum, that Lucas found both the Dutch-language paper *De Grondwet* and the extensive collection of semicentennial memoirs and other writings that were collected by celebration organizer Gerrit Van Schelven. Since 1988 the archives of the museum have been located at the Joint Archives of Holland (on the campus of Hope College) where they are available alongside the archives of the college and Western Seminary. Similar collections of Van Schelven papers and other immigrant materials are collected at Heritage Hall on the campus of Calvin College.

Both repositories — Heritage Hall at Calvin College and The Joint Archives of Holland at Hope College — serve as the leading repositories documenting the Dutch immigration to the Midwest in the nineteenth century and the story of the various settlements over the last 150 years. Any individual interested in Dutch immigration to the United States and the Midwest would be well advised to consult one or both of these repositories.

Many people contributed to the process of reissuing this volume. Foremost, the Dutch American Historical Commission began the dialogue, moved the process forward, and agreed to contribute financially to the publication effort. Members of the Commission appear below. After I agreed to assist in piloting the project through, members of the staff at the Joint Archives of Holland, the A. C. Van Raalte Institute for Historical Studies, Heritage Hall at Calvin College, and Charles Van Hof of William B. Eerdmans Publishing Company were very helpful. Dr. Robert Swierenga coordinated the collection of new translations available only in Dutch in the original volume and also created the new extensive index. The translations themselves are the result of hours of work by Dr. Herbert Brinks, Ellie Dekker, Dr. George Harper, Dr. Nella Kennedy, and Zwanet Janssens. They have helped make these Dutch-language pieces available to the general reader, and we deeply appreciate their efforts. Jerome Kemp, of Stow, Ohio, assisted by optically scanning the text. Dr. Elton Bruins, Ellie Dekker, Lori Trethewey, and I reviewed the materials before submission to the publisher.

It is a fitting tribute to Professor Henry Lucas and to the Sesquicentennial Celebration of Dutch immigration to the Midwest that the Dutch American Historical Commission can offer this reprinted edition of *Dutch Immigrant Memoirs and Related Writings*.

LARRY J. WAGENAAR, Associate Professor
Director, The Joint Archives of Holland
Hope College
May, 1996

MEMBERS OF
THE DUTCH AMERICAN HISTORICAL COMMISSION

Herbert J. Brinks	Heritage Hall, Calvin College
Elton J. Bruins, Treasurer	A. C. Van Raalte Institute for Historical Studies, Hope College
Donald J. Bruggink	Western Theological Seminary
Conrad J. Bult, Secretary	Calvin College
Peter DeKlerk	Calvin Theological Seminary
Jon Huisken, President	Hope College
Henry P. Ippel	Calvin College
Zwanet Janssens	Heritage Hall, Calvin College
Paul M. Smith	Western Theological Seminary
Robert P. Swierenga	A. C. Van Raalte Institute for Historical Studies, Hope College
Larry J. Wagenaar	The Joint Archives of Holland, Hope College
Henry Zwaanstra	Calvin Theological Seminary

INTRODUCTION TO THE REVISED EDITION

FOR FORTY YEARS this unique collection of nineteenth-century travel accounts and reminiscences of Dutch immigrant pioneers has enlightened and stimulated their children's children. The newcomers, few of whom had ever sailed the seas or even ventured more than a day's journey from home, here recount in vivid detail their frightening experiences crossing the Atlantic Ocean and then being crammed like "herring in a vat" on Erie Canal boats en route to Michigan and the Midwest. Some lost loved ones to the briny deep or buried them in the forests of Michigan in the first desperate years. But all attest to God's grace and the blessings of peace and prosperity. Here they raise their Eben-ezer (the banner — "God with Us"), which was the constant theme of the Old Timers.

At times of remembrance on the occasions of the twenty-fifth (1872), fortieth (1887), fiftieth (1897), and sixtieth (1907) milestones of the founding of the various colonies, the surviving pioneers penned their memoirs. Especially in 1897 for the semicentennial celebration in Holland, Michigan, Gerrit Van Schelven, postmaster and editor of the *Holland City News* and a member of the program committee, encouraged many of his fellow first settlers all across the United States to retell for posterity the stories of the transplanting. For the better part of three days at the celebration that drew 25,000 visitors, the pioneers, mostly common folk — farmers, businessmen, and clerics — read their accounts in various churches in Holland. Those who could not attend sent their writings. Most were subsequently published in *De Grondwet,* Holland's Dutch-language newspaper.

Henry S. Lucas, great-grandson of a Holland colony pioneer, compiled this anthology in 1955 at the behest of Hendrik Prakke, a Dutch scholar and editor of the Van Gorcum Publishing Company of Assen, Drenthe. Lucas, the nestor of Dutch-American historians in the years after World War II, was born in Jamestown, Michigan, in 1889 of Christian Reformed parents. His ancestors, to whom he dedicated the collection, were born in Graafschap Bentheim, Germany, and helped to establish the Christian Seceder *(Afgescheiden)* church there. They emigrated in the first wave of 1847 and pioneered in the Graafschap, Michigan, settlement. The illustrious Lucas family history captivated young Henry from an early age, and he took an abiding interest in the history of Dutch immigration to North America. It became his avocation, while his vocation was professor of medieval European history, especially of the Low Countries.

In 1947 Lucas wrote for the Holland centennial commission a memorial souvenir booklet, *Ebenezer — 1847-1947,* which recounted the early history of the Dutch immigration. By 1951 he had completed a full-length history, *Netherlanders in America,* which the University of Michigan Press published in 1955 and the William B. Eerdmans Publishing Company reprinted in 1989. This invaluable book is the only detailed account of Dutch settlement written from an American perspective, in contrast with the two-volume work of the same title that Jacob van Hinte published in Groningen in 1928, which reflects the Old Country interpretation of the American experience.[1] In 1955 Lucas completed his studies of Dutch immigration with the publication of this two-volume collection of primary documents. He was then sixty-six years of age and six years from his death in 1961.

That Henry Lucas would contribute so extensively to his ethnic heritage is somewhat of an anomaly because he moved outside of his tradition personally, professionally, and religiously. Unlike other Christian Reformed collegians, he bypassed Calvin College, the denominational school, as well as the nearby sister institution of Hope College, and instead opted to attend a Nazarene institution, Olivet College (Michigan), from which he graduated in 1913. Then, after completing graduate studies in history by earning the M.A. degree from the University of Indiana (1915) and the Ph.D. degree from the University of Michigan (1921), he again passed over "onze school" and joined the faculty of the University of Washington in Seattle, where he taught until his retirement.

Even more remarkable is that Lucas at the age of fifty-eight years in 1947 left the Reformed faith for the Roman Catholic Church. This was the very year he published *Ebenezer,* the first of his Dutch immigration trilogy. The religious conversion was both of mind and heart. As Lucas explained in a spiritual autobiography edited by Catholic prelates, he became disillusioned with contemporary Protestantism. While he cherished the "sound doctrine, consistent worship, and serious conduct" of his Calvinist forebears, he found Protestant modernism wanting. "As I found my path into the world, away from my first religious influences, I was frequently disturbed by the opinions expressed in 'up-to-date' pulpits," Lucas noted. "I was weary of the personal ex cathedra

[1]Jacob van Hinte, *Nederlanders in Amerika. Een studie over landverhuizers en volkplanters in de 19e en 20ste Eeuw in de Verenigde Staten van Amerika,* 2 vols. (Groningen: P. Noordhoff, 1928), published in English as *Netherlanders in America: A Study of Emigrants and Colonists in the Nineteenth and Twentieth Centuries in the United States of America,* ed. Robert P. Swierenga, trans. Adriaan de Wit (Grand Rapids: Baker Book House, 1985).

pronouncements of liberal preachers. . . . It is no exaggeration," Lucas continued, "that, taking all Protestant groups in the United States into consideration, there is not one traditional doctrine, not even the basic one that God exists, that can fairly be said to be held by all of them."[2]

Lucas's academic studies had guided him into Catholic philosophy through the domain of *Kulturgeschichte*. He immersed himself in the writings of the *devotio moderna;* then the Pietist Calvinist theologians Gijsbertus Voetius and his students Jodocus van Lodenstein, Bernardus Smijtegelt, and Wilhelmus à Brakel; followed by their spiritual successors Johan Huizenga and Abraham Kuyper. A pilgrimage to the Gothic cathedrals of Europe and the museums of Flemish primitives and Italian Renaissance masterpieces further convinced Lucas that Protestants had made "a cultural error" to reject the "Holy Catholic, Apostolic Church, now triumphantly, yes, gloriously existing through these nineteen centuries." Catholic worship, he confessed, especially the liturgy and Mass, "was most satisfying."[3]

Lucas's mentors, Christian Reformed cleric Dr. Henry Beets, Netherlands consul Willard Wichers of the Netherlands Museum in Holland, and Peter Theodore Moerdyke, historian at the Museum, continued to encourage and assist him after he left the Reformed faith, as the author acknowledges in the foreword to this work. His new religious affiliation also accounts for Lucas's commendable care to include three key documents on the Dutch Roman Catholic immigration to the Fox River Valley of Wisconsin. After all, Catholics comprised nearly one-fifth of the nineteenth-century Dutch immigration to North America and they nearly equaled in numbers the renowned Seceders.

The 114 documents in this collection cover the first sixty years of the Dutch settlements, 1846 to 1907, but the major emphasis justifiably is on the initial group migration and the founding of the colonies. Common themes are the fearful ocean crossing and unpleasant inland journey over the Erie Canal and Great Lakes, the privations the pioneers suffered, the valued leadership of the dominies, and above all the many expressions of gratitude for God's providential care. Piety was a hallmark of Seceder faith, as these writings attest.

In terms of geographic coverage, Lucas gave the Holland colony center stage, with sixty-three documents, or fifty-five percent of the book. The major satellite villages are also generously represented — Graafschap, Groningen, Zeeland, Drenthe, Vriesland, North Holland, Noordeloos, Beaverdam, Ravenna, and Overisel. But Grand Haven, Muskegon, and Kalamazoo are largely ignored, and only four entries relate to Grand Rapids, the major Dutch urban center. Clearly,

[2]"Henry S. Lucas," in *They Heard His Voice*, compiled by Bruno Shafer, O.F.M. Cap., edited and translated by Berchmans Bittle, O.F.M. Cap. (New York: McMullen Books, 1952), 147-56 (quotes 150, 154, 151).
[3]Ibid., 154, 156.

the decision to focus on the first wave of immigrants dictated an overemphasis on the Holland area, at the expense of other equally important settlements in Michigan, Iowa, Illinois, and Wisconsin. For example, the perceptive reports of Bernardus de Bey, pastor of Chicago's First Reformed Church, published in Groningen in the 1860s and 1870s, deserved consideration for their insights into Dutch immigrant life in a major urban center and for the vivid firsthand reports on the devastating Chicago fire of 1871.

While one can understand Lucas's concentration on the Holland colony, there is no excuse for slighting Holland's sister colony of Pella, Iowa, which was established the same year. Henry P. Scholte, Pella's founder, was the leader at Leiden University of the Afscheiding of 1834, and his reports on the Pella settlement are noteworthy. Pella also mothered daughter colonies throughout the West — in northwest Iowa, eastern Kansas and Nebraska, southwestern Minnesota, and eastern South Dakota. Lucas lamely dismissed the Pella story on the grounds that there was only "one sketch of Pella worthy of a place in the collection" (vol. 2, p. 40). But this cannot be the case. Lucas was obligated to include Scholte's *Eerste stem uit Pella* [First voice from Pella] (February 1848), published in English by Jacob Van Der Zee in the *Iowa Journal of History and Politics* in 1911, or Scholte's *Tweede stem uit Pella* [Second voice from Pella] (Fall 1848), which was not translated or published until 1968 in the *Annals of Iowa*.

Both of Scholte's reports were published and read widely in the Netherlands, drawing thousands to consider emigration to the Midwest, which Scholte portrayed as a place of refuge from God's imminent destruction of Europe, including the Netherlands. These unique American letters detailed the advantages of the Iowa prairies that awaited the plow without the need to hew wood, and described Dutch farming methods, craftsmanship and dress, and the ease with which the people were integrated into the political life of frontier Iowa.

For a sharply critical view of Scholte's leadership by a Frisian pioneer settler, Lucas should have considered Sjoerd Aukes Sipma's *Belangrijke berigten uit Pella*, published in Dokkum in 1849. This priceless account provides factual information about life on the Iowa frontier and reveals various facets of cultural conflict between the Dutch and Native Americans, and also among the Hollanders themselves. Another detailed account of farming on the Iowa prairies is the pamphlet by Jan Nollen, *De Hollanders in Iowa: Brieven uit Pella, van een Gelderschman*, published at Arnhem in 1858, which also could have been included with profit.

Including critical reports such as Sipma's would have balanced the filiopietistic character of this collection. The contributors overly praised the accomplishments of the pioneers and tended to ignore their failures and squabbles. In the warm afterglow of a life lived out, the elderly memorialists touted the triumphs but diminished the disappointments.

Several of the papers in chapter XI, "What Americans Thought about Dutch Americans," suffer from superficial Yankee stereotyping and add little of value. Deleting the recollections of Edward Cahill, George E. Holm, and Anna C. Post might have provided valuable space for more accounts by Dutch clerical leaders. Theodore de Heer's 1907 puffery, "Our Hollanders in Michigan," is equally expendable. Far better to have included the lengthy letter Van Raalte sent from Detroit on January 30, 1847, to his brother-in-law Antonie Brummelkamp, entitled "Holland in America, of de Hollandsche kolonizatie in der staat Michigan," which closely argues the rationale for the crucial decision to settle in western Michigan rather than in Wisconsin, as originally intended. Shedding additional light on this important issue are the letters of Van Raalte, Cornelius van der Meulen, and Seine Bolks penned in 1849 to C. G. Moen and published together in a pamphlet.

Other writings that Lucas might have included with benefit are C. van der Meulen's 1847 letter, "Aan al mijne geliefde vrienden in Nederland" [To all my dear friends in the Netherlands], which offers a frank portrayal of the difficulties of the April 1847 migration from Goes; and the Reverend Gerrit Baay's *Brief* [Letter] of January, 1849, from Alto, Wisconsin, to his "dear friends in Holland," which describes life in early Alto. Or again, J. Berkhout's "Brief uit Noord-Amerika," sent from Pella in 1848, recounts in heartrending detail the fraud and deceit he and his wife suffered in trying to proceed from the docks at New York to Pella via St. Louis. Friends published his horror story in 1849 "as a warning word . . . to all who are contemplating to emigrate to America, and advise to give it a second thought before they fully decide to venture out."

Admittedly, readers of document collections can more easily second-guess an editor's selections than make wise choices themselves. Generally, I applaud Lucas for his selections. He clearly captured the best of the 1897 memoirs that were published in *De Grondwet*. Nevertheless, unvarnished accounts written at the time of the transplanting are preferable to recollections put to paper in old age after memories fade and an "official" version has evolved from oft-told tales.

The twelve letters of Arnold Verstegen (chapter XXIV, number 79) are invaluable for describing the settlement at Little Chute, Wisconsin. Indeed, they are the only extant letters from this seminal Dutch Catholic colony of 1847. But they are problematic, because the originals have been lost. Only nine of the reputed twenty originals have survived as seven complete letters and two fragments. Henri A. M. van Stekelenburg of Vught, Netherlands, in the 1980s compared the surviving originals with the published versions in Lucas's *Memoirs,* and concluded that the English translations are "very free." The Verstegen letters, in Van Stekelenburg's opinion, have been "mishandled and linguistically polluted."[4] Van Stekelenburg also located an additional one-page Verstegen letter dating from 1882.

Herbert J. Brinks in *Dutch Immigrant Voices: Letters from the United States, 1850-1930* (1995) published the thirteen Verstegen letters: four copied verbatim from Lucas, eight newly translated by Maria de Groot, and the newly discovered 1882 letter that Brinks translated (pp. 43-62). De Groot's translations are barely half the length of the letters Lucas printed in 1955, which the Reverend Matthias van der Elsen had translated and published in the *Annals of St. Joseph* (1943-1944). It is not known whether Van der Elsen worked with the originals, but his version of Verstegen's account rings true. The wealth of detail about family matters, church life, prices of land and crops, and farming conditions on the Wisconsin frontier could only have come from Verstegen or an immediate member of his family. Hence, the lengthier Lucas version of Verstegen's correspondence, while questionable from a specialist's viewpoint, provides an authentic record of early life in Little Chute.

Dutch Immigrant Memoirs is an indispensable resource for all students of immigration and of pioneer days on the American agricultural frontier. The more than one hundred first person accounts describe the immigrant experience and explain its meaning as no other documents, except personal letters, can do. The writers, who went forth in faith and trust in God, penned their captivating stories of the struggles, hardships, and triumphs of migration as a testimony to succeeding generations. Together with Brink's collection of Dutch "America letters" and the comprehensive historical surveys of Van Hinte and Lucas, those descendants and all persons interested in the story of the Dutch immigration can now readily assemble the essential library.

ROBERT P. SWIERENGA

---

[4]These comments are quoted in Herbert J. Brinks, *Dutch Immigrant Voices: Letters from the United States, 1850-1930* (Ithaca, N.Y.: Cornell University Press, 1995), 43-44.

CONTENTS

CHAPTER XII

LIFE DURING THE EARLY DAYS OF THE DUTCH SETTLEMENT

CHAPTER XIII

AN OFFICIAL REPORT ON THE DUTCH KOLONIE IN MICHIGAN, 1849

CHAPTER XIV

EXCERPTS FROM A CONTEMPORARY DIARY

CHAPTER XV

VAN RAALTE'S VIEW OF THE HISTORY OF HIS UNDERTAKING, 1846-1872

CHAPTER XVI

AN HISTORICAL ACCOUNT BY A FIRST SETTLER

FOREWORD

To the reader moved by the labor and triumph of plain men and women who left their ancestral homes to brave unknown dangers in lands utterly strange to them the memoirs and related writings here made available for the first time should possess unique interest. Not because of faultless rhetoric or the embellishment of poetic fancy, [for these memoirs and related writings do not possess such qualities], but simply because these documents express the plain truth of hard experience gained in the virgin woods of Michigan and Wisconsin or on the prairies of Iowa and other states or in the villages and towns of the great American frontier will readers be attracted to what these Dutch and Friesian and Bentheim immigrants and their children have recorded.

The history of immigration from the Netherlands to United States presented in these writings began in 1846 when Albertus Christiaan van Raalte and his family, accompanied by a shipload of Hollanders, on September 24 or 25 sailed from Hellevoetsluis in the *Southerner* and arrived in New York on November 17. This proved to be the vanguard of a steady flow of immigrant Netherlanders of the Reformed faith who settled in Michigan, Ohio, Illinois, Indiana, Wisconsin, Iowa, Minnesota, the Dakotas, New York, New Jersey, and other states. In 1848 three shiploads of Catholic Hollanders led by the Dominican father Theodorus van den Broek started the tide of Catholic immigrants who settled in the Fox River country in Wisconsin, later to scatter to other states in the American Midwest.[1]

In these days when it is the fashion to posit economic forces as the sole ultimate basis of social and political organization and action, the reader may ask what motives impelled these Hollanders to seek homes in the

---

[1] For the history of Dutch immigration see J. van Hinte, *Nederlanders in Amerika* [Groningen, 1928], 2 vols; A. Hyma, *Albertus C. van Raalte and His Dutch Settlements in the United States* [Grand Rapids, 1947]; H. E. Dosker, *Levensschets van Rev. A. C. van Raalte, D.D.: Een der Vaders der Scheiding in Nederland en Stichter der Hollandsche Kolonien in den Staat Michigan, Noord Amerika. Uit Oorspronkelijke Bronnen Bewerkt* [C. C. Callenbach: Nijkerk, 1893].

primitive regions of the United States then being opened to settlement. Were their reasons not economic – difficulty after the Napoleonic wars of making a living in the Netherlands, the pressure of a too numerous population, the stagnant character of industry and commerce, the disastrous potato blight during the 1840's? To this question stated in this manner, the historian must in all fairness answer emphatically in the negative. This is most certainly the case with immigrant Netherlanders who held to the Reformed faith.[1]

Most of the Dutch immigrants who came to America during the decade following 1846 held to the teachings four centuries ago taught by the reformers in Geneva. Since the creation of the kingdom of the Netherlands in 1813, after the disasters of the French Revolution and the dictatorship of Napoleon, this Reformed faith, revitalized, found expression in the hearts and minds of plain people in almost every part of the realm Finally, in 1834, came the Secession [*Afscheiding*] of these devout folk under the leadership of such dominies as Hendrik de Cock at Ulrum, Hendrik Pieter Scholte at Genderen, Antonie Brummelkamp at Hattem, and Van Raalte. These ministers broke with the official Reformed Church which in their eyes had compromised itself by embracing the thought of the Enlightenment so influential in Dutch ecclesiastical circles during the preceding decades. Statistically it can be shown that these people led by Van Raalte and Scholte, with the exception of the Catholic immigrants, constituted almost the entire number of Hollanders who established themselves in the above mentioned states before the Civil War.

Clearly, reasons of religion must have exercised an emphatic influence upon the decisions of these people, for the poverty of the day bore with equal gravity upon the poor among the Seceeders [*Afgescheidenen*], who remained faithful to the old Reformed Church, and also upon the Catholic portion of the population. Yet, as a perusal of the available statistics and a study of the literature of the time reveals, only Seceders and Catholics in any number came to this country during the period stated.

Besides the example of vigorous dominies like Van Raalte and Scholte who exhorted their followers and counselled them, what practical religious reasons impelled these people? First of all was the endeavor of the State for a brief space of time to restrain the Seceders, and to subject them to police measures, fines, and imprisonment. Next, there also was the problem of discrimination, for only too frequently the public resented the

[1] This point is demonstrated in the writer's *Netherlanders in America*: *Dutch Immigration to the United States and Canada* 1789-1950 [to be published by the University of Michigan Press, Ann Arbor, Michigan]. Bibliography in this study supplements that given by Van Hinte.

presence of people who had severed ancient ecclesiastical ties. But, dominant as the religious motive may have been, it would be a mistake to ignore the economic situation. The sources frequently speak of economic and social motives as well as religious. The knowledge that in America lay vast areas of virgin soil wholly unoccupied, to be purchased at a pittance, also attracted these people. There, the emigrants believed, they could live in untrammeled freedom. Economic problems would be few. Religious restrictions were not imposed. Without restraint they could organize their religious life and educate their children according to the precepts of the faith they cherished.

The Catholic portion of the immigrants who flocked to the Fox River region in the Green Bay area of Wisconsin was no less zealous in their faith. They too experienced difficulties at the hand of the state. They were not permitted an organization of bishops, which hampered the free development of the Catholic Church in the Netherlands. Nor were they allowed to establish a system of education in conformity with the traditional principles of their faith. They were not, however, restrained as were the Seceders in establishing their parishes. So, while the religious motive to emigrate to America was strong in the breasts of Dutch Catholics it was not so all consuming a reason with them as it was among the Seceders.[1]

The Dutch immigrant came to this country not simply to acquire a new culture and let his own, based upon centuries of thought and labor, pass away into indifferent desuetude. The truth is he came possessing a rich inheritance of culture, something he could not forget as he embraced the life he found in America. Cherishing his own culture, he contributed vitally to the new life surging on the prairies and in the forests of the Midwest. He had as much to give as to receive, and the life of America was enriched by his contributions. It is with the history of this life and these contributions that the present collection of memoirs and other papers is concerned.

At first the immigrant in his daily toil found little leisure or incentive to write down his experiences. But he could not keep from thinking about his position in life since he left his friends and relatives in the socially and culturally compact village communities in provinces like Drente. Frequently, when sitting around the kitchen fire with friends, his conversation turned to days of old – the life he had left and the fortunes that had

[1] M. J. M. van der Heijden, *De Dageraad van de Emancipatie der Katholieken* [Nijmegen, 1947]; W.G. Versluis, *Geschiedenis van Emancipatie der Katholieken in Nederland van 1795-Heden* [Utrecht, 1948].

been his since he had arrived in what he had pictured as a land of blessings. Although he could write and indeed spent much of his leisure reading the Bible and especially the Psalter and the Heidelberg Catechism or perusing some comforting writer like Wilhelmus à Brakel [d. 1711], Alexander Comrie [d. 1774], Bernardus Smytegeld [d. 1739], or Abraham Hellenbroek [d. 1731], his toil-worn hands failed to express in literary form the thoughts that surged in his soul. Like their brethren of the Reformed faith, the Catholic Dutch immigrant, we may be sure, had similar thoughts At most, perhaps, and like the Hollander of the Reformed faith, he penned a letter on some political or religious question to the Dutch newspapers in this country. But as the years of their sojourn lengthened, the immigrants sought to cast up in writing their spiritual and material accounts, and concluded they had been blessed abundantly.

Not until the twenty-fifth anniversary of their settlement in western Michigan approached did the immigrants from the Netherlands make their first attempt in an official way to recall the events of Holland's founding.[1] Plans were made to celebrate it in fitting fashion. A large crowd assembled on September 17, 1872. Special music was provided, dignitaries assembled, and a parade was organized in which, among other features, surviving first settlers were conveyed in an ox-drawn wagon. Over the speaker's platform, erected just outside Holland on the road which led toward New Groningen, between the Dutch and American flags appeared in large letters the word Eben-Haezer [for the meaning of this expression see 1 Samuel 7, 12], the name A. C. van Raalte, and the Netherlands coat of arms with the motto *Eendragt Maakt Magt*.[2] Dominie Cornelius van der Meulen opened the program with prayer whereupon followed the noble thought of Psalm 66, 3, from the Dutch Psalter. Next came the speeches of which Van Raalte's recapitulation of the history of the settlement from its inception in 1847 was the most noteworthy. This address has become a little classic; it is to be regarded as the fountain source of the historiography of Dutch immigration. Likewise in Zeeland, on the following day, September 18, the pioneers celebrated at which occasion Dominie van der Meulen gave an appropriate address in true pioneer fashion.[3] Similar exercises were held in the settlements of Overisel and Vriesland.[4]

With the example of these popular and successful celebrations before

[1] *De Hope*, Sept. 25, 1872; *De Grondwet*, Sept. 24, 1872.
[2] H. S. Lucas, *Ebenezer 1847-1947: Memorial Souvenir of the Centennial Commemoration of Dutch Immigration to the United States held in Holland, Michigan, 13-16 August 1947* [New York, 1947].
[3] *De Hollander*, Sept. 25, 1872.   [4] *De Hope*, Sept. 25, Oct. 2 and 9, 1872.

them, for the festivities at Holland were estimated to have attracted as many as 5,000 persons, the habit of organizing fitting commemorations soon became established. In 1887 the community of Zeeland celebrated the fortieth anniversary of its beginnings with fitting ceremony in which the pioneer monument which still graces an open square in the city was unveiled.[1] As if to make sure the commemorative mood would not pass into oblivion Dingman Versteeg in 1886 produced a remarkable book entitled *De Pelgrim Vaders van het Westen*, a kind of classic now become impossible to find except in two or three libraries.[2] Few immigrant groups boast so interesting an account of their ideals and striving. Certainly western Michigan possesses no other treatise so moving and vital as this picture of pioneer life in 1885.

Dominie Roelof T. Kuiper [b. 1826, d. 1894] from Wildervank had arrived in Graafschap in 1879 and soon inspired the pioneers with deep affection for their past.[3] He encouraged them to compose their memoirs for the edification of future readers. His efforts bore ample fruit, for by 1882 Evert Zagers, Egbert Frederiks, Tede Ulberg, Rieks Bouws, and P. Schut had written their noteworthy sketches. To Kuiper's efforts while pastor at Graafschap from 1879 to 1889, we are indebted for some of the most important contributions presented in this collection.

When in 1897 the Semi-Centennial celebrations were planned, the city of Holland naturally presented itself as the leader of that event. The authorities in a preliminary announcement stated their object in a truly commendable spirit: "As regards the character of the coming celebration, it is desired that it shall be conducted in a cosmopolitan spirit. This will be in accordance with the record which the immigration from Holland has thus far made for itself. A peculiar feature of many of these colonists has been that they preserved their identity, and retained many of their national characteristics without refusing to become fully incorporated with our body politic, preserving their individuality without refusing to be absorbed into the national life. The Hollanders who came to these shores in 1847 and since, and their descendants, are still bound together by many common interests; therefore, it is desired that this jubilee celebration shall witness a coming together from North and South, from East and West. It is not a celebration of Western Michigan, much less of

[1] *De Hope*, Aug. 10, 24, and 31, 1887.

[2] D. Versteeg, *De Pelgrim Vaders van het Westen: Eene Geschiedenis van de Worstelingen der Hollandsche Nederzettingen in Michigan benevens eene Schets van de Stichting der Kolonie Pella in Iowa* [C. M. Loomis and Co., Grand Rapids, Michigan, 1886].

[3] R. T. Kuiper, *Eene Stem uit Amerika over Amerika* [G. J. Reits, Groningen, 1881].

any particular locality. We will come together from different colonies and settlements in various states, not with a spirit of rivalry, but as brethren with common interests which we all hold dear."

In accordance with a resolution adopted by the Common Council of the City of Holland on July 7, 1896, elaborate plans were made to celebrate the event in fitting manner. The city was decorated in gala fashion, with flags and bunting. The best music of the day was secured and an elaborate parade was prepared, to be held on Wednesday morning August 25. The celebration, attracting thousands of spectators, was an immense success. An unforgetable feature of this event for which the historian is deeply grateful was the program of papers prepared for this occasion to be read on August 26, the second day of the celebrations.

The preparation of this part of the program was entrusted to Gerrit van Schelven who, born in the Netherlands in 1842, had come to this country in 1855. He speedily acquired a ready use of the English tongue, engaged in business which he lost in the Holland fire of 1871, served in various political capacities, published the *Holland City News*, was postmaster of Holland, and died in 1927. Being a pioneer, he was intimately acquainted with the history of the Michigan settlement [or *de Kolonie* as the settlers frequently referred to it]. As that settlement in a very real sense was a kind of cultural capital of Hollanders in America, he was equally well posted on the history of most Dutch settlements in other states. Because of his interest in pioneer history, it appears, the Semi-Centennial Commission which had been appointed by the Common Council of Holland named a sub-committee to implement its intention and put Van Schelven in charge of "Speakers and Historical Papers." Associated with Hollanders in other settlements, he was instrumental in collecting a large number of memoirs from pioneer immigrants in practically every community in which Hollanders had settled.

The Commission announced its desire to secure "reminiscences and recollections, from a historical standpoint, by any one that has something to contribute toward enabling posterity to obtain a better conception of the event and the times we commemorate." The Commission had commendable intentions about all papers contributed, for they informed the public that "at the close of the celebration all of said papers are to be deposited with the Commission, with a view of their compilation and publication." "The reading of these papers," they announced, "is to commence on the morning of the second day, consecutively or simultaneously, from one or more stands, or in one or more of our large churches.... If necessary, or desired, this feature of the celebration can be extended into the third day."

An extraordinarily large number of papers were presented, proof of the interest pioneer immigrants and their friends had in their own history. Some of the addresses were ex tempore, others were delivered from notes or from brief outlines. Addresses in English were given in the Christian Reformed Church at the corner of Ninth Street and College Avenue [the historic Van Raalte church]. Papers in the Dutch tongue were read in the First Reformed church on Ninth Street and Central Avenue, the Third Reformed church on Twelfth Street, and the Christian Reformed church on Central Avenue. Each speaker was allowed twenty minutes.

An impressive series of meetings was arranged. On Wednesday August 25 at 2:30 P.M. addresses with appropriate music were presented.[1] Among the features of this program was a humorous song *De Teleurgestelde Landverhuizer*, or the *"Disappointed Immigrant,"* specially prepared for this occasion and sung by Van Lente's Choir. Its six stanzas are an interesting document relating to the tribulations of immigrants and possess considerable historical value.

Vol moed en vuur en weltemoe
Trok men naar 't verre Westen toe,
Daar dolf men, 't was de moeite waard,
Het goud bij schoppen vol uit d'aard.
Doch de verwachting was te groot:
Voor tarwe at men korenbrood.

Men zei: „Daar loopen, lieve wijf,
De varkens met het mes in 't lijf;
De peren hangen om en rond
Gebraden voor uw fijnen mond."
Doch de verwachting was te groot,
't Was korenpap en korenbrood.

Ja, zeg mij, of het armer kan:
Men smeerde met de kaars de pan,
En menig weeldrig lekkerbek
Moest leven als een ware vrek.
En voor het sponzig heerlijk brood
At men er kost zoo zwaar als lood.

[1] *De Grondwet*, Aug. 24 and 31, 1897.

Waar toch, waar kon het beter zijn?
De beken vloeiden zelfs van wijn
Maar ach! men dronk, dat Neerland zat,
Voor Javakoffie, roggenat.
Hun uitzicht was wat al te stout,
Doch vond geen dronkenlui in 't woud.

Maar eindlijk wendt zich, dank zij God,
Hun arm en deerniswaardig lot;
Herschapen uit een wildernis,
Is het een land, als 't heden is.
Was de verwachting eerst te groot,
Men heeft er nu zeer goed het brood.

Thans viert men feest na vijftig jaar,
Men is hier vroolijk bij elkaâr,
En over Gode's doen voldaan,
Heft men Hem, blij, een danklied aan.
Men juicht: Gods goedheid is zeer groot,
Voor armoê vindt men nu het brood.[1]

While the titles of many of the papers read at these meetings have been recorded, it is impossible to draw up a complete list of them. Some, like the one on Nebraska announced by Jan Trompen, probably were presented but appear to have been lost. A very large number, however, were collected, in accordance with the Commission's plan. At the meetings it was again announced that these addresses, including the papers that were not read, were to be published in a special volume, a plan never carried out. Years later, starting December 20, 1910, Van Schelven began their publication serially in *De Grondwet* under the title *Historische Schetsen uit het Koloniale Leven.* This series came to an abrupt close with the June 22, 1915, issue although Van Schelven expressed his intention to resume the series in the autumn of the same year, a hope never realized. Of the plan to issue these papers in a substantial volume nothing further was heard.

Under this title Van Schelven published memoirs and other writings drawn from a variety of sources. He republished, for example, those written twenty years earlier by Evert Zagers, Egbert Frederiks, Rieks

[1] F. M. Knobel, „Holland City en de Hollandsche Amerikaan," *Vragen Van Den Dag*, XXI [1906], 556-567.

Bouws, and Tede Ulberg. Most of his collection, however, was composed of papers read or prepared to be read at the Semi-Centennial celebrations. The manuscripts of these addresses ultimately became the property of the Netherlands Museum of Holland, Michigan.

For years after the passing of the Semi-Centennial celebrations Van Schelven continued to urge Hollanders and also Americans who had had a part in Dutch settlement to write their memoirs. He succeeded in collecting a considerable number written after 1897, many of which were published in *De Grondwet*. Among these also are the sketches read at the Sixtieth Anniversary of the founding of Zeeland held in that place in 1907.[1] From the souvenir printed to commemorate that event are included in the present collection Cornelius van Loo's *Jannes van de Luyster* and Jacob den Herder's *Sketch of Zeeland's History*.

There·also were other commemorative celebrations at this time, for example, the one held in Orange City, Iowa, in September 1895. A parade was organized on that occasion, and a series of articles was penned, subsequently published in *De Volksvriend* of September 19, 1895, by men like Henry Hospers and Antonie J. Betten. A few years later an enterprizing publisher produced a *Historical Atlas of Sioux County* wherein appeared several series of pioneer memoirs by Hendrik Jan van der Waa, Arie van der Meide, Dominie James de Pree, D. Gleysteen, and Joe Rexwinkel.

There were other celebrations in western settlements, like that of Holland in Nebraska in 1910 to commemorate the first arrival of Hollanders in that state, but no written memoirs appear to have been produced at most of those occasions.[2] So, for example, the people of Sioux Center, Iowa, on May 17, 1947, held services to call to mind the organization of the first congregation. Part of the ceremony consisted in the planting of a tree on an appropriate spot. A dominie commented on the third verse of the first Psalm, whereupon some words were spoken at the graves of Dominie and Mrs. James de Pree who contributed so much to the spiritual life of Sioux Center during its early days, and the services were concluded with singing Psalm 116, 7 [from the Dutch Psalter].[3]

The reader will note few contributions in these pages from Catholic Hollanders. This was due, not to any indifference on the part of these people, for they too, like most pioneers, were intensely interested in

---

[1] *De Grondwet*, Aug. 27, 1907; *De Hope*, Aug. 27, 1907; Theo. De Veer, „Ons Hollanders in Michigan," *Eigenhaard*, 1907.

[2] *De Volksvriend*, June 30, 1910.

[3] *De Volksvriend*, May 29, 1947.

their experiences. That memoirs like those read at the celebrations in
Holland were not prepared for the celebrations held in Hollandtown and
Little Chute is unfortunate. But the pioneers of those places fittingly did
remember their origins. At Hollandtown on June 22, 1898, following a
Solemn High Mass at which Catholic organizations from nearby places
assisted, there was a program of music and speeches and the splendid
services were concluded by the archers' guild shooting the king bird, a
festive custom to which the community of Hollandtown still clings with
great affection.[1]

At Little Chute, largest Dutch Catholic community in this country,
much enthusiasm developed as the dates of celebration approached – June
14, 15, and 16, 1898. On a splendid arch erected in the open square before
St. John's Church appeared the legend "Let us Praise Men of Renown".
On the posts of this arch were inscribed the names of the priests who had
served the parish, beginning with Theodorus J. van den Broek. Three
other arches were erected: one, on which was inscribed the word "Welcome" and the dates "1848-1898", near the place where the main festivities were to take place; the second in Main Street, a simple arch
bearing in front the legend "Holland-Amerika", and on the back, also in
Dutch, "Fifty Years of Toil and Progress"; and a third on the corner of
Grand Avenue and Main Street bearing on its sides the names "Father
van den Broek", "Libera", and "Maria Magdalena" [the last two being
names of the ships in which the settlers came to America], and the words
"Holland-America". There was fitting music, flags in great display, priests
everywhere in evidence, elaborate floats, representative Catholic societies,
and other features.[2]

Although the people did not use these occasions to put their thoughts
into writing, it has been possible to find two memoirs which in some
measure fill the vacant gap: the first, an account written by John Verboort
in 1898 of the founding of Hollandtown in 1848; the second, an autobiographical sketch touching the history of Hollandtown and Little Chute
by Chrysostom A. Verwyst, published in 1916. Fuller, and more specifically illustrating the development of Little Chute, is the series of letters
written by Arnold Verstegen, a storekeeper in Little Chute, to his father-
in-law in the province of Noord-Brabant, from 1850 to 1880.

Preparing for publication the texts drawn from these sources presented

---

[1] For the announcement, see *De Gids* [De Pere, Wisconsin], Nov. 20, 1897. [Reprint in
University of Wisconsin Library].

[2] *De Volksstem*, June 22, 1898 [*Supplement*]. A copy of this issue is preserved in the Bishop's
Chancery in Green Bay, Wisconsin.

many a problem. Most of the accounts were written by people who never had attempted any systematic literary composition. Van Schelven obviously corrected many of the manuscripts, some of them written in almost indecipherable hand. The present editor has examined much of the literary material relating to these documents left by Van Schelven and now reposing among the papers belonging to the Netherlands Museum in Holland, Michigan. A few compositions were so disorderly written and so illegible that the attempt to produce a readable text had to be abandoned. In some cases as, for example, Gerrit van Oostenbrugge's account of the settlement at South Holland, Illinois, the text was completely reorganized, although as much of the author's language as possible was retained. To indicate all changes effected in the diction and spelling of this memoir would have been a difficult and useless task.

Other problems presented themselves, sometimes so serious as to argue against including some of the texts in this collection. Writers frequently omitted Christian names, neglected giving dates, or failed to give exact place references. Particularly difficult in this respect were the papers of G. W. Renskers and J. van Erve. Only because of the intrinsic value of these writings as historical sources was the labor undertaken of transcribing them and producing a more or less satisfactory text. But in spite of all such problems the reader is assured that no unwarranted liberties have been taken with the statement of fact or with the language of the documents. No attempt has been made to correct major grammatical and syntactical faults. It seemed preferable to let them stand just as they appeared in the original memoirs. Nor has it seemed fitting to reproduce these slips and incoherencies in the translations appended to a number of the memoirs. The controlling idea in making these translations was to present the original text as faithfully as possible.

The reader will discover that no notes have been appended to these texts. To provide such notes appeared precluded by the size of these volumes and expense of publication. For references to the various personages mentioned in these texts, to the many events alluded to, and to titles of pamphlets and books the reader is referred to J. van Hinte's two-volume *Nederlanders in Amerika* and to my own *Netherlanders in America: Dutch Immigration to the United States and Canada* 1789-1950, soon to be published by the University of Michigan Press.

My interest in the history of Dutch immigration to America dates from my youth spent in Graafschap, Michigan. During the years which followed I read everything I chanced to find dealing with the subject. I perused *De Grondwet* and *De Wachter*. Not until 1947 did I begin to formulate

plans for the publication of these memoirs and related writings. The
Netherlands Pioneer and Historical Foundation of Holland, Michigan,
for years had held an annual observance on February 9 to commemorate
the settlement of Holland and the Kolonie. As the hundredth anniversary
of the founding of Holland approached, it was decided by the members
directing the Foundation to secure the services of an historian to write
an account of all phases of Dutch immigration to the United States.

In 1947 the Foundation and the Centennial Commission of the City of
Holland invited me to assume this task. An appeal by these bodies to the
President of the University of Washington was favorably received and I
was given a quarter's leave of absence to study the files of newspapers and
other materials preserved in the Netherlands Museum in Holland,
Michigan. On the basis of the researches made during the spring of 1947
and during previous years I have been able to prepare the following
titles: first the forty page pamphlet *Ebenezer* 1847-1947: *Memorial
Souvenir of the Centennial Commemoriation of Dutch Immigration to the United
States Held in Holland Michigan,* 13-16 *August* 1947 which was published
in New York in 1947. This profusely illustrated booklet was followed by
by a larger and more serious work, a volume entitled: *Netherlanders in
America: Dutch Immigration to the United States and Canada* 1789-1950
which in 1951 was accepted for publication by the University of Michigan
Press.

The present title, while a kind of afterthought, must be regarded as also
falling within the scope of what the Netherlands Pioneer and Historical
Foundation and the Centennial Commission of Holland had originally
envisaged. Now was the strategic moment to publish a collection of
immigrant memoirs and related writings. This was the thought of all who
in any way were acquainted with these accounts, not only in this country,
but also in Belgium and in the Netherlands.

Numerous persons have helped me in collecting these accounts and in
the tedious labor of criticism, but unfortunately space precludes naming
all of them. First, I wish to mention the late Dominie Henry Beets of
Grand Rapids, Michigan, who for years took an active interest in my
researches while they were little more than a hobby. His encouragement
was an ever vital source of inspiration. To Mr. Willard Wichers, Director
of the Midwestern Division of the Netherlands Information Service at
Holland, Michigan, I owe a considerable debt of gratitude for help and
suggestions. To Mr. Peter Theodore Moerdyk, Historian of the Netherlands Museum in Holland, Michigan, I am obliged for much helpful
assistance. For advice which culminated in the publication of the present

volumes I wish to thank Dr. Hendrik J. Prakke of the Van Gorcum Press at Assen in the Netherlands.

In addition to the interest shown by all these persons and by many others, I owe a debt of gratitude to a number of friends whose financial assistance made the publication of these volumes possible. Among them are Dr. Arie van der Spek, Netherlands Consul in Seattle, Mr. Frans M.W. van Schaik of Everett, Washington, and Mr. Carl Remeeus of Milwaukee, Wisconsin. I also wish to thank the University of Washington for making available to me a grant from its Agnes H. Anderson Research Fund. I am also indebted to the Social Science Research Council for a grant-in-aid, which enabled me to collect these memoirs during the initial stages of my work, and to the American Philosophical Society of Philadelphia for a grant-in-aid from their Penrose Fund to meet some of the expenses incurred in the final stages of the preparation of these memoirs for publication. Miss Maya van der Spek assumed the burden of typing most of the memoirs at the beginning of this task. And a grant from the Research Fund of the Graduate School of the University of Washington paid the expenses involved in retyping the manuscript in final preparation for the press. Sincere thanks are due to these people and agencies; and last but not least to my wife, Edna Stonebrook Lucas, whose active interest has ever been an unfailing source of encouragement in a long and arduous task.

The Hague, Summer 1954.

Chapter I

BEGINNINGS OF THE
"NEW EMIGRATION" FROM THE NETHERLANDS TO
THE UNITED STATES, 1846

I. APPEAL TO THE FAITHFUL IN THE
UNITED STATES IN NORTH AMERICA MAY, 25, 1846

[In 1846 Antonie Brummelkamp and Albertus C. van Raalte published the pamphlet *Land-verhuizing, of Waarom Bevorderen wij de Volksverhuizing naar Noord-Amerika en niet naar Java?* Amsterdam: Hoogkamer en Cie, at the close of which appeared an appeal *Aan de Geloovigen in de Vereenigde Staten van Noord-Amerika*, dated May 25, 1846. Copies of this appeal dated June 1846 were carried by some of the emigrants who handed them to Isaac N. Wyckoff in Albany. A translation was placed in the *Christian Intelligencer* of October 15, 1846, as explained by the Rev. Thomas de Witt (1791-1874), minister at the Collegiate Reformed Church in New York, in the note here following.]

The following is a translation of the "Appeal to the Faithful in America" issued by Rev. Messrs. Brummelkamp and Van Raalte, in behalf of the Christian brethren who have Separated from the Established Reformed Church, who purpose emigrating to America, which I promised last week. I have been spared the trouble of translating it myself as I have just received this translation from the pen of Mrs. S., a member of Dr. Isaac Wyckoff's church in Albany, who emigrated from Holland a short time since. A view of the history of the Secession, and of its present state, will be given hereafter, in the course of reminiscences of the Fatherland, to be published in your columns.

Thomas De Witt.

To the Faithful in the United States of North America:
Beloved brethren and sisters in the Mediator between God and man, the Lord Jesus Christ the Son both of God and Man, who is over all, God blessed for ever; who with us, though by nature dead in trespasses and sins, by the riches of God's mercy, are born again into a living hope, by faith in God's Son, our crucified, but also risen and sitting at the right hand of God, and now expected, according to the working of His mighty power, whereby He will be glorified in us who believe – grace be to you, and peace from God our Father and from the Lord Jesus Christ by the Holy Spirit.

Brethren and sisters, though separated from you by the ocean, we have a word to you. We, by the great mercy of God our Saviour, ministers of God's word, servants of the blood-bought Church of God, ask for the exercise of the communion of saints, and call upon your compassion towards many of the Lord's children, towards many poor and needy of your fellowmen.

But that you may be able to grant us some confidence, we will endeavor to make you better acquainted with our persons, circumstances, and purposes.

After having completed our studies at the University at Leiden, more than ten years since, we entered into the ministry of the Word, and being partakers of the true and living faith, and through God's Spirit partaking a revival of His children, we soon found ourselves standing in opposition to our national, or world-church, which in many instances is nothing but a mere State machine, dependent upon worldly government, and supported by the State fund, with a minister of public worship at its head. Because we rather choose to obey the Word of God, than the despotic rules and regulations of their Church government, which estranges itself more and more from God's truth, we, together with some more ministers, were troubled and hindered in the ministry of the Word. The consequenes of this were that amidst much reviling and persecution, viz., fining, quartering, and imprisonment – [for in this country it is not permitted to preach the gospel to more than twenty persons at one time – the preaching of the gospel also is made dependent from its being acknowledged by the government as a distinct religious body in the community, and it is limited within buildings appropriated for that purpose by such bodies] – these have formed themselves in every part of the Netherlands small congragations, entirely independent from the government-congregations small and poor according to the world, but, for the most part, out of the middle class of citizens, and consisting in the whole of members who know and feel their forlorn and condemnable condition before God, who take refuge only in the blood of reconciliation, and who desire nothing better but to live during the time of their indwelling in the flesh, according to the will of God, that they may be a sweet savor of Christ, to the praise of God the Father.

Since two years we were ministering to those congregations, lowly and soberly, according to the outward appearance, as many of the vital concerns of those congregations are greatly suffering from the social oppression; for though our members are bound to pay, together with all the other inhabitants, their equal share in the taxes which are imposed upon the public for the support of the church of the land, and of the superstition, yet, not being willing to sacrifice the liberty of our congregation, we judiciously would refuse to accept any subsidies of the land's treasury, if ever such would be offered to us – but we have no fear at all that we shall be brought into the temptation, having been compelled, as we are – in order to get our civil acnowledgement in the community, and through it, the liberty of preaching in church buildings – to promise never to claim any support of the public fund, neither for our churches nor poor. In consequence of this, the cares of the churches, parsonages, for the support of the widows and the poor, for ministers and the training of laborers in the word, are very oppressive; the more so as the means of the faithful are rather small, while many, and especially among the more wealthy children of God, are yet lingering behind in the Established Church. This languishing and outward wretched condition of many of our members, and thousands of our fellow-citizens – which stands near related to the deplorable material state of this country, occasioned by the superabundance of its population, and the consequently mutual pressing – the poor, decaying condition of trade and handicraft – the diminution of wages – the invasion of rights of conscience – and, finally, the quite exhausting tributes or taxes which are daily required to balance our enormous State's debt – by all this we see that our middle class disappears, the wealth of the wealthy increases, and the laboring classes, often, notwithstanding their best efforts, are quite unable, according to the expressed will of God, "that every man should work that he might eat", to get any kind of fixed and sufficient employment by which to make their scanty living, much less to provide for their houses, and to lay something aside in behalf of the widow and fatherless, and the promotion of God's kingdom upon earth. These sad realities have, for some time past, urged us to look for some other part of our globe, as an habitation for many of our Christian countrymen, especially for many of those of our Christian fellow-citizens. In consequence of their inactive and impoverished condition, they find themselves, with their children, reduced to rest embarrassment, if not to the practice of some of these the conscience-defiling traffics, and seek resort to a country where the work awaits the man, and not man the work – where there is no such super-abundance of population as to occasion mutual and continual repulsing, but where God's beautiful creation is still ready to receive men. The more we are forced to look out for such a new habitation, in consequence of the utter failure of all our efforts, during several of the past years, to find employment and livelihood for the multitude of the destitute – and we feel ourselves, moreover, bound to do so, as it is our conviction that idleness or inactivity, not less than slavish labor, usually begets stifling cares, or becomes the exciter of man's inward corruption, the great source of so many deplorable sins, by which our own spiritual interests are endangered, and the general concerns of God's kingdom slighted and injured; by which matrimony is avoided, licentionsness cherished, our offspring neglected, and a stream of social and civil pollution is flowing in the midst of us; by which sin to the one becomes a trifle, and to the other, is a cause that he passes his days sighing and with a spotted conscience.

Though they see more and more in this country the necessity of emigration, yet the nobility are mightily opposed to it, on account of the general loss which they expect from it, at least in case the way does not lead to one of the Dutch owned colonies, for which colonies our Christian people are sorely afraid, as much in consequence of the unhealthy climate, as on account of the oppressive couse of the Dutch government, in relation to religious liberty. For all these reasons we have turned our eyes towards the United States of North America. Our heart's desire and prayer to God is, that on one of those uninhabited regions there may be a spot where our people, by the culture of the ground [for it is this quiet mode of life we prefer above all, and the greatest part of the emigrants are either husbandmen or industrious mechanics], may find their temporal subsistence secured, and be able also to save their families from the miseries of a declining state of community. Especially we would desire, that they, settling in the same villages and neighborhoods, may enjoy the privilege of seeing their little ones educated in a Christian school – a privilege of which we are here entirely deprived, as the instruction given in the state's schools may be called but a mere general moral one, offensive to neither Jew nor Roman Catholic, and the free schools are quite interdicted. We neither may nor wish to endure this privation any longer. Furthermore, it is our desire to take an active part in the promulgation of God's truth among the heathen, as here with many, by the lack of power, there arises the lack of will. To our great satisfaction, we have heard that in the interior of America, together with all the privileges of religious and scholastic liberty, there is still a great abundance of fertile ground and profitable labor to be found. But as there is not much fund to be expected by mechanics nor either by husbandmen, we are not able to defray all the necessary expenses, neither can we look to defray all the necessary expenses, neither can we look for aid to any of the wealthy of our countrymen, for the above-mentioned reasons. Though a bright and free path of rescue for so many sorely afflicted and godly families is indeed brought within our view, yet still it remains rather inaccessible, at least we have already been obliged to send away many entreating, godly, needy, miserable fellow-creatures, to see them sink still deeper in want and destitution. God commands us that we must love our neighbor not in words only, but in deed and truth; that whatsoever our hand finds to do, we should do it with all our might; it is in accordance with those principles that we boldly apply to you, beloved brethren and sisters, beseeching you to grant us your aid and assistance in this precious work, to rescue many members of the body of Christ – many fellow creatures from a really great distress, which, by the present condition of the land, threatens to become more distressing still, and more pernicious for the welfare of the rising generation. We entreat you to aid and assist us with your counsel, with your wealth, and with whatsoever the Lord our God has entrusted to you. Such we beseech of you with perfect boldness, assured as we are, that it shall work together for your salvation, and that your good works shall be rich in fruits of thanksgiving unto God. We ask it confidently, not presuming that either your hearts or hands, by any prejudice, will be fenced against a Dutch colony on North America's ground, as also this work is to our hearts a very dear and precious task. Once more, dearly beloved brethren and sisters O! do assist us, that we may become mutually acquainted in God, through Christ, in performing good works, that we may together rejoice in these new and sweet bonds of Christian love and charity.

The following has already taken place here. Besides a few single families and persons who removed previously, there left in the autumn of last year a company of about thirty persons, out of our neighborhood and elsewhere, all respectable citizens and husbandmen. Their destination was to Macrean, or Decator, in Vandalia, State of Illinois. We hope they have succeeded in finding a livelihood. Then a small Society has been formed, with the purpose of promoting emigration – to prevent as much as possible the separation of the emigrants from one another, and to secure, by their remaining united, the interests both of religion and education of the young. By means of funds furnished by this Society, those families of clever, industrious mechanics, Christian people, who, with fear and trembling, were anticipating the winter season, have been enabled to make their way to one of the seaports of America, there to make, by industry and economy, provisions for their remaining parents and friends, in aiding them to liquidate their affairs in the native land, as also to procure them the means of going thither among their Dutch Christian countrymen. At this moment a number of no less than forty Christian persons, for the most part farmers, are quitting the land of their natvity, and it is especially those whom we would recommend to you, to aid them with your counsel. They would make their journey either over the lakes or along the Ohio to Milwaukee in Wisconsin, to the Dutch Christians settled there. Let them know which way or mode of travelling is the most secure and with the least expense for those of our people who may follow. This will be as much as the Lord will enable us to help along with their most necessary expenses. May it please the Lord to move in the hearts of the godly in the United States, the bowels of their compassion that they may confirm the hope and the prospects of many distressed and faithful Christians in the Netherlands, of rescue out of so many anxious cares, to the praise of God in Christ Jesus. We beseech you, therefore, do come to our aid! Though we feel that your sholders are, probably, laden with many burdens and calls for charity, yet, in the other hand, we are sure that the Christians in America are graciously spared from that distressful decline in business, and also from those heavy taxes or duties under which our people are bowed down. Moreover we know that union makes power and that in the kingdom of God the penny of the poor widow is of great importance.

If you should think it judicious to circulate, by means of some of your American papers, this our petition among the faithful, scattered throughout the states, you would greatly oblige us, being confident that, by the goodness of God, the voice of prayer shall, for his Son's sake, come, here and there, to the hearts of his people. In the full conviction that the kingdom of God does not consist in word, but in power – that we ought to love one another in deed and in truth – that we have to bear each other's burdens – that the commandments of God not only may, but must be attended to, cost what it will, and that we therefore are not permitted to seperate the injunction to work and to eat – that every Christian is in duty bound to provide for his house, wherever such may be; yea, more, that he ought to be enabled to visit the widow and the fatherless in their affliction, and to serve the kingdom of the Lord of his substance- that he ought to keep himself undefiled before the world – that he is not to bring up his childeren in a mere general moral way, but in the nurture and admonition of the Lord – and being assured, moreover, that though we are surrounded with manifold distressing obscurities, and often go astray, yet, that we desire above all things to serve the Lord all the time of our lives – we lay this our petition before you, and humbly recommend it to the Lord who reigneth and dwelleth in the hearts of the children of men.

We close with the supplication of our hearts, that the God and Father of our Lord Jesus Christ, the God of our salvation, by His almighty power and the riches of His mercy, may make both you and ourselves diligent and abounding in obedience; and that the great unspeakable truth, that we have in God, for all eternity, a reconciled God and Father in Christ, who has thrown all our sins behind his back, and who never more shall be angry with us – may be to our souls the sweet sourec of comfort and happiness – that the hope of life may enable us to go on our ways rejoicing, and that we, having our hearts burning with love, carry forth in ourselves the image of God, and live to be a blessing upon the earth.

Your most appreciable and well-wishing brethren in Christ.

A. C. van Raalte, V.D.M.

A. Brummelkamp, V.D.M.

Arnhem, June 1846

2. A. C. VAN RAALTE'S LETTER

TO G. G. VAN PRINSTERER, SEPTEMBER 21, 1846

[The following letter, preserved in the Van Prinsterer Correspondence in the National Archives in The Hague, reveals Van Raalte's idea about Dutch immigrant settlement in America's Midwest.]

Arnhem, 21 September 1846

Hoog Welgeboren Heer en Geliefde Broeder!

Zoo denk ik den vaderlandschen bodem te verlaten; de stem en behoeften der naar Noord Amerika vertrekkende broeders dringt mij daartoe; de hoop dat langs dezen weg vele in bange handen zuchtende broeders redding vinden vervrolijkt mij dit pad; en de behoeften van mijn gezin, vooral de behoefte aan schoolonderwijs leveren nevens andere drangredenen mij eenen scherpen spoorslag daartoe. Ofschoon ik gesterkt in God mijn Vader die mij om Zijns Zoons wil zal helpen gemoedigd mijn pad betrede, toch krenkt mij de scheiding mijn hart; mijn harte keert zich als om van wege liefde tot het mij zoo dierbare volk van God; ik ben blijde dat ik het liefhebbe en toch mijn harte doet mij zeer. Ik gevoel veel behoefte aan gemeenschap der Heiligen, ach dat het volk één ware! Verlies van God en bloedbanden en verguizing was voor mij niet de in nadruk bittere beker welke ik op den vaderlandschen grond gedronken heb! Maar neen! de scheiding, verwijdering, ja verbittering tusschen het volk Gods, ach dat het volk één ware! Te midden van mijne smarten echter hebt gij, Broeder, mijne ziel vertroost [duid mijn vrijmoedig schrijven niet ten kwade, bij het scheiden is mij zulks behoefte]! Gij hebt u onzer niet geschaamd en ofschoon op verschillend standpunt staande, vond ik in u te midden van smaad en verguizing eene broederliefde die warmte afgaf en men moet zelve het pad der smaadheid betreden om het kunnen beoordelen wat het in heeft daar eenen Broeder te vinden. God bekrachtige u en wees tot sterking en tezamen binding der broederen. Mijn hart en gebed is voor u, daar vraag ik uwe wederliefde, uwe voorbede vraag, de voorbede van de broederen die 13 October, D.V. zullen vergaderen; ik had gehoopt hen mijn laatst vaarwel te kunnen toeroepen, doch het uitstel der vergadering heeft mij zulks onmogelijk gemaakt. Nu dat zij voor mij bidden! Ik kan wel van harte betuigen dat het mijnen wensch is steeds in liefde voor Gods troon aan de dierbare Nederlandsche kinderen Gods te gedenken, ja, ik wil bidden dat God ze vereenige en vereenigd doe werken opdat zij als een stad op een berg mogen blinken en zoo schoolen geopend worden en door Gods liefde in ijver en liefde ontvlamd dienaren des Woords zullen worden uitgezonden, zal ik ofschoon verre verwijderd verkwikt worden en God danken. Onder Gods zegen zullen wij hier of daar in Amerika wel spoedig tot een buurtschap of dorpje zijn aangegroeid en wij hoopen daar van vermogende Broeders, bedrukte weduwen, weezen, en gezonkenen te ontvangen en den Broederen aldaar in dit liefdewerk te dienen, God geve dat hierdoor de gemeenschap zoo onderhouden [zal] worden dat de wereld gedwongen zij te erkennen dat wij elkander liefhebben; ik bid u ter onderhouding dezer zalige gemeenschap, wil ons zenden een exemplaar van de nu en dan uitkomende schriften der vereeniging ter bevordering van Christelijke lectuur, enz.; zoo zal ons gebed voor Neerlandsch volk voor de Neerlandsche vrienden in den Heere worden verlevendigd, en dit werk der liefde zal u zelve ook het gebed voor ons in het hart geven. Ja bid voor ons, voor mij dat ik niet geesteloos moge zijn maar het dierbare mijner roeping moge zien opdat ik voortdurend tot den einde mijns levens moge arbeiden zonder verslapping tot bekeering en opbouw en volmaking van het dierbare volk van God. Bid voor mij, ach! Ik heb zooveel noodig. God zegene U en uwe gade en stel U ten zegen op aarde.

Hoogwelgeboren Heer!

Uwen U liefhebbende en zeer hoogachtende Broeder in Christus,

A. C. van Raalte.

Ps. Heeft U ook adressen van aanbeveling voor mij onder den vrienden, zoo ja den 23 en 24 dezer is mijn adres de H.H. Hudig en Blokhuizen, cargadoors te Rotterdam alwaar het schip de *Santhener* in lading ligt waarmede ik hoop den 25sten te vertrekken. Vergeef mijn haastig schrijven, vele drukten verhinderen mij.

[Translation]

Arnhem 21 September 1846

Noble sir and dear brother!

So then I am thinking of leaving my fatherland! The voice and the needs of the brethren departing for North America urge me to do so. The hope that in this way many of our brethren in oppressed and straitened circumstances may find relief cheers me in my chosen path. And the needs of my family and especially the need of school instruction give me, besides other urgent reasons, keen incentive for this. Although strengthened in God my Father who for His Son's sake will encourage me in my course, severing my ties, wounds my soul. It is as if my soul holds me back because of affection for the people of God so dear to me. I am happy that I have this love for them, but nevertheless my soul is in pain. I deeply need the communion of the saints. O that the people were one! Loss of God and of ties of blood and abuse was emphatically not a more bitter cup which I have drunk on the soil of my fatherland. No, the schisms, the estrangement, yes even the embitterment among God's people – O that the people were one! Brother, in the midst of my pains you have comforted me [do not think ill of my candor, for at this moment of separation I deeply feel the need of such freedom of expression]. You have never been ashamed on our account. Although you have assumed a different standpoint, I have ever found in you amidst scorn and abuse a warmly radiating brotherly love. One must himself tread the path of scorn to be able to judge what it means to find a brother. May God strengthen you to be a means to bind the brethren together. My soul and my prayer are for you; I ask for your affection in return. I beg your intercession, the favor of the brethren who will meet on October 13, *deo volente*. I had hoped to be able to give them my last farewell, but the postponement of the meeting has made this impossible for me. Now this is for my prayers. From my heart I can testify that it is my wish always to remember in charity my beloved Netherlands children of God before His throne. Yes, I shall pray that God unite them and cause them to work together that they may shine like a city on a hill, so that schools be opened-that servants of God's Word, zealous and filled with His love, shall be sent forth. Should this happen, though far distant, I shall be heartened and I shall thank God. Under God's blessing at some place in America we soon shall grow to become a community or a village. There we hope to receive, sent by brethren of means, oppressed widows, orphans, and depressed persons. There we hope to serve the brethren in this work of charity. God grant that through these means the world may be led to acknowledge that we love each other. I pray that, to the end that this blessed communion may be maintained, you from time to time send me a copy of the newly published writings of the society for the development of Christian reading matter, etc. In this way will our prayer be quickened for the people of the Netherlands and for our Netherlands friends in the Lord. This work of charity will likewise stir you to pray for us. Yes, pray for us, for me that I may not become spiritless, but that I may discern the beloved object of my calling, and that I until the end of my life may labor without weakening for the conversion, the upbuilding, and the perfection of God's beloved people. Pray for me, alas! I need so much. God bless you and your wife and make you to be a blessing on earth.

Noble sir,

Your affectionate and respectful friend in Christ,

A. C. van Raalte

P.S.   If you have any addresses to recommend for me among our friends, my adress on the 23d and the 24th is Messrs. Hudig en Blokhuizen, ship-brokers at Rotterdam where the ship *Santhener* [the *Southerner*] is loading with which I hope to sail on the 25th. Pardon my hasty writing; many pressing things are hindering me.

3. RECEPTION OF THE FIRST IMMIGRANTS IN AMERICA, 1846-1847

[When on December 17, 1846, Van Raalte and his followers on *The Southerner* arrived in New York harbor their coming had been anticipated by members of the Reformed Church in America. Among those who took a charitable interst in them and their plans was Thomas de Witt (1791-1874) pastor of the Collegiate Reformed Church in New York. At Albany Isaac N. Wyckoff (1792-1869) was especially active in assisting the immigrants at very turn. Their many acts of charity were recorded in the *Christian Intelligencer,* official organ of the Reformed Church in America. Besides reporting the welcome accorded the immigrants and the practical assistance given them in New York and Albany, the paper also published the proceedings of the meeting held on January 22, 1847, in the session room of the Presbyterian church in Detroit, which named committees in each of several towns of Michigan, besides Detroit, to assist Hollanders journeying to the proposed settlement on Black Lake in Ottawa County.]

A. The *Christian Intelligencer*, October 8, 1846

A Society has just been formed in our Reformed Dutch Churches at Albany, named The *Protestant Evangelical Holland Emigrant Society*. This was organised in consequence of an appeal received from Holland by the Rev. Dr. Isaac Wyckoff, in reference to a contemplated emigration of a large number of people, mainly connected with the secession from the old Established Reformed Church, who strictly adhere to the faith of their fathers. During my recent short visit to Holland, I became partially acquainted with this movement, and found it commanded deep interest, and that large numbers are ready to enlist in it. Very many of them are of the class who struggling by honest industry to obtain a mere living, and stand in need of aid to take the preparatory steps to leave their own country and make their settlement in America. A few individuals of their number some time since, settled in our Western States, and have written to them in language of encouragement and promise. I have brought with me an appeal in pamphlet form, to their countrymen in Holland, stating the character of the proposed step, and vindicating it, to which is annexed an address to the faithful in the United States [*Aan de Geloovigen*]. It is signed by Albertus C. van Raalte and Antonie Brummelkamp, both ministers from the Reformed Church, seperated from the Established Reformed Church, in behalf of their brethren. When at Utrecht, I had a short interview with the Rev. Hendrik P. Scholte, who is one of the committee appointed to proceed to America this fall, in order to make the necessary inquiries and investigations, and take preparatory steps, by the purchase of a well selected tract of land in one of the Western States [probably Iowa], and other means. He told me that he probably would reach New York in the latter part of October or beginning of November, when I hope to see him at my house. Dominie Scholte was one of the first to raise the banner in vindication of the truths of the Standards of the Church, and in apposition to the course of ecclesiastical courts in relation to them. He became subjected to suspension from the office by the ecclesiastical court, and then continuing his ministrations, he was subjected to repeated fines and imprisonment, until a few years since the King allowed the privilege of separate worship without molestation. He is evidently a man of vigorous mind as well as zeal. I met, while in Holland with Count St. George, of Geneva, on his return from the General

Assembly of the Free Church of Scotland. He told me that he was with Scholte during his literary course at the University of Leiden; that after his graduation he entered into the army, when he became converted, where he also knew him, as well as after entering into the ministry. He speaks highly of his whole character, moral, intellectual and spiritual. I shall next week translate the address to the pious in America, in the pamphlet before mentioned and subsequently present farther information. On the arrival of Ds. Scholte the subject may be presented in a more definite and satisfactory form. The object proposed by the society recently formed at Albany, viz, to aid the pious poor in taking the necessary steps to obtain a settlement here, is one which commend itself to my best judgment and feelings, and to the promotion of which I stand ready to contribute what little share of influence I may possess. It is peculiarly commended in all its associations and bearings, in the religious character it presents to the ministers and members of the Reformed Dutch Church in America. This short notice must suffice for the present.

Thomas de Witt

B. The *Christian Intelligencer*, November 26, 1846

Messrs. Editors: – I have read with much interest the article in reference to a contemplated emigration of Christian people from Holland to our Western States. From the *Appeal to the Faithful in the United States* in behalf of those who purpose to emigrate, the following appears among other things.

1. That they have separated from the National Church in Holland, that they might enjoy greater liberty of conscience, but are still subjected to serious difficulties, arising from the connection of the Church from which they separated with the State.

2. That the decayed conditions of trade and handicraft, the diminution of wages, the enormous taxes imposed by the government, together with the superabundant population, render it extremely difficult for many to make even a scanty living, much less to make provision for the future wants of their families, or appropriate any thing for the purpose of Christian benevolence.

3. That they have turned their eyes to our Western States, as the place where they may settle in villages and neighborhoods, and be exempt from those veils under which they now Labor, procure the necessary temporal subsistence for their families, and enjoy those priveleges as to religion and education, which they so much desire.

4. That those contemplating emigration, are mostly industrious, mechanics, and husbandmen of small means, and that many among them are in circumstances to need the aid of the benevolent in their removal to the interior after their arrival in New York.

Now I might say, and would say, in behalf of all the faithful in Illinois, to these Christian people: Come on, friends. Though we have no money to bestow, we can direct you to suitable locations, give employment to your mechanics, furnish land for you farmers to cultivate till they shall get lands of their own, and aid you in various ways, so as to make your circumstances comfortable, and expedite those important objects you have in view in leaving your native country.

It is probable that the society formed in Albany will make such arrangements, as that these people shall be transported to their respective destinations, at the cheapest possible rate, while similar measures will be adopted by a society formed in Holland to aid their emigration to New York.

To complete the arrangement, it seems to me, that there should be a society or committee in that section of the country to which it is probable they will emigrate, to afford them the necessary assistance in regard to providing their location, employment, etc, etc.

It appears from the Appeal that some few families are already located in this State. Probably Illinois presents more inviting locations on all accounts for such emigrants than any other State in the West. The religious denominations to which they are attached, has an existence here already. Five of our Reformed Dutch Churches are established in eligible places. In the vicinity of each, if not immediately adjoinuing, are tracts of neighborhoods or villages. Our own people, I am pursuaded, would cordially welcome these emigrants to their respective settlements and afford them all the aid in their power.

I throw out these suggestions, that those whose business it may be to seek locations for the emigrants may have their attention directed to some places which we, Dutch folk in Illinois, think would be eligible for the settlement of these Christian people.

                                                                Yours, S

C. The *Christian Intelligencer*, December 3, 1846

Rev. Albertus C. van Raalte, of Arnhem, in Holland, with his family and emigrants to the number of a hundred souls, adults and children, reached here by the *Sultana* [erroneous for *Southerner*] from Rotterdam, on Wednesday, the 18th of November. They left for Wisconsin the next day by the way of Buffalo and the lakes, being fearful to make any delay on account of the close of navigation being at hand. They expect some to join them this winter, by the way of New Orleans. Mr. van Raalte is one of the signers of the *Appeal to the Faithful in America,* a translation of which was published in the *Christian Intelligencer.* Rev. Hendrik P. Scholte, of Utrecht, who was expected this fall, has deferred it till next spring when he expects to bring his family with him.

D. The *Christian Intelligencer*, December 31, 1846

It was stated three or four weeks since, that the Rev. Albertus C. van Raalte and a company of emigrants amounting to the number of more than one hundred persons, had arrived within this city. As it was about the close of navigation on the lakes, and winter was about to come, they pressed immediately on, towards Wisconsin. Within two days, three vessels have arrived from Holland with emigrants; two of them containing upwards of one hundred each, and the third about thirty. The voyages have been long and stormy; In two of the cases, between sixty and seventy days, and in the third, between fifty and sixty. The length of passage has brought them here in the midst of winter, in utter uncertainty of definite place of location, when traveling, if attempted, is far more costly, and far less opportunity for temporal employment can be found. The emigrants are generally pious people, adhering to the true faith of the Reformed Dutch Church, as expressed in her standards, who have struggled with difficulties and trials in adherence to their faith, while seperating from the Established Church. They generally have depended on their industry for the support of their families, and with scanty means have crossed the ocean which in many cases have been exhausted. An elder in one of our churches who kindly visited the respective companies of emigrants, and gave them such aid, and counsel as he could, in the hurry and exigency, speaks of them with deep interest, as a people evidencing attachment not only to the evangelical doctrines of our church, but also true experimental piety, and that his heart has been warmed in his intercourse with them. By a postcript to a letter from Buffalo, received at the office of the *Christian Intelligencer*, it appears that four or five of the families which came with Ds. van Raalte remained at Buffalo, in circumstances, which will require the aid of christian charity during the winter. The company which arrived about ten days since went on, after one intermediate day, to Albany. I have just received a private letter from the Rev. Isaac Wyckoff of Albany, from which I take the liberty to take the following abstract: "Some eighty persons arrived here about Wednesday night. They were so hurried through the city that their baggage was left behind, and they were two days destitute of beds to lie on or food to eat. One woman died of exhaustion at the depot, in the car. I have spent Thursday and Friday, and part of this day [Saturday], in attending to the Holland emigrants, which are now with us. The expenses of a large proportion of them for the winter will have to paid by the association or, they must go the poor house. There were among them the most lovely and noble Christians I have ever seen. They remind me of the fathers – their faith is like Abraham's." Dr. Wyckoff alludes here to an Association formed at Albany last month, when a few emigrants have arrived, and letters from Dss. van Raalte and Brummelkamp to Dr. Wyckoff stated the proposed emigrantation of larger numbers. Its object is to give advice and aid against customary imposition on the emigrants, and in case of necessity, supply their pressing wants. The company which arrived three or four days since, remain here, deliberating as to their course. The far greater part will doubtless continue there during the winter, and most of them will be dependent on charitable contributions, or industrious employment if it could be procured. At the meeting of our ministers on Monday morning last, this subject was a topic of conversation. It was deemed advisable to appoint a committee of judicious and well adapted laymen, to visit the emigrants now here, or who may arrive, give them advice and council, guard them against imposition, and to inquire into their condition. That committee consists of Messrs. James Forrester, Jacob Brinkerhoff, Benjamin Wood, and R. J. de Jong, who will report to the minister next Monday morning.

It is greatly to be regretted that these worthy people should have reached here in the midst of inclemency of winter, rendering their difficulties and discouragements greater. But Providence has so ordered it, and they are among us, with the strongest and most impressive claims, as descendants from Hollanders, or as ministers, members and friends of the Reformed Dutch Church. It is also to be regretted, that in view of the contemplated emigration, the way has not been previously prepared by the appointment of a judicious committee from Holland to visit the United States, to make thorough inquiry, obtain a place of settlement and open the avenue for an easy access, with the best economy of means.

When in Holland last, I learned of a projected emigration among the *Afgescheidenen* or Seceders, and obtained the pamphlet issued on the subject of Dss. van Raalte and Brummelkamp, from which the translation of the *Appeal to the Faithful in America* inserted a few weeks since in the *Christian Intelligencer*, was extracted. The only person interested in the movement, whom I visited, was the Rev. Hendrik P. Scholte, of Utrecht, with whom I had a very short interview. I urged upon him the importance of such preparatory visit, with which he accorded, and it was then his purpose, [as I understood him] as a member of such committee, to visit the United States last fall. The circumstances of his family have prevented him. In a note which I received from him by Ds. van Raalte, he alludes to the purposed emigration to some extent next spring. I have just written to him, urging the importance of such a preparatory visit, not leaving the emigrants, on their arrival here, in uncertainty as to their destination. The whole subject is one of interest, calling for wisdom, while the case of the worthy poor emigrants among us, presents a strong, and I would hope, resistless appeal to the friends of Christ and "His little ones" in the bosom of our Church. Rarely has such an appeal met them, and surely it will meet with a response. We ask the attention of our ministers and out Christian brethern throughout the whole Church to it.

Thomas de Witt

E. The *Christian Intelligencer*, December 31, 1846

The following paragraph, related to the condition of some of our Dutch brethern recently from Holland, is extracted from a letter recently received from N. Lyman of Buffalo:

"Please have the goodness to say to some of your influential Dutch friends in your city, that there is in Buffalo a company of five families, consisting of about thirty souls, young and old, who are lately from Holland, and who have been prevented from going west for want of means to do so, and are very destitute of means to obtain food and fuel. Clothing they do not need. There are a few persons in our little forsaken Dutch church here, who can speak to them in their mother tongue, and who are using every exertion to make them confortable, and save them from starving. One of the men tells us that he saw Dr. de Witt in Holland, and conversed with him there.

"These families arrived here just at the close of navigation. I suppose that by making known their condition, some people in New York will be prompt to assist them. They are a class of people deserving attention.

"Respectfully yours,

N. Lyman"

Contributions for the relief of these strangers may be left with the clerk, in the office of the *Christian Intelligencer*. – Eds

F. The *Christian Intelligencer*, January 7, 1847

Among the worthy poor emigrants recently arrived from Holland, who expect to remain here during the winter and proceed to the west during the spring, there are a few mechanics and several farmers. They are anxious to obtain employment, both in view of occupying their time and economizing their small means they have brought with them. A few of them are entirely desitute. Cannot our friends procure for them some employment?

Acknowledgement. – The subscriber gratefully acknowledges the receipt of twenty dollars from a lady, and of fifteen dollars, also from a lady, both members of the Collegiate Reformed Dutch Church, transmitted after reading the statement in the *Christian Intelligencer* of last week, in relation to the Emigrants recently arrived from Holland. These sums will be carefully appropriated to relieve the necessities which may occur among the worthy emigrants, recognized as Christ's little ones. Contributions from others are respectfully solicited, and will be thankfully acknowledged

Thomas de Witt

New York, January 5, 1847

G. The *Christian Intelligencer*, February 4, 1847

The Netherlands Society, for the protection of emigrants from Holland.
  Public attention has lately been arroused to the destitute and unprotected condition of emigrants arriving on our shores, who, until within a short period had no point where to apply for advice and protection; consequently, they too often fell into the hand of designing persons, whose chief object was to plunder them of the little money they possessed, and under the pretence of friendship, offering advice which too often led to ruin.

Information having been received that some ten thousand emigrants were about leaving the Netherlands for this country, affords us much pleasure to observe, that a few gentlemen, natives of Holland, have formed an association, called the "Netherland Society", which must be of great advantage to their protection and guidance, as well as for others who may here after migrate from that part of Europe, whence they arrive equally strangers to our language and our customs, and requiring the aid which will now be extended for their welfare, and especially to protect them against the innumerable frauds which emigrants have heretofore been the victims of.

The Society solicits the aid of Hollanders and the descendants of Hollanders, at the same time observing that the object is not to promote emigration, but rather to assist and protect those who may of themselves wish to make this the country of their adoption. The Society will require funds, as it will be necessary to forward many of them on their arrival to the West, and elsewhere, at the expense of the Society, as they will not be encouraged to remain about the city, where they might become a charge on the public charity. Others will be provided with good and respectable situations; the sick will also be provided for in a suitable manner, and the destitute assisted to earn their living.

The industry of this class of emigrants, and their patience and power of endurance, will recommend them to the favorable consideration of all; and their national cleanliness will make them desirable domestics, and in a measure, remove the difficulties so much complained of in procuring good servants.

We most emphatically recommend the Society, which will alleviate much distress. Few persons enjoying the comforts of the domestic circle, who have never left the homestead of their ancestors, and whose path has been smooth and happy under our free institutions, can realize the feeling of the emigrant – a wanderer from home and country, from near and dear relations, whom he probably will never meet again – driven by stern necessity to try his fortune in another land, and frequently quite desitute. Surely such misfortunes must call forth the sympathies of every feeling heart and induce benevolent individuals of all countries to aid the Netherlands' Society in carrying out their laudable plan of operation.

We shall be happy to receive any donation forwarded to us through this Society, and acknowledge the receipt through the *Christian Intelligencer*.

H. The *Christian Intelligencer*, February 11, 1847

It being understood that there was a probability of a large emigration from Holland in the course of this year and thereafter, and the agent of the first emigrants being in this city, after having explored the western part of this State with a view to the settlement in it, a meeting was convened at the session-room of the Presbyterian church, on the evening of Friday, the 22nd inst at which were present a number of citizens of Detroit, and of other portions of the State.

Rev. Mr. Ova P. Hoyt, of Kalamazoo, Rev. Mr. Andrew B. Taylor, of Grand Rapids, and Mr. Theodore Romeyn, of Detroit [having been appointed a committee, by a previous meeting, held at the office of Judge Shuball Conant, in Detroit] submitted certain resolutions through Mr.

Romeyn, who gave to the meeting a statement of the origin of the present movement in Holland, and of its probable importance. The interference of the government with the exercise of religious and exclusive control of education, accompanied by inhibitions to teach or worship, except according to certain arbitrary ordinances, conjoined with the intolerable taxation and other civil oppression – had led to such a state of feeling among a nation like the Dutch, always attached to their religion, and distinguished for their opposition to arbitrary power, that now large masses of the people were ready and anxious to leave. This emigration proceeding from such motives, and embracing men of various and diversified pursuits, would bring a most valuable class among us, if they selected our State as their resting place. Michigan has been much misrepresented abroad, and the agent of these colonists had come here possessed against us, and inclined to go elsewhere. But he had met sympathy, countenance and aid, and was disposed to commence his colonization here. By so doing he was entitled to our cooperation; and a little sacrifice by individuals, a little advice and attention to emigrants, might be of inestimable advantage. Several hundred of them were already in the United States, and many more would soon arrive. After these and other remarks, Mr. Romeyn submitted, as the report of the committee, the following resolutions:

Resolved, That this meeting has heard with much interest of a large prospective emigration from Holland to this country, proceeding from a love of civil and religious liberty, and stimulated by the oppresive interference of that government with education and the exercise of religion, it commends itself to our admiration and sympathy. We pledge ourselves to co-operate, as far as we can, with those who elsewhere may aid and sustain this movement; and, if these emigrants make their abiding place in Michigan we will extend to them the hand of fellowship and friendship. We admire the past history and character of the people of the Netherlands. For their faith and independence they struggled for more than thirty years against the powers of Spain and Germany. They stood side by side with our English ancestors in arduous conflicts for freedom in civil and religious matters. They gave an asylum to the persecuted Puritans. They aided in the settlement of our most important state. In their industry, their enterprise, their frugality, their integrity, their love of country, their devotedness to their faith and to freedom in their civil institutions, we recognize those qualities which entitle their descendants to our respect and welcome.

Resolved, That a committee of seven be appointed, who may associate with them such others as they deem expedient, and whose duty it shall be to aid, in every practicable way, the emigrants who may reach our limits, and to correspond with such associations or committees as may be found elsewhere; and in other ways, to invite, encourage and direct the settlement of these emigrants within our State.

Resolved, That we recommend the appointment of committees and associations for a similar purpose, at such other points as may be deemed desirable by the Rev. A. C. van Raalte, the agent and pioneer of this movement, and whom we cheerfully recommend as a gentleman of energy, talent, piety, and disinterested zeal.

The resolutions were unanimously adopted.

The following persons were appointed the committee at Detroit: Theodore Romeyn, Shuball Conant, Rev. George Duffield, D.D., E. C. Seaman, Hon. A. S. Porter, E. P. Hastings, and J. W. Brooks.

Mr. van Raalte having suggested the expediency of committees at the places hereinafter designated, and gentlemen being present from those parts of the country, the following were appointed: –

For Marshal – Hon. John D. Pierce and Hon. H. W. Taylor, of the House of Representatives, and Samuel Hall.

For Kalamazoo – Rev. Ova P. Hoyt, William Denison, and Hon. N. A. Balch, of the Senate.

For Grand Rapids — George Young, John Ball, and Rev. Andrew Brown Taylor.

For Grand Haven – Rev. William M. Ferry, Henry Pennoyer, and Thomas W. White.

For Allegan – Hon. John R. Kellog, E. B. Bassett, Ezra C. Southworth, and F. J. Littlejohn.

For Saugatuck – S. D. Nichols, William Carley, and William G. Britton.

It was further resolved that the proceedings of this meeting be published in the papers of this city, and that the country papers generally be requested of publish them.

Rev. Mr. van Raalte, in a most touching and impressive manner, expressed his gratitude for the sympathy and aid proffered to his countrymen, and his gratification at having thus far succeeded in the preparatory steps for the settlement in a land where labor would meet with its reward, and civil and religious freedom be secure.

After an interesting and appropriate reply from Hon. John Ball, the meeting was adjourned.

Shuball Conant, Chairman

N.A. Balch, Sec'y

I. The *Christian Intelligencer*, March 11, 1847

Rev. A. C. van Raalte, formerly from Arnhem, Holland, reached here
with his family and a number of emigrants in November last, at a time
approaching the close of navigation on the lakes and canals. He felt urged
to proceed immediately with a view to make investigations, in reference
to a place of permanent settlement for himself, and others expected to
emigrate from Holland, and then proposed to go as far as Wisconsin.
On reaching Detroit, he was kindly received by ministers and Christians
there; provision was made for the temporary accommodations of his
family, and letters of introduction were given to him to ministers and
laymen in the interior of the State and farther west. He writes, that he
was uniformly received with kindness, and that Evangelical Christians
cherished and expressed a lively interest in the proposed settlement of
religious emigrants from Holland. Our readers will remember the insertion in the *Christian Intelligencer*, two or three weeks since, of an account
of the proceedings of a meeting held at Detroit, in reference to this
movement, and with a view of giving counsel and aid to Ds. van Raalte
in this enterprise. At this meeting, Rev. Andrew B. Taylor, our missionary
at Grand Rapids, Mich., was present and took part. A most respectable
committee was formed, consisting of six citizens of Detroit, of established
christian character and standing, and some of them holding high position
in society. Ds. van Raalte, although originally intending to go farther
west, has determined, after careful investigation in the State of Michigan,
and conferences with the most judicious friends, to cast his lot in that
State. A document from the Detroit committee, addressed to the Rev.
Dr. Isaac Wyckhoff of Albany, has been received, which is of considerable length and full of interest. It first enters into an extended comparative
view of the advantages of different points for settlement and after showing
this comparative estimate, draws the conclusion that settlement in the
State of Michigan would be decidedly most eligible. In relation to the
selection mady by Ds. van Raalte, the committe say: "Knowing these
things to be so, we have felt that we would be acting from no selfish
umpulse, but from disinterested and philanthropic motives, when some
of us advised and all approved the determination of our friend, Mr. van
Raalte, to cast the lot of himself and his people within our borders. In
the particular location which has been preferred by him, we have no
more interest than you would have in his settlement on the borders of
Lake Erie; merely because it chanced to be within your own State. We
have listened to his explanations; we are so convinced of his fidelity and

industry, and of the comprehensiveness of his views, and of his knowledge of the wants of his countrymen, that we would have much hesitation in expressing a dissent from his conclusion, if our judgment were not entirely satisfied. He has selected Black lake and river, on the eastern coast of Lake Michigan, and in the western part of Ottawa county between the Kalamazoo and Grand Rivers." The committee then proceeds to describe the district of country in which the selection for settlement has been made, and show its advantages. Ds. van Raalte has proceeded with his family to enter the woods, and prepare the way for settlement.

In a letter dated February 17, from Rev. Mr.Ova P. Hoyt, at Kalamazoo, who has taken great interest in the enterprise, it appears that Mr. van Raalte and his family then at his house were then about to proceed to the land he had purchased and to make a clearing, with the view of erecting a cottage. His family will reside, in the mean time, with a missionary laboring among the Indians, about six miles from that place. Mr. van Raalte, by necessary expenses incurred in traveling purchase of land, etc., has reduced his means to about $ 400. A decent cottage will cost at least $ 300, and he will need cattle, implements, etc.

Rev. Mr. Hoyt proposes to raise among his own people and in the vicinity, provisions sufficient to support his family and the colonists who may be associated with him in the settlement for at least six months, and inquires whether sufficient may be contributed here to build his cottage, so as to leave him the little means he has to commence his farming; otherwise, he may be greatly cramped. He speaks like the gentlemen at Detroit, in high commendation of Ds. van Raalte and his family.

The Detroit committee speak in their letter of the importance of obtaining a considerable tract of land at the location selected, in prospect of the proposed emigration, now while the price of land is cheap, and before the commencement of the settlement gives rise to an advance of price. As the means are not in hand to make the purchase in ready payments by Ds. van Raalte, the inquiry is made, whether persons among us possessing ample means would not advance capital for such purpose, say to the amount of five thousand dollars, giving the assurance that it would be a safe and soon a profitable investment.

I received by the *Cambria* a letter from the Rev. Hendrik P. Scholte, of Utrecht, to whom allusion has before been made. He accords with the suggestion I made to him in a letter of the mistake which had been made in the emigration in the fall so as to arrive here in winter, amid many inconveniences, and also of the importance of guarding future emigration so as to find the best facilities. From this letter it appears, that a considerable emigration may be expected in the spring, most of which will be to this port, and some by the way of New Orleans to St. Louis. The mind of Ds. Scholte appears to be directed to settlement as far west as Wisconsin or Iowa. An association has been formed in [the provinces of] North and South Holland, Utrecht, etc., who have means in hand for a considerable purchase. Many of the emigrants will be poor, and it will be important to help them on their way with as little trouble and expense as practicable, and to guard them against imposition. I trust that Ds. van Raalte has recently written to Ds. Scholte in relation to his investigation and plans and that this will lead to a full concert in their operation. Ds. Scholte proposes leaving with his family about the first of April and may be expected here in May. We must wait till then to find the development of the course of settlement by the religious emigrants from Holland.

The committee make the following important suggestion, on the supposition that the location selected in Michigan will be the one in which the religious emigrants from Holland will centre: – "The emigration should, as far as practicable be directed to one point. New York is doubtless the most appropriate. At this, and if necessary at other ports on the Atlantic, there should be a committee to whose care the emigrants should be directed, and should help them, with such co-operation as may be required at Albany, as far as Buffalo. Here there should be an efficient and disinterested committee; great care should be taken in its selection. It is the point where there will be the most responsibility and the most danger. Then they speak of the routes for emigrants to reach the place of settlement, and then add, "some of us will at all times be prepared and willing to act. In every case, clear definite written contracts for their transportation etc., to be executed, and the evidence of them be preserved, and copies transmitted to the appropriate committees. On the Erie Canal and lakes, there is often great imposition."

The above suggestion is a most important one, and I submit it to the consideration of my Christian brethren in the ministry and in the Church, to organise at once such an efficient committee, ready, with the opening spring, to attend the case of emigrants that may arrive. It is evident that individuals cannot meet the exigencies which may occur. The excellent Christian brother, Mr. James Forrester, who has alone given so much time and pains to meet the wants of poor emigrants during the past winter, will gladly co-operate with other brethren who may be disegned. But it would not be practicable to do much, unaided, by every effort he might employ; and surely, after the burden he has borne during the last winter, so cheerfully and disinterestedly, he should be strongly aided. It has been my pleasure to come in contact with "God's poor blessed children" among these emigrants, to be the almoner of those kind friends who voluntarily and unsolicited sent in their contributions after reading the simple statement in the Intelligencer. At some future time I may relate some of these cases. In this, whatever time and care may have been called for, I have found a rich reward. I leave this matter of organizing a committee with my brethren.

This movement, in the emigration from Holland, is one of great interest. There is wisdom necessary in conducting it, and next summer will witness the character it will assume here. The interest in it has been felt and practically manifested in Evangelical christians of other denominations in Michigan. *Surely, surely*, it becomes the *Reformed Dutch Church in America*, in remembrance of her ancestry, and the common standards of faith and worship, to advance this movement with peculiar interest, and, as the providence of God may open the way, to throw in a large measure of sympathy and co-operation. We should bear in mind the appeal once made by Mordecai to Queen Esther: *For if thou altogether holdest thy peace at this time, then shall enlargement and deliverance arise to the Jews from another place, but thou and thy father's house shall be destroyed; and who knoweth whether thou art come to the Kingdom for such a time as this?*

T. d. W.

ACKNOWLEDGEMENT. – I acknowledge the receipt of the following sums, in addition to what I have before acknowledged, for the relief and benefit of poor worthy emigrants from Holland: – Mrs. M. F. T., $ 5; Miss. A. B., $ 10; Chas. C. Broadhead, of Utica, $ 20.

Thomas de Witt

March 10, 1847

J. The *Christian Intelligencer*, March 17, 1847

Mr. Editor: – I was gratified to find, by an article in your paper of the 11th inst., over the initials of our respected friend, the Rev. Thomas de Witt, that the emigrants from Holland can now be directed to a settlement of his countrymen under the charge of the Rev. Albertus C. van Raalte, in the State of Michigan. I am likewise very much pleased with the arrangements made for their reception, and the handsome manner in which Mr. Hoyt has come forward in the hour of need in behalf of Mr. van Raalte's settlement.

Allow me, Mr. Editor, to state what has been done by the *Netherlands*

Society for the Protection of Emigrants from Holland. At a late meeting of the directors of the Society, Pieter Hodenpyl, Esq., was appointed *General Agent*. This gentleman is to devote his whole time to attend to the best interests of the emigrants. The business of this Society will be transacted at the house, No. 114 Greenwich Street.

The Society, formed by natives of Holland, who have the interests of their countrymen at heart, had but a faint idea of the service the Society could render their countrymen. While every nation emigrating to this country was provided with organised societies for their protection, the Hollander alone has been at the mercy of those who would be most likely to deceive and mislead him.

When the Netherlands Society was formed it was more with the view of benefitting the countrymen who arrived, than those who were already among us. You will be surprised to learn that Mr. Hodenpyl's time has been almost exclusively employed attending to the interests of these people. He has proved a most vigilant and efficient officer of this Society. In no instant has an applicant been turned off without benefit of some sort. Some hundred and fifty have been aided and advised since the formation of this Society. Within the short period of eight or ten weeks, many, through the personal influence of Mr. Hodenpyl, have been provided with permanent situations; others, with farms to work on shares; mechanics furnished with employment; and female domestics with good places amongst respectable and pious families, where their morals will be properly cared for.

The agent has now on his books many applicants for farmers, mechanics and domestics. The Society will, however, use their best efforts to persuade the emigrants to emigrate to the West, as we believe their best interests will thus be consulted. The sick have been provided for by the Society; the destitute will be aided in reaching their adopted home; and those in good circumstances will be advised and directed.

The agent has made contracts with responsible persons, under bonds and penalties, well secured, for the fulfilment of their contracts, to convey emigrants to their distant homes without unnecessary delays. Baggage will be weighed by the agent, their weight marked on each pakage. No pains will be spared to guard the emigrants from impositions. The agent, will, in all cases, forward the emigrants with as little delay as their interests will require. Mr. Joseph Smith, a native Hollander, will, on the first day of May [1847] open a house for accomodating emigrants, at a very low charge, not to exceed 50¢ per day, or two dollars and fifty cents per week. He has for that purpose, taken a large and commodious house on the corner of Greenwich and Cedar Streets. He will give bonds for the proper treatment of persons recommended to him by the Society. Arrangements have also been made with consignees of vessels to prevent persons from boarding vessels other than those authorized by the Society.

The Society have entered into correspondence with eminent persons in Holland, to aid and advise the emigrants and prevent them from leaving Holland at the season of the year when they must remain in the city at expense and this expend the means to carry them into the interior. It would be much to the interest of emigrants not to go to New Orleans, as the expense to reach the West is greater than from this city and there is danger of reaching there at a sickly season. The heat even in May is greater than at any period of the summer in Holland. Besides, the Mississippi produces cholera, morbus, and many foreigners die ere they reach their location, while others are so debilitated as to be unfit for labor for months after their arrival. The agent is also in correspondence with influential persons in those towns through which the emigrant must pass on his way to the West. Five thousand Hollanders are soon expected to arrive. Five vessels are daily expected. The avenues to the West not being opened, the lakes still unnavigable, these emigrants will necessarily be detained here for some weeks. To provide for the needy, funds will be required – more than the Society can at present control. We trust that the wealthy descendants from Hollanders will promptly come to our aid, by becoming members, or by donations, to enable us to do the utmost good, to lighten the burden of our care for strangers in a strange land. We make this appeal with the more confidence, as we sincerely believe that they will never fall a charge to the Society a second time.

You will observe, Mr. Editor, that the wishes of the friends of the emigrants are already accomplished, and their interests properly cared for. We shall be happy to act in concert with any gentlemen who may take an interest in the matter. Any respectable person can become a member of the Society by paying annually in advance two dollars. This two dollars constitutes a life member. It is gratifying that while we have been employed in devising means to benefit the emigrants, they have not been neglected in the interior. We will give those engaged in this laudable undertaking of providing a home for the emigrant our hearty co-operation. Will you be kind enough, Mr. Editor, to call the attention of the public to the Society, and solicit funds, which should be sent to the agent, Mr. P. Hodenpyl, the Editor of the Christian Intelligencer, or the Rev. T. de Witt, particularly naming that it is for the "Netherlands Society for the Protection of Emigrants from Holland." By giving this an insertion in your valuable paper, and calling the attention of your readers to it, you will greatly aid the object of the Society.

John F. van Eden Hollermann
President of the Netherlands
Society

K. The *Christian Intelligencer*, March 25, 1847

In the last *Christian Intelligencer* is a communication from the "Netherland Society for the Protection of Emigrants," recently formed. The objects which they have in view are of great importance, viz., to guard the emigrants against imposition on their arrival here, provide suitable places for the passing accomodations, aid them in finding means of employment, and facilitate their removal westward, at the cheapest rates, which guards against imposition. In the prosecution of these objects, the Society deserves approbation and co-operation. It is under the direction of native Hollanders resident here. It appears from their statement, as well as from what we have learned from other sources, that a strong tide of emigration is setting in from Holland, and that large numbers may be expected in the course of this spring and summer. The scarcity now spread in various parts of Europe, increasing the strong pressure heretofore felt as to the means of living, will doubtless increase the spirit and amount of emigration from various quarters. Until, now, emigration from Holland has been quite limited, in very small numbers; but as the spirits is now awakened and extended, it is probable that larger numbers, promiscuously from various classes will leave for America. It is proper that I should distinctly state the precise object I have had in view, in the appeal to our Churches. Sometime since, a number of members of the Reformed Church adhering to the doctrines of the Reformation and the Standards of our Church, and who had separated from the Established Church [in Holland] on account of the pervading defection, entertained the purpose of removing to America and forming a settlement in one of our Western States, there organise their churches, etc. A pamphlet on this subject in the spring of 1846 at the close of which is an *Appeal to the Believers* [*de Geloovigen*] *in America*. That appeal, translated, was published in the *Christian Intelligencer* last fall. Late in the fall, at an unpropitious season, a considerable number of such emigrants arrived, some of whom reached Michigan and Buffalo, a considerable number remained in Albany, and also a considerable number in this city. Intimations of a large number of this character ready to emigrate in the spring, have been given. The appeal to our Church, on account of our ancestry and common faith and standards, has been felt as a strong one. The contributions which have been furnished have enabled us to administer to the cases of pressing want and affliction and will be so appropriated to those here remaining or who may hereafter arrive. It is important that this precise point connected with the appeals I have made, and to which, without personal solicitation in any case, such kind responses have been given, should be kept in mind. The "Netherland Society," just formed, occupies broader grounds as to the whole emigration which may occur. The measures for protection and counsel which they propose, are important, and as such the religious emigrants of the Reformed faith to whom we advert, may take the advantage of. The position occupied by the "Netherland Society" is therefor an important one in the prosecution of the measures proposed, and commends itself to the favorable consideration of the community.

T. d. W.

ACKNOWLEDGEMENT. – I acknowledge the receipt for the relief of the poor worthy emigrants from Holland, collected from the following persons: Rev. D. Ch. Hopewell, Rev. A. P., $ 5; J. P., $ 5; R. C. V. W., $ 5; Mrs. A. R. S., $ 5; J. P. L., $ 5; P. A., $ 3; T. J. V. W., $ 3; I. R. A., $ 2; J. A., $ 2; V. W. B., $ 2; P. N. B., $ 1; A. H., $ 1; cash 25ℓ ; making the sum of $ 41.25. Also $ 10 from S. B., of Kingston, Ulster Co.,; and $ 5 from a lady member of the Collegiate Church.

Thomas de Witt

March 22, 1847

L. The *Christian Intelligencer*, May 6, 1847

Messrs. Editors: – Hoping that there are some yet among our denomination who would gladly aid the Hollanders, whom a kind Providence, has cast on our shores, permit me, through the medium of your columns, to say, that there is now a most pressing need of the exercise, of their benevolence. There is now, and has been for some time, a most painful state of want among these devoted brethern. Their provisions have failed them, and *some have been subsisting on bran*. If this state of things continue, they will be scattered over the land, and become the prey of every rogue in whose hands they may chance to fall, or if they remain, Black River must afford them only a resting place for their bones. The sufferings which they, and especially their selfdenying leader, have already endured, in erecting their temporary dwellings on the ground chosen as their new home, have been exceedingly great. And such they must necessarily continue to be, even under the most favorable circumstances with which their settlement can be made. The settlers in the neighboring region have acted a generous part toward them, and many are still willing to do for them; but owing to the difficulty of access to them, and their destitution of means of conveyance, a great portion of the generous aid offered to them is of no avail. *They must buy at their* nearest village, which is some twenty miles distant, and then be conveyed to their settlement, in the midst of a forest.

The circumstances are such as will render any donation, though as small as the widow's mite, a matter worthy of a cheerful acceptance. Cannot, and will not, the pastors of the churches scattered through the country, act as agents, and make an effort for them? Or shall we suffer them, to our reproach, to perish in our midst, and thus fulfill the predictions of their oppressors at home? "Whose hath this world's good, and seeth his brother have need, and shutteth up his bowels of compassion from him, how dwelleth the love of God in him?"

Yours, in haste,

A. B. Taylor

Grand Rapids, April 26, 1847
Donations may be left with Rev. Dr. de Witt, of New York, or at this office. – Ed.

M. The *Christian Intelligencer*, May 13, 1847

A number of communications have recently appeared in the *Intelligencer*, upon the subject of the present unusual emigration from Holland to this country. The most of these, however, have appeared over a single respected name; so that while they have exhibited the great importance of the subject, they have afforded but an imperfect test of the extent of the interest it has awakened. A proper sympathy in the embarrassments of a stranger in a strange land has indeed been exhibited in the formation of the *Netherland Society for the Protection of Emigrants*, which was noticed some weeks since, and in the donations of individuals, which have been ackowledged from time to time. But there is a peculiar ecclesiastical sympathy demanded by the movement, which notwithstanding the appeals of the earnest writer alluded to, seems to have been, as yet withheld. Upon this point I wish to make a few remarks. The agency which these emigrants may be made to exert in extending the bounds and influence of our Church, should make them objects of the deepest interest of all who have her welfare at heart.

It is familiarly known that attempts have been making, through a long course of years, to effect the establishment of the Reformed Dutch Church in some of our Western States; and whatever may be the ultimate success of those attempts, it is also well known that one difficulty has constantly threatened their failure. We have always wanted proper material upon which to work. We are the "Dutch" Church; and the Dutch Church I hope we may continue to be, so long as the memory or ouf origin can be perpetuated. Yet this name with the character which accompanies it, has always retarded our growth among the heterogeneous population of the West. Presbyterian, Methodist, Baptist churches spring up everywhere and flourish. Our missionaries have preached, and surely with as great talent as the missionaries of either of those other churches, and what is the result? Their congregations ard yet without exception, dependent upon the society whose benevolence called them into existence. A few families from New York or New Jersey have constituated a nucleus at each station, which has throughout grown but little. These remarks are far from being designed to question the propriety of continuing the present efforts, but only to exhibit the two things of which I spoke: our Church's desire to extend its limits; and the difficulty which has always interfered with the accomplishment of that desire. The desire certainly remains. Who of us does not wish to see the Reformed Dutch Church exerting its wholesome influence among the various elements of this order which will long continue to convulse the West? Is it not something, then, that the difficulty is removed, that the very material for which we have so long been wishing, are gathering themselves at the very point where we wish to employ them? The descendants of Hollanders among ourselves, the writer proceeds, will, with few exceptions, continue to cultivate the rich land, which their ancestors have the judgment to select. But Holland itself freights its ships with pioneers, and sends pious men, with their ministers, to occupy our desolate places. Here is the wonder of the movement; they are pious men. An evangelical party, we are informed, has recently separated from the corrupted Church in Holland. And these are the men who are now emigrating to the United States. They come just as our forefathers came three hundred years ago, bearing the same name, speaking the same language, cherishing the same Bible, and catechism, and confession; to do for the heart of our country what they did for its shores to soften the wilderness into the garden of the Lord. They seek, indeed, homes of comfort. So did the first pilgrims. But, like them, they have for the great object of their search "freedom to worship God." We are not to look upon them, therefore, as mere adventurers;

they are God's instruments for doing this work, and, so far as we are
laboring to establish the Church which we love, in our Western States,
they are our helpers. The passage of years will work the same changes in
their case, which have been wrought in our own. The language which
they bring with them will be exchanged for the prevailing language of
our country; and the Reformed Dutch Church, firmly grounded in a
colony of Hollanders, will be prepared to make adherents of those who
are of a different ancestry. Now let those who have been contributing and
laboring for years in behalf of the Western Mission of our Church, decide
whether this movement has not the strongest claims upon their sympathy.
Surely it cannot be a little thing in the view of the Christian of any name,
that among the armies of errorists which are swarming our shores, there
is a band of five thousand that love the true doctrine of the Cross. But
especially does it concern us, that they come to extend our names, our
institutions, and our faith. But what shall we do? Does the matter require
action? Yes. Let us first arouse ourselves to a proper appreciation of the
importance of the movement. If any are sympathizing in these views, let
them make an expression of their sympathy. The subject has been before
us for months; but either the Church has felt no interest in it or it has
maintained a strange disguise of indifference. Nothing has been done,
except by two or three individuals interested in the object, and the few
who have made them their laborious almoners. But, more than this,
nothing has even been said. So far we seem in this matter to be encouraging the standing reproach upon the character of the Dutch Church,
that it does not become in earnest till the time for action is past.

If we become in earnest upon this subject we shall find something to
do. The immigrants of whom we speak are the cheapest missionaries,
they support themselves. But they need to be established. There are rigors
inseparable attending the early settlement of the colony in the wilderness.
Cannot something be done toward softening these? If there can, let us
not be backward in attempting it. We have it in our power to aid at the
moment of their greatest difficulty, those, who, when once established,
will never cease to be a blessing to ourselves. Let us not draw back from
the work. Let it not be said, that while other denominations will compass
sea and land to make their proselytes, the members of the Reformed Dutch
Church have not enough regard for their origin, nor love of their name,
nor love of their faith, to lend a helping hand to their own brethren, when
they come to advance the interest of their own religion.

4. AREND JAN BRUSSE'S REMINISCENCES

[The following document relating to emigration from Arnhem to Milwaukee, Wisconsin, in 1846 fills an important place in this collection. It tells how the Dutch immigrant's first attention was focused upon Milwaukee before it was diverted to Michigan by Van Raalte. This account, based upon a manuscript preserved in the Netherlands Museum, was first published in the *Wisconsin Magazine of History*, XXIX (1946).]

When I was a young man, aged about twenty-two years, from what I noticed of the general condition of the class of people to whom I belonged, I plainly saw that my temporal prospects for life were not very promising in the Netherlands; and so I concluded to go to America, if I possibly could get there. I then had no idea that my parents and the rest of my family would break up and also go to America; but my mother, not being willing to let me go alone, induced father that we all go together. Our family consisted of father and mother: Jan Brusse, and his wife Grada, with their seven children, Arend Jan, Gerrit Jan, Dersse, Willem, Berend, Janna, and Hendrik.

On the first day of June 1846 we left our home at Dinxperloo, province of Gelderland, for Rotterdam; by way of Arnhem and the Rhine. At Rotterdam we took passage on the sailing vessel *De Hollander*. There were 100 passengers on board, of whom one-half were Hollanders; the others were Germans. Of the ten families of Hollanders seven came from Aalten, Varseveld, and Dinxperloo, from what is known as de Achterhoek. The others came from Velp near Arnhem and from the province of Zeeland.

Of the many Hollanders on board the ship I had only been intimately acquainted with Rademaker and family, from Varseveld. He was one of the elders of the Reformed [*Afgescheiden*] Church of Varseveld, a gifted and devout Christian. Of this church I had been a catechumen till I left for America, and of which I still retain many blessed memories. On board the ship everything was about as inconvenient and as untidy or dirty as it could be. We were herded together almost like cattle. We had to provide our own provisions for the voyage. There was little chance for cooking. The stove, or range, or whatever you might call it, had only two or three holes, where the many families could do their cooking. The water for drinking and cooking was nasty. I yet imagine that I can smell it. Those who did attempt cooking on the stove were not always particular about the fire. At one time through someone's carelessness the ship took fire, and but for its timely discovery might have turned out very serious. We had only one severe storm that was considered really dangerous.

There was no death, nor any serious sickness among the passengers, and when we left the ship there was one more passenger than when we boarded it.

After being forty days on the Atlantic Ocean we landed at Boston. Our aim, and that of the seven families mentioned above, was to reach Milwaukee, Wisconsin. But how to get there was a serious question. There we were, strangers in a strange land; we understood nobody, and nobody understood us. I could speak a little German, and so could Roelof Sleijster, one of our fellow passengers. Well, as best we could we made a bargain with a German agent to get us to Milwaukee. Through our ignorance we knew nothing of the route we were to travel. This was in 1846, hence we were among the very first that left old Holland to open the way to the West.

At Boston we were put into the cars of a freight train that slowly took us to Albany. Arriving at Albany we had to stay there for a day, and stopped at a German hotel. While there the Rev. Dr. Isaac N. Wyckoff passed by. Hearing us speaking Dutch, he stopped and took some of us to his home. There Sleijster who had been a theological student at Arnhem gave Dr. Wyckoff a letter from the Rev. A. C. van Raalte and the Rev. A. Brummelkamp [dated Arnhem, June 1846] directed *Aan de Geloovigen in de Vereenigde Staten van Noord-Amerika* [To the Faithful in the United States of North America]. Through this medium the Hollanders became acquainted with the Reformed Church in America.

At Albany we got on an immigrant canal boat. The horses going nearly always on a walk; in the day time, I walked a good deal of the time by the side of the boat. It was a slow and tedious way of traveling. Our daily fare on the boat was bread and milk, which we bought along the route of the canal. After being a week on the canal boat we reached Buffalo. From there, as steerage passengers on a steamer, we came to Milwaukee late in July 1846.

The only Hollander we met in Milwaukee was a saloonkeeper by the name of Wessink. He told us that times in Milwaukee were dull and advised us to go into the country among the farmers. There was a farmer at his place from near Kenosha who had come to Milwaukee for help on his big farm, or farms, it being wheat harvest time. Through this Holland saloonkeeper we made a bargain with the farmer. He promised to give us work through the harvest, and after that was finished we were to continue working for him, or take his farm and work it. We hired a team and followed the farmer to within sight of Kenosha, where at the semblage of a house, we unloaded our goods and took possession.

This farmer had a large field of wheat. He was to give every one of the family work, or to those of us that could work. He tried us, to see what we could do. My brother Gerrit did not like the appearance of things; so he went to work for another farmer. The rest of us were set to work. I and two other hands were sent into the fields with cradles to cut grain; it was the hardest work I ever did. I found that this farmer was a dishonest rascal. When his grain was cut, we had to leave, without getting a cent for our hard and honest work. We again hired teams and went back to Milwaukee. By this time our purse was getting light and I had to do something. I got work tending a bricklayer, made mortar, carried brick, etc.; and again I was cheated out of my pay.

In Milwaukee I had become acquainted with a Zeelander, a painter, by the name of Lukwilder, who had been in this country for years. He persuaded me to go into the painting business with his boss, and I did so. After having worked at this for a number of weeks, painting made me sick and I had to quit. Again I got no pay for this work. I felt that I was yet far from the promised land. In fact I was almost ready to exclaim, as I later heard Dominie Hendrik Geert Klijn exclaim [the gentle dominie] when a boat of Hollanders destined for Holland, Michigan, stopped at Milwaukee longer than he thought necessary, and he seemed to think there was a sinister motive in this delay, "O dit goddelooze Amerika" [Oh this wicked America!]

Milwaukee was then a town of 6,000 people. On the Northwest part of the town away from the Milwaukee River bottoms [which then were covered with stumps, and in the spring stood under water, but now form the center of that beautiful city] there was a commons where most of the Hollanders who had come with us across the sea were living in cabins. So we settled there. I helped build our cabin 16 feet square, out of rough common lumber. The boards were lapped and nailed on like siding, without anything else being added inside or out, and the roof was of the same material. There was also a so-called upstairs which was reached by climbing a homemade ladder. Not much of a manse this – and it was certainly an uncomfortable dwelling during a storm or in weather below zero.

We few Hollanders there keenly felt being deprived of the public ministry of the gospel of Jesus Christ to which we had been accustomed in Holland. As a substitute I suggested to our Holland friends that we meet on Sunday afternoons for worship in our cabin. To this they all agreed. This was the beginning of social life and public religious meetings among the Hollanders of Milwaukee.

Aside from prayer and song and the reading of Scripture, I made use of a volume of Hellenbroek's sermons from which some sermon was read. This certainly was a day of small things as far as means and outward form are concerned, but God's presence surely was felt.

Later in the fall of this same year, 1846, other families of Hollanders from the Old Country came to Milwaukee, so that by winter we had quite a settlement of Hollanders *op den Hollandschen berg* ["on Dutch hill"] as the Hollanders used to call it. I do not know who was the owner of that land, but we were not disturbed.

A great bereavement befell us – my mother, who for years had been in poor health, died in October, three months after our landing. Care of the family devolved upon my sister Dersse, now Mrs. William Giebink of Waupun, Wisconsin, the only one of us children except the writer now living. On October 9, 1850, my father died from the effects of cholera which at that time was prevalent in many parts of the country. So after a short stay, after great privations and many hardships incident to a new country, both parents passed away.

That first winter in Milwaukee I had no steady employment, but my brother Gerrit who was a tailor readily got all the work he could do. In the summer of 1847, the Rev. Pieter Zonne with a number of families came from The Netherlands to Milwaukee. We rented a hall, and for over a year he preached to the Hollanders without pay. Zonne was certainly a talented preacher, whose ministry I greatly enjoyed. The population of Hollanders *op den Hollandschen berg* kept increasing all the time I lived in Milwaukee, but all of them were comparatively poor. In Scripture parlance, they were the hewers of wood and drawers of water for the well-to-do Yankees.

In Milwaukee I kept working at whatever I could find. Soon I began to go to an evening school, and for two years I attended a collegiate institute. It was my desire to enter the ministry of the gospel. I was given the opportunity to study at the Rochester University and Theological Seminary. There I was ordained to the ministry of the gospel of Jesus Christ. God indeed has ever been good to me.

Before I left Milwaukee in 1850 the Hollanders had learned that Uncle Sam had cheap and fertile lands which invited occupation. Some accordingly left for the timber lands of Sheboygan County, where they each claimed a quarter section of land. These Hollanders at once started to turn the wilderness into fruitful fields and in time came to own their splendid farms.

When I left Milwaukee *de Hollandsche berg* began to assume a different

appearance. Streets were laid out, lots were sold cheap, the humble cabins
of the first pioneers were replaced by more pretentious and desirable
dwellings, and we Hollanders realized that we really had come to a better
country. We have great reason to be thankful to our heavenly Father for
having led us to this land of plenty.

Now at the age of eighty – five years as I look back with my mind's
eye to the first Hollanders as they came to this country, most of them
poor, uneducated, and lacking in practically all of the civilities of
American social life, I see them and their children, educated, enterprising,
thrifty, and prosperous, equal in every way in social as well as in business
life to any class of people in this broad land. May God continue to bless
the Hollanders and their descendants in America, who remain true to the
faith of our fathers.

P.S.   I ought to state by way of explanation, that as my life and labors
were among English-speaking people who pronounced my name "Bruce"
instead of "Brusse", the newer spelling and pronunciation were adopted.
Letters addressed to "Brusse" were invariably returned to the sender and
for that reason I chose the form "Bruce".

5. HENRY COOK'S AUTOBIOGRAPHICAL SKETCH

[This autobiographical sketch by Henry Cook, or Hendrik Kok, who accompanied Van
Raalte on the *Southerner* in 1846, written more than fifty years after the event, reproduces
faithfully some of the experiences of Van Raalte's band of pioneer imigrants. Henry Cook
died on April 30, 1919.]

The folowing is a short story of my life. I was born on March 11, 1831,
near Hardenburg in the Province Overijsel in Netherlands. This is near
the German Hanover. Father owned a small farm. The country at that
place was a sandy upland and poor. Much of the uncultivated land in
those parts is covered with heather, as in Scotland, from four to six feet
tall. It has a beautiful purple blossom and provides a fairly good pasture
for young stock, but it is a poor milk producer.

During 1845 and 1846 there was a good deal of unrest because of
religious repression. Times were hard so that the common people could
scarcely provide for their families. A large company of these people made
plans to emigrate to America under the leadership of Dominie A. C. van
Raalte. Uncle Egbert Dunnewind, Hendrik Oldemeyer, and other
neighbors sold their possessions and prepared to leave friends and fatherland in the hope of bettering their lot and especially provide their children
a chance in life. This was in the fall of 1846. So we started for Rotterdam,
and, travelling mostly by water, passed near The Hague. Although we

did not enter the city we saw from a distance its streets lined with beautiful groves and shade trees.

When we arrived at Rotterdam we found people from various parts of the Netherlands ready to embark under the leadership of Van Raalte. We were about a hundred in number. This was the first shipload of emigrants who were destined to begin the founding of the Holland settlement in Western Michigan. Our ship of three masts, the *Southerner*, to us looked large enough to plough through the waves with ease. But we soon discovered this belief was ill founded.

We sailed from Rotterdam on September 24, 1846. After sailing 54 days we landed in New York a little after dark. I was eager to step ashore, but mother said, "No, we are in a strange land; you must wait till morning." A woman, one of our group, died in mid ocean, and was wrapped in blankets and lowered into the water. Our captain was an American whose home was in Baltimore. From him and the sailors we learned a litte English. Each morning the sailors distributed water. The heads of families stepped forward in turn and received an amount in proportion to the size of their households. I remember how one morning when father's turn came he said, "Negen". The man passing out the water said "Why don't you say, 'nine?'". When the weather was calm dominie and Mrs. van Raalte and the captain would sit in front of the cabin and sing hymns. One I remember ended with the words:

> O that will be joyful to part no more
> on Canaans's happy shore!

I never forgot these words even though at the time I did not know their meaning.

In a day or two we left New York for Buffalo and from there by railroad to Detroit. On a Sunday our train stopped at a town and some of our company got off to see what the place was like. Our train started leaving us behind. Not knowing what to do, we walked about and passing a church we noticed some men standing outside it. We went to them and tried to tell them about our trouble, but they could not understand us. So one of the men took some silver money from his pocket and offered it to us. But we protested we were no beggars. Finally they seemed to understand our plight and put us on the next train which came along and overtook the train which was carrying the rest of our group.

At Detroit we stayed for a while. A kindly gentleman, Mr. Theodore Romeyn of Dutch descent had been notified of our coming. He took us to a large building, a kind of hotel in which we were assigned a large upper room. When Sunday came we found time dragging heavily and so sent a committee to order a good dinner. But we waited a long time expecting to be called. So we sent down another committee to see why we had to wait. They were told that the first committee had ordered no dinner. So we had much trouble with the English language; the older ones of our company made slow progress, but the youngsters learned quickly.

From Detroit we went to St. Clair where we spent most of the winter. The first night in St. Clair we witnessed a heavy snowstorm. In the morning I saw cows with bells wading in the snow, which I disapproved of strongly because in Holland cows were kept in warm stables and were given warm drink in very cold weather. A large steamboat was under construction in St. Clair, and the men in our group were given such work in the boat yard as they could perform, and so they were able to support their families.

In St. Clair I learned a little more English. One time I accompanied some of our men to a blacksmith shop in order to grind an axe. A boy and a man were standing idly in the shop; they looked at us with some curiosity and the man said to the boy, "Kick him!" The boy's boot hit my shins, which made such an impression that I never forgot the meaning of that simple word. I have frequently wondered what ever became of that rude man and boy. But on the whole the people were very kind to us.

We stayed in St. Clair until some time in February 1847 if I recall correctly. Van Raalte who had gone on ahead after leaving his family in Detroit wrote to us from Allegan, where he had during most of the time been a guest of John R. Kellog, that he had secured a location on Black Lake between Grand River and Kalamazoo River and asked us to proceed to Allegan by way of Kalamazoo. So we were loaded into sleighs [if I recall correctly we were five families at that time] and were taken to Detroit where our good friend Mr. Romeyn again greeted us. After staying in Detroit a day or two we proceeded to Kalamazoo where we arrived on a Saturday evening. The Rev. Mr. Ova P. Hoyt, a Presbyterian clergyman, who had been notified of our coming took us to a general store. Some kindly ladies brought us food sufficient to last over Sunday. Monday morning the owners opened their store. Our party bought some things for our use after which we left in sleighs for Allegan. At noon we stopped for lunch in Otsego, but I have forgotten who paid for it. Toward evening we came in sight of Allegan, a very small and quiet town. There was but one house on what we now call the Southside; it was where the Oliver home now stands. The first object to attract my eye was the steeple of the Presbyterian church, like many spires we had seen in every small town or village while travelling westward. We were taken to John R. Kellog's house after which he conducted us to a vacant house on the corner of North Cedar and Monroe Streets, where the Episcopal rectory now stands. Here we stayed for sometime during which food was provided by the Kellog home.

After a brief stay we left Allegan by sleigh and set out for what was to be the Holland Colony on Black Lake. Men had been sent some time before this from Allegan in oder to build some shanties for the first families to occupy until they could secure land and build their own homes. The road to Saugatuck was fairly good. But beyond Well's tannery in that place we had to make our way through the virgin forest for some ten miles. We stayed in Saugatuck while the men went out each day through the deep snow, finding land for their families. During this time we were dependent on supplies brought by oxen from Allegan. These ox teams were welcome when our povisions ran low.

I remember how one day when father and I and some other men, after working a whole day on what were to be our new homes returned by way of the Indian village on Black Lake. We wanted some flour but found it hard to make the Indians understand what we wanted. But after making some signs they understood us and gave us a small quantity of it. Father secured 40 acres on the county line between Ottawa and Allegan counties, twenty acres in Holland Township and twenty in Laketown Township. I helped my father build a shanty which was to serve as a home. This was in the spring of 1847. Sometime in April or May I went to Allegan in order to earn money for the support of our family.

In Allegan I first worked for Mr. John R. Kellog. During the fall my brother John and I worked for farmers digging potatoes and husking corn. During the winter of 1847-48 I worked for Mr. Wilkes, doing chores and helping in his hardware store. They were fine people and very good to me. But I did not like to get up early in the morning to start the fire and do other things. Accordingly I made an agreement with another Dutch boy – Engbertus van der Veen who now lives in Holland – whereby he was to do the household chores every other morning. In his very first turn Engbertus, seeing nothing handy in which to remove the ashes, used the wash basin. That proved the last and only morning I could sleep a little late, for Mr. Wilkes made it very clear to me that I was the one to start the fire in the morning.

By this time I had learned enough English to understand what was said, but there were times when I failed to grasp the meaning of words. Thus one day Mr. Wilkes said to me, jokingly, "Henry, do you know what horse-radish is?" "Yes sir, I think so." "Well," he said, "it is what you put on a horse when you hitch him to a wagon!" Luckily they did send me for some horse-radish that day. Next I went to live for a while with Judge Ely. Mrs. Ely was of Dutch descent and spoke our language so that our Hollanders called upon Mr. and Mrs. Ely for advice. The judge, a very good man, helped our people in many ways. In 1852 I went to work for Mr. N. B. West in a sash and door factory and stayed with him until 1890 when Mr. Baker and I bought him out. After a while Hiram and George de Sano joined our business whereupon we began to manufacture furniture. In 1900 I sold my interst in the firm to them.

Father in the fall of 1847 built a good log house with a cellar under it. He overworked, fell sick just as our family moved in, and died on December 29, 1847. Thereupon we brought our mother to Allegan where she died in August 29, 1861. Our only sister, Hermina, also died in Allegan, on October 11, 1849. Two little brothers, Harm Jan and Jan Harm, about three and six years respectively died in the summer of 1847. Brother John died in Allegan in August 1898.

Chapter II

BEGINNINGS OF HOLLAND, MICHIGAN 1847

6. EGBERT FREDERIKS' PIONEER MEMORIES

[Egbert Frederiks (d. October 11, 1888) from Noord Barge near Emmen in the province of Drente accompanied Van Raalte to America in 1846. His account, *Pionier Herinneringen*, written in 1881, presents much reliable information about the early history of Dutch Settlement in Michigan. The text of this article appeared in the *Jaarboekje van de Hollandsche Christelijke Gereformeerde Kerk voor het Jaar* 1882 (Grand Rapids 1881), and was reprinted in *De Grondwet*, December 20, 1910.]

Meermalen opgewekt op mijne levenservaringen op reis naar Amerika, en uit onze eerste tijden van ons verblijf alhier iets mede te deelen, gevoelde ik wel de lust en zag ik wel het nut er van in, vooral ook ter herinnering aan ons opkomend geslacht; maar als ik er mij toe zette ontzonk mij soms de moed omdat ik het niet konde doen zooals ik wel wilde en de zaak het wel vorderde. Doch als nu al onze oude settlers zoo denken en doen als ik reeds telang gedacht en gedaan heb, vrees ik dat veel aan de vergetelheid zal overgegeven worden, wat toch wel waardig is in gedachtenis te blijven. Ik wensch van mijne ervaringen in alle eenvoudigheid mede te deelen zoo goed ik het kan, en hoop dat anderen er door opgewekt mogen worden om de hunne mede te deelen, wellicht dragen wij dan op die wijze iets bij tot een leerzame geschiedenis van onze Hollandsche nederzetting in het land onzer vreemdelingschap, onzen God tot eer, en onzen kinderen en volgende geslachten misschien tot een groot nut en genot.

Het was in het jaar 1846, dat door het schrijven van eenige leeraars in de Christelijke Gereformeerde Kerk in Nederland, over het wenschelijke eener emigratie naar Noord Amerika, bij velen de genegenheid en lust ontwaakte om daaraan gevolg te geven. Een werkje van de leeraars Ds. A. C. van Raalte, Ds. A. Brummelkamp, en Ds. H. P. Scholte kwam ook mij en mijne vrouw in handen, en had de uitwerking op ons beiden, dat wij van stonden aan met die zaak werkzaam werden en gedurig gedrongen werden om den Heere te vragen, wat wij hadden te doen. Toen onze familie en vrienden hiermede bekend werden, ontbrak het niet aan afrading en tegenstand, doch als wij hen dan mededeelden, wat er in ons omging, hoe wij er onder verkeerden, en wat reden ons bewogen, dan zeiden zij tenslotte: „Welnu! gij moet het dan ook maar zelve weten." Toch ging het niet gemakkelijk om tot een besluit te komen. Wij beseften

ten volle, dat er groote bezwaren aan de gewichtige onderneming verbonden waren. Wendden wij ons dan met dezelve in den gebede tot God,
dan gevoelden wij telkens een nieuwe aandrang van op te trekken, en
kwamen eindelijk tot het besliste besluit, om onder opzien tot den Heere,
om Zijne leiding en ondersteuning, de groote reis te ondernemen.

Wij woonden te Noord Barge, gemeente Emmen, provincie Drente.
Wij hadden het genoegen, dat Evert Zagers en vrouw met ons in hetzelfde geval verkeerden en gelijktijdig met ons tot hetzelfde besluit
kwamen. Wij vertrokken te zamen van Noord Barge over Koevorden
naar Hasselt, 3 uur van Zwolle aan het Zwarte Water in Overijsel gelegen. Daar was Ds. W. H. Frieling toen voorganger bij de gemeente,
door wien wij in alle liefde werden ontvangen, maar waar ons een zware
beproeving overkwam. Mijne vrouw, doorgaans zwak, werd zoo ongesteld, dat wij dachten, dat zij sterven zou. Wij werden radeloos. De tijd
van vertrek van Rotterdam, waar wij Ds. van Raalte dachten te ontmoeten, en met wien wij reizen zouden, was bepaald. Op aanraden van
broeder Zagers en de andere vrienden, vroeg ik mijne vrouw wat wij
zouden doen? „Wel", zeide zij, „kiest de gebaande wegen." Zij bedoelde
daarmede de reis voort te zetten. In eene groote ziekenstoel werd zij in
het schip gebracht, en daar op een bed gelegd, en naast haar een ziekelijk
kindje. Dat was eene zware beproeving, maar de Heere maakte het zoo
wel, dat toen wij te Rotterdam aankamen, mijne vrouw weer volkomen
hersteld was. Dat wij toen zeer verblijd waren en vroegen, „Wat zullen wij
den Heere vergelden voor Zijne weldaden?" laat zich gemakkelijk begrijpen.

Te Rotterdam vonden wij, volgens afspraak, Ds. van Raalte met de
zijnen en andere vrienden van verschillende plaatsen, die de reis zouden
mede maken. Van Rotterdam tot Hellevoetsluis, zoo lang wij tusschen de
vaste wallen door voeren hadden wij weinig kreuk; maar toen wij van
Hellevoet maar pas in zee waren, werd de eene na de andere zeeziek,
zoodat bijna geen enkele der passagiers frisch bleef. Doch dat was het
ergste niet. Toen wij 14 dagen op zee waren geweest stierf ons zieke kind,
en nu moesten wij zien, dat het lijkje in zee werd neegelaten. Dat was een
gevoelige smart voor het ouderhart. Doch de Heere gaf ons met onderwerping te mogen zeggen: „Hij doet wat goed is in Zijne oogen." Broeder
Evert Zagers trof nog eene zwaardere slag; zijne vrouw, anders zoo
frisch en in staat anderen te dienen, werd ziek en stierf, haren man als
weduwnaar met een zeer jong kind op den grooten Oceaan, op reis naar
een vreemd land, achterlatende. Wat indruk dat sterfgeval op bijna alle
schepelingen uitoefende, laat zich begrijpen. Doch de Heere sterkte ook
Zagers in zijn lot.

Na zeven lange weken op zee doorgebracht te hebben [wij deden de reis met een zeilschip] kwamen wij eindelijk behouden te New York aan. Spoedig werden wij gewaar, dat wij in een vreemd land waren, waar alles ons vreemd voorkwam, maar ook dat wij als een zeer vreemd soort van menschen werden aangezien. Vooral onze kleeding, inzonderheid onzer vrouwen groote gluiphoeden, die zij toen nog droegen, verschafte ons veel bekijks. Gelukkig konden wij niet verstaan wat men al van ons zeide, maar ongelukkig konden wij ons niet doen verstaan om iets te koopen, zoodat het groote moeite baarde om met alles klaar te komen. Hadden wij Ds. van Raalte niet tot leidsman gehad en die niet weder zijne vrienden, zooals Ds. de Wit en anderen, dan hadden wij ons onmogelijk weten te redden. Nu kwam met 's Heeren hulp toch alles terecht.

Van New York vervolgden wij onze reis met eene stoomboot naar Albany. Na op de boot gegeten te hebben, vertrokken wij per spoortrein van daar naar Rochester, waar wij een nacht overbleven. Verder reisden wij per spoor naar Buffalo, waar wij weder overnachten moesten. Daar het in November en koud en er geen kachel in de cars was, zaten wij te bibberen van de koude totdat wij in eene daar tegen ons overstaande spoorwagen eene kachel ontdekten, die aanmaakten, en ons daarbij verwarmden. Te Rochester geraakte Ds. van Raalte in moeite met een Duitscher, over de vracht van een trunk, waarmede de Duitscher echter doorging. Van daar reisden wij naar Detroit, waar wij veertien dagen zijn gebleven. 't Was koud, wij waren de eerste nacht in een pakhuis gelogeerd, maakten van onze kisten een bedroom, zoo goed wij konden, maar leden dien nacht veel van de koude. Den volgenden morgen betrokken wij met vier huisgezinnen een klein huisje. Als wij 's avonds onze bedden hadden uitgespreid was er de geheele vloer mede bedekt. De levensmiddelen waren er goedkoop. Wij gaven vier dollars voor een barrel meel en betaalden maar anderhalve cent voor een pond vleesch. Brandhout moesten wij duur betalen, veertien shillings voor 't cord.

De kapitein der boot, waarmede wij van Buffalo gekomen waren, liet te St. Clair eene nieuwe stoomboot bouwen. Hij onzen behoeftigen toestand merkende, stelde ons voor, om met hem mede te gaan, om bij hem te werken. Onze verdiensten zouden zijn: huisvesting, de kost, brandhout, een en ander uit den winkel, en ieder een paar laarzen. [Tot nu toe hadden wij altijd nog klompen gedragen.] Wij besloten met ons 10 huisgezinnen om mede te gaan. Voor woning was er een oud pakhuis voor ons in gereedheid gemaakt, dat wij betrokken. Er werkten zoo ongeveer 30 man op die werf, bij welke wij zoo wat dribbeljongens waren en het om loopend werk verrichtten. Op zekeren dag waren wij daar getuige van een droevig ongeluk. Twee mannen stonden te zagen aan een lang en zwaar stuk hout op schragen, de onderste zager wilde het met een handspaak van elkander buigen, maar het hout slipte van de schraag en viel op den man, dat hij onmidellijk dood was. De man liet eene vrouw, en zes kinderen na. Nadat zijn lijk bij zijne weduwe te huis was gebracht werd het werk gestaakt en des avonds eene lijkrede gehouden, waarvan wij echter niets konden verstaan. De kapitein, die zich over ons had ontfermt, bleek ook bij deze gelegenheid een goed man te zijn. Hij schonk de bedroefde weduwe dadelijk $ 200.

Terwijl wij naar St. Clair vertrokken, was Ds. van Raalte, na eenig toeven te Detroit, verder doorgereisd naar het doel waarop het gemunt was. In Januari ontvingen wij een brief van hem, dat hij ons wenschte te zien om de voorgenomen plannen met 's Heeren zegen ten uitvoer te brengen. Met vijf huisgezinnen besloten wij om dadelijk aan zijne uitnoodiging gevolg te geven. Per slede reisden wij weder naar Detroit, ontvingen daar van Mr. Theodore Romeyn, een man van Hollandsche afkomst, die ook Hollandsch verstond, eenige inlichting en aanbeveling aan Ds. [Ova P.] Hoyt te Kalamazoo. Van Detroit reisden wij met het spoor naar Kalamazoo. Met eenige moeite gelukte het ons Ds. Hoyt te vinden, die na den brief van Mr. Romeyn gezien te hebben, dadelijk vrouwen en kinderen van het station liet halen en zorgde, dat wij allen des nachts uitnemend verzorgd werden. Ach wat waren die menschen goed voor ons! Zij zorgden voor alles, zelfs voor de reis naar Allegan, die per slede moest gedaan worden en dat alles behoefde ons niets te kosten. Hoe gaarne wilden wij met hen spreken, maar wij konden niet. Den volgenden morgen bedankten wij hen, zoo goed wij konden, zeer hartelijk voor de liefde ons bewezen en reisden verder met de slede, die Ds. Hoyt voor ons besteld had, over Otsego naar Allegan. Daar was Ds. van Raalte met vrouw en kinderen bij Mr. [John R.] Kellog gelogeerd Van weerszijden blijde, dat wij elkander weder zagen, werden wij zeer vriendelijk ontvangen. 't Was Zaterdag avond. Men herbergde ons uitmuntend tot Maandag, toen betrokken wij te zamen een huis van Mr. Kellog. Toen het bekend was, dat er Hollanders waren overgekomen kregen wij veel bezoek en ieder bracht wat om in onze behoeften te voorzien. Vooral genoten onze vrouwen veel dienst van eene Mrs. [Lydia Baxter] Ely, die ook van Hollandsche afkomst was en onze taal verstaan en spreken kon, en hoe goed was dit voor ons mannen, die zouden doorreizen en onze vrouwen hier achterlaten. Wij zagen nu, dat zij door de goedheid des Heeren onder deze menschen wel bezorgd waren. Daar Bernardus Grootenhuis met zijne vrouw reeds vooruit waren gegaan naar de plaats ter vestiging, door Ds. van Raalte uitgekozen, ten zuid-oosten van de Black Lake in Michigan, werd besloten,dat wij hen zoo spoedig mogelijk zouden natrekken.

Den 9den Februari, Dinsdags morgens, gingen wij op reis naar de plaats onzer bestemming. Het was een afstand van 24 uren, maar meest door het bosch, langs ongebaanden weg. De reis werd per slede gedaan. Ons reis-gezelschap bestond uit Ds. van Raalte, Evert Zagers, Willem Notting, J. Lankheet, Jan Laarman, en Egbert Frederiks, en de vrouw van Willem Notting. Na een langen en moeielijken tocht kwamen wij des avonds ge-lukkig goed en wel bij de hoeve van Mr. Isaac Fairbanks aan, waar wij allervriendelijkst werden ontvangen en geherbergd, en drie weken hebben gelogeerd, totdat wij zelf een onderdak hadden gereed gemaakt. Des daags gingen wij eten bij Ds. George N. Smith en des nachts gingen wij slapen bij Mr. Fairbanks op de vloer. Ons leger was wel wat hard, maar er was niet beter te krijgen. Met een deken onder en een deken over, slechts de jas en laarzen uitgetrokken, genoten wij dan toch soms een goeden nachtrust. Om ons tegen de Februari koude te beveiligen stookten wij den geheelen nacht het vuur.

Vreemd keken wij daar soms in onze omgeving rond. Behalve Ds. Smith en Mr. Fairbanks en hunne gezinnen, waren onze buren Indianen. Som-migen hadden reeds een blokhuis en een kleine clearing, waarin zij wat verbouwden, doch de meesten woonden in tenten, van schuin in den grond gestoken stokken, en van buiten met matten van biezen gedekt. In het midden was de stookplaats. Op een afstand van 2 tot 2½ mijl van Ds. Smith was de „Indiaansche stad", zoo noemde men eene verzameling van zulke hutten aan den zuidelijken oever van de Black Lake. Zij leefden van de jacht en visschen, en van het fabriceeren van maple suiker, dat zij zeer goed verstonden en die zij te Allegan of te Saugautuck verkochten. Zij deden ons geen kwaad, maar schenen toch geen goed vertrouwen op ons te hebben, want zij waren wat schuw voor ons. Wij bezochten hen wel eens in hunne tenten en zagen hen dan wel eten met een door hen zelf gemaakte houten lepel. De vrouwen droegen hunne kleine kinderen door-gaans op den rug. In de kerk waren zij veelal niet zeer eerbiedig; daar de vrouwen dan hare kinderen bij zich hadden, bevorderde dit de stilte niet.

Traden wij maar even buiten de kleine hoeve van Mr. Fairbanks, dan waren wij van alle zijden omringd van een nog maagdelijk woud, waarin het wild gedierte nog een bijna ongestoord verblijf hield, en dan keken wij met verbazing op tegen de ontzachelijke woudreuzen van misschien een paar eeuwen oud. Sommigen honderd voet hoog en zes voet in door-snede dik, groeiende op een heuvelachtigen bodem van verschillende grondsoorten: en gewassen doorsneden van beken en kreeken, die gevoed werden door tal van springen of fonteinen, maar alles nog even woest en wild, nergens beter geschikt voor, zou men denken, dan ter woning voor het schuwe gedierte des wouds. En toch, hier was het, zei Ds. van Raalte, dat eene stad en tal van dorpen moesten verrijzen en eene uitgestrekte Hollandsche Kolonie moest ontstaan, waar wij en onze kinderen een onbekrompen bestaan zouden hebben, en onzen God vrij en onbelemmerd zouden dienen, en Hem voor Zijne goedertierenheden danken. Wij, eenvoudige Drentsche lui, hadden wel niet zulke verheven idealen, maar geloofden er toch veel van, en toogen met lust en moed, onder een gedurig opzien tot den Heere, aan het werk.

Ons eerste werk was een blokhuis te bouwen tot onze gezamenlijke woning. Dat was hard werk. Wij waren geen boomkappen gewoon, onze gereedschappen waren weinig en gebrekkig, en daar wij geen ossen bezaten, moesten de logs gerold, gesleept, of gedragen worden naar de plaats waar wij bouwden. Het ergste was nog, dat wij geen planken of shingles voor het dak hadden, zoodat wij dat moeilijk zoo dicht konden krijgen, dat ons de regen niet hinderde.

Toen wij het eerste blokhuis gereed hadden, lieten wij onze vrouwen van Allegan overkomen en hebben toen met vijf huisgezinnen samen gewoond, t.w. Zagers, Notting, Lankheet, Laarman, en Frederiks. Wij leefden onderling in vrede en hadden alle dingen met elkander gemeen. Wat er nog was gekocht en van Allegan medegenomen of door Amerikaansche vrienden medegegeven, werd aan den gemeenschappelijken disch gedeeld, maar spoedig werd onze tafel zeer sober. Aan meel en aardappelen, vleesch of vet was niet te denken. Tarwe, zemels, en corn werd het eenige voedsel, en koffie? gebrand corn werd als zoodanig gebruikt. Om dit eten te bereiden was zelfs nog moeielijk. Bij gemis van een kachel werd van tarwezemels pannekoek gebakken boven het vuur, en brood er van aan bollen gaar gemaakt in de asch, of in een pot met een ijzeren deksel, met onder en boven vuur gebakken. Met het corn waren wij eerst verlegen om dat te bereiden, totdat de Indianen ons leerden hoe zij het deden, nl., eerst in een pot met houtasch en water boven het vuur het week maken en dan na het afgewasschen te hebben in schoon water gaar te koken. Doch hoe sober die kost ook was, zij smaakte ons goed en wij waren er zeer dankbaar voor. Er was niets anders, zelfs Ds. van Raalte heeft meermalen zich met dien kost moeten vergenoegen. De Heere gaf ons moed en deed ons hopen en in de hope arbeiden op een betere toekomst. Intusschen werden wij nog bitter bedroefd, daar de vrouw van W. Notting, kort nadat wij hier gekomen waren, overleed en dus als eerste in de nieuwe Kolonie werd begraven. Daar wij meer Hollanders verwachtten en hoe langer zoo meer moed kregen, dat de Heere het ons wel zou doen gelukken, gingen wij bij voorbaat roads uitkappen en van de gekapte boomen loghuizen bouwen.

Toen wij met het tweede loghuis gereed waren, kwamen Jan Binnekant, Teunis Keppel, en Hein van der Haar van St. Louis naar hier toe. Ook van hen, die te St. Clair waren achtergebleven, kwamen er over en weldra velen uit onderscheidene provinciën van het oude vaderland, zoodat er geen doen aan was om voor die allen zoo spoedig huizen in gereedheid te krijgen. Men woonde met zoovelen in een huis samen als 't maar kon, maar de menigte werd te groot, zoodat sommigen zich moesten behelpen in loverhutten van hemlocktakken, maar helaas! dikwijls ten koste van hunne gezondheid. Het voorjaar en den zomer van 1847 was ook nog vochtig. Wij hadden veel regen en nu gebeurde het dikwijls, dat wij in onze slecht gedekte woningen, evenmin als in de loverhutten, eene plaats konden vinden om droog te blijven. Dit werkte schadelijk op onze gezondheid. Velen werden ziek en waren daarbij verstoken van geneeskundige hulp [er was geen dokter te verkrijgen] en leden ook nog gebrek aan alles wat zieken noodig hebben. De ligging was slecht, het voedsel schadelijk, de verpleging gebrekkig. Ach! wanneer ooit een volk arm en ellendig was, dan zijn wij het in dien eersten zomer geweest. Wij werden zwaar beproefd. Wel zal er bij dezen of gene in het hart zijn gekomen: „Maar zijn wij dan daarom hier gebracht, om in deze woestijn te sterven, waren dan in het oude vaderland geen kerkhoven? Ach! waren we er toch maar gebleven!" De sterfte was groot, de begrafenis kon soms niet eens welvoegelijk geschieden. Er zijn ouders geweest, die hunne kinderen eigenhandig hebben moeten begraven.

Ds. van Raalte deed in die bange dagen wat hij kon, om het lijden van het volk te verlichten. Hij bewerkte, dat er een dokter kwam, met wien hij de zieken te paard langs reed, om hen van geneesmiddelen te voorzien. Het was een bange tijd. Er zijn veel gebeden en smeekingen in dien tijd tot den Heere opgezonden. Er was veel genade noodig om staande te blijven: maar de Heere heeft ook veel genade gegeven; zelfs te midden van al die ellende hoorde men nog roemen van de goedertierenheden Gods, en deed men de bosschen weergalmen van Zijn lof. Immers, hoe schamel onze woningen, hoe sober onze tafel, hoe eenvoudig onze kleeding, hoe zwaar ons werken en onze beproevingen waren, toch was de Heere ons goed in het land onzer vreemdelingschap. Ja, de Heere was met ons, ook daar het scheen, dat Hij tegen ons was. Wij bleven gelooven dat wij met Hem waren opgetrokken en hadden in zoo vele gevallen

Zijne voorzorg en hulp ondervonden, dat wij door dit geloof op Zijne beloften bleven hopen, dat ons het licht uit de duisternis zou opgaan en betere tijden bleven verbeiden.

Allengskens ging het volk, nadat zij uit onderscheidene provinciën van Nederland overkwamen, zich naar verschillende oorden in de bosschen verspreiden. Ds. van Raalte koos zich eene woonplaats in de nabijheid der plaats, van welke hij geloofde, dat aan 't oostelijk einde der Black Lake aan den zuidelijken oever, eene stad, de stad Holland, zou verrijzen. Hij stelde ons aan het werk om wegen uit te kappen, en velen begonnen er hutten en huizen te bouwen. Des Zondags [het was in den zomer van 1847], hielden wij godsdienst onder de boomen bij zijn huis. Ds. van Raalte stond dan te preeken bij een tafel en het volk zat daar rondom voor hem; op omgekapte boomen en op planken daarover gelegd. De Zondagen waren ons tot eene ware verkwikking en de kernachtige prediking, die wij dan mochten hooren tot bemoediging, onder onzen arbeid en in ons lijden. Daar echter het kerk houden in de open lucht, was 't ook onder de boomen, op den duur niet gaan kon, werd er besloten eene kerk te bouwen. Deze moest, bij gebrek aan andere bouwstoffen, natuurlijk even als de huizen, een blokhuis worden. Ten zuidoosten van de stad Holland, waar ook Ds. van Raalte zijn woning had, is van bekante hemlock boomen, met veel moeite, arbeid, en kosten een gebouw tot stand gekomen, dat een geruimen tijd tot het houden van den openbaren godsdienst is gebruikt geworden. Door de sterfte, waarvan ik gemeld heb, waren er eenige onverzorgde weezen achtergebleven. Om deze te verzorgen ging men ook een weeshuis bouwen, doch dit bleek weldra niet noodig te zijn, daar medelijdige kindervrienden de arme weezen onder zich verdeelden, en voor hun opvoeding zorgden. Ja, ook in dit opzicht werd ondervonden, dat de Heere geen rijke fondsen van goud noodig heeft om Zijne beloften te vervullen, dat Hij de weduwen en weezen in hunne verdrukkingen staande houdt. Hij heeft hen in de arme kolonie, waar bijna allen gebrek hadden, voldoende weten te onderhouden, en verzorgers en verzorgden later rijkelijk gezegend.

Daar nu het volk door gedurige inkomst van emigranten al meerder werd en zich naar verschillende zijden uitbreidde kwamen er ook eenigen in met middelen om in de behoeften te voorzien en onderscheidene handwerkslieden en mannen van onderneming, zoodat een en ander wat meer en beter konden worden ingericht en geregeld. Groote moeielijkheid was het altijd om de nieuwe en toenemende bevolking van het noodige te voorzien. Alles moest zeer ver worden gehaald, b.v. van Allegan, Saugatuck, of Singapore, zelfs van Grand Haven en Grand Rapids. Dat zou nu weinig bezwaar zijn, maar toen was het heel wat anders. Toch was het overal tusschen de kolonie en die plaatsen, 8 uren gaans naar Grand Haven, Grand Rapids, en Allegan nog al bosch, en dat zonder wegen. Om die plaatsen te vinden waren er op zekere afstanden van elkaar, boomen met eene bijl aangeblest en van merken voorzien, die voor handwijzers moesten dienen om de richting naar en van die plaatsen aan te geven. Zoo'n reis nam een dag heen en een dag terug. En menigeen heeft zoo'n reis gedaan om op zijn rug een zak vol flour te halen om met de zijnen het leven te houden.

De geheel onbemiddelden hadden 't in het eerste jaar bovenal moeielijk, doch de nood leert de hand uit den mouw steken, en de zorg voor vrouw en kroost doet al wat ongemakken verduren. Velen gingen ver van huis naar Engelschen [„Amerikanen"] uit om werk te zoeken en keerden dan met wat geld of een dragt flour en spek en sommigen met een koetje of kalfje weer naar huis.

Zoo zijn Evert Zagers en ik met nog twee anderen in de maand Mei van 1847 er ook uit op gegaan, en na wat verdiend te hebben, weer gekeerd. Het was een wonderlijke tijd. Het scheen, dat wij allen iets hadden van den geest, die onzen leidsman bezielde, Ds. van Raalte, die nimmer twijfelde aan den goeden uitslag, en ook wij bleven er aan gelooven onder opzien tot den Heere.

O ik zou er nog zoo veel meer van kunnen vertellen, maar het wil niet zoo geregeld meer voor den aandacht komen. Anders was er nog veel te zeggen van het houden van vele vergaderingen, van ontwerpen, van uitgevoerde en geslaagde maar ook van gansch in 't water gevallen plannen, zoo als b.v. het bouwen van een schip, het oprichten van een zeepfabriek, het darstellen van een zaagmolen, en al die dingen meer, maar er moet ook wat voor anderen overblijven.

Anders was er ook nog te vertellen van het uitkappen der wegen in de stad, het overbruggen van de kreeken en rivieren met loggen naast elkander te leggen. Van het invoeren van koeien, varkens, kippen, enz, die de eenigszins bemiddelden van de Amerikanen gingen koopen, maar de minder bedeelden gingen verdienen met arbeiden. Daar men geen hooi had kunnen winnen, moesten de koeien des winters grootendeels leven van de takken der boomen, die men omkapte. De varkens konden zich wel redden, die werden vet van de overvloed van beuken noten, die zij in de bosschen vonden.

Ziet daar iets van onze geringe opkomst. O als wij nu eens terug denken, hoe arm en behoeftig ons volk in den beginne hier was en wat het later door den zegen des Heeren is geworden, wij hadden het onmogelijk kunnen denken. Het uitgestrekte en toen ongerepte woud is uren gaans in het rond, in vruchtbaar land herschapen. Huizen en schuren, kerken en scholen allerwege gebouwd, boomgaarden geplant met fruitboomen en wijnstokken; tal van paarden en koeien en ossen en schapen grazen in de weiden: hadden wij toen maar gebrekkige handgereedschappen, thans zijn er tal van machines aangeschaft. Toen moesten wij dagen reizen om iets uit den winkel te halen, nu hebben wij zelfs meer dan een op onze dorpen. En wat meer dan dat is. Toen vooral die wat ver van het bosch in gingen, verstoken van de openbare samenkomst. Nu hebben wij tal van leeraars, die ons den vollen raad Gods verkondigen en die wij gemakkelijk kunnen bereiken in onze wel ingerichte kerken die des zomers door schuiframen verkoeld en des winters door kachels verwarmd worden.

Och! hoedanigen behoorden wij met onze kinderen nu niet te zijn voor den Heere, die toch dit alles bewerkt heeft. Helaas, wij hebben niet aan de verwachting beantwoord. Och! dat de Heere Zijnen Geest eens mocht uitstorten tot bekeering en verlevendiging. Bidde toch die bidden geleerd heeft. De Heere wil er toch om aangebeden zijn en om verzocht worden en Hij is een Verhoorder van het gebed. Moge Hij nu mijne eenvoudige mededeeling ook daartoe zegenen, dan is mijn wensch vervult.

[Translation]

I have repeatedly been urged to relate my experiences on my journey to America and give some account of the earliest years of our stay here. I felt a desire to comply with these suggestions, and naturally saw how useful such an account would be to recall these events to the minds of our children now growing up. But whenever I tried to write about our life in the earliest years my courage failed because I could not accomplish this as well as I wanted to do it and as I thought the subject demanded. But if all our old settlers think and act as I long have thought and acted I fear that much worthy to be remembered will be forgotten. I want to tell of my experiences in as plain a manner as possible and as well as I can, and I hope that others thereby may be roused to write about their experiences. In this way we as strangers in the land of our sojourn most likely will contribute something to the rich history of our Dutch settlement and perhaps we may greatly serve our God, our children, and our further descendants and probably give them some pleasure.

It was in the year 1846 that the writings of several dominies of the Christian Reformed Church in the Netherlands dealing with the desirability of emigration to North America roused among many a desire to follow their suggestions. Pamphlets by the dominies Albertus Christiaan van Raalte, Anthony Brummelkamp, and Hendrik Pieter Scholte came into our possession and so influenced my wife and myself that we from the first became preoccupied with this project of emigration and frequently were led to ask God what course we were to take. When our relatives and friends heard of this there was no lack of discouraging advice and even of opposition. But when we told them what our innermost experiences were, how we were influenced by them, and what our reasons for acting thus were, they finally said, "Well, it is your own affair!" But it was not an easy matter to come to a decision. We understood very well that there were great difficulties associated with this weighty undertaking. With these questions in mind we repeatedly turned to God in prayer, but we constantly felt renewed urging to emigrate. Finally we came to the firm decision to undertake the great journey with eye fixed upon the Lord, under His leadership and with His support.

We were living at Noord Barge near Emmen, in the province of Drente. We were comforted by the fact that Evert Zagers and his wife were under the same conviction and at the same time had also come to the decision to emigrate. We left Noord Barge together, and traveled by way of Coevorden to Hasselt, distant three hours from Zwolle and situated on the Zwarte Water in Overijsel. Dominie W. H. Frieling was leader of the congregation at that place. We were charitably received by thim, but a sore trial came to us there. My wife, never strong, now became so seriously ill that we thought she might die. We did not know what to do. The date of departure from Rotterdam where we thought to meet Dominie van Raalte with whom we were to journey, was set. At the suggestion of Brother Zagers and other friends, I asked my wife what we should do? "Well," she replied, "choose the way already indicated." [Psalm 66, 3, in the Dutch Psalter]. By this she meant we should continue the journey as planned. She was brought aboard ship in a large sickchair and placed upon a bed, and next to her an ailing child. That was a sore tribulation, but the Lord guarded so well over her that when we arrived in Rotterdam she was completely recovered. That we then were happy and asking "How shall we ever repay the Lord for His kindness?" one can well imagine.

At Rotterdam, according to agreement, we found Dominie van Raalte and his followers and other friends gathered from various places, who were to make the voyage with him. From Rotterdam to Hellevoetsluis we experienced little difficulty so long as we traveled between the banks; but hardly had we moved from Hellevoet when one after another became seasick. But that was not the worst, for on the fourteenth day of our voyage our ailing child died, and we had to see them lower its little body into the waves. That was a grievous blow for the hearts of its parents. But the Lord moved us to resignation and to be able to say, "He does what is good in His eyes." Brother Zagers met with a yet sadder blow – his wife, ever vigorous and able to help others, fell ill and died, leaving her husband a widower with a very young child. The impression her death made upon all the passengers can readily be imagined. But the Lord also strengthened Zagers to bear his tribulation. After passing seven long weeks on the sea [we made the voyage in a sailing ship] we finally arrived in New York. Speedily we noted that we were in a strange land where everything seemed odd to us, but also that we ourselves were looked upon as a very strange kind of people. Our clothing, and particularly the large poke bonnets of our women drew much attention. We could not understand what the people said about us. Unfortunately we could not make ourselves understood when we wanted to buy something so that it was with the greatest difficulty we could get what we wanted. Had we not had Dominie van Raalte or his friends to guide us, as for example Dominie Thomas de Witt, we would not have known how to make our way. But with the Lord's help everything turned out well.

From New York we continued our journey per steamboat to Albany. After having eaten on the boat we left by train for Rochester where we spent one night. Next we traveled by train to Buffalo where we had to spend a night. It was November and the weather was cold. As there were no stoves in the cars we were shivering from the cold until we noticed a stove in a car standing on the tracks opposite ours and built a fire around which we warmed ourselves. At Rochester Dominie van Raalte had differences with a German over a trunk and the German ran away with it. From Rochester we journeyed to Detroit where we stayed fourteen days. It was cold; the first night we were lodged in a storage house; we improvised as well as we could a bedroom with our trunks, but that night we suffered much from the cold. The next morning four of our families moved into a small house. When in the evening we had spread out our beds the entire floor was covered. Food was inexpensive. We paid $ 4 for a barrel of meal and paid a cent and a half for a pound of meat. Firewood was expensive, 14 shillings per cord.

The captain of the boat in which we came from Buffalo had ordered a new steamboat to be built at St. Clair [Michigan]. Noting our poverty he suggested that we go to work for him. Our pay would be: housing, food, firewood, some articles from a store, and each of us was to have a pair of boots. [Until this moment we had been wearing our wooden shoes.] An old storage house was gotten ready for us to live in. As many as 30 men were working on the wharf, but compared to them we were only flunkies. On a certain day we witnessed a sad accident. Two men were sawing a long and heavy piece of wood resting on jacks. The sawyer who stood under the piece of wood tried to move it with a canthook but it slipped from the jack and fell upon him so that he was killed instantaneously. That was a grievous misfortune. He was survived by his wife and six children. His body was carried to his widow and placed in their house. All work was suspended and in the evening there was a sermon of which, however, we understood nothing. The captain, who appeared to be a good man, gave the grieving widow $ 200.

When we left for St. Clair Dominie van Raalte, after spending a few days in Detroit, traveled ahead to carry out the purpose he had in mind. In January we received a letter from him. He wanted to see us, with God's blessing to carry out the plans that had been formed. Five families decided to act upon his invitation immediately. By sleigh we journeyed back to Detroit. From Mr. Theodore Romeyn, a man of Dutch descent who also understood Dutch, we received directions and also a letter of introduction to Dominie Ova P. Hoyt in Kalamazoo. With little trouble we found Dominie Hoyt who, after reading Mr. Romeyn's letter, immediately ordered the women and children be brought from the station and saw to it that we were well cared for that night. How good those people were toward us! They looked after all our needs, even for the journey to Allegan which had to be made by sleigh, and all without any expense for us. How gladly we would have spoken with them, but we could not. The following morning we thanked them as well as we could for the kindness they showed us, and we journeyed by way of Otsego to Allegan in the sleigh Dominie Hoyt had ordered for our use. There Dominie van Raalte with wife and children was staying with Mr. John R. Kellog. We were all happy to see each other and were received in friendly fashion. It was Saturday evening. They took good care of us until Monday when we all moved into one of Mr. Kellog's houses. When it became known in Allegan that some people had arrived from Holland we had many visitors and each person brought us something we needed. Mrs. Lydia Baxter Ely, who also was of Dutch origin and understood our tongue and spoke it, was especially helpful to our womenfolk. This was a happy turn in events for us men who were to journey ahead and leave our wives here. Now we perceived that they would be well cared for through God's goodness. And as Bernardus Grootenhuis and his wife had already gone on ahead to the place of settlement chosen by Dominie van Raalte it was decided that we would follow them as soon as possible.

On Tuesday morning, February 9, we left on the final stage of our journey. It was a distance of 24 miles, mostly through woods, along a poorly marked out road. The journey was made with a sleigh. Our group was composed of Dominie van Raalte, Evert Zagers, Willem Notting, J. Lankheet, Jan Laarman, Egbert Frederiks, and Willem Notting's wife. After a long and difficult journey we fortunately arrived safe and sound at the farm of Mr. Isaac Fairbanks, where we were received in the most friendly manner and were given lodging where we stayed for three weeks until we had prepared our own shanty. Every day we had our meals at Dominie George N. Smith's house and at night we slept at Mr. Fairbank's house. Our bed was not very comfortable, but none better was to be found. We took off our coats and boots, slept on a blanket laid out on the floor, and covered ourselves with another blanket. In spite of such an uncomfortable bed we sometimes enjoyed a good night's rest. To keep ourselves warm in the cold February nights we kept a roaring fire going all night.

It was a strange sight that greeted us. With the exception of Dominie Smith and Mr. Fairbanks and their families, our neighbors were Indians. Some of them had built log houses and had made a little clearing where they raised a few things, but most of the Indians lived in tents made of slanting sticks stuck into the ground and covered with mats made of reeds. In the center of these tents were fireplaces. At a distance of from 2 to 2½ miles from Dominie Smith's was the Indian Village, as we called the collection of such tents, situated on the south shore of Black Lake. The Indians lived by hunting and fishing and made maple sugar, something they understood very well, and sold their product at Allegan and Saugatuck. They never did us any harm, but nevertheless did not trust us and appeared to fear us. Sometimes we visited them in their tents and saw them eat with wooden spoons of their own making. The women always carried their children on their backs. In church they often were not respectful, since the fact that the women then carried their children with them did not make for quiet.

Beyond Fairbanks' small clearing we beheld surrounding us on all sides a virgin forest teeming with wild life as yet wholly undisturbed. We viewed with astonishment the mighty giant trees which perhaps were two centuries old, some of them a hundred feet tall and six feet in diameter, all growing on a rolling terrain of various kinds of soil; and the dense underbrush cut up by streams and creeks fed by springs and bubbling waters, a desert wild, fit only as a home for the timid creatures of the forest. Nevertheless this was the place, declared Dominie van Raalte, where a city and a number of villages should rise, where an extensive Dutch Kolonie should be planted, where we and our children would enjoy and untrammeled existence, serve our God freely and without restraint, and thank Him for His gracious kindness. We plain folk from the province of Drente, of course, did not have such exalted ideals, but nevertheless we believed in a good deal in what he kept before our eyes, and so courageously went to our labors with frequent prayer to God.

Our first task was to build a log house to serve as our common dwelling. That was hard work. We had no experience at cutting down trees. Our tools were as few as they were defective. As we had no oxen we rolled the logs or dragged or carried them to the place where we were building our house. And worst of all, we had no boards or shingles with which to make the roof so that we had difficulty in getting it tight enough to keep out the rain.

As soon as we had finished our first log house we asked our wives to come from Allegan. From that moment the five of our families lived together, that is, Zagers, Notting, Lankheet, Laarman, and Frederiks. We lived together in peace and had all things in common. Whatever had been purchased and had been brought from Allegan or had been given by American friends was served up in a common dish; but soon our table became very meager. Meal and potatoes, meat or fat were not to be had. Wheat, bran, and corn constituted our only food; and coffie – roasted corn – was used in its place. Even to prepare such food was a difficult matter. Because we had no stove, pancakes made of bran were baked above the fire. Bread prepared from bran was baked in round pieces placed in the hot ashes or in a pot provided with an iron cover and placed in the fire. We did not know how to prepare the corn until the Indians taught us – first softening it in wood ashes and water placed above the fire and finally, after washing it in clean water, cooking it. Although this was plain fare, it tasted good to us and we were very thankful for it. There was no other food to be had; even Dominie van Raalte had to satisfy himself with such fare. The Lord gave us courage and hope and in that hope to labor for a better future. Meanwhile we were in bitter grief because Willem Notting's wife died shortly after her arrival here. She was the first of our group to be buried in the new colony. Because we were expecting other Hollanders and our confidence steadily increased that God surely would cause us to succeed we went ahead chopping out roads and building loghouses from the trees we cut cown.

As soon as we had finished our second loghouse, Jan Binnekant, Teunis Keppel, and Hein van der Haar arrived from St. Louis. Also, others who had stayed behind in St. Louis now arrived, soon to be followed by many persons from various provinces in the fatherland so that it was impossible to provide houses for them as fast as they were needed. People crowded together in houses, but so great was the number of newcomers that some of them had to be content with shelters made from hemlock branches. Alas! this frequently at the loss of their health. The spring and summer of 1847 were quite wet. There was much rain and it frequently happened that we could not find a place in our poorly roofed loghouses, not to mention the huts covered with hemlock branches, where we could keep dry. This was injurious to our health. Many became ill, and, what made matters worse, they could not have medical attention [a doctor was not to be had]. They lacked everything sick people needed. The beds were poor, food was bad, and care of the sick was inadequate. If ever a people were poor and miserable, we were the ones during that first summer. The thought rose in the souls of many, "Why have we been brought here – to die in the wilderness, and were there no cemeteries in our fatherland? Alas! had we but remained there!" Many people died, so many that funerals sometimes could not be conducted decently. There were parents who had to bury their children with their own hands. In those fearsome days Dominie van Raalte did all he could to lighten the suffering of the people. He managed to secure the services of a doctor whom he accompanied, on horseback, to provide the sick with medicines. That was a dreadful time. Many a prayer and pressing petition were offered to the Lord. Determination was needed in order to stand firm, but the Lord gave much of His grace. Even in the midst of all that misery were to be heard praises of God's kindness, and the people filled the woods with the echoes of praise offered to Him. For no matter how miserable our dwellings, how bare our table, how simple our clothing, how hard our labors and tribulations, yet in all this God was good to us in this land in which we were strangers. Yes, the Lord indeed was with us even when it appeared that He was against us. We remained steadfast in our faith that He had come with us and that we had experienced His help and providence in so many instances. Through such faith in His promises we persisted in our hope that light would shine for us out of this wilderness and that better times would come.

Gradually the people as they came from various provinces in the Netherlands began to settle at several places in the forest. Dominie van Raalte chose a place to live near the east end of Black Lake, and on its south shore the city of Holland was to rise. He set us to work chopping out roads; and many of us began to building huts and houses on that site. Sundays [this was in the summer of 1847] we held religious services under the trees near his house. Dominie van Raalte stood behind a table which served as a pulpit and his listeners sat around him on logs on which boards were placed. Those Sundays truly were an inspiration for us because of the spiritually pithy sermons we were privileged to hear for our encouragement to labor and endure. However, because holding services in the open, even though under trees, could not continue very long, it was decided to build a church. This church had to be built of logs, exactly as in the case of our houses, for we lacked all other building material. Southeast of the city of Holland, near the spot where Dominie van Raalte's house stood, a structure was erected of squared hemlock logs. It cost us much difficulty, labor, and expense, but it served for a considerable time as the meeting house for holding public religious services. The mortality I have mentioned above had left us a number of abandoned orphans. To care for these we went to work to build an orphanage; but this soon proved an unnecessary undertaking, for sympathetic friends took them into their homes. Yes, also in this respect it was discovered that the Lord does not need rich funds of gold in order to carry out His promises that he will support widows and orphans in their distress. He knew how to maintain them in all need, in our poor Kolonie where nearly every person lived in poverty. He abundantly blessed not only those who cared for the orphans, but later also showed His rich favors to those who were cared for in this manner.

Our people steadily increased in number because of immigration, and settled in various places. Some came bringing financial means, and a number of craftsmen and men of enterprise arrived. It became possible to expand our activities and arrange things in better detail. Great difficulty was experienced in providing for the newcomers and for the increasing population. All goods had to be carried from a great distance, for example, from Allegan, Saugatuck, or Singapore, some even from Grand Haven and Grand Rapids. Today this would cause little worry, but at that time it was a very different matter. The country everywhere between the Kolonie and those places, a distance of eight hours to Grand Haven, Grand Rapids, and Allegan, was covered with woods and there were no roads. To be able to find those places trees at certain distances from each other had been marked by means of an axe, provided with blazes or marks intended to serve as guides indicating the direction to and from these places. A journey to any one of these places and back required one whole day. Many a person made such a journey carrying on his back a bag of flour needed to keep his flock alive.

Those completely without financial means experienced much hardship in the beginning, but necessity is a hard teacher and concern for wife and children teaches a person how to endure privation patiently. Many a settler went far away from home to look for work among the English [that is, "Americans"] and returned with a bit of money or a load of flour and pork; and there were some who returned leading a cow or a calf.

Thus Evert Zagers and I and two other persons went away from home in the month of May of 1847 and returned after having earned some money. That was a wonderful time. It seemed that we all had caught something of the spirit that inspired our leader Dominie van Raalte who never had a doubt of the success of our settlement, and we too persisted in our faith, under God's guidance.

Many things could still be told about the numerous meetings, of projects, of plans some of which were carried out while others failed, such as, for example, the building of a ship, forming of a soap factory, erection of a sawmill, and many other matters; but I must leave something for others to tell. Otherwise I could tell about how the roads in the city were chopped out, how bridges made of logs placed alongside each other were built over creeks and rivers. I could also tell about the importation of cows, pigs, chickens, etc., which those who had a little money purchased from Americans but which the poorer people paid for with their labor. At first people had no hay, and during winter the cattle lived mainly on the branches of trees we chopped down. Pigs could readily take care of themselves, feeding on the great quantities of beechnuts which they found in the woods.

Such are a few facts about our simple origins. When we think back upon those times and reflect how poor and needy our people were in those beginning days and what through God's blessing they became in later days, we could not have imagined it. The virgin forest for many hours' distance has been converted into fertile land. Houses, barns, churches, and schools have been built in every direction, orchards with fruit trees and grape vines have been planted, numbers of horses, cows, oxen, and sheep are grazing in the pastures. Where in the beginning we had only defective handmade tools, now our people have acquired machinery of many kinds. At first we had to travel days to get anything from the stores; today we have more than one store in each of our villages. And there is one matter more important than all this. At first people who lived far away in the woods could not readily come to religious meetings.

Today we have a large number of ministers who fully proclaim God's counsel, and we can readily go to our churches traveling along our well laid out roads, to churches in summer cooled by windows that can be raised and in winter warmed by stoves.

What a thankful people we and our children should be before the Lord who has worked all these things! But alas! we have not come up to what might be expected of us.

O, that the Lord would pour out His Spirit to convert our people and to revive their faith! Pray, you who have learned to pray. The Lord wills that prayer and petition be made to Him, and He is the nearer of all prayer. May He bless my simple story. That is my wish.

7. EVERT ZAGERS' ACCOUNT

[Like Egbert Frederiks, Evert Zagers from Noord Barge in the province of Drente accompanied Van Raalte on the *Southerner* in 1846. This relation, entitled *Mededeeling*, of the greatest value for the history of Holland and the Dutch Settlement, was first published in *Jaarboekje voor de Hollandsche Christelijke Gereformeerde Kerk in Noord Amerika voor het jaar* 1883 [Grand Rapids 1882], subsequently reprinted in *De Grondwet*, October 24, 1911.]

Het jaar 1846 is een onvergetelijk jaar voor velen alhier, wegens eene beslissing toen door hen genomen, waaraan zij vroeger nooit hadden gedacht en die hen later menigmaal deed zeggen: „het is van den Heere geschied." Gelijk er toen velen door kleine geschriften van Ds. H. P. Scholte, Ds. Anthony Brummelkamp en Ds. A. C. van Raalte werden bekend gemaakt met America, en hoe goed het voor velen zoude zijn om daar naar toe te trekken, zoo ontwaakte ook bij mij de begeerte om met andere broeders en zusters, met wien ik veel verkeerde en die zooals ik, bovendien hoopten nog een beter vaderland te vinden, naar Amerika mede te trekken. Doch daar ik gehuwd was en eene vrouw en een kind van vijf jaar had, was er destijds nog al meer reisgeld noodig als nu, en ik bezat nagenoeg niets. Met mijne beurs raadplegende, dan werd mij ernstig geraden om al mijne emigratieplannen maar geheel uit het hoofd te zetten. Wie toch volstrekt geen geld had, kon onmogelijk in Amerika komen. Doch behalve met mijn beurs raadpleegde ik met God, en werkelijk kreeg ik op mijn biddend worstelen, in de zaak geloof, dat de Heere mij zou helpen en in mijne behoefte voorzien, en Hij heeft mij niet beschaamd gemaakt.

Ik wist dat onder hen die ook wilden vertrekken, menschen van middelen waren. Inmiddels was mijn oog op hen geslagen, doch ik had den moed niet om hun mijn toestand te openbaren, zooals ik echter beken, dat ik wel gedaan moest hebben.

Na ernstig mijne zaak den Heere aanbevolen te hebben, besloot ik, tegelijk met Egbert Frederiks van Noord Barge en eenige vrienden uit het Graafschap Bentheim, met vrouw en kind mede te gaan.

Wij kwamen tezamen met Ds. A. C. van Raalte en vele anderen, te Rotterdam bijeen, maar nu bleek het dat ik niet in staat was de overtochtskosten te kunnen betalen. Doch nu toonde de Heere mijn gebed te willen verhooren, door de harten van eenige vrienden te neigen, dat zij aanboden om mij de overtochtskosten voor te schieten.

Dit was voor mij en mijne vrouw eene verrassende uitkomst. Dankbaar en verwonderd aanbad ik de trouwe en goedheid Gods, en nu scheen al onze zwarigheid geheel geweken en in goede hoop en met goede vooruitzichten gingen wij scheep en op reis.

Ik werd op het schip aangesteld om kok te zijn en mijne vrouw moest oude en jonge vrouwen en kinderen helpen, en zou dan in de week 30 stuivers [d.i. 60 cents Amerikaansch] verdienen. Dit gaf ons goeden moed, dat alles wel terecht zou komen. Maar ach! het duurde niet lang of mij trof de zwaarste ramp mijns levens. Ik zelf werd zeeziek, zoodat ik mijn werk als kok niet meer verrichten kon, doch dit was niet zoo erg. Erger was het, dat mijne vrouw weldra doodelijk ziek werd en helaas! na weinige dagen stierf. Haar lijk werd in de zee neergelaten. Dit was voor mij een verpletterende slag. Ik stond, ik weet zelf niet meer hoe, maar geheel verlegen, als weduwnaar met een zoontje van 5 jaar oud en geen middelen, of ik moest ze van anderen ontvangen. Toch liet zich de Heere ook aan mij niet onbetuigd. Mijn hulpbehoevende toestand deed mij veel bidden, dat de Heere mij mocht ondersteunen en voor mij en mijn kind mocht zorgen. Hij heeft mijne verzuchtingen verhoord.

Behouden te New York met het zeilschip aangekomen, reisden wij spoedig met een stoomboot over Albany, Rochester, en Buffalo, naar Detroit. Het was in de maand November 1846, en dus reeds winter. Ons voornemen was om naar Wisconsin door te gaan, maar dat kon niet meer van wege het ijs, dat de wateren onbevaarbaar had gemaakt. Wij stonden dus daar zeer verlegen. Wij hadden geen middel om te overwinteren, en ook geen werk om er de kost mede te verdienen en hierdoor werd het ons bang om 't hart. Doch de Heere betoonde zich weer over ons te ontfermen. Een scheepskapitein, die te St. Clair eene stoomboot liet bouwen, onzen toestand bemerkende, bood aan om ons allen daar heen mede te nemen en werk te verschaffen. Ons loon zou zijn: huisvesting, de kost, en brandhout voor de kachels. Met tien huisgezinnen ondernamen wij de reis en maakten van het aanbod gebruik. Onze woning was een oud pakhuis.

Wij hadden het er tamelijk goed, maar toch niet naar onzen zin. Al wat wij zagen en hoorden was ons vreemd. Toch schikten wij ons zoo goed wij konden, in dien vreemden ongewonen toestand, blijde dat wij maar onderdak en wat te eten hadden, hopende op betere tijden en verandering van omstandigheden, die wij biddend te gemoet zagen. Dagelijks spraken wij over onzen leidsman Ds. A. C. van Raalte, die met Bernardus Grooten-huis in Detroit was gebleven en vervolgens met zijn huisgezin naar Allegan was doorgereisd.

Na eenige weken ontvingen wij een brief van hem waarin hij mede-deelde dat hij eene plaats ter vestiging voor ons Hollandsch volk had gevonden, niet in Wisconsin maar in Michigan. Spoedig daarop ont-vingen wij weer een brief, waarin hij ons verzocht om allen over te komen, om ons met hem in een bosch te gaan vestigen en daar eene nieuwe kolonie aan te leggen. Wij hadden slechts een gezin onder ons, dat middelen bezat en waardoor wij allen op reis moesten geholpen worden. De moeder van dat gezin was de weduwe Laarman.

Zij vroeg ons wat wij oordeelden? Zij dacht het best om aan het ver-zoek van Ds. van Raalte gehoor te geven en vroeg of wij met haar mede wilden gaan. Daar wij van haar afhankelijk en veel aan haar verplicht waren, en ook niet wat beters wisten te doen, besloten wij met haar mede te gaan. Nadat wij dus besloten hadden, ontvingen wij een derde brief van Ds. van Raalte, waarin hij onderrichtte hoe wij van St. Clair naar Allegan reizen moesten. Ach, wij waren met alles zoo onbekend. Hadden wij Ds. van Raalte niet tot onzen raadsman en hulp gehad, er zouden weinigen van de eerste emigranten hier terecht gekomen zijn.

Op Ds. van Raalte's inlichting gingen wij met vier andere huisgezinnen van St. Clair per slede op reis naar Detroit, een afstand van 60 mijlen. Vijf huisgezinnen bleven te St. Clair. Te Detroit begaven wij ons op ge-geven raad naar Mr. [Theodore] Romeyn, die ons iets naders van de plannen van Ds. van Raalte mededeelde en onderrichtte aangaande de reis. Hij gaf ons een adres en brief mede aan Ds. [Ova P.] Hoyt te Kalamazoo, die ons dan wel verder zou voorthelpen.

Mr. Romeyn zorgde dat wij met onze personen en bagage op de spoor-trein kwamen, en na hem voor zijne moeiten en goede diensten bedankt te hebben, spoorden wij naar Kalamazoo, verder liep er nog geen trein.

't Was avond toen wij er aan kwamen. Daar stonden wij weder zeer ver-legen, want hoe met onze Hollandsche taal in eene Engelsche stad, dominee Hoyt te vinden. Met veel moeite gelukte het ons eindelijk Ds. Hoyt te vinden en hem den brief van Mr. Romeyn over te geven. Ds. Hoyt liet dadelijk een paard voor de slede spannen en onze vrouwen

en kinderen van het depot halen. Wij werden bij eenige burgers ingekwartierd en van het noodige verzorgd. Den volgende dag werd er een
slede besteld en om acht uur gingen wij reeds weer op reis naar Allegan.
Onze goederen bleven in het depot te Kalamazoo, die zouden ons worden
nagezonden. Ds. Hoyt met dank voor zijne goede zorgen afscheid genomen hebbende, vervolgden wij onze reis.

Te Otsego was het juist middag. Bij eene herberg aangekomen werden
wij daar vriendelijk ontvangen en in eene verwarmde kamer bij den
kachel gebracht. Daar zittende kwam de kastelein bij ons en vroeg: Of
wij geen dinner lusten? Onze maag zei: Ja, wel graag; maar onze beurs
zei: pas op, dat kost geld. De kastelein scheen noch het Hollandsch van
onze maag, noch van onze beurs te verstaan en vroeg alweer, of wij geen
dinner lusten? Wij alweer Ja wel... maar.... Doch de man kon het maar
niet in 't verstand krijgen en bleef aanhouden, zoodat onze geldschieter
eindelijk zeide: Kom laat ons maar eten gaan. De maaltijd smaakte ons
heerlijk en onze maag gevoelde zich zeer wel, maar ons gemoed een ietwat bittere nasmaak er van, door de gedachte: wat zou dat nu wel kosten?
Wij vroegen den kastelein: wat wij hem nu schuldig waren? maar hij
wist niet wat wij meenden. Nu trachten wij het hem met gebaaren en
wijzen met de handen duidelijk te maken, doch die gestikulatien scheen
hij ook nog niet te begrijpen, want in plaats van ons te beduiden wat hij
moest hebben, haalde hij een handvol geld uit zijn zak en zeide het ons
toehoudende, „To take it!" „No, no!", zeiden wij, en gaven al weer te
kennen wat wij moesten geven. Eindelijk begreep hij ons en zeide met
zeer begrijpelijke gestes: „Nothing, nothing!" Dat wisten wij nu ook
reeds, wat dit beteekende en werd dan met hartelijke dankzeggingen beantwoord. Voorwaar dat was alweer tot aanmoediging in den levensstrijd
van moeite en ontbeering, die wij te gemoet gingen.

Na dus verwarmd en verkwikt te zijn, beklommen wij weder de slede
en reisden wij voort naar Allegan, waar wij op Zaterdagavond, den 6den
Februari 1847 aankwamen en waar wij door Ds. van Raalte met de zijnen
zeer hartelijk werden verwelkomd. Wij hadden elkander in zes weken
niet gezien en waren hartelijk blijde elkander weer te mogen ontmoeten.
Grootenhuis was met zijne vrouw en kinderen reeds vooruit gegaan,
naar de eerste plaats van onze bestemming.

Maandag, den 8sten Februari hielden wij vergadering en werd er besloten: dat de vijf mannen, die er waren, en eene der vrouwen mede
zouden gaan naar het woud, en dat juffrouw van Raalte en de andere
vrouwen met de kinderen vooreerst te Allegan zouden blijven. Nadat nu
de vrouwen en kinderen te Allegan bezorgd waren, maakten wij aan-

stalten voor de reis door het woud zonder weg, anders dan die door gebleste boomen werd aangewezen.

Het was een harde zet, om zoo in een vreemd land, vrouw en kinderen onder vreemden achter te laten en zelf op te trekken naar een ongerept woud, waarin de wilde dieren huisden en Indianen woonden, met slechts een paar blanken.

De Heere gaf ons moed op den ingeslagen weg voorwaarts te gaan, en Hij zorgde boven verwachting. De vrouwen en kinderen die achterbleven ondervonden te Allegan veel dienst en hulp van eene Mrs. [Lydia Baxter] Ely, eene afstammelinge van eene Hollandsche familie, die nog wat Hollandsch verstond en spreken kon. Dat was voor hun een groote troost en voor de mannen tot veel geruststelling. Met vijf mannen en eene vrouw verlieten wij Allegan den 9den Februari 1847 en des avonds laat arriveerden wij bij den Indiaanschen dominee, zooals wij den zendeling Rev. George N. Smith noemden, en bij Mr. Isaac Fairbanks, die daar bij hem woonde om de Indianen de landbouw te leeren.

Daar troffen wij ook Grootenhuis en zijne vrouw weer aan en werden wij zeer vriendelijk ontvangen. Twee van ons gezelschap werden gelogeerd bij Rev. Smith, al de anderen bij Mr. Fairbanks.

Daar zijn wij 14 dagen geweest; wij veroorzaakten de goede dominee en zijn medehelper vrij wat ongerief, want zij waren beide maar zeer klein behuisd. Zij woonden in blokhuizen, doch zij vervulden de wet Christi, „draagt elkanders lasten", op uitnemende wijze.

Wij aten bij den dominee en sliepen des nachts bij Mr. Fairbanks op den vloer. Intusschen bouwden wij zelf een loghuis, en toen wij dat gereed hadden, lieten wij de vrouwen en kinderen van Allegan overkomen. Met zes huisgezinnen betrokken wij ons eerste blokhuis. Vóór wij in eigen woning waren, hadden wij het voor het uitwendige goed. Sommigen hadden nog wat vleesch gekocht en ook was er van Amerikanen wat medegegeven, dat, even als door de eerste Christenen, als een gemeenschappelijk deel werd opgegeten. Maar weldra volgden moeielijker dagen.

Zoolang men nog met de slede hier kon inkomen, werd ons tarwezemels voor pannekoek en brood en ook gepeld corn aangebracht, maar toen de sneeuw weg ging, raakte onze voorraad op, en daar er intusschen nog meer vrienden van de achtergeblevenen te St. Clair overkwamen, kregen wij gebrek. Om deze te kunnen huisvesten, bouwden wij een tweede loghuis. Daar er nu ook van andere plaatsen overkwamen, moest er nog een gebouwd worden. De nood en schaarschte maakte ons zuinig en vindingrijk om ons te redden zoo goed wij konden, en de Heere gaf ons moed en lust om te volharden, hoe zwaar onze beproevingen ook waren. Toen in 't laatst van Maart, of in 't begin van April de sneeuw weg ging, begonnen sommigen uit te zien om een stukje land voor zichzelven te koopen, om zich op eigen land te vestigen.

In de maand April hielden wij veel vergaderingen om over de plannen van kolonisatie te spreken. Op zekeren tijd kwam Ds. van Raalte bij ons in de vergadering en sprak op zijne gewone indrukwekkende manier: „Wel mannen, het ijs is gebroken, en wij moeten voorwaarts. Daar is veel volk op weg om naar hier over te komen. Zie hier de brieven."

Maar wat nu voor ons en voor hen die komen, hier in het bosch te beginnen? werd er gevraagd. „Wel", zeide hij, „in de eerste plaats moet er zoo spoedig mogelijk een blokhuis, of althans eene woning gemaakt worden aan den mond van Black Lake, bij Lake Michigan, en daar moet ge met alle man maar naar toe om te zien hoe ge daar maar het best een bergplaats voor de menschen en hunne goederen in orde krijgt."

Gewoon om altijd en in alles zijne wenken en bevelen op te volgen, gehoorzaamden wij ook nu. Twintig of dertig manschappen, ik weet het niet juist meer, maakten zich gereed, maar het ging niet zoo gemakkelijk om er te komen en om des middags eventjes naar huis te gaan eten, daar viel niet aan te denken. Wij moesten ons gebak van tarwezemels, ons gekookt corn en koffie van gebrand corn medenemen, om er drie dagen te kunnen blijven.

De reis daarheen ging niet gemakkelijk. De afstand van vijf mijlen nam ruim een halven dag. Toch zijn we alle moeilijkheden doorgemarteld. Ter bedoelde plaats gekomen, zagen wij daar eene menigte planken liggen, die er aan het strand gespoeld waren. Wij wisten eerst niet of wij die wel nemen mochten, doch spoedig dachten wij er geen kwaad mede te doen, als wij die tot ons doel gingen gebruiken en gingen ze nu naar boven slepen of dragen, zoo hard wij konden. Ondertusschen werd het avond, wij hadden honger en onze leden verlangden naar rust. Wij zetten eenige planken schuinsch tegen elkander en maakten alzoo een nachtverblijf. Vuur gemaakt hebbende, gingen wij daar rondom zitten, kookten water voor koffie, en deden onze buidels open om te eten. Nadat de sobere spijzen door het gebed waren geheiligd, aten wij te zamen met verheuging des harten en spraken wij onderling over de wondere wegen en goedertierenheden des Heeren en na Hem hartelijk gedankt en met Psalmgezang geloofd te hebben, begaven wij ons ter ruste zoo goed dat lukken mocht.

Des anderen daags zou het nu aan het bouwen gaan, maar wij hadden geen enkele goede timmerman onder ons. Ons gereedschap bestond uit eenige bijlen, twee oude handzagen, eenige booren, dat was alles wat wij hadden, ook maar weinig spijkers en moesten ons dus wel van houten pennen bedienen om den boedel aaneen te hechten. Ach! Onze armoede deed zich bij alles gevoelen. Wat aan middelen ontbrak, werd vergoed door moed. Onzen hoofdleider bij het werk was Jan Kolvoord, een moedig jongeling naar het in- en uitwendige beide.

Toen wij den tweeden dag den avond hadden en onze buidels eens nazagen en onze manschappen telden, merkten wij dat we eten te kort kwamen. Wij overlegden wat nu te doen. Sommigen ook zeiden dat eenigen naar huis moeste hem wat op te halen. „Ja," zeiden anderen, „als daar maar wat te halen was. Wat er is heeft men bitter hard noodig." Eenigen spraken om het werk maar op te geven en terug te keeren. „Wel neen," zei Jan Kolvoord, „laat ons blijven en maar moed houden. De Heere zal wel zorgen. Ik zie mijne twee zusters en broeder te gemoet van Grand Haven en die brengen alles mede, wat wij naar het lichaam noodig hebben. Ik heb hen geschreven, dat in Holland [de stad Holland in April 1847] niets te krijgen was, en zij dus van alles uit Grand Haven moesten mede brengen, en als zij nu van avond of van nacht eens overkwamen, dan waren wij immers gered. Laat ons uitzien en wachten." „Zij komen over de Lake," zei Jan, „en dus moeten zij noodzakelijk hier passeeren." Dit gaf moed.

Wij besloten een groot vuur aan te maken en brandend te houden, als een baken voor de komenden, als zij kwamen, en voor ons, om hen beter te kunnen waarnemen.

Wij waren allen op wacht en op den uitkijk. Eindelijk omstreeks 10 à 11 uur daar hoort men wat bonzen in het water, als van de riemen van een platboot, de ooren gespitst en de oogen gericht naar den kant van waar het geluid komt, daar ziet men werkelijk iets op het water drijven. Om de komenden niet te verschrikken, was het niet raadzaam dat een ander riep, daarom riep Jan Kolvoord: „Bertus Kolvoord, zijt gij daar?" Wij hoorden daarop: „Ja," en kort daarop: „Jan, zijt gij daar?" Hij antwoord woordde: „Ja, Bertus! zijn mijne twee zusters ook aan boord?" „Ja!" klonk het weer over 't water. „Welnu," zei Jan, „dan moet gij hier aanleggen."

Spoedig was nu de platboot voor den wal en werd aan de passagiers verteld waartoe wij daar waren en waarom wij hen zoo zeer verlangden. „Hebt gij ook een barrel flour en spek mede gebracht?" zei Jan. „Ja!" zeide zijn broer. „Welnu dan is 't alles in orde, vrienden," zei Kolvoord.

Dat was eene verrassende uitkomst. Vroeger slechts zemels zonder vet, nu hadden wij weer flour en zelfs spek er bij.

Dadelijk gingen nu de zusters Kolvoort aan 't pannekoeken bakken voor ons volk en ieder at tot verzadiging met een dankbaar hart. Hoe wij dien nacht gesteld waren, dat kan ik niet in woorden uitdrukken. Wij aanbaden en dankten God met een verruimd hart.

Den volgenden dag gingen wij weer vlug aan 't werk, doch om 2 uur na den middag hadden wij geen spijkers meer en moesten wij onzen arbeid voor eerst staken tot men spijkers had. Tot zoover heb ik den bouw van de loods aan de Lake mede bijgewoond.

In de kolonie nu, door nieuw over gekomenen volkrijker geworden, werd het in Mei vrij wat drukkend. Wij hadden niets om van te leven. Met ons vieren besloten wij naar Allegan te gaan, om te vernemen of wij daar ook werk konden krijgen.

Wij melden ons aan bij Mr. [Elisha Dickinson] Ely, wiens vrouw Hollandsch verstond en maakten haar met onzen toestand en begeerte bekend. Zij deelde dit mede aan haar man. Mr. Ely ried ons, bij monde van zijne vrouw, om naar Kalamazoo te gaan, daar zouden wij misschien werk kunnen krijgen aan den railroad, die van daar gelegd werd. Wij namen dezen raad ter harte. Dat wij geen geld hadden, durfden wij niet te zeggen. Den volgenden dag reisden wij verder. Wij liepen tot op den middag, werden moede en hongerig tevens. Wij keerden bij Amerikanen in. Gaven te kennen dat wij honger hadden, maar geen geld hadden om brood te koopen. Het eerste begrepen zij wel, het tweede niet. Zij gaven ons meer dan brood en wij gevoelden ons weer verkwikt en versterkt. Nu wilden wij hen beduiden, dat wij hen niet betalen konden, dat ging moeielijk, eindelijk schenen zij het te begrijpen en zeiden, „Nothing!" Wij wisten wat dat beteekende en gingen hen nu op z'n Hollandsch hartelijk bedanken.

Wij reisden nu verder naar Kalamazoo. 't Was avond. Wij stonden verlegen zonder in staat te zijn om onzen toestand bekend te kunnen maken. Terwijl wij daar zoo stonden komt er iemand op ons toe en vroeg: „Zijt gij Hollanders?" „Ja", zeiden wij. „Ik ook", zei de man. Wij vroegen of hij ook een huishouding had? „Ja," zei hij, „met mijne zuster." „Kunnen wij dan van nacht bij U blijven?" vroegen wij. „Ik heb geen ruimte", zei de man. „Och," zeiden wij, „wij willen ons wel behelpen, al moeten wij ook op de vloer slapen." „Dat moet ik ook," zeide hij. „Maar kom, ga maar mee, gij moet toch ook wat te eten hebben." „Ja," zeiden wij, „wij hebben wel behoefte, maar geen geld." „Welnu," zei hij, „ik heb nog wat, en zal nog wat koopen, en dat zullen wij te zamen deelen."

Wij gingen met hem mede en hebben tweemaal bij hem gegeten, belovende als wij wat verdiend hadden, hem te zullen betalen. Wij vroegen of hij geen werk voor ons wist. „Neen," was zijn antwoord, „ik ben hier ook nog vreemd, het mocht zijn aan den railroad, daar ben ik nog niet geweest."

Des anderen daags gingen twee van ons naar de boeren en vonden werk. Ik en Egbert Frederiks gingen naar den railroad, maar konden er geen werk krijgen. Nu keerden wij terug naar Kalamazoo doch konden daar ook niet aan den gang komen. Moedeloos gingen wij nu weer terug naar Allegan en klaagden opnieuw onzen nood aan Mr. Ely en zijne goede vrouw. Zij werden met ons verlegen, doch raadden ons te blijven om te zien of er zich geene gelegenheid voordeed. Wij lieten ons raden en bleven. Mr. Ely en vrouw deden wat zij konden. Wij kregen soms een dag te werken bij de burgers te Allegan. Als wij zoo bij die menschen in 't werk waren, dan gingen zij druk tegen ons praten, doch wij konden er niets van verstaan en moesten elkander alles door wijzen beduiden. Zoo brachten wij daar eenige dagen door.

Toen kwam er een boer, vijf mijlen van Kalamazoo wonende, te Allegan, om van daar een span ossen te halen. Van dezen vernam Mrs. Ely, dat hij wel twee Hollanders gebruiken kon. Wij, bij hem aangediend, besloten met hem mede te gaan. Laat in den avond en zeer vermoeid kwamen wij met hem op zijne plaats aan. Des anderen daags morgens werd ons gezegd wat wij moesten doen, maar wij verstonden er niets van. Er moest dus een van de drie zoons mede om ons bij 't werk te brengen, en door voordoen te onderrichten. Die jongens losten elkander alle uren af. Wij hadden het er tamelijk hard. Zij lieten ons lange dagen maken. 't Was in de maand Mei. Des morgens met zons opgang waren wij met 't eten klaar en tot des avonds, dat de lamp werd opgestoken, moesten wij arbeiden. Daar de man godsdienstig scheen, aan tafel bad, en wij 't er overigens goed hadden en wat verdienden, hoopten wij op beter en bleven. 's Avonds als wij naar bed gingen, bogen wij onze knieën en klaagden den Heere onze dwaasheid en blindheid en onkunde in alles, en smeekten Hem om verstand en wijsheid en besturing in- en uitwendig. De huisgenooten bemerkten er iets van en kregen daardoor achting voor ons. Zij verzochten ons mede naar hunne kerk te gaan. Wij deden het, doch konden er niets van verstaan.

Dit een en ander werkte gunstig op de Amerikanen, zoodat zij ons gaarne wilden onderwijzen en terecht helpen. Al droegen wij ook onze gewone Hollandsche kleeding, en al volgden wij ook onze oude gewoonten dit deed ons geen kwaad. Zij beschouwden ons als godsdienstige lieden, en kregen een goeden dunk van de Hollandsche emigranten. Dit nam toe, toen zij zagen dat ons volk in het algemeen zoo handelde.

Het gebeurde namelijk zoo nu en dan, dat er anderen en meer bemiddelden uit de kolonie over kwamen om koeien te koopen, en als zij dan daar bij de boeren moesten blijven en daar mede eten, dan schroomden onze ouden zich niet, om eenvoudig en oprecht voor hun godsdienst uit te komen. Zij baden aan tafel, zooals zij in hun eigen huis gewoon waren. Dat heeft er veel toe bijgedragen dat de Amerikanen [gelijk Ds. Isaac N. Wyckoff in 1849] met zooveel ophef van onze eerste nederzetters spraken als van den volk dat veel overeenkomst had met de eerste Christenen.

Als ik daar aan denk, hoe wij toen gesteld waren en ons gedroegen onder elkander en in den vreemde, dan dekt schaamte mijn aangezicht, als ik op ons heden zie. Als wij toen bij elkander kwamen was het spoedig, dat wij elkander naar onzen geestelijken toestand vroegen, en mocht men dan van elkander hooren, dat wij ons zelven als verloren zondaar hadden leeren kennen, dat wij Jezus zochten of hadden gevonden, o, dan waren wij blijde met elkander en dankten God voor Zijne genade aan ons bewezen en voor Zijne trouw die wij in zoo vele opzichten ondervonden.

Ach! wat is er thans veel veranderd, maar helaas niet verbeterd. Wel zijn onze akkers opgeruimd en zijn wij in het tijdelijke vooruitgegaan, maar wij hebben veel van onzen vroegeren ernst en godsvrucht verloren. Toen gingen onze gesprekken veel over den Heere en Zijnen dienst, nu dikwijls over het nieuws van den dag, waar onze harten koud bij worden.

Ik heb dit medegedeeld in hope dat het iets bijdrage tot de kennis van de geschiedenis onzer eerste nederzetting en tot verbreiding van den lof des Heeren, die ons in alles zoo boven bidden en denken heeft geholpen en gezegend. Hem zij de eere.

[Translation]

The year 1846 is one that can never be forgotten by the settlers in this community because in that year they made a decision which they had never even dreamed of taking but which later caused them to say, "It was inspired of God." Just as many others at that time through the brochures of Dominie Hendrik Pieter Scholte, Dominie Anthony Brummelkamp, and Dominie Albertus C. van Raalte, became acquainted with America and heard how good it would be for many people to emigrate to that region, so also there rose in me a desire to go to America in the company of other brothers and sisters with whom I lived intimately and who like myself also hoped to find a better fatherland there. But as I had a wife and a child of five more money was needed for travel than now [?], and I possessed next to nothing. Consulting my purse, I was earnestly advised to put out of my mind all plans to emigrate. One who had absolutely no money could not possibly go to America. But I consulted not only my purse, but also God; and positively after wrestling in prayer I obtained faith in this matter that God would help and provide me with all I needed; and I must state that He never has made me ashamed.

I knew that among those who intended to emigrate were persons who had some money and I secretly looked to them for help, but I did not have the courage to tell them of my circumstances, which as I now confess I should have done.

After having earnestly recommended my cause to the Lord, I decided at the same time with Egbert Frederiks from Noord Barge and some friends from the Graafschap Bentheim to emigrate with my wife and child. At Rotterdam we joined Dominie van Raalte and many others; but now it became clear that I was not able to pay my expenses of the voyage. But the Lord showed He was willing to hear my pleas by inclining the hearts of several friends so that they offered to advance the money needed for my passage. To me and my wife this was an unexpected surprise. Thankful and filled with wonder, I prayed to the faithfulness and goodness of God and now all our difficulties seemed to depart entirely, and in good hope and with bright prospects we boarded our ship and began our voyage.

On board ship I was appointed to cook; and my wife was to help the older women and also the younger who had children and we were to receive for this 30 stuivers a week [that is, 60 cents American]. This gave us courage and hope that all would work out well. But alas! This lasted but a short time, for the most grievous misfortune of my life struck me. I myself became seasick so that I could not do my work, but this was not so unfortunate. Far more serious was the illness of my wife who suddenly died. Her body was lowered into the sea. For me this was a crushing blow. There I stood, wholly unable to decide what to do – a widower with a little son of five and without any means – unless I got help from others. But the Lord now also did not leave me without a witness of Himself. My desperate needs caused me to pray constantly that the Lord might support me and care for me and my child. He indeed heard my lamentations.

Arrived safely in our sailing ship at New York, we soon journeyed by steamboat over Albany, Rochester, and Buffalo to Detroit. It was in the month of November 1846, and therefore winter. Our intention was to continue to Wisconsin, but that was difficult because of the ice which made it impossible to journey by water. Thus we were greatly perplexed. We had no money, nor could we readily find work in the winter. This filled us with fear. But again the Lord took pity upon us. A ships' captain who was having a steamboat built in St. Clair, noting our poverty, offered to take us with him to that place and to provide us with work. Our pay was to consist in shelter, food, and firewood for the stoves. Ten of our families took advantage of this offer and we went on our journey. Our dwelling was an old warehouse.

Although we fared well, we were not entirely satisfied. Everything we saw and heard was strange. Nevertheless we adjusted ourselves as well as we could in these surroundings, glad that we had shelter and something to eat and hoping for change in circumstances and praying for better times. Daily we talked about our leader Dominie van Raalte who had stayed with Bernardus Grootenhuis in Detroit and who soon after with his family journeyed on to Allegan.

After several weeks we received a letter from him in which he wrote that he had found a place where our Dutch people could settle – not in Wisconsin, but in Michigan. Soon thereafter we received another letter in which he asked all of us to come and settle with him in the woods and there establish a new kolonie. We had only one family in our group with any money, which was to help us all on our journey. The mother of that family was the widow Laarman. She tought it best to accept the suggestion of Dominie van Raalte and asked if we were willing to go with her. Because we were dependent upon her and were obligated to her and also because we knew of nothing better to do, we decided to go with her. Having thus decided, we received a third letter from Dominie van Raalte in which he instructed how we were to travel from St. Clair to Allegan. Oh! we were so unfamiliar with everything. Had we not had Dominie van Raalte to advise and help us few of the first emigrants would have arrived here.

Following Dominie van Raalte's instructions we traveled with four other families by sleigh from St. Clair to Detroit, a distance of 60 miles. Five families stayed in St. Clair. Following instructions we went to Mr. Theodore Romeyn who was more particularly informed about Dominie van Raalte's plans. He gave us a letter of introduction to Dominie Ova P. Hoyt at Kalamazoo, who was to help us farther on our journey.

Mr. Romeyn saw that we with our trunks were put on the train. After thanking him for this trouble and his good services we traveled to Kalamazoo beyond which point no trainswere running. It was evening when we arrived. Again we stood not knowing what to do, for how were we to find Dominie Hoyt in an English city where we could speak only our Dutch tongue? With great difficulty we luckily at length found Dominie Hoyt and handed him the letter written by Mr. Romeyn. Dominie Hoyt at once ordered a horse to be hitched to a sleigh to bring our women and children from the depot. We were lodged with some of the citizens and were provided with what we needed. The following day a sleigh was ordered and at 8 o'clock we went on our way to Allegan. Our baggage remained in the station at Kalamazoo and was to follow us at once. We took our departure, after thanking Dominie Hoyt for all his kind care, and continued our journey.

At noon we arrived at Otsego. Coming to a tavern, we were kindly received and taken into a warm room and given a place beside a stove. While we were sitting there the waiter came and asked if we wanted something to eat. Our stomachs urged us to say, "Yes, gladly," but our purses warned, "take care, for that costs money." The waiter appeared not to understand the Dutch of our stomachs nor that of our pocket books and again asked if we did not want dinner? Again we stammered, "Yes... but...." The man could not understand this and kept insisting until our companion who had the money finally said, "Come, let us have something to eat." The food was good and we ate heartily; but our conscience left a somewhat bitter aftertaste, for we asked ourselves, "How much will this cost?" We asked the waiter how much we owed him, but he did not understand our question. We tried to tell him with gestures and motions of the hands, but he did not seem to comprehend these gesticulations, for instead of indicating to us how much he wanted he drew a handful of money out of his pocket and offering it to us said, "Take it." "No, no!" we replied, and again we asked what we were to pay him. Finally he understood and in spirited manner said, "Nothing, nothing!" We had learned what that signified and thanked him sincerely. Truly this again was an encouragement for us in the struggle we were facing with poverty and privation.

After we had warmed ourselves and been refreshed we again mounted our sleigh and journeyed further to Allegan where we arrived on Saturday evening, February 6, 1847, and were heartily welcomed by Dominie van Raalte and his company. We had not seen each other in six weeks and were sincerely happy to see each other again. Grootenhuis and his wife and children had gone on ahead to the place of our destination.

On Monday, February 8, we held a meeting and decided that the five men of our company were to go to the woods and that Mrs. van Raalte and the other ladies with the children were for some time to remain in Allegan. After the women and children were cared for we made preparations for the journey through the "woods without roads" other than those indicated by markings or blazes cut on the trees.

It was a hard thing for us to leave wife and children among strangers in a strange land and trek into the virgin forest where wild animals roamed and Indians anda few whites lived. But the Lord gave us courage to go forward along the way marked out and He provided beyond expectation. The ladies and children who remained in Allegan received much help and colsolation from a Mrs. Lydia Baxter Ely, descendant of a Dutch family, who understood and spoke some Dutch. This was for them a great comfort, and to the men it gave peace of mind. With five men and one of the ladies we left Allegan on February 9, 1847, and late in the evening we arrived at the houses of the "Indian dominie", as we called the missionary the Reverend George N. Smith, and of Mr. Isaac Fairbanks who lived near him and taught farming to the Indians. There we also met Grootenhuis and his wife who received us in the most friendly fashion. Two of our group were lodged with Reverend Smith, the rest with Mr. Fairbanks There we spent 14 days. We caused the good dominie and his wife a lot of trouble because they had only a small house. They lived in log houses, but they fulfilled the law of Christ: "bear ye one another's burdens" in striking manner.

We had our meals at the dominie's and at night we slept on the floor at Mr. Fairbanks'. Meanwhile we built a log house for ourselves, and when it was finished we had our women and children come over from Allegan. Six families occupied the first log house. Before we had our own house we were quite comfortable, at least externally. Some of us had bought some meat and besides, some food had been given by Americans, which as in the case of the first Christians was consumed as a common portion. But soon followed difficult days. So long as it was possible to come to the settlement by sleigh, we had bran from which we made pancakes and bread, and also had shelled corn; but when the snow thawed our supplies gave out. Meanwhile some of our friends who had stayed at St. Clair arrived, and we soon were in want. To take care of these friends we built a second loghouse. When others followed them we had to build still another. Our needs and the scarcity of supplies forced us to be saving, made us inventive, and we did everything we could think of in our determination to persevere. To this end the Lord gave us keen desire and courage, no matter how difficult our trials. When toward the close of March and in the beginning of April the snow melted some of the settlers began to look about for land on which to establish themselves.

We held many meetings in April and discussed plans of settlement. One day Dominie van Raalte came to one of our meetings and spoke in his usual impressive manner. "Well, men," he said, "the ice has broken, and we must go forward. There are many people now on their way to this place. See, here are their letters."

"But how are we here in the woods to provide for ourselves and for those who are coming," it was asked. "Well," he said, "First, a loghouse or at least some kind of shelter must be built at the mouth of Black Lake at Lake Michigan. All hands must go to that place to see how best you can erect some sort of shelter for the newcomers and their belongings."

Accustomed at all times and in all things to follow his suggestions and instructions, we obeyed him. Twenty or thirty men – I do not remember exactly – made themselves ready to go, but it was difficult to get there, and to take off a few moments to go home and have something to eat and drink was out of the question. We had to carry with us a supply of baked wheat bran and coffee made from burnt corn to last for three days.

This proved a difficult journey, a distance of five miles, which required a half day. But we overcame all difficulties on the way. At the indicated place we noted a large number of boards lying on the shore deposited there by the waves. At first we hesitated to make use of them, but some of us decided we would do no wrong in using them in building our shanty. We began to carry them up from the shore as fast as we could. Soon it was evening and we were hungry and longed for rest. We put up several boards against each other in a slanting manner. This was to serve as a shelter for the night. We sat around our fire, boiled water for our coffee, and opened our bundles. After we had sanctified our simple food with prayer we ate together and spoke with each other about the wonderful ways of the Lord and of His goodness. After thanking Him sincerely and praising Him with psalms we went to sleep, as well as that was possible.

Next day we intended to start building, but there was not a single good carpenter among us. Our tools were a few axes, two old handsaws, and some one-inch augers. We had few nails and had to depend upon wooden pegs in fastening the boards together. Our poverty was apparent in all we did and had. But whatever we lacked so far as our means were concerned we made up with courage. Our leader in this task was Jan Kolvoord, a courageous youth in respect to the outer man as well as to the inner.

When on the evening of the second day we looked into our bundles and counted the men in our company we noted that we did not have enough food. In talking over what was to be done it was suggested that a few of us return home and get some food. "Yes," was the reply, "if there is any to be had there. For the little they have is sorely needed by them."

A few talked about quitting and going back home. "Let us not do this," said Jan Kolvoord, "let us stay here and keep up our courage. The Lord surely will provide. I hope to see my two sisters and my brother coming from Grand Haven and they will bring with them everything that is needed so far as our bodies are concerned. I have written them that nothing was to be had in Holland [the "*stad*" Holland in April 1847] and that they would have to bring all necessaries with them from Grand Haven. If they should chance to arrive this evening or during the night we would be saved. Let us therefore watch and wait. They are coming by way of the Lake," said John, "and so will have to pass at this point." His remarks instilled courage in our hearts.

We decided to build a big fire and to keep it burning, to serve as a beacon for those who were coming – if indeed they were coming – and to enable us to see better. We were all on the outlook and waiting. Finally, about 10 or 11 o'clock we heard some splashing in the water like that of the oars of a flatboat. With our ears intent and our eyes directed toward the spot from which the noise came we actually saw something on the water. Not to frighten the newcomers, it was best that one who was not a stranger should call to them. So Jan Kolvoord called, "Bertus Kolvoord, are you there?" We heard an answer, "Yes," and soon another question, "Jan, are you there?" He responded, "Yes, Bertus, are my two sisters aboard with you?" "Yes," was the reply from over the water. "Well," said Jan, "this is the spot where you must anchor."

Soon the flatboat was ashore. We told the passengers why we were at that spot and why we were so eagerly waiting for them. "Have you brought a barrel of flour and pork with you?" asked Jan. "Yes," replied his brother. „Then everything is in order," said Kolvoord. That was a surprising turn in events. For we had only bran without fat; now we once more had flour and even some pork. The Kolvoord sisters at once began baking pancakes and we ate all we wanted, and with a thankful heart. I cannot express in words the feelings we had that night. We worshiped God and thanked Him out of a full heart. The next day we went on with our work, but at two o'clock in the afternoon we had no more nails and had to discontinue our efforts until we could get some. That was the last of my part in the building of the receiving shed at the Lake.

By this time, because of immigration, the population of the Kolonie had so increased that in May conditions became oppressive. We were without food. Four of us decided to go to Allegan, to see if we could find some work. We stopped at Mr. Elisha Dickinson Ely's whose wife understood Dutch and we told her about our trouble. Mr. Ely, thus informed, advised us to go to Kalamazoo where we might possibly find work at the railroad under construction at that point. We accepted this advice, but we did not dare tell anyone that we were penniless. Next day we journeyed further. We walked until noon, tired and hungry. We stopped at a house belonging to some Americans. We told them that we were famished but that we had no money to buy bread. The first part of our statement they understood, but not the second. They gave us more than bread and we were strengthened and refreshed. Now we tried to tell them that we could not pay them, but that was difficult. Finally, they appeared to understand and replied, "Nothing!" We knew what that meant, and thanked them sincerely in the Dutch manner.

We resumed our journey and arrived at Kalamazoo in the evening. But we were helpless and could not tell anyone about our needs. Some one came to us while we were standing there and asked, "Are you Hollanders?" "Yes," was our answer. "So am I," replied the man. We inquired whether he had a home. "Yes, with my sister." "Can we stay with you to-night?" "I have no room," came the answer. "Oh, we can sleep on the floor, if necessary." "So must I," he said, "but come with me, for you must have something to eat." "Yes; however, we have no money, but we are hungry." "Well," he said, "I have a little money; I'll buy some food and we will share it."

We had two meals with him, and promised, as soon as we had earned something, we would repay him. We asked if he knew where we could find work. "No," was the reply, "I also am a stranger here. Perhaps you can find work at the railroad, but I have not tried there."

The next day two of us called on some farmers and obtained work. Egbert Frederiks and I went to the railroad where there was no work. We returned to Kalamazoo but could not get work there either. Discouraged, we returned to Allegan where we again laid our troubles before Mr. Ely and his kind wife. They did not know how to help us, but advised us to stay to see if some opportunity should come. We accepted this suggestion. Mr. and Mrs. Ely helped us as much as they could. Occasionally we got a day's work in Allegan. Whenever we worked for any of these people they began talking to us, but we could not understand them and had to resort to signs. So we spent several days in Allegan.

Then came a farmer, living five miles from Kalamazoo, to Allegan to get a yoke of oxen. From him Mrs. Ely learned that he could make use of at least two Hollanders. Having been recommended, we decided to accompany him. The next morning, we were told what we were to do, but we could not understand a word of what was said. One of our host's three sons had to show us by example what was expected of us. The sons relieved each other every hour. We had to work pretty hard. It was May. Our breakfast was finished at sunrise, and we had to work all day until evening when the lamp was lit. As our host seemed devout and said grace at table and we were otherwise well treated and, besides, were earning a little, we were hoping for the best and stayed. In the evening when we went to bed we knelt and complained to the Lord about our folly and blindness and ignorance in all things, and begged Him for understanding and wisdom and direction in matters external. The members of our host's family noted something of this and began to respect us. They asked us to go to church with them. We accepted their suggestion but we could not understand the services.

This and other acts made a favorable impression upon the Americans so that they gladly sought to teach us and help us. Although we still wore our ordinary Dutch clothing and adhered to our old customs this did us no harm. They regarded us as religious people and had a good opinion of Dutch immigrants. This impression deepened when they noted that our people generally conducted themselves in this manner. For it happened from time to time that when others with money came from the Kolonie to buy cows and had to sit at table with these farmers they did not hesitate to profess their faith simply and uprightly. They offered prayer at table just as they did at home. This custom caused Americans [like Dominie Isaac Wyckoff in 1848] to speak about our first settlers with much praise. They said that the faith of our people resembled that of the first Christians.

When I reflect upon our spiritual condition in those early days and how we conducted ourselves not only among our people but also among strangers, shame comes to my face as I think of the present. Whenever we came together we talked about our spiritual welfare. We had learned to regard ourselves as lost sinners who were seeking Jesus. We were happy among ourselves and thanked God for His grace shown us and for His faithfulness which we experienced in so many ways.

Alas! how things have changed; but they have not become better. Our fields indeed have been cleared and we have gone foreward in material matters, but we have lost much of our early earnestness and piety. In those first days our conversation often was about the Lord and His worship; today we often talk about the news of the day, which leaves our hearts cold. I have written this account in the hope that it may contribute something to the knowledge of the history of our earliest settlement and to the extension of the praise of God who has helped and blessed us beyond what we could ask in prayer. To Him be all the glory.

Chapter III

EMIGRATION FROM BENTHEIM.
FOUNDING OF GRAAFSCHAP, MICHIGAN, 1847

8. LAMBERTUS B. SCHOLTEN'S
MEMORIES OF EARLY DAYS IN GRAAFSCHAP

[Lambertus Scholten, born in 1861, died 1953, spent all his days in Graafschap, Michigan, living most of his years on his father's homestead two miles southwest of Graafschap. This accurate and extensive account was especially prepared for inclusion in this collection.]

Our family, so far as its American origins are concerned, dates from the emigration of Berend Hendrik Scholten [born May 26, 1817] to the Dutch colony in Ottawa and Allegan counties in western Michigan. The Scholten family, which lived from time immemorial in the purely Dutch communities along the Netherlands border of the ancient county [or Graafschap] of Bentheim, originally went by the name of Wolbert, not Scholten. Berend Hendrik Scholten's father was Lambertus Wolbert who died before Berend Hendrik came to America. Lambertus was an officer of some kind at Haftenkampf, the place of his birth, being charged with official and administrative matters. From this post he was given by his friends and acquaintances the name of Scholte, one usually given to officials of this character. He was the father of three sons: Berend Hendrik, the youngest and the founder of our family; Albert, the oldest son, who went by the name of Klooster, in accordance with a local custom whereby men frequently adopted the names of their wives' families; and Hendrik, the second son, who for a similar reason went by the name of Kraker. Albert Klooster also came to America where, however, he was known as Albert Scholten. Hendrik Kraker never came to this country, but his sons did emigrate; and they founded the Kraker family in this country represented by some of the numerous Krakers at present living in Michigan. After settling in this country the letter *n*, first affixed to the name Scholte by the Yankees, was definitively added to form the name Scholten which has ever since remained the customary form.

Mother Scholten, Berend Hendrik's wife, was Hendrika Lucas, youngest daughter of Steven Lucas, born in the Graafschap Bentheim on December 13, 1833. She had three brothers, Hendrik, Jan, and Harm, and two sisters, Wilhelmina and Dina. Two reasons impelled the Lucas family, like many other Dutch families in Bentheim, to come to America. One of these was economic, for times were difficult and people found it hard to make a living. The second motive in emigrating was religious, for the policy of the government in Bentheim toward religion was practically the same as in the Netherlands. No unauthorized religious gatherings of more than two persons were permitted. To enforce this policy the government sent its police into the homes of the people, broke up meetings, and fined the violators of the law governing the holding of unauthorized religious meetings.

During the summer of 1846 these people heard that Dominie Albertus C. van Raalte of Arnhem was planning to emigrate with a group of needy and oppressed Hollanders. The Graafschappers also decided to found new homes in America, but, as they could not get ready in time to accompany Van Raalte, they did not leave Bentheim until March 15, 1847. Journeying to Rotterdam, they boarded the sailing ship *Antoinette Marie* on April 4. After an uneventful voyage of 49 days they arrived in New York on May 23.

This company, composed of 104 persons, did not all come from the Graafschap. A number, 34 in all, from the province of Drente in the Netherlands had joined them. From New York they came up the Hudson River to Troy and thence by canalboat proceeded to Buffalo. The boat was so heavily loaded that there was scarcely room enough for everybody. Some of the group accordingly preferred to walk. They came by boat over Lake Erie to Detroit, then over Lake Huron by way of Mackinac through Lake Michigan to Macatawa, then serving as harbor for Holland which had been founded by Dominie van Raalte during the late winter and spring. They arrived at Macatawa Beach on June 20, but anchored off shore in Lake Michigan as it was not possible for the boat to enter Black Lake through the shallow outlet. The members of the party were brought ashore in rowboats by solicitous sailors who also showed them how to make shelters from evergreen boughs under which they spent a few days until they could decide what steps they should take next.

These hastily constructed shelters gave the immigrants some little protection from the wind, but not from the heavy rain that beat down upon the branches and leaves which formed the roof over their heads. Nor could they keep off the countless mosquitos that assailed them. But they thanked God they had arrived in their new homeland. After resting at Macatawa for several days, several of the men on June 26 out for the "city" of Holland to see Dominie van Raalte who at that moment happened to be too ill to give them personal attention. But he secured for them the help of Jan Rabbers who had repeatedly accompanied immigrants on inspection trips in the forests around Holland. Walking along trails used by the Indians, they explored the region three miles south and one mile west of Holland. Here several of the Graafschappers decided to found their homes. They chose their claims and Dominie van Raalte forwarded their applications to Detroit. The price of this land was $ 1.25 per acre. The settlers at once moved on to their claims, thinking to receive their titles in due course. But they could not always follow the surveyors' lines and so some of them built their simple homes on property that was not their own. Van Raalte suggested they purchase the property on which they had mistakenly erected their homes and where they had begun to clear away the woods. On one of the hills commanding a fair view over the surrounding country they founded the village of Graafschap, from which the entire farming community took its name, after the Graafschap Bentheim they had left.

The following were the first settlers who founded homes in Graafschap, Michigan: Jannes Rutgers and family; Steven Lucas and family; Geert Zaalmink and family; Derk Zaalmink and family; Lambert Tinholt and family; Lucas Tinholt and family; Hendrik Kleiman and family; Arend Klomparens and family; Lambert Kropschot and family; Hendrik Brinkman and family; and the Notting family. With these families had come a number of unmarried persons: Jan Klomparens and his father; Arend Jan Neerken; Geert Heneveld; Jan Hendrik Lemmen; Gerrit Jan Speet; Jan Harm Wiegmink, brought up in the Derk Zaalmink family; Gerrit Bouws; Kasper Lahuis; Geert Frerks; Hilligje Poppen; and Jannigje Meyer – seventy souls in all. Accompanying these Graafschappers were a number of people from the province of Drente: father Hunderman and his son Klaas; Berend ter Haar and wife; Hindrikus Stokking and wife; Hendrikus Strabbing; Hermanus Strabbing; and Hendrik Hofmeyer and family – thirty four souls.

Some time after these people had begun to make their homes in Graafschap arrived Berend Hendrik Scholte, at a date we cannot now recall. With him came a group of about 25 other young men, of whom I remember the names of the following: Jan Harm Slenk; Berend Lugers, Berend Stegink; Jan Hendrik Poppen; and a man named Bruidschot with his wife. In those days ocean going immigrant ships indeed provided some supplies for their passengers but no cooks. The ship's cook was required to provide only for the crew. As the Graafschappers had to do their own cooking, they arranged with Mrs. Bruidschot to take charge of this work for them. In return, they agreed to pay her traveling expenses.

Father Scholten bought 60 acres of government land southwest of the village of Graafschap. On this property which was covered with a dense hardwood forest of large trees he built a log house, assisted by Jan Harm Slenk. Here they made their home, but, being in great need of money, during summers they worked for the Yankees on their farms near Martin, Plainwell, and Kalamazoo. When not so engaged they worked hard to clear their own property. During all this time father Scholten and Slenk prepared their own meals and did their own housework. This lasted until father married Hendrika Lucas. To this union were born ten children: Susan who married James C. ver Heulen; Hanna who married Teunis de Frel; Truida who married Albert Tien; Lambertus, author of this sketch, the husband of Grietje Boone, daughter of Jan Hendrik Boone, son of Egbert Boone who arrived in the Kolonie shortly after Van Raalte; Albert, husband of Siena Slenk; Dina who married Cornelius J. Kievit; Hattie who married the Reverend Douwe R. Drukker; Minnie who married David Postmus; and Fenna and Hendrica who died at 21 and 18 respectively.

Such in brief is the history of our family as I vividly recall it in this the eighty-fifth year which the Almighty in His infinite goodness has granted me. But my memory also goes back to those distant days when much of the country around Graafschap was uncleared and pioneer conditions still obtained. The virgin woods were thick with hardwood trees such as maple, beech, elm, some birch, and an occasional sycamore. There also were many softwood trees such as white pine, basswood, and hemlock. So dense was the forest of heavy timber that little brush could grow among the trees.

On one occasion father, with the help of Arend Jan Neerken and Jan Harm Slenk, felled a giant pine fully six feet in diameter. Slenk lay down across the stump but his head and feet did not touch the bark. The roots of this stump resisted decay for a long time and may even today be found deep in the ground. The wood of this tree provided beautiful shingles for father's house and barn. But as a rule the trees were smaller, although many were as much as three or three and a half feet in diameter.

Clearing the woods was a laborsome task. The trees had to be felled with axes, in windrows which usually ran in a north-south direction. After lying for a year or two they would be sufficiently dry to burn, especially when a strong summer wind from the south would blow up a hot blast which reduced whole windrows of big logs to ashes.

Our first crops were pitifully small. We planted corn and potatoes among the stumps. At first it was hard work to turn up the ground filled with the roots of the many trees. The hardwood stumps decayed very soon and after a year or two we were able to burn them by piling dry brush around them and setting fire to them during the dry months of summer. In this way as the years passed we were able to create fields, and so the country became dotted with farms. We prepared the ground by means of the hoe, and that was the only tool we had at first to cultivate the little patches of soil among the stumps. The ripe grain we cut with cradles, the grass with scythes.

For drawing logs, pulling stumps, and plowing we used oxen. Later the settlers bought horses in Allegan or Kalamazoo. Our cows were turned out to pasture in the woods, and to enable us to find them we fastened bells on their necks. Horses were not common till about 1860; they proved a great convenience in traveling on roads. Almost from the beginning most of our Dutch settlers had chickens and also pigs which fed on beechnuts in the woods, even in winter when there was little or no snow.

During those early days P. A. Kleis of Holland acted as a peddler and drayman, bringing such articles into the Kolonie as the Hollanders needed. His usual route to Kalamazoo – covered by a wagon drawn by a yoke of oxen – started from Holland and passed through Allegan, Otsego, and Gun Plains. During those first pioneer days there was much demand for cats to war on the multitude of small wild life so harmful to farmers. Kleis imported cats from Kalamazoo and sold them to the Hollanders who placed orders with him. Moving slowly through the Kolonie with his yoke of oxen, he would call out "katten te koop" [cats for sale!]. But many necessaries were bought in the stores at Singapore on the mouth of the Kalamazoo River where they had been brought by boat from Chicago. Our people secured lumber from the mills in Saugatuck.

No matter how hard we might work at clearing the woods and preparing fields, our settlers could not raise enough food for themselves, and so they were forced to buy many things including such articles as had to be manufactured. In nearby Saugatuck, a settlement at the mouth of the Kalamazoo River which had come into existence before the Hollanders arrived with Dominie van Raalte, there were merchants who could supply us with goods they brought down the river. Among the business men of Saugatuck were Butler, owner of a hotel; Morrison, a dealer in furs; Wallin Brothers, who also dealt in furs and later moved to Grand Rapids; and Lamoureaux, a fur dealer who had a store at Richmond a small place on the river a short distance [about two miles] east of Saugatuck. From these people the Graafschappers bought much of their necessaries. Many a Hollander carried a sack of flour on his back all the way from Saugatuck or Singapore to his home near Graafschap. Born and

Company in Allegan made wagons from whom Wallin Brothers secured their stock which they sold to the Hollanders who paid for them by delivering hemlock bark or cordwood. The Wallins had full trust in the honesty of our people, giving them extensive credit, and never regretted placing their trust in them. Hemlock bark usually was peeled in spring or early summer, about the time for planting corn. It was not very pleasant work felling the tall hemlock trees and stripping their bark because the woods were filled with countless multitudes of mosquitoes which attacked the men while at work. The bark usually was delivered during winter.

Our first houses were simple log structures, shanties we whould call them today, with two or more rooms on the ground floor and an attic [*zolder*] above. The roofs at first were covered with bark, but soon these were replaced with pine shingles. Wooden latches secured the doors, but these in time gave way to iron latches, supplied among other hardware articles by the stores in Saugatuck. Our barns also were log shanties but larger and taller than our houses. The stables were made in the same manner. We were happy when we had a cow or two, a pig, and a yoke of oxen.

We had a vigorous church life from the beginning. Our pioneers frequently met for worship at the house of Willem Notting, a shoemaker by trade. But they also went to Holland where Dominie van Raalte held services every Sunday. This was during 1847 and the early part of 1848, until our first log church was built. It was a most simple structure. A row of benches on each side of the room, an aisle between, and a plain pulpit made up the interior. The dominie lived in a lean-to constructed on the north side of the building, the length of the church being parallel to the road which ran from east to west and still exists. Whenever he needed more room, during week days, he moved some of his things onto the platform around the pulpit. This structure stood on the hill in Graafschap just west of the present imposing church edifice.

Here the first settlers met for their religious services. They sang the psalms in Dutch in full notes without musical accompaniment. The road on which the church was built ran parallel, east and west, to the road between sections 6 and 7 of Fillmore Township. The curving road which at present joins the east end of the road on which the church was built was never provided for in the original plans. It simply was a much frequented path used by the settlers who came to church. Its curve was due to the fact that our people traced a path which would avoid the swamp to the south.

Soon after they had estabished themselves on their claims around the village of Graafschap, some of the settlers, not being accustomed to the rigors of pioneer life, died. They were buried in the cemetery just southeast of the church, toward the foot of the hill. These deceased were: Lambert Tinholt [1849]; an infant of the Neerken family, Geejse Kropschot, Geert Kamps, Roelofje Schrouw, and Hendrik Brinkman [1850]; Wilhelmina van Zanten, Gerrit Bouws, Hendrikje Klomparens, Derk Oudeginkel, and Jan Hendrik Lubbers [1851]; Berend Bos, Janna Lamping, Johannes Hovinga, Trutje Lucas [wife of Steven Lucas], and Steven Lucas [an infant son of Hendrik Lucas] – [1852]; and Hendrika Rutgers, wife of Hendrik Lucas [1853]. This swampy burying ground at the foot of the hill proved unsuitable and a new cemetery was laid out one mile north of Graafschap. Later a marble shaft was raised over the final earthly resting place of our first dead in the village of Graafschap. Their names were recorded on its sides. For many years the passerby could not see this simple monument as he traveled along the road into the village, for the church stables used to stall the horses when the people came from far and wide to services on Sunday hid it from view. In recent years, when the automobile supplanted the horse-drawn buggies, the stables were torn down and the shaft could be readily seen. In 1938 this shaft was moved to the side of the road and a suitable bronze plate with the names of the first deceased firmly secured to a large boulder was placed by its side.

As indicated, the parsonage was altogether too small for the needs of any minister. So unsatisfactory was this arrangement that Dominie Seine Bolks, who arrived from Hellendoorn in the province of Overijsel in the Netherlands, refused to accept a call extended by the congregation.

During the first days of the settlement our pioneers, not having horses and buggies, came afoot to church. Frequently they came in their ox-drawn wagons. This condition lasted till the 1860's. During the religious troubles when several churches disapproved of Dominie van Raalte's policy of union with the Reformed Church in America and our Graafschap church was one of the congregations to withdraw, people came long distances in the Kolonie to attend our services. They came afoot, through the forest along difficult paths, through bogs, and over creeks.

Later, however, when prosperity came, after nearby Holland had become a busy city and the wooded country around Graafschap had been converted into a well kept farming community, the present church was erected to replace the old structure of logs. In this building two generations of Graafschappers have worshipped. There were sermons on Sunday mornings and afternoons. From every part of the "Graafschap" farmers came in their buggies. The men with the older boys and girls attended morning services, but the whole family appeared in the afternoon. Frequently, at least during the earlier years which I well remember, families took lunches to church. About 1870 there was a kitchen equipped with a stove in the nearby schoolroom; there, the members of the congregation had hot coffee – prepared by the ladies – for which they paid a cent per cup.

Sermons were about an hour in length. The morning sermon was usually based upon a section in the Heidelberg Catechism, the afternoon sermon on some Bible text. For years in our Graafschap church we had a leader [*Voorganger*] who led in the congregational singing. He also read a chapter from the Bible, especially when the dominie was infirm from old age or sickness, and the Confession of Faith. When dominie was absent, the *Voorganger* would read a sermon from the works of some famous minister like Hellenbroek. Catechetical instruction was given systematically, generally by the elders but sometimes by the dominies. The younger children came about 2 o'clock in the afternoon. The older children and girls from 16 to 20 came about 4 o'clock, the boys in the evening. Such instruction was imparted from October till April, when farm work became urgent. There also was a singing school which was opened and closed with prayer.

Another important feature of our religious life was systematic house visitation [*huisbezoek*]. Every home was visited once a year by the minister and one of the elders. The itinerary was made known at Sunday service and the exact time was announced so that the entire family would be home when the visitors called. During these visits members of the family were questioned regarding their religious life and were asked to make known anything that burdened their conscience or any difficulties in matters of faith or discipline or any church troubles. These visits were opened and closed by prayer, the dominie offering the opening, the elder the closing prayer at the first family visited, and vice versa at the next.

There were a few special services during the year, at Christmas and the last day of the year [*Oud jaar's dag*]. Our people adopted the American Thanksgiving Day, but also kept the traditional Prayer Day in the spring as they has been accustomed to when still in the Old Country. In addition, there were prayer meetings during the winter months.

Instruction of the young was ever in the minds of our pioneer Graafschappers. No district schools were organized before about 1861. But during all those early years a school was attached to the church in Graafschap. For years after the 1860's "Hollandsche School" was maintained in connection with the church. In it the children received instruction in the Bible, biblical history, and the three R's – all in the Dutch language. Pupils were charged ten or twenty-five cents per month to pay the salary of the *meester*, as we called the teacher. One such teacher was Meester van Ooyen, a rather wrathy disciplinarian who originally had come from Burum in the province of Friesland. By 1900 the custom of holding such a school had been given up, although in the public schools some effort was made to instruct the children in the elements of the Dutch language. During all these years, of course, our young people learned English in the public schools. But Dutch or rather the Dutch dialect of the western parts of Bentheim for years was heard almost exclusively, even on the playgrounds of the public schools.

The old log church, erected at the beginning of the settlement, for a while also served as a school. But about 1870 an unused church building which stood on Thirty-Second Street in Holland Township on what is now U.S. Highway 31 and had been abandoned by those Hollanders who had joined the Presbyterian Church was moved to Graafschap. This *Schotsche Kerk*, as it was generally called, was placed on skids and drawn by ten yoke of oxen. This building was long used as a schoolhouse and also as a meeting place for the young people. Later it was sold and became a village blacksmith shop. A chapel was erected on the east side of the church, which until recent years met the needs of the young people. This was sold before 1930, and a new one was erected on the north side of the church. Besides this chapel which seats a hundred persons, the building has four Sunday School rooms and a sewing room in the basement.

Of our earliest dominies, Hendrik Geert Klyn and Maarten A. Ypma who served our church respectively from 1848 to 1851 and 1852 to 1855, I have no personal knowledge as I was born in 1861. But I have vivid memories of Dominie Douwe J. van der Werp who served us from 1864 to 1872. I had catechism under him. The present imposing church structure commanding a wide view of the Graafschap countryside was finished during the early years of his pastorate. The bell whose peals are sweet music in my ears and rouse the tenderest memories in my breast – how could it fail to do so when most of the years of my life I heard its sweet notes every day, morning, noon, and night! – was installed about five years later.

This bell for years has been a noteworthy village institution. To all Graafschappers its peals announced the 7 o'clock morning, 12 o'clock midday, and 6 o'clock evening hours by which our farmers and villagers alike regulated their daily work. Usually the bell ringer was also the janitor who was elected in an annual meeting of the church which paid him for his work. On Sunday mornings he rang the bell one hour before services, again thirty minutes later, and at the opening of the service both in the morning and afternoon. At funerals he tolled the bell – one stroke for each year the deceased had lived. Often the people counted them and thought sadly about the brevity of this life, its fleeting character, and how all men must soon appear before their Creator.

Our people were a hard-working and sober lot, devoted to the task of conquering the forest and building homes for themselves and their children. Few of them at first left the community to find their fortunes elsewhere. But I recall distinctly a certain Bowman, a Graafschapper, who returned from Virginia just before the opening of the Civil War. His stories about the mistreatment of slaves, even their cruel mutilation, made a deep impression on me as he told them on my father's farm.

Graafschap was not a very large community, and good farming land was strictly limited. After years of steady immigration all available good soil was appropriated, and many families were trying to wrest a living from poor sandy soil. To the southeast lay Collendoorn [now also known as East Saugatuck] where until about 1869 Chicago speculators owned kilns in which they manufactured charcoal which enjoyed a ready market and was shipped to many places. Many Graafschappers moved into this region where at first a Dutch Presbyterian church was established. This soon failed and its minister, Dominie J. R. Schepers in 1870 took charge of the Christian Reformed church which had been organized.

While the Graafschappers were expanding in the direction of Collendoorn their attention was called to Virginia where at the suggestion of Dominie van Raalte a colony of Hollanders was to be established. A number of Graafschappers, Harm Lucas, Vredeveld, and Hendrik Koert with his wife and five children, accompanied by Evert Sprik from Drenthe and a number of others went to investigate the proposed site of the new colony, but returned with a very adverse verdict about the suitability of Virginia as a place for Dutch immigrants to settle. The Virginia colony proved a miserable failure and practically none of the Hollanders who had gone there in high hopes stayed.

In 1882 some Graafschappers turned their attention to the still virgin woods in Wexford and Missaukee counties. Harm Lucas, Hendrik Lucas, Jan Lemmen, Jan Eppink, Geert Piers, and a number of others went north to investigate the possibilities of a settlement in the pine woods east of Cadillac. This resulted in the founding of the present entensive Dutch colony at Lucas in Missaukee County. A large number of Graafschappers

established themselves on farms in that region. This settlement may be
regarded as an offshoot of Graafschap, Michigan, but Netherlanders from
various parts of the Kolonie and others who came directly from the Old
Country also settled there.

9. RIEKS BOUWS'
HOW I SPENT MY EARLIEST YEARS

[An immigrant from Bentheim, Rieks Bouws (b. 1832, d. 1909) arrived in Graafschap,
Michigan, in the early summer of 1848. Written in 1881 under the title *Iets uit het Leven van
de Kinderen der Eerste Settlers*, this account was published in the *Jaarboekje van de Hollandsche
Christelijke Gereformeerde Kerk in Noord Amerika voor het jaar* 1882 (Grand Rapids, 1881). Later
it was reproduced in *De Grondwet*, February 14, 1911, under the heading *Hoe ik de Eerste
Jaren Doorbracht*.]

Toen in den jare 1847 de emigratie naar Noord Amerika meer en meer
toenam, werden ook in het Graafschap Bentheim, de pinnen uitgetrokken
om naar de nieuwe wereld te verhuizen. Eenigen van onze familievrienden
en goede bekenden gingen in dat jaar op reis om zich aldaar te vestigen.
Onder hen was eene ongehuwde broeder van mijn vader, met name
Gerrit [Geert] Bouws. Hij was weduwnaar en had twee kinderen, mij en
mijn overleden broeder Jan. Ook hij oordeelde het goed om het oude
vaderland te verlaten en zich in de nieuwe wereld te gaan vestigen.

In 't voorjaar van 1848 gingen wij den 12den April van huis, den 16den
van Bremerhaven met een zeilschip op reis en kwamen den 6den Juni te
Quebec, van waar wij met een stoomboot naar Buffalo voeren, en van
daar reisden wij over Detroit, met welke gelegenheid weet ik niet meer,
naar Chicago en van Chicago deden wij de reis met een zeilschip over
Lake Michigan tot naar den mond van Black Lake, die echter zoo ondiep
was dat wij niet konden invaren. Op eenigen afstand van den mond werd
ons goed in een platboomde roeischuit overgebracht en gingen wij ook
daarin over. In den mond van Black Lake werd het echter zoo ondiep
dat de roeischuit voor een gedeelte moest ontladen en over de zandbank
heen gewerkt worden. Toen wij daarover waren werd het goed weer in-
geladen en nu ging het kleine Lake op Holland af. Soms werd geroeid,
soms daarenboven door mannen de boot voortgetrokken, tot wij kwamen
ter plaatste van onze bestemming, waar de boot werd gelost en wij
jongens haasten om vrienden en bekenden te zoeken en *de stad* in te gaan.

Het was den eersten Juli 1848 ongeveer 17 maanden geleden, dat men
begonnen was om de eerste boomen voor het aanleggen van de straten
der stad uit het ongerepte woud uit te kappen. Zoo hier en daar zagen
wij een huisje tusschen de boomen staan, onder deze ook een winkel waar

wat te koop was, in de nabijheid waarvan een koffiemolen aan een boom was vastgespijkerd, waar de koffieboonen gemalen werden. Wij zagen verder zoo hier en daar nog een planken shanty of een blokhuisje tusschen de boomen verscholen, en bleven maar al naar de stad Holland zoeken. Eindelijk vroegen wij: „Vader waar zou de stad nu zijn?" „'k Weet het niet jongens" zei vader. Toen wij eindelijk eenigen bekenden aantroffen vroegen wij dezen: „Waar is de stad Holland?" „Wel," zeiden dezen, „Gij zijt er midden in, hier, hier is Holland!" Dat viel ons af en was voor ons jongens eene bittere teleurstelling. Wij hadden verwacht in eene mooie stad te zullen komen en nu stonden wij er midden in een bosch waar wij niet geloofden dat ooit een stad zou verrijzen. Er waren slechts weinige boomen gekapt en de logs [boomstammen] lagen er nog in alle richtingen dwars in den weg.

Holland beviel ons niet; wij verlangden naar Graafschap, waar onze familie en oude kennissen woonden. Eenigen van ons gezelschap moesten naar Zeeland, en toen wij van dezen afscheid genomen hadden, daar zij naar 't oosten het bosch inmoesten, trachtten wij in zuid westelijke richting bij onze vrienden te komen. Zonder gids zouden wij hen onmogelijk hebben gevonden, een trouwe leidsman nam het op zich ons er te brengen. Wij gingen het bosch in, doch onderscheidden weg nog steg; er mochten vroeger menschen langs gegaan zijn, maar van wagensporen waren geen teekens. Onze leidsman alleen was in staat den koers te houden; hij kon dan door het oog te houden op gemerkte boomen in het woud die, op zekere afstanden van elkander, met een bijl waren aangeblest en die voor handwijzers moesten dienen. Dit was me een reisje! Eerst gingen wij over zandige boomrijke heuvels, weldra kwamen wij op mokkigen bodem, nu omhoog dan omlaag, meer dan eens liep onzen weg door een kreek, en daar omgewaaide boomen dwars over den weg lagen, moesten wij er nu eens over heen klimmen, dan eens onder door kruipen, of waar ze soms kruiselings over elkander gevallen waren, moesten wij alle beide om aan de andere zijde te komen.

Eindelijk kwamen wij ter bestemder plaatse, te Graafschap! Ja, zoo is later die country wel genoemd, maar het was er toen nog veel minder dan te Holland. Wij waren bij oude Graafschappers [uit het Graafschap, Bentheim] die in het vorige jaar hierheen getrokken waren, teweten, onze oom Gerrit, die echter ongehuwd was, en Johannes Rutgers, Steven Lucas, Lambert Tinholt, Lukas Tinholt, Hendrik en Geert Zahlmink, Berendjen Brinkman, Geert Arends, Albert Klomparens, Arendjen Neerken, Geert Heneveld, ook de gebroeders Hermanus en Hendrikus Strabbing uit Drenthe, en eenigen meer.

't Was wel een blijde ontmoeting, maar ook al niet weder zonder gevoel
van teleurstelling voor ons jongens, dat wij onze vrienden daar in zulke
ellendige huisjes zagen wonen. Ellendige blokhuisjes midden tusschen,
ja nog gedeeltelijk onder de boomen, klein en bekrompen, en zoo slecht
bedekt dat ze hen niet voldoende tegen den regen beschutten konden, het
dak was òf van gekloofd hout uit eiken- of pijnboomen, òf ook van
hemlock en lindeboomen schors, die door de droogte kromp en nu het
regende door het water geen voldoende beschutting gaf, zoodat het
meermalen gebeurde dat beddegoed en kleederen doornat werden. Hier
moesten wij met hen huizen en hoewel onze eerste indrukken teleurstelling
waren, wij schikten ons weldra in den toestand, en daar wij zagen hoe
wel te moede onze familie en vrienden in hunne nederige omstandigheden
waren, waren wij het spoedig ook met hen in de hoop op betere tijden.

Maar er moest wat gedaan en verdiend worden, en wat nu te beginnen,
hier in het woud. Om ons wat te laten verdienen daarvoor was het volkje
hier te arm, zij moesten er zelf op uit om elders werk te zoeken, en buiten-
dien, het werk dat eerst aan de orde was, was voor jongens van 14 tot
18 jaren ook veel te zwaar. Boomkappen en korten en kloven of met de
logger en handspaak in de logs te arbeiden, dat ging niet. Eenige jonge
menschen, jongelingen en meisjes waren dan ook reeds van hier, den
weg naar Kalamazoo uitgegaan om daar, of in de omliggende streken,
onder de Amerikanen, werk te zoeken. Drie weken na onze aankomst
gingen wij er met ons zessen, 4 jongens en 2 meisjes, waarvan de jongste
14 en de oudste 18 jaar ook op af. Ik was toen 16 jaren oud, maar zeer
klein van persoon. Een der jongens was reeds daar een korten tijd geweest. Onze kleeren en goed tot verschooning in een kussensloop of
reiszakje gedaan en aan een stok op den rug, of in een doek gebonden,
onder den arm dragende, namen wij de reis aan. Wij moesten den eersten
dag vijf en twintig mijlen te voet gaan eer wij om werk behoefden te
vragen. Er woonden wel eerder Amerikanen, maar die waren zoo kort
te voren begonnen, dat zij zelf nog niet veel hadden om van te leven. In
den beginne was de weg zeer ongebaand en moesten wij maar goed uit
onze oogen zien en op de gemerkte boomen letten om niet verdwaald te
geraken, doch hoe verder wij van huis kwamen, hoe beter de weg werd.

Nadat wij te Allegan den eersten nacht bij vrienden overgebleven
waren, vervolgden wij den volgenden dag onze reis, want wellicht
moesten wij nog tien, twintig, ja dertig mijlen verder eer wij hopen
konden te slagen een dienst te krijgen. Dat was waarlijk een moeilijke
tocht. Niemand van ons verstond iets van de taal die hier werd gesproken.
Alleen konden wij door het vertoonen van het adres op een brief en met

bijvoeging: „Road Kalamazoo?" naar den weg vragen, en verstonden dan het Amerikaansche „Yes" of „No", om te weten of wij nog in de rechte koers liepen, doch wij hielden moed en werkelijk ging het alles goed. De Heere heeft kennelijk voor ons gezorgd en door ons, voor onze ouders, die wij al spoedig tot grooten steun mochten wezen. Mij gelukte het eenen dienst te krijgen, een ander wat verder op naar Kalamazoo. een ander in de omstreken dier plaats, een der meisjes in Kalamazoo zelf, en weldra waren wij allen geplaatst, de eene hier, de andere daar, mijlen van elkander, allen bij Amerikanen, zoodat wij geen enkel Hollandsch woord meer hoorden. Wat die menschen met elkander spraken daar verstonden wij niets van, en als zij dan tot ons spraken, begrepen wij het evenmin en konden geen antwoord terug geven. Gij kunt begrijpen welk een leven dat in den beginne voor ons was en welk eene harde leerschool wij door moesten. Men moest ons alles met wijzen en voordoen verduiden, maar de menschen waren geschikt. Zij deden dit gaarne en hielpen ons voort zooveel zij konden.

Spoedig leerden wij eenige Engelsche woorden uit het dagelijksch gebruik spreken, en de namen der dingen kennen die dagelijksch voorkwamen, zoodat het bij het werk al spoedig begon te gaan. Maar toch daar wij tot een gedurig zwijgen veroordeeld waren, dewijl wij wisten dat men ons niet verstaan kon, o! dat was eene penitentie! Welk een vreugde en welk een genot als het ons trof dat wij eenen Hollandschen jongen ontmoetten, zooals soms gebeurde dat iemand dien weg langs kwam, of als wij Zondags eens met twee of meer bij elkander konden komen. Wij gevoelden ons dan allen als broeders en zusters. Als men zoo een week of zes of acht had doorgeworsteld, begon men, ook al naardat men vatbaar was, het wat gemakkelijker te krijgen met de taal en wat te gewennen aan het volk en in dien toestand. Na dus, vier, vijf, of zes maanden gediend te hebben, ging men dan wel eens weer naar huis om zijne ouders eens een bezoek te brengen. O, met welk eene blijdschap wij dan elkander weder ontmoetten, laat zich wel begrijpen. Met groote vreugde zagen wij dan ook de veranderingen die er in dien korten tijd dat wij weg geweest waren, gemaakt was, hoeveel boomen er waren gekapt, hoe de wegen waren verbeterd en hoe ook reeds eenige betere huisjes waren gebouwd. Wij kregen met de ouden moed dat er in dit woud misschien van ons nog wel wat worden kon. Na eenige dagen of weken te huis vertoefd te hebben, namen wij opnieuw onze nu weer wat verstelde kleerbundels aan den stok en gingen weer denzelfden weg op, doch niet altijd weer naar dezelfde plaats. Nu wij wat met de taal terecht konden, gingen wij daar wij nieuwsgierig waren om meer plaatsen te leeren kennen, veranderden wij nog al gedurig eens, en naar dat wij grooter werden en met het werk beter terecht konden, verdienden wij ook meer. Zoo hebben wij dat 4 à 5 jaar volgehouden, dat wij meest onder de Amerikanen dienstbaar waren.

In dien tijd was het in de kolonie ook vrij wat veranderd en verbeterd, zoodat onze ouders ons niet meer missen konden. Elk had er zich op toegelegd om een eigen erf te krijgen en had daarvan zooveel gekapt en geschoond als hij kon, zoodat er al mooie plaatsen begonnen te komen. Men was reeds begonnen ossen aan te schaffen om mede te werken in het bosch, om het hout bij elkander te krijgen enz., alsook om te ploegen. Doch daar deze ossen eene Amerikaansche opvoeding en dressuur hadden gehad, konden er onze ouders niets mede uitrichten, omdat die dieren, hoe geschikt en gewillig ook, hen niet konden verstaan, zie, daarom ook werd het behoefte, dat wij te huis kwamen om met de ossen te werken. Maar als dan de oudere broeders om die reden naar huis kwamen, gingen de jongere er wel weer op uit, om net zoo te doen als hunne broeders en zusters gedaan hadden. Dit verkeer in den vreemde begreep men nuttig, ja, noodig te zijn, niet alleen om ossen te leeren mennen, maar vooral om in het maatschappelijk leven mede voort te kunnen. Vele jonge menschen gingen dan ook, ter plaatse waar zij dienden, de scholen bezoeken en oefenden zich zoodanig in de Engelsche taal, dat zij zich in alle goede zaken goed konden redden en maar weinigen van onze tegenwoordige jeugd met vele van die ouden kunnen meten.

Dat de ouders in het bezit van ossen en koeien kwamen, hadden velen ook aan de vlijt en spaarzaamheid van hunne kinderen te danken. De kinderen achtten dit aan hunne ouders verplicht en zoo werkten beiden samen tot gemeenschappelijk welzijn.

Op die wijze was men onder veel ontbering met inspanning en door moeilijken arbeid onder 's Heeren zegen wat vooruit gekomen, en nu 't eenmaal aan den loop was, vond men daarin vanzelf aanmoediging. De huisjes werden verbeterd, hier en daar zag men er een schuurtje bij verrijzen, het vermeerderde en de welvaart nam gestadig toe. Des winters, als er op den akker niets te doen was, was toch jong en oud in de bosschen om er wat te verdienen. De eene met loggen te zagen, de andere met kuipstaven te maken, een derde met cord hout voor de kachels, een vierde met wat anders, en wie ossen had kon door het vervoeren van het hout naar het water, soms goed wat verdienen. 't Was noodig ook, want ofschoon er wel wat verbouwd werd om van te leven, kwamen er door de uitbreiding en ontwikkeling van zaken zoo vele behoeften, dat men altijd arm bleef aan geld. Ja, men kreeg bijna zelf geen geld te zien – 't was allemaal "store pay".

Daar er nu ossen en bekwame bestuurders waren, moesten er behalve de zelfgemaakte sleden ook wagens, ploegen, eggen, en andere gereedschappen zijn; hoe zou men het alles gekregen hebben, indien de kinderen niet tot het welzijn van het huisgezin hadden medegewerkt. Maar zie, dat was in die dagen opmerkelijk. De vreeze des Heeren, die beginsel der wijsheid is, scheen destijds veel meer oud en jong te bezielen dat dit *nu* wel het geval is. Onze vrome ouders, zij waren en leefden werkelijk vroom. Zij hielden bij al hun werk God in erkentenis en waren nauwgezet in huiselijke en openbare godsdienst. Dit vervulde ons jong volk met eerbied en liefde en deed ons degenen die over ons gesteld waren hoog achten en trouwe bewijzen om des Heeren wil.

Met genoegen en dankbaarheid herinner ik mij nog gaarne die dagen en als ik dan zie, hoe wij sedert in het maatschappelijke tijdelijke leven, zijn vooruitgegaan, en eene toen niet verwachte welvaart genieten, maar helaas! in het geestelijke veel van onze ernst en nauwgezetheid hebben verloren, dan word ik beschaamd; dan is het mij alsof God, onze Weldoener, ons vraagt: „is dat nu uwe weldadigheid jegens uwen vriend en uwe dankbaarheid voor al zijne trouw!" en dan wensch ik het geestelijk leven dier dagen O! zoo hartelijk terug. Moge de Heere het geven, en oud en jong als toen, door Zijnen geest bewerken!

[Translation]

When in the spring of 1847 the number of emigrants to North America was constantly increasing there were some people in the Graafschap of Bentheim who pulled up their stakes in order to found homes in the New World. Some of our acquaintances and friends of the family in that same year also went to settle there. With them was a brother of my father; his name was Gerrit [Geert] Bouws. My father was a widower with had two children, my now deceased brother John and myself. Father also judged it advisable to leave our fatherland and establish himself in the New World.

In the spring of 1848, on April 12, we left our home and on the 16th left Bremerhaven by sailboat on our voyage to Quebec where we arrived on June 6. From there we went by steamboat to Buffalo. We next traveled by way of Detroit to Chicago; but by what means I have forgotten. From Chicago we went by sailboat over Lake Michigan to the mouth of Black Lake which, however, was so shallow that our ship could not move into it. At some distance from the mouth of the lake our baggage was placed in a flat-bottomed rowboat, and we passengers also got into this boat.

But the waters at the mouth of Black Lake were so shallow that our boat had to be unloaded. Only with much effort could it be moved over the sand bar. When we had passed over this bar our baggage was again placed in the boat and we proceeded up the small lake to Holland. At times the boat was propelled by oars, sometimes pulled by the men until we reached our destination where the boat was unloaded and we boys hurried off to the city to hunt up friends and acquaintances.

It was July 1, 1848, about 17 months after the first settlers had begun to cut down the trees of the virgin forest in laying out the streets of the city. Here and there we noted a small house standing among the trees. Among these we saw a store in which a few articles were offered for sale, and near-by we saw a coffee grinder nailed to a tree where people might grind their coffee beans. Farther away we descried here and there, half hidden among the trees, an occasional plank shanty or a small loghouse. We kept on searching for the city of Holland. Finally we asked, "Father, where is the city supposed to be?" "That I do not know," replied father. At length we asked some people we met, "Where is the city of Holland?" "Well," they answered, "you now are in the midst of it "here, here is Holland!" Those words were a bitter disappointment for us boys. We had expected to come to a beautiful city, but now we stood in the midst of a forest where we believed no city ever would arise. Only a small number of trees had been cut down and the logs were lying in every direction impeding our movements.

We did not like Holland at all. We wanted to go to Graafschap where our relatives and old friends were living. Some of our group who had to go to Zeeland had to travel through the woods to the east. We tried to move into a southwesterly direction in order to reach our friends. Without a guide it would have been impossible to find them, but a reliable person took it upon himself to take us to them. We went into the woods, but we could see no sign of a road. It was possible that people had gone this way before us, but there were no traces of wagons. Our guide was the only person who knew how to hold to the right course. This he did by keeping his eye upon the marks made upon trees at certain distances. These trees had been indicated by blazes cut into the tree trunks, which were to serve as markers of the way. This indeed was a journey! First we traveled over sandy hillocks covered with trees, but soon we reached bottom lands and had to move forward now through swampy ground, now over solid earth. More than once we had to cross a creek on wind-fallen trees, now creeping, now clambering through them, and where trees had fallen in various directions over each other we did both.

Finally we arrived at the end of our journey at Graafschap! Yes, that's what the area was called, but at that moment it was even more wild than Holland. We now were among old Graafschappers [from Graafschap Bentheim] who had arrived here during the previous year. These were our uncle Gerrit [who was not married], Johannes Rutgers, Steven Lucas, Lambert Tinholt, Lukas Tinholt, Hendrik and Geert Zahlmink, Berendjen Brinkman, Geert Arends, Albert Klomparens, Arendjen Neerken, Geert Heneveld, also the brothers Hermanus and Hendrikus Strabbing from Drente, and a few others.

This was a happy meeting; but it was not without its disappointment for us boys that we beheld our friends living in such miserable loghouses. Wretched shanties among the trees, sometimes partly under the trees, and provided with roofs which could not keep out the water. These roofs were made of split slabs of oak, pine, hemlock, or basswood bark that had shrunk while drying, but this did not give adequate protection when it rained so that it often happened that bedding and cloting were thorough ly wet. It was in these shanties that we had to live with our friends, and although our first impressions were of disappointment we soon adjusted ourselves to the situation. When we noted that our relatives and friends were living amid these lowly circumstances we like them began to hope for happier times.

We had to get busy to earn some money; but what were we to undertake here in the forest? To earn a penny among our people was out of the question, for they were poor and themselves had to look for work and, besides, the work first in order was much too heavy for boys of fourteen or eighteen. Cutting down trees, sawing up logs, splitting wood, working among logs, and moving them with cant hooks was out of the question. A few of our young people, boys as well as girls, had already left for Kalamazoo and parts nearby to find work among the Americans. Three weeks after our arrival a group of six of us, four boys and two girls from fourteen to eighteen, followed their example. I was sixteen, but small for my age. One of the boys had already worked among strangers. We packed our clothing and clean underwear in pillow cases or in bundles hung by a stick over our shoulders or wrapped in a cloth and carried under our arms, and so we went on our journey. The first day we had to travel 25 miles afoot before we thought it worth while to ask for work. The first were Americans, living along the road; but they had begun farming so recently that they had accumulated hardly enough to live on. The road at first was very rough and we had to keep a sharp eye to note the blazed trees in order not to be lost. But the farther we went from home the better the trail became.

After we had spent the first night in Allegan we continued our journey on the next day, for we knew that in all probability we might have to walk 10, 20, even 30 miles before we could hope to find work. That surely was a difficult journey. None of us understood a word of the language people spoke here. Only by showing them an address on a letter and by adding, "Road Kalamazoo?" could we enquire about directions. We understood that the American "Yes" or "No" meant that we were on the right or wrong road. But we kept up our courage and everything went well. Clearly the Lord cared for us and by means of us for our parents whom we were to help a great deal.

I had the good fortune to find work, another of us found work in Kalamazoo, a third in another place nearby, one of the girls obtained something in Kalamazoo, and so we all soon were earning something, the one here, the other there, miles apart, all alone with Americans so that we never heard a single word in the Dutch language. We understood nothing of what these people talked about among themselves and of course when they spoke to us we could not answer. You can imagine what kind of life this was for us in the beginning and how hard a teacher experience was for us. They had to show us what to do by means of sigs and by example, but these people were kindly inclined toward us. They gladly helped us as much as they could.

Soon we learned some commonly used English words as well as the names of common objects so that we got along pretty well with our work. But that we were often forced to be silent because we could not understand was hard penance. How happy we were and what a comfort it was when we met some Dutch youth who came along the road, or whom we met on Sundays. On such occasions we felt that we were all brothers and sisters. After we had struggled through six or eight weeks in this manner, we began, in proportion as we were quick to learn, to become acquainted with the language and somewhat accustomed to the people and the circumstances under which we lived among them. After having worked, four, five, or six months in this fashion we went home to visit our parents. How happy we were to see each other once again! With satisfaction we noted the changes that had taken place in the short time that we had been away, how many trees had been cut down, how the trails had been improved, and that several better houses had been built. We and our parents together had hope that we might perhaps make something of ourselves in this wood. After spending several days or weeks at home we again went on our way with our mended and cleaned clothing placed in bundles and attached to a stick, down the same trail but not to the same place. Now that we were better acquainted with the language we went where we could earn most. In this manner we worked among Americans for four or five years.

During those years there were many changes and improvements in the Kolonie, so that our parents needed our help. Each settler had acquired his farm, had chopped down as many trees as possible, and had cleared as much land as he could so that some of the farms began to present a pleasant appearance. We had begun to acquire oxen for work in the woods, to bring together the logs, etc., and also for plowing. But as these oxen had been brought up among Americans, our parents could not use them because the animals would not obey. For no matter how willing, they could not understand our parents, and that was one reason why it was necessary for us to stay at home to work with the oxen. But while the older brothers returned, the younger brothers and sisters left home, repeating what the older ones had done before them. Living among strangers was beneficial, even necessary, not alone to learn how to drive oxen but especially how to get along with the people among whom we were now living. Many of the younger folk even went to school at the place where they worked. In this way they became proficient in their use of the English language so that they could take care of themselves in all proper transactions. Few of the youth in the present can do this better than the youth of that day.

Parents acquired possession of oxen and cows, due to the industry and thrift of their children, who believed they were obligated to do this for their parents, and so both worked together for their common advantage.

In this manner – with much privation, effort, and hard work, and with the Lord's blessing-the settlers made progress. A beginning had been made and this was sufficient to give them encouragement. Houses were improved here and there, small barns were being built, and prosperity spread and increased steadily. During the winter when work on the farms was impossible old and young alike went into the woods in order to earn a little cash. Some peeled hemlock bark, some made tub or barrel staves, some cut cord wood for stoves, and those who had a yoke of oxen could earn a wage by hauling wood to creek, river, or the lake [for shipment to market]. There was great need for work of this kind, for while enough food was raised on the clearings many new demands were felt as the community developed. People always were money poor. We hardly ever saw money and transactions were usually settled in store pay.

When oxen came into general use and our people knew how to drive them, there was a demand for home made sleighs, wagons, plows, harrows, and other tools and equipment. How would all these objects have been acquired if the children had not helped their families on the road to prosperity? Such loyalty in those days was a remarkable thing. The fear of the Lord, which was the basis of wisdom in those days, seemed to animate old and young alike far more than in the present. Our parents truly were a pious folk. In all their labors they never forgot God; at all times they practiced their faith meticulously, in private as well as in public. This filled us, the younger folk, with love and respect and caused us to esteem those who were above us.

I recall those days with pleasure and thankfulness, especially when I consider what progress we have made in the temporal aspects of our social life and what welfare we are now enjoying. But alas! we have lost much of our former seriousness in spiritual life and have become lax. When I think about this I become ashamed; for it seems to me it is as if God our Benefactor is asking us, "Is this your kindness toward your friend, is this your thankfulness for all His steadfastness?" Then I begin to wish so earnestly that the spiritual life of those days would return. May the Lord grant this and as in those days lead old and young alike through His Holy Spirit.

10. KASPER LAHUIS' PIONEER MEMORIES

[Kasper Lahuis was born on September 14, 1828, at Vorwold in the county, or Graafschap, of Bentheim in the kingdom of Hanover. In 1847 he sailed in the *Antoinette Marie*, with the first group to emigrate from Bentheim to the Michigan Kolonie. His account, read at the 60th anniversary of the founding of Zeeland held in 1910, was subsequently published in *De Grondwet*, August 1, 1911, under the heading *Pioneer Herinneringen*.]

Schrijver dezes is geboren op 14 September 1828 te Vorwold, Hannover, uit ouders niet van de hoogere klas naar de wereld, want zij vonden hun bestaan in het bebouwen van een klein stuk lands, en in timmer en metsel-werk. Tot op 18 jarigen leeftijd werkte ik te huis, in het boeren en tim-meren, doch naar de eigenaardigheid van de plaats, was het regel als iemande wilde medegerekend worden, dan moest men 3 à 4 jaren buiten de plaats wezen. Ten einde op te kunnen treden als timmerman werd van hem verwacht een ossenkop op het achterste part van een wagen te kunnen uitwerken. Ook mijn doel was zulks te leeren, doch na beproe-ving om werk te vinden in Drenthe, was dit eene mislukking.

In dien tijd was de landverhuizing naar Amerika reeds begonnen. Ds.

van Raalte en gezelschap waren toen, in 1846, reeds vertrokken, en de straatliedjes: „Mijn geluk is daar, in Amerika," werden alom gezongen. En ik zong ook mee.

Zoo omstreeks 15 Februari 1847 vraagde ik vader en moeder om hunne goedkeuring om naar Amerika te gaan, en om dan na 4 à 5 jaren met een welgevulde geldzak terug te keeren. Zulks werd toegestemd, op conditie om van 's koningswege verlof te ontvangen, en zulks zelfs te bewerkstelligen. Dit scheen mij echter niet zoo rooskleurig toe, als te zingen: „Mijn geluk is daar, in Amerika."

De klompen uit, en de schoenen aan, ging ik op reis naar Nieuwenhuis, en bracht mijn verzoek in om vrijstelling van den militairen dienst ten einde naar Amerika te kunnen gaan en aldaar mijn geluk te zoeken. Vriendelijk, doch niet zeer bemoedigend, was de taal van den ambtman. Onder anderen zeide hij, als ge naar Holland wilde gaan, om daar een rijke vrouw op te zoeken, dan weigeren we zulks niet; maar naar Amerika! ten slotte zeide hij, ik zal uw verzoek opsturen aan den landdrost, en die beslist.

Eenigszins met gebogen hoofd ging ik over Wilsum huiswaarts, onder het diepe besef, dat God is rechter die 't beslist.

Volgens afspraak met dien ambtman moest ik met 14 dagen terug komen, en tot mijne verbazing waren alle papieren gereed, om vrij en ongehinderd te kunnen reizen.

Na de kosten betaald te hebben, stak ik de papieren in mijn zak, en ging huiswaarts, zeggende tot mijzelven, wat heb ik toch begonnen, vader en moeder, vrienden en bekenden nu te gaan verlaten! Dit deed mij zeer gevoelig aan, waarover geen woorden zijn te vinden om het te uiten.

Te huis komende, en de uitslag hoorende, werden mijne ouders ook gevoelig aangedaan, maar de gedachte van vader, wij komen ook nog in Amerika, hielp, ook in het maken van mijn trunk en om die op te vullen voor de reis.

Intusschen werd het afgesproken met buurman Steven Lucas, die ook Amerika voor zich en zijn gezin had gekozen, om bij hen als onder zijne huisgenooten te worden gerekend. Ook dit troostte ons allen, en zoo kwam alles in gereedheid, om op 15 Maart 1847 ingescheept te worden te Rotterdam.

Na afscheid genomen te hebben van ouders en vrienden en in gezelschap te zijn van Steven Lucas, Jannes Rutgers, Berend Brinkman, Hendrik Kropschot, Geert Heneveld, A. J. Neerken, Lambert en Lucas Tinholt, Albert Klomparens, Nakken en anderen, als ook Hundeman, B. ter Haar, [Hindrikus] Stokking, en anderen uit Drenthe, vertrokken wij van Coevorden, per wagen, naar de Hasseldevaart, alwaar de boot gereed lag die ons te Rotterdam bracht, alwaar het zeilschip, de *Antoinenette Marie*, voor ons gereed lag. Met groote verwondering stonden wij het schip te bezien, want zoo iets hadden wij nog nooit gezien. Nadat wij de noodige levensmiddelen, welke bepaald werden door de maatschappij, aangekocht en aan boord gebracht hadden, vertrokken wij naar Hellevoetsluis. Daar gekomen zijnde moesten wij voor anker liggen, want de wind was ons tegen om het zeegat te kunnen ingaan.

Na verloop van 3 à 4 dagen hielpen wij met vroolijke aangezichten, en onder een luchtig deuntje als jonge lieden de ankers ligten, en zeilden het zeegat in. Tot belooning voor onze diensten kwam de kapitein op het dek met een bittertje, zeggende dat dit hielp tegen zeeziekte.

Bemerkende de rolling van ons schip, zoo gingen we naar beneden, en o wee, zeeziekte was alles wat we hoorden en zagen. Doch al heel spoedig kwam ons onze proviand goed te stade, en zoo verliep de eene dag na de andere, onder het steeds aangroeien van levendig gezelschap.

Veertig dagen verliepen er dat we niets zagen als lucht en water, en zoo nu en dan een schip. Terwijl het ongeduld toenam, kwam Lambert Tinholt met moedgevende woorden en sprak tot het volk, zeggende: „wees getroost, want we zullen binnen kort land zien." Met diepen ernst staarden we hem aan, en dachten, hij heeft even als Jacob met God geworsteld en waarlijk; des avonds zagen we land. En zoo kwamen we te New York aan, in het land waarvan we hadden gezongen.

G. Nakken, die zijn been in een val op het schip had gebroken, werd overgebracht naar Staten Eiland, en daar moesten we hem achter laten. Later hebben we niets meer van hem gehoord, zoo ik meen.

Daar de plaats onzer bestemming Michigan was, zetten wij, per kanaal, onze reis onder veel tobben en lijden voort. Zoo viel o.a. Kropschot in het kanaal, en Geert Heneveld redde hem. Eindelijk gelukte het ons de haven onzer begeerte te bereiken, en het was de „Indianen stad" waar we onze voeten aan wal zetten. Hier hielden wij „house cleaning". Hilligje Poppen, later de vrouw van Evert Zagers, deed het werk voor mij zonder belooning. Van hier ging elk tot zijn bestemming.

Te Groningen, bij Jan Rabbers, was mijn tehuis. Platbooten maken, ter vervoering van levensonderhoud, aangekocht door Hendrik de Kruif, was ons eerste werk. In het vervoeren hiervan werden wij bijgestaan door Paul Stavast en Koo Vinke. De tocht liep langs de Kalamazoo River en de kust van Lake Michigan tot Holland en Groningen. In den winter van 1847 en 1848 werkte ik als timmerman, onder opzicht van Mr. Isaac Fairbanks, aan de zaagmolen van Jan Rabbers, te Groningen. Daar kwamen Ds. van der Meulen en ouderling Van de Luyster mij opzoeken, om mijn zielenheil te bevorderen, en daarop werd ik toegelaten tot de gemeente van Zeeland.

Als timmerman hielp ik de huizen bouwen voor B. Kamps, B. J. Poes, en E. Everts.

En nu iets anders. Nadat het op drie achtereenvolgende Zondagen afgekondigd was dat er huwelijksbelofte bestond tusschen Kasper Lahuis en Fennigje Kamps, en dat ieder die daar iets tegen had de gelegenheid had van te verschijnen, zijn we, den 19 Juli 1848, in den huwelijksstaat bevestigd door Ds. Ypma van Vriesland na een korte preek, in het kerkgebouw te Drenthe.

Wij namen toen onzen intrek bij H. Kamps, te Zeeland. Op 2 November 1848 namen we intrek in een huisje zonder vloer of zolder, in section 14, Holland Township. Op 7 Maart betrokken we ons eigen opgericht huis. De eerste 10 à 15 jaren waren jaren van armoede en gebrek. Cornbrood en corn koffie dekte onze tafel. Opgehouden door de prediking van Ds. van der Meulen, gelijkheid met anderen, en onbekend met ons goede land, deed ons de lasten des levens geduldig dragen. Van een koe en kalf zijn we geklommen tot 30 à 35 stuks vee; van een paard tot 7 à 8. Het opklieren van ons land ging met veel moeite gepaard, want we waren in alles zoo groen. Als we zaaiden dan kwamen de herten en aten het op, tot op twee roeden afstand van het huis. De eekhoorns en ander wild gedierte moesten we bevechten, indien we wat corn wilden inzamelen. 's Zaterdags avonds waschte moeder de kleeren van de kinderen, als ze sliepen, om op Zondag schoon te zijn. Ja, ons leven was in de eerste tijd een leven van worstelen.

Ons vaste vertrouwen dat die plaats van God ons was beschikt, en moed om er door te komen, bleef ons bij. Wilden we alle onze ontberingen optellen, we zouden er vele kunnen opnoemen. B.v., onze ossjes waren opgegroeid, zoodat ik er mede begon te werken, en terwijl ik en S. de Koeijer op de jacht waren, vonden we er een dood in het bosch liggen, en dat wel de beste.

En zoo snelden onze jaren door. Onze kinderen groeiden op, en moeder zeide: „Ik ben altijd blij dat het voorjaar daar is, want dan kunnen de kinderen zonder schoenen loopen." Dagen van genot en moeite hebben we doorgeleefd. Te zamen hebben we 200 acres land opgeklierd, etende van des zelfs vrucht.

Na 46 jaren op het land te hebben gewoond, dachten we het werd tijd voor ons om te rusten, en in April 1897 hebben we ons woonhuis in de stad Zeeland betrokken. Terwijl ouderdom en grijsheid daar zijn, en 82 en 83 jaren bereikt hebbende, zoo wacht ons nog een stap, en zullen ook wij bijgezet worden bij zoo vele pioniers die reeds zijn heengegaan, en met wien we een en hetzelfde lot gemeen hebben gehad.

En als wij nu onze levensgeschiedenis zoo nagaan, mogen we dan niet zeggen, wat een veelbewogen leven. Denk slechts aan Zeeland, dat nog gouvernements land was toen ik bij Jan Rabbers kwam, en nu een city met zoo vele mooie en kostelijke gebouwen. De omgeving toen was een donker bosch, en nu een vruchtbare landstreek met al hare schoone boerderijen. Ds. Christiaan van der Veen zeide eens: „Ik ben blij dat ik in dezen tijd geleefd heb," en we zeggen het hem achterna.

[Translation]

The writer of this sketch was born on September 14, 1828, at Vorwold, Hanover. His parents did not belong to the higher class, according to the way the world reckons this, for they made their living tilling a small piece of land and in carpentering and in masonry.

Until my 18th year I worked at home, at farming and carpentering. But a peculiar feature of this neighborhood was the rule that if one wanted to stand well with his fellows he had to work in some place a distance away, for a space of from three to four years. To be a carpenter one was expected to be able to carve the head of an ox on the rear end of a wagon. I also wanted to learn how to do this. But after looking about in Drente for a chance to work, I had to give it up.

At that time emigration to America had already begun. Dominie Albertus C. van Raalte and his company had sailed in 1846. Everywhere people were singing songs in the street, "My fortune's there, in America!" I too sang such songs.

About February 15, 1847, I asked father and mother for their approval to emigrate to America. After four or five years I would return with pockets well filled with money. They agreed to my request on condition royal consent was obtained. They even offered to help obtain this. To secure such permission did not seem so easy as to sing, "My fortune's there, in America!"

I discarded my wooden shoes, put on my dress shoes, went to Nieuwenhuis, and presented my plea to be excused from military service in order to go to America, there to seek my fortune. The official's language was friendly but not encouraging. Among other remarks he said that if I wanted to go to Holland to find a rich wife, my request would not be refused – but to America! This was quite another matter. Finally he said, "I'll send your petition to the bailiff who will decide."

Somewhat depressed, with bowed head I went home by way of Wilsum. I was under the profound conviction that God was judge and that He would decide.

In accordance with my agreement with the official I had to return within 14 days. I was amazed that all my papers were in order, and I was free to go on my journey.

I paid the fee for the papers which I thrust into my pocket and started homeward, saying to myself, "What is this I have begun, leaving father, mother, friends, and acquaintances!" This thought moved me greatly. But I can find no words to express this thought adequately.

On my return home I told my parents that I had been granted permission. They were deeply moved. But father's thought, "We'll also go to America," helped, even in getting ready my things and filling my trunk for the journey.

Meanwhile we agreed with our neighbor Steven Lucas, who himself and his family had also chosen to emigrate to America, that I should go with him, to be counted as one of his family. We all were comforted by this arrangement. Finally we were ready to board ship in Rotterdam on March 15, 1847.

After taking our departure from our parents and friends, we left in the company of Steven Lucas, Jannes Rutgers, Berend Brinkman, Hendrik Kropschot, Geert Heneveld, Arend Jan Neerken, Lambert en Lucas Tinholt, Albert Klomparens, G. Nakken, and others, besides Hendrik Hundeman, Berend ter Haar, Hindrikus Stokking [Stokken] and others from Drente. We traveled from Coevorden by wagon to the Hasselt Canal [i.e., Zwarte Water] where our boat lay ready to take us to Rotterdam. There the sailing ship, the *Antoinnette Marie* was waiting for our arrival. We marveled at the sight of the ship, for we had never seen anything like it. After we had bought such necessary provisions as the shipping company prescribed and brought them aboard we left for Hellevoetsluis. Arrived at that place we were forced to lie at anchor, for the wind prevented us from putting out to sea.

After a delay of three or four days, with gleeful faces, and singing airy songs after the manner of young people we raised anchors and sailed away to sea. As compensation for our trouble the captain came on deck and offered us bitters telling us that it was effective against seasickness.

Noting the rolling motion of the ship we went below. Woe was us, seasickness was to be seen on every hand. But it was not long until our provisions began to appeal to us. So passed each day, and the spirits of our company rose and became lively.

Forty days passed during which we saw nothing but sky and water, only now and then some ship. While our impatience was mounting Lambert Tinholt spoke words calculated to comfort us. He said, "Be comforted, for soon we'll see land." With great seriousness we stared at him and thought that he like Jacob had struggled with the Lord. And indeed, that same evening we beheld land. And so we arrived in New York in the land of which we had been singing.

G. Nakken, who while on the ocean had fallen and broken his leg, was taken to Staten Island where we had to leave him. We never heard any more about him, if I remember correctly.

As Michigan was our destination we continued our journey by canal, and with much trouble and suffering. For example, Lambert Kropschot fell into the canal and was rescued by Geert Heneveld. Finally we were fortunate to reach the haven of our desires. This was the Indian village where we put our feet ashore. Here we cleaned our clothing. Hilligje Poppen, later wife of Evert Zagers, did this work for me without compensation. From this place each of us went to his destination.

I stayed with Jan Rabbers in Groningen. Our first job was to make flatboats. These were bought by Hendrik de Kruif and were used to convey foodstuffs up the river. In this work we were assisted by Paul Stavast and Koos Vinke. These flatboats sailed along Kalamazoo River and the shore of Lake Michigan to Holland and Groningen. During the winter of 1847 and 1848 I worked as a carpenter under the direction of Mr. Isaac Fairbansk, at Jan Rabbers' sawmill at Groningen. While there, Dominie Cornelius van der Meulen and Elder J. van de Luyster looked me up and enquired into my religious welfare, after which I was admitted to the congregation in Zeeland.

In my capacity as carpenter I helped build the houses of B. Kamps, B. J. Poes, and E. Everts.

And now something else. After it had been announced on three successive Sundays that a promise of marriage had been made between Kasper Lahuis and Fennigje Kamps and that persons having any reason to urge against this marriage should make their appearance we were married on July 19, 1848. Dominie Maarten A. Ypma of Vriesland after a brief sermon performed the ceremony in the church at Drenthe.

First we lived with H. Kamps in Zeeland. Then, on November 2, 1848, we moved into a small house without any floor or stairs in section 14 in Holland Township. On March 7 [1849] we moved into our house, built with our own hands. Our first 10 or 15 years were years of poverty and short-comings. Johnnycake and coffee made from corn graced our table.

We were comforted by the preaching of Dominie C. van der Meulen. The spirit of equality among our people and our common ignorance of our country helped us to bear life's burdens patiently. In the beginning we had one cow and one calf, finally we had as many as 30 or 40 head of cattle; and where at first we had but one horse we came to have seven or eight. Clearing land was accomplished with great difficulties, for in all the work related to it we were so inexperienced. The deer ate everything we sowed up to within two rods of our house. We had to be vigilant against squirrels and other creatures if we wanted to have any corn for ourselves. On Saturdays mother washed our children's clothes while the children were abed so they might be clean on Sundays. Yes, during those first days our life indeed was a life of struggle.

We had a firm conviction that our farm was the place provided for us by God, and our courage to survive never left us. If we wanted to list all our privations, it would be a long one. For example, our oxen had grown up so that I had begun to work them. But one time, while I and S. de Koeijer had gone hunting, we found one of them, the best, lying dead in the woods.

And so our years rushed by. Our children grew up, and mother used to say, "I am always happy when spring comes, for then the children can go barefoot." We have lived through days of comfort and through days of hardship. Together we have cleared 200 acres of land, and we have eaten the fruits of this labor.

After having lived 46 years on our farm, we decided it was time for us to take a rest. And so in Arpil 1897 we moved into our house in the city of Zeeland. Meanwhile age has brought its gray hairs and we have attained our 82d and 83d year. One more step yet awaits us. We shall be laid aside along with so many of the pioneers who have gone beyond and with whom we have shared one and the same portion in life.

As we review our life's history we may not say it was a lamentable one. Think how Zeeland which was government land at the time I went to live with Jan Rabbers, has now become a city with many beautiful and expensive houses. The country roundabout then was a dark forest. Now it is a fertile countryside with mani fine farms. Dominie Christiaan van der Veen once remarked, "I am happy I have lived during this time," and we repeat this sentiment after him.

11. C. L. STRENG'S
HOLLANDERS AT SINGAPORE, MICHIGAN

[This account entitled *De Hollanders te Singapore*, written in 1913, appeared in *De Grondwet*, January 27, 1914. It relates some experiences of the Hollanders who stayed at Singapore near the Settlement of Graafschap. Concerning the author little can be ascertained beyond the fact he wrote this account at Montague near Muskegon.]

Ons huisgezin bestond uit acht personen – grootmoeder, vader, moeder, en vijf kinderen. Wij verlieten onze betrekkingen in Nederland, op den 17den of 18den Maart 1847 en vertoefden op ons schip, te Amsterdam, omstreeks zes weken, en vertrokken toen naar New York, waar wij in de maand Juli aankwamen.

Van daar ging het met een stoomboot naar Albany; van Albany met een kanaalboot naar Buffalo – een heele week. Van Buffalo met een stoomboot naar Milwaukee – bijna twee weken.

Op die reis zagen wij wat van den Amerikaanschen geest; op een Zondagmorgen, toen de boot brandhout laadde te Cleveland, kwamen er boeren om melk te verkoopen. Er was een Duitscher op de boot die melk kocht, en toen hij de melk had, wilde hij er niet voor betalen, waarop de boer zoo boos werd, dat hij dien Duitscher een geheelen emmer met melk over het hoofd wierp.

Toen wij in Milwaukee aangekomen waren, zochten wij een zeilschip op om ons naar de Hollandsche Kolonie over te voeren. In plaats van naar de Kolonie, bracht de kapitein ons naar Saugatuck. Er waren zoowat 40 of 50 landgenooten op het schip, die zich spoedig verspreidden naar Chicago, Holland, en omstreken. Wij, die daar bleven, hadden de belofte verkregen, om in een pakhuis te mogen logeeren. Wij namen daar gebruik van op echte Amerikaansche manier. Met den avondtijd namelijk, toen wij bereid waren om de nachtrust te beginnen, werden de bedden uitgespreid op den vloer aan eene kant van het gebouw, en hierop legden wij ons neder, de eene naast de ander, op eene rei, met een weinig ruimte tusschen de gezinnen, hetwelk – waren we toen gephotografeerd geworden – een aardige photografie zoude geweest zijn, zoo als die veertig of vijftig personen daar naast elkander op den vloer lagen. Doch het zoude met een flash light moeten gebeurd zijn, omrede er geen gaslicht was – allen kaarsen.

Zoo verkeerde ons huisgezin zes of zeven weken in dat pakhuis, en waren de laatsten van de landverhuizers om te vertrekken, omrede vader en moeder beiden door koortsen werden aangetast en, uithoofde van zwakte, niet konden vervoerd worden. Wij, als kinderen echter, hadden een aangenamen tijd, door ons te vermaken met in de bosschen te spelen en in het zand te rollen, hetwelk heden ten dage een outing zoude genoemd worden. Wij hadden als kinderen ook buren, namelijk de kinderen van Indianen, die met hunne ouders, in de omgeving, in zoogenaamde wigwams woonden. Local option was toen onbekend, zoodat de Indianen met hunne squaws niet zelden in hoog beschonken toestand, in hunne canoe's de rivier overstaken naar hun wigwams.

't Hoofd der Indianen was een man, die Pritchard heette, die Fransch, Engelsch, en Indiaansch sprak, en die voorgaf dat hij een phrenologist was. Hij gaf bij zekere gelegenheid eene verklaring van het hoofd van mijn jongste broer en ook van het hoofd van de zoon van Jelte Bakker, en gaf eene omschrijving van hunne karakters, en bracht hiervoor 10 cents in rekening voor ieder kind. Hij had een zoon van omstreeks twaalf jaar oud, en vertelde ons, dat die zoon Protestant, doch dat hij zelf Katholiek was.

Toen wij daar in het pakhuis aangeland waren, moesten wij voort beginnen met kooken en bakken. Er was een store in de nabijheid, toebehoorende aan eene Nichols, waar een zekere Kibble bediende was. In die store konden wij sommige dingen koopen, doch, onder meer, geen kachels. Behoefte hebbende aan een kachel, begaven vader en moeder zich daarom naar Singapore, om er een te koopen bij Stockbridge and Carter, die daar een grooten store hadden, bovendien hadden zij een boarding house en een zaagmolen, en betaalden hun werkvolk in half geld en half winkelwaren.

Bij hen konden wij bijna alles krijgen, wat wij in dien tijd noodig, hadden. Daar kochten mijne ouders een kachel, een barrel witte boonen, een barrel gedroogde appelen, een barrel crackers en andere dingen om mede te beginnen. De company bezorgde alles vrij aan den mond van de Kalamazoo rivier met een roeiboot, en die boot was zoo zwaar geladen, dat toen dezelve bij ons pakhuis aankwam, de grootste voorzichtigheid moest gebruikt worden bij het ontladen. In weerwil hiervan kwam er een klein ongeluk voor. Jan Kerkhof namelijk, die ons bij 't ontladen de behulpzame hand bood, had het ongeluk een weinig aan de eene zijde van de boot te stappen, en voor het voorkomen kon worden, liep de boot half vol water. Dat was het eerste ongeluk.

Vader had twee barrels zoogenaamd witmeel, in Milwaukee gekocht. Toen de eerste geopend werd, was het roggemeel in plaats van witmeel. Dat was het eerste bedrog dat ons in Amerika trof; de andere barrel was goed. Toen begon het kooken en bakken. Ons eerste brood – niet bekend zijnde met zuurdeeg – was zoo zwaar als een steen, toen het uit den oven kwam, doch wij hongerige kinderen aten het als koek. De kachel moest in de open lucht staan, in het zand, dus er was geen gevaar voor lucht brood te zullen hebben.

Mijn vader had, eer hij ziek werd, te midden van het bosch, aan den oever van Lake Michigan, op zoowat een mijl ten westen van Douglas, een boerderij gekocht. Mijn vader nam Jelte Bakker met zijn gezin, met vier jonge mannen, die hij overgebracht had, met zich mede, en zoo waren er achttien personen, die den winter moesten doorbrengen in een huisje van zoowat vijftien bij dertig voet groot. Dus geen ruimte voor een parlor.

In het voorjaar van 1848 begonnen wij suiker en stroop te maken, want wij hadden veel maple boomen.

In de maand April 1848 vertrok Bakker en zijn gezin naar Port Sheldon, halfweg tusschen Holland en Grand Haven.

Het voorjaar begon met zeer warm weder, zoodat het reeds in Mei te heet was om in de zon te werken. Het was een warme zomer, maar in 't laatst van September zette de koude reeds in. Wij werden bijna allen door koortsen aangetast. Mijn grootmoeder stierf en de volgende week mijn vader, en mijn moeder bleef als weduwe met vijf kinderen achter.

In die dagen waren er geen predikanten om een lijkrede te houden. Mijn grootmoeder en vader werden beiden door Amerikaansche vrienden op onze boerderij begraven. Wij hadden een goede vriend in Steven Morrison, de postmeester van Saugatuck, die bij de ter aarde bestellingen de aanspraak maakte. Ook Mr. A. Steginga, een broer van den kapitein van het Kolonie schip, was er bij tegenwoordig; deze had ook een boerderij gekocht, zoowat een half mijl zuid van de onze gelegen.

Kort daarna begonnen wij des Zondags, ten onzen huize, godsdienst-oefening te houden, waarbij een buurman, zekere Van der Velde, voor-ging. Deze godsdienstoefningen werden een paar jaren voortgezet. Daar er bij dien tijd echter verscheidene gezinnen te Singapore woonden – waaronder ook Mr. Verrij, die in het huwelijk trad met een dochter van Mr. Brouwer en die later met Professor Cornelius Doesburg trouwde – begonnen de Hollanders godsdienst te houden te Singapore, waarbij Jan Poes voorging. Mijn oudste broer en ik gingen dan des Zondags-morgens, ter bijwoning dier godsdienstoefening, te voet naar den mond van de rivier langs den oever van Lake Michigan. Hier lagen altijd canoes, voor algemeen gebruik bestemd, en met een dezer staken wij dan de rivier over. Van hier trokken wij dan de zandbergen over naar Singapore; een afstand van zoowat drie mijlen. De godsdienst bestond in een preek te lezen en Psalmgezang.

Later kwam Rense Polsma – die ook bij ons te Saugatuck in het pakhuis had gelogeerd, en die later in het huwelijk trad met Mrs. Jacob van der Veen – en ging voor bij de godsdienstoefening. Dit hield men vol tot zoowat 1855. Omtrent dien tijd aanvaardde Christiaan van der Veen de betrekking van klerk in de store van F. Stockbridge.

In al de jaren van 1847 tot 1856, heb ik maar een preek gehoord, door een Methodistisch leeraar gedaan, die kwam om het nachtmaal te vieren in het schoolhuis, waar ik drie maanden ter school ging. Ook heb ik een of twee maal ter kerk geweest te Holland, bij gelegenheid van een bezoek aan mijne zuster, Geertruida Pfaff, aldaar. Dat was eene wandeling van 14 of 15 mijlen te voet, en dan 's Maandags weer op dezelfde wijze terug.

Eens predikte Ds. H. G. Klijn voor de Hollanders in Welch's leer-looierij, op twee mijlen afstands van Singapore en drie mijlen van onze boederij. Mijne moeder woonde die predikatie bij. 't Was de eerste die zij in negen jaren gehoord had.

In den winter van 1848 en 1849 ging ik en mijn jongste zuster drie maanden nabij Singapore ter school. Dat was zes mijlen loopens iederen dag, want geen dag bleef ik thuis, al lag de sneeuw ook twee voet of meer diep, en al leefden de bosschen ook van beeren, wolven, wild cats, enz. Deze drie maanden was de eenige schooltijd, die ik in Amerika gehad heb. Ik was toen 14 jaar oud.

De winter van 1847 en 1848 was de zachtste die ik ooit beleefd heb. Het ijs was niet meer dan vier duim dik in de Kalamazoo rivier, en de dochters van Jelte Bakker namen er gebruik van om schaatsen te rijden. Het was toen iets bijzonders voor Amerikanen om vrouwen schaatsen te zien rijden.

Met meergenoemde Nichols hadden we te dier tijd een contract gemaakt om honderd cord vier voet's hout te maken en aan den mond der rivier te leveren. Eerst kappen, dan met de ossen naar de rivier brengen, dan op een platboot laden, dan er mede de rivier afvaren, ontladen, en vier voet hoog opstapelen. Daar kregen we $ 1.12 per cord in store pay voor. We waren blij om dat te krijgen. Later schilden we hemlock bark, waarvoor we $ 3 per cord ontvingen. Toen kregen wij moed en zagen kans om vooruit te komen. 't Was toen wat anders dan nu, en toch klagen de menschen in onzen tijd nog.

Toen ik 14 jaar oud was, kreeg ik den post van mail carrier. Het bestond hierin: om driemaal per week naar het postkantoor te gaan en couranten en brieven te bestellen bij een onze buren, op 3 mijlen ten zuiden van ons. Eerst moest ik naar Saugatuck, dan heen en weer naar dien buurman, circa tien mijlen, en daar kreeg ik 6 centen voor, of 18 cents per week.

Ook hebben wij een tijd beleefd, dat wij circa zes weken lang niets anders hadden dan boekweitmeel en alle dagen pannekoeken aten. Op zekeren nacht geraakte er een platboot met leder geladen, in de rivier vast, en mijn broer werd gehuurd om te helpen om dat leder van de platboot te halen en door het water aan land te dragen en naderhand [daar de leege platboot toen weer vlot was] weer op te laden. Dit werk duurde zes uren, waarvoor hij nooit geen cent gehad heeft, in weerwil van het feit, dat we het zoo hard noodig hadden.

Dieven waren er toen niet, maar we kregen dikwijls bezoek van Indianen. Eens kwamen er 's avonds te tien uur nog twee om eten vragen, die, na hunne magen gevuld te hebben, ons met een „Bonjour" weer verlieten. In de winter van 1848 kwam er eens een circa 80 jarige squaw om eten vragen en om zich te mogen verwarmen. Somtijds kwamen er dronken buren binnen, die in de koude niet verder konden komen, en die we dan op bedden tegen den vloer moesten laten overnachten. We hadden verscheidene gevallen van dezen aard in de negen jaren, dat we te Saugatuck woonden.

En, om deze herinneringen niet te lang te maken, zal ik afbreken, met de hoop, dat de lezers, hieruit duidelijk wordende het verschil tusschen die tijden der eerste settlers en nu, dankbaar zullen zijn voor de zegeningen, die hun thans ten deel vallen.

[Translation]

In our family were eight persons – grandmother, father, mother, and five children. We left our home in the Netherlands on March 17 or 18, 1847, and lived on our ship in Amsterdam for about six weeks after which we left for New York where we arrived in the month of July.

From there we went by steamship to Albany. From Albany we traveled by canalboat to Buffalo, a journey which lasted two weeks. On that journey we witnessed something of the American spirit. On a Sunday morning while our boat was taking on firewood at Cleveland some farmers came to sell milk. A German on our boat bought some but refused to pay for it. The farmer was so angry that he threw a pailful milk over his head.

Arrived in Milwaukee we looked for a sailing ship to take us to the Dutch Kolonie on the other side of the Lake. But instead of taking us to the Kolonie, the captain took us to Saugatuck. There were about 40 or 50 fellow countrymen on our boat who scattered to Chicago, Holland, and other places. Those of us who stopped [at Saugatuck] had been promised to be able to stay in a storehouse. We made use of our lodging in genuine American fashion. When evening came and we were ready to begin our night's rest we spread our beds out on the floor along the side of the storehouse. On them we lay down, the one next to the other, with a little space between the families. These 40 or 50 persons lying on the floor in this fashion would have presented a curious effect, if we had had a picture taken of us. Such a photograph would have had to be taken with a flashlight because there was no gas light, only candles.

In this manner our family lived six or seven weeks in that storehouse. We were the last of the families to leave because father and mother both suffered from the fever and were too weak to be moved. We children, however, had a happy time playing in the woods and rolling in thes and. Today this would be called an "outing". We also had as neighbors the children of Indians who with their parents lived in wigwams. "Local option" at that time was unknown. Frequently Indians with their squaws in drunken condition crossed to their wigwams on the other side of the river. The chief of the Indians was a vertain Pritchard who spoke French, English, and Indian. He represented himself as being a phrenologist. On one occasion he made an analysis in writing of the head of my youngest brother and also of the head of Jelte Bakker's son. For this service he charged ten cents for each child. He had a son about twelve years old and told us the boy was Protestant, but that he himself was Catholic.

As soon as we were lodged in the storehouse we had to begin cooking and baking. There was a store in the neighborhood; it belonged to a man named Nichols for whom a certain Dibble was working. In that store we were able to buy many articles, but not stoves. As we needed a stove very much father and mother went to Singapore in order to buy one from Stockbridge and Carter. These people had a large store, kept a boarding house, ran a sawmill, and paid their help half in cash and half in store pay. At that store we could buy everything we needed. My parents purchased a stove, a barrel of white beans, a barrel of dried apples, a barrel of crackers, and other articles needed in starting housekeeping. The company delivered all these articles free to the mouth of the Kalamazoo River. The rowboat carrying them was so heavily laden that when it reached the storehouse it had to be handled with the greatest care while being unloaded. While helping us Jan Kerkhof stepped to one side which tipped the boat so that it was half filled with water. This was our most serious accident.

Father had bought two barrels of wheaten flour in Milwaukee. When the first barrel was opened it was found to contain rye meal instead of white flour. This was the first fraud practiced on us in America. The second barrel was as represented. We at once began cooking and baking. Our first bread was as heavy as stone [for we were not acquainted with the use of yeast]; but being hungry we children ate it as if it were cake. Our stove had to be set up out of doors, in the sand.

Before he fell sick, my father had bought a farm in the midst of the woods, on the shore of Lake Michigan, about one mile west of Douglas. To that farm my father took Jelte Bakker and his family and four young men whom he had brought overseas. During that winter there were 18 persons lodged in a house of about 15 by 30 feet. So there was no room for a parlor. During the spring of 1848 we began we began to make sugar and sirup, for we had a large number of maple trees. In April 1848 Jelte Bakker and his family moved to Port Sheldon, midway between Holland and Grand Haven. In spring the weather turned warm so that already in May it was too hot to work in the sun. The summer too was warm, but cold weather set in during September. Most of us were suffering from fever. My grandmother died, followed in the next week by my father. My mother thus was left a widow with five children. In those days there were no ministers to hold funeral services. My frandmother and my father were buried on our farm, by American friends. We had a good friend in Mr. Steven Morrison, postmaster at Saugatuck, who made an address at the funeral. Mr. A. Steginga, brother of the captain of the colony's ship, also was present. He had bought a farm about a half mile south of our's.

Soon after this we began to hold religious meetings at our house at which a neighbor, a certain Mr. van de Velde, served as leader. These meetings continued for a few years. Other families had settled at Singapore, among whom was Mr. Verrij who married a daughter of Mr. Brouwer. This daughter later became the wife of Professor C. Doesburg. These Hollanders began to hold services at Singapore under the leadership of Mr. Jan Poes. On Sunday mornings my oldest brother and myself attended these meetings. We went afoot along the shore of Lake Michigan to the mouth of the river where always lay a number of canoes intended for general use, and with one of which we crossed the river. Thence we proceeded over the sand hills to Singapore. These religious services consisted in the reading of a sermon and the singing of psalms. Next came Mr. Polsma to lead these meetings. He had lived with us in the storehouse in Saugatuck and later married Mrs. J. van der Veen. These services were held until about 1855. At about that time Christiaan van der Veen [later Rev. van der Veen] began to work as a clerk in F. Stockbridge's store.

During all those years from 1847 to 1856 I heard but one sermon, by a Methodist preacher who came to celebrate communion in the schoolhouse where I attended school for three months. Once or twice I attended church in Holland, when I visited my sister Geertruida Pfaff who was living there. That was a journey afoot of 14 or 15 miles, and on Monday, the same distance returning. Once Dominie Klijn preached for the Hollanders in Mr. Welch's tannery two miles distant from Singapore and three miles from our farm. Mu mother attended that service. It was the first she had heard in nine years.

During the winter of 1848 and 1849 my youngest sister and I attended school near Singapore for three months. That was a walk of six miles daily, for I never missed a day in spite of the fact that the woods were alive with bears, wolves, wild cats, etc. These three months were the only schooling I had in America. At that time I was 14 years old.

The winter of 1847 and 1848 was the mildest I ever experienced. The ice in the Kalamazoo River was no more than four inches thick. The daughters of Jelte Bakker took advantage of this to go skating. This was something extraordinary for Americans who were not accustomed to seeing ladies skating.

We made a contract with Nichols [the storekeeper] to produce and deliver at the mouth of the river 100 cords of wood four feet long. First, we had to chop down the trees and cut up the wood, next, with our oxen we had to take the wood to the river, then load it on a flatboat and convey it down the stream and unload it, and finally pile it up in rows four feet high. For all this labor we received $ 1.12 per cord and were paid in store pay. Later we peeled hemlock bark which brought us $ 3 per cord. Earning this money kindled our courage, for we saw we had a chance to get ahead. In those days conditions were very different from those obtaining a the present time, but nevertheless today people complain.

When I was 14 I obtained the post of mail carrier. The work it entailed was as follows: three times a week I had to go to the post office and deliver papers and letters to one of our neighbors who lived three miles from us. First I had to go to Saugatuck, next proceed to our neighbor, then return, a total distance of about 10 miles for which I received 6 cents, or 18 cents per week.

There also was a time during which we had no food other than buckwheat flour when every day we ate pancakes made from it. One night a flatboat loaded with leather was stranded in the river. My brother was hired to unload the flatboat, carry the leather through the water, and afterwards, when the flatboat was floating again, reload the leather. This was a job which lasted six hours. But he never was paid for this work in spite of the fact that we needed this money desperately.

There were no thieves. Frequently Indians called upon us. On one occasion at ten o'clock in the evening two of them called, asking for something to eat. After being served they left us merely saying, "Bonjour". During the winter of 1848 an 80 year old squaw stopped to ask for some food and to be permitted to warm herself. Sometimes drunken neighbors stopped because they could not travel further on account of the cold. These we kept for the night, letting them sleep on beds stretched out on the floor. We had many such incidents during the nine years of our residence at Saugatuck.

I now shall cut short my account, in the hope that readers, having formed a clearer conception of the differences in the times in which our first settlers lived and those of the present, will be thankful for the blessings which at present are their's.

Chapter IV

FOUNDING AND EARLY HISTORY OF
OLD GRONINGEN AND NEW GRONINGEN 1847-1856

12. JAN HENDRIKS STEGINK'S
RELATION OF MY JOURNEY TO AMERICA

[This relation of the earliest history of Groningen and Zeeland was prepared for the Semi-Centennial celebrations in Holland, Michigan, held in August 1897 and published in *De Grondwet*, February 10, 1914. The author emigrated from Drente in 1846, sailing in the *Isabella Bath*.]

Het was in den zomer van het jaar 1846, dat er in het zuidelijke gedeelte van de provincie Drente sprake ging, dat Ds. A. C. van Raalte toebereidselen maakte om het Hollandsche grondgebied te verlaten, en naar Amerika te vertrekken, met emigranten uit de provinciën Overijsel en Gelderland.

Hierover werd onder de arbeidende klas veel gesproken, doch men had weinig inlichting van het „hoe?"

Hierop kwamen eenige brieven in druk van lieden die uit de provinciën Groningen en Gelderland reeds naar Amerika waren getrokken. Die gaven wat meer inlichting over Amerika: wat het was voor de arbeidende klasse, het ruimere bestaan, dat daar onder Gods zegen kon verkregen worden niet alleen, maar dat de mindere klasse ook land in eigendom kon krijgen.

Dit wekte velen op, die wel met noesten arbeid hun brood hadden, doch aan eigendom niet konden denken. Een paar familiën uit de gemeente Emmen, Drente, met name Evert Zagers en Egbert Frederiks, reisden naar Van Raalte om verdere informatie in te winnen, en besloten met nog een paar familiën in en bij Coevorden, de reis met Van Raalte te ondernemen. Zij vertrokken, naar ik meen, in September 1846 en nu was er sprake dat ook Jan Rabbers uit de gemeente Emmen voornemens was Van Raalte te volgen.

Dit verwekte bij anderen ook onderzoek, doch men kon weinig inlichtingen inwinnen. De zaak werd meer overwogen en bij velen een gebedszaak gemaakt.

Door een vriend die voornemens was de reis mede te doen onderricht zijnde zoveel hij wist, werd de zaak ons ernstig voor het tijdelijke en geestelijke. Wij mochten den Heere vragen om licht in die gewichtige zaak, en besloten met vrijmoedigheid het land der vaderen te verlaten.

Ons gezelschap van Drente bestond uit zes hoofden van gezinnen en vier vrijgezellen, met de vrouwen en kinderen, vier en twintig in getal; twee hoofden van gezinnen waren Graafschappers van geboorte.

Door schrijven om informatie te verkrijgen aangaande de overvaart van Rotterdam naar New York, kregen wij bericht, dat er plaats was voor ons op een emigranten-schip, dat bestemd was naar New York, en hetwelk den 13den October van Rotterdam zou vertrekken. Wij maakten ons reisvaardig en namen afscheid van bloedverwanten – vader, moeder, broeders, en zusters.

Het scheiden viel aan onze zijde veel gemakkelijker, dan aan de zijde van hen, die wij verlieten. Het is wonderlijk hoe een volk, dat geen reizen gewoon was, zulk eene groote reis durfde ondernemen. Het meerendeel had nog nimmer een schip gezien, was nog veel minder er op geweest. Maar waar de Heere de harten neigt en gewillig maakt, daar is geen tegenstand.

In den vroegen morgen van den 6den October verlieten we onze woonplaats, en gingen naar Buinen, gemeente Borger, drie uren van Assen, alwaar wij tijdig aankwamen om van daar naar Meppel te vertrekken. Van Meppel gingen wij, per Meppeler beurtschipper naar Amsterdam. Aan de pier of afvaartplaats te Meppel openbaarde zich de vijandschap tegen Amerika. Spotters hadden zich aan den steiger vergaderd, om al spottende ons uit de provincie te doen vertrekken.

Den 8sten October kwamen wij des morgens te Amsterdam aan. Tegen den avond verlieten wij Amsterdam per trekschuit naar Rotterdam en kwamen in den morgen van den 9den aldaar aan.

Onze reisgenooten, Jan Rabbers en anderen, hadden een overlandreis gemaakt over Dedemsvaart tot Hasselt, vandaar over de Zuiderzee en het Haarlemmer Meer per zeilschip naar Rotterdam, en kwamen den 10den daar aan.

Toen wij aan het schip kwamen dat onder „de Boompjes" ten anker lag, was het meerendeel onzer medereizigers ter plaatse. Het waren Gelderschen en Overijselschen, een paar familiën uit Utrecht en een gezin Friesen. Al spoedig kamen wij met onzen reisgenot Jan Kolvoord in gesprek. Zoo ik meen, waren er maar twee familiën onder de honderd zes en twintig personen, welke de reis medemaakten, die van de Groote Kerk waren.

Er was nog veel drukte om de provisie in te koopen, want den 13den zouden wij van Rotterdam vertrekken. De Nederlandsche regeering had toezicht, dat, volgens de wet, zeker aantal ponden levensmiddelen aan boord moesten zijn.

Den 13den van Rotterdam naar Hellevoetsluis vertrokken zijnde gingen wij den 14den onder zeil en zagen de meesten onzer het vaderland en de plaats waar wij het eerste levenslicht aanschouwden, nooit weder.

Uithoofde van tegenwind waren wij vóór den 28sten niet uit het Engelsche kanaal. Den 23sten November kregen wij een storm, die den volgenden dag in een orkaan ontaarde, en wel van zoo'n hevigen aard, dat een oude kok, die vijf en twintig jaren lang den oceaan bevaren had, getuigde nog nooit zoo iets bijgewoond te hebben. De luiken waren allen dicht, want bestendig was er water op het dek.

Het volk was echter bijzonder bedaard. Men hoorde lezen en bidden, ja zelfs werd den 130sten Psalm gezongen. Wij hadden een student van Van Raalte aan boord, zekere Mannes Mensing, die alle dagen twee keeren bijbeloefeningen voor het volk hield. Dit voorrecht mochten wij genieten, dat, al was het ook 's Zaterdags winderig, wij er 's Zondags nimmer door werden gestoord. Twee kinderen zijn op den oceaan gestorven en een toen wij voor New York ten anker lagen.

Na eene reis van een en zestig dagen, kwamen wij den 19den December te New York aan. Het aardrijk was met sneeuw bedekt. Den 22sten verlieten wij het schip, *Isabella Bath* genaamd, en onder kommando van kapitein Kellie. Wij vertoefden een nacht te New York en verlieten den 23sten de stad. Daar de Hudson rivier dichtgevroren was, vertrokken wij per trein naar Albany, waar wij laat aankwamen. Even voor dat wij hier aankwamen, stierf de vrouw van Jan Rabbers.

Uit hoofde van het ijs kon de ferry boat ons niet over de rivier brengen. Wij liepen daarom over het ijs en kwamen allen gelukkig behouden in de stad aan, waar we in de herberg vertoefden tot den 26sten. In de herberg konden wij geen slaapplaats bekomen. Een ieder zocht een plaatsje om te slapen, waar hij althans geen gevaar had om door een ander op het lichaam getrapt te worden. Ik zocht het onder de eettafel op den vloer, een ander in een hoek, een ander op een stoel, enz.

Dewijl onze goederen niet eer kwamen, huurden wij eene woning en waren met vijftien personen te zamen. Het voornemen was naar Buffalo door te trekken, doch koude en ziekte verhinderden ons verder te gaan.

Binnen veertien dagen na onze aankomst, was ons gezelschap van vier en twintig tot negentien verminderd.

Wij wisten niet waar Van Raalte zich zou neerzetten. Men dacht dat dit in Wisconsin zou zijn, doch wij kregen spoedig berichten van Detroit, Michigan, dat de keuze was om aan de Black Lake, in Ottawa County, Michigan, zich neer te zetten.

Hij verzocht eenige mannen ten spoedigste naar hem over te zenden,

om toebredselen te maken voor hen, die in het volgend voorjaar uit
Albany zouden optrekken, alsook voor diegenen welke voornemens
waren om uit Nederland over te komen. Van ons gezelschap gingen er
heen: Jan Kolvoord, Willem Kremers, Jan Stegeman en zoon, de gebroeders Hendrik, Jan, en Harm Plaggemars, en ik meen nog een of twee
meer.

De kerstdagen waren voor ons niet heel aangenaam, doch wij schikten
ons in ons lot. Daar den 26sten onze goederen gekomen waren, moesten
wij het noodigste voor huiselijk gebruik hebben, en dat bestond in een
kachel en zijn toebehoren. Jan Rabbers en schrijver dezes werden opgedragen om in die behoefte te voorzien.

Moeilijk was die opdracht, daar wij niets verstaan konden. Doch wij
kochten een kachel, en de prijs er van werd ons op de vingers voorgeteld.
Des avonds waren wij verblijd, dat wij, na eene moeitevolle reis van 74
dagen, in onze gehuurde woning de huiselijke godsdienst wat meer onbelemmerd mochten waarnemen. De Heere beschikte ons al spoedig
vrienden. Velen van de oude burgers van Hollandsche afkomst konden
nog Hollandsch verstaan en spreken. Zij zochten ons op, vergezeld van
Rev. I. N. Wyckoff, die als stadszendeling bestendig werkzaam was voor
het welzijn van ons emigranten. Naar ziel en lichaam, met raad en daad,
tijdig en ontijdig, altijd was hij behulpzaam en wekte velen op tot liefdadigheid voor behoeftige gezinnen.

Velen van ons gezelschap kregen, spoedig na aankomst te Albany,
werk. De jeugdigen een dienst in of buiten de stad; die een ambacht
geleerd had, kreeg werk om in zijne behoeften te voorzien. Die lust had
om naar de Sabbatschool te gaan, werd verzocht des Zondags tusschen
de vóór- en namiddag-godsdienstoefening in de kerk te komen waar Rev.
Wyckoff leeraar was. Daar was een ouderling, die Hollandsch verstaan
en spreken kon.

Met vijftien personen betrokken wij onze woning. Spoedig verminderde het getal. Een werd ziek en kwam in het armhuis; twee gingen bij
de boeren, buiten de stad werken; den 26sten Januari 1847 vertrokken er
zeven naar Buffalo. In April kwam dominee van Raalte, uit Michigan,
predikte voor ons en was hen behulpzaam, die naar Michigan wenschten
te vertrekken. Op eenige uitzonderingen na, vertrok het volk. Schrijver
dezes moest, wegens huiselijke omstandigheden, blijven, en zag het gezelschap met betraande oogen na. In het laatst van Augustus vertrokken
wij met ons vieren; vier bleven er achter. Een mijner vrienden werd op
de kanaalboot ziek. Met elf dagen waren wij in Buffalo en moesten wegens
ziekte blijven tot het voorjaar van 1848.

In het laatst van April 1848 maakten wij ons gereed voor de reis naar Michigan. Wij vertrokken per stoomboot naar Chicago, vandaar per zeilschip naar Grand Haven, vandaar per rivier boot naar Grandville, en toen per ossenwagen naar de Kolonie, zonder weg, door geulen en gaten.

Soms werden de wielen van den wagen gespannen met een keten, om door de diepe geulen te komen. Hier en daar een bles aan een boom was het teeken dat men volgen moest. Nadat wij den 30sten April 1848 te Grandville waren aangekomen, gingen wij met ons drieën den eersten Mei naar de Kolonie. Vroeg namen wij de reis aan. Soms moesten wij over omgevallen boomen loopen, om over het water te komen. Des namiddags bereikten wij het eerste bolkhuis van Jakob Borger, in section 10 Dit was het eerste van de Kolonie.

Het tweede huis was dat van Willem van de Luyster, op de n.w. quarter van section 17, town Zeeland. Vandaar kwamen wij aan den n.o. hoek van Zeeland, en naderden het eerste plankenhuis, dat van Van de Putte. Vandaar naar Groningen, over de hoogte, die langs de swamp loopt, in sectie 24, dicht op het dorp aan, waar circa dertig huizen stonden, alle blokhuizen op twee na.

Nu terug naar Zeeland. Wij waren op het middelpunt van Zeeland, eer wij een blokhuis zagen. Dit was van De Kruif. Dan ontwaarden we er nog eenigen, zooals die van De Naaie, Van der Vliet, en Vijn. De andere blokhuizen stonden aan de zuidzijde van het dorp. Men was bezig met het bouwen eener kerk, omtrent waar Dr. Baart's huis staat. Vóór dien tijd werd de dienst verricht in het huis van Jan Wabeke.

De straten waren, op eene uitzondering na, onberijdbaar. Oost van de kerk stonden de boomen nog op den stam. West van de kerk waren aan de noordzijde nog geen huizen, dan tegenover de kerk, op het halve lot ten noorden van het plein, voor de kerk. Zoo ik meen, is op den tweeden Zondag in Mei de kerk ingewijd. Door den grooten toevloed van landverhuizers dien zomer, werd zij te klein, en in het najaar werd er eene nieuwe gebouwd, van gekante cederloggen en zestig bij veertig voet groot. Het was toen nog zoo genoegenlijk niet 's avonds langs de straten van Zeeland te gaan. Men moest voorzichtig loopen om niet te vallen. Doch een pelgrim wandelde zijn pad met blijdschap des avonds langs de hobbelige wegen.

[Translation]

In the summer of 1846 rumor spread in the southern part of the province of Drente that Dominie Albertus C. van Raalte was making preparations to leave the Netherlands and sail to America with emigrants from the provinces of Overijsel and Gelderland.

Many a person of the laboring class talked about this plan, but we had little information about how it was to be carried out. Soon letters from people who had already emigrated to America from the provinces of Groningen and Gelderland appeared in print. These letters gave us some more information about America and what emigration meant for the laboring class, namely not only that a better economic existence could be had there under God's blessing, but also that those of the poorer class could actually acquire their own farms.

These reports roused many of us who earned our bread with hard toil but who could not possibly dream of owning farms. A couple of families from the parish of Emmen, Drente, namely Evert Zagers and Egbert Frederiks, went to consult Dominie van Raalte in order to gain further information. They decided to undertake the voyage with Van Raalte and a few other families living in or near Coevorden. They departed, if I remember correctly, in Setember 1846; and soon there was talk that Jan Rabbers from the parish of Emmen also had formed plans to follow in the footsteps of Van Raalte.

News of these decisions roused others to seek information, but little that was substantial could be had. So the matter was further discussed; and many made it the subject of prayer. A friend who formed the intention to emigrate told us all he knew about the undertaking, and so the question of emigration became for us a serious sprirtual and temporal concern. We approached the Lord for light in this weighty undertaking, and came to the decision that we could leave the land of our fathers with a clear conscience. Our company from Drente consisted of the heads of six families and four unmarried persons, besides women and children. Two heads of families were natives of the Graafschap of Bentheim.

In response to our letter for information concerning passage from Rotterdam to New York, we were informed that there was space for us on an emigrant ship sailing for New York and that its sailing date was October 13. We got ourselves ready and took leave of our relatives – father, mother, brothers, and sisters. Parting from them was much easier for us who were leaving than for those who were staying behind. It is remarkable how people totally unaccustomed to travel were bold enough to undertake such a long voyage. Most of us had never seen a ship, had never been on one. But when the Lord inclines men and makes them willing there is nothing to stop them.

In the early morning of October 6 we left our home and proceeded to Buinen, parish of Borger, three hours from Assen where we arrived in good time to leave for Meppel. From Meppel we traveled by market boat to Amsterdam. At the pier at Meppel people displayed enmity toward America. Mockers had collected at the pier in order to cover us with insults as we were leaving the province. We arrived in Amsterdam on October 8. Toward evening we left Amsterdam by canalboat for Rotterdam where we arrived on the morning of the 9th.

Our companions, Jan Rabbers and others, had traveled across the country by way of Dedemsvaart to Hasselt from which place they went by sailing ship over the Zuider Zee to the Harlemmermeer and thence to Rotterdam where they arrived on the 10th.

When we arrived at our ship which was lying anchored at the "Boompjes" most of our fellow travelers had already gone aboard. They were Gelderlanders, people from Overijsel, a few families from Utrecht, and one familie from Friesland. Soon we met our companion Jan Kolvoord. If I recall accurately, there were but two families out of the total of 126 persons in this company who belonged to the Reformed Church.

We were very busy buying provisions for the voyage. The Dutch government exercised some supervision in this matter, namely, that there should be a certain quantity of provisions for each passenger on board ships. On the 13th we left Rotterdam and on the 14th our ship set sail from Hellevoetsluis, and the most of us never again saw our fatherland and the place where we were born.

Because of contrary winds we did not get out of the English Channel before the 28th. On November 23 we had a storm which on the following day developed into a tornado so severe that an old cook who had sailed the ocean for twenty-five years declared he had never seen anything like it. The hatches were closed to keep out the water on the deck. The passengers were peculiarly calm. They were engaged in reading and praying; some sang Psalm 130 [from the Dutch Psalter]. Aboard with us was one of Van Raalte's students, Mannes Mensing who held Bible exercises twice each day. To us it appeared a special privilege that while it was windy on Saturdays, on Sundays it was quiet. Two children died on the ocean, and a third while we lay at anchor in New York.

After a voyage of sixty-one days we arrived in New York on December 19. The ground was covered with snow. On the 22d we left our ship, the *Isabella Bath* under the command of Captain Kellie [Kelly?]. We spent one night in New York and continued our journey on the 23rd. As the Hudson River was covered with ice we went by train to Albany which we reached late in the day. Just before we arrived Jan Rabbers' wife died.

The ferry boat could not carry us over the river because of the ice. So we crossed over walking on the ice and arrived safe and sound in the city where we stayed in a hotel until the 26th. But we could find no place to sleep in the hotel. Each person tried to find some spot to sleep where he was in no danger of being stepped upon. I found such a place under the table, another in a corner, another on a chair, and so forth.

As our baggage was slow in arriving we hired a house into which fifteen of us moved. Our intention was to proceed to Buffalo, but cold weather and sickness prevented our doing this. Within fourteen days after arrival our group of twenty-four had dwindled to nineteen.

We did not know where Van Raalte intended to settle. Some of us thought he would do so in Wisconsin, but soon we received news from Detroit, Michigan, that he had chosen a spot on Black Lake, in Ottawa County, Michigan. Van Raalte asked that some of the men be sent over to him as soon as possible in order to make preparations to receive the people who would come from Albany in the following year and also those who were still planning to emigrate from the Netherlands. Of our group those that left for Michigan were Jan Kolvoord, Willem Kremers, Jan Stegeman and son, the brothers Hendrik, Jan, and Harm Plaggemars, and, I believe, one or two more.

The Christmas season was not a very pleasant one for us, but we adjusted ourselves to circumstances. Our baggage arrived on the 26th, and we had to acquire some needed kitchen equipment, that is a stove and the things that went with it. Jan Rabbers and I were instructed to provide these things. This proved a difficult task, for we could not understand the language of the people. But we did buy a stove, and the price was computed for us on fingers. We were happy when in the evening, after a difficult journey of 74 days, we were able to have more unrestricted household religious services. The Lord soon provided friends for us. Many of the old citizens [of Albany] were of Dutch origin and still could speak and understand Dutch. Accompanied by the Reverend Isaac N. Wyckoff who was appointed as a missionary to look after the needs of us immigrants, they called on us. He roused the people to perform acts of charity for needy families. He helped us in every way, according to our spiritual and physical needs, at all times giving advice and setting an example.

A number of our group soon found work in Albany. The young folk found employment in the city or outside the city. Those who had mastered some craft earned enough to provide themselves for all their needs. Those who wished to attend Sabbath School were invited to come to Wyckoff's church on Sunday, between morning and afternoon services. There was an elder in that church who understood Dutch and spoke it.

We, a total of fifteen persons, moved into our house. One of us fell sick and went to the poorthouse; two found work with farmers outside the city; and on January 62, 1847, seven departed for Buffalo. In April Dominie van Raalte came to us from Michigan. He preached for us and helped those of us who wanted to go to Michigan. With few exceptions the members of our group departed. For family reasons I had to remain. With tearful eyes I saw my friends depart. Four of us left at the close of August. Four remained. One of my friends fell ill on the canalboat. In eleven days I was in Buffalo where on account of sickness I remained until the spring of 1848.

At the close of April 1848 we got ready for our journey to Michigan. We left by steamboat for Chicago, thence by sailboat to Grand Haven, by river boat to Grandville, and by oxwagon from that place to the Kolonie, without road and through deep mud and holes. At times chains were fastened to the wheels in order to draw the wagon through the holes and mud. Occasional blazed trees indicated the road we had to follow. After we arrived at Grandville on April 30, 1848, the three of us departed for the Kolonie on May 1. We started early in the morning. At times we had to walk over logs in order to get across the water. In the afternoon we reached the first loghouse, that of Jacob Borger, in section 10. This was our first glimpse of the Kolonie.

The second house was that of Willem van de Luyster, on the northwest quarter of section 17, Township Zeeland. From there we reached the northeast corner of Zeeland and soon came to the boardhouse of Van de Putte. Next we went to Groningen, along the high ground which runs along the edge of the swamp, in section 24, near the village [of Zeeland] where stood about thirty houses, all but two constructed of logs.

Now, to resume what we were saying about Zeeland. We were in the center of Zeeland before we saw the first loghouse. This belonged to Hendrik de Kruif. Next we noted some others, those of De Naaie, Van der Vliet, and Vijn. The other loghouses occupied the south side of the village. Men were busily engaged building a church, about where Dr. Baart's house now stands. Before this church was finished services were held in Jan Wabeke's house.

The streets with few exceptions were impassable for wagons. East of the church the trees had not been cut down. No houses had yet been erected to the west of the church nor on the north side of the village except on the half lot north of the open place opposite the church. If I remember correctly the church was dedicated on the second Sunday in May [May 9, 1847]. Because of the great influx of immigrants during that summer this church was too small and a new one 40 feet wide and 60 long was erected in the autumn. At night it was not easy to pass along the streets of Zeeland without stumbling, and one had to keep his eyes on the path. Nevertheless the pilgrim wandered happily along the rough streets after dark.

13. J. D. WERKMAN'S MEMORIES OF MY JOURNEY FROM THE NETHERLANDS TO NORTH AMERICA

[This narrative entitled *Mijne Herinnering van de Reis van Nederland naar Noord Amerika*, written in 1911, was first printed in *De Grondwet*, January 21, 1913.]

Het was in het jaar 1847, ik meen wel den 11den Maart, dat mijne ouders met vier kinderen vertrokken van het dorp Uskwert, provincie Groningen. Wij vertrokken met een wagen naar Delfzijl, waar het schip waarmede wij de reis zouden maken ten anker lag. Wij moesten echter nog ongeveer eene week wachten aleer het schip gereed was om uit te gaan. Het schip was niet groot, en er waren maar zes en dertig passagiers aan boord, groot en klein; allen Nederlanders. Dit was ook het geval ten aanzien van het scheepsvolk, zoodat, wat dit aangaat, wij een plezierige reis hadden. Wij waren zeer spoedig met elkander bekend.

Een ieder had moeten zorgen voor zijn eigen proviand, waarvan zij eene opgaaf van de Compagnie ontvangen hadden, met het oog beide op wat en hoeveel voor ieder persoon noodig was. Deze proviand bestond uit hard scheepsbrood, gepelde gerst, en vleesch. Het was voorwaar een zeer harde en flauwe kost. Ik heb mijne ouders vaak hooren zeggen: dat, als zij die reis ooit weer moesten maken, zij dan wel zorgen zouden voor aardappelen en pekelharing.

Het drinkwater was ook zeer slecht en was gedaan in wijnvaten, en dat gaf er eene flauwe en onaangename smaak aan.

Wij hebben op onze reis veel storm gehad, en velen van de passagiers waren zeeziek, ik geloof wel dat mijne moeder de gehele reis zeeziek is geweest. Natuurlijk onder die onstandigheden was er weinig eetlust, anders dan om pekelharing, die niet te verkrijgen was.

Na een reis van negen en veertig dagen zijn wij den 7den Mei allen behouden te New York aangekomen. Van New York hebben wij onze reis voortgezet met een kanaalboot, waar wij ingepakt waren als haring in een ton. Dit veroorzaakte veel ontbering, doch na eene reis van veertien dagen zijn wij met een stoomboot uit Buffalo vertrokken en zijn eindelijk te Milwaukee, Wisconsin, aangekomen. Hier hebben wij ongeveer drie maanden gewoond. Het was toen hier een tijd dat alles goedkoop was.

Mijn vader en J. van der Werp [met wien wij de geheele reis gemaakt hadden], hebben voor twaalf dollars aan lumber gekocht, waarvan zij een huis bouwden, waarin beide hunne gezinnen hebben gewoond tot wij Milwaukee verlieten. Zij kochten ook te zamen een koe voor twaalf dollars, met een groot vet kalf er bij. Zij verkochten het kalf aan den slager voor vier dollars, zoo dat de koe hun slechts acht dollars kostte.

Het arbeidsloon was ook laag, zoodat een arbeider niet meer dan 75 cts. per dag kon verdienen, en dan was er nog altijd geen werk te krijgen. Vader zeide meermalen, dat indien hij de helft van den tijd maar werk had, hij dan nog goed had kunnen leven. Toen werd hun gezegd, dat te Grand Haven, Michigan, het arbeidsloon hooger was, en dat zij daar gemakkelijk één dollar per dag verdienen konden. Daarom zijn zij met een zeilschip verhuisd van Milwaukee naar Grand Haven. Bij onze aankomst aldaar was er geen huis te bekomen om in te wonen, en wij hebben ons een tijd lang moeten behelpen, door in een pakhuis, dat aan het dock bij de rivier stond, te wonen. Wij waren echter niet de eenige bewoners van het pakhuis, want het leefde er van ratten, en dat wel zoo erg, dat zij des nachts over ons heen liepen. Mijn broer, die toen een baby was, hebben zij toen een stuk uit den wang gebeten. Een kachel konden wij niet in het pakhuis hebben, zoodat die buiten stond en daar moest het eten gekookt worden. Het gebeurde eens dat vader laat van zijn werk thuis kwam. Moeder had een pot met eten op den kachel laten staan om het warm te houden tot vader's thuiskomst.

Intusschen was het donker geworden en was het vuur in den kachel uitgedoofd, en van deze gelegenheid wist een opgedaagd varken gebruik te maken. Toen moeder nu later om den pot eten kwam, stond het varken met zijn voorste pooten op den kachel en at zoo uit den pot.

En wat het werk en loon aanging, ja, zij vonden werk tegen één dollar per dag, maar het was een nat en koud baantje, vooral laat in het voorjaar. Zij moesten namelijk lumber, die in vlotten de rivier afkwam, uit het water halen en aan boord van schepen laden.

Toen de winter naderde moest er natuurlijk een huis gezocht worden, om in te wonen, en zij trachten ook om ander werk te krijgen. Vader en Van der Werp vonden beiden werk en een huis te Nortonville, op eenige mijlen ten noorden van Grand Haven.

Zij werkten in een zaagmolen en kregen twaalf dollars in de maand en vrije woning; dat wil zeggen, één huis voor de beide gezinnen. Hier hebben wij dien winter gewoond, en er was nog een ander Hollandsch huisgezin in diezelfde streek, met name Brouwer.

Des Zondags hadden wij godsdienst bij ons aan huis, en dan werd er geregeld een preek gelezen. Van der Werp was de voorganger. Wij zijn hier blijven wonen tot het voorjaar 1848, en hoewel hun loon niet groot was, toch hadden vader en Van der Werp acht en veertig dollars bij de afrekening te goed. Doch er was geen geld in kas, zoodat zij, in plaats van geld, een span ossen kregen.

Ook wat zij vroeger ontvangen hadden, was geen geld, maar store pay. Aardappelen hadden wij den geheelen tijd zonder moeten doen. De molenbaas had aardappelen besteld in Chicago, maar het schip waarmede zij vervoerd werden, was aan strand geslagen. Zoodoende was het drie keer per dag spek en brood; zeker een goede kost voor gezonde menschen. Wel had men vaak zin aan een verandering, maar zulks was niet te verkrijgen. Van Nortonville verhuisden wij terug naar Grand Haven, en hebben daar nog een paar weken vertoefd om ons gereed te maken om – zooals men het toen noemde – naar de Hollandsche Kolonie te vertrekken.

Wij – de familiën Werkman en Van der Werp, altijd nog te samen – hebben Grand Haven verlaten, met hetgeen wij dachten noodig te hebben om de wildernis in te kunnen gaan.

Op een stillen nacht hebben wij onze reis begonnen met een platboot, met een paard er voor gespannen, langs het strand van Lake Michigan en zijn allen behouden aan den mond van Macatawa Bay aangekomen. Daar werden wij met ons goed aan land gezet, want een haven was er toen nog niet.

Na aankomst aan den mond van Macatawa Bay, zijn wij met een kleine platboot, met pak en zak, Black Lake opgevaren, maar de boot was zoo erg lek, dat alle man, toen wij een eind van wal waren, water uitscheppen moest, teneinde dezelve boven water te houden.

Na Black Lake overgevaren te zijn, voeren we Black River op, en kwamen des avonds laat nabij wat men nu Oud-Groningen noemt, aan, waar het goed aan wal werd gebracht, en de kisten rond in een vierkant gezet, en daar tusschen werden bedden gespreid. Daar hebben wij des nachts geslapen, en tegen den morgen begon het regenen alsof het uit de lucht goot, zoodat wij allen doornat werden. Dit was in Mei 1848.

Toen zijn wij een pad opgevolgd, en dat leidde ons naar de woning van Jan Rabbers, die pas een blokhuis betrokken had, dat aan de rivier stond, ter plaatse waar nu het kerkhof van Groningen is. In dit blokhuis [dat later nog gebruikt is als een school] hebben wij ons weer gedroogd, en na een goed maal gegeten te hebben, zijn wij weer te voet op reis gegaan naar Nieuw-Groningen, alwaar een klein blokhuis was, dat door ons tijdelijk kon bewoond worden. Het dak was bedekt met hemlock bark en het was door de zon zoo rond getrokkenen en zoo open, dat het binnenin huis even nat werd als buiten, wanneer 't regende.

Bij zulk een gelegenheid werd alles op één hoop gepakt, opdat het niet nat zou worden. Jan Rabbers met nog een ander [die naar ik meen, Rikken heette] waren toen bezig met het bouwen van een zaagmolen die later bekend was als Borger's molen.

Vader en Van der Werp hebben toen land uitgezocht, en hebben te zamen een blokhuis gebouwd, en het duurde slechts een dag of wat of het huis was klaar. Zij hadden lumber genoeg weten te krijgen voor een vloer en zolder. Het dak bestond uit planken, met slabs over de naden heen gelegd, en er waren gaten gezaagd voor de ramen en een deur. Daar er geen ramen noch glas te bekomen waren, moest het zoo maar door de beide gezinnen betrokken worden. Des nachts werden er eenvoudig beddelakens voor de opening van deur en ramen gehangen. Onder was slechts één kamer, en zoo ook boven. Het onderste diende als een kamer voor dagelijksch gebruik. Het bovenste werd gebruikt als een slaapkamer waar allen slapen moesten.

In den zomer van 1848 kwamen tot ons uit Nederland T. Huizinga en gezin, en ook mijn grootmoeder met haar gezin. Deze alle hebben eerst bij ons ingewoond, zoodat wij, groot en klein, ongeveer 25 personen telden, die allen hetzelfde huis bewoonden. In het najaar hebben.T. Huizenga en mijne grootmoeder een huis voor zichzelven gebouwd, en het volgende voorjaar heeft ook mijn vader een eigen huis gebouwd, zoodat Van der Werp en gezin toen de eenige bewoners van het eerstgebouwde huis waren.

Deze buurt – in sectie 14, Holland Township – kreeg al spoedig den naam van Groninger streek. Om kort bij elkander te wonen, was deze streek zoo uitgelegd, dat het 160 roeden achteruit meette, en daar ieder 40 acres land had, was ieder stuk slechts 40 roeden breed.

Het waren dagen van veel moeite en groote ontbering, want in den eersten tijd was er niets om iets uit te maken. 't Is waar, er was hout genoeg, maar al wat men er mee kon doen, was het te verbranden. Het land moest klaargemaakt worden voor landbouw, en dit was zwaar werk, te meer, omdat allen onervaren waren in deze zaak. Mijn vader heeft op vier acres de boomen neergehakt en zoo groen verbrand. Om dit te doen moest men iedere tak van den boom hakken en op het vuur leggen. Later ging het beter, want toen werden de boomen op streepen geveld, en als het dan een jaar gelegen had, werd het in brand gestoken, en dan brandde meest al het kleine hout er uit.

Er was in den eersten tijd niet veel te bekomen, want het moest alles ingevoerd worden, en er waren nog geen wegen. De eerste reis die mijn vader naar Grandville heeft gedaan, met ossen, nam hem vijf dagen.

Wanneer men voor een beek of moeras kwam, moest men de beste plaats uitzoeken om er over of door te komen, en zoo ging alles zeer langzaam.

Het gebeurde, zoo ik meen, in den winter van 1849-50, dat mijn ouders maar één ijzeren pot hadden om het eten in te koken. Mijn moeder had die op een zekeren avond vol water laten staan, en daar het dien nacht zeer koud was, was die pot stuk gevroren. Nu moest er een ander voor in de plaats komen, maar er was er nergens een te komen zelfs niet in de geheele kolonie. Gij zult misschien zeggen: toch wel in de stad Holland? Er werd altijd wel gesproken van de „stad", maar terecht werd door een onzer gezegd: „Een stad van boomen."

Maar er moest toch een pot wezen, en mijn vader ging te voet naar Grand Haven, en kwam den volgenden dag des avonds laat weer thuis, met een pot op den rug.

De meeste menschen, die hier kwamen, waren arm, en de enkelen die nogal bemiddeld waren, waren ook spoedig uitgeput, want er waren wel uitgaven maar geen inkomsten. Eerst konden de armen nog wat ver- dienen bij hen die bemiddeld waren, maar dat hield ook spoedig op. Dus klom de nood somtijds hoog, en er waren ook verscheidenen die ver- huisden, velen naar Grand Rapids, Kalamazoo, en Grand Haven. Zij vertrokken omdat, zooals zij zeiden, zij niet gewillig waren langer honger te lijden. Ook mijne ouders hadden het zeer arm. Ik herinner mij nog dat mijn moeder het laatste flour-meel verbakt had en dat er geen geld was om meer te koopen. Des morgens toen wij zaten te eten, zeide vader tot moeder: „Gij hebt altijd een groot geloof, maar waar is nu uw geloof?" Moeder antwoordde daarop: „Ja waarlijk God is Israël goed" en wat er meer volgt van Psalm 73 : 1. Zij had dus nog een sterk vertrouwen, dat de Heer uitkomst zou geven. Mijn vader moest dien dag naar Zeeland en ik ging met hem. Onder weg ontmoetten wij Jans Alting, en na wat met elkander over den toestand in de Kolonie gesproken te hebben vertelde vader ook zijn nood.

Daarop zeide Alting: „O, dat is niet zoo erg; ik heb nog wat geld, en wij zullen bij H. Keppel aangaan, want ik heb gehoord, dat die juist een vracht flour-meel aangekregen heeft. Ik zal een barrel flour-meel voor mij zelven en ook een voor u koopen, en gij hebt ossen zoodat gij de prijs van de flour weer met de ossen bij mij kunt verdienen." Dat was weer eene groote uitredding, en de Heer ontving de eer. En heb ik ooit een blij

mensch gezien dan was het mijn moeder. Zoo werd gedurig Gods red-
dende hand ondervonden.

Hierna heeft mijn vader eene harde beproeving moeten ondergaan. Ik
denk het was in de maand April in het jaar 1852, dat mijn moeder kwam
te overlijden. Vader bleef dus over met zes kinderen, de oudste [een
meisje die de vallende ziekte had en die geen oogenblik alleen vertrouwd
was] was ongeveer 12 jaren oud, en de kleinste slechts zes weken. Het
was voorwaar een harde weg voor vader, maar ook voor ons als kinderen, want wij hebben te zamen veel moeten lijden en ontbeeren. De
kleinste was bij een ander uitbesteed, maar de overigen moesten zich
dagelijks zelf helpen. Vader was bijna alle dagen van huis om wat te verdienen, en na ongebeer een jaar weduwnaar geweest te zijn, is hij weer
getrouwd. Toen is het langzaam beter geworden op tijdelijk gebied, zoo
voor ons eigen gezin als in het algemeen. Er begon uitvoer te komen van
boschproducten, zooals kuipstaven, bark, lumber, railroad ties, en zoo
al, en dat gaf werk en bracht handel en nijverheid. En alzoo zijn de toestanden op tijdelijk gebied hoe langer hoe beter geworden.

[Translation]

It was in the year 1847, I believe it was on March 11, that my parents with
four children left the village of Usquert in the province of Groningen.
We left by wagon for Delfzijl where the ship in which we were to make
our voyage lay at anchor. We had to wait, however, for about one week
before the ship was ready to leave port. The ship was not a big one; there
were only 36 passengers both adults and children, and all were Netherlanders. The sailors also were Dutch, a fact which made our voyage a
pleasant one. Soon we were well acquainted.

Each person had to provide his own food. The company had prepared
a list which specified what food and how much was required for each
person. These provisions consisted of hard ship bread, barley, and meat.
This truly was unpalatable and tasteless food. I have heard my parents
comment that if they ever would have to make that voyage again they
surely would provide themselves with potatoes and herring. Drinking
water likewise was of poor quality; being kept in winevats, it had an
unpleasant taste. We had much stormy weather on this voyage and many
of the passengers were seasick; I believe that my mother was ill during
the entire passage. Naturally under such circumstances we had little
appetite except for herring which, however, was not to be had.

After a voyage of 49 days we arrived safely at New York on May 7.
From New York we continued our journey by canalboat in which we

were packed like herring in a vat. This caused much discomfort, but after a journey of 14 days we left Buffalo by steamboat and finally arrived at Milwaukee, Wisconsin. There we lived about three months. That was a time when everything was inexpensive. My father and J. van der Werp [with whom we had made the entire journey] built a house with lumber for which they paid $ 12. Both families lived in this house until they left Milwaukee. They bought a cow and a large fat calf for $ 12. They sold the calf to a butcher for $ 4 so that the cow cost them only $ 8.

Wages also were low so that a workingman could not earn more than 75 cents a day, and at times it was difficult to find work. Father often said that if he had had work half the time he could have lived well. They heard that wages were higher in Grand Haven, Michigan, and that in that place they could readily earn a dollar per day. For that reason we went by sailing ship from Milwaukee to Grand Haven. On our arrival we could not find a house so we had to be satisfied with a pack house at the dock by the river. We were not the only inhabitants of the pack house, for it was infested with rats, so many that they ran over us while we were sleeping. They bit a piece out of my baby brother's cheek. We were not permitted to have a stove in the pack house. We set the stove out of doors and we had to prepare our food there. One night father came home late from his work, and mother kept his food on the stove so that it would be warm when he returned. It had grown dark and the fire in the stove had died down. A wandering pig knew how to make use of this opportunity. When mother went out to get father's dinner she found the pig, with front legs on the stove, eating the food. So for as work and wages were concerned they earned a dollar a day. But it was a wet and cold job, especially during the closing months of the year. Their task was to lift the lumber which came down the stream on rafts out of the water and load it on the ships.

When winter approached we naturally had to find a house. Father and Van der Werp found one and also some work in Nortonville, a few miles north of Grand Haven. They worked in a sawmill at $ 12 a month, including free housing, that is to say one house for two families. Here we lived during the winter. There was one other Dutch family in this place besides us, named Brouwer.

On Sundays we had religious services in our house, when a sermon always was read. Van der Werp was the leader. We lived there until the spring of 1848, and although wages were small father and Van der Werp had $ 48 when final settlement was made. But as the company had no cash on hand, instead of money, they received a yoke of oxen. From the beginning they had been paid in store pay. We had to do without potatoes during this period. The boss of the mill had indeed ordered potatoes but the boat transporting them went ashore. So we had bread and pork three times a day, certainly good fare for healthy persons. Often we would have liked a change but this was impossible.

From Nortonville we moved to Grand Haven where we spent a few weeks in order to get ready to go to the Dutch Kolonie, as people then called it. We two families – Werkman and Van der Werp always together– left Grand Haven with the things we thought we needed in order to settle in the wilderness. We began our journey one quiet night in May 1848. In a flatboat drawn by a horse along the shore of Lake Michigan and arrived safely at Macatawa Bay. There our possessions were carried ashore, for a harbor had not yet been prepared.

After our arrival at the mouth of Macatawa Bay we moved up Black Lake with our possessions in a small flatboat. But the boat was so leaky that all hands had to bail out water to keep it afloat. After sailing up Black Lake, we proceeded up Black River and at night arrived at what now is called Old Groningen where our things were set ashore. Our boxes were arranged in the form of a square inside which we put our beds. There we slept the following night. In the morning it began to rain. It poured out of the skies and everything was thoroughly wet.

We followed a path which led us to the house of Jan Rabbers who recently had moved into a loghouse which stood by the river; at the place now occupied by the Groningen cemetery. In this loghouse [which later was used as a school] we dried ourselves. After having had a good meal we went afoot on to New Groningen where there was a small loghouse ready to be occupied. Its roof was made of hemlock bark which had so shrunk in the sun that when it rained it was as wet within the house as without. Whenever it rained all goods were places in one pile in order to keep them dry. Jan Rabbers and another person [who, I believe, was called Rikken] were busy building a sawmill, later known as Borger's Mill.

Father and Van der Werp selected their land, and together built a log-house, a job which required ony la few days' labor. Somehow they se-cured lumber for the floor and the ceiling. The roof was composed of boards with slabs laid over the cracks where they joined. Openings were sawn to serve as door and windows. But as window frames and glass for them were not to be had the two families moved into this unfinished house. At night bed sheets were hung across the openings intended for the door and the windows. There was only one room below and one room upstairs. The lower floor served as daily living room; the room above was our common sleeping space.

During the summer of 1848 Tamme Huizinga and family from the Netherlands joined us. My grandmother and her family also came over. This family at first lived with us so that, counting the fullgrown and the children, we numbered about 25 persons, all living in the same house. During the autumn Tamme Huizinga built a house for himself. My father also built a house the following year so that Van der Werp and his family alone continued to live in the house we had built together.

This neighborhood – section 24, Holland Township – soon was known as the Groningen community. To live near each other, the land was so laid out that each 40 acre piece was only 40 rods wide but 160 rods deep.

That was a time of great difficulty and self denial, for in the early days of the community we had nothing to sell. True, there was plenty of wood, but we could do nothing with it but burn it. The land had to be cleared for farming. This was hard work, especially as we all were inexperienced in clearing land. My father cut down the trees on a four acre piece and burned them while still green. To do this it was necessary to cut each branch from the tree and lay it on the fire. Later, our methods improved. Then trees were felled to lie in windrows, and after lying there drying for a year were set afire. This was a successful method not only for the felled trees but also for most of the undergrowth.

During the earliest days necessaries could not be acquired because everything had to be imported, and roads did not yet exist. My father's first trip to Grandville was made with oxen and required no less than five days. Whenever we came to a creek in a swamp we had to search out a place to cross over or to wade through, and so travel was very slow.

It happened, if I remember rightly, during the winter of 1849-50 that my parents had but one iron pot in which to cook their food. One evening my mother had failed to empty it of water, and as it was very cold that night the pot cracked from the frost. We had to have a new pot, but nowhere in the entire Kolonie could we find one. Perhaps you are asking, "certainly you could have gotten one in the city of Holland?" We always talked of the "stad", but one of us quite correctly called it "a 'stad' of trees." But we had dire need of an iron pot, and my father went afoot to Grand Haven returning late the following evening carrying a pot on his back.

Most of the people who settled here were poor. The few who had some wealth soon had spent all, for expenditures were constant but there was no income. At first the poor could earn something working for the better-to-do, but this soon came to an end. Our need sometimes became very great and many moved away to Grand Rapids, Kalamazoo, and Grand Haven. They went away because, as they said, they no longer were willing to suffer from hunger. My parents were very poor. I still remember that my mother on one occasion had used the last bit of flour and there was not a penny to buy more. While we were having breakfast father said to mother: "You always have a firm faith, but where now is your faith?" Mother replied, "yes, truly God is good to Israel," and what further follows in Psalm 73 : 1 [in the Dutch Psalter]. Clearly she had a firm faith that God would provide deliverance. That day my father had to go to Zeeland, and I went with him. While on the way we met Jans Alting. After we had talked at some length about conditions in the Kolonie, my father told Alting of his great needs. To this Alting remarked, "Oh, that is not so serious. I still have a little money. We will stop at Huibert Keppel's, for I have heard that he has just gotten a load of flour. I'll buy a barrel of flour for myself and also one for you. You have a yoke of oxen, so with them you can earn the price of the flour you owe me." This indeed was a deliverance, and the Lord received the praise. If ever I have seen a happy person, it was my mother. In this way me many times felt God's protecting hand.

After these experiences my father had to pass through a sore trial. It was in the month of April, I believe, in the year 1852 that my mother died. My father was left with six children; the oldest [a girl who suffered from epilepsy and could not be left alone for even a moment] was about twelve and the smallest only six weeks. This was a hard road for my father, and also for us children, for together we suffered deeply in our penury. Care of the youngest was entrusted to people who were not members of the family; the others had to shift for themselves. Father was away from home every day, in order to earn something. He remarried after having been a widower for about a year. Soon things improved in a material sense, for our family and also for others in general. It became possible to export wood products such as barrel staves, bark, lumber, railroad ties, and similar articles. Trade and industry grew and we all had work.

14. ABRAHAM STEGEMAN'S
HISTORICAL SKETCH OF GRONINGEN

[Born in New Groningen on May 4, 1857, Abraham Stegeman in 1883 became a minister in the Reformed Church after attending Hope College and New Brunswick Theological Seminary. His youth was spent in Groningen, which enabled him to write this detailed account of the founding and early history of Groningen. Written for the Semi-Centennial celebrations at Holland, Michigan, in August 1897, this *Historische Schets van Groningen,* with the notes by John Kolvoord and Gerrit van Schelven added, was printed in *De Grondwet,* January 3, 1911. The author died on February 10, 1899.]

Albert Borgers, een der eerste bewoners van Groningen, schreef 1 December 1847 een brief aan zijn vader te Nieuw Stadskanaal, provincie Drente, Nederland, welken brief door zijn vorigen leeraar, Postein, aldaar in druk gegeven werd: „Waarom ik hierheen trok, en wat ik verwachtte, dat vind ik hier – volledige vrijheid van alle dwangwetten tegen den Woorde Gods, en zelfs grootte begunstiging van alle zijden; goed land in overvloed; 80 akkers hebben wij gekocht voor 3 gulden per akker."

Dit uittreksel geeft te kennen het tweeledig doel der emigratie naar Amerika in de jaren wiens jubelfeest we nu vieren. Sommigen gevoelden meer den aandrang van het eerste; anderen meer dies van het laatste doel. Sommigen bedoelen niets anders dan hun tijdelijk voordeel. Maar wat ook de oorzaak der emigratie, Gods bedoeling was alhier een volk te planten, dat ten zegen zoude zijn van Amerika op godsdienstig en burgerlijk gebied.

Voor velen is Groningen bijna in de vergetelheid geraakt, zoo onbeduidend is het op 't oogenblik, en zoo weinig trekt het uiterlijk den aandacht; doch in de eerste jaren van zijn bestaan was het in 't geheel niet onbeduidend maar van veel beteekenis. Het werd in December van het jaar 1847 reeds onder de zes dorpen gerekend, daar Borgers in den boven aangehaalden brief zegt: „Wij hebben al zes Hollandsche dorpen, en deze zijn, Holland, Groningen, Zeeland, Vriesland, Drenthe, en Graafschap." En in Augustus 1848 schreef Hendrik van Eyck in zijn dagboek: „Daar de meeste kolonisten ver landwaarts in trekken, en dit voor den boerenstand – uithoofde dat het land aldaar goedkooper en veel beter is – ook verkieselijker is, zoo worden er hier en daar nieuwe dorpen aangelegd, welke reeds scholen, kerken en predikanten hebben of te verwachten hebben. Drie mijlen van de stad [Holland] heeft men het dorp Groningen, aangenaam gelegen, ter plaatse alwaar de Black River ophoudt bevaarbaar te zijn. Een houtzaagmolen, welke door het water van eene beek in beweging wordt gebracht, geeft dit dorpje reeds eene aangename levendigheid, en onderscheidene menschen werk. Een nieuwe school is er in aanbouw. Men heeft er eene bekwame onderwijzer, en heeft reeds een predikant beroepen. Twee à drie mijlen verder ligt 't dorp Zeeland."

Nu moet men echter niet vergeten, dat het dorp waarvan hier melding gemaakt wordt, niet is het New Groningen alwaar de tegenwoordige school en chapel staan, maar het geen later toen New Groningen ont-wikkelde, Oud Groningen genoemd werd, en welker middenpunt men vindt alwaar vroeger vader Manus Stegeman woonde, en nu Jan Stege-man woont. De loten van het dorp aldaar lagen aan weerszijden van de lijn tusschen sections 23 en 26, voor een vierde van een mijl.

In de eerste jaren lag het dorp aan den weg die toen van Holland naar Zeeland leidde, langs de plaats van Albert van Hazenkamp, naar de Black River, welke men doorwaadde of met een ferry overstak, per plaatse alwaar de creek van 't noorden zich oplost in de Black River.

Men bereikte de plaats ook langs de Black River, over welke rivier, op platbooten, de meeste immigranten kisten, en de levensbehoeften der kolonisten te Groningen, Zeeland, Vriesland en Staatsland aangevoerd werden. Aan de plaats alwaar men de Black River overstak, werd een dok gebouwd, alsmede het waterhuisje, dat „Castle Garden" genoemd werd, bewoond door de familie Van de Laare, die ook voor de overtocht der reizigers zorgden.

Jan Rabbers wilde dat de publieke weg van Holland naar Zeeland door Oud Groningen zou loopen, en daartoe bouwde hij, grootendeels op eigen kosten, een lange brug over de rivier op de lijn tusschen sections 23 en 26, recht west van het dorp; maar door het hooge water stroomde dezelve weg. Daarop werd de weg en de brug verlegd ter plaatse alwaar deze nu zijn.

Dit was in het jaar 1857, en daarmede werd de ondergang van Oud Groningen en de opgang van wat later New Groningen genoemd werd, verzekerd.

De naam werd aan dit plaatsje gegeven zeer waarschijnlijk door het nog al talrijk getal Groningers, alhoewel er van het begin al aan een mengel-moes van Drentenaars, Zeelanders, Overijsselschen, en Graafschappers woonden. Het ontstaan van het plaatsje, het uitleggen van de loten, de daarstelling van school en gemeenten, de bedrijvigheid in handel moet grootelijks toegeschreven worden aan Jan Rabbers.

Jan Rabbers met vijf andere huisgezinnen, waaronder J. H. Stegink, H. Wassink en H. Jekel behoorden, verlieten Emmen, provincie Drente, Nederland, in het jaar 1846. Den 14den October gingen ze scheep en kwamen den 19den December te New York aan. Te Albany stierf Rabbers' vrouw.

In Mei 1847 kwam hij in de Kolonie aan. Gedurende den zomer was hij bezig in het uitzoeken van land en het terechtbrengen van immigranten. „Hij verdwaalde nooit."

Vele Drentenaars en Vrieslanders genoten zijne leiding. Hij opende in den zomer van dit jaar reeds een winkeltje, in een blokkenhuis, hetwelk op het tegenwoordig kerkhof stond. Hij was een man middelmatig in grootte schraal van lichaamsbouw, en roosachtig in uitzicht; een man van groote bekwaamheid, algemeen vertrouwde godsvrucht en grooten invloed; een man van groote idealen en utopische verwachtingen; een man met een vlug verstand, vindingrijk, vernuft, en groote ondernemingsgeest. Hij had ook de moed om te trachten zijne idealen tot verwezelijking te brengen.

Er bestond groote behoefte aan een zaagmolen. Het aanbrengen van bouwmaterialen van elders kostte te veel moeite. Door zijne leiding der immigranten had Rabbers reeds een plaats voor een houtzaagmolen aan de creek, tegenover het tegenwoordige schoolhuis, uigezocht. Hij aanvaarde een compagnieschap met Rikking, een Hoogduitscher. Rabbers vond de bemiddelde menschen gewillig om hem in zijne onderneming te steunen, zelfs zoo, dat eenmaal zijn dienstmeid in haar schort $ 500 van een dier menschen ophaalde. De onbemiddelden gaven hun werk uit liefde, of in de hoop om in eigen behoefte aan planken te voorzien. In den zachten winter van 1847–1848 werd alreeds met het bouwen een aanvang gemaakt. De vader van Isaac Fairbanks, van Holland, was de contractor.

De dam werd door het volk opgeworpen en de volgende personen namen daar aan deel: Teunis en Harm Ratering, Gerrit Derks, de broeders Van de Laare, Pieter Wissekerke, Arnold Barendse, Willem de Jong, Berend de Vries, en meer anderen.

Deze molen was in het eerst zeer lomp gemaakt, op zijn meest kon men er maar enkele duizende voeten, gedurende de vier en twintig uren, mede zagen. Deze molen gaf echter aan vele menschen werk. Kasper Lahuis, H. en J. ten Have, Berend Jan Veneklaasen en Hendrik van Eyck zijn enkele namen der personen die aan deze molen werkten. Maar daar de machinery gedurig brak en de dam niet bestemd was voor den sterken aanvoer van water ten tijde van den opdooi en van zware regens, brak hij gedurig door. Nieuwe leeningen van geld moesten er gemaakt worden, om het gebrokene te herstellen. Daar dit echter herhaaldelijk voorviel, werden de eigenaars in geldelijke moeilijkheden gewikkeld, zoodat de 12 crediteuren Jan Rabbers, Albert Borgers, en A. Niemeijer als volmachten aanstelden, en later de geheele affaire aan Albert Borgers en Tamme Huizinga overdroegen die dezelve nog voor een tijd voortzetten. Er werd veel geld door deze affaire verloren.

In de herfst van 1849 begon Jan Kolvoord een nieuwe affaire. Hij had tijdelijk in Allegan vertoegd en aldaar het draaien, d.i. draaiwerk uit hout te vervaardigen, geleerd.

Hij was toen reeds van overtuiging dat de huismeubelen ietwat fraaier moesten worden. Schrijver dezes herinnert zich, dat er in de huizen van dien tijd niets anders dan eigengemaakte meubelen gevonden werden. Kolvoord zette een fabriekje op aan het beekje nabij New Groningen, een weinigje ten noorden van het brugje aldaar.

De machinery werd door een overschot waterwiel in beweging gebracht. Dit fabriekje was een profetie en voorlooper van de groote fabrieken, die heden in Holland en Zeeland gevonden worden. Dit fabriekje werd echter al zeer spoedig in een korenmolen veranderd, waaraan destijds een dringende behoefte was.

Derwaarts wendden zich van heinde en verre de boeren, menigmaal de vrouwen en kinderen met pakjes corn op de schouders. Dat corn was misschien met de hand gepeld, op lakens in de zon gedroogd, en gedurig moesten ze dan nog een of twee dagen wachten eer het gemalen was.

Toen de molen van Jan Rabbers in de handen van Borgers en Huizenga overgegaan was, was de ondernemingsgeest van Rabbers nog niet uitgestorven. Daar Kolvoord's molen geen genoegzame toevloed van water ontving en hij door ondervinding geleerd had, dat een lange dam te veel kostte, begon hij een flourmolen te bouwen aan dezelfde creek waarop de zaagmolen stond, ongeveer 200 roeden zuidwest van het tegenwoordige kerkhof. Rabbers was nu in compagnieschap getreden met Cornelius de Roo, vader van C. de Roo, van de Walsh de Roo Milling Company.

Opdat men nu gedurende het geheele jaar genoegzaam water zoude hebben, maakte men een dam en sluis in de rivier, op eenige roeden afstands, west van de brug bij 't kerkhof, alwaar nu een kolk water gevormd werd. Van deze kolk werd een kanaal gegraven naar de molen, en het water door dit kanaal gevoerd, bracht de molen in beweging. Jan van Eenenaam van Zeeland was de eerste molenaar. Aan deze molen werd ook later een pelmolen toegevoegd. Deze molen werd zoo zeer begunstigd dat men al spoedig plannen maakte om een groote stoommolen te bouwen. Het gebouw van drie verdiepingen was bijna voltooid [G. Slenk en P. Zalsman aannemers] de stoomketel en machinerie waren te Grand Rapids aangekocht, doch nog niet verzonden, toen zeer plotseling, C. de Roo op 1 September 1855 aan bloedloop overleed. Dit maakte een einde aan deze nieuwe onderneming. Nooit is het gebouw voltooid.

De machinerie werd niet verzonden. De molen heeft echter zooals hij was nog jaren daarna in werking geweest. Jan Rabbers stierf in 1860. De weduwe de Roo huwde met D. C. Oggel die nog voor een tijd lang de affaire voortzette, met C. van Eekelenburg als molenaar. Deze molen bracht een groote levendigheid aan de plaats. Rabbers had al spoedig een grooten winkel opgericht, op een lot recht west van Stegeman's huis. In 1854 verkocht hij de store aan Jan van Eenenaam, terwijl Rabbers nu een huis bouwde naast de molen. Op hetzelfde lot waarop Van Eenenaam's store stond, werd een shingleshop geplaatst, alwaar Machiel de Puit en Thomas de Witt werkten.

Jan Hendrik Veneklaasen, die als steenbakker uit Rijssen, provincie Overijsel, Nederland, gekomen was, maakte in 1848 reeds een aanvang met het steenbakken, op de plaats, tegenover de farm alwaar nu Benjamin van Raalte woont. Hij en zijne zonen Berend Jan, Jannes, en Pieter brachten deze bakkerij later over nabij Oud Groningen, in het jaar 1853.

De eerste standplaats aldaar was noord van de brug bij 't kerkhof, aan de westzijde van den weg. Hier maakte men met de hand zoo ongeveer van vier tot vijf duizend steenen daags, en een 100,000 gedurende het seizoen.

De yard en gebouwen welke nu het eigendom van B. J. Veneklaasen werden, werden in 1865 aan de overzijde van den weg gebracht, maar al spoedig begon men behoefte te gevoelen aan een grootere hoeveelheid klei. Men wilde nu ook op veel grootere schaal beginnen en zelfs tot het uitvoeren van steen overgaan. De Kolonie had eindelijk een railroad verkregen. Een compagnieschap werd aanvaard tusschen B. J. Veneklaasen en Bolks, welke op de tegenwoordige standplaats nabij Zeeland, met machinerie door stoomkracht gedreven, het vervaardigen van baksteen voortzetten. Bolks trad later uit de compagnieschap, en deze werd nu zoo veranderd, dat de geheele affaire bleef in de handen van de familie, het talrijk zonengeslacht van B. J. Veneklaasen, die nu nog en op veel grooter schaal aan drie yards, n.l. te Zeeland, Hamilton, en te Cloverdale de affaire voortzetten.

In de vorming, voortzetting en uitbreiding werd een degelijke ondernemingsgeest en een ijzeren wilskracht geopenbaard. Gedurende al de jaren van het bestaan dezer affaire hebben velen aldaar hun brood verdiend. Zeeland's groei is daaraan eensdeels te danken.

In hetzelfde jaar toen J. H. Veneklaasen zijne steenbakkerij te Groningen begon, kwam August Jansen, nu in West Pullman, Illinois, woonachtig, zich in de Kolonie vestigen. Hij was een schoenmaker van ambacht, en zag de behoefte onder de kolonisten aan leer. Het looien van vellen had hij als knecht aan de leerlooierij te Saugatuck en Grand Rapids geleerd. Door den ondernemenden Rabbers werd hij aangespoord en bewogen een leerlooierij op te richten en twee akkers grond werden aangekocht in de nabijheid van de plaats alwaar Rabber's zaagmolen stond.

Het gebouw werd zeer doelmatig ingericht. De vooruitzichten op

succes waren goed. Het hemlock bast had men bijna voor niets. Het dagloon was slechts 75 centen en de huiden goedkoop. Maar, de handel was
slap. De schoenmakers in de onmiddellijke omgeving hadden maar weinig
leer noodig. Zoo nu en dan verzond men wel een kleine hoeveelheid leer,
maar niet genoeg om de affaire een succes te doen zijn. Bovendien, door
de gedurige uitspoeling van den dam, waardoor de kuipen vol water
liepen en de liqueren bedierven en om andere redenen was deze onderneming gedoemd een failure te zijn. Jansen is later nog voor een geruimen tijd als slager te New Groningen bezig geweest.

Nadat Jansen's onderneming een failure was geworden, ondernamen
Lukas Aling en Toon Baart een leerlooierij op te richten, en wel op de
plaats alwaar nu de enginehouse, van de tegenwoordig in werking zijnde
brickyard van Veneklaasen and Sons, staat. Deze onderneming werd ook
niet met succes bekroond, daar het gebouw spoedig in asch werd gelegd.

Reeds vroeg in de vijftigen begon Andries Steketee, een oom van de
Steketee's te Holland, Grand Rapids, en Muskegon, handel in staven.
Hij bouwde een dock aan de Black River, naast de zoogenaamde Scholten's
Brug, kocht de staven, vervoerde ze op platbooten naar Holland, alwaar
ze gebruikt of per zeilschip naar andere oorden overgebracht werden.
Deze handel heeft veel tot den voorspoed der Kolonie bijgedragen. Nu
kon men iets uit de eikenboomen maken, die als reuzen onder het andere
geboomte – beuk, maple, elm, ash, hickory – alom te Groningen,
Noordeloos, Noord Holland, Ebenezer, Drenthe, Vriesland, enz., te
vinden waren.

Nu zag men dan ook al spoedig, schuins door de bosschen, over onbe-
schrijfelijk slechte wegen, van alle oorden de zwaarbeladen wagens en
sleden met ossen bespannen aankomen. Men zag gedurig karavanen van
die wagens en sleden van ver uit Drenthe en Vriesland langs de wegen
trekken, de stilheid der bewoners langs die wegen verstorende door het
geroep aan de luie, trage, maar menigmaal afgebeulde viervoeters.

Van af het jaar 1855 tot ongeveer het jaar 1865, was het de gulden eeuw
van Groningen. Deze stavenhandel in verband met de flourmolen van
Rabbers en De Roo en de steenbakkerij van Veneklaasen gaf veel bedrijvigheid. Steketee verkocht in 1857 zijn plaats en handel aan Hendrikus
Scholten, die denzelve jaren lang voortzette en die in verband daarmede
een winkeltje hield, alwaar ook de dorstige en vermoeide ossendrijvers
lafenis konden krijgen.

Een bewijs van het doen van goede zaken door Scholten wordt gezien
in het groote steenen gebouw, dat hij op zijne standplaats bij de brug
liet bouwen.

Gerrit J. Boone, G. Huizinga, en J. de Vries aanvaardden in 1867 een compagnieschap tot het oprichten van een zaagmolen. Deze molen werd gebouwd eenige roeden zuidoost van Scholten's Brug, alwaar nog de vervallen overblijfselen van 't gebouw en de machinerie te zien zijn. Tweemalen, de eerste maal in 1871 en de tweede maal in 1877 werd het gebouw in de asch gelegd. Deze molen is in werking geweest voor een twintigtal jaren en heeft veel bijgedragen tot de voorspoed van het volk en het ontginnen van de boschlanden. De prijzen der loggen waren goed, van heinde en verre werden deze per slede des winters, en ook op met het door den opdooi verhoogde water der rivier des voorjaars aangebracht. De bosschen werden nu aangesproken en de groote brand van 1871 hielp bovendien tot het wegruimen der omgehakte boomen. Die brand, toen zoo verschrikkelijk en zoo zeer betreurd, om de ontzachelijke verliezen er door geleden, werd later beschouwd als de krachtige hand Gods tot het wegruimen van zoo vele bosschen en tot het herscheppen van dezelve in schoone landerijen.

Met het verleggen van den weg van door Oud Groningen naar New Groningen zag ook Jan van Eenenaam de noodzakelijkheid in om van standplaats te veranderen. Albert Borgers en H. ten Have hadden de loten van 't dorp New Groningen in 't jaar 1858 uitgelegd. De school was daar als middenpunt van het district gebouwd en Anesus J. Hillebrands was in 1857 schoolmeester geworden. Hij was altijd een ijveraar voor Groningen's voortuitgang en bloei. Van Eenenaam bouwde den winkel welke aldaar nog heden ten dage als winkel dienst doet. Spoedig daarop werd de smederij van Willem Huizinga van Oud Groningen naar Nieuw Groningen overgebracht en Klaas Boer vestigde zich daar als wagenmaker. Nu bloeide New Groningen, welke naam aan de plaats gegeven werd door A. J. Hillebrands, toen de postoffice aldaar gevestigd werd.

Dominee Cornelius van der Meulen werd den 1sten October 1847 te Oud Groningen, onder aan de brug, een weinigje ten zuidwesten van 't tegenwoordige kerkhof, gehoord te prediken over de woorden, 2 Cor. 1 : 10: „Die ons uit zoo grooten dood verlost heeft en nog verlost; op welken wij hopen, dat Hij ons ook nog verlossen zal." Hij had een stump tot predikstoel en de toehoorders zaten mede op stumps en afgehakte boomstammen. De nog bijna aan elkaar sluitende boomkruinen, met de daar doorbrekende blauwe lucht, vormden het gewelf.

De godsdienstige gestemdheid van die eerste dagen, zoo zeer geprezen en zeker niet ten onjuiste, had echter ook wel eens haar schaduwzijde. De godsdienst werd wel eens gebruikt als middel tot het bevorderen van stoffelijke, of zelfzuchtige en utopische plannen. Het doel van den beginne af aan scheen te zijn om Groningen tot een voornaam centre te maken. School en kerk moesten daartoe medewerken. De bewoners van Groningen waren met de Zeelandsche gemeente verbonden. Deze gemeente had de handen meer dan vol om haren leeraar, dominee C. van der Meulen, te onderhouden.

Maar, wat gebeurd er? In het jaar 1848, volgens het dagboek van H. van Eyck en volgens anderen, in het jaar 1849, werd er te Groningen een leeraar beroepen, n.l. J. H. Budding. Er was aldaar nog geene gemeente georganiseerd. Te Zeeland had men de regel aangenomen, dat al degenen die als ouderlingen en diakenen uit Nederland vertrokken waren, en zich bij deze gemeente aansloten, ook aldaar in die betrekking zouden fungeeren. De uitkomst was, dat men al spoedig een veel te groot getal ambtsdragers had. Op 12 Juni 1849 besloot men dat allen hun ambt zouden neerleggen en dat er uit hen een zeker getal ouderlingen en diakenen zouden gekozen worden. Dit geschiedde. Ouderling Niemeijer werd niet herkozen. Vermoedelijk waren Niemeijer, Rabbers en H. van Duren de hoofdpersonen in het daarstellen van godsdienstoefeningen, want Niemeijer was het, die aldaar geduriglijk de godsdienstoefeningen leidde, door een predikatie voor te lezen.

Doordat Ds. Budding, zonder eene roeping naar eene gemeente, in Amerika gekomen was en door de Kolonie rondzwierf en op onderscheidene plaatsen, en ook te Groningen, preekte, zoo koesterden de Groningers de hoop, dat indien zij hem beriepen, hij zijn lot onder hen zou werpen. Ds. Budding's verschil van opvatting der waarheid enz., waardoor hij niet in één kerkverband met de alreeds hier gevestigde leeraars kon leven, gaf misschien ook een stoot aan deze zoo onkerkrechtelijke handeling.

Maar men had mis gerekend. Ds. Budding bedankte. Hij deed dit op eene hem alleen eigene wijze. Des voormiddags had hij in het schoolhuis gepreekt. Des middags waren ze samen bij een der aldaar wonende broeders en 's namiddags maakte hij bekend, dat hij bedankte voor de roeping, omdat ze hem niet begeerden, daar zij noch bij voor- of nagebed bij het middagmaal voor hem gebeden hadden.

In het najaar van 1850 gingen de Groningers eigenwillig te werk, in het verkiezen van twee diakenen. Vermoedelijk waren A. Niemeijer en Jacob R. Schepers ouderlingen. Nu was men georganiseerd.

De kerkeraad te Zeeland van de stichting dezer nieuwe gemeente gehoord hebbende, schreef een brief aan de broeders te Groningen, hen vermanende en waarschuwende tegen zulk eene onkerkelijke handeling

„in strijd met den Woorde Gods". De uitwerking van dezen brief was, dat de Groningers op Zeeland's kerkeraad verschenen zijnde, verzochten „dat terwijl de gemeente nu eenmaal gesticht was, ze maar zoo te laten voortgaan."

Er werd besloten om Schepers te Zeeland te laten voorgaan wanneer Ds. van der Meulen niet tehuis was, en alle veertien dagen eens op 't Groningsche dorp voor te gaan. Schepers had in Nederland voor de Heilige Bediening gestudeerd, maar was om de een of andere rede niet tot zijn doel gekomen. En de Groningers dachten op deze wijze een dominee te verkrijgen. Schepers predikte voor een geruimen tijd te Groningen. Hij gaf echter geen voldoening, werd niet geördend en ging daarop over tot de Schotsche Kerk.

Het schoolhuis brandde af. A. J. Hillebrands vertrok naar Wisconsin. De aanhangers der gemeente dropen zoo gestadig de een na den ander af en keerden terug naar Zeeland. Het was een verloren zaak geworden. Toch bleef de begeerte naar eigene diensten steeds levendig; want in December 1855 kwam er op den kerkeraad te Zeeland, „een verzoek van het dorp Groningen om aldaar des Zondags godsdienstoefening te mogen houden, daar het te ver was voor de vrouwen om naar Zeeland te gaan." „Geoordeeld: daaromtrent geen bepaalde regel te stellen. Zij mogen wel bij elkander komen om elkander te stichten." Hieraan werd gehoord gegeven, daar men nu in het schoolhuis, nu te New Groningen gebouwd, te zamen kwam. Deze samenkomst werd later in een biduur veranderd, alwaar J. H. Stegink gewoonlijk de leiding had. Catechetisch onderwijs werd ook alhier gegeven door den leeraar der gemeente, die dan gewoonlijk des avonds voor het te zamen gekomen volk een bijbellezing hield. Dominee Seine Bolks oefende door de bijbelverklaringen een grooten invloed over het volk uit. Gedurende het verblijf van Dominee Willem Moerdijk in Zeeland's gemeente, werd de chapel te Groningen gebouwd, welke nog voor catechisatiën en begrafenisdiensten gebruikt wordt.

Men begon te Groningen reeds vroeg met schoolonderwijs aan de kinderen te bezorgen. Schooldistricten waren er nog niet. De kinderen hadden behoefte aan onderwijs en dat was rede genoeg om de handen ineen te slaan om een schoolhuis te bouwen. A. J. Hillebrands, die zijn lot onder hen geworpen had, werd als eerste schoolonderwijzer gehuurd. Dat eerste blokken schoolhuisje stond eenige roeden west van Frank Brummel's huis. De haard was in het midden van het gebouw. Aan het eene einde van het gebouw woonde Mr. Hillebrands en aan het andere einde was het schoollokaal, zonder muur tusschen beiden. Alhier hebben ter school gegaan Jantje Niemeijer; Dirk, Jan, en Jantje Broek, later huisvrouw van G. J. Boone; Juriën de Vries, Hendrik en Jochem van Dijk; Naatje, Christina, en Mary Sakkers; Berend en Pieter Kleis en anderen. Dit schoolhuis brandde af, als ook het grootere en doelmatiger gebouw dat spoedig daarop de in de nabijheid van Rabbers' en De Roo's flourmolen werd opgericht. A. J. Hillebrands vertrok hierop naar Wisconsin. En nu waren de kinderen tijdelijk van onderwijs verstoken.

De school inspectors van Holland Township, op het verzoek der stemgerechtigden te Groningen, belegden eene vergadering aan Rabbers' zaagmolen op den 23sten Mei 1853 tot het organiseeren van School District No. 2, later No. 3. A. Steketee werd verkozen tot voorzitter en de volgende personen als eerste ambtenaren voor 't nieuwe district, n.l. A. Steketee, moderator, J. H. Stegink, assessor en H. van Eyck, director.

Niettegenstaande de groote oppervlakte van het district waren er maar 26 kinderen in de schooljaren, in het jaar 1853. Jan Boer was de eerste schoolmeester, die drie maanden voor $ 12 per maand, in een afdak van een schuur in de nabijheid van Rabbers' zaagmolen, de jeugd onderwees. Alhier hebben ter school gegaan, Roelof en Hendrik Evers; Dirk, Harm, en Jan Borgers; Jantje Rabbers; Bonel de Vries; Wolter van Huil; J. D. Werkman en anderen.

De driehoek land, tegenover de store te New Groningen, werd aangekocht en daarop een schoolhuis gebouwd van 20 × 30 voor de som van $ 100.

Eene bijzonderheid dient hier aangemerkt te worden, n.l. dat er een zeer nauwkeurig geschreven contract gemaakt werd tusschen de Board en de aannemers. Men wist toen reeds, in het jaar 1853, op wettige wijze en in de Engelsche taal zaken te doen.

En hier is een lijst van de onderwijzers, die in geregelde opvolging van elkander, in de eerste jaren schoolgehouden hebben: Thomas C. Kenworthy, in 1854; C. Doesburg, in 1855; Thomas C. Kenworthy, in 1856. Van hem werd gezegd, dat hij altoos des morgens het onderwijs aanving met knielend te bidden. A. J. Hillebrands kwam in 1857 weer als schoolmeester te Groningen terug en bleef aldaar in die betrekking tot het jaar 1870. In 1867 begon men een select school, alwaar desverkiezenden hunne kinderen konden laten onderwijzen. In deze school gaven James Brandt in 1867-68, R. Hyma in 1868-69 en Mr. Bacon in 1869-70 onderwijs. In 1870 geraakte A. J. Hillebrands buiten de school, na een geweldigen strijd tusschen zijne voor- en tegenstanders. Sedert dien heeft de school opgeheven. De vele onderwijzers in deze school werkzaam geweest, hebben niet vruchteloos gearbeid. Deze school behoeft niet voor eenig andere school in deze omgeving ten achteren te staan, ziende op de afgeworpene vruchten – de ware toets van succes. Met een zekere trots zouden wij een lange lijst namen kunnen geven van degenen die als kinderen aan deze school den eersten stoot ontvingen tot verstandelijke ontwikkeling en later plaatsen van nut en eer in maatschappij, school en kerk verkregen.

Op Oud Groningen, dat is op het origineele dorp, hebben de volgende huisgezinnen van af het jaar 1847 tot 1855 gewoond: Jan Rabbers, Harm Krans, Pieter Karsten, Cornelis Weniger, Willem en Adriaan van de Laare, Pieter Sakkers, Pieter Daane, A. J. Hillebrands, H. van Duren, Manus Stegeman, B. J. Veneklaasen, C. de Roo, J. van Eenenaam, en wellicht nog anderen; en in de streken van wat destijds bij Groningen behoorde: A. Borgers, J. Wener, A. Niemeijer, B. J. de Vries, J. Aalting, H. Vredeveld, G. Kamps, Jan Jekel, H. Lubbers, J. van der Werp, H. Werkman, T. Huizinga, Salomon de Koeijer, Kasper Lahuis; en later Evert Zagers, J. H. Stegink, A. Westveer, P. van Belois, en A. van Duine.

In de nabijheid van Rabbers' zaagmolen woonden de Weduwe ten Have en kinderen, Pieter Meins Boekhout, H. ten Have, Dirk de Pau, Jan Koster, en anderen.

Janna Weniger, dochter van Cornelis Weniger, was de eerste die te Groningen geboren werd en wel zooals gezegd werd, onder den blooten hemel. Zij werd ook het eerst in Zeeland's gemeente gedoopt.

Het eerste kerkhof werd aangelegd op een stuk land, hetwelk later bewezen werd aan speculanten te behooren, en lag ruim $\frac{1}{4}$ van een mijl zuidoost van het middenpunt van Oud Groningen, op het land dat nu aan J. Stegeman en de weduwe H. Brummel behoort. Aldaar liggen er velen begraven – Abraham en Adriaan van de Laare [laatstgenoemde werd door een tak van een boom gedood, en bij zijne begrafenis sprak Ds. C. van der Meulen over de woorden: „Het behaagde den Heere hem te verbrijzelen"], zijne weduwe, later de huisvrouw van B. J. Veneklaasen, eene dochter van Poppen, A. van Zwaluwenburg, Aaltje Ensing, huisvrouw van M. Stegeman, en de familie Pieter Meins Boekhout, welke in korten tijd uitstierf.

De eerste dokter op Groningen was een Amerikaan, Dr. C. D. Shenick, die in 1849 zijn practijk aldaar reeds uitoefende en die in dat jaar een township office ontving. Hij genoot de achting en het vertrouwen van het volk in 't algemeen.

Op het tegenwoordige kerkhof rust het stoffelijk overschot van den tweeden dokter, N. R. Parsons, op wiens grafsteen wij de volgende inscription lezen: „Dr N. R. Parsons. Born at Enfield, Connecticut, August 20, 1819. Died March 5, 1860, aged 40 years."

Among my scraps I find the following, which appeared in the *Holland Daily Sentinel*, and has a bearing on the early history of Groningen:

Hamilton, Michigan
October 27, 1899.

Cornelius de Roo, Esq., Holland, Michigan.

Dear Sir:

Last week my mother died and you may know or remember that she was the oldest miller that the Dutch Colony had. My father built a small stone mill on a small creek in Groningen and when he found the power was too small he would go to Allegan and work at this trade as a turner, and my mother would run the mill and grind what she could with the water there was. I have heard her tell about grinding from 70 to 100 bushels of corn and rye a week. Of course I do not remember how long or how many years my father owned the mill, but I know that in time he sold it to John Rabbers and the mill was moved down the stream where, as you know, milling was carried on for a number of years. How your father got an interest in the business you may know better than I do. After my father sold out his mill machinery he then put turning machinery in the building in Groningen, and made chairs and bedsteads, and mother has told also how she helped put up chairs. My father died in or about 1855. You might call him and mother the pioneer millers and makers of furniture, but time and death now claims them both. I write this to you as a matter of history of milling in our Colony.

Respectfully yours,
John Kolvoord

As additional information, Mr. de Roo tells us that the second mill referred to by Mr. Kolvoord [the Rabbers' mill] was located at what was formerly the village of Old Groningen which was located on the Zeeland road about half way between Holand and Zeeland and to the south of the highway. There is now only one farmhouse on the spot but formerly there were a number of houses there and the village was regularly platted into streets and lots. Mr. de Roo states that his father purchased an interest in that mill early in 1855 and died the same year. This mill did a thriving business in the early colony days and was for some time the only mill in the Colony, the next one being built by Mr. Alderd Plugger at Holland. The waterpower of the Rabbers' mill finally failed and the machinery was sold, part of it going to a town in the northern part of the State, and some of it was purchased by Mr. Conrad P. Becker of Holland. The remains of the old mill dam of that mill and the millrace leading to it are still in existence. – Gerrit van Schelven.

[Translation]

Albert Borgers, one of the first settlers of Groningen [Michigan], wrote a letter on December 1, 1847, to his father at Stadskanaal, province of Drente, the Netherlands, which letter was published there by his former pastor, a man named Postein. He wrote, "Why I came here and what I expected to find – that I found, namely complete freedom of all compulsory laws against the Word of God; even great favors shown me on all sides; and excellent land in abundance of which we have bought 80 acres at the rate of three guilders per acre."

This excerpt clearly states the two-fold motive of the emigration to America in those years which we now are commemorating. Some of the emigrants were more interested in the first motive, others were more concerned in the second. Some thought exclusively of their temporal advantage. But whatever may have been the cause of the emigration, it was God's intention to plant in these parts a people who would be a blessing to America in religious as well as in civil matters.

To many, Groningen has become almost a memory, for at the present moment it seems insignificant and its actual appearance is such as to attract no attention; but during the first years of our settlement it was by no means of little importance; on the contrary it was a place of much consequence. For in December 1847 it was already numbered among the six villages, as Borgers states in the above mentioned letter, "Already we have six Dutch villages, and these are Holland, Groningen, Zeeland, Vriesland, Drenthe, and Graafschap." And in 1848 Hendrik van Eyck wrote in his *Diary*, "As most of the settlers are moving in to the outlying parts of the Kolonie [for the farmers this is desirable because land in those parts is not only cheaper but also of much better quality], new villages are being built. These already have schools, churches, and pastors or are expecting to have them soon. Three miles from the 'stad' [Holland] is the village of Groningen, pleasantly situated at the spot where the Black River ceases to be navigable. A sawmill, turned by the water of a creek, already is imparting a pleasing and lively activity to this little village and is providing work for a number of persons. A new school is being built. A competent teacher has been obtained and the people have already called a pastor. Two to three miles further is the village of Zeeland."

At this point it must be emphasized that the village we are mentioning here is not the New Groningen [Nieuw Groningen] where the present school and chapel stand, but what later when New Groningen began to develop became known as Old Groningen [Oud Groningen], the central point of which was where formerly father Manus Stegeman used to live and where Jan Stegeman at present lives. The lots of the village lay on each side of the line between sections 23 and 24, for a distance of a quarter of a mile.

During the first years this village lay along the road which at that time led from Holland to Zeeland, past the farm of Albert van Hazenkamp, to the point on Black River where a creek joined it. Those using this road would either wade across the stream or cross over on a boat.

People reached this place [Groningen] by rowing up Black River. Most immigrants, for example, transported their baggage and necessaries on flatboats for the settlers at Groningen, Zeeland, Vriesland, and Statesland [Drenthe]. A dock was built at the point where people were wont to cross Black River. There also was built *het Waterhuisje*, which was called "Castle Garden" and occupied by the Van de Laare family.

Jan Rabbers was determined that the public road from Holland to Zeeland should pass through Old Groningen. To accomplish this he built, mainly at his own expense, a long bridge over the river on the line separating sections 25 and 26, directly west of the village. But high water carried this bridge away. Consequently the course of the road was altered so as to cross the river at the spot where the bridge [Scholten's Brug] is to be found. This change, which took place in the year 1857, assured the decline of Old Groningen and the growth of what later was called New Groningen, which name was given because of the many Groningers among the settlers, in spite of the fact that from the beginning a medly of people from Drente, Zeeland, Overijsel, and Graafschap also lived there. The origin of this place, the laying out of building lots, organization of school and church community, and the development of trade must be ascribed mainly to the energy of Jan Rabbers.

Rabbers, accompanied by five other families among whom were those of Jan Hendriks Stegink and Harm Wassink, and Hendrik Jekel who was unmarried, left Emmen, province of Drente, the Netherlands, in the year 1846. On October 14 these people boarded ship and arrived in New York on December 19. Rabbers' wife died at Albany.

In May 1847 Rabbers arrived in the Kolonie. During that summer he busied himself looking up land for the immigrants and getting them settled. "He never lost his way in the woods," it was said of him. Many an immigrant from Drente and Friesland profited from his advice. In the summer of 1847 he opened a small store in a loghouse which stood on the spot at present occupied by the cemetery. He was of average height, spare of frame, of florid complexion; a man of great ability, one generally trusted, pious, and exercising great influence, with broad ideals and utopian expectations; a man quick to understand, resourceful, ingenious, and capable of assuming leadership. He also had the courage to try to bring his ideas to realization.

There was great need for a sawmill. Bringing building materials from a distance was too costly and difficult. Through his leadership among the immigrants he soon picked out a place for a sawmill on the creek, at a spot opposite the present schoolhouse. He formed a partnership with Rikken, a High German. Rabbers found some persons who had a little money and were willing to support his venture. Such was the confidence he inspired that on one occasion his hired girl received $ 500 from one of these persons and, carrying it in her apron, brought it to him. Those who had no money freely gave him their work on the basis of charity or in the hope of being provided with lumber for their own needs. Building of the mill was begun during the mild winter of 1847-48. The father of Isaac Fairbanks of Holland was contractor. The following persons took part in constructing the dam: Teunis and Harm Ratering, Gerrit Derks, the Van de Laare brothers, Pieter Wissekerke, Arnold Barendse, Willem de Jong, Berend de Vries, and some others.

The mill, as it was first constructed, was a crude affair. At its best it could saw only a few thousand feet each twenty-four hours. But it gave people an opportunity to work. Kasper Lahuis, H. and J. ten Have, Berend Jan Veneklaasen, and Hendrik van Eyck are a few of the people who worked in this mill. The machinery frequently broke. And as the dam was not strong enough to hold back the large volume of water at the time of thaw and heavy rains, it often gave way. Money had to be borrowed to pay for repairs. The owners fell into debt and the twelve creditors named Jan Rabbers, Albert Borgers, and A. Niemeijer to serve as administrators with full authority. Later they transferred the mill to Albert Borgers and Tamme Huizinga who continued the business. Much money was lost in this venture.

In the autumn of 1849 Jan Kolvoord began a new undertaking. He had spent some time in Allegan and had learned woodturning. He had convinced himself there was a demand for better furniture. The writer of this sketch recalls that in the houses of that day the settlers had only handmade furniture produced by themselves. Kolvoord built a mill on a small creek near New Groningen, a little north of the [present] bridge. The machinery of this mill was turned by an overshot waterwheel. That insignificant factory was a prophecy and forerunner of the large factories today to be found in Holland and in Zeeland.

Kolvoord's small mill soon was converted into a cornmill, for the people were in great need of cornmeal. To this mill from far and near the farmers and not infrequently women and children carried packages of corn on their backs. It usually had been shelled by hand and dried on bed sheets. After being brought to the mill the people had to wait a day or two before it could be ground.

Rabbers' enterprising spirit was not quenched after his mill passed into the hands of Borgers and Huizinga. As Kolvoord's mill lacked the necessary volume of water to operate efficiently and as Rabbers had learned from experience that a long dam cost too much money, the latter began construction of a flourmill on the creek on which he had built his sawmill, about 200 rods southwest of the present cemetery. Rabbers now was acting in partnership with Cornelius de Roo, the father of C. de Roo at present associated with the Walsh de Roo Milling Company [of Holland, Michigan].

That a sufficient amount of water for this mill might be guaranteed throughout the entire year, the company laid a dam in the river and dug a sluice a few rods west of the bridge by the cemetery. Here they formed a millpond. A canal was dug from the millpond to the mill which insured sufficient volume of water to turn the mill wheel. Jan van Eenenaam of Zeeland was the first miller. Later, a barley mill was added to the business. This mill was such a success that its owners conceived plans to build a larger one run by steam. The three story building to house it was nearly completed [G. Stenk and P. Zalsman were the contractors] and the boiler and machinery had been purchased in Grand Rapids, but had not yet been delivered, when suddenly C. de Roo died of dysentery on September 1, 1855. This put an end to the new undertaking. The building was never finished.

While the new machinery for this mill was never delivered, the old mill operated many years after. Jan Rabbers died in 1860. The widow of C. de Roo married D. C. Oggel who continued the business for many years with Cornelius van Eekelenburg. This mill attracted much activity to Groningen. At an early date Rabbers had erected a large store on a

lot directly west of Manus Stegeman's house. In 1854 he sold this store
to Jan van Eenenaam and built a house next to his mill. On the lot on
which Van Eenenaam's store stood was erected a shingle mill in which
Machiel de Puit and Thomas de Witt were employed.

Jan Hendrik Veneklaasen, brickmaker, who had emigrated from Rijssen
in the province of Overijsel in the Netherlands, as early as 1848 began to
make bricks opposite the farm on which Benjamin van Raalte is living at
present. Veneklaasen and his sons Berend Jan, Jannes, and Pieter in 1855
moved this business to Old Groningen. Its first location was north of the
bridge near the cemetery, on the west side of the road. Here they made
by hand something like 4,000 or 5,000 bricks each day, about 100,000
during a season.

The present yard and other buildings, the property of Berend Jan
Veneklaasen, were moved to the other side of the road in 1855, but soon
it became necessary to find a location where there was a sufficient supply
of clay. The management wanted to expand the business and begin to
ship bricks to distant places. For the Kolonie finally had acquired a railway. A company was formed by Berend Jan Veneklaasen and Bolks who
established the factory at the present location, employing steam driveu
machinery. Later Bolks left the company which then became the family
property of Veneklaasen and his sons. The business is still active and is
operating on an expanded scale, having three yards, at Zeeland, Hamilton,
and Cloverdale. Such was the enterprising spirit and the iron will
exhibited in the formation, advancement, and expansion of such a business.
During the years of the existence of this brick factory many a person has
earned his bread by working there.

The same year Veneklaasen opened his brick factory in Groningen
arrived August Jansen [at present living in West Pullman, Illinois], a
shoemaker by trade who believed the people of the Kolonie were in need
of leather. He had learned how totan hides in tanneries inSaugatuck and
Grand Rapids. Rabbers, ever enterprising, urged him to start a tannery.
Two acres near Rabbers' mill were purchased as a site and a tannery was
built and adequately equipped. Prospects for success seemed excellent.
Hemlock bark could be acquired for practically nothing. Wages were
75 cents a day and hides were cheap. But business demand was feeble.
The shoemakers in the immediate neighbourhoud had little need for leather
From time to time small batches were sent to market, but the volume was
not sufficient to make the undertaking a success. Besides, the dam
frequently gave way so that the vats were filled with water, which ruined
the tanning fluids. And there were other reasons why this undertaking

was doomed to failure. For a considerable time thereafter Jansen lived in New Groningen busily employed as a butcher.

After the failure of Jansen's business Lukas Aling and Toon Baart opened their tannery on the spot where the engine house of Veneklaasen and Sons' brickyard now stands. Nor was this undertaking crowned with success, for the building in which it was housed soon burned.

Early in the 1850's Andries Steketee, uncle of the Steketees of Holland, Grand Rapids, and Muskegon, began his business in staves. He constructed a dock on the Black River next to Scholten's Brug, bought staves, shipped them on flatboats to Holland where they were consumed, or were shipped by sailboat to distant places. This business contributed much to the prosperity of the Kolonie. Now people were in a position to make some money from the oak trees which grew everywhere. These oaks stood like giants among the beech, maple, elm, ash, and hickory trees in every direction in Groningen, Noordeloos, Noord Holland, Ebenezer, Drenthe, Vriesland, and elsewhere. Those days one could see coming through the woods, along indescribably bad and crooked roads, heavily loaded wagons and sleighs drawn by oxen. Caravans of such vehicles from distant Drenthe and Vriesland disturbed the quiet of the people living along these roads, such was the noise of the drivers who drove the slow, lazy, and all too abused four-footed creatures.

The golden age of Groningen lasted from 1855 to about 1865. The stave business of Andries Ateketee, the flourmill of Rabbers and De Roo, and Veneklaasens' brickyard brought much activity to this community. In 1857 Steketee sold this factory to Hendrik Scholten who continued it for many years. He opened a small store in connection with this business and offered refreshment to thirsty and weary drivers of oxen. Proof that Scholten conducted a profitable business is to be seen in the spacious brick house which he built next to his place of business at the bridge.

In 1867 Gerrit J. Boone, G. Huizinga, and J. de Vries formed a company to build a sawmill. It was erected a few rods southwest of Scholten's Brug, where the decaying remnants of the building and fragments of the machinery may still be seen. Twice this mill burned down, the first time in 1871, the second in 1877. For twenty years the activity of this mill brought prosperity to the people and greatly encouraged clearing of the woods. The price of logs was favorable. From near and far they came by sleigh during winter, or werde floated down the river swollen with the thawing snows of springtime. The forest now was stripped of its timber, and the great fire of 1871 advanced the work of clearing by burning the cut-down trees. That fire, a frightful ordeal, was a deeply regretted event because of the great losses it caused. But later it was regarded as the hand of God which burned away so much of the woods and helped to convert wild lands into splendid farms.

When the new road was laid through New Groningen so that it by-passed Old Groningen Jan van Eenenaam thought it necessary to move his place of business. In 1858 Albert Borgers and H. ten Have surveyed the lots in the village of New Groningen. The school was the central point of the area. Anesus J. Hillebrands became the first teacher. He was ever an energetic worker for Groningen's growth and progress. Van Eenenaam erected the store which still stands on the original spot. Soon also Willem Huizinga's smithy was moved from Old Groningen to New Groningen and Klaas Boer established himself in the latter place as wagonmaker. Thus New Groningen flourished. Its name was given by Hillebrands when the postoffice was established there.

Dominie Cornelius van der Meulen preached a sermon on October 1, 1847, at Old Groningen, below the bridge, a short distance southwest of the present cemetery. His text was drawn from 2 Corinthians, 1, 10: "Who delivered us from so great a death and doth deliver; in whom we trust that he will yet deliver us." A stump served as pulpit. His hearers sat on stumps or on logs. Above the branches of the trees they saw the blue sky as if it was the ceiling.

Religious life, during the first days so highly praised and assuredly not unjustly, sometimes had its defects. Religion served occasionally to advance material, or selfish and utopian ends. The object from the first was to make an important center of Groningen. The church and the school were to help to attain it. The settlers of Groningen were united ecclesiastically with the church in Zeeland which had great difficulty in supporting its pastor Dominie van der Meulen.

But, what happened? In 1848, according to the diary of Hendrik van Eyck and according to others, the people in Groningen called Huibertus Jacobus Budding to be their pastor. It is to be noted that no congregation had yet been organized. In Zeeland the rule had been adopted that those who emigrated from the Netherlands as elders or deacons and who had joined that congregation should continue to function as such. The result soon was apparent. There were altogether too many such office holders. On June 12, 1849, it was decided that all these people should surrender their dignities and that from among them a given number of elders and deavons were to be chosen, and this was carried out. Elder Niemeijer was not reelected. Apparently Niemeijer, Rabbers, and H. van Duren were the chief persons to lead religious services [in Groningen]. For it was Niemeijer who frequently led the meetings by reading somesermon.

Because Dominie Budding had emigrated to America without being called to serve any congregation and was traveling about the Kolonie holding religious services in various settlements, it was hoped he would cast his lot in with them in Groningen. An invitation was extended to him. Since his divergent conception of what constituted correct church practices made it impossible for him to live in one church fellowship with other ministers, he declined the invitation. He made known his decision in his own peculiar fashion. He had preached in the schoolhouse during the morning service. He and several others had lunch at the house of one of the brethren. In the afternoon he made his announcement. He declined their call because, he declared, they did not want him, for they had not mentioned him when saying grace at mealtime.

In the fall of 1850 the Groningers proceeded on their own initiative to elect two deacons. It appears that A. Niemeijer and Jacob R. Schepers were chosen elders. Now a congregation was organized! The consistory at Zeeland, hearing of the formation of this new congregation, wrote to the brethren in Groningen, begging and warning them not to persist in such an unecclesiastilac proceeding "contrary to the Word of God." The consequence of this letter was that when the Groningers appeared before the consistory in Zeeland, they suggested that "as the congregation now had been organized it would be best to allow it to continue."

It was decided that in the absence of Dominie van der Meulen, Schepers was to lead in Zeeland, and was to conduct services in the village of Groningen every fortnight. In the Netherlands Schepers had studied for the ministry but for some reason had not reached his goal to become a minister. For a considerable time Schepers preached in Groningen. He did not please the people and when he failed to be ordained he went over to the Scottish [Presbyterian] Church.

The schoolhouse burned down and Hillebrands moved to Wisconsin. The supporters of the congregation steadily dribbled away and rejoined the congregation of Zeeland. It was a lost cause. Nevertheless there was always a lively desire to have separate services in Groningen, for in December 1855 there was presented at a meeting of the Zeeland consistory a "petition from the village of Groningen that religious services be held there Sundays because the distance was too great for the women to walk." "Decision: no definite rule is to be established. These people may meet for mutual edification." This was agreed to, and they henceforth met on Sunday evenings in the new schoolhouse in New Groningen, at which meetings Jan Hendriks Stegink usually led. Catechetical instruction also was given there by the pastor of the congregation who, usually, on the evening before his services read a portion of the Bible and discussed it for the assembled people. Dominie Seine Bolks by means of these Bible discussions exercised much influence among the people. The chapel at New Groningen was erected while Dominie Willem Moerdyk served in the Zeeland congregation. This building is still being used for catechetical instruction and funeral services.

Very early the people of Old Groningen took an interest in schooling for their children. As yet school districts were not organized. The little ones were in need of instruction, which was reason enough to plan the building of a schoolhouse. That first schoolhouse, composed of logs, stood a few rods west of Frank Brummel's house. A fireplace was erected in the center of the building. One end of the building served as the house of the teacher, the other was the schoolroom. There was no wall between the two. Among those who attended this school are Jantje Niemeijer; Dirk, Jan, and Jantje Broek, later wife of G. J. Boone; Jurien de Vries; Hendrik and Jochem van Dijk; Naatje, Christina, and Mary Sakkers; Berend and Pieter Kleis; and others. This schoolhouse was destroyed by fire, and likewise the larger and more suitable building which later was built near Rabbers' and De Roo's flourmill. Hillebrands then moved to Wisconsin. For a while the children had to get along without schooling.

The school inspectors of Holland Township at the request of the voters in Groningen held a meeting at Rabbers' sawmill on May 23, 1853, to organize School District No. 2 [later No. 3]. Andries Steketee was chosen to preside and the following persons were elected to serve as officers of the new district: A. Steketee, moderator, Jan Hendriks Stegink, assessor, and Hendrik van Eyck, director.

Notwithstanding the extensive area of the school district there were but 26 children of school age in 1853. Jan Boer taught school for $ 12 per month, in a lean-to of Rabber's sawmill. Among those attending this school were Roelof and Hendrik Evers; Dirk, Harm, and Jan Borgers; Jantje Rabbers; Bonel de Vries; Walter van Huil; J. D. Werkman; and others. Finally, the triangular plot of land opposite the store in New Groningen was purchased, and on it was erected a schoolhouse of 20 by 30 feet which cost $ 100. It is interesting to note that a precise contract was drawn up between the school board and the contractors. Already at that time, in 1853, these people knew how to make binding contracts in English.

We here add a list of the teachers who followed each other during the first years: Thomas C. Kenworthy in 1854; C. Doesburg in 1855; Thomas C. Kenworthy again in 1856. Of Kenworthy it is related that he always began his instruction in the morning by kneeling in prayer. Hillebrands returned [from Wisconsin] to Groningen to serve as teacher and continued in this capacity until 1870. In 1867 a "select school" was organized to which anyone who wished could send his children. The teachers who taught in this school were James Brandt in 1867-68, R. Hyma in 1868-69, and a Mr. Bacon in 1869-70. Hillebrands was turned out [of the originally established school] in 1870 during a vigorous contest between his supporters and his opponents. Thereafter this school was discontinued. The many teachers who taught here have not labored in vain. This school in no way was inferior to any other in this region. With some pride we could draw up a long list of names of those who as children received their first impulse toward rational development and who later attained important and honorable posts in society, church, and school.

At Old Groningen, the original village, the following families lived from 1847 to 1855; Jan Rabbers, Harm Krans, Pieter Karsten, Cornelis Weniger, Willem and Adriaan van de Laare, Pieter Sakkers, Pieter Daane, Anesus J. Hillebrands, H. van Duren, Manus Stegeman, Berend Jan Veneklaasen, Cornelis de Roo, Jan van Eenenaam, and most likely some others. In the area which at that time belonged to Groningen lived Albert Borgers, J. Wener, A. Niemeijer, B. J. de Vries, J. Aalting, H. Vredeveld, G. Kamps, Jan Jekel, H. Lubbers, J. van der Werp, H. Werkman, Tamme Huizinga, Salomon de Koeijer, Kasper Lahuis, and, at a later date, Evert Zagers, Jan Hendriks Stegink, A. Westveer, P. van Belois, and A. van Duine. In the neighborhood of Rabbers' sawmill lived the widow Ten Have and her children, Pieter Meins Boekhout, H. ten Have, Dirk de Pau, Jan Koster, and some others.

Janna Weniger, daughter of Cornelis Weniger, was the first child to be born in Groningen – "under the blue sky" – as it was said. She also was the first of the children to be baptized in Zeeland's congregation.

The first cemetery was laid out on a plot of land which later proved to belong to some speculators. This was fully a quarter of a mile southeast of the central point of Old Groningen, on land at present belonging to Jan Stegeman and to the widow Brummel. Many lie buried there – Abraham and Adriaan van de Laare [the last named died as the result of a blow from the branch of a tree]. At his funeral Dominie van der Meulen spoke using as text "It pleased the Lord to break him in pieces" [Isaiah 53, 10]. His widow, a daughter of Poppen and later the wife of Berend Jan Veneklaasen, A. van Zwaluwenburg, Aaltje Ensing wife of Manus

Stegeman, and the family of Pieter Meins Boekhout [which died out early] likewise were buried here.

The first doctor in Groningen was an American, Dr. C. D. Shenick, who practised his profession there in 1849 in which year he was elected to a township office. He possessed the confidence of the people.

In the present cemetery also rest the material remains of the second doctor of Groningen, N. R. Parsons. On his gravestone we read the following inscription: "Dr. N. R. Parsons. Born at Enfield, Connecticut, August 20, 1819. Died March 5, 1860, aged 40 years."

15. ALBERT STEGEMAN's
TWO MONTHS OF EARLY PIONEERING

[The Stegeman family of which Albert Stegeman (d. 1901) was a member emigrated from the province of Groningen in October 1846, sailing in the *Isabella Bath* which arrived in New York on December 21. This account based upon memory and composed fifty years after the events it describes contains valuable information about Holland's first days. To this address printed in *De Grondwet*, April 18, 1911, Gerrit van Schelven, editor, added a few notes relating to the history of the Stegeman family.]

Fellow Citizens: We have come together here to-day to commemorate the departure from the Fatherland and the settlement in this place fifty years ago, an event that has wrought a great change for most of us, and, speaking for myself, was of great moment. For here I have found that liberty, that freedom, that independence, that elbow-room which my soul had craved from childhood. Here I found the field and the co-laborers in my life's work; here I found a people composed of all the nations of the earth, bringing with them their heredity, characteristics, and personalities to be blended and molded into a people such as this world has not known before, and of which it is our priviledge to form a part.

It was the intention of our people to start at the same time and in the same ship with Rev. A. C. van Raalte, but all the space was taken before our application was received, so we had to wait for the next craft to sail, thirty days later.

We left Rotterdam about the middle of October, and arrived in New York on December 21, 1846, oud long and stormy sea voyage covering sixty-two days. – We found this new continent, the land of our future home, clad in its wintry garment and wrapped in a mantle of snow – cold and forbidding.

Having to leave the ship which had been our home for over two months, in a strange land mid a curious crowd, speaking a language of which we could not understand a word, hustled hither and thither not knowing where, for the immigrant station at Castle Garden was not in existence then, we then and there for the first time in our life felt what it was to be lonely in a crowd.

The next day we left New York, arriving at Greenbush in the eve of December 24. We found the Hudson frozen over and crossed it on the ice. Here we went into winter quarters, intending to remain till spring. About the middle of February we received a letter from Van Raalte requesting all the able-bodied men to come on at once to Black Lake in Western Michigan – that being the place selected to locate his Colony – to help build log or block-houses and make roads, leaving the women and children to follow in the spring after the opening of navigation. A few of the men responded and we started.

In our party were the two Plaggemars, Kolvoord, Hofman, one other, and father and I, seven in all. We went by rail as far as the Niagara Falls, crossed the river in a skiff below the falls, mid ice and foam, and as I looked up at its great torrents of water coming thundering down from above, its ice-covered surroundings, its clouds of mist, its towering banks on either side, its whirling water below, – it filled my youthful breast with awe and admiration as I had never felt before. It seemed as though I had been trasported to a wonderland. From the falls we started for Detroit on foot, walked all the way except twenty five miles, when we hired a farmer to take us.

Arriving at Windsor in Canada, tired and footsore, we found the Detroit River full of ice, so that the ferry boat was not running. Being ancxious to get over to the Detroit side, we hired a man to pilot us across. Each of us was provided with a sixteen-foot board fence, which we were to carry under our arms so that in case we should fall through between the cakes of ice, it would hold us up; and when we came to an opening too wide to jump across, they were used to make a bridge. Thus we picked our way from cake to cake, some of them being on the move, till we reached the Detroit landing.

Here we were directed to find a Reverend Duffield, at whose house we met Van Raalte, who gave us the needed information and directions. On the following morning we left Detroit by rail for Kalamazoo. From there we got a ride on a pair of bobs with a man who was going to Allegan after lumber.

We remained in Allegan three days with old friends and relatives who had already come over with Van Raalte. From here we started with Mr. E. J. Harrington, Sr. with an old-fashioned low-kneed sled drawn by a yoke of oxen, through the woods on a newly cut-out unbroken road through snow and slush, walking nearly all the way and arriving at our destination late in the evening.

We found here two log shanties, located between where Van Raalte's residence stands and Mr. Grootenhuis' place. One was assigned to our party, the other being occupied by the few men and one woman who came here before we did and by whom these had been built.

Our furniture consisted of an old stove, a pot, and kettle; not a chair or table. Our beds were made of hemlock boughs, laid in a pile across one end of the shanty with a few blankets spread over them. To remain warm during the cold March nights we had to keep a fire all night, taking turns in filling the stove with such wood as we could find or dig from under the snow. Our food consisted of whole corn, middlings, and some pork. Being the youngest, most of the cooking fell to me, and I can assure you that I possessed all the primitive simplicity of our ancestry. The middlings were made into bread, very much resembling the hoecake of the South, and eaten when hungry without butter. The corn was boiled in water and ashes, and when tender it was taken to the brook, soaked, and washed till free from lye and hulls [in a measure at least], and eaten with a little pork grease. But when hunger calls, the simplest or plainest food is relished and we are the better for it. Would that our present civilization paid less homage to appetite; it would aid us in purifying our lives. During my stay here I carried the mail once a week to Manlius, on foot, through rain and shine, snow, water, and mud.

As spring approached, and the snow began to disappear the Indians opened their sugar camps, and the pioneers began to select land for their future homes. About this time Van Raalte came out to show us the lands that were for sale. One day we went with him to where Zeeland is now located. Starting in the morning we crossed the Black River on the ice, tramped through the woods all day, and on our return found the river swollen, overflowing its banks, and the ice covered by water, rendering it unsafe to cross.

We followed the stream till finding a tree which by being cut down fell across the stream, but not being very large was partly covered by water, on which we managed to get over, most of us straddling it, holding on with both hands, as it lay shaking and trembling in the swift current – dipping us to our waists in the icy waters of Black River. Not a very agreeable baptism. Our leader Van Raalte was a small but brave man and during the day, as he lead us through the woods, compass in hand, clad in a longgreat coat and top boots, he reminded me of a picture I had seen in my childhood of Napoleon the First. As we came to large fallen landing trees, covered with snow, he would lean down and roll over them, of his feet. Before dark we found ourselves safely back to our shanty home, plus the days' experience and a suit of wet clothes.

My stay in Holland was a brief one. About the first of May, hearing that mother and the rest of the family had arrived at Grand Haven, a few of us started for that place to meet them. There I hired out, after returning to Holland to get my clothes. Since that time I have made only an occasional visit here.

Though not located among you, I have watched your growth with a good deal of interest, and on the whole I can say, "You have acquitted yourselves well!" In a material sense you have succeeded where others have failed. By your industry and perseverance you have changed this region from a wilderness to one of the most propserous and productive in the state. Socially you stand abreast with any community in the nation of which you have become a part. And educationally – yonder institution, Hope College, and those who have graduated therefrom, speak volumes where I could lisp but sentences. Morally and religiously – let your daily life voice your eulogy.

And now as I am about to leave you for the sunset clime of the Pacific coast, let my best thoughts and wishes remain with you and yours follow me, and both go on till they circle the globe, freighted with good will to all creatures wherever found. Not that we should love kindred less, but humanity more. In our prosperity and superior advantages let us not forget the less favored children of earth, feeling as one of old that "the world is our country, and to do good our religion."

Note – The Stegeman family, of which the writer is one, consisted of father John Stegeman, mother and seven children: Jennigje, whose first husband, Jan Hulst, was drowned in Chicago Creek, who was later married to Jacob de Frel; Wilhelmina, married to Hendrik Manting; Hendrikje, married to Wiepke Diekma; Jan and Martin who are both living, the former in California and the latter in Allegan; and Albert, the writer of the above reminiscence. In the course of time after leaving Holland, Albert became one of the leading citizens and merchants of Grand Haven and was junior member of the firm of Cutler, Worts, and Stegeman. Afterwards he moved to Allegan and organized the Grange Store on the co-operative plan, which soon became historic as the greatest establishment of its kind in the west. In 1897 he went to California where he was extensively engaged in the raising of fruit and died in 1901. – Gerrit van Schelven.

16. ALBERTUS KOLVOORD'S PIONEER RECOLLECTIONS

[The Kolvoord family emigrated from the province of Groningen in 1846, sailing in the *Isabella Bath*, arrived in Michigan in the spring of the following year, and settled in Groningen. These *Pioneer Recollections* were written toward the close of Albert Kolvoord's life and published in the *Holland Evening Sentinel*, November 16, 1940.]

Ninety-three years ago, Holland, Michigan, and vicinity was not as we see it today; the younger generation of the present time has no conception of the hardships, struggles, and privations that the hardy *voortrekkers* [pioneers] experienced in their battle to create a home for themselves and posterity. In 1847 the territory in which Albertus C. van Raalte and Cornelius van der Meulen and their countrymen settled was literally a wilderness, bordered by shifting sand dunes on the west and interspersed with tangled forests, swamps, creeks, and marshes toward the east. There were no railroads, not even a decent, country dirt road to provide communication to a distant settlement. Food was the great requirement and that meant work and more work. Before corn, potatoes, or grain could be planted, the trees had to be hewn down laboriously and the limbs cut off to provide space for the prospective crop. After the corn and grain had been harvested, then came the problem of preparing it for food.

My father, Jan Kolvoord, was a member of the second small group that followed Van Raalte and assisted in building log huts and roads and clearing land. Father and his fellow countrymen from the Netherlands arrived in the vicinity of Holland, Michigan, on March 10, 1847 and in the summer of that year we find him on the north shore of Black Lake, making shingles by hand at five shillings, 65 cents, a day. What is now Holland city did not have a clearing large enough to grow a patch of potatoes. Soon after, Jan Kolvoord bought 20 acres of land in New Groningen, Ottawa County, through which a small creek [where the State Fish Hatchery is now located] flowed into the Black River. Seeing the possibilities of utilizing the water power, he built a dam and a small gristmill, with an overshot water wheel to operate the millstones. He also built a long reel, or bolster, for separating the bran and middlings from the flour after the grain had been ground. The wheat in those days was cut with a sickle, threshed with a flail, and the chaff separated from the grain with a winnow. This information I have from the lips of pioneers who went to the mill with a pack of wheat or corn on their shoulders, and also from my mother who used to do the grinding in father's absence.

As father was a turner and cabinet maker by trade, he sold his gristmill machinery to Jan Rabbers, his brother - in - law who had constructed a dam farther down the main stream and thus became father's successor as a miller. Jan Kolvoord now turned his attention to making furniture for which there was a growing need in "De Kolonie" as thevarious Dutch settlements were known collectively. The village of Holland was called "de stad". By using the gristmill building and the overshot waterwheel for power he ran his woodlathes and other machinery for making chairs, tables, bedsteads, and other furniture.

As I was born in New Groningen, Ottawa County, on February 18, 1856, I well remember the lay of the land and the location of our various neigbors. I recall the Rev. van Raalte's house at the east end of Holland. Going east and north we came across a creek, and thence we came to a swamp; from this, going to the high lands, we came to a place where lived a man by the name of Ver Wey. Nearby lived an Indian, short of stature, who had very crooked legs. We children were afraid of him although he was harmless.

Father east and north, we came to Scholten's Bridge, a place of much activity. Staves were brought here and loaded on a scow. By means of poles the boat was pushed to Holland on the Black River, where staves were loaded on sailing vessels and shipped to Chicago and Milwaukee. At the bridge was the beginning of Groningen. Here lived at that time Gerrit J. Boone, Jan H. Boone, J. de Vries, and Berend J. Veneklaasen who at this time was operating a brickyard. He mixed the clay with sand and water by means of a long pole full of wooden pins. This pole was pulled round and roung by a horse until the clay and sand were well mixed and ready for the molds.

Going south from here, we came to the cemetery; then on to the corner where lived Mannes Stegeman and Brummel. To the west was the flour-mill of Jan Rabbers at this time operated by Cornelius van Eecklenberg. Rabbers died early in 1860. East from Stegeman's corners lived Hendrik van Eyck, Berend J. de Vries, B. Kamps, Hyma, Wissink, and a few others.

Coming back to Veneklaasen and going north, there was De Katte with his two bachelor sons Adriaan and Willem. Next lived Tamme Huizinga and then came the creek on which stood Jan Kolvoord's former gristmill and remodeled furniture factory. The mill stood back of the house, a story and a half building with basement and over-shot water wheel at the end. Next to Kolvoord's house lived Anesus J. Hildebrand, our schoolteacher, next was H. ten Have and then Klaas Boer, blacksmith and wagonmaker. Next to him was the schoolhouse and across from the school was the store kept by Jan van Eenenaam. The main part of this store is still there at the present time. To the south lived a Mr. Jansen, tanner by trade; to the east was Borger's mill operated by steam. There was also a dam but this was not used for power. North of the school and next to it lived Gerrit Derks; going north and east from there was Zeeland. By going west we came to Mr. Sterken, J. Blink, D. J. Werkman, G. H. Huizinga, Kasper Lahuis, Mr. de Kooyer, Tamme van den Bosch, and others.

Of all places named, I cannot remember any loghouse, for the people, as I recall, had frame houses. The road lay through the woods with large trees quite near the road and with small clearings farther back. At this time there was a stagecoach running between Holland and Grand Rapids, operated by Gerrit Haverkate. The post office was kept by Jan van Eenenaam. There was no church in Groningen, but all went to Zeeland where services were held in a log building. The first minister in Zeeland was Cornelius van der Meulen and the second, Rev. H. Stobbelaar. These are my remembrances of New Groningen in 1865.

My father died Nov. 6, 1856, the year that I was born, leaving mother with four small boys, Johannes, Jan, Klaas, and Albertus. Having no means of support, I have often been asked "How did you get along?" Well, first of all we needed kind friends and good neighbors. The fact of the matter is that all the pioneers were poor, and every one was helpful and all knew each other's needs and were willing to divide with each other. This was especially so during sickness and death.

I can remember only one time we were hungry. We children got up in the morning and all cried because there was no food. Mother gave us a slip of paper with which we went to the small mill father once owned, and the miller gave us a sack of meal. On our way home, the sack broke and some of the meal was spilled on the ground. We scraped it back into the bag as best we could and with it some sand. About noon we had something to eat, and to this day I have never forgotten the sand between my teeth.

I also remember a man coming to our home with a quarter of beef on his shoulder. He told mother he had heard we were in need, and said all he could get for beef was two cents a pound, so he concluded to give the beef to us, for which mother thanked him. I have heard it said many times that there was no market for anything that could be turned into money, so the pioneers of those days had enough to eat. Fish and all other food was plentiful, but for clothing and such things they suffered.

Mother's second marriage was to Cornelius Bliek, and to this union were born Lena Maria Bliek and Alice Bliek. A brother of Bliek, named Hendrik, always stayed with us and went wherever we went, and was part of our support. Again our mother became a widow, and in 1885 we all moved to Overisel, Allegan County, except Johannes, the eldest who was taken into the home of Geert Lubbers, an uncle, living in Drenthe, whose wife, Maria, was a sistre of father. This came about as follow. On his way home from school in New Groningen Johannes and another boy were wrestling in a friendly manner, when the teacher came along and stopped them, and two days later gave him an unmerciful whipping so that he would not go to that school again.

Johannes was a good student and, after finishing the district school in Drenthe, he attended Hope College until 1871 when he lost his school books in the big Holland city fire. This ended his college career, and he then taught school in Drenthe and North Holland and also in Orange City, Iowa, where he later became county superintendent of schools. In 1886 he became connected with the Review and Herald Publising Co. of Battle Creek, Michigan, in capacity of editor and translator. His death occured April 16, 1936.

Jan, next in age, had a good supply of common sense. The only schooling he had was obtained in a district school, yet his natural business ability enabled him to build and conduct a general store in Hamilton. After selling out the store, he engaged in the sawmill and planingmill business which he operated until the supply of timber gave out. He also secured an interest in the Hope Flourmill and afterward built and operated the flourmill known as the Kolvoord Milling Company. He was elected representative to the Michigan Legislature and alter was appointed postmaster at Hamilton. He died Dec. 1, 1936.

Klaas, the third in age, was a farmer in Overisel Township. He died Oct. 30, 1933, in Hamilton.

Albertus, commonly known as Bert, the youngest of the four Kolvoord boys, is the only surviving member of the family. In 1865 mother was married to Jan Dubbink and to this union was born Gerrit Hendrik Dubbink. The Rev. Gerrit H. Dubbink was a graduate of Hope College and served as pastor of Third Reformed Church of Holland for nine years. For six years he was Professor of Theology in the Western Theological Seminary of the Reformed Church in America. He married Margaret Janet Kollen, May 29, 1895, and his death occurred July 26, 1910, at Holland.

We lived in Groningen until March 6, 1865, and then moved to Overisel Township in Allegan County, and, as I remember, we had six head of cattle. That winter of 1865 was mild, hardly any snow. On the day we moved it was warm and the birds were out in great number. The place we moved to was a loghouse. On April 1, I became a hired man at nine years of age. My wages were $ 12 a year, two pounds of wool, and three months' schooling; the first of December in school and the first of March out again.

Brothers Jan and Klaas did about the same, but suffice it to say we were all in demand. The first place I stayed for two years. The second year I got $ 18 and two pounds of wool, which was for mother because she spun her own yarn and did her own knitting. The third year I got $ 22.50 and three months' schooling. After that mother became a widow again, and we all came home, working on the farm and clearing land. We worked hard on the farm and never had much schooling, not over four months a year at the most.

About 1872 Jan went to Saugatuck and became interested in milling, or rather worked in a mill for George P. Heath, who had obtained a threshing machine on a mortgage. This threshing machine required five teams of horses to furnish power. We operated this machine three years on the farm and elsewhere with success. We tought the outfit for $ 100. The first year with the threshing rig we made over $ 300 clear profit. Three hundred dollars meant something in those days. We kept doing this three years during the threshing season. It was very hard work, but we were used to it, and it got us away from the humdrum of farm life.

Some one wanted me to act as clerk in a store. This was to my liking and I stayed there a year at a salary of $ 2 a week and board. This was quitte a step up from where I began.

Having had no chance for an education, I went for three years to Hope College and graduated from the preparatory department. This was in 1878. Then I clerked for six months in Hamilton. After this I clerked in a store in Cadillac, and for four months in a drug store in Fife Lake. On returning to Hamilton I became interested in the store business. I had $ 300 in cash and William ter Avest had $ 600 in cash, making $ 900 between the two of us. With this we bought out John Kolvoord's and Siebe Bakker's store and contents for $ 4,200 leaving us a debt of $ 3,300. Ter Avest mortgaged his farm for $ 1,500 and I borrowed from a farmer and gave my note for $ 700 with my good looks as security.

Storekeeping at that time was not what it is to day. Butter and eggs were our principal stock. We bought from farmers such produce as they had to sell, including beef, pork, maple sugar, wood, and shingles, but never used any money in the trasanction. It was all in trade for groceries, dry goods, boots, and shoes. We had a general store and did a trading business. I went to Muskegon once each month and there sold our butter and eggs, pork, or anything that was needed in that market. Muskegon was a sawmill town, a good place to sell such products as we had. With the money thus collected we paid our wholesale grocer, but it took a lot of patience and hard work.

It also required lots of credit extended to us by the wholesale grocers. In the 12 years of struggling and hard work with butter and eggs, the principal stock in trade, we have had as much as two tons of butter on hand at one time looking for a market. There were no creameries and butter came in by the tons. It was a drug on the market so we had to work it over and ship it out. In those days prices were from 8 to 15 cents for butter and eggs. Eggs were not graded and therefore had no standing in the market for goodness or quality.

We never could take a discount from the wholesale grocers. For example, I recall a certain bill was due on a specified date or they would take possession of the store. I told my wife what was coming. Well, as luck would have it, I got sufficient money to pay on the day set. When I went home for dinner at noon she asked me "What luck?" I told her I had the money. She said, "I prayed for it," and it was greatly appreciated by me.

We kept on doing business as best we could, until a competitor went into bankruptcy. A representative from the wholesalers came in and said, "So-and-so has gone into bankruptcy and we have lost considerable money. You too, owe us quite a sum. How much do you owe?" I told him I did not know but a great plenty. He asked for my books, which he compared with our inventory and when finished said, "It amounts to over $ 5,000, quite a sum," with which I agreed. I told him we had doubled the size of the store and gave him our last yearly invoice which showed we were doing a good business. "Well," he said, "we will talk it over and let you know," but we never heard from anyone, thanks to Amos S. Musselman, the representative. I was in the store business twelve years, and butter and eggs drove me out. In 1892 I had a chance to sell and got enough money to pay my creditors 100 cents on the dollar and had a little left, for which we were thankful.

In 1894 three of us bought a flourmill in Allegan, run by water power, for $ 13,500. The terms were $ 100 each month on the principal and interest as accrued from month to month. One of the three was a miller, another a good man at the door, and my job was that of salesman. This was not a small job. For 18 years I traveled as far north as Traverse City and Cadillac and I covered the trade every 30 days. In 1912 a competing mill was combinet with ours and we formed a stock company of which I became manager. The World War came on and wheat became scarce in 1917 and brought a high price. In the month of August we did over $ 85,000 business. The government took flour for $ 15 a barrel; this was a banner month. I sold out my interest in 1920. There were at one time 22 flour mills in Allegan County alone, but at present the mill in Wayland is the only one doing business.

Chapter V

FOUNDING AND EARLY HISTORY OF ZEELAND FROM 1847

17. CORNELIUS VAN DER MEULEN'S ADDRESS AT ZEELAND SEPTEMBER 18, 1872

[Born at Middelharnis, the Netherlands, on December 15, 1800, Cornelius van der Meulen (d. 1876) became a leader among the Seceders and emigrated to Michigan where with his followers he became the founder of Zeeland. This *Hoofd Inhoud der Rrede Uitgesproken op het Vijf-en-Twintig Jarig Feest te Zeeland* was delivered on September 18, 1872, on the twenty-fifth anniversary of the founding of Zeeland. The address, preserved in a typed copy among Gerrit van Schelven's papers, reposes in the Netherlands Museum. It is the earliest historical account of the community of Zeeland.]

Waarde Vrienden en Landgenooten. – Heden een vierde van een eeuw doorgeleefd in dit land. Wie had het kunnen of durven denken, dat wij elkander dezen morgen zouden begroeten?

Wij zijn onder de gespaarden en zijn nog levend hier. Velen die met ons overkwamen en zich hier nedervestigden, rusten in hunne graven, wier gedachtenis echter in zegening blijft, en waarvan velen reeds het eeuwige feest vieren. Wij kunnen allen niet opsommen. Weest tevreden met de eerste kerkeraadsleden die van ons zijn weggenomen door den dood: B. Kamps, J. van de Luyster, E. Niemeijer, J. Kruid, M. Westrate, J. Rabbers, R. M. de Bruyn, A. Borgers, allen ouderlingen; dan de diakenen, J. Hovink, A. van den Berg, J. Wabeke, J. Boes, W. van Loo, – te zamen dertien in getal. Derhalve, wij zijn uitgedund. Nog enkelen zijn hier die met ons kunnen gedenken de daden des Heeren en een traan plegen voor onze dierbare vaders en broeders, die rusten op den Gods akker, waarvan verre de meesten zeer zalig en ruim den tijd met de eeuwigheid verwisseld hebben. Ja, die den grooten strijd hebben afgestreden, en nu als gekroonden wandelen. En behalve deze waardige mannen, zijn er nog zoovele dierbaren die in het stof der aarde rusten. Wij hebben graven op deze plaats die voor ons dierbaar zijn. Hunne bewoners baden, weenden, streden en arbeidden met ons, en zijn reeds afgelost. Het is ons niet mogelijk om heden hun voorbij te gaan, die met ons deelden in al het zuur en zoet des levens. Doch wij mogen ook heden morgen onze blikken slaan op sommigen uwer, die hier kwamen als spelende jeugd; die nu mannen en vrouwen, vaders en moeders zijn geworden. En anderen die hier kwamen in de kracht van het leven, zijn oud geworden, en voor het meerendeel versleten door den harden arbeid en de zorgen des levens. Vele beproevingen zijn doorgeworsteld. In 1851 was een jaar van vele ellenden. Een mislukten oogst, door den aanhoudenden regen. Wat nog overschoot werd door het ongedierte verwoest. Daarbij kwam nog sterfte aan het rundvee.

In 1858 werden wij bezocht door zware ziekten, vooral bloedloop, waardoor velen te grave daalden, vooral van het jeugdig geslacht; zoodat in sommige huizen, twee en drie kinderen werden weggerukt. Uit een school distrikt van 123 kinderen zijn 45 gestorven; thans telt die school weder ruim 200.

En toch mogen wij elkander heden toeroepen, „Tot hiertoe heeft ons de Heere geholpen."

Dewijl wij op den dag van gisteren deelnamen aan de feestviering in het naburig Holland, en wij daar hoorden een uiteenzetting van de geheele geschiedenis onzer landverhuizing van den Eerw. Dr. van Raalte, zoo zou ik vrijheid hebben om daar volkomen in te rusten. Wij beschouwden het als een geheel voor onze nederzetting. Doch elk leeft ook plaatselijk iets bijzonders. Zoo kan ik vrijmoedigheid krijgen om ook in onze geschiedenis in te dalen. Doen wij het heden, en laat ons overwegen:

1. Wat ons bewoog tot de landverhuizing?
2. Is dat doel bereikt?

Wat ons tot de landverhuizing bewoog is gisteren krachtig ontwikkeld door Dr. van Raalte. Wij zullen dat niet over doen. Wij ook gevoelden ons zeer ongemakkelijk, door de wederrechtelijke behandeling in Nederland.

Toen wij op den grooten Oceaan waren, werd dit duidelijk bevestigd door onzen kapitein. Wij praaiden eens een schip, en er werd aan onzen kapitein gevraagd: Wat hebt gij geladen? Hij riep terug uit al zijn macht: „Valsche munt, die in Nederland niet meer gangbaar is." Ik denk hij was de tolk des harten van velen in Nederland.

Daarbij kwam een benauwde bezoeking van schaarschheid van brood. Vooral onder de mindere klas. Het gerucht deed zich hooren: aan de andere zijde van den oceaan is ruimte voor beter bestaan; allen die daarheen getrokken zijn stuurden berichten over dat wij het vrije Amerika bijna vergelijken kunnen met het beloofde Canaan. Ook werd ons medegedeeld dat godsdienst daar in eere was; de Waarheid vrij kon beleden worden, en uitgeoefend.

Er kwam een beroering onder het volk, overal sprak men over Amerika. Men las in den Bijbel, en landverhuizing was niet alleen geoorloofd, maar het was het doel, plan en bevel des Heeren: „Wees vruchtbaar en vervult de aarde." Men zag den loop der geschiedenis met Gods gemeente op aarde, hoe zij, als het ware, haren gang gehouden heeft als de zon, en dat de Heere nu aan het tijdvak ook aan het westen vervuld wat beloofd en toegezegd was. Wij werden bereid om daarheen te trekken, ons geslacht daarover te planten, waar de Heere Zijn waarheid zou doen bloeien, en het nageslacht Zijn werken roemen. Ik hoorde eens bij die gelegenheid te Arnhem, Ds. van Raalte tot mij zeggen, toen ik hem tegenstond in zijne beoordeeling over de landverhuizing: Gij zult de landverhuizing zoo min stoppen als gij den Rijn in zijnen stroom kunt keeren. Dat ondervond ik dan ook spoedig in mijn eigen hart en oordeel.

Alles werd voor- en toebereid. Op eens hoorden wij: De oude Van de Luyster gaat met zijne familie en met allen die in zijne gemeente Borselen wonen, als zij willen, naar Amerika gaan; voor de armen zal hij de onkosten voorschieten. Dat gaf een opspraak door het geheele Zeeland en verder in Nederland. Daarop volgden bewegingen en navragen, en eindelijk wij hielden in Goes vergadering, waarop uitgenoodigd werden allen die deel wilden nemen in het naar Amerika gaan. Na een en andermaal de zaak behandeld te hebben, werd besloten te organiseeren, een bestuur te benoemen, een reglement te maken, en Ds. C. van der Meulen te beroepen om als hun herder en leeraar mede te gaan, die dan ook zeer bereid was dit beroep aan te nemen, die zich gevoelde even als Jesaja: Zend mij.

Alles was in beweging, wij namen drie schepen aan, te Antwerpen twee, en een te Rotterdam, en verlieten Zeeland in April 1847. Twee derden reisden naar Antwerpen en een derde naar Rotterdam, waar ik toe behoorde. De afspraak werd gemaakt, dat die van de drie schepen eerst in Amerika aanlandde, zijn reis zou nemen naar Michigan, waar Ds. van Raalte gesettled was, welken wij reeds bericht hadden toegezonden, dat wij kwamen en dat hij voor ons volk loodsen zou opslaan, opdat wij een schuilplaats hadden als wij daar aankwamen. Die van Antwerpen vertrokken hadden het voorrecht om dadelijk af te varen. Ons gezelschap van Rotterdam had het lot een grooten oponthoud te hebben, door een wet uit Amerika, welke bepaalde hoeveel ruimte elke passagier moest hebben in het schip, waartoe wij te Hellevoetsluis belet werden af te varen en wij een tweede schip er bij kregen, of liever dit in gereedschap werd gebracht, hetwelk een oponthoud baarde van zes weken en waar wij door des Heeren hand zwaar bezocht werden. Van ons gezelschap stierven er 26 aan het roodvonk. Dit dompelde ons in eenen diepen rouw. Op den 27sten Mei 1847 voeren wij af en landden den 4den Juli te New York aan. Op zee moesten wij nog drie personen door den dood missen. Bevolgens op den landreis te Buffalo en Cleveland, brachten wij nog drie ten grave. In het laatst van Juli landden wij aan de Black Lake in Michigan waar wij onze oude vrienden ontmoetten, met vele aandoening en ontroering van ons hart en met dakbaarheid aan God voor zijn bewarende liefde.

In zooverre was ons doel bereikt. Zie nu onzen eersten toestand. Afgereisd en afgemat vielen wij in de wouden van Michigan. De oude vader Van der Luyster was eerst aangekomen en had drie secties land gekocht. Een gedeelte van Sectie 19 werd tot dorp gekozen en uitgelegd. Blokhuisjes of houten tenten opgeslagen, die door ons betrokken werden, waarvan ook ik een zou bewonen, dat ook door mij zelven en anderer hulp is opgebouwd.

Jakobus de Hond en vrouw hebben op het dorp den eersten rustdag doorgebracht. Daarop zijn wij gevolgd. Landverdeeling, kiezen, en verder opzoeken was aan de orde van den dag. Wegen maken, huizen bouwen, boomen vellen, was het zesdaagsche werk. De rustdag riep tot rust. Dan vergaderden wij in de open lucht. Onze zitplaatsen waren de omgehouwen boomstammen. De preekstoel was een boomstan, en van drie latten, waarop een plankje gelegd werd, en wel zamengevoegd, lag mijn staten Bijbel. Hadden wij dagen van zorg en vele beproevingen en kwade ontberingen. Op den dag des Heeren werden wij verkwikt en versterkt. O, wat was het ons dikwijls goed onder den blauwen hemel. Op deze wijze vierden wij de godsdienstoefeningen tot in den maand November, toen wij van wege de koude het niet meer konden uithouden. Toen nam ik het volk in mijn blokhuis, dat spoedig verwisseld werd door het grooter blokhuis van Mr. Jan Wabeke. Daarop volgde een groot blokhuis dat voor kerk moest dienen, hetwelk geplaatst werd waar nu het platte steenen gebouw van Dr. Baart staat. Toen kwam men overeen om een kerk te bouwen van beter loggen zestig bij veertig voeten; hetwelk gebeurde. Dit werd door ons betrokken met blijdschap in den Heere en wij gevoelden ons rijk en vergenoegd.

Onze blijdschap werd verhoogd. Wij kregen in en rondom ons eenige Drenthsche huisgezinnen en Noord en Zuidwest van ons dorp eenige Groningsche familieën, allen op enkele na, uit de Christelijke Afgescheidene Kerk, daar wij dadelijk op het innigst mede vereenigd waren, en wij zamen een gemeente organiseerden, en wij kunnen zeggen, als broeders samen woonden. Zoo vervlogen de jaren 1847 en 1848 en 1849 brak aan, voor ons tot veel opbouwing en versterking. Een gezelschap Zeeuwen en anderen kwamen over, waaraan wij behoefte hadden, aan de personen en gaven, zoowel als aan de hulpmiddelen, welke zij medebrachten, want het was bij ons uitgeput. Alleen waren wij voor, door ons arbeid en landontginning. En dan is dat gezelschap onder de leiding van Ds. H. G. Klijn later nog tot eenen bijzonderen zegen geweest. Zij hebben op dat schip een lading overgebracht, daar zij en wij de waarde zelf niet van geweten hebben op dat oogenblik. Geen schip heeft zoovele predikanten overgevoerd, ten minsten, die het naderhand geworden zijn en die thans de gemeenten bedienen. Ds. Adriaan Zwemer, en straks zijn oudste zoon, de twee zonen van Jan de Pree, Peter en Jakobus, dan de twee zonen van J. Moerdijk, waarvan een, Pieter, professor is in Hope College en Willem, leeraar in Zeeland; dan Ds. Jakobus Huyszoon te Paterson; en mogelijk zijn er nog wel meer. Doch genoeg, het was een rijke lading. Nu zijn wij zoo al door gesukkeld. Het is al wonderlijk geloopen. Onvergetelijke dagen die wij hier doorgeleefd hebben. En de prediking van zulk een geschiedenis roept ons luide toe in dit feest uur: God heeft voor ons gezorgd, Hij heeft ons doorgeholpen en was ons mild, vriendelijk en goed. En nu volgt:

2. Wat is het heden?

Ons antwoord is: wij zijn opgewassen in dit land; wij zijn vermenigvuldigd; ons vee is bij duizenden vermenigvuldigd; onze bosschen zijn herschapen in vruchtbare akkers. Zoo is het op elk gebied van vooruitgang. Doch het grootste, wat een schaar van jeugdigen die hier geboren zijn en opgroeien. Wat een menigte die in hunne jeugd hierkwamen zijn nu mannen van kracht, zelfs in regeering en bestuur; vooral ook in de scholen en kerken. Wat een wisseling in 25 jaren! Het is nauwelijks geloof- of denkbaar. De mannen die nu gesteld worden onder de meest gegoeden, waren in het begin ossendrijvers die op de Grand Rapids wat handel dreven, een paar reizen in de week. Nu hebben wij dit niet meer noodig, dewijl de spoortrein elken dag oost en westwaarts menschen en goederen vervoerd. In een uur naar de Grand Rapids en in weinige uren naar Chicago; en in tien minuten in Holland, waar wij onze Hooge School hebben met al hare vertakkingen, minstens zeven professoren, die in vele wetenschappelijke vakken kweken voor de maatschappij, school, en kerk. Dan al die georganiseerde school distrikten, om de jeugdigen op te voeden. Neen, ik overdrijf niet. Het is geen menschelijke roem of grootspraak. Het is dankzaak. En dat ik het met vrijmoedigheid uitspreek is, om den Heere de eere te geven. God heeft het gedaan, dies zijn wij verblijd. En wat noopt ons dit heden, tot ware name dankerkentenis aan God? Geven wij dan Hem de eer. Gevoelen wij het, dat Hij ons tot hiertoe geholpen heeft. Ons oog zij in de toekomst op Hem geslagen. De Heere zij voor ons alles. Ebenezer, steen der hulp. Er moet dankolie op. Komt dan rond den steen, giet uwe dankbare harten uit, als familiën, als volk, als gemeente.

Het is op te merken hoe de Bijbel heiligen hunne dankbaarheid hebben uitgeoefend. Noach stichtte een altaar, na den vloed, en offerde van de vruchten. Jakob goot olie op den steen die hem tot hoofdpeluw verstrekt had. En wat een muziek met trommelende maagden geleid door Mariam, die het heerlijk lied zongen nadat zij door de Roode Zee waren doorgegaan. Denkt aan het Ebenhaezer door Samuel opgericht. En van de feesten van Israël zoo dikwijls herhaald. Zij gedachten Gods daden. En zouden wij Hem vergeten? Neen, het zij ons feest van dank voor ons en ons geslacht, opdat zij nog dankoffer plengen op onze graven. En eens wordt er door ons, met voor- en nageslacht, een eeuwig feest gevierd, waar wij allen Zijne wonderlijke leidingen zullen herdenken en Hem eeuwigen lof en dank zullen toebrengen.

[Translation]

Dear friends and fellow countrymen. – Today we have lived a quarter of a century in this country. Who of us had dared to think that we would greet each other here this morning?

We are among those who have been spared, we are still among the living of this community. Many of those who came across the sea with us and settled here are now resting in their graves. Their memory remains a blessing. Many now are celebrating their eternal feast. We can only summarize this history. Let us content ourselves by naming the first members of our consistory who have been taken away by death: Berend Kamps, Jannes van de Luyster, E. Niemeijer, Jan Kruid, Marinus Westrate, Jan Rabbers, Robbertus M. de Bruyn, Albert Borgers, all elders; and the deacons Jacob Hovink, E. van den Berg, Jan Wabeke, Jan Boes, and Willem van Loo, a total of thirteen. So we have declined in numbers, yet a few are here who can recall to memory the deeds of the Lord, and drop a tear in thinking of our beloved fathers and brothers now resting in God's acre. They have exchanged the temporal for the eternal in a blessed manner, and to their advantage. Yes, such may be said of those who have fought the good fight and who now are walking as crowned of the Lord. And besides these worthy men there are till so many other beloved ones who are resting in their graves. In this place we have graves which are dear to us. These people resting in them prayed, wept, struggled, and labored with us, and now already are among the redeemed. Today we cannot pass by these people who shared with us the sweet as well as the sour of this life. But this morning we are privileged to note some of you who came here as playing childeren who now have become men and women, fathers and mothers. And others who came here in the full possession of the strength of maturity have become old. Most of them have worn out their lives in the hard struggle and in the cares of life. We have passed through many trials. The year 1851 was full of misery. The perpetual rain ruined the crops. Whatever remained was drestroyed by the rodents. Then also came mortality among the cattle.

In 1858 we were visited with severe sickness, especially dysentery which carried many of the youth to their graves. In some families as many as two or three chidlren died. Out of 123 children in one school district 45 died. Today the school of that district has fully 200 children.

And in spite of all this we may say to each other, "Hitherto hath the Lord helped us" [1 Samuel 7, 12].

Because yesterday we took part in the celebration in neighboring Holland and on that occasion heard an exposition of the entire history of our emigration from Dr. A. C. van Raalte, I would feel free to rest content with what he said. We thought of his address as of one that applied to our entire settlement. But each person also has special roots in his own locality. For that reason I take the liberty here to discuss our history. Let us do this; let us consider the following:

1. What moved us to emigrate?
2. Have we attained our purpose?

What moved us to emigrate was forcefully developed by Dr. van Raalte [see No. 59]. We shall not repeat it. We also were uncomfortable because of the unjust treatment we experienced in the Netherlands. This was clearly confirmed for us by our captain when we were out on the mighty ocean. We hailed a ship, and our captain was asked, "What are you carrying?" He replied with all his strength, "False coin no longer valid in the Netherlands." I believe he truly interpreted what was in the hearts of many in the Netherlands.

In addition to this attitude there was the sore trial of scarcity of bread, especially among the common people. Rumor was current: on the other side of the ocean there is room for a better existence. All who had gone thither reported glowingly about America so that we compared it with the promised Canaan. It also was told to us that worship was held in honor there, that the Truth could be freely confessed and exercised.

There was agitation among the people. Everywhere they spoke about America. They read the Bible, and it appeared that emigration was not only permitted, but it was the purpose, plan, and command of the Lord: "Be fruitful and multiply and replenish the earth...."[Genesis 1, 28]. We beheld the history of God's church on earth, how, as it were, it kept to its course like the sun and that the Lord in the present age fulfills in the West what He promised. We were ready to emigrate thither, to plant our people there where the Lord would cause His truth to flourish and where our descendants would praise His works. On one ocasion at Arnhem Dominie Van Raalte said to me when I raised objections to his judgment on the question of emigration, "You will not be able to stop this emigration any more than you can stop the Rhine in its course." That too, I soon realized and that also came to be my judgment.

While making every possible preparation, we heard the rumor, "Van de Luyster and his entire family is going to America. He will take with him, if they are willing, all the members of the congregation in Borslesen, and to the poor he will advance their expenses." Report of this intention spread throughout Zeeland and also in the Netherlands. There was much activity following this news and many were the questions asked. Finally we held a meeting in Goes which all who wanted to go to America were invited to attend. After repeated discussions it was decided to form an organization, elect officials, draw up a series if rules, and invite me to accompany them as pastor and teacher. I was quite ready to accept this call; I thought even as did Isaiah, "Send me" [Isaiah 6, 8].

There was much activity among the emigrants. We secured three ships, two at Antwerp and one at Rotterdam in which I was to sail. It was agreed prior to sailing that the emigrants of the first of the ships to arrive in America would at onze proceed to Michigan where Dominie van Raalte had settled, to whom we had sent notice that we were coming and asking him to have some sheds built for our people to serve as a shelter when we should arrive. Those who were to leave from Antwerp were the first to sail. Our group at Rotterdam was held back because our ship was kept in port by an American law which laid down how much space there had to be for each passenger on each ship. This prevented our leaving Hellevoetsluis. So we secured a second ship. This delayed us six weeks, which caused us sore trial at the hand of the Lord. For of our group 26 persons died from scarlet fever. This plunged us into deep sorrow. On May 27, 1847, we sailed out of the harbor and arrived at

New York on July 4. Three of our group died on the ship. During our journey to Buffalo and Cleveland three more went to their graves. At the close of July we landed at Black Lake in Michigan where we met our old friends, an occasion of much emotion and deep stirring of the heart which provoked tankfulness to God for His loving care.

So far we had attained our goal. Tired and exhausted after our journey, we moved into the forests of Michigan. Old father Van de Luyster, the first to arrive, had bought three sections of land. A part of section 19 was chosen to be the village site, and the plat was drawn up. Loghouses or wooden "tents" were erected and we moved into them. I was to occupy one of these, which I myself constructed with the help of others.

Jakobus de Hond and his wife were the first to spend a Sunday in the village. We were the next. Division of land, choosing land, and looking for land was the order of the day. Making roads, building houses, and felling trees was our weekly work. The Sabbath called us to rest. Then we gathered under the open sky. Our seats were the cut-down trunks of trees. A tree stump served for a pulpit. On it were placed three laths and a small board on which lay my States' Bible. We had our days of sorrow, many trials, and many hardships. On the Lord'sday we were quickened. Oh how great was the comfort we so often experienced there under the blue sky! In this manner we had religious services until in the month of November when it became so cold that we could no longer meet under the sky. Then I brought my people into my loghouse. Soon this was exchanged for the larger loghouse belonging to Mr. Jan Wabeke. Next we had a spacious loghouse which was to serve as a church. It was built on the spot where now stands the low stone building occupied by Dr. Baart. Then we came to the decision to erect a new church of better logs, 40 by 60 feet, which was duly carried out. We began using this building happily, in the spirit of the Lord. We thought we were rich and were well contented.

Our happiness increased. For a number of families from Drente came to live near us. To the north and southwest of our village settled a number of families from the province of Groningen, all, or practically all of them, belonging to the Christian Reformed church [that is, the *Christelijke Gereformeerde Kerk* in the Netherlands, not to be confused with the Christian Reformed Church which later [1856] came into existence in Michigan]. We were immediately bound to them in the most intimate fashion. Together we formed a congregation, and we can truthfully state that we lived together as brothers. Thus speedily passed the years 1847 and 1848. Dawned the year 1849, one that strengthened us and helped us in our upbuilding. Another group of Zeelanders and a number of other persons arrived from the Netherlands. We needed these people, their creative capacities, and also their resources, for our own means were exhausted. The only progress we had made was the clearing of land through our own labor. In addition, the group which arrived under the leadership of Dominie Hendrik Geert Klijn [or Klyn] later proved a particular blessing. They carried a cargo on their ship the value of which at that moment neither they nor we knew how to estimate. No other ship brought over so many ministers, or at least people who later became ministers and who at present are serving congregations. Among them were Dominie Adriaan Zwemer and his eldest son now soon to follow in his steps; the two sons of Jan de Pree, Pieter and Jakobus; the two sons of Jakobus Moerdijk of whom Pieter is professor in Hope College and Willem is pastor in Zeeland; Dominie Jakobus Huyszoon [or Huyssoon] now at Paterson, New Jersey; and perhaps there are a few others. But enough, that was a rich cargo! And so we have struggled through our difficulties. This has been a wonderful course. Unforgettable are the days through which we passed. And the spiritual preaching of such a history calls to us loudly in this hour of commemoration: God has looked after us, He has helped us, He has been kind, friendly, and good. And now we consider:

2. What is our present condition?

Our answer is: we have grown up in this country; we have multiplied; our cattle have increased by the thousands; our forests have been converted into fruitful acres. Thus it has gone in every aspect of our progress. But the greatest point is: what a host of young people who were born here and who are now growing up! What a number of those who came here in their youth now have become men of power, even in business and government, and especially in school and church! What a transformation in 25 years! It is hardly to be believed. Those who among our people today are regarded as the most prosperous in the beginning were drivers of oxen, men who carried on their business in Grand Rapids, making that trip a couple times a week. No longer do we need oxen to carry our products to distant market, for now the train daily transports goods and passengers eastward and westward. In one hour we are in Grand Rapids, and in a few hours in Chicago, and in ten minutes in Holland where we have our college, a school where instruction is imparted in all branches, under at least seven professors who prepare their pupils in many scientific matters, for school, for church, and for society. Further, let us note our numerous organized school districts for the upbringing of our youth. No, I am not exaggerating. This is not mere human praise or empty boast. It is a matter for which we must be thankful. I say these things in a spirit of candor, for it is to give honor to God. He has wrought all these things, for which we are happy. And what urges us to express a true and warm thankfulness to God? Let us give Him all honor. Let us feel the force of the fact that "Hitherto the Lord hath helped us" [1 Samuel 7, 12]. Let our eye ever rest on Him. May the Lord be all things unto us. Ebenezer, stone of help! On that stone let us pour the oil of our thanksgiving. Gather around that stone; pour out the thanks of your hearts, as families, as a people, and as a congregation.

It is well to note how the holy men in the Bible have expressed their thankfulness. Noah raised an altar after the flood and made an offering of the fruits of the field. Jacob poured oil upon the stone which had served him for a pillow. And what music rose from the maidens with their drums, led by Miriam as they sang the glorious song after they had passed through the Red Sea! Think of the Ebenezer stone raised up by Samuel! Think of the great feasts of Israel we so often read of! These people never forgot God's deeds. Should we forget them? No, let this be a feast of thankfulness for us and for our descendants, that they may pour out libations of thanks upon our graves. Some time for us and for our descendants there will be an eternal feast at which we all will recall His wonderful guidance and give Him everlasting praise and thanks.

18. PIETER VAN ANROOY'S
LAND AND SEA JOURNEY OF THE ZEELANDERS IN 1847

[Van Anrooy's account of the voyage of the *Kroonprins van Hanover* concerns the experiences of the Zeelanders under the leadership of Jannes van de Luyster. Van Anrooy and several of his friends and relatives settled in Fillmore Township one mile east and a quarter mile south of Graafschap. Written to be read at the Semi-Centennial celebrations in Holland in August 1897, this account under the title *Land en Zeereis der Zeeuwen* appeared in *De Grondwet*, March 21, 1911.]

In het jaar 1846 heerschte er een algemeene zucht naar Noord Amerika, en vooral in de provincie Zeeland, zoodat er gedurig vergaderingen gehouden werden in de stad Goes en er eene Commissie benoemd werd om te zien hoe daarin te handelen. Na voorloopig ingelicht te zijn, vergaderde men opnieuw, en toen waren er tegenwoordig belangstellenden uit het land van Axel en uit het land van Cadzand, doch meestal uit het land van Goes, Zuid-Beveland.

Deze vergadering werd mede gehouden te Goes en toen werd er eene vaste commissie aangesteld om verder de zaak te regelen. Deze commissie bestond uit Jannes van de Luyster, J. Verhorst, Willem Houtkamp, en Jan Steketee, en er werd besloten om drie schepen te nemen, twee van Antwerpen en een van Rotterdam.

Elk schip had een leider. Op het eerste schip was Jannes van de Luyster van Borselen; en op het tweede Jan Steketee, van Nieuwdorp. Die beide schepen zijn van Antwerpen afgevaren. Op het derde schip, *Prinses Sophia*, waren Johannes Kaboord en Ds. Cornelius van der Meulen van Goes. Deze zijn te Rotterdam scheep gegaan.

Den 6den April 1847 is het gezelschap van Goes op reis gegaan, 's morgens om 3 uren, met een schuit. De naam van de schipper was Arnold Narebout, en aan boord waren de volgende huisgezinnen: Johan Frederik van Anrooy, Johannes Hoogesteger, Willem van de Luyster, Jan den Herder, Pieter ver Lee, Pieter Daane, en de kinderen van Jannes van de Luyster. Om 1 uur waren wij te Antwerpen aangekomen. Daar werd het gezelschap eenige dagen opgehouden, want het schip dat de compagnie voor ons bestemd had, de *Plato*, was een oud schip, zoodat onze commissie het afkeurde. Toen liet de compagnie het volk wachten, zoodat de commissie kostgeld vraagde van de compagnie, wat het was over de tijd, volgens het contract. De compagnie betaalde 1½ frank de man daags, en leverde een ander schip dat goedgekeurd was door de commissie. De naam van dit schip was *Kroonprins van Hanover* en de naam van de kapitein was Mennen.

Toen al het volk aan boord was, werden er twee koks benoemd en nog drie assistent-koks; de twee koks waren R. Schilleman en Johan F. van Anrooy, die kookten en zorgden voor het eten. De drie assistenten waren Isaac Cappon, Tobias Potters, en Kommers. Het volk had hun eigen proviand. Aan boord was een fornuis met twee koperen ketels, daar het water en ander eten in gekookt werd. Wanneer de koks, met de hulp van de assistenten, het eten aan ieder huisgezin hadden uitgedeeld, dan kwam er een uit het gezelschap in het midden en bad voor al het volk. Allen aten dan gelijk, en als dat geëindigd was, kwam er een en die las een hoofdstuk voor uit den Bijbel. Vervolgens werd er een Psalmvers gezongen en gedankt. En zoo werd dit volgehouden totdat wij in New York aankwamen. Des Zondags werd er geregeld gepreekt door den student Jan van de Luyster en Cornelius van Malsen. Er waren ook 18 Duitschers aan boord.

Op de reis van Antwerpen naar Vlissingen heeft het gezelschap twee kinderen door den dood verloren. Den 4den Mei werd het anker geligt, des morgens om 4 uren, en 's avonds om half zes zagen wij voor 't laatst de vuurtoren en de lichten van Engeland. Op zekeren nacht, terwijl wij nog in het Engelsche kanaal waren, ontkwamen we ter nauwernood een groot onheil, doordat een ander schip op ons aan vaarde en wij elkander amper passeerden.

Op de zeereis hadden vier sterfgevallen plaats; het eerste was op Zondag 9 Mei een kindje van Willem van de Luyster; den 10den Mei de vrouw van Abraham Zomer; den 17den Mei het jongste kind van Pieter Daane; en den 4den Juni een kindje, wiens naam niet is aangeteekend. De begrafenisdiensten werden geleid door den student Jan van de Luyster en Cornelius van Malsen. Het lijk werd in een stuk zeildoek genaaid, met wat steenkolen aan de voeten, en door de matrozen op een plank gelegd, op de verschansing gelegd, en in de tegenwoordigheid van het volk liet men dan het lijk zachtjes van de plank afgleiden.

Een der scheepsgenooten, de Wit, had het ongeluk, door dat het schip zoo overhelde, om te vallen en zijn schouder uit het lid te krijgen. Gelukkig hadden wij een dokter aan boord, Dr. van Nus.

Den 4den Juni hadden wij land gezien en den 5den Juni 's morgens om 1 uur is de loods aan boord gekomen. Zondag 6 Juni 'smorgens om 4 uur werd het anker uitgeworpen in de Hudson rivier en 's avonds om 10 uur zijn wij te New York aangekomen. Eer wij te New York aan wal mochten stappen, kwamen er dokters aan boord en vraagden aan de kapitein of er zieken aan boord waren. De kapitein antwoordde: „Hoe zouden er zieken aan boord kunnen zijn, dit volk doet niets dan bidden en psalm zingen."

Te New York ontmoetten de commissie en het volk Ds. Hendrik P. Scholte, die zeide, dat zij bij Ds. Albertus C. van Raalte, in Michigan, in de bosschen, niet konden leven wegens het klimaat, dat er niets te krijgen was om van te leven, en dat het beter was dat ze allen naar Iowa gingen om dat daar beter land was.

Het volk verliet New York den 7den Juni, per stoomboot, naar Albany, en zijn daar den volgenden dag aangekomen. Aldaar is de commissie naar Dr. Wykoff gegaan, om de zaak te onderzoeken met betrekking tot Michigan. Dr. Wykoff gaf de commissie een brief mede naar Mr. van der Poel te Buffalo. Deze commissie bestaande uit Mr. Steendijk en Cornelius van Malsen gingen met den trein naar Buffalo om de zaak te onderzoeken en in orde te krijgen. Te Albany is er nog een kind overleden en daar begraven. Den 11den Juni werd de weduwe Van Laare door een zware ziekte aangetast, waaraan zij den 12den Juni overleed. De kanaalboot waarmede men naar Buffalo zou gaan was blijven liggen, ten einde de vrouw ten grave te kunnen brengen. Allen waren tegenwoordig bij de begrafenis. Den 18den Juni zijn wij te Buffalo aangekomen. Aldaar ontmoette het volk de commissie, Mr. Steendijk en Cornelius van Malsen, alsmede Mr. van der Poel, en toen was de zaak weer in orde, en het volk was blijde, want men wilde naar Michigan.

Den 19den Juni is het gezelschap met een stoomboot van Buffalo naar Michigan gegaan, en zijn den 26sten Juni aan den mond van Black Lake aangekomen. De stoomboot bleef voor anker liggen, en toen moesten de goederen en het volk met kleine booten aan wal gebracht werden, en toen kwamen de Indianen met hunne canoe's bij de boot; zij zagen er nog al vriendelijk uit. Toen Dr. van Nus, die in Nederland onder dienst geweest was, de Indianen zag, ging hij dadelijk naar zijn kist en haalde daar een degen uit, en begon langs de kust te marcheeren, zoodat de Indianen hem zien zouden.

Het volk moest dien nacht, tusschen de kisten, in de open lucht, hun verblijf houden. Zondagmorgen 27 Juni is het volk met de platboot naar de stad Holland gevaren. Het was middag toen wij in Holland aankwamen. Toen het volk aan wal stapte keken zij verbaast op, omdat het nog al bosch was, en zeiden: Is dat nu stad Holland? De Zeeuwen hadden drie planken loodsen laten bouwen. Een dezer stond in River en de andere twee in Achtste straat. Ds. Maarten Ypma, met zijn gezelschap Friesen, had 's daags te voren een dezer loodsen betrokken, maar ze moesten er wel uit. Het volk echter haalden wat planken bijeen en bouwden hier een soort afdak van, zoodat de dominie toch weer onder dak kwam. Ds. Ypma preekte dienzelfden namiddag voor het volk, in de open lucht, en na de preek waren allen in de weer om hunne goederen onder dak te krijgen. Tegen den avond nam elk zijn bed en legde dit op den vloer, en als het morgen was, werden die bedden weer opgenomen, ten einde des daags weer ruimte te hebben.

Naardien de emigratie in 1847 al zoo groot was dat er geen huisvesting genoeg was in de loodsen zoo nam men hemlock takken en zette die schuins tegen elkander en dan een laken er om toe; maar als het regende werd alles anat. Het gevolg was veel koortsen en ziekte en sterfte. Het gezelschap van Jannes van de Luyster hadden de pokken medegebracht in de Kolonie. De man die aangetast was, was Cornelius de Nijs. De pokken breidden zich in erge mate uit, zoodat er vele menschen aan bezweken en grafwaarts werden gebracht.

De vrouwen moesten nu eten kooken en brood bakken, en daar er geen kookkachels waren namen de mannen een paar takken met een dwarsstokje er aan, en die werden in den grond gezet, en dan werd er een dwarshout ingelegd, en daar konden de vrouwen hun potten aan hangen met een ketting, die zij nog van Nederland hadden mede gebracht. Zij hadden ook nog eenij zeren pan met een deksel, daar konden zij hun brood in bakken. Die pan werd in de heete asch gezet, en dan wat heete asch en vuur op het deksel gelegd, en zoo kreeg de vrouw brood.

Toen wij enkele dagen in de stad waren, kwam er een platboot aan met aardappelen, tarwemeel, korenmeel, boonen, en andere eetwaren. Het volk was dan ook spoedig bij de boot en in een oogenblik was dezelve ledig. Het eten in den beginne was maar schraal. Vleesch of spek was er in 't geheel niet te krijgen. Witte boonen en boonensoep was een hoofd-artikel, ook korenmeel in de pan gebakken, zonder vet. Doch de Heere gaf het volk kracht, moed en lust. Sommigen hadden nog enkele vet-kaarsen mede gebracht uit Nederland, daar zij de pot of pan mede smeerden. Anderen hadden niets zoodat zij de pot of pan met water nat maakten. Doch het volk was tevreden met het geen zij hadden en waren vol moed, zoodat bidden en danken en Psalmzingen door de bosschen heen klonk. De oude heer Jannes van de Luyster, met behulp van Ds. van Raalte, zocht spoedig een streek uit voor de Zeeuwen, en men koos de section waar nu de stad Zeeland is, met de omliggende bosschen. Daar er toen geen wegen waren van Holland naar Zeeland hebben Van de Luyster en de Zeeuwen een blokhuisje gebouwd aan de Black River, een kwart mijl oost van Scholten's brug. Dit noemde men *het Waterhuisje*, en 't was het hoofdkwartier van de Zeeuwen en daar overnachten zij. Wanneer men 's morgens gebeden en gegeten en gedankt en een Psalm gezongen hadden, dan ging Van de Luyster met het volk met de bijl op den schouder den bosschen in om wegen uit te hakken naar de plaats die hij uitgekozen had. De goederen werden van Holland met een platboot naar *het Waterhuisje* gebracht. De bemanning der platboot waren Jan van de Luyster, kapitein, Pieter van Dieke, Cornelius van Laren, en Pieter van Anrooy.

Op zekeren morgen toen wij op de rivier waren zagen wij in de verte twee dieren in het water. Zoo als het toescheen waren zij aan het vechten. Toen wij er nader bij kwamen zagen wij dat een Indianen hond een hert beet had. Wij namen onze lange stokken en sloegen het hert dood, sleepten het in de boot en sneden het den hals af. De hond liep weg, huilende en blaffende door de bosschen. Bij onze terugkomst te Holland was het volk blijde met de vangst. Toen werd het hert afgehakt en uitge-deeld zoo goed als wij konden en dat was het eerste vleesch dat daar gegeten is. Den volgenden dag toen wij weer voorbij diezelfde plaats voeren met de platboot, waren wij wel wat bevreesd voor de Indianen,

omdat wij hun hond het hert hadden afgenomen en toen zeide de kapitein:
„Jongens, kijk goed uit of ge geen Indianen ziet." En zoo hebben wij
verscheiden dag op de rivier gevaren. Spoedig werden er wegen uitgehakt en kwam er langzamerhand verandering.

Pieter ver Lee en mijn vader, Johan Frederik van Anrooy, waren meer
genegen om zich zuid van de stad Holland te vestigen, en Ver Lee kocht
120 akkers aan den weg naar Graafschap van Hendrik de Jonge, die daarop naar Illinois is gegaan. Toen moesten zij alle morgens naar de plaats
toe om een blokhuis te bouwen en 's avonds weer terug naar de stad. Zij
hadden een Indianen pad gevonden door de bosschen en dat was hun
weg naar hun land. Op een keer toen zij weer naar de stad moesten,
dachten zij dat ze konden wel wat nader loopen als dat Indianen pad,
want het slingerde zoo veel heen en weer. Zoo gedacht en zoo gedaan;
maar jawel, zij kwamen in een moeras terecht. Het werd donker en zij
wisten niet meer waarheen of hoe zij gaan moesten. Zij begonnen te
roepen, maar er kwam geen antwoord, en zetten de reis voort door het
moeras, over boomen en takken, en kwamen ten laatste, laat in den nacht,
oost van de stad te lande bij iemand die daar pas gevestigd was. Den
volgenden dag namen zij weer het Indianen pad.

Toen het blokhuis zoowat klaar was, en toen er een weg gemaakt was,
zoodat de ossenwagen er door kon, zijn zij daar gaan wonen. Ver Lee
had twee koeien gekocht; die moesten 's daags in de bosschen den kost
zoeken; een van de koeien had een bel aan. Tegen den avond, als zij de
bel niet hooren konden, gingen Ver Lee en Van Anrooy het bosch in, of
zij de bel ook hooren konden. Eens moesten zij op de koeien uit want zij
waren des avonds te voren niet te huis gekomen. Zij hadden eenigen tijd
in het bosch rondgeloopen, en toen kwamen zij bij een kliering en zagen
een blokhuis. Ver Lee zeide tegen Van Anrooy: „Johannes, wel schepsel
nog toe, hier woont ook volk, want ik hoorde ze praten; toe, gaat eens
vragen wie hier woont." Van Anrooy zeide tegen Ver Lee: „Gaat gij
maar." Ver Lee ging en toen hij wat nader bij kwam zag hij dat hij bij
zijn eigen huis was.

[Translation]

During the year 1846 there was a general desire to emigrate to America.
This craving was especially marked in the province of Zeeland; hence the
frequent meetings held in the city of Goes. A committee was named to
determine how to proceed. After having gathered preliminary information, a new meeting was called. Present were people interested
from the Land of Axel and from the Land of Cadzand; but most of

those who attended were from the Land of Goes in Zuid-Beveland.

At this meeting held at Goes a definitive committee was appointed to make further plans. Members were Jannes van de Luyster, J. Verhorst, Willem Houtkamp, and Jan Steketee. It was decided to secure three ships, two from Antwerp and one from Rotterdam.

Each ship had a leader. Jannes van de Luyster from Borsselen was the leader of the first. Jan Steketee from Nieuwdorp headed the second ship. Both of these ships sailed from Antwerp. Leaders on the third ship, the *Princess Sophia* were Johannes Kaboord and Dominie Cornelius van der Meulen. These people boarded ship in Rotterdam.

Our group left Goes on April 6, 1847, in a canal boat at 3 o'clock in the morning. The skipper's name was Arnold Narebout. The following families were on board: Johan Frederik van Anrooy, Johannes Hoogesteger, Willem van de Luyster, Jan den Herder, Pieter ver Lee, Pieter Daane, and, in addition, the children of Jannes van de Luyster. We arrived at Antwerp at one o'clock. There our group was obliged to wait a few days because the ship which the company had provided, the *Plato* was found to be so old that our committee rejected it. The company then made our people wait, so our committee asked the company for money to pay expenses inasmuch as our delay extended beyond the term set in the contract. The company paid 1.50 franks each day per man and provided another ship which was approved by the committee. The name of this ship was the *Kroonprins van Hanover*, that of the captain was Mennen.

When all our people had gone aboard we named two cooks and three assistant cooks. The two cooks were R. Schilleman and Johan F. van Anrooy who did the cooking and had charge of the food. The three assistants were Isaac Cappon, Tobias Potters, and a man named Kommers. Our people furnished their own provisions. On board was a large stove with two copper kettles in which our water and food were to be cooked. After the cooks aided by the assistants apportioned the food to each family, one of our passengers would stand in the middle of the group and say grace. They all ate together and when finished someone would read a chapter from the Bible. Then followed a verse from one of the Psalms, which was followed with the offering of thanks. This became the routine until we reached New York. On Sundays we always had sermons given by the students [for the ministry], Jan van de Luyster and Cornelius van Malsen. There also were 18 Germans on board our ship.

On the voyage from Antwerp to Flushing [Vlissingen] two children belonging to our group died. The anchor was weighed on May 4, at 4 o'clock in the morning, and at 5.30 in the evening we had our last glimpse of the lighthouse and the lights of England. One night while we were still in the English Channel we barely escaped a great disaster when another ship bore upon us and we scarcely were able to pass each other.

There were four deaths on our voyage. The first was a child of Willem van de Luyster on Sunday May 9; next, the wife of Abraham Zomer, on May 10; next the youngest child of Pieter Daane, on May 17; and the last, on June 4, a small child whose name is not recorded. Funeral services were conducted by the students, Jan van de Luyster and Cornelius van Malsen. The remains in each case were wrapped in sail cloth, placed on a board, and laid upon the ship's railing by the sailors. Then in the presence of the passengers the remains were gently dropped into the water.

One of our fellow passengers, a person named De Wit had the misfortune, when the ship lurched, to fall and dislocate his shoulder. Luckily we had a doctor on board, Dr. van Nus [J. J. M. C. van Nuys].

We saw land for the first time on June 4 and on the 5th at one o'clock in the morning the pilot came on board. Anchor was cast in the Hudson River on Sunday, June 6, at 4 o'clock in the morning. At 10 o'clock in the evening we arrived in New York. Before we were permitted to step ashore, doctors came aboard and enquired of the captain whether any sick passengers were on the ship. The captain replied, "How could there be sick people on board this ship; these people do nothing but pray and sing psalms."

At New York the people and their committee met Dominie Hendrik P. Scholte who told them that they would not be able to live with Dominie Albertus C. van Raalte in the woods of Michigan on account of the climate, that there was no food to be had there, and that it would be better that all should go to Iowa because land was of better quality in that state.

Our group left New York on June 7, by steamboat, for Albany, and arrived there on the next day. There the committee called on Dr. Issac N. Wyckoff in order to investigate the question of going to Michigan. Dr. Wyckoff gave the committee a letter for Mr. van der Poel in Buffalo. This committee, composed of Mr. Steenwijk and Cornelius van Malsen, proceeded by train to Buffalo in order to investigate and arrive at a decision. At Albany another child died and was buried there. On June 11 the widow Van Laare became seriously ill and died on the 12th. The canalboat in which we were to travel to Buffalo was halted out of respect for the funeral. All were present at the services. On June 18 we arrived at Buffalo. There we met the members of the committee and also Mr.

van der Poel. The question had been settled; we were pleased, for we wanted to go to Michigan.

On June 19 the group left Buffalo by steamboot for Michigan and on June 26 arrived at the mouth of Black Lake. It lay at anchor while our baggage had to be brought to shore in small boats. Then the Indians came in their canoes. They appeared to be quite friendly. When Dr. van Nus [J. J. M. C. van Nuys], who had seen military service in the Netherlands, saw the Indians he rushed to his trunk and took out of it a sword. He marched up and down the shore brandishing it so that the Indians could well see him.

That night our people had to sleep among their boxes under the open sky. On Sunday morning, June 27, we proceeded to Holland by flatboat. It was midday when we arrived. When we stepped ashore, we looked about in astonishment because everywhere we saw nothing but woods, and we asked, "Is this, then, the city ['stad'] of Holland?" The Zeelanders had ordered the building of three board sheds. One of these stood on River Street, the other two on Eighth Street. Dominie Maarten A. Ypma and his party had arrived the previous day, and they had occupied one of these sheds, but they had to make room for us. But the people assembled some boards and constructed a kind of lean-to, and so the dominie and his folloswers had a roof to protect them. That same afternoon Dominie Ypma preached a sermon for us in the open air. After the sermon we all went busily to our task of bringing our baggage into the sheds. When evening came each one of us laid out his bed on the floor, and when morning came the beds were taken up so that during the day we might have room in the sheds.

Because the immigration of 1847 was quite large so that it was impossible for all to find lodging in the sheds, the newcomers [erected shelters by] setting hemlock branches against each other and covering them with bed sheets. But when it rained everything became wet and as a result there was much fever, sickness, and even death. Jannes van de Luyster's following brought the pox into the Kolonie. One person infected was Cornelius de Nijs. The pox spread so much that many persons succumbed and were carried to their graves.

Food had to be prepared and bread baked, but as the women had no cook stoves the men stuck sticks cut from branches into the ground and fastened crosspieces to them on which the women could hang their pots. The chains they used for this purpose had been brought from the Netherlands. They also had an iron pan with a cover in which they baked their bread. The pan was covered with hot ashes and fire, and thus the women baked their bread.

After we had been in the "*stad*" several days, a flatboat arrived loaded
with potatoes, flour, cornmeal, beans, and other things to eat. At once
the people were at the boat and in a moment everything was sold. In the
beginning food was meager. Beef and pork were not to be had. Navy
beans and soup made from them, also cornmeal baked in a pan and without
grease, were the chief articles of diet. But the Lord made us happy, gave
us strength and courage. Some of us had brought candles from the
Netherlands; with them we greased our pots and pans. Some had nothing
whatever and moistened their pots and pans with water. But we were
content with the little we had andre were full of courage. And hence the
woods echoed with the sound of prayer and thanksgiving, and with the
singing of Psalms.

The elderly Jannes van de Luyster, with the help of Dominie van Raalte
soon chose an area for the Zeelanders to settle. The spot they chose is the
present "stad" of Zeeland, with its adjoining woods. As there were no
roads between Holland and Zeeland, Van de Luyster and the Zeelanders
built a small loghouse on Black River, a quarter of a mile east of Scholten's
Bridge. This loghouse was known as *het Waterhuisje*. This was head-
quarters for the Zeelanders, a place where they could pass the night. In
the morning, after prayer, breakfast, thanks, and the singing of a Psalm,
Van de Luyster and his people went into the woods with axe on shoulder
to cut out trails to places they had chosen for their homes. Supplies were
brought by flatboat from Holland to *het Waterhuisje*. The men who
managed the flatboat were Jan van de Luyster, captain, Pieter van Dieke,
Cornelius van Laren, and Pieter van Anrooy.

One morning when we were on the river we noted in the distance two
animals struggling in the water, apparently fighting. Drawing near, we
saw that a dog belonging to the Indians had seized a deer. We killed the
deer with long sticks, dragged it into the boat, and cut its throat. The
dog ran away, barking and yelping through the forest. When we got
back to Holland our people were glad because of this catch. The deer
was cut up and the meat was parceled out as well as was possible. That
was the first meat we had to eat since our arrival. The following day,
when we passed by this place in our flatboat, we were afraid of the
Indians because we had taken the deer away from their dog, and our
captain said, "Boys, keep a sharp lookout for Indians", and so we made
many a trip on the river. Before long roads were cut through the woods,
and all aspects of our life changed gradually.

Pieter ver Lee and my father, Johan Frederik van Anrooy, were inclined
to settle on land south of Holland. Ver Lee bought 120 acres situated

along the road to Graafschap from Hendrik de Jonge who thereupon moved to Illinois. Each morning they had to walk to their property in order to build a loghouse. In the evening they returned to the *"stad"*. They had found an Indian trail through the woods which served as a path to their land. One time when they were returning to the *"stad"* they thought they could find a way shorter than the Indian trail which zigzaged back and forth. But they soon landed in a swamp. Night came and they lost all sense of direction. They called, but there was no answer. Continuing, they walked through the swamp over fallen trees and branches and finally, late in the night and east of the *"stad"*, they arrived at the house of someone who had recently settled there. Next day they kept to the Indian trail.

When the loghouse was nearly ready and a road had been cut out sufficiently wide to permit oxen to pass along it, they went to live on their land. Ver Lee purchased two cows. Each day they had to forage in the woods. One of the cows had a bell attached to its neck. Toward evening, if we could not hear this bell, Ver Lee and Van Anrooy went into the woods listening for it. One day they had to search the woods, for the cows had not returned the night before. The two men walked around in the woods for some time and came upon a clearing and saw in it a loghouse. Ver Lee exclaimed to Van Arnooy, "Johannes, I declare! there are some people living here, for I heard them talking. Go and ask them who is living here." To which Van Anrooy replied, "Why don't you go?" Ver Lee went to the loghouse and when he came near it he saw it was his own house.

19. JACOB DEN HERDER'S
SKETCH OF ZEELAND'S' HISTORY

[This sketch entitled *Historische Mededeelingen aangaande het dorp Zeeland en Omgeving* was read at the Semi-Centennial celebrations in 1897 and published in *De Grondwet*, April 29, 1913. It gives much information about Zeeland and the surrounding community. The author, born in 1834, settled in Zeeland, became schoolteacher, owned a bank, held political offices, and died in 1916.]

Elk land en volk heeft, op grootere of kleinere schaal, deszelfs bijzondere en eigenaardige geschiedenis, terwijl ook iedere plaats, dorp, of gemeente, ja zelfs elk persoon zulks in meer beperkt bestek heeft.

En, waar eene tijdsruimte van een halve eeuw over dezelve vervlogen is, wordt het voor ons eene dure roeping om eens bedaard stil te staan en een blik terug te werpen op dat afgelegde pad, ten einde men voor zich en voor het nageslacht de sporen der goede en trouwe voorzienigheid Gods moge herdenken en naspeuren, om dezelve der vergetelheid te ontrukken.

Het is dan met dat doel, en met het oog daarop, dat wij eene korte schets wenschen te leveren van „Zeeland en deszelfs Stichters." En dewijl Zeeland niet alleen de naam is van het dorp, maar ook van het township, waarin dorp Zeeland grootendeels gelegen is, zoo gevoelen wij ons verplicht, eerst eene korte beschouwing te geven van het township en daarna van het dorp en hare gemeenten.

Tot in de maand Augustus 1847 was dit township, dat later Zeeland genoemd werd, ook de plek waar wij thans vergaderd zijn, zoowel als de aangrenzende townships, eene woeste wildernis, dicht begroeid met velerlei soorten van hard en zacht geboomte van verschillende dikte, sommigen tot zelfs zes voet in doorsnede, die meest allen tot eene lengte of hoogte van boven de honderd voeten opgroeiden, en zoo dicht bij elkaar stonden dat men nauwelijks de axe of bijl zwaaien kon om een begin te maken met ze af hakken. Die wouden waren van eeuwen herwaarts de schuilplaats geweest van beeren en wolven, vossen en ander klein wildgedierte, benevens de vreedzame doch zeer vlugge en schuwe herten; ook waren er nog enkele van de oorspronkelijke boschbewoners, de Indianen, van den Ottawa stam, of tribe, die hun levensonderhoud vonden met jagen en visschen, doch die niemand onzer eenig leed aandeden. Hun voornaam tehuis in onze nederzetting was een dorpje, toen de Indianenstad geheeten, gelegen aan de zuidkust van Black Lake, van waar zij oost en noordwaarts een Indianen voetpad of *trail* door het dichte woud uitgespeurd hadden naar Grand Rapids, waarvan dan ook door onze eerste pioniers niet zelden gebruik gemaakt werd, want rijwegen ontbraken; op die *trails* ontmoette men dan somtijds met een beangst hart, van die oorspronkelijke boschbewoners, die tot de jacht gewapend waren met geweer, bijl, *tomahawk*, mes [*bowie knife*], enz., en waar wij dan ook beleefdelijk voor hen ter zijde traden, zoodat een ieder zijn weg ongestoord mocht voortzetten.

Wat de ligging en grondslag van town Zeeland betrof: hare oppervlakte was van de noordoost tot de zuidwest hoek doorsneden door een moeras of swamp, omzoomd aan beide zijden met heuvelen, en begroeid met elmen-boschjes en ander zacht geboomte. Deze moeras was gemiddeld omtrent 160 roeden in breedte, en was voor den meesten tijd des jaars bijna ondoordringbaar, en de schuilplaats van velerlei afschuwelijke slangen, enz. Ook was section 19, waarin het dorp Zeeland thans gelegen is, aan de zuidzijde doorkruist door een bijna ondoordringbaar moeras, die om het hout waarmede zij begroeid was, *cedar swamp* geheeten werd, welke lage landen, schijnbaar zoo geheel waardeloos, toch allen langzamerhand, door den noesten vlijt en ijver der nederzetters, in de meest vruchtbare velden herschapen werden.

Het overige gedeelte van het township, hoewel doorsenden met enkele heuvelen, is van een vruchtbaren grondlsag, doch vereischte helden moed en reuzenkrachten, zoowel als volharding om tot vruchtbare velden herschapen te worden. Ja, weelderig groeide het geboomte doch droeg geenerlei eetbare vruchten, zoodat noch het geboomte boven ons, noch de grond onder ons, eenige hulp of uitkomst verschafte; ook had het hout geene waarde voor ons in die eerste jaren.

De eerste stappen ter bewoning dezer woeste streken werden door den staat genomen, in het jaar 1832; door uitmeting in townships en sections; elk township bevatte 36 sections land, op rijen van zes naast elkaar, en elke section bevatte 640 acres land. Na die staats uitmeting tot townships en sections, moesten van lieverlede ook de sections tot kleinere afdeelingen uitgemeten worden.

Als landmeters in deze omgeving diende Bernardus Grootenhuis van het naburig Holland als ook Cornelius Voorhorst van het naburig Overisel; ook is schrijver dezes als jongen daaraan behulpzaam geweest in kettingslepen.

Wegens de geringe bevolking werden eerst eenige uitgemeten townships gecombineerd tot een township, om onder beheer te zijn van township-ambtenaar, als voorgeschreven door de staatswet; zoo was het dat dit township van 36 sections, dat later tot town Zeeland georganiseerd werd, bij de aankomst der Hollanders in deze streken in 1847 nog een deel van Georgetown uitmaakte, daarna in 1848 van town Ottawa, in 1849 van town Allendale, en is gedurende het jaar 1850 tot 10 Juni 1851, gecombineerd geweest met town Holland, tot het in dat jaar daarvan afgezet en tot een afzonderlijk township door de Board of Supervisors georganiseerd werd.

De eerste speciale town-meeting werd gehouden in de blokkenkerk te Zeeland, op 14 Juli 1851; dewijl bij dien tijd een genoegzaam getal der bejaarde manspersonen de vereischte stappen om Amerikaansch burger te worden genomen hadden, werden bij die gelegenheid de volgende ambtenaren gekozen: tot supervisor, Elias G. Young; tot town clerk en treasurer, Robbertus M. de Bruyn; tot school inspector, Dominee Cornelius van der Meulen; tot highway commissioner, Willem Regenmorter; tot justices of the peace, Johannes G. van Hees, Elias G. Young, en Johannes Nieuwendorp; tot directors of the poor, Jan de Pree en

Hessel O. Yntema; tot constables, Willem Kremer, Hendrik de Kruif en George H. Baert. Bij deze verkiezing werden er 141 stemmen uitgebracht.

Sedert dien tijd zijn de twee eerstgenoemde ambten tot op heden bekleed geworden door de volgende personen: als supervisor heeft Elias G. Young, 1½ jaar gediend; Johannes G. van Hees, 21 jaren; Robbertus M. de Bruyn, 2 jaren; Jacob den Herder, 3½ jaren; Cornelius van Loo, 11 jaren; Christian den Herder, 6 jaren; en Willem D. van Loo, thans in functie, 13½ jaar. Als township clerk, heeft Robbertus M. de Bruyn, 5 jaren gediend; Jacob den Herder, 20 jaren; John Boer, Albert Bolks, Gerrit Bolks, en Albert Lahuis – ieder een jaar; Henry Bosch, 7 jaren, en Jakob van den Bosch, thans in functie, 10 jaren.

Dit township [Zeeland] maakte van af den tijd van deszelfs organisatie, als nu, een deel uit van Ottawa County.

Onder de county ambtenaren die in den loop dezer 50 jaren gefungeerd hebben, vinden wij van Zeeland's burgers de namen van Pieter van den Berg, die gedurende de jaren 1863 en 1864 het ambt van county clerk en register of deeds bekleedde, en van Jacob den Herder, die in 1868 en 1869 als een van de drie county poormasters diende; Cornelius van Loo van af 1869 voor zes jaren register of deeds, en de thans fungerende register of deeds, Peter Brusse.

Ook diende genoemde Cornelius van Loo als county superintendent of schools en was voor eenige jaren voorzitter van de Board of supervisors van Ottawa County. Ook was hij van af 1881 gedurende vier jaren vertegenwoordiger van het 1ste district van Ottawa County, in de Wetgevende Kameren van dezen staat.

Ook heeft Jakob den Herder in 1876 het ambt bekleedt van Presidentiale Elector, of lid van de elf kiescollegeleden voor dezen Staat, in den heet bevochten politieken kampstrijd tusschen Rutherford B. Hayes en Samuel J. Tilden en zijne stem uitgebracht voor den Republikeinschen candidaat, Hayes, die daarop ook door het kiescollege der geheele Vereenigde Staten, welke uit 369 stemmen bestond, met slechts eene stem meerderheid, verklaard werd verkozen te zijn tot het ambt van president der Vereenigde Staten. Verder heeft hij nog gedurende de jaren 1889 en 1890 het ambt bekleedt van Staats Senateur. Genoeg hiervan.

De geschatte waarde van township Zeeland, na deszelfs afzetting van Holland, verschijnt eerst in 1852 en was toen; Vaste of onroerende goederen, $ 35,580; roerende, $ 4,309; terwijl vijftig jaren geleden de geschatte waarde van geheel Ottawa County, met inbegrip van Muskegon township, slechts de totale som van $ 295,661.36 bedroeg.

Doch van af den tijd dat de eerste nederzetters, in 1847, de wouden van township Zeeland indrongen, werd deels door de natuurlijke ligging des lands en deels wegens afkomst der nederzetters uit de verschillende provincies van Nederland, het township plaatselijk en gemeentelijk, eerst onder drie benamingen verdeeld, namelijk; Zeeland, Vriesland, en Drenthe. De twee laatstgenoemden waren samen tijdelijk onder het herderlijk opzicht van Ds. Maarten Ypma, tot dat Ds. Roelof Smit in 1851 te Drenthe aanlandde, toen Dominee Ypma de gemeente Vriesland alleen ging bedienen.

Doch dewijl mijn bestek meer tot Zeeland zich beperkt, zal ik mij ook tot die plaats en gemeente meer bijzonder beperken.

Zooals gezegd is, werden de plaatsen of gemeenten genoemd naar de namen der provincies in Nederland. Daardoor was het dat, dewijl velen der allereerste nederzetters west van de Zeeland *swamp* uit de provincie Zeeland, Nederland, kwamen, ook de gemeente van meet af en later ook het dorp en township, den naam van Zeeland verkreeg, te meer ook nog doordien zij [de Zeeuwen] als georganiseerde gemeente uit Nederland overkwamen, welke in het begin van 1847 gevormd werd in de stad Goes, Provincie Zeeland, Nederland, op welke vergadering tot ouderlingen gekozen werden, Jannes van de Luyster en Johannes Hoogesteger en tot diakenen Jan Steketee en Adriaan Glerum en op welke vergadering ook tot herder en leeraar beroepen werd Ds. Cornelius van der Meulen, die ook bereidwillig die roeping aannam.

Deze organisatie en roeping geschiedde met het oog op het spoedig vertrek uit Nederland naar Noord Amerika, niet wetende waar men zich in dit groote land vestigen zou, maar met het vaste voornemen, om waar des Heeren hand hen ook leidde, toch zooveel doenlijk bij elkaar te blijven en het gemeentelijke leven voort te zetten.

In de maand April van het jaar 1847 dan, verlieten wij, namelijk de Zeeuwsche afdeeling, het land onzer geboorte, het oude, dierbare Vaderland. Wij kwamen met drie zeilschepen over den grooten oceaan, in drie afdeelingen; een afdeeling onder opzicht van Ds. van der Meulen en Jan Kaboort, dat van Rotterdam scheep ging; het tweede onder Jannes van de Luyster en het derde [ons ingesloten] onder Jan Steketee, welke beide laatsten zich van Antwerpen inscheepten.

Na eene zeereis van 30 tot ruim 60 dagen, en een zeer vermoeiende landreis van New York herwaarts van omtrent vier weken, en na nog drie à vier weken toevens in het naburige Holland, terwijl de hoofden der huisgezinnen de dichte bosschen indrongen om geschikte landen ter vestiging uit te speuren, kwamen velen in de maand Augustus en September in deze nabijheid, of plaats, zich voor goed vestigen, en zetten het gemeentelijk leven in 's Heeren naam voort, onder den naam van gemeente Zeeland.

De eerste godsdienstoefening te Zeeland, werd gehouden den derden Zondag in Augustus in het half voltooide blokhuis van Jan Steketee, door een preek uit een der oude schrijvers voor te lezen.

Slechts zeer weinigen konden dezelve bijwonen, want wij waren nog maar een klein getal, en de geopende wegen waren er ook nog niet, men moest maar, zoo goed men konde, de bosschen doorkruisen. Dat was dan, hoe donker en woest ook de omgeving, ons nieuw tehuis voor de toekomst.

Spoedig besloeg deze gemeente eene oppervlakte van alles wat in town Zeeland, west en noord van de Zeeland *swamp* gelegen was, en van een groot gedeelte van town Holland gelegen ten oosten van Black River. Wel poogde men ook een paar mijlen ten westen van Zeeland eene gemeente te stichten onder den naam van Groningen, doch dat leidde al spoedig schipbreuk. Later, in 1873, is echter wegens de groote distantie en toeneming der bevolking, in het noordoostelijk gedeelte der gemeente nog eene nieuwe gemeente gevormd onder den naam van Beaverdam.

Zooals gezegd is, waren de overgekomene leiders der eerste gemeente, Ds. Cornelius van der Meulen, Jannes van de Luyster, Johannes Hoogsteger, Jan Steketee, en Adriaan Glerum, doch dewijl er van verschillende gemeenten uit Nederland, toen, en ook spoedig daarna zich ettelijke personen vestigden die ook in gemeentelijke bediening als ouderlingen in Nederland gediend hadden, zoo aanvaarden dezulken van stonden aan bij hunne aankomst hier, ook dat ambt onder het aangenomen begrip: „eens ouderling, blijft ouderling", waardoor dat ledental zoodanig toenam, dat het getal ouderlingen tot ruim 20 klom, en men tot de overtuiging kwam, dat er een andere weg moest worden ingeslagen, dat dan ook op vreedzame wijze geschiedde doordien zij allen schriftelijk hun ambt neerlegden, waarna op eene gemeentevergadering, gehouden op 12 Juli 1849, onder leiding van onzen leeraar, Ds. van der Meulen, zes ouderlingen en vier diakenen uit de gemeente en door de gemeente werden gekozen. Tot ouderlingen: Jannes van de Luyster, Johannes G. van Hees, Q. Huyser, H. Krans, Johannes Hoogesteger, en Albert Borgers. En, tot diakenen: Jan Steketee, A. Glerum, J. van der Werp, en J. Hovink.

Gaarne zouden wij terug gaan om te wijzen op de oorzaak dezer emigratie beweging en op de voornaamste leiders, doch dewijl mijn schets zooveel mogelijk tot Zeeland zich moet beperken, moet ik mij ook in dezen beperken tot de prominente leiders van die plaats.

Vooraan onder de leiders van de eerste settlers van Zeeland, stond dien trouwen Ds. Cornelius van der Meulen, als een vader voor zijn gemeente, als een vader ook voor velen die hij door zijne trouwe dienst onder die moeilijke worstelingen door het Evangelie gevoed heeft. Doch dewijl de levensschets van dien bekwamen dienstknecht Gods aan iemand anders is opgedragen, stap ik hiervan af en wijs op een andere pilaar van den tempel onzer gemeente en nederzetting, namelijk, op de reeds genoemde eerwaardige vader, Jannes van de Luyster, die van af den tijd van zijn uitgaan, of afscheiding van de staatskerk in Nederland, in 1834, tot aan den dag zijns doods te Zeeland, in Amerika, gedurende een tijdperk van 44 jaren, onafgebroken als ouderling de gemeente Gods te Borselen, Nederland, en te Zeeland, Michigan, gediend heeft. Zijn vromen handel en wandel maakte hem voor oud en jong steeds zijner bediening als ouderling dubbel waardig, en al was hij ook, naar sommiger meening, wat eng in zijne opvatting der waarheid, toch was hij ook ruim genoeg om, waar hij bij verschil van gevoelens, ook oprechte godsvrucht zag doorstralen, dezulken de hartelijke broederhand te drukken. Ook was en bleef hij onder al de woelige kerkelijke verwikkelingen en oneenigheden, een trouwe voorstander der Gereformeerde Kerk, leer, en dienst der vaderen, en een biddend onderzoeker der waarheid, en een ernstig voorbidder voor land en volk, en der gemeente Gods, die hem zoo dierbaar was.

Hij bezat ook als landman een veelzijdig welontwikkeld verstand, en had in zijn jeugd een goede kweeking genoten. Maar, zijn lust en streven was bovenal om de vrucht en kracht der waarheid gedurig en bij vernieuwing aan zijn hart te mogen genieten. En waarin hij vooral boven velen uitmuntte, was zijne Christelijke menschlievendheid. Zijn huis stond in Nederland altijd open voor allen die schuilplaats behoefden, maar vooral voor de arbeiders in 's Heeren wijngaard; en niet slechts tot herberging derzulken, maar voor jaren lang werd zijn huis en schuur steeds als kerk tot godsdienstofening gebruikt, tot er later eene kerk gebouwd werd. Hij beoefende de les van Paulus betreffende ouderlingen: „gaarne herbergzaam."

Nog in Nederland zijnde bezat hij eene groote boerderij met deszelfs omslag van roerende goederen, welke hij bij zijn vertrek uit Nederland [want hij was ten volle besloten tot het vertrek naar Noord Amerika] verkocht voor de som van zestig duizend gulden – omtrent $ 20,000.

Hij begreep echter dat door zijn vertrek uit die jeugdige gemeente, die onder zijnen invloed en leiding gesticht en aangegroeid was, doch meestal uit de arbeidende klasse bestond, vele huisgezinnen in groote armoede zouden gedompeld worden grooter dan ooit te voren, daarbij kwam dat, voor hem en zijn gezin, wat zijne financieele toestand betrof, er toch geenerlei behoefte bestond om zulk eene onzekere onderneming te gaan wagen, wat hem dus bewoog om dien stap te nemen, moge voor velen een raadsel schijnen, tenzij men moet veronderstellen, dat wegens de rampspoeden die Nederland toen troffen, hij duidelijk de steeds toe-nemende armoede en algemeene achteruitgang tegemoet zag, en vooral ook dat de smaad en verguizing door de vijanden des Heeren, welke hij met zijn gemeentje, die de staatskerk verlaten hadden, steeds te verduren hadden, hem verlangend deed uitzien naar een oord warm en vrij en onbelemmerd naar Gods Woord en de inspraak des gewetens den Heere konde dienen; of ook dat een verborgen aandrift hem onweerstaanbaar bewoog, om gelijk een Moses van ouds al was het dan ook op kleiner schaal, in 's Heeren hand te dienen ter redding en uitkomst van de be-hoeftige huisgezinnen zijner gemeente, wier heil hij steeds als ouderling op zijn harte droeg.

Zeer waarschijnlijk droegen alle drie dezer reden bij om hem bereid-vaardig te maken zijne bezittingen veil te hebben en ze te wagen ter redding van een tiental behoeftige huisgezinnen, die hem geenerlei waarborg tot terugbetaling konden aanbieden, dan eenvoudig eene schriftelijke belofte dat zij zoo spoedig de Heere hen in staat stelde, zij de voorgeschotene gelden zouden terug betalen.

Zijn door hooger hand bewogen menschlievend hart overzag eindelijk alle hinderpalen; doch dat ging niet zonder eene hevige worsteling, gelijk een Jacob met den Engel te Pniël. Treffend schoon luidt zijne nagelatene mededeeling desaangaande; hoe hij in den vroegen morgen van 1 Januari 1847 worstelde met zijnen God om licht en kracht en genade, ten einde 's Heeren goedkeuring te mogen ondervinden. En ziet, de Heere kwam hem voor met „de kostelijkste Zijner beloften", zoodat hij van toen af ten volle besloten was zijne voorgenomen plannen door te zetten. En nu zou men natuurlijk meenen, dat de aandrang om mede verlost te mogen worden, vooral bij die arbeidende huisgezinnen ontstaan was. Maar neen, hij zelf overtuigde en drong die huisgezinnen aan om de, vooral voor hem veel gewaagde stap met hem te ondernemen. Ja, voor sommi-gen van dat getal bood hij zelfs aan en betaalde niet alleen de geheele reiskosten met inbegrip van levensonderhoud, voor de geheele reis, maar moest hen ook voorzien van noodige deksel en kleederen om die groote reis te kunnen ondernemen; daarbij kwam nog, dat sommigen hunner door de werkelooze winterdagen, waarin zij niets hadden kunnen verdienen, in schuld waren geraakt bij hunne winkeliers, en dewijl hij het denkbeeld niet konde verdragen, dat iemand hunner als een bank-roetier zijn vaderland zou verlaten, zoo schoot hij de benoodigde gelden ook daartoe hun voor; en toen hier in deze dichte wouden gekomen zijnde het bleek, dat er niets voor hen te verdienen was, dan door de wouden te vellen, die hij aangekocht had, zoo namen velen hunner ook toen alweer naar dien rijken boschbankier voor levensonderhoud de toevlucht.

De lezer mocht misschien opmaken dat Van de Luyster een roekelooze verkwister was van de middelen en gaven, waarmede de Heere hem zoo ruimschoots begiftigd had, doch zij en wij die hem van nabij gekend hebben, zijn wel overtuigd van zijne opofferende behulpzaamheid, maar tevens ook van zijn zuinigheid en spaarzaamheid, steeds beoefende en leerde hij aan anderen de les van zijn dierbaren Heer en Meester er mocht niets verloren gaan, telkens ook waarschuwende tegen de ver-kwisting zijner gaven. „Zuinigheid" was steeds zijn motto, en verstrekte voor hem en de zijnen tot veel nut. Daarbij nam hij dagelijks de toevlucht tot die Fontein van alle genade die hem steeds zoo troostvol en kracht inboezemend bezielde, zoodat hij op dat ingeslagen pad steeds voortging, want hiermede eindigde nog zijne gulle overgegevenheid niet; hij kocht namelijk van den staat Michigan ruim twee sections land aan in sections 9, 18, 19, en 30 en bood ieder der huisgezinnen, die hij over gebracht had, 20 akkers land meer of min aan, om tegen inkoopsprijs en de nevens-gaande onkosten, van hem over te nemen, op voorwaarden dat zij twintig jaren tijd zouden hebben tot terugbetaling. Zij die zulk een aanbod aannamen, kregen op eens een koopacte, en zij gaven weder-keerig een hypotheek daarop, die tegelijkertijd de door Van de Luyster voorgeschotene reiskosten insloot, zoodat de som der hypotheek meestal van vijf tot tienmaal grooter was dan de prijs des lands. Dat maakte dan zoodoende zijne securiteit of waarborg uit; daar nevensgaande nam hij nog een „note" of schuldbekentenis in de volgende bewoording en in de Hollandsche taal door hem zelf geschreven:

„Als vrijgekochten des Heeren, beloven wij, N.N. en S.S. zijne vrouw, aan Jannes van de Luyster, zoo spoedig de Heer ons in staat stelt te betallen de som van .... Dollars, met jaarlijksche rente tegen zeven ten honderd."

Gedaan te Zeeland, November 1847.

Doch slechts vijf huisvaders van dat getal hadden den moed dit ver-nieuwde edele aanbod met deszelfs verplichting te aanvaarden, en welke ook allen, na verloop van tijd, aan die belofte voldaan hebben, terwijl van de anderen sommigen in gebreken gebleven zijn, en hunnen weldoener met ondank bejegend hebben, en sommigen door den dood al spoedig weggenomen waren.

Wij kunnen en mogen niet anders dan, met het oog op het edele en zelf opofferende beginsel en de eere Gods en het tijdelijk en eeuwig welzijn zijner arme medemenschen dat hem bezielde, getuigen dat Jannes van de Luyster wel met recht voor een der eerste drie helden kan prijken welke zich in die eerste tijd in deze nederzetting vestigden, en als zulks mag en moet aangeteekend blijven. Want daarbij kwam nog dat hij niet alleen zorgde voor den engen kring van de huisgezinnen, welke hij zoo vaderlijk geholpen en gered had, maar op velerlei wijze heeft hij, beide op burgerlijk en op kerkelijk gebied, naar zijn vermogen, ja, zelfs boven vermogen, hulp en bijstand verleend, totdat zijn ruim kapitaal geheel versmolten was en hij met de zijnen, even gelijk de andere uitgeputte pioniers zich voor een geruimen tijd met cornbrood, polka-boter, en rogge-koffie veeltijds moesten vergenoegen, en in armoedigen toestand zich moest behelpen.

Ter staving dezer bewering is nog in het bezit van een zijner klein-kinderen een dagboek aanwezig, waarin door hemzelf alles aangeteekend werd, hoe hij niet alleen die geredde huisgezinnen verzorgde en voort-hielp, maar hoe hij ook op ongeloofelijke wijze behulpzaam was op ieder gebied van ons maatschappelijk bestaan.

En wat dat schitterend karakter nog te meer deed prijken, was de gulle hartelijke instemming en medewerking zijner waardige vrouw, die met een bezadigd christelijk gemoed de handelingen van haren nobelen echt-genoot steeds ondersteunde, dewijl zij bewust en overtuigd was van het verheven christelijk beginsel dat haar geliefden man tot alles bewoog, want die nieuwjaarsmorgen-worsteling van haar man was ook haar niet onbekend en gaf haar moed en geloof voor de toekomst.

Zijn naam was alreede als ouderling in Nederland in eer en achting en is steeds onbevlekt gebleven tot aan het einde zijner nuttige loopbaan, en zal voor zijn talrijk nageslacht, zoowel als voor de velen, die hij uit armoede en verachting gered heeft en voor de gemeente Zeeland, die hem zoo dierbaar was, steeds in de grootste achting en eere blijven. Maar toch bovenal komt de Heere de lof, eere, en dank toe, dat Hij Jannes van de Luyster tot zulk een nuttig instrument verheven heeft; immers zelf-verheffing scheen hem vreemd te zijn.

Hij ontsliep in zijnen Heer te Zeeland, den 13den Maart 1862 in den ouderdom van 67 jaren, Psalm 27 : 37: „Let op den vrome en zie naar den oprechte, want het einde van dien man zal vrede zijn."

De derde leidsman van die verhuizende komplotten, diaken Jan Steketee, was ook een man met een gezond verstand van christelijke be-ginselen en een vast karakter. Het zijne was een van de drie eerste huisgezinnen – de andere twee waren die van Christiaan den Herder en Jacobus de Hond – die de wouden indrongen en hunne tenten te Zeeland opsloegen. Doch dewijl zijne oudste zoons, gelijk vele anderen, tot levensonderhoud naar naburige plaatsen moesten vertrekken om voor zich en hunne ouders wat te verdienen, al spoedig bespeurden, dat er voor hun groot huisgezin veel beter vooruitzicht was in de naburige plaats Grand Rapids, zoo vertrok hij met zijn gezin in 1851 derwaarts, en dewijl de oudste zoons reeds in Nederland eene goede opvoeding en onderwijs genoten hadden, maakten zij een gunstigen indruk op hunne werkgevers en kwamen al spoedig in winstgevende betrekkingen. Later is hij tot deze nederzetting teruggekeerd en heeft met zijne vrouw hunne laatste dagen rustig in Holland, Michigan, gesleten.

Onder hen, die ook mede tot den opbouw van Zeeland gediend hebben, waren vooral Johannes G. van Hees, Robbertus M. de Bruyn, Huibert Keppel, Arie van Bree, en vele anderen.

Eerstgenoemde kwam in 1848 te Zeeland aan. Hij was een man met een helder doorziend en ontwikkeld verstand en gezond christelijk karakter, die ook nog vrij wat middelen bezat en besteedde, door aan vele der Zeelandsche arme pioniers werk te verschaffen, want zijne zachte handen als bakkersbaas, stonden er niet naar om de woudreuzen te vellen. En daar hij te Rotterdam in Nederland alreede als ouderling gediend had, werd gij gedrongen deze betrekking hier onder ons voort te zetten, dewijl de gemeente aan zijne edele gaven en bekwaamheden behoefte had. Hij heeft dan ook tot het jaar 1862 de gemeente in dat ambt tot veel nut gediend; daarbenevens bekleedde hij gedurende eene reeks van twintig jaren, zooals reeds gezegd is, den post van supervisor van township Zeeland. Eindelijk werd ook dien pionier langzamerhand gesloopt en uitgeput, tot hij in het jaar 1891 de rust is ingegaan.

In Robbertus M. de Bruyn kreeg Zeeland een bijzondere steun en de vervulling van eene dringende behoefte, namelijk, in het onderwijs der jeugd. Als een man met de daartoe zeer gepaste gaven en bekwaamheden bedeeld, met een zeer voorbeeldigen wandel en nederige, doch tevens schitterende godsvrucht, was hij jaren lang biddende werkzaam onder de kinderen der gemeente, met hun te onderwijzen in de benoodigde wetenschappen en met tegelijkertijd op echt christelijk fundament dat gebouw op te trekken, totdat eene bijzondere lichaamkwaal hem noodzaakte deze betrekking neer te leggen en hij naar het naburig Holland vertrok, en korte jaren daarna de kroon der heerlijkheid ontving.

Wat vader Huibert Keppel betreft, die den hoogen ouderdom van 93 jaren bereikte, hij heeft van zijn komst te Zeeland in 1848 af, door zijnen ondernemenden en welberaden geest, op financieel gebied wellicht meer dan iemand anders voor den opbouw van Zeeland met gezegenden uitslag werkzaam geweest, eerst met voor lange jaren kuipstaven uit de eiken boomen te laten maken, welke hij met zeilschepen naar Chicago overbracht, daardoor aan velen werk verschaffende en hierdoor in het levensonderhoud van velen voorzag, al waren de loonen van 50 cents per dag ook niet groot; en daarna in 1871, in gezelschap van Wopke van Haitsma en Jakob den Herder, te Zeeland een graanmolen van ruime capaciteit te bouwen. Vele jaren diende hij ook de gemeente Zeeland als diaken. Eindelijk moest ook hij, wegens ouderdom, van het werkzame leven afstappen en het aan zijn zoon overlaten.

Wat de vierde dier mannen, Arie van Bree, betreft, hij is steeds van af 1850 als ouderling tot zijn laatste stonde een echte sieraad onder ons geweest, zoo in zijn lieftallig karakter als in leer en wandel; ook hij kwam in 1848 als ouderling uit het oude vaderland.

Verder tellen wij onder hen, die tot de handelsontwikkeling in de eerste jaren behulpzaam waren, de namen van Dr. George H. Baart, Klaas Smits, Johannes Busquet, en Jan Rabbers. Laatstgenoemde die, hoewel te Groningen wonende, toch onder de gemeente Zeeland behoorde, was een man, die een werkzamen en veel ondernemenden geest bezat. Hij bouwde met Albert Borgers, te Groningen, onder vele ontbeeringen, moeielijkheden, en teleurstellingen, een water-zaagmolen, die voor eenigen tijd vrij wat bouwstof vervaardigde, doch, uithoofde van de zwakheid van den dam, die telkens bij hoogen waterstand doorbrak, was deze molen, na korte jaren, onnut. Daarop bouwde hij in die buurt een graanmolen, ook door waterkracht gedreven, welke echter door gebrek aan water veeltijds niet gebruikt kon worden; en, dewijl er een grootere en door stoom gedreven molen in het naburig Holland was opgericht, zoo verviel al spoedig ook die onderneming. Gebrek aan kapitaal en aan rijpe ondervinding voor al dat werk waren ongetwijfeld de voorname reden der mislukkingen. Overspanning en uitputting sloopten al spoedig ook dien ijverigen pionier, zoodat hij in het jaar 1860 reeds door den dood weggenomen werd.

Onder het getal van hen, die ook ieder van een tot drie behoeftige huisgezinnen uit Nederland meebrachten, die zich te Zeeland vestigden, waren Jan de Pree, Jan Smallegange, en Jan en Gillis Wabeke.

Dan, als eene bijzonderheid, in betrekking tot het overhelpen van arme huisgezinnen uit Nederland, kan nog gemeld worden, dat gedurende de jaren 1852 tot 1854 die eerste pioniers van hunne armoede, zoowel te Zeeland als in de naburige plaatsen, gemeentelijk gelden bijeen brachten om arme huisgezinnen uit Nederland over te laten komen: wanneer er dan een genoegzaam bedrag bijeen was, werd er van Classis wege [want het was eene kerkelijk zaak geworden], om geloot ter beslissing welk huisgezin nu gered zou worden, nadat verschillende belanghebbende vrienden namen daartoe ingediend hadden. Waaruit duidelijk te bespeuren is, dat, hoewel men hier ook met veel tegenspoeden en ontbeeringen te kampen had, men toch vergenoegd was niet alleen, maar benevens ook bij de aangename vrede en vrijheid die men genoot, ook de gegronde hoop koesterde voor het welslagen der toekomst, waarin men dan ook niet teleur is gesteld geworden, want de Heere was met ons. En, hoewel er waren, die het zware werk van boschland te ontginnen, en ook den moed ontbrak om het armoedige boschleven te doorstaan, en daarom de vlucht namen naar naburige plaatsen, toch bleef de massa standvastig voortworstelen, aangemoedigd door den trouwen dienst van hunnen beminden leeraar, Ds. van der Meulen, die, waar en wanneer telkens vernieuwde tegenspoeden zich opdeden, zijn volk, vooral ook des Zondags van den kansel, door zijne moedgevende en vertroostende prediking wist aan te moedigen en aan te dringen tot standvastigheid.

Onder de omstandigheden die later veel bijgedragen hebben tot den opbouw en voorspoed van Zeeland, was het bouwen van een zaagmolen door de gebroeders Peter, Gerrit, en Cornelis Vyn, en verder door het bouwen van den Chicago and West Michigan Railway, die in 1871 is gebouwd en het ter zelfder tijd bouwen van den ruimen graanmolen, reeds genoemd, en het spoedig daarop bouwen van een steenbakkerij, een mijl ten westen van het dorp Zeeland, door B. J. Veneklaasen en Zonen, en het nog later oprichten van een meubelfabriek op groote schaal, en het bouwen van andere fabrieken, zaagmolen, schaafpomp, wagenfabrieken en andere ondernemingen van handel en welvaart, te veel om op te noemen, zoodat Zeeland, zelfs gedurende de laatste vier jaren van algemeene stremming en achteruitgang in den handel in dit land, groote reden tot dankbaarheid gehad heeft omdat de drukking zoo weinig armoede of ellende onder ons veroorzaakte, en vooral ook, omdat gedurende de vervlogene 50 jaren van haar bestaan, geen algemeene rampen de plaats of hare inwoners getroffen heeft.

De zwaarste algemeene ramp was in den herfst van 1856, toen eene gevaarlijke ziekte van bloedloop, vele kinderen en ook enkele bejaarden ten grave gevoerd heeft. Vele andere dingen en zaken konden nog vermeld worden, maar mijn taak is beperkt en zal dus ook ruimte aan anderen overlaten.

Maar dewijl het godsdienstige en gemeentelijke leven der eerste nederzetters, hare geschiedenis geheel doorstraalde, moeten wij nogmaals tot dat gedeelte daarvan terug, want de ondervinding heeft het bewezen, dat ook hier in deze woestijn, de satan geen vreemdeling was, en door allerlei listen, gelijk bij onzen Heiland van ouds, zoo jongen als ouden poogde te verstrikken, en dat het hem, jammerlijk genoeg, maar al te dikwijls gelukte, want twist en tweedracht kwam telkens te voorschijn. Doch, dan vinden wij ook, als eene bijzonderheid, dat nagenoeg alle geschillen onder hen door de kerkelijke rechtbanken van kerkeraad en Classes ver- effend werden, want hoewel het grootste gedeelte der oude settlers een goed vroom volkje was, toch was het donkere woeste woud nog tot geen paradijs herschapen. Wel hoorde men niet zelden de wouden weer- galmen met Psalmen ter eere Gods maar de kerkeraad's notulen van die tijden toonen ook aan dat, gelijk reeds gezegd is, twist en verdeeldheid niet zelden de vrede kwam storen, wat daartoe bijdroeg of mede oorzaak was, zal ongetwijfeld deels ontstaan zijn uit verschil van kweeking en op- voeding, dewijl onder de gemeente Zeeland zich vestigden eene menge- ling van al de provincies uit Nederland, hoewel de Zeeuwen hier onge- twijfeld de meerderheid uitmaakten; doch treffend was het, hoe het wijs beleid en de rijpe ondervinding, gepaard met godsvrucht van hunnen trouwen leider en der bekwame leden van den kerkeraad hen meest altijd wist tot eenheid en vrede te brengen.

Wat echter de moeilijkste taak zoo hier als in andere gemeenten scheen te zijn, was de verschillende godsdienstige richtingen waarin zij in Nederland gekweekt en onderwezen waren, waaruit menigwerf gods- diensttwist en verdeeldheid voortvloeide en eerlang tot botsing en on- herstelbare scheuring leidde.

De eerste verwijdering begon in 1851, toen enkele Drentsche huisge- zinnen de richting van Ds. Roelof Smit van het naburige Drenthe gingen volgen en zich daar tot eene gemeente vormden. Daar benevens droeg vooral bij de scheuring in het naburig Graafschap en elders over de kerkelijke verbintenis met de toen zoogenoemd Dutch Reformed Church of America, welk kerkgenootschap al vele jaren in den staat New York en omgeving gevestigd was. Onze voornaamste leiders waren genegen om zich kerkelijk daarmee te vereenigen; doch sommigen meenden reden te hebben om dien weg niet te mogen inslaan en gingen voort om, hoewel zich niet organisch, toch met de Christelijke Gereformeerde Kerk van Nederland aansluitende, aan de godsdienst, vorm, en beginselen daar- van strikt vast te houden; daarbij is in 1881 de vrijmetselaars beweging begonnen, die in vele gemeenten, alsook te Zeeland, de verwijdering uit de Reformed Church grootelijks vermeerderde.

In het voor of tegen dezer beweging zal ik niet treden, vooral ook niet omdat de gewetensovertuiging aangaande godsdienstige begrippen en opvattingen zulk een teedere zaak is. Immers, de meeste oude settlers verlieten het oude vaderland ook, opdat zij den Heere naar inspraak huns gewetens vrij en onbelemmerd mochten dienen, en daarom weerhoud ik mij van de fijne twistpunten over die kwestie, zoowel als van de namen der leiders en bestrijders van die beweging mede te deelen, want beide partijen meenden toen en meenen nog uit oprecht godsdienstig beginsel zijne opvatting of zienswijze te moeten vasthouden, maar wat, en wie ook de voorname oorzaak van die jammerlijke scheuring moge geweest zijn [God weet het], toch is het een zeer bejammerenswaardige toestand, zonder eenig vooruitzicht op heeling. Maar daadzaak is het, dat vooral voor hen, hier te Zeeland, zoowel als voor hen op andere plaatsen, die met ons deze jammerlijke broederbestrijding en verwijdering en scheuring hebben doorleefd, en nog moeten bespeuren en niet anders dan met weemoed kunnen herdenken en moeten aanzien, te meer wanneer men denkt aan die eerste jaren van vrede en eenheid. Durven wij nog met het gezicht van dat alles met den dichter van ouds in den geloove zingen: „Maar de Heer zal uitkomst geven?" Verlangende zien wij uit naar die stonde. Ja, vele veranderingen zijn sedert die eerste pioniersjaren ook op godsdienstig gebied te Zeeland als elders langzamerhand ingekropen. Te wenschen ware het, dat ze meestal gunstige veranderingen waren geweest, en nu mag de eene tegenover de andere al staan roepen, gelijk van ouds: „Des Heeren tempel, des Heeren tempel, des Heeren tempel is deze," maar zoolang wellust, weelde, wereldzin en mammon de boventoon aanheffen, zal zoo min bij de eene als bij de andere de strikste rechtzinnigheid in leer, zeer weinig van die oude nederige vroomheid te weeg brengen. Alleen de zoele, vruchtbaarmakende regen des Geestes kan ons redden; laten wij ook daarnaar maar biddend uitzien.

Nogmaals terug naar de eerste jaren onzer onderlinge samenleving en vergun dan, als eene der velen, ook mijne ouderlijke woning te beluisteren, en wat verneem ik daar; des morgens en des avonds allen biddend gekniel, den dag beginnende en eindigende; bij sommigen ook met psalmgezang; daarbij bij elke maaltijd overluid bidden en danken. Ook werden al de kinderen geleerd om, al ware het dan ook in zoogenoemde formuliergebeden, des morgens bij 't opstaan en 's avonds met te bed gaan voor zich knielende luid op te bidden.

Dan, beluisteren wij de gesprekken der vrouwtjes bij hun kopje koffie of thee, en ook daar maakt men kennis met elkaar met te verhalen wat de Heere al voor hun gedaan had, en over Zijne Vaderlijke leiding. Dat

waren met recht zoete gezelschappen, wat men nu noemt „a good time",
maar o, wat een verschil van velen thans. Doch er waren ook al weer
belemmeringen in dezen, want bijvoorbeeld, wanneer mijne geliefde
moeder [die niets anders dan plat Zeeuwsch kon spreken] met hare vrome
buurvrouw, de vrouw van onze waardige ouderling Harm Krans, in
gesprek kwam [die niet anders dan plat boere Drentsch geleerd had te
spreken] zie, dan zaten zij bij tijden zoo vast in de war, dat ze met weemoed moesten afbreken. En dat was ook vooral het geval in gesprekken
met de boere-Friesen. Tusschen beiden zij hier ook opgemerkt, dat die
moeilijkheid niet alleen ondervonden werd bij de godsdienstige gesprekken der oude lui, maar evenzeer onder het jeugdige geslacht, hetwelk vooral onder hen het gebruik der engelsche taal bespoedigde, want
dan kwamen wij allen op een spoor; al was het eerst ook gebrekkig.
Toch bleven de godsdienstoefeningen tot 1887 toe uitsluitend in bijna al
de gemeenten in de Hollandsche taal, met uitzondering, dat in Zondag-
schoolonderwijs al spoedig de engelsche taal indrong, maar toch hield
men vast aan de oude taal en dienst der vaderen. Ook werd op verre na
niet de Bijbel en godsdienst onder de trouwe leiding van den waardigen
onderwijzer, Robbertus M. de Bruyn, uit onze school verbannen of
geignoreerd; maar ook echter weer niet in dier mate alsof dag aan dag de
school een catechisatiekamer was, maar de geest en beademing der godsdienst was steeds aanwezig. Het catechiseeren geschiedde voor vele jaren
voor de schoolkinderen, door den leeraar op elke Woensdagnamiddag
van een tot vier ure. Eindelijk heeft men, in betrekking tot den tijd, zoo
nu en dan veranderingen aangebracht; of ze verbeteringen geweest zijn,
betwijfel ik nog wel. Indien men echter meent dat de schoolkinderen en
de jeugd over het algemeen toen zondelooze engelen waren, maar ach,
dan klinkt de verontwaardigde klachte en bestraffing van dien trouwen
dienaar Gods, de eerwaarde Van der Meulen, mij nog in het oor, waar hij
met zijn stok op de tafel of bank sloeg: „Gij schijnt waarlijk eerder zoovele jonge duivelen te zijn, dan engelen of verbondskinderen."

Ja strijd was het en strijd blijft het; en gelukig ook, indien de strijd
blijft tegen den vorst der duisternis en voor Koning Jezus en Zijn rijk,
totdat het heerlijk tijdperk daagt, waarin stoorlooze vrede zal genoten
worden; en daarom, houd moed.

De dag van heden [dit heugelijke feest] geeft ons een nasmaak van onze
eerste gelukkigste tijden van vrede en liefde, ook onder druk en ellende,
maar ook een voorsmaak van dat heugelijke vrederijk waarin al de vrij-
gekochte pelgrims, daar zonder druk of ellende, onafgebroken het feest
des Lams ongestoord en voor altoos zullen vieren. Moge dat ons aller
deel zijn!

[Translation]

Each country and each people possesses in greater or less degree a special history. Such likewise is the case of every village or community; yes, each person possess such history although in a limited manner. When a period of half a century has passed it becomes our duty to pause a moment and cast a backward glance along the path that has been trod, so that we may recall God's good and faithful providence and reclaim it from oblivion for ourselves and our successors.

This is our aim in presenting a brief sketch of *Zeeland and its Founders*. And as Zeeland is not only the name of a village, but also of a township in which most of the village of Zeeland is situated we are obliged to write a brief description of both township and village.

Until August 1847 this township, later named Zeeland, including the spot where we are now gathered, as well as adjoining townships was a wild waste with a thick growth of hard and softwood trees of various dimensions, some as much as six feet in diameter, most of them more than a hundred feet tall, and standing so close together that one could scarcely swing an axe to begin cutting them down. For centuries the woods had been the haven of bears and wolves, foxes, and other small animals as well as the fleet and timid deer. There also were original dwellers of the forest, Indians, who belonged to the tribe of the Ottawas. They made their living by hunting and fishing but never harmed us in any way. Their most important abode in our settlement was a small village, then called *Indianen stad* ["Indian Village"] situated on the south shore of Black Lake. From that place there extended eastward and northward an Indian trail which led through dense jungles to Grand Rapids. Of this trail our first pioneers made frequent use, for there were no wagon roads. On these trails we sometimes ran onto the original inhabitants of the woods armed with gun, axe, tomahawk, and knife. Politely we kept out of their path so that each of us could continue unhindered on his way.

So far as the character of the township of Zeeland was concerned, its surface was divided by a swamp which extended from the northeast to the southeast. Each side was flanked with hills covered with elm and other softwood trees. This morass was 160 rods wide on the average, impenetrable during most months of the year, the abode of horrible snakes and other creatures. Another impassable swamp divided section 19 on which Zeeland is situated. From the wood growing in it this was known as the Cedar Swamp. These low lying lands at first seemed to be totally valueless, but gradually through the unwearying industry of the settlers they were converted into the most fruitful fields.

The remaining part of the township, although cut up by several hills, was fertile. Only with heroic courage and gigantic strength as well as persistence was it possible to reduce these woods to cultivation. The luxuriant growth of trees bore no fruit. Nor did the ground under our feet contribute to our needs, neither did the wood have any value during our first years.

The first steps toward the settlement of people on these wild lands had been taken by the state in the year 1832, when it divided the area into townships and sections. Each township consisted of 36 sections laid out in rows of six next to each other. Each section contained 640 acres. After the survey of townships and sections had been effected, further sub-divisions were to be made gradually, when needed. The subdividers of this region were Bernardus Grootenhuis in neighboring Holland and Cornelius Voorhorst in nearby Overisel. The writer of these pages, as chain-puller, also helped these surveyors.

At first several of the surveyed townships, on account of their scanty population, were combined to form one township, to be under the super-vision of a township official, as prescribed by state law. Hence this township which, when the Hollanders arrived in 1847, formed part of Georgetown Township, was joined to Ottawa Township in 1848, to Allendale Township in 1849, and was combined with Holland Township during 1850 until June 10, 1851, when it was organized as Zeeland Township under its own board of supervisors.

The first special meeting of the township was held in the log church in Zeeland on July 14, 1851. By that date a sufficient number of male persons of mature age had taken the necessary steps toward becoming American citizens who could legally transact business. They elected as supervisor Elias G. Young; as town clerk and treasurer Robbertus M. de Bruyn; as school inspector Dominie Cornelius van der Meulen; as highway commissioner, Willem Regenmorter; as justices of the peace, Johannes G. van Hees, Elias G. de Young, and Johannes Nieuwendorp; as directors of the poor, Jan de Pree and Hessel O. Yntema; as constables, Willem Kremer, Hendrik de Kruif, and George H. Baart. A total of 141 votes were cast in this election.

Since that date until the present the first two offices mentioned were held by the following persons: supervisors, Elias G. Young who served 1½ years; Johannes G. van Hees, 21; Robbertus M. de Bruyn, 2; Jacob den Herder, 3½; Cornelius van Loo, 11; Christiaan den Herder, 6; and

Willem van Loo, present occupant, 1½ years. As township clerk Robbertus M. de Bruyn served 5 years; Jacob den Herder, 20; John Boer, Albert Bolks, Gerrit Bolks, and Albert Lahuis, each one year; Henry Bosch, 7 years; and Jacob van den Bosch, present occupant, 10.

From the moment of its organization until the present the township of Zeeland has formed part of Ottawa County. Among the number of county officials during the course of these 50 years we note the names of the following citizens of Zeeland: Pieter van den Berg, who during 1863 and 1864 functioned as clerk and registrar of deeds; Jacob den Herder, who during 1868 and 1869 served as one of the three county poormasters; Cornelius van Loo who was registrar of deeds for six years following 1869; and, finally, Peter Brusse the present registrar of deeds.

Van Loo served as county superintendent of schools, and also was presiding officer of the board of supervisors of Ottawa County. For four years following 1881 he represented the first district of Ottawa County in the Legislature of this state.

Jacob den Herder filled the post as presidential elector in 1876, that is, he was member of the electoral college of Michigan in the contested political struggle between Rutherford B. Hayes and Samuel J. Tilden. Den Herder cast his vote for Hayes who finally was chosen President by a majority of one in the electoral college of the United States [which was composed of 369 votes]. Den Herder also held the office of state senator.

The first assessed value of the township of Zeeland after it was separated from that of Holland, in 1851, was as follows: real estate $ 35,580, and movables $ 4,309, while 50 years ago the total estimated value of Ottawa County [including the present Muskegon Township] was $ 295,661.36.

From 1847 when the first settlers moved into the woods the township of Zeeland was devided roughly into three areas. This was due partly to the natural features of the township, but also to the fact that the settlers came from various provinces in the Netherlands. These three communities were Zeeland, Vriesland, and Drenthe. The second and third were for a short time under the pastoral care of Dominie Maarten A. Ypma until Dominie Roelof Smit arrived in Drenthe in 1851. Thereafter Dominie Ypma had charge only of Vriesland. But as my theme is Zeeland, I shall restrict my remarks to it.

As I remarked, the communities in our settlement were named after the provinces of the Netherlands. Hence, as many of the first settlers who lived west of the Zeeland Swamp came from the province of Zeeland that name was applied to the village and township of Zeeland. Specially significant in this connection is the fact that the Zeelanders came over as an organized religious community formed in a meeting held at Goes in the province of Zeeland early in 1847, at which time Jannes van de Luyster and Johannes Hoogesteger were chosen elders, and Jan Steketee and Adriaan Glerum were elected elders. The members of this meeting called Dominie Cornelius van der Meulen to serve them as their pastor, an invitation he accepted.

The formation of this organization and the calling of the pastor were effected because the members intended soon to emigrate to North America. They had no idea at that moment where they would settle in this spacious country. But they were determined, under God's guidance, to stay together and to perpetuate the religious bond in which they were already living.

In the month of April 1847 we Zeelanders left the land of our birth, our beloved fatherland. We crossed the vast ocean in three sailing ships each carrying a part of our group. One of them was under the leadership of Dominie van der Meulen and Jan Kaboord; this ship sailed from Rotterdam. The second group was under the direction of Jannes van de Luyster. The third [with which we sailed] was under the guidance of Jan Steketee. The last two sailed from Antwerp.

After voyages of from 30 to 60 days and a tedious journey of about 4 weeks from New York to this place, and after staying in nearby Holland for three or four weeks while the men searched the dense forest for suitable lands on which to settle, finally many of us in August and September 1847 settled in this neighborhood. Here, then, it was that we continued our religious community life in the Lord's name, and called our settlement Zeeland.

The first religious services in Zeeland were held on the third Sunday in August [Aug. 15] in the half finished loghouse belonging to Jan Steketee. On that occasion was read a sermon by one of the old theologians. Only a few were able to attend this service. As yet there were no roads; and people, in order to go to any place, found their way as well as they could by traveling through the woods.

Soon our parish covered all the area in Zeeland Township west and north of the Zeeland Swamp and also a large part of Holland Township, which lay east of Black Lake. An effort was made to establish a congregation separate from that of Zeeland, a few miles to the west. It was called Groningen, but this soon failed. Later, in 1873, on account of the distances and the increase of population a new congregation in the northeast part of our township was formed under the name of Beaverdam.

As we have stated, the leaders of our first congregation, who had come over with us, were Dominie van der Meulen, Jannes van de Luyster, Johannes Hoogesteger, Jan Steketee, and Adriaan Glerum. But a number of ohter persons from various parts of the Netherlands came over to us as elders and continued to serve as such under the principle "once an elder, always an elder." The number of elders so increased that there were more than twenty. To remedy this situation, the elders were induced to submit a written resignation. This step was followed by a meeting of the consistory on July 12, 1849, under the direction of Dominie van der Meulen, at which six elders and four deacons were elected from the membership of the congregation. The new elders were Jannes van de Luyster, Johannes G. van Hees, Quirinus Huyser, H. Krans, Johannes Hoogesteger, and Albert Borgers. The newly chosen deacons were Jan Steketee, Adriaan Glerum, J. van der Werp, and Jacob Hovink.

Chief among the leaders of the first settlers of Zeeland was the trusted Dominie van der Meulen. He was as a father to his congregation and to his many followers who led a life of bitter struggle. He nourished them with the food of the Gospel. But the writing of a sketch of that able servant of God has been assigned to other hands and so I point to another pillar of the temple of our congregation, namely our already mentioned and honored Jannes van de Luyster. From the time when, in 1834, he left the state church in the Netherlands until the daty of his death at Zeeland in America, for a period of 44 years he served continuously as elder of the Lord's congregation at Borsselen in the Netherlands and at Zeeland in Michigan. His pious life and example made his services as elder doubly valuable. Although some have thought his conception of the truth was somewhat narrow, nevertheless he was broad enough to extend the hand of friendship to those who manifested sincere piety even though their ideas differed from his. In church bickerings and dissensions he remained ever faithful to the Reformed Church, its doctrines, and its order of service. He was a devout investigator of the truth and prayed earnestly for his country, his people, and God's church.

As a farmer Van de Luyster had a well developed intelligence. In his youth he had received a sound education. He excelled his fellows in Christian charity. In the Netherlands his house ever was open to all who needed protection, and expecially to laborers in the Lord's vineyard. For years his house and barn served as a place for religious services until, finally, a church was erected. He followed the counsel of the apostle Paul concerning elders, "given to hospitality" [Romans 12, 13]. He owned a large farm with much movable property. This he sold for 60,000 guilders – about $ 25,000 [exactly $ 24,000].

Van de Luyster realized that he had to care for the poor of the congregation. Its members belonged to the laboring class. These people
would fall into abject poverty if he abandoned them. Such was his
wealth that there was no reason for him to risk so much in so dubious an
undertaking. Why he decided to emigrate might well appear an enigma
unless it was due to the calamaties which overtook the country. He noted
the poverty of the people. He was impressed by the reproach and derision
heaped upon him and his followers when they left the state church. This
condition induced him to look for some haven where they might worship
freely in accordance with the word of God. An irresistable desire impelled
him, like a Moses of old, to serve the Lord by helping needy families of
his congregation. These were the reasons why he sacrificed his property
to help some of those who possessed nothing and could give no guanrantee of repayment beyond a written promise stating that as soon as the
Lord made it possible they would repay him.

His charity surmounted all obstacles. This was not accomplished
without a grave struggle, like that of a Jacob with the angel at Pniël
[Genesis 32, 30]. Striking is his statement of how in the early morning of
January 1, 1847, he struggled with his God for light and strength and
grace that he might experience God's favor. And, behold, the Lord
appeared before him with the most precious of His promises. From that
moment he was determined to carry out his plans. It may be thought that
the plan to be delivered from the obstacles first rose among the toiling
families. This was not the case, however, for Van de Luyster himself
urged these families to emigrate, a step which appeared hazardous to
them. For ten families he advanced traveling expenses, including food,
clothing, and other things needed on the journey. Further, some of the
families had fallen into debt when work was not to be had during winter
monthw. He could not bear the thought that they should leave as
bankrupt people, and so he supplied them with the money they needed
for their debts and the journey. Later, when these people had settled in
the forest and it was apparent they could earn nothing except by felling
trees on the land he had bought, they received help from the rich "banker
of the woods" [boschbankier].

The reader may perhaps form the idea that Van de Luyster was a
careless waster of the means with which the Lord richly endowed him.
But those of us who knew him are convinced not only of his readiness to
help others, but also that he was most thrifty. He taught others the lesson
of his Lord and Master that nothing must be lost. He warned people
against squandering the money he gave them. For him and his followers

this proved beneficial. Daily he sought refuge at the Fountain of all grace which gave him comfort and strength and enabled him to continue in the way he had begun. His liberality was not exhausted by these kindnesses. He bought from the state more than two sections of land in sections 9, 18, 19, and 30, and offered 20 acres, more or less, to each of the poor families he had brought from the Netherlands. In twenty years they were to repay him the original purchase price and, in addition, all incidental expenses. Those who accepted these conditions were given a bill of sale. In return they gave a promissory note the amount of which included the traveling expenses Van de Luyster had advanced for their journey. Such a note constituted a mortgage, the sum of which was five or ten times as much as the original cost of the land. This, then, was his security. In addition, he caused these people to sign a promissory note which he drew up in the Dutch language and in his own hand:

"As redeemed of the Lord we, N... N... and S... S... his wife, promise to pay Jannes van de Luyster, as soon as the Lord makes it possible for us, the sum of ... dollars, at an annual interest of seven per cent. Done at Zeeland ..., Nov. ... 1847."

Only five persons of all those who purchased land from Van de Luyster, had the courage to accept this new obligation. These five in the course of time met the terms of this noble offer. Of the others, some never paid their benefactor and treated him with ingratitude. Others, speedily claimed by death, likewise failed to make payment.

Jannes van de Luyster must be held as one of the three first heroes who established this settlement; not only did he care for the immediate circle of families he aided and rescued in so fatherly a way, but as citizen and church member he extended help according to his means and frequently beyond his means. This used up his capital, and like the rest of the exhausted pioneers many a time he had to be satisfied with johnnycake, subtute butter, and coffee made from rye. In support of this statement there is a diary, still in the possession of one of his grandchildren, in which he noted with his own hand how he cared for these families and also how he was helpful in advancing the welfare of the community.

What caused his character to shine even beautifully was the cooperation of his worthy wife who supported the acts of her noble husband with a sober Christian conscience. She was certain that her husband was moved by Christian principle. She knew what struggle he had on that New Year's morning; they too gave her courage and faith.

As elder, Van de Luyster's name had been held in respect in the Netherlands. His reputation never tarnished; his many descendants as

well as the descendants of all those he aided in their poverty will honor
him. Above all, the Lord deserves praise and thanks that He raised up
Jannes van de Luyster to be so useful an instrument. He died in the Lord,
in Zeeland on March 13, 1862, aged 67 years. "Mark the perfect man, and
behold the upright; for the end of that man is peace." [Psalms 37 : 37.]

The third leader of the emigrating group, deacon Jan Steketee, likewise
was a person of character and Christian principles. His family was one of
the three first who invaded the forest and raised their tents in Zeeland.
[The two other families were those of Christiaan den Herder and Jacobus
de Hond.] Steketee's oldest sons sought employment in Grand Rapids.
They had had the advantage of a good education in the Netherlands and
on this account made a favorable impression upon the people for whom
they worked. Because of better prospects for work, Steketee and his
family moved to Grand Rapids in 1851. Later he and his wife returned to
the settlement and spent their last years in Holland, Michigan.

Among the others who contributed to the building of Zeeland, to
mention only a few, were Johannes G. van Hees, Robbertus M. de Bruyn,
Huibert Keppel, and Arie van Bree. The first of these old settlers arrived
in Zeeland in 1848. He was a man of insight, and Christian character. He
spent his resources giving the pioneers of Zeeland work cutting down
the giants of the forest. Being a baker, his hands were unit for chopping
down trees. In Rotterdam he had served as elder, and in that capacity,
until 1862, he ably served the congregation of Zeeland. For more than
20 years, he was supervisor of Zeeland Township. Finally this pioneer
also entered his rest, in 1891.

In De Bruyn Zeeland had a citizen who answered a pressing need, the
education of its youth. He was a man of ability, proper gifts, splendid
example, modest, pious, and upright. For years he worked prayerfully
among the children of the community teaching them in the necessary
branches and in genuine Christian fashion. Finally ill health forced him
to lay down his task and he retired to Holland where after a few years he
received his crown of glory.

Concerning Huibert Keppel it is to be stated that this enterprising person
reached the high age of 93 years; he served Zeeland from the moment of
his arrival in 1848 in financial matters more effectively than any other
person. First he made a business of mnaufacturing barrel staves from oak
trees, which he shipped to Chicago, thereby providing work for people
when wages, fifty cents per day, were modest. Later, in 1871 in company
with Wopke van Haitsema and Jacob den Herder, he erected a large
grain mill in Zeeland. He served the Zeeland congregation as deacon.

Finally, because of age, he had to abandon his labors and transfer his business to his son.

The fourth of these men, Arie van Bree, was elder from 1859; until his last days he was an orrnament because his amiable character shown not only in his faith but also in his conduct.

Further, among those who helped build our business life during the first years we name George H. Baart, Klaas Smits, Johannes Busquet, and Jan Rabbers. Last named, although residing in Groningen, belonged to the congregation of Zeeland. He possessed an industrious and enterprising spirit. In company with Albert Borgers he erected a sawmill at Groningen, hampered by many difficulties. For a time this mill produced a considerable amount of lumber. But because of the weakness of the dam which repeatedly broke through when water was high the mill became useless. Thereupon he built another mill nearby, also driven by water. From lack of water this mill often was idle. When a larger mill driven by steam was erected in nearby Holland this enterprise also came to naught. Inexperience and lack of capital undoubtedly contributed to this failure. Strain and exhaustion undermined the strength of this pioneer whom death claimed in the year 1860.

Among the number of those who brought from one to three needy families to Zeeland from the Netherlands were Jan de Pree, Jan Smallgange, and Gillis Wabeke. Later there was much charitable effort to bring poor people from the Netherlands to this country. In Zeeland and elsewhere money was collected for this purpose. Names of needy families were presented by their friends in the Kolonie. Whenever enough money was collected the Classis [for this had become a church activity] cas lots. From this it is clear that in spite of difficulties, the people were confident the settlement would succeed. There were some who could not take on the labor of clearing woodland. They lacked the courage to face the hard conditions of forest life. Hence they moved to neighboring places. But most of the people perservered, encouraged by their beloved pastor Dominie van der Meulen. He inspired their spirits, especially in his Sunday sermons, and steeled their determination.

Among the factors that later contributed to the prosperity of Zeeland was the erection of a sawmill by the brothers Peter, Gerrit, and Cornelius Vijn, the laying of the tracks of the Chicago and West Michigan Railroad in 1871, the construction of a grist mill, the erection, by B. J. Veneklaasen and Sons, of a brickyard one mile west of the village, the opening of a large furniture factory, and other ventures such as a sawmill, a planing mill, a pump factory, a wagon shop, etc. Hence during the past four years of depression we have been blessed in having little poverty and misery. The most serious calamity we experienced came in the fall of 1856 when an epidemic of dysentery bore many children and a few aged people to their graves. Many other matters might be retailed, but I must limit myself, for other speakers are to follow me.

As religion colored the life of this community we must point out that here too Satan was no stranger. By all manner of deceits as in the Netherlands he sought to mislead young and old, in which unfortunately he was successful. There were dissensions and quarrels. But most of these were smoothed away by the consistories of the churches and by the Classes. The old settlers were good and pious people. One frequently heard the strains of psalms sung to the praise of God. But the minutes of the church records tell of differences due partly to varying degrees of education and partly to the diversity of the people who formed the community of Zeeland. Although the majority of the people who settled here had come from Zeeland, many had come from other provinces.

The first estrangement to be noted began in 1850 when some families in Drenthe formed a separate congregation under Dominie Roelof Smit. He also contributed to the schism in neighboring Graafschap and elsewhere in rejecting union with the Dutch Reformed Church of America, which organization for many years had been established in New York and other states. Our most prominent leaders wanted to unite with that church; but some of our brethren believed they could not do so. Although these people did not organically unite with the Christian Reformed Church in the Netherlands, they adhered strictly to the form and the principles of that group. In addition, there was the anti-Masonic movement which began in 1881, and increased the number of those who abandoned the [Dutch] Reformed Church.

Into the pro and con of this movement I shall not enter, for questions of conscience concerning matters of religion are a delicate matter. Most of the old settlers had left the fatherland because they could not worship in accordance with the dictates of their conscience. Hence I refrain from discussing the fine points of the conflict. Nor will I comment on the leaders of the movement or discuss their opponents, for each party believes it was acting on pure religious principles. But whatever may have been the chief cause of this schism [God knows how it started], it was unfortunate, and is without any prospect of being healed. The truth is that we who have lived through this schism recall it with sadness, especially when we think of the peace and unity we had in the beginning. May we say with the poet of old, "But the Lord will give deliverance"

[Psalm 42, 5, from the Dutch Psalter]. With longing we are looking forward to that hour. Today one may stand up against his brother as of old and shout, "The Lord's temple, the Lord's temple, this is the Lord's temple!" But so long as sensuality, luxury, and conformity with the ways of the world and mammon have the upper hand the strictest adherence to correct doctrine will not promote the old time humble piety. Only the warm, fruitful rain of the Spirit can save us.

Turning once more in retrospect to our common life during the first years, let me recall what was to be heard and seen in my parental home. Morning and evening we knelt in prayer, thus beginning and ending the day. Some of the settlers also opened the day with the singing of psalms. Grace was said before and thanks were given after meals. Children, on rising in the morning and also at night, were instructed to kneel and recite prayers aloud.

And when we listened to the talk of the women at their cup of coffee or tea, there too they spoke of what the Lord had done for them and of His fatherly guidance. Those were really blissful meetings. What in these later days is called "a good time," really is something very different. There were difficulties in exchanging thoughts; for example, when my beloved mother [who could speak nothing but the broad Zeeland dialect] talkes with her neighbor, the wife of our elder Harm Krans [who spoke only the Drente dialect of farmers], the two had such difficulties that they would hardly understand each other. Such too was the situation when in talking with Friesian farmers. Also, it is to be noted that difficulties were experienced among the older folk in conversation about religion. This difficulty hastened the adoption of the English language. So we all learned to speak one language, although imperfectly. Nevertheless, religious services until 1887 continued to be held exclusively in Dutch in all congregations. The only exception was in the Sunday School into which the English language early made its inroads. Nevertheless the people adhered steadfastly to the old language and to the order of religious service of our fathers. The Bible was not neglected or banned from our schools, something the faithful leadership of Robbertus M. de Bruyn would not countenance. But is was not stressed in such a manner that the school became merely a catechetical agency. For many years catechetical instruction was imparted to the children by teachers every Wednesday afternoon, from one to four o'clock. If it is thought the youth of that time were sinless angels we are mistaken. For the words of our trusted pastor Dominie van der Meulen still sound in my ears. On one occasion he struck his stick upon the bench saying, "You truly seem like so many young devils rather than angels of the children of the Covenant."

Yes, it was a struggle; lucky if it is waged against the prince of darkness, for Jesus and His Kingdom – until that glorious time when perfect peace shall be had. And for that reason, let us keep up our courage.

This day, this memorable celebration, gives us an aftertaste of our earliest and happiest times of peace and charity, under the pressure of misery. But it also gives us a foretaste of that realm of peace in which all the redeemed pilgrims, without the pressure of misery, forever will celebrate the feast of the Lamb. May that be our portion!

20. ALBERTUS G. VAN HEES' LIFE OF HIS FATHER

[The author of this sketch, born in Rotterdam April 16, 1838, on August 16, 1847 emigrated to the United States. The family arrived in Michigan on August 16, 1848, when they settled near Zeeland where Albertus died on September 13, 1891. This sketch of his father Johannes George van Hees appeared in *De Grondwet*, May 16, 1911.]

Johannes George van Hees werd geboren den 2den December 1809 in de Graaf, provincie Gelderland. Daar hij zijn vader verloor toen hij slechts vijf jaren oud was, zoo moest hij al heel vroeg voor zijn eigen onderhoud zorgen, en vertrok naar Rotterdam, toen hij vijftien jaren oud was. Eenige jaren later huwde hij met Neeltje de Vries en werd broodbakker van beroep.

Daar hij lid van het Hervormd Kerk genootschap was en niet verge-noegd was met de toenmalige toestand en de prediking der meeste leeraars, zoo sloot hij zich aan bij de Afgescheiden gemeente aldaar, die spoedig daarna door Ds. Cornelius van der Meulen bediend werd. Hij nam een actief deel in de vestiging en aanbouw van de gemeente, en als ouderling moest hij mede de vervolging van dien tijd verduren. Zelfs werd hij als bakker in zijne klandizie bekort, en omdat hij des Zondags zijn winkel niet open had, werden de glazen menigmaal stuk geworpen. Dit geschiedde terwijl de politieagenten er bij stonden te lachen. Ging hij de straat door, dan moest hij de scheldnamen van de „Nieuwlichters" verdragen.

Daar het vooruitzicht voor het arme volk in Nederland maar bang was, en zooals vader placht te zeggen, „dat het er donker uitzag voor kerk, school, en maatschappij," zoo nam hij het in ernstige overweging mede iets te doen tot bevordering van de landverhuizing naar Noord-Amerika. Hoewel hij vele emigranten met raad en daad had bijgestaan in betrekking tot het inschepen en logies te verleenen en Ds. Hendrik Pieter Scholte verscheidene vergaderingen bij vader aan huis gehouden heeft, zoo kon hij voor zichzelven nog niet besluiten.

Zes weken na de afvaart van Ds. Cornelius van der Meulen echter, besloot hij ook om met en door de leiding des Heeren de reis naar Noord Amerika te aanvaarden, en met zijn vrouw en eenige zoon, en zijn vrouws vader, Gerrit de Vries, oud 82 jaar, hun vaderland te verlaten. Zij scheepten zich in op den 16den Augustus 1847 op een walvischvaarder, genaamd de *Sabina*, met enkele andere huisgezinnen uit Zuid Holland en Utrecht. Na tien dagen gewacht te hebben te Hellevoetsluis op een gunstige wind, besloot de kapitein om uit te varen. Daar echter de noordoost wind zoo hevig opstak en ons tegen was om de Noordzee in te gaan, zoo besloot de kapitein terug te keeren; en daar hij bang was om met het havenhoofd of pier in botsing te komen, zoo liet hij de drie ankers te gelijk neder, die allen hun ketens afsnapten, zoodat we met het achterschip over het havenhoofd geslingerd werden, met dit gevolg, dat we nog vier weken te Hellevoetsluis moesten wachten naar nieuwe ankers uit Amsterdam. Na vijf en een halve week te Hellevoetsluis vertoeft te hebben, staken we eindelijk zee in.

Wij hadden verder een vlugge en voorspoedige overkomst. Daar ons schip te Sagg Harbor, Long Island, tehuis behoorde, zoo kwamen wij, na 21 dagen op zee geweest te zijn, aldaar aan. Hier werden wij over-gepakt in twee sloepen. Terwijl men hiermede bezig was, was Gerrit te zoek geraakt, daar Robbertus M. de Bruyn hem had mede genomen het land in. Maar spoedig daagden zij op met hun zakken vol met Ameri-kaansche appels. Den volgenden dag, Zondag 22 October, kwamen wij te New York aan. Van daar per stoomboot naar Albany, alwaar vader in kennis kwam met Ds. Wyckof, die twee jaren later de Kolonie bezocht en vier dagen bij vader logeerde.

Vandaar gingen wij op de kanaalboot naar Buffalo. Op deze reis moesten wij ons vele ontberingen getroosten. Den tweeden morgen bekromp moeder het hart daar het heel koud was en geen vuur aan boord, zoodat men zelfs geen warm voedsel of drinken kon krijgen. Daarop zond vader De Bruyn en Ruitenberg naar wal. Zij gingen naar een farmhuis langs het kanaal en vonden juist een ketel kokend water op de kachel, waarvoor zij een fooi op tafel legden en het mede naar de boot namen, zoodat het heele gezelschap koffie kon drinken. Na een warme kom koffie gebruikt te hebben greep moeder weer moed.

Na dertien dagen kwamen wij te Buffalo. Van daar zouden wij op een stoomboot naar Milwaukee, maar daar De Bruyn en vader niet bewillig-den om op die boot te gaan, van wege de vuile toestand, zoo werden wij ingescheept in een andere boot naar Chicago. Daar aangekomen zijnde, vernamen wij dat voormelde boot door brand was vergaan voor Milwaukee en dat slechts enkelen waren ontkomen. Hierin was des Heeren hand over ons opmerkelijk te zien.

Het was vader's doel om naar Pella, Iowa, te gaan, alwaar vele van zijn vroegere vrienden heengetrokken waren. Doch daar er geen gelegenheid was om per wagen de landreis in den winter naar Keokuk te aanvaarden, zoo moesten wij te Chicago overwinteren.

Daar vader niets te doen had, en zijne boeken nog ingepakt waren, zoodat hij ook geen leesstof had, zoo besloot hij zijn ouden vriend Ds. van der Meulen te Zeeland, in Michigan, nog eens te bezoeken en daarna verder naar Pella te gaan. Deze reis aanvaardde hij in gezelschap van Jacob Borgards, in de tweede week van Februari 1848. Ze gingen te voet en volgden de kust van Lake Michigan. De reis nam dertien dagen. Daar er nog geen brug was over de Kalamazoo rivier en het ook niet dicht bevroren was, zoo werden zij door een Indiaan in een canoe een voor een over gezet. Zij vertoefden een week in de Kolonie bij Ds. van der Meulen en Ds. van Raalte. Beiden kochten tachtig akkers land in section 3, Town Zeeland, en zoo viel het voornemen om verder naar Pella te gaan, in duigen.

De terugreis nam hen zeven dagen, over Allegan, Kalamazoo, Battle Creek, naar St. Joe en zij kwamen goed en wel, doch vermoeid, den 9den Maart bij de hunnen. Op den 3den April scheepten wij in naar Grand Haven, en van daar op de stoomboot *Daniel Ball* naar Grandville. Dewijl de weg nog ongebaand was naar de Kolonie, moesten wij te Grandville vertoeven tot 15 Augustus 1848 toen wij met drie ossenwagens de reis aannamen door het bosch, over bergen en door de swamps, zoodat het eene span ossen het andere moest helpen. Wij kwamen des avonds bij Jakob Borgards aan. Vader en moeder gingen door naar Ds. van der Meulen. Grootvader en wij overnachten aldaar en kwamen 16 Augustus te Zeeland. Dus zijn wij juist een jaar op reis geweest.

Vader had in Juni veertig akkers land gekocht nabij het dorp en een huis laten bouwen. Ook liet hij een paar akkers met wortel en tak uit-roeien, dat menig gouden willempje gekost heeft. Het dagloon was gering, een halve dollar voor een arbeider en voor een timmerman 75 centen; doch daar hij van dertig tot veertig man aan het werk had, vier of vijf maanden lang, moest hij alle week, en aardige som uitbetalen aan loon. De planken voor het huis zijn allen van Grand Haven gehaald per platboot langs de lake.

Toen vader's geld op was, moest hij zelf de hand aan den ploeg slaan en Gerrit moest de ossen drijven. Met vele ontberingen hebben mijne ouders te kampen gehad. Ook waren zij veeltijds ongesteld van wege de ongezonde lucht en dampkring, veroorzaakt door de lage landen en bosschen. Echter heb ik vader maar eens moedeloos gezien. In 1851 kwam vader met betraande oogen uit het dorp, daar hij vernomen had dat hij 52 dollars tax moest betalen, en dat bedrag niet aan hand had. Maar moeder had nog een spaarpenning en zoo brachten zij met hun beiden die som bijeen.

In het voorjaar van 1851 kwam de eekhoorn plaag, die het koren en de aardappels uit den grond haalden zoo spoedig het geplant was.

En zoo zijn wij door de bewarende en ondersteunende hand des Heeren er door gekomen.

[Translation]

Johannes George van Hees was born on December 2, 1809, in Graaf in the province of Gelderland. Having lost his father when but five, he had to care for himself and went to Rotterdam when he was fifteen. Some years later he married Neeltje de Vries, and became a baker.

He was a member of the Reformed Church, but, being dissatisfied with the doctrine of most of its pastors, joined the church of the Seceders [*Afgescheidenen*] in Rotterdam which soon there fater was served by Dominie Cornelius van der Meulen. He took an active part in the establishment and upbuilding of that congregation. As elder he had to undergo the persecution of the day. As a baker he was deprived of his clientele. And because he would not keep his shop open on Sundays his windows often were broken. This happened even while the police stood by laughing. Whenever he appeared on the street he heard the insulting epithet of "Nieuwlichter" [that is, "Newlighter"].

Because the future was dark for poor people in the Netherlands and because, as father used to say, "prospects for church, school, and society were not good" my father thought seriously of doing something to promote emigration to North America. Although he helped many emigrants with advice and other matters, particularly in securing passage and in lodging them, and although Dominie Hendrik P. Scholte held many meetings in father's house, father himself could not make any decision to emigrate.

Six weeks after Dominie van der Meulen sailed, father also decided to emigrate to North America – through God's guidance – taking with him his wife and only son and his wife's father Gerrit de Vries who was 82 years old. On August 16, 1847, they sailed in a whaler, the *Sabina*. With them were several families from Zuid-Holland and Utrecht. After waiting ten days at Hellevoetsluis for a favorable wind the captain decided to set sail. But as the northeast wind was so violent that the ship could not enter the North Sea the captain ddecided to return. Fearing he would collide with the pier he dropped the ship's three anchors, but their chains snapped, with the result that the ship's stern was thrown over the pier. We had to wait four more weeks before new anchors arrived from Amsterdam. After staying five and a half weeks in Hellevoetsluis we finally sailed out to sea.

For the rest, we had a speedy passage. After sailing 21 days our ship put in at its destination, Sagg Harbor in Long Island, where we were transferred to two sloops. While we were being transferred we lost sight of Gerrit [de Vries]. Robbertus M. de Bruyn had taken him along into the country; both soon returned with their pockets full of American apples. On the following day, Sunday October 22 [Sunday fell on October 24], we arrived in New York. Thence we went by steamboat to Albany where father met Dominie Isaac N. Wyckoff, who two years later paid the Kolonie a visit on which occasion he stayed at father's house.

From Albany we proceeded by canal boat to Buffalo. On this journey we suffered great hardship. On the second morning mother suffered from a heart attack. It was quite cold and there was no heat on board our boat and it was impossible to get warm food or drink. So father sent De Bruyn and Ruitenberg ashore. They went to a farmhouse standing by the side of the canal. Entering, they found a kettle of boiling water on the stove. They put a small sum of money on the table, took the kettle with them to the boat, and so the entire group had warm coffee whereupon mother again took courage.

In thirteen days we arrived in Buffalo. Our plan was to proceed by steamboat to Milwaukee. But as De Bruyn and my father were unwilling to take passage in the ship because of its filthy condition, we took passage in another ship bound for Chicago. On arrival we learned that the first boat had been destroyed by fire near Milwaukee and that only a few of its passengers had been spared. In this the Lord's hand was clearly visible.

It was father's intention to go to Pella, Iowa, where many of his earlier friends had gone. But as there was no opportunity to go by wagon to Keokuk, we were constrained to spend the winter in Chicago.

As father had nothing to do and because his books were not yet un- packed and he had no reading material, he decided to look up his old friend Dominie van der Meulen at Zeeland, Michigan, and after that move on to Pella. Accompanied by Jacob Borgards, he went to Michigan in the second week of February 1848. They traveled on foot, following the shore of Lake Michigan, a journey of thirteen days. At the Kalamazoo River there was no bridge, nor was the ice sufficiently thick to support them. An Indian helped them across in a canoe. They spent a week in the Kolonie, staying with Dominie van der Meulen and Dominie van Raalte. Father and Borgards each bought eighty acres of land in section 3 in the Township of Zeeland, and so the intention of going to Pella was given up.

The journey back required seven days, over Allegan, Kalamazoo, Battle Creek, to St. Joseph. Fatigued, but in good health they came back to their families, on March 9. On April 13 they took ship for Grand Haven and from there proceeded by the steamboat *Daniel Ball* to Grandville. Since there was as yet no road to the Kolonie, they had to stay in Grandville until August 15, 1848, when with three oxwagons we undertook the journey through the forest, over hills, and through swamps. Such were the difficulties of the road that each yoke of oxen had to help the others. In the evening we arrived at Jakob Borgard's. Father and mother continued on their way to Dominie van der Meulen. Grandfather and the rest of us spent the night at Borgards' and reached Zeeland on August 16. So we spent exactly one year on our journey.

Father bought forty acres of land near the village of Zeeland and built a house on it. He also had a few acres cleared root and branch, which cost many a golden guilder. Wages were low, a half dollar for a workman and 75 cents for a carpenter. But since he had 30 to 40 men working for him he paid out a considerable sum for wages. The boards for his house all were brought by flatboat from Grand Haven along the Lake.

When father's money was gone he put his hands to the plow and Gerrit [de Vries] had to drive the oxen. My parents had to contend with much hardship. Often they were ill from the unhealthy air and the mist, due to the woods and the swampy character of the country. But only once have I seen my father despondent. In 1851 he came home from the village with tear filled eyes, for he had learned that he owed $ 52 in taxes, and he could not pay. But mother had saved some money, and so they were able to produce the sum that was needed.

In the spring of 1851 came the pest of squirrels which dug the corn and potatoes out of the ground as soon as they were planted. And so, under God's protecting and supporting hand, we had our measure of success.

21. HENDRIK BRINKS'
BRIEF LIFE SKETCH OF ROELOF BRINKS

[Roelof Brinks emigrated from Noord Barge in Drente in 1846, settled near Zeeland in 1878, moved to Sioux County, Iowa, and in 1883 to Harrison, South Dakota. This sketch, written by his son Hendrik was published in *De Grondwet*, February 6, 1912, where it bears the title *Korte Levensgeschiedenis van Roelof Brinks.*]

Roelof Brinks werd geboren te Noord Barge, gemeente Emmen, provincie Drente, Nederland, in het jaar 1820. In het jaar 1846 verliet hij zijn vaderland en ging in gezelschap van vele landgenooten naar Noord Amerika. Aan boord ziek geworden zijnde, moest hij te Buffalo, New York, in het hospitaal achterblijven. Na een tijd van vier maanden daar te hebben doorgebracht, werd het hem door Gods goedheid vergund om het hospitaal te verlaten. Nog zwak zijnde sukkelde hij de country in om werk te zoeken. Hij vond een farmer, die iemand noodig had om te ploegen. De boer spande de paarden voor de ploeg en hield zelf de lijnen, terwijl vader de ploeg hield. Na een keer rond gekomen te zijn gaf de boer ook de lijnen aan den „green Dutchman". Een broeder van den boer, die aan de andere kant van de fence aan het ploegen was, zei: „Them horses will give him...." [een dik woord], maar dat kwam anders uit. Door de frissche voorjaarslucht werkte de natuur mede om de krachten op te bouwen en de sterken.

Na daar eenige maanden te hebben doorgebracht, nam vader het besluit om zijne vrienden in Michigan te bezoeken, en als ik het wel heb, was het Johannes G. van Hees die hem $ 100 leende om 80 akkers land te koopen, dat was toen de prijs van 80 akkers. Vader kocht 80 akkers ten oosten van Zeeland, in sectie 20.

Daarna kwam hij in kennis met Jantje Hulst van West Drenthe, toen ter tijde „Staatsland" genaamd, en den 15den Juni 1848 werden zij in den echt verbonden door Ds. Cornelius van der Meulen te Zeeland. Zij gingen op hun land wonen en scharrelden er langzaam vooruit. Het werk bestond meestal uit boomen te vellen en hun land op te clearen.

Na twee à drie jaar op het land te hebben doorgebracht, kreeg vader een aanbod om te Millpoint [nu Spring Lake] als foreman op te treden in een log kamp en moeder als kok. Dat scheen hun goed toe om wat geld te verdienen en zoodoende hun schuld aan Mr. van Hees af te betalen, maar och wat eene teleurstelling stond hun te wachten! Moeder werd aangetast door de driedaagsche koorts, zooals men die ziekte toen noemde. Zij keerden toen naar hun ouders in de Kolonie terug, doch op reis daarheen begon ook vader aan diezelfde ziekte te lijden en sukkelde daaraan een geheel jaar.

De armoede die nu heerschte was vreeselijk; ik weet nog goed, dat men moeder vroeg om brood, maar er was niets in huis. Vader moest in den zomer naar Kalamazoo om in den oogsttijd wat te verdienen, ook om

$ 7 interest voor de $ 100 schuld te betalen. Maar later kwam er wat ver-ademing; toen begon Johannes Busquet en later ook Huibert Keppel, staven te koopen en daar heeft vader veel geld mee gemaakt.

Toen kwam er in 1858 een vreeselijke ziekte onder de kinderen en ook onder sommige oude menschen, en zij hebben toen binnen 24 uren 3 kinderen verloren. Moeder en ik lagen ook aan den oever des doods; vader alleen bleef gespaard.

Ik zou er nog veel meer van kunnen zeggen, en hoe Mr. Roozenraad door Gods goedheid hen in hun armoede heeft geholpen. Moeder zei, dat ze dat nooit zou vergeten.

In het jaar 1878 zijn zij met hun huisgezin naar Sioux County, Iowa, vertrokken en in het jaar 1883 hebben zij zich metterwoon gevestigd in Douglas County, Zuid Dakota, nabij Harrison, waaronze ouders zijn ontslapen en de zalige rust zijn ingegaan.

[Translation]

Roelof Brinks was born in 1820 at Noord Barge, in the parish of Emmen, province of Drente in the Netherlands. Accompanied by many fellow citizens he left his fatherland in 1846 and emigrated to North America. He fell sick while on his voyage and was forced to stay in a hospital in Buffalo, New York. After three or four months' illness he was permitted by God's goodness to leave the hospital. Weak in body from his long confinement he wandered about the countryside looking for work. He found a farmer who needed a man for plowing. The farmer hitched his horses to the plow and held the reins while my father guided the plow. After driving his team around the field once, the farmer gave the reins to the "green Dutchman". The farmer's brother who was plowing on the other side of the fence which separated them remarked, "Them horses will give him...." [an ugly word], but the outcome was far different. Fresh spring air and nature cooperated in restoring his strength.

After spending several months at this kind of work, father decided to look up his friends in Michigan. If I recall correctly it was Johannes G. van Hees who loaned him $ 100 with which to purchase 80 acres of land. [This sum was the total cost of this land.] The property father bought lay in section 20, east of Zeeland.

Thereafter he became acquainted with Jantje Hulst from West Drenthe, at that time known as "Statesland", [this was Staphorst] and on June 15, 1848, they were married by Dominie C. van der Meulen. They moved onto their land and gradually forged ahead. Their work consisted mostly in felling trees and clearing the ground.

After spending three or four years on their farm father received an offer to serve as foreman in a logging camp at Mill Point [now known as Spring Lake]. Mother was to serve as cook. This seemed a good opportunity to earn some money and pay off their debt to Mr. van Hees. But what disappointment there was in store for them! Mother fell sick of the three day fever, as this malady then was called. They returned to her parents in the Kolonie, but on the journey father also came down with the same illness and suffered from it for an entire year.

The poverty which reigned was dreadful. I recall very clearly that when we asked mother for bread there was none in the house. Father went to Kalamazoo in the summer in order to earn some money during harvest time. He had to pay $ 7 interest on the $ 100 debt he owed. But later we breathed more easily, for then Johannes Busquet and later also Huibert Keppel began to buy barrel staves. Father made much money selling staves.

Then in 1858 a terrible mortality appeared among the children and also among some of the older folk. My parents during that time lost three children within 24 hours. Mother and I lay at the brink of death. Father alone was spared.

I could relate many more matters, especially how Mr. Roosenraad through God's goodness helped them in their poverty. Mother said she would never forget this.

In 1878 my parents and their children moved to Sioux County, Iowa. Later, in 1883, they established themselves in Douglas County, South Dakota, near Harrison. There our parents passed away and entered into their blessed rest.

22. SIETZE BOS' OUR FIRST SETTLEMENT

[This autobiographical sketch entitled *Onze Eerste Nederzetting* which appeared in *De Grondwet*, January 24, 1911, presents much information about the settlement at Zeeland and other places in the Dutch *Kolonie* of Michigan.]

Ofschoon ondergeteekende beter met boerengereedschappen dan met de pen weet om te gaan, heeft hij toch eindelijk toegegeven aan het verzoek van vrienden, om eens in een korte schets te vertellen, wat mij en die met mij betrokkenen, bij onze komst in dit land zoo al is wedervaren. Misschien is het niet onaangenaam voor oude settlers, nog eens aan die kommervolle dagen te worden herinnerd, en het zal voor latere settlers zeker geen kwaad kunnen te vernemen hoe de eersten hebben moeten zwoegen om te komen waar ze nu zijn. Het staat te vreezen, dat de weelde van heden, bij de uitkomst minder voordeelig zal zijn, dan wel de bekrompenheid van ons begin.

In het jaar 1847 ging een van mijne vrienden scheep om naar Noord America te vertrekken. Ik had er veel onder te doen; maar wist niet wat er van te zeggen. Na veel peinzen en gedurige gesprekken met hem, zeide ik eindelijk: „Welnu, als het Gods wil moge zijn, dan hoop ik het volgende jaar ook bij u te komen." „Dat hoop ik," sprak mijn vriend Bartel van Dijk. Hij vertrok en ik bleef, als boerenknecht van 20 jarigen ouderdom, met een slecht vooruitzicht in de toekomst. Die toestand en mijne halfgegevene belofte veroorzaakten mij veelvuldige gedachten in dat jaar.

Hoe bedenkelijk zulk eene onderneming ook zij, toch kwamen wij gereed en vertrok ik met mijne ouders, twee broeders en eene zuster in het jaar 1848. De landverhuizing was toen echter eene geheel andere zaak dan wel nu. Wij vertrokken den 18den Maart naar Amsterdam, waar wij moesten blijven tot den eersten April. Vandaar gingen wij naar Den Helder en die tocht geschiedde met 36 paarden. Dat was een aardig gezicht! Als ik het wel heb, was dat een afstand van 36 uren, dien wij in drie dagen aflegden.

Den 6den April gingen wij in zee. Nu had ik gelegenheid om Gods machtigen arm te zien, op eene geheel andere wijze dan wel vroeger op het land. Veel zuchten werden er geloosd en veel gebeden opgezonden, dat God ons in de begeerde haven mocht brengen.

Dat gebeurde dan ook in den tijd van 42 dagen. Den 18den Mei 1848 waren wij te New York. Er was vreugde dat wij aan den vasten wal waren, maar ook droefheid ontbrak er niet, want een zevental had het tijdelijke met het eeuwige verwisseld. Wij vertoefden daar een dag en gingen toen met eene stoomboot naar Albany. Daar aangekomen in den morgen, moesten wij al weer aan het overpakken in een kanaalboot, die door twee paarden getrokken werd en die ons in 13 dagen naar Buffalo bracht; maar dat was een levendje vol ellende.

Den 1sten Juni te Buffalo aangekomen, gingen wij over in eene groote stoomboot, die ons in vier dagen over de Lake Michigan naar Chicago bracht. Daar aan wal gezet, waren wij echter nóg niet in de Kolonie Holland waarheen men ons brengen zou. Na twee dagen daar stil te zijn geweest, gingen wij met een zeilschip naar Grand Haven; doch tóch ook dat was nog geen Holland. Van Grand Haven gingen wij weer in een schip naar Holland; maar dat was een verschrikkelijke reis. De schepelingen geleken meer op duivels dan op menschen en het weer was zeer ruw. Als ik aan die reis denk, gaat mij nog een koude rilling over de leden. Ik geloof niet dat ik ooit meer gezucht en gebeden heb dan toen, dat God die ons tot zoo ver gebracht had ons toch nu niet aan de golven mocht prijs geven.

Eindelijk kwamen wij aan de kust van Holland, maar nu kon het schip niet aan wal komen; dus, alweer nieuwe ellenden. Hieruit werden wij gered, doordien Koo Vinke ons met een platboot te hulp kwam. Ik moet u tusschen beiden zeggen, dat gij u geen al te groote gedachten van die platboot moet maken; want het waren maar eenige balken en daar wat posten dwars over gelegd. Nu ging het aan een overgooien van het schip op de platboot, op eene zoo ruwe manier, dat men het niet zonder huivering kon aanzien. Doch, hoe het ook ging, wij kwamen goed en wel te Holland aan den wal. Ons eerste logies was een hok, 6 mijlen van de stad Holland, waarheen Koo Vinke ons den volgenden morgen zou vervoeren gelijk hij dan ook deed.

Weldra werden wij opgezocht door Bartel van Dijk, die een jaar voor ons vertrokken was, zooals boven gemeld is. Die ontmoeting was eene blijde verrassing, te meer nog, omdat wij in den jongsten tijd in zulk een vreemd en ellendig gezelschap hadden verkeerd. Van Dijk bracht ons naar zijn huis, dat een uur van Holland verwijderd was. Deze vriend had, zoo ik meen, toen twee stoelen en een kist tot tafel en een klein huisje, zoodat wij op den vloer moesten slapen; doch dat was toen al heel goed ook.

Ik ga met mijn verhaal een stap terug. Toen wij in Holland kwamen, vroeg iemand van ons nieuw gezelschap: „Waar is de stad Holland?" „Wel", werd er geantwoord, „Gij zijt er midden in." De antwoorder heeft daarbij zeker gedacht: „Gij zijt midden in het bosch, waar men eene stad hoopt te bouwen, met den naam van Holland." Althans het was rondom zwaar bosch, en in het midden daarvan stond eene smitswerkplaats, die uit wat palen en bast van boomen was samengesteld. Wat wij er over dachten, dat men in Amerika aan zulk eene woeste plaats de naam van „stad" gaf, louter op grond dat men dacht er eene te zullen komen, kunt gij wellicht beter gevoelen, dan door mij gezegd zou kunnen worden.

Wij keeren tot ons verhaal terug. Toen wij bij Van Dijk waren, moesten onze kisten gehaald worden. Gelukkig was er in de nabijheid een boer, die een wagen en een paar ossen had en die ging er met ons op los. Dat ging er echter vreemd door. Het ging over hoogten en laagten, over heuvels en dalen, over omgevallen boomstammen en door waterpoelen heen. Wij hadden nu wel vooreerst onderdak; maar goede raad was toch duur, omtrent onze verdere toekomst. Wij hadden geen geld en geen werk en alzoo den donkersten nacht voor oogen.

Wij gingen naar Ds. van Raalte en die dacht, dat wij maar naar de stad moesten gaan, om daar den bast van de boomen te halen, als waarmede een man zoowat 50 cents per dag kon verdienen. Toen wij terug kwamen, ontmoetten wij echter een boer, Harm Brinks, die wilde wel wat bosch neer hebben. Wij geraakten met hem in accoord en werkten twee dagen voor hem. Toen kwam Marling van wat men toen Zeeland noemde. Deze broeder zeide tot ons, dat wij land moesten koopen. Dat klonk ons natuurlijk vreemd in de ooren: wel schuld, maar geen eten en geen geld, en dan nog praten van land te koopen! Marling wist ons echter te vertellen dat Van Hees, van Grandville, ons wel 40 acres zou willen verkoopen op de voorwaarde, dat wij er op bouwden en de interest betaalden. Er waren nog twee meer zonder geld: Jan Bos, mijn neef en Jan Lamer, en benevens dezen Jan Vork, Klaas Hofman, en Derk Kok, doch deze laatste drie hadden wat geld.

Wij begaven ons echter allereerst naar Ds. C. van der Meulen, die destijds op Zeeland woonde en er een jaar geweest was. Wij gingen met ons vijven: ik, Jan Vork, Klaas Hofman, Jan Bos, en Jan Lamer vonden ZEw wel te spreken. Hij was blijde dat er meer nieuwe landverhuizers waren. Hij ging den volgenden dag met ons het bosch in, om dat te bezien en drongen 4 à 5 mijlen daarin door. Op eenen afstand van 4 mijlen ontmoetten wij het huisgezin van Jacob Borgers, wonende in een huis van wat stokken en eenige planken. Hij had vier weken daar gewoond en men was heel wel te moede. Zulke ontmoetingen geven troost in de ellenden; want ik verzeker u, dat het eene moedbenemende bezigheid is, met zulk eene donkere toekomst voor oogen, door het bosch, over bergen en door zwampen te sukkelen, zonder te weten, of onze beslissing ten goede of ten kwade zal zijn. Waarlijk het was eene wonderbare beschikking van God, die allen moed gaf. Er waren eenigen met geld, maar de meesten waren arm. En toch hoorde men niemand klagen, maar hoe ellendig het er ook bij stond, steeds was men blijde. Men zong Psalmen in dien nacht van jammer en ellende.

Wij gingen dan naar Zeeland terug en den volgenden morgen gingen wij met ons vieren op reis naar Granville, n.l.: Marling, J. Bos, J. Lamer, en ik. Dat was een afstand van misschien 20 mijlen, en al bosch. Op drie mijlen afstands vandaar, kwamen wij bij een Amerikaanschen boer en dezulken vonden wij er zes. Eindelijk kwamen wij te Grandville bij Van Hees, waar wij den nacht overbleven in een goed huis en sliepen voor het eerst op een goed bed. Doch het was maar voor eenen nacht. Wij kochten echter 40 akkers land van hem, gelegen op zoowat drie mijlen afstands van Zeeland; maar wat moesten wij nu met die 40 acres zwaar bosch? Wij waren zoo pas uit Nederland gekomen en aan geen boomkappen gewoon; maar moeten is ook wat. Ik en mijne broeders waren nog jong, maar onze vader was oud en versleten; zoo moesten wij met ons drieën er op af.

Ons eerste werk was, dat wij stokken of palen in den grond zetten, bast van boomen er om toedekten en bladeren opraapten voor ons leger, en klaar was ons huis. Nu aan het kappen, maar dat ging raar. De eene boom viel zus en de andere zoo. Toen wij twee à drie dagen bezig waren geweest, kwam mijn jongste broer onder een omvallende boom en kreeg de heup uit het lid. Daar lag hij, hij trok het haar uit het hoofd, van wege de pijn. Wij hadden geen dokter en geen mensch ter hulpe, dan neef Bos. Er werd besloten dat ik vader en moeder zou halen, om op onzen broeder te passen; en dat gebeurde, al viel het moeielijk.

Op onze reis van drie mijlen, die wij met onze ouders moesten maken door het wilde bosch, woonde er zoo hier en daar een op dezelfde wijze als wij. Het gebeurde zelfs dat wij ze hoorden Psalmen zingen, eer wij wisten dat er iemand in de nabijheid woonde. Trouwens, dat ging in die dagen zoo gemakkelijk dat wij, alleen door het bosch gaande, gedurig zingende of biddende: „Heere, wat wilt Gij dat ik doen zal?" onzen weg voortzetten. Wij waren dikwijls in groot gevaar van te verdwalen, daarom droegen wij eene bijl mede, om een merk aan de boomen te maken, om het pad weer terug te kunnen vinden.

Zoo kwam ik dan ook met vader en moeder terug, tot de 40 acres, die wij bezig waren voor den landbouw in gereedheid te brengen. Wij hadden echter nog geen ander huis, dan dat wij voor ons drieën hadden opgericht en mijn broer Machiel lag op ons bed van boombladeren. Er moest nu allereerst een betere woning komen en ja wel, wij deden als zoowat iedereen: wij zetten een klein huisje van boomstammen, en toen die op elkander lagen, was er een Mr. van Buren, die hier al een jaar geweest was, deze moest het maar verder voor ons afwerken.

Nu was ons huisje klaar, maar er moest wat verdiend worden ook. Wij gingen met ons drieën op Grand Rapids los; ik, mijn oudste broer en mijn neef, die hier al een jaar geweest was. Mijne ouders bleven bij mijn jongsten broer in huis. Grand Rapids was toen een dorp en verdiende nog volstrekt den naam niet van eene stad. Daar aangekomen, waren wij alweer niet weinig verlegen, omdat wij geen Engelsch verstonden. Wij kwamen dan aan het kanaal, waar sommigen bezig waren aan het werk. Gelukkig was daarbij een voor ons onbekenden Hollander. Wij vroegen hem of hij ook werk voor ons wist; doch wij kregen weinig inlichting, maar hij verwees ons naar Jan Roost, bij een wagenmaker. Jan Roost gezocht en gevonden hebbende, verwees ons naar Frans van Driele die aan het kanaal werkte. Toen wij hem zeiden dat Roost ons tot hem had gezonden, vroeg hij wat wij geleerd hadden, en na van ons verstaan te hebben dat wij boerenknechts waren geweest, oordeelde hij dat wij naar Willem Lageweg moesten gaan, het eenigste Hollandsche huisgezin,dat wij daar dezen nacht moesten blijven en dan bij een boer zien te komen. Zoo gezegd zoo gedaan. Bij Lageweg onderrichtte men ons, waar boeren woonden en als wij geen werk konden krijgen, dan konden wij maar weer terug komen.

Welnu, den volgenden morgen gingen wij aan den loop, en toen wij omtrent eene halve mijl hadden afgelegd, verhuurde zich mijn broer voor $ 10 in de maand. Mijn neef en ik kregen drie mijlen verder ook werk tegen 75 cents per dag. Toen wij daar drie weken gearbeid en gedaan hadden, ging ik en mijn neef weer werk zoeken bij een ander. Ook gelukte dat. Mijn neef bedong $ 11 in de maand en ik verhuurde mij weer voor 75 cents per dag. Drie dagen later kwam de boer van mijn neef mij de boodschap brengen, dat mijn neef ziek was en dat ik komen moest. Ik ging aanstonds en het was 9 uur des avonds. Zoodra ik hem zag, begreep ik, dat hij spoedig het tijdelijke met het eeuwige zou verwisselen. Na nog een weinig met hem gesproken te hebben, stierf hij reeds om 1 uur en te 2 uur ging ik op reis naar Zeeland, waar zijn broer woonde, want hij zou den volgenden dag ter aarde besteld worden.

Des morgens te 4 uur was ik weer bij het dichte bosch, en zoo als ik daar in kwam, hoorde ik ietwat in beweging, waardoor ik niet weinig verschrikte. Ik wist immers dat hier allerlei wild toehield, als: beeren, wolven, herten, wilde katten, slangen en wat niet al? en, in de klauwen van ongedierte te vervallen, dat deed mij natuurlijk huiveren. Wat er op dat oogenblik in mij omging, kan ik niet beschrijven. Toen ik dan van den schrik bekomen was, vernemende dat het twee herten waren, reisde ik voort onder aanbeveling van mijn lot aan den Heere. Ik kwam dan ook goed en wel te huis, tegen den middag. Ik trof mijne ouders aan in ons nieuwe huis, dat nu klaar was en zij waren in het gebed vóór het middag eten. Er vloeiden tranen van vreugde toen wij elkaar ontmoetten.

Nu ging het aan een vragen en vertellen, en daar ik nog al goeden moed had, werden mijne ouders verblijd. Ik had voorts nog de treurmare van het overlijden van mijn neef aan zijnen broeder te brengen, en den volgenden morgen ging ik met hem op reis, om zijn broer ter aarde te bestellen. Al zulke dingen zijn veel erger in den vreemde, dan daar, waar men te huis is, doch zij dringen ook sterk om zich met al zijne nooden naar God te wenden. Gelukkig als men den weg heeft leeren kennen, waarlangs men tot Hem kan komen.

Mijn neef en ik kwamen goed en wel aan het sterfhuis. Het huis was vol, met een leeraar uit Grand Rapids in het midden. Maar het was alles Engelsch. Hollanders waren daar nog niet dan mijn broer Jan. Wij konden dus zien hoe zij deden, maar verstonden niet wat zij zeiden.

Na de begrafenis verhuurde ik mij bij dien boer voor $ 11 per maand, en omtrent vijf weken later, gingen mijn broer en ik weer naar huis, om onze families te bezoeken. Die reis deden wij op een Zaterdag en des Zondags gingen wij naar Zeeland ter kerk, waar Ds. C. van der Meulen toen stond. Dat deed ons goed. Wij gevoelden ons weer als te huis; want rond Grand Rapids gingen wij naar geene kerk, omdat wij er niets van verstonden. Zoo vaak als wij daar bij elkander waren, gingen wij in de schaduw der boomen wat lezen en zingen met elkander.

Den volgenden zomer ging het echter beter. Er kwamen telkens meer Hollanders en nu begon Frans van Driele des Zondags te lezen, terwijl zoowat om de maand Ds. van Raalte, van Holland, of Ds. van der Meulen, van Zeeland, of Ds. Ypma van Vriesland, kwamen prediken.

Ik keer met mijn verhaal naar huis terug. Wij hadden wat geld verdiend en dat kwam goed te pas, want wij hadden een huisje, maar nog geen huisraad. Allereerst kochten wij twee stoelen en, des Maandags, keerde ik met mijn broeder weer terug naar Grand Rapids, om wat te verdienen, blijde en goedsmoeds. Toen wij een volgende keer terug kwamen – want wij gingen om de vijf weken ons geld naar huis brengen en de familie bezoeken – had men te huis een kachel gekocht en een paar zitbanken gemaakt, en klaar was nu de huishouding.

Het had echter moeite gegeven, om die kachel te huis te krijgen. Ossen waren daar niet en alzoo moest men de kachel twee mijl dragen. Dat was erg, maar er was geen andere gelegenheid. Mijne moeder en zuster gingen er daarom ook op los, om te doen, wat een paar sterke mannen geen kleinigheid genoemd zouden hebben. En ja wel, zij brachten de kachel aan een paar stokken goed en wel te huis. Zoo men dat thans van eene moeder en dochter durfde vragen, zou men al voor heel ontaard worden aangezien. Daar viel ook nog op die reis een dubbel bewijs van Goddelijke zorg waar te nemen. Wat dat was? Toen moeder en zuster de kachel naar huis droegen, liep er een zwarte beer voor hen op het pad, zonder dat zij er door verschrikt werden, want zij kenden toen nog geene beeren.

[Translation]

The undersigned, knowing better how to handle farmers' tools than to hold a pen, nevertheless has yielded to the request of friends to tell in a short sketch what we and those with us experienced when we first came to America. Probably it is not unpleasant for old settlers to be reminded of the distressing times gone by, nor can it do later settlers any harm to hear how the earliest settlers have had to labor like slaves in order that later settlers have come to be what they now are. We fear that the luxury of the present in final reckoning will be less of an advantage perhaps than the poverty of our beginning.

In 1847 one of my friends boarded ship for North America. His departure moved me, but I did not know what to think of it. After much reflection and repeated conversation with him, I finally remarked, "Well, if it may be God's will, I hope to be with you next year." "That also is my hope," replied my friend Bartel van Dijk. He departed, but I stayed – a farmer's helper, twenty years of age, and with slight prospects for the future. This condition and my half-made promise caused me to think about emigration many times that year.

However hazardous such an undertaking might appear, we finally got ready, and in 1848 I departed with my parents, two brothers, and one sister. In those days emigration was a very different matter from what it now is, however. On March 18 we left for Amsterdam where we were forced to wait until April 1. Next we went to Den Helder, our ship being drawn by 36 horses. That was an interesting spectacle. If I recall correctly, that was a distance of 36 hours, which we made in three days.

On April 6 we sailed. Now I had occasion to see God's mighty arm, in a manner very different from formerly on land. Many were the sighs uttered, the prayers offered that God would bring us to our desired destination. And this was granted us in the space of 42 days. On May 18, 1848, we were in New York. We were happy to stand on firm ground, but there also was sadness, for seven of our group had exchanged their temporal lot with their eternal. After spending a few days there we proceeded by steamboat to Albany. We arrived there in the morning, and we had to transfer our baggage into a canalboat drawn by two horses which brought us to Buffalo. But that was an experience full of hardship.

On June 1 we arrived in Buffalo, and there boarded a large steamship which in four days carried us by way of Lake Michigan to Chicago. There we were landed, but we were not yet in the Kolonie of Holland to which they had contracted to take us. After waiting two days in Chicago we proceeded by sailing ship to Grand Haven, but we were not yet in Holland. At Grand Haven we again boarded a ship, this time for Holland. That was a dreadful voyage. The sailors acted more like devils than human beings, and, besides, the weather was rough. Whenever I think of that voyage cold chills run down my back. I believe that I have never sighed and prayed more than at that time, that God who had brought us so far would not let us become the victims of the waves.

Finally we arrived at the harbor of Holland, but our ship could not make land, and so there were new problems. We were delivered from them by Koo Vinke who came to get us in his flatboat. You must not form too favorable a notion concerning that flatboat, for it was made of a few beams with some poles laid upon them crosswise. They began to throw our bagage from the ship upon the flatboat and in so rough a manner that one could not watch without shuddering. But, no matter how rough all this was, we finally stepped ashore in Holland. Our first lodging was a rude structure, six miles from Holland to which Koo Vinke took us on the following day.

Soon Bartel van Dijk looked us up. As related above, he had immigrated the year before. Our meeting was a happy surprise, especially because during recent months as we had lived in so strange and miserable a society. Van Dijk took us to his house, an hour's distance from Holland. This friend, as I recall, had two chairs, a box which served as a table, and a small house. We had to sleep on the floor, but that seemed good to us.

Now I retrace my steps for a bit. When we arrived in Holland someone of our company asked, "Where is the 'stad' Holland?" "Well," came the answer, "you are in the midst of it." That person no doubt thought, "You are in the midst of a forest where, it is hoped, a city named Holland will be built." On every hand we saw dense woods, and in the midst of it there stood a smith's place of work made of poles and bark of trees. What we thought of the idea that people in America gave the name of "city" to such a waste place, purely on the ground that they hoped to build one – you readily can imagine better than I can express in words.

We now return to the theme of this account. One thing to be done when we were staying with Van Dijk was to have our boxes taken to his house. Fortunately there was a farmer nearby who had a wagon and a yoke of oxen and who set out with us. That was a curious trip. We jogged over elevations and holes, up hill and down, over logs and through pools of water. Of course, for the time being, we had a roof; but it was not easy to find good advice concerning our future. We had no money and no work, and we faced a most uncertain prospect.

We went to consult Dominie van Raalte, who was of the opinion that we should go to the "stad" to peel bark which would bring us 50 cents per day. On our return we met a farmer, Harm Brinks, who wanted to have some of his woods felled. We came to an agreement, and worked two days for him. Then came Marling from what at that time was called Zeeland, who advised us to buy some land. Naturally that sounded like strange advice: debt, nothing to eat, no money, and talking about buying land! Marling knew that Van Hees, in Grandville, would sell us 40 acres on condition that we would build on it and pay interest. There were two other men also without money, Jan Bos my cousin, and Jan Lamer. Besides these, there were Jan Vork, Klaas Hofman, and Derk Kok, who had some money.

We first went to see Dominie van der Meulen in Zeeland where he had been living a year. The five of us called on him – I, Jan Vork, Klaas Hoffman, Jan Bos, and Jan Lamer – and found him in a talking mood. He was pleased that there were new immigrants. The following day he went into the forest with us as deep as four or five miles. At a distance of four miles we met the family of Jacob Borgers living in a house made of some sticks and a few boards. After living there four weeks he was pretty well fagged out. I can assure you that it was discouraging, having only a dark prospect before us, to clamber over hills and wade through swamps without knowing whether our decisions would turn out well or otherwise.

We returned to Zeeland and the following morning four of us, Marling, Jan Bos, Jan Lamer, and I, went to Grandville. That was a distance of perhaps 20 miles and entirely through the forest. Three miles from Grandville we found an American farmer. We found six such farmers in all. Finally, we arrived at Van Hees' in Grandville where we spent the night in a good house and where for the first time we slept in a good bed. But that was only for one night. However, we bought 40 acres of land from him, about three miles from Zeeland. But what were we to do with these 40 acres which were covered with heavy timber? We had only recently come from the Netherlands and were not accustomed to chopping down trees. But something had to be done. My brothers and I were young but our father was advanced in years and worn out. So the three of us went to work.

Our first task was to place sticks in the ground, cover them with the bark of trees, and gather leaves for our beds – and our house was ready. Then we began chopping; but not with skill. One tree fell this way, another fell that way. After we had been occupied in this manner for two or three days my youngest brother was caught under a falling tree and dislocated his hip. He lay on the ground pulling his hair from his head on account of the pain. We had no doctor, not a person to help us other than our cousin Jan Bos. We decided to get father and mother to take care of our brother. This was accomplished, but with difficulty.

Along the three-mile trail through the dense forest which we and our parents traveled there were some people living in the same manner as ours'. We heard them singing psalms before we realized anyone was living nearby. That was a common occurrence those days. For we often plodded alone in the forest singing or praying, "Lord, what wilt Thou that I do?" [Luke 18, 41]. We often were in great danger of getting lost. To prevent this we always carried an axe with which to blaze trees. This enabled us to find our path if perchance we lost it.

Finally father, mother, and I returned to the 40 acres we had been busily engaged in getting ready for farming. We still had the house the three of us had constructed, and my brother Machiel lay sick abed. First of all, a better house had to be built. Like most other settlers we erected one of logs. After we had put them in their place Mr. van Buren who had lived here [in the Kolonie] for a year was given the task of finishing the house.

It was not enough that our house was finished; we had to earn some money. Three of us went to Grand Rapids – I, my oldest brother, and my cousin who had come here a year ago. My parents stayed at home with my youngest brother. At that time Grand Rapids was only a village and in no way deserved to be called a city. Arrived there we were embarrassed, for we could not understand English. We went to the canal where some men were busy working. Fortunately among them was a Hollander whom we did not know, however. We asked him if he knew where we could find work. He could not give us any information, but directed us to Jan Roost who was working for a wagonmaker. Jan Roost sent us to Frans van Driele who also was employed at the canal. When we told him that Roost had sent us, Van Driele asked us what work we could do, and learning that we were farmer's hands, judged it would be best for us to go to Willem Lageweg, the only Dutch family nearby. We could stay with Lageweg for the night after which we should try to find work on a farm. Lageweg showed us where farmers were living and told us that if we found no work we could come back to him.

The following morning we went on our way, and after traveling about a half mile my brother obtained work at $ 10 a month. Three miles further my cousin and I also found work at 75 cents a day each. After working there three weeks my cousin and I began searching for other work, and we succeeded. My cousin asked for $ 11 a month and I again was offered 75 cents per day. Three days later the farmer for whom my cousin was working came to tell me that my cousin was ill and that I had to come and see him. I left at once; it was nine o'clock in the evening. As soon as I saw him I knew he was about to die. After speaking with him, he passed away at one o'clock. At two I left to go to Zeeland where my brother was living, for my cousin was to be buried on the next day.

At four o'clock in the morning I arrived at the dense forest. I heard some noise, something was moving, and I became frightened. For I knew all kinds of wild animals lived here – bears, wolves, deer, wildcats, snakes, and what not. The thought of falling into the clutches of wild animals made me shudder. I can scarcely describe my thoughts at that moment. When I overcame my fright I noticed that the moving animals were two deer, and I went on, after recommending myself to God's care. Toward midday I arrived home. My parents were in their new house which now was finished. They were sitting at table saying grace before eating. Tears of joy flowed when we saw each other.

Questions and answers followed; and as I gave evidence of courage, my parents were happy. I also had the duty of bringing the sad news of my cousin's death to his brother. The following day accompanied by the latter, I went on my way to help bury his brother. All such experiences are much sadder in a foreign land than at home. But they also induce us to turn to God in such moments when we need Him. Fortunate is the man who has learned the way by which he can go to Him.

My cousin and I finally arrived at the house where his brother had died. The house was full of people and a minister had come from Grand Rapids. But the services were entirely in English. There were no Hollanders there but my brother John. We could indeed see what the people were doing, but we understood nothing of what they were saying.

After the funeral I again found work, this time at $ 11 per month. Five weeks later my brother and I went to see our family. This was on a Saturday. The next day Sunday we went to church in Zeeland where Dominie van der Meulen was preaching. That proved to be an inspiration. We felt as if we were at home. For at Grand Rapids we went to no church because we could not follow the services. As often as we met we sat down together in the shadow of the trees in order to read and sing.

The following summer we got along better. Hollanders were constantly arriving [in Grand Rapids]. Frans van Driele read sermons on Sundays. About once a month Dominie van Raalte from Holland, or Dominie van der Meulen from Zeeland, or Dominie Ypma from Vriesland came to preach for us.

And now I turn my attention to home. We had earned a little money, something useful, but although we had a house, we had no furniture.

First we bought two chairs. On Monday my brother and I returned to Grand Rapids to earn something, happy and full of good cheer. On one occasion when we returned to our parents – we did this about every five weeks to take our money home and to visit the family – we found they had bought a stove and had made a couple of benches and so our house-keeping was in order.

They had had difficulty, however, in getting the stove home. They had no oxen, and so they were forced to carry the stove a distance of two miles. That was a hard task, but there was no other solution. My mother and sister decided to do this job, something a couple strong men would think only a trifle. They put the stove on a pair of poles and so brought it home. If we would ask a mother or a daughter to do something like that today we would be considered quite inhuman. On mother's and sister's trip to get the stove there was a doubly obvious proof of God's marvelous care. What was this? When mother and sister were carrying the stove howeward, a black bear ran across the path in front of them. But they were not alarmed, since they were unaware that bears could be dangerous.

23. CORNELIUS VAN LOO'S
ZEELAND TOWNSHIP AND VILLAGE

[The author published this sketch of the early history of Zeeland and the township by tha. name in the *Historical and Business Compendium of Ottawa County, Michigan*, Vol. I (1892) Van Loo, originally from Driewegen on the island of Zuid-Beveland, settled in Zeeland during its first days and was prominently associated with the business activities and public life of Zeeland until his death in 1927. The author was Republican in politics and was known for his outspoken opinions.]

The territory included within the bounds of the township of Zeeland was in 1845 part of the township of Polkton. That was in the good old days when three men constituted the board of supervisors of Ottawa County. Timothy Eastman was supervisor. The total assessment was $ 12,359 and the total tax $ 41.78 on fourteen descriptions of land. One of these descriptions was the south-west quarter of section 28. On the east half of this quarter Jan Hulst settled, arriving there for permanent residence on June 8, 1847, being the first settler in the township. His son, Jan Hulst Jr., still lives on the same farm. One week later Hilbert Mast arrived and settled on the east section. The above named Jan Hulst left his home in the Netherlands March 2, 1847, left the port of Hellevoet March 19, and arrived at Baltimore, Maryland, April 27. From there the journey was over land to his farm, occupying six weeks.

The first settlers at or near the village were: Jan Steketee in July 1847, Jacobus de Hond, and Christiaan den Herder of whom the latter arrived on August 16, 1847, and settled on the south-west quarter section 17. He brought with him a load of lumber and immediately placed it on end in the shape of a bell tent under which the family passed the first night in the wilderness. At that time the township was part of Georgetown Township, Asa A. Scott being supervisor; in 1848 it was part of Ottawa Township, C. B. Albee, supervisor; in 1849 part of Allendale Township, Grosvenor Reed, supervisor; in 1849-50 part of Holland Township, Henry D. Post, supervisor.

At a session of the legislature in 1850 Zeeland was organized as a separate township, and the first meeting was held July 14, 1851, and the following persons were elected township officers: supervisor, Elias G. Young; clerk and treasurer, Robbertus M. de Bruyn; directors of the poor, Hessel O. Yntema, Jan de Pree; highway commissioners, Milan Coburn, Robbertus M. de Bruyn, Sietse op 't Holt; justices of the peace, J. Nieuwendorp, Elias G. Young, Johannes G. van Hees; constables, Hendrik de Kruif, George H. Baart, Willem Kremers. Number of votes cast, 93.

First general election held under the new constitution of 1850 was also held in 1851, when sixty-five votes were cast, 57 Democratic and 8 Whig. In 1852 the presidential election was held, and 141 votes cast, 131 were Democratic and ten Whig.

In October 1853 Arie van Bree was appointed agent for the sale of spirituous liquors under the new liquor law at an annual salary of $ 15. A stock of $ 20 worth of liquors was procured which he was scarcely able to sell under the stringent provisions of the law. The total number of accounts allowed against the town the first year was $ 111.99.

December 26, 1850, the first school district was organized, and the first school meeting was held in the Reformed church building January 7, 1851. Johannes G. van Hees was elected moderator, Robbertus M. de Bruyn, director, and Hendrik de Kruif, assessor. One dollar tax was voted for each child between four and eighteen years of age.

At the first meeting of the board of school inspectors Elias G. Young was examined and licensed as teacher, and a week later Madame Young also. August 15, 1851, Rev. Cornelius van der Meulen visited the Zeeland school, and Robbertus M. de Bruyn visited the Vriesland school in district number two, then recently organized. This was the first official school visitation had in the township.

The first highway in the town was laid out November 23, 1849, excepting the state road from Grandville to Holland, angling through the town and long since taken up. C. B. Albee and Frank B. Gilbert were the commissioners that laid out the first highway with Timothy Eastman, surveyor. In March 1851 Henry D. Post and James Walker, commissioners, and Bernardus Grootenhuis, surveyor, laid out and recorded fourteen highways in the town providing an outlet to most of the settlers.

The first child born was one of Cornelius Weninger, though the first of which there is an official record was Wouter van Nuil, September 18, 1847, and, according to the church record, baptized in October.

The first couple married were Jan Wabeke and Martina Glerum, December 1, 1847, by Rev. Cornelius van der Meulen, at the house of the latter. The witnesses were Jannes van de Luyster and Jan Stekeete. All the parties to this interesting ceremony are now deceased.

In Vriesland the first couple to enter into the bonds of matrimony were John van Zoeren and lady, both still living.

Jan Elsma on section twenty-two was the first settler in that part of the town in July 1847. He is still living and knows what house building means. First he made himself comfortable under a brush tent, then in a log house, next a frame, and now he inhabits a substantial brick building. He is a typical old country Frisian, quaint, individual, religious, patriotic, and republican, as all Frisians are, loyal to all that is noble, beautiful, and true.

The first settlers of Zeeland all came from the land of William the Silent, bringing with them the love of liberty, civil and religious, of that great prince. The secession of a large body of Christians from the dead formalism of the state church in the Netherlands led to persecution by fine, imprisonment, loss of employment, and obliquy. Free church and free schools, freedom to worship God according to the dictates of their own conscience, and a desire to improve their temporal conditions, finally led them to forsake the land of their birth and to try their fortunes in a new world.

Early in 1847 three meetings were held in the little city of Goes in the province of Zeeland to consider the matter. It was decided to emigrate in a body. They organized themselves into a church society and elected Jannes van de Luyster and Johannes Hoogesteger as elders. It was further decided that they ought not to go without a minister, and extended a call to Cornelius van der Meulen of Goes, who accepted the call.

Three vessels left the Netherlands with the emigrants on board; the first under leadership of Jan Steketee, the second of Rev. Cornelius van der Meulen, and the third of Jannes van de Luyster, arriving here at different times during the summer of 1847. So it may be said that the Reformed church of Zeeland was organized in the old country, and came here as a church, the only known instance of the kind, with the exception of, perhaps, the pilgrim fathers.

In the eastern part of the township the first settlers were mainly from the province of Friesland, and also brought a minister with them, the Rev. Maarten Anne Ypma. The large family of Van Zoeren, however, came from Gelderland, and from this fact their neighborhood is still called *De Geldersche Buurt*. It will be noticed that the early settlers perpetuated the names of the different provinces when they came here, by applying them to the localities where they settled. Thus we have Holland, North Holland, Vriesland, Overisel, Graafschap, Old and New Groningen, Drenthe, Zeeland, and names of towns as Niekerk, Zutphen, Borculo, Harderwijk, etc.

Jannes van de Luyster the proprietor of the village of Zeeland, bought of the United States government the entire section nineteen, on which the village is mainly located. He also bought section seventeen, which was settled mainly by his children, and peasantry of his farm in the old country, whom he brought with him.

Jan Wabeke, father of the late Rev. Cornelius Wabeke, also brought a number of poor families with him.

Jan Smallegange did the same in 1849 whereof the writer then ten years old was a humble member and who will hold the name of Smallegange in grateful remembrance while memory lasts.

Of the sufferings, privations, and struggles of these early settlers no one not familiar with pioneer life can form any conception. Locating in a dense wilderness without means, without roads, unacquainted with the language or institutions of the country, inexperienced in the severe toil required to clear up heavy timber land, suffering from diseases incident to the living around the swamps and to the process of acclimation. Many gave up the struggle and moved to Grand Rapids, Kalamazoo, Grand Haven, and other places, some to return again when better days dawned. The majority, however, were "stayers", chief of whom was the old minister, Van der Meulen.

Poor as any other of the settlers with a family to support, he was at once minister, doctor, land-looker, and judge. When worn and tired and discouraged, the colonists came out of the woods from different directions on Sabbath mornings, the old saint of God would preach to them with a pathos and a fervid eloquence now seldom heard, and would send them back in the evening to their humble cabins with new courage, with firmer purpose and more unfaltering trust, to renew the struggle in the forest and hew out a home and competence. Before any one had a decent house to live in these sturdy men of Puritan mould built a church of hewn timbers, 40 by 60 feet, the most substantial and most comfortable building in all the settlement. Nor was the school forgotten, for though school district No. 1 was not organized, in a legal way, till December 26, 1850, yet a school was taught long before that, part of the time by a man who came there to sell fruit trees, and afterwards by Robbertus M. de Bruyn, father of Rev. Pieter de Bruyn, who was probably the first Hollander qualified to teach school in Ottawa County. And let us note here while speaking of schools that it has ever been the endeavor of the settlers in this township to have a free school of American type. They have never been led off into sectarian or parochial bypaths, not even to the idea of a school taught in the Holland language for which it seems our fellow citizens of the same nationality in other localities have a penchant. While not ashamed of the land of their fathers but proud of their ancestry and loving the language in which their forefathers worshipped God, wooed their brides, and recited the deeds of Tromp and De Ruyter, Mauritz and William the Silent to their wondering children, yet they do not believe in a Holland or a France, an Ireland, or a Germany in free America. Again, while clinging to their church and their doctrines with tenacity and respecting their ministers and giving them generous support, yet must it be said in justice to Zeeland's inhabitants, that they are as free from sectarian spirit and bigotry as any equal body of citizens in the United States. They are most intensely jealous of their right to think for themselves on every subject; loyal to the core to the land of their adoption, and thorough believers in its free institutions. In proportion to their means they are generous to prodigality toward suffering humanity and lead all other Holland communities in support of domestic and foreign missions.

Quite a number of young men of our township served in the civil war; among those killed were Dirk Keppel, Gerrit van Bree, and Alexander Jonkheer. The township paid out $ 25,180,30 for the support of the war for the Union. The township also paid large sums toward the opening of Holland harbor.

The disastrous fire of 1871, when Holland was laid in ashes, taxed the generosity to the utmost, while at a township meeting held in 1880 a sum of $ 800 was raised for the relief of the sufferers by the fires in the state during August and September of that year.

The Russsian famine of the present winter again touched the sympathies of the people, and almost without effort, over 300,000 pounds of flour was collected and sent forward on its errand of relief and mercy.

Zeeland village is situated on the west line of the township, and was platted in 1849. At present it contains 780 inhabitants. School district number one, which includes the village, has a school census of 468. The village has three churches, the Reformed, and the First and Second Holland Christian Reformed, a fine two story school building with six school rooms, two furniture stores, two clothing stores, five general and one grocery store, one book store, two butcher shops, two wagon and smith shops, one hotel, one tannery, one cooper's shop, two flour exchange and feed stores and a fine furniture factory, which turns out over $ 1,000 worth of suites and side boards every week. The village is on sections 18 and 19, township 5 north, range 14 west, on the Chicago and West Michigan Railway, and is twenty miles southwest of Grand Rapids, twenty-six from the county seat. On section three is situated Beaverdam church and postoffice and two stores; on section 15 the Reformed church building of Vriesland, one of the largest and finest church buildings to be found outside of a village or city. A fine brick school building stands just across from the church, and on the opposite corner is the fine store of Den Herder and Tanis, and the Vriesland cheese factory near by. On the corner of section 34 is the Drenthe Christian Reformed Church, a brick school house and the large store of H. Bakker and Son. On the opposite corner is a general store in which is kept the Drenthe postoffice, with a blacksmith shop and wagon shop in the immediate vicinity.

The population of the township outside of the village of Zeeland is 2,236, making a total in the town of about 3,000. In 1854 it was 912. In 1874 it was 2,576. Since the first presidential vote, which stood Democratic 131, Whig 10, there has been a great change in the politics of the town, receiving its first impetus in the trying period of the war, and constantly fostered by discussion and effective work. It may safely be stated that there is more politics to the square foot in Zeeland, year in and year out, than in any other locality in the state. In 1876 the vote stood: Republican 296, Democratic 147; 1880, Republican 348, Democratic 132; 1884, Republican 371, Democratic 162; 1888, Republican 430, Democratic 184. The reasons for this condition and political complexion of the town are: first, the Democratic party's record on secession and rebellion, finance and tariff; second, the intense jealousy with which the Zeelanders regard their civil and religious rights and our public school system, all of which they regard in constant danger from the Catholic hierarchy which, together with the liquor interest of the country, is a standing menace to free institutions.

Chapter VI

EMIGRATION FROM DRENTE.
HISTORY OF DRENTHE, MICHIGAN

24. HERMANUS STRABBING'S MEMORIES

[Emigrating from Drente in the autumn of 1846, Strabbing settled in Graafschap in 1847, later living in Sheboygan, Wisconsin. His *Ervaringen* which present a true and vivid picture of what emigration and settlement meant, was published in *De Grondwet*, November 14, 1911.]

Het was in het voorjaar van 1846, toen wij aan het aardappels planten waren, dat ik eerst van Amerika hoorde spreken. De *Drenthsche Courant* had het nieuws verspreid, dat Ds. van Raalte spoedig daarheen zou vertrekken. Men wist niet, wat hij daar zou doen. Velen zeiden, dat hij daar de heidenen het Evangelie zou verkondigen. Ik had nooit gehoord, dat er uit onze omgeving naar Amerika waren vertrokken, wel uit Duitschland, maar die waren uit groote armoede teruggekeerd.

Op den 12den Augustus was er een markt te Zwolle en daar vertelde mij mijn neef, dat zijn broeder en zuster met Van Raalte naar Amerika gingen. Hij beklaagde hen bitterlijk, maar ik zweeg want ik wist niet wat te zeggen. Er waren gedachten in mij gaande die ik niet durfde uit te spreken. Niet lang daarna, in het laatst van September, was ook mijn oudste broeder gereed om te vertrekken. En hij drong er ook mij toe aan om mee te gaan, er aan toevoegende: „Als ik nog zoo jong was als gij, zou ik in Amerika nog wel wat kunnen worden." Maar ik had geen licht in de zaak en kon daarom niet dadelijk beslissen. Doch ik zocht licht en vond het daar, waar in alle dingen licht te vinden is, namelijk in het gebed. Het duurde wel een langen tijd, maar het werd mij steeds duidelijker, dat de vinger Gods ook mij daarhenen wees.

Het was op den 7den Januari 1847 dat ik ten vollen besloten was om naar Amerika te vertrekken. Ik had mij weer verhuurd als knecht bij boer Riddering, waar ik reeds vier jaar gediend had, maar onder voorwaarde dat ik vrij zou zijn als ik besloot naar Amerika te gaan. Vrouw Riddering was blij, toen ik haar mijn besluit te kennen gaf want, zeide zij, „wij gaan er ook heen na eenige maanden." Zij raadde mij dat ik dadelijk mijne vrienden en huisgenooten met mijn besluit moest bekend maken. Dat deed ik dan ook. Ik ging dienzelfden avond nog naar moeders huis waar ook twee van mijn broeders aanwezig waren. En daar begon een strijd waar ik niet op gerekend had. Zij waren er zeer op tegen dat ik zou vertrekken. Ja, hunne harten waren ontstoken. Maar toen ik hen

vertelde hoe ik tot deze overtuiging gekomen was, en met elkander gezongen te hebben Psalm 25, 2, opgevolgd door gebed, was de tegenstand
geheel ten einde. Van dat oogenblik af aan erkenden zij dat er een hoogere
hand in was, die zij niet konden of wilden keeren.

Het was op den 27sten Maart, dat wij van huis vertrokken. Mijn
broeder Hendrikus was ook besloten mee te gaan. Op de Zuiderzee was
de vaart schoon maar op het Haarlemmermeer hadden wij een geweldige storm, zoodat bijna allen ziek waren. Toen wij in Rotterdam
kwamen, was het schip nog niet geladen en wij moesten verscheidene
dagen wachten. Op den 13den April voeren wij af naar New York en
arriveerden aldaar op den 21sten Mei, na een voorspoedige reis.

In New York bleven wij niet lang, maar gingen per stoomboot naar
Albany en Troy, alwaar wij overgezet werden op de kanaalboot. Dat was
niet naar onze smaak want het was daar bekrompen en nauw. Wij hadden
bijna geen plaats om te zitten. Aan nederliggen, om te rusten of te slapen,
was niet te denken. En of wij daar al tegen protesteerden, 't hielp ons
niet. Zij gaven voor dat zij ons niet verstonden en wij moesten maar
tevreden zijn.

Te Buffalo werd het beter. Daar werden wij weer overgezet op een
stoomboot die ons voor de haven van Black Lake bracht, juist een
maand nadat wij in New York waren aangekomen. Eenigen van ons gezelschap, waaronder ook Hindrikus Stokking en K. Hundeman, verlieten zoo spoedig mogelijk de boot en liepen langs het strand, en kwamen
nog dienzelfden avond aan bij onze neef Egbert Frederiks, die in een
klein blokhuisje woonde, in de nabijheid waar nu de Bush Lane piano
fabriek staat.

Hier vertoefden wij eenige dagen. Maar wij waren gekomen om te
werken, want daar moest het van komen zooals wij wel wisten. Bij een
zekere godsdienstoefening onder de boomen zeide Ds. van Raalte:
„Jongens en meisjes, straks komt de winter en er is hier niet veel te
verdienen. Ik rade u aan om achter Kalamazoo te gaan waar er dit jaar
een groote oogst is en veel werk." Wij wachtten niet lang om die raad
aan te nemen. In ons gezelschap waren onder anderen, Hilligje Poppen,
Geesje Kropschot, Evert Zagers, Willem Kremers en Hendrikus Kuipers.

Op den 10den Juli gingen wij op reis. 't Was geen gemakkelijk pad –
overal door het dichte bosch. Aan den avond van den eersten dag kwamen
wij te Allegan en bleven dien nacht bij Willem Smid. Wij hadden
cornmeal pudding voor *supper*, sliepen tegen de floer en *johnnycake* voor
breakfast en waren blij dat onze snoeren in zulke liefelijke plaatsen gevallen waren.

Den volgenden dag kwamen wij op onze bestemming op de Dry Prairie, eenige mijlen achter Kalamazoo. Wij kregen al spoedig werk, wij verdienden goed geld en genoten beste *boarding*. Dit laatste was zoo uitstekend dat wij onder elkander zeiden: „Dat kunnen die menschen nooit zoo uithouden." Ons werk scheen hun ook naar den zin te zijn, want toen de oogst voorbij was, verlangden zij dat wij zouden blijven. Op den Zondag kwamen wij bij een in een kamer, ons daartoe met blijdschap afgestaan. Evert Zagers was gewoon die vergaderingen te leiden en werd al spoedig door de boeren onderscheiden als de *priest*.

Maar hoe gezegend ook de zomer werd doorgebracht, wij kregen verlangen om zoo spoedig mogelijk naar de Kolonie terug te keeren. En dat deden wij allen, de eene wat vroeger en de andere wat later. Toen wij daar aankwamen vonden wij veel ziekte en er waren gedurende de nazomer velen gestorven, zoodat de anders blijde ontmoeting met droefheid gepaard ging en de toekomst donker scheen. Een zeker huisgezin, met name Hofmeijer, bestaande uit vijf personen, was geheel uitgestorven. 't Waren ontmoedigende en beproevende tijden, maar de Heere hield staande en gaf de noodige lust en moed en kracht, om elkander te helpen en te blijven vertrouwen dat Hij, die ons zoover had geleid en ondersteund, het verder zou welmaken ook onder verlies en beproeving.

In den winter van 1848 hebben wij, bijgestaan door onze neven, Frederiks en Kuipers, de 8ste straat van Holland City uitgehakt – een halve mijl lengte; ook twee loten behoorende aan den vader van Engbertus van der Veen en de oude Mr. Doesburg. Dat was voor April van dat jaar. Op den 20sten April, stierf onze broeder Jan Strabbing, toen gehuwd met de weduwe Hidding – later Mrs. Hekhuis. In diezelfde maand bouwden wij ons blokhuis in Graafschap [section 7, Fillmore], waar wij later het grootste gedeelte van ons leven doorbrachten in het genot van de vele blijken van Gods gunst en trouw. Er zouden vele bladzijden kunnen gevuld worden met de wondervolle ondervindingen aldaar opgedaan, hoe de Heere leidde, uit nooden verloste en gebeden verhoorde. Maar onze ondervindingen zijn ook al de ondervindingen van velen met ons en daarom zwijgen wij liever, echter niet nalatende onzen hemelschen Vader voor Zijn trouwe zorg en leidende liefde, genoten op al den weg, dankende te aanbidden.

[Translation]

It was in the spring of 1846, while we were planting potatoes, that I heard folks talk about America. The *Drentsche Courant* had spread the news that Dominie van Raalte soon would emigrate to America. People did not know what he intended to do there. Many said he would bring the Gospel to the heathen living there. I had never heard that any people from this region had ever left for America; I had heard that some had done so from Germany, but most of these had returned in the greatest poverty.

At the market in Zwolle on August 12 my cousin told me that his brother and sister were emigrating to America with Van Raalte. He was bitterly sorry for them; but I dared say nothing, for I did not know what to think of it. Not long after, in the latter part of September, my oldest brother was ready to depart. He urged that I also should go with him, adding, "Were I as young as you I could readily amount to something in America." But I saw no light on the proposition and so could not come to an immediate decision. But I sought light and I found it where in all things one finds light, namely in prayer. It was long in coming, but it became constantly clearer to me that the finger of God was also pointing the way for me to America.

By January 7, 1847, I was fully determined to emigrate. I had hired myself to farmer Riddering for whom I had worked for four years, but on the condition that I would be free to go to America should I decide so to do. Mrs. Riddering was pleased when I told her my decision, for she said, "We also intend to go there in a few months." She advised me to acquaint my friends and relatives immediately with my decision, which I did. That same evening I went to my mother's house where two of my brothers also had come. A struggle began upon which I had not counted. They were very much opposed to my departure. They argued passionately. But when I told them how I had come to this conviction and after we had sung together Psalm 25, 2 [from the Dutch Psalter] and had joined in prayer their opposition ceased completely.

We set out on March 27. My brother Henry had decided to go with me. We had a pleasant voyage on the Zuider Zee. But we ran into a mighty storm on the Haarlemmermeer and nearly everybody was seasick. On arrival in Rotterdam we learned that our ship had not yet been loaded and so we were forced to wait many days. On April 13 we set sail for New York where, after a prosperous voyage we arrived on May 21.

We did not stay long in New York, but proceeded by steamboat to Albany and Troy where we were transferred to a canal boat. We did not like our accomodations, for they were crowded and small. We scarcely had any room to sit. To lie down, rest, or sleep was out of the question. Our protests availed nothing. The crew acted as if it could not understand us, with which we had to be satisfied.

At Buffalo we had better accomodations. We were transferred to a steamboat which delivered us at the harbor of Black Lake, exactly one month after we had arrived in New York. Some of our company among whom were Hindrikus Stokking and Klaas Hundeman went ashore as soon as they could and walked along the shore. On that same evening they arrived at our cousin Egbert Fredericks' who was living in a small loghouse not far from where the present Bush and Lane piano factory stands.

We stayed here a few days. But we had come to work, and it was from work we would derive our living, as we well understood. At a certain religious meeting under the trees Dominie van Raalte stated, "Boys and girls, soon it will be winter. There is little chance to earn anything here. I advise you to go to Kalamazoo and beyond where harvests this year are ample and where there is much work to be had." We quickly acted on his advice. In our group were, among others, Hilligje Poppen, Geesje Kropschot, Evert Zagers, Willem Kremers, and Hendrikus Kuipers.

On July 10 we went on our way. Our path was a difficult one – everywhere it led through dense woods. On the evening of the first day we arrived at Allegan where we spent one night at Willem Smid's. We had cornmeal pudding for supper, slept on the floor, and had johnnycake for breakfast. We were happy that our lines were cast in such pleasant places [see Psalm 16, 6].

Next day we arrived at our destination, at Dry Prairie, several miles beyond Kalamazoo. We soon found work, earned good money, and had good board. This last was so extraordinarily good that we said to each other, "These people will never be able to keep this up!" They seemed to like our work, for when the harvest was finished they wanted us to stay. On Sundays we met in a room which they gladly let us use. Evert Zagers usually acted as leader and our hosts soon were referring to him as the "priest".

But however happily we spent our summer, we began to yearn to go back to the Kolonie as soon as possible. That was something we all did, some sooner, some later. When we returned we found much sickness. So many had died that what would have been a joyful meeting turned out to be one of sadness. The future seemed somber. One family, that of Hofmeijer, composed of five persons had completely died out. These were discouraging times, and trying; but the Lord stood by and gave us needed desire, courage and strength to help each other, and to remain steadfast in the conviction that He who had guided and supported us would take care of us even though we might experience losses and have sore trials.

In the winter of 1848, with the help of our cousins, Frederiks and
Kuipers, we chopped out Eighth Street of Holland City – a length of a
half mile, and also two lots belonging to the father of Engbertus van der
Veen and to the aged Mr. Doesburg. That was in April 1848. On April 20
our brother Jan Strabbing died; he had married the widow Hidding,
later Mrs. Hekhuis. In that same month we built our loghouse in Graafschap [section 7, Fillmore]. There we spent most of our years, in the
enjoyment of God's evident favors and trust. It would be possible to fill
many pages on the wonderful experiences we had there: how the Lord
guided us, helped us in distress, and answered our prayers. Our experiences were the experiences of many like ourselves. And for that reason
we pass them by silently, not without prayer to our heavenly Father, and
thanking Him for his faithful care and guiding love which we experienced
all the way.

25. MRS J. H. BOONE'S
JOURNEY AND ARRIVAL OF TAMME VAN DEN BOSCH

[The author, Grietje, daughter of Tamme van den Bosch from Havelte, later from Witten,
in Drente, arrived in the Michigan Dutch settlement in the late spring of 1848. Her relation
under the title *Reis en Aankomst van Tamme van den Bosch*, written in 1910, appeared in *De
Grondwet*, February 27, 1912. She married Jan Hendrik Boone and lived in or near Groningen
during most of her life, dying in Zeeland in 1916.]

Er werd in dien tijd, na de vervolgingen, veel over Amerika gesproken
en in onze omgeving waren dan ook verscheidene huishoudingen, die
ook naar Amerika wilden. Drie zoons van Tamme van den Bosch wilden
ook gaarne mede en vader zeide tot moeder: „Dan moeten wij ook mede;
daar is de godsdienst vrij en dat is het toch wat wij begeeren. „Ja," zeide
moeder, „maar ik kan er nog niet toe overgaan want een van onze
kinderen kan niet mee en om die achter te laten, dat is wat."

Vader en moeder hadden negen kinderen, waarvan Ds. Koene van den
Bosch de oudste was en die kon niet meegaan.

Het was dan alles klaar op moeder na. Op zekeren morgen zei moeder
bij het opstaan: „Vader, ik ben nu gereed om naar Amerika te gaan."
„Wel," zei vader, „hoe is dat toch?" Moeder antwoordde: „Ik heb den
Heere gebeden, dat hij mij mocht los maken, als het Zijn wil was dat wij
naar Amerika moesten en Hij heeft mij los gemaakt en mijn gebed
verhoord; ik ben gereed."

Als ik mij wel herinner was dat in de maand Maart 1848 en den 1sten
Mei waren wij klaar om met verscheidene huisgezinnen op reis te gaan.
Deze waren: A. J. Hillebrands, Berend Kamps, Evert Evers, Diekema,

Schepers, Roelof ten Hake, H. Vredevelt, H. Pijl, Berend Jan Poes, E. Eding en de weduwe Essing.

Wij verlieten ons vaderland om den godsdienst en verder ook voor het welzijn van de kinderen. Wij waren het eenige huisgezin op het dorp Witten bij Assen dat tot de Afgescheidenen behoorde. De buren brachten ons en ons goed naar de boot en o! wat was dat afscheid hard, ik zal het nooit vergeten.

Wij hebben een tamelijk goede reis gehad. De naam van ons schip was *Scandica* en wij zijn 35 dagen op zee geweest. Eens hebben wij nog een flinken storm gehad, zoodat de luiken des avonds alle gesloten werden. Gedurende de reis zijn er drie kinderen op het schip gestorven.

Ons voornemen was om naar Zeeland te gaan en toen wij aldaar aan-kwamen, verleende Jan Steketee ons onderdak, totdat vader een huis gebouwd had. Vader was slager en kocht nu en dan een koe of os, die hij slachtte en dan bij het pond verkocht; ook verkocht hij flour. Vader hield dat een of twee jaar vol, gedurende welken tijd wij het goed hadden en daarna kocht hij land in section 13, voor zichzelf en zijn drie zoons, die vader hielpen bij het omkappen der boomen.

In het eerste jaar van ons verblijf op de farm kwam er niet veel van het planten en wat er geplant was, werd opgegeten door de *coons* en ander wild gedierte.

In het tweede jaar plantten wij vrij wat koren en dat stond heel goed, doch in het najaar begonnen wij allen aan de koorts te lijden. Ds. Cor-nelius van der Meulen kwam gedurig bij ons; hij was onze dokter, do-mine en vader. Ik zal nooit vergeten hoe goed hij voor ons was. Eens kwam hij bij ons, terwijl wij allen ziek te bed lagen. Daar wij erge dorst hadden, vroegen wij hem om ons wat water te geven. Hij zei: „Dit water is zoo lauw dat ik naar de bron zal gaan om frisch water te halen." Toen hij terug kwam, zei hij: „Dat ziet er niet mooi uit, het koren is rijp en allen zijn ziek." Maar de Heere maakte het nog weer wel; vader werd beter en ging het koren van de stronken plukken en bracht het daarna in een zak naar huis en wij kinderen dopten het dan af, zoodat wij nu koren hadden voor brood en wij een varken konden mesten. Den Heere komt de lof en dank er voor toe, dat Hij het zoo wel gemaakt heeft tot op dit oogenblik toe.

[Translation]

At that time, after the prosecutions by the state, there was much talk about America. Among our acquaintances there were many families who wanted to go to America. Three sons of Tamme van den Bosch also wanted to go. My father said to my mother, "Then we too must go with them; the practice of religion is free there, and that is what we desire." "Yes," said mother, "but I cannot decide, for one of our children is not able to go with us, and to leave him here, that is asking too much of me." Father and mother had nine children of whom Dominie Koene van den Bosch was the oldest; and he was the one who could not go with us.

Everything was in readiness, except mother. On a certain morning mother said on rising, "Father, I now am ready to go to America." "Well," said father, "how did this happen?" Mother replied, "I have prayed to God, that He might give me freedom to go. He has given me this freedom, He has heard my prayer, I am ready to go to America!"

If I recall well that was in the month of March 1848. On May 1 we were ready to depart. A number of families were going to accompany us. These were Anesus J. Hillebrands, Berend Kamps, Evert Evers, Diekema, Schepers, Roelof ten Hake, H. Vredevelt, H. Pijl, Berend Jan Poes, E. Eding, and the widow Essing.

We left our fatherland for the sake of religion and also for the welfare of the children. We were the only family in the village of Witten near Assen which belonged to the Seceders [*Afgescheidenen*]. Our neighbors took us to the boat. Oh! to part from them was so hard; that is something I shall never forget.

Our voyage was tolerably comfortable. The name of our ship was *Scandica*. It was a voyage of 35 days. Once we ran through a stiff storm so that the ship's hatches had to be closed each night. Three children died on this voyage.

Our intention was to proceed to Zeeland. When we arrived, Jan Steketee offered to take us in until we built a house. Father was a butcher. He also sold flour. He bought cows or oxen which he butchered and sold by the pound. Father kept this up for two years during which time we got along very well. Thereafter he bought some land in section 13 for himself and his three sons who helped father chop down the trees.

During our first year on the farm we raised very little. Whatever was planted was eaten by coons and other wild pests. In the second year we planted a considerable patch of corn, which produced very well. But in the fall we all began to suffer from the fever. Dominie van der Meulen frequently visited us. To us he was doctor, dominie, and father. I shall never forget how kind he was. On one occasion he visited us when we were all sick abed. As we were very thirsty we asked him to give us some water. He said, "This water is so warm. I'll go to the spring and get fresh water." Returning, he remarked, "Things don't look well; the corn is ripe and all of you are sick." But the Lord healed all things and father recovered. He picked the ears of corn from the stalks and carried them to the house where we children shelled them. So we had corn from which to make johnnycake and also to fatten our pigs. To the Lord is due all praise and thanks because up until the present moment He has done all things well for us.

26. ADRIAAN KEIZER'S
DRENTHE'S HISTORY TO THE PRESENT

[Serving the Christian Reformed congregation at Drenthe from 1896 to 1898, Adriaan Keizer became fully acquainted with the community of Drenthe. This account, presented here only in translation, was written in 1897, was published under the title *Drenthe's Wording en Opkomst tot Heden*, and appeared in *De Grondwet*, March 7, 1911.]

Drenthe you will find in the southern part of Ottawa County, in the southern part of Zeeland Township. Its church, the center of the population, stands on the northwest corner of section 35.

During the first years there was some difference of opinion as to what should be the name of this place. The first settler, who came from Staphorst in Overijsel, wanted to have it called Staphorst. But most of the settlers, coming from the province of Drente, desired to have the name of Drenthe. In 1848 the community was known as Drenthe, and later this name was given to the postoffice station.

The first settlers in the township were Jan Hulst and family. He left his home in Staphorst, Overijsel, on March 2, 1847, sailed from the harbor of Hellevoetsluis on March 19, and arrived at Baltimore, Maryland, on April 27. He spent six weeks in traveling from Baltimore to that piece of woods where he chose to have his home, two miles west of the village Drenthe, on section 28.

Eight days after Hulst's arrival, came Hilbert Mast, also from Staphorst. He established himself in the southeast part of the same section. Soon thereafter came J. Jansen from Utrecht and Arend Smeding from Hoogeveen, both with their families. Among the others who came during that same year are the following persons whose children in considerable number still live in Drenthe and belong to its most respected families: Cornelius van der Stadt, D. Broekman, Jan Wiggers, Johannes op 't Holt, Hendrik Lanning, Jan Riddering, Hessel Yntema, Hendrik Hunderman, Willem Kremers, S. Kaslander, J. Rijgel, Jan Kamps, M. Grenewits, Jan Euvink, Jacob Neijenhuis, M. and J. Regenmorter, Ulke de Vries – all of whom excepting two were heads of families.

Berend ter Haar and his family arrived after New Year's 1848 from Holland, Michigan, where he had been working for a half year.

In the course of the next year, 1848, arrived among others, A. Lubbers and H. Hunderman with their children.

Of these first settlers the following are still living: Berend ter Haar, Cornelius van der Stadt, M. Grenewits, and J. Jensen's widow. Of the children who came over with their parents are still living A. Lanning, H. Yntema, H. Wiggers, K., G. and J. Hunderman, J. Rijgel, H. Kamps, Mrs. L. de Kleine, Mrs. J. op 't Holt, and Miss. Geesje Euvink.

The reasons why these people emigrated from the Netherlands were not the same in every case, but the most important was the temporal welfare of their children. These newcoming settlers found no inhabitants here. But a few miles northeast in so-called Indian Creek [Indianen Beek] some Indians were living. In Drenthe, however, there were a few traces of Indian dwellings.

The houses of the first settlers in Drenthe were of the same sort as in other settlements. Here too they lived under branches covered with leaves. After that they had loghouses. During this time some of them lived in holes dug in the ground. Such were these simple loghouses that six men could erect one in the course of a day. Furniture was most scanty. Any kind of a box served as table. A block of wood passed for a chair. Even among the more well-to-do there were no exceptions.

During the first days of the settlement the people used the food they brought with them, some of it from the ship in which they had sailed. Most of the food needed was brought from Grand Rapids, but only those articles that were needed most. The men traveled far from home in order to earn some money. Under such circumstances the women and children could accomplish little, chopping down trees and clearing the land. Willem Kremers carried the first three apple trees of the settlement on his shoulders all the way from Allegan and planted them a quarter of a mile from the village where they may still be seen. They have grown to be large trees and bear fruit. Grand Rapids was the market for Drenthe. Concerning the products of the first years it may be stated that in the first fall [1847] blight affected the potatoes. In the summer and fall of 1851 squirrels destroyed all the corn and potatoes. So great was the multitude of these destructive creatures [caused by the exceptionally mild winter which preceeded] that they invaded the houses and at times actually made away with the food placed on the tables. This again happened in 1854, with the result that some left the settlement. That not more left was due to the advice of Dominie van Raalte not to abondon their farms.

The first store where the farmers exchanged their products for groceries and other things was run by Geert van der Schouw, one and three quarters miles north from the village. The first store to be opened in the village proper was that of Klaas Hulst. The present store keepers, Bakker and Son, on the southeast corner, and J. Riddering, on the northeast corner, have had no less than thirteen partners or predecessors in the immediate neighborhood of the village.

In addition to these two stores there is a harness shop belonging to Cornelius Verhulst. Formerly it belonged to Frits van Houten. There also are a smithy belonging to R. de Vries whose immediate predecessor was Hindrikus Stokken [or Stokking] and a wagon making shop on the property of K. van Essen, successor of A. Boer, the first person to be engaged in this kind of business in Drenthe.

One-half mile north of the village is the creamery, a flourishing business. During the summer an average of 20,000 pounds of milk are received here daily, during the winter, 15,000 pounds. Through the telephone office in J. Riddering's store the people of Drenthe have contact with every part of the United States.

So far as population statistics are concerned, these were never kept; but we do know that the Drenthe congregation in early days numbered no less than 45 families. The first child to be born in Drenthe was Rikus Wiggers, at the home of Huibert Mast, a few days after his parents' arrival in their forest home. The first couple to be married was Jan Tanis and Arendje Broekman, by Dominie Maarten A. Ypma.

Among the varieties of illnesses during the first years were hot and cold fevers and dysentery. A half dozen died from cholera. Of the first to die in the settlement were Bouke Yntema on Oct. 7, 1847, and a little later three of Ulke de Vries' children. Then followed Lammert Floris, Neeltje Kruithof, and Altje ter Haar. Of the seven men and youths of Drenthe who served in the Civil War, four perished on the field of battle.

The first doctor to call on the sick was C. D. Schenik from Groningen. The first doctors to be stationed at Drenthe were Willem van den Berg and Ypes. The present physician, Dr. E. de Spelder had as many as seven predecessors in Drenthe. The present population of the community according to the postoffice is 300 but the congregation has a membership of 655. Membership of the church is drawn from an area larger than that served by the postoffice.

During the first days of the settlement, the newcomers received letters addressed to Grand Rapids, some to Holland, and others to Zeeland. The first person to carry mail for Vriesland and Drenthe was Jan Elsma.

In 1876 Drenthe had its own postoffice, at the house of H. van den Bosch. Later the postoffice was housed successively in the two stores of the village, at present in the store of Bakker and Son. It is a fourth class postoffice at which yearly over $ 100 in stamps are cancelled.

As early as 1848 the people of Drenthe had a school, three months per year, jointly with those of Vriesland. Miss. Fijl, from Allegan, was the first teacher. In 1853 Drenthe was organized as a separate school district, its first teacher was Elias de Jong. At present the number of children is below 100. There are two teachers in two rooms. The term is ten months. The attractive school building, a brick structure, was built in 1884, next to the church.

At first the congregation of Drenthe was united with that of Vriesland. But it became a separate congregation in 1848. In 1851 they invited Dominie Roelof Smit fròm Nieuw Leusen in the province of Overijsel. But in 1853, followed by two thirds of the congregation, he abandoned the Reformed Church and joined the Associate Reformed Church of North America. He served this congregation until the date of his death, on May 27, 1886. His following thereupon united with the Christian Reformed Church. The members of the Reformed Church who in 1853 refused to follow Dominie Smit showed remarkable growth and in 1861 invited Dominie Roelof Pieters to be their first minister, who was followed by Jakobus Huyssoon in 1865, Willem Moerdyk in 1869, and Christiaan van der Veen in 1876. This group, with few exceptions who joined nearby congregations, in 1886, also broke with the Reformed Church and joined the Christiaan Reformed Church. The first pastor of this congregation was Dominie Henry van der Werp, succeeded by Egbert Broene in 1886, and in May 4, 1896, by Adriaan Keizer. The congregation at Drenthe numbered 45 families, 70 communicants. The present congregation has 145 families, 290 communicants, a total of 655 souls.

Among the persons born in Drenthe who have graduated from various schools, the following may be named. Professor Douwe B. Yntema, Hope College; Professor A. J. Poppen, Tokio, Japan; Dr. Henry Kremers, Holland, Mich.; Dr. E. Hoffman, Grand Haven, Mich.; Dr. T. Holman, Chicago, Ill.; Dr. J. Poppen, Forest Grove, Mich.; Dr. H. van den Berg, Milwaukee, Wisc.; Dr. J. de Vries, Overisel, Mich.; Dominie H. Kremers, Rusford, Minn.; H. Kamps, candidate, called to New Holland, S. D.; Mrs. A. van der Wagen, missionary at Fort Defiance; K. Poppen, student at the University of Michigan; Nicholas Boer, Henry Boer, John Wiggers, Nicholas van Duren, and Nicholas van Dam, all students at Hope College.

We conclude with the remark that also in Drenthe there are spots where, as it were the soil is moistened with the sweat of toil, also with the tears of afflliction and of thankfulness.

27. HENRY KREMERS'
MEMORIES OF THE BEGINNING OF DRENTHE

[The author, a physician, born in 1850, the son of Willem Kremers, spent his youth in Drenthe, and was thoroughly acquainted with the community. His father emigrated from Drente in the fall of 1846, sailed in the *Isabella Bath*, and in 1847 became one of the founders of Drenthe. Editor Van Schelven's note contains what seems to be a complete list of the group that walked from Buffalo to Detroit.]

Verzocht zijnde door Mr. G. van Schelven om een weinig mede te deelen van het begin van Drenthe, kan ik niet weigeren aan dit verzoek te voldoen; en hoewel een deel van hetgeen ik zal schrijven mij door anderen is medegedeeld, zoo is het nochtans waarheid.

Mijn vader, Willem Kremers, geboren in 1820 te Noord Barge, gemeente Emmen, Nederland, verhuisde naar Amerika in 1846 en kwam den 7den December 1846 te New York aan.

De reis, die met een zeilschip gemaakt werd, duurde 63 dagen – een zeer bange en moeielijke reis. In dit gezelschap waren Jan Rabbers, Jan Kolvoord en anderen, wier namen ik nu niet meer kan herinneren. Ds. van Raalte en zijn gezelschap waren hen een weinig vooruit. Men ging van New York per boot naar Albany en kwam daar in kennis met oud Hollanders – Dr. Isaac N. Wyckoff en anderen, die hen zeer behulpzaam waren en met goeden raad bijstonden.

Dit gezelschap had het geluk dat ze in den winter reisden, en alzoo de reis met die ellendige kanaalboten ontkwamen, want het kanaal van Albany naar Buffalo was bevroren. Men reisde met den spoorweg naar Buffalo en daar vond men werk. Met zeer hard werk verdiende men 50 cents per dag, met hout te hakken.

Ds. van Raalte was toen al in Michigan en had de plaats reeds uitgekozen om een Hollandse Kolonie te planten. Hij schreef dringende brieven dat allen die de reis konden maken, zo spoedig mogelijk naar Michigan moesten komen. Jan Rabbers, mijn vader, en enige anderen hadden reeds in Nederland kennis met Ds. van Raalte gemaakt, en waren zeer begerig om te gaan.

Met negen man [geen vrouwspersonen] ondernamen zij de reis naar Michigan. Men besloot om 300 mijlen door Canada te voet af te leggen en alles wat ze bezaten op de rug mee te dragen. Hun bezittingen waren dan ook niet groot, en met zeer weinig geld in de zak, begonnen zij deze moeielijke reis. Maar het viel niet mee. Met veel sneeuw, harde vorst, en veelal slechte wegen was de voortgang traag en vervelend. Men huurde ten laatste een bobslede en verkortte alzo de reis. Men arriveerde allen in goede gezondheid te Detroit, na met levensgevaar over de Detroit rivier gepasseerd te zijn. Men had brieven aan de heer Theodore Romeyn, een oud Hollander, die hen logies bezorgde, en hen den volgenden dag aan het station bracht. Men ging per spoorweg naar Kalamazoo, met wat nu genoemd wordt de Michigan Central. De spoorweg was nieuw en de reis duurde de gehele dag — 12 uren. De trein liep dan ook zeer langzaam. Als het 'up grade' ging, verliet men den spoorwaggon en liep te voet mede daar men het zitten moede werd. Ik deel dit mede om aan te toonen wat een vooruitgang er in die 60 jaren gemaakt is. Den volgenden dag reisde men per slede naar Allegan alwaar Judge Kellogg allen in zijn huis nam en hen in zijne woning op de vloer van den keuken liet slapen.

Er was niets in de geheele Kolonie dan een paar huizen in Fillmore Township, en wel die van Mr. Isaac Fairbanks, een agent van het gouverment, en die van George N. Smith, een zendeling onder de Indianen. Er was ook een blokkerk, gebouwd voor de Indianen. Mijn vader was nieuwsgierig om de godsdienst onder de Indianen eens bij te woonen. Vandaar begaf hij zich op zekeren Zondagmorgen naar die blokkerk. In weerwil van het feit, dat het gehoor bestond uit slechts een enkele Indiaan, preekte reverend Smith, die in het Indiaansch sprak, alsof er een goed gehoor was. In den namiddag preekte Ds. van Raalte voor de weinige Hollanders.

Kort na aankomst van mijn vader en zijn gezelschap, begon men wegen te maken door de dichte bosschen. Allen hielpen. Het werk werd gratis verricht. Later bouwden ze een cedar-loggen-huis voor Ds. van Raalte. Men droeg de loggen uit het moeras en maakte ze vierkant. Daarna werden ze op elkander gelegd en aan de hoeken verbonden. Bijna alle boeren woningen waren in het begin uit loggen gebouwd, maar de loggen werden niet vierkant gemaakt.

De eerste werkstaking [*strike*] kwam hier voor, toen men op zekeren morgen, bij het bouwen van het huis voor den dominee, het werk neerlegde. Met mooi praten echter gelukte het van Raalte de meesten ertoe te bewegen het werk weer op nieuw te hervatten en het huis te voltooien.

Met het begin van het voorjaar kon er niets binnengebracht worden. Black Lake was vol ijs en het was niet mogelijk om van Allegan iets in te brengen. Er waren geen bruggen en alles was vol water. Men had dan ook niets te eten dan corn. Dit kon niet gemalen worden, want er was geen molen. Men kookte het daarom den geheelen dag om het zacht te krijgen. Gedurende circa zes weken had men bijna geen ander voedsel dan corn. Met het inzetten van goed weer vertrok mijn vader naar Kalamazoo en werkte daar een jaar lang voor de boeren.

In het voorjaar van 1848 kwamen er verscheinene Drenthers naar Amerika over, en vestigden zich hier, en vader voegde zich bij dit bekende volk. Men koos goed land uit, tien mijlen ten oosten van Holland gelegen. Ik zal de namen van eenigen van die eerste beginners opnoemen: de familien Opholt [Op 't holt], Wiggers, Neijenhuis, Ensink, Lanning, Riddering, Lubbers, Hunderman en Kamps. Dezen zetten zich in het oostelijke, anderen, uit de provincie Overijsel afkomstig namen het westelijke gedeelte in bezit. Hier vond men de familien Hulst, van Spijker, Boer, Seinen, Dazeman en anderen. Deze, of sommigen er van, waren niet tevreden met den naam Drenthe, maar kozen de naam Staphorst. Mr. Jan Hulst was de kampioen van dit gedeelte en had aan een boom op zijn farm een plank vastgespijkerd, waarop het volgende opschrift voorkwam, „Hier begint Staphorst." De oude groot-vader Hunderman streed hard voor Drenthe, en eindelijk koos men in de naam.

Van die eerste settlers hadden de meesten weinig of geen geld. De familien Lanning, Riddering en Lubbers waren misschien de uitzondering ook Lanning kocht 640 acres land; de weduwe Riddering kocht 640 acres. Deze verschaften werk aan anderen, mijn vader niet uitgezonderd. Mij is dikwijls vertelt, dat ze ook geld uitleenden op weinig of geen securiteit, en vaak het geleende niet terug kregen. Maar men deed nog al veel voor elkander en ik heb hun of hunne kinderen nooit horen klagen over het uitgeleende en niet terugbetaalde geld.

Dit oosten en westen werd georganiseerd tot eene Gereformeerde gemeente, welke bediend werd door leeraars van de omliggende gemeenten, Ypma, Van der Meulen, Bolks, Van Raalte, en anderen. Ook door Ds. Budding, die sommige dagen onder hen doorbracht, en op den Zondag voor hen predikte. Er wordt nog al veel vertelt van deze wonderlijke man, zijne buitengewone preekgaven en scherpe menschenkennis en ook van zijne 'notions'-kuren, zou ik zeggen. Bijvoorbeeld, het volk zou zitten wachten in de kerk, maar geen Budding daagde er op. Gelogeerd bij mijn vader, die in dien tijd nog ongehuwd was, meldde de kerkeraad zich daar aan, om te zien waarom hij [Budding] niet kwam. Deze kregen dan ten antwoord dat de Geest niet gewillig was. Met lang praten bewoog men hem er toch eindelijk toe om op te treden.

Maar, men wilde een eigen leeraar hebben. Het gezelschap van het westen was bekend met zekere Ds. Roelof Smit van Rouwveen. Deze werd beroepen, en gaf gehoor aan de roeping. De dominee was een goed en vreedzaam man, maar had niet de gelegenheid gehad om lang op school te zijn, en beviel het oosten niet, met het gevolg, dat men in de grootste moeite kwam. En, nog al eigenaardig van oons Hollandsch volk, werden ze zeerverbitterd op elkander, en de gemeenten scheurde in tweeën.

Het westen sloot zich aan bij de United Presbyterian church, en werd hierna genoemd de Schotsche gemeente. Het oosten bleef bij de Gereformeerde Kerk, en was zonder leeraar tot 1861 toen kandidaat Roelof Pieters hun beroep aannam.

Ds. Smit bleef leeraar van de Schotse gemeente tot aan zijn dood. Velen van zijne aanhangers hadden hem verlaten en zich gevoegd bij de Afgescheidene gemeente te Vriesland. Later, met de afscheiding van 1882 ging de Gereformeerde gemeente over tot de Afgescheidene Kerk en de afgescheidene gemeente te Vriesland brak op, en de meestte inwoners van Drenthe werden opnieuw vereenigd in een gemeente, en is nu een sterk bloeiende gemeente van de Christelijke Gereformeerde Kerk.

Die scheuring tusschen het westen en oosten, verwekte zulk eene verwijdering, dat ze zeer weinig gemeenschap met elkaar hielden. Men hield ieder zijn eigen school[Hollandsche] er op na. Men had ieder zijn eigen kerkhof, en ik herinner nog dat een van de afgescheidenen verzocht om een begraafplaats op het kerkhof der Gereformeerde gemeente, omdat ze het beste kerkhof hadden. Dit werd geweigerd, en hij kreeg bovendien ten antwoord: „Gij wilt niet bij ons zijn in het leven, en wij weigeren u te hebben als gij dood zijt." Dit was echter het antwoord van een individu. Toch, de tegenstand was zoo groot dat het geweigerd werd.

De publieke school echter kon men niet scheiden, en hier moest men met elkander in aanraking komen. Dit hielp dan ook om meer verdraagzaam te worden, en na een 60 jaren is dit alles vergeten en het volk vereenigd.

[Zoover wij ge-informeerd zijn, bestond het gezelschap van negen man, hierboven gemeld, uit Jan Rabbers, Willem Kremers, Hendrik Plaggemars, Jan Kolvoord, Abraham Slaghuis, Jan Stegeman, Gerrit H. Wolterink, Gerrit J. Hofman, en Rekkers. — G. v. S.]

[Translation]

Having been asked by Mr. Gerrit Van Schelven to contribute a short account of the first days of Drenthe, I connot refuse, although whatever I may write is being stated in the sketches drawn up by others; but this does not lessen the truth of what I have to say.

My father Willem Kremers was born in Noord Barge in the parish of Emmen in the Netherlands and emigrated to America, arriving in New York on December 7, 1846. This voyage by sailing ship lasted 63 days, a very fearful and difficult passage. In this company were Jan Rabbers, Jan Kolvoord, and others whose names I cannot exactly recall. Dominie Van Raalte and his group had sailed a little earlier. They proceeded from New York to Albany where they became acquainted with Knickerbocker Hollanders — Dr. Isaac N. Wyckoff and others who proved most helpful to us by giving good advice.

The group had the good fortune to travel in winter and so avoided the wretched canal boats, for the canal from Albany to Buffalo was covered with ice. They journeyed by train to Buffalo where they found work, earning 50 cents per day at hard labor — chopping wood.

Dominie Van Raalte had already gone to Michigan and had chosen a site for a Dutch kolonie. He wrote urgent letters to all who could to hasten to Michigan. Jan Rabbers, my father, and a few others had already formed some acquaintance with Dominie Van Raalte in the Netherlands and were eager to go to him.

Nine men [no women accompanied them] undertook the journey to Michigan. They decided to travel the 300 miles through Canada on foot and carry their possessions on their backs. With very little money in their pockets they started on their difficult journey, one slow and tiresome, for there was much snow, the frost was severe, and the roads at many points bad. Finally they rented a sleigh and so shortened their journey.

They all arrived safely in Detroit, after passing, in great danger of death, over Detroit River. They carried letters addressed to Theodore Romeyn, Knickerbocker Hollander, who found lodging for them. On the next day he took them to the station. They proceeded by train to Kalamazoo on what now is known as the Michigan Central. The railway was new and the trip lasted the entire day — 12 hours. The train was very slow. When it had to go up grade the passengers climbed out of the coaches and walked by the side of the train because they were tired of sitting. I record this in order to indicate how much progress has been made in the past 60 years. The following day they went bij sleigh to Allegan where Judge John R. Kellogg took them all into his house and let them sleep on the floor of his kitchen.

There was nothing whatever in the entire Kolonie axcept a few houses in Fillmore Township — those belonging to Mr. Isaac Fairbanks, agent of the United States government, and to Geaorge N. Smith, a missionary to the Indians. There was a church of logs, built bij the Indians. My father was curious to attend a regilious meeting of the Indians. So one Sunday morning he proceeded to their log church. In spite of the fact that the audience consisted of only one Indian, Reverend Smith preached as if a large audience sat before him. In the afternoon Dominie van Raalte preached to the handful of Hollanders there.

Soon after the arrival of my father and his group, they began to make roads through the woods. Everybody lent a hand. The work was gratis. Later they built a house of heavy cedar logs for Dominie van Raalte. They carried the logs out of the swamp and squared them. Next, the logs were placed one upon another and fastened at their ends. In the beginning nearly all farmers' houses were made of logs, but the logs were not squared.

The first strike occurred in this place, when on a certaain morning the men who were building the house for the dominie quit working. But Van Raalte was able with persuasive talk to induce most of them to resume their work and finish the house.

At the beginning of spring nothing could be brought into the Kolonie. Black Lake was covered with ice and nothing could be shipped in from Allegan. There were no bridges and there was water everywhere. The settlers had nothing to eat but corn. This could not be ground, for there was no mill. They boiled the corn a whole day in order to soften it. For about six weeks they had practically no food but corn. With the advent of good weather my father went to Kalamazoo where he worked for a year as farmer's hand.

In the spring of 1848 many immigrants arrived from Drente and settled here. Father joined these people with whom he was acquainted They chose good land, ten miles east of Holland. I shall give the names of the first settlers: the families of Op 't Holt, Wiggers, Neijenhuis, Ensink, Lanning, Riddering, Lubbers, Hunderman, and Kamps. Some of these settled toward the east, others toward the west. These latter came from the province of Overijsel. Among them were the families of Hulst, Spijker, Boer, Seinen, Dazeman, and others. These people, or at least some of these were displeased with the name of Drenthe and chose instead Staphorst. Mr. John Hulst was the champion of these people. He nailed a board to a tree standing on his farm carrying the following inscription, "It is here that Staphorst begins." Old grandfather Hunderman fought hard for the name Drenthe, and finally the people chose that name.

Most of these first settlers had little money. The families of Lanning,

Riddering, and Lubbers probably were exceptions. Lanning bought 640 acres; the widow Riddering also secured 640 acres. They provided work for the others, my father not excepted. I have been told repeatedly that they loaned money on little or no security and that they never were repaid the amount loaned. It should be remembered that these people did a great for each other; and I have never heard them or their children complain that such money was never repaid.

The east and west parts of the settlement were organized as a congregation of the Reformed Church. Services were held by ministers from the outlying congregations – Maarten A. Ypma, Cornelius van der Meulen, Seine Bolks, A. C. van Raalte, and others. Also by Dominie Huibertus Jacobus Budding who spent some days in the settlement and preached to them on Sundays. Many things are told about that curious person – his extraordinary gifts as a preacher, his keen insight into human nature, and also his notions [kuren] as I would describe them. For example, the people would be sitting in the church, but Budding would not appear. He was lodged at my father's – my father was not married at that time – and the consistory called to see why Budding did not appear. The reply was that the spirit was not willing! After much talk they finally persuaded Budding to mount the pulpit.

But, the people desired to have their own pastor. The people living in the western part of the settlement were acquainted with a certain Dominie Rudolf Smit from Rouwveen, Overijsel. He was invited and accepted their call. The dominie was a good and peaceable man. But he had not had the opportunity of extended study. Nor were the people in the east part of the settlement pleased with him and the greatest difficulties arose. Very characteristically of our Dutch people, they became embittered toward each other, and the congregation was rent in two factions.

The western faction joined the United Presbyterian Church, and thereafter was called the Scottish congregation. The eastern faction remained faithful to the Reformed Church and had no pastor until 1861 when Roelof Pieters, then candidate for the ministry accepted their invitation.

Dominie Smit remained pastor of the Scottish congregation until his death. Many of his adherents had left him and had joined the Christian Reformed Church at Vriesland. Later, at the time of the secession in 1882, the Reformed Church went over to the Christian Reformed Church. The Christian Reformed church at Vriesland then broke up and most of the people of Drenthe were united again into one congregation which at present is a strong, flourishing congregation of the Christian Reformed Church.

That schism between the eastern and western factions produced such an antagonism that they had very little to do with each other. Each faction kept its own Dutch school. Each had its own cemetery. I recall that one of the Christian Reformed on one occasion asked for the privilege of a burial in the cemetery of the Reformed group because the latter had the best cemetery. This request was refused. The answer given him was, "You do not want to be with us in life, and we refuse to have you with us in death!" This, however, was only the answer of an individual. Nevertheless, the oppositon was so keen that the request was refused.

It was impossible, however, to have a schism in the public school. There the people could not avoid each other. This fact made them become more tolerant toward each other. Now, after 60 years all this has been forgotten, and the people have been united.

[So far as we have been informed, the group of nine men mentioned above was made up of Jan Rabbers, Willem Kremers, Hendrik Plagge-mars, Jan Kolvoord, Abraham Slaghuis, Jan Stegeman, Gerrit H. Wolterink, Gerrit J. Hofman, and Rekkers. – Gerrit van Schelven.]

Chapter VII

FRIESIAN EMIGRATION IN 1847.
FOUNDING AND HISTORY OF VRIESLAND, MICHIGAN

28. TEDE ULBERG'S NOTES ON THE FIRST SETTLERS
IN THE DUTCH KOLONIE IN MICHIGAN

[In 1847 Tede Ulberg from Minnertsga in Friesland settled in the forest of the country henceforth called Vriesland. His account gives some idea of the thoughts that surged in the mind of emigrants about to undertake the great adventure of settling in a foreign land. Ulberg wrote this article at Vriesland in 1882 under the title *Uit de Portefeuille van de Eerste Settlers in de Hollandsche Kolonie in Michigan.* It was published in *Jaarboekje voor de Hollandsche Christelijke Gereformeerde Kerk in Noord Amerika voor het Jaar* 1883 (Grand Rapids 1882).]

Indien ik nu ingevolge verzoek een korte mededeeling van mijn ont-moetingen herwaarts en hier in Amerika zal doen aan de lezer van het *Jaarboekje,* dan komt het mij 't best voor – om zulks eenigermate regel-matig te doen – allereerst mede te deelen hoe ik met mijn gezin naar Amerika gekomen ben.

Dat is op deze wijze toegegaan. In de leiding die de Heere met mij in het oude Vaderland gehouden heeft was ik sterk overtuigd, dat Hij wat bijzonders met mij voor had, maar ik wist niet wat. Ik deelde mijne ge-dachten mede aan den predikant onzer gemeente, Minnertsga, Friesland en aan vrome menschen. Ik had begeerte om leeraar te worden, maar ik wist niet of de Heere mij daartoe geroepen had. Onze leeraar, die mij goed kende, raade mij aan om mijne begeerte aan de Classis te Franeker bekend te maken en tot dat einde mijn weg en werkzaamheden in ge-schrift mede te deelen. Ik deed zoo, en na bovendien onderscheidene vragen aan de Classikale vergadering beantwoord te hebben, moest ik naar buiten, ten einde zij met elkander over mij zouden kunnen raad-plegen. De uitslag was dat de Classis mij aannam, en nu werd mij gezegd, dat ik in eene volgende samenkomst der Classis een voordracht moest houden over 2 Cor. 8 : 9: „Want gij weet de genade van onzen Heere Jezus Christus, dat Hij om uwentwil is arm geworden, daar Hij rijk was, opdat gij door zijne armoede zoudt rijk worden." Maar ik zeide dat dit wel wat veel gevergd was van mij, een onbestudeerd man. „Ja, ja," werd gezegd, „maar wij verwachten van U wat meer, en gij zijt ook alreeds 42 jaren oud." „Welnu," antwoordde ik, „als dat dan in den weg des Heren is, dan hoop ik, dat Hij mij geestelijk licht en wijsheid zal schenken, maar is het niet in zijn weg, dan wensch ik dat Hij mijne gedachten op dat punt tot dwaasheid make."

Nu wenschte ik een boek daarover te hebben. Ik zocht ook alles af om een preek over dien text te kunnen lezen, maar nergens vond ik daarover een preek. De tijd naderde. Ik was op zolder. Nu lag ik eens een wijle op de knieën en, kreeg ik weer wat, dan schreef ik dat op. De predikant van onze plaats komt bij mij, en ik verzocht hem te mogen voorlezen wat ik had, en dan zou hij geheel oprecht zeggen, of het verband en de ver- deeling goed was. „Ja," zegt hij eindelijk, „alles is goed." Daar kwam ik dus goed af. De Heere schonk mij verder licht en de preek kwam in gereedheid. Mij werd ook gegeven dat ik haar met vrijmoedigheid in de Classis mocht uitspreken en toen werd gezegd: „Tede, gij kunt tot de studie overgaan, wat ons als Classis betreft."

Ik zeide tot mijn predikant: „als ik niet meer licht krijg, kan ik er toch niet toe overgaan. Ik heb nog zoo veel aanvallen." „Dat is Satan's werk," zeide hij. „Mogelijk," zeide ik, „maar dan zijn zijne listen mij onbekend."

Op de volgende provinciale vergadering waren er twee verzoeken. Predikanten en ouderlingen hadden – buiten mij – een verzoek voor mij tot de provincie gericht. Over het verzoek van een ander werd afwijzend beschikt. Het verzoek voor mij werd toegestaan. Ik kwam er te meer door in de engte, want de begeerte was er, maar de vrijmoedigheid kwam niet.

In dien tijd begon het volk naar Amerika te gaan. De gedachte kwam in mij op: „Zou ik ook naar Amerika moeten?" Ik wist dat de Heere wat bijzonders met mij voor had, maar ik wist niet wat. Ik had geen neiging om naar Amerika te gaan, want dan moest ik verreizen wat ik had en als ik studeerde dan kon ik dat behouden. Mijne vrouw zeide: „Als gij naar Amerika gaat, dan weet ik heel goed, dat ik hier blijf." De menschen wilden er ook niet van hooren dat ik naar Amerika zou gaan. Ik woonde dien avond den kerkeraad te Sexbierum bij en hoopte nog wat licht te ontvangen, maar alles bleef duister. Ik ging naar huis en mijne bede was: „Och Heere, geef mij de overtuiging in mijne ziel welken weg ik heb te kiezen." Ik kwam 's nachts thuis, ging bij tafel zitten en bad om licht en opening in mijnen weg; dat ik overtuigd mocht wezen wat te doen. En eindelijk, ja, ja, ik werd klaar in mijne ziele overtuigd; wij moesten naar Amerika. Ik zeide: „Heere, moeten wij heengaan, ach het is tegen mijn zin. Och geef mij ook nu nog een teeken uit Uw Woord." Er lag een Nieuw Testament op tafel. Met mijn geschockt gemoed nam ik het, sloeg het open en las: „Het boos en overspelig geslacht verzoekt een teeken en het zal geene teeken gegeven worden." Ik viel achterover in mijn stoel en zeide: „Heere wat woord is dat! O Gij zijt rechtvaardig, ik heb altijd gevraagd, dat Gij overtuigend licht in mijne ziele zoudt schenken – Gij deed het en nu verzocht ik weer een teeken uit Uw Woord bovendien, Gij deed recht: Hun zal geen teeken gegeven worden. Mij kwam voor: „Indien gij Mij gelooft om de woorden, gelooft mij dan om de werken die ik doe, dat ik van den vader gezonden ben." Helaas, nu was ik als de Jooden! Maar ik kwam tot ernstige schuldbekentenis en de Heere stelde mij gerust. Ik vertelde aan mijne vrouw geheel de omstandigheid, en zij zeide: „Als dan alles zoo klaar is, dan ga ik mede."

Dien nacht had ik weinig rust gehad, en 's morgens stond ik buiten bij onze steenen hut. Onze buurman zou een hut van hout bouwen.... Hij kwam met zijn vader; zij bezagen het nog eens en de koop was gesloten. Onze predikant was krank. Des Zaterdags ging ik naar hem toe om alles mede te deelen, maar de bolloopsters hadden hem alreeds met alles bekend gemaakt.

„Wat hoor ik nu?" zeide hij. „Gaat gij naar Amerika? Alles verkocht? Nu weet ik niet meer wat ik van de bevinding der heiligen denken moet!"

Ik vertelde hem alles omstandig. „O broeder," zeide hij, „indien ik er een roeping heen had, ik verkocht ook alles en ging met u mede." De menschen verwonderden zich en vraagden: „Baas naar Amerika?" Mijn buurman wilde ook meegaan.

Ik vraagde: „Maar hebt gij al met den Heere geraadpleegd?" „O ja," zeide hij, „dat heb ik gedaan." „Welnu, laten wij dan samen bidden om vrijmoedigheid."

24 Mei 1847 stapten wij zoo uit ons huis en lieten alles achter, behalve de bedden. Wij kwamen aan boord van het zeilschip *Doggerbank*. Spoedig ontdekte ik, dat er waren bij wie de vreeze des Heeren niet was. Toen ik er een opmerkzaam op maakte, dat hij niet mochte vloeken, zeide hij „Welnu, ik doe het niet in huis, maar op het schip wel." Des Zondags hadden wij tweemaal godsdienstoefening aan boord en dan las ik preeken. Toen wij in het Kanaal waren werd er nog een groot huisgezin van 17 personen opgenomen, waarvan de vader Parelberg heette, een vroom man.

Eindelijk kwamen wij in Albany. Wij verstonden geen woord Engelsch. De vraag was: waar zullen wij heen? Ik zei: „Laten wij onder die luik gaan", want het regende hard. En welk een gelukkige geschikking! Toen wij daar stonden kwam er een Hollander bij ons, een jongeling uit Utrecht. „Kom," zeide hij tot mijne vrouw, „geef mij Uw kind en volg me maar, ik zal u naar een plaats brengen, waar meer Hollanders zijn." Toen wij daar waren, vraagde ik: „Wie weet waat Ds Ypma is?" „Die is in April alreeds naar de kolonie Vriesland in Michigan gegaan." „Is hier ook eene Klaas de Vree?" „Ja, die woont in Franklin Straat."

Wij ontmoetten zijn zoon, die ons van blijdschap omhelsde en bij zijn ouders bracht. Ons meisje M. zeide: „Nu zijn wij thuis." Wij kwamen boven De Vree te wonen en leefden in gulle vriendschap met elkander.

Maar ik was schoenmaker en had geen werk en toch moesten wij eten. In zulke omstandigheden is een Christen vaak niet zonder gebed. Op een Zaterdagmorgen ging ik met een zwaar gemoed buiten Albany op de bergen. Toen ik daar op den berg was viel ik op mijne knieën, stelde onzen toestand den Heere voor en zeide: „Och Heere, wij zijn hier in een vreemd land, in het midden van menschen wier spraak wij niet kennen; maar Gij zijt diezelfde God als die gij waart in Nederland. Aan U heb ik mij voor tijd en eeuwigheid overgegeven, och geef dat ik nu ook het Jakobsdeel mag hebben, brood om te eten en kleederen om aan te trekken."

Er kwam geen uitkomst. Ik ging boven op den berg en knielde weder en toen kreeg ik zoo klaar deze woorden: „Uw brood is zeker en uw water gewis."

Ik ben nu 78 jaren, maar de Heere heeft die belofte altijd niet alleen trouw aan ons vervuld, maar ook zooveel nog bovendien aan ons geschonken. Ik werd ziek maar de Heere verloste ons uit alle nooden gedurende de negen maanden dat wij in Albany waren.

In Albany woonden wij in het midden van Ieren. Die menschen zijn over het algemeen verbazend onverschillig. Ds. Wyckoff kwam gedurig en wilde ons daar weg hebben. Wij lieten die Ieren voor hetgeen zij waren en omdat wij ons niet met hen bemoeiden, bekommerden zij zich ook niet om ons. Het ging er overigens soms schrikkelijk bij hen over weg. Eens was er een groot rumoer naast ons, een dochter sleepte hare moeder bij de haren de deur uit en schopte en sloeg haar. Bij een andere gelegenheid vocht een man met zijne vrouw. Zij bloedde hevig en stierf kort daarna. Hoe ongelukkig als in huisgezinnen de vreese des Heeren gemist wordt.

Eindelijk kwamen wij op een kanaal boot of trekschuit, om naar de kolonien in Michigan te gaan. Wij waren vijf weken onderweg en kwamen eindelijk in Grandville aan. Wij gingen naar een oude store. Klaas de Vree en Albert Kroes waren bij ons en wij allen waren onrustig omtrent het heden en den dag van morgen.

„Hoever zijn wij hier nog van de Kolonie en van Ds. Ypma", vroegen wij. „Vijftien mijlen", was het antwoord. Wij hadden geen eten en namen dus ook geen mede toen wij op reis gingen naar Vriesland, want 15 mijl dachten wij, dat is slechts 5 uren. Maar, eilieve, den gehelen dag reisden en dwaalden wij in de uitgestrekte bosschen en eerst 's avonds om vijf uur kwamen wij op goed geluk bij de oude Lanning, te Drenthe, aan. Zij zetten ons eten voor maar eten kon ik niet, alleenlijk drinken.

En daar heb ik het eerst in de kolonie geschreid, want toen was men op
een zeker punt in het kerkelijke in de war. Om den anderen Zondag
namelijk, zou Ds. Ypma daar preeken en men verstond elkander niet.
Ik kon dien twist niet hebben en dacht: „Zij zijn hier pas en nu hebben
zij-het al met elkander in de war. Wat wil dat worden?"

L. Dijkstra had een blokhuis opgericht en die kwam bij Lanning. „Zijt
gij dat, Tede?" „Ja man, kent gij mij?" „Persoonlijk niet, maar ik heb al
vaak van u gehoord."

Toen wij een weinig met elkander gesproken hadden, zei ik: „Ik zou
zoo gaarne naar Ds. Ypma willen gaan." „Kom dan maar met mij", zei
Dijkstra.

O, die ontmoeting met Ypma en de juffrouw was zoo hartelijk en ik
was zoo door en door blij, dat ik alle armoede in eens vergat! Ik was
volkomen gerust want ik was bij het Volk. Daar bleef ik dien nacht en
den volgenden dag gingen wij naar de blokkerk bij Kaslander. Wij allen
waren blij in de kerk. Na de kerk wilde Ulke de Vries mij mede hebben.
O vrede, wat was het daar arm! Geen tafel, geen stoel. Blokjes waren
stoelen en de kist was tafel. Er waren er die geld genoeg hadden, maar
meubelen waren hier niet te krijgen. Geert van der Schouw haalde vervolgens ons volkje van Grandville. Van daar tot hier overal boomen en
daardoor konden wij zoo gemakkelijk verdwalen. Dan waren er ook
geen bruggen. De wagen door ossen getrokken en mijn vrouw met een
kind in den arm er op, ging zoo de beek maar in, en verscheidene keeren
riep zij: „Ik ga dood tusschen al die kisten hier!"

Toen kwamen wij eindelijk in de Kolonie op ons land, 20 acres, dat ik
reeds in Nederland gekocht had voor 20 gulden. De staten hadden vroeger
dit land in Michigan van de Indianen gekocht voor een schelling de
acre en dan haalden zij jaarlijks een gedeelte van dat geld van Mr.
Camplace te Grand Rapids.

Hier in de Kolonie scheen het ons nog veel donkerder toe dan in
Albany. Menschen hoorde men niet. Wij kwamen gedurig bij Ds. Ypma.
Die man heeft wat uitgestaan! Een dag, het was in 1849, heeft hij bepaald
niets kunnen krijgen; er was niets. Des nachts had hij zijn huis gesloten
met een deken en een kist er voor want men was ook nog bevreesd voor
wolven; beeren waren er soms ook.

Hier in de nabijheid waren menschen, die gedurig last van beeren
hadden. Eens op een avond dreunde de grond van het gebrul en een
oogenblik daarna zagen wij een beer, die een van hunne dikke varkens
uit het hok gehaald, tusschen de voorpoten had en daarmede wegging.
Maar ook moesten die beesten zulke tochten wel eens met hun leven

boeten, schoon niet iedereen het hart had om ze dood te schieten. Zoo waren er eens verscheidene mannen bij die lieden, waarvan ik zoo even sprak. Men zou den beer vangen. Tot dat einde had men dicht bij het huis een groot gat gegraven, wat dunne planken en stroo er over gelegd en daarop een klein varkentje geplaatst. Maar beer om scheen het te begrijpen en waagde zich niet op die verleidelijke brug. Hij kwam er bij en liep er omheen, maar meent gij, dat een dier mannen het hart in het lijf had, om hem van onder het venster langs dood te schieten? Niet een, en de beer kwam er heelhuids af.

De Engelschen schoten er wel. Eens waren wij op een middag bij hen. Zij noodigden ons en wij schikten aan. De vrouw des huizes zeide: „Mr. Ulberg, do you like beef?" „Yes ma'am." Even daarna vraagde zij: „Do you know what it is?" „No ma'am." „It is pork of the bear." Wel, als ik het niet geweten had – het smaakte lekker – dan had ik het gegeten voor vet schapenvleesch.

Wij kwamen te wonen in de „citadel", een huis van palen recht opstaande van boven tot beneden en boven er op een dikke laag modder en mitsdien bomvrij, waarom het dan ook een „citadel" genoemd werd. Daar waren wij zoolang tot ons blokhuis klaar was. De familie Van Zoeren kwam ook nog bij ons „of wij hen konden herbergen?" „Ja wel, maar wij kunnen het u niet beter geven dan wij zelven het hebben. Gij moet op den grond slapen."

Dat was alles best. Nu regende het alle dagen, mijn boeken gingen uit den band. Overal en alles was water. Mijn volk begon te murmureeren en ik zelf ook. Degenen die uit een fatsoenlijke stand kwamen, hadden het meest te lijden. Wij kregen een stuk zout spek en kookten soep.

„Maar," zeide mijn vrouw tot de timmerlui bij ons blokhuis, „zijn dat geen siepels [uien] in het bosch?" „Welzeker." „Zijn ze goed?" „O ja."

Ik haalde toen siepels uit het bosch en wij kookten ze in de soep, maar toen zij opgeschept was en wij ze zouden eten, helaas het was geen eten. Ik riekte het wel toen ik thuis kwam en zei als de zonen der profeten: „de dood is in de pot" – en had ik nu maar het geloof van den profeet gehad, dan zou ik er zeker nog wat flour in geworpen hebben, maar dat geloof had ik niet en wij konden die soep niet eten.

„Toen wij nog in de „citadel" woonden hadden wij vijf kinderen bij ons, en die kinderen hebben weten dat men nu den een eens en dan den ander moet bestraffen, want da schreeuwt eens de een en dan de ander. Mijn buurman, Van Vliet, zeide: „Laat de kinderen maar schreeuwen, want dan hoor ik nog dat er menschen zijn en anders hoor ik er niets van."

Vervolgens kregen wij nog een grootte behoefte. Het geld was op, alles op. Mijne huisgenooten murmureerden, ik raakte van het pad af en murmureerde ook. Maar met een bezwaard gemoed ging ik naar buiten en stond bij een omgevallen eikenboom en stelde biddend mijne behoeften den Heere voor. Toen kwamen zoo helder in mijn hart de woorden: „de jonge leeuwen hongeren [lijden armoede staat er, maar ik kreeg de woorden zoo, hongeren] maar die den Heere vreezen hebben geen gebrek aan eenig goed." „Ja, Heere", zeide ik, „dat is voor uw volk maar niet voor mij." Gij ziet hoever ik reeds van het rechte pad was. Toen was het alsof tot mij gezegd werd: „Ben Ik niet de God van Albany op den Berg? Heb Ik u niet beloofd, dat uw brood zeker en uw water gewis zoudt zijn?" O, daar viel ik; de Heere stelde mij in de ruimte, omringde mij met vrolijke gezangen en toen werd, zooals men dat wel eens noemt, het verbond tusschen den Heere en mij vernieuwd.

Vervolgens kwamen wij in ons blokhuis. Ik sprak daar van vroolijke gezangen. Des avonds, als het mooi weer was, zaten wij op de fonda-menten van het niet afgebouwde gedeelte. Ik had het fluitspelen geleerd en den Heere beloofd, dat ik niet anders dan psalmen spelen zou. Kwamen mij wereldsche deuntjes voor den geest en zou ik neiging gevoelen om die te spelen, dan moest ik steeds weer naar de door mij aan God gegeven belofte terug. Op die fondamenten zaten wij, ik speelde en mijn vrouw en kinderen zongen allen vroolijk psalmen. Dat klonk heerlijk in het bosch.

In 1849 kwamen bij ons de predikanten Ypma, Van Raalte en Wyckoff. Wij waren verblijd ook met Ds Wyckoff, vermits wij ZErw. zoo goed kenden uit het dagelijksche verkeer in Albany. Toen deed Ds Wyckoff de vraag: „Of het volk zich niet zou willen vereenigen met de Dutch Reformed Church?" Op die vraag werd eerst niet geantwoord.

„Onze kerk biedt voordeelen aan", zeide hij. „Gij zijt nu nog in uwe kindschheid, maar als gij mannelijke jaren krijgt en het staat u dan bij ons niet aan, dan kunt ge ons de broeder hand reiken en op uzelven staan. Gij hebt ook een rondreizenden predikant noodig; gij kunt er een uit Holland, of van waar ook, beroepen en onze Board geeft daarvoor $ 200, en als de gemeenten dan ook nog daarvoor iets kunnen doen, dan gaat het gemakkelijk."

Ik ben nog de eenige levende van die vier aan wie zulks het eerst werd voorgelegd. Twee weken later was het Classis. Toen heeft Ds. van Raalte een man uitgemaakt. Er waren namelijk ouderlingen en anderen, dien het voorstel van Ds Wyckoff uitmuntend beviel. Zij zeiden: „Wij moeten het doen en het is niet noodig om er de gemeenten naar te vragen."

Ds. van Raalte zeide: „Broeders, dat is mis, ik waarschuw u. Blijkt het van achteren verkeerd, dan hebben wij de schuld. Stellen wij het aan de gemeenten voor en mocht het verkeerd zijn, dan is ook de schuld mede voor de gemeenten."

In 1851 kwam er alreeds roering in betrekking tot de aansluiting. Wij vergaderden in een blok schoolhuis te Vriesland. Ik was uit het Oosten gekomen en men vroeg mij, vermits ik 9 maanden in Albany geweest was, wat ik er van wist?

„Wat ik er van weet," zeide ik, „kan ik zeggen." [1] „Ik heb daar nog nooit over den Catechismus hooren preeken, ook in de kerk van Ds. Wyckoff niet." [2] „Zij hebben daar geen feestdagen. Toen ik in Albany was, vraagde ik mijn baas eens: hoe komt dat zoo baas, dat er hier geen catechismus gepredikt wordt?" „Dat weet ik niet, wordt er in Holland uit den Catechismus gepredikt?" „Ja." [3] „Ook ben ik er nooit geweest dat er in de gemeente gedoopt werd, dat geschiedde in de consistorie-kamer en bij rijken ook wel aan huis. Ik heb er het Avondmaal eens mede gehouden en toen zaten de zwarten geheel afgezonderd." Ik vraagde later: „Waarom zou men dat zoo doen baas dat de zwarten geheel af-zonderlijk en niet mede bij de avondmaalstafel zitten?" „Wel, als uw vrouw eens stierf en gij zoudt een ander nemen, zoudt gij dan een zwarte willen hebben?" „Neen, dat juist niet. Maar het is hier toch een geheel ander geval. Als eens alle geslachten der aarde voor den rechterstoel van Christus zullen verschijnen, zal dan alle onderscheid niet weg zijn? Bij God is geen aanneming des persoons; mogen wij zulk een onderscheid maken in het godsdienstige?" De baas antwoordde niet.

Toen wij hier een jaar in de Kolonie geweest waren, ontmoette ik Ds. Pieter J. Oggel, die mij vraagde: „Wat dunkt u baas, zou het met de Kolonie opgaan?" „Ik denk ja", zeide ik. „Maar", vraagde hij verder – want die predikanten vragen nauwkeurig – „wat reden hebt gij daar-voor?"

Ik zeide: „Daarvoor heb ik twee redenen. [1] De menschen zijn bij het heengaan niet te raden gegaan met vleesch en bloed, maar hebben het aangezicht des Heeren gezocht. [2] Als God een volk planten en opbou-bouwen wil, dan laat hij dat vermenigvuldigen en weinigen sterven. Dokters zijn er niet, de eene helpt den ander en alles gaat immers goed."

„Dat is waar," zeide Ds. Oggel, „als het volk nu maar in des Heeren wegen wandelt." Ds. Oggel predikte in een blokkerk en wij hadden zegen.

Toen wij nog in de citadel woonden, stond alles nog vol boomen. Eens toen ik van ons te bouwen blokhuis weer naar onze woning zou gaan, verdwaalde ik en bleef lang uit. Mijn vrouw werd zeer bevreesd en stond met de lantaarn buitenshuis en riep: „Zijt gij daar?" Ik zeide: „Ja." Welk een groote behoefte hebben wij aan licht in natuur en in genade, want toen ik het licht maar zag was ik gerust en spoedig thuis.

Dat verdwalen gebeurde vaak. Ds. Ypma kwam ook eens uit eene woning in de nabijheid, hij liep tweemaal om een omgevallen boom en komt, na lang geloopen te hebben, weer bij hetzelfde huis. „Hoe wonderlijk", dacht hij, „zijn hier twee gelijke huizen?" Oude Van der Kooi kwam ook eens eindelijk bij zijn eigen huis en kon niet zien, dat het zijn eigen was.

Nu had ik in dien tijd werk genoeg, maar geen leer. Ik zeide tot mijn vrouw: „Ik ga naar Grand Rapids." Zij zeide: „Wat zult gij er doen, gij hebt geen geld." Ik zeide: „De Heere zal voorzien." „Ja," zeide zij, „maar hoe?" Ik zeide: „Dat weet ik niet."

Ik liep er heen, nam een paar schoenen mede, die te groot waren en verkocht die te Grandville voor $ 1.50 – had eenige boekjes over de Rechtvaardiging, die ik verkocht en kreeg dus wat geld. Daarmede ging ik naar de looierij en zocht leer uit voor drie maanden. Ik wilde betalen maar had veel te min. Ik liep weg en zie, daar is er iemand die mij op zekere voorwaarden een menigte centen gaf. Toen ging ik naar de looierij, keerde mijn jaszak op de tafel om en ziede: "All gold my friends." "No, no," riepen de Engelschen, "we want no penny from you." Zij wilden mij het leder op crediet geven, maar namen ten slotte op mijn aanhouden toch de pennies aan en ik was geholpen. Met een blij en dankbaar hart keerde ik huiswaarts.

Na verloop van jaren zouden wij weder een nieuw blokhuis hebben en dan de boomen geschild. De timmerman zei: „Doe het niet, zet er eenvoudig planken om heen." Mijn buurman had geld in een zaagmolen, kon wel hout, maar geen rente in geld krijgen. Hij zeide: „Gij maakt stevels voor mij en dan krijgt gij hout, zooveel gij noodig hebt." In orde. Nu moesten er shingles en spijkers enz. wezen. Alles kostte mij $ 3 aan geld en overigens betaalde ik alles met schoenen en stevels.

Ja wonderlijk, de Heere maakte alles voor ons te recht. Nu ben ik 78 jaar en door de genade Gods, die mijne eeuwige en trouwe Vader in Christus is, sta ik nog tot op dezen dag. Wij hebben zes kinderen, vier en veertig kleinkinderen en vijf achter-kleinkinderen. En nu terugziende op den weg, dien de Heere ons leidde, mogen wij met geheel ons hart zeggen: „Ebenhaezer – tot hier toe heeft ons de Heere geholpen."

[Translation]

If pursuant to request I am to write a short account of my experiences on my journey hither and while here in America for the readers of the *Jaarboekje* [yearbook], it seems best – to do this in a more or less systematic manner – first to relate how I and my family came to America.

This happened in the following manner. Under the Lord's guidance shown me in my fatherland I was strongly convinced that He had in mind some particular purpose for me, but what this was I did not know. I communicated my thoughts to the pastor of our congregation at Minnertsga in Friesland and also to other pious persons. I had the desire to become a minister, but I did not know whether the Lord had called me. Our pastor who knew me well advised me to state my desire to the Classis at Franeker and to that end present a written statement of my activities. This I did; and after having answered a number of questions asked by the classical body, I was invited to step outside the room so they could discuss among themselves what answer they should give me. The outcome was that the Classis accepted me, and I was asked to prepare a discourse on 2 Cor. 8, 9, "For you know the grace of our Lord Jesus Christ, that being rich he became poor for your sakes: that through his poverty you might be rich", to be given before the next meeting of the Classis. But I pleaded that this was asking a little too much from me, a man who had never studied much. "Yes," it was argued, "but we expect more from you, and, besidedes you are 42 years old." „Well then," I replied, „if that is in accord with the way of the Lord, I hope He will give me spiritual light and wisdom; but if it is not in accord with His way then I wish he would make my thoughts on that matter to be foolishness."

Now I wanted some book dealing with this theme. I looked everywhere to find some sermon on that text, but nowhere could I find one. The time drew near. I was up stairs. I would lie on my knees a while and, when some thoughts came to me, I wrote them down. Our pastor came home; I asked him to listen to what I had written and he was to tell me truly whether the context and the divisions of the text were proper. "Yes," he said, finally, "everything is proper." I had succeeded. The Lord granted me additional light and my sermon finally was finished. I delivered it before the meeting of the Classis. Then I was told, "Tede, so far as the Classis is concerned, you may proceed with your studies." I said to my pastor, "If I do not get more light, I shall not be able to begin my studies. I still have so many doubts." "That," he assured me, "is Satan's work." "Possibly," I replied, "but if so I do not know his tricks."

At the following provincial meeting two requests were presented. The pastors and the elders without my knowledge had addressed a request in my behalf. The petition of the other person was not accepted. I was more troubled than ever, for while I had the desire to go ahead, I did not possess the necessary courage. At that time the people began to talk about America. The thought rose in my mind, "Should I too have to go to America?" I knew that the Lord had some special intention regarding me, but what it was I did not know. I had no desire to go to America, for I would need to spend all I owned, and if I studied I would be able to keep it. My wife said, "If you go to America, then I know very well that I will stay here." Nor would the people listen to my idea of going to America. That night I attended a meeting of the consistory at Sexbierum, hoping to acquire some more light, but everything remained dark as ever. I returned home with the prayer, "O Lord give me the necessary conviction which way I am to go." I returned during the night, sat by the table, and prayed for light and for information which way to go, that I might be convinced as to what I should do. And, finally, I had clarity; we should go to America. I said, "Lord, if we must go, alas! it is against my desire. Give me one more indication from out of Thy Word." A New Testament lay on the table. Deeply moved, I opened it and read, "An evil and adulterous generation demands a sign, and no sign shall be given unto it...." [Matthew, 12, 39]. I fell back in my chair and said, "Lord, what a thing is Thy Word! Thou art just, I have always prayed that Thou might give light to my soul. Thou didst grant my prayer, but again I sought a sign out of Thy Word. Thou didst write, 'and no sign shall be given unto it.'" The thought then came to my mind, "if you believe Me, believe My words, believe in Me also because of the works I do, that I have been sent of the Father. [See John 5, 23-38] Alas! To me it seemed like the Jews! But I came to an earnest acknowledgement of my guilt, and the Lord comforted me. Thereupon I told my wife all these things, and she replied, "If, then, everything is so clear, I shall go with you."

That night I had little rest, and in the morning I stood outside by our little brick house. Our neighbor was planning to build one like but of wood.... He appeared with his father and we discussed his buying my house instead of building an ew one. They examined the house, and the sale was completed. Our pastor was sick. On Saturday I called on him to tell him what had happened, but the gossipers had already informed him. "What do I hear now," he asked. "Are you going to America? Sold everything? Now I no longer know what to think of the faith of saints!" I told him everything. "Brother," he said, "if I had a calling to go to

America, I would sell everything and go with you." People marvelled and asked, "You are going to America?" My neighbor also wanted to go with us. I asked him, "But have you consulted the Lord?" "O yes" was his reply, "that I have done." "Well, then, let us pray together for courage."

On May 24, 1847, we left our house taking nothing except our bedding. We boarded the sailing ship *Doggerbank*. Soon I noted that some of the crew did not have the fear of the Lord. When I called the attention of one of the men to the fact that he might not swear, he replied, "Well, I do not swear at home, but I do it on board ship." Every Sunday we had two services, and I read sermons.

When we were in the English Channel a large family of 17 persons came aboard. Father of this household was Parelberg, a pious man. Finally we arrived in Albany. We did not understand a word of English. The question was, "Where shall we go?" I suggested, "Let us stand by that shutter," for it was raining hard. What a lucky move! For while we were standing there along came a Hollander to stand by us, a young man from Utrecht. "Come to my wife," he said, "give me your child and follow me, I shall take you to a place where there are Hollanders." When we came to the place he had in mind, I asked, "Who knows where Dominie Ypma has gone?" "He left in April for the Kolonie Vriesland in Michigan." "Is there a Klaas de Vree here in the city?" "Yes, he is living in Franklin Street."

We met his son who hugged us with delight and took us to his parents. Our little girl M. said, "Now we are at home." We took upstairs rooms and lived in generous friendship with De Vree. But I was a shoemaker. I had no work, and yet we had to eat. Under such circumstances a Christian has recourse to prayer. On a Saturday morning, greatly depressed, I went outside Albany into the hills. On one of the hills I dropped on my knees, and spoke to the Lord about our circumstances, and said, "Lord, we are here in a strange land, amid people whose language we do not understand. But you are the same God as you were in the Netherlands. To you I have surrendered my temporal and eternal lot. Do but give me my Jacob's portion, bread to eat and clothes to wear." An answer came. I climbed to the top of the hill. Again I knelt and then the words came to me clearly, "Your bread is sure, your water certain." [Isaiah 33, 16].

I am now 78 years old, but the Lord has fulfilled that promise not only faithfully, but he has provided more. I fell sick, but the Lord delivered us from all our distress during the nine months we lived in Albany in the midst of Irish people who for the most part were astonishingly wicked and indifferent. Dominie Wyckoff frequently came to us and wanted to move us from that place. We left those Irish severely alone and, because we paid no attention to them, they took no notice of us. Sometimes there were frightful rows among them. Once there was a violent uproar next to us. A daughter dragged a mother by her hair out of the hosue and kicked and beat her. On another occasion a man fought with his wife. She bled profusely and soon died. How unfortunate when the peace of the Lord is not to be found in homes!

Finally we sailed in a canalboat to go to the settlements in Michigan. Our journey lasted five weeks, and finally we arrived in Grandville. We went to a store. Klaas de Vree and Albert Kroes accompanied us, and we were restless about our needs for today and tomorrow. "How far are we from Vriesland and Dominie Ypma?" we asked. "Fifteen miles," came the answer. We took no food with us, for we thought "15 miles is only 5 hours." But we traveled the entire day, and walked about in the boundless woods. It was five o'clock in the evening when with good luck we arrived at the house of the aged Lanning in Drenthe. They placed food before us, but I could not eat, only drink. Then I wept for the first time in the Kolonie, for the people were at odds over a certain point in church matters. On the next Sunday Dominie Ypma was to preach, but the people were divided.

L. Dijkstra had built a loghouse and he now came to Lanning's place. "Is that you, Tede?" "Yes, do you know me?" "Not personally, but I have often heard about you." After we had talked a little while, I said "I would like very much to go to Dominie Ypma." "Just come with me", was Dijkstra's reply. That meeting with Ypma and his wife was most cordial. I was so very happy that I forgot all poverty! I was completely at peace, for I was with my people. I stayed with them that night, and on the next day we went to the log church at Kaslander's. We all were happy in the church. After services Ulke de Vries wanted me to come with him. How poverty stricken it was in his house! No table, no chair. Blocks of wood served for chairs and a box was their table. Some of the people indeed had enough money, but furniture was not to be had. Next, Geert van der Schouw brought our families from Grandville. A dense forest covered the region between Grandville and Vriesland and so it was easy to get lost. There were no bridges. Our wagon was drawn by oxen. On it sat my wife holding a child in her arm. She was frightened when the wagon plunged into the creek. Many times she cried, "I shall die among all these boxes!"

Finally we were on our own land in the Kolonie, 20 acres which I had bought for 20 guilders in the Netherlands. The United States government had bought this land from the Indians at the rate of a shilling per acre. Each year they received a portion of this money from Mr. Camplace [Campau?] in Grand Rapids. Here in the Kolonie prospects seemed darker than in Albany. The forest was silent. We heard no human sound. We often called on Dominie Ypma. How much that man endured! One day in 1849 he was completely without food; there simply was none to be had. At night he closed his house by spreading a blanket before the door and placing a box in front of it, for the fear of wolves as well as bears.

In our neighborhood people were troubled by bears. One evening there was the growl of a bear which soon put in its appearance. It had dragged a big hog out of a sty, carrying it between its front paws and making away with it. Sometimes bears lost their lives in such forays, although not everybody was sufficiently courageous to shoot them. On one occasion a group of men were at the house of the people I referred to above for the purpose of trying to catch the bear. They had dug a deep hole near the house, placed thin planks over it, covered the planks with straw, and placed a small pig upon the straw. But Uncle Bear seemed to understand this was a trap, and refused to risk going over to the alluring bait. He walked up to the hole and walked around it, but do you think any of these men had the nerve, standing by the window, to shoot him? Not a one of them, and the bear scaped with his whole hide.

The English [that is, Americans] did shoot bears. Once we had lunch with some of them who invited us to their table. The housewife asked, "Mr. Ulberg, do you like beef?" "Yes ma'am." After a few moments she asked, "Do you know what it is?" "No ma'am." "It is the meat of a bear." If I had not known it [for it was tasty] I would have taken it for mutton.

We lived in the "Citadel", a house made of upright logs which were covered with a thick layer of mud, and for that reason bombproof wherefore the house was called the "Citadel". We lived here until our loghouse was finished. The Van Zoeren family came to us asking if we could give them shelter. "Yes, but we cannot give you better accomodation than we ourselves have. You'll have to sleep on the ground." That was well. But it rained every day so that the covers came off my books. There was water everywhere, and everything was soaked. My family began to complain, and so did I. Those who had belonged to a more respectable class suffered most. We managed to get a piece of salt pork from which we made soup. "But," said my wife to the carpenters

working on our loghouse, "are those not onions out there in the woods?"
"Of course." "Are they good?" "Oh yes!" I got some onions [leeks]
from the woods and we cooked them in the soup. But when it was served
we could not eat it. When I came into the house I said like the sons of
the prophet, "There is death in that pot." Had I only had the faith of the
prophet I surely would have thrown some flour into the soup, but such
faith I did not have, and so we could not eat that soup.

While we were living in the "Citadel" we had five children with us, and
those children learned that some of them had to be punished, for now
and again one of them would cry. My neighbor Van Vliet remarked,
"Let the children cry, for when they cry I know that there are human
beings around."

We had another great need. Our money had given out. There was none
left. My family complained. I too got off the straight path and also found
fault. But in a heavy mood I went outdoors, stood by a fallen oak tree,
prayerfully recommended my needs to the Lord. Clearly the words came
to my heart, "the young lions are hungry [suffer poverty, it is written,
but I read the word 'hungry'] but those who fear the Lord shall lack
nothing." [Psalms 34, 10] "Yes, Lord," said I, "that is for your people,
but not for me." You see how far I already was from the straight path!
Then it was as if I heard the words, "Am I not the God of Albany on
that hill? Have I not promised that your bread would be sure, your salt
certain?" O, there I fell; the Lord placed me in the open, surrounded
me with joyful songs and then, as it has been expressed, the covenant
between the Lord and me was renewed.

Finally we moved into our loghouse. There I sang joyful songs. In the
evening in fair weather we sat on the foundations of the part that had not
yet been finished. I had learned to play the flute and had promised the
Lord that I would play nothing but psalms. Whenever worldly tunes
came to my mind I returned to my original promise I made to God. On
that foundation we sat, I played and my wife and children all sang joyful
Psalms. This filled the woods with pleasant echoes.

In 1849 the ministers Maarten A. Ypma, A. C. van Raalte, and I. N.
Wyckoff came to us. We were pleased to see Dominie Wyckoff because
we knew him so well from our daily relations with him in Albany. He
posed the question whether the people would want to join the Dutch
Reformed Church? To that question at first no answer was made. "Our
church offers advantages," he declared. "You still are in your youth, but
when you arrive at your mature years if you are not pleased with the
union, you can extend a brotherly hand and stand by yourselves. You

are in need of a visiting missionary pastor, you can invite one from Holland or from any other place. Our Board will provide $ 200 for that purpose, and, if the congregation can contribute something, the object will be attained more easily."

I am the only living person of the four before whom this proposition was first placed. Two weeks later a meeting of the Classis was held. On that occasion Van Raalte showed himself a man of leadership. For there were elders and others who were pleased with Dominie Wyckoff's proposal. They said, "We must accept, and it is not necessary to ask the congregations about this matter." But Van Raalte urged caution, "Brothers, that is wrong, I warn you. If this thing later appears wrong then it will be our fault. Let us place it before the congregations for decision. Should it be wrong then the congregations will have to share part of the guilt."

Already in 1851 there was objection to the union. We met in a log schoolhouse in Vriesland. I had come from the east [New York], and was asked, since I had lived 9 months in Albany, what I could say on the matter. "What I know about it," I replied, "I can relate: 1. I never heard any preaching on the Catechism, not even in Dominie Wyckoff's church. 2. They do not keep the feastdays. When I was in Albany, I asked my boss 'how is it that they do not preach on the Catechism here?' 'I do not know; do they preach on the Catechism in Holland?' 'Yes," was my answer. 3. Nor have I ever seen any baptism in the midst of the congregation. That took place in the consistory room, also, if the people were rich, at their homes. I once participated in the Lord's Supper when the colored folk sat apart from the whites. Later I asked, 'Why this custom that the colored people are kept entirely apart at the Lord's table?' 'Well, if your wife should die and you should remarry, would you take a colored woman?' 'No, not exactly that. But this is a totally different matter. When all peoples of the earth one time shall appear before Christ's judgment seat there surely will be no distinction drawn? With God there is no preference of persons; may we then make this distinction in religious life?' My boss made no reply."

After we had lived a year in the Kolonie I met Dominie Pieter J. Oggel, who asked me, "What do you think, will the Kolonie succeed?" "Yes, I believe it will", was my response. "But," he asked fruther [for these ministers ask exact questions], "what reason have you for your conclusion?" I answered, "I have two reasons. 1. These people when they emigrated did not proceed taking counsel with flesh and blood, but they have sought the face of the Lord. 2. When God wants to establish a people He lets them increase and permits few to die. There are no doctors here, each person helps others, and everything goes well." "That is true," said Dominie Oggel, "if the people only walk in the Lord's ways." Dominie Oggel preached in the log church, and we were blessed.

While we were still living in the "Citadel" the surrounding country was covered with trees. Once when I was going from the place where we were planning to build our loghouse to our dwelling I lost my way and did not return home. My wife was frightened. She held a lantern in her hand and, standing in our doorstep, called, "Are you there?" I shouted "Yes." How much we need light in nature and also in grace, for when I saw the light I was at peace and soon back home.

Getting lost was a fequent occurrence. Once Dominie Ypma, on leaving a house in the neighborhood, twice circled a fallen tree, and after much walking came back again to the same house. "How strange," he thought, "that there are two similar houses." On one ocasion old Van der Kooi finally came to his house but could not tell whose it was.

At that time I had plenty of work, but no leather. I said to my wife, "I am going to Grand Rapids." She asked, "What will you do there, you haven't any money?" I replied, "The Lord will provide." "Yes, but how?" "That I do not know." I proceeded to Grand Rapids, took with me a pair of shoes which were too big and sold them in Grandville for $ 1.50. I also had several booklets on Justification which I sold and thus acquired some money. I went to the tannery and picked out enough leather to last me three months. I wanted to pay for the leather, but had not nearly enough money. So I walked away. But, behold, there stood someone who let me have some money. Then I returned to the tannery, emptied my pockets on the table and said, "All gold, my friends." "No, no," cried the English [that is, "Americans"], "we want no penney from you." They wanted to let me take the leather on credit. But, finally, on my insistence they accepted my money, and I was well served. With a happy and thankful heart I returned home.

After the passage of years we wanted a new loghouse, made of trees from which the bark was peeled. The carpenter said, "Don't do that, just nail boards over the logs." My neighbor had invested money in a sawmill. He could get all the wood he wanted, but no interest on his money. He said to me, "You make boots for me and I shall provide you with wood, as much as you may need." Agreed. But shingles and nails, etc., had to be bought. All these cost me $ 3. For the rest, I paid everything with boots and shoes.

Yes, marvelously, the Lord made all things straight for us. Now I am

78 years old. Through the grace of God, my eternal and trusted Father in Christ, I am able to stand until the present day. We have six children, 44 grand children, and 5 great-grandchildren. And now looking back upon the way along which the Lord has led us, may we with all our heart say, "Ebenezer – hitherto hath the Lord helped us." [1 Samuel 7, 12].

29. HENDRIK FRERIKS' MY EXPERIENCES

[Born in Bentheim, Hendrik Freriks settled in Vriesland in 1848. His *Ervaringen* were published in *De Grondwet*, March 5, 1912.]

De ondergeteekende is geboren te Veldgaar, koningrijk Hanover, graaf-schap Bentheim, in 1834. Ik ben den 20sten November 1847, met mijn vader, twee zusters en één broeder naar Rotterdam vertrokken. Wij zijn daar tot 5 Maart 1848 gebleven en zijn den 7den Maart 1848 aan boord gegaan van het zeilschip *Wijglehausen*, kapitein Warniekeim, om de reis naar Amerika te ondernemen.

Wij hebben 64 dagen op den Atlantischen oceaan gezwabberd en hebben veel storm gehad. Op Paaschmaandag zijn twee masten en de boegspriet van ons schip weggeslagen; toen waren wij in nood. Alle mannen die timmeren konden, moesten helpen om de gebroken stukken af te nemen en nieuwe weer op te zetten, toen de storm bedaard was.

De kost aan boord was slecht; het brood dat wij kregen was zoo hard, dat men de hamer er bij gebruiken moest om het stuk te slaan.

Gedurende de reis zijn drie personen gestorven en is één kind geboren. Wij hebben vele soorten visch gezien en ook de groote walvisch. Den 10den Mei zijn wij de haven van New York binnengezeild en vandaar zijn wij met een stoomboot de Hudson rivier opgevaren naar Albany. Van-daar gingen wij met een kanaalboot langs het Erie kanaal naar Buffalo. De kanaalboot was ongeveer 40 voet lang en er waren ongeveer 60 per-sonen aan boord met hun toebehooren. Er was 's nachts geen plaats voor allen om te slapen, zoodat velen hun nachtverblijf moesten zoeken op de kisten of ergens anders, maar niet op een bed, zoo als wij nu hebben. Deze reis duurde acht dagen.

Van Buffalo gingen wij met een stoomboot naar Chicago, een reis van vijf dagen, en vandaar met een zeilschip naar de haven van Holland en van de haven met een platboot naar Holland.

Holland was toen nog niet veel besetteld, bijna alles was nog bosch. Ds. van Raalte was toen al in Holland en wij zijn naar hem gegaan om inlichting te krijgen, waar wij goed land konden vinden. Hij is met ons gegaan naar wat nu Vriesland is en heeft land voor ons gekocht van het gouvernement voor $ 1.25 de akker. Toen wij het land gekocht hadden, zijn wij er zoo spoedig mogelijk heen gegaan. Wij zijn met een platboot van Holland gegaan naar "het waterhuisje", wat nu Groningen is en van daar zijn wij verder gebracht met een wagen, getrokken door ossen.

Het was den 16den Juni 1848 toen wij hier aankwamen, waar ik thans nog woon. Het was in dien tijd nog alles bosch en wild gedierte, zooals beeren, wolven, herten en meer andere soorten van wilde dieren in overvloed.

De eerste nacht dat wij hier waren hadden wij geen onderdak; het heeft den geheelen nacht geregend. Mijn vader en broeder hebben onder den wagen gelegen en ik op den wagen en toen de morgen aanbrak had geen van ons veel droogs meer aan.

Den volgenden dag hebben wij een hut gebouwd van takken, om daarin te wonen. Daarin hebben wij zes weken gewoond en in die zes weken hebben wij een log huis gebouwd. Er ontbrak ons in dien tijd van alles. Alle huismeubels die wij hadden, waren een kachel en twee stukken pijp en een elleboog.

In den herfst, toen de bladeren van de boomen begonnen te vallen, kwam de wind door het bosch en toen begon het moeilijk te worden om de kachel aan te houden. Onze schoorsteen was een gat door de loggen, op zij naar buiten. De wind woei er soms in en dan konden wij het in huis niet uithouden van den rook, zoodat wij maar besloten om de pijpen door den zolder te steken en de rook tegen het dak te laten gaan, want wij hadden geen pijpen genoeg om boven uit het dak te komen. Het was zeer moeilijk om nieuwe pijpen te krijgen, daar wij daarvoor naar Grand Rapids moesten loopen. Die reis heb ik meer dan eens te voet gedaan.

Het wild gedierte heeft ons meer dan eens den oogst bijna geheel vernield. De beeren hebben ons dikwijls de varkens uit het hok gehaald en vaak hebben wij elkaar geholpen om de beeren te verdrijven.

Het eerste graan, dat wij hier verbouwd hebben, hebben wij zelf in huis gedorschen, door het met handen vol over een blok te slaan. Wanneer wij het gedorschen hadden, zagen wij zoo goed als mogelijk was om het graan bij elkaar te krijgen, en om het schoon te krijgen brachten wij het naar buiten in den wind en schudden het heen en weer in een schotel of iets dergelijks.

Onze eerste leeraar was dominee Maarten Ypma, die ons elken Zondag Gods Woord verkondigde. En mogen wij ten slotte ook God danken dat hij ons door alle wederwaardigheden heen tot hiertoe gezegend heeft. En laat ons met den dichter van ouds zeggen:

Voorgeslachten kwijnen henen
En wij bloeien op hun graf.
Ras zal 't nakroost ons beweenen,
't Menschdom valt als bladeren af.

[Translation]

The undersigned was born at Veldgaar in the kingdom of Hanover. With my father, two sisters, and one brother I left for Rotterdam on November 20, 1847. We stopped there until March 5, 1848, and on March 7 we went on board the sailship the *Wiglehausen*, captain Warnekeim, in order to go to America.

For 64 days we sailed on the Atlantic Ocean driven hither and thither by much storm. On Easter Monday [April 23] two masts and the bowsprit of our ship were carried away by the waves. That was a moment of danger. All men among the passengers who had any skill at carpentering were required to remove the broken pieces and install new parts as soon as the storm abated.

Our food on board this ship was poor; our bread was so hard that we had to use a hammer to break it.

During our passage three persons died and one was born. We saw many kinds of fish, also one large whale. We entered the harbor of New York on May 10 and thence we went by steamboat up the Hudson River to Albany. From there we proceeded by canalboat along the Erie Canal to Buffalo. This canalboat was about 40 feet long and carried about 60 passengers and their possessions. During nights there was not enough room for each passenger to lie down to sleep. Many of the passengers had to spend their nights lying on trunks or on other objects, but not abed as we do nowadays. This journey lasted eight days.

From Buffalo we went by steamboat to Chicago, a trip of five days, and from that place we went in a sailing ship to the harbor of Holland and from there in a flatboat to Holland.

Holland was not much of a settlement, nearly everything still was forest. Dominie A. C. van Raalte was living in Holland at that time and we called on him for information where we could find good farm land. He accompanied us to what now is Vriesland and bought land for us from the government at $ 1.25 an acre. As soon as we had bought this land we settled on it. We traveled in a flatboat from Holland to *"het Waterhuisje"*. At present this is Groningen. From that place we went by wagon drawn by oxen.

We arrived on our property on June 16, 1848, where we are still living. At that time the country was covered with forest in which roamed numbers of wild animals such as bears, wolves, deer, and other kinds.

During the first night after our arrival we had no roof over us. It rained the entire night. Father and brother slept under the wagon, and I on top of it. When morning came our clothes were pretty well soaked.

The next day we built a hut made of branches, to serve as a house. In this we lived six weeks during which time we built a loghouse. In those days we had to do without everything. Our furniture consisted in a stove and two pieces of pipe and one elbow piece.

When fall came and the wind blew through the woods it became difficult to keep the fire burning in the stove. Our chimney was simply a hole through the logs on one side of the house. At times the wind blew into the stove so that we could not stay in the house on account of the smoke. We decided to extend the pipes through the ceiling and let the smoke rise against the roof, for we did not have enough pipe to form a chimney on the roof. It was difficult to secure new pipe, to get it we had to go afoot to Grand Rapids. More than once I made the trip afoot to that place.

Wild animals destroyed practically all our crops. Often bears carried our pigs out of the sty. Often we had to work together to drive the bears away.

The first grain raised by our efforts we threshed in our house. Taking it in handfulls we beat it over a block of wood. After threshing we were as careful as possible to collect all the grain. To clean it of chaff we brought it outdoors and shook it back and forth in the wind using a saucer or some similar object.

Our first pastor was Dominie Maarten Anne Ypma who every Sunday proclaimed God's Word to us. May we in concluding now also thank God for having helped us trhough all vicissitudes up until the present moment and for having bldessed us. Let us repeat with the poet of old:

Generations fade away
And we bloom upon their graves
Soon our children will weep o'er us,
For we too are falling like the leaves.

30. ANNE DE VREE'S MY EXPERIENCES

[Emigrating from Sexbierum in Friesland in 1846, after tarrying in Albany, New York, De Vree arrived in Vriesland in the spring of 1848 where he spent most of his life as a farmer. His *Ervaringen*, written in 1910, were published in *De Grondwet*, February 20, 1912.]

Als ik mij wel herinner was het in 't jaar 1846, dat ik voor het eerst hoorde van Noord-Amerika. Vader was een van de eerste Afgescheidenen in Nederland en had om der waarheidswille ook al heel wat moeten lijden; en hoewel het toen niet meer zoo erg was met de vervolging als vroeger, werd er toch met verlangen uitgezien naar een plaats waar meer vrijheid van godsdienst heerschte.

Nu moet men wel in het oog houden dat dit niet de eenige reden was. [Ik houd van de geheele waarheid]. Neen, men wilde ook, o zoo graag, wat meer ruimte voor het lichaam, dat is, wat ruimer bestaan voor het tijdelijke leven. Daarom werd naar een andere streek gezocht en zoo werd Amerika het toevluchtsoord.

Mijn geboorteplaats is Sexbierum, Provincie Friesland, Nederland, en van daar uit ving onze reis aan. Wij gingen per as, dat is met de wagen, naar Harlingen, dat een uur gaans verwijderd was. Van daar met de boot over de Zuiderzee naar Rotterdam. Dit was in den herfst van 1846. Het plan was om met Ds. van Raalte te reizen, doch er waren zoo velen die met den goeden man wilden reizen, dat het schip hen niet kon herbergen en dat was ook ons lot, wat eene groote teleurstelling voor ons was. Doch weldra werd een ander schip gevonden, een nieuw schip, dat voor de eerste maal een reis zou doen naar Amerika. Dit was geen groote stoomboot, zooals er nu varen, maar een gewoon zeilschip.

Nu wil ik eene ervaring vertellen, die ik had als kind van nog geen 7 jaar, want ik werd pas 7 jaar toen wij eenige dagen op zee waren. Vader en moeder waren de stad [Rotterdam] in, om nog het een en ander te koopen voor de reis, en mijne zuster, die een paar jaar ouder was dan ik, zei tot mij: „Laten wij ook de stad eens bezien." Dit beviel mij en wij gingen de eene straat in en de andere uit en hadden reeds heel wat van de groote stad gezien, toen wij tot elkander zeiden: „Wij moeten terug naar het schip." Maar wij waren het niet eens over den weg dien wij moesten gaan. Ik zeide, dat wij deze straat moesten nemen en mijne zuster zeide, dat we de andere moesten inslaan. „Ik ga deze straat in", zei ik; „en ik ga die andere nemen", zei zij, en zoo geraakten wij van elkaar af. Het gelukte mij om het schip weer te vinden, maar Jantje bleef weg.

Gij die kinderen hebt kunt wel begrijpen hoe vader en moeder zich gevoelden, toen zij gewaar werden hoe het er bij stond. Men deed al wat men kon om haar weer te vinden; het werd reeds donker en den volgenden morgen zou het schip vertrekken. Wij brachten zeer bange uren door doch de Heere gaf uitkomst. Ongeveer te negen uur des avonds werd er van de wal geroepen „Zijn hier ook ouders die een kind hebben verloren?

Gij kunt wel begrijpen, dat dit geen tweemaal behoefde geroepen te worden. De verlorene was terecht gekomen; een heer en jufvrouw hadden haar gevonden en hadden haar beloofd voor haar te zullen zorgen, indien zij vader en moeder niet weer kon vinden. Die lieden hadden zelf geen kinderen en als ik daar nu nog over denk, dan zeg ik: wat is de Heere goed. Wij konden weer gerust slapen.

Den volgenden morgen, 19 October, verlieten wij Rotterdam naar Hellevoetsluis en van daar de groote zee in. Alles ging in het eerst zeer voorspoedig op zee; wij hadden mooi weer en de wind achter ons, dus alles ging naar wensch en de kapitein zei: „Als het zoo voortgaat, zijn we in drie weken in New York". Maar dit kwam anders uit, want nu volgde storm op storm en zoo hevig, dat wij niet vooruit, maar geweldig achter-uit geslagen werden. Alles in het schip moest vastgemaakt worden, zoo zelfs dat wij 's avonds, als wij naar kooi gingen om te slapen, onze kleeren oprolden en er een touw om bonden en het dan aan de bedde-plank, of liever de kooi vastmaakten, opdat zij niet ergens in een andere hoek van het ruim terecht kwamen. Eens werd de storm zoo erg, dat geen passagier naar boven mocht, de luiken werden dichtgenageld en 's nachts gaf de kapitein zelfs order om de groote mast om te kappen. Doch toen de nood op het hoogst was, gaf de Heere weer uitkomst; het schip begon weer te rijzen en de storm begon te bedaren; er was gebeden en er werd gedankt. Daarna hebben wij nog wel storm gehad, doch niet meer zoo erg.

Ik zal nu sommige noemen, die met ons naar dit land reisden: H. Stegink, die ouderling geweest is van de Eerste gemeente van Zeeland, en Jekel, ook van deze gemeente; Jan en Bart Kolvoord met hun twee zusters; de oude Michmerschuizen en zijn gezin en een zekere Jan Snoek. Ik weet al de namen niet meer en de naam van het schip is mij ook ont-gaan; ik weet wel dat het maar een zeilschip was en niet een van de groote stoomers van dezen tijd. Hoe het ook zij, na 65 dagen op den grooten oceaan te hebben rondgevaren, kwamen wij te New York aan. Dat er blijdschap was, toen onze oogen land zagen, behoef ik zeker niet te zeggen, vooral niet tot hen die in dien tijd over het groote water zijn gekomen. Toen wij het eerst New York zagen zei de een tegen den andere: „Amerika is wit." Men wist niet dat het sneeuw was en dus ook winter, want het was 23 December.

Wij waren dus in Amerika, maar wat nu te doen? Vader's beurs was leeg, ten minste er was geen geld meer om ver te reizen. Vader wist dat er een dominee de Witt in New York was en het gelukte ons ook om dien te vinden. Ds. de Witt dacht het best om naar Albany te gaan; hij dacht dat vader daar het best terecht kon en hij gaf een brief mede aan Ds. Wyckoff.

Zoo vertrokken wij van New York naar Albany met de stoomboot de Hudson Rivier op. Ik weet niet meer hoe ver, doch wel weet ik, dat de boot in het ijs vast raakte, zoodat wij de boot moesten verlaten en met den spoortrein, die toen pas was aangelegd, verder gingen tot Albany, waar wij laat in den avond van 24 December 1846 aankwamen. Wij moesten over het ijs om in Albany te komen, want de ferryboot was vast-gevroren in het ijs. Maar de Heere was met ons en leidde ons veilig, zoodat wij allen behouden aan wal kwamen.

Dien nacht was ons hotel een groot pakhuis; het zal licht zoo goed geweest zijn als de plaats waar onze Heer en Zaligmaker geboren werd. Hier vierden wij dus ons eerste Kerstfeest in dit land. Vader ging al spoedig Ds. Wyckoff opzoeken en vond in hem een warm vriend en goed raadsman. Al ras kregen wij een betere woning, en vader en mijn oudste broeder kregen al spoedig werk, en zoo werd er in onze behoefte voor-zien. Er was te Albany toen nog geen Hollandsche gemeente, maar wij gingen toch naar de kerk. Hoewel wij het niet konden verstaan, waren wij toch op de plaats waar Gods Woord verkondigd werd, en wij konden dan alleen maar meezingen, wanneer de wijze van den 134sten Psalm gezongen werd: „Dat 's Heeren zegen op u daal".

Wij werden al spoedig gewaar, dat wij in Amerika ook wel ziek konden worden. Dienzelfden winter nog kregen wij eerst de mazelen, toen de roodvonk en daarna nog de pokken en toch, uit dat alles redde ons de Heere en Hij spaarde ons het leven.

Na een jaar en drie maanden in Albany gewoond te hebben, vertrokken wij vroeg in het voorjaar van 1848 naar het Westen. Onze bestemming was naar de plaats waar Ds. Ypma woonde; dit is waar nu Vriesland is. Wij reisden van Albany naar Troy, van daar met de kanaalboot naar Buffalo en verder met de boot naar Detroit. Vervolgens naar Milwaukee en van daar naar Grand Haven en verder naar Grandville.

Nu waren wij weer op vasten wal en met een span ossen voor een wagen gingen wij langs ongebaande wegen het bosch in. De meesten van ons liepen, maar die op den wagen zaten hadden moeite om er op te blijven. Wij zagen dien dag niet veel anders dan boomen, hier en daar een kleine opening, of zooals men toen zeide, clearing – dit beteekent een plaatss waar de boomen weggeruimd waren.

Toen het avond werd, konden wij niet verder; wij ontdekten een kleine clearing, waar een log shanty stond en besloten hier te overnachten. Deze hut was gebouwd door Johannes Groen, den vader van Ds. Groen. Hij was een schoenmaker en had een paar beestenhuiden in de hut hangen, die een alles behalve aangename geur nalieten. Ik weet nog heel goed, dat ik tot moeder zei: „Hier lust ik geen eten." Buiten werd een goed vuur gemaakt en die niet in de hut konden, sliepen bij het vuur. Wij waren maar een mijl meer van mijn oom Ds. Ypma en toch moesten wij hier overnachten. Den volgenden morgen gingen wij weer op reis en nu waren wij dan ook weldra op de plaats onzer bestemming.

Onze reis van Albany, New York, naar Vriesland had ruim drie weken geduurd en nu waren wij in het Westen. Wij kinderen waren erg teleurgesteld, daar wij meenden dat het Westen een groote stad was en nu zagen wij niet anders dan hier en daar een log huis. De pastorie waarin mijn oom woonde was ongeveer 14 bij 16 voet, met een klein afdak aan eene zijde en hier moesten wij bij in, vader en moeder en zeven kinderen, en hier bleven wij tot ook voor ons een huis gebouwd was. Hierbij wil ik het voor deze keer maar laten.

[Translation]

If I recall accurately it was in the year 1846 that I heard for the first time about North America. My father was one of the first Seceders [*Afgescheidenen*] in the Netherlands and for the sake of the truth had to suffer a great deal. And although bitterness toward the Seceders was not as keen as it had been, people were earnestly looking for some place where there was greater freedom of religion.

The reader must keep in mind that this was not the only reason for emigration. [I believe in telling the complete truth.] No, people also were eager for greater physical freedom, that is broader material basis for living. This was the reason why people looked eagerly for some other region, and so America became a haven of refuge.

My birthplace is Sexbierum in the province of Friesland, the Netherlands, and from that place we undertook our journey. We traveled by wagon to Harlingen, a distance of one hour. From there we went by boat over the Zuider Zee to Rotterdam. This was in the fall of 1846. Our plan was to travel with Dominie A. C. van Raalte. But so many wanted to travel with that good man that the ship could not accommodate them all. Nor could we be given space, which was a great disappointment for us. But soon another ship was provided, a new one which was to make its first voyage to America. It was not a large ship, such as today crosses the ocean, but an ordinary sailing ship.

Now I want to tell of an experience I had as a child [I became seven after we had been a few days at sea]. Father and mother were in the city [Rotterdam] to buy a few things for our voyage. My sister who was a few years older than I said to me, "Let us go to see the city." I liked this idea and we walked about from one street to another. Finally, when we had seen a good deal we said to each other, "Now we have to go back to our ship." But we could not agree upon the way to the ship. "I'll take this street", said I; and "I'll take the other one", were her words. And so we separated. It was my fortune to fined our ship, but Jantje did not return.

You who have children can well understand how father and mother felt when they understood what had happened. Everything was done to find my sister. It was growing dark and our ship was to sail the following morning. We spent most anxious hours, but the Lord gave deliverance. At about nine o'clock a voice from the shore was heard, "Are there any parents here who have lost a child?"

You can well understand that it was not necessary to ask this question a second time. Our lost sister had come back to us. A lady and gentleman had found her and had promised to take care of her should she not find her parents. These people themselves had no children, and whenever I think about this event, I think, "How good is the Lord." We were able to sleep calmly.

The following morning, October 19, we left Rotterdam for Hellevoet-sluis where we sailed into the North Sea. At first our voyage was calm; the wind was fair and from the stern. So everything was going as well we could wish, and the captain remarked, "If this continues we'll be in New York in three weeks!" But this did not happen, for we passed through repeated storms, so violent that we made no progress but were driven back. Everything on board had to be fastened down. In the evening when we went to our bunks to sleep we rolled our clothing and tied it to our beds. We even fastened our bunk so that we would not be shifted to some other part of the ship. During one storm, such was its violence that no passenger was permitted on deck, the hatches were nailed down, and during the night the captain gave orders that the main mast be cut down. But when distress was greatest, the Lord again brought relief. The ship began to sail more smoothly, the storm abated, the people prayed and gave thanks. After this we had other storms but none was as violent.

Now I shall give the names of some of those who made this voyage with us. They were H. Steging [Jan Hendriks Stegink] who became elder of the first congregation in Zeeland, Jekel, the brothers John and Bart Kolvoord and their two sisters, the aged Michmerschuizen and his family, and one Jan Snoek. I do not recall the names of all the passengers, nor do I remember the name of the ship [it was the *Isabella Bath*]. However that may be, after 65 days sailing on the ocean we arrived in New

York. That we were happy when our eyes beheld land I surely need not state, especially not to those who crossed the ocean at that time. When we first beheld New York we were saying to each other, "America is white!" We did not realize it was snow that gave the city this appearance, for it was winter, and December 23.

So then we had arrived in America, but what were we to do? Father's purse was empty, at least it did not have money for us to travel much farther. Father knew there was a dominie named Thomas de Witt living in New York. Fortunately we were successful in finding him. He was of the opinion we had better proceed to Albany, for he thought father could better make his way there, and he gave him a letter of introduction to Dominie Isaac N. Wyckoff.

We left New York by steamboat and went up the Hudson River. I cannot recall how far we steamed, but I remember that we were caught in ice so that we had to travel further by railroad which had just been finished. We then proceeded to Albany where we arrived late in the evening of December 24, 1846. To get into Albany we had to walk over the ice, because the ferryboat was frozen fast in the ice. But the Lord was with us and guided us, so that we all arrived safely.

That night our hotel was a large packhouse. It certainly was as large as the place in which our Lord and Saviour was born. Here then we observed our first Christmas in this country. Father went to look up Dominie Wyckoff and found in him a warm friend and a wise counsellor. Soon we had a better place to live in and father and my oldest brother quickly obtained work so that we were provided for in our daily needs. There was no Dutch congregation in Albany at that moment, but we nevertheless went to church. Although we could not understand the services, we were comforted by the knowledge that we were in a place where God's Word was proclaimed. But we could follow one of the hymns for we recognized the tune of Psalm 134, 3 [in the Dutch Psalter]: "The Lord's blessing descend on you."

It was not long before we learned that we could become sick also in America. During that first year we had measles, scarlet fever, and the pox. But in spite of all, the Lord delivered us and spared our lives.

After living a year and three months in Albany we left for the West early in the spring of 1848. Our destination was the place where Dominie Maarten A. Ypma lived. That is the present Vriesland. We went from Albany to Troy, and from there by canalboat to Buffalo and thence by boat to Detroit; next to Milwaukee, thence to Grand Haven, and then to Grandville.

Now we had again set foot firmly ashore and with a yoke of oxen hitched to a wagon we moved along unmarked roads into the forest. Most of us walked, but those who rode on the wagon had difficulty to keep their seats. That day we saw almost nothing but trees, here and there a small opening in the forest where a log shanty had been built at one of which we decided to spend the night. This loghouse had been built by Johannes Groen, father of Dominie Johannes Groen. He was a shoemaker and had hung up a couple of cow hides in this loghouse, which gave forth an unpleasant odor. I remember very well that I said to my mother, "Here I cannot eat any food." A large fire was kindled out in the open, and all who could not find shelter in the loghouse slept around the fire. We were only a mile from my uncle, Dominie Ypma, but in spite of this short distance we had to spend the night where we had stopped. The next morning we went on our way, and soon arrived at our destination.

Our journey from Albany, New York, to Vriesland had required fully three weeks; and now we were in the West. We children were greatly disappointed, for we had imagined that "the West" was a large city. Now we beheld only a loghouse here and there. My uncle's parsonage was about 14 by 16; it had a small lean-to on one side. Here father, mother, and seven children had to live with my uncle and his family until our own loghouse was finished. With this I will close my remarks.

31. JOHN H. KARSTEN'S LIFE SKETCH
OF HENDRIK WILLEMS DAM AND LUMMIGJE DAM

[This account by a son of Lummigje Dam (*nee* Kruis) presents much information about one of the pioneer families which settled in Vriesland during 1847. Written in 1910 by John H. Karsten at the request of the surviving members of the family, it was published in *De Grondwet*, April 30, 1912].

Hendrik Willems Dam and Lummigje Dam, *nee* Kruis, with their six children and one grandchild immigrated from Terband, a hamlet near the beautiful city of Heerenveen, Netherlands, in the year 1847, to the United States of America, and settled in Vriesland, Ottawa County, Michigan, in that same year. The reasons for leaving their native land were mainly financial.

In the great religious revival which swept over the country in 1830 and succeeding years they took part. Freedom of public worship was denied those who left the State Church, and persecution followed. Soldiers were sent and quartered upon the families of those who united with the secession from the State Church. The subjects of this sketch were compelled to lodge and board four soldiers in their comparatively small home. However, when they left for this country freedom of worship had been proclaimed, and they were allowed to build houses of public worship. It can therefore not be truthfully said of them that they left Holland for the sake of religious freedom.

Mr. and Mrs. Dam belonged to the well-to-do middle class of society. Social conditions, however, were fast forming in which this middle class would be crushed out. Sliding down into the poor class, the proletariat, stared them in the face and they decided to escape this fate and move to a land where every man had an equal chance with his fellow man.

Before we relate the history and experiences of their journeying from the old country to their new home in the wilds of Michigan, the following should be stated in order clearly to understand the names mentioned:

Mrs. Dam was twice married. The name of her first husband was Harm Karsten. They had six children: Pieter, Wieger who after a short married life died in Groningen near Zeeland in the early fifties, Jentje who married Reinder Meyering who served in the Second Michigan Cavalry in the War of the Rebellion, Hendrik who died at the age of 74 years on the old homestead in Vriesland, where the family settled in 1847, and Jan H., who became a minister of the Gospel in connection with the Reformed Church in America.

After being a widow about two years, Mrs. Karsten was married to Hendrik W. Dam. Two children were born to them, both daughters, one of whom died in infancy. The other is Annigje, who was married to Nicholas Haan, who enlisted during the Civil War in the First Michigan Mechanics and Engineers.

Hendrik Willems Dam was born November 21, 1804, and died January 29, 1866. Mrs. Hendrik W. Dam was born May 12, 1798, and died August 5, 1888. Both lie buried in the Vriesland cemetery.

On April 26, 1847, the family left its home near Heerenveen, Vriesland. On the day of their departure the premises were crowded with people to see them leave. Immigration to America was at that time a great event. It was a venture into the unknown. Some admired, some pitied, some ridiculed it as a foolish act and undertaking. In a small sailing vessel they went first to Koudum, Vriesland, to meet the family of Hessel O. Yntema, with whom through correspondence they became acquainted and with whom they were to make the journey to America.

They stopped a short time at Stavoren and Hindeloopen, then crossed the Zuider Zee. In due time they reached Amsterdam, whence the ocean voyage was to be made on a sailing vessel, *de Noord-Hollander*. The goods were stowed away in the ship's hold, and all was ready to leave Amsterdam with about 159 passengers. But the ship was detained six weeks for the following reasons: Tidings had just come from the United States that every person on board an emigrant ship should have a specified number of cubic feet of fresh air. There were entirely too many passengers on board the ship to satisfy the requirements of this new law.

Reverend Pieter Zonne, leader of a company of immigrants, objected to sailing with so many persons on board and brought the matter before the proper court in Amsterdam. He won his case, whereupon two vessels divided the passengers between them.

The families of Hendrik W. Dam and Hessel O. Yntema were transferred with others to the *Albatross*, of Amsterdam, captain Kryn Hazenoot, a fine Christian gentleman. They left June 1, 1847, the vessel according to the custom of those days being drawn by horses through the canal from Amsterdam to Nieuwediep. After a prosperous, pleasant voyage of 42 days they reached New York.

From here they traveled by nightboat to Albany. In Albany they were transferred to a canalboat, towed by horses to Buffalo. From Buffalo they proceeded by propeller, via the Lakes to Chicago, stopping a short time in Milwaukee.

In Chicago they were delayed one week, the wind according to the captain being adverse to getting out of the harbor. Then on a sailing vessel they left for Black Lake, where they arrived on a beautiful afternoon. Their goods were transferred from the vessel, which anchored a distance from the shore, to an open flatboat on Black Lake [now Macatawa Bay], and paddled to what was then already known as "the City" [Holland] though nothing but primitive woods met the eye. Reverend A. C. van Raalte, the leader of the immigration, had been there only a few months.

Many of our fellow passengers stopped in Chicago. Forty of them went to Holland. There was no shelter prepared for them. Tents of brush were quickly erected, while only the bare ground served as a resting place for the night. After a short time the family moved to Groningen. There Pieter, Wieger, and Hendrik worked some time for Jan Rabbers who was building a dam across a little stream for the purpose of securing water power for a sawmill.

The father, not a strong man, physically, and the youngest son Jan, then only 14 years old, guided only by blazed trees, walked to Vriesland to build a house on a tract of 60 acres which had been paid for in the old country to a committee of which Reverend Maarten Anne Ypma was

president. Ypma with two or three families had been there only
about six weeks and lived in a log house something like 16 by 24 feet.
There was no room for the two new comers, so they went to their land
nearby, built a tent of brush, and slept on the bare ground with only a
blanket for cover. On Saturday evenings they returned to their family
at Groningen.

It was soon decided to move the whole family to the farm at Vriesland.
Popke Steginga, a man with some means, owned an ox team and moved
the family. The trip was made without mishap, due perhaps more to the
instinctive intelligence of the oxen than to the driver, who had been a
seafaring man in Holland all his lifetime.

The family arrived at their destination on the last day of August 1847.
Having brought a quantity of linen with them from Holland, a tent of
linen was erected adjoining the tent of brush. Immigrant boxes served
as tables, sections of tree trunks as chairs, and the bare ground as bedsteads. In this tent the family lived ten weeks, till the beginning of
November.

The log house was built of small trees set on end in a trench. The entire
house was made without a single board, except the door. There were no
shingles. After the day's work the men sat around the fire making boards
about two feet long, for the roof. These were put on the next day. When
the roof was half covered the family moved. There was no floor except
hardened clay with shavings on top. A roughly constructed chimney let
down some distance in the room served as a ventilator to draw out the
smoke. At times, while yet in the tent, the whole family was sick with
chills and fever, and no doctor. The food problem was a difficult one.
In the old country the housewives did no baking. They did not know
how to bake bread, and what they did bake was more fit for cannon balls
than for a human stomach.

There was no opportunity to earn any money to meet daily expenses,
limited as they were. Hence the men built a fence of small trees around
a section of land about three miles from home, east of the Drenthe
church, owned by Mr. Lanning.

About three miles west of the Drenthe church there was a small grove
of pine trees opposite the homestead of a man by the name of Geert
Lubbers. Of these the father, Hendrik and Jan, made shingles and as
such, they had, as we believe, the distinction of being the first shingle-
makers in the Colony.

Many interesting experiences of privation and happy deliverances might
be related, but we forbear for fear of being too lengthy for a record of

the family. The third generation already is very numerous, numbering not far from 150 descendants from the first pioneers. The fourth generation begins already to call for recognition. Most of them are engaged in agricultural pursuits.

The above record has been made by the Rev. John H. Karsten, son of Harm Karsten and his wife Lummigje Dam, at the suggestion of the surviving members of the family.

32. HENDRIK DAM'S DESCRIPTION OF MY JOURNEY

[Departing Koudum in Friesland in April 1847, Dam arrived in Vriesland during the follo-wing summer. Dams' relation closes with the 11th of July, 1847, and was continued in 1909 by Hessel O. Yntema who spent most of his years living in Vriesland near the community of Drenthe. This sketch appeared in *De Grondwet*, November 5, 1912.]

Den 21sten April 1847 zijn wij van Koudum, Friesland, vertrokken naar Amsterdam, waar wij den 22sten aankwamen en waar wij dadelijk aan boord gingen van het schip *Noord Holland*. Op dit schip zijn wij geweest tot 28 Mei wegens een pleidooi met de reeders van de schepen, die meer geld vroegen dan het accoord was. [De tonnage van het schip was te klein, volgens de wet, gerekend met het getal passagiers dat aangenomen was, zooals mij verteld is.]

Eindelijk, door er iets bij te geven, zijn wij dadelijk doorgegaan op het schip *Albatross* van Amsterdam, waarna wij spoedig vertrokken. Den 30sten waren wij te Alkmaar en den 1sten Juni aan het Nieuwe Diep van waar wij het ruime sop op moesten, en daar er des morgens nog geen matrozen genoeg aan boord waren, moesten wij wachten tot 's avonds 6 uur. Circa een uur later verlieten wij den vaderlandschen bodem.

Wij hadden een gunstigen wind. Kort na onze afvaart zongen wij Psalm 84 : 3 en 89 : 7, den Heere aanbevelende hen die wij achtergelaten hadden en zij die met ons op de wateren dobberden.

Den 2den Juni ging het voor den wind en wij hadden mooi weder. Sommigen waren een weinig ziek en slaperig. Des avonds om 9 ure konden wij het vuur van de Engelsche en Fransche kusten zien en zoo zijn wij bij nacht door het Kanaal gegaan.

Den 3den Juni mooi weer; om 12 uur kregen we tegenwind; toch was het stil weder; tegen den avond stak de wind op. Den 4den Juni ging het voor den wind met mooie koelte. Om 5 uur zagen wij weer land, de krijtbergen langs de Engelsche kust namelijk. Den 5den Juni ging het weer voor den wind, maar het schip slingerde geweldig; toen waren wij in de Spaansche wateren. Den 6den Juni weer voor den wind. Velen waren zeeziek. Men zou niet gelooven dat een zoo groot schip zoo kan slingeren, aangezien het 16 voet diep door het water ging. Wij ondervonden wat de dichter zegt in een Psalm: Zij dansen en waggelen gelijk een dronken man. Tot nog toe koel weder.

Den 7den Juni nog al mooi weer en voor den wind. De Heere maakt tot nog toe onzen weg voorspoedig. Wij zeilen tot nog toe West Zuidwest en hebben in drie dagen geen land gezien.

Den 8sten Juni de wind noordelijker met eene mooie koelte. Het zeilt nu beter als voor den wind en hebben nu 15 zeilen bij.

Den 9den Juni zagen wij groote visschen, die het scheepsvolk Noordkapers noemt; wij hadden het schuins in de wind. Den 10den tegenwind en wij konden geen koers houden, maar mooi weer en een kleine koelte. Wij zagen drie schepen met landverhuizers, die met ons zeilen. Den 11den stil weer. Den 12den sterke wind. Den 13den [Zondag] nog sterke wind en veel zeeziekte. Toch kon de een den ander nog helpen met eten en drinken kooken. Den 14den was de wind wat stil en toen begon men als 't ware wat op te leven en toen zagen wij weer land [Azores eilanden]; het zijn hooge bergen. De stuurman vertelde ons, dat wij er nog geen vijf mijlen van verwijderd waren. Den 15den goed weer. Den 16den mooi weer met een zachte koelte. Daarna het water bij de maat, maar voldoende. Den 17den en 18den voor de wind, maar stil weder. Den 19den schuins voor de wind met een mooie koelte; door den zegen des Heeren zijn allen gezond. Den 20sten [Zondag] mooi weer; toen werd er twee keeren een preek gelezen. Den 21sten verloor onze vriend, R. Polsma, een kind van 2½ jaar oud; de begrafenis was aandoenlijk. Het geschiedde aldus: Het lijk werd in een stuk zeildoek genaaid, met een zak zand aan de voeten; daarna op een plank gelegd, waar het zachtjes afglijdt en in de diepte weg zinkt. Ook hier zal het waarheid worden, dat ook de zee hare dooden zal opgeven, zooals wij dat lezen in de Openbaring. Polsma was kleermaker en kwam van Workum, Friesland. Hij was een man die den Heere vreesde.

Gedurende dezen dag zagen wij, op korten afstand van het schip, een grooten visch. Den 22sten schuins voor den wind en een mooie koelte; des namiddags hadden wij een schip met landverhuizers naast ons; groot en klein was dadelijk op dek. Zij vroegen elkaar, waar ze heen moesten en beider bestemming bleek New York te zijn. Het was een aangenaam gezicht; spoedig daarna waren wij uit elkanders gezicht en hebben elkaar niet weer gezien.

Den 23sten [Woensdag] voor de wind en zachte koelte. Den 24sten stil met tegenwind. Den 25sten voor de wind met zachte koelte; des namiddags begon het hard te waaien, zoodat zij zeilen moesten bergen. Den 26sten nog harde wind. Den 27sten [Zondag], voormiddag, een mooie koelte; des namiddags stil, zoodat wij nog godsdienstoefening konden houden. Den 28sten stil en in de wind; nu bedaarde de zeeziekte. Den 29sten de wind west; dat heeft men over het algemeen op deze hoogte. De eerste 14 dagen zeilden wij bijna zuidwest, later bijna noordwest.

Den 30sten, des morgens omstreeks zeven uur, overleed er eene vrouw van omstreeks 40 jaar, na eenigen tijd ongesteld geweest te zijn. Zij is om half elf in de diepte begraven. Eerst werd er gezongen Psalm 103 : 7 en 8 en daarna werd er gebeden. Kapitein en stuurman waren er bij tegenwoordig. Toen het zingen en bidden klaar was, werd de plank aan het hoofdeinde opgeligt en zakte het lijk zacht naar beneden tot het in de diepte verdween. Daarna werd er gezongen het 9de vers van Psalm 108.

De wind was zuidwest en er heerschte een mooie koelte. Wij zeilden koers; het schip voer tien uur in vier uur – $7\frac{1}{2}$ mijl per uur. De kapitein en boven-stuurman zijn burgerlijk godsdienstig. Aan den avond van dien dag werd er een preek gelezen over Prediker 12 : 7, het eerste deel.

Den 1sten Juli. De wind west en een mooie koelte zoodat onze weg begint te korten; als het zoo voort gaat, hopen wij in drie dagen land te zien. Des avonds om tien uur schonk de vrouw van Bartelt Luten de geboorte aan een dochter; moeder en kind wel. Men gaf het den naam van het schip *Albatross*. De kapitein zorgde voor eten en versterkende middelen, dat haar door de beide stuurlieden gebracht werd, en dien tengevolge had de vrouw, onder den zegen des Heeren, niets te klagen.

Den 2den. De wind zuidelijk; het schip liep snel. Den 3den, de wind Oost Noordoost; des namiddags liep het schip bijna tien mijl per uur. Den 4den, stil weer. Den 5den, de wind west, een mooie koelte. Wij moeten zeggen; de Heere is met ons. Het dieplood wijst aan 120 vademen – 720 voet. Den 6den stilte. Den 7den stil weer. Toen hebben wij zeer groote visschen gezien. Men noemt ze Boschkoppen. Den 8sten stil weer en zeer vlak. Den 9den geen wind en de zee vlak en effen; zulks is zij nu reeds 3 dagen. Zaterdag, den 10den, kregen wij de loods aan boord. Zondag, den 11den Juli, des voormiddags, kwamen wij te New York binnen. Het anker werd uitgeworpen en wij lagen stil. God baande door de breede stroomen, enz.

Den 11den Juli 1847.

Het bovenstaande geschreven door Hendrik Dam.

De kapitein van de *Albatross* was een bijzonder medelijdend man en deed veel om de passagiers te gerieven.

Van New York zijn wij, na twee dagen per stoomboot gereisd te hebben, te Albany aangekomen. Vandaar naar Buffalo [door het Erie Canal] met een kanaalboot getrokken door paarden. Dit nam 9 dagen. Van Buffalo zijn wij per stoomboot over Lake Erie naar Detroit gevaren. Vandaar langs de Michigan kust door Lake Huron, dan door de Straits of Mackinaw in Lake Michigan, waar wij de westkust langs vaarden naar Milwaukee; verder naar Chicago, waar mijn toen jongste broeder, van 1½ jaar oud, begraven is. Van Chicago zijn wij langs de oostelijke kust van Lake Michigan gevaren, naar den mond van Black Lake. Van Buffalo naar Holland, Michigan, nam omstreeks drie weken, daar de boot vele landingen maakte.

Door zoogenaamde platbooten werden passagiers met toebehooren, aan land gebracht. Vader huurde een platboot, waarop wij en ook Pieter Damstra en vrouw Black Lake op vaarden naar de Black River. Een gedeelte varende bij nacht, stootte de boot op een boom in het water en bekwam een lek, zoodat wij er over haast af moesten. Na herstelling van het lek vaarden wij verder de rivier op en kwamen eindelijk aan het zoogenoemd Oud Groningen [tusschen Holland en Zeeland] aan. Hier overleed, blijmoedig in den Heere, de jeugdige vrouw van Pieter Damstra. De wederwaardigheden daar in de tenten zullen anderen daar wel opgeteekend hebben. Na eenigen tijd daar geweest te zijn, gingen wij per ossenwagen het bosch in, naar den zoogenaamden hoogen berg, drie mijlen west van Drenthe, Michigan. Ik herinner mij de lange pijnboomen daar dicht bij den berg, waar ons twee mannen ontmoeten. Nog eenige uren voortgereisd hebbende, kwamen wij eindelijk aan de plaats onzer bestemming. Er was een kleine clearing zoogenaamd, van een akker, op de zuidwest quarter, van section 26, Zeeland Township, nabij waar nu de Drenthe creamery staat. Dit was in Augustus 1847. Wat mijn vader en moeder ondervonden hebben, kan moeielijk beschreven worden. Want binnen tien maanden na onze aankomst te New York, zijn overleden drie broeders, een zuster en de vrouw van Pieter Damstra, die ook bij ons als huisgezin was.

[Translation]

We left Koudum, Friesland, on April 21, 1847, for Amsterdam where we arrived on the 22d and immediately boarded our ship, the *Noord Holland*. We spent the next days until May 28 on this ship on account of a lawsuit with the shipping company which was asking more money than had been agreed upon. [The ship's tonnage was too small according to the law which demanded a certain proportion of tonnage to the total of passengers accepted, as was told me.]

Finally, by paying something in addition we secured passage on the ship *Albatross* of Amsterdam, in which we soon departed. On the 30th we were at Alkmaar and on June 1 at Nieuwediep at which place we were to put to sea. But as in the morning there were not enough sailors aboard, our departure was delayed until 6 o'clock in the evening. About an hour later we left our fatherland behind us. We had a favorable wind. Soon after our departure we sang Psalms 84, 3, and 89, 7 [from the Dutch Psalter]. We recommended to our Lord all those we were leaving behind and also those who were sailing with us.

On June 2 we sailed before the wind and had pleasant weather. Some of us were sick and sleepy. During the evening at 9 o'clock we saw the flicker of light from the lighthouses along the English and French coasts, and so we passed trough the Channel during the night.

On June 3, fair weather. At 12 o'clock we had contrary winds, but it was quiet. Toward evening the wind rose. On June 3 we sailed before the wind; the weather was cool. At 5 o'clock we saw land, the chalk cliffs along the English coast. On June 5 we again sailed before the wind, but our ship rolled heavily; we were then in Spanish waters. On June 6, we again sailed before the wind. Many were seasick. One would not think so large a ship could roll so heavily, seeing that it drew 16 feet of water. We experienced what the poet wrote in Psalm 107, 27, "They reel to and fro, and stagger like a drunken man...."

On June 7, fair weather, and again sailing before the wind. The Lord until now prospered our voyage. We still were sailing west southwest, and hadn't seen land in three days. On June 8 the wind was from a more northerly direction. The ship sailed more calmly, before the wind, and with 15 sails.

On June 9 we saw large fish, by sailors called "Atlantic whales". The wind was from the south. On the 10th contrary winds, and we could not hold to our course, but the weather was fair and slightly cool. We saw three ships carrying emigrants sailing in the same direction. On the 11th quiet weather. On the 12th strong wind. On the 13th [Sunday] strong wind and much seasickness. Nevertheless the passengers were in a condition to help each other in preparing food and drink. On the 14th the wind was quieter, and the passengers began to show some spirit. Then we saw land, the Azores Islands, high mountains. The steersman said that we were not five miles from them. On the 15th good weather. On the 16th fair weather and slightly cool. From this moment water was measured out for us, but in sufficient quantities. On the 17th and 18th sailing before the wind, weather mild. On the 19th wind from port side, weather cool and pleasing. Because of the Lord's blessing all were well. On the 20th [Sunday] weather fair; on that day twice a sermon was read.

On the 21st our friend R. Polsma lost a child $2\frac{1}{2}$ years old. The funeral was a moving experience. It took place as follows. The body was sewed in a piece of sail cloth. A bag of sand was placed at the feet. Next, the body was laid on a plank from which it was gently allowed to slide down into the water and sink away into the deep. Here too will the truth be manifest, that the sea will give up its dead, as we read in Revelation 20, 13. Polsma was a tailor and came from Workum, Friesland. He feared the Lord.

During this day, at a short distance from our ship we saw a large fish. On the 22d we sailed with the wind from portside; the temperature was pleasantly cool. In the afternoon a ship laden with emigrants appeared beside ours. Everybody, large and small, immediately came on deck. We asked each other's destination which for them also appeared to be New York. It was a pleasant thing to see this ship. Soon, however, we passed out of sight and we did not see each other again.

On the 23d [Wednesday] sailing before the wind, cool weather. On the 24th it was quiet, but with contrary breeze. On the 25th sailing before the wind, wether mild. In the afternoon a stiff breeze began to blow so that we had to roll up our sails. On the 26th still a stiff breeze. On the 27th [Sunday] in the morning pleasant and cool. During the afternoon it was calm so that we could have religious services. On the 27th quiet and a moderate breeze. Seasickness declined. On the 29th the wind came from the west, something usual in this latitude. During the first 14 days we sailed in a southwesterly direction, thereafter practically in a northwesterly.

On the 30th, about seven o'clock in the morning, a woman died, aged about 40. She had been ill for some time. She was buried in the sea at half past ten. First we sang Psalm 103, 7 and 8 [from the Dutch Psalter]. This was followed by prayer. The captain and steersman attended the services. When the singing and prayer were finished the upper end of the the board was lifted and the body gently sank into the sea and sank from sight. Then we sang the ninth verse of Psalm 108 [from the Dutch Psalter]. The wind now was from the southwest, and the temperature was mild. We followed course. The captain and first steersman had some appreciation of relegion. On the evening of that day a sermon on Ecclesiastes 12, 7, part 1, was read.

July 1. The wind was from the west, the temperature pleasant, and our voyage was growing shorter. If our progress continued in this manner we should see land in three days. During the evening at 10 o'clock Bartelt Luten's wife gave birth to a daughter; mother and child doing well. The daughter was given the name Albatross, after that of our ship. The captain provided food and stimulants which were brought to her by both steersmen and so the woman, under God's blessing, had no reason for complaint.

July 2. A southerly wind, and our ship progressed well. On the 3d the wind was east northeast. During the afternoon our ship made about ten miles per hour. On the 4th, calm. On the 5th, a west wind, temperature pleasant. We confessed, "the Lord is with us." The deep lead registered 120 fathoms – 720 feet. The 6th, calm. The 7th, likewise calm. Then we saw large fish called porpoises. The 8th calm and smooth. On the 9th no wind, the sea calm and smooth. So it was for three days. Saturday, the 10th, a pilot came on board. On Sunday, July 11th, in the morning we entered the harbor of New York. The ship's anchor was dropped, and our voyage was finished. "God prepared for us through the waste waters and vasty tides," etc. [Psalm 66, 3, from the Dutch Psalter].

The above account was written by Hendrik Dam.

The captain of the *Albatross* was an exceptionally sympathetic man, and actively promoted the comfort of his passengers. From New York we sailed by steamboat and in two days arrived in Albany. From there we went to Buffalo [through the Erie Canal] on a canalboat which was pulled by horses. This was a journey of nine days. From Buffalo we went by steamboat over Lake Erie to Detroit. From there along the Michigan coast through Lake Huron, next through the Straits of Mackinaw into Lake Michigan and proceeding along the west coast to Milwaukee, then to Chicago where my youngest brother, a year and one-half old, was buried. From Chicago we proceeded along the east coast of Lake Michigan to the mouth of Black Lake. From Buffalo to Holland, Michigan, was a voyage of about three weeks, for the boat stopped at many points.

Passengers and their baggage were landed in so-called flatboats. Father hired a flatboat on which we and also Pieter Damstra and wife sailed up Black Lake and to Black River. While we were sailing during the night the flatboat ran onto a tree lying in the water and sprang a leak so that we had to leave the boat in haste. After having repaired the leak we sailed further up the river and finally arrived at so-called Old Groningen [between Holland and Zeeland]. Here died, happily in the Lord, the youthful wife of Pieter Damstra. The adversities experienced there in the tents [loghouses] no doubt will have been described by others. After spending a little time there we went into the forest by ox wagon, to the so-called high hill, three miles west from Drenthe, Michigan. I recall those tall pine trees near the hill. After having journeyed a few hours we finally arrived at our destination. There was a small clearing of one acre, in the southwest quarter of section 26, Township Zeeland, not far from the spot on which stands the present Drenthe creamery. This was in August 1847. What my father and mother experienced here can be described with difficulty. For within ten months after our arrival at New York, three brothers, one sister, and Pieter Damstra's wife who also lived with us a member of our family, died.

Chapter VIII

ORIGENS OF NORTH HOLLAND NOORDELOOS
AND BEAVERDAM [SOETERMEER] 1848-1849

33. PIETER G. VAN TONGEREN'S NOORD HOLLAND

[A son of Jan van Tongeren, one of the first settlers of North Holland in 1849, Pieter spent most of his years in that place and so speaks with authority. His sketch was published in *De Grondwet*, July 25, 1911.]

In 1848 zeide Ds. van Raalte tegen mijn vader, Jan van Tongeren, „Er moet 5 of 6 mijlen noordoostelijk van de stad Holland zeer goed land liggen, zooals de Indianen mij gezegd hebben."

In het voorjaar van 1849 settelde mijn vader op de plaats waar later Eildert Nienhuis' zaagmolen stond, 2½ mijl noord van Holland. In den herfst van datzelfde jaar liepen Van Dijk, Van Tongeren en schrijver dezes in een noordoostelijke richting langs een Indian trail cranberries zoeken en plukken. Toen wij nabij de townline tusschen Holland en Olive kwamen, rustten Jan J. van Dijk en Jan van Tongeren een poos. Ik, als jongen van 10 jaar, ging wat verder en kwam in een mooi bosch terecht, alwaar geen hemlock was. Ik keerde terug en vertelde wat ik gevonden had, waarop mijn vader tot Van Dijk zeide: „Dan is dat het land, waarvan Ds. van Raalte tot mij gesproken heeft." Ze stonden op en gingen zien en ja wel, het was zoo. Dit nu werd wat later Noord Holland is genoemd. Wij waren toen ruim ½ mijl west van waar nu de Gereformeerde Kerk staat.

Dat het spoedig algemeen bekend werd, dat daar zulk mooi land was, blijkt hieruit, dat men nog in datzelfde jaar begon met log huizen te bouwen. Het eerste blokhuis was van Jan Kramer, een broer van Lambert Kramer, welbekend in Noordeloos. Het tweede was van mijn vader, Jan van Tongeren, op de plaats waar nu het huis van Minne P. Stegenga staat, tegenover de kerk, in township Olive.

Dien eerste winter was wildbraad ons voorname voedsel, want herten waren er in groot getal. Dit hertevleesch kwam goed van pas, want geld hadden we niet, ook geen vee of varkens en al hadden we die bezeten, er was geen hooi of voeder. De hertejacht in die eerste jaren vergeet ik nimmer. Noord Holland had als eerste jagers – Steven Coleman, Boer Veldheer, Otto G. van Dijk, E. W. Kooijers en anderen. Het aantal herten dat zij gekregen hebben, loopt in de honderden. Ik zelf heb er een 70-tal geschoten. Zoover ik mij herinner heeft het geen levens gekost, zooals nu in de noordelijke bosschen.

Op 2 Januari 1850 betrokken wij het huis. Het was ongeveer 10 bij 20 voet, doch groot genoeg voor zes personen, vader, moeder en zoon; en dan waren er ook nog drie kostgangers: H. Brouwer, Wiger van der Kolk en Geert Raak. De koe moest er ook in, dus was het een echte Noach's ark.

Des Zondags moest het huis ook somtijds dienen voor kerk, want godsdiensthouden werd niet vergeten, hoe eenvoudig ook. Ik herinner mij nog dat eens op een keer de ouderling er niet was en mijn vader wat ziek was, ik als jongen van 11 of 12 jaar oud een preek lezen moest. In die eerste jaren bleef er niemand die niet ziek was 't huis. Dit moet gezegd worden van de eerste settlers.

Waren er ook wegen hoegenaamd niet; alles moest gedragen worden, door bosschen en moerassen en over boomen. Onze eerste kachel werd op een kleine handslede heengebracht, en later de andere huismeubelen ook. Er kwam echter langzamerhand verandering, er werd een road geopend en meer huisgezinnen kwamen er in. Hein van der Haar, met zijn roode ossen, kwam nu en dan van de stad Holland. Het derde huis was dat van Gerrit van Dijk, op de plaats waar thans Jan Meijer woont.

In den zomer van 1850 kwamen er meer gezinnen bij, zoo dat aan 't einde van dat jaar de volgende aldaar woonden: Jan van Tongeren, Jan Kramer, Jan G. van Dijk, P. J. Kuiper, Brouwer, Jan Spijkerman, Jan Veldheer en Jan van der Kolk. Spoedig daarop kwamen ook nog de volgende families: Jan Slag, Jan C. Smit, Evert Luidens, Van den Berg, Kerst Weener, Ten Have, M. P. Stegenga en anderen, zoodat er na 5 jaar heel wat inwoners waren.

Zooals we zeiden, de eerste godsdienst werd gehouden bij Van Tongeren; later bij Kerst Weener, Otto G. van Dijk en Jacob van Dijk en daarna, in 1856, in de school. De eerste predikatie werd gehouden door Ds. A. C. van Raalte. Zijn tekst was uit Matt. 6 : 10: „Uw koninkrijk kome." Ik herinner nog deze woorden: „Vrienden, gijlieden zijt hier begonnen in een nieuw settlement. Ik zou van 's Heeren wege wel wenschen dat gij geen boom durfdet neerhouwen voor en aleer gij God gevraagd had om de komst van Zijn rijk."

Het eerste nachtmaal is gehouden bij K. Weener en werd bediend door Ds. Maarten A. Ypma. De stichting der eerste gemeente had plaats, zooals Jan C. Smit mij verhaalde, bij Van Dijk aan huis. Zoo ver ik vinden kan, zijn er geen notulen gehouden, doch naar het mij voorkomt, moet zulks zijn geschied in 1851; zeker niet later. De eerste ouderling was Alexander Hartgerink en de eerste diaken, Jan van Tongeren; beiden zijn bevestigd door Ds. C. van der Meulen.

Het eerste kind dat in Noord Holland geboren is, was Gerrit Jan Spijkerman. Dit was 22 April 1851. De eerste volwassene aldaar overleden, was Jan van der Kolk, in Mei 1855. Het lijk werd door Jan Spijkerman op een ossenwagen naar Holland gebracht ter begrafenis. Het eerste paar dat getrouwd is, waren Jan ten Have en Trijntje van Dijk, 26 Juli 1854, door Ds. Ypma. Mrs. ten Have is nog in leven.

De eerste publieke school is gebouwd in 1856 en de eerste teacher was Herman Grebel. In de hoogste klas waren: Katherina van Dijk, Ale P. Stegenga en Peter G. van Tongeren; allen nog in het leven.

Nog eenige bijzonderheden met betrekking tot het gemeentelijke. In 1855 kwam er een persoon met name Jacob Duim. Hij beweerde prediker of oefenaar te wezen en de eenige die de ware leer nog had. „Het volk", zoo zeide hij eens, „is in de woestijn en daarom kunnen de kinderen niet gedoopt worden. De leeraars zijn Baalpredikers, en geen leiders, maar verleiders; doch hij zag nog een lichtstraal in Zwitserland", enz.

Het gevolg was, dat het meerendeel hem volgden, de gemeente versplitterde en anderen naar Noordeloos gingen. De kinderen werden niet gedoopt, zoodat toen Ds. Engelbert C. Oggel in 1866 als leeraar in Noord Holland kwam, er 75 kinderen ongedoopt waren. Dit duurde ongeveer vijf jaar, toen de gemeente als het ware gereorganiseerd werd en Duim's aanhang tot vijf of zes huisgezinnen verminderd was. Bij zijn dood in 1879, waren slechts twee huisgezinnen hem trouw gebleven.

Het eerste kerkgebouw werd opgericht in 1862 en het tweede, dat nog in stand is, in 1867. De inwijding had plaats op 5 Februari 1868. De eerste leeraar was Ds. Engelbert C. Oggel, die 14 October 1866 door Ds. C. van der Meulen en zijn broeder, Prof. Pieter J. Oggel, bevestigd werd en de gemeente 3½ jaar bediend heeft. Het eerste huwelijk door ZEw. ingezegend was dat van schrijver dezes en Jentje Brouwer, 28 Februari 1867.

De tweede leeraar was Ds. Balster van Ess. Hij kwam in Februari 1870. Onder zijne bediening genoot de gemeente in 1876 en 1877 eene groote verlevendiging en velen kwamen tot de belijdenis van Christus. In laatstgenoemd jaar werd de Sabbatschool georganiseerd. Na de gemeente ruim 14 jaren bediend te hebben, nam hij een beroep aan naar Roseland, Illinois, en is aldaar overleden.

In 1856 werd er een zanggezelschap opgericht. Onder de leden waren: Jan ten Have [leider], Jan Spijkerman, Albert van Dijk, Kerst Weener, Otto van Dijk en P. G. van Tongeren.

Ook kunnen we nog kortelings melden, dat er door J. Brouwer een ashery, door Veldheer, Oostenrijk en Heiboer een zaagmolen en door

H. Pelgrim een kaasfabriek opgericht is; deze echter zijn allen verdwenen.

Aan den burgeroorlog, 1861-65, namen de volgende, te Noord Holland tehuis behoorende personen, als vrijwilligers deel: Wouter Weener, gesneuveld te Stone River; alsmede Broer van Dijk, Jan Hofman, Bartel van der Zwaag, Arend Brouwer, Willem Frik, Derk P. Stegenga, Jan Dunnink, Willem de Fouw en Peter G. van Tongeren.

Van al de settlers die in 1850 in Noord Holland zich vestigden zijn er, voor zoover ik weet, nog acht in leven.

34. ANTHONY ROSBACH'S
SETTLEMENT IN NOORDELOOS

[This account written by Anthony Rosbach under the title *De Nederzetting in Noordeloos Michigan* was published in *De Grondwet*, February 21, 1911. Although the community began its existence as early as 1848 it was not until 1856, upon the arrival of Dominie Koene van den Bosch from Noordeloos in the Netherlands, that it received the name of Noordeloos.]

Geschiedenis doorleven en geschiedenis schrijven zijn twee zaken, die niet altijd te zamen gaan. Het is gewoonlijk de taak van het nageslacht om de geschiedenis der vaderen te beschrijven, en hoewel daardoor wellicht de beschrijving meer onpartijdig en meer nauwkeurig wordt, ligt er toch niet het eigenaardige in, hetwelk de mededeeling van persoonlijke ervaringen medebrengt. Nochtans willen ook ons, het nageslacht der pioniers, de smarten van het hart, als wij denken aan de worstelingen onzer vaderen; en hoe zij zich hieral in den vreemde een weg baanden door de wildernis en te midden van moeite en ontberingen, omringd van wilde menschen en dieren, de eeuwenoude wouden herschiepen in een vruchtbaar veld.

Zoo is het ook, dat wij in het ter neder schrijven van de geschiedenis der nederzetting te Noordeloos, liefst zaken verzwijgen die minder aantrekkelijk zijn en alleen datgene aan de vergetelheid ontrukken wat dienen kan tot eer van de Hollanders in Amerika.

De grondslagen van Noordeloos werden gelegd in 1848. Het was in den loop van dat jaar, dat een gezelschap van jongelieden uit de provincie Groningen het oude vaderland verlieten, in „de Kolonie van Van Raalte" aankwamen en hun intrek namen bij vrienden te Oud Groningen. Van hier gingen zij op verkenning uit, noordwaarts in om land te zoeken. Zij waren geboren en opgevoed op de vette kleigronden van Groningerland en toen zij den „klei berg" beklommen welke de zuidelijke grens van Noordeloos uitmaakt, was al spoedig hun uitroep: „hier moeten wij land hebben." Hier was het dan ook, dat zij zich vestigden.

Het gezelschap bestond uit P. A. van Dyk en vrouw, Melis [Meus] Hulsebos en vrouw, J. de Slachter en P. Bos.

Zij togen aan het werk en bouwden een huis van loggen in de noordoostelijke hoek van section 15, Holland Township. Bij hen voegde zich Alexander Hartgerink, die een quarter section gouvernementsland verkregen had voor militaire diensten bewezen in den Mexikaanschen oorlog, en hieruit zien wij, dat althans een Nederlander van geboorte de oorlog tegen Mexico medegemaakt heeft.

Dit land was de northwest quarter van section 11 en is omstreeks het middenpunt van Noordeloos geworden.

Spoedig kwamen er meer kolonisten en werden er meer log huizen gebouwd verder noord en oost. Zoo kwamen onder anderen de volgende personen met hunne gezinnen: T. Bos, C. Weninger, Liesveld Blankenzee, G. J. Renskers en W. van den Berge; in 1852: A. van den Bosch; in 1853: B. W. W. Kooijers en P. van den Bosch; in 1854: H. Willink; in 1855: H. Diepenhorst en P. Verduin.

Velen van hen waren reeds vroeger in Amerika gekomen, maar kwamen nu van andere plaatsen om zich alhier te vestigen; sommigen zijn ook weder spoedig vertrokken.

De settlers hebben zich ook hier als op andere plaatsen vele ontberingen moeten getroosten, maar hebben door Gods goede hand over hen, nimmer broodsgebrek gehad. Storegoederen moesten te voet, of per ossenwagen gehaald worden van Holland en Zeeland. Het was eerst in 1865 dat de eerste winkel begonnen werd door Adriaan Wagenaar. De bosschen bestonden voor het meerendeel uit beach, maple en ash, en veel kostbaar hout werd er in de eerste tijden verbrand, omdat men niet wist wat er mede te doen. Later werd er door Jan Vogel een zaagmolen gebouwd bij de *creek* tusschen Van den Bosch en Diepenhorst.

Op maatschappelijk gebied heeft Noordeloos het zijne bijgedragen tot den bloei dezer kolonie, maar het is voornamelijk op kerkelijk terrein, dat het plaatsje een rol gespeeld heeft in de geschiedenis der nederzetting.

De eerstkomenden waren Godvreezende lieden, die niet alleen om een tijdelijk bestaan, maar ook om meerdere godsdienstvrijheid te verkrijgen, zich een heenkomen zochten in het nieuwe werelddeel.

Zij sloten zich aan bij de gemeente te Zeeland en namen de godsdienst waar, in zoo ver een reis van 3 à 4 mijlen door de bosschen zulks toeliet. Doch zij ondervonden dat op den duur de afstand te ver zoude zijn, zoodat men spoedig rijp werd voor het organiseeren eener eigene gemeente. Dit geschiedde in het jaar 1855, toen Diepenhorst en Verduin kwamen, met A. van den Bosch de zaak aanvatten. De stichting der gemeente geschiedde door Ds. Cornelius van der Meulen, van Zeeland. Nu kwam de vraag op, hoe de nieuwe gemeente te noemen. Men besloot haar de naam te geven van Noordeloos, dewijl het plan was om een beroep uit te brengen op Ds. Koene van den Bosch van Noordeloos, Provincie Zuid-Holland, Nederland. C. Weniger gaf eenige acres grond en een loggen-kerk werd opgericht op de plaats waar later het woonhuis van G. A. A. Rosbach gebouwd werd. In 1856 werd het beroep op Ds. Koene van den Bosch uitgebracht. Het beroep werd door hem aangenomen en eerlang mocht de gemeente zich verblijden in het bezit van haren leeraar. De bevestigingsrede werd uitgesproken door Ds. Cornelius van der Meulen, en daar het kerkgebouw te klein was om de schare te bevatten, geschiedde dit in de open lucht, onder de boomen des wouds, terwijl een boerenwagen als kansel dienen moest. Het was een plechtig uur en de bosschen, wiens stilte vroeger door niets werd afgebroken dan het geluid der wilde dieren of het woest geschreeuw van den Indiaan, weergalmden nu van de statige toonen der Psalmen Davids. In den namiddag deed Ds. van den Bosch zijn intreerede in de kerk. Hij was een ijverig predikant en werkte met veel zegen onder het volk.

Met den leeraar kwamen over P. Heyboer en gezin, de familie Vogel en anderen, die veel hebben toegebracht tot de ontwikkeling der nederzetting. Door P. Heyboer werd eenigen tijd les gegeven aan de kinderen in de Hollandsche taal, zoodat ook voor de opvoeding der jeugd werd gezorgd.

Het zou aangenaam zijn als hier de geschiedenis der nederzetting kon worden afgebroken, maar er gebeurde iets dat van groote beteekenis is geweest voor de toekomst der Kolonie, en niet mag verzwegen worden. Ds. van den Bosch kreeg al spoedig na zijn aankomst bezwaar in de Dutch Reformed Church, met welke de Hollanders zich vereenigd hadden. Zijn bezwaar bestond in hoofdzaak hierin, dat naar zijn inzien, in practijk de Kerk de gereformeerde grondslagen verlaten had. Velen hier en op andere plaatsen deelden met hem dit bezwaar en zochten verruiming in de afscheiding.

Den 14den Maart 1857 leverde Ds. van den Bosch zijne acte van afscheiding in bij den kerkeraad te Zeeland. Zestien lidmaten scheidden zich met hem af en werden gevormd tot de eerste gemeente der Afgescheidene of Christelijke Gereformeerde Kerk in Amerika. Zij bouwden een kerkje op de zuidoostelijke hoek van section twee, nabij het woonhuis van Ds. van den Bosch. Later werd het verplaatst, en halve mijl het westen in, nabij Diepenhorst. De gemeente nam steeds in getalsterkte toe en naar mate dat zij groeide, brak de gemeente die gebleven was af, en hield na eenige jaren op te bestaan. Zulks is in het kort de geschiedenis van de nederzetting te Noordeloos.

Veel is er in den tijd van haar bestaan doorleefd. Vele tranen, beide van blijdschap en droefenis, zijn gestort en ook hier zijn vele gebeden opgezonden tot den troon der genade.

35. P. HUYSER'S FROM SOETERMEER TO SOETERMEER

[Four brothers of the Huyser family, of whom this author was one, emigrated from Zoetermeer near The Hague to Michigan and settled in the woods northeast of Zeeland. This place briefly was known as Soetermeer, soon, however, was called Beaverdam. This sketch appeared in *De Grondwet*, May 28, 1912.]

De ondergeteekende, P. Huyser Sr., tot 25-jarige leeftijd opgevoed te Soetermeer, Zuid Holland, besloot in Augustus 1847 naar Amerika te gaan en vertrok met het driemast zeilschip, de *Sabina*, kapitein Staal, van Rotterdam naar Helvoet, waar wij wegens tegenwind 4 weken moesten wachten. Op een Zondagmiddag zijn wij door een stoomboot naar zee gebracht en den volgenden morgen waren wij in het Engelsche Kanaal.

Na een zeer voorspoedige reis van 21 dagen kregen wij op een Zondagmorgen om 9 uur New York in 't zicht, en door ons Hollandsch gezelschap [bestaande uit mijn twee gehuwde broeders Quirinus en Johannes, Johannes George van Hees en gezin, Robbertus M. de Bruin, De Ruitenberge, A. van den Berg en vrouw en Van Wingere] werd toen gezongen Psalm 66 : 3 : „God baande door de woeste baren", enz.

Nadat het anker gevallen was, gingen wij aan wal en brachten een bezoek aan Ds. Thomas de Wit. Des Maandagsavonds zijn wij met de stoomboot naar Albany gereisd en van daar met de kanaalboot naar Buffalo, waar ik met mijn beide broeders heb overwinterd. In het voorjaar van 1848 kwam mijn broeder Cornelius uit Nederland over en hebben wij onze reis naar Michigan verder doorgezet. Met de boot gingen wij naar Chicago, alwaar ik Robbertus M. de Bruin ontmoette, die gereed stond om met den storekeeper, Alderd Plugger, naar de Kolonie te vertrekken.

Wij zijn toen nog dienzelfden dag afgevaren en werden den volgenden morgen om 9 uur aan den mond van de Kalamazoo rivier afgezet. Wij brachten onze bagage over op een platboot, die in de Kolonie thuis behoorde; en toen begon de grap. Vier onbedreven schippers, waarvan twee aan een lange lijn trokken en twee aan het roer stonden. Telkens zaten wij vast op het zand en dan moesten wij over boord springen en tot het middel in het water staande, de boot oplichten en over de zandbank duwen. Na hard werken kwamen wij na verloop van drie uren aan de plaats onzer bestemming, de monding van Black Lake en vervolgens heeft Jacobus Vink een paard voor onze boot gespannen en ons zoo naar de zoogenaamde stad gebracht. Wij plaatsten onze bagage onder zware hemlock boomen en over omgevallen boomen springende, bereikten wij een klein hotel van Jan Binnekant, op de plaats waar nu de Holland City Bank staat. In wat nu de Achtste straat is, zagen wij niets dan klein planken of blokhuisjes; overigens was alles bosch.

Toen zijn wij gegaan naar den vader der Kolonie, den hooggewaardeerden Ds. A. C. van Raalte, dien wij in zijn tuin vonden.

Daarna zijn wij naar het dorp Zeeland gegaan, steeds door het bosch, waar wij nog eens erg schrikten toen wij meenden een jonge beer te zien, doch het bleek slechts een stekelvarken te zijn.

Toen wij aan het waterhuisje kwamen, de plaats waar de goederen voor Zeeland werden afgehaald, moesten wij zeer voorzichtig over een boom kruipen om niet in de rivier te vallen. Wanneer men met een ossenwagen hier langs kwam, moesten de ossen door de rivier zwemmen. Na zoo nog 3 mijlen door het bosch te zijn gesukkeld, kwamen wij eindelijk door de goede hand des Heeren in welstand te Zeeland aan, waar wij terstond den waardigen Ds. C. van der Meulen bezochten, die juist met nieuw overgekomenen in het bosch was om land aan te wijzen ten noordoosten van Zeeland.

Den volgenden dag is ZEw. daar ook met ons heen gegaan en heeft hij ons ieder ook 40 akkers aangewezen. Al wat wij zagen was niets dan boomen van 60, 80 en 100 voet hoog, van allerlei soort.

Ons eerste werk was nu om boomen om te hakken en plaats te maken voor een blokhuis. Daar ik twee getrouwde broeders verwachtte, die ook spoedig kwamen, hebben wij dat blokhuis ingericht met twee vertrekken, die zij ook terstond betrokken. Ik had hun echter 10 akkers gegeven, waar zij een „shanty" opsloegen en waarin zij gingen wonen.

Schrijver dezes was nu in het bezit van 40 akkers land en een blokhuis met twee vertrekken, doch ik had geen hulp om mij bij te staan. Zoo werd het mij eene behoefte om den Heere te smeeken dat hij ook in deze in zijn gunst mocht voorzien, en de Heere heeft ook in deze mijne bede verhoord, zoodat ik 20 April 1851 in het huwelijk ben getreden met Trijntje Kok. Wij zijn terstond naar ons sober eigendom gegaan, waar wij nu 58 jaar onafgebroken hebben gewoond.

Wij hebben groote ontberingen moeten doorstaan, maar op den Rustdag mochten wij, onder leiding van Ds. van der Meulen, weer troost en moed ontvangen. Want er was veel waarmee wij te kampen hadden; niet alleen met de zware en lange boomen, maar ook met het wild gedierte, daar de herten des nachts de boekweit afweidden en de coons en stekelvarkens het corn vernielden. Wanneer het corn in de aar begon te komen haalden zij de stammen naar beneden en aten de aar af. Ik had eens een acre zomertarwe gezaaid en toen het tijd was om te maaien stonden alleen de stengels en de aren kon ik uitgepeld vinden op de dikke stompen, die er overal tusschen stonden. Doch de Heere heeft ons door al deze en nog vele andere moeilijkheden heengeholpen, zoodat wij wel vragen mogen: „Wat zal ik den Heere vergelden voor Zijne weldaden, aan ons bewezen?" [Psalms, 116, 12].

En ten slotte: Kon Jacob zeggen: „Met mijn staf ben ik over de Jordaan gegaan", enz. [Genesis 32 : 10] zoo kan ik ook zeggen: „Met een schip ben ik over den oceaan gegaan en nu ben ik tot twee heiren geworden", daar wij nu met kinderen, behuwd-, klein- en achterkleinkinderen 73 zielen tellen.

Chapter IX

EARLY DAYS IN OVERISEL, MICHIGAN

36. P. SCHUT'S ACCOUNT OF MY JOURNEYS

[The author about whom nothing seems known lived in Overisel and in 1891 wrote these *Reisverhalen* published in the *Jaarboekje voor de Hollandsche Christelijke Gereformeerde Kerken Noord Amerika voor het Jaar* 1891 (Holland 1890).]

Ik schrijf zooals dit in mijn geheugen is bewaard gebleven, sints mij het een en ander is verteld. Het doel is om de eerste dagen en den strijd der oude kolonisten in gedachtenis te houden. Moge het eene niet vrij zijn van humor en plooit het uwe lip in een lach, gij zult het andere lezende, den ouden niet vergunnen dat zij soms iets zoo aardigs ondervonden, dat zij het lachen niet geheel hebben verleerd.

I

Van Holland naar Grand Haven

Het was in 1847. Vele familien woonden in stad Holland onder de takken van boomen. 18 huisgezinnen waren zoo gelukkig een onderkomen te hebben in een groote loggen loods van pl.m. 20 × 30 voet groot. Alles was in wording. Vele vrome menschen hadden met Ds. van Raalte de reis naar Amerika gemaakt. Schoon de leider der kolonisten dit wist, wist hij ook dat het edelste het eerste nagemaakt wordt en dat onder de goedgezinden ook wel slechten binnensluipen zouden. Om nu het ergste te voorkomen had hij een twaalftal constables aangesteld, onder welke ook H. G. M., mijn zegsman. Dat deze maatregel niet overbodig was zal weldra blijken.

Men was nog in de pas genoemde loghut, te midden van kisten en pakken, toen men aan Van Raalte klaagde over bedreven diefstal. Van Raalte, die alles tegelijk was, gevolgd door twee constables, zou de goederen onderzoeken en ja, men vond de gestolene goederen op den bodem van eene kist, die aan twee gehuwde personen behoorde. Zij waren de dieven.

Nu moest men er mee naar Grand Haven, want daar is de jail en de rechter. Hoe er te komen? Dit was niet zoo gemakkelijk te beantwoorden.

De wegen ongebaand, de scheepvaart in slechten staat. Men heeft geen paard, geen wagen, geen os zelfs. Ook geen geregelde boot, alleen eene platboot, een vaartuig van tweeduims planken saamgespijkerd, van ruwe constructie en twijfelachtige sterkte. Daarmee zal men dan over de Lake naar Grand Haven.

Spoedig heeft men de dieven met hunne bagaadje in de boot gebracht; H. G. M. en J. R. moesten mee gaan. Een zekere E. wilde ook juist naar Grand Haven en hij stapt in. Van Raalte is de leidende geest. Zonder hem had niemand den moed de Lake over te steken. Hij, die zelf geen vrees scheen te kennen, wist door zijne tegenwoordigheid in 't gezelschap moed in te boezemen. Twee mannen vatten de riemen. Ds. zit als stuurman aan 't roer. De Black Lake uit. En nu gaat het de groote Lake Michigan in.

Aanvankelijk gaat het prettig. Om den tijd wat te korten doet een der mannen de vraag: „Dominé hoe zit het eigenlijk, draait de zon of de aarde?" Dominé geeft geen antwoord. „Misschien heeft Dominé het niet gehoord, vraag hem nog eens", zegt de roeier tegen zijn kameraad. Nog eens weer dezelfde vraag gedaan. Eindelijk zegt de dominé: „Ik geloof dat er veel menschen in den hemel zijn die geloofden dat de aarde draait; en ik geloof ook dat er vele menschen in den hemel zijn die geloofden dat de zon draait." Meer niet.

Nu wist men nog niets en men gevoelde zich wel een beetje verlegen over zijn eigen niets beteekenende vraag en het zoo karakteristieke antwoord.

De beide roeiers zien eindelijk eens achterom. Het gaat zoo ontzettend ver van den wal en de lucht in 't westen niet pluis. J. R., die liever hitsen wil dan bijten, zegt tegen zijn scheepsmaat: „Zeg eens aan dominé dat hij niet zoo ver van wal moet steken." Dominé stoort zich hieraan niet; nog altijd gaat het verder van den wal. De lucht wordt dreigender. Nog eens gezegd: „Dominé, gij moet niet zoo ver de Lake in, zie eens in 't westen." Nog helpt het niet.

„Weet ge wat," zegt J. R. tegen H. G. M.; „als wij blijven voortroeien, stuurt dominé ons naar de diepte om daar te vergaan. Wij moesten zeggen dat als hij niet naar den wal wil sturen, wij niet langer gaan roeien." Zoo gezegd zoo gedaan. Het hielp niet of Dominé al zei: „Als wij dichter bij den wal komen, raken wij in de branding en onze boot gaat uit elkaar." Hij moet toegeven, de mannen zijn niet te overreden. Nu recht naar den wal en zooals Ds. van Raalte voorspeld had, ook recht in de branding en de boot sloeg uiteen. Zij bereikten allen behouden het land, druipnat door de hooge zeeën. Ds. van Raalte echter niet; vlug als hij was en alles

berekenende, sprong hij over en tusschen de golven door en was verge-
lijkenderwijze droog gebleven. Nu lachte hij zijne heldhaftige matrozen
hartelijk uit. Zij konden dit wel niet te goed velen, maar 't was hunne
schuld. Nu zoo goed en zoo kwaad als het ging het goed op den nek en
met de beide dieven het pad gezocht en den weg naar Grand Haven
ingeslagen.

Niet zeer lang duurt het of het gezelschap komt voor de rivier. Deze
moet men doorwaden. De dieven weigeren en zij worden er door gedragen. Ds. ziet het aan en zegt: „Jongens, je bent nu toch nat; draag mij
er ook even door."

De beide roeiers van straks zijn aan de overzijde der rivier. De een
fluistert den ander in 't oor: „Ga gij maar om dominé te halen en denk er
om, hij heeft ons straks zoo uitgelachen, als gij midden in de rivier zijt,
dan struikelt ge en gij weet de rest wel."

M. gaat om dominé te halen, terwijl J. R. op de dieven moest passen.
Als een echte coelie draagt hij dominé op zijn nek. „Hou mij goed vast!"
zegt dominé. „Ja", is het antwoord, „gij moet mij vasthouden." Ziet,
midden in de rivier begint het lastdier te struikelen en voorover kopje
onder in het water. Na wat proesten en blazen zegt de dominé: „Had ik
het niet gedacht!" Meer niets.

Nu gaat het op Port Sheldon aan waar men den nacht verblijft. Des
anderen morgens wilde Ds. van Raalte met eene boot naar Grand Haven,
waar men nog 12 mijlen vandaan is. Hij leent eene boot, een dikke stok,
een beddelaken en verandert de roeiboot in een zeilscheepje, maar het
gezelschap was door de geledene schipbreuk van den vorigen dag zoo
geschokt, dat het niet meewilde. Alleen H. G. M. kon zooveel moed verzamelen, dat hij met Ds. in de boot stapte, denkende: als gij het waagt
dan doe ik het ook.

Daar glijdt het bootje heen; een goede bries zwelde het zeil en met twee
uren waaren zij goed en wel, na een prachtige vaart, te Grand Haven.
De rest van het gezelschap kwam over eenige uren, doodmoede, ook ter
plaatse en weer moesten zij het zich laten welgevallen, dat dominé hen
om hunne lafhartigheid uitlachte.

Hoe men terug kwam is mij niet verteld. Wel dat de dieven, eer zij nog
voor den rechter werden gebracht, Ds. van Raalte op gruwelijke wijze
vervloekten, dat hij zeer geduldig verdroeg. Zij werden uit de kolonie
verbannen en op belofte, dat zij niet weer de voeten in Holland zouden
zetten, op vrije voeten gesteld.

Wat u wellicht het meest heeft aangetrokken is de kalme moed, de onverzettelijke wilskracht en de praktische zin van hem dien men, en terecht,
de Vader der Kolonie noemt.

II

Van Overisel naar Saugatuck en terug

Het moet in den winter van 1849 en 1850 geweest zijn. De sneeuw lag diep, de wegen waren nog ongebaand, toen een vijftal mannen besloot, om in het belang hunner gezinnen en buren, een reis naar Saugatuck te doen of liever zich gedwongen zag derwaarts te gaan.

De vrouwen hadden geen naald of draad, geen lint of band meer. Koffie, thee en suiker waren reeds lang vergeten of nog niet gekende artikelen. De nood klom tamelijk hoog, want men kon geen boezelaar meer verstellen, geen knoop of trens meer zetten.

De moeders waren in de laatste dagen zuinig geweest en hadden zeer excellente boter gemaakt. Van te voren was reeds beproefd om bij Ds. Seine Bolks, die toen in een log hut ten zuiden van het dorp woonde, samen te komen.

Zoo geschiedde het. Eerst heeft men samen gebeden. Men bad toen meer dan nu. Ds. Bolks zegt: „Jongens, ik blijf van avond op, tot ge weerom komt en ik zal de koffie klaar hebben." Moedig en verheugd door de gulle hartelijkheid stapt het vijftal er heen, ieder zijn mandje met boter in den arm.

Men neemt een zuidwestelijke richting. Er zijn geen heiningen in den weg, tenminste niet voor de eerste vier mijlen. Is dit nu wel gemakkelijk – men mist ook het genot om langs de heiningen over gebaande wegen te gaan.

Eerst gaat men op Mr. Schoner [Anton Schorno] een oud settler, een Duitscher, aan. Vandaar naar de „townline". Hoeveel de weg gekronkeld heeft weet ik niet, maar dat de vijf mijlen zeer verlengd zijn geworden, daar men de „Indian Trail" of des houthakkers voetpad niet kon volgen, is zeker en waar men geen van beiden had, moest men zelf den weg vinden om de putten en poelen heen.

Verder naar Saugatuck is de weg meer gebaand; maar ons gezelschap is moede eer zij nog dien weg hebben bereikt. In den avond, toen men de lichten begon op te steken, kwamen zij in Saugatuck aan.

De boter op de toonbank gezet, wordt met een mesje door gesneden, want er mag geen haartje in zitten. De moeders hebben flink opgepast. De boter kan de toets doorstaan en dan voor zooveel centen? Neen, daaraan dacht men niet, geld te ontvangen. Het was alles ruilhandel. Geld is alleen de basis voor de ruiling. De winkelier heeft alles in zijn macht. Hij geeft precies wat hij goedvindt. Een ieder ontvangt nu zooveel naalden, soelden, garen, lint, knoopen, enz., het allernoodigste, en daarvoor heeft men nu 14 mijlen geloopen door diepe sneeuw en langs ongebaande wegen!

Zoo spoedig mogelijk is het stukje „corn" brood veroverd en neemt men de terugreis aan. Het is niet raadzaam om den weg, dien men in den morgen gegaan is, in den avond te bewandelen. Zij kennen hem niet zoo goed en de laatste 4 à 5 mijlen is hij geheel ongebaand. Niet zonder gevaar kan men zich in de bosch begeven. Verdwalen en op de sneeuw vernachten na zulk een vermoeiende reis zou zeer noodlottig kunnen worden. Daarom besluit het gezelschap over Graafschap te gaan. Dit is wel 4 mijlen verder en maakt den weg tot 18 mijlen, maar hij heeft ook dit voordeel, dat men altijd op beter bekend terrein is en hier en daar de hutten van eerste settlers voorbijgaat. In nood kan men dan allicht een onderkomen vinden.

De terugreis wordt aanvaard. Het waren krachtige mannen en toen moet men zeer sterk geweest zijn. Ik geloof altijd dat de Heere, in wiens kracht de reis over de wateren gedaan werd, hier in de eerste worstelingen bizondere lichaamskracht en zedelijken moed verleende.

Reeds is ons gezelschap de Graafschap voorbij. 't Is reeds laat maar nu is elke schrede een nader bij huis en dan de gedachte der blijde ontmoeting geeft nieuwen moed. De vrouw te verblijden met zulk een schat, alleen te waardeeren in zulk een tijd, is zoo'n blijde gedachte.

Het is ongeveer negen uur. Een van het gezelschap is zoo uitgeput, dat hij niet dan met de grootste moeite verder kan komen. Men sleept tot Mr. Hellenthal's woning zich voort en besluit aan te kloppen en te zien of hij misschien ook iets voor hen heeft te eten. Zoo gezegd, zoo gedaan, Aangeklopt, de deur der gastvrije hut wordt geopend en Hellenthal ziet ons gezelschap voor zich, beschenen door het flauwe schijnsel der vetlamp. Zij verklaren hem, dat zij gaarne wat willen uitrusten en wat te eten hebben, indien hij misschien iets in huis heeft. Hellenthal had ook geen overvloed; hij zegt: „Vrouw, heb je nog wat in huis?" En de vrouw heeft niet anders dan droog „corn" brood, dat anders voor den volgenden dag was bestemd. Alles heeft men in die dagen voor elkaar over.

Spoedig is de koffie van gebrande rogge opgezet en na met de meeste hartelijkheid gegeten en gedronken te hebben, spreekt men reeds over vertrekken. Het gezelschap zou gaarne hebben overnacht, doch een had zijne vrouw in zulke omstandigheden achter gelaten, dat hij wel moest en wilde, al bleven de anderen ook. Dat lieten de overigen niet toe, en na samen gedankt en gebeden en elkander aan de hoede des Heeren bevolen, stapt straks het gezelschap de deur uit – Hellenthal leent hen zijn lantaarn om bij het schijnsel daarvan beter het pad te vinden. Helaas! dit genot is slechts kort. Nog 2½ mijl van Overisel gaat de lantaarn uit. Indien ergens, dan hadden zij op dezen weg licht noodig.

Toen zij zoo in het donker langs een gebaand pad eene mijl zijn voortgesukkeld, vinden zij eene halve mijl wel den weg uitgekapt, maar de boomen dwars over het pad. Mr. F., een van 't gezelschap, die dat eind weg mee uitgelegd had, ging telkens een eindje vooruit om het terrein te verkennen, daar hij de gaten beter wist. Riep hij straks: „Jongens, hierheen!” dan moesten zij op hem af. Maar zoo moede en stijf waren zij, dat ze haast zich meer over de boomen lieten vallen dan er over klommen. Men zette zich er op neer, legde eerst het eene dan het andere been er over. Het gaat naar huis en zoo zij er door zijn, is het slechts eene mijl tot het punt van gezamenlijke uitgang, Ds. Bolks „loghut”.

Ook deze ellende werd overwonnen. 't Is reeds middernacht. Ds. Bolks zit nog met zijne vrouw te wachten. De koffie is klaar, volgens belofte. Nog eenigen tijd vertoefd en straks gaat het gezelschap uiteen, om ieder zijne wachtende jonge vrouw en kind in de eenvoudige hut op te zoeken. Gij kunt u die ontmoeting voorstellen. Ik schets ze u niet. Dat de ouden met sterke banden aan elkander zijn verkleefd, laat zich begrijpen. Dat de Heer hen heeft geholpen en staande gehouden in dien bangen tijd, willen zij gaarne met een traan in het oog dankend erkennen. Of het jeugdig geslacht den strijd der ouden weet te waardeeren en den zegen God, hun in die ouders geschonken, wij mogen het wellicht evenzeer betwijfelen, als dat we hen daartoe opwekken.

Ik wil hier mijn wensch nog uitdrukken, dat de oude settlers, die hier en elders nog leven, met nauwkeurigheid de verschillende exploits mogen aanteeken. Wij leeren daaruit de hulpe Gods, den volhardenden moed der ouden waardeeren, en het zal ons jong geslacht helpen de voorrechten van heden hooger te schatten.

Chapter X

SETTLEMENT AT GRAND RAPIDS, RAVENNA AND JAMESTOWN

37. FRANS VAN DRIELE'S FIRST EXPERIENCES

[Born at Middelburg in Zeeland in 1816, Frans van Driele emigrated to Michigan in 1847, arriving in Grand Rapids in the following year where he spent the rest of his years ever influential among the Hollanders in Michigan and other communities. Though of limited education Van Driele wrote copiously on theological topics printed in *De Hope* of Holland and on other subjects in *De Volksvriend* of Orange City, Iowa. The following sketch, *Eerste Ervaringen* was an address delivered at the Semi-Centennial celebrations in Holland in August 1897 and printed in *De Grondwet*, November 26, 1912. Following this sketch is a *Postscript* or *Nalezing* which in its original form was delivered at the Fortieth Anniversary of the settlement at Zeeland, printed in *De Grondwet*, April 4, 1911.]

Ge zult zeker wel gelezen hebben, dat er te Zeeland een groot feest is geweest [1887]. 't Was veertig jaar geleden dat de Hollanders, meest Zeeuwen, zich daar hebben nedergezet. Ik ben daar ook tegenwoordig geweest. Uit Grand Rapids waren er minstens 300 opgekomen en men berekend het geheel getal op 4 à 5 duizend. Allen hebben zich vergast aan de welvoorziene tafels en den geheelen dag door werden er redevoeringen gehouden, afgewisseld door gezang.

In de eerste plaats verheugde het mij, dat al de broeders vereenigd waren, even als op begrafenissen. Wel, dat is dan ook goed, want op het feest hiernamaals zullen wij zeker eeuw uit eeuw in vereenigd zijn.

Dan, in de tweede plaats, waren er menschen tegenwoordig die nog al zwak zijn en zich den meesten tijd onwel gevoelen om naar de kerk te gaan, of anderen, wien den lust daartoe ontbreekt. Dezulken hadden nu eene goede kans, een en ander te hooren.

Vervolgens was het waarlijk een aangenamen dag, broeders te spreken, die men in geen jaren ontmoet had. Het maakte bij die gelegenheid dan ook geen onderscheid, tot welk „huisgezin" men behoorde.

Nu dan, „de Heere heeft ons ruimte gemaakt". Let wel, de Heere heeft het gedaan; Hij heeft lust en kracht en wijsheid geschonken, om al die boomen te vellen en die wildernis in een vruchtbaar land te herscheppen. Waar men vroeger zich verloor in de bosschen, zou iemand, die in geen jaren daar geweest is, verdoold raken in de uitgestrekte velden.

Ik herinner mij nog, – 't was in de maand Februari 1849 – dat ik met een oude vriend een reisje maakte naar „de Kolonie". Het werd donker, zoodat wij bij het naast gelegen huis een lantaarn leenden om de blessen van de boomen te vinden, waarlangs de road was afgebikt; doch de kaars was zoo klein, dat zij spoedig uitgebrand was. Daar stonden wij, in den donker, te zweeten van angst. Wij wisten niet meer of wij oost, west, zuid of noord gingen; doch de Heere gaf spoedig ruimte en wij kwamen aan een „opening", dicht bij waar wij dien nacht zouden vertoeven.

„De Heere heeft ruimte gemaakt." Thans heeft men goede wegen; paarden in plaats van ossen; in een uur tijds rijdt men nu van hier met den spoortrein naar Holland, daar men vroeger een dag toe noodig had.

In 1848, 1849 en 1850 en ook nog een weinig later, kwam hier te Grand Rapids menige jongeling en jonge dochter uit de Kolonie, om te werken voor een klein loon. Zij waren eenvoudig gekleed, doch helder en stuurden in den regel hunne verdiende penningen naar hun ouders die, ofschoon boeren, het in die dagen maar schraal hadden.

Thans hebben die boeren, de meesten althans, flinke huizen, groote schuren, paarden en koeien op stal, graan op zolder, geld aan kas en sommigen in de bank; en de jonge dochters verdienen hooge loonen, willen nu liefst niet zoo hard werken en gaan vrij prachtig gekleed, om de zes weken een nieuwen hoed en om de twee maanden een nieuwe *dress*.

Wij zijn gewassen in dit land, gelijk de kinderen Israëls in Egypte. Zoo wat vijf jaren geleden telde ik te Vriesland, binnen een afstand van ongeveer drie mijl, nagenoeg vijftig kinderen in vijf huisgezinnen.

Wij zijn gewassen niet alleen in getalsterkte, maar wat meer is – en dit is van groot belang – in de stad Holland is niet alleen wat men voor maatschappelijk welzijn noodig heeft, maar ook voor onze verstandelijke ontwikkeling en voor ons zielenheil; een college en een seminarie, waar vele jonge menschen gekweekt worden en welke reeds tal van jaren goede vruchten hebben opgeleverd, niet alleen dokters en schoolmeesters en advokaten, maar inzonderheid vele dienaars des Evangelies. Dit is alles een zegen van den Allerhoogsten.

Daarbij zijn wij ook zoo gewassen, dat er aan den mond van Black Lake groote schepen kunnen in en uitvaren. En toch, bij al die zegeningen, is er nu iets treurigs. Op die zelfde Black Lake varen nu stoombooten, des Zondags zoowel als in de week met honderden menschen, die aan de parken aldaar den dag des Heeren ontheiligen met varen, springen, zwemmen, enz. En mogelijk zijn daar ook wel van onze jongere verbondskinderen onder, die zich op dien dag bij de gelederen der pleizierzoekers voegen. Zoo nu en dan komen er zelfs klachten, dat er oudere christenen zijn, die het niet heel nauw nemen om op den Sabbat ook eens pret te hebben, zooals zij dat noemen, aan die parken.

Mogelijk vraagt ge, hoe maken die jonge menschen het nu; zenden ze nog geld naar hunne ouders in de Kolonie? Antwoord: Er zijn niet veel boeren meer wier kinderen te Grand Rapids, noch op andere plaatsen dienen, daar de nood hen niet langer dringt. En dan hebben zij, die hier en elders dienen, tegenwoordig hun geld ook hard noodig; want als men mooi en naar de mode gekleed wil gaan, dan kost dit geld. Vandaar dat er nog al geklaagd wordt, dat de jeugdigen maar schrale offers brengen voor de Kerk, voor armen en het Godsrijk – die zorg schijnen zij aan de ouderen, de gehuwden, over te laten.

Nu moet ge wel verstaan, vele ouden zijn dood. Er is bijna een nieuw geslacht, dat niet zoo voorbeeldig is en bij velen van ons, oudjes, valt ook niet te roemen; zoodat het mij soms wel eens toeschijnt alsof de voornalige ernst des levens gemist wordt.

Het is nu 50 jaar geleden dat God ons als eerste settlers dit land deed beërven, waarvan niet alleen wij, maar ook onze kinderen en klein-kinderen thans inwoners en burgers zijn. En ons ook onder alle moeilijk-heden dezes levens gezegend en welgedaan heeft, daar velen onzer van arm rijk geworden zijn. En, wat meer is, dat velen onzer hier het brood des levens gevonden hebben en alzoo ook erfgenamen des eeuwigen levens geworden zijn.

Nu is het waar, dat velen onzer in die eerste jaren menigen zweetdroppel lieten vallen en menigen traan hebben gestort; nochtans heeft God er ons tot hiertoe doorgeholpen, waardoor wij dan ook op dezen dag geroepen worden om Hem eer, lof en dank toe te brengen voor al het goede dat wij van Hem hebben ontvangen, zoo in de natuur alsook in de genade die Hij aan ons bewezen heeft.

Tranen zijn er natuurlijk gevallen toen wij onze dierbaren ten grave brachten; ook tranen van teleurstelling in die eerste jaren, omdat alles niet aan onze verwachting voldoet.

Mijne eerste tranen vielen in het begin van October 1847 te Wawarsing, Ulster County, New York. En wel onder deze omstandigheden. Mijn geheel kapitaal had ik verreisd en met slechts 50 cents in den zak, ont-moette ik gelukkig een oud vriend. Ik verwachtte dat hij mij met blijd-schap zou ontvangen en zeggen: „Wel Frans, ik ben blijde u te ont-moeten." In plaats hiervan was het mij toegevoegde van geheel ander gehalte en wel: „Wat moet gij hier doen?" De tranen liepen langs mijne wangen. „Gij schreit, maar," hernam hij, „het is ernst, ik weet niet wat gij hier moest komen doen." „En", vervolgde hij, „de vraag is ook nog: wat wilt gij doen?" „O", antwoordde ik, „al was het koeienwachter." „Zoo, nu, dan is er geen nood." En des anderen daags reeds kreeg ik, door bemiddeling van hem, werk aan het kanaal.

Na verloop van negen maanden had ik genoeg oververdiend om, in gezelschap van de familie P. de Pree, de reis naar het thans bestaande Holland te aanvaarden, een reis die toen ter tijde per kanaal- en stoomboot, ruim vier weken duurde.

In het begin van Juni 1848 kwamen wij in „de stad" Holland aan. Er waren toen alhier een klein getal woonhuizen en een wind-houtzaagmolen en voor de rest was het meestal bosch. In dat bosch heb ik de eer genoten om een drietal boomen – het was echter alleen om de bark te doen – omver te hakken. De vierde, ook een hemlock, viel slechts ten deele, daar hij in de takken van een anderen boom bleef hangen. En dat kostte menigen zweetdroppel en wel zoo, dat ik doornat bezweet was vóór de boom ter aarde lag, in aanmerking nemende dat het voor mij ongeveer een halven dag hard werkens was om een niet heel dikken boom neer te vellen. Bij zulk zwaar werk vielen niet alleen menige zweetdroppels, maar ook niet weinige tranen.

Den derden dag kwam ik weer in het bosch en keek met een droevig gezicht naar mijnen nog steeds hangenden boom. Er was echter nog een ander persoon in het bosch, die ook bezig was met boomen omver te hakken en het geluk had er een te doen vallen, die juist boven op de mijne terecht kwam en hem ter aarde en binnen mijn bereik bracht. O, welk een blijdschap was er toen in mijn hart.

Eenigen tijd daarna vertrok ik van Holland naar Grand Rapids en verhuurde mij den 5den Juli 1848 aldaar als kanaal-arbeider tegen $ 16 per maand en de kost. Het waren echter lange dagen, van half zeven 's morgens tot zonsondergang. Geld was er niet; onze betaling bestond in store pay. Mijne slaapplaats was in een shanty – in drie kribben boven elkander, op stroozakken. Deksel hadden wij niet; het was warm genoeg.

Mijne kameraden bestonden uit een 14 à 15tal Ieren, tamelijk goed voor hun doen. Des avonds bogen wij allen de knieën. Ieder bad voor zichzelven. Zij vroegen mij hierop of ik Katholiek was. Ik antwoordde, dat een goed Protestant ook bad als hij ter ruste ging.

Na zoowat vier maanden aan het kanaal gewerkt te hebben, verhuurde ik mij aan M. L. Sweet and Clements, op een flourmolen, tegen $ 10 en de kost per maand. In deze capaciteit heb ik 15 jaar gewerkt.

Den 24sten Maart 1849 huwde ik met de Weduwe Postma. Zij had een meisje van 6 jaar, die later met Willem Kotvis is gehuwd. Ons huwelijk werd ingezegend te Vriesland, door Ds. Maarten Ypma. Ik denk dat ik de eerste Hollander van Grand Rapids was die in het huwelijk trad. Onze weddingtrip van Vriesland naar Grand Rapids, een afstand van zoowat 24 mijlen, werd te voet afgelegd, want $ 11 voor een ossenteam kon er

niet op overschieten. Wij huurden een man voor $ 1.50, om ons doch-
tertje te helpen dragen.

Bij onze aankomst te Grand Rapids konden we, uit gebrek aan woningen, geen huis huren. Daarom namen wij onzen intrek in het basement der Eerste Gereformeerde kerk aldaar. Een gedeelte hiervan werd
door ons als woonhuis gebruikt, terwijl het ander gedeelte door ons ter
houding van godsdienstoefeningen werd afgezonderd.

Nu werd mijn loon tot $ 14 per maand verhoogd, maar – eigen kost
koopen. Gij begrijpt „Schrale Hans” werd keukenmeid. Toch, wij waren
vergenoegd en tevreden. God zorgde voor ons en we leden geen gebrek.

's Zondags werd er in den voormiddag godsdienstoefening gehouden
in het basement in de Eerste kerk, in het Engelsch; daar konden wij
niets van verstaan. 's Namiddags werd er een preek gelezen in de Hollandsche taal. Doch spoedig vertrok Ds. Andrew Taylor, die de Engelsche
oefeningen leidde en toen kregen wij de gelegenheid om driemaal daags,
des Zondags namelijk, eene Hollandsche preek te lezen. Later kwam
Ds. Cornelius van der Meulen van Zeeland om de vier weken preeken;
en ook Ds. Ypma van Vriesland kwam om de vier weken, zoodat wij
toen iedere 14 dagen prediking hadden. Ds. Ypma kwam dan te voet
van Vriesland en dan betaalden wij hem, en ook eveneens Ds. van der
Meulen, ieder $ 4. De laatstgenoemde reed met een wagentje bespannen
met twee versleten ponies; en, in betrekking tot die ponies kan het
volgende gemeld worden:

Ds. van der Meulen had bij zekere gelegenheid weer bij ons gepreekt
en op de terugreis te Beaverdam komende, vroeg hij aan Mr. Dunnink
of hij niet iemand wist die een poosje op de ponies zou willen passen. Op
de vraag: „Zullen zij anders op den loop gaan?” antwoordde Ds. van
der Meulen „Neen, maar als er niemand bij is, vallen zij wel eens omver.”
Bij een andere gelegenheid vroeg de dominee Mr. P. Benjaminse en
schrijver dezes, of wij des anderen daags niet met hem naar Zeeland
wilden rijden, en zoo ja, dan moesten we zorgen dat wij des morgens te
zeven uren te Grandville waren. Wij namen het aan en op genoemden tijd
vertrokken wij ook van daar. Na ongeveer drie mijlen gereden te hebben,
moesten wij afstijgen en daarna tot de knieën door den moddder en met
een zweep in de hand hadden wij al dat wij doen konden om de ponies
voort te zweepen, laat staan zelf te rijden. Te Beaverdam komende,
waren we genoodzaakt om twee van de vier zakken meel, die wij aan
boord hadden, achter te laten. Kort nadat wij Beaverdam verlieten, ontmoeten wij een span ossen, welke ons en de ponies des avonds om half-
acht op Zeeland brachten. Dat was een reis van ongeveer 17 à 18 mijlen.

Later, toen wij als gemeente gevestigd waren, kwam er een stroom van Hollanders met attesten en om belijdenis te doen. Bij gelegenheid dat er een dominé bij ons was, hadden we soms kerkeraadsvergaderingen die tot 12 à 1 uur in den nacht duurden om die menschen aan te nemen; en, de dominé moest bovendien des Zondags driemaal prediken; en dat alles voor $ 4 begrijpt u. Doch, wij konden niet meer geven en o, die dominé's waren dan ook zoo blijde, daar zij dan weder een weinig geld in handen kregen.

Wij verkeerden in die dagen alles behalve in een rijken toestand, maar wij waren tevreden en vergenoegd en opgeruimd; alles was even eenvoudig, de kleeding van de vrouwen en jonge dochters even als alles anders; men droeg toen geen hoeden met bloemen, maar eenvoudig caps, zooals men die noemde, en verder calico dresses. Mannen en jongelingen insgelijks; geen witte overhemden met staande kragen, daar wist men toen niet van. Het gebeurde soms dat als ik een nieuwe blauwe overall gekocht had tegen 25 of 37 cents, ik die eerst een poos gebruikte om des Zondags mede naar de kerk te gaan. En, dat was nu geen nederige hoogmoed; wij wisten niet beter en bovendien, wij waren geldeloos. Ook de dagloonen waren slechts van 62½ tot 75 cents en de betaling dan nog meestal store pay. Het was hard werken om aan het eten te blijven en voor huishuur te zorgen. Doch, wij leefden vergenoegd en er was innerlijke godsdienst. En, wat de jonge menschen betreft, zoo als later bleek, toen wij een gemeente waren en toen zij belijdenis des geloofs aflegden, dat waren halve professoren. Zij hadden flinke bijbelkennis: waren goed onderwezen in den Catechismus en zij waren in het *Kort Begrip* goed te huis.

Wat ons kerkelijk leven aanging, dat was alles in zijn kindsheid, zoo als ik hier laat volgen. Wij waren van den 5den Juli 1848 tot Juli 1849, nog niet als gemeente georganiseerd, doch niemand liet de onderlinge bijeenkomst na. Wij waren allen als een van hart en zin. Wij erkenden elkander als ware geloovigen. G. Dalman en schrijver dezes waren de leiders. Ongeveer op het laatst van Juli 1849 oordeelden wij, dat wij twee ouderlingen moesten hebben en dan als eene gemeente georganiseerd te worden. Wij maakten des Zondags aan de broeders bekend, dat zij aanstaanden rustdag hun briefje in het kerkzakje zouden doen, met de namen van twee personen er op, die men als ouderlingen begeerden.

Den volgenden rustdag, na kerktijd, zagen Dalman en schrijver dezes, de briefjes na, met den afloop dat wij bevonden, dat wij beide met algemeene stemmen tot ouderlingen verkozen waren. Dit maakten wij 's namiddags bekend en verzochten daarna Ds. van Raalte om ons den volgenden Zondag te bevestigen en te verklaren dat wij de Tweede Gereformeerde Gemeente waren. Aan dat verzoek heeft Ds. van Raalte voldaan en nu waren wij als gemeente gevormd, zonder dat iemand een attest bracht of belijdenis deed. Ook zonder navraag van de Classis. Er is hier ook geen notulen van gehouden. Later mocht men, om als lidmaat tot de gemeente toegelaten te worden belijdenis doen of een attest hebben. Ook in het beroepen van een leeraar handelden wij zonder goedkeuring van de Classis. Wij wisten niet beter. In het beroepen van een leeraar hadden wij geen formaliteiten. Wij hebben twee á driemaal een beroep gedaan en dan was het altijd zoowat de hoofdzaak: kom over en help ons; en, wat het traktement aanging: de arbeider is zijn loon waardig. Men zal een dorstenden os niet muilbanden. In het beroepen van een dominé vroegen wij geen goedkeuring van de Classis of dat wel zoo mocht. En dat scheen toen alles in orde te zijn.

En nu, mijne vrienden, ik moet eindigen. God geve, dat we niet alleen goede burgers mogen zijn van dit ons aangenomen vaderland en dat gij, jongelingen en jongedochters en kinderen, eenmaal ons Eeuwfeest mogen vieren, maar inzonderheid, dat wij ook goede burgers en inwoners mogen zijn en worden van het hemelsche vaderland dat Boven is.

Bij mijn 82sten verjaardag:

Ik ben geboren te Middelburg, provincie Zeeland, Nederland, den 6de Juni 1816. Toen ik den leeftijd van 12 jaar bereikt had, verloor ik door den dood mijn vader. Van mijn 12de tot mijn 15de jaar ben ik op een blikslagers winkel werkzaam geweest. Van mijn 15de tot mijn 20ste jaar was ik bakkersknecht te Middelburg. In 1836 vertrok ik naar Axel en diende daar vier jaren. In 1840 vertrok ik als bakkersknecht naar Yzendijke en diende daar een half jaar en verkeerde het overige half jaar zoo wat bij vrienden en bekenden, toen ik mij in 1841 weer als bakkersknecht te Goes verhuurde. In 1842 begon ik met garen en band, boeken, enz. rond te gaan en was dus in plaats van knecht nu baas, of liever koopman. Dit heb ik met eenig succes volgehouden tot 1847 en had toen zooveel oververdiend dat ik de reis naar Amerika kon doen, zonder iemand lastig te vallen.

Den 6den Augustus 1847 vertrok ik van Hellevoetsluis met het schip, *Charles Hummerston*, en den volgenden nacht verdaagden wij op het strand te Calais op de Fransche kust, in den mond van 't engelsche kanaal. Wij werden allen door visschersschuiten gered en te Calais aan wal gebracht.

Te Calais vertoefden wij twee weken en werden toen naar Havre, Frankrijk, getransporteerd. Ook daar moesten we weder een week of iets meer verblijven, tot wij eindelijk in het laatst van Augustus met de *Robert Parker* naar New York vertrokken, alwaar wij in het laatst van September eindelijk gelukkig arriveerden.

Toen ik 19 jaar oud was deed ik belijdenis in de Hervormde kerk te Middelburg, Nederland, doch alleen in vorm, want ik verstond er niets van wat ik beleed. Later toen de Heere mijne oogen door genade opende, deed ik andermaal belijdenis in de Groede, provincie Zeeland, en sloot mij in 1841 bij de Afgescheiden Kerk aan.

Den 5den Juli 1848 arriveerde ik te Grand Rapids en den volgenden Zondag werd ik verzocht om voor de weinige Hollanders die er toen waren een preek te lezen. Er waren slechts drie families met hunne kinderen en twee jongelingen. John Roost en Josua Elenbaas en Mrs. A. Kroes, thans Mrs. J. Pauels, die zoover ik weet, maar alleen meer in leven is.

Er waren in de eerste bijeenkomst nog 8 à 9 meisjes meer aanwezig, waarvan sommigen nog in leven zijn.

Ik heb het preeklezen zoowat een jaar volgehouden voor wij als gemeente werden georganiseerd, hetgeen in den zomer van 1849 onder den naam van Tweede Gereformeerde gemeente plaats had.

G. Dalman en mijn persoon werden als ouderlingen verkozen. In 1876 werd ik als ouderling bij de Vierde Gereformeerde Gemeente gekozen, doch toen Ds. Lammert Hulst zich met die gemeente afscheidde, stond ik buiten, totdat er weder eene nieuwe Vierde Gereformeerde Gemeente werd georganiseerd, waar ik toen weer als ouderling werd gekozen, bij welke gemeente ik thans nog behoor en hoop er bij te blijven, totdat de Heere mij oproept in Zijne Gemeente hier Boven, waar geen ouderlingen noch diakenen zijn zullen, maar waar we allen als Gods kinderen Hem eeuwig in volmaaktheid zullen dienen.

[Translation]

You surely will have read that there was a great celebration at Zeeland [1887]. It was forty years ago that Netherlanders, for the most part Zeelanders, settled there. I also was present at that celebration. At least 300 attended from Grand Rapids; the total was estimated from 4,000 to 5,000. These people were entertained at well-set tables. During the entire day there were alternating speeches and singing.

First, I was pleased that all the brethren were in harmony, even as at funerals. That, of course, is a good thing, for at the feast in the hereafter we surely will be united throughhout all ages. Second, there were people in attendance who were physically weak, not feeling well enough most of the time to attend church services, and others, who had no desire to attend such services. These people now had a good chance to hear each other. Next, it truly was a pleasant day for brethren to speak to each other, brethren that had not seen each other in years. On that occasion it made no difference to which "household" they belonged.

Now then, "the Lord has given us space." Note well, the Lord did this, He granted us the desire, strength, and wisdom to chop down the trees and recreate the wilderness into fruitful farming land. Where formerly we used to be lost in the forests, today one who had never visited this country would become lost among the extensive fields.

I remember very well – it was in the month of February 1849 that an old friend and I made a trip to the Kolonie. It was getting dark. At the nearest house we borrowed a lantern in order to see the blazes on the trees which marked the road. But the candle was so small that it soon was burned out. There we stood in the dark, perspiring from fear. We could not tell whether we were going north, east, south, or west. But the Lord directed us and we came to a clearing, not far from the place where we were going to spend the night.

"The Lord made room." Today we have good roads, horses in place of oxen. In one hour one rides by train from Grand Rapids to Holland. Formerly one needed an entire day for this journey.

In 1848, 1849, and 1850, and later came many a young son or daughter from out of the Kolonie to look for work, and at a small wage. They were simply clothed, but they were intelligent and usually sent their earnings home to their parents who as farmers usually were not any too well off. Today farmers, at least most of them, have comfortable houses, large barns, horses and cows in their stables, grain stored up, money saved and sometimes in the bank. Now young daughters are earning good wages, and they usually do not work very hard and go about beautifully clad and buy a new hat every six weeks and a new dress every two months.

We have grown up in this country, like the children of Israël in Egypt. About five years ago I counted in Vriesland, within the distance of about three miles, about fifty children in five families. We have grown not only in numbers, but into something of much greater importance. The city of Holland possesses not only everything necessary for its social progress but also everything for its intellectual development and our spiritual advancement. It has a college and a seminary in which many young students are being trained. For years these institutions have produced excellent fruit not only in medical men, school teachers, and lawyers, but especially ministers of the Gospel. This in all respects is a blessing of the All Highest.

In addition we have so grown that at the mouth of Black Lake large ships sail in and out. And yet all this progress is not without its dark side. On that same Black Lake today steamboats, on Sunday as well as on week days, are carrying hundreds of people to the parks dishonoring the Lord's day by boating, diving, swimming, etc. Possibly among these groups of pleasure seekers are to be found some of our younger children of the Covenant. From time to time we hear complaints that some Christians of more advanced years are none too strict and seek pleasure at these parks on the Sabbath.

Possibly you are asking, "How are these young people getting along, are they sending their earnings to their parents in the Kolonie?" Answer: Not many farmer's children are to be found in Grand Rapids, nor in other places, for necessity no longer urges them. And besides, those who nowadays are earning wages here and there themselves need their money very much, for if they want to be well dressed and follow the fashions, that costs money. Hence the complaints that the younger folk make only slight contributions to the church, for the poor, and for God's kingdom. This they appear to leave to the older folk, to the married people.

You should well grasp the fact that many of our older folk have left us and have gone beyond. A new generation, practically, has come into existence; hence it is not vain imagination that among many of us older folk we have little cause for praise, and so sometimes it appears to me that our onetime seriousness has vanished.

Fifty years ago God bequeathed to us as first settlers this country in which we, our children, and our grandchildren are dwellers and of which we are citizens. He also blessed us and caused us to prosper in spite of all of life's difficulties, for many of us who were poor have become well-to-do. And what is more, many of us here have found the Bread of Life and so also have become heirs to the life eternal.

It is true of course that our people have moistened the ground with many a drop of sweat and have wept many a tear. Nevertheless God has helped us through all this. For this reason today we are called to give Him honor, praise, and thanks for all the good we have received from Him, not only in the natural order, but also the grace He has shown us. Naturally, tears have fallen when we brought our beloved ones to their graves. There also were tears of disappointment during those first years, for nothing ever fully meets our expectations.

I shed my first tears in the beginning of October 1847 at Wawarsing,

Ulster County, New York, and under the following circumstances. I had exhausted my entire capital in journeying hither. I had only fifty cents left in my pocket, but fortunately I met an old friend. I expected he would receive me with joy and say, "Well, Frans, I am glad to see you." But instead of this what he said was of a very different nature – "What are you doing here?" Tears ran down my cheeks. "You may weep," he continued, "it is a serious matter. I really don't know why you should come here. And, the question is, "what do you intend to do?" "O," I replied, "if I could find work simply as a cowherd." "If that is all you want, you will have no trouble." Next day, through his help, I found work on the canal.

After nine months I had saved enough money to undertake the journey to Holland with the P. de Pree family, a journey which in those days required fully four weeks. In the beginning of June 1848 we arrived at the "*stad*" Holland. Here we saw a small number of houses and a sawmill driven by wind, and for the rest practically nothing but forest. In that forest I enjoyed the honor of chopping down three hemlock trees, but this was only for the sake of the bark. The fourth tree, also a hemlock, lodged in the branches of another tree. To bring that tree down to the ground cost many a drop of sweat and I became thoroughly wet. It required a half day's labor to fell a moderately big tree. Such labor brought forth many a sweat drop and not a few tears. On the third day I returned to this tree and looked sadly at the way it had lodged. But there was another worker there who also was busy chopping down trees. He dropped one which landed right on mine and brought it down with it. How happy I was!

Soon after that I left Holland for Grand Rapids and on July 5, 1848, found work as a laborer on the canal at the rate of $ 16 per month and board. But the days were long, from 6:30 in the morning till sunset. There was no money, and we were paid in store pay. I slept in a shanty on a straw tick. There were three bunks, one above the other. We had no blankets, for the weather was warm. My friends were 14 or 15 Irishmen who conducted themselves fairly well, considering everything. When evening came we all knelt in prayer. Each prayed by himself. They asked if I was Catholic. I answered that a good Protestant also said his prayers when he went to bed. After working about four months on the canal I hired myself out to M. L. Sweet and Clements, to work in their flour mill at the rate of $ 10 [cash] per month and board. In this capacity I served them for fifteen years.

On March 24, 1849, I married the widow Postma. She had a daughter of six who later married Willem Kotvis. Our marriage was blessed by

Dominie Maarten Ypma, in Vriesland. I believe I was the first Hollander in Grand Rapids to enter the matrimonial estate. Our wedding trip from Vriesland to Grand Rapids was made afoot, a distance of about 24 miles, for we could not afford $ 11 for the services of a yoke of oxen. We paid a man $ 1.50 to help carry our daughter.

On our arrival in Grand Rapids we could not rent a house, owing to the prevailing scarcity. For that reason we found a place to live in the basement of the First Reformed Church. A part of this basement was given us as a dwelling, the rest was set aside for our religious services. My wages were raised to $ 14 per month, but I had to provide my own food. You can well imagine how "Poor Hans" became kitchen maid. But we were contented. God cared for us and we suffered no want.

On Sunday morning religious services in English were held in the basement of the First Reformed Church; but of this we could understand nothing. But the Reverend Andrew Taylor soon departed. He had led services three times each Sunday. Now we had the opportunity of hearing a Dutch sermon read. Later Dominie Cornelius van der Meulen came from Zeeland every four weeks. Dominie Ypma from Vriesland also came to us once every four weeks and so we had Dutch services every two weeks. Dominie Ypma walked all the way from Vriesland and we paid him and Dominie van der Meulen $ 4 for their services. The last named drove a team of worn out ponies.

On one occasion after he had preached for us and when on his way home he had reached Beaverdam, Dominie van der Meulen stopped at Mr. Dunnink's and asked if some one would watch his ponies. To the question, "Would they run away?" the dominie replied, "No, but if no one is watching them, they may fall down." On another occasion the dominie invited Mr. P. Benjaminse and me to ride with him to Zeeland the next day. We were to be at Grandville at 7 o'clock in the morning. We accepted this invitation and at the stated hour left Grandville. After having ridden three miles we had to get off the wagon. Then, wading knee deep in the mud and with whip in hand, all our efforts were consumed in urging the ponies forward. At Beaverdam we were forced to leave four sacks of meal which we were carrying in his wagon. After leaving Beaverdam we met a yoke of oxen whose driver helped us and our ponies to get to Zeeland where we arrived at 7:30 in the evening. This was a journey of 17 or 18 miles.

Later, after we had been organized as a congregation, a stream of Hollanders came to us, some carrying letters of church membership, others to make their profession of faith. If a dominie were present we would have a consistory meeting which might last until 12 or 1 o'clock at night. After such a meeting the dominie would have to preach three times on Sunday, and all that for $ 4. But, we could not pay more. Those dominies were so glad to have a little money in their hand.!

In those days we were contented and well satisfied and happy. Everything was plain, the cloting of the women and the young girls like everything else. Then they wore no hats decked with flowers, but plain caps, as they were called, and in addition, calico dresses. Similar plainness characterized the men and the boys; they did not wear white shirts and stiff collars. Such things were not heard of in those days. It happened occasionally that I wore to church a newly purchased blue overall which had cost no more than 37 cents.

This was no pride in our humility; we simply had no other ideas and, besides, we were penniless. Our daily wages were from 62½ to 75 cents, and we ordinarily were given store pay. We had to work hard to provide ourselves with food and to pay the house rent. Nevertheless we were satisfied and there was a deep inner piety. And our young people, as was evident when we were organized as a congregation, were exceedingly well instructed when they made their profession of faith. They gave evidence of having good acquaintance with the Bible, were well instructed in Catechism, and were well at home in the *Kort Begrip* [a commonly used introduction to the Reformed faith].

Our church life was still quite elementary as I shall explain below. We were not yet organized as a congregation from July 5, 1848, to July 1849, but everybody attended services. We were all of one heart and one mind. We recognized each other as truly being of the faithful. G. Dalman and the writer were the leaders. About the close of July 1849 we came to the decision to elect two elders and to be organized as a congregation. We asked the brethren to put their votes containing the names of those they wanted to serve as elders into the collection box next Sunday.

On the following Sunday, after services, Dalman and the writer scrutinized the ballots and found that we had been unanimously elected as elders. We announced this fact at the afternoon services. We asked Dominie van Raalte to confirm us in our functions on the following Sunday and to proclaim us to be the Second Reformed Church [of Grand Rapids]. To this request Dominie van Raalte agreed. So we were constituted a congregation without anybody presenting a letter of membership or making a profession of faith, as normally would have been necessary. Nor was there any inquiry made by the Classis. Nor were any minutes kept. Later, to be admitted to the congregation, people either presented letters of membership or made their profession of faith. Also in calling a minister we acted without approval from the Classis. We just were not acquainted with the proper legal formalities. We issued two or three such calls. Our appeal always was, "Come over and help us!" So far as salary was concerned the idea simply was "the laborer is worthy his pay." One was not to muzzle the ox! In so inviting dominies we never asked the Classis if this was proper. But such seemed to be entirely in order.

Now, my friends, I must conclude. God grant that we not only may be good citizens in this our adopted country and that you young men and young women may sometime celebrate our eternal Centenary, but also that we may become good citizens and inhabitants of the heavenly fatherland which is Above.

[Added at my 82nd birthday]. I was born in Middelburg, province of Zeeland, the Netherlands, on June 16, 1816. When I reached my twelfth year death robbed me of my father. From my twelfth to my fifteenth year I worked in a tinsmith's shop. In 1836 I went to Axel where I worked five years. In 1840 I went to Yzendijke where I worked as baker's apprentice for a half year. The next half year I lived with friends and acquaintances. Then I became a baker's apprentice at Goes. In 1842 I began to sell yarn, ribbon, books, etc., from house to house. Instead of being an apprentice I now was a master, or merchant. This business I followed with some success until 1847. By that time I had saved enough to pay for my voyage to America without having to borrow anything from anybody.

On August 6, 1847, I left Hellevoetsluis in the *Charles Hummerston*, and on the following day we arrived at Calais on the French coast at the entrance of the English Channel. We were saved by fishing boats which brought us ashore at Calais [where we had met with shipwreck]. There we stayed two weeks and then were taken to Le Havre, France. There too we had to spend a week or longer. Finally, in August, we left in the *Robert Parker* for New York where we arrived safely at the close of September.

When I was nineteen I made my profession of faith in the Reformed Church in Middelburg. This was merely a form, for I did not understand anything of what I professed. Later when the Lord through His grace opened my eyes, I made another profession, at Groede in the province of Zeeland and in 1841 I joined the church of the Seceders [*Afgescheidenen*].

On July 5, 1848, I arrived in Grand Rapids. On the following Sunday I was invited to read a sermon for the small number of Hollanders there.

There were only three families and their children, besides two young men, Jan Roost and Josua Elenbaas, and Mrs. A. Kroes [now Mrs. J. Pauels] who alone of this group is still alive. At this first meeting some eight or nine girls were present, some of whom are still living.

I kept up my reading of sermons for a year until the congregation was organized, which took place in the summer of 1849, under the name of the Second Reformed Church. G. Dalman and I were chosen elders. In 1876 I was chosen elder of the Fourth Reformed Congregation. But when Dominie Lammert Hulst separated from that congregation, I was deprived of this office until a new congregation was organized when I again was chosen elder. I still belong to this congregation and I hope to remain a member of it until the Lord will call me to His congregation above where there will be neither elders nor deacons but where we all as children of God will serve Him eternally and perfectly.

38. ADRIAAN PLEUNE'S MEMORIES

[One of the settlers who attempted to form the Dutch community at Ravenna in Muskegon County in 1848, Adriaan Pleune soon moved to Grand Rapids where he lived several years leading an active and prominent life among the Hollanders of that place. For a time he taught in a school maintained by Hollanders for the purpose of teaching reading and writing the Dutch language and inculcating Christian principles. His sketch entitled *Ter Gedachtenis*, written for the Semi-Centennial celebrations at Holland in August 1897, was printed in *De Grondwet*, May 13, 1913.]

Oorzaak van ons vertrek en verlaten van Nederland was om meerder of beter brood in Amerika te vinden; en door de godsdienstige toestanden werd dat nog bespoedigd. Veel werd er over dat goede land gesproken en uit de brieven die kwamen uit Amerika, van die ons voorgegaan waren, bevestigd. Dit alles werd door mij gadegeslagen en ter harte genomen met begeerte om daar ook te mogen wezen of te mogen komen. Ik was toen nog ongehuwd en werkte voor mijn moeder die weduwe was. Ook waren mijn militaire dienstjaren nog niet vervuld; ik was van de lighting van 1842.

Menigmaal sprak ik tegen anderen mijne begeerte uit om in dat vrije land te mogen wezen en Ds. Huibertus Jacobus Budding, leeraar in de stad Goes, met wien ik hartelijk gemeenschap had, bleef niet onbekend met deze mijne begeerte. Middelen die vereischt werden hadden wij niet; zoodat iets bijzonders moest voorvallen zouden wij ooit in Amerika komen. Nadat ik mijn paspoort ontvangen had bleef ik nog een jaar voor mijn moeder werken en trad den 29sten Maart 1848 in het huwelijk met Neeltje Pleune geboren Slootemaker.

Het gebeurde in het begin van de maand Juli 1848 dat ik een brief ontving van Ds. Budding uit Gorkum, met den inhoud, dat indien ik nog begeerte had en wenschte naar Amerika te gaan hij mij daartoe in de gelegenheid stelde door de reiskosten te willen betalen en ons verder van levensmiddelen te voorzien. Wij voeren met een zeilschip en moesten ons voorzien van eigen proviand.

Met blijdschap maakten wij gebruik van dat aanbod en ik reisde daarop naar Gorkum om met den dominé over een en ander te spreken die reis aangaande. Dat zelfde aanbod werd door hem ook gedaan aan C. van Sliederegt en gezin en J. Verwijs en gezin. Laatstgenoemde is niet mede-gegaan – in diens plaats kwam Jakob Gouw en gezin die in Goes woonden.

Wij maakten ons dan gereed tot de reis maar moesten van vriend en vijand, direct en indirect, veel tegenstand ondervinden. Te Hellevoetsluis kwam P. van Dijke, vergezeld van een diaken, bij ons om ons terug te halen, met belofte van na een jaar hetzelfde met ons te doen dat Ds. Budding deed, want dan zou hij, Van Dijke, ook gaan wat evenwel niet gebeurd is.

Op 29 Juli 1848 kwamen wij te Rotterdam, maar omdat het schip nog niet gereed was en de wind ons tegenliep, was het eerst den 12den Augustus dat wij Hellevoetsluis verlieten met het schip de *Garonne* van Baltimore.

In het gezelschap dat met Ds. Budding, vrij van overvaartskosten reisden, waren: De Vries en gezin, J. Gouw en gezin, C. Rosenraad en gezin, Maarten Oogbruin, een dienstmeisje en schrijver dezes met zijn vrouw.

Langzaam voer het schip omdat de wind ons tegen was, zoodat wij na 30 dagen op zee geweest te zijn, nog niet halfweg waren.

Geregeld hadden wij bidstonden waarin de dominé ons voorging.

Op 24 September kwam de loods aan boord, die gebood meer zeil bij te zetten hoewel de wind hevig woei. Het gevolg was dat de boegspriet kort aan den voorsteven van het schip afbrak en tegen de zijde van het schip aansloeg; gelukkig echter liep niemand er eenig letsel bij op. Den volgenden dag landden wij frisch en gezond in die groote stad New York aan.

Nu in New York zijnde, begonnen onze zorgen. De belofte van Ds. Budding was, vrij overvaart naar New York. Wij zongen wel en ook wel hartelijk:

God baande door de woeste baren
En breede stroomen ons een pad. [Psalm 66 : 3].

Maar toch, de gedachte, hoe zal het met ons in New York gaan en dan waar heen bleef niet achter. Ds. Budding deed wel al wat hij kon voor ons, maar ziet, de moeite die hij voor ons maakte kwelde ons ook, omdat de tijd in New York verlengd werd doordien wij niet wisten waarheen wij zouden gaan. Die oud Hollandsche heeren met wien Ds. Budding handelde, zeiden ons wel dat we maar gerust zouden zijn, maar we durfden de uitkomst niet afwachten. Toen werd ons voorgesteld te reizen naar Michigan, Kent County, Township Ravenna; daar was het o zoo goed. Ik zal het niet goed noemen, want daar was niets van dat goede te vinden. Goed was het land en goed bezet met dikke en dunne boomen. De eenige farm in het township was van James Roloffsen, met 10 acres gecleard land.

Wij verlieten dan de stad New York op 5 October na 10 dagen aldaar vertoefd te hebben, met een gezelschap bestaande uit een elftal personen en gingen zoo arm als wij waren, op reis naar Ravenna in Michigan.

Ik had nog 15 stuivers aan hand van de kollecte op het schip waarom ik den dominé vroeg en die hij mij ook gaf, want van mijn eigen had ik niets. Jakob Gouw had een rijksdaalder. C. van Sliederegt, die zijne erfenis aan zijn zwager in Nederland verkocht had, had plus minus 100 gulden.

Den 27sten October, na 22 dagen op reis te zijn geweest, kwamen wij te Ravenna; daar liepen de vette varkens aan den weg; om het schaap gaf de boer niet als hij de wol maar had!

Al de ellende op die reis [en al bij water] staat gelijk aan de dagen der reis, toen wij van Buffalo naar Milwaukee voeren. Wij hebben weggeworpen brood en vleesch gegeten, hoewel het niet bedorven was. Maar, genoeg van de zeereis en ook van de landreis.

Nu zijn wij in dat goede Ravenna. Den berg afgaande in een wagen bespannen met ossen, ontmoetten wij Mr. Hoogstraaten, een man uit Amsterdam afkomstig, en vroegen hem in allen ernst waar toch de stad of het dorp Ravenna gelegen was, waarop hij antwoordde: „Indien gij naar het dorp vraagt, dat is hier." Ik kan dat zeggen niet vergeten. Daar waren daar alreede, behalve Mr. Hoogstraaten, J. d'Ooge, Adriaan d'Ooge, Pieter G. Hodenpyl, Vos en Winkel, C. Borrendamme en nog een paar anderen, bewonende de stallen van de ossen die den winter te voren bij de zaagmolen aldaar waren gebruikt.

Het was eene laagte tusschen de heuvels, waardoor een groote kreek liep; de weg naar Muskegon loopt er doorheen. Niets was er voor ons om in te wonen; wij moesten maar dadelijk planken gaan dragen van den molen, om een afdak voor ons te maken.

Des middags kwamen wij aan en na den middag werd onze woning gebouwd en des avonds werd het door ons, elf personen sterk, gezelschap betrokken. De planken lagen zoo maar op den grond; ons beddegoed er op; de een naast den ander; geen kachel. Wij maakten eerst vuur in een put in den grond en daarna in eenen ijzeren pot of ketel; wij schoven de planken op het dak een weinig open en lieten op deze wijze de rook er uit, en in deze slechte loods heeft ons gezelschap, natuurlijk insluitende vrouwen en kleine kinderen, verblijf moeten houden tot 18 Januari 1849.

Wij spraken wel tot hem, die mede in betrekking stond tot die welke in New York zoo aannemelijk tot ons had gesproken en zoo veel goeds van die plaats had gezegd, maar kregen ten antwoord dat wij nu maar roeien moesten met die riemen die wij hadden.

Veertien dagen waren wij zonder brood. Wij maakten van een blikken emmer een rasp en kregen van James Roloffsen nu en dan wat corn, dat we in water weekten en dan raspten en er dan pap van kookten. Dan gebeurde het dat wij niets als hertenvleesch hadden zonder zout; op zekeren dag hadden wij niets anders dan knollen en dat zonder zout. Dat duurde zoo voort totdat de weg goed was om met een slede over de sneeuw te rijden.

Den 18den Januari 1849 betrok ieder gezin een eigen woning, maar die woningen waren nog niet warm genoeg om zelfs een beest in te stallen en daar moesten menschen gedurende een strengen winter gepaard met buitengewoon veel sneeuw in doorbrengen. In zoo'n woning beviel op den 28sten Januari 1849 mijne vrouw van ons eerste kind Pieter. Geen geld, geen dokter, geen kleeding en bovendien kreeg mijn vrouw verzweering in beide borsten. Beide jong zijnde wisten wij weinig of niets.

Ik kan aangaande ons verblijf in Ravenna, Ds. Budding's komst aldaar, zijn zorg voor ons en wat hij raadde omtrent de Kerk en kerkgemeenschap niet uitweiden.

Na een weinig meer dan zeven jaren in Ravenna gewoond te hebben, werd ik geroepen van de Gereformeerde kerkeraad van Grand Rapids, om de kinderen onderwijs te geven om in de Hollandsche taal te lezen, dat ik aannam en van 1856 tot 1863 waarnam en toen voor deze betrekking bedankte. Hierop keerde ik naar de boerderij terug en ben tot heden toe nog op de farm.

[Translation]

The cause of our departure and our leaving the Netherlands was to have more and better food in America. This desire also was stimulated by the religious circumstances. Much was being said about that excellent land, and letters which came from America written by emigrants who had preceeded us confirmed this news. I noticed all these things, and took them to heart because I desired to go to America. At that time I was unmarried and worked for my mother who was a widow. My military service was not discharged; I belonged to the quota of 1842.

Many a time I spoke of my desire to emigrate to that free land and Dominie Huibertus Jacobus Budding, pastor in the city of Goes, with whom I enjoyed an intimate acquaintance, knew all about my desires. We had no means to emigrate so that something especial would have to happen if ever we would go to America. After I had received my passport I continued to work for my mother and on March 29, 1848, I married Neeltje Pleune, nee Slootemaker.

It happened at the beginning of the month July 1848 that I received a letter from Dominie Budding from Gorcum. It stated that if I still desired to go to America the dominie would provide for a chance to do so by paying our traveling expenses and by providing us with the necessary provisions. We were to have passage in a sailing ship and had to provide our own food.

We were glad to take advantage of this offer. So I journeyed to Gorcum in order to talk with the dominie about various matters concerning the voyage. A like offer was made by the dominie to C. van Sliederegt and J. Verwijs and their families. Verwijs, however, did not accompany us. In his place came Jakob Gouw and family who lived in Goes.

We made ready for the journey, but met with much opposition, directly as well as indirectly, from friend and also from enemy. At Hellevoetsluis P. van Dijke, accompanied by a deacon, came to get us from the ship. He promised to do for us excactly what Dominie Budding was promising, because he, Van Dijke, also planned to go to America within one year, which, however, never happened.

On July 29, 1848, we arrived at Rotterdam, but as our ship, the *Garonne*, from Baltimore, was not yet ready and the weather was contrary it was not until August 12 that our ship sailed out to sea from Hellevoetsluis.

In the group whose expenses were wholly paid by Dominie Budding were the following: De Vries, J. Gouw, and C. Rosenraad and their families, a serving girl, Maarten Oogbruin, and also the writer and his wife.

Slowly the ship made its way, for the wind was contrary. After we had been on the ocean for thirty days we were not yet half way across.

We regularly had prayer meeting in which the dominie led.

On September 24 a pilot came on board. He commanded that more sail be put out notwithstanding the heavy wind. The result was that the bowsprit snapped off at the stem and struck the side of the ship. Fortunately no one suffered any injury. The following day we landed in a fresh and healthful condition in the great city of New York.

Now being in New York, our sorrows only began. Dominie Budding's promises were to provide free passage to New York.

We of course sang, and with cordial sentiments, the 3rd verse of the 66th Psalm [from the Dutch Psalter]:

> *God prepared through barren wastes*
> *Through spacious streams for us a path,* etc.

But the thought of how we would get along in New York and then where we were to go next rose in our minds. Dominie Budding did all he could for us. But his efforts in our behalf made us uneasy, for our stay in New York became extended and we did not know what our destination was to be. The old Dutch gentlemen with whom Dominie Budding dealt kept telling us not to worry, but we did not dare to await their decision. Finally it was suggested that we should go to Michigan, Kent County, Township Ravenna. There, they said, prospects were very good. I refuse to call the place good because there was nothing good to be found in it. The land was excellent, that is, covered with an excellent growth of trees, both thick and thin. The only farm in the township was that of James Roloffsen, which had ten acres of cleared land.

We left New York on October 5 after we had lived ten days with our group of eleven persons, and left, poor as we were, on our journey to Ravenna in Michigan.

I still had fifteen stuivers [thirty cents American] which I received from a collection on board the ship. The dominie had asked for this collection, the proceeds of which he gave me because I had no money whatsoever. Jakob Gouw had a rijksdaalder [$ 2.50 American]. C. van Sliederegt who had sold his share in an inheritance to his brother-in-law in the Netherlands had about 100 guilders.

On October 27, after traveling 22 days we arrived at Ravenna. There the fat pigs were grazing along the road; for the sheep the farmer did not care, if only he had their wool!

The misery we experienced on our journey [entirely by water] was as great as the misery we experienced on the journey from Buffalo to Milwaukee [?]. We ate discarded bread and meat, although these were not spoiled. But, enough of the voyage by sea and also of the journey by land.

Now we are in good Ravenna. In all earnest we asked Mr. Hoogstraaten, originally from Amsterdam, who was coming down hill in a wagon drawn by oxen, where the village of Ravenna was to be found. He replied, "If you are looking for the village, here it is." I can never forget those words. In addition to Mr. Hoogstraaten others had arrived, namely J. d'Ooge, Adriaan d'Ooge, Pieter G. Hodenpyl, Vos en Winkel, C. Borrendamme, and a few others. They were living in stables designed for oxen which had been used at the sawmill during the preceding winter.

This was a low stretch of land between hills, through which ran a large creek [Crockery Creek]. The road to Muskegon passes through it. There was no house for us to move into. Immediately on arrival we had to fetch boards from the mill in order to build a lean-to.

We arrived at noon. During the afternoon we erected a house and when evening came we, eleven persons in all, moved into it. Boards lay on the ground, on them was scattered our bedding, and there was no stove. We built our first fire in a hole in the ground. Later we used an iron pot or kettle. We shoved aside the planks forming the roof and in this way made an opening for the smoke. In this miserable hut our group, the women and children excepted, had to live until January 18, 1848.

Of course we spoke with the person who represented those in New York who had spoken of this project in so attractive a manner. But his answer was simply that "we had now to row with such oars as we had."

For fourteen days we had no bread. We made a grater from a tin pail. From James Roloffsen now and then we got some corn which we soaked in water and thereupon grated so we could prepare soup from it. On one occasion we had venison, but without salt. One day we had nothing but turnips, and without any salt. Such were conditions until snow came and one could ride in a sleigh.

On January 18, 1849, each family moved into its own house. But those houses were not sufficiently warm to make even an animal comfortable. In such houses human beings had to live during a cold and snowy winter. In such a dwelling my wife, on January 28, 1849, gave birth to our first child, Pieter. No money, no doctor, no clothing. In addition my wife suffered from a festering infection of the breasts. As both of us were young we were quite inexperienced.

I cannot further extend my comments about our stay in Ravenna, about Dominie Budding's arrival, about his care for us, and about what he advised concerning church and church membership.

After having lived more than seven years in Ravenna I was invited to go to Grand Rapids by the consistory of the [Second] Reformed Church of Grand Rapids, to instruct the children in reading and in speaking the Dutch language. I accepted this invitation and busied myself in this task from 1856 to 1863 when I resigned. Thereafter I returned to my farm on which I have busied myself every since.

39. ADRIAAN HAGE'S EXPERIENCES

[The author of this account emigrated from Zeeland in 1849, settled in Grand Rapids, but soon moved to Grandville. His *Ervaringen*, published in *De Grondwet*, February 20, 1912, presents a reliable picture of the trials of the Dutch immigrant.]

Als lid van de Oud-Settlers Vereeniging wensch ik iets mede te deelen over mijn vertrek uit Nederland, de zee en landreis, en eenige jaren hier in Amerika.

Geboren den 16den November 1841 op een boerenplaats, Kralenhoeke genaamd, in de provincie Zeeland, Nederland, verloor ik op zes jarigen leeftijd mijn vader. Mijne moeder, die met zes kleine kinderen bleef zitten, meende op de plaats te moeten blijven en met Gods hulp te trachten zich er door te slaan. Maar de Heere dacht anders.

Mijne moeder had een broeder, Dirk van Farowe, die met vele anderen uit de Hervormde Kerk was getreden. Deze Dirk van Farowe woonde op het dorp Nieuwerkerk en bezat daar een groote boerenschuur, waar de leeraren Van Dijk, Budding en Cornelius van der Meulen kwamen prediken. Daar men niet in grooter getale dan 19 personen mocht bijeen-komen moest mijn oom veel boete betalen. De godsdienst was hem meer waard dan het geld, zoodat hij de dominees maar liet prediken en steeds boete behaalde, wat hem veel geld heeft gekost.

Daar Ds. van der Meulen met vele anderen naar Amerika was ver-trokken, wenschte ook mijn oom te gaan naar het land waar vrijheid van godsdienst heerschte en met hem ongeveer 20 huisgezinnen, meest arme menschen.

In het voorjaar van 1849 kwam mijn oom bij mijne moeder en zei: „Ik ga naar Amerika en wensch, dat gij met uwe kindertjes met mij gaat; ik zal voor u doen wat ik kan." Mijne moeder besloot dat het beste was om mee te gaan en in het laatst van April scheepten wij ons in op het schip *Maria Magdalena* en kwamen na een zeereis van 48 dagen, waarop niet veel bijzonderheden voorvielen, in redelijken welstand te New York aan. Wij zouden met den trein verder gaan tot Buffalo en waren pas op den trein, toen een jongentje van vier jaren dat aan het oog van de ouders was ontsnapt, van het platform onder de wielen viel, zoodat het terstond dood was. O, wat waren die ouders treurig gesteld! Dat was de eerste ramp op de landreis.

Toen wij te Buffalo aankwamen werd mijne moeder zoo erg ziek, dat zij in een stoel van het hotel naar de boot moest worden gedragen. Op reis beterde moeder weer wat aan, zoodat zij, toen wij in Milwaukee aankwamen, weer van de boot in een hotel kon worden gedragen. Een broeder van mijne moeder, die bakker van beroep was, kwam in Milwaukee in kennis met iemand van hetzelfde beroep die hem aanraadde daar te blijven, dan kon hij daar werk krijgen. Toen hij daar twee dagen geweest was kreeg hij de cholera en stierf. Dat was de tweede treurige ervaring.

Wij vertrokken nu verder naar Grand Haven en van daar naar Grandville, waar wij den 28sten Juni 1849 aankwamen. Mijn oom was van plan om daar een paar dagen te blijven, om wat uit te rusten en ons te reinigen, waaraan veel behoefte was, om dan verder Zeeland en Ds. van der Meulen op te zoeken om te zien, of hij zich daar kon vestigen. Maar de Heere dacht anders. Toen wij daar twee dagen geweest waren brak de vreeselijke ziekte, de cholera, onder ons uit en binnen 36 uren werden er 15 menschen ten grave gebracht. Dit was een vreeselijke toestand. Onder de dooden waren mijne grootmoeder, twee zusters en mijn oom Van Farowe. Mijn oom werd op Zondagmorgen aangetast en was binnen drie uur een lijk. O, wat eene teleurstelling was dit, nu onze leidsman weg was. Wij konden niet langer in het dorp blijven; de Board bouwde shanties voor ons op den oever van de rivier en van een tot drie gezinnen leefden in een shanty. Daar zijn nog drie personen gestorven, zoodat wij in een paar dagen achttien dooden hadden.

Toen de cholera over was vertrokken velen naar Grand Rapids. Mijne moeder kon dat niet doen, daar nog een van mijne zusters lijdende was aan waterkanker in den mond, waaraan zij later is gestorven. Wij bleven daar tot in het laatst van September. Mijne moeder wilde ook gaarne naar Grand Rapids, maar wist niet hoe zij het aan moest leggen, daar zij zwak was.

Op zekeren morgen toen moeder bezig was goed uit te spoelen in de Grand rivier, kwam de boot voorbij en een jongen sprak haar aan in het Hollandsch. Zij gaat naar de aanlegplaats en verzocht hem om met den kapitein te onderhandelen, om ons naar Grand Rapids te brengen. Dit gelukte en des namiddags om vier uur zijn wij te Grand Rapids. Wij werden aan land gezet in het bosch en daar stonden wij eenzaam en verlaten. Wij zagen in de verte wel huizen doch konden daar niet komen. Mijne zuster kon niet gaan van zwakheid. Toen wij daar ongeveer een half uur geweest waren kwam er een man die ons aansprak, doch wij konden hem niet verstaan. Hij beduidde ons toen met gebaren om te gaan zitten en na een half uur kwam hij terug met een paard en wagen, waarmee hij ons naar een huis aan South Division straat bracht. Die man, Dr. Plat, trachtte nog mijne zuster te genezen maar het was te laat; eene week later stierf zij. Ik leed aan dezelfde kwaal maar werd weer beter. Wat een zware slag voor mijne zwakke moeder; binnen twee maanden tijds verloor zij haar moeder, drie kinderen en twee broeders.

Wij bleven daar tot in het begin van Januari 1850 toen mijne moeder in het huwelijk trad met Dingeman Minderhoud. Zij werden getrouwd door Ds. Maarten Ypma, toen leeraar te Vriesland, ten huize van Sterrenberg te Grandville.

Dit gaf mij gelegenheid om in kennis te komen met vele van de eerste settlers van Vriesland en Drenthe. Wij kwamen te wonen ongeveer drie mijlen ten zuiden van Grandville aan den Vrieslandschenweg, alwaar mijne moeder nu 45 jaar geleden is overleden. De begrafenis werd geleid door Ds. Adriaan Zwemer, toen leeraar te Vriesland. Anderhalf jaar later stierf mijn vader Minderhoud; beiden rusten nu op de begraafplaats te Grandville. Van allen die toen met ons zijn overgekomen, zijn nu maar twee meer in leven, dat is mijn persoon en mijn broeder, C. Hage, harnessmaker te Grandville.

[Translation]

As a member of the Old Settler's Society I wish to tell something about my departure from the Netherlands, my voyage on the ocean, my journey on land, and my first years here in America.

Born on November 16, 1841, on a farmstead named Kralenhoeke in the province of Zeeland, the Netherlands, I lost my father when I was six years old. My mother who was left with six children thought she had to stay on the farmstead and with God's help try to make a success of it. But the Lord thought differently.

My mother had a brother, Dirk van Farowe, who like so many others had seceded from the Reformed Church. He lived in the village of Nieuwerkerk [Schouwen], and being a farmer owned a large barn in which the ministers Van Dijk, Huibertus J. Budding, and Cornelius van der Meulen were in the habit of preaching. Inasmuch as no more than nineteen persons were permitted to assemble for such a religious service my uncle had to pay heavy fines. But to him the faith was worth more than money. So he let the ministers preach in his barn and he kept paying fines.

Inasmuch as Dominie van der Meulen, accompanied by many Netherlanders, had emigrated to America, my uncle also wanted to go to the land where there was freedom of religion. He wanted to take with him about twenty families most of whom were poor people.

In the spring of 1849 my uncle came to my mother and said to her, "I am going to America, and I would like to have you and your little children go with me. I'll help you as much as I can." My mother decided it was best to go with him. At the close of April we boarded ship, the *Maria Magdalena*. After a voyage of 48 days during which few striking events took place we arrived in tolerably good condition in New York. We had planned to go by train to Buffalo. We had just boarded the train when a small boy of four who had escaped the watchfulness of his parents fell from the platform and landed under the wheels of the train. He died instantly. How sad were his parents! That was the first misfortune during our land journey.

On our arrival in Buffalo mij mother became very sick so that she had to be carried in a chair from her hotel to the boat. She improved during the voyage so that when we arrived in Milwaukee she could be carried in a chair to a hotel. There my mother's other brother, who was a baker, made the acquaintance of another baker who advised him to stay in Milwaukee where he could readily find work. After two days in Milwauke he contracted cholera and died. That was our second sad experience.

Next we proceeded to Grand Haven, and from there to Grandville where we arrived on June 28, 1849. My uncle Dirk's plan had been to pass a few days there, to rest and refresh ourselves, something we needed very much. Thereafter we were to look up Dominie van der Meulen in order to find a place for us to settle. But the Lord thought otherwise. After we had been two days in Grandville cholera again broke out among us. Within 36 hours fifteen were brought to their graves. This was a dreadful thing. Among the dead were my grandmother, two sisters, and my uncle Van Farowe. My uncle was seized on Sunday morning and was dead within three hours. What a disappointment was this, for our guide had passed away! We were not permitted to stay in the village [of Grandville]. The [village] Board built shanties for us on the shore of the [Grand] River. From one to three families lived in one shanty. In those shanties three more persons died so that in only a few days death claimed eighteen persons.

As soon as the cholera ceased many of the group went to Grand Rapids. My mother could not go with them, for one of my sisters was suffering from gangrene in the mouth, which later caused her death. We stayed in Grandville until the end of September. My mother also wanted to go to Grand Rapids, but she did not know how she could do this seeing that she was so weak.

One day, when mother was busy rinsing clothes in Grand River, a boat passed by. A young man on the boat called to her in the Dutch tongue. She walked to where the boat docked and asked him to arrange with the captain of the ship to carry us to Grand Rapids. This was agreed upon, and at four o'clock in the afternoon we arrived. We were put ashore in a wood. There we stood, lonesome and abandoned. In the distance we saw many houses, but they were too far away for us to walk to them. My sister was too weak to walk the distance. After we had been there about a half hour a man appeared who spoke to us, but we could not understand what he said. He indicated by motions that we should sit down. After a half hour he returned with a horse and a wagon with which he took us to a house on South Division Street. That man, Dr. Plat, sought to cure my sister, but is was too late; one week later she died. I suffered from the same sickness, but I recovered. What a heavy blow for my weak mother! For within a space of two months she lost her own mother, three of her children, and two of her brothers.

We stayed in that house until the beginning of January 1850 when mother was married to Dingeman Minderhoud by Dominie Maarten A. Ypma, then pastor at Vriesland, at Sterrenberg's house in Grandville. This gave me an opportunity to become acquainted with many of the first settlers of Vriesland and Drenthe. Finally we went to live about three miles south of Grandville, on the road to Vriesland. There my mtoher died forty-five years ago [1865]. The funeral sermon was preached by Dominie Adriaan Zwemer, at that time pastor at Vriesland. One year and a half later my father Minderhoud passed away. Both father and mother now rest in the cemetery in Grandville. Of the entire company that came over with us only two now are living – myself [Adriaan] and my brother C. Hage, harness maker at Grandville.

40. ADRIAN JOHNSON'S
HOLLANDERS IN GRAND RAPIDS

[The author of this historical sketch, Adrian Johnson (Adriaan Jansen) emigrated from the Netherlands and settled at Ravenna, in Muskegon, a settlement with which Van Raalte had no relations, for it was an enterprise based on speculation. When failure appeared imminent, the Hollanders abandoned Ravenna and went to Grand Rapids. There Johnson lived many years and wrote this account for the Semi-Centennial celebrations in Holland in 1897. It was published in De Grondwet, November 11, 1913. The note at the close, added by Gerrit van Schelven, a valuable contemporary bit of evidence, is also reproduced here.]

To write a historical paper on any subject one should have some documentary resources to draw from, but as I have none, I have to write mostly from my own memory, and from what I could gather from other old people.

When I arrived in Grand Rapids on the 5th day of August 1849 I found a few Hollanders here, namely, Frans van Driele, Louis Lageweg, Barteld Luten, John Roost, Josiah [Josua] Elenbaas, John Hendricks and family, Paulus d'Ooge, Adriaan Semeyn, and a few others, and some young girls who were working as domestics.

I could not learn the name of the Hollander who first arrived in Grand Rapids, but her history was told me by Thomas B. Church, who is dead now, but who was well known among the Hollanders.

In 1847 a young girl came here by stage from Kalamazoo [the only means of transportation we had at that time] and was left at the National Hotel. She could not speak a word of English, and she went to work for a family by the name of Peasley. The girl was melancholy and seemed to be in distress about something. Mrs. Peasley tried to find out her trouble, but as she could not talk with the girl, she called in some foreigners who were in Grand Rapids at that time. None of them could speak her language, and Mrs. Peasley finally called Mr. Church, who had some knowledge of a few foreign languages, but he could not understand the girl. He told Mrs. Peasley he would write to Ds. van Raalte and tell him about the girl. When Ds. van Raalte came to Grand Rapids Mr. Church took him to Mrs. Peasley's to the girl, and as soon as she heard her native tongue she forgot all who surrounded her and embraced and kissed the little man in the presence of all. Then they started a conversation, in which she stated that her lover had written her that he was in Grand Rapids, and had sent her money to enable her to remove to this country and that he had directed her to comd to Grand Rapids. She did not find her lover, nor anybody else whom she could talk to. Mr. Church suggested to Ds. van Raalte [as there was also a Grand Rapids in Wisconsin], that he correspond with somebody in Grand Rapids, Wisconsin, and find out whether there was such a young man in that city. Shortly after this the young man came, took his bride, and they went their way rejoicing.

I have cited this episode to show the difficulties which the first emigrants had to contend with, and the services of the eminent Van Raalte were needed everywhere.

The first Holland settlers of Grand Rapids were but a small body among the Americans, and some of the sharp Yankees would often take advantage of the Hollanders' ignorance of the English language.

I recollect that my father worked for a man who kept a general store, where he had to take all his earnings out in trade. One day my mother

wanted some meat, not seeing it in the store [she had to point at everything she wanted], she asked a Holland neighbor how to say "spek en
vleesch" in English. Her friend told her to call for "pork and beef," and
my father and mother went to the store, repeating on the way the names
of the much desired articles. When they came at the store and asked for
it, the storekeeper pretended he did not understand them, and he showed
them white beans and clover seed!

I met a friend of mine the other day. We were talking about olden
times, and he told me how he one day met an American who asked him,
"Dutchman, you want work?" Thinking the man asked him if he had
work, he answered "no". A few days later another man asked if he
wanted work, and by way of inducement told him that he would pay
"cash", which was a great inducement, as most of us were paid in store
orders, but my friend told him that he did not want to work for "kaas",
being under the impression that he would be obliged to take his pay in
cheese, the man hailing from the province of Zeeland, where they
pronounce the word "kaas" somewhat like the English word "cash".

But it must be said to the honor of the Americans that they used a
great deal of patience with us and they preferred the Hollanders to the
English-speaking laborers who were here, because the Hollanders were
industrious and honest.

Money was scarce in those days. We all had to take our pay in store
orders. I myself worked nine months for one man, my wages being $ 8
per month and board, and all the money I received during that time
was $ 6.

The first marriage ceremonies, as near as I can ascertain, were performed
by Rev. Martin Ypma from Vriesland, the contracting parties being
Klaas Kloosterhuis and Lamigjen Vredeveld, and Roelof Kloosterhuis
and Diena Mulder. They were married at the house of Frans van Driele.

I do not know much about the first births and deaths, for the records
of Kent county were destroyed by the fire in 1857, but I was told that
the first death that occurred was of a man of the name of Bos. He died in
Parish Township, and as the people knew of no burying ground, they
buried him right there on the farm. He was afterwards taken up by
friends and interred in a burying ground. Many Hollanders were buried
in the potter's field of the Fulton Street cemetery, and their resting places
will never be found or known until the day of resurrection.

The first sad calamity happening to a Holland family here was an
accident which befell a promising young man by the name of Cornelius
Stoutjesdyk. He came to Grand Rapids with his parents in 1849, being

11 years old. After being here a while, he hired out as an apprentice to learn the mason trade with Mr. Louis Davidson. On the 22nd day of June 1857 he fell from a four-story window of the Lovett block, which was then in course of erection, to the sidewalk below, and was picked up dead. This event spread sadness among the Holland settlers, for, as I have said before, he was a very promising young man, and had a bright future before him. He was but 19 years old and engaged to be married to Mary Adriaanse. Almost the whole population, Hollanders and Americans, attended the funeral, the services being conducted by the venerable Rev. H. G. Klyn, and I never attended a funeral before or since where there were so many tears shed as at this one, it being the first calamity of that kind which ever happened in Grand Rapids, and it is still remembered by many old settlers.

One of the early noted Holland settlers was Peter J. G. Hodenpyl, who came to this country in 1840, and was professor in languages in Rutgers College, in New Brunswick, New Jersey, from 1842 to 1846. He came to Ravenna, then in Ottawa, now in Muskegon County, in 1846. A man by the name of Edmond B. Bostwick had bought a number of sections of land there with the intention of starting a Holland colony. Hodenpyl, formerly having been connected with a foreign emigration bureau in New York, and being acquainted with Mr. Bostwick, was prevailed upon to come to Ravenna to start the colony.

Some Hollanders of Grand Rapids went out there; and Rev. Huibertus Jacobus Budding came to this country with some Holland emigrants, who after arriving in New York sent them also to Ravenna. The first Hollanders who went there from Grand Rapids were Johannes Hendricks, Paulus and Adrian d'Ooge, Cornelius Borrendamme, and a few others; but they never bought any land. The Hollanders who came with Rev. Budding to Ravenna were Adriaan Pleune, Cornelius van Sliederegt, Jacob Gouw, Jacob de Waal, and some others whose names I have forgotten. They took up a piece of land, but had nothing to begin with, not even a thing to eat, and at first endured many hardships. They lived on turnips boiled in water wihtout salt or seasoning whatever, for fifteen days. They all lived in the same log shanty, which had been used for stabling oxen, and they built a fire in the center of the shanty, and having no soap to wash with, the smoke soon made them look like darkies, so in the midst of their misery they had to laugh at one another's appearance. I myself went there in January 1851 and found these people settled on their land. I had nothing to eat but dry johnnycake for a month. But as these people had taken up their land on contract and were not able to pay interest, they all left the settlement and the improvements which they had made upon it, and came to Grand Rapids. I bought Van Sliederegt's contract for a calf, an old silver watch, two geese, and a jackknife; but as they all moved to Grand Rapids, I went with them and have never seen the land since. Thus the Holland colony in Ravenna was a failure. I have inserted this bit of history in this paper, because it has some connection with the early settlers of Grand Rapids.

Since 1848 the Holland population of Grand Rapids has increased from a very few to about 25,000. And from the gathering of a few people [we had not yet organized a congregation], in the stone church on East Bridge Street, where Frans van Driele lived in one end of the basement and services were held in the other, we have now twenty-five organized congregations. The Hollanders had the honor of building the first brick church in Grand Rapids.

The old Holland settlers, with the exception of a few, have all saved money enough to live comfortably in their old age.

As I am not a historian, nor a student of history, nor even a scholar, because my parents were poor and my education was very limited, this paper is, of course, very incomplete. But I hope the committee will be satisfied.

[In the issue of *De Grondwet*, of July 4, 1911, appeared an article on "The Early Settlement of Ravenna, Michigan," by Professor Martin Luther D'ooge [No. 41 of these *Memoirs*]. It is this same effort at colonization that reference is made to in the foregoing article. The *Grand River Eagle*, in its issue of February 1, 1849, also makes mention of the enterprise set on foot by Mr. Hodenpyl, as follows:

"We have taken some pains to find out the present situation and future prospects of the Holland colony, established at Ravenna, on Crockery Creek, in the northern portion of Ottawa County.

"There are about eighty souls, all told, but they are pioneers of large numbers who will follow them the coming spring. Many of the present settlers have purchased land, and are preparing for spring crops.

"Mr. Hodenpyl, who leads the colony, is an enterprising man and an educated gentleman. He is erecting a grist mill at Ravenna for the purpose of giving aid to the infant colony.

"There are three agents in Holland for the purpose of bringing out emigrants early next season, to make their future home among us, and, from the high toned recommendations of the country by those already located, no doubt thousands will follow.

"A large number of small frame buildings are to be put up on the road leading from Steel's Landing to Ravenna, ready for settlers the coming spring. Each of these buildings to be placed a quarter of a mile from the other, and five acres of land to be cleared off and fenced about each house. This land is to be cleared off forty rods along the road, and twenty rods back, so that half of the forest will at once disappear along the public highway for a distance of three miles, commencing one mile south of the mills at Ravenna and extending three miles toward Steel's Landing." – Gerrit van Schelven.

41. MARTIN L. D'OOGE
EARLY SETTLEMENT AT RAVENNA, MICHIGAN

[Emigrating from Zeeland in 1851, the D'Ooge family was induced to settle in the speculative Ravennna colony in Muskegon. Martin L. D'Ooge in 1897 penned the following sketch of the settlement's failure. Having been a part of this venture during youth, D'Ooge was especially fit to write this sketch which appeared in *De Grondwet*, July 4, 1911.]

In the spring of 1851 my father, Leonard d'Ooge, then a resident of New York City, was induced by Mr. Edmond B. Bostwick, of Grand Rapids, who was on a visit in New York, to make tour of the western part of Michigan, with a view to locating and joining others in forming a settlement. The spot to which he was directed was called Crockery Creek, later named Ravenna, in Muskegon County.

The result of this trip was that in the fall of the same year my father took his family to this lonely spot in the Western wilderness. We went from Buffalo to Milwaukee by propeller, and thence by steamer across Lake Michigan to Grand Haven, from where we went by a small steamboat to Steele's Landing, on Grand River. Here we found Mr. Steele, who drove us and our belongings in a lumber wagon over twelve miles through the heart of the forest to our destination.

At Ravenna we were welcomed by Mr. and Mrs. Peter J. G. Hodenpyl and hospitably entertained for a few days in their log house. However, the earliest beginnings of a settlement had already been made by James Smith and his brother, Mr. Mortimer Smith, the "Doctor", as he was generally called. The Smith brothers had acquired a large tract of land, covered with a magnificent pine forest which they were cutting down and converting into lumber. For this purpose they had built a dam in Crockery Creek, and erected a small sawmill.

There was only one road that led to Grand Rapids, a distance of about twenty miles, and it was from this place that all supplies had to be brought. In the spring of the year this road for several miles was almost impassable, and the difficulty of getting the necessities of life was almost insurmountable. For weeks the only articles of food were cornmeal and potatoes, and not always an abundance of these. The advent of a barrel of flour in their or the neighboring Bennett settlement was a great event, and people for miles around would come to the lucky family to buy or borrow a few pounds of this luxury.

In the course of the first year my father put up a gristmill, to grind the corn that was raised in the neighborhood. But not enough grain was brought to the mill to keep it running for more than half of the year, and soon the stores were sold out and the mill turned into a carpentershop. During its existence, however, it furnished meal to the early settlers of Muskegon, who, in the winter months had to go to Grand Rapids by way of Ravenna to get their provisions. I can still remember the teams of J. Ryerson and Morris, of Ruddiman, and of other lumbermen, loading bags of meal to take to Muskegon.

Little by little the surrounding country began to be cleared for farms. On the main road to Grand Rapids a number of families, newly arrived from Holland, came to settle and made openings in the dark forest. I recall particularly the names of Van Sliederegt, Pleune, Gouw, and Hoog-straaten. Sturdy, honest, hardworking men they were, and many were the hardships they endured. There was no school. For a few weeks Mrs. Hopenpyl, one of the noblest and most efficient women I have ever known, gathered the children about her to learn the elements of education. Her home was also the place where on Sundays occasionally we gathered to-gether for a simple religious service.

As traffic and travel increased between Muskegon and Grand Rapids – and it was quite impossible to traverse the distance between them in one day – the necessity arose for a place where travellers could stop over night. My parents were the first to provide such a shelter.

The mail service between these places was a weekly one, and a single bag, carried on the back of a man, was the only outfit. The mail was carried by my father for one year on his back on a contract let to him by a Mr. Fletcher, who resided in Grand Haven. In connection with this service my father sometimes bought cattle in Grand Rapids, which he drove him-self to Muskegon to be slaughtered and sold for the use of the mill hands.

Bears and wolves were frequently heard and seen around the settlement, especially in the winter. My father encountered a pack of wolves one winter night, while on his way home and owed the preservation of life to a lantern which by its light kept the wolves a few yards away from him at bay.

Shortly after our removal to Grand Rapids, in 1853, the sawmill of Mr.

Smith was burnt, but it was rebuilt soon after on a larger scale. The surrounding country, which was very fertile, especially towards the South and East, rapidly developed and new settlers came in. From about 1858 Ravenna came to be a small village. So far as I know, none of the descendants of those early pioneers have remained in this section, but have moved away, chiefly to Grand Rapids. The fruits of their toil and struggle still abide, to be enjoyed by those who have come after them.

42. SKETCH OF THE FIRST REFORMED CHURCH OF JAMESTOWN [FOREST GROVE], MICHIGAN

[Moving eastward from Drenthe during the years following the Civil War (1861-5) the Hollanders began to settle in Jamestown Township, in 1869 founding the First Reformed Church at Forest Grove, later followed by the organization of the Second Reformed Church in the village of Jamestown, also in Jamestown Township. This sketch first appeared in *The Zeeland Record*, August 27, 1915.]

Before the organization of a church in Forest Grove, many of our earlier Holland settlers of this vicinity attended religious services in Drenthe each Sunday. The children were also sent to catechism there, and it was a long walk for many of them. So it was decided to organize a congregation here.

In Juni 1869 a committee of two clergymen and to elders from Holland were appointed to investigate conditions here; and these having been found favorable for organizing a Reformed congregation, after suitable investigation, such a congregation was organized here on September 15, 1869. The necessary funds for building not being in readiness, the first meetings of the members of the congregation were held in the school house; and religious services have also been held at the different homes previous to services being held in the school house. The members of the first consitory were elders Willem A. Veenboer and Hendrik Van de Bunte and deacons Dirk Smallegan and Evert van Bronkhorst; the latter, however, was not destined to live very long after coming to America, and was the first person to be buried in our present cemetery. After his death, Jan Bos was chosen to fill his position as deacon. The first year's financial report shows that Dirk Smallegan was the first treasurer and the total receipts for the first year of the existence of this congregation being $ 21.46; total disbursements being $ 16.85. This is somewhat less than the receipts of the present day, as the collection for current expenses now every month is between $ 40 and $ 50, besides $ 100 monthy for pastor's salary and collections for the various funds, such as for the Board of Publication, Western Theological Seminary, Church Building Fund,

Widow's Fund, also Foreign, Domestic, and Arabian Missions, etc.

The church building was erected during the summer and fall of the year 1873, Jacob Strick hauling the first load of lumber for the new building. The dimensions of the first church were 36 feet by 50 feet. Later an addition was built to accommodate the increasing congregation and still later, in 1905, a fine large chapel was annexed.

The church was dedicated December 17, 1873. The first pastor of this congregation was Rev. John van der Meulen, who remained for nine years, from 1875 to 1884. After he left, Rev. Willem Wormser was called and he was here from 1885 to December 1889; following him, C. C. A. L. John was our pastor from June 1890 until February 1892; after being vacant for ten months, Barend W. Lammers became our pastor and remained for almost eleven years, from December 1892 to November 1903. Then, after issuing calls to different pastors, Pieter Paul Chef came from Grand Rapids to take charge of affairs in March 1905 and remained until January 1910. After several calls, our next pastor was Marinus E. Broekstra from 1911 to July 1914. Now after having been vacant for a little more than a year, but always having been supplied with pastors from other churches or students from the seminary, we again have our own pastor, Nicholas Boer, who with his family came from Passaic, New Jersey, in July 1915. Boer has been in the ministry for fifteen years, his first pastorate being in the Reformed Church in Jamestown where he went in 1900, remaining there two years and eight months; he has held successive pastorates [and also successful] in the Bethany Reformed Church in Grand Rapids for four years; then in the Fisrt Reformed Chruch in Chicago for three years; following which he has served the First Holland Reformed church in Passaic, New Jersey, for five and one half years; now he has come to Forest Grove, having come back almost to his starting point, this church in Forest Grove being called the First Reformed Church of Jamestown, while the congregation in the village of Jamestown is the Second Reformed, having been organized later and many of its members formerly having belonged here.

Our church at the present time consists of nearly one hundred families. The total number of communicants is two hundred twelve, and the total number of baptized members is two hundred sixty as shown in the annual report of the different churches as published this spring. Since this report was published, however, thirty-three more have been received into our church on confession of faith.

The total enrollment in the Sunday school is two hundred fifty, divided into fourteen classes. Our first Sunday school superintendent was James

Brandt who performed his duties as such for eight years, from the time of organization although at first catechetical classes were held after services and his actual years of service as superintendent were from September 30, 1874 to 1882. Following him, Arend Bos was superintendent until 1884. And since that time, from October 1884, until now, S. Yntema has very ably filled that position, and for nearly thirty-one years, he has been our superintendent. There are few, if any, who could have been more faithful than he; and nothing except sickness prevents him from Sunday school, so he has had very few absent marks during all these years. And even though he is advanced in years, Mr Yntema still retains all his faculties; and we hope he will be able for many more years to perform the duties of Sunday School superintendent.

There have been many men during the forty-six years of the existence of this congregation who have been members of the consistory and all performed their duties to the best of their ability, but there are too many to mention. The members of the present consistory are Elders S. Yntema, Herman van de Bunte, Willem van Bronkhorst, and John Kamer; deacons, Lucas Kremers, Bert Shoemakers, Cyrus Keizer, and Albert Bos.

Chapter XI

WHAT AMERICANS THOUGHT ABOUT
DUTCH IMMIGRANTS

43. HENRY GRIFFIN'S VISIT TO THE KOLONIE IN JULY 1948

[As County Clerk of Ottawa County Henry Griffin visited Holland and Zeeland during July 1848 in order to receive the declaration of intention to become citizens from those Netherlanders who were ready to take this step. His letter to *The Detroit Free Press*, July 10, 1848, is here reproduced because of the wealth of information it contains about the settlement fifteen months after its first beginnings.]

County Clerk's Office
Grand Haven July 10, 1848

Mr. Editor:

Sir: – Having spent the past week among the Hollanders at Black River, and believing some farther account of them may intrest the public, the following is at your disposal. About 300 of these people have filed in my office the report and declaration of intention to become citizens of the United States, from the age of twenty-one and upwards, the average being about thirty-five years of age. I think it worthy of notice that only six individuals of the whole number made a mark, two in 100 who could not write their names. In order to enable these emigrants to do this conveniently, at the request of Rev. A. C. van Raalte, and others, I met the people in their three principal settlements; first at Holland city, then at Zeeland village and Statesland [Drenthe]. They have taken up nearly all the government land in the two southern tiers of surveyed towns 5 and 6, in Ottawa County, and also a portion of Allegan, where they have purchased some of the Indian farms with small improvements, and paid at the rate of $ 5 per acre. Many of those who cut the first tree on their farms last fall and winter have from 5 to 10 acres cleared and in crops of corn, potatos, etc. that look well; and a few have from 20 to 40 acres cleared and planted.

Holland City is pleasantly situated, high, dry and level, the streets partly cleared out. I should think there were about 200 houses of all descriptions, from the rude hut covered with bark, to the well finished and painted frame house, every lot occupied having a fine garden and yard, in front of the house a gate, and at every window on the street the neat white curtain. Here are already several stores and provision groceries where goods are sold as cheap as in any county or village in Michigan. And here is in building an extensive windmill establishment to drive four gang of saws amounting to 60 [the meaning of this passage is uncertain]. I attended their church at this place, in two of their services, and estimated their number at 500 souls, thirteen of whom were Americans; in the evening the Rev. McPason of Comstock addressed the Hollanders very appropriately, which was interpreted by their minister, the Rev. A. C. van Raalte. They have an English school in this church which is large, about 40 by 60 feet, and before leaving the place I assted them in organizing a district school, greeable to our Primary School Law system.

Zeeland village is located about six miles east of Holland city on Sec. 19 T. 5 R. 14, laid out in one acre lots sold to settleers at $ 7 per lot, and has probably 100 houses built, principally of white cedar, with a fine garden upon every occupied lot,; it is only about one year since this place was commenced. They have a neat church built of white cedar timber in which a Holland school is kept, well furnished with books, slates, and blackboards, and appeared to be conducted, by their Holland teacher, with ability; there are at present only three Americans here. From Zeeland, I traveled to Statesland, „Drenthe" as it is called, some six miles farther east, but 12 in rounding the large swamp in Town 5 Range 14. This is exclusively a farming community with about 70 farms at present. They have a fine tract of land, principally all timbered with the sugar maple. New settlers are going in every day and they all appear happy and contented; there are few very poor among the Hollanders and they are all provided for by contribution in their churches every Sabbath. Much more might be said in relation to this interesting Colony, but lest my communication be to long I shall close.

I had the pleasure of dining with the Hon. F. J. Littlejohn, in the forest, between Port Sheldon and Black Lake. I left him with compass in hand executing his commission, and venture to say he will give a satisfactory account of himself in a few days.

Most truly yours,

H. Griffin

44. THE DUTCH IN MICHIGAN 1853

[In the autumn of 1853 a reporter for the *New York Tribune* wrote an account of his visit to the Dutch settlement in Michigan. He noted curious facts about the progress the Netherlanders had made since February 1847. This letter will ever remain a source of prime importance for the history of the community. It was printed in the issue of October 8, 1853. It has been impossible to determine the name of the author who signed his initials D. C. H.]

Detroit, Saturday, Oct. 8, 1853.

I have just returned from a visit to the Kalamazoo Valley region and a trip to the Holland colony. Left the Michigan Central Railroad cars at Kalamazoo, a most flourishing town, and the center of an extensive trade with the farming districts in that vicinity, and took the stage for Allegan village, passing through the village of Otsego, which begins to show signs of progress. Reached Allegan, the county site, the next day, and spent several days there most agreeably. The village is beautifully situated on a peninsula formed by the Kalamazoo. There is an excellent water power, many manufaturing establishments, a considerable traffic by merchants with the people of the adjoining towns, and a large quantity of lumber exported to the mouth of the river, and thence to several lake ports. The lumbering business is now a most profitable one on account of the large demand in Illinois and Wisconsin for timber, boards, shingles sash, etc. But he harbour at the mouth of the Kalamazoo is a miserable one. In the summer season the bar across the mouth of the river is about five feet deep and impassable for the larger crafts. The products of Allegan industry are obliged to be taken outside the bar by lighters, thus greatly increasing the cost of the transportation and detaining the vessels. Otherwise the harbor is naturally a most excellent one, the river being navigable for steamboats to Allegan and quite deep at both sides of the bar. The river widens into a lake at Newark village. Hundreds of lives are annually lost by gales on the lake and several wrecks occur at the mouth of the Kalamazoo. A vessel and her crew were reported missing when I was leaving Allegan County on my return to Detroit. With a good harbor and a railroad from Kalamazoo the products of Michigan would obtain good markets and the resources of Allegan County would be greatly increased and its business extended.

While at Allegan I took a jaunt to the Holland Colony, twenty-two miles to the northwest, accompanied by the coroner of Allegan, in a team of the sheriff's, and arrived at Holland city in six hours, taking the Bee Line Road. Passed through a fine farming country, some of the best timbered land in the state, and except at the village of Holland [Black Lake] where the land is piney, the soil is of much the same quality throughout the Colony. The settlement in the neighborhood of Black Lake was commenced by the Rev Mr A. C. van Raalte in February 1847 by some of the friends of a party of persecuted Hollanders, who had spent the preceding winter at Detroit and Allegan until they could make preparations to clear the lands they had purchased.

The Colony is composed of three organized townships: Fillmore, in Allegan County, and Holland and Zeeland in Ottawa County. In 1850 the two last townships had a population of 1829 and the former 600. These towns are subdivided into settlements on the basis of the colonial church organisation, each place having a church of its own, with schools convenient of access to all the children of the settlers. We give the names of the settlements, and the dominies who officiate as pastors over the Dutch Reformed Churches:

Holland Stad – The Rev. A. C. van Raalte
North Holland – No pastor
South Holland - The Rev. R. Schepers
Zeeland – The Rev C. van der Meulen
Vriesland – No pastor
Drenthe
Overyssel – No pastor. Allegan County
Graafschap – The Rev. Ypma. Allegan County

Mr. Schepers, who preaches in South Holland, is connected with the Associated Reformed Church. The Rev. Mr. Roelof Smit in Drenthe is a Presbyterian, and the other churches in the Colony are connected with the Reformed Dutch Church of North America.

Holland village, which is considered the great emporium of the Colony, has about 700 inhabitants, and the village of Zeeland 500 or 600. The lack of a harbor has materially retarded the growth of the Colony, although the entrance to the Black Lake is well situated naturally for a harbor, the Black Lake being from 30 to 70 feet deep. The harbor is almost or quite inaccessible in the summer months of business season, but can be entered with difficulty during the spring and fall seasons by small craft, lighters, etc. Black Lake is from 6 to 7 miles long and from 1 to 2 miles wide. The last Congress granted a small appropriation for widening the channel of the Lake and opening its entrance into Lake Michigan, designing to make it 250 feet wide and 12 feet deep. A job is now under contract and will remain unfinished until a larger appropriation is granted. The harbor having failed, the want of shipping facilities at the village of Holland has checked the growth of the place, and has tended to scatter the new comers to other places in the vicinity, Grand Haven, Mill Point, Grand Rapids, Allegan, Kalamazoo, etc., who all look with hope to permanent harbor improvements at Black Lake. As soon as a harbor is made they all design to return to the Colony, which will double the population in 12 months, the Colony now numbering about 4,000 inhabitants.

The Harbor Appropriation is being expended in commencing a Harbor in concordance with a plan previously reported and approved by the Topographical Engineers, which would cost $ 105,000. The work this season has been the erection of shops, clearing grounds for proposed cut, getting machinery, and building a bridge-pier to receive materials for two solid piers. Should another appropriation be made the excavation of het new channel will probably be the first work which will be undertaken. The harbor, if completed according to plan, will be the best on Lake Michigan, of easy access, perfect safety, and abundant capacity. But as it now stands, not more than one bridge-pier, of 50 feet, can be built in an unfinished state this season.

Black Lake was at no remote period a deep bay of Lake Michigan. The proposed improvement will be to cut a new channel through the point of sand which has gradually formed and closed its entrance, and protect it with two piers.

The farming lands of the Colony are all heavily timbered with beech, maple, oak, etc. Soil a heavy clay loam, except a sandy belt of four or five miles in width along Lake Michigan. They are excellent lands for wheat, corn, and grass. The clearings are now five or six miles long, leaving only small strips of timber between them, and soon the whole colony will be one open space, resembling the prairies of Kalamazoo and St. Joseph counties, Illinois, Wisconsin, and Minnesota. The Hollanders are a very industrious and frugal people, and persevere, under the difficulties incident to western life, with the most unflagging energy. On many of the half-cleared farms, in the midst of freshly felled logs and brush, you will see stalwart corn, pumpkins and potatoes raised, the lands never being allowed to be idle from the moment the log hut or backwoodsman's house or shanty is erected. The Hollanders adapt themselves to the manners and customs of the western people with a striking aptitude, and a "goaheaditiveness" which puts to blush the many gentlemen farmers who tarry for years around the neigborhood of western villages.

The manufacturing establishments of the village of Holland are two steam sawmills [one with a gristmill attached] capable of manufacturing 6,000,000 feet of lumber per year, an ashery, and two tanneries. They have also seven stores in the village, three of which are kept by American traders, Messrs. Post, Bailey and Harrington. Quite a number of native-born Americans reside in the Colony, mostly having dealings with the colonists or employed in industrial pursuits. A few years ago when the emigrants moved to their new homes, some Alleganians went among them and taught them the mysteries of woodchopping, the Hollanders not being versed in the art, and in their haste to clear the forest, five or six would be hacking away at one tree; others would attempt to saw the tree down and some would use chisels. But, with the assistance of Yankees, space enough for small farms was cleared.

One of the relics of the first establishment of the Colony is a dilapidated wind sawmill which has been abandoned to give way to modern improvements and Yankee ingenuity.

Outside of Holland village, in other portions of the Colony, there are: a sawmill with lath machine attached, two tanneries, a water gristmill, and an oil mill for the manufacture of rape oil. In spite of all the disadvantages of shipment, Black Lake exported products to the amount of about $ 40,000 last year. The principal articles of export are staves, bark, lumber, and shingles. The exports this season will be 2,000,000 feet of lumber, [which is rafted down Black Lake] and 1,000,000 staves.

De Hollander is the name of the colonial paper published at Holland, edited by Mr. Hermanus Doesburg, a classical teacher by profession, who is also a master of the art of printing, and is assisted in the typographical department by two of his sons. He is a public spirited citizen and manfully advocates the interests of the colony.

The colonists are generally well educated in their own language, and many have acquired a good acquaintance with the English, French, and German languages, besides possessing a knowledge of the classics. There are ten or eleven district schools in the Colony where the rudiments of an English education are taught. There are also several schools where the scholars are taught the Dutch language.

A high school has been established at Holland, for the benefit of the colonists, by the Reformed Dutch Church, under the charge of Walter T. Taylor, A. M. a classical teacher of repute from Geneva, New York, who is principal; and a beautiful site has been selected for buildings, which will probably become a permanent institution of character and influence.

Quite a railroad feeling has sprung up in the Colony. Holland is advocated as the termination of the Oakland and Ottawa Railroad instead of Grand Haven, the Lake being reached in fewer miles from Grand Rapids, over an easier route to grade, and if a Lake Shore Railroad to Chicago is even built in connection, the distance from Grand Haven to Black Lake, 25 miles, is saved, while Holland would be equidistant to the people of the Kalamazoo and Grand Rivers. Holland is at the terminus of the proposed Kalamazoo, Allegan, and Holland Railroad, and the Harbor at Holland, when finished, will be navigable to all kinds of Lake craft and be an excellent haven for vessels seeking protection during a storm. The people of Ottawa, Kent, and Allegan counties are already agitating other railroad routes. The mouths of the Grand, Black, and the Kalamazoo rivers are nearly opposite the cities of Milwaukee, Racine, and Kenosha. Before many years the capitalists on the Michigan side of the Lake expect that branches will be made by the Southern and Central Roads to the north-western portion of the state.

Another addition to the colony is expected in the spring, under the charge of Dominie Wijnand Gardenier, with a flock from the province of Zeeland, the Netherlands.

The half-annual Classis of the Reformed Dutch Church of Lake Michigan was in session at Zeeland on the 28th and 29th ult., representing delegates from twelve churches, consisting entirely of the new emigration from the Netherlands. The Rev. Mr. Cornelius van der Meulen, presided, and the Rev. Mr. van Raalte acted as scribe. The usual church business was transacted. Delegates were present from Chicago, Milwaukee, Kalamazoo, Grand Rapids, Grand Haven and the Colony churches of Michigan. The meeting is said to have been quite an interesting one. One of the Colony preachers, the Rev. Mr. Seine Bolks, is stationed at Grand Haven.

The Colony is of more interest as a nucleus of future growth than for present numbers or wealth. It was the first, and with the exception of the colony in Pella, Iowa, the only Colony of Hollanders in the United States emigrating *en masse* for religious and political motives. The people have sufficient similarity of feeling and principle to act together as a body. They represent a large and influential class of the people of Holland, and retain a connection with them. They are connected with the Reformed Dutch Church of the United States, and exert more influence upon future emigration to America than all the other settlements in the States united.

The colonists are indebted for their present location and to much assistance on their first arrival in Michigan to the Rev. Dr. Duffield, Robert Stuart [now dead,] E. P. Hastings, Shubal Conant, Theodore Romeyn of Brooklyn, [formerly of Michigan,] John R. Kellog and Elisha Ely of Allegan; Gen. Lewis Cass, John Ball of Grand Rapids; Mr Colt of New York [formerly] of Kalamazoo, H. Pennoyer, the Rev. Ova P. Hoyt of Kalamazoo, and many other citizens of Michigan, and friends of western emigration in different parts of the country, and return to them sincere thanks for the interest they manifested in their behalf. They are much pleased with the Michigan climate, as it is about the same with Holland.

I returned to Allegan and got back to the Biddle, Detroit, on the 5th instant, *en route* for New York, after enjoying a most delightful taste of Western rural life and its pleasures.

45. HENRY J. BROWN'S RECOLLECTIONS

[The Rev. Henry J. Brown, minister in St. Philip's Parish (Episcopal) in Chicago was a student at Holland Academy in Holland, Michigan, in 1859. When revisiting Holland in the summer of 1905 he penned the following *Recollections of an Early Student at the Holland Academy* which appeared in *The Holland Ckity News*, later reprinted in *De Grondwet*, January 14 and 21, 1913.]

Forty-five years ago Holland was a town of about five hundred people. I remember it as if a few years ago. A wayward boy, listless, fond of company, a wise parent thought best to put me down to study in the woods of the Holland Colony. The change from Battle Creek to this quiet, crude spot was like a dream. Two years I remained under gracious influences, which were the moulding of my life. Now, when life's work is well behind, and absent all these years, I return as if waking out of a Rip Van Winkle slumber of more than two score years to see what God has done.

When last my boyish eyes rested on the town, war clouds burst upon the land and the flag was bathed in blood. After, followed the most startling period of the world for discovery and invention; population of the United States rose from twenty to eighty millions; Battle Creek from three to eighteen; Kalamazoo from four to thirty; and Grand Rapids from five to ninety thousand people.

In the spring of 1859 the country around Holland was wild beyond description. There was not even a corduroy road, but a lumber trail, from Allegan. I rode from Allegan on the surveyor's wagon, who was laying out a state road from Allegan to Muskingdom [Muskegon]. Three miles out of Allegan, beech, pine, and hemlock forests interspersed with cedar and cypress swamps, continued all the way to Holland. At Rabbit River, midway, was a lumber camp. Beyond this, for miles, was heard chopping, and an opening, covered with stumps, appeared among great trees. A loghouse with blue smoke curling, cheered the weary wilderness ride. Around this clearing a few more openings, and this was Overisel.

How grand the stately pines, how dense the underbrush off towards "Saugertuk!" In that direction was a pigeon roost. These wild birds gleaned wheat fields hundreds of miles, but nested in this thicket. They flew in great clouds and broke branches in settling down. Enterprise soon netted profits by netting pigeons for Chicago market. Black squirrels were so thick among beech trees that three were shot off one tree. They have gone entirely. Wild beasts infested dense cedar and cypress swamps.

Once I was footing it in from Allegan by night. Wolves got after me three miles east of Rabbit River. I had walked from Kalamazoo, and thought to make Holland by midnight. At first I heard a bark, or yelp, ahead; then to one side; then a number of yelps behind. Suddenly it struck me they were wolves. Tired as I was, the sprinting was marvelous, including many tumbles and the mad rush through the river. A great mastiff rushed furiously out from the lumber camp, but I was so glad that I could have hugged the noble animal. At Rabbit River were food, rest, and refuge. The bounty on these beasts was six dollars, the hide was worth three.

West of Holland the forest came right up to the town. A trail ran along the shore to the finest beechnuts and wintergreen berries heart could wish. In the autumn bright tinted leaves covered the ground like a velvet carpet. When very busy and tongue-sore from hulling nuts suddenly a big black bear stood before my wild eyes. Nutting suddenly ceased. Such time as I made would fill the Hope College team with envy. Just my luck to tumble over every log, expecting every tumble to see the great red mouth and glistening teeth of the wild monster upon me. I dared glance back at the bear; old bruin was making equal speed the other way. Then my spirits came back and I shouted and thought how much I would like to have a gun. An Indian, whom I met spearing through bunches of reeds on the ice for muskrats, told me that he had just had his partner slain by a bear caught in a lair near Saugatuck. The Indian was hemmed in the bush and neither he nor his dog could struggle free.

The first week I was in Holland a bear stole a hog weighing two hundred pounds. He dragged it over a fence in the outskirts of the town that was six feet high. I must not pull "the fox's tail too long", but I will not deduct a single pound from the weight of that hog, even to save veracity. Of course I did not weigh the hog, nor the bear, but there may be those who will bear out the story. This is the only theft in Holland that I heard of in two years residence. Often deer would wander down the runway, just west of town, to the waters' edge, whilst boys were bathing. Venison was plentiful all winter, Indians bringing it in for sale.

There were a few Indians yet in the county. They made maple sugar, which they packed into birch baskets. It was delicious. They seemed to have an art of blending spruce or wintergreen flavor with it. I came upon a hut once full of these birch baskets and sap troughs. A noted chief – was it Pokagon or Macsaubee – ranged this region. They were inoffensive, the expiring embers of a woodland life fast passing away. Midsummer their women brought in berries: such blackberries and blueberries never will be seen again. They also brought in many of the cruder furs. Woman, as usual among them, did all the work.

Wandering far off into the tickest forest I lost myself once and remained in a wigwam over night. Ugh! I washed and scrubbed at dawn. Millions of mosquitoes, fleas, and bugs. The old Indian snored the night through Next day he went six miles to set me on my way again. Such was the wilderness of this county at that time. How bewildering now to look out of the cars upon rolling fields, farm houses, splendid cattle, and country churches, nestling so peacefully among the hills.

How dreary the view of Holland as we drove into it. After much jolting, pitching, shaking up, and wonder at the forests, we were told that Holland was near. We strained our eyes through the trees and lo! the turn of a sandy knoll opened the town to view. Around the edge were a tangle of fallen hemlock branches and trunks charred and black. In the midst stood Van Vleck Hall, then one year old. No beautiful shade trees. I helped clear up and burn hemlock trunks. All was bleak sand. A walk lead up to the Hall, on each side of which were rows of unhealthy pinks.

But most cheering was the long white church, standing all alone. It seemed very large, then, with no buildings near; and, to me, to whom the world was so small, but to whom the world would grow so large, in the roaming of forty-five years – there it stood, symbol of law and of hope, true foundation of all the miraculous prosperity since. I felt kind of home-like to see so large a church. People, who out of poverty, would make the finest building a church, surely would warm toward a stranger boy. They did. My eyes moisten when I recall all the kindness of those two years from those honest but large hearted people to me, the first American student to break through that environment of forest wilds. Most of them are gone and a second generation follows; but of those hardy pioneers we must say, "their works do follow them."

Main street was about as sandy as could be. Sawdust covered the middle of the way. Rows of one-story cottages lined the sides. They were painted with queer blendings of dark red, orange, and green. Men painted their own dwellings. There were no horses; ox teans every where. I can yet hear the *gee, haw* and *wo* ringing through woods and on the streets. Those were the only words I could understand. Women wore short dark woolen skirts, white caps, and some of them wooden shoes. How do I remember the women so well? I had just come from mother's care, and mother's love was in my heart in those new scenes. I had never seen wooden shoes; hoop skirts, hair puffed on the side or forehead, or chignons hanging behind in nets were the fashion in the home I had left. But I found mother's love and woman's tenderness behind a strange tongue, even as I had left them behind.

A lumber wagon ran as a stage form Holland to "the Rapids" [Grand Rapids], once or twice a week. A boat, the *Rapaljih*, J. Pauels skipper, before a north or northeastern scudded to Chicago. We students footed it out and into town.

There were two American families – Henry D. Post and Manley D. Howard. Post kept postoffice and general store; over on the opposite corner, where the bank now stands, Howard dwelt. On the southwest corner was Pfanstiehl's grocery. Van der Veen's hardware store was on the northeast corner. Herold's shoe shop was further down. Along the lake was the only hotel, a saw mill, a tannery, a blacksmith and wagon-maker's shop, etc.

Ds. van Raalte lived at the eastern end of town in a very comfortable frame house. I met a short man, horseback, dressed in white overalls, strong voice, nervous, quick, and shortspoken. He did not seem sympathetic, but resolute and thoughtful. He was a man of extraordinary faith and devotion. He could look out of woods and swamps by faith to see what industry and thrift could do. Nor did he falter from doubt or fear to lay foundations out of all proportions to their surroundings. Holland now justifies his shrewd foresight, and grumblers went with wolves and bears from this redeemed waste.

Settled in the Academy, I went to Vrouw Kroes for supper. She could speak English a little, and soon filled my plate. This language everyone could understand. Nineteen of us boarded at her house where the Episcopal church now stands. She was a mother, and nothing nobler need be said of her. Meals began with a psalm, a chapter from the Bible, a prayer, and oftentimes a hymn to close, at morning and evening, all in the Holland tongue. Noon was much briefer in its worship, students took turns in prayer. Some prayers were dolefully long for hungry boys in front of savory meals.

Theirs was that noble emulation oftentimes among ambitious students, of who could best remind the Lord of what was needed in all the vineyard, and long ranges were ventured into the realms of heathen darkness. Ah me, we need to smile; twenty-nine of these Academy students have gone by faith to teach the pagan world! God heard their prayers! Many of those students have finished life's work. Memory brings back voices, merry laughter, and "those angel faces which oft I've seen but now have lost a while."

There was not a piano in town accept, perhaps, at Howard's. There was not a musical instrument at the Academy except a tune fork – that Kriekard, who led the singing, had. Cornelius Doesburg taught school.

There was one saloon in town. I say only one drunken man in two years, and he was not bad! It was market day and possibly he celebrated a famous bargain. Every six months people who had anything to sell or to show came to town to market. That was a holiday, and religion, politics, and business were talked up on every corner, which was better than getting a corner on the market.

What skating, hunting, swimming! The winter of 1860 was very cold; skating was all the way down to Lake Michigan, and for miles along the shore. One night half way up Black Lake, all alone, I fell into an air hole, I threw my arms over the ice, and never knew how I got out, I came out so fast. My clothes were frozen, so that they had to be thawed to get them off. Nothing was known of the escape lest Academy authorities might forbid such dangerous sport thereafter. Old Holland skates were brought out, the blades turned up in a great circle over the toes. The pride of skating was to swing over the ice, leaning over so that a hankerchief could be caught up. With long strides this swaying motion would be kept up from shore to shore. Arend van der Veen, now physician in Grand Haven, used to glide over the bay with a short stemmed pipe, puffing away, his hands in his pocket and bundled in short jacket. His silhouette still haunts my memory through all the years.

Amid this isolation we learned that the election of Lincoln had taken place, but we knew little of the real situation while each hour sounded the destiny of a nation, almost an epoch, in the world's history. News of tremendous throbbing and roaring came into our forest-bound life, but none knew how near earthquake shock and volcanic eruption political throes were.

Early on April 12 William and Peter Moerdyk and myself started out at early dawn for a fifty mile tramp. Never was there a more beautiful day. We passed through Overisel and breakfasted at Rabbit River, with birds twittering and fluttering, and early spring flowers signaling forth a new season. We sang and laughed as we communed in nature's forest solitudes. We dined and rested at Allegan, then on for Kalamazoo by nightfall. But when we arrived all was excitement. Bells rang, everywhere "Star Spangled Banner" was sung, flags were flying, earnest groups gathered, hot angry speeches mingled with drum and fife. No one stopped long to explain. Simply: "Rebels fired on Sumter." A thrill of patriotism was passing over the land. Speeches strained not after rhetoric or elocution, illustration or humor. Men were earnest. Blood was up! Lips compressed, fierce light burned in eyes. At my parents' home in Battle Creek I sought to crawl in a lower window to surprise them in the morning. I just had my body in when an old pepperbox revolver gleamed under my nose. I soon made myself known. My father was so excited over the news of Sumter that he could not sleep. Sleepy as I was from that fifty-one miles tramp, he kept me to day dawn earnestly telling the war's break with the first gun at Sumter. That father's patriotic heart lies cold with a generation gone, and I, an old man, strive to sing a far off song to new Holland! The Colony sent a whole company to bloody fields, many to die or to suffer, maimed and halt, for the liberty they prized.

And now I come back to Holland after forty-three years, to see forest wilds gone, pioneers gone, commerce, industry, railways, electric cars, telegraphs, education, refinement, and a most beautiful city where I heard the owl hooting and the wolf's howl near half a century ago. Patient industry that stole from ocean and dyked into garden spots of Europe, have transformed crude nature into a region abreast of any in the State for material wealth, intellectual activity, and moral grandeur. But the hardy pioneers gave their lives. Here and there a lingering oak stands to confirm my story. The land has been redeemed, but graveyards are filled, and I would gratefully engrave their deeds upon their stones.

46. EDWARD CAHILL'S OLD COLONY DAYS IN HOLLAND

[Edward Cahill, later a judge in Lansing, Michigan, for several years following 1854 lived in Holland. His *Old Colony Days in Holland* was published in *De Grondwet*, September 25, 1911.]

I have been asked to furnish a brief account of my sojourn in Holland sixty years ago when the Colony from Old Holland was laying the foundation of what has since become one of the most prosperous settlements ever made by emigrants in Michigan.

In the winter of 1853 and 1854 my father, being in poor health, sold his farm on Grand Prairie about three miles west of Kalamazoo and began to look about for a new home. Before deciding where he would settle my mother wanted to visit her two brothers, Doctors Wells R. Marsh and Charles P. Marsh, who were then living in Holland, practicing their professions.

Accordingly my father and mother drove in a sleigh from Kalamazoo to Holland for a visit. It is easy to imagine that the journey, though for the most part through a wilderness, was an easy and pleasant one in the winter. As a result of this visit my father and mother decided to make Holland their future home. They returned to Kalamazoo to settle up their affairs, packed their household goods upon wagons, and early in April of 1854 started upon what we children, two boys and four girls, regarded as a long and venturesome journey. The famely rode in an old ark of a carriage, very comfortable on good roads but not well suited to spring travel over the kind of roads we had in the then sparsely settled protions of Michigan. I was a boy of ten and I remember that I preferred to walk or to ride perched upon one of the wagons with goods rather than to be smothered in the family ark. Our first day's journey was to Allegan where we were hospitably entertained at the home of Jacob B. Bailey, who had a sawmill at Holland and whose acquaintance, I assume, my parents had made on their visit a few months before.

I remember very little of the incident of our stay in Allegan, beyond the fact that Baily had two daughters, whom I thought very pretty and whom I afterwards knew as charming women. One of them married a Mr. Breeze for many years a successful and highly respected lawyer in Kalamazoo. A younger sister married Mr. George H. House, a successful insurance man who lived for some years in Lansing and later in Saginew.

I do not recall that we had any difficulties with the roads until we left Allegan. From there on and until we drew near to Holland the settlements were few and the road ran through an almost unbroken wilderness. Much of the way it was only recently cut out and the marks of travel wove in and out among the stumps of giant trees whose roots – the size of a man's leg – made travel a slow and tedious process. Then there were deep holes where the goodswagons were mired and long corduroy stretches over marsh and swamp. I know not how many hours we were on the road, but I remember it was long after dark before we reached Holland, about twenty-five miles from Allegan.

My father had rented a house in which in a few days we were settled. My boyish recollections of it is that it was quite a sizable house with a hall running through it from south to north. On the east side of the hall was a parlor and bedroom on the west side, a dinning room, kithcen, and bedroom. The roof was quite steep and the bedrooms on the second floor were open to it. The partitions between the rooms were of tough unplaned boards, standing on end and reaching only about seven feet, and it was a favorite amusement for us children to toss our shoes from one room to another over the partitions, regardless of where or upon whom the missile would fall.

Our house was on what was then – and still is – Main Street of the street of the straggling village which, as I remember, ran east and west. If so the house fronted south. And in front and rear there were comfortable porches where during the summer the family generally gathered. At the back of the house was a good-sized garden, which we soon had planted with all kinds of vegetables for our own use. I remember that at the foot of this garden we discovered a spring of delicious soft water, a novelty to us. This we housed in and from it obtained our family supply.

Our house was located a short distance, rather less than a block, west of the corners, which I can best describe by telling how they were occupied. On the corner east of us was a residence occupied by Manly D. Howard, with whom when we first reached them, I think, both my uncles boarded. Directly across the side street to the east was Henry D. Post's store. Across Main street south was Peter Pfanstiehl's general store. The last time I was in Holland there was little left to identify my old home. The house itself had gone and on the lot where it stood was a business block [Engine House No. 1]. On the corner where Howard lived was a fine building occupied by a bank.

There were three general stores at that time, Peter Pfanstiehl's, Alderd Plugger's, and I am not sure about the name of the other. It was on the north side of Main Street several blocks further east. There were two flourishing sawmills, Bailey's [built by Oswald D. van der Sluis], which was at the east end of the Lake and had in connection with it a three or four story, rude, unpainted frame structure known as the Boarding House, in which his employees lived, and on the south side of the Lake about half a mile from our house was White's mill, if I remember right.

The only newspaper was printed in the Dutch language and was edited and published by Hermanus Doesburg, who had two sons, I well remember. Doesburg also kept a small school for instruction in the Dutch language, which I attended for a time. There was in those days a large frame building [the Orphan House] standing on the square where I think Hope College now stands, in which a Walter T. Taylor with one or more assistants had a school for instruction in English. Whether it was a public or private school I do not know [this was the beginning of the Holland Academy, now Hope College], but I remember Mr. Taylor very well. He was an elderly man with a long gray beard and a severe aspect. I know I stood in great awe of him [and so did all the boys that had passed once under his rod], for he greatly resembled the prophet Elijah, whose picture was in our family Bible. I think he closed his last term in June 1854 and was succeeded as principal by a Presbyterian [or perhaps Dutch Reformed] minister, whose name I cannot recall. He was, I think, American born, although he may have been of Dutch descent. If any of the old settlers remember him, I wish they would supply his name as he was a good man and a fine teacher. Associated with him in the school was a Mr. James A. Ostrom, who was a a favorite teacher of

mine. I have now a small copy of *Pilgrim's Progress* which he gave me as
a reward for merit in school. At least it was so inscribed on the front leaf
under his own signature. As a further mark of his confidence, although
I was but eleven years old, he used occasionally to assign me to hear some
of his younger classes in reading. I doubt whether that was a prudent
thing to do. He is, however, long past criticism in this world. Years
afterwards, in Kalamazoo, at his house, I made the acquaintance of his
niece, whom I afterwards married, and we last month celebrated the
forty-seventh anniversary of our marriage.

My doctor uncles had a practice extending over a wide territory, including all the settlements of the Colony – Zeeland, Graafschap, Overisel,
Holland, etc. I used often to ride with one of them on these trips and
never failed to go in at places where he called, because I soon learned that
the hospitable *huisvrouw* was sure to have something put away that she
knew would please a hungry boy. It was there that I permitted myself to
drink coffee, which I was not allowed to do at home. That was always
ready or quickly made ready whenever a visitor called.

Speaking of hospitality, I have never since seen that virtue better
exemplified than in the old Colony days. I remember an old man and his
wife, who kept a bakery on the corner near where Mr. Gerrit J. Diekema's
first law office was when I was last in Holland. There was a small shop
in front and the bakery and living rooms were at the back. We boys used
to play about their corner a good deal. Its popularity was due largely to
the fact that the good old lady [Mrs. Jan Binnekant] was liable at almost
any time to bring out a batch of freshly baked cookies for the boys who
happened to be there. I never remember going into the house of one of
my boy friends without getting a treat of some kind from the good
mother.

One other thing impressed itself indelibly on my recollection and that
was the immaculate cleanliness of the houses. The native American in
those days had grown up in a crude and somewhat haphazard way. He
had never been trained or had the time to put the polish on himself or
his surroundings. The American housewife cleaned house occasionally
and generally to the disgust of her husband. But those Hollanders had
just come from an older and denser civilization, where cleanliness and
orderliness were necessities, and when they brought their habits into the
wilderness, they shone like a lamp set in a dark place.

There were only a few native American families in Holland in those
days. Henry D. Post and Hoyt G. Post, Manly D. Howard and his
family, Dr. Wells R. Marsh and his family, Dr. Charles P. Marsh, a

bachelor, the teachers I have alluded to, and our own family are the only ones I can recall who actually lived there. I think the sawmill owners were Americans but lived elsewhere. I know Mr. Bailey for some time continued to live in Allegan.

Soon after we settled there, Mr. Howard and my father formed a partnership and started to build a sawmill on the north side of Black Lake where they had bought considerable land. They planned also to lay out a town and build a settlement there. They had the mill well under way in August when my father was suddenly taken ill, and on the 3rd day of that month, 1854, passed away. My mother was thus left with six children, the eldest being less than thirteen, and with very little except the wild land in which my father had invested the money realized from the sale of his farm. It can be easily realized that this sudden loss of our protector and guide was a terrible tragedy to all of us. My mother's father and mother and several of her brothers and sisters lived in Kalamazoo, and so, after a few months of loneliness, she determined to go back to her old home, which she did in the spring of 1855.

I will conclude these hastily written lines with a brief reference to the remarkable man who founded the Colony and was as long as he lived its first citizen. I refer, of course, to Dominie van Raalte. In the sixty years that have passed since I knew him three generations have been born and have grown or are growing to manhood and womanhood in the Colony. Most of these never saw the Founder and only knew him by tradition. He was a great man, whom everybody who came within the circle of his influence respected and loved. He had a gentle but most persuasive personality. He was a gentleman of the old school; but he was more than that, for he was one who loved his fellowmen and labored unselfishly for their good. May his memory be forever kept green in the Colony which he founded and which has done so much for the welfare of this State of their adoption!

47. ISAAC FAIRBANKS' RECOLLECTIONS

[Isaac Fairbanks was born at Pelham, Massachusetts, on November 10, 1818, and moved to Michigan settling in Kalamazoo County in Richland Township from which place in 1844 he moved to Old Wing Mission in what soon was to be called Fillmore Township. His close association with the Rev. George N. Smith and with the Hollanders who settled in the region qualified him to pen an authoritative memoir for the Semi-centennial celebrations in 1897. These *Recollections*, preserved in manuscript form in the Netherlands Museum, Holland, Michigan, accompanied by *Notes* which he penned later, subsequently edited by P. T. Moerdyk, constitute a unique authority for the rise of the Dutch community in the Black Lake region.]

For the history of the first settlement of the city of Holland and the surrounding townships in Ottawa and Allegan counties in the state of Michigan, and for about three years prior to said settlement, I make a statement of some facts that came within my personal knowledge.

In the autumn of 1844 I moved from the township of Richland, county of Kalamazoo, with my wife and one child, to a place called by the Indians, Old Wing, which is on section 3 in the now township of Fillmore. At that time Fillmore was attached to the township of Manlius. At Old Wing there was, by government appointment, a mission established for the Ottawa tribe of Indians.

My first occupation was building a dwelling house for the missionary and teacher, the Rev. George N. Smith, who received his appointment from the United States government.

There was also an appointment to said mission by the government, a Farmer and an Interpreter. Before I had completed the dwelling house for said missionary, I received the appointment of Farmer at a salary of $ 400 per year. The salary of the missionary was the same. The Interpreter's salary was $ 100 per year.

My appointment as Farmer gave me a good opportunity to form an acquaintance with the Indians. They were receiving annually, from the government, about $ 8 per capita in money and in addition they received pork, flour, and tobacco. Joseph Wakazoo was the chief. His family consisted of a wife and 3 daughters and one son. His wife's name was Tabita; the eldest girl was named Mary; the next Catherine; the next Tenis, and the youngest, a son, was named Joseph. Nacauba appeared to be next to the chief. He had 3 sons, Louis, Joseph, and Francis. I remember other names, to wit: Peter Wakazoo, who was a brother to the chief; Musquogwun, Chingwa, Shinacosha, Shawshawgwa, Showbatese, James Pricket [the interpreter], Robert McShinley [who was a dealer in furs], and John S. Claymore, [the last three named were half bloods.]

Chief Joseph Wakazoo died and his brother Peter Wakazoo was the chief thereafter. The Mission was in charge of the Congregational Church. The Indians were nearly all Catholic and, if they had been permitted, would rather have had a Catholic for their missionary and teacher. They were pleased to have their children learn to read and write, and for that purpose, near the dwelling of their missionary and teacher, Rev. George N. Smith, on section 3, they had a building for school, meeting, and council purposes, which was built of logs hewed on the outside and the inside, about 24 by 30 feet in size.

The Indians, at their village on the south shore of Black Lake, about one mile west of the city of Holland, had a frame building about the same size, where they met for meetings when visited by a Catholic priest. They also had at said village a cemetery which was fenced. The fence was about ten feet high, constructed of logs set close together, set in the ground endwise. The Indians were not willing to comply with the requirements of civilized life. They preferred to gain a living by hunting, trapping, and fishing. They had small clearings where they planted corn, potatoes, and squash. They left the largest trees on the ground and planted their crops between them. I persuaded some of them to clear off the large trees so that I could plow their lands. The government furnished for their use one yoke of oxen, an ox-cart, plows, harrows, and chains. They had objections to settling for a permanent living on their farms. That by doing so they would become the slaves of their cattle and hogs. They had rather have their meat by hunting, and when they wanted some meat, take their rifles and get it, and when they returned to their wigwams lie down and rest instead of waiting upon and feeding dumb brutes.

They did not like the practice of hotels in charging the traveler for something to eat. They were a merry lot of fellows to work with especially when we got them to a logging bee. There was no reservation of land here for the Indians. They bought their land from the government. They made boats of birch bark, large enough to carry quite a number of persons and they were so light that two persons could carry one. The best reason that I know why the Indians left and went to Grand Traverse where the settlement of the place was less, was that the settlement of this place by the Holland Colony interfered with their mode of living.

Before the settlement of the Holland Colony, Holland, Zeeland, Fillmore, Overisel, and Laketown were almost entirely unsettled, and heavily timbered with valuable timber. The trees so shaded the ground that the sun's rays were prevented from reaching the ground. The roads which were very few were almost impassable. It was a hard day's work to go with the oxen and cart from the mission settlement to the Indian village and return the same day, and it took about two days to go with the oxen and cart to the Kalamazoo River at New Richmond. We had no road to Grand Haven. When we went to Grand Haven we would go to Point Superior and take the Indian Trail or take the shore of Lake Michigan. I remember that at one of the annual payments of the Indians at Grand Haven, we had to wait a day or two and could not proceed with the payment for the reason that the chief had taken too much *scuta-wabo*, or fire water, and he skillfully dodged every question as to where he obtained it. We had the same law then that we have now, that it was not lawful to sell intoxicating liquor to an Indian, and when the pay master would ask the chief where he got the liquor he would not tell, but would respectfully commence a speech about his trials and difficulties with his people.

At Point Superior there was the frame of the sawmill and several dwelling houses. At Port Sheldon there was a splendid hotel and several other buildings.

Our cattle and Indian ponies found a good living in the woods not only summers but winters, and kept in good condition without hay or grain.

Of the character of the Indians I can say that they were kind and law abiding, and in their manner of life their wants were provided for. They would cheerfully feed the hungry with the best they had without money or price. Their greatest enemy was intoxicating liquor.

I now refer to January 1st, 1847, when Dominie van Raalte with John R. Kellogg me gave a call, and with the missionary George N. Smith waded through the snow which was then about 2 feet deep, from the mission to Black Lake, when the site for Holland City was selected. I remember the time from the practice of the Indians of firing a salute near our dwellings to usher in the new year and I remember those pioneers who came to erect the first shanties during the same winter. They found a place to sleep at night on the floor of my log house. I had a large fire place in one corner and firewood was plenty and the fire was kept burning day and night for several weeks. I think the first shanty was built on the east half of the South east quarter of section 28 and the next on the west half of the south east quarter of said section 28 in the township of Holland Town 5 north of range 15 west.

Few if any of those pioneers are left to tell of their hardships. It was evident to me that when they left their native land, their trust in God came across the ocean with them, and when springtime came their songs of praise could be heard in the woods, and I well remember the earnestness manifested by Dominie van Raalte, not only to care for temporal wants but also to make Holland a godly town. The further development of the settlements was convincing evidence that the God whom they trusted was with them. The first township meeting of Fillmore was held at my house on the first Monday in April 1849. The number of votes cast at said meeting was seven, with the following call list: Isaac Fairbanks, Benjamin Fairbanks, Anton Schorno, George Harrington, George N. Smith, Homer E. Hudson, and Andrew Drew. Isaac Fairbanks was elected supervisor, Benjamin Fairbanks, clerk, and Anton Schorno, treasurer. There were no defeated candidates.

[Notes]

Incidents in the history of the first settlement of the Holland Colony in the north part of Allegan and the south part of Ottawa counties in the State of Michigan. As allegations without evidence are worthless, I propose to state such facts as came within my personal knowledge and observation.

During the winter of 1846-47, about New Year's in 1847, I was living in Fillmore Township, Allegan County, with my small family. The place was then called Old Wing. There was at that moment about two feet of snow on the ground. I then held an appointment from the United States government as Farmer for the Indians; for which post I received a salary of $ 400 per year.

The government had established a Mission at that place, known as Old Wing Mission, which was in the care of the Congregational Church. The Rev. George N. Smith was appointed by the government to serve as missionary and teacher of the Indians at a salary of $ 100 per year. James Pricket, a half blood, was Interpreter at a salary of $ 100 per year. These salaries were paid regularly.

Insurmountable obstacles hindered the success of the mission. Being of the Catholic faith, the Indians desired to have a Catholic missionary and teacher. But as the Mission had been assigned to the Congregational Church, the Indians were force to accept this arrangement or not have any missionary or teacher. Notwithstanding this obstacle, the Indians refused to abandon their Catholic faith. The Mission evidently was a failure so far as civilizing and christianizing the natives.

When I moved to Fillmore Township it was for the purpose of establishing a home for myself and family. About New Year 1847 I heard a rap on my cabin door and for the first time met the Rev. Albertus Christiaan van Raalte and if I mistake not John R. Kellogg from Allegan, and learned from them that a colony of Hollanders from Europe were about to establish themselves in the vicinity of Old Wing Mission. With joy I extended to them a warm welcome in my cabin after a tramp with them toward Black Lake, through the snow in company with the Rev. George N. Smith.

The following arrangements were made. About six or eight Hollanders, detailed to build the first shanties, were to have lodging in my cabin. As I had a large fireplace I kept a fire burning day and night for several weeks until they had erected their shanties. The Rev. George N. Smith furnished them a room in which they prepared their food. Bernardus Grootenhuis and his wife attended to the cooking.

I now propose to correct statements I saw in a late issue of the *Workman*, a paper published in Grand Rapids. Its author appears to have had more zeal than knowledge. 1. The Indians did not, as he states, live on a reservation, but bought their land from the United States government. 2. They were not forced to sell their lands, but sold them at a fair price. 3. The statement the Dutch pioneers crowded the Rev. George N. Smith out of his house and bed is false. 4. The first Farmer of Old Wing Mission was Dr. Goodrich of Allegan; next, Francis Mills of Gull Prairie, a personal friend. Mills was a brother-in-law of Mr. Smith who presented his name for that post. His salary was $ 400 and not $ 500 as reported. He did not retain his position very long because of his defective eyesight, and he did not occupy that post at the time of the first settlement of the Hollanders. 5. I have yet to learn the Indians were imprisoned or abused by the Hollanders, or that the Mission endured one of the ten plagues sent to the Egyptians for their sins. 6. Regarding the suggestion Mrs. George N. Smith receive a pension from the citizens of Holland, I hope and trust her relatives will provide for her in her declining years, for she was most kind in surrendering her best room. And I trust the relatives will erect a suitable monument at Mr. Smith's grave.

My first labor was to build a house for Mr. Smith. In 1845, at the earnest request of the Indians, I was nominated Farmer for Old Wing Mission. For the first three months of that year while Mr. Smith and his family were on a visit to the East I had full charge of the Mission. But my appointment was delayed for this period of three months during which I never received payment for my labor. During the next two years I served as Farmer and received my pay quarterly.

After having lived in the society of the Dutch people of the Colony for half a century I cannot believe the allegations above made against the character of the Hollanders until it is substantiated by competent evidence.

48. EDWARD J. HARRINGTON'S
EARLY REMINISCENCES

[Son of George S. Harrington who was associated with the settlement of Holland from the first days, Edward J. Harrington was especially qualified to present much information of the Dutch community during its earliest days. His *Early Reminiscences* were published in *De Grondwet*, February 25, 1913.]

The way my father George S. Harrington and his family came to locate in Michigan was as follows: Father had a homestead in Cayuga County, New York, when all at once he got an attack of the western fever, as it was called. He had a sister in Michigan, and, with a growing family of boys, it did not seem to be a bad idea to adopt Horace Greely's advice and go West. But unfortunately he fell prey to the machinations of a land-shark, who offered to exchange our homestead of 100 acres for 200 acres at Green Lake in the northeast corner of Allegan County 100 acres lying on each side of the road. It seemed a good proposition, and father accepted. He took a warranty deed of the land, sold his household effects, and we started on our emigrant journey, passing through Canada. This was in the fall of 1845. Our journey led to Oswego, New York, when we took the propeller *New York* through the Welland Canal and the Straits to Chicago and thence by boat to St. Joseph, Michigan. Here father bought a team and we drove to Gun Plains in Kalamazoo County.

Our first intimation of trouble came when we passed a farm where the owner, named Samuel Maynard, was digging potatoes. This was about 8 or 10 miles from Paw Paw. Here we were treated with true western hospitality. As we left, he called out, "Where are you going?" We were getting too far away from eastern conventionalities for the question to seem surprising. We answered, and he said, "Have you an abstract of the land?" Upon father's answering in the negative, he said, "Well, you had better get one at once, as many people are being fleeced by land-sharks. You can stay here a week, if you want to, and it won't cost you a cent. You can unload your stuff on the barn floor." We stopped a while and dug potatoes with him.

Father went to the office of Judge John R. Kellogg in Allegan, a well known figure in those days, and we found that unfortunately Maynard's suspicions were too well founded. The so-called land agent did not own a foot of land, a portion of his so-called farm lying in the middle of Green Lake. Kellogg wrote to him, and father went to see him. He changed color, and said, "There must be some clerical error. I will make it right with you tomorrow." But during the night, he hired a man and team to take him away, and that was the last seen of him.

Now, having no land, we had to go work by the day. Father worked for Judge Kellogg. About the time that Ds. van Raalte came here, Kellogg advised father to preëmpt a piece of government land, which he did. This land was bought for ten shillings an acre; it is situated on the county line, south of the city of Holland, and known by all as the Harrington homestead. Kellogg hired father to come down here, with the first band of colonists, and we arrived here in the latter part of February 1847 with an ox team. The wages at this time were $ 2 a day for a man and team.

Isaac Fairbanks, one of first settlers in what is now Fillmore [Township] took us in. He had a shanty with a fireplace, built of sticks and clay. He helped us build our log house. Mrs. Fairbanks was hospitable. Mr. Fairbanks was popular with the people. They called him the "old squire".

I went to school with the young Indians, of whom at that time there were a great many. They were not good students. Most of them were Catholics and they had a small Catholic church at what was long known as the Indian Village. The priest was a goodlooking man and was very popular with them. There was also a Congregationalist clergyman, Rev. George N. Smith. One of his daughters afterward married an Indian by the name of Wolfe, and one of the daughters of that marriage, Mrs. Wilson, afterwards became a reporter for the *Grand Rapids Herald*.

There were several small Indian clearings near Ds. Smith's. Most of the Indians lived in tents and tepees. Squire Fairbanks and Rev. Smith were neighbors and their place was called Old Mission. There were about 24 or 30 small houses there, all occupied by the Indians; also a church, about 24 by 30 feet, built of lumber, and a schoolhouse built of hewn timber. The Dutch and the Indians got along fairly well together; but, of course, their relations at times became somewhat complicated by the characteristic differences in aim between tillers of the soil and hunters. The Dutch settlers put up fences, which the Indians did not like, and their pigs, which roamed about in the woods, got into the Indian's corn.

Deer were plentiful. I only shot one full-grown buck; but my brother George shot a great many. He still enjoys his deer hunt. The meat sold for three cents a pound, the hind quarter, and one cent a pound for the fore quarter, and it was frequently given away outright. The tallow was used to make candles.

It was difficult to make a living in those days, unless one had some cash reserve to fall back on. Those who had money generally lost it and had to go to work with new grit and determination. It was hard work to get the land cleared and to dispose of the green logs. We planted potatoes in between the logs and raised good crops; did not raise wheat right away; had to contend with squirrels, woodchucks, crows, etc. We liked to hunt these animals.

Our flour we got from Allegan at first, until after a while Jan Rabbers had a mill at New Groningen. Oswald van der Sluis also ground corn in the sawmill which he built at the head of Black Lake.

After a while I became an expert logger, and was in good demand to show the Hollanders how to clear their land, and what timber would make good shingles and fence rails. We cut down the basswood trees for building purposes.

Prices were low. Grain and corn sold for fifteen cents a bushel; patatoes from twelve to fifteen cents; wheat from forty to fifty cents. But gruadally conditions improved.

The Hollanders, as they became better known, became more popular and their trade was much appreciated in Allegan, Singapore, and Saugatuck, where they left many a golden *willempje*, a Dutch coin worth about four dollars.

Judge Kellogg was one of the best friends of the Dutch, and employed a great many of them. Henry Pennoyer at Grand Haven was equally kind to them. Our family got along very well with our Dutch neighbors. My mother herself was an Amsterdam woman, being a Van Alstyne on her father's side and a Visser on her mother's. I could read some Dutch and frequently acted as interpreter.

Isaac Cappon and I worked together a great deal in those days. His mother, being a Zeelander, was neat and a good cook. We enjoyed going over there and eat her pancakes which were the size of a dinner plate. My mother also was a good cook and they enjoyed coming over and sampling her American dishes. And right here I want to give an incident of those early days.

Cappon said to me one day, "Jerome, I want to go to Kalamazoo." I asked, "What do you want to go there for?" He said, "I have a girl there," and he gave me her name. I replied, "I will go with you."

We started to walk all the way to Kalamazoo. It was wintertime and slippery. We took the Kalamazoo River Road and traveled to Pine Creek, two miles west from Otsego. We were very tired and stopped at a Pine Creek house and the next day we went to Kalamazoo and put up at an inn there. I told the landlady to leave the door open during the night, inasmuch as Cappon went to see his girl. The two had crossed the Atlantic in the same ship.

On our return trip we met a man by the name of Warner Sample, and he walked along with us. We got down west of Allegan and there we saw a skunk. I said, "Boys, let's kill him!" I looked for a club; but Cappon found one first. He ran after the skunk and struck him. At that early day Cappon did not know the nature of the animal. The skunk retaliated, hitting Cappon in the right eye. I was sorry, for I thought Cappon would suffocate. I had no idea it would be so bad. He had on a nice new broadcloth suit and a good cap. The clothes were ruined. He buried them a while to get rid of the smell, but could never use them afterwards. The smell annoyed him so much that he became desperate and threw away his cap in the creek.

Pretty soon we arrived at De Boe's half-way house. I was hungry and suggested going in and having something to eat. Cappon said, "I am not going in, I smell so," but I persuaded him to go in. I asked for a cup of coffee and something good to eat and the old lady said she could get it for us. All this time Cappon kept out of sight behind the stove. Mrs. De Boe and her daughter Mary busied themselves preparing our lunch. All at once Mrs. De Boe screamed, "Oh! Mary, run! run! the skunks are after our chickens again." Mary ran, and Cappon looked blue. I said to the old lady, "My friend has just killed a skunk; that's what you smell." She said to me, "Oh! you rascal!" She knew me well enough to realize that I must have had something to do with it. We ate our pancakes and coffee and started out again. Cappon said, "You don't get me into another house, no matter how hungry you get."

There was much teaming from Saugatuck, Hamilton, and Allegan, and as I had a good ox-team I did a good deal of the hauling. The roads however were awful. Anton Schorno did a thriving business at Hamilton, selling groceries. In due time Overisel on the east and Laketown on the south were set off as separate townships.

One more incident is worthy of mention. The old man Kronemeyer, who lived on the bee line, had a hard time of it; but at one time, in the latter part of the 1850's, he made a big haul. There was a large bounty on wolves, and one day one of the Kronemeyer boys came across a nest of young whelps. He called his father, who got his gun and first shot the whelps and then the old wolves when they came. There were seven wolves in all, and each brought $ 20 or $ 25. That helped the old man Kronemeyer. He was a hard worker, and so were his boys.

In 1865 I moved to Holland, bought the dock of Alderd Plugger, at the head of Black Lake, and engaged in the bark and stave business.

49. GEORGE E. HOLM'S
RECOLLECTIONS OF HOLLAND IN 1852

[George E. Holm lived in Byron Township in Kent County south of Grand Rapids at the time the Hollanders settled in the Black Lake region. This account, published in *De Grondwet*, February 28, 1911, presents with great fidelity the appearance of Holland in 1852 when the author visited the village.]

Anent the semi-centennial celebration at Holland yesterday are a few recollections of my own which may not be uninteresting to your readers.

At the time the Holland Colony was established by Rev. A. C. van

Raalte in 1847 I was a farmer's boy in the township of Byron in Kent County where father had been a resident 2 years and I remember very well the coming in of the Colony and the coming out of the foreign settlers among the farmers of Byron and parts adjacent for such things as they needed to work with or live on, to wit: oxen, cows, corn, pigs, potatoes, sheep, etc., before they had raised anything of their own, and I remember also that our farmers were always very glad to see them, for a purchase by the newcomers of anything we had to sell always brought gold, the ten guilder gold piece being the most common, in exchange for what they bought. The farmers in those days seldom saw any gold, or but very little money of any kind, and you may well guess that the curious, oddly dressed strangers from over the sea were welcome guests to those of our region who had anything to sell.

I also remember with what wonder my boyish eyes watched the peculiarities of these, to me, queer people and with what amazement I would see them haul out their leather purses and count out the gold for every purchase; nor was it long before nearly every farmer had exchanged something or other for some of their golden guilders. In my boyish mind the Hollanders were a mine of wealth – they were overflowing with sacks and bags of gold and they at once became to me a wonderful people. Whenever I saw one of them he became a magnet which collected the curious boy about him, that I might study his ways, his dress and hear him talk, for was he not a man who had recently sailed over the great ocean all the way from Holland, to become a citizen of Michigan and help found a remarkable colony at Black Lake? If he had dropped out of the moon he could not have interested me more and to visit him in that wonderful settlement and see him at home became one of the leading ambitions of my backwoods life. It was so much talked about and for the first year or so we saw some of them often; and now and then some adventurous young man whom I knew had actually "been to Holland", so it seemed as though, if I did not go there also, there would be a void in my life which nothing else could possibly fill. It would be so much like visiting a foreign country, you know.

Pictures of Holland in my old geography always had a windmill prominent in the foreground. Would this Holland in Michigan have a windmill? Verily, how could I ever enjoy life unless I went to see? Yes, I would go; but when or how was left to the years of waiting which fill so large a space in every boy's life who has some big thing to do and watches out for time to bring him his opportunity. So my time came at last, 5 years later, in the fall of 1852. I was 18; I was my own man; I had some well-earned money in my pocket and I had not forgotten Holland and would visit this foreign country and see these curious people in their own famous colony.

At that time there was far from being any sort of a decent road from Grandville to the Colony. I was an expert woodsman and cared little for roads when I wanted to go anywhere but I must have a comrade, and so for company persuaded a young farmer friend about my own age, Otis Freeman by name [I think he is living yet], to be my companion during the voyage, and together we shouldered our rifles and struck out westerly through the woods to find a way or make one to Holland.

Think of that now, ye scorching cyclers who think nothing of a run down there and back the same day awheel, or ye happy Ottawa Beachers who leave your pleasant homes in Grand Rapids and alight at your cottage door 6 miles beyond Holland in an hour! Behold the changes time has wrought – and how little is it you know of the pleasures of pioneering!

Freeman's people had dealt a good deal with the Hollanders. My friend Ote could talk with most of them quite well and, besides, he knew some of the Zeeland farmers. At the cabin of one of them was where we brought up at the end of our first day's jaunt, tired, wet, and hungry, for a damp November snow had been coming down all day and our tramp had been through bush and brake without much thought or care for the roads. Indeed, the most welcome road was the unblazed forest path, for the roads of those days in that region at that season of the year were double roads, that is to say there were always two, where you found one, and one of them was usually a foot or two below the other. Therefore the woods walking was much more preferable.

Our good host's name was Yntema. He had a son about our age, whose given name was Otto, who had mingled with the Yankees enough to speak English very well, and I remember we were made very welcome, indeed; also that the provender was abundant and good, and that the evening passed very pleasantly. The young visitors were entertained by the exhibition of many quaint and curious things which had been brought from the old country, not the least among which that interested me was a huge Bible published in 1647 – just 200 years prior to the settlement of the Michigan Holland Colony. Its staunch covers were half an inch thick and it was bound and clasped all over with silver, and if I remember right its central clasp was fastened with a lock and key. And the pictures that were in that book! Why, I almost think I am looking at them yet. And in it, as a part of it, there was also a wonderful map, showing what was known of the Americas, for the Western continents had then only been discovered 155 years. Except for the Holy Land I had never seen any kind of a map in a Bible before. This one showed Newfoundland with a strip of Canada as far west as the Niagara Falls, the ocean coast from the St. Lawrence River to Florida, the Gulf of Mexico, Mexico, Southern California, the northern part of South America, and the West Indies. There have been some changes in American maps since that day!

Mr. Yntema also had a watch which was nearly related to this venerable book in point of age – a watch purchased by his great-grandfather nearly a century and a half before and which [according to our notes made at the time] "still regulates the sun and tears the moon wide open."

His daughter, a rosy cheeked young maiden of 16, showed us many old-country articles of head gear, one single ornament of gold being valued at $ 250, together with many other things to us quaint and queer, because we had never seen the like before. She then opened a large cupboard and exhibited some 300 Sunday School books, which the children of New York had given to the children of the Drenthe settlement, whatever that was. The books she said "were the best of all" – and thus do worthy pioneers find many aids.

But I must not linger too long, though, indeed, my 5 years' dream of a foreign shore was now being realized and my weariness had faded completely out. We retired betimes and were up before the sun, for the strange city was still half a dozen miles away and that was the acme of my dream. Our kind host and his family gave us pleasant coffee and the simple breakfast of their people, while Otto accompanied us a mile on our way to be sure we took the right path, bade us a cheery good-bye, urging us to call on our return and tarry yet another night. Now, as some of the descendants of this family are doubtless living in that township yet, I desire to thank them again for the pleasant and profitable evening spent with them in their pioneer cabin on November 17, 1852.

We struck the village of Holland at the head of Black Lake at about 10 o'clock in the morning and, as we did not leave it until near 4 in the afternoon, we had ample time to do the town. Yes, and as sure as I am an honest historian, there was the Dutch windmill! Surely I was on the dikes of the old land, only, perhaps, this one was not built for pumping! It was nearly a mile to the hotel, and I therefore reserved its examination until after dinner, as, unlike the erratic Don Quixote, I could not think of attacking a windmill on an empty stomach.

Holland village at that time was 5 years old and contained 600 or 700 inhabitants. There were 7 stores, 2 hotels, a bakery, a tinner's shop, a tailor shop, a clock and watch repairing and jewelery shop, besides various mechanical shops, and wagon and blacksmith shops, such as became any new village where there are no idlers. It also had a church which cost $ 800, a schoolhouse, and a printing office. We were in most of these places during the day, concerning some of which permit us to speak later on. In the printing office we found 2 intelligent lads 14 or 15 years of age and I still have among my relics some dead copy in the Dutch language which one of the boys gave me, which at that time was a great take for me, being in a foreign language. Candor compels me to say I have never read it.

As soon as we had put away our dinner we made for the windmill. You could not keep me away from it another moment. Indeed, it was a wonderful thing to me. It was a sawmill and I think there was also a simple run of stone for grinding corn, and as the mill was not running that day it was open for inspection. I went all over it. The tower must have been 75 or 80 feet high, for it is down in my notebook that I climbed 9 pairs of stairs or ladders, before I came out on the balcony which surrounded its cap on a level with the pinion of those mammoth wings, which had a sweep of at least 100 feet. The framework of these great sails was light, except the main arms, and covered with sail cloth, when in operation, arranged in some way so they could be furled when there was too much or too little wind to run the mills properly, or when idle as at the time of our visit. From the balcony I could see Lake Michigan 6 miles away. It was the first view I ever had of it – and that was another big thing – though I had sailed its entire length some 17 years before when less than half a year old.

This giant windmill was one of the joys of my journey, nor have I ever seen anything since in that line equal to it. I brought it away with me and have it in memory still, though in my subsequent visits to Holland in after years I was never able to tell where it stood. I do not think I was there again for nearly 25 yeras, and then everything was changed. My trip had not been in vain. I had found the windmill and my last view of it, as we left the village that afternoon, I thought very like the pictures in my old geography, as it stood in relief against the western sky and the great lake beyond.

Another thing which interested me was a monstrous clock in the watch-maker's shop. The sun, moon, and some of the stars circled round its honest face from east to west in quiet succession, while it also had a calendar arrangement which told us the year, month, and day, and I shall long remember the day I was there – November 18, 1852. My notebook says so, and I'll make my "happy David" [affidavit] it is true, as it was the first rare thing of the kind I had seen, and you may be sure I was going to remember it. Calendar clocks are now as common as mosquitos, but they were not 45 years ago.

I remember, also, that we made several attempts to buy something, but as the tinner had no tin side saddles, or the wagonmaker any carriage plows, or the blacksmith any ready-made snow shoes, we went as we came empty-handed except for rifles and supplies of the staff of life procured from the bakers.

To look back at it now, our boyish pranks were at once impertinent and silly, but it was such fun to see those honest mechanics stare at us when they came to understand our absurd requests. They were men who never joked, if, in fact, they knew what a joke was. Their lives had been, and were, too much in earnest for any such nonsense, and if it were possible I would even now beg their several and collective pardon for any annoyance we possibly gave them that November afternoon. If they thought of us the second time after we were gone, they probably voted us a pair of harmless lunatics who did not know what we were talking about, and so suffered us to go in peace. Perhaps it was the windmill that had loosened our tongues. I have often been called a windmill since, but, somehow, never took much pride in it; not as much as I ought to have done, considering how many years I had yearned to see one.

The weather that afternoon was not the most pleasant of Noveeber days. There were occasional snow squalls, the sky was heavily overcast, and toward night it set in for a heavy storm, but this did not balk us of our intent to camp that night on the bank of Black River.

At that time many of the houses in the village of Holland were built of logs, though, perhaps a majority of those in the immediate village were frame. They were all a good deal scattered. Very few of them were helping "hold 'tother fellow up." And as to Dominie van Raalte's church, that was something very grand for the time in an architectural way. We were fortunate enough to find it open with the sexton in attendance cleaning up, sweeping out, and dusting and so, without let or hindrance, we walked in. The sexton greeted us pleasantly, but I do not recollect that we attempted any conversation with him. The church was a block-house, built of square-hewn timber, and for size was, perhaps 50 by 70. Inside it was very like other churches [though at the time I was not very familiar with them], except that in the roof were 2 great ventilating flues. I remember to have thought them very warm-blooded worshipers, but perhaps they were not much used in winter or perhaps that was the plan in the old home country – but doubtless they knew their needs much better than I – so we departed without suggesting any alterations. I presume there are many of the present residents of Holland who will remember this pioneer church.

One more thing before leaving the village on our return trip. We had quite a pleasant chat with the 2 bright boys we found in the printing office, both of whom spoke English fluently. They had great faith in the future of Holland, and, as I remember, were strong in the faith that Congress would soon grant them a sufficient appropriation to make an elegant harbor there – one of the best, in fact, on the Michigan shore – but if alive now those lads must be looking for it yet, as I do not recall that Congress has ever done any such thing. Nature long ago seems to have done its full share to that end, but mighty little help has it had from any other source, as such meager appropriations as have ever reached that point have been but driblets, scarce sufficient to keep the sand out of the nose of their still prospective excellent harbor; and yet, perhaps, enough for some congressman to harp on when he wanted the Holland vote. I told the boys I hoped they would get it, but that I did not believe it would bother them very soon, as Frank Pierce was president, and I never took any stock in his desire to improve the rivers and harbors of the North. I think they must be waiting for that appropriation yet.

But, as this is not a political essay, we will hasten on through the snow storm to our camp on Black River, remarking as we leave the pioneer village that we do not remember to have found but two streets in it, and these we named respectively Stump Street and Mud Street, for reasons which would have been apparent had you traveled them in the fall of 1852. Our camp on Black River was an improvised affair. I don't know how far it was from the village, but we arrived there just on the edge of a dusky, stormy evening, and under the arching hemlocks and cedars, where storms or snow never come, soon had a roaring fire going. Our camp was near a deserted clearing with the ruins of a shanty thereon, from which we laid in an ample supply of fuel and prepared to be comfortable.

For beds we abstracted some of the roofing of the aforesaid shanty, to wit: Two huge slices of hemlock bark about 4 feet long and 3 feet wide. These had curled up quite a bit like a concave lens and when laid up "slantingdicular" against the roots of a tree, with a big fire in front and a covering of hemlock boughs ten feet above you, became a warm, dry nest – fit for any explorer returning from a foreign shore. We camped thus for the fun of the thing – not because we had to – and, behold, even to this day that camp is called "The Camp of the Valley".

Our next business was supper, and two or three squirrels and a partridge which our rifles had gathered in were soon dressed and broiled on crotched sticks, with no salt or seasoning except ashes and smoke. As we broiled we caught the savory drippings on large slices of Dutch bread, and as these drippings dripped deliciously what more was wanting to make that repast such as many another weary explorer, on occasion, would be glad to get? It was a rare treat. As we had nothing to hurry us and no dishes to wash up or table to clear away, we broiled and ate, and ate and broiled for nearly 2 happy hours, making the wild woods resonant with shout and song. Had there been any settlers within a mile or so they must have thought pandemonium had broken loose down by the sluggish river. It was a great lark.

It must have been about 9 o'clock when it became apparent we were to have company. The lads in the printing office, when we told of our camping idea, had warned us of the wolves, but what did we care when we heard them howl either in answer to the delicious odor of our broiled game supper or the song and shout of the campers. It did not matter. The branches hung low on the trees which embowered us and wolves do not climb trees. We had a good fire, plenty of ammunition, and so let the varmints howl, if it pleased them. Noise seldom kills anyone, and your wild wolf is as big a coward as your human one, if you face him and tell him you do not care a fig for his music. I had camped among them before and all we cared about it was that it meant a watchful night for two weary young fellows who had been on their feet since 5 o'clock in the morning. All there was of it we must woo Nature's sweet restorer as the homeopath doctor gives his pills – alternately. So we took turns standing guard through the long night, and if we took an occasional shot at gleaming eyes in the woodsy blackness beyond the circle of our campfire it was more with the expectation of scaring than killing any of the fierce howlers with which we were surrounded. We kept our fire going and did not even climb a tree.

At about 3 o'clock we broiled and devoured the balance of our game, and were ready for marching orders at the first crack of day. We saw no sign of wolf after daylight, except tracks in the snow at a safe distance all about our camp, which we left without regret.

At 10 o'clock we secured a breakfast at a Hollander's cabin on the far frontier of the Colony, and that night lodged with a Yankee friend within 5 or 6 miles of Freeman's home, mine being several miles further on.

And thus it was that not until about noon of the 4th day from our starting out I sat down with Ote to dinner in his own home, as I had often done before, and while we did ample justice to what was set before us entertained the family with the history of our grand expedition to Black Lake. Such was Holland 45 years ago, and one of the ways of getting there. For myself, I felt abundantly paid for my trip and I have never been there since without thinking of my youthful visit or looking in vain for Stump Street or Mud Street or in my mind wondering whither had flown the mighty windmill, which was such a marvel of unchained power in my boyish eyes.

Once, more, than twenty-five years after my first visit, being booked for a stump speech at Holland I prefaced my talk with a lively reference to the old-time tramp and what I saw, and how it impressed me at the time, with pleasant comments on the progress they had made, to the great delight of my audience. In that audience sat many a grand gray head who was there when I came out of the woods with my rifle in November 1852.

And now it is 50 years since they first came, and 45 since I first visited them, and today the stranger would be very far from taking that thriving city for a foreign port.

The wild woods where we camped, begirt with howling wolves, have been swept away. The small openings in the woods here and there miles apart, where the pioneer colonist started his farm, have melted into each other, and the bright village of Zeeland now stands where, possibly, not a tree was cut on that stormy November day in 1852 when my friend and I made our tramp to the famous Colony.

At that time Grandville was a smart village and it was a somewhat mooted question whether Grandville or Grand Rapids was to be the coming city of the Grand River valley. It is not so mooted now. Holland has long since taken its place among the thriving cities of Michigan. With its college, its extensive business houses and immense factories, its more than healthful and pleasant summer resorts, there is no reason in the world – when they get that harbor appropriation the printer lads spoke of in 1852 – why this city, founded upon principles of the staunchest integrity and ever maintained along the same line, should not be the Chicago of Michigan, with a port sufficient for all the commerce of the Great Lakes. Yet another fifty years – though we be not here to see – Holland will remain, nor is there any reason why it should not be the principal lake-shore city on the eastern coast of Lake Michigan. That is where I put it and I'm not going to take it back.

50. ELVIRA H. LANGDON'S SCHOOL REMINISCENCES

[The author (Mrs. Cooper) was first lady schoolteacher in Holland, from 1849 to 1850. Later she moved to Nebraska where from Hastings she wrote this letter dated August 20, in connection with the Semi-Centennial celebrations in August 1897. It was published in *De Grondwet*, December 17, 1910.]

I have only recently learned of the Pioneer Day at Holland, and I wish to be identified with the pioneers so much, that I cannot express myself. My work in Holland is not forgotten by me and I feel desirous that it should be recorded somewhere.

It was in the middle of the century, 1849, that I was employed by Henry D. Post to teach the first school taught by a woman in Holland. In addition to this I also organized the first English Sunday School in Holland. It was kept up six months and then dropped, owing to sickness and cholera.

I boarded in Mr. Post's family, and at that time we were the only American residents. Dr. C. D. Shenick lived a few miles away. I sometimes felt lonely, and imagined I had privations; I had not yet lived in Nebraska. I was treated with great respect by man, woman, and child because I was the *schoolvrouw*.

The biggest day I saw in Holland was June 1, 1850. It was Sunday morning, and three boats came sailing over Black Lake to the Indian village where they halted and pitched their tents. They were under Major Bowes, U.S. topographical engineer, sent to survey the surroundings in view of making a harbor, which Ds. van Raalte was desirous to secure. The arrival of these boats with the American flag unfurled was a sight to rejoice the hearts of the people, for they now felt prosperity was near. The surveying party remained about six weeks and as they were intelligent gentlemen they added materially to social life. After Bowes and party left we – that is, Mr. Post's family and myself – fell back into our monotonous living.

Some of us were ill a good deal. It began to be shaky times and we shook. I had fever and ague some but kept in school. Some tried quinine and some tried other remedies; the best was plenty of cold water and a sweat. As cold weather came on we all got better.

We only had mail once a week. A woman came with a bag and got our letters, taking them to her husband who took them to the stage terminus twelve miles from Holland and brought back return mail.

My first journey to Holland was tedious. I went from Allegan to Singapore by stage where I stopped a week with a family who owned a tannery until I could get word to Mr. Post, twelve miles distant. There was no team or roadway to convey me through the woods. When my escort arrived we went in an open democrat wagon, traveling on the beach of Lake Michigan. The sleet and snow made slow traveling for the horses and they had to rest often. Once I tried walking for a change but a big wave from the lake caused me to hurry back into the wagon. Finally we reached the mouth of Black Lake. There I was refreshed with a cup of coffee from the *vrouw* of the boat house. I was here transferred to an open boat, with my big trunk, shaking with fear lest we would be spilt in the lake. We reached Holland in safety about dark,thankful to be on dry land once more.

There was no schoolhouse in Holland but I had a small, comfortable room in which to open school. I adopted methods in teaching suited to children who were ignorant of the English language. I used oral teaching entirely at first, as I perceived they retained these ideas better than when required to study. My Sunday School was also on a simple plan.

Rev. Dr. Isaac N. Wykoff of Albany, New York, visited the Colony in 1849 to confer with Dr. van Raalte on the subject of connecting the Holland churches with the [Dutch] Reformed Church of America. He called on me in my little school and on his return sent me quite a Sunday School library which helped me a great deal as my little people began very soon to read English.

The Ottawa Indians that were here decided to move to Grand Traverse, thus vacating the Indian village. Two old Indians, Pricket and Poneat, lingered as if loth to leave their hunting ground. They were friendly and often brought us presents of fish. Mr. Post dealt with them and we had no fears of mischief. One young Indian boy expressed a wish to go to school. I welcomed him but when he was given a book he soon left.

The sawmill of Oswald D. Van der Sluis and the ashery were built while I was in Holland. I might mention also the death of President Taylor, a national event of such importance that Henry Pennoyer of Grand Haven, knowing that Post and Van Raalte could not get the news by mail for some days, kindly sent a man on foot a distance of 22 miles to convey the sad news.

The families of Post and Van Raalte often exchanged coffee visits. The latter was fine in conversation. Once he entertained us by relating his experience in the old country in being tried for schism. He had many trials with his people. He lost an infant and conducted the funeral service himself in English. Mr. Post and myself were there to sympathize with them as Mrs. Post was ill. We were the only American present.

Hoyt G. Post went to visit his home and I began to think of a change but how to get out of Holland was a query. I could not go back the way I came and there was no livery and only one horse in Holland. Finally a farmer from Allegan came to take home a hired woman and I engaged passage with him. It was a very hot day, the 12th of August. The *vrouw* and myself walked some of the way and picked blackberries. A few miles from Allegan the horse tired out so badly that Mr. Prouty, our driver, said we must abandon the wagon, while he did the same. I tried to keep up with the woman but was so tired. My journey from Holland was as hard as when I went there. I was at last welcomed at Judge Ely's. After I rested a few days I went to Kalamazoo by stage and took the cars from there for Marshall and other points to visit. All were eager to learn about the Hollanders, as the enterprise of the new Colony was much talked of. The first agricultural fair of Michigan was held that year at Ann Arbor, which I attended.

When ready to return to Holland I learned from Mr. Post that the people had voted to raise no money for school or town purposes but that there was enough money on hand to pay me for the winter term. As my baggage was in Holland I went back and taught until spring when I was relieved from my labors and my name stricken from the pay roll. That winter I taught in a lone house built for orphans. During the winter nothing unusual happened. The 16th of January was the darkest day I ever saw. It seemed to forbode disaster. I never lost interest in Holland, though I dare say I would find none of my Holland friends who would remember the schoolma'm.

Though I cannot be present at the Semi-Centennial yet in my prairie home I think of you and unite in wishing continued prosperity and blessing to your city.

51. ANNA C. POST'S REMINISCENCES

[Anna C. Post (*nee* Coatsworth), wife of Henry D. Post, like her husband witnessed the beginnings of Dutch settlement at Holland. Title of her account as printed in *De Grondwet*, March 28, 1911 is *Reminiscences Written in* 1881, 1897, *and* 1891.]

Early in July 1848 [it was toward the end of our wedding tour] we left the rude hotel at Singapore near the mouth of the Kalamazoo River where we had been waiting a week for favorable weather to enable us to reach our new home in Holland. It was near sunset when we went to the bank of the river and embarked in an Indian mackinaw boat. The captain and crew consisted of but a single person – an old Frenchman named Joseph Victor.

We reached the mouth of the river just as the lamps in the lighthouse

were being lighted. The swells of Lake Michigan, meeting the current of
the Kalamazoo River, caused waves which seemed very dangerous to me
on this my first voyage in an open boat. Stephen D. Nichols, the lighthouse keeper, kindly tossed a little package to us, which I found to
contain a few crackers and a herring. Captain Victor threw a tow-line to
Mr. Nichols, and he pulled our boat through the waves and over the bar.
He then cast off the line; and we were alone on Lake Michigan.

The old Frenchman spread his sail and for a time we sailed away to the
north, on our right hand the sand hills crested with dark pines and on
our left the boundless expanse of water. Soon the wind died away and
old Victor furled his sails and took up his oars. Our progress then
became very slow.

How vividly even now I recall my feelings as the light of the harbor of
Kalamazoo River faded in the distance. There was something so fearful
as being on Lake Michigan in the darkness and in a small boat; and, to
add to my uneasiness, the old man had frequent recourse to a jug under
his seat [the light of the stars was sufficient for me to see this.]

At two o'clock in the morning, just as the moon was rising, we reached
the mouth of Black Lake. A boatman by the name of [Jacobus] Vinke
lived in a little house on the shore of the lake; and, being aroused by the
shouts of our captain, he came out with a lantern in his hand, accompanied
by his wife. The tow-line was thrown out to them and they drew us over
the bar and into Black Lake. I ought, perhaps, mention that this was about
a quarter of a mile north of the present harbor. I noticed now how smooth
and still the water was, with nothing to break the silence save the dip of
the oars.

At daybreak we landed on the beach at the head of Black Lake, where
the stave factory [Pfanstiehl's dock] is now located. It was almost an
unbroken wilderness with but here and there a log cabin or a rough,
temporary house. A footpath led up from the lake to the building which
was to be my home. It is necessary to mention that Hoyt G. Post, my
husband's brother, was already here. The first thing which attracted my
attention on the morning of my arrival was the singing in all the little
houses near us. I soon learned that my neighbors sang psalms after
every meal.

It may be interesting to describe the first call I received after my arrival
in Holland. In the afternoon of the first day my husband and his brother
went out for a short walk, leaving me alone. I heard a slight noise and at
once went downstairs. An Indian stood just over the threshold, holding
in his extended hand a strip of raw meat. He advanced toward me and I

receded. He then laid the meat on the table and departed. Hoyt explained on his return that the Indian was a friend of his who was about to leave the place and that he had brought the tenderloin of a deer as a parting gift.

I very soon made the acquaintance of the Rev. and Mrs. A. C. van Raalte. I was struck with his youthful appearance, as he had been described to me by a mischievous friend, who had met him at Lansing the previous winter, as a venerable looking man with a long white beard. In those early years they were our most intimate acquaintances; and the pleasant visits with them are among the brightest recollections of those times. Van Raalte possessed rare conversational powers and every sentence he uttered was worth remembering. His noble wife was a lady of culture and refinement.

When I had been here a few days, Hoyt told me there was a very pleasant Dutch lady quite near, who could speak English a little. I was anxious to see her, but I did not understand more than half dozen words of the Dutch language; yet I went to visit her. She was a very sweet looking woman, who met me with a cordial smile of welcome and gave me a seat and a little footstove to put my feet on, the first one I ever saw. She soon brought me tea in a tiny porcelain cup. You can imagine the difficulty we had in making ourselves understood. For instance, she took hold of my arm and smilingly said, "you got not much spek." I had seen "spek te koop!" on barrels, and on inquiry, had been told it meant "pork for sale", so I knew "spek" was pork. I said, "yes, we got plenty 'spek' in the cellar." Then gently taking hold of my cheek, she said in a much louder tone, "No, no, you got no spek!" It then flashed upon my mind that she wished to say I was thin. That excellent woman is still living and she could doubtless tell of my blunders during that call. My visit was here interrupted by a messenger who said I had a caller and must come home immediately. I went at once and found one of the very few American residents then in the Colony. She had walked several miles to see the "new Yankee woman". I recollect that in the course of the conversation she told me I had better take off my rings and go to work.

In the early settlements many visitors were attracted here by curiosity. We had been here but a few weeks when the Rev. McPason of Galesburg, Kalamazoo County, and Elder Meppin of Gull Prairie came on a Saturday afternoon, bringing a letter from Judge Booth of Allegan. The next morning being Sunday, we all went to hear Van Raalte preach in the log church. In the afternoon Rev. McPason preached the first sermon in English ever delivered in Holland. After the services we were invited to tea at Rev. van Raalte's.

I remember about this time there was quite a sensation caused by the arrival of a family from Paris. They rented a log cabin opposite us and the frequent appearance of an unusually beautiful boy with long, dark curls and large, lustrous eyes made me the more anxious to meet his mother. Mrs. van Raalte and myself, armed with an interpreter, soon went to call on her. We found a fine looking French lady, dressed very neatly with a snowy kerchief crossed on her bosom and a becoming cap upon her head. We exchanged bows and courtesies in abundance; and there was some *parlez-vous-ing* with our interpreter. At length casting a scrutinizing glance upon us, she said to the interpeter, "Where were these ladies educated that they do not speak French?" A few more bows, and the interview ended. This French lady is still with us and last spring celebrated her 90th birthday.

We had constant accessions of pleasant families from the Netherlands – among them Mr. Pieter F. Pfanstiehl, Mr. Hermanus Doesburg, and others too numerous to mention. By this time we had become sufficiently acquainted with the Dutch language to be understood.

Ex-Governor Slade of Vermont originated a society about 1846 or 1847 for the purpose of supplying the West with competent schoolteachers. Miss. Elvira H. Langdon, a well educated woman, came out under the patronage of this association. She was the first lady teacher in Holland and was a member of our family for two years. She was a pleasant social companion and added much to Holland society. About 1850 Mr. Walter T. Taylor and his family came from Geneva, New York. They brought the first piano. Mr. Taylor was the first teacher in the Holland Academy. Society was soon after still farther increased by the arrival of two physicians, one with a wife and two daughters. Also, Elias G. Young and family of Grand Rapids. Among the number mentioned there were several good singers; and as Hoyt played the flute, the shores of Black Lake often resounded with music from pleasant parties going to or coming from Lake Michigan. The social condition of Holland for three or four years remained very much as I have described it; then there was an addition of several more American families [those here leaving about the same time] and society began to assume the character it has since attained.

When we came to Holland in 1848 we found a band of Ottawa Indians. They had a village a mile from town on the south side of Black Lake. It consisted of loghouses and a church surmounted by a cross. A burying ground was neatly enclosed with a picket fence and full of graves which were marked with black crosses upon many of which hung garlands of paper flowers. East of us in Fillmore they had their farms which they cultivated under the direction of Isaac Fairbanks. There the missionary, Rev. George N. Smith, lived among them and preached to them through an interpreter.

It was my privilege to be invited to spend the first New Year's Day after we came to Holland at the home of Rev. Smith. I had never met Mrs. Smith and the family, so I looked forward with pleasant anticipations to the day. It dawned bright and clear. There had been quite a fall of snow during the night, so that every bush and tree was covered with a white mantle. We had been told that a sleigh would be sent for us, and breakfast was no sooner over than the tinkling of bells called me to the door. There was our sleigh and a pair of Indian ponies, driven by a strong well-built Indian named Joseph Pricket.

We were soon ready, and with beating heart I got into the sleigh with Mr. Post, and we started on our journey. There was no road, only an Indian trail. The three miles were soon past and we landed in safety at the door of the missionary. After a cordial welcome and introductions to the members of the family we were invited to accompany Rev. Smith to the schoolhouse and hear him preach to his flock, as was his custom on that day. A number of Indians and squaws with blankets over their heads – some had bright-eyed papooses fastened to a board, which they carefully set against the wall near a small box stove – gathered to listen to the message of salvation. It was a scene never to be forgotten. The first hymn given out was the familiar one:

> *Oh for a thousand tongues to sing*
> *My great Redeemer's praise!*

Rev. Smith spoke in English, and the Indian who had brought us to the station stood by his side and repeated it in his own tongue. The Indians had hymn books in their own language. After service was over we went to the home where dinner had been prepared in our absence. There were five Indians at the table with us and our host explained that they belonged to the family of a chief. The Indians were coming and going all day, bringing little gifts to members of the family who all spoke Indian when in conversation with them. I do not remember having heard the Indians speak our language. The day was soon past and the same Indian who came for us in the morning brought us home in the twilight through the grand old forest by the light of the moon.

This was my first acquaintance with our Indians, though I saw more of them afterwards. In the spring or summer of 1849 they took up their dead that were buried in the Indian village and prepared to leave Holland for the northern part of Michigan on the west side of Traverse Bay. They went in their mackinaw boats. Rev. Smith and his family soon prepared to follow them to Grand Traverse. It seemed then as great an undertaking as going to China or Japan now. They came and stayed a week with us, waiting for a vessel to come from Chicago to take them to their distant home. A schooner, named the *Merrill*, came after much delay. When their goods were all on board and the wind was favorable, they prepared to go. Rev. Isaac N. Wykoff, of Albany, New York, was visiting at Rev. van Raalte's and he with Rev. and Mrs. van Raalte, Henry D. Post, and myself accompanied them as far as Lake Michigan. Before parting prayer was offered and a hymn sung. We bade them farewell and returned to Holland in a small boat, while they proceeded on their journey.

As I look back to my first meeting with Van Raalte – he looked so young with no beard – and recall the striking incidents of that time and each successive year, the faces that were familiar and have passed away now, the changes and progress and improvements down to the present day, it seems to my mind a wonderful panorama.

It was in the winter of 1847 that Van Raalte first visited this tract of land where our city now stands. I have been told by a person who was with him when he first looked at the land that he knelt down in the snow and prayed for guidance and direction from above.

Let us look for a moment at the prospect before him. The ground was covered not only with snow, but with a most magnificent growth of forest trees of immense size – sugar-maple, oak, hemlock, a great variety, several of them six feet in diameter. The people who had come with the dominie [as we called him then] knew nothing about chopping down these great trees. They were store-keepers, carpenters, tailors, gold-smiths, shoemakers, and builders of windmills; and when I asked my near neighbor his vocation, he replied, "*bosselmaker*" [borstelmaker], meaning brushmaker.

The dominie knew the character of his people, knew they were active, steady, persevering, and that they could learn. They also were actuated by the same motive which had brought their leader here. So the beautiful forest did not deter him from his purpose. He came not to this wilderness to seek his own, or to secure any possible worldly advantage. The motive that brought him here was a noble one – that they might enjoy more religious freedom. It was on the occasion of the marriage of his son that the dominie at the wedding feast related among other reminiscences that when the bridegroom was an infant he, the dominie, had been thrown into prison for preaching contrary to the law. He had chosen America as the land of his adoption because here he could enjoy perfect religious freedom. There were great trials and privations to be endured, but in the darkest hour he seemed to see with prophetic eye the future success of his labors. I have heard him say when we were passing through the darkest days, "If my head were laid low, the place would still go on. My work can not be in vain, because I have built in faith." His wife was a noble helpmate, worthy of a place in history along with him. The remembrance of home and kindred often intruded itself and Mrs. van Raalte often spoke of the trial of leaving early and well-remembered friends, but she always added, "It is the Lord."

A volume could easily be filled with reminiscences of those early days, but a glance must suffice to show the contrast between our privileges now and those enjoyed by the early settlers. Our mail in those days came only once a week on Thursday afternoon. How eagerly we watched for *Vrouw* Willem Notting to come with the mailbag on her back. Her husband would go to Manlius in Allegan County and bring the bag on his back to his home in Graafschap. He would be tired out. His good wife would them bring it the last three miles to Holland. I frequently assisted my husband, who was postmaster, in opening and making up the mail in those days. There were not as many love letters written then, for the postage was higher. As yet we had no roads. Now the mail comes every few hours, but we do hardly appreciate it as much as when it came only once a week.

I cannot refrain from alluding to our system of lighting at that time. We used the tallow candle. My husband thought I must learn to make mold-candles, so in one of his journeys to Allegan he purchased some candle molds. I filled it in good orthodox order, a wick in the centre and then full of hot tallow. I put them out doors against a large tree close by the door. Very soon I heard the rustling of leaves and I ran to the door just in time to see a hungry-looking Indian dog jumping over logs and brush with the candle molds and candles in his mouth. He ran so fast that it was useless to think of pursuing him and I was left to meditate on the light that failed.

The supply of milk for the family seems a trifling thing now, but in those days it involved a good deal of labor. Our milkman was a milk-woman. We did not have the cow brought to the door and milked in our presence, but good *Vrouw* Arends brought the milk in pails, which hung from a yoke carried across her shoulders. I would say: "Good morning, *Vrouw* Arends, are you well?" and she, while dipping out my supply of milk, would respond to my inquiry thus, "Beter hoeft het niet te wezen," meaning it need not be any better, but it was better after a while, for she got a horse and wagon.

It was at the quarter-centennial anniversary of this settlement in 1872, that Dr. van Raalte paid a tribute to the citizens of the United States who received and aided the colonists. Among the names he mentioned were General Lewis Cass, Dr. Isaac Wyckoff of Albany, Judge John R. Kellogg of Allegan, and many more names I have forgotten. But it was General Robert Stuart of Detroit who first directed his attention to the present location. Van Raalte's object was to secure a site for a society of religious people, which should form a centre of education and religion.

The first church services were held in the open air. It was a place near where the old Van Raalte home still stands; a place cleared by falling trees and forming a hollow square. This was in May 1847. In the autumn of that year the first church was built in the village. The log church was where Pilgrim Home Cemetery now is.

One aim of the Dutch emigrant was education, step by step from our public school to the Academy, now Hope College, which has a name and a place among the colleges of our land. Van Raalte had noble helpers, but to him belongs the honor of laying the foundation. As I write the names of Dr. Philip Phelps, Hope's first president, Dr. Abel T. Stewart, Dr. T. Romeyn Beck, Dr. Charles Scott, all faithful men who have passed away.

As I recall the incidents of those early days, it seems like the stories of the original settlement at Plymouth – the voyage across the sea, the forest life, the great sickness and privation of those days, the religious zeal and strong faith of those Dutch pilgrims. Hope College and Theological Seminary crown the educational system which is the outgrowth of their religious faith. The first lecture ever delivered here was by Dr. Philip Phelps and his subject was "Omens, Signs, Auguries, or Prognostications." It was interesting and deserves mention as being the first of a series given under the auspices of the Fraternal Society of Hope College.

And now, the wilderness has been made to blossom like the rose and a change has been wrought which at first thought seemed impossible. Let us not forget that these people were Christians, that they trusted in One who heard and answered their prayers. They brought their religion overseas with them. I remember the first morning after my arrival hearing from the little loghouses all around us the singing of psalms and on inquiry was told it was the beautiful custom to sing after each meal or before it.

We have taken a hasty glance at Holland as it was in the beginning of our history, when paths not deserving the same of roads winding through the thick forest among trees and over logs led among the scattered huts, some built of logs, some of boards, and some of boughs and bark. I remember going to see a sick person and noticed that the bedstead upon which he lay was made of twigs of a tree with the bark on them.

We were at that time surrounded on all sides by an unbroken forest, isolating us as completely from the world outside as if we were on an island in the ocean. How different is the picture as we now see it: our city surrounding; our fine bay; numerous vessels and steamers engaged in a lucrative trade with the great shipping centres; railroads diverging in many different directions; telegraph lines giving us the means of sending messages which contrast strongly with good *Vrouw* Notting's weekly mail; our shops and factories giving employment to a large and increasing population; our beautiful streets lighted with electricity and lined with well-constructed buildings; our many pleasant homes, our churches, and our schoolhouses – all of these go to make up our Holland of today. Someone has said and truly, "Holland owes her proud position today, by God's blessing, to the careful and successful labors of those to whom the great work of organizing and shaping the growth of the new settlement was committed."

Van Raalte was spared to see his labors crowned with success. The people who came with him from the fatherland were blessed with high educational advantages; they were prosperous in their enterprises, comfortable in their homes, and respected as worthy citizens of their adopted country.

Contemplation of this subject for a few moments is well calculated to fill our hearts with gratitude to Him who has so blessed and prospered us in the past that we can safely trust the future in the hands of Him who has brought us thus far and so signally blessed us in spiritual as well as temporal things. Many congregations in our Western States owe their existence under Providence to this important centre. How many ministers of the Gospel and teachers have gone from among us and are now laboring in distant lands. In China, Japan, Arabia, and India are noble workers among the heathen whose names are familiar to us all. Here in our College a few years ago several native Japanese were educated. They were baptized and became members of Hope Church [the Second Reformed Church in Holland] and afterwards returned to their native land to spread the gospel among their own people. These influences have earthly limit, but spread wider and wider until the final result can only be known in eternity. The event of Van Raalte and his people settling in this locality in 1847 has had a great influence upon the history of our country in general, sufficient to warrant my choosing this subject and calling it "A History-Making Event".

Chapter XII

LIFE DURING THE EARLY DAYS OF THE DUTCH SETTLEMENT

52. MRS. CORNELIA SCHADDELEE'S
HISTORICAL RECOLLECTIONS

[Daughter of Jan Slag who arrived in Holland on July 4, 1847, Mrs. Cornelia Schaddelee lived in Holland all her life. Her *Historical Recollections*, especially concerned with the earliest history of Holland, appeared in *De Grondwet*, May 2, 1911.]

In *De Grondwet* are published a series of historical compilations, bearing upon the early days of the settlement of the Hollanders in Michigan, and it is my desire to add a few personal observations and experiences. In doing so I am fully convinced that it was the Lord who did encourage the pioneers, and gave wisdom to the leaders for such a gigantic undertaking of bringing a poor people [for poor they were, with perhaps a few exceptions] into the wild forests of Western Michigan.

It was in many instances no small affair for parents with a large family of children to come here under such circumstances. Many of them died and were buried on the shores of Lake Michigan and Black Lake. They were the first sacrifices of what was to follow, by reason of the malarial atmosphere of those early days. Still, these casualties always will happen when there is immigration on a large scale.

The people, as well as their great leader, the Rev. Albertus C. van Raalte, whom the people in general looked upon as father and counsellor, were unitedly full of courage, with a hope for the future that their labor should not be in vain and that they should finally succeed in reclaiming these dense forests into a fruitful landscape.

Did they succeed, many a reader will ask? Yes, and their hope and expectations have not been in vain. The children of these *stoere* pioneers are deriving the abundant benefits from this undertaking. Many of them are prosperous and independent farmers, while others are well-to-do in manufacturing or mercantile business.

Although but a young girl during the period of this early pioneer life, I have been personally identified with the experience, struggles, and adversities our parents, neighbors, and friends had to endure and to contend with. I also remember well the many prayers sent up to God in the family circle, and by the Christian people when assembled together, either in the open air or in their log church. In both these cases they petitioned their heavenly Father, under whose protection they were, to help and encourage them from day to day.

And when I think of the sufferings and privations we had to endure in these first years, and how God graciously has protected these first families with the many children, I have reason to say with the psalmist of old, "Bless the Lord, O my soul, and all that is within me, bless His holy name." [Psalms 103, 1].

It was on July 4, 1847 that the family of Jan Slag, consisting of father, mother, and eight children, besides an aged uncle and aunt, arrived on the sailing ship, *De Snelheid* of Amsterdam, Captain Gorter, at the port of New York, and today I am the only surviving member of that large family. We went direct from New York to the projected Holland Colony in Michigan. Arriving at Chicago, a little schooner was to transport our family and that of Jacob van der Veen across Lake Michigan, a distance of 110 miles, to Black River, now called Macatawa. Arriving there our little craft could not get into the so-called harbor, as the entrance was barred up with sand, and the schooner therefore anchored near the beach. But suddenly and without warning there arose a storm from the northwest, so that the captain found it necessary at once to get away with his ship from the beach. With all possible speed and hurry chests, trunks, and baggage, passengers and all, were placed in a yawl and rowed toward the beach; but as the waves were making fast the yawl could not get near enough to the beach to discharge her cargo, and the chests and baggage were thrown in the water and the children carried ashore on the shoulders of the sailors. There we stood, on the shore of Lake Michigan, 4,500 miles away from the motherland, with no other covering over our heads than the blue sky above, and still six miles from our destination. How to get there, was the question. The sun was going down, and night was upon us. The children became sleepy. On the beach were boards lying at random. These the menfolk gathered up, and constructed a kind of protection against the cool night air, behind which we laid the children down to sleep.

At midnight we heard a loud voice, calling out that they were ready to transport immigrants to Holland. The conveyance was an open flatboat, propelled by two men, with long poles. We went on board, and in the morning arrived at the head of Black Lake, near where the Scott and Lugers lumberyard is now located, and landed there.

All that was to be seen was a few booths, constructed of sticks driven into the ground, and branches of trees overhead, in which a few families lodged for the time being. Our family could find no shelter and were obliged to make a similar booth. Soon the womanfolk set up a howl, when they discovered squids creeping up their limbs. The different families managed to keep a campfire going night and day, to serve as a beacon during the night for other immigrants who might arrive, and also to ward off wild beasts.

The womanfolk of the two families deemed it advisable that their husbands should go to the village, to rent two dwellings, if possible of two stories. In the meantime they, the women, were to attire themselves so as to be ready when their husbands returned to go and view the houses they thought to occupy. Upon their return they reported: 1st, that there was no village with any dwellings to be seen, except a few log cabins; 2nd, that there were no eatables to be bought, because there were none; 3rd, that in following an Indian trail through the woods, they came at last to a spot where Van Raalte and his family lived in a little log cabin.

After listening to this report, some of the little band commenced to cry, while others cheered them up. Soon we provided ourselves with somewhat of a more permanent shelter for the time being.

My father and two of my elder brothers were ship carpenters, and father having some means to buy building material with, they went to Saugatuck, eight miles south of the harbor, to make their purchases. The reader might ask: how did they bring that lumber and other building material from there to Holland? They made a raft of boards, piling them crosswise and, in this way, with a line fastened to the raft they pulled it along the shore of Lake Michigan and thence to Holland.

But how about cooking, in the absence of stoves and other utensils? I will tell you. Two stakes were driven in the ground, about six feet apart, with a crosspiece, and a chain with kettle and pot, or both for that matter, and a hole in the ground to serve as an ashpot. In this way our parents managed the housekeeping. Soap for washing purposes was made of wood ashes.

And now as to our first Sunday here in the woods of Michigan. The church we attended was on Van Raalte's premises. The path leading thereto was an Indian trail. The building itself was the open air, with the blue skies as cover. The pulpit was a box, on which the speaker stood, and the seats for the audience were felled trees. The sermon on this occasion made a deep and lasting impression upon young and old. We were told that it was the directing hand of God that had brought us here, that our Heavenly Father would safely guide us further and keep us under His protection and care.

Of the first arrivals several died. My father made many coffins, not so elegant as they are now made. The material at hand dit not admit this. A few boards, taken out of the water, was all that could be obtained. No charges for the coffins were made. The people at that time tried to help each other as much as they could. Nearly our whole family soon became sick with malarial fever, of which my uncle and aunt died. The rest, by the mercy of God, soon became better again.

The first winter was very mild, and this was also a special blessing from our God. In the fall of 1847, and during that mild winter, father and my elder brothers commenced to put up a large frame building, and in the spring of 1848 our family occupied it, partly as a dwelling and partly as a general store.

For our large family of boys and girls our parents had provided abundant wearing apparel, bedding, and clothing, and other necessary articles, all of which they had brought with them from the Old Country. When we commenced to unpack the several chests and trunks it was amusing to see the Indians, who happened to pass by from their village, a little ways west from us. The women folk, with their papooses on their back, looked at our goods, and laughed, and seemed to enjoy themselves greatly.

Soon thereafter our store was opened. The Indians came nearly every day to buy something. They were good customers, and very honest. On one occasion mother gave them a cup of coffee, with a piece of bread. They were sitting around the fire, and occasionally would throw a few crumbs of bread into the fire, and then laugh. They seemed to enjoy themselves, and we thought those performances were a part of their religion, which of course we could not understand. These Indians were a good-hearted people, and never molested any of us. They always liked to talk with father, whom they called "the old gentleman." Once they brought him a piece of plug tobacco, rolled in a nice silk handkerchief. They were very good neighbors to us.

The second year, 1848, father bought two waterfront lots where the Chicago boat landing is now located, with the intention of establishing a ship wharf there. Soon thereafter, with my two oldest brothers, they laid the keel for a coaster – a small vessel intended for the coasting trade. When it was finished the Americans that lived here baptised it *The Flying Dutchman*, by reason of its speed. In the course of time several other and larger vessels were built there. Some years later, in the sixties, there was also laid the keel of what was intended to be a missionary ship, but the project was too visionary and never got any further than the keel.

In the fall of 1847 the people commenced to build a church of logs, at the southwest corner of the churchyard now called Pilgrim's Home Cemetery. The way to get there was not on a cement sidewalk. The road lay partly through low ground, and trees were chopped down and laid lengthwise along the so-called road. Over those trees, people who went to church had to walk single file. The young folk of those days, the girls included, soon practiced to jump over those logs as swift as a squirrel. Sometimes it happened that a deer jumped right in front of us going in a different direction.

In those early days there was much sickness and many died. In some instances death carried off both parents, leaving their orphan children pitiful circumstances. These however were kindly provided for in private families. But as the number of these orphans increased it was deemed best to erect an orphan house, and one Sunday morning Van Raalte suggested to his congregation to open a subscription list at once for that purpose, and invited every one present to come forward to his pulpit and subscribe as much as each one would give toward erecting such a building. The writer, a girl of fifteen at that time, also went forward and told the dominie, "money I have not, but I have gold earrings and other jewelry at home, which is new and has never been worn." The answer of the dominie was, "Yes, my child, such a gift is very much appreciated and welcome." When I came home from church I told my sisters what I had done, and they also were willing to give their jewelry for such a good cause. The next day, Monday, Van Raalte came to our house, as he often did to see mother, who suffered with rheumatism, and in his conversation with mother, he said, "*Moedertje*, I have come to collect the jewelry of your girls, which they subscribed toward erecting an orphan building."

Mother was taken by surprise and said that these ornaments did not belong to the children, but to their parents, and that the children were as yet too young to dispose of the same. But the dominie answered that mother should view it as a blessing that the Lord put this willingness into the hearts of the girls to give away needless ornaments for necessary use as an offering to the Lord. All contradiction came to an end and the dominie received the new gold earrings and other ornaments. With this example of charity Van Raalte went to others for the same purpose. Although that orphan house was erected it has never been used for that purpose. The number of orphans not increasing to any extent, they were all placed in private families.

As I review that past I cannot but observe the guiding hand of our heavenly Father and how he has graciously guided us through the trying period of our early colonial life, and in closing this collection of historical reminiscenses I would exclaim with the poet of old, "Bless the Lord, O my soul, and all that is within me, bless His holy name." [Psalms 103, 1].

53. REIJER VAN ZWALUWENBURG'S LIFE SKETCH

[Born in 1832 Reijer van Zwaluwenburg in 1850 left Kleine Musschard in Gelderland, and established himself, with his parents, brothers, and sisters south of Holland, Michigan. His *Levenschets* printed in *De Grondwet*, May 30, 1911 presents an accurate picture of pioneer conditions among the Duth settlers from 1850. The author died in Holland, Michigan, September 15, 1913.]

Omstreeks het jaar 1813 ging er een bevel uit van Napoleon I die destijds heerscher was over Nederland, dat de mannelijke oudste van elk geslacht een tweede naam, of, zooals dat toen genoemd werd, een *van* moest opgeven. Voor dien tijd was het voldoende, dat men van elk kind dat geboren werd, aangifte deed aan het gemeentehuis; dan werd de datum van de geboorte en de naam opgeschreven in het gemeenteboek, en als tweede naam kreeg het kind de naam van den vader. Zoo staat b.v. mijn grootvader aangeschreven te Oldebroek, Nederland, als Reijer Aartzoon, zijn broeder als Willem Aartzoon en hun vader als Aart Reijerzoon; en mijn vader die in 1802 geboren werd weder als Aart Reijerzoon. Toen de nieuwe inschrijving kwam gaf Willem Aartzoon, die toen de oudste was van de familie, den naam op van Willem van Zwaluwenburg „omdat de familie toen op Zwaluwenburg woonde". Zwaluwenburg was in dien tijd een beroemde heerlijkheid met verscheidene welbebouwde en vruchtbare boerderijen die er toe behoorden. Bij mijn geboorte in 1832 werd mijn naam niet meer opgeschreven als Reijer Aartzoon, maar als Reijer van Zwaluwenburg.

Nu iets over ons verhuizen naar Amerika en de eerste jaren hier. Den 16den Mei 1850 zijn wij vertrokken van de Kleine Musschard, provincie Gelderland, naar Michigan, Noord Amerika. Dat is, vader en onze tweede moeder en hun kind, 1 jaar oud en vijf broeders en zusters: de schrijver dezes, 18 jaren oud; mijn zuster Lubbigje, 16; Hendrikje, 14; broeder Gerrit, 10; en broeder Jacob, 7 jaren oud.

Wij zijn per as van huis naar Harderwijk gegaan en vervolgens met een veerschip naar Amsterdam en met den trein naar Rotterdam. Daar hebben wij twee weken moeten wachten, omdat ons schip niet klaar was; van daar naar Hellevoetsluis. Wij hadden maar een klein schip, 12 zeelieden in al. De eerste nacht op de Noord Zee was het aardig ruw. In het Engelsche Kanaal was het schoon weder. De eerste twee weken op zee hadden we veel storm en zeeziekte, maar geen ongelukken.

Na een lange reis van 52 dagen op zee kwamen wij in het laatst van Juli te New York aan. Van daar per stoomboot naar Albany; tien dagen op de kanaalboot naar Buffalo; met de stoomboot naar Detroit; met den trein naar New Buffalo, Michigan; met de stoomboot naar Chicago; met een zeilschip naar de mond van Black Lake; en eindelijk per platboot naar Groningen, Michigan.

Westelijk Michigan was toen nog al bosch. Rev. A. C. van Raalte's Kolonie was gevestigd in Ottawa en Allegan counties. In 1847 waren de eerste Hollanders daar gekomen en de Indianen hadden hunne kampen waar nu de stad Holland is; er was toen alhier geen bebouwbaar land. Toen wij kwamen, drie jaren later, waren de Indianen meestal vertrokken en was men al begonnen met het land schoon te maken. In Nederland hadden wij gehoord van Van Raalte's Kolonie. Vader had twee brieven gehad van een vriend dien toen te Groningen werkte; anders wisten wij niets van Amerika af en zoodoende kwamen wij rechtstreeks naar Groningen.

Dikwijls denk ik nog aan die eerste ontmoeting daar te Groningen en de groote vooruitgang die er sedert dien gemaakt is. Daar, een weinig over de brug van het nu oude Groninger kerkhof, zagen wij vader Veneklaasen met zijn zoon, de blauwe overalls opgerold tot over de knieën. Zij stonden in de klei met een schop in de hand en als het ware met handen en voeten de klei bewerkende om er steen van te bakken. Zij waren in Nederland steenbakkers geweest en dit was het begin van de groote steenbakkerij, die hoofdzakelijk door den zoon, Berend Jan, is uitgebreid en nu voortgezet wordt door de gebroeders Veneklaasen, kleinzonen van dien vader Veneklaasen.

De eerste settlers waren hier al drie jaren geweest. Velen waren gestorven door ontberingen, daar er geen huizen waren en geen voedsel; en ook door de Michigan koortsen, die in dien tijd hier zoo algemeen waren. Anderen, die wat geld hadden medegebracht, hadden land gekocht en geleefd, doch weinig of niets gemaakt en moesten om wat eten te hebben naar de omliggende plaatsen, ten einde iets te verdienen – naar Grand Rapids, Kalamazoo, Singapore of Grand Haven. Sommigen gingen alleen en lieten vrouw en kinderen op het land, anderen gingen daar wonen. In dien tijd was het nog niet zoo zeker, dat de strijd die er begonnen was tegen die groote wouden, een strijd zou zijn van overwinning. Hier en daar waren enkele akkers omgehakt en een loghuisje gebouwd. Doch wat een woesternij! Haast geen wegen, meest paden door de bosschen kenbaar door blessen aan de boomen. Het omhakken der boomen was nog niet zoo erg – dat kostte van drie tot vier dollars per akker; maar al die boomen op te branden – dat kostte van acht tot tien dollars per akker, hoewel de meesten dat zelf deden. In het voorjaar, zoo spoedig als het maar wat droog was, begon men te branden, ten einde nog een of twee akkers schoon te maken om corn in te planten. In den zomer op nieuw aan het branden, om in den herfst tarwe te zaaien. De takken te verbranden was niet zoo erg, maar die dikke harde boomen twee of driemaal door te hakken, om ze bij elkander te rollen om zoo te kunnen verbranden [want alleen wilden ze niet branden], en dat in den heeten zomer – dat was hard werk. En dan had men nog al die stompen en wortels; men kon geen tien voet rechtuit ploegen of de ossen stonden stil en wij moesten de ploeg los maken uit de wortels. Dikwijls denk ik nog aan die eerste jaren.

Gelukkig voor ons waren wij zoover altijd vrij gezond geweest. Sommigen echter waren wel wat zeeziek geweest en het was aan hen te zien, dat zij zeer vermoeid waren van de lange reis. Zoowat drie weken waren wij hier en toen kregen wij koortsen en na enkele dagen meer, kregen wij allen de koorts, „de Michigan koorts", die er veel heerschte. Moeder heeft dagen gelegen, dat wij dachten elken dag de laatste te zijn. Vader had vier of vijf maal de koorts en toen werd hij slaperig; wij moesten hem wakker maken, anders sliep hij maar door. Na een of twee dagen gelegen te hebben, konden wij hem niet weder wakker krijgen en 's avonds stierf hij. Twee weken daarna stierf mijn halfbroeder, anders zoo'n gezond kind van bijna twee jaar oud. En twee maanden daarna stierf tante, vrouw van den Berg, vader's zuster, nalatende drie weezen. Van dien tijd af tot aan het volgende voorjaar hadden wij gedurig koorts.

Toen vader stierf, hadden wij $ 400 en volgens vader's plan en dat van zijn vriend, die vader's raadsman was, hebben wij 40 akkers land gekocht, dicht bosch, en daar een huis op gebouwd. Omstreeks November gingen we daarin wonen, op Nederlandsche wijze zonder kachel, maar met een vuurplaats en bakoven. Gelukkig was het dien winter een zachte winter. Het broodbakken ging zeer gebrekkig. Van November tot Mei hadden wij een barrel flour gehad, overigens korenmeel [in water gebakken, zonder het te rijzen] en aardappelen en een weinig spek.

Omstreeks Maart trouwde moeder weder. Wij hadden onze zinnen er op gezet om bij elkander te blijven en ons home te behouden, maar toen het voorjaar werd zagen wij wel dat het niet kon. Ons geld was op, onze kleederen waren versleten en daar was in onze omgeving niets te verdienen. Had ik werk kunnen krijgen, of wat kunnen verdienen, dan had ik dat gedaan, maar daar was toen niets te verdienen in de Kolonie.

Om dezen tijd kregen wij schrijven uit Nederland van oom K. Stange, dat als wij terug wilden komen, hij ons de reiskosten wilde sturen; dan konden wij daar bij de familie wezen. Maar wij hadden al veel gehoord wat een goed land het hier was om geld te verdienen, en wel wetende wat het in Nederland was bij de familie, hebben wij allen daar hartelijk voor bedankt.

In Mei ging mijn oudste zuster dienen te Grand Rapids; nu waren wij met ons vieren. Ik had gedurende den winter wat boomen gekapt en plantte tusschen de loggen in wat corn en aardappelen, maar er waren dat voorjaar zooveel eekhoorns, dat toen ik ging zien of het corn ook groeide ik maar twee plantjes vinden kon; de eekhoorns hadden al het zaadcorn uit den grond gehaald. Dat deed ons besluiten om op te breken.

In die dagen waren er veel kinderen in de Kolonie, die hun vader en moeder door den dood verloren hadden, en dan werden gewoonlijk die weezen opgenomen door menschen, die ze verzorgden tot dat wij 16 of 18 jaar oud waren. Zoo waren ook de kinderen van tante van den Berg opgenomen, maar daar konden wij niet aan denken – wij wilden onszelven vrij houden en onafhankelijk blijven. Ik weet ook niet dat wij ooit een cent gehad hebben, waar wij niet voor betaald hebben.

Bij dezen tijd was ik 19 jaren oud geworden en daar ik de oudste was en de eenige die wat helpen kon, zoo rustte thans alles op mij. Nu waren er wel die ons raad wilden geven en daar wilde ik ook wel naar hooren, maar raad was niet genoeg; wij moesten geld verdienen, en zoo zijn wij uit elkander gegaan, eerst met de gedachte om naderhand weder samen te komen, maar dat is nooit gebeurd.

Mijn jongste zuster, die altijd nog ziekelijk was, kwam bij een buur. Daar zou zij de kost verdienen en ik zou zorgen voor kleeren en school-boeken. Mijn jongste broeder liet ik bij moeder en betaalde haar twee dollars in de maand kost. Dit was wel niet veel, maar voor hen een groote hulp. Ik moest werk gaan zoeken bij wat men toen noemde „Engelschen", want bij de Hollanders was niets te verdienen; ze hadden wel werk maar geen geld. Mijn broer Gerrit, die toen elf jaren oud was, en ik, en een goede vriend, Jan de Vries, [vader van Dr. Bernard de Vries, van Holland], die wat Engelsch kon spreken, gingen op reis van Groningen naar Singapore en van daar nog vijf mijlen verder, wat men nu noemt New Richmond. Daar bleven wij overnacht. 's Morgens moest ik 50 cents betalen voor ons beiden. Ik had maar 35 cents en moest vragen om mij te borgen voor 15 cents. Wij gingen een mijl verder en kwamen bij Mr. Mann, in Manlius. Die had een kleine zaagmolen en had werk voor mij. Onze vriend verhuurde mij voor $ 10 in de maand; broer Gerrit ver-huurde hij bij een buurman voor kost en kleeding en ging toen weder terug naar huis. Zoo waren wij daar; konden geen woord Engelsch verstaan en nog minder spreken.

Toen het avond werd, riep Mr. Mann mij. Hij had twee blikken emmers in de eene hand en met de andere hand wees hij naar de koeien, die wij konden zien grazen in de weide. Ik wist wat dat beteekende, nam de emmers en ging de koeien melken. Telkens als hij mij werk bestelde, moest hij altijd mee om het mij te wijzen. Ik had 's avonds niets om mij bezig te houden en ging maar vroeg naar bed, en kon 's morgens gemakkelijk, zonder geroepen te worden opstaan. De eerste morgen toen Mr. Mann opstond en mij dacht te roepen, had ik de vier koeien al gemolken; dat was goed naar zijn zin.

's Avonds en Zondags waren broer Gerrit en ik altijd bij elkander. Toen kon ik er wat van verstaan wat het is om alleen in de wereld te zijn, zonder een tehuis. Veel dacht ik er over na, of er geen andere gelegenheid voor ons was, maar er was naar mijn oordeel geen andere weg open om een eerlijk bestaan te vinden.

Mr. Mann en zijne vrouw waren zeer goed voor mij. Mijn werk was niet zwaar en al spoedig werd het wat beter. Ik werd wat bekend met mijn werk en de omgeving en ook met de taal. Toen ik er een maand geweest was, betaalde Mr. Mann mij $ 10. Wat was ik rijk! In Nederland was dat 25 gulden en moest ik er een half jaar voor werken. Ik vroeg Mr. Mann om drie of vier dagen verlof. Dat kregen wij zonder moeite en gingen naar de Kolonie.

Onze reis was door de bosschen, te voet 26 mijlen, en wij hadden een dag noodig om dat te loopen. Ik ging eerst mijn 15 cents schuld betalen. Moeder betaalde ik twee maanden kostgeld voor mijn jongste broertje en kocht wat kleeren voor hem en voor mijn jongste zuster en mijzelven. Er was plaats genoeg voor mijn 10 dollars. Ik had dan ook niet veel over toen wij terug gingen, maar wij gevoelden ons zoo blijde en opgeruimd en dachten dat wij al heel wat Amerikaansch waren geworden. En zoo kwamen wij terug te Manlius.

Ik had het er zeer goed; vader en moeder hadden niet beter voor mij kunnen wezen. Mijn werk was niet zwaar – de vrouwen in huis helpen, in de schuur en vier koeien melken. Maar de Zondagen waren er zoo lang; wij waren gewoon 's Zondags naar de kerk te gaan. Dat was mij een bijzonder genot geweest; en hier was geen kerk. Toen wij er twee of drie Zondagen geweest waren, zeide Mrs. Mann dat er in het schoolhuis gepredikt zou worden. Wij gingen daar heen; ik kon er niets van verstaan dan enkele woorden, zooals Jezus en Jeruzalem en dat was mij toch zoo aangenaam, dat ik kon mijn tranen niet weerhouden. Dat er in deze streek geen kerk was, was mede een van de reden dat wij al spoedig van daar naar Kalamazoo gingen, alwaar eene Hollandsche gemeente was.

Bij Mr. Mann was ons eerste tehuis in dit land. Zuster Lubbigje, die te Grand Rapids werkte, kwam het volgende jaar ook bij Mr. Mann; zuster Hendrikje ook; en nadien is broer Jacob er ook geweest.

De eerste twee jaren hadden wij alles gemeen; nadat wij ouder werden, zorgde elk meer voor zichzelven.

In het voorjaar van 1852 ben ik naar Kalamazoo gegaan en vond daar eene Hollandsch sprekende Gereformeerde gemeente. Die zomer werkte ik aan de steenbakkerij. Den volgenden winter heb ik weder in Manlius gewerkt en pijn loggen gemaakt. Bij dezen tijd was ik wat Amerikaansch geworden, en, gelijk vele jonge menschen, altijd uitziende naar wat beters. Er waren twee huisgezinnen in Holland, Michigan, met wien ik kennis gemaakt had, die uit Galena, Illinois, gekomen waren en daar het hun in Holland niet beviel, weder terug gingen. Die vrienden hadden niet veel moeite om mij te overtuigen, dat het voor mij daar ook beter was. In Augustus 1853 gingen wij op reis met de boot naar Chicago; van daar met de trein naar Freeport, dan 50 mijlen met de wagen naar Galena.

's Avonds kwamen wij te Freeport aan en moesten in het hotel blijven. Ik voelde in mijn zak en mijn geldbeurs was er niet. Die had ik op den trein verloren. Hier was ik in een vreemde plaats en geen cent in mijn bezit; maar die bekenden hebben voor mij betaald. Ik had wel niet veel geld verloren; toch zooveel dat, als het mij niet beviel, ik weder in Michigan had kunnen komen; en nu moest ik er blijven tot dat ik zooveel verdiend had. Hier heb ik zeven maanden in een store gewerkt, als hulp-klerk, maar het beviel mij daar niet. In Maart was ik weder te Kalamazoo. Mijne financieele zaken waren wel niet verbeterd, maar ik had veel geleerd. Te Kalamazoo heb ik toen een jaar en een half gewerkt aan de ijzergieterij.

Ik had al lang begeerte gehad om belijdenis te doen en mij nader te verbinden aan Gods gemeente, doch persoonlijke bezwaren hadden mij terug gehouden. Nu werd de begeerte zoo sterk dat ik belijdenis deed en toegelaten werd in volle gemeenschap. Ik werd dan ook zeer versterkt in het geloof van onzen Verbonds God en in de gemeenschap der heiligen.

Nu was het zoo geheel mijn begeerte en streven om zelf een home te hebben, en om deze tijd dacht het mij, het zoude wel goed voor mij zijn, als ik mij wat vaster nederzette. Ik was al hier en daar geweest en wat bekend geworden met handel, maar ik dacht daar had ik geen aanleg voor. Zoo was dan boer worden voor mij het beste. In de bosschen in de

Hollandsche Kolonie was het land goedkoop en het was ook zoo mijn verlangen om te leven in de nabijheid van een Hollandsche kerk. Om van die dichte reuzen wouden echter een boerderij te maken, was gemakkelijker gezegd dan gedaan. Harden arbeid was ik niet bang voor.

In dien tijd waren er verscheidene Hollandsche meisjes die in Kalamazoo dienden bij de Engelschen en die even als ik, ook wel een home wilden hebben. Zoo was het mijn geluk, dat ik zonder veel moeite en zoo geheel volgens mijn keuze, een meisje vond, Sara Kools, die het met mij waagde. Nu was het in dien tijd niet zoo als nu, dat men eerst een goed huis en wel gemeubeld moet klaar hebben, eer men een meisje durfde vragen om te trouwen. Daar werd niet eens over gesproken. Wij hadden ieder zoowat evenveel – en dat was niet veel. Wij waren beiden nog jong: mijn aanstaande was 19 jaren en ik 23. Zij was op dertienjarige leeftijd in Amerika gekomen met haar vader, Abraham Kools, een broeder en drie zusters. Zij kwam met $ 24 schuld. Het eerste jaar was zij tehuis; het tweede jaar verdiende zij 50 cents per week en het laatste jaar $ 1.26 per week. Zij had daarvan in dien tijd haar schuld betaald en geld genoeg over om haar eigen bruiloftskleederen te koopen – een bewijs van Hollandsche nijverheid, eerlijkheid en zuinigheid. Wij zijn 's Zondags avonds in de kerk te Kalamazoo door Ds. Wijnand Gardenier – de vader van Kolonel Gardener, – getrouwd, den 4den November 1855. Den volgenden Maandagmorgen gingen wij op reis naar Holland, een reis van twee dagen , met een lumber wagen, met maar eene zitting. Mijn vrouw en ik moesten op onze kist zitten.

Het eerste jaar werkte ik voor M. D. Howard; in den winter loggen uit het bosch halen en in den zomer aan den zaagmolen. Aldaar bij die zaagmolen is ons eerste kind Alice geboren. In den herfst van dat jaar hebben wij 80 akkers land gekocht, in section 16, Fillmore Township, allemaal bosch. Eerst wat boomen omgehakt en toen midden in het bosch, een mijl van de naaste buur, een blokhuisje gebouwd. Daar zijn wij in den herfst van 1856 gaan wonen, vier mijlen van kerk en store en post office en geen wegen. Enkele tijden van het jaar konden wij met de ossenwagen bij huis komen, doch de meeste tijd moesten wij wat wij noodig hadden op den rug dragen. Omdat het land laag was hadden wij boomen omgehakt daar wij over liepen, anders moesten wij door het water. Als wij samen naar de buren of naar „de stad" wilden, moesten wij te voet gaan en de baby dragen. Toen er twee babies waren, moesten wij er elk een dragen. Wij gingen naar het bosch wel met beider toestemming, toch was het wel wat hard voor mij dat ik mijn jonge vrouw in geen beter omstandigheden kon plaatsen. Maar wij dachten het kon

niet anders. Wij waren jong en gelukkig met elkander. Jezus zegt:
„Deze twee," dat is man en vrouw, „zullen een vleesch zijn," maar nu
zijn wij menschen nog zoo onvolmaakt, dat er tijd en ondervinding toe
noodig zijn om „een" te worden. Het ligt zoo in de natuur van onze
schepping, zoo als God ons geschapen heeft, dat de jonge jaren de beste
zijn, dat onze levens te zamen gevormd worden en zoo een worden.

Wat denk ik veel aan die tijden. Ik had niet anders te doen dan boomen
om te hakken en zoodoende een opening te krijgen, waardoor de zon ons
kon beschijnen. Er was in die dagen veel wild in de bosschen – herten
en wolven en enkele beeren, daar toen veel jacht op werd gemaakt.
Dikwijls hoorden wij de wolven enkele roeden van ons huis. Als mijn
broer Jacob wat laat van school tehuis kwam, hoorde hij ze vaak. Op
zekeren nacht hoorden wij een geweldig leven enkele roeden van huis.
In den morgen ging ik zien wat het geweest was en vond daar wat
beenderen van een hert dat de wolven verslonden hadden. Wanneer ik
's morgens vroeg naar buiten ging, zag ik dikwijls herten brousen waar ik
den vorigen dag boomen had omgehakt. Ik had een goede rifle en kon
wel een spreeuw uit den hoogsten boom schieten, maar in het herten
schieten had ik niet veel geluk; ik was te haastig en heb er maar een gekregen. Herten schieten moet ook geleerd worden en dat leert men,
door het veel te doen. Op zekeren dag was ik in het bosch op de jacht
en op eens was ik dicht bij een groot hert. Toen kreeg ik de „buck fever".
Misschien zult ge vragen, wat soort van koorts is dat? Laat ik u mijn
ondervinding mededeelen. Ik liep over een kleine heuvel aan de zijde
van een laagte en daar voor mij, enkele roeden van mij af, zag ik een
grooten buck grazen tusschen de takken van een omgewaaiden boom.
Ik dacht, als ik nu voorzichtig ben en raak hem op de rechte plaats, dan
is hij de mijne en legde de rifle aan tegen een boom. Ik stond iets hooger
dan het hert en meende de rifle voorzichtig te laten zakken en als het de
rechte hoogte bereikt had, dan te schieten. Ik had mijn gezicht goed aan
het geweer, maar zag zoo sterk op het hert en dacht niet aan mijn vinger
die begon te beven; en daar ging het geweer af, zoowat twee voet over
het hert heen. Zoover had het hert mij niet gezien, maar nu keek het op
en stond mij aan te zien. Ik wilde spoedig weder laden; het kruid kreeg
ik er goed in, maar mijne handen beefden zoo, dat ik de kogel er niet
goed in kreeg en hij bleef halfweg zitten. Ik was druk aan het stampen
met de laadstok en toen ging het hert heen. Ik ging naar huis en besloot,
dat herten schieten mijn werk niet was.

Bij eene andere gelegenheid had ik eene ontmoeting met een crane
roost, of rijger nesten. Het was een donkeren dag en ik was in een donker

hemlock bosch. Op eens hoorde ik een geweldig leven; ik had nooit zulk een leven gehoord. Ik had wel eens bij een wilde duiven roost geweest, alwaar er duizenden dicht bij elkander zijn en die ook een geducht leven maken, maar een crane roost had ik nooit aangetroffen. De oude rijgers kwamen om de jongen eten te brengen. Ik liep wat terug, maar dacht, als ik nu tehuis kom, dan kan ik niet eens zeggen waar ik bang voor geworden ben. Ik kon maar niet begrijpen waar dat leven vandaan kwam. Wolven waren het niet; een beer ook niet; Indianen konden het ook niet zijn. Ik had mijn rifle wel bij mij, maar ik was geen Nimrod genoeg om daarop te vertrouwen. Eindelijk besloot ik om te gaan onderzoeken. Ik ging niet ver of ik ontdekte dat het rumoer boven in de boomen was. Ik ging een weinigje verder en ziedaar, het waren rijgers! Twee of drie honderd rijgers kunnen al heel wat leven maken.

Op zekeren morgen zou mijn broer naar een van de buren gaan. Hij ging het bosch in, maar was spoedig terug en zeide dat er een beer in het bosch was. Ik zeide: „O, dat is geen waarheid, ge zijt bang geworden." Broer zeide: „Ga maar eens zien, zulke groote voetstappen in de losse sneeuw." Ik nam mijn rifle en ging, en jawel, daar dicht bij de clearing waren de groote sporen van zijn voeten – zoo groot als kleine paarden-hoeven – in de sneeuw. Ik volgde die op zoo lang als het licht was en ik de clearing kon zien, maar toen ik in het duistere bosch kwam en geen clearing meer kon zien, stond ik stil en dacht, als die beer eens van achter dien dikken boom kwam! Ik zag om, maar kon niets meer van de clearing zien en die groote voetstappen waren daar zoo duidelijk in de sneeuw. Ik wist goed dat het een beer was. Ik zag nogmaals vooruit; het scheen of het bosch meer duister werd. Ik dacht, laat de beer gaan, ik ga naar huis.

Het gebeurde eenmaal dat wij op een familiepartij waren, bij Harm Lucas. Hij woonde twee mijlen west van ons door het bosch, zonder pad; de weg rond over Graafschap was het vijf mijlen. 's Morgens waren wij die vijf mijlen te voet gegaan. Onze baby, die toen een jaar oud was, hadden wij gedragen en waren voornemens om des avonds door het bosch terug te komen. Ik was in dat bosch wel bekend en zoolang ik de boomen kon zien wist ik goed waar wij waren; maar het was wat later geworden als wij gedacht hadden en toen wij iets meer dan een mijl in het bosch waren, werd het zoo duister, dat wij geen boom meer konden zien. Nu was er aan de eene zijde van ons een groot bosch en wij waren in groot gevaar, als wij verder gingen om daar in te dwalen. Wij overlegden om maar te blijven waar wij waren en gingen daar zitten, bij een dikken omgewaaiden boom. Wij hadden geen matches en konden geen vuur maken en moesten maar wachten tot het weder daglicht werd. Ik was wel wat bezorgd dat wij wolven zouden hooren, maar wij hebben niets bijzonders gehoord. Toen het licht werd waren wij spoedig tehuis.

Omstreeks dezen tijd had ik zaken te doen te Kalamazoo. Dit zouden wij thans kunnen doen met de telefoon; doch toen waren wij vier mijlen van de postoffice en de mail kwam maar eens of tweemaal in de week. Zoo dacht ik om maar te voet te gaan en ging Woensdagavond naar een vriend van mij in Overijsel; Donderdag morgen van daar naar Kalamazoo; 47 mijlen; Vrijdag naar Prairie Round, 14 mijlen en terug naar Kalamazoo, Zaterdag weder naar Overijsel. Dat was in drie dagen 122 mijlen. Ik was Zondagmorgen zoo stijf en mijn beenen waren zoo zeer, dat ik van daar haast niet tehuis kon komen en dat was maar drie mijlen. De reis had mij maar elf cents gekost.

[Translation]

About the year 1813 an order went forth from Napoleon I who at that time was ruler of the Netherlands that the oldes male of each family should assume a second name or, as it was called at that time, a *van*. Before that time it was sufficient to present a newly born child at the courthouse. On such an occasion the date of birth and the name were inscribed in the register. As second name the child was given the name of its father. So, for example, my grandfather in inscribed in the register at Oldebroek, the Netherlands, as Reijer Aartzoon, his brother as Willem Aartzoon and their father as Aart Reijerzoon, and my father who was born in 1802 as Aart Reijerzoon. When the new law was instituted Willem Aartzoon, then the oldest member of the family, assumed the name Willem van Zwaluwenburg "because the family at that time was living at Zwaluwenburg." Zwaluwenburg was a noted seigniory, with many well managed and fruitful farms. At my birth in 1832 my name was not inscribed as Reijer Aartzoon but as Reijer van Zwaluwenburg.

Next, something about our emigration to America and my first years here. On May 16, 1850, we departed from Kleine Musschard, province of Gelderland, the Netherlands, and emigrated to Michigan, North America. That is, father and our second mother and their child, one year old, and five brothers and sisters: the writer, 18 years old, my sisters Lubbigje, 16, and Hendrikje, 14; and brothers Gerrit, 10, and Jacob, 7.

We went to Harderwijk by wagon, next by ferry boat to Amsterdam and thence by train to Rotterdam. There we were forced to wait two weeks because our ship was not ready. Next we went to Hellevoetsluis. We had a small ship – twelve seamen in all. Our first night on the North

Sea was pretty rough. In the English Channel the weather was fair. During our first tweo weeks on the ocean there was much storm and seasickness but no accidents.

After a long voyage of 52 days we arrived in New York in July. From there we went by steamboat to Albany, by canalboat to Buffalo in ten days, by steamboat to Detroit, by train to New Buffalo, Michigan, by steamboat to Chicago, by sailing ship to the mouth fo Black Lake, and finally by flatboat to Groningen, Michigan.

Western Michigan at that time was one vast forest. Dominie A. C. van Raalte's Kolonie was founded in Ottawa and Allegan counties. The first Hollanders had come here in 1847, and the Indians had their wigwams where the "stad" Holland now is, and there was no cleared land. When we arrived three years later the Indians for the most part had departed and the settlers had begun to clear the land. When still in the Netherlands we had heard about Van Raalte's Kolonie. Father had received two letters from a friend who worked in Groningen [Michigan]. We had no knowledge about America other than what was conveyed by them and so we came directly to Groningen.

Often I think of what we saw then in Groningen and compare it with the great progress that has been achieved since those days. There, a little beyond the bridge by the present Groningen cemetery we saw father [Hendrik Jan] Veneklaasen and his son Berend Jan in overalls which had been rolled up above their knees. They stood plying their shovels and working the clay with their hands and feet to bake bricks. They had been brickmakers back in the Netherlands, and this was the beginning of the extensive brickyard expanded mainly by the efforts of the son. This business at present is being continued by the Veneklaasen brothers, grandsons of the first father Veneklaasen.

The first settlers had been here three years. Many of them had died from privation, for there were no houses nor was there food. And, besides, there were the Michigan fevers so common at that time. Others who had come with some money had bought land and although they had survived had progressed only little. To secure food they had to go to such neighboring places as Grand Rapids, Kalamazoo, Singapore, or Grand Haven. Some of these men went alone to these places, leaving wife and children on their land. In those days it was not a certainty that the struggle begun against the vast forest would result in victory. Here and there a few acres had been chopped down and a loghouse had been erected. But what a waste! Hardly any roads, mostly trails through the woods to be followed by tracing the blazes on trees. Chopping down trees was not so serious a job – it cost from $ 3 to $ 4 an acre; but to burn all those trees cost from $ 8 to $ 10 an acre, although most settlers did this work themselves. In springtime, as soon as it was dry enough, they began burning in order to have one or two acres cleared for planting corn. During the summer they renewed their burning in order to sow wheat. To burn the branches was no hard job, but to chop those thick tree trunks through twice or three times and to roll them into piles [for, lying singly, they would not burn at all] in order to burn them – that was hard work, especially during the heats of summer. The next obstacles were the stumps and the roots of the trees. It was impossible to plow straight as much as ten feet without halting the oxen in order to pull the plow out of the roots. Often I think about those first years.

Fortunately for us we had until now enjoyed good health. Some of us had been somewhat seasick, and it was evident from our appearance that we were weary from the long journey. About three weeks after our arrival here we all had the "Michigan fever," which was quite common. Mother lay abed for days so that we thought each day would be her last. After father had had the fever four of five times he became sleepy. We had to awake him, for if not he simply would sleep endlessly. After two days in bed we could not rouse him and one evening he died. Two weeks later my half-brother, a very healthy child of nearly two years, died. And, two months later my aunt, Mrs. van den Berg, father's sister, died leaving three orphans. From that time until the following spring we frequently had fevers.

When father died we had $ 400. Following father's plan and the plan of his friend who was father's adviser we bought 40 acres of land, a dense wood, and built a house on it. We moved into it about November. Following Dutch custom the house had no stove but simply a fireplace and an oven for baking. Fortunately that winter was a mild one. Baking bread was a primitive matter. From November until May we had but one barrel of flour. Besides this we had cornmeal [baked in water, without benefit of rising], some potatoes, and a little pork.

About March mother remarried. We had made up our minds to stay together, to maintain our home together, but when spring came we began to see that this was not possible. We had no more money, our clothes were worn out, and in our neighborhood there was no chance to earn anything. Had I been able to get work or to earn anything I would have done so, but at that time one could not earn anything in the Kolonie.

About this time we received a letter from my uncle K. Stange in the Netherlands. He offered to send us our travel expenses if we wanted to return, and wrote that we could stay with his family. But we had heard a great deal about how good a country this was to earn some money, and knowing what conditions were like in the Netherlands among the relatives we declined with thanks.

In May my oldest sister Lubbigje went to Grand Rapids to earn some money as a maid. Now there were four children left in our household. During the winter I had chopped down some trees. I planted some corn and potatoes among the logs. But that spring there were so many squirrels that when I went to look for corn I found only two plants. The squirrels had dug all the seed corn out of the ground. This failure caused us to decide to quit living together.

At that time there were many children in the Kolonie whose fathers and mothers had died. These orphans usually were adopted by people who looked after them till their 16th or 18th year. The children of my aunt Van den Berg were taken care of in this way. But we could not follow this example, for we wanted to be free and remain independent. I cannot recall that we ever received one cent which we did not repay.

I now was 19 and being the oldest of the children and the only one able to help, everything rested on me. People were ready with advice to which I was quick enough to listen, but such advice was not enough. For we needed money, and so we separated, with the idea of coming together again at a later time, but this never took place. My youngest sister Hendrikje who always was sickly found a place with a farmer. There she would earn her board but I was to provide clothes and schoolbooks for her. I left my youngest brother Jacob with my mother, paying her $ 2 a month for board. That was not much money, but it helped them greatly. I had to look for work among the "English" as they were called by us, for among the Hollanders there was no chance to earn anything. They of course had work to offer but they had no money. My brother Gerrit, who then was eleven, and I and a good friend Jan de Vries [father of Dr. Bernard de Vries of Holland, (Michigan) who could speak a little English proceeded on our trip from Groningen to Singapore and five miles beyond to what today is called New Richmond where we spent a night. In the morning I had to pay fifty cents for our lodging. But I had only thirty-five cents and asked to be allowed to pay fifteen cents later. We went a mile further to a Mr. Mann, in Manlius, who owned a small saw-mill and offered me some work. Jan made arrangements with him and I was to earn $ 10 per month. He succeeded in placing brother Gerrit with a neighbor; he was to receive board and clothes. Then he returned home. There we were; we could not understand or speak a word of English.

When evening came Mr. Mann called me. He had two tin pails in one hand. With the other hand he pointed to his cows which we could see grazing in the pasture. I knew what that meant, so I took the pails and milked the cows. Whenever he indicated some work he always went with me to show me how. Having nothing to keep me busy during evenings I went to bed early and so when morning came I could easily get up without being called. The first morning when Mr. Mann rose and thought to call me he found that I had already milked his four cows. He was pleased with this.

During evenings and on Sundays brother Gerrit and I were always together. It was then that I could understand something of what it meant to be alone in the world, to be without a home. I thought a good deal about whether there was not some other opportunity but in my judgment there was no other way open for us to earn an honest existence. Mr. and Mrs. Mann were very good to me. My work was not difficult. Soon I got along better, for I was becoming acquainted with my work and also with the language.

After one month Mr. Mann paid me $ 10. How rich I was! In the Netherlands that was 25 guilders, and there I would have to work a half year for such a sum. I asked Mr. Mann for three or four days' leave which he granted and we went to the Kolonie. Our way was through woods, afoot a distance of 26 miles, and we needed one whole day to make the journey. First I went to pay my fifteen cent debt. I paid mother two month's board money for my youngest brother and bought some clothes for him and for my youngest sister and myself. There were demands enough for my ten dollars. Accordingly I had little left of it when we returned, but we were happy and in high spirits. We thought we had already become quite American. And so we arrived back in Manlius.

For me this was a very good place. Father and mother could not have been better for us. My work was light – help the women in the house, work in the barn, and milk four cows. But our Sundays were so long! For we were accustomed to going to church on Sundays. That was for me a special delight, but there was no church. After we had been there two or three Sundays Mrs. Mann told us there would be preaching in the schoolhouse. We went to hear the service, but we cuold understand only a few words of it such as Jesus and Jerusalem, but this was so pleasing to me that I could not hold back my tears. The fact there was no church in this part of the country was one of the reasons why we soon left for Kalamazoo where there was a Dutch congregation.

Our first home in America was at Mr. Mann's. Sister Lubbigje who worked in Grand Rapids went to work for Mr. Mann the next year; sister Hendrikje likewise, and later brother Jacob also. During the first two years we had all things in common. As we grew older each one of us cared more for himself.

I went to Kalamazoo in the spring of 1852, where I found a Dutch speaking Reformed congregation. That summer I worked in a brick factory. The next winter I again worked at Manlius, cutting pine logs. By this time I had become somewhat American and, like many a young person, was ever looking for something better. I had become acquainted with two families in Holland, Michigan, who had come from Galena, Illinois. As they were not getting along very well in Holland they had decided to go back to Galena. These friends easily convinced me that it would be better for me to do so also. Accordingly, in August 1853 we went on our journey, by boat to Chicago, from there by train to Freeport, and then we were to travel 50 miles by wagon to Galena. We arrived in Freeport in the evening, and had to stay in a hotel. I felt in my pocket but could not find my pocketbook. I had lost it on the train. Here I was, in a strange place and without a cent, but my acquaintances paid for me. I had not lost much money, but it was enough to pay for my return to Michigan if I did not like it in the new place. Now I had to stay until I had earned enough to pay for my return. Here I worked in a store as assistant clerk, but I did not like this at all. In March I was back in Kalamazoo. My financial affairs had not improved much, but I had learned a great deal. Then I worked a half year in an iron factory in Kalamazoo.

For a long time I had had a desire to make my profession of faith, to unite myself more closely with God's church, but personal scruples held me back. My desire now became so great that I made my profession and was admitted to full communion. And I was greatly strengthened in faith in our covenant God and in the communion of the saints.

It now was my desire and my striving to have my own home, and I thought it would be well for me if I established myself more permanently. I had traveled around a little and had become somewhat acquainted with business, but for these things I thought I had no capacity. So then to become a farmer seemed best. Land was cheap in the woods of the Dutch Kolonie and it was my desire to live near a Dutch church. To convert those dense forests into a farm was easier to say than to do. But I was not afraid of hard labor.

At that time there were many Dutch girls serving as maids in the homes of the English ["*Americans*"] in Kalamazoo. Like myself they too desired a home. Luckily and without much effort, and entirely according to my desires, I found a girl, Sara Kools, who decided to risk it with me. In those days it was not as it is at present – that one must have a good house well furnished before he dare ask for a girl's hand. No mention was ever made of such a thing. Each of us had about as much as the other, and that was not much. We both were young, my fiancee was 19 and I was 23. At thirteen she had come to America with her father Abraham Kools and with one brother and three sisters. She came with a debt of $ 24. The first year she had spent at home, the second year she earned fifty cents a week, and during her last year she earned $ 1.26 per week. From these earnings she had paid her debt and had saved enough to pay for her own wedding clothes – proof of Dutch industry, honesty, and thrift. We were married Sunday evening on November 4, 1855, by Dominie Wijnand Gardenier, father of Colonel Gardener. Next Monday morning we left for Holland, a journey of two days, in a lumber wagon provided with but one seat. My wife and I had to sit on our trunk.

During the first year I worked for Manley D. Howard, in the winter hauling logs out of the forest, in the summer working in the sawmill. There near the sawmill our first child Alice was born. In the fall of that year we bought eighty acres of land, entirely wooded, in section 16, Fillmore Township. First we chopped down some trees. Next, in the midst of the woods, a mile distant from the nearest neighbor, we built a loghouse. There we went to live in the fall of 1856, four miles from church, store, and postoffice, and without any roads. Only a few times a year were we able to come to our house with ox wagon, but usually we had to carry our necessaries on our backs. Because our land was low we had chopped down trees for the purpose of walking over them and so avoid the water. When together we wanted to visit the neighbors or go to the "stad" we always had to go afoot and carry the baby. When there were two babies we each had to carry one. We had bought our farm in the woods with each other's consent. It was hard for me that I could not place my young wife in better circumstances. We had the idea there was no other possibility. We were young and happy in each other. Jesus says, "These two," that is, man and wife, "shall be one flesh" [Matthew, 19, 5]. But we human beings are still so imperfect that we need time and experience to become "one". It is a feature of our creation, as God has formed us, that our youthful years are our best ones during which our lives are formed together and so become one.

How often I think of those times! There was nothing else to do but chop down trees in order to have an opening through which the sun could shine down upon us. In those days the woods were filled with deer, wolves, and some bears, which were much hunted. Frequently we saw the wolves come within a few rods of our house. When my brother Jacob came home late from school, he would hear them. One night we heard a great noise a few rods from our house. When morning came I went out to see what had taken place. I found the bones of some deer which had been devoured by the wolves. Often in the early morning when I went out of doors I saw deer browsing where on the day before I had cut down some trees. I had a good rifle and was able to shoot down a sparrow in the highest trees. But I had little luck in shooting deer; I was too hasty and succeeded in getting only one. Shooting deer is something which must be learned, and one learns to do this by practicing it. One day when hunting in the woods, I came upon a large deer. Then I got "buck fever". Perhaps you ask, what kind of fever is that? Let me tell you my experience. I was walking over a small hill along the edge of some low ground. There through the branches of a wind-fallen tree I saw a large buck grazing. I thought that if I were careful and shot him in the right spot he would be mine. I steadied my rifle against a tree. I stood a trifle above the deer, and intended to shoot after lowering my rifle. I had placed my eye carefully for aiming the gun. I looked so intently at the deer that I forgot my finger which soon began to tremble and off went my gun, the bullet passing about two feet above the deer! Until this the deer had not seen me, but now he looked up and gazed at me. I tried to reload my rifle, but my hands trembled so much that I could not insert the bullet properly and it stuck half way in the barrel. While I was busy stamping with my ramrod the deer ran away. I went home, concluding that hunting deer was not my calling.

On another occasion I ran onto a crane roost, that is crane's nests. It was a dark day and I was standing in a dark hemlock wood. Suddenly I heard a great noise. Never had I heard such an uproar. I of course had been near a roost of wild doves where thousands of them sit together and make a tremendous noise, but a crane roost I had never run into. The old cranes were bringing their young something to eat. I ran back, but had the thought that when I got home I would not be able to tell why I had been frightened. I just simply could not imagine where that noise came from. There were no wolves, nor was there a bear, nor could it be Indians. I was carrying my rifle, but was not enough of a Nimrod to have any confidence in it. Finally I concluded to investigate the business. Before going far I discovered that the din was in the tops of the trees.

I went a little farther and, behold, they were cranes! Two or three hundred cranes can make a lot of noise.

One morning my brother was to go to one of the neighbors. He walked into the woods, but soon came back, saying that there was a bear there. I said, "Oh, that isn't possible, you merely became afraid." Replied brother, "Just go and see, large footprints in the freshly fallen snow." Taking my rifle I went to the spot, and indeed there in the snow near the clearing were tracks made by feet as large as the hooves of horses. I followed these tracks as long as I could see. But when I reached the dense woods and couldn't see our clearing any more I stopped and thought, "Suppose that bear should come from behind that big tree!" I looked around but could see nothing more of our clearing and those large tracks in the snow seemed so clear. I knew these were the tracks of a bear. I thought, "Better let the bear go his way. I had better go home."

It happened one time that we were on a family visit at Harm Lucas's. He lived two miles west of us, directly through the woods. There was no path and the way around through Graafschap was one of five miles. We had left in the morning and had walked the distance, five miles. We had carried our baby in our arms. It was our intention to return in the evening, along the path through the woods. I was well acquainted with the woods and so long as I could see the trees I knew where we were. But it had become later than we intended and when we were a little more than a mile in the woods it was so dark that we could not see the trees. On one side of our place there was a large woods and we were in great danger of being lost if we proceeded farther. We decided to stay in that spot and sat down beside a large windfallen tree. Since we had no matches, we could not start a fire, and so had to wait until daybreak. I was fearful that we would hear wolves, but we heard nothing in particular. Soon after dawn we went home.

About this time I had some business in Kalamazoo. Today we can take care of such a thing over the telephone. But at that time we were four miles from the postoffice and mail came only once or twice a week. I thought it best to go afoot to Kalamazoo, and left on Wednesday evening to stay with a friend in Overisel. Thursday morning I traveled on foot to Kalamazoo, a distance of 47 miles; Friday I went to Prairie Round, a distance of 14 miles, and back to Kalamazoo, and Saturday back again to Overisel, in three days a total of 122 miles. Sunday, morning after my return, my legs were so stiff and sore that I could hardly get home, and that was a distance of only three miles. That trip cost me but eleven cents.

54. GEERT S. DE WIT'S EXPERIENCES

[Born in 1831 at Eenrum in the province of Groningen, Geert S. de Wit arrived in the Michigan Settlement in June 1848, at length establishing himself on a homestead in Fillmore Township in Allegan County. His reminiscences, entitled *Ervaringen*, appeared in *De Grondwet* June 25, 1912.]

De schrijver werd den 10den April 1830 te Eenrum, Provincie Groningen Nederland, geboren.

Den 20sten Maart 1848, op 17 jarigen leeftijd, vertrokken wij naar Amerika. In een zeilschip voeren wij van Zoutkamp naar Amsterdam en van daar naar Hellevoetsluis. Daar moesten wij een dag of wat wachten, om het schip verder voor de reis gereed te maken en alles voor het kooken in orde te brengen, want een ieder moest voor zijn voedsel zorgen. Er werd op toegezien, dat een ieder genoeg had en vandaar werd alles gewogen. Het drinkwater echter kregen wij van het scheeps-bestuur; dat werd ons dagelijks toegedeeld, naar de persoon en getal. Dat ging altijd niet zoo vlot, want de een moest op de ander wachten en dan geraakte bij zoo'n gelegenheid het geduld wel eens ten einde.

Wij hebben twee of drie op het schip overledene personen, ter zee moeten begraven; hunne namen kan ik mij niet meer herinneren.

Na 41 dagen op zee gedobberd te hebben, kwamen wij te New York aan. Vandaar reisden wij met een stoomboot naar Albany en vandaar per kanaalboot naar Buffalo. Van hier reisden wij met een stoomboot verder naar Chicago. Te Chicago werden wij in een zeilschip overgebracht om naar Holland, Michigan, over te varen, maar daar wind en golven te sterk waren, bracht men ons naar Grand Haven en den volgenden dag terug naar de Black Lake. Hier werden wij overgeladen met ons goed op een platboot en die platboot moesten wij, daar de haven van Black Lake vol zand was, er door trekken. Eindelijk binnen de haven en de boot weder vlot, zetten wij de reis over Black Lake naar Holland en zooals wij dachten, naar de stad Holland, voort. Maar, in plaats dat wij een stad vonden, vonden wij een ondoordringbaar bosch. Alleen Achtste en River straten waren uitgekapt, zoodat er een ossenteam door kon passeeren.

Wij vroegen naar de stad en men zeide ons, dat we er midden in waren. Hierop keerden we rechts om en kwamen terug aan den oever van Black Lake, en bleven dien dag en den daaropvolgende nacht hier vertoeven en onder een aantal tegen elkaar opgezette planken overnachtende. Het was nu zoowat 20 Juni, de rechte datum weet ik niet meer; na eene reis van circa drie maanden. Ik stond toen onder toezicht van Pieter Naber en was toen 18 jaren oud geworden.

Den volgenden morgen trokken wij met een ossenwagen het bosch door naar de plaats die nu East Holland genoemd wordt. Daar woonden toen eenige huisgezinnen, te weten: Simon Sluiter, Willem Mulder en Mr. Holman, door wien wij liefderijk onder dak genomen werden. Holman is later naar Kalamazoo vertrokken. Ook woonde daar toen een huisgezin met name Molog, die allen in 1847 hier gekomen waren en die toen juist bezig waren met het oprichten van een loghuis. Het vereischte een dag om met de ossen door het bosch te komen en East Holland te bereiken.

Na hier een paar dagen rondgezien en het land in den omtrek eens een weinig in oogenschouw genomen te hebben, vertrokken de oudsten te voet naar Grand Rapids, om daar, indien het hun aanstond, land te koopen. Johannes Naber, Pieter Naber, Egbert Pilon en Jan Kramer kochten daar ook land. Dit land was gelegen in section 35, Holland township, Ottawa County.

Maar wij jongelieden zijn toen naar Kalamazoo geloopen. Ons gezelschap bestond uit: Jacob Sluiter, Albert Kapinga met zijn ondertrouwde vrouw Afkie en nog een meisje, Cornelia genaamd, een zuster van de vrouw van Johannes Naber, Cornelius Noorhuis, Jan de Fuiter en mijzelven.

Den eersten dag liepen wij tot zoover als Allegan en overnachten daar ten huize van de weduwe Kok. Des anderen daags kregen wij gelegenheid om met een boer mede te rijden naar Cooper, op zes mijlen ten noorden van Kalamazoo gelegen. Daar kregen C. Noorhuis, Cornelia en schrijver dezes werk bij daar wonende boeren. De anderen zetten de reis door naar Kalamazoo, vonden daar werk en bleven daar eene maand.

Korten tijd later verhuurden Jacob Sluiter en ik ons te Kalamazoo, aan Govenor Epaphradatus Ransom om op de farm te werken, daar nu selderij verbouwd werd en die toen ter tijde [een paar jaar later] verkocht werd aan Den Bleyker, een bemiddelde boer uit Texel, Nederland.

In den herfst heb ik aan de Michigan Central Railroad gewerkt, tegen een loon van 75 cents per dag en 25 cents per dag voor kostgeld. Maar toen de winter inzette en alles met sneeuw bedekt was, was het werk aan de railroad gedaan en toen was het maar een donker vooruitzicht voor mij die geheel alleen en zonder familie was. Maar de Heere heeft toen ook voor mij gezorgd en ook uitkomst geschonken.

Ik hoorde dat er een boer was, die een knecht moest hebben, maar die woonde 15 mijlen van Kalamazoo en ik kende de weg niet en evenmin de naam van den boer. Ik ging evenwel op reis, liep in zuidelijke richting en vroeg zoo nu en dan eens waar ik „Zuid Prairie" kon vinden, niet wetende, dat de streek waar ik heen moest Round Prairie heette, waar het dorp Schoolcraft in gelegen is, in het zuidelijk gedeelte van Kalamazoo County en dat ik eigenlijk te Schoolcraft wezen moest. Al voortloopende slaagde ik er toch in, om te circa drie ure in den namiddag het dorp te bereiken. Daar gekomen, vroeg ik de weg naar het huis van een boer, die vijftien paarden bezat en die een knecht noodig had. Men antwoordde mij, dat dit Andrew Y. Moore moest wezen, wiens boys hier ter school waren. Naar de school dus en daar gevraagd naar Mr. A. Y. Moore's boys. Deze verwezen mij naar een huis, een half mijl ten oosten van Schoolcraft gelegen. Daar aangekomen, was ik welkom en bleef daar tot den volgenden herfst.

Mr. Moore was de vader van Kolonel Moore, van het 25ste Regiment Michigan Infantry, onder onze Hollandsche boys welbekend. Daar heb ik het eerst een groote machine gezien, die door zestien paarden gedreven werd. Deze machine maakte de tarwe schoon en deed ze in zakken. Later werd dezelve naar California gezonden, omdat het de kosten niet loonde, om er hier zulk eene groote machine op na te houden. Daar was het 't eerst dat ik gewaar werd, dat de Heere ook aan deze plaats was en ook mijne gangen kende en mij niet aan mijzelven overliet.

In den zomer kwamen er meer Hollanders om hier werk te zoeken en dan kwamen wij Zondags samen in de schuur en riepen den naam des Heeren aan. Wij hadden ons bedroom in den schuur en zoodoende een plaats voor gebed en onderzoek van het Woord en dat bleef voor mij niet ongezegend, iets dat ik thans beter besef dan toen.

Mijn volgende plaats was een mijl oost, bij een boer, Darnel Bruss genaamd, een goed man, die met zijn gezin er huisgodsdienst op na hield en superintendent van de Zondagschool van de Presbyteriaansche Kerk was.

En zoo zijn er vier en een half jaren verloopen dat ik daar als vreemdeling verkeerd heb. Ik had toen een eigen span paarden en werkte voor mijzelven op het land van eene weduwe, eene zuster van mijn ouden boer, Mr. D. Brigs.

Ik ging alle jaren eens naar de Kolonie, om mijn vrienden te bezoeken. De eerste keer nam ik een span ossen mede voor Pieter Naber en het volgende jaar een span voor Johannes Naber. Bij een andere gelegenheid bracht ik een paard mede, hetwelk ik verruilde voor 40 acres land in Fillmore Township, dat later mijn homestead is geworden.

Geld was er in die dagen niet en zoo kreeg ik ook geen geld voor mijne ossen. Alles ging op goed geloof door, vertrouwende dat er betere tijden zouden aanbreken. En, wij zijn niet beschaamd uitgekomen, in weerwil van het feit, dat alles zonder bewijs en zonder interest werd omgezet.

Daar, zoo als ik reeds gezegd heb, ik voor mijzelve werkte, moest ik bij anderen in kost gaan en zoo nu en dan een nieuw kosthuis zoeken en dat voldeed mij niet meer. Daarom begon ik uit te zien naar een vrouw en ging dien winter naar Kalamazoo, om als teamster werk te zoeken. Ik ging, na aankomst aldaar, in kost bij Albert Kapinga en vrouw. Daar kwam ik in kennis met Maria Meijaard, met wien ik op den 10den April [mijn 23sten geboortedag; zij was 20 jaren oud] 1853 in de kerk door Ds. Cornelius van der Meulen in den echt verbonden werd.

Hierop zijn wij gaan wonen op 14 mijlen oost of zuidoost van Kalamazoo, in Climax Township, op een farm van een advokaat uit Kalamazoo. Daar heb ik alle krediet voor een advokaat verloren. Hij wilde zijn deel wel hebben, maar niet doen zooals het contract luidde. Daar zijn wij twee jaren geweest.

In den herfst van 1856 hebben we ons huisraad op een wagen geladen en zijn naar de Kolonie vertrokken om daar ons fortuin te zoeken.

Wat het beteekent, in een dicht bosch te beginnen, dat weten allen die het doorworsteld hebben – hard werken en armoede.

Ik had echter zeven jaren onder de Amerikanen verkeerd, de landtaal vrij goed geleerd en ook hoe het werk hier gedaan behoorde te worden, en dat kwam later goed te pas. Maar er was ook een keerzijde aan, zoodat ik met Azaf moest zeggen: „Mijn voeten en mijn teeën waren tot mijn leed, van 't spoor der godsvrucht afgegleen." Want, en in zonderheid de laatste twee jaren, was ik meest in slecht gezelschap. Daar ik de farm had opgegeven, moest ik nu wat anders beginnen. Ik kwam toen in kennis met zekeren Mr. Kamfiel en kwam met hem overeen om een breaking team te koopen, om het land, dat nog nooit geploegd was, op te breken. Wij hadden voor dit doel vijf span ossen met mijn paarden voor op als leiders. Maar Kamfiel was een goddeloos mensch of zonder God, en als men den eersten Psalm leest, dan ziet men hoe gevaarlijk het is met zulke lieden om te gaan. Daarom was het, dat wij besloten om naar de Kolonie te gaan.

Toch moet ik even melden, hoe wij door de Yankee's behandeld werden. Eens nam ik mij voor om een vracht flour naar de Kolonie te brengen. Vijf mijlen ten noorden van Allegan, geraakte mijne slede met die vracht er op, in het bosch, waar er nog geen road uitgekapt was, vast. Uithoofde van de diepe sneeuw, kon ik niet uitmaken, hoe de boel eigenlijk vast zat. Natuurlijk wilde ik, indien mogelijk, doorgaan. Ergo zette ik de paarden nog eens goed aan, met dien afloop, dat ze de disselboom braken en de slede even vast zat als ooit. Noodwendig moest ik hulp gaan vragen bij het eerste het beste huis dat er in de omgeving te bereiken was. De man was gelukkig te huis en deze ging dadelijk met mij terug en hielp mij de slede los en de disselboom weer in orde maken. Toen echter was het avond en kon Hamilton niet meer bereiken. De goede man nam mij mede naar zijn huis, voorzag mij van voedsel en liet mij ten zijnen huize overnachten. Hij had maar een stal en die moest dienen voor zijne ossen, maar hij besloot zijn ossen te laten loopen en zette mijne paarden op hunne plaats op stal. Den volgenden dag betaalde ik hem en zette mijne reis door.

Toen ik met de vracht flour in Holland kwam, kon ik geen koopers vinden. Had ik cornmeel gebracht, zeide men, dan had ik koopers genoeg kunnen vinden, maar voor meelbloem was er te Holland geen markt. Na lang wachten verkocht ik de flour eindelijk aan Mr. Schaddelee Sr., tegen $ 3,25 per barrel, en zelf had ik er $ 3 per barrel voor betaald te Galesburg, vijftien mijlen van Kalamazoo. Mijne verdiensten op die vracht flour bedroegen $ 2,50 en hiervoor had ik een reis van 65 mijlen moeten afleggen.

Maar, om terug te komen op onze reis naar de Kolonie: Wij kwamen in het eerste gedeelte van December 1856 op de plaats onzer bestemming, namelijk te Fillmore, Allegan County, Michigan, aan.

Wij dachten naar Albert Kapinga te gaan, maar het werd ons te vroeg duister. Daarom bleven wij dien nacht bij Jannes van den Beldt, dicht bij ons land, met wien wij later jaren buren zijn geweest. Den volgenden dag vonden wij een huis kort bij, dat aan Isaac Fairbanks toebehoorde en door Indianen was gebouwd en bleven daar den eersten winter, omdat de winter ons overviel toen wij met een loggen huis aan 't bouwen waren.

In het voorjaar bouwden wij een shanty en begonnen onzen moeielijk-heden-arbeid om land te klieren in een groen bosch. Wij kapten de boo-men om en lieten dezelve zoo veel mogelijk op hoopen vallen, en tusschen die omliggende boomen planten wij corn en aardappelen. Dat ging nog al, maar 't was moeilijk werk, omdat er weinig grond was om 't geplantte te bedekken. Vandaar gebruikten wij hiertoe bladeren en wat er maar te vinden was.

De Heere echter zegende ons werk met een goede crop aardappelen. Het corn was echter niet zoo goed. Bij het planten van dat corn kapten we met een bijl een gat in den grond en in zoo'n gaat plantten we het tusschen wortels en stompen in. Onder zulke omstandigheden was er aan cultivatie geen denken.

Het volgende jaar ging het al wat beter en daar wij zelf ossen hadden, hadden wij al gauw wat land schoon. Het derde jaar was alles een mislukking. Wij hadden toen een paar acres met tarwe, die mooi stond, maar in de maand Juni hadden wij een harde nachtvorst, waardoor al de tarwe bevroor, zoodat wij het afmaaiden voor hooi. Aardappelen en corn in den grond. En, daar de boekweit ook bevroren was, oogstten wij dat jaar niets dan alleen knolrapen. Zoodoende bestond toen ons dagelijks voedsel gedurende dien winter, uit bijna niets anders dan johnnykoek en knolrapen. De varkens moesten we, uithoofde van gebrek aan voeder, slachten om ze uit den weg te krijgen.

Dat jaar gaf de Heere echter nog uitkomst. Wij hadden nog eiken boomen en maakten, hierin geholpen door Egbert Bol, hieruit staven en zoo waren er weer twee huisgezinnen gered.

In dien tijd kwam er zoo nu en dan nog wel een Methodistisch leeraar bij ons in het schoolhuis preeken [ook Mr. Clapper kwam wel eens om revival-meetings te houden]. En daar wij nog geen belijdenis gedaan hadden en altijd dachten, dat er vele kinderen Gods onder de Methodisten zijn, zoo gingen ook wij en velen van het Hollandsche volk dikwerf naar het schoolhuis om naar die predikaties te luisteren.

Niet lang na dezen kwam Ds. van Raalte ons bezoeken en hij beloofde bij zijn vertrek, eens spoedig terug te zullen komen. Korten tijd later kwam ZEw. dan ook, in gezelschap van twee ouderlingen, ons wederom eens bezoeken en na wat gepraat en eenige vragen gedaan te hebben, besloot men om ons beiden aan te nemen en onze vier kinderen te doopen, dat ook kort hierna in het schoolhuis [toen bekend als het district van Broek] plaats had en waren toen leden van de gemeente van Holland, die nu bekend is als de gemeente aan Negende Straat. Later is de kerk in Fillmore aan de county lijn gebouwd, bekend als Ebenezer tot op dezen dag.

Maar wij keeren terug naar het leven op het land met deszelfs moeie-lijkheden. Gedurende een van de eerste jaren, bij gelegenheid van een mislukking van den oogst, gingen wij, zes man sterk [vergezeld van eene vrouw, die als kok diende] naar Laketown om daar wat te verdienen door cordhout te kappen voor H. Walsh, die in Holland een „general store" had. Wij hadden daar een shanty gebouwd en bleven daar van Maandag tot Zaterdag. Mijn vrouw moest zoodoende al dien tijd met vier kinderen en het vee alleen te huis blijven.

Zoo sukkelden wij den winter door. In het voorjaar en voor de scheep-vaart aangevangen was, was de nood soms nog erger. Maar, de Heere heeft altijd gezorgd.

Van jaar tot jaar werd de clearing grooter. Het duurde echter ver-scheidene jaren eer wij genoeg voor onszelven en ons vee konden ver-bouwen. Vandaar werden we soms genoodzaakt om het vee, zoodra in het voorjaar de sneeuw weg was, het bosch in te zenden, om eigen kost te zoeken.

Had je de ossen bijvoorbeeld, dan later noodig, dan moest je ze gaan opzoeken. Bij zekere gelegenheid ging ik even na den middag, met zulk een doel de bosch in, maar kon de ossen nergens vinden. Tegen het vallen van den avond begon het te regenen en overviel mij de duisternis, zoodat ik den weg niet meer vinden kon en genoodzaakt werd om in het bosch [waarin dien tijd nog vele wolven zich ophielden] te overnachten. Daar alles natgeregend was, kon ik geen vuur ontsteken. Dien ganschen nacht heb ik achter een boom gestaan, den Heere bescherming afsmeekende.

Toen het licht weer aanbrak, kon ik de weg wel weer vinden en kwam des morgens, een halve mijl ten zuiden van Jan Kleinheksel's woning, weer het bosch uit. Nadat ik het bosch uit en circa een mijl op reis naar huis terug, voortgeloopen had, trof ik tot mijne vreugde mijne verloren ossen aan, die hier langs den weg liepen te grazen.

55. KASPER LAHUIS' PIONEER CLEARING

[This description, devoted entirely to the character of the Dutch immigrant settler's clearing, vividly presents the immense difficulties with which the Hollanders unaccustomed to clearing the virgin forest had to contend. *De Pionier Clearing*, composed for the Semi-Centennial celebrations of 1897, was published in *De Grondwet*, October 28, 1913.]

Daar ik door omstandigheden verschoond werd om mijne beschouwing op het Vijftig-jarige Feest te Holland uit te spreken, zoo zend ik u bij dezen eenige opmerkingen. Niet omdat ik denk dat er niet genoeg gezegd en geschreven is, of in den waan verkeer iets beters te kunnen daarstellen, neen, zulks niet, maar terwijl ook onze naam staat onder die 47tigers, zoo hebben ook wij die geschiedenis doorleefd. Op onze schoongemaakte boerderij hebben we ruim 46 jaren zoet en zuur gesmaakt. Wij hebben dikwijls bij het opruimen der bosschen in doodsgevaar gestaan. Wij waren toen nog betrekkelijk jong doch dragen nu grijze haren.

Hoe vreemd was het voor ons toen we onze voeten aan wal zetten in Juni 1847, in wat men toen al „stad Holland" noemde. Waarlijk men zou haast zeggen dat wij onbekwaam waren tot het wegruimen van de donkere bosschen die voor ons lagen. Doch waar een wil is daar is ook een weg werd weer bevonden waarheid te zijn. Vastberadenheid en een vast geloof in den weg van Gods Voorzienigheid, zie dit noemen wij het eerste begin van de Pioneer's Clearing. Die vastberadenheid en dat vertrouwen was wellicht niet aller deel, toch zeggen we niet te veel wanneer we zeggen, dat de eerste nederzetters beslist zich voorgenomen hadden:

hier zullen we wonen met de gezellinne onzes levens en onze kinderen,
om onder Gods zegen ons brood te hebben.

Moed doortintelde de eerste nederzetters, terwijl boomen van twee tot
zes voet in doorsnede en 30 tot 60 voet hoog voor hen stonden. Als
Nederlanders op Amerikaanschen bodem de boomen om te hakken op
Amerikaansche manier, daarvan had men nog geen begrip. Niet zelden
stond men voorover gebogen om toch laag aan den grond den boom om
te hakken; dikwijls werd rondom den boom gehakt, zoodat men hem
dikwijls zag vallen waar hij niet begeerd werd, zoo zelfs, dat de woningen niet altijd verschoond bleven en dien ten gevolge den boel erg
door elkander viel. Het was een moeilijk werk en vereischte mannen van
moed om takken en boomen op te ruimen en het is een wonder, dat de
moed bijbleef en er niet meer ongelukken waren te betreuren bij al deze
onkunde in het vellen van het woud.

Als een bewijs van de onkunde die er bestond kan dienen, dat waar soms
zware boomen naar een of andere kant overbogen, men dan aan den
tegenovergestelden kant de eerste keep maakte en ook hoe men, Nederland's bodem, die zonder stompen is, nog steeds in het oog houdende,
men begon om de boomen met wortel en al uit te roeien en in de begeerte
om land zonder stompen te hebben, geene moeite ontzag om ze groen uit
te roeien, ja soms een sloot te graven naast een groene boom om er deze
in te begraven. Toch waren er gelukkig Amerikanen van geboorte onder
ons, die onderricht gaven. Kleine kepen en groote spanen, de bijl iedere
keer terug in de plaats waar zij uitkwam, de boom gehakt ter hoogte van
's man's halve lengte, was het motto van elk die besefte: we staan als
Nederlanders op Amerikaanschen bodem en wij willen Amerikanen
worden.

Moed en vastberadenheid in het voornemen om het land schoon te
krijgen, bezielde de pioniers. Het vaste plan om ieder de clearing uit te
breiden, deed onder ons bevestigd worden: langzaam maar zeker voorwaarts. Moed bezielde den man die de takken van onder de sneeuw trok
en ophoopte om ze in het voorjaar te verbranden. Het oploggen was zeer
moeilijk, daar alles groen was. Met groote moeite werkte men de loggen
rond de stompen om ze op te hoopen te krijgen. Ossen waren nog zeer
schaarsch en het viel den Hollander zeer moeilijk om dezelve zonder
teugels te besturen. Het is gebeurd, dat terwijl een man een juk ossen
kocht en onderricht ontving om ze te kunnen besturen, dat de oude
vader daar bij staande en hoorende wat er gezegd werd, tot zijn zoon
zeide: „schrijf op, jongen", om het geheugen te hulp te komen. Het was
soms zeer moeilijk om de opgehoopte boomstammen verbrand te krijgen.

Niet zelden werd des avonds nog eens opgestookt, waaraan moeders en dochters mede hielpen.

De eerste vrucht was meestal tusschen de boomstammen geteeld en als het niet door het wild gedierte vernield werd, dan had men een vollen oogst. Door herten, raccoons, eekhoorns, enz., welke er in groote menigte waren, werd veel schade aangericht; niet zelden gebeurde het, dat op slechts een paar roeden van huis door de herten schade werd aangericht. Eekhoorns werden bij honderdtallen geschoten en toch verminderden ze niet.

Het ploegen ging met groote moeite gepaard en beteekende soms niet veel, doch waar men slechts de sporen van de ploeg kon zien, gaf het belooning in de opbrengst van vruchten en waar dikwijls de ploeg vastliep en teruggetrokken moest worden, hielp dit toch voor een volgende keer.

Men leerde echter al spoedig de Amerikaansche methode van omhakken van het hout, om het dan na een of twee jaren aan het vuur over te geven en op te ruimen. Langs dezen weg hebben de pioniers akker aan akker onder de ploeg gebracht, is de woestijn in een vruchtbaar land herschapen. Ook de boschbranden, door een of ander ongeluk ontstaan, heeft veel land onder bebouwing gebracht.

Wij herdenken den worstelstrijd van de vroegere en latere pioniers. Een terugblik doet ons goed; de Heere heeft geholpen, moed en kracht gegeven, bewaard waar het gevaar dreigde. Menigwerf werd datgene wat wij meenden tegen ons te zijn, voor ons; wij zeggen: „Ebenhaezer". Laten wij niet vergeten, bij alles wat wij zien en hooren, de farms, opgeruimd door oud en jong, zijn de wielen aan den maatschappelijken wagen. De pioneer's clearing is de grondslag van onzen welvaart.

Wij verheugen ons in den dag van heden, een halve eeuw ligt achter ons. Is het te veel wanneer wij, die de donkere wildernis aanschouwd hebben en nu zien dorpen, steden en landerijen met huizen en schuren, zeggen dat een veelbewogen leven achter ons ligt? Laat ons eindigen in Hem die moed gaf, die ondersteunde in de moeilijke taak van de pioniers; waren dezen niet staande gebleven en gezegend door een machtige hand, we zouden niet aanschouwen wat we nu zien.

Onder alle ontbering was tevredenheid het gezegende deel der pioniers. En nu zien we reeds iets van de uitkomst. Velen genieten thans de vruchten van al die ontberingen en moeiten en kunnen leven van de opbrengsten van wat ze met harden arbeid gewonnen hebben. Er zijn nog velen in leven van degenen, vroeger of later gekomen, die medehielpen aan het in orde brengen van de landerijen en die de moeiten en ontberingen mede hebben doorworsteld.

Laat ons alle zeggen met hart en mond: „Uit Hem, door Hem en tot Hem zijn alle dingen."

[Translation]

On account of circumstances I have been excused from appearing in person to present my thoughts at the Semi-Centennial celebrations in Holland. Nevertheless I am sending you these few observations. I do this not because I think that not enough is being said or written on the subject of our history not because I am under the illusion that I could write something better than is being prepared by others. No, not at all, but simply because my name is mentioned as being one of the immigrants of 1847 who has had a part in this history. We have tasted not only the sweet but also the sorrow of life's experiences on the farm which we have cleared with our own hands. Frequently, while clearing away the woods, we have been in danger of death. At that time we were rather young but today our hairs are gray.

How strange things appeared to us when in June 1847 we set our foot ashore at the spot people already were calling "stad" Holland. In truth people might remark that we were unfit to undertake the task of clearing the sombre woods that lay before us. But where there was a will there also was a way, a saying once again proved to be true. Resolution and a firm faith in the way of God's providence – this we would say was the first beginning of the pioneer's clearing. Such resolution and confidence most likely was not held by all the settlers. But we are not affirming too much if we declare that these people had formed the resolution, "here we will live with our wives and our children and here, with God's blessing, earn our bread."

Courage animated our first settlers when they beheld trees two to six feet in diameter and thirty to sixty feet high standing before them. These Netherlanders just arrived on American soil did not have the slightest idea how to chop down trees in the American manner. Often they stood bent over in order to cut the trees off at the ground level, frequently they cut around the trunks of the trees with the result that the trees did not fall where they were desired. Sometimes such trees fell on houses thereby throwing everything in confusion. It was a difficult task requiring men of courage to clear away trees and branches. It was a wonder that the courage of these people did not languish and that there were not more accidents due to their lack of knowledge in clearing the forest.

Our settlers lacked skill in all this pioneer forest work. Sometimes in felling leaning trees we undercut on the wrong side. Keeping in mind conditions in the Netherlands where there were no stumps, some of us in our desire to have a field without stumps tried to dig green trees out of the soil. And sometimes we even dug ditches to bury the logs of the trees we felled. But, fortunately, there were native Americans living among us who showed us how to clear forests. Making waist-high undercuts and backcuts and using wedges effectively was the motto of every one of us who grasped the idea that "we Netherlanders on American soil want to become Americans."

The fixed determination of each to expand his clearing illustrated the motto "progress slow but sure". Courage inspired a man to pull the branches out of the snow and pile them up that they could be burned in the springtime. Heaping up green logs was a hard job. It required much labor to gather them from among the stumps and work them up into heaps. At first oxen were scarce, and the Hollanders had great difficulty in driving them without reins. On one occasion when a father bought a yoke of oxen and was told how to drive them, on hearing the directions that were given and afraid of forgetting them, commanded his son to "write it down, boy!" Often it proved difficult to burn piled up logs. After burning all day the fires were again stirred at night, in which task mothers and daughters usually helped.

Our first crops grew among logs. If they were not destroyed by wild animals we had a full harvest. Much damage was inflicted by deer, raccoons, squirrels, etc., which swarmed in the woods. Frequently deer came within a couple of rods from houses destroying plants. Squirrels were shot by the hundreds but they nevertheless increased in number. Plowing was an operation of great difficulty. Frequently it amounted to only the slightest stirring of the soil. But the least trace of a furrow produced crops. And whenever the plow stuck in the soil and had to be pulled back a second attempt might succeed better.

We soon mastered the American method of chopping down trees which were burned within one or two years, after which whatever was left was cleared away. In this manner our pioneers subjected acre after acre to the plow. And so the wild waste was transformed into fruitful fields. Forest fires, started by some accident, also cleared much land.

We commemorate the struggle of our pioneers, the earlier ones as well as the later. To cast a backward glance is instructive for us. The Lord has helped us, has given us courage and strength, has protected us whenever danger threatened. Many a time when things seemed to be against us, they really were in our favor. We say "Ebenezer" [1 Samuel, 7, 12]. Let us never forget the fact that in all we see and hear, the farms cleared by old as well as young are the chief means of our social well-being.

We rejoice in the present day. A half century lies behind us. Are we making too much of our past when we who have looked upon the sombre forests now behold villages, towns, and farms with houses and barns and say that an eventful life lies behind us? Let us praise Him who gave us courage and sustained us in our difficult task of being pioneers. If we had not stoof firm and had not been blessed by a mighty hand we would not see what we now behold.

To be satisfied was the pioneer's blessed portion, in spite of all privations. Today we are witnessing some of its results. Many now are enjoying the fruits of those privations and now we can live on what the pioneers have won with their hard labor. Many of those are still alive who came during the earlier or later days and helped create our farmlands and who struggled through all difficulties and privations. Let us then all say with heart and soul, "For of Him, and through Him, and to Him, are all things; to Whom be glory forever" [Romans 11, 36].

56. WILLIAM VAN EYCK'S
TRANSPORTATION IN COLONIAL DAYS

[The wooded isolation of the settlers of Holland and the surrounding Dutch Kolonie, especially during the first years after 1847, seemed insuperable and presented grave problems. William van Eyck, son of Henry van Eyck, spent his days in Holland and witnessed the conditions described in the following sketch written in 1897 and printed in *De Grondwet*, August 13, 1912.]

The ways and means of transportation in any country, in any age, furnish a very satisfactory index to material progress and development. Good roads have come to be recognized as factors in government, while the locomotive, the ocean greyhounds, intelligent electrical machines – even the unpretentious bicycle – have revolutionized the realm of economics and bade defiance to the predictions of the most skillful economic doctors. The number of horses displaced by the bicycle was enormous. The bicycle, it may be said, has abrogated some of the laws of political economy. And what will the further result be now the horseless carriage and the airship are added to the list of realities!

It is true that in the sphere of intellect there may be the highest attainments while at the same time the material interests lag; yet the ways and means of locomotion, of transportation, whether they be rude or highly refined, remain, obviously, characteristics – distinguishing marks – of a civilization.

In these days of rapid transit, of distance annihilating lightning expresses, telegraphs, and telephones, when "old times have gone, old manners changed," it is pleasant to look back through the mist of fifty years and contrast the quaint, unwieldy boats and vehicles of our fathers with the steamships – veritable floating palaces – the railroad, the telegraph, and telephone of today.

Fifty years ago the expression: "Distance lends enchantment to the view" meant more than it does today. Although Robert Fulton's *Clermont* plied the Hudson as early as 1807, forty years before, the steamship was yet in its infancy. There were a few steamers running between New York and Liverpool and on the rivers and the Great Lakes; but by far the great bulk of traffic and transportation was carried on by sailing vessels. There were a few railroads in Massachusetts and New York, but of a very primitive kind. The government had constructed several important western highways; there were so-called "territorial roads" even in Michigan. The Erie Canal had been opened, but the magnetic telegraph had only just been invented and the news of Polk's nomination telegraphed from Baltimore to Annapolis. But all those agencies which have since grown so great were as yet in their experimental stage – the exceptions, not the rule – so that, when the Hollanders came to America, in the forties, the whole American continent still lay in the gloom and loneliness of the era of long distances. We of to-day can scarcely realize the pall of solitude that hung over the frontier settlements of this country fifty years ago. Imagine the present generation waiting for satisfactory election returns for months! Imagine the news of the Battle of Waterloo or of Gettysburg reaching us two months after the encounter! Yet such was the case fifty years ago.

Then, one unbroken forest of tall pines and monster oaks stretched from Kalamazoo to Grand River. Grand Haven and Grand Rapids were small trading posts in the depths of the forest; Port Sheldon, a typical "Deserted Village". No roads connected those small points except an old Indian track or a trail blazed through the woods. In 1847 there were a few shivering Frenchmen at Port Sheldon, and a few stragglers at Singapore and Saugatuck, while the bosom of Black Lake was disturbed only by the wind and the red man's canoe. The Reverend Mr. Smith, missionary among the Indians, and Mr. Isaac Fairbanks, wo taught the Indians agriculture, were the only white men in the vicinity of Black Lake when the first Hollanders arrived. There was no Chicago and West Michigan Railway then, no *Lizzie Walsh*, *City of Holland*, or *Soo City* then – not even a *Fanny Shriver*.

But then as now the great waterways were there and almost all transportation was carried on by water. Travel by land was almost impossible, for the extremely dense forest with its close undergrowth and the swampy soil made it hazardous – in fact, often impossible – to travel on foot, not to speak of wagons and teams. This explains why the emigrant, who had crossed the ocean in the sailing vessel – not a steamboat – the voyage frequently lasting ninety or one hundred days [an exaggeration], continued the journey west by water. Many of the Hollanders who came to America during the forties and fifties made the entire trip from their homes in the Netherlands to their new homes in America by water. Landing at New York, they sailed up the Hudson, then through the Erie Canal to Buffalo, thence over the Great Lakes to the mouth of the Black Lake, where Macatawa and Ottawa Beach are today. From the mouth they proceeded to "de stad" by means of scows of flatboats, which were propelled by sails when the wind was high, but more often by means of long poles with which the men on board pushed the scows along the shore – a very laborious process, to be sure. The settlers at Groningen and Zeeland went up Black River, beyond the present Scholten's Bridge to Groningen, where they finally disembarked.

Those of the Hollanders who went farther west, sailed down the Ohio, or up the Mississippi from New Orleans, to St. Louis or to Keokuk, whence they continued the journey by land to that western Dutchman's Jerusalem – Pella, Iowa.

In 1846, when Dominie van Raalte arrived, the Michigan Central Railway terminated at Kalamazoo; the Michigan Southern reached as far west as Hillsdale; while from Detroit to Pontiac was the beginning of the Detroit, Grand Haven, and Milwaukee Railway.

The story of these early ventures at railroading forms an interesting bit of history. The romantic episode of Governor Mason and Theodore Romeyn, with their trunkful of bills, the failure on the part of the State when it undertook the work of building railroads, and the curious blunders of the projectors have in the light of subsequent developments acquired the aroma of fiction.

The construction of the roads in itself is interesting. Wooden stringers about five by seven inches were placed on ties or crossbeams sunk into the ground. On the wooden stringers was spiked down a flat iron bar, called "strap rail", about one-half inch thick, somewhat like a wagon tire. Th. M. Cooley, [Justice of the Supreme Court of Michigan], says, "The railroad with its little cars of stagecoach fashion was doing what it could to help the procession of emigrants move into Michigan. It carried baggage at the risk of the owner, but its speed was not such as to put life at much risk except perhaps when a broken strap rail ran a snakehead up through the car floor." That accidents were none too uncommon on those early roads, and that late trains were something regular, does not require a violent stretch of the imagination. The average speed was far greater than that of the stagecoaches, and those railroads, primitive as they were, wherever they went, superseded the old reliable stage lines.

With the heavy forest and swampy soil the project of roadmaking was the problem of those early colonial days in Michigan. The utter want of experience proved the great obstacle to progress in this line. On the plains of Iowa, Nebraska, Kansas, and the Dakotas roads may be said to have existed from the beginning. All that the settlers needed was the proper direction, when they could strike out over the prairie wherever they wanted to go. Roads could be made simply by driving over the same track a few times. Very little bridging was necessary. But in Michigan where the country in its primitive shape was a swamp full of gigantic trees resembling those of the Carboniferous Age, the labor of opening roads and building bridges was a herculean task. The amount of work and money devoted to roads and bridges was enormous. It is safe to say that for years more than one third of the time and energy of the Holland colonists of Allegan and Ottawa Counties was expended in the construction of roads and bridges. First, trees were felled and stumps removed so as to admit of the passage of wagons. Log bridges were thrown across streams and in boggy places logs were laid crosswise over the way, making that excellent road called, from its pronouncedly ribbed appearance, "corduroy". In 1847 the State made an appropriation of 400 acres of land for the purpose of building a bridge across Black River at Holland. The work was afterwards completed under the supervision of Dominie van Raalte and Jan Binnekant. A little later, the business men of Grand Rapids helped in the construction of the Grand Rapids road – a bee line – in order to obtain more of the colony trade. A stage was put on this line, running through Groningen, Zeeland, Jennison, and Wyoming [now Grandville], with the Half-way House at Mrs. de Regt's, in the southeast corner of Blendon township. Still later, a road was constructed by a commission appointed by the Governor, from Allegan to Holland and northward, called the Allegan, Muskegon, and Grand Traverse Bay State Line. This road entered the Village of Holland by what is now called State street.

At first there was little order or system in roadmaking. People helped each other as best they could, with the same spirit that prompted the scheme of the "colony store" and "colony vessel"; but it was only when highway taxes became prominent and a force of highway commissioners elected that more rapid and systematic progress was made.

Considerable local traveling was done on foot. In 1847 Messrs. Teunis Keppel, Hein van der Haar and Jan Binnekant, a committee of three for a party of colonists that had come by way of New Orleans and St. Louis, came all the way from Chicago on foot. Trips of twenty miles or more to Allegan, Grand Haven, or Grand Rapids were made on foot. In 1848-49, many emigrants who had landed at Grand Haven walked to Holland. Business trips to "The Haven" and "The Rapids" were usually made on foot; that was the cheaper, often the quicker – sometimes the only – way of traveling.

The ox played an important role in those early days. The horse was considered beyond the reach of common people. Besides, the slow, patient ox was admirably adapted to the bad roads and stumpy fields, and the shouts of *whoa*, *haw*, and *gee* mingled on all sides with the sound of the woodsman's ax and the crash of the falling tree. The ox was the locomotive of those days and was only gradually displaced by the horse when roads improved and the woods were removed. For years people drove to town with a yoke of oxen and on market days the streets were lined with ox teams. Mr. Gerrit J. Haverkate divided with Edward J. Harrington Sr., the distinction of having introduced the first yoke of oxen and the first span of horses.

The mails of those days would simply create a panic in the business world of today, if we should all at once be subjected to the same delays and slow carriers. For years, the western mail from New York and New England had come along the shore of Lake Erie in winter, by boat over the lake in the summer, and from Monroe to Chicago by stage. In 1838 there was a weekly stage from Jackson to Kent [now Grand Rapids]. Mails were exceedingly slow and postage was sometimes as high as 25 cents on a single letter so that it cost a fellow a pretty penny if his best girl lived in another town. In 1846 the Rev. George N. Smith and Isaac Fairbanks were obliged to go to Saugatuck for their mail, or to Grand Haven by Indian trail, or along the Lake Shore for mail and the Indians' pay. In 1848 a postoffice was established in what is now Holland City, and was called "Black River". Henry D. Post was the first postmaster. The mail came once a week from Manlius [New Richmond], then the nearest postoffice, Willem Notting and his *vrouw* were the first mail carriers carrying the mail on their backs. Later, when a post office was established, at Zeeland, a private carrier, Keesje van den Hoek, brought mail to Vriesland and Drenthe, receiving eight cents apiece for carrying letters.

The most interesting part of the subject clusters around those heroic men who braved the weather, roads, forest, and all – the stage drivers. Rich in anecdote and thrilling experience is the lore of those jolly fellows. Their daily trips averaged between twenty and thirty miles. The roads were of the roughest kind, full of stumps and through densde forests. Swamps, morasses, sink holes, sand, and clay obstructed and delayed travel. No graded and graveled roads. In winter, the snow was frequently six feet deep; and, until the advent of the spring wagon, the heaviest kind of lumber wagon, covered with canvas like a gypsy's served as a coach. Perhaps, in after years, when our citizens shall have nothing better to do, they may duplicate the old stage between Holland and Grand Rapids, with its jolts and corduroys, just as the elite of New York and Philadelphia every summer reproduce the tallyho of a hundred years ago.

The first regular mail carriers and stage drivers were Jan Trimpe, Jan van Dyk, and Gerrit J. Haverkate, while Pieter F. Pfanstiehl was one of the first who held the contract for carrying mail to and from Kalamazoo. Among the other early drivers may be mentioned M. Visser, S. Hofstra, James Westweer, Roelof Bongaerts, C. de Young, Willem ten Hagen, and Richard van den Berg.

The stage drivers were the important men of their day. They connected the settlement with the outside world. They carried passengers, freight, packages to the express offices and anything else that was portable. They were the lightning express of their day; but they did wonderfully well if they succeeded in reaching their destination after a whole day's travel on the road. They braved all sorts of weather, drove through sleety rain and howling snowstorms, often stuck in the mud, and as often capsized. Their lot was hard and the pay small.

Mr. Haverkate, the first regular driver on the Grand Rapids line, made the trip up and down semi-weekly, stopping at the Half-way House of De Regt, about two miles and a half west of Hudsonville.

Among the other drivers on that line may be mentioned S. Hofstraat, Cornelius de Young, C. Blom Sr., and Adam Westma. De Young was driver during the war – 1862-64 – and was succeeded by Cornelius Blom. Adam Westma was the last stage driver, and with him the line died when the Grand Rapids branch of the Chicago and West Michigan Railroad reached Holland.

P. F. Pfanstiehl and his son Captain Peter Pfanstiehl, men to whom this locality owes so much in the line of shipping facilities, had charge of the Kalamazoo and Grand Haven line, the trip up and down taking six days – one day from Holland to Allegan, the next from Allegan to Kalamazoo, the third from Kalamazoo to Allegan, the fourth from Allegan to Holland the fifth from Holland to Grand Haven, the sixth, the return from Grand Haven to Holland. This stage line was discontinued when the Allegan and Grand Haven Railroad reached Holland in 1868.

One of the early merchants of Holland described the transportation of his wares as follows: "Before Holland harbor was built, goods came by vessel to Saugatuck or Grand Haven, whence they were brought forward to Holland by team. We were obliged to lay in a stock of goods in the fall before the close of navigation, to last until May following. We bought on credit, six months sometimes elapsing before we could pay. We often bought bark and staves at Groningen, loaded them on scows there and shipped them to the mouth of Black Lake, the trip taking a whole day and more. At the mouth the staves and bark were unloaded and piled on the beach. Frequently while thus piled the water and the wind would cover them over with sand."

"I lost", the merchant continued, "three or four hundred dollars' worth in that way during the Crimean War but I made the loss good by the rise in prices incident to that war. At the mouth of Black Lake we would watch for a vessel bound for Chicago. The vessel, when sighted, would be signaled and stopped and would cast anchor about a quarter of a mile from shore. Then a rope was stretched from the vessel to a scow on which the bark and staves had again been piled, and by means of that rope the scow was pulled toward the vessel and the bark and staves were loaded."

The merchant in charge of such a cargo would frequently go along with the vessel to Chicago, to sell the staves and bark, and return by another vessel with a supply of store goods.

Sometimes it happened that the harbor was entirely barred with sand and the water in Black Lake and the river would be very high, although usually light craft could enter. The old channel ran where Ottawa Beach Hotel now stands, and considerably north of the present pier. At one time the Government spent about $ 6,000 in building a pier west of where Macatawa Park Hotel is now, but the job was given up. A little later, Alderd Plugger, L. Schaddelee, Pieter F. Pfanstiehl, John Roost, and others took up the matter of harbor improvement and soon the present harbor was begun. A little trench was dug and the water allowed to widen the trench into a channel. One of those present when that work was performed afterward declared: "It was a magnificent sight; the pressure of the water was tremendous." When this channel was completed larger vessels could enter the harbor and go as far as Holland. The lake trade grew considerably during the sixties and freight and passenger rates were reasonable; but, when the railroad from Allegan in 1868 and the railroad from Chicago and Grand Rapids in 1871 reached Holland, most of the transportation was done by railroad. It was much quicker by rail; and time, with business men, is always the essence of a transaction. The advent of the first railroad in 1868 also brought a more expeditious mail service, and an express office, with Otto Breyman agent, at a salary of $80.

The incidents of life on the frontier are generally very similar: the same phenomena present themselves with only slight differences – the same long distances, the same trackless woods or plains, the same familiar ox team as in every new settlement. What applies to the early settlements in Michigan applies with equal propriety to those in Wisconsin. The settlers at Pella, Iowa, had the same experience as those in this state, except that the forest primeval was not so primeval in that region as in Michigan; but, so long as they had no railroads there, the settlers were obliged to travel by stage, and the mails came the same way from stations miles away.

The settlers in Sioux County, Iowa, had little to contend with in the way of swamps and jungles, and roadmaking was no problem for them; but for a time they had to go sixty or seventy miles to and from Juction City, now Le Mars, the nearest railroad station. The settlers in Nebraska, Kansas, and in Douglas, Charles Mix, and Campbell counties, South Dakota, had the full benefit of improved railroad appliances to their nearest station; but the journey from the station was all the way from twenty to seventy miles. The horse had by this time completely supplanted the ox, for on the plains the slow and steady ox was not a prime necessity, as among the stumps and logs of Michigan, and in Dakota and North-western Iowa all local transportation was carried on by horses, the ox doing the plowing and heavier farm work.

It is beyond the province of this sketch to enter into the details of the different ways and means of transportation of fifty years ago and of the present. To do justice to the subject would involve a reproduction of that noble exhibit in Transportation Building at the World's Fair.

When the Hollanders emigrated from the Netherlands to the settlements in America all the giant agencies of transportation of today were in their infancy. The ocean voyage fifty years ago took many weeks; now, it takes from six to ten days. The inland trip from the seaboard was a pilgrimage of weeks' duration; now, it can be done in thirty or forty hours. The journey from "the Haven" or "the Rapids" took from twelve to twenty-four hours; now, it takes only one hour. The transmission of a letter from New York to the settlements took three or four weeks; now, only two days at the longest. Then, such a thing as people miles apart talking over a wire was not so much as an iridescent dream. In those days, a President would be inaugurated before the election news had reached the frontier settlements; now, the telegraph scatters the news broadcast within twenty-four hours.

One of the brightest chapters in the world's history is that which records the progress in the means of transportation during the past fifty years. For ages the horses, stagecoach, the sailing vessels were the only common carriers. During the past half century, the steamship, the railroad, the electric road, the irrepressible bicycle, and the telegraph and telephone have practically annihilated a hitherto impassable gulf, rescued civilization from the shell of seclusion and division, and wedded humanity into a closer brotherhood. It is not a common occurrence now for a whole nation to die of hunger, as was frequently the case in former years; now, the telegraph spreads the news of famine and straightway the trains and the steamship speed on their mission of mercy and relief. It is during the past fifty years that these agencies of speedy communication and transportation have been perfected; and we share the benefits. What advancement in the line of transportation the future has in store for us we know not, but this is certain – that to do as well as our fathers have done we must do better.

In the noon-day splendor of the present "great things", let us not forget the "small beginnings" whence they grew. Let us rather "think on these things."

Chapter XIII

AN OFFICIAL REPORT
ON THE DUTCH KOLONIE IN MICHIGAN, 1849

57. ISAAC N. WYCKOFF'S REPORT

[In 1849 the Board of Domestic Missions asked the Rev. Isaac N. Wyckoff to visit the newly founded Dutch settlements in Michigan and Wisconsin, which resulted in the union of the immigrant churches with the Reformed Church of America. The report published under the title *Report of a Visit to the Holland Colonies* (New York, 1850) will ever remain an instructive document in the history of Dutch immigration.]

The undersigned begs leave respectfully to report the fulfillment of his mission, to the Board of Domestic Missions of the Reformed Protestant Dutch Church of North America.

Agreeably to your wishes and instructions after I had fulfilled the objects of my delegation to the Rev. the General Assembly of the Presbyterian Church convened at Pittsburg, I went on my way to the Holland Colony. I would first of all gratefully acknowledge the goodness of God and the kindness of Christian men in all my journey. Not a day has my health been in any wise impaired – not a day have I been hindered by stress of weather from prosecuting my mission. Everywhere the kindest personal attentions, and the best facilities for travelling have been offered by the Christian brethern. My journey was made from Pittsburgh by public conveyance through Beaver Canal, and by stage to Cleveland, by steamboat to Detroit, by railroad to Kalamazoo, by mail wagon to Allegan, and then by the voluntary and gratuitous favor of Judge John R. Kellogg's team and man, to the Colony. Such interest as Judge Kellogg [a New Englander] and his family have shown to our Holland brethern, ought to be recorded here. He hospitably entertained Mrs. A. C. van Raalte and children for three months while a house was erecting in the wilds of the Colony for her reception. He has several times given up his kitchen, and other parts of his dwelling, and the whole of another house he owns to accommodate the Hollanders as they weregoing through. He has preserved and defended the emigrants from imposition and oppression, and stood by them, as they gratefully express it, *met raad en daad* ["counsel and deed"] in all their difficulties.

He traveled with the Rev. A. C. van Raalte to examine lands and greatly contributed to the selection of the glorious country which the Colony now occupies. The Dutch Church thanks him, and may God bless him and his for such kindness!

It was a novel ride and not without peril, from Allegan to the Colony. With a noble span of horses and a wagon made for the purpose we hardly reached the place in eleven hours "with whole bones". How then must the colonists have struggled with ox teams and such wagons as they could get to reach the place.

My reception, as your messenger, by the Colony was almost literally with a shout of joy. There had been sorrow in the colony over many things and not least over the fact that the Dutch Church [which they had hoped would have reached the poor emigrants, flying in poverty from persecution, with sympathizing hearts and open arms] had seemed to take almost no interest at all in them. With the exception of a few individual brethren, they mourned that the Dutch Church counted them strangers, and had no word of encouragement, no hand of help for them. The reaction, therefore, was electrical. To think that we at last felt for them [cared for them, were willing to help them though late] shot through every heart, and there were many thanksgivings to God for His work of love, and many benedictions on the head of your representative. "Out of their deep poverty" shone "the riches of their liberality" to your commissioner. They feasted us with all they had – but it was mainly a change in pickled pork and fine potatoes. But they begin to have butter and eggs and when time permits they can get fine fish out of the lake.

It did not enter into my commission to examine their physical circumstances, and yet I doubt not that both you and many others will be pleased to know some particulars of their locality, progress of settlement, and condition; and I am happy to be able to satisfy so just a curiosity in a way that will gratify every benevolent heart. I arrived on Thursday evening June 1st [really, on May 31]. My plan was to assemble the ministers on Saturday [June 2], make your overtures, and be ready to start for Wisconsin on Monday [June 4]. But brother Van Raalte could not consent to so early a departure. First, the ministerial brethren could not be assembled till Monday, for expresses had to be sent for all. And second, I must see every settlement in order to give a fair account. The appearl was so earnest and reasonable that I consented to remain. On Friday [June 1], then, I visited the *city* of Holland. On Saturday [June 2], I walked from morning to night along Indian trails from one clearing and settlement to another in the vicinity. On Monday [June 4] the Classis met. On Tuesday mounted on the doctor's horse [the only horse in the colony] without a saddle, and Dominie van Raalte and others walking and leading the way, we went forth to visit the several country churches, swam the Black River, halted at Groningen, the nearest province, proceeded on a trail to Zeeland, spent the night with Rev. Cornelius van [der] Meulen's congregation. Wednesday, started early, went by the church of Drenthe, where we dined on butter and bread and coffee, and started for Vriesland, but got lost in our way, and had to employ a good woman as our guide. We at last found Rev. Maarten Anne Ypma, and after looking over his province and being hospitably entertained, and spending the night with him, we returned through the rain next morning to the city.

In my route I gathered the following statistics: The city with its environs contains 235 houses: Groningen, 30; Zeeland, 175; Drenthe, 45; Vriesland, 69; Overyssel, 35; Graafschap, 50. In all about 630 houses, which, at an average of five souls to a house will make the population over 3,000 souls. Some of the farms have two acres chopped and cleared, others five, and so on up to eighty; so that it may be fairly estimated that there are now three thousand acres cut and in progress of clearing.

The face of the country, which I had supposed was very flat, is pleasantly diversified with hill and valley, lake, and stream. The streams are fed by large cranberry marshes, which being themselves supplied by springs, send forth clear and healthy waters. I saw no lands which cannot be easily drained, so as to make them excellent for hay culture. It is a remarkable provision of nature that along the several rivers of Michigan there are broad tracts of natural meadow, affording abundance of pasture for summer and hay for winter. If the character of the forest is a proper index of the quality of the land on which it grows, then the soil is of the most fruitful kind. The trees are wonderful to a dweller on the Hudson. Many and many an oak have I seen from two to three feet in diameter, straight as an arrow, and having from nine to twelve post-cuts of eight feet each, before you reach the limbs. There are thousands of white pines that will yield from two to three thousand feet of clear inch boarding. I measured the stump of an oak five and a half feet in diameter. Three men [I being one] could only touch the tips of our fingers around an ancient sycamore. The most beautiful sugar maples grow on the heavy soils. Black walnut and curled and birds' eye maple and wild cherry trees, all of great dimensions, are plenty, and in many parts hemlocks of the most stately proportions. Where ever the land is sufficiently cultivated, the wheat is splendid, rank in growth and rich in color. Potatoes and turnips of the best quality will be abundant this year, and probably also Indian corn. The prospects of agriculture are full of hope and promise. The heart of the people rejoices amidst all their privations, in the mercy of God, which has given them such a goodly land and such great progress

A most cheering fact further encourages the people. It was anticipated from the dark color of the water in the river and lake indicating that it drained a soil deeply filled with vegetable matter, or flowing from muck swamps of great depth, that the location would be unhealthy. In the first year that dark anticipation seemed to be considerably realized, for not a few sickened and some died. But just as soon as the people became properly housed, this fear entirely subsided, for directly the colonists enjoyed an unusual average of health. During my whole visit I did not see or hear of a sick person, and this fact is the more conclusive, as this spring has been uncommonly wet and all the lower grounds have more or less surface water upon them. The early sickness was evidently owing not to badness of climate and air but to exposure to the inclemency of the elements and want of nourishing food.

I ought perhaps to mention in this connection that the Colony has uncommon natural advantages. There is a water power on the Black River driving two sawmills, to which a gristmill will soon be added, and at other points shingle and lath factories, and whatever else requires water power may be added. And there is scarcely on the face of the whole earth a more beautiful harbor for all manner of vessels than the Black Lake. It is about five miles long and varies from a quarter to a mile and a half broad and has a depth varying from seven feet within twenty feet of the city strand, to twenty, thirty, fifty, and even eighty feet. Like all the rivers on the eastern shore, its outlet is obstructed by the sandbars of the Michigan, but let a channel and haven once be formed, and it is the general opinion of all disinterested persons it will be the most desirable harbor and wintering place on all the western side of the peninsula.

For one thousand dollars a pier and plank road of five hundred and sixty yards can be constructed, which will immediately increase the trade ten or one hundred fold. A corps of engineers of the general government is now on the lake making an exact topographical survey of the lake and waters of the Michigan at its mouth. Colonel John R. Bowes, the experienced and gentlemanly leader of the corps, spoke in the highest terms of the beauty and facilities of the lake and harbor.

An enterprising gentleman has just finished and set in operation a steam sawmill that draws up its logs out of the lake and is doing a good business. A company have constructed a wind sawmill which operates well and is capable with an ordinary wind of driving six saws. At annery is in progress of erection, which will find inexhaustible quantities of quercitron and hemlock bark in the neighborhood; and within the limits of the city is a shipyard, which will be prepared to build all kinds of craft, and the live oak for the hulks and for plank, and the magnificent pines for masts and spars, are in sight on the shores of the lake.

From this description of the physical circumstances of the colony I will turn to the direct object of your commission, which was to inquire into the religious and ecclesiastical relations of this people, to express to them the sympathy of our church, to make an overture for church relation and to offer such aid in their straitness as might be necessary and desirable. To obtain this information Rev. van Raalte deemed it would be expedient to assemble the ministers and the elders of the churches. Accordingly he dispatched letters and messengers to the several ministers and consistories inviting them to a conference with me on Monday June 5th. Quite a large company attended and having opened the conference with prayer and a psalm we spent nearly the whole day in giving and receiving information and comparing ideas. From the assembled brethren I obtained the following facts and statistics. There are seven congregations and four ministers tacitly constituting the Classis of Holland.

			Families	Commu-nicants
1	Church of Holland	Van Raalte	225	250
2	Zeeland	Van der Meulen	175	225
3	Friesland	Ypma	69	125
4	Overyssel	Bolks	35	80
5	Graafschap	[Has called Rev. Mr. H. G. Klyn who is on his way to America]	50	100
6	Drenthe	[Has made a call but without success]	45	79
7	Groningen	[Has as yet made no call]	30	63

Five of these congregations have erected houses of worship, that of Zeeland is 45 by 60 feet, built of handsomely squared cedar logs with a cupola and bell, and is quite an ornamental building. The Holland house was first built and was more hastily and less neatly constructed. The others are comfortable log houses.

Of all these communicants in these churches it may be said they are praying and hopefully converted persons. Their religious habits are very strict and devout. They do all things with prayer and praise. They sing and pray in the morning, after their dinner, and after their supper. They pray when they meet for business. At a bee [or meeting for common work] they pray. The common council of the city opens its sittings with prayer. The appearance and tone of piety is purer and higher than any thing I have ever seen and seemed like the primitive Christians and most beautiful.

The colony is paying as much attention as possible to schools and Christian education. They have a Dutch school and English school in the city. At Zeeland, a Dutch school, and will soon have an English one and all the rest will follow. The teachers "must" be godly persons, who besides teaching reading and writing, must see that the children are prepared on the Catechism, and that they are taught to sing the Psalms. The ministers catechise all the children once a week, and if they are hindered, the elders take their place.

The pecuniary resources of the church are very low. The funds of the people, which were very limited, have been exhausted in the purchase of land, and in making their improvements, private and public, until there is nothing left. The pastors have had but little support, some of them literally none, from their churches. They have been obliged to struggle, and work, and suffer wants, just as these people have done. But they live in faith and hope of better times. They rejoice that the Lord has kept them alive and given them joy over their flocks in the drak and untrodden wilderness.

At the classical meeting it was soon made known that the brethren were a little afraid of entering into ecclesiastical connection with us although they believe in the union of brethren and sigh for Christian sympathy and association. They have so felt into the quick the galling chain of ecclesiastical domination and have seen with sorrow how exact organization according to human rules leads to formality on the one hand and to the oppression of tender consciences on the other that they hardly know what to say. I protested, of course, that it was the farthest from our thoughts to bring them in bondage to men or to exercise an ecclesiastical tyranny over them. And I stated that they would be most perfectly free at any time they found an ecclesiastical connection opposed to their religious prosperity or enjoyment to bid us a fraternal adieu and be by themselves again.

On comparison of doctrine a perfect agreement with our standards was found. In the order of their churches they believe each church and consistory shall direct and manage its own concerns; and incline to the idea that an appellate jurisdiction of superior judicatories is not so scriptural as kind and fraternal conferences and advice. Each of their churches appoint as many elders as seem desirable and they are always in office until they are dismissed as guilty and unworthy of removed by death. As the result they agreed with these explanations to join our Synod. It was deemed best that they should not emerge themselves into our existing Classis of Michigan, but unite as a separate Classis with our Northern Synod. They will, however, correspond by delegates with our classes there. To this agreement I saw no insuperable objection and I would report the Classis of Holland accordingly.

On the subject of missionary aid the brethren expressed most singular and honorable objections. They thought it seemed best that the obligation of the churches to support them as pastors should not be impaired by the hope of foreign aid and that until the churches were able suitably to take care of their pastors, they must suffer with their people. That they were all sadly poor was true but they saw no example in the Scripture, in which a suffering church or people asked for aid, and therefore did not feel at liberty in their correspondence to dot it. But there was a precedent in the Scriptures in which, when it was known that the churches of Judea suffered, other churches sent them supplies not as by solicitation but out of brotherly love and bounty. If therefore our churches, knowing by this report how straitened they were, would out of their love and symptathy send a free gift to the Colony to be appropriated as the ministers and elders should deem the necessities of the saints demanded they would receive and acknowledge it with all gratitude in the Lord.

I felt that this was taking high and holy ground and I hope it may be considered within the powers of the missionary board to meet their hallowed scruples in this matter. And whether the board can do this or not there is one form in which they can minister to the necessity of the emigrants and in this form I adventured to take the liberty to pledge their aid. There are scattering companies of Hollanders at Kalamazoo, Grandville, Grand Haven, Allegan, and a number of surrounding places, which the brethren in the Colony endeavor to supply. Bu this supply is extremely inconvenient and laborious for them. For example, Allegan is thirty miles and Kalamazoo still further from the Colony. The ministers have no horses, and to walk afoot thirty miles out and preach three times on the Sabbath is very exhausting work when they must clamber their way often by blazed trees and along Indian trails. The bretheren very much wished they had a missionary or itinerant brother who should have

these small and scattered flocks under his soled care. I promised that as
soon as they could call a suitable man and report to you, you would put
him on the footing of your most favored country missionaries. The Rev.
Mr. Klyn will come through New York. He has sacrificed much to this
service. [The Graafschap to which he is called is struggling with difficulties.] Any token of love from you or the New York churches to him
will be very opportune.

The length of time necessarily spent in Michigan had already thrown
me a week beyond my engagement to return and it became out of my
power to visit the settlements and churches in Wisconsin. I made a visit
to Milwaukee and spent the Sabbath with the churches there. There are
about sixty Holland families, comprising seventy-five communicants
mostly located on the south side of Milwaukee River, where they have
built a very decent house of worship. They have no minister at present,
and they compelled me to attempt to preach to them in the Holland
language. Then I ascertained that there is a church in the neighborhood
of Sheboygan under the care of the Rev. Peter Zonne embracing about
eighty families and perhaps the same number of communicants.

At Waupun, six miles from Fond-du-lac, the head of the Winebago
Lake, there is a settlement of thirty families or more and a regularly
organized church under the care of the Rev. Mr. [Gerrit] Baay, containing more than forty members.

There is also a rising settlement eight or ten miles out of Milwaukee,
consisting of sixteen families who have neither organization nor minister.
I am informed by letter from Mr. B. of the willingness of himself and
church to connect themselves with our church and their thankfulness for
any aid our missionary board may please to give. I have written to him,
advising him to join the Holland Classis until a Wisconsin Classis can be
formed.

On my return, I ascertained, that there was a sufficient number of
Holland emigrants at Buffalo, to form a respectable church; – that they
had been just ready to organize under the ministry of the Rev. Cornelius
van Malsen, a most godly and estimable young man, when it pleased God
to remove him by death, and that no other movement has since been
made among them. There is also an organized church at Pickleville and
Pultneyville, eighteen miles from Rochester, under care of the presbytery
of Steutren, to which the Rev. John Visscher has been sent as a missionary
by the Home Missionary Society of the Old School Presbyterian Church.

There is another organized church of Hollanders at Rochester under
care of presbytery, to which the Rev. A. B. Veenhuysen ministers. Your

commissioner felt a disagreeable emotion at the thought, that these Holland brethren, agreeing with our church in every particular of standards, doctrine, and government, should have been so long neglected by us, that at last they must fall into the hands of strangers to their language and customs. But still, thanks are due to God, and to our Presbyterian brethren, that the poor people were provided with the bread of life.

On the whole I consider the Holland colony in Michigan most wisely located in divine providence. There are many excellent men in the state who cordially favor its interests. The state has enacted a law appropriating 3,000 acres of land to make roads in the colony and 4,000 for the erection of a pier and other facilities for convenience. The ministers and the city council importuned me till I could not refuse to promise them as soon as possible to negotiate for them the loan of a thousand dollars on the whole property of the city, consisting of eleven contiguous eighty acre lots for the purpose of building this pier. A spirit of brotherly kindness and philanthropy reigns among these colonists which must be as acceptable before God as it is beautiful before me. A case will illustrate this. Two godly parents having six children both died leaving no relations or support for their orphans. Immediately six families adopted each one of the orphans, to bring them up in all respects as their own and one of their families [brother Van Raalte has six of his own]. It is a most remarkable community and God will sustain and bless it and I feel that it will be a blessing and an honor to us to be His instruments in this matter.

In conclusion if I have been more particular and prolix in the report than is usual, I think you will pardon me. I judge you wish not for generalities but for particulars and I have endeavored to furnish them. My journey has been very fatiguing but if you should have as much pleasure in hearing and ministering as I have had in observing and detailing we shall all be amply repaid for this effort of Christian benevolence.

> Respectfully Submitted,
> Isaac N. Wyckoff
> Deputy of the Missonary Society

Chapter XIV

EXTRACTS FROM A CONTEMPORARY DIARY

58. HENDRIK VAN EYCK'S DIARY

[The following excerpts from a manuscript diary kept by Hendrik van Eyck, now preserved in the Netherlands Museum, present an exceptionally detailed view of the Dutch settlement in Michigan during its earlier years.]

Maandag den 26 April [1847]. Ik gevoel het gewicht van het standpunt waarop ik geplaatst ben. Van mijne moeder, het dierbaarste wat ik op aarde bezit, van mijne beminde broeders, lieve zusters en verdere betrekkingen heb ik een hartroerend afscheid genomen. Van mijnen vaderlijken meester L. Pessink te Zwolle en diens overige huisgenoten; van alle vrienden en vriendinnen; J. Montijn, den leeraar mijner jeugd; van de plek mijner geboorte Oldebroek, in de provincie Gelderland gelegen, van het eenvoudige oord mijner kindsheid, dat oord, dien kring waar mijne kinder- en jongensjaren in vroolijke droomen over de toekomst henen rolden. Het is avond, wij schepen in. Goedsmoeds varen wij af. Zwolle is spoedig uit ons gezicht verdwenen.

Hasselt en Zwartsluis voorbij gestevend zijnde loopen wij uit in de Zuiderzee bij Genemuiden; het is nu reeds morgen van 27 April. Stormachtig weder. Aanhoudende tegenwinden. Wij passeeren langs de Geldersche kusten. Elburg zien wij nog van verre. Wij zijn genoodzaakt te ankeren in het gezicht van Harderwijk tot 's avonds van den 28 April.

29 April. Arriveeren wij te Amsterdam, liggen in het Noord-Hollandsch Kanaal. Vele onaangename verschijnselen doen zich op. Wij kunnen nog niet vertrekken, nog niet aan boord van ons schip en moeten maar zoolang aan het tolhuis over het IJ in stallen verblijven...

Den 2 Mei. Wij wonen de godsdienst bij aan boord van het schip *Noord-Holland*, onder de leiding van Ds. Zonne...

22 Mei, 1847. Ingevolge eene geslotene overeenkomst met de Heeren Ponselet en Zonen, stappen wij aan boord van het schip de *Snelheid* gevoerd door kapitein J. J. Gorter, om met dien bodem de reis naar de nieuwe wereld te doen...

23 Mei. Zijnde Pinksterzondag vangen wij den togt, na voor het laatst Nederlandsch hoofdplaats bezocht te hebben, aan en trekken door het kanaal langs onderscheidene dorpen, waaronder Ilpendam, enz. tot Purmerend, een net stadje met veel handel. Wij zouden er den nacht over

verblijven en hebben dus den tijd om hetzelve te bezichtigen...

1 Aug. Een reisje [van New York] gedaan naar New Jersey waar insgelijks vele Hollanders woonen, welke ons zeer vriendelijk onthalen...

15. Aug. Te Throgsneck in West Chester County blijf ik eenige tijd aan het werk, hetwelk mij in het eerst zeer moeijelijk viel, zijnde ik nog niet tot mijn vorige sterkte gekomen, bovendien het werk wat afgewend.

5 Sept. Het werk af zijnde verliet ik dezen oord en vertrok van hier met de stage naar Williamsburg, waar ik mij in den spoorwagen plaatste en de reis over een dorp, Haarlem genoemd, naar New York voortzette. Wij kwamen behouden te New York aan, waar ik bij mijne vrienden Liesveld mijnen intrek neem en New York nader bezichtig...

Schralenburgh, 9 Sept. Ging ik de stad alweder verlaten om in de buurtschap Schralenburgh, gelegen in Bergen County in New Jersey State te gaan wonen. Hier is eene gemeente van de oude Hollandsche Gereformeerde Kerk, welke de oude regelen en formulieren van eenigheid dier gemeenten nog behouden en gebruiken, hoezeer de Hollandsche taal in hunne eeredienst niet meer gebezigd en in hunne scholen niet meer geleerd wordt. In den dagelijkschen omgang spreken de menschen nog bijna algemeen de oude Nederduitsche taal. Er bestaat insgelijks een gemeente Seceder, welke afgescheiden is van eerstgenoemde Church...

25 Nov. Ik geniet alhier vele vriendschap van den achtingswaardigen leeraar der Reformed Dutch Church, de Rev. Cornelius Blauvelt. Zijn huis staat altijd voor mij en de overige hier zijnde Hollandsche emigranten open. Menige avond in gesprek aan zijn huis doorgebragt en met het zingen van een Hollandsche psalm en gebed besloten, zal mij voor altijd onvergetelijk zijn en mij met achting aan dien waardigen godsman doen denken...

19 April [1848]. Uit het westen dezes lands ontvangen brieven doen mij besluiten het tegenwoordig verblijf weder verlaten. Den 17n April verliet ik Schralenburgh, het oord waar ik den winter met zoo veel genoegen en het genot van zoo veele onverdiende vriendschap heb doorgebracht. Met weemoed had ik daags te voren van den waardigen leeraar C. Blauvelt afscheid genomen... In New York neem mijnen intrek bij mijne vrienden Liesveld...

6 Mei. Na een verblijf van 17 dagen ben ik dan eindelijk vast besloten, om naar het westen te reizen. Wij gaan den 4 Mei aan boord van de stoomboot *North America* en komen den volgenden morgen te Albany aan. In het jaar 1653 werd er de eerste Hollandsche Ger. Kerk gebouwd. Dezelve staat nog in State Street. Er zijn van deze gemeente nog zeer vele leden, kerken en predikanten, onder derwelke laatste vooral uitmunt,

Isaac N. Wijckof wegens zijne goede gezindheid jegens de Hollandsche landverhuizers en zijne geleerdheid zeer beroemd...

10 Mei. Wij kunnen bijna niets vorderen, het kanaal bevat geen water genoeg om alle booten door de sluizen te laten...

Buffalo, den 18 Mei, Gisteren avond arriveerden wij alhier. Dus hadden wij na eenen vervelenden togt langs het Erie kanaal eindelijk Buffalo bereikt...

Erie, in Pensylvania, den 20 Mei. Nadat wij des avonds van den vorigen dag van onze togt naar Niagara te Buffalo terug gekomen waren, gingen wij aan boord van de stoomboot *General Harrison* en stevenden het meer Erie op...

Beaver, 24 Mei. Dezen morgen arriveerden wij alhier. Wij vertrokken den 21n van Erie met eene kanaalboot, op welke wij ons ellendig behelpen moesten, omdat er de helft te veel volks op was, zoodat er naauwelijks plaats om te staan, laat staan om te zitten of te liggen, was. In onzen weg zagen wij vele oorspronkelijke bosschen, veele korts ontginde landerijen, overal vruchtbare gronden. Het kanaal strekt ten bewijze, dat de Amerikanen in onderneming en volvoering van grootsche plannen voor geen volk der wereld behoeven te blozen. Zijnde hetzelve op vele plaatsen door de vaste rotsen, over kleine, maar zeer laag liggende rivieren, heen gewerkt is, in het laatste geval schijnt het eene groote goot te zijn; op eene plaats liep het ter hoogte van 180 voeten boven de grond heen, hetwelk een gezicht op levert, als of men door de lucht voer. Onderscheidene dorpen beginnen te ontwikkelen langs het kanaal. Beaver ligt aan de river Ohio...

Cincinnati, 27 Mei. Wij arriveerden heden alhier na eene reis van over de 400 mijlen op de Ohio rivier...

Mississippi, 31 Mei. De boorden van de Mississippi vertoonen natuur in alle deszelfs oorspronkelijke ruwheid. De verschijnselen van eene dikwijls buiten zijne oevers tredende geweldige stroom, herinnerden mij de vele rampen welke mijn dierbaar vaderland dikwijls om dezelve oorzaak heeft moeten ondergaan. Door den vloed uit den grond gerukte boomstammen liggen hier en daar opeengehoopt of drijven den stroom af. Lage prairies meestal met kort en digt woud begroeid, maakt het tooneel niet zoo schoon of zoo verscheiden als langs de overschoone Ohio...

St. Louis, den 4 Juny, Den eersten Juny arriveerden wij te Saint Louis in den staat Missouri en zochten dadelijk onze voormalige landgenooten op en namen onzen indrek bij een derzelve... Er worden alle jaren eenige honderden, het vorige jaar meer dan duizend, huizen aangebouwd. Eene verbazende menigte Hoogduitschers hebben zich hier gevestigd, gelijk wij die gedurende onze reis overal zeer veel aantroffen. In St. Louis, gelijk in alle Amerikaansche steden, zijn zeer veele kerken. Hoogduitsche, Methodisten, Lutherschen en Katholieken rigten er alle jaren in menigte op. Als ook de Presbyterianen, Engelsche Methodisten en andere gezindheden. Er zijn hier nog veele afstammelingen van de Fransche kolonisten, welke hunne taal nog spreken. Ons verblijf hier zal misschien niet heel lang zijn...

7 Augustus. Na een kortstondig verblijf op het land, eenige mijlen van de stad in den staat Missouri, kom ik heden weder in St. Louis. Het land is zeer vruchtbaar en wordt zonder bemesting bebouwd en bezit vooral in de nabijheid der stad reeds eene hooge waarde. Boeren hofsteden [farms] vindt men hier ter groote van 300 en meer acres. De staat is over het algemeen weinig bewoond. In het westelijke gedeelte zijn nog eenige Indiaansche volkstammen, van welk ik er eenige in St. Louis zag. Zij zijn blank van huid. Alleen hebben zij zich door beschildering somstijds afzigtelijke vormen aangenomen. Sommigen hebben het hoofd en haar rood geplekt, anderen hebben het aangezicht zwart gevervd met 3 à 4 witte strepen over elke wang. Het haar wordt meest kaal van het hoofd geschoren, alleen laten zij eene kuif haren op het hoofd staan, welke tezamen gebonden en met vederen versierd wordt.

8 Aug. Alles in overweging nemende, de ongezondheid van het luchtgestel, enz., besluiten wij St. Louis te verlaten en nemen plaats op de stoomboot *Anthony Wayne* en stevenen de Mississippi op.

Peru, den 10 Aug. Na eene genoegelijke togt van twee dagen kwamen wij alhier aan. Het was nacht toen wij de Mississippi verlieten en de Illinois rivier opstoomden. Beardstown is eene nieuwe welvarende plaats aan deze rivier. Peoria is eene zeer schoone plaats aan een plein door de Illinois gevormd meer. Peru zal denkelijk in welvaart toenemen, naarmate de doorvoer langs het kanaal van Chicago tot St. Louis in belang toeneemt. Tot hiertoe hadden wij bijna niets anders dan bosschen ter wederzijden van de rivier gezien. Dezen morgen werden wij aangenaam verrast door het verschijnen eener heerlijke prairie, welke eene verhoogde streek langs de rivier had. Dit scheen mij een dijk te zijn. Ik waande mij op eens in Nederland verplaatst te zijn en de heerlijke Hollandsche weiden te zien. Het heerlijkst groen geschakeert met prachtige bloemen verrukten mij dermate, dat ik er als aan geboeid was...

Chicago, den 14 Augustus. Hedenmorgen arriveerden wij na eenen langzamen togt alhier. De reis was anders niet onaangenaam en zelfs soms zeer vermakelijk geweest. De schoonste prairies van onafzienbare groote, somtijds afgewisseld door schoone, snel ontwikkelende dorpen of kleine bosschen, waren verukkelijk fraai. Onder de plaatsen langs het kanaal munt vooral uit Ioliet [Joliet], aan beide zijden van het water liggende. Wat digter naar Chicago komende vonden wij veel rundvee grazende op die onafzienbare vruchtbare weiden. Aan Chicago rivier gekomen zijnde, waar groote stoomwerktuigen het kanaal van water voorzien, werden wij door eene stoom sleepboot naar hier gesleept. Het kanaal is uitmuntend gebouwd en is veel beter ingerigt dan de andere Amerikaansche vaarwaters die ik zag. Het is ook gemakkelijk dat men er niet zoo vele locks [schutsluizen] heeft dan in het Erie kanaal, daarbij zijn de bruggen hoog en boven het water gebouwd en is het kanaal zelve breeder en regelmatiger aangelegd dan de andere canals, langs welke ik gereisd heb.

Den 16 Aug. Chicago is binnen weinige jaren van niets tot eene tamelijke groote stad aangegroeid en bevat nu ongeveer 25,000 zielen. Koophandel en fabriekwezen bloeijden er ongemeen. Er heerscht eene drukte en bezigheid als in de grootste koopsteden der oude wereld. Ik vond hier onderscheiden Hollanders welke ik vroeger gekend had. Het ging hun hier wel. Veel handel wordt hier in timmerhout gedreven, enz.

Lake Michigan, den 20 Augustus. Tot gisteren morgen werden wij door tegenwind verhinderd onze reis voort te zetten, doch toen werd de wind gunstiger en wij zeilden uit in het meer. Eene kleine storm beliep ons, welke mij en sommige onzer reisgenooten zeeziek maakte; hierbij kwam het slechte onthaal dat wij aan boord genoten. Slechte spijs en het slapen op eene kist in het ruim, alwaar ik door het menigvuldige water dat in het schip kwam naauwelijks droog kon liggen, deden mij zeer naar land verlangen. Tegenwind verhinderde ons de mond van Blackriver te bereiken.

Grandhaven, den 21 Augustus. Heden morgen liepen wij de Grandriver in, doch daar wij met de schipper overeengekomen waren om ons aan de mond der Black river te brengen, zoo bleven onze goederen aan boord, alsmede de andere passagiers om derwaards gevoerd te worden. Ik had echter geen zin om weer zee te kiezen en zal mijn vriend Mulder te Port Sheldon bezoeken en vervolgens verder te voet naar Black Lake gaan.

Holland aan Black Lake, den 22 Aug. Nadat ik gisteren mijn vriend J. G. Mulder bezocht en bij hem den nacht had doorgebracht, kwam ik heden middag in de Kolonie aan. Al aanstonds zocht ik mijn voormalige vrienden en bekenden op. Doch iets dat mij zeer ter neder sloeg was,dat ik bijna geen huis intrad of er waren zieken in; somtijds vijf of zes in eene woning. Kwaadaardige koortsen heerschten overal, de menschen zagen er uit als waren zij uit het rijk der schimmen op de wereld wedergekeerd. Het was ook juist het ongezondste getijde des jaars toen wij hier kwamen.

Vele voormale vrienden en bekenden waren reeds niet meer. Onder de sukkelingen, ontberingen, ongewoonheid des klimaats, enz., hetwelk koortsen en andere landkwalen verwekten en in de hand werkte, waren zij bezweken. Dat velen, welke zich in een aardsch paradijs, in een lui-lekkerland in Amerika waanden te zullen worden binnengevoerd, en nu eene woeste wildernis, ondoordringbare bosschen, bijna geen menschelijk wezen, of geen de minste sporen van bewerking, geen ordentelijk woonhuis te zien kregen, dat velen daarop den moed al aanstonds lieten vallen, baarde mij weinig verwondering. Dit alles, gevoegd bij de afgematheid door de lange reis, eerst ter zee en dan nog zoo lang te lande en de schadelijke dampen uit de pas opgeklierde landen, wekte te zamen ten verderve van den emigrant.

Bij onze aankomst waren de koortsen wel algemeen heerschend, doch de sterfgevallen waren niet buitengewoon veel en in geene vergelijking met die des vorigen jaars. Ook is het thans voor den eerst aankomende gemakkelijk, dat er reeds huisvesting te bekomen is. Ook is er geen gebrek aan de noodige levensmiddelen. Er zijn huizen te huur, boarding houses [kosthuizen] te bekomen. Winkels zijn er ook genoeg.

Den 28 Augustus. De reeds uitgelegde stad een weinig doorgeloopen hebbende en ook een weinig van het omliggende land, trek ik er een kort verslag van tezamen.

In het eerst is het geen zeer opwekkend gezicht steeds hier en daar een huis gebouwd te zien of nog in aanbouw, in kleine openingen van het bijna ondoordringbaar woud, omringd door boomstompen, welke ter hoogte van twee à drie voeten boven den grond staan. Alom staan deze stompen nog op de straten, in de tuinen, enz., in zulk eene menigte dat men zelfs bij dag, gestadig voor zich heeft te zien en des avonds in den donker, alle behoedzame voorzichtigheid behoort in het werk te stellen, teneinde in geene, ver van aangename, aanraking met die onverzettelijke stijfhoofden te komen, doende de minste botsing tegen dezelve, niet zelden den wandelaar met blauwe schenen te huis komen.

Slechts langs eene straat staan de huizen gebouwd, eenigen aan Black Lake uitgezonderd. Het aantal in die straat is dertig. Hier en daar staan er nog wat afgezonderd. Ik denk dat e1 in het geheel zoo wat 50 zijn. Men gaat echter druk voort met den aanbouw van huizen, het klieren van land, enz. Er zijn in de Kolonie bij de 4,000 menschen. Zij wonen wel 20 mijlen in het rond. De boeren trekken meer landwaarts in. De stad wordt op een schrale zandgrond aangelegd, doch allergeschikst gelegen aan Black Lake voor den handel en de oprichting van fabrieken. Eene stoomzaagmolen zal er worden gebouwd. Eene windmolen is reeds afgetimmerd. Nog zijn er op een uur afstands twee zaagmolens, welke door waterkracht gedreven worden. Dat er nu voortaan geen timmerhout behoeft aangevoerd te worden van elders is een zeer voordeelige zaak voor de Kolonie; nu toch blijft het geld onder de Hollanders en levert den werkman arbeid en bestaan. Doordien in het eerst alles van andere plaatsen moest komen, zooals bouwmaterialen en levensbehoeften, ging al het gerede geld weg en er kwam niets terug, zoodat er groote schaarste aan geld in de kolonie, welke veele anders voor de opkomst en bloei derzelve onontbeerlijke werkzaamheden en ondernemingen zoo lang reeds teruggehouden heeft en wie weet hoe langen tijd nog wel doet uitstellen.

De mond van de Black River, welke geheel door het zand uit Michigan Lake volgespoeld is, zoodat geen vaartuigen in of uit kunnen, moet worden opengemaakt, en met piers of hoofden ver in het meer gewerkt, tegen verdere verstopping beveiligd worden. Zonder dit kunnen koophandel, neeringen en handteeringen niet bloeien en geen tak van nijverheid welvaren. Nu brengt die zoo uitnemend voor bevaring geschikte stroom, de stad der kolonie niets aan dan ongezonde, door het stilstaande water veroorzaakte, dampen.

De opvoeding der jeugd is mede nog in een slechte toestand, zijnde er in het geheel geen schoolgebouw in de stad. De penningen tot oprichting van dusdanig lokaal en tot onderhoud van een geschikte en bekwame onderwijzer zijn niet te bekomen.

Ter opening van de rivier en tot het daarstellen van bruggen en wegen zijn door den staat 7,000 acres land gegeven; doch dezelve zijn nog niet te gelde gemaakt.

De Eerw. Heer A. C. van Raalte heeft door zijn voorbeeldelooze ondernemingsgeest, verstandige vlijt en onvermoeide arbeidzaamheid, in den aanleg en uitbreiding der Kolonie ten toon gespreid, een duurzaam gedenkteeken gesticht, dat de laatste naneef nog met dank aanschouwen zal. Aan hem toch is men naast God de oorsprong en aanvankelijke ontwikkeling verschuldigd. Zijn standvastige geest, zijn onvermoeide werkzame ijver, zijn doordringend verstand, zijn voorbeeld en zijn bestuur is als het ware de ziel der Kolonie. Men is echter nog voor een gedeelte onkundig wat men dezen weldoener in zijn volle waarde en verdiensten verschuldigd is. De toekomst zal dit eerst ten heerlijkste doen uitblinken. Ook als zielsverzorger in de zedelijke belangen van het volk verdient ZEw. allen lof, zijnde hij een vrij en onbekrompen prediker van het Evangelie, dringende met allen ernst aan op een geloof werkdadig in liefde, op zedelijke verbetering en op een geheiligden wandel. God bekroone zijn werk met zijnen rijken zegen!

Daar de meeste kolonisten ver landwaarts intrekken, en dit voor de boerenstand, uithoofde dat het land aldaar goedkooper en veel beter is, ook verkieselijker is, zoo worden er hier en daar nieuwe dorpen aangelegd, welke reeds scholen, kerken en predikanten hebben, of te verwachten zijn. Drie mijlen van de stad heeft men het dorp Groningen, aangenaam gelegen ter plaatse alwaar de Black rivier ophoud bevaarbaar te zijn. Een houtzaagmolen, welke door 't water van eene beek in beweging wordt gebracht, geeft dit dorp eene aangename levendigheid en onderscheidene menschen werk. Eene nieuwe school is in aanbouw. Men heeft er een bekwame onderwijzer en heeft reeds een predikant beroepen. Twee à drie mijlen verder ligt het dorp Zeeland. Het ligt in een vruchtbaren grond en bevat reeds 80 huizen. Alles is er geregeld: het onderwijs der jeugd, de godsdienst, een predikant, eene nieuwe kerk, de oude te klein bevonden zijnde voor de menschen, welke nu bijna voltooid is. Een schoolonderwijzer, een doelmatig schoolgebouw zijn zaken, welke dit dorp nu zelfs verheffen boven de stad. Verder in het staatsland woonen veele boeren welke het daar zeer wel gaat, veel land hebben zij al geklierd en sommigen hebben het afgeloopen oogstgetijde al aanmerkelijke hoeveelheden vruchten ingezameld, waaronder al veel aardappelen en mais, met hetwelke zij al veel kunnen toebrengen ter voeding van het overige gedeelte der Kolonie.

Twee à drie dorpen liggen er insgelijks op eenigen afstand. Onder deze is het dorp Hellendoorn onder de leiding van Ds. Bolks aangelegd, het voornaamste. Algemeen wordt goede ligging en de vruchtbaarheid van den grond geroemd. De overige dorpen zijn insgelijks in snelle ontwikkeling en aanvankelijke bloei. Het Vriesche dorp heeft een predikant, Ypma genaamd, en het Drentsche heeft een beroep naar eenen in Nederland afgezonden. Dit voorbeeld hebben ook de Graafschappers gevolgd,

Eene indiaansche stam heeft eene vestiging en kleine stad [city] op eene mijl afstands van de stad. Zij zijn er onder het bestuur van de missionaris Smith, doch hebben eene soort van Roomsche godsdienst oefening, waarin zij door Fransche zendelingen zijn onderwezen. Zij zijn van de stam der Ottawas welke nu bijna vernietigd is, doch in vroeger tijden was het eene sterke stam, welke een groot gedeelte van Michigan en Illinois voor hunne jachtgronden in bezitting had. Hunne zeden en gewoontens hebben door het verkeer met de beschaafde wereld veel van het oorspronkelijk natuurleven verloren. Echter hebben ze nog veel dat hun onderscheidt. Zij trekken bij zomertijd hier vandaan naar meer woeste streken, waar betere jachtgronden zijn. De jacht en het tappen van suiker maken hunne hoofdbezigheden uit. Voor het eerste is hier bijna geene gelegenheid meer, naardien het wild schaars is en der menschelijke nabijheid gestadig ontwijkt. Het laatste is hier nog al eene goede zaak doordien er nogal veele suiker maple is. De Indiaan maakt een opening in de stam des booms waaruit een vogt zijpelt, hetwelk door kooking eene heerlijke suiker oplevert. Deze Indianen zijn eenigszins koperkleurig en hebben sluik zwart haar. Zij zijn gehard in het verduren van koude en andere ongemakken des levens. Zullende zich ter nederleggen om te rusten of zich door den slaap te verkwikken, wikkelen zij zich in een deken, welke hun altijd ter kleedij verstrekt en leggen zich in het zand neder. Ik zag sommige derzelve aan Michigan Lake liggen bijna geheel naakt, terwijl eene snerpende wind op het strand aanwoei en hun gestadig met water bespatte. Hierbij kwam nog dat het zand zeer vochtig was. Het is aangenaam te zien hoe handig zij zijn in het maken van kano's [canoes]. Dit zijn uitgeholde boomstammen, welke over het algemeen zeer smal en lang zijn. Toen men mij er voor de eerste maal mede overzette bij Port Sheldon, bekroop mij niet weinig de vrees voor omslaan, doch met eenen bekwamen roeijer heeft men geen gevaar te duchten. De Indianen maken ook schuiten van berkenbast, welke zeer kunstig met harst digtgemaakt worden. Met deze wagen zij zich zonder vrees op het soms zeer stormachtige meer en hebben geen andere vervoermiddelen om hetzelve over te steken. Deze schuitjes zijn zeer licht te dragen. Dat is zeer gemakkelijk, kunnende dezelve op hunne tochten over land medegenomen en door één man gedragen worden, teneinde men er gebruik van kunne maken wanneer zij eenige rivier aantreffen, welke zij er dan mede oversteken en zoo zonder omwegen hunne reis voortzetten. Onze wilden zijn nog een gering overblijfsel van den eertijds zoo sterken en geduchten stam der Ottawa's, naar welke deze county dezelfs naam draagt.

Den 11 September. Heden eene diep treurige dag voor mij. Gisteren ontving ik berigt van mijnen vriend, J. G. Mulder, dat ZEd. ernstig ziek was en mij verzocht hem te bezoeken. Ik ging, hoezeer ik mij zelf ongesteld gevoelde, er dezen morgen naar toe, doch vond bij mijne komst te Port Sheldon, dezen mij zoo dierbaren vriend, reeds overgegaan in de eeuwige rust. Hij overleed den zelfden morgen om 4 uur. Smartelijk viel mij deze slag daar ik hem als een braaf mensch had leeren kennen, als een vriend zelfs in nood had leeren hoogschatten en als een broeder beminnen.

Onwillekeurig wekte het in mij zeer ernstige gedachten. Gedachten aan mijne eigene sterfelijkheid en onsterfelijkheid, aan mijne eigene voorbereiding voor het volgend leven, opdat mij de dood geen koning der verschrikking, maar een engel des vredes moge zijn.

Den 4 July. De gedenkdag van de Onafhankelijk verklaring der Vereenigde Staten van Noord Amerika. Ds. van der Meulen viert dezelve met ons op eene godsdienstige wijze. ZEW. verhaalde in eene hoogst gepaste redevoering de ontdekking van America door Columbus, Americus Vesputius en anderen; wijdde vervolgens zijne rede aan de bloei en opkomst dezer Ver. Staten, derzelver glorierijke onafhankelijk verklaring, de moeijelijke vrijheidsstrijd onder den braven Washington zoo luisterrijk volgehouden en zoo heerlijk ten einde gebracht. Hoezeer in het klein werd er in het dorp Zeeland geïllumineerd, de Americaansche star banner waaide voor the Zeeland Hotel; de jeugd gaf zijne vreugd door het schieten met geweer en pistolen te kennen. Hartelijke gebeden en dankzeggingen werden aan den grooten bestuurder van volken en staten opgezonden...

1850, January 1. Zoo licht dan de eerste morgen eener nieuwe halve eeuw aan...

22 January [1851]. Al weder een jaar van mijnen levenstijd vervlogen...

25 Juny. Zeer verblijdend was het voor mij een mijner vrienden uit de plaats mijner geboorte te zien overkomen, welke ook door familie betrekking eenige nadere betrekking op mij had. Het was n.l. J. van Zwaluwenburg een volle neef mijns moeders. Veel hoorde ik van hem aangaande mijne nadere aanverwanten verhalen. Veel hoorde ik hem vertellen van allerlei zaken sinds mijn afwezen voorgevallen; al hetwelk mij niet weinig genoegen aanbragt.

Augustus. Omstreeks dezen tijd kwam mijn neef A. van Zwaluwenburg met zijn gezin uit Nederland, hetwelk mij zeer veel genoegen gaf, zijnde hij een braaf en ondernemend man, welke zich hier juist in zijn element bevond. Wij besteden onze meesten tijd met praten over het verlaten oord onzer geboorte, over allerlei zaken hier, enz. Nevens dit zochten wij ijverig naar goed land.

Sept. 1. Nadat alle plannen gevormd waren kochten wij eindelijk land, daarop zoude een huis gebouwd worden, enz. Doch aller menschen lot is de wijze handen des Oppermagtigen. De mensch overdenkt zijnen weg doch de Heer bepaald zijnen gang. Tot mijne groote ontstelling zag ik zijne constitutie langzamerhand verminderen, zijne krachten afnemenen, den waarlijk beminnenswaardigen man, na eene slaap van twee etmalen overgaan in den langen duister diepen doodslaap. De 23n Augustus eindigde de zalige zijn aardsche leven; was toen wij dachten dat zijne werkkring eerst regt zou aanvangen, reeds aan het einde zijns loopbaans. Zoo onnagaanbaar zijn de wegen die de alwijze voorzienigheid met deszelfs kinderen houdt. Zijn doen is majesteit en heerlijkheid...

Den 8 Juny. Verguizing, liefdelooze en onrechtvaardige oordeelvellingen zijn mijn deel. Men praat elkander na en toont dus zijne Jehus' ijver voor de strengste orthodoxie, zoodat ik bijna in elk mij omringend persoon een vijand moet vermoeden. Hoe bang is dit voor mij, daar ik zoo met al mijn hart in elk mensch een vriend zou willen ontmoeten! Menschen die nimmer met mij over godsdienstige onderwerpen gesproken hebben, gaan mij maar zoo uit de hoogte veroordeelen, zoeken mij bij alle gelegenheden te benadeelen en als een dwaalgeest te brandmerken. Ook eene door mij aangeknoopte verkeering met een meisje is daardoor reeds in het niet gelopen. Smartelijk als mij dit valt, wensch ik evenwel de kwaadstokers niet te haten...

In mijne eenzaamheid den 3 July 1851. In den eersten dezes betrokken zijnde van het dorp, woon ik deszelfs nabijheid alleen; daar zal ik mijne dagen in eenzaamheid gaan doorbrengen. Afgezonderd van het gevoel der wereld, meer buiten het bereik van laster en leugen, welke toch in Groningen [hoe klein en onbeduidend dit anders moge zijn] zulk eene schrikbarende hoogte heeft beklommen...

9 July. Blijdschap en verootmoediging wisselen zich beurtelings af in mijn gemoed...

Den 22 Augustus. Ik las eene leerrede van wijlen den zaligen Lavater, over de Christelijke vriendschap en gemeenzaamheid met veel genoegen en stichting...

31 Aug. Heden avondmaal! God de levende en levendmakende vader geeft aan dood en doemschuldige zondaren het leven, de verzoening en eeuwig zalig gelijk in zijn Zoon Jezus Christus.

Den 15 Sept. Een door mij zeer hoog geschat persoon maakt zich aan eene zware zonde schuldig, valt diep. Hoezeer leert dit menschelijke zwakheid, de argelistigheid van het menschelijk hart en de diepe afhankelijkheid van Gods wederhoudende genade en het licht des geestes...

1 January 1852. De tijdstroom golfde weder een jaar ons voorbij en vloot voor altijd in de zee van het verledene.

Allen dobberen wij te gader,
Door een wijs bestuur geleid
In het bootje van het heden
Op de zee der eeuwigheid. - A. Fokke Simonsz.

Den 4n July 1852. De gewigtigste dag mijns levens, eene geheele verandering in mijne zaken, in mijne betrekking, enz. Hoezeer ben ik doordrongen van het gevoel omtrent het belangrijke van hetzelve. Dezen dag die in den Amerikaansche Almanak zulk eene voorname plaats is aangewezen, door de verklaring der onafhankelijkheid, heeft insgelijks in mijn Dagboek de voornaamste rang. Op dezen dag werd ik plegtig door heilige banden des huwelijks verbonden aan Hilligje Kamps door den weleerw. Heer S. Bolks die te Zeeland de plaats van den weleerw. Ds. C. van der Meulen vervulde. Indrukwekkend was de plechtigheid voor mijn gemoed...

Den 5 April 1853. Na eene genoegelijke echtvereeniging doorgebragt in het stille en aangename huiselijk leven van negen maanden, schonk ons de liefderijke hemelsche Vader een pand onzer teedere liefde. Wat ik toen gevoelde laat zich niet beschrijven...

20 April 1853. Onze dochter ontving bij den heiligen doop den naam Alida.

15 April 1855. Heden werd ons eene andere dochter geboren. God was ook weder een redder uit den nood. Hoezeer wij liever een zoon zouden gehad hebben, was ook toch daarom de kleine even welkom. Wij noemen haar Hendrica. God spare haar en doe haar leven vóór Zijn aangezicht!

7 April 1856. Heden werd ik met bijna algemeene stemmen als Superviser aan het hoofd des bestuurs onzer Township geplaatst. Ik gevoel het gewigt dezer betrekking levendig, het vertrouwen door het volk in mij gesteld, met eene gewillige volwaardigheid uitteoefenen met regt en onpartydigheid. De belangen van het algemeen als mijne eigene te behartigen, regt en geregtheid te handhaven, onder opzien tot den grooten Albestuurder is mijn pligt! God schenke mij daartoe de zoo noodige wijsheid en krachten!

26 September 1856. Op heden werden wij weder verblijd door de geboorte van een derde dochter. Hoezeer teleurgesteld in onze hoop en verwachting op een mannelijk zaad, berusten wij in Gods beschikking en heetten de kleine al weder hartelijk welkom en zijn dankbaar voor de voordeeligen opgroei en vermeerdering onzer kleinen. God drukke het gewigt van derzelver opvoeding en opleiding op onze harten. Opdat wij ze naar ons vermogen in biddend opzien tot Hem mogen opkweeken in Zijne vrees tot verheerlijking Zijns naams, tot onze blijdschap en vreugde. Mogten zij opgroeijen tot sieraden in de maatschappij, tot nuttige en voorbeeldige leden der kerk op aarde en zoo rigten voor den hemel! Wij noemen haar Bertha.

Dit te leren uit het sterfgeval eenes vriends kan niet anders dan een zaad zijn, hetwelk hoezeer smartelijk, ook voor het tegenwoordige rijke vruchten kan opleveren in de toekomst. De oorsprong alles goeds, de God der liefde, geve dit uit genade om Zijns Zoons onzes Heeren Jezus Christus wil.

Groningen [Ottawa County] den 13n October. Heden vestigde ik mijne verblijfplaats alhier om de administratie eener houtzaagmolen waar te nemen...

[Translation]

Monday, April 26 [1847]. I feel the significance of my decision. I have taken a touching farewell of my mother – dearest earthly possession – my beloved brothers, dear sisters, and other acquaintances. Also from my father-like teacher L. Pessink at Zwolle and the members of his household; from all my friends both men and women; from J. Montijn, teacher of my youth; from Oldebroek in Gelderland, the place of my birth and home of my simple childhood, that place in which my youthful days rolled away in dreams about the future. It is evening. We are moving away in a happy frame of mind. Soon Zwolle passed out of sight.

Having sailed past Hasselt and Zwartsluis, we enter the Zuider Zee at Genemuiden. It now is the morning of April 27. Stormy weather. Contrary winds. We are moving along the coast of Gelderland. We still see Elburg in the distance. We are forced to cast anchor within sight of Harderwijk, until the evening of April 28.

April 29. We arrive at Amsterdam, are in the Noord-Hollandsch Kanaal. Many unpleasant things happen. We cannot yet depart, nor go on board our ship and are required to stay in the stalls at the toll house on the other side of the IJ....

May 2. We attend a religious service on board the *Noord-Holland*, led by Dominie Zonne....

May 22, 1847. Following an agreement reached with Messrs. Ponselet & Zonen, we board the ship *Snelheid*, commanded by J. J. Gorter, and are to sail to the New World in that ship.

May 24. It is Pentecost Sunday and we depart after first having paid a final visit to Holland's capital. Our ship is being pulled along the canal past some villages, among which Ilpendam, etc., until we reached Purmerend, a neat little town with much trade. We were to pass the night there and so have time to visit it....

August 1. Made a trip [from New York] to West Chester County where many Hollanders live who receive us in friendly fashion....

August 15. I am working some time at Throgsneck in West Chester

County. This work was very hard at first as I have not recovered my former strength and had been unaccustomed to work.

Sept. 5. My job finished, I left this place and departed for Williamsburg where I boarded a train and continued my journey by way of a village called Harlem to New York. We arrived safely in New York where I stayed with my friends, the Liesvelds, and take a closer look at New York.

Schralenburg, Sept. 9. Again left the city in order to live in the community Schralenburg in Bergen County, state of New Jersey. Here is a congregation of the old Dutch Reformed Church which remains faithful to its ancient rules and confessions although the Dutch language is no longer employed in their services and is no longer taught in their schools. But the people in their daily intercourse quite generally speak the old Dutch language. Likewise, there is a Seceder church here, which has separated form the above enamd church....

Nov. 25. In this place I enjoy the candid friendschip of the respected minister of the Reformed Dutch Church, Rev. Cornelius Blauvelt. The doors of his house are constantly open, welcoming me and the other Dutch immigrants living here. Many an evening I have spent here in conversation which we close with the singing of a Dutch psalm and saying a prayer in the Dutch language. This will always remain an unforgetable experience with me and always cause me to think with respect of that worthy man of God....

April 19 [1848]. Letters received from the West lead me to decide to leave this place. On April 17. I left Schralenburgh, the place where I spent a pleasant winter and where I experienced the comfort of many an unearned friendship. Sadly, on the day before, I took leave of the worthy pastor Blauvelt.... In New York I went back to my friends, the Liesvelts....

May 6. After spending 17 days with them I finally decided to go West. On May 4 we left on board the steamboat *North America* and on the following morning arrived at Albany. The first Dutch Reformed Church here was built in 1653. It still stands in State Street.... Of this congregation there are many members, churches [sic], and ministers, of whom the last, Isaac N. Wyckoff, is especially well known, bedause of his kindliness toward Dutch immigrants and because of his learning.

May 10. We can scarcely make any progress, for the canal carries too little water to permit boats to pass trough the locks....

Buffalo, May 18. We arrived here yesterday evening. So after a wearisome journey along the Erie Canal we finally reached Buffalo....

Erie, in Pennsylvania, May 20. After we had returned form our trip to Niagara [Falls] at Buffalo on the day before we boarded the *General Harrison* and steamed up Lake Erie.

Beaver, May 24. Arrived here this morning. We left Erie by canal boat on the 21st. It was a difficult trip because there were more than a half too many passengers so that there scarcely was any place stand, let alone place to sit or to lie down. On our journey we saw much primeval forest, many recently cleared farms, and at every hand fertile land. This canal shows now Americans need not blush when compared in imitiative an daccomplishment with any other people in the world. The canal at many points has been dug through great rocks, through small and low lying rivers which make the canal look like a great trough. At one point the canal was 180 feet above low ground, which gave the appearance that we were passing through the air. Various villages are beginning to develop along the river. Beaver is situated on the Ohio River....

Cincinnati, May 17. Today we arrived here after a journey of over 400 miles on the Ohio River....

Mississippi, May 31. The banks of the Mississipi reveal nature in its original harshness. The phenomena of a mighty stream which frequently overflows its banks cause me to recall my beloved fatherland which often and for the same reason has had to suffer from so many disasters. Trees torn out of the ground by the force of the water lie here and there, piled up or else float down stream. Low areas, as a rule, are covered with small trees and are thickly wooded. This renders the sight less fair or less varied than what was to be seen along the most beautiful Ohio....

St. Louis, June 4. On June 1 we arrived in St. Louis in the state of Missouri and at once looked up our former citizens and found lodging with them.... Each year several hundred houses are built, last year more than a thousand. An astonishingly large number of High Germans have settled here, as we often noted at many other points on our journey. In St. Louis, as in all American cities, there are a good number of churches; High Germans, Methodists, Lutherans, and Catholics are building a large number each year. The same is true of the Presbyterians, English Methodists, and other groups. There are here many descendants of French settlers who still speak their tongue. We shall probably not tarry here long....

August 7. After a brief stay in the country, several miles from the city and in the state of Missouri, I return to St. Louis. The soil is very fertile, grows crops without manuring, and, near the city, land sells at a good price. Farms here are of 300 acres and more. This state is generally thinly populated. There still are several Indian tribes in the western parts of the state, of whom I saw some in St. Louis. They have a light complexion. But they have adopted unsightly appearances by means of paint. Some have colored head and hair red, others have painted their faces black with 3 or 4 white stripes over each cheek. They usually shave their heads but leave a knot of hair on the top of the head, tied in a knot and decorated with feathers.

August 8. Taking all things into consideration. the unhealthful character of the atmosphere, etc., we decided to leave St. Louis and board the steamboat *Anthony Wayne*, and sail up the Mississippi.

Peru, August 10. After a pleasent journey of two days we arrived in this place. It was dark when we left he Mississippi and sailed up Illinois River. Beardstown is a new and prosperous town, situated on this river. Peoria is very beautiful place built on a space of level ground by the Illinois River. Peru probably will prosper as the flow of commerce along the canal from Chicago to St. Louis increases in volume. Until now we have seen practically nothing but woods on each side of the river. This morning we were agreeably surprised to see a beautiful prairie stretching along the higer ground by the river. This higher ground to me appeared to be a dyke. I at once thought I was in the Netherlands and was seeing beautiful Dutch pastures. The fairest green grass interspersed with beautiful flowers so impressed me that I was entranced.

Chicago, August 14. This morning, after a tedious journey, we arrived in this place. The journey, in other respects was not unpleasant. The fairest and unbounded prairies, occasionally marked by rapidly developing villages or by small woods were charmingly beautiful. Among the towns on the canal Joliet, situated on both sides of the water, is especially to be noted. As we draw nearer Chicago we see large numbers of cattle grazing on boundless fertile pastures. After our arrival at the Chicago River, where giant steam pumps supply the canal with water, a tug pulled us forward. This canal was well constructed and is better equipped than other American canals I have seen. Traffic is facilitated because there are not so many locks as in the Erie Canal. Besides, the bridges are built high above the water, and the canal itself is broader and better constructed than other canals along which I have traveled.

August 16. Chicago in a few years has developed from nothing into a fairly large city, and at present has about 25,000 inhabitants. Commerce and industry are developing in extraordinary fashion. One notices a bustle here like that in the largest commercial centers of the Old World. Here I found many Hollanders whom I had known some time ago. They were all doing well. There is much trade here in wood for building purposes, etc.

Lake Michigan, August 20. Until yesterday morning contrary winds prevented us from continuing our journey, but the wind changed, and we sailed out to sea. We passed through a slight storm which made me and some of our travel companions sick. Our discomfort was increased by the wretched service offered by our ship. Poor food and sleeping on a trunk in the hold, where much water poured into the ship so that I could scarcely remain dry, made me long for land. Adverse winds kept us from reaching the mouth of Black River.

Grand Haven, August 21. This morning we sailed up the mouth of Grand River. As we had agreed with the skipper to be brought to the mouth of Black River our baggage was left on board. The passengers also stayed on board in order te be taken there. But I had no desire again to travel by sea and instead shall visit my friend Mulder at Port Sheldon and then proceed afoot to Black Lake.

Holland on Black Lake, August 22. After visiting my friend J. G. Mulder yesterday and spending the night with him, I arrived in the Kolonie at noon today. I immediately looked up my former friends and acquaintances. But something at once depressed me – in nearly every house I entered there were sick people, sometimes as many as five or six in one dwelling. Evil fevers were rampant, people looked as if they were ghosts returned to this world. It was the most unhealthful moment of the year.

Many former friends and acquaintances were dead. They had died because of the struggles, privations, unusual climate, etc., which brought on fever and other maladies customary in these parts and helped bring on their death. Many a person had thought he was emigrating to an earthly paradise, a happy dreamland in America. But now they beheld a wild waste, impenetrable woods, practically no fellow human beings, nor the least trace of farming or other activity, nor saw anywhere a house fit to live in. That many at once gave up courage did not surprise me. All these things, besides weariness because of their long journey first by sea and then by land, and the harmful vapors rising from the newly cleared lands combined to work harm for the immigrant.

At the moment of our arrival the fevers were quite general, but the number of deaths was not especially large and in no away comparable to the mortality of the preceding year. Today it is possible for a new arrival to find a place to live. Nor is there any shortage of food and other necessaries. There are houses to be rented, and one can find boarding houses. There also are enough stores.

August 28. Having now walked through the town, which has already been laid out, and also having seen something of the surrounding country, I can make the following observations. First, it is not surprising to see here and there a house built or one in building, standing in a small opening in the practically impenetrable forest, surrounded by stumps two to three feet high. One meets with stumps everywhere on the streets, in the gardens, etc., in such numbers that even in daytime one must watch where he walks, and during dark take every precaution not to run onto these immovable objects, for the least contact with them is likely to cause the wanderer to return home with blackened eyes.

The houses are built only along one street, excepting the few along Black Lake. Their number in that street is thirty. Here and there are, some standing apart. I believe there must be about 50 in all. But the people are busy building houses, clearing land, etc. There are about 4,000 people in the Kolonie. They live within a circumferance of 20 miles. The farmers are moving into the more remote parts. The city is being built on light sandy soil, but at a point advantageously situated on Black Lake, from the standpoint of commerce and industry. A sawmill is to be constructed. A windmill has been finished. In addition, within one hour's distance there are two sawmills propelled by water power. It is most advantageous to the Kolonie that in the future no wood for building purposes will have to be shipped in from other places. Henceforth the Hollanders will keep their money at home, and this will provide a means of livelihood for workingmen. In the beginning all building materials and foodstuffs had to be brought from other places. For these things the immigrant paid out money, none of which ever returned; consequently money became very scarce in the Kolonie. This kept back many activities and exterprises indispensable for the growth of the community and which, we cannot tell how long, may well continue to retard them.

The mouth of Black Lake has been completely filled with sand washed up out of Lake Michigan. Ships can neither enter nor pass out unless the channel is cleared of sand and a breakwater is constructed far out into the water so as to prevent any future interference with ships. Without such improvements no trade or craft will be able to flourish nor any branch of industry develop. At the present moment the stream [Black River] and the Lake, so well adapted to commerce, can produce for the city of the Kolonie nothing but unhealthy air, caused by the stagnant waters.

Education of the youth is still in a primitive state as there is no school building in the city. It has been impossible to find the necessary capital to erect and maintain such a building and to employ a competent teacher.

The state has set aside 7,000 acres for the opening of rivers, building of bridges, and laying out of roads. But no money has yet been realized from this source.

Dominie van Raalte has erected a permanent memorial, revealing intelligent industry and unwearied labors in laying out this Kolonie and in expanding it. His future descendants will thank him for this. To him, next to God, the people are indebted for its original conception and early development of it. His firm spirit, his untiring energy, his penetrating intelligence, the force of his example, and his guiding skill are the soul of the Kolonie. People, however, are only partially aware to what extent they are indebted to this servant. But the future will make this clear. He also deserves all praise as shepherd of souls in spiritual matters. For he is an untrammeled preacher of the Gospel, emphasizing earnestly a faith fruitful in charity, stressing moral improvement and sanctified conduct. May God richly crown his labors!

Most of the settlers are moving deeper into the woods. For farmers this is most advisable as the land there is cheaper and also of better quality. Here and there new villages are being created which already have schools, churches, and ministers, or expect to have them. Three miles from "*de stad*" is the village of Groningen, pleasantly situated at the point at which Black River ceases to be navigable. A sawmill, driven by water from a creek, provides a number of people with work. A new schoolhouse is in process of building. They already have a competent teacher, and have invited a minister. Two to three miles further is the village of Zeeland, situated on fertile ground; it already has 80 houses. Everything has been regulated there: eduction for the youth, religion, a minister, and a new church, the older one having been found to be too small for the people, now nearly finished. Having a teacher and a proper schoolhouse are matters which raises the prestige of the village as compared with the "*stad*". Farther east, in Statesland, there are many farmers who are getting along very well. They have cleared much land. During the past harvest season they have garnered considerable crops, especially potatoes and corn. By means of these they can contribute markedly to the food supply of the rest of the Kolonie.

Two or three other villages also are situated some distance away. Among these the most important is Hellendoorn, under the leadership of Dominie Bolks. Its excellent location and the richness of its soil are generally praised. The rest of the villages likewise are developing rapidly. The Friesian village [Vriesland] has a minister named Ypma.

The village of Drenthe has sent an invitation to some minister in the Netherlands. The people of Graafschap likewise have followed this example.

An Indian tribe has settled here and has a small place ["stad"], a mile distant from Holland. They are under the care of the missionary Smith, but they have a kind of Catholic religious service in which they are instructed by French Missionaries. They belong to the Ottawas, a tribe now nearly destroyed. Formerly, however, they were a poverful tribe possessing a large part of Michigan and Illinois as their hunting area. Their morals and customs have lost much of thier nature life manner through contact with the civilized world. However, they still have many distinguishing characteristics. In summer time they move from here to more primitive areas where hunting is better. Their chief occupations are hunting and tapping for sugar. For hunting this region presents few opportunities, for wild animals have become scarce and steadily flee the presence of human beings. Tapping for sugar is a good buseness in view of the many sugar maple trees. The Indians cut an opening in the trunk of a tree, from which flows the sap which on cooking produces a splendid sugar. These Indians are of a copper color and have shiney black hair. They readily endure cold and other discomforts. When they lie down to rest or to sleep they wrap themselves in a blanket, which they always carry as part of their clothing, and lie down in the sand. I saw some of them at Lake Michigan lying in the sand, in almost a nude condition. A sharp wind blew upon them and sprayed them with water. The sand on which they lay was very damp. It is a pleasure to note how clever they are in making their canoes. These are hollowed out logs, generally very narrow and long. When for the first time I was transported over the water at Port Sheldon I was afraid of tipping, but one does not have to fear if the paddler is capable. The Indians also make boats from birch bark, the holes of which are cleverly sealed with resin. With canoes they do not hesitate to cross lakes. Such canoes are easy to carry and to transport over land. They use them in crossing rivers when on journeys. These wild folk are but a small remainder of the one time powerful tribe of the Ottawas after whom this county was named.

September 11. Today a sad day for me. Yesterday I received a message from my friend J. G. Mulder that he was seriously ill and that he wanted me to visit him. Although I myself did not feel well, I went to see him. But when I arrived at Port Sheldon I found that my beloved friend had already gone to his eternal rest. He died that same morning at 4 o'clock. This was a hard blow for me, for I had come to know him as a splendid man and had learned to appreciate him in time of need and to love him as a brother. His death raised serious thoughts in me. Thoughts about my own mortality and immortality, about my own preparation for the hereafter, that to me death may not be a king of terrors but an angel of peace.

July 4. Commemoration of the Declaration of Independence of the United States of America. Dominie Van der Meulen celebrated it with us in a religious fashion. He recounted in a most fitting manner the discovery of America by Columbus, Americus Vesputius, and others. Next he described the flourishing growth and rise of these United States, their glorious Declaration of Independence, their difficult fight under brave George Washington who persevered so brilliantly and brought the struggle to a glorious conclusion. Zeeland was illuminated. The American stars and stripes waved over Zeeland Hotel. The young folk proclaimed their joy by shooting guns and pistols. Hearty prayers of thanksgiving were sent up to the great Ruler of peoples and of states....

1850, January 1. Thus we see the light of the first morning of a new half century....

January 22 [1852]. Again another year of my life's span has flown....

June 25. Most happy was I over the arrival of a friend from the place of my birth and also a relative. He was J. van Zwaluwenburg, a full cousin of my mother. He told me a great deal about my close relatives and what had happened since I had left. All this pleased me much.

August. About this time my cousin A. van Zwaluwenburg with family came from the Netherlands which pleased me greatly, for he was a good and enterprising man who found himself here in his proper element. We spent most of our time talking about our place of birth and about all kinds of matters. At the same time we eagerly looked for some good land.

September 1. After forming all our plans we finally bought some land on which a house was to be built, etc. But the lot of all people is in the wise hand of the Almighty. Man thinks about the way he will travel, but the Lord really determines it. To my great distress I noted that his health gradually declined, his strength failed.

The lovable man after a slumber of forty-eight hours passed away into his long dark death sleep. On Aug. 3 the pious man closed his earthly life. When we thought that his work was only beginning it really was coming to the end of its course. So inscrutable are the ways an all-wise Providence has with its children. His acts are majesty and glory....

June 8. Abuse, uncharitable and unjust judgements, are my share. People are repeating gossip, revealing a Jehu's eagerness for the most strenuous orthodoxy, so that in each of my friends I must suspect an enemy. How fearful this is for me, in view of my desire with all my heart to regard each person as a friend! People who never have spoken to me about religious matters are judging me on the basis of prejudice, seek to harm me in all matters, and to brand me as a heretic. A relation with a girl begun by me has already come to naught. Although this is painful for me, I do not, nevertheless, want to hate those who speak evil of me.

In my loneliness, July 3, 1951. Being the first in this village to be involved, I am living near it, but alone. There I'll pass my days in loneliness. Separated from the ill will of the world, beyond reach of lies and slander which, however slight and insignificant this may appear, has reached a fearful point in Groningen.

July 9. Happiness and humiliation alternately fill my soul.

August 22. I read with great comfort and edification a sermon by the late, blessed J. K. Lavater on Christian charity and friendship.

August 31. Today communion! God the living and vivifying Father extents life to dead and doomed sinners, reconciliation and eternal salvation through His son Jesus Christ.

Sept. 15. A person highly esteemed by me makes himself guilty of serious sin, falls deeply. How hard it is for this human weakness to grasp the deceitfulness of the human heart and its dependence upon God's grace and the light of the spirit....

January 1, 1852. Time's stream has again engulfed a year which vanished for all time into the sea of the past.

> *We all are floating together,*
> *Guided by a destiny wise,*
> *In our little boat of to-day*
> *On the sea of eternity.* – A. Fokke Simonsz.

July 4. 1852. The weightiest day of my life, a complete change in my affairs, in my relations, etc. How I am impressed with the feeling of the importance of the same! This day which in the American Almanac occupies an important place because of the Declaration of Independence likewise has a most important place in my *Diary*. On this day I was bound in holy bonds of matrimony to Hilligje Kamps, by Dominie Seine Bolks who at Zeeland was taking the place of Dominie C. van der Meulen. The ceremony was impressive.

April 5, 1853. After a pleasant period of married life of nine month our beloved heavenly Father gave us a token of our tender love. What I at that time experianced I cannot describe.

April 20, 1853. Our daughter received the name Alida, in holy baptism.

April 15. 1855. Today another daughter was born to us. Once more God delivered us out of our great need. However we may have wanted a son, our little one was not the less welcome. Her name is Hendrica. God spare her, and may she live a holy life in His sight!

April 7, 1856. This day I was elected, almost unanimously, Supervisor, to serve as head of our township government. I grasp the importance of this office conferred upon me by the people. I shall endeavor to discharge my duties with justice and impartiality. It is my duty, under prayer to the All-highest Ruler, to treat the interests of the public as my own, justly and uprightly. To this end may God grant me the necessary strength and wisdom to do this!

September 26, 1856. This day once more we were made happy by the birth of a third daughter. However much we had hoped for a son, we resign ourselves to God's decision and so we heartily welcome our little one. We are thankful that out children are growing up, that they increase in number. May God impress upon our hearts our duty in regard to bringing them up. That we, according to the measure of our ability, prayerfully looking up to God, may educate them in fear of Him, to the glory of His name, to our joy and happiness. May they grow up to be an adornment in society, useful and exemplary members of the church on earth and so directed heavenward! Her name is Bertha.

To learn all this from the death of a friend can only be a seed, however sad, to bear fruit in the future. May the source of all good, the God of love, grant us this out of His grace for the sake of our Lord Jesus Christ.

Groningen [Ottawa County], October 13. Today I took up my residence here in order to take over the administration of a sawmill....

Chapter XV

VAN RAALTE'S VIEW OF THE HISTORY
OF HIS UNDERTAKING, 1846-1872

59. VAN RAALTE'S COMMEMORATION ADDRESS, 1872

[To commemorate the twenty-fifth anniversary of the founding of Holland, Michigan, and the surrounding Dutch Kolonie, fitting ceremonies were prepared. A striking celebration took place on September 17, 1872, when Van Raalte delivered his *Toespraak* (Address) in the woods one mile east of Holland. This *Toespraak* was printed in *De Hope* of September 25, 1872, and reprinted in the September 1, 1897, issue of the same paper. A translation of the *Toespraak* was published by H. S. Lucas in his *Ebenezer 1847-1947* (New York 1947). The *Toespraak* is the first summary of the Settlement's history thus far produced.]

Met eene mengeling van ontroering, dank en vreugde, staat de gebeurtenis onzer landing als vreemdelingen in een vreemd land, voor onzen geest. Het baarde uit de diepten van nood een geroep tot God en Zijne hand bracht ons alhier. Een vierde van een eeuw is doorworsteld; en ziende op de uitkomst en vrucht, begeeren wij dankend en juichend te belijden: „De Heer heeft groote dingen bij ons gedaan; dies zijn wij verblijd." En onze opvolgers, wien wij de erve overgeven, begeeren wij toe te roepen: „Vergeet het niet, 't is God die het ons bewees!"

Veroorloof mij iets van de geschiedenis onzer verhuizing, zoo invloedrijk op uw lot, mede te deelen. Voor omstreeks vijf-en-dertig jaren hadden velen onzer in ons geboorteland een vreeselijke worsteling voor godsdienst vrijheid. Na smadelijke en alle burgerrechten verkrachtende vervolgingen gedurende jaren, verkregen wij een even smadelijke als onrechtvaardige vrijheid.

Langs dien weg verkregen wij veel kennis van den zinkenden toestand van velen. Hierdoor werd in 1845, na vruchtelooze pogingen om de op stoffelijk gebied zinkende huisgezinnen op te beuren, in Arnhem eene organisatie tot stand gebracht, om, door goede berichten daartoe genoopt, zoodanige familiën naar Amerika over te helpen. Gelijktijdig werd onze voorstelling van zoodanige kolonizatie in de zoogenaamde Haagsche Heeren meeting verguisd. Zoo sterk was de band van liefde voor Neerlands belang, dat ik mijzelven aan Ds. [Otto G.] Heldring verpandde, onder zekere conditiën, naar Java's hooglanden te willen gaan, doch Nederland durfde op Java geen vrijheid laten tieren.

Ofschoon ons doen, uitgekreten als onvroom en trouweloos aan Vaderland en Kerk, opzien, tegenstand en laster baarde, toch verwekte het bij velen dorst, hoop en vurig verlangen om een ruimer en vrijer veld voor zich en zijn geslachte te vinden. Als een adem Gods ging het over het gansche land. Gelijktijdig werd men rijp in Zeeland onder Ds.[Cornelius] van der Meulen, in Utrecht onder Ds. [Hendrik P.] Scholte, in Vriesland onder Ds. [Maarten A.] Ypma, in Overijssel onder Ds. [Seine] Bolks. Het verdedigingspamphlet, 't welk Ds. [Anthony] Brummelkamp en ik onder den titel: *Waarom wij emigratie naar Noord Amerika en niet naar Java bevorderen*, in 't licht gaven, verhaastte alles; en in mijn hart was de overgave om zelve den beker te drinken, in overtuiging dat het was ijsbreking ten nutte van eenen stroom, breed en diep; in de zekerheid en vurige begeerte, dat dit in vrijheid's worstelingen gekweekte volk, getrouw aan God en roeping zijnde, veel nuttiger, invloedrijker en gelukkiger, in deze nieuwe wereld zijn zou, dan in de oude, waar wij rust en burgerrechten als bij vergunning moesten genieten, en zoo velen met zorg en kommer naar eene voor zich en de zijnen brood en ruimte gevenden werkkring zuchtend moesten uitzien. Tegelijk ziende, dat het planten van christen kolonisatieën Evangelisatiewerk was.

In September 1846 waren de schepen van Holland naar Amerika gevuld met emigranten, en tot mijne bemoediging in dat hartbrekend uur, schreef mijn dierbare broeder, Ds. [Anthony] Brummelkamp, mij: „de duizende kinderen Gods in Nederland vergezellen u op den oceaan met hunne gebeden." Er was eene machtige roering in de harten. Vele duizenden maakten zich voor het volgend jaar gereed.

't Geloof, dat als God roept tot werk, Hij er ook Zijn eigen arm toe leent, schraagde mij onder stormen en in 't gezicht van onwetendheid en onvermogen. In December hieven wij, in 't gezicht der haven, onze dankpsalmen voor behoudene landing aan, en werden in New York bemoedigd door de vriendelijke deelneming van Ds. [Thomas] de Witt en den ouderling [James] Forrester. Wij zijn niet vergeten de moeiten van eene emigrants landing, en evenmin Gods vriendelijke Vaderzorg voor ons door veler liefde arbeid, als bijvoorbeeld van Dr. [Isaac N.] Wyckoff, te schenken. Waarlijk zij waren ons als engelen Gods.

Het winterweder en 't gebrek aan spoorwegcommunicatie verplichtte mij de mijnen in Detroit achter te laten. Ook daar vonden wij de hartelijkste deelneming bij Dr. [George] Duffield, Ds. West en den Heer [Theodore] Romeyn en anderen. De gemeenschap met den bejaarden christen [Robert] Stuart, Presbyteriaansch ouderling en opzichter over het Illinois kanaal, gaf mij veel licht over het land en mijn werk.

Vooral het verkeer in de pioneer woningen, het crediet dat oppassend geldeloozen verkregen, het vrolijk werken van allen, niet zoo zeer om brood als wel om in goede omstandigheden te geraken, de bijzondere beschaving der inwoners, de in het oog loopende ontwikkeling en liefde voor school en Sabbat, hadden voordeeligen invloed. Het kwijnen echter en het opbreken van vele settlements, deed mij goede marktprijzen, middelen van vervoer en werk voor geldeloozen noodzakelijk zien. De werkman was mijne eerste zorg en kracht. De kennis der beide rivieren, de Grand River en Kalamazoo met de schoonste gelegenheden en overvloedige arbeids-gelegenheden, bepaalde mijne keuze van settling aan het Michigan Meer, tusschen de beide rivieren, wanneer het persoonlijk onderzoek zou blijken, dat wij niet door kaarten en Landoffice-onderricht misleid waren.

Mijn onvergetelijke vriend, de heer Kellogg, van Allegan, bracht mij te paard, met enkelen zijner vrienden, allen reeds overleden, ten huize van den predikant, den Eerw. heer [George N.] Smith, den arbeider onder den hier wonenden stam der Ottawa Indianen, die mij herbergde en vele diensten bewees in de verkenning dezer landstreek; door wiens invloed de Indianen mij met zorg ten dienste stonden, veel inlichting gaven en zelfs verheugd waren, als ze mij door het staan achter op hunne sneeuwschoenen, te gelijk de beenen opheffende, van het uitputtend zinken in de sneeuw bevrijden en mijne reizen vergemakkelijken konden. Dezen toch gingen mijne krachten te boven; zodat een maal Ds. [George N.] Smith mij op mijne bede in de sneeuw achterliet, daar wij verdwaald waren, doch door hondengeblaf terecht komende, mij nog met veel moeite naar zijn huis wist te halen; in welken onvergetelijken nacht ik mij zeer in Gods zorg verheugde, hoewel ik door overspanning weinig of geen slaap genoot.

Ofschoon de Amerikanen de plaatsen langs de rivieren aanbevolen en meestal de inbreking alhier te gewaagd beschouwden; ofschoon de Hollanders de wouden ontvloden en het mij zelven grooten strijd kostte mij en de mijnen aan de ongeriefelijkheden van zulk eene inbreking te onderwerpen: nochthans, de combinatie van zoovele voorrechten, ofschoon ze eerst langzaam konden ontwikkelen, lieten mij geen twijfel over, wat mijn plicht was. Ik wist dat de rijke boschgronden de beste gras- en wintertarwe-landen zijn. Dat verre weg zwaardere marktprijzen dan elders in het Westen, en wel nabij voor alles van wege fabriek en scheepvaart, konden verkregen worden. Dat de landstreek aan de zijde van Michigan meer bevrijd was door den water invloed van te strenge vorst en bij uitnemendheid de landstreek voor de fruitteelt was. Geen plek konde ik vinden, waar gelijk aan deze landstreken langs de be-

woonde rivieren vol van fabriekwezen en molens, de tien duizenden
werk konden vinden, zonder gevaar van verstrooiing; en waar wij te
gelijk verzekerd waren van eene gelegenheid om staag bij voortduring
land te kunnen bekomen, zonder belemmering, voor eene groote verscheidenheid in settlementen. Ik koos in nadruk, met veel beslistheid de
landstreek om den wille der verscheidenheid, zeker zijnde, dat zou de
Nederlandsche emigratie tot een kracht ontwikkelen, dan moesten wij
tot steun bij elkander kunnen blijven; dan moesten wij die verscheidenheid voor arbeidsman en kapitaal en vooral voor eene toekomstige ontwikkeling hebben.

Ik zag in mijne geest niet alleen eene berging voor den stroom arbeiders,
doch ik zag ook de schepen der Hollanders, groeiende visscherijen, ook
eene schoone haven en 't geen er bij groeien moest, alsmede landstreken
gewijd aan fruitteelt. Vooral ook de rijkste landelijke dorpen, waarvoor
ik God toen al dankte. Ik was hoopvol dat ook de onzen molens en
fabrieken zouden drijven.

Mijn settling tusschen beide rivieren was om de voordeelen van beiden
voor ons volk te verzekeren, – wij konden de bevolkte streken niet
missen – en tegelijk er een middenpunt voor samenbindend gemeentelijk
leven en werk voor Gods Koninkrijk te doen geboren worden.

Meer dan verwacht is ontvingen wij! Boven bidden en denken heeft de
Heer geschonken! Wie kan zonder verbazing al de dorpen en townships,
bedekt met de rijkste boerderijen, bezoeken. 't Wordt moeijelijk om de
waarde onzer schepen, visscherijen, molens, fabrieken en fruitteelt over
deze landstreken op te sommen. En nog beginnen de bronnen pas te
vloeijen en anderen liggen nog ongeopend, als b.v. onze steenmijnen en
ijzerbedden – zoo gunstig gelegen, wijl we navigatie en een centrum van
spoorweg communicatie bezitten. Voorwaar, God heeft groote dingen
aan ons gedaan!

Ook de wensch des harten naar de geboorte van een te zamenbindend
gemeentelijk leven en werking voor het Koninkrijk, is ons gegeven. Reeds
tellen onze gemeenten in Michigan alleen 26. Reeds 33 leeraren en 15
schoolmeesters zijn van ons uitgegaan. Illinois, Iowa, Wisconsin, zoowel
als Michigan, ja, zelfs de oostersche gemeenten zijn door deze gave gezegend. Onze plantigen in Minnesota, Nebraska en Kansas zijn er aan te
danken. In Virginia geniet men de prediking en reeds een jeugdig invloedrijke kweekhof er door. Zelfs mogen wij ons verheugen, dat ook
Indie onzen dierbaren broeder [Enne J.] Heeren bezit. En dat wij in ons
midden den Japanees mogen kweeken, welke drie, zoo wij hopen, toege-
rust werkende, onder Gods hand een rijken zegen zullen zijn. God gaf

ons in ons midden een samenbindend werk en leven. Zijn naam zij er voor geloofd en ook inzonderheid dat Hij ons in 't harte gaf een dankoffer te brengen ten nutte dier kweeking nu reeds $ 20,000 beloopende, zoodat men deze gave toenemend schat, als voorrecht en roeping, als kroon, kracht en lust.

Wij gaven u iets van de redenen onzer setting alhier, doch keeren wij terug tot de geschiedenis zelve. In de laatste dagen [really, second week] van Februari verzamelden wij ons volkje – B[ernardus] Grootenhuis en familie, Laarman en familie, E[gbert] Frederiks, [Willem] Notting, [Evert] Zagers, [Frans] Smit, Lankheet, etc., uit Detroit en St. Clair, en zonden tijding naar de onzen door het land verspreid. Wij vertrokken naar Kalamazoo, waar wij vele vriendelijkheid genoten, inzonderheid van Ds. [Ova P.] Hoyt. Wij trokken over Allegan naar onze verkorene legerplaats, latende de mijnen onder het onvergetelijk dak van den heer Kellog en zijne gade, van wie ons volk zoo veel genoot.

Naast het huis van Ds. Smith legerde men zich in de kerk der Indianen. Het eerste werk was een ossen wagenpad te maken, langs Hellenthal's, Kampers', Van Duren's en Van der Haar's farms, waarin wij ondersteund werden door den trouwen, kundigen Amerikaan, Mr. [Edward J.] Harrington. Doch in het Cedar Swamp, op den nu Zeeuwschen weg, werd de taak te zwaar en men moest langs de hoogten van Van der Haar's farm en mijn huis een weg naar de landing zoeken. De eerste loghuizen, niet beter dan ossenschuren, werden gebouwd waar nu Van der Haar's schuur staat; dezen dienden tot woning en een plaats voor raadsvergaderingen. De eerste vergadering, die ik nimmer vergeet, openende met gebed, had ik in nadruk besef van 't werk en de toekomst voor ons. Daarna werd gebouwd het lang door Van Lente bewoond loghuis: gelijktijdig begon nu 't werk van Grootenhuis, Laarman en ook het bouwen van mijn huis, van allen dezen is niets meer in aanwezen, behalve het huis 't welk ik bewoon. Zeer tijdig kwamen in Maart tot sterking van hart en hand de gezelschappen van St. Louis, [Teunis] Keppel, [Hein] van der Haar, [Jan] Binnekant bekend door 't werk. Van Albany, de Kolvoords en anderen. De bijzondere gezelschappen in verwachting van vrienden, zochten bijzondere plaatsen voor buurtschappen of dorpen te vormen, welke landzoeking met het gezelschap van Plaggemars, Stegeman, Oldemeijer, Dunnewind, over het ijs der rivier 't noorden indringende, ons eenmaal in groot levensgevaar bracht. Een zeer zware zoele regen brak het ijs op en sneed ons af van alle hlup. Wij hadden moeten omkomen van gebrek en koude; het weder veranderde, 's avonds bevroren onze kleeren; en ziedaar, iets boven waar nu Boone's molen staat, hadden Indianen door een langen dunnen boom te vellen, hangende op tegen boomstammen stuitende ijsschotsen, voor ons een brug ge-maakt, die ik aanwees als het eenige voorhanden zijnde middel te redding van een gewissen dood. Doch het was mij een brug! enkelen schreeuw-den, weenden van vreeze toen ik ze in ernst daartoe gebruikte. Tegen alle verwachting ontkwamen wij allen den dood. Ik genoot een blijde, dan-kenden nacht, die te koud was om in bed warm te worden in mijn open huis.

Vroeg in 't voorjaar kwam [Jan] Rabbers en zijn gezelschap en velen onzer weten zijn helpend werken in Groningen. Bijkans gelijktijdig kwamen de Vriezen onder Ds. [Maarten] Ypma, die toonden te weten wat goed land was. Drenthe en Graafschap waren zwaar vertegenwoor-digd in de settling van het eerste jaar. In het laatst van Mei bracht ik mijne eigene familie binnen door de ongebaande bosschen en nog ver-wekt het in mij dank aan God, dat mijne nu in de ruste gegane gade, dadelijk het onafgemaakte huis betrok met psalmgezang.

De Zeeuwsche organizatie, onder leiding van Ds. [Cornelius] van der Meulen en den ouderling [Jannes] van de Luister, die bij uitnemendheid georganizeerde en met gelden bedeelde vergadering, had in tijds woord gezonden loodsen voor hen op te slaan. Met een drietal scheepsladingen grondden ze het sterke uitgebreide settlement van het Zeeuwsche Dorp, hetwelk tastbaar bestemd was om de nederzettingen tot een geheel en uitgebreid te maken. De plaatsen welke men verkoos, werden van zelve genoemd met zoodanige namen als die, door welke de gezelschappen bekend waren. Het tweede jaar trok Ds. [Seine] Bolks met zijne Over-ijsselsche vrienden, die een klein jaar te Syracuse vertoefden, binnen en grondeden ten zuidoosten ons Overijssel. De townships 5, north ranges 14, 15 en 16 kregen op mijn verzoek vereenigd den naam van Holland, waarvan Zeeland naderhand werd afgezet. Onze landing plaats, aan 't hoofd van Black Lake, droeg den algemeenen naam, de *Lake*. De plaats bestond uit de Zeeuwsche loodsen, enkele loghuizen en een stoorplaats, doch van sommigen hoorde men alreeds van een gaan naar „de stad". De wegen door het gebrek aan bruggen, waren een behulp en al het werk er aan besteed ging daardoor, met uitzondering van enkele hoofdlijnen, geheel verloren. De invoer was allerbezwaarlijkst bij land. Langs het strand met platbooten naar de monden van Grand River en de Kalamazoo moesten onze provisiën komen, 't werk toen van wege de zandbar aan onze haven geschiedde met veel moeite en schade. Geen wonder dan dat de landende emigranten, in brieven reeds onderricht dat ze in de stad Holland aankwamen, bewilderd vroegen naar de stad Holland, of naar winkeliers, bakkers, etc., en dat de teleurstelling groot was, te vernemen dat dit alles nog maar bestond in de verwachting.

De moeilijkheden waren velen, doch het Psalmgezang van onder de takken en in de hutten gaf iets onverklaarbaars voor den oppervlakkigen aanschouwer. Er was bij zeer velen hoop op God en bewustheid van een edelen bedoeling. Ook het zoet genot van volkomene onbelemmerde vrijheid, een leven zonder schrik of vrees voor overtreding van een menschelijk gebod, zonder vrees voor smaad van menschen was dierbaar en om het bij den naam te noemen, 't was als een gedurig feestmaal, dankbaar genoten. Rondom mijn huis, neergehakte boomstammen tot zitplaatsen hebbende, genoten wij de eerste predikplaats in de lucht: ook daar hielden wij de algemene publieke vergaderingen, waar onze algemene belangen met meerderheid van stem werden geregeld. Eerst in 't najaar leerden wij door Mr. H[enry] D. Post onze regering gieten in den landsvorm en verkoren onze beambten.

In het laatste gedeelte van dien eersten zomer stegen onze beproevingen ten hoogsten toppunt, daar de geheele nederzetting een ziekbed werd en er zeer velen, ofschoon er op algemeene onkosten geneesheeren ingeroepen waren, stierven, vooral door gebrek aan goede huizing en weltoegemaakte en passende spijzen. De toestand was hartbrekend en ontmoedigend en vorderde tegenover het gevoelige van 's menschen natuur een pijnlijk geweld. Nimmer was ik nader bij het zinken, dan toen ik in die opeen gepakte loodsen, waar elk gezin zich binnen weinige voeten vierkants moest behelpen, den ganschen tijd een mengeling van alle huiselijke bezigheden van handel, ziek zijn, sterven en dooden toe schikken zag. Geen wonder dat men in dat heete uur van beproeving sporen van wanhopige onverschilligheid zag veld winnen. God gaf verandering! de zieken werden gezond, het najaar was allerliefelijkst en de winter was buitengewoon zacht, zoo dat elk kon bouwen en werkende zijne maaltijden in de open lucht kon gebruiken. De menigte ging naar het land en voor een groot deel bleef op de Landing plaats het kranke en behoeftevolle. De kerk werd om den wille der farmers gebouwd buiten de zoogenaamde stad. Op den hoek van het kerkhof stond onze onvergetelijke logkerk, te gelijk ook schoolhuis, die niet vóór 1856 met de eerste kerk in Holland verwisseld werd, als wanneer er een te talrijke schare woonde om door het swamp ter kerk te gaan.

Onze volksplanting was met godsdienstbeginsel bezield. Zij sterkte zich in God. Zoolang zij er van doordrongen blijft is zij veilig. En het zoet genot der onafhankelijkheid en volle vrijheid, 't welk wij dronken met volle teugen, gaf vreugde en kracht in 't hart. Inzonderheid de vreugde van den Sabbat, de hartsterkende kracht der waarheid, het gebed en 't genot van 't tezamen leven en werken van vele naburige gemeenten heeft gesteund, bemoedigd en doen volharden in een zwaar en moeielijk werk. Gods reddingen in het tijdelijke waren vele; elke dorpkring en familie heeft eene geschiedenis. Volgende sprekers zullen wel het een en ander melden.

Na 25 jarigen worstelstrijd mogen wij in weerwil van alle zonde, ellende en zware tucht toch een uitnemend schoonen feestdag genieten. Want God heeft opgebouwd en wij leven in blijde bewustheid, dat God ons heeft welgedaan en geschonken heeft de wenschen des harten. Wij begeeren nu Hem te prijzen als den Hoorder der gebeden. Wij wenschen Zijn naam te boven als onzen genadigen drager, Almachtigen helper en onzen God die menigvuldig vergeeft.

Waar nu die stof van lof Gods geboren werd, mijn dierbare vrienden! daar leeft ze in 't hart over dood en graf; we zullen dan onze vreugde in de geschiedenis behouden, doch onder volmaakter vreugde toonen. Dierbaren die ons opvolgen zullen in de erve! wij zijn gereed haar u met vreugde over te geven. Doch vergeet niet, wij ontvingen haar van God. Wij ontvingen haar als kweekhof Gods voor de eeuwigheid, als een werkplaats voor Godsrijk, wij ontvingen haar biddend uit Gods hand en begeerden Gods doel met die erve te bereiken.

Die erve zal in uwe hand bloeien in welvaren zoo God Zijn dag, de Christus Gods Zijn rijk en werk uw dierbaar levensdoel blijven. De zonde, die schandvlek der natiën, is de verteerende roest uwer vreugde en kracht. Verzaking van 't gebed wordt verzaking van God en 't geloof. Wij vertrouwen betere dingen, o jeugdigen! dan zoodanige verwoesting onzer erve. Zij blinke in uwe handen als Gods stad op aarde. En God geve u een Godewijdend, Godlovend, zeer blijde half eeuwfeest onzer settling in 1897. En deze erve zij u in alle eeuwigheid dierbaar als de plek waar gij u zelven leerdet kennen, uw God vondt, Zijne vergeving omhelsdet, en Hem leerdet loven. Dat zij zoo.

Chapter XVI

AN HISTORICAL ACCOUNT BY A FIRST SETTLER

60. ENGBERTUS VAN DER VEEN'S LIFE REMINISCENCES

[Engbertus van der Veen, born in Amsterdam, April 1, 1828, died in Holland, Michigan, August 20, 1917, lived in Holland from its first days, managed a hardware store on the corner of Eighth and River streets, and served for some years as mayor of the city. His *Life Reminiscences*, published in pamphlet form in 1915, are here reproduced, corrected in spelling. The text has been rearranged and repetitions have been omitted.]

I, Engbertus van der Veen, was born in the kingdom of the Netherlands in the city of Amsterdam on the first day of April 1828. My father's name was Jacob, my dear mother's Anna C. née Ruiter, both of them born in Amsterdam. All I know of my grandmother is that when six years old she was left an orphan. I was eight when she died. My father also was eight when his father died, and 15 when his mother passed away. He served in the cavalry, married my mother as soon as he was discharged, and, being an expert coppersmith, managed a coppersmith's shop and store in which he sold tin and copper ware. Amsterdam was a seaport with docks for trade with ports to the east and west in Europe. Merchantmen came and went, carrying cargoes to the East Indies and the West Indies. There were warships in the harbor and, on shore, barracks for soldiers, both infantry and cavalry. Amsterdam also had parks and places of amusement, which made that city an enjoyable place to live in.

Those were the good old days when emigrants crossed the ocean in sailing ships; my father sailed with his family on May 27, 1847, to this happy country, America, in the *Snelheid* under the command of Captain J. J. Gorter. After a voyage of 49 days we arrived in the harbor of New York, and in sixteen days traveled from New York to Chicago, going by steamboat up the Hudson to Albany, by canalboat on the Erie Canal to Buffalo, and by steamboat over Lake Erie and Lake Huron, through the Strait of Mackinac and over Lake Michigan to Chicago. The last part of the journey was made in a sailboat to the mouth of Black Lake, now called Macatawa Park. The vessel came to anchor at the entrance and a yawl landed the passengers with their trunks, boxes, and other possessions on the beach. As there was no harbor the men carried all the goods over the beach to a flatboat lying in Black Lake to take us to the place where Dominie van Raalte had settled. At midnight we landed at the foot of

Fifth Street in what was called the City of Holland, really a dense forest of big trees – timber of all kinds. The air was full of malaria caused by the swamp, stagnant water, and dirty waters of Black Lake – a place of sickness and death. The night was dark, so we built a brush fire partly for light, partly on account of the damp air. We could not see how dismal and fearful our surroundings were. The moaning sounds of the western pine, the night birds squawking and shrilly breaking into weird cries, the hooting of owls, and the croaking of a multitude of strange creatures made a painful impression on our family just arrived from Amsterdam, and filled our hearts with dismay. However, the dawn of the first morning was welcome. Slowly the immigrants already settled here awoke from their slumber and made their appeareanc throught the openings of the places in which they rested at night – little square log houses or huts made from branches placed against each other or leaning against fallen trees.

Kees de Witt, an old soldier who served in the army of Napoleon I, and his wife, had erected a tent just long and wide enough for two and so low that they had to creep on their hands and knees to get in and out. Nearly all the people we met had come from the rural districts of The Netherlands. Their dress and appearance were foreign to us who had come from the cities. Thier dialects and their habits of speech were new to us. "Oh! oh!" cried mother, "I wish we were back in Amsterdam! Why did we come here?" She took courage, however, hoping soon to leave these miserable surroundings, for she remembered that some gentlemen in New York had told father that Dominie van Raalte's settlement was a large city, well populated, with many homes. She said to father, "First before all else go to the city and rent a good house with a nice lawn, near a brook with running water in which we can wash and rinse our clothes and bleach them on the lawn." So father went to Dominie van Raalte's abode, a plain board shanty, to find out where the city was and learn all the particulars about the location. Meantime mother comforted herself with the thought that she would soon be settled in a good house with everything as pleasant as in Amsterdam.

Father came back with a downcast look, saying that Dominie van Raalte thought we might find a vacant log house among the Indians who had a village near Black Lake on the present Diekema farm. Here stood a few small houses, a log church, and a cemetery nearby in which stood a large cross made of square timbers. Some of the settlers looked upon this cross with suspicion and contempt. On the beach the Indians built their canoes. "Horrid," cried mother in agony. "What! a vacant log house and one that has been occupied by the Indians? O, what shall we do?" A cry of distress sprang from her agonized soul, followed by weeping. We remained in the woods without preparing any shelter, waiting for a boat to come and take us back to our old home across the ocean. We had left our boxes and trunks, all unopened, on the beach, ready to load them upon a ship. There they remainded about two months in rain and sun. No ship appeared, and we were left to our fate.

After father came back from Dominie van Raalte, in deep disappointment, the children asked for bread. All we had was dried ship's biscuit. I had been taken sick when on the Erie Canal and came near dying. When we landed at Black Lake I was so weak I could not walk. I had neither doctor nor medicine, and death would have been welcome. But the Lord did wonderfully. On the flat bottomed boat at midnight near the point at Central Park I felt a change and was cured. I had had nothing to eat for many days, but now my appetite returned. I asked for bread, but there was nothing. So we had to wait until something turned up. We did have some beans, however. Water was supplied by a spring, and for days we had bean soup.

After a while father found a vacant house in the woods near the place we had landed. It was built of logs each about eight inches in diameter. The walls were about $3\frac{1}{2}$ feet high, the whole being covered with a peak roof.

Small trees used in place of rafters had been fastened on the logs and thatched with hemlock brush. Into that shelter we moved from our open air abode. This was our first lesson in training for the life of a colonist. My father opened a box containing a large table upside down, unpacked the feather beds and valuable articles such as china and crockery which had been tucked carefully between the table legs. The table was placed in the center of the room; our beds were spread out on the ground, for there was no floor. Water pitcher, bowls, plates, umbrellas, and other objects gave some impression of civilized life and reminded us somewhat of our life beyond the sea. Evening and night came as before and also the strange and unbearable variety of sounds. Again there was that horrid hooting and croaking. We placed an open umbrella in the door of our dwelling to keep any unlawful intruder, man or beast, from walking in. By this time the hemlock branches had dried out and began shedding their leaves which dropped in what we were eating and drinking. Our house looked like a large bird cage because of the chinks between the logs and hemlock branches. One afternoon a thunderstorm came up. The bolts roared like heavy cannon; the rain poured down while father, mother, aunt, and children tried to keep themselves dry under umbrellas. I took shelter under the table. Plates, pitchers, and other objects that would hold water were placed in the beds to keep them dry. But everything was soaking wet, for the rain came pouring in torrents through the brush which formed the roof.

After waiting in vain for a boat or vessel to take us from this place, father opened a box of coppersmith's and tinner's tools – only a few taken from the shop in the old country. We had some tin plate and solder rivets, etc. A fallen tree was chosen for a work bench. The news spread that a tinshop and store had been opened, and so the first hardware store in Holland City was a settled fact. One day while at work seated on our tree, soldering, there came a pretty girl of fifteen, carrying a leaky pail. I repaired it and she paid for the work. I looked at her again, following her with my eyes when she walked away – and she was gone. Six years later we became close friends, and for years thereafter we were each other's joy and happiness.

Marriage customs in those days were interesting. Two Sundays before the ceremony the minister announced from the pulpit before the congregation our intention of marriage. The purpose of this declaration was to enable anyone who had any lawful objections to the proposed marriage to state his reasons. This, according to the custom, was said to be "under the law." No one appeared, which showed we were in good standing; and on Saturday afternoon before the marriage at 5 o'clock, the appointed hour, we were to be at the house of Dominie van Raalte. It happened that I was busy that afternoon making stovepipes for C. Hoffman, who helped me while I worked on them. He wanted me to help him get ready his stove, but before I had finished it my pretty bride came in to see where I was and tell me it was past the time when we were to present ourselves before the dominie. I laid down my tools, washed myself, and changed my clothes – all in a hurry – and we were on our way, walking to the spot where the knot was to be tied. I don't remember what became of Hoffman, his stovepipe, or stove – all I know is that we were late, but not too late for the solemn words to be pronounced by Dominie van Raalte who also gave advice and encouragement, closing with a prayer.

Lighthearted and happy, I went with my bride to the house of her cousin Herman Verbeek, with whose family she was staying. We talked and had supper. Not being so well posted as was my bride, I looked upon her as my lawful wife – the dominie had said so – and I thought the ceremony had been duly performed, although I did know that we were expected to come before the pulpit in church on the following day, during the Sunday service, for benediction. But oh, no! – my better half told me that the ceremony on the next day would complete our marriage, and that I would have to go back to my little room over our one-story 12 by 20 hardware store, to which early in the morning I had said "goodby, old bed, I won't come back to you again." I told her that if she understood it thus I would wish her good night, and so I went back to the hardware store where five hours before I had been making stovepipes.

All summer, up to the date of our marriage, I had boarded with my bride's cousin Herman Verbeek, with whom we were to stay for a few days until we began housekeeping. Sunday morning I went to his house for breakfast, and met my sweetheart. We went to the log church near the cemetery, and Dominie van Raalte pronounced the benediction. The soldier Kees de Witt placed the pillows on the floor before the pulpit on which we knelt to receive the benediction. Kees received his tips from the bridegroom and was happy. This was the final part of the ceremony, and now our marriage was in perfect order. Monday evening a few friends, Dominie and Mrs. van Raalte, Mr. and Mrs. Reitsma, Mr. and Mrs. Meengs, Herman Verbeek, and my sisters Christina and Hannah came to celebrate our wedding. My bride had prepared a wedding cake and served it with coffee, and we had a pleasant time. According to the custom no presents were given, which made everybody comfortable and free to enjoy the event. Our clothes were neat and plain. Our furniture was simple – only a cook stove and no carpet on the floor. Four couples in all were married that day – John de Vries, Klaas Mulder, Gerrit J. Hesselink, Pas and myself. Three of us paid Dominie van Raalte his dues in cash, but one of the bridegrooms promised some corn, and the dominie said that would be all right.

About four weeks after our arrival in the woods, while father stood near a tree that had fallen on our tin shop, an old lady by the name of Slag came on a dead run stating excitedly that a man had just come with a drove of milk cows. Twelve dollars would buy one. "Just think of ti – 30 guilders for a milk cow; she is worth only that much for beef." Father went to see this man, and bought a black cow. It became my duty to feed her. For an hour in the morning, and several times during the day I led her from tree to tree so she could eat the leaves. At other times we kept her tied to a tree, believing such treatment would be sufficient. But what did city folk know about cows? At best we had two or three scanty meals a day and thought a cow ought to be satisfied with only a few leaves. One morning we looked through the openings between the logs of our hut to see if the cow still was tied to the tree. We saw her rope, but the cow had gone; and so before breakfast I had to go into the woods to look for her. But it was not until afternoon that I found her pasturing with other cows near the river. Klaas Hinderman told me that she had been there all day. From that time we let her feed at will. We made a tin bell for her so we could readily find her. She went dry in the fall, and we took her to Mr. I. van Dyke at Port Sheldon, where she died during the winter, and this put an end to our interest in cows.

Not many days after we arrived in Holland Bart Slag and I took a stroll through the woods and walked to the Indian village. When Bart saw the Indians he started on a run, thinking they would kill him. I looked around but was not a bit afraid of Indians. I had a greater fear of wild beasts, and in my imagination, seeing terrible beats, I too ran away. On one occasion Abraham Slaghuis came running out of the woods. Thinking he had heard a fearful roaring, he believed he had escaped violent death. A few days later he again heard the same roaring and, more courageous than before, went to look for the beast but found it was only a night owl whose hooting had frightened him. Others had similar experiences. Some of the settlers thought they had seen a monstrous black animal, but upon looking a second time saw it was a blackened stump of a tree that had frightened them. On another occasion when people who had been frightened met a bear, the latter quietly ambled away.

Our neighbors had come from different parts of the fatherland. Each spoke his own dialect – to us quaint-sounding words from Friesland, Groningen, Drente, Zeeland, Graafschap, etc. We understood few of these words. A Zeeland girl came to me one morning and said, *"Guns, lang me een zulvertje"* [Come, give me a match]. We had some old country matches made of flax stems, eight inches long with one end dipped in sulphur. I said "no," not knowing if I had hit it correctly or not. She looked at me and talked fast and loud, perhaps calling me names and I don't know what else. I felt embarrassed. She then drew Mrs. Dok's attention who said, "he doesn't understand you. I will talk to him." She was a Zeeland woman but could also talk like city folk. "Boy," she said "will you give me one of your old country matches?" I gave her one. "Don't you see," she said, "that he did not understand you?" One Graafschap boy told me that I did not speak pure and correct Dutch because what he called a *boxse*, I called a *broek*, both words meaning trousers. He said it was plainly written in the Bible, in the parable of the prodigal son where he said to his father [Luke 15, 29] "Thou hast never given me a kid [*bok* in Dutch] that I might make merry with my friends." I laughed, and pointed out his mistake, and those who heard of it agreed I was right.

A Jew from Groningen tried to be sweet on my stepmother, my father having died January 9, 1849. In one of his visits he told some story about his wife before she died – that she had a bale of gold, as I understood him. Afterwards, I learned that he meant a lot of good clothes. When I heard him say he had a 'bale of gold,' I thought it meant a coffee bale filled with gold money, and said to myself "what a liar that old Jew is, how he does boast!" He was rejected, however, and my stepmother in 1852 married Rense Polsma who went to the war in the fall of 1861. With him went my brother Arend, then only seventeen. Polsma died in a hospital in 1862, but my brother returned in 1865.

The colonists suffered much in the fall of 1847. We had neither food nor money. For days some of our people had nothing to eat but pork. Others had nothing but beans while some had only ship's biscuit. The strong and healthy among the men walked to Singapore or Allegan or Grand Haven to buy provisions, carrying them home for their families. But the weaker and helpless colonists had to make the best of it. Dense forests without roads, low land, swamp, and river made it almost impossible to reach any market with oxen or horses. It was 24 miles to Allegan, 30 to Grand Rapids, 22 to Grand Haven, and 14 to Singapore. One day farmer Anton Shorno, who lived eight miles from Black Lake, came to Holland with some salt pork, and sold all of it at eight cents a pound. Dear old lady Slag bought a small piece of about two pounds, paying eight stuivers [i.e. eight Dutch cents] for it.

Aart Vissers, the baker, managed to buy some flour and made bread which he sold at ten cents a loaf. Father bought all he could, and so we ate bread soup saltpork. Mr. Luther ate noting but pork for three days; others were fortunate if they had anyting else to eat. Some merchants from Allegan loaded a scow with potatoes and other provisions and floated it down the Kalamazoo River to Lake Michigan and along the shore to the mouth of Black Lake. There they loaded a yawl the with provisions from the scow and came to Holland with small quantities, thus making the settlers believe their supply was limited. This enabled them to charge a dollar for a bushel of potatoes which at home had cost but eight or ten cents. They sold their groceries at the same rate. Everybody, however, was glad to get something toe at and willingly paid any price asked.

A plan was formed to open a co-operative colonial store. All goods were to be bought at wholesale and sold to customers at cost with a small percentage added. A committee was appointed to collect money in the form of a loan, to be returned with interest. Loaning money for this enterprise was considered a noble cause. The sums so collected were entrusted to a committee of two, Bernardus Grootenhuis and Mr. Elias Young, an elder from Grand Rapids, who were commissioned to buy merchandise in New York. They bought a lot of dry goods, groceries, shoes, Yankee notions, and other articles. They paid for some of these things in cash, and charged the rest to "Dominie van Raalte and Company." The first committee purchased a vessel in which to transport to Black Lake the goods that came from Chicago. This vessel also was to transport articles purchased from the settlers by the Company and carry them to the Chicago market. Shingle bolts, bark, oak staves, cord wood, and other wood products would be exchanged for necessaries. The co-operative company secured the sailboat *Knickerbocker*. Ale Stegenga and his son Wipke were placed in charge of the vessel; Jannes van de Luyster Jr. acted as local agent. The harbor at the mouth of Black Lake was choked with sand. When the vessel came in from Chicago she dropped anchor off shore in Lake Michigan. One of the crew was sent ashore in a yawl. A messenger was sent to the local agent in Holland. The goods had to be transported over the sand choked entrance and loaded in a boat and brought to Holland. Whatever the committee had bought from the settlers was shipped to Chicago by the same means. The local agent was busy managing this business which included sending scows to the mouth of the lake. A board structure on a lot near the present *De Grond-wet* office served as the store. Grootenhuis was manager, Verhorst and Jim Westveer clerks. The committee was handicapped by lack of funds. Their management was without system, and the co-operative enterprise incurred expenses which made the goods exceptionally expensive.

Binnekant and Houtkamp then started a general store, accepting shingle bolts, staves, and bark in exchange for store goods. This store was located at the foot of Second Street, near the Lake. Stores also were opened by Henry D. Post and others. With such competitors the colony store could not flourish, and the enterprise was a failure. The *Knickerbocker* was sold; and the remaining store goods were distributed among those who had loaned the money. The balance due was charged against Dominie van Raalte who was burdened with this debt for a long time. Finally the brethren in the East helped him out of these difficulties.

The strange climate, malaria, moisture in the woods and swamps, stagnant water in the pools, improper food, and lack of shelter under-mined our health, and many died. My sister Anna was seriously ill. Dr. J. J. M. C. van Nus who had just arrived from the old country was called. He gave her some medicine which did not help her. Father remarked to the doctor that he gave only a small dose. The doctor replied that this was true, saying he had only a limited supply and had to ration it that everybody might have some. My sister died along with four others that same night – and there was not a soul available to help the sick, for nearly everybody was suffering.

Father sent me to Dominie van Raalte, as his house was headquarters for everything, to tell him that my sister had died and to ask if he knew where we could obtain a coffin. The good man made ready to go with me, but first took a bowl of fresh milk. It was early in the morning and we walked through the woods until we came to a brush shed occupied by a carpenter who had a few rough boards from which to make a box. Two men carried the box on their shoulders to our place. After placing my sister in a sheet, they laid her in the box and nailed on the cover. This done, they carried the coffin on their shoulders and, followed by my father and myself, buried it near Fourth Street and River Street, without any ceremony whatever.

The settlers grieved deeply, for they could not bury their dead decently. Thus when his wife died, unable to find materials for a coffin or anyone to help him in his bereavement, Notier de Reft had to dig a hole near his hut, wrapped his wife's body in a bed sheet, and buried it with his own hands. There were others who buried their friends and children in the same manner.

Several doctors came to Holland, but they were not the best. Their intention was to fill their pockets. When their ignorance became apparent they went away. My father also fell sick, and the doctor gave him a tablespoon of brandy every hour until father refused to take any more. He felt he was becoming intoxicated. Soon it became clear that the physician was only a horse doctor. Another doctor came to Holland bringing with him a lot of sheep, for, as he said, he cured the sick by giving them mutton. He sold his mutton at a good price, collected handsomely for his services, and went away with pockets well filled, after which other doctors also came and went.

Our never-to-be-forgotten Dominie van Raalte was loved and trusted by all. His untiring zeal and readiness to help comforted the sick. Every morning he received patients in his house, administering medicine with a tablespoon. Around him were bottles of quinine, blue pills, and rhubarb. The log kitchen served as a waiting room; the sick sat on a long board bench. In turn they went into the room where the dominie dispensed his medicines and gave advice, and this went on day after day.

I have often wondered if he ever received any pay for his medicines.

Whenever anything unusual happened such as the arrival of a wagon or a boat with something for sale, the fact soon became known. One day a boat loaded with fresh meat came to the landing place, and many hastened to the spot. Everybody was eager to buy, but the owner of the boat insisted upon providing the sick before selling anything to the others. Those who had sick folk in their tents secured fresh meat at a high price. The rest who were in good health went home happy that they had actually seen fresh meat.

After a short while we moved into a small house made of rough boards, owned by Jannes van de Luyster. The house had one room with a low ceiling. A ladder thrust through an opening in the ceiling gave access to the room under the rafters. The little room on the ground floor was occupied by four families with their children. The upstairs under the rafters served as sleeping quarters. Our beds were spread out on the boards, and the four families laid down side by side their feet toward the opening. It was my good fortune to lie near Boudewijn Dertro and his wife Maria. Their evening dialogue was most amusing. Maria had no trouble in falling asleep, and soon snored to beat the band. "Quit that snoring," cried Boudewijn, "or I will kill you!" Then he would give her a vigorous shaking. But Maria did not like being interrupted. When she again began snoring there was another verbal barrage. Maria often talked to me and told me how much fun she had had when as a young woman she went to circuses and dances. Poor soul, she died before New Year's. Her husband tanked the Lord openly, saying "I thank you, Lord, that I am delivered of her". But his joy was short lived, for soon after he also closed his eyes, never to open them again.

There was much amusement over our scratching which began with the plague of Egyptian lice. The woods and huts were all filled with the pests, and no remedy could be found so long as we lived herded together. The lice had been brought in by the immigrants. When in spite of the vermin we began to fall asleep, we found comfort in dreaming of the past in our fatherland. Only when in my imagination I was back in Amsterdam, could I find joy and comfort. Then I saw the royal palace, bands of musicians, soldiers on horses, infantry marching through the Kalverstraat to the Dam. Again I walked in the Pantoffel Parade in the Keisersgracht, again I was in the Boter Markt where I saw the Jew Smoel with his tray full of cookies and Sara with her can of pickles. Once more I heard drums and trumpets. There at the Duivelshoek I again saw the dog shows. And then there was the Munt, the famous old tower.

There I found my friends, old chums, and told them I had lived in America – in the howling wilderness, shut off from civilization – and how happy I was to be back again! In my dreams I kicked the very stones in the street, to be sure I was not dreaming, and that I was back again in my beloved Amsterdam. But when I awoke, great was my disappointment, for it was only a dream! The night birds would scream, the owls hoot, and the surroundings looked so desolate that I felt as if I had been banished from my friends, robbed of the joy of life.

Five of the first settlers – Dominie van Raalte, Jan Binnekant, Jan Rabbers, Jan Stegeman, and Jan Kolvoord – each bought on contract eighty acres of the land which originally had been intended for the use of the city and its surroundings, for pastures, vegetable gardens, etc. Four of these men intended to speculate and make a little money. "No," said Dominie van Raalte, "it was understood before we bought this land that no person could buy more than eighty acres of state's land, and that this land should be reserved as colony land, for the benefit of the settlers." At first they objected, but finally they turned the land they had bought over to five trustees selected by the people at a citizen's meeting. My father was one of these trustees. As soon as the trustees received the money from the sale of the land, they bought more land on contract, paying a little down in order to secure all the land for miles around to distribute to the immigrants who were arriving each week. Thus, it was hoped, a large Dutch settlement would come into existence. All this caused Dominie van Raalte much labor and no end of trouble. The state lands in Drenthe, Vriesland, and surrounding country also were secured, at least so thought the dominie. But certain speculators who dug the canal in Grand Rapids received from the state land warrants which had been appropriated by the legislature for the payment of the canal. Seeing the immigrants settling on the choice lands of the region, they hurried to the state Land Office in Ionia. They selected the lands for which the dominie had repeatedly visited the Land Office. This caused Dominie van Raalte much difficulty and expense, all of which afterwards raised the purchase price of the land. The dominie employed lawyers, and traveled from place to place to obtain information, but with no result. The land officers obliged their countrymen; the Hollanders lost the land. Finally, however, the dominie succeeded in securing title to the disputed land.

Meanwhile the city had to be surveyed and platted, a job given to Mr. E. B. Bassett from Allegan. With compass and chain he laid out the blocks, lots, streets, and public market places. First he ran a line through

Eighth Street from east to west limits and platted the city north from
that line to First Street – after the model of Allegan, and unfortunately
without making provisions for alleys. After he finished this part of the
city he became ill and went home, but soon sent Mr. John Dumont to
survey and plat the part south from Eighth Street. After he laid out the
streets and blocks, he sold his compass and chain to his helper Ben
Grootenhuis. With the help of a man named Van Dam, Grootenhuis
surveyed the lots in each block. The surveying finished, the plat was
brought to the county clerk's office where it was registered as the village
of Holland. The five trustees sold the first house lots for $ 15 each, but
soon raised the price to $ 48 for corner lots and $ 38 for the lots between.
The money thus received was divided among three funds: one for the
salary of a minister and for church expenses; another for constructing a
harbor and to encourage navigation; and a third for the improvement of
the corporation and payment of its debt.

The trustees, knowing what benefit factories brought their communities,
started a shingle mill. They had little success, however, for they were
without capital, had no acquaintance with markets, and lacked the means
of transporting their product. A good many settlers, however, made
shingles for their own use. Henry D. Post and Dominie van Raalte
started an ash factory to make black salt for the Chicago market. Mr.
John Littlejohn and other citizens of Allegan talked against the Dutch
settlers, wishing they would move away. They feared heavy taxes to
support such a crowd of paupers. No! and again, no! Mr. Littlejohn!
Although you are considered an intelligent man, little do you understand
the history and character of the Dutch, a people zealous, enterprising, and
perservering. Our ancestors by hard work converted the bottom of the
sea into fertile fields. Over land and sea they are known as daring and
patriotic people with deep appreciation for statesmanship. Should their
children eat pauper's bread provided by the citizens of Allegan? No!
As true children of the old Dutch stock they possessed the courage and
perserverance to transform this land covered with timber and interspersed with soggy marshes into a countryside dotted with farms,
villages, and factories, and now blessed with railroads and steamboat
lines which bring our products to market, and all this by the grace of
our God! To Him be the praise!

The principal motto of Dominie van Raalte was "My fellow countrymen, unite, inform, and elevate yourselves; aim at a lofty standard of
life; cultivate knowledge; lay an adequate foundation for your colony
according to a well developed plan, that you may be a great people among

the other groups of this land. Be diligent in educating your children; don't hold a calf in higher esteem than your own child." Before this settlement was organized into school districts, the promoters of education hired a Yankee school teacher, Mr. Hoyt from Kalamazoo; paying him a salary of $ 30 a month. The children went to school in the log church on the cemetery grounds. The older children, and also some of the younger, went to school in a room in Mr. Houtkamp's house on East Eighth Street. This house was built for Mr. Houtkamp by Mr. R. Schelleman in the winter of 1848. The teacher was a Methodist who commenced his daily task with prayer. Our text books were Bibles, on each page two columns – one in Dutch, the other in English. We had to read in English and, by looking on the other column, tell the meaning of what we were reading.

The principles to govern our life in a consecrated Christian commonwealth as laid down by our leaders were: to educate the young, build seminaries and common schools, organize local government, establish factories, open navigation, construct a harbor, and build roads. Town meetings were the order of the day. These gatherings were held in Binnekant's home and hotel on the northwest corner of Eighth and River Streets. The first was a simple beginning, for the colonists had nothing; and sacrifice and labor were needed to start the wheels of our common life. Here young and old met on a basis of equality to discuss all questions of local importance. The consistory, composed of the elders and deacons, constituted the highest court, chiefly to maintain discipline.

The French and Yankee settlers on Point Superior who had vacated the place in 1836 had left a few empty houses. Jan Binnekant moved one of them to his lot on the corner of Eighth and River streets, and this became the first hotel. Arie van Zoeren, H. Meengs, G. Zalsman, H. Geuring, Mr. Bosdijke, and Hein van der Haar were among the earliest boarders in the first Holland Hotel. Binnekant, the landlord, himself asked grace before each meal which was closed by all singing a psalm in chorus.

This hotel, as we have noted, was the place for public meetings, and many an enterprise had its birth in this building. Everybody had the privilege of bringing new propositions before the meeting, which were disposed of to the best interests of all. At first meetings were held in the open air, and always opened with prayer. Committees were appointed for different tasks. Volunteers were asked to open roads, cut down trees in the school yard and the public square, and open the harbor at the head of the lake by digging out the sand bar. The first public worship was held in the open air near the dominie's kitchen. The men had to stand up, but women, children, and the physically weak sat down on logs and fallen trees. The dominie stood and preached on a rude platform. Everyone came to these meetings unless something serious prevented. It was the only place where all the people could meet each other in common friendship after a week of hard physical labor. The boys and young men came to see the girls, to hear a sermon and join in the worship; but the older people longed for the words of truth and the communion of saints. Through the week, evening services were held at Binnekant's hotel, Bible study at the dominie's house, and prayer meetings in the little red schoolhouse on East Eighth Street. The settlers were sincere Christians, God loving men and women. The Lord's house was their joy – a fountain to fill their hearts and minds with strength from above, encourage them to perservere, and do all things charitably, trust in God who would give them better days and crown their affairs with success. Dominie van Raalte's preaching proved a blessing, the tie that bound men's hearts in love and caused them to place their trust in Him, that He would care for them and help them.

The trials, exertions, and severe physical toil during the week caused many an exhausted person to fall asleep at Sunday services, but the resourceful dominie knew how to rouse them. Whenever it rained we worshiped in the dominie's log kitchen. Occasionally the Old Country students Jannes van de Luyster and Cornelius van Malsen preached. The former on one occasion preached from 2 Kings 4, 8-12, how Elisha entered the house of a Shunemite woman and how she treated him. He laid much stress on how in a little chamber she set a bed, table, chair, and candlestick.

During the summer of 1847 the settlers built a log church on the cemetery grounds. Gerrit J. Kroon was the architect. By the close of autumn it was so nearly finished that a room in the front of the building could be used for worship. Two old-fashioned cookstoves – Premium No. 9 – were set on each side of the room, their stovepipes being passed through the side walls. While being transferred, the two cross plates which supported the covers were lost. Father made two new ones out of sheet iron, but these soon warped from the heat, and so the room filled with smoke. But the room was warm and the smoke mattered little. First comers occupied the seats nearest the stoves, hugging the stove between their legs and remaining in that position throughout the sermon. The dominie stood on a little platform which had been erected near the partition. In the morning he preached a sermon; in the afternoon service he asked questions from Scripture. By the next summer the entire building was finished, with pulpit and pews according to custom. It was a satisfaction to have order in our worship. The first communion was celebrated out of doors behind the dominie's house, the communicants standing in a circle with the dominie and elders in the center. It was a solemn sight – in the midst of the discomforts of our life to remember the death of our dear Saviour and partake of His holy sacrament. How they testified that the Lord was good! The new church was provided with communion tables, children were baptized in front of the pulpit, and when marriages were solemnized with benediction – usually on the Sabbath – Kees de Witt, the janitor, laid the pillows before the pulpit for the couples to kneel on. Most everyone rewarded the good old man with a tip.

On New Year's morning we went to church to hear the New Year sermon. How well I remember the dominie preached on New Year's Day of 1850 in that old log church from the gospel of Luke, 16, 2 [last part]: "Give an account of thy stewardship, for thou mayest no longer be steward." The dominie preached with great earnestness, warning his hearers to take these words to heart. To me the truth came with great force – it seemed a matter of life or death itself. From the depth of my soul I cried out, beseeching the Saviour for mercy. I went home penitent, meditating upon my sins and upon the redeeming love of the Saviour to save souls of such even as me.

In the afternoon of that day we had a meeting of a different nature. It concerned the renting of pews. In front of the pulpit a table had been set boards placed upon carpenter's horses. Elder Aldred Plugger took the chair while C. Hoffman acted as clerk. The consistory managed the affair. Deacon Teunis Keppel acted as auctioneer. Standing on a pew he asked, "How much for a seat in this pew?" "Six dollars," offered three persons. "Who will pay more than six, who?" "Seven dollars!" "Who more than seven?" The lucky person had to appear before the chairman and pay the money. Everybody knew that the amount had to be paid at once, but with the consent of the consistory purchasers might pay their sums later to the treasurer, Aldred Plugger, in his store. Sometimes the bidding became lively and some of the bidders were swept away in the excitement. So Lambert van Dis, Dirk Maurik, and others were loaded with seats at a high price. For the young people who had little recreation this was pleasant amusement, as to them any commotion was welcome. Yes, those young men were not as careful as they ought to be, for over the church door was written the admonishment, "Beware of your feet when you enter the House of the Lord."

The spirit of the Massachusetts Pilgrim fathers ruled the settlement, and many felt the sting of discipline as severe as any inflicted by the Blue Laws of Connecticut. The dominie and consistory exercised extensive ruling power, settling disputes, applying justice, rebuking people. Mrs. Fannie D. had gossiped about a neighbor woman who complained to the consistory. The penalty was public confession in church. I felt sorry for her. An elder had noticed a young lady, Sesine S. who improperly exposed her neck. So a cloth was placed over the offending neck and thus modesty was restored. Mr. Hermanus Doesburg published an article in the newspaper about the dominie and the consistory. The article was headed *The Pope and his Cardinals*. Doesburg was punished by being denied admission to the Lord's Supper. The time came for Holy Communion when according to custom all sat near the table. An elder stood at each end to keep unworthy persons from sitting down and prevent infraction of the regulations. One of the elders who did not know a reconciliation had been effected with the consistory saw Doesburg take his seat among those who intended to receive Holy Communion. Taking Doesburg by the shoulders, with much patience, he requested him to leave the table, which created great commotion. Doesburg became very excited, stood up and declared he understood that on the day before all had been forgiven. Thereupon the members of the consistory corroborated his statements; and peace was restored whereupon Doesburg was permitted to sit down.

In the 1850's, perhaps it was in 1855, a circus came to our city and spread its tents in a vacant lot opposite the Grand Haven House, Mr. C. van der Veere's hotel on the corner of Sixth and River Streets. What a great scandal this was, violating the morals of the community and insulting its Christian charter! The elders, J. Labots and Teunis Keppel, stood near the entrance of the tent to note all who went in. Those who entered could be sure they would be required to make a strict accounting. The children were interested in the circus, but their fathers told them that it was a sin to see the performance. The circus men wandered among the stumps, swearing and using vulgar language, saying "What a d----d hole this is."

Our life was plain; even in church on Sunday the clothing of the people was simple. No one went thirsty during services, for a pail full of water with a dipper in it stood ever ready at the door. The dominie's two sons Bertus and Ben brought to church an Old Country jug filled with water. The churchgoers brought with them their noonday meal, consisting mostly of bread. This they ate in the church, washing down their frugal repast with water from the pail.

In 1854 our people began the building of a new church on the corner
of College Avenue and Ninth Street. Jacobus Schrader was the architect;
Herman Verbeek, Gerrit Slenk, and Piet Zalsman the principal carpenters.
The sills, crossbeams, and heavy timbers were hewn in the woods. The
flooring, wall boards, ceiling, and pew boards were planed and matched
by hand. For weeks Piet de Vries and others planed the floor boards. Ben
Grootenhuis, assisted by his son Johannes, painted the structure in 1856.
When the new building was finished we moved from the log church in
the cemetery. Thus the members, who belonged to the Reformed
Church, built this church with great zeal, with cash earned by hard labor
and saved by rigid economy. The church was dedicated, but the members
failed to incorporate the church body according to law. Teunis Keppel,
an old settler, and his followers, immigrants of later years, never paid a
cent toward expenses. They took advantage of the fact that the church
body had never been incorporated, and seceded. They told the minority
they should leave the church and surrender the building. Keppel and
the rest of the consistory held the keys; they were determined to keep the
structure for their own following, forgetting, as men of common sense
would not, that the consistory were acting as trustee for the members.
But according to law, inasmuch as the members were not incorporated,
they were only a religious society and the majority ruled. Keppel was
ambitious to perpetuate his own name. The consistory and the majority
of the members, in the interest of purity of doctrine and peace of
conscience, separated from what they declared was the wicked church
in the East [*Breken met het Oosten*] – Break with the East was Keppel's
motto]. Thus they expelled a minority of their own brethren without
refunding them a cent of their hard earned money, without a church
building of their own, to drift, for themselves. Time came for the Classis
to meet, according to the minutes of the latest session – that is, before
Keppel's secession. Its sessions were to be held in our historic church,
but Keppel and his followers said the church was theirs. On the morning
of the day the Classis was to convene the consistory locked the double
door with a logging chain. The leaders Van den Berg and Derk te Roller,
one on each side of the doors, stood like sentinals guarding the entrance.
Other members of the consistory, supported by a group of their faithful,
stood within calling distance. By their gestures they showed themselves
ready to resist any attempt to open the church door. Keppel, dressed in
his best, walked inside the church yard from the gate to the church door,
up and down, looking excitedly in all directions, his fists clenched as if
ready for combat. Dominie Nicholas Steffens, Dominie Pieter Lepeltak,

Professor Philip Phelps, and other members of the Classis gathered on the sidewalk near the church gate. Seeing no agreement could be reached, they organized as a Classis then and there and adjourned to the Third Reformed Church. I went home, leaving the scence with a heavy heart, saddened to see how selfish men could act in the name of Christianity.

Teunis Keppel kept the church keys; and when the janitor, Dirk Sluiter, had to ring the bell he went to Keppel who accompanied him to the church, opened the door, and kept watch lest the ejected members should claim their church. After the janitor had rung the bell, Keppel locked the door. How well did Solomon declare that "the evil doers fear even when there is no pursuer".

In one of the public meetings held during 1850 in Binnekant's hotel, it was resolved to purchase a bell for public use. A subscription list was opened and money was pledged to secure the bell we desired. The bell, bought in Troy, New York, arrived in good condition. A committee constructed a frame about ten feet high and set it up in the woods at the corner of College Avenue and Tenth Street. Gerrit Alberts, the watchmaker who had served as a soldier under Napoleon I, cast the metal sockets for the yoke because, as he claimed, he could construct them in such a way as to permit the bell to swing freely. To Hermanus Doesburg was assigned the task of ringing the bell. He was required to ring it on Sundays before church time, throughout the week for town and church meetings, in case of fire and burials, and four times each day at 7, 12, 1, and 6.

When the church was completed in 1856 this bell was placed in the tower. That faithful bell still rings out in silver tones from that old tower, reminding me of the days gone by and filling my soul with emotion. And that old copper rooster on the steeple – how I did work on it, making a good pattern and constructing in its bowels the apparatus that would enable it to respond to the winds from every direction! In these 48 years it had never disappointed my expectations, for even today it notes every change of wind. May it remain faithful to the purpose for which I made it. Good old church, blessed house of the Lord, you remind us old settlers of our cash offerings, our united labors, our perserverance in building you, also the comfort and Christian fellowship we enjoyed in those good old days when we worshiped in that blessed place of consecration and in communion with the Lord's people. Its very walls speak of the outpouring of the Holy Spirit and the abundant conversion of souls in the revival meetings of 1869 and later.

When in 1846 Dominie van Raalte arrived in New York he found friends among the descendants of the original settlers [Knickerbockers] on Manhattan Island. From them he heard how the first Dutch governor Pieter Minuit had purchased that island from the Indians for $ 24, one mill per acre. These friends learned from Van Raalte that an immigration of Reformed Christians, persecuted by the authorities for leaving the State Church, was on the way. Being faithful to Reformed teaching and also warm Christians, these friends sympathized with the immigrants who were displeased because the State Church in the Netherlands had drifted from the traditional precepts of the Reformed Church, many of its ministers teaching that Jesus was merely a good model to follow, and that salvation came simply from doing good deeds. The Knickerbockers helped the immigrants with advice and money. They advised Van Raalte to settle on the cheap and unoccupied lands in the West where there was room enough to found a new Netherlands. They gave him letters of recommendation to friends in Albany, Buffalo, Detroit, and other places; and they treated him with respect. At Detroit the dominie found friends who were eager to help. The state legislature of Michigan was in session and friends in Detroit introduced him to Mr. John R. Kellog, a member of the Legislature, who advised him to settle in Ottawa County, near Black Lake. The dominie left his family in Detroit and went to inspect the suggested site. So satisfactory appeared the region that he decided to found his colony there. He sent for his family. The immigrants came in large companies, eager to establish homes. The people founded and built churches and elected consistories. They thought it best to unite with the old Dutch Reformed Church in the East. A committee was sent to talk over the matter with the committee in New York representing the Reformed Church, and it reported that all was satisfactory. Thus was brought about the union with the Reformed Church in America, which provided a bond of Christian fellowship and an opportunity for higher education in the college at New Brunswick in New Jersey. The brethren in the East helped relieve the suffering of the settlers, and this endeavor springing from Christian love was a factor in the success of the colony. These friends sent clothes and other necessaries to the ministers for the use of the settlers. They even sent books. It was through Dominie van Raalte's influence that the Pioneer School, later Hope College, was founded in Holland. The brethren in the East sent Mr. Walter T. Taylor, who came with his family, and as principal took charge of the Pioneer School.

The first troubles in our church life began when Richard Baxter's *Call to the Unconverted* was distributed among the people. This book taught that everybody should discharge his obligations in Christian work, lead a consecrated life, and give freely of his resources to further the good cause. Some of the members declared they could not tolerate such doctrine, for they thought it was heretical to place such confidence in the merit of outward works. They believed that those ordained to eternal life would be saved by grace. In addition, there was misunderstanding of the motives of the brethren in the East, which created suspicion and caused the secession of 1857. A young farmer from Graafschap said to me when he noticed I had a book, "What! Have you also one of those Baxter books? I despise the doctrine, and use such books for scrap paper when I shave."

Work on the harbor and opening roads was on a voluntary basis, without pay. We cut trees although we had never seen an axe in our lives. We chopped around tree trunks, thinking that the best way to fell them. This was dangerous, for a tree standing on the center of a stump might fall in any direction, endangering the lives of the choppers. The roads were made just wide enough for a team of horses. If two teams happened to meet, they turned out into the woods the best they could. In low places logs were laid side by side across the road, such a construction being called a "log bridge," or "corduroy road". Riding over such a bridge in a lumber wagon drawn by oxen was a severe trial. The shaking made me sick in my stomach. I chopped down trees on my father's property on the southeast corner of College Avenue and Eighth Street, where we intended to build a house. I began chopping a dead hemlock tree two feet six inches in diameter, which had no limbs. Like others, I chopped around the trunk. As the outside had rottted and was soft I soon reached the center of sound wood only a few inches in diameter. The tree began to sway a whip lash, and I started on a dead run. Fortunately, it fell in another direction. On another day I chopped a green birch tree 16 inches in diameter. To my horror, when it began to fall, I saw my brother Christian coming. I shouted with all my might. He thought I wanted him to run toward me. Fortunately, the tree lodged in another tree and my brother was saved from certain death. Trees standing near houses were dangerous, and cutting them down was entrusted to Indians and Yankees who knew how to fell trees in any direction. A large tree stood close to the house of John Kolvoord on Eighth Street near Columbia Avenue. Mr. Gerrit Wilterdink thought he had acquired the art of felling trees. But the Kolvoord family, not trusting his skill, stood outside the house to watch him while he worked. Bart Kolvoord, John's brother, looked at the tree and said, "It is a dangerous thing to chop down so big a tree." He was right, for Wilterdink failed to drop the tree away from the house, and it crashed through the roof crushing the stove and furniture.

A resolution was adopted to open a road between Holland and Zeeland, to be done by volunteers. Trees were cut down in mid-winter during a heavy fall of snow. Fires were built which enabled us to keep warm while we ate our frozen bread and drank water from the streams. The Cedar Swamp east of the city limits was filled with water and cedar logs were piled in the road to make it passable. Next was hewn a road leading through the low land across the brook to the log church. This likewise was accomplished by volunteer labor. Everybody turned out whether he knew how to chop down trees or not. I chopped down a tree near the brook, about 12 inches in diameter. The tree was crooked, and, when it came down, the lower part swung around my head and I escaped by a hair's breadth. Once Kees Kuit, brother-in-law of G. and Jacob van Putten, was chopping down a tree when a man cried "Look out!" Kuit dropped behind a big log and the tree fell over him. Jacob van Putten scolded the man for his thoughtless shouting, for he should have waited till the tree started to fall before giving his warning. I remember that the dominie's team of black oxen, driven by Cornelius van Herwijnen, pulled logs and stringers which were needed to make a firm road bed. Thus was finished this important road, the one over which so many of the settlers went to church for worship, to be married, or to carry their dead to their final resting place.

Step by step the settlers built their town in accordance with their ideas of comfort and happiness. Eighth Street was the first thoroughfare to be opened. Trees were cut down and piled high in the Public Market, or Fish Market, by the church, or in the school yards. These piles of logs and brush burned readily during the dry weather of the following summer. A fire started in the woods and, whipped by a strong wind, spread to the woods everywhere. The pine and hemlock trees were aflame to their very tops. This was on a Saturday morning, and everybody turned out to keep the fire from spreading to the few dwellings already standing. People carried water and covered their possessions with sand. Hermanus Doesburg and I were asked to keep watch during the night to keep the log fences around the school yard from catching fire. All Sunday the people fought the fire, so there was no public worship that day. People carried their clothing and furniture into the streets and open spaces, thinking things would be safer there than in the houses. But in spite of the fact the fire raged on all sides, the Lord's protection was marvelous.

The fire burned the brush and wood around the houses and even swept under the house belonging to Mr. V. Verhorst, situated near the City Mills, but not one house was lost. Finally it began to rain and the fires were extinguished. We were very thankful for the fires because the town looked much better than when the brush and logs covered the ground on all sides.

The first water-driven sawmill in the Colony was built at Groningen, three and one-half miles northeast of Holland. This neighborhood was named Adam and Eve after two settlers everybody knew at that time. But in Holland Jacobus Schrader erected the first windmill to be constructed in the Colony. It was built according to Old Country models. Willem Flietstra and Piet and Geert Klaver, millwrights by trade, did all the work. This mill was situated near the Grand Haven Bridge on River Street, but it never sawed much lumber.

Oswald van der Sluis arrived from Arnhem in the summer of 1848. He erected a sawmill near the lake on Fourth Street. This mill, which operated a one-frame saw, produced a good deal of lumber. Mr. Bosdijke, a gentleman of rank, came from Amsterdam by way of Canada. In 1849 he installed two sets of small millstones with which to grind wheat and corn. This was our first flour mill but its operation soon came to an end when Bosdijke returned to the Old Country. One time the dry logs, brush, and rotting wood which still lay in great quantities near the houses caught fire. A wind rapidly spread the blaze, endangering the mill. I heard a noise near Binnekant's hotel, and saw Mrs. Binnekant ringing a dinner bell, shouting "Fire! Fire! Van der Sluis' mill is burning. Help! Help!" Everybody rushed with ropes, shovels, and pails to put it out. A pail brigade was formed, a successful way of extinguishing the flames.

Dominie had planned to build a house for orphans. To pay for it he collected the jewelry the ladies had brought with them from the Old Country. There were strings of beads fastened by hooks and eyes of gold, gold ear rings, finger rings, gold and silver head pieces used by those colonists who had come from Groningen, Friesland, and Zeeland. These articles were called "vanities", not becoming Christians. From the money thus raised a house was erected, the beginning of a good cause. But the orphans were placed in private families and the house was not needed. The children fared well, better than if they had been placed in the orphanage.

On at least one occasion were the blue laws applied. Instead of going to church one Sunday, Joos ver Planke and Kees Dok played in the woods and broke the windows of the orphanage. Deacon Keppel made a complaint before Justice of the Peace Henry D. Post. The court – the first jury trial in Holland – was held in a small house next to Binnekant's hotel, and old John Trempe served as chairman of the jury and I was one of the jurors. As we talked about the case one of the jurors said he had been told some one had heard that, while the boys were in bed, Kees had said to Joos, "I'll whip you if you tell what we have done." This settled the case. "Guilty," said the foreman of the jury. Joos being too young to be sent to prison, the judge made his father pay a small fine. But Kees was sent to the county jail in Grand Haven for thirty days. When the sheriff and his wife heard the grounds on which the boy had been sentenced, they laughed heartily. No lawyer had been employed to defend him, and it was only a jury's verdict that had sent this young villain to jail for thirty days on account of the crime of breaking a pane of glass seven by nine inches. The sheriff entertained the boy as a member of his family until the thirty days were finished.

Our Indian neighbors were very good people so long as they trusted our honesty. Nevertheless they were Indians, and ugly when drunk. One afternoon when I passed a saloon two young Indians came out of that dirty place, their faces covered with paint. They had feathers and squirrel tails on their beaver skin caps and were drunk. One carried a dagger in his hand and shouted in his Indian language, "Here is a white man", and rushed at me. But I was sober and, as my legs were willing, I ran away. But I always was on good terms with them. One spring morning a young brave, all trimmed up in Indian style and accompanied by a young squaw, came into our store. They bought a cook stove and paid for it in gold, telling me they would call for it. From time to time the Indian came to look at the stove until, late in the fall, he took it away.

One Sunday our dominie announced from the pulpit that a chief had complained that the settlers had taken away their sugar troughs, and that the Indians were revengeful. He demanded that we punish the guilty persons and that the troughs be returned. The dominie told him that this had happened perhaps by mistake or through ignorance. After the announcement the dominie advised that those who had taken the troughs should return them. The people had taken them home for feeding their hogs.

One day a family chanced upon a dressed deer hanging on the limb of a tree. They took the venison home and salted it in a keg. When the Indians noticed their deer was gone, they came to the house. The Indians opened the locked door and found the venison. They seemed to be able to recognize their property. When the family came home they found the door open and some of the venison on the table, cut into little pieces. The family understood this meant revenge, and without delay hastened to settle with the Indians.

The majority of the first settlers were Christians, but yet imperfect, which showed itself in many ways – on one occasion especially in a political election in the township of Zeeland which had been organized in 1850. The southeastern part of the township at Drenthe was known as Statesland, while the country beyond from Forest Grove to Jenison formed one township. The first town meeting in Zeeland Township was held in the log church at Zeeland. Early in the morning of the day of the caucus Dominie Van Raalte, accompanied by such as had the right to vote and also by some friends and boys, went to Zeeland, walking the entire distance, climbing over fallen trees, and wading through water. They arrived in time for the meeting. Dominie van der Meulen was in the pulpit, acting as chairman. Soon there was great excitement, and Dominie Van Raalte stood on the pews appealing to the men, saying "Brothers! Brothers!" The Zeelanders, supported by their friends from Statesland, wanted all the offices to the exclusion of the men from Holland. The dominie's exhortations calmed the spirits just in time to prevent hard blows.

After the caucus we went home in a body. Some of the office seekers were angry and jealous, complaining that the Zeelanders had captured the best offices. Pieter van den Berg said, "Holland is ignored." Others said, "Well, Well! that old Jan Hulst from Statesland, justice of the peace! That man with such a rebellious character! He is more for war than peace!"

The Zeelanders and Stateslanders were angry at the men from Holland. They declared that the Pope and his Cardinals of Holland [Dominie van Raalte and the consistory] had come to Zeeland to impose their rule, and that they were selfish. The expression "Pope and his Cardinals" was frequently employed by malcontented spirits, especially in the editorials of *De Nederlander*, a weekly paper published for a short time by men who gloried in publishing vicious articles.

The last day of the year always was a happy holiday. A society had been formed to raise a fund to help needy people in the Old Country to emigrate. Members paid their weekly assessed amount into a fund. On the last day of the year they drew lots to determine who might have some friend or family come over with all expenses paid. Persons so helped would refund this sum which in turn would be used to help others. The drawing took place in Aldred Plugger's store which was filled with fragrant odors coming from the bakery in the kitchen in anticipation of the evening festival. At this gathering we saw happy faces, much in the spirit of the old custom in the fatherland. What a comfort it was to see everybody in good spirits when New Year's day drew near! Everybody behaved modestly. We had no saloons to make us unhappy. Will we ever behold the day when the evil saloon is banished from our land? May the Lord grant it! The first building lots were sold on the agreement that no saloon was ever to be built upon them. Of course there were people who had whiskey at home; when friends called they were given drinks which made them merry. There were too many people of this sort, but there were no saloons.

The homes of Toon van der Wal, Captain Gerrit J. Havekate, and old Bongars, and the blacksmith shop belonging to Hindrikus Stokking were resorts of the thirsty ones; and everybody knew this. One time a smart fellow told Jan Knoll a butcher and a friend of the bottle, that after the vendor had delivered a deed the purchaser was free to do as he liked with the property. The agreement not to open a place for the sale of liquor was not binding and could not be enforced, he stated. So Knoll opened a saloon in the second story of his house on Central Avenue between Seventh and Eighth streets. Jan Vissers opened the front room of his bakery on the southeast corner of Central Avenue and Eighth Street for the accomodation of church-going people who wanted to smoke and drink beer on Saturdays. The room was always full of good Christians who smoked, drank beer, and talked about sermons, the Bible, and Christian comfort. The more strict called this place the "church saloon". These brethren came to see the sinfulness of their ways, which resulted in breaking up the "church saloon".

Dominie Van Raalte preached against places of temptation and deeds of wickedness. He was an eloquent and pious minister, his sermons were powerful and instructive. And although not perfect, he was a wise and loyal leader, serious, inspiring courage, and ready to give advice to all who asked for it. He was first to donate cash to promote any good cause in the church. May his name and influence long be a blessing to the community. The first sermon the dominie preached in English was at the funeral of Abraham Cahill in the house built by Jan Slag on the lot where the present Engine House no. 1 is located. The text of the sermon was from the Lamentations of Jeremiah 5, 16: "The crown is fallen from our head: woe unto us, that we have sinned!" The sermon could have been spoken in better English, but it was uttered with power, for the dominie dwelt on the thought how through sin, we have lost our crown of holiness, and being lost through sin, the penalty of sin is death, but that through God's grace, through Jesus, our blessed Saviour, full redemption and a heavenly crown are offered to penitent sinners.

The settlers stretched as far as possible what little they possessed. For our narrow circumstances demanded careful use of money. From tin plate I had on hand I made, among other articles, a square basin supported by three small legs and provided with a little handle, to hold live coals when placed in a wooden foot stove, following Old Country style. One day Mr. Hindrikus Stokking, the blacksmith from Drenthe, called on mother and stated that he could sell some foot stoves if I would make some. So one day early in the morning, accompanied by Elder Broek, I set out for Drenthe, carrying a lot of basins tied together with a rope and slung over my shoulder. We walked through the woods, climbing over fallen trees, traveling up and down hills, wading through low land and brooks, and crossing large streams until at last, late in the afternoon, we arrived at the house of a widow, the mother of a number of children. They were friendly and glad to see us. Mr. L., an old widower, was visiting in the house, and seemed to take a leading part in the household affairs. He was sweet on the widow and must have had some under-standing with her which afterwards resulted in marriage. The girls were busy – some churned, others came in with the cows, and everybody worked. The cows, the house, and even the air out of doors carried the odor of wild leeks, a green plant which grew plentifully in the woods during springtime. The milk and butter, in fact everything, had the unpleasant taste of leeks.

It was spring and evenings were long. The front door of the cookstove was open and the glow of fire lit the room. We ate by the light of a candle, and, as soon as we had finished our supper, Mr. L. suggested that instead of reading a chapter from the Bible we should sing a psalm. Next came a prayer of thanksgiving during which for the sake of economy the candle was put out because, as he said, our eyes being closed, we would not need any light. The evening passed pleasantly. "Good night," said one of the daughters and, lighting the candle, she mounted the ladder to go to her bed on the second floor. Thinking the girls would let the candle burn longer than necessary, Mr. L. said, "Girls, blow out the light." "Yes, yes," they replied, and all was dark. After that we went to bed, and, being young, I soon was in sweet dreamland. It was dark when I awoke but the rooster's crow announced the dawn. How often in life's journey – in dark hours of sorrow, in trouble, and in trial – the Lord has given His children the faith to see the signs of glorious morning! This is only a part of our experiences; hitherto hath the Lord helped us, 1903.

CONTENTS

Chapter XVII

THE BURNING OF HOLLAND, OCTOBER 9, 1871

61. GERRIT VAN SCHELVEN'S THE BURNING OF HOLLAND

[Gerrit van Schelven, citizen of Holland, was eye witness of the catastrophe which wiped out most of Holland and in which he lost his property. This description from his pen appeared in the *Report of the Pioneer and Historical Society of the State of Michigan*, IX (1886).]

The southern tier of townships in Ottawa County, constituting, with a part of Allegan County, the Holland Colony, with the city of Holland as its commercial, social and educational center, were on the eve of celebrating the first quarter-centennial of their settlement.

During a period of nearly twenty-five years they had enjoyed comparatively, a continuous prosperity, marked not so much by the accumulation of capital or wealth, as by a steady and healthy growth of both the agricultural districts and Holland City as its natural market. A variety of resources, a diversity of soil, a growing manufacturing interest, with shipping facilities by both water and rail, had combined in making Holland a prosperous and flourishing little city of about 2,400 inhabitants.

The purport of this paper is to make brief historical mention of the fire of October 9, 1871, whereby in a short space of two hours the labors of a generation were destroyed, hundreds of families rendered houseless and homeless, and many a worthy old settler, upon the evening of a well-spent life, left in straitened circumstances, from which he has never been able to recover.

For weeks preceding this eventful October night we had experienced an uninterrupted drought. In most every direction from the city the woods were on fire and had been for several days. By hard labor the southeastern part of the city was saved from these forest fires during the week preceding the conflagration, the locality immediately south of Hope College and the old Orphan House being at that time particularly exposed.

During the afternoon of Sunday, October 8, the atmosphere was unusually warm for that season of the year. At intervals fine ashes were showered over and into the city. The very skies seemed to betoken the advent of the impending calamity. These proved afterwards to be the first messengers of the burning of Chicago on that same Sunday, as was subsequently explained.

The effect of this long drought and of the atmosphere at this time, seemed as it were, to prepare all the combustible material in and around the city for that awful which was awaiting it.

The greater part of the southwest addition, but recently platted and sparsely settled, was nothing less than a wooded wilderness, and the ravine along Thirteenth street was filled with logs and timber.

At 2 o'clock in the afternoon the wind turned southwesterly and began gradually to increase. The fire alarm was rung, and from this time on the fighting of the fire all along the timbered tracts south and southwest of the city, was kept up uninterruptedly. As night advanced the wind increased in force, until at midnight it blew a hurricane, spreading the fire and the flames with an alarming velocity toward the doomed city. The huge bark piles at the Cappon and Bertsch tannery in the western and the Third Reformed Church in the southern part of the city, were among the first points attacked; from thence on, the devastating fire fiend had a full and unmolested sway. The burning shingles and siding of this new and large church edifice and the flaming fragments of bark were blown towards the center of the town, sweeping everything in their northward course. At this fatal moment the wind turned more westerly and thus forced the fire toward the center and more eastern parts of the city-this sealed the fate of Holland.

Within the short space of two hours, between one and three o'clock, of Monday morning, October 9, 1871, this entire devastation was accomplished. No one unless he has been an eye-witness of such a scene, can conceive its terror or its awfulness. We shall not attempt to describe it. The entire territory covered by the fire was mowed as clean as with a reaper; There was not a fencepost or a sidewalk plank and hardly the stump of a shade tree left to designate the old lines.

The grounds at Hope College, somewhat isolated as they were, seemed to be the only spot where one could escape with his life. Many took to the waters of Black Lake, escaping in small boats.

The fierceness of the wind and the rapidity with which the fire spread, may be inferred from the fact that over two hundred and fifty dead horses, cattle and swine were found in the burned district, and that a cancelled bank check, partly burned, drawn by the firm of De Jong, Van Schelven, and Oggel, upon Nathan Kenyon, banker, was picked up on one of the farms in section four of the township of Tallmadge in this county, a distance of twenty-five miles.

The break of day on that Monday morning presented a scene, the memory of which will outlive all other recollections in the minds of its victims, and a faint idea can only be given in this sketch by furnishing a few statistical incidents.

The loss of human life was limited to one aged widow woman, Mrs J. Tolk. Over three hundred families were left without shelter. The number of buildings destroyed are about as follows: dwellings, 210; stores, shops, and offices, 75; manufactories, 15; churches, 5; hotels, 3; miscellaneous buildings, 45; docks and warehouses, 5; one tug and several other boats. Amount of property destroyed, $ 900,000. Amount of insurance, $ 35,000. Of this insurance only a small part was recovered, inasmuch as many companies had been rendered insolvent by the Chicago fire.

Neither was the calamity limited to the city. The damage and devastation in the surrounding township of Holland, as well as in the townships of Fillmore and Laketown, in Allegan County, were great. The recollection of the writer is that in these localities seventy families were burned out, and the relief work performed during the winter that followed, includes also the care of that number of families, besides feed and shelter for their stock. No mention is made of the thousands of rods of fencing destroyed all through this locality, or the damage done to standing timber.

A minute description of the fire district is not expected in this sketch. Suffice it to say that the heart of the city, including the entire business portion thereof was destroyed. A better idea of the general ruin might perhaps be obtained by stating what remained of the once thriving and prosperous city. A strip of houses along the extreme western and southern parts of the city, all south of Tenth and east of Market and nearly the entire first ward. In addition to this and in the order of their relative importance, we might also make particular mention of Hope College, Plugger Mills, Heald's Planing Mill, Union School, First Reformed and True Reformed churches, both our railroad depots and the townhouse. Insignificant as this array may appear now, it created at the time a sort of nucleus around which clustered the faint hopes for the future of Holland. And especially was this so in the case of Hope College, not so much for the money value of the buildings but for what these buildings represented historically, and for the connecting link it had left between the Holland colonists and their true and most faithful friend who had stood by them from the very hour of their arrival upon American soil, under whose fostering care they had gradually developed from the emigrant into the American, and to whom this calamity was to furnish a new field, for them to again demonstrate that same generosity and attachment-I refer to the *Reformed Church in America*.

Hunger and the want of shelter, drove most of the people into the country, to the extent that the flames and smoke from the surrounding fires permitted them to do so. In their flight they were not handicapped with many cares, for whatever had not been buried in the ground had been consumed by the fire. All day long the roads leading east out of the city were lined with refugees.

But we must hurry on. We feel a longing to quit these scenes of destruction. There is something in store, in connection with this calamity, which to a certain extent alleviates much that is painful in comtemplating so much misery.

The general conflagrations of the 8th and 9th of October embraced not only Holland and Chicago, but also Peshtigo, Manistee, the Port Huron district and several other localities, and that is a matter of history that co-extensive with this widespread ruin, were also the sympathies and charities of our fellow-men.

It will undoubtedly be remembered, when the news of the burning of Chicago had reached New York, how James Fisk in his novel but effective way at once gathered in a trainload of provisions and supplies, and how with lightning speed he sent them on to relieve the thousands of Chicago's refugees, scattered over the open prairies. So it was here.

Hardly had the people of Holland, on the following Tuesday morning, awakened from their first slumbers after so much anxiety and despair, and while they were yet casting around for a relic or a landmark to designate the spot where once had been their home, and with no indication of what the succeeding morrow was to bring – but that the generosity of their neighbors was already seen and felt in their desolate home.

The surrounding fires had cut off all railroad communications. The bridge on the line of the Michigan Lake Shore Railroad had been destroyed so that no trains could enter the city. Penetrating as far as they could toward the northern banks of Black River the friends from the neighboring city of Grand Haven had unloaded a timely supply of provisions and other stores, the variety of which was not the least striking feature. These stores consisted, not only in what the grocery and the bakery could supply, but the kitchen and the pantry had also been emptied – a loaf of bread partly cut, a solitary biscuit, doughnuts; a remnant of a roast, a part of a ham, etc., – creating in the minds of the hungry recipients the indelible impression that this contribution – *so timely forwarded* – was the spontaneous act of sympathising friends and generous hearted neighbours.

These supplies as they were spread out before that hungry population, spoke more eloquent than words, and proved more forcible than any oral message which accompanied them, that our neighbours felt for us and appreciated our condition, and so feeling and appreciating did not hesitate or delay to act.

At the same time it should be stated here that few of the many incidents, following in the trail of this catastrophe, affected the burned out people of Holland more deeply than the receipt of these first supplies. It was relief mingled with so much that was painful; and in order to understand this we should imagine these people, regardless of their prior condition or home comforts, and clad in the garments of destitution and misery, standing in line each awaiting his or her turn to receive supplies according to the number in his or her family. It was this which brought home to them a realizing sense of their true condition, and how, for the present, they were thrown upon the charities of their fellow men.

On the afternoon of the next day, a meeting of the citizens was called to discuss the general situation. Among those present was Dr. A. C. van Raalte. Those of you who were acquainted with this great leader of the Holland emigration, may form an idea of what was said by him on that occasion, and of the inspiring effect it had upon the people. One of his closing sentiments was expressed in the following language: "With our Dutch tenacity and our American experience, Holland will be rebuilt." And mark the coincident, how a similar sentiment was expressed on that same day, by Joseph Medill of the Chicago *Tribune*, in the first issue after the fire, when he wrote: "With Christian faith and western grit, Chicago shall be rebuilt."

As the news of our destruction became generally known among our immediate neighbors and surrounding places, aid and relief was liberally forwarded. The Board of Supervisors of Ottawa County, just then in session, visited us, and made ample provisions for a destitution which was to be feared during the approaching winter, but which aid, thanks to a generous public, was never needed. A new assessment roll of Holland City was ordered by the board, to make the valuations correspond with the new order of things.

A local relief committee was appointed by the citizens, consisting of the following persons as near as we can recollect them: Dr. B. Ledeboer, Chairman, Henry D. Post, Secretary, Kommer Schaddelee, Treasurer, Rev. Drs. A. C. v. Raalte, Philip Phelps, C. Scott, A. T. Steward, R. K. Heald, Dr. S. L. Morris, H. Meengs, J. O. Doesburg, G. Wakker, E. Herald, and G. v. Schelven.

The township of Holland appointed as their relief committee W. Diekema, Jan Hendrik Boone and D. Miedema, and a similar committee was also appointed for the burned district in Allegan County.

At Grand Rapids a general relief committee was appointed by Governor Baldwin to distribute aid through the western part of the State. This committee consisted of Messrs. T. D. Gilbert, Wm. A. Howard, N. L. Avery, H. Fralick, and R. M. Collins.

An address was published by Dr. van Raalte and others to the people of this State, setting forth the extend of their calamity. Also another addres was issued by the secretary of the Holland Relief Committee refuting the slanderous reports that "the Hollanders refused to aid in extinguishing the fire for the reason that it was Sunday, and that the churches would not permit their bells to be rung, fearing that it would disturb the congregation."

Governor Henry E. Baldwin made a tour of inspection of the several burned districts in this State, including Holland, to satisfy himself as to the necessity of furnishing State aid. The abundance of voluntary relief, however, rendered this unnecessary. In his message to the Legislature, at the extra session in March 1872 he made mention of the aid distributed through the Grand Rapids relief committee, and a similar committee appointed by him for the eastern part of the State in the Port Huron district.

The labors connected with the receiving and distributing of supplies were kept up during the greater part of the winter. Lumber and building material, hardware, provisions, clothing, household goods and furniture, were shipped in large quantities. The liberality of the railroad companies in furnishing free transportation was an important item. It is a source of regret to the writer of this sketch that the short notice given to prepare the same did not allow him to furnish an approximate statement of the amount and kind of aid recieved. It would been have so appropriate to do so at his time. Through the instrumentality of Rev. John L. See, of New York, treasurer of the Board of Education, and the Reformed Church, a cash fund of about $ 40,000 was collected, mainly from among the friends of the Holland Colony in the east. The sister colony in Pella, Iowa, was not among the last to contribute. Our kin across the sea also responded. But it is impossible and it would be manifestly unjust to the others, to further single out individuals or localities in this general outburst of good will and charity.

The distribution of all this bounty devolved upon the local committee at Holland. To do this in the spirit of its donors and with fairness and equity was a task requiring all the ability and discrimination they could muster, and more too, it was a noble, though thankless labor.

The work of re-building Holland once begun, was kept up uninterruptedly. The rebuilding Chicago, however, created a large demand for all kinds of building material and a corresponding increase of prices. The effect of this upon Holland proved very disastrous. It added materially to the cost of every new building and enterprise, thereby creating, in nearly every instance, an indebtedness beyond the shrinkage in values, caused by the panic of 1873, reducing the assets and valuation of the rebuilt city fully fifty per cent., without lessening in the least the liabilities and incumbrances.

The result of this was – and it is among the most painful reminiscences in the history of the *Burning of Holland* – that the men of push and of enterprise, who had been instrumental in making Holland City what it was, up to October 9, 1871, and who had again placed their shoulders to the wheel, and who, in doing so, had assumed large financial responsibilities, were unable to face the distressing period that followed the panic of 1873. The tide of events crippled them seriously, and caused a general depression to the newly rebuilt but poverty stricken place, which depression lasted for years. It was a cruel but unavoidable fate that awaited these men, and it seemed as though the new growth and prosperity of the town were made to hinge upon the completion of their downfall. It has since been accomplished; and Holland City of today has fairly begun to assume her old-time position; but many of the men who in the past had contributed to her fair name and prestige have not been permitted to share in the new work.

As we commemorate this evening the semi-centennial settlement of Ottawa County, we delight in paying tribute to the memory of the men who sowed that others might reap. So in contributing this sketch of the *Burning of Holland*, we bespeak a kind word for these resolute men, who at an advanced age were made to suffer that others might profit. Brave as they were they could not outweather the storm, but ultimately were wrecked upon the shores of an honest and honorable ambition.

62. A CONTEMPORARY ACCOUNT OF THE HOLLAND FIRE

[The following relation of the burning of Holland on October 9, 1871, was published in a joint issue of *De Grondwet*, *De Wachter*, and *De Hollander* on October 12, 1871].

Holland was, en is niet. Holland's Ramp. Dagen van Angst, Nood en Lijden! Wij hebben thans eene der moeijelijkste en droevigste taken voor ons, welke ons immer werden opgelegd. Ons hoofd weigert geregeld te denken en onze handen neder te schrijven de bijzonderheden der ijselijke reeks van rampen, welke ons getroffen heeft. Wij kunnen al de bijzonderheden niet mededeelen, en moeten ons zeer beperken. Door de goedwillendheid van de uitgevers der *Hope* zijn wij in staat gesteld dit blaadje

uit te geven, en wij brengen bovengenoemden hiervoor onze welge-
meende dankbetuiging.

De Almagtige heeft gesproken, en de uitwerking dier stem is geducht.
Onze geliefde stad Holland kan gezegd worden, niet meer te zijn. Het
geheele handelsgedeelte ligt in puinhopen, geheele straten zijn weggevaagd, elke business man heeft alles verloren en er zijn tusschen de
200 en 300 huizen verbrand. Het schoonste gedeelte onzer stad is thans
een onaanzienbare vlakte vol rookende en smeulende puinhopen.

Gedurende de afgelopene week woedende er in den omtrek, vooral in
de rigting van Graafschap, groote boschbranden. Reeds werden sommige
plaatsen der stad gevaarlijk bedreigd en den nacht van Woensdag op
Donderdag van verleden week werd besteed in eene wel geslaagde poging
ter redding der HOPE drukkerij, Dr. Crispell's woning, en de College
gebouwen. Sedert dien tijd bleef heet vuur voortsmeulen, hier en daar
schuren en huizen in onze omgeving vernielende. Doch er scheen geen
gevaar voor ons te zijn. Zondag namiddag begon het echter zeer hard uit
het zuiden te stormen, eer de namiddag godsdienstoefeningen ge-eindigd
waren, werden de alarmklokken geluid. Nog echter scheen het gevaar
meer de omliggenden, dan wel de stad zelve te bedreigen. Ware de wind
in die rigting gebleven, dan was Holland er nog, doch van 11 uur tot
1 uur draaide dezelve westwaarts en nam toe in hevigheid, zoodat het
bijna een orkaan werd. De zoogenoemde kreek, laagte, welke opgevuld
was met neergehouwen, doode en half verrotte boomen en allerlei tuig
was spoedig eene vlammenzee. De wind joeg de vonken regen naar
Sprietsma's en Elferdink's looijerij, en in een ander oogenblik naar de
groote stoomlooijerij van Cappon en Bertsch, welke onmiddellijk in
lichterlaaije brand stond, benevens minstens 2 à 3,000 cords bark er bij,
en vandaar sloeg de brand over naar de 8ste straat en liep van daar voort
door de geheele straat door River straat door een aantal zijstraten alles
weg zweepende en wegvagende wat in het spoor van den wind was. Een
weinig meer zuidwaarts sloeg de vlam in de 3e Gereformeerde kerk en
van daar in Hope Church en de nieuwe Methodistische kerk en van daar
naar andere gedeelten der stad. De vlammen verspreidden zich met ongeloofelijke snelheid, en in minder dan een uur tijds lag het grootste en
schoonste gedeelte van Holland in asch. Wij kunnen zeggen, dat het geheele handelsgedeelte totaal verbrand en dat zeven achtsten der stad
vernield is. De schade is niet te berekenen, en is tusschen de $ 800,000 en
een millioen dollar. Tusschen de 150 en 200 huisgezinnen zijn van huis,
kleederen, meubelen, in een woord van alles beroofd en moeten zelfs het
brood der liefdadigheid eten. Er komen ruimschoots levensmiddelen aan

uit de omliggende plaatsen, vooral uit Grand Haven en Grand Rapids, welker burgers wij ten hoogste verpligt zijn voor hunne overgrote mildadigheid. Ook vernemen wij dat er te Grand Rapids, Kalamazoo, en zelfs te Detroit gelden ingezameld worden en kleederen bijeenvergaard voor onze van alles beroofde burgers. De nacht van Zondag op Maandag, de nacht toen Holland vernield werd, die nacht van onuitsprekelijken doodsangst en lijden zal nimmer vergeten worden. Voor zooverre wij vernemen zijn er geene menschenlevens te betreuren en zijn er geene personen bij den brand omgekomen behalve Sara Ooms, de wed. Jacob Tolk, die vermist werd en wier beenderen men gevonden heeft.

Holland was en is – wij kunnen het in vele opzigten zeggen – niet meer. De stad, als stad, is vergaan, en slechts een kleine buitenrei van huizen is overgebleven. Geheel het fabriekswezen en de handel is weggevaagd, en alles moet van den grond weder opgebouwd worden. Het schouwspel is op heden nog ijzelijk en hartbrekend. Waar de stad stond, is eene groote vlakte, bedekt met ruikende puinhopen en met menschen gravende in de ruïnen om nog iets te vinden, en zoekende naar hetgeen men begraven had. De welvarende plaats is thans in een oogenblik arm, hulpeloos, geheel ontbloot van alle inkomsten en moet thans door de omliggende plaatsen voorzien worden van de noodige levens behoeften. De omstandigheden zijn verpletterend, en nog kan men den vollen omgang van de ijselijke reeks der jammeren niet goed beseffen. De arbeid van een 25 tal jaren is weggevaagd. En wat de toestand nog oneindig verergert is de gegronde vrees dat, door den vreeselijken brand welke de groote wereldstad Chicago, zoo goed als met wortel en tak uitgeroeid heeft dat de brandwaarborgmaatschappijen bankroet zijn en dat dus velen onzer burgers, die door het weinige hunner verzekerde panden, weder dan aan den gang zouden kunnen komen, ook die hulp zullen moeten ontberen en dus, totaal arm, hulpeloos en van alles bloot, met niets op nieuw zullen moeten beginnen.

In dezen nacht van dikke duisternis zijn ons echter nog eenige flaauwe lichtstraaltjes overgebleven. De moed heeft onze burgers niet begeven, en reeds hier en daar is men druk bezig met het oprigten van kleine loodsen en het aanbrengen van timmerhout en planken. Onze vriend J. van Landegend, thans voor de tweede keer uitgebrand, E. van der Veen en vele anderen zijn reeds druk te werk. Op eene volksvergadering, die op Dinsdagmiddag gehouden werd, werden algemeene betuigingen gehoord van een voornemen om op nieuw te beginnen. Er werden comité's aangesteld, om giften te ontvangen en uit te deelen.

Ook in andere plaatsen onzer nederzettingen zijn woonhuizen, schuren, heiningen enz. enz. verbrand. In Graafschap en Noordeloos zijn vele huizen en schuren verbrand. Te Collendoorn is de kerk en pastorie afgebrand. Tusschen Groningen en Zeeland heeft ook de brand hevig gewoed, en het dorp Zeeland werd eenigen tijd gevaarlijk bedreigd.

Onder de publieke gebouwen, welke in den nacht van Zondag op Maandag alhier verbrandden, zijn de 3de Gereformeerde Kerk en pastorie, de 2de Gereformeerde (Amerikaansche) kerk, de nieuwe Methodistische kerk, de Protestantsche Episcopale kerk.

De 1ste Gereformeerde kerk, rondom door een zee van vuur omringd en thans omgeven met puinhopen, is voor de tweede keer op eene zonderlinge wijze gespaard gebleven. De Union school, de Hope drukkerij, en de College gebouwen zijn staande gebleven. De pastorie der 3de Gereformeerde kerk bleef gespaard, ook het Townhuis. De Ware Hollandsche Gereformeerde kerk en pastorie bleven staande. Onder de fabrieken zijn Plugger's zaag- en flourmolen, Heald's ploegfabriek en ijzergieterij staande gebleven. De depots der beide spoorwegen bleven gespaard.

De 8ste straat of Main street is schoongevaagd aan de zuid zijde van af de plaats waar E. Herold's woonhuis stond tot aan Mr. G. Wakker. Aan die zijde zijn verbrand de woningen van E. Herald, I. Cappon, J. Parks, F. Kieft, W. Blom, Wed. Klijn, Wed. Tolk, E. van der Veen, H. Wiersema, A. Verplanke, H. Meeng's 2 gebouwen, Beukema's salon, *Gazeteer* drukkerij, City Hotel, E. van der Veen's ijzerwinkel, J. Duursema's store, P. Sakker's meubelwinkel, Sprietsma's schoenenwinkel, D. Bertsch's store, Nibbelink's vleeschhal, Koningsberg's saloon en woonhuis, Mrs. Wheelers modewinkel, de Weerd's vleeschhal, de Weerd's woonhuis, P. van Landegend's sigaarwinkel, het postkantoor, Van der Haar's vleeschhal, N. Zalsman's winkel, Joslin en Breyman's juwelierswinkel, E. Herold's schoenen en laarzenwinkel, Pessink's City Bakkerij, J. Alber's woonhuis, Alber's juwelierswinkel, Van Landegend's hardware store, Doornink en Steketee's store, P. Boot's woonhuis, J. Doesburg's apotheek, de woonhuizen van A. Vennema en W. Brouwer, K. Schaddelee's office en twee woonhuizen, toebehoorende aan Mr. E. J. Harrington.

Aan de noordzijde der 8ste straat is dezelve schoon gevaagd vanaf de plaats waar het prachtige woonhuis van Mr. P. van den Bosch stond tot aan het woonhuis van Mr. G. van Schelven, dat staande is gebleven. Aan deze zijde is verbrand: woonhuis van P. van den Bosch, H. Koning's woonhuis en store, E. Winter's smederij, E. van Zee's woonhuis, J. Roost, een huurhuisje, J. Binnekant's Pioneer Bakkerij en boekwinkel,

Hollander drukkerij, G. H. van Winkel [?], M. D. Howard's woonhuis, H. D. Post's apotheek, winkel, en woonhuis, H. Bennett's restaurant, C. Hofman's woonhuis, J. W. Bosman's kleerwinkel, Kroon en Everhard's ijzerwinkel, Wed. J. Vervenne's zadelmakerswinkel, Kanters en Co's store, Bosch en Co's store, City Bank, De Jong, Van Schelven en Oggel's store, een oud gebouw van J. Koning, J. O. Bakker's schoen-en laarsenwinkel, Cloetingh's boekwinkel, H. Walsh apotheek en woonhuis, Labarden en Zoon's meubelwinkel, U. de Vries zadelmakerswinkel, modewinkel der gezusters van den Berge, A. Geerling's woonhuis, H. Vaupell's zadelmakerswinkel en woonhuis.

River straat is uitgebrand aan de westzijde van de woonhuizen van H. Uiterwijk en M. Russel, de huizen tusschen hier en den hoek van de River en 10de straat zijn blijven staan. Vanaf de hoek van River en 10de straat tot aan het woonhuis van Kraai, niet ver van de Grand Havenbrug. Aan deze zijde zijn verbrand: een huurhuis toebehoorende aan P. Pfanstiehl, Mr. J. Roost's winkel en woonhuis, Koffers en Gringhuis' winkel, Dr. Nichols tandarts kantoor, de nieuwe schoen- en laarzenwinkel van W. Elverding en Co., woonhuis van P. Pfanstiehl, de schuur van het City Hotel, M. D. Howard's kantoor, De Kraker's vleeschhal, Werkman, Geerlings en Co's store, huurhuis van D. T. Werkman, M. P. Visser's nieuwe store, *American Exchange* en schuur, Holland Brouwerij; H. Gezon's woonhuis; woonhuis van E. Nienhuis, 3 à 4 huisjes van ons onbekende personen; en E. Kraaï's woonhuis.

Aan de oostzijde der straat is verbrand: het oude fabrieksgebouw van Verbeek en Co., H. W. Verbeek en Co's meubelwinkel, W. van Putten's apotheek, D. te Roller's kleermakerswinkel, *De Grondwet* drukkerij, H. Meeng's winkel, G. Lauder's portret gallerij, Aling's winkel, Flieman's wagenmakers winkel en smederij, Wilson's barbierswinkel, Butkan's woonhuis, een huurhuis van T. Sullivan, Storing's saloon en woonhuis, een huurhuis van H. van der Haar, City Mills, een oude smederij, American Hotel, R. P. Ferris woonhuis, R. van Kampen's woonhuis, Arnold's woonhuis en M. Clark's woonhuis.

In Lake straat is verbrand: O. I. Pfanstiehl's shingle, stave, and bolt fabriek, E. J. Harrington's kantoor en nieuw dok, een gedeelte van het zijspoor van den Michigan Lake Shore spoorweg, en R. P. Ferris's zaagmolen. Bij deze straat zijn verbrand de aan de docks liggende tug *Day Spring*, de oude *Mayflower* en 3 à 4 scows.

Aan Fish straat is verbrand: aan den westzijde de huurhuizen van K. van Haaften en B. van Rij, aan de oostzijde A. Geerling's huurhuis en Teunis Keppel's woonhuis.

Aan Marktstraat is verbrand: aan de oostzijde, het huurhuis van de Wed. Nies; livery stable van H. Boone; de woonhuizen van L. D. Visser en J. Paulus; huis en schuur van D. de Vries.

Aan de westzijde: het woonhuis van P. Nagelkerk, huurhuis van H. Keppel, een klein huisje, Helling en Busch naaimachinewinkel, Bostwick's portret gallerij en woonhuis, de oude store van Mrs. H. C. Knol; woonhuis van K. Mulder, schuur en huurhuis van Weduwe H. G. Knol, huis en schuur van P. Kleis, woonhuis van Mrs. Jacobs.

Aan Pinestraat verbrand aan de westzijde: de woonhuizen van H. J. Peckler, Mrs. Minderhout, Rev. W. H. Bronson, en M. van de Vrede. Aan Maple straat is verbrand de looijerij van Sprietsma en Co.

Aan de 1ste straat is verbrand: W. K. Flietstra's stoomzaagmolen en J. de Feyter's woonhuis. Aan de 2de straat: de woonhuizen van P. de Kraker, G. Dalman, een klein huisje, en [een van] E. Sawyer. Aan de 3de straat: de woonhuizen van H. Beukema, G. Raak, twee huizen en schuur van C. Blom Sr. en J. Louwis.

Aan de 4de straat: de woonhuizen van C. de Wit, G. Gringhuis, P. Pfanstiehl, J. de Spelder, Weduwe Winters, en Burke. Aan de 5de straat: het woonhuis van Symonds, het nieuwe baksteenen huis van P. Winter, en de woonhuizen van W. Finch en J. Fliemen.

Aan de 6de straat is verbrand aan de noordzijde: woonhuis en zeepfabriek van M. Mehr, woonhuis van P. Gunst, Wesleyaansche kerk en de woonhuizen van P. Pfanstiehl en J. Verschure. Aan de zuidzijde: de woonhuizen van M. de Feyter, Bouman, A. Meerman, de Weduwe Mulder, 2 huizen van de Weduwe H. G. Knol, G. Bos, W. J. Scott, en A. Verschuur. Aan de 7de straat is verbrand aan den noordzijde: de woonhuizen van L. van Dis, Heetebrij, L. ter Beek, J. M. Reidsema, G. IJskes, Mrs. Vinke, P. Bouman, P. van der Stel, A. Rot, Kamferbeek, B. Volmari, de Weduwe H. G. Knol, H. de Vries, baksteenen huis van T. A. Berkompas, huis en machineriewinkel van G. H. Brooks, huis van J. Trimpe. Aan de zuidzijde: schuur van T. Keppel, 2 woonhuizen van J. Smit, Ds. C. van der Veen, J. de Peyster, W. Joslin, P. Geense, P. van Geenen, J. Labots, P. J. Kamperman, Weduwe Kooijers, en het nieuwe huis van D. J. Werkman.

Aan de 9de straat is verbrand aan de noordzijde: Cappon en Bertsch's groote stoomlooijerij, de woonhuizen van I. Kramer, G. Boot, 2 huurhuizen van F. van der Veen; 1 huurhuis van H. Wiersema, S. Reidsema, M. van Regenmorter, J. Verplanke, J. van de Roovaard, J. Kramer, J. Nibbelink, W. C. Nibbelink, W. Verbeek, A. Meerman; huurhuizen van H. Boone en R. Takken, A. Westveer, J. Albertis' huur en livery stable; P. de Vries, P. de Koning, R. Oostema en K. van Haafte.

Aan de zuidzijde dier straat zijn verbrand: de woonhuizen van S. Schmidt, J. R. Kleyn, C. Dok, E. Everhard, J. D. Everhard, H. Vergter, D. Verschuur, A. Woltman, R. Schilleman, Prof. C. Scott, Verbeek en Co's huurhuisje, G. van Putten, D. te Roller, J. Schoon, C. Vorst (2 huurhuisjes), G. Steketee, en H. W. Verbeek.

Deze straat is schoongezweept aan de noordzijde van de Cappon's looijerij tot aan den hoek van de 9de en Cedarstraat en aan de zuidzijde van J. R. Kleyn tot aan J. W. Bosman's huis bij de 1ste Gereformeerde kerk.

Aan de 1ode straat is verbrand aan de noordzijde: huurhuisjes van Hermanus Boone en Mrs. C. B. Baily, woonhuis van M. Mulder, de oude en nieuwe Methodist Episcopaalsche kerken, de woonhuizen van Mrs. Broadmore, P. de Vries en H. Barendregt, de groote en nieuwe schaaf- en ploegfabriek van H. W. Verbeek en Co., schuur van G. van Putten, Grace Episcopaalsche kerk, en het woonhuis van J. Duursema. Aan de zuidzijde dier straat is verbrand: de woonhuizen van J. Elverdink, S. Davis, Hope (2de Gereformeerde) kerk, en het woonhuis van W. H. Deming.

Aan de 12de straat is verbrand aan de noordzijde: de woonhuizen van J. Boersema, F. van Rij en Westerhof. Aan de zuidzijde C. de Jong's groot en prachtig baksteenen huis, en de 3de Gereformeerde kerk en pastorie.

Dit is eene nauwkeurige lijst van al het verbrande. Van de kerken zijn verbrand 2de en 3de Gereformeerde, Methodist Episcopal en Wesleyan Methodist. Alleen de 1ste Gereformeerde en de ware Hollandsche Gereformeerde kerken zijn overgebleven, waaraan men zien kan de oude ligging der stad, en deze zijn: Plugger's zaag- en flourmolen, het townhuis, de 1ste Gereformeerde kerk, Ware Hollandsche Gereformeerde kerk, Union school, Collge gebouwen, *Hope* drukkerij en de beide *depots*.

Chapter XVIII

A DUTCH JOURNALIST'S VISIT TO THE KOLONIE IN 1907

63. THEODORE DE VEER'S OUR HOLLANDERS IN MICHIGAN

[The author, a Dutch journalist, visited Zeeland at the occasion of its sixtieth anniversary celebrations. His spirited article appeared in *Eigenhaard*, 1907.]

Daar bloeit in 't westen van Michigan, op 'n twintig mijl zuid-west van Grand Rapids, 'n klein proper stedeke van echt oud-vaderlandschen naam. Zeeland werd het er gedoopt.

'n Zonnig welvarend plekje in groot weelderig farmerland, in 't land van geel golvende akkers, van verre grazige weiden, van bloeienden tuin en boomgaard. 't Zal een tweeduizend nu tellen van flinke energieke menschen, van degelijke arbeidzame bewoners, geboren en in hoofdzaak uit Nederlandschen stam.

En alles, alles wijst er op voorspoed, op 'n maar immer gestadig „vooruit". Daar zijn houtzagerijen, worden meubelen en huisraad gemaakt, is een staande-klokkenfabriek – nog wel de grootste ter wereld, malen twee stoommolens het graan, is 'n wagenfabriek, 'n fabriek van deuren en ramen, daar zijn banken en groote winkels, daar heeft 'n elk 'n vrijstaande woning met z'n plekje tuin er om. En buiten de ruime hoofdstraat zijn 't er al lanen, koel onder wijdschaduwend geboomte.

In dat nijvere, dappere Zeeland nu, in dat stedeke uit Zeeuwen geboren, was 't voor kort een glorieus gefeest, haar brave „Old Folks" ter eere. „Old Folks' Day" maar van een wel bijzonder karakter; de zestigste jaardag immers der kolonie werd gevierd. Een plechtig gevoelvol eerbewijzen aan die moedige mannen en vrouwen, die zich toen dorsten nederzetten in dat donkere onbekende land.

„21 Augustus 1907", het was 'r het festijn aan die kranige „sturdy" pioniers van 1847, 1848 en 1849, die pelgrimvaders van West-Michigan, gewijd. Vierde tien jaren het naburig Holland haar halve eeuwbestaan, bij 't twaalfde lustrum ging 't kleiner Zeeland voor in 't glorievol herdenken der Neerlandsche emigratie naar dat groote vrije gewest.

Dankbare hulde aan die helden die er leden en worstelden, hun leven zelfs er lieten in den reusachtigen ongelijken strijd met intense oerwildernis, met verraderlijke ziekten, met nijpend hongerend gebrek. Weet de „old country" wel van dien moed en de bovenschrijfelijke volharding?

Zestig jaren zijn voorbij sinds die nobele pionier, Dr. A. C. van Raalte, naar die „land of liberty" kwam. Hoe zwaar en droevig somber waren de tijden toen in 't oude vaderland. 't Was er 'n reactie na Fransche heerschappij, een reactie die, en wel niet het minst, zich ook in de Kerk deed gevoelen.

Vrijheid om God te kunnen dienen naar eigen denken, dat recht was,. werd niet erkend. Vanaf de Kerkreorganisatie van 1816 door Koning Willem I waren Staat en Kerk één. En slaafsche onderwerping werd geëischt aan Synodale heerschappij. Geen afwijking van die Kerk, geen verschil in Godsdienstige overtuiging werd door dien Staat geduld. Kon een spanning in deze haast wel uitblijven? Sterker en sterker moest wel de agitatie groeien. Honderden en honderden wilden breken met het opgedrongen régime. En de breuk kwam, 'n afscheiden van het Hervormd Genootschap, een Kerkelijke revolutie.

Hendrik de Cock in Ulrum, H. P. Scholte in Doeveren, hoewel ter zelfder tijd, toch afzonderlijk van elkander, waren deze predikanten, de eersten die de scheiding opwierpen, als voorstanders der Gereformeerde leer.

Eene schorsing van deze beiden bleef natuurlijk niet uit. Men was nu eenmaal niet vrij in 't dienen van zijn God. Eens toch de vonk, woekerde dra het wijde vuur der revolutie. Overal in den lande doken „afgescheidenen" op. Men begon zijn eigen dienst in schuren en in het open veld. Dat was 1834. Maar 'n oud politiereglement uit den „Code Napoléon" had onder de bestaande Grondwet zijn kracht nog niet verloren. Geen vergadering van meer dan negentien personen mocht zonder toestemming van plaatselijke autoriteit gehouden worden. Zoo werd toen voor den dienst der „afgescheidenen" die toestemming ontzegd.

't Gevolg laat zich begrijpen. De diensten hadden toch plaats en beboetingen waren aan de orde. Maar 't bleef bij geen beboeten; – inkwartiering, gevangenisstraf, hunne bijéénkomsten ruw uitééngejaagd door de gewapende macht, eigendommen verbeurd verklaard en zij zelven soms ruw, wreed behandeld. 't Gepeupel keerde zich op hen, op die verachte sekte van afgescheidenen. Uitgeroeid moesten ze worden en 't talrijke brandstichten begon. En zaken verliepen; ja op de scholen ging zelfs de domme vervolging door. En waarom? Omdat ze in godsdienstige overtuiging van de rest der natie verschilden. Daarom werden in die verlichte negentiende eeuw, in een Christelijk land, Christenen dusdanig achtervolgd, werden de lijnen hen zoo eng getrokken, dat den volgelingen der Gereformeerde leer het leven bijkans onmogelijker werd. En wat baatte alle protest, met dat politiereglement nog van kracht?

Drukkender al werden de tijden, ook op maatschappelijk gebied, waar aardappelziekten den oogst van het volksvoedsel dreigde te vernietigen en 'n algehele „malaise" den horizon van vooruitzicht verdonkerde. Toch, de strijdenden hielden nog stand, en onder hen de edele pionier, de groote leider en vader van alle tegenwoordige Hollandsche nederzettingen in het Westen van Michigan, de predikant Dr. A. C. van Raalte.

Maar 't was duidelijk, iets moest er worden gedaan. En zoo, in de winter van 1845 op 1846, kwamen de leidende mannen, H. P. Scholte in de eerste plaats, in Amsterdam te zamen om de questie van landverhuizing te bespreken. Een comité werd uit hen daar benoemd, om met het gouvernement te onderhandelen over de kolonisatie op de Hooglanden van Java, doch zoveel werd hun hierbij in den weg gelegd, dat men 't oog op „ergensanders" richtte. De Kaap de Goede Hoop leek velen een veilig oord en er werd ook wel door hen over gedacht, totdat Amerika als het toekomstland door hen werd aangenomen.

In de lente van 1846 dan, voordat eenig systeem van emigratie nog tot stand was gekomen gingen A. Hartgerink en J. Arnold, door hunne vrienden en hun Kerk uitgerust, naar het groote Noord-Amerika om er 'n voorlopig onderzoek daar in te stellen en den broederen thuis 't rapport te zenden. En 'n uitvoerig verslag van de reis en ondervindingen in dat nieuwe werelddeel, – een lijvig document waarvoor 'n port van elf gulden was betaald, – werd met voldoening in Nederland gelezen.

De zomer van datzelfde jaar zag Rev. Thomas de Witt uit New York, gezonden door de Generale Synode van de „Reformed Dutch Church in America", op een officiële missie naar 't oude vaderland.

Welken invloed heeft dit bezoek gehad op de voorgenomen landverhuizing? 't Is niet moeilijk na te gaan. In zijn rapport aan de General Synod in 1847 zegt hij: „When in Holland I received information of a rising spirit of emigration to America and especially among the seceders (afgescheidenen) from the established church. Soon two important colonies from this class will be founded in the west."

Over emigratie naar Amerika werd nu algemeen gesproken, al drukker kreeg men 't over „de West" en dan noemden ze Texas, Michigan, Wisconsin en Iowa, als geliefkoosde plekken. Zoo dan vertrok op 14 September 1846 een Amerikaanse tweemaster de *Southerner* uit Boston, onder kapitein Crosby van Rotterdam en bracht over de breede Atlantische, Dr. A. C. van Raalte en de eerste emigranten bestemd voor groot Amerika. Hier voor mij, op mijn schrijftafel ligt 't lijstje met de namen van bijna al die moedige pelgrims.

O! het deed hun zielsleed, het smartte hen zoo dien geboortegrond te moeten verlaten, ze stuitte hen zoo, die godsdienstige onverdraagzaamheid. Toch, ballingschap met vrijheid boven 'n vaderland zonder dat.

En dien verguisden „afgescheidenen", waarvan ik niet dan onder diepsten eerbied hier schrijf, dien kloeken mannen en vrouwen wachtte daarginds in een woeste Indianenstreek dat reuzenwerk; zij legden daar dien schoonen grondsteen der huidige bloeiende „Dutch settlements", de trots van Michigan.

Neerland, dat waren Uw dochteren en zonen; trotsch moogt ge, neen! moet ge op hen zijn!

Hoe het Dr. Van Raalte en den zijnen verging? Te ver zou 't mij hier voeren waar alleen mijn doel 't maar was 'n beknopt „hoe" en „waarom" der emigratiebeweging van 1847, 1848 en 1849 te geven, in verband als hiermede staat de groote Zeeuwen-Trek en mijn „Old Folks' Day" in Zeeland. Genoeg zij 't dus vooreerst dat, na veel moeite en gezwerf, de krachtige pionier en zijn mannen, op den twaalfden dag van Februari 1847, zich in de ongerepte wouden van West Michigan aan den rand van het Black Lake nederzetten.

Onderwijl had ook in de provincie Zeeland de „afscheiding" al meer en meer zich verbreid en in Goes was de beweging in vollen gang toen de eerste tijding van Van Raalte uit West Michigan daar werd ontvangen. Een tweehonderd vervolgden kwamen er in die plaats te zaam om over 't nieuws te onderhandelen, en toen er daar de plannen voor den Trek naar Noord-Amerika werden vastgesteld, organiseerde zich de „meeting" tot 'n gemeente der Afgescheiden Kerk.

In massa zou men emigreeren en een predikant zou de gemeente vergezellen op den langen moeilijken tocht. Een beroep werd daartoe gedaan op Ds. Cornelius van der Meulen, leider der worstelende gemeente in Goes. En dat beroep werd aangenomen, Van der Meulen stond gereed.

Drie schepen vol emigranten kozen kort daarop zee. Dat onder leiding van Jannes van de Luyster en 't schip onder Jan Steketee vertrokken uit Rotterdam, het derde onder Ds. Cornelius van der Meulen zeilde van Antwerpen weg.

O, 't was pijnlijk dat afscheid van 't vaderland, 't was met zoo'n hartezeer dat ze die Zeeuwsche kusten verlieten. Velen onder hen waren uit Borselen op Zuid Beveland en toen op dien Zaterdagmiddag van de Luyster's schip vol zeil in 't zicht daar kwam stonden 'n dertig of meer achtergeblevenen op den dijk. Ze wuifden hun laatst vaarwel aan al die dorpsgenooten, en ver over 't water ging 't: „Wij komen ook!" Dat was de laatste boodschap.

De lange, lange zeiltocht was begonnen, de reis van maanden op 't onstuimig watervlak. En ieder maakte het zich maar zoo goed als dat toendertijd kon. Voor 't voedsel moesten ze zelf zorgen. Op het achterschip stonden een paar fornuizen, daarop konden de vrouwen, voor zoover ze niet te ziek waren, haar eigen potje koken. Wel genoeg water was aan boord maar zoo tegen 't eind der reis was 't niet altijd meer frisch. En dan die honderden andere kleine ongemakken aan het reizen toen verbonden!

't Langst was Steketee onder weg, 63 dagen bleef zijn schip op den Oceaan. Jannes van de Luyster deed het in 54 dagen. C. van der Meulen in 45. Op verschillende tijden van den zomer 1847 kwamen ze dan aan den mond der Hudson aan.

't Eenig bestaand geval, met uitzondering der oude „Pilgrim Fathers", dat 'n godsdienstige sekte als reeds georganiseerde kerk de nieuwe wereld betrad.

De Hudson werd nu opgezeild tot Albany. Hier gingen de emigranten op de Kanaalschuit die, door twee paarden getrokken, twee weken lang door het Erie-kanaal werd gesleept naar Buffalo. Niet alleen hadden ze weer onge makken op die reis, maar zelfs tot twee maal toe ook nog brand aan boord.

Van Buffalo weer op zeilschepen over de Groote Meren naar Chicago en daar weer op andere schepen over Lake Michigan naar Black Lake, en hun nieuw tehuis. Een volle maand van New York naar Black Lake, 't kleine zijmeer van groot Lake Michigan.

Ondertusschen had Dr. Van Raalte in Juni 1847, bericht gekregen uit Albany, dat 'n groote Zeeuwenemigratie 't tot daar al had gebracht en dat ze na lange en ernstige beraadslaging besloten waren zich in Michigan neer te zetten.

Verschillende blokhuizen werden nu terstond voor hun ontvangst aan 't Black Lake opgetrokken opdat als de $\pm$ 400 vermoeide reizigers in de wildernis daar aankwamen, ze 'n onderdak zouden hebben. En in Juli kwamen ze dan ook aan en vonden er de veilige plaats bij Dr. A. C. van Raalte en zijn „sturdy" pioniers. Verre van rijk, laten wij gerust zeggen arm, waren wel de meesten dier nederzetters. En „malaise", èn vervolging had hen schier alles ontroofd.

Toch, één was er onder die niet uit armoe het vaderland had behoeven te verlaten en dat was Jannes van de Luyster. Bemiddeld grondeigenaar als hij was, verkocht hij z'n landerijen voor f 60,000 om zich aan te sluiten bij de landverhuizers niet alleen, maar nam hij nog 17 gezinnen bestaande uit 70 personen met zich waarvoor hij overtocht, kleeren en voedsel betaalde.

Na een hoognoodige rust ging men nu op onderzoek naar 'n geschikte plaats voor vestiging en werd eindelijk, ten Oosten van waar Dr. Van Raalte zich had gevestigd en wat hij Holland had gedoopt, door Jannes van de Luyster de plek van het huidige Zeeland in de wildernis gekozen.

Als eerste blanke „settler", in wat nu is het oordschap Zeeland, kwam op 8 Juni 1847 al 'n zekere Jan Hulst. Deze Jan Hulst had 2 Maart 1847 z'n woning in Nederland verlaten, was 19 Maart uit de haven van Helle-voetsluis gezeild en 27 April in Baltimore gekomen. Vandaar was hij zes weken over land naar zijn plek onderweg geweest. Zijn plek, de bijna ondoordringbare wouden.

Zoo vonden 't ook de Zeeuwen daar, – wildernis en Indianen. Hier zouden ze voortaan wonen in die dichte woestenij, zonder iets, zonder wegen, onbekend met de taal van het land, onbekend met 't harde, moeilijke werk, vereischt om die bosschen om te hakken. Arm, honge-rend, sliepen ze er onder den blooten hemel. 't Water uit de poelen dron-ken ze en ziekten als cholera, typhus en pokken braken uit. En malaria sloopte de lichamen, toch al zoo verzwakt door ongezond voedsel en onvoldoende beschutting. Dat lijden, dat gebrek, die strijd, – kunnen we er ons maar even waarachtig indenken?

Velen gaven wel den strijd op en togen naar de steden als Grand Rapids en Kalamazoo. Maar de meerderheid toch waren „stayers". Met hun ouden predikant Van der Meulen aan 't hoofd beven ze vechten tegen de wouden, tegen de verraderlijke moerassen, tegen 't hun vreemd klimaat, met 'n alles verzettenden wil. Arm als eenig ander van hen, met 'n gezin nog tot onderhoud, was Van der Meulen er predikant, geneesheer en rechter te gelijk. En wanneer afgemat, afgewerkt, ontmoedigd, de kolo-nisten dan uit 't woud kwamen op Zondagmorgen, wist hij ze op te beuren met 'n zeldzame welsprekendheid en 'n enorme kracht, zoodat ze 's avonds terug zouden gaan naar hun blokhutten, frisch in moed om den strijd in 't woud te strijden en 'n „home" er zich vrij te hakken.

Die menschen daar moesten met weinig, of in 't geheel geen kennis van ontginnen, uit oerwoud akkers maken. Velen van hen wisten zelfs geen bijl aan den steel te zetten en bij 't hakken van een boom deden ze net als de ratten en wekten van alle kanten, zoodat tot 't uiterste zoo'n boom bleef staan en ze nooit vooruit wisten, naar welken kant hij vallen zou.

Een klein bewijs, hoe weinig idee de menschen in 't vaderland toen hadden van wat hun hier te wachten stond, levert wel 't feit, dat sommige gezinnen groote zuurkoolsteenen hadden meegesleept, die ze werkelijk dachten, hier te kunnen gebruiken, en dat menige Fries niet zonder z'n scheepshaak uit z'n provincie was gegaan.

Het maken van wegen en 't bouwen van bruggen over stroompjes en over moeras was zwaar werk in die vroegere dagen, en met de weinige ervaring nam 't meer dan den halven tijd dier „settlers" in beslag.

Heel langzaam vorderde 't werk. Gevelde boomen moesten eerst worden verbrand en dan nog bleef de stronk met wortels 'n heele karwei. Langzamerhand werden aardappels en koren verbouwd en hadden ze hier en daar koeien.

De Indianen, in hoofdzaak „Ottawa's", waren gelukkig den „Dutchmen" goed gezind en hielden zich rustig en ordelijk, en wat wilde beesten betrof waren er enkele beren, wolven, vossen en wilde katten, die met 't vellen der bosschen al gauw verdwenen.

Maar van verdienen was natuurlijk nog geen sprake, geld kwam er niet in. En al 't vervoer ging op den rug, menige vrouw die haar koren twee of drie mijl ver moest dragen om 't daar te laten malen. Anderen weer maakten hun eigen meel in 'n oude koffiemolen. Eerst later konden ze ruimer gebruik van den ossenwagen maken, vooreerst ging alles nog over de primitieve „Indian trail."

Wilt ge hooren hoe die pelgrims er soms kwamen? Dit is wat één der ouden U thans nog verhaalt: „M'n vader en moeder gingen uit Nederland den 22sten Maart 1849. Van New York zeilden ze de Hudson rivier tot Albany, toen op de kanaalschuit naar Buffalo, van daar over de meren naar Milwaukee en over Lake Michigan naar Grand Haven, dan weer op de rivierboot naar de Grandville en eindelijk met 'n ossenwagen naar Zeeland. 't Was 25 Mei toen we daar aankwamen. Mijn jongere zuster, geboren op de boot in Buffalo, was toen elf dagen oud. Ik zal zoo wat tien jaar geweest zijn en m'n broer twaalf. Te voet moesten we 18 mijl door de wouden. Vader liep natuurlijk ook, en ook moeder moest dat heele eind te voet, terwijl haar 11-dagen-oud kindje in den schoot van 'n oude vrouw op den ossenwagen lag." Uit zulk kostelijk, krachtig hout waren die arme verschopte menschen. 'n Soort postkantoor, dat ze Black River genoemd hadden, werd in 1848 door hen opgericht en kwam hier de „mail" eens per week. In 1849 werd door Jannes van de Luyster het dorp Zeeland uitgelegd en kort daarop, in 1850, werd Zeeland 'n eigen township, waarop ze 14 Juli 1851 hun eerste townmeeting hielden.

't Was wel altijd nog tobben en zwoegen; maar vooruitzicht teekende zich toch. Tegenover het simpele kerkje op de markplaats kwam een schoolgebouwtje, 't getal huisjes groeide al aan en 't klimaat begon meer en meer te wennen. Zoo langzamerhand werd opgewerkt: 't dorpje werd grooter en belangrijker, industrie vestigde er zich en bloeide en 't dorp bleef geen dorp meer, 't werd stad, 't werd „city". Dat gebeurde den winter van het vorig jaar. En nu, geen stad van haar grootte in Michigan overtreft de „city of Zeeland" in belangrijkheid van haar industrie. Alles en alles is er „thriving". Moge 't lang zoo blijven, er is meer dan voor gewerkt: er is voor gestreden, een strijd schoon, grootsch, geweldig, titanisch!

Die gebeurtenisvolle zestig jaren werden nu voor kort herdacht. 'k Zou niet weten dat ik ooit 'n prettiger en mooier feest van dien aard in mijn leven heb meêgemaakt dan dien Zeelandschen „Old Folks' Day".

's Morgens vroeg al was ik met de electrische uit Holland City gekomen. Druk vlaggenbesierd vond 'k de straten, de winkels, de woningen van de jarige kranige stad. Vlaggedoek overal, de vlag van het nieuwe vaderland en de vlag van 't moederland. Die laatste was er toch heusch nog niet vergeten. Waar de „Stars and Stripes" uitwapperden daar woeien ook meê de „schitterende kleuren van Nederlands vlag" en waar 't hier en daar kon was ook met 't „oranje" van de groote „Zwijger" versierd, of fladderden de oranje wimpels. In de winkelkasten hingen prenten van Zeeuwsche kleederdracht of hadden ze poppen in 't Zeeuwsch costuum gekleed.

En de U.S. Post Office pronkte voor die feestelijke gelegenheid met, op wit doek in vette letters, de woorden „Post-Kantoor".

Het – laat ik 't hier nu ook zoo eens noemen – Oranjezonnetje beloofde 'n prachtige dag en feeststemming was alom al aan 't groeien. Overal op den weg die prettige feestgezichten, dat feestdiscours, dat feestgelach. Van verweg uit andere Staten waren ze gekomen zelfs, die Holland-Amerikanen, om toch bij deze „dag" te kunnen zijn.

Maar de oude marktplaats zou het brandpunt der ware vreugde blijken. 'n Kleurige eerepoort riep er U al 't jubelend „welkom" toe.

Maar in koel geschaduw van dicht ahornlover waren spreekgestoelte en eeretribune en stonden gereed de lange tafels, waar straks voor die ouden van dagen 't gastmaal zou worden gediend.

Daar was ook het simpele withouten kerkgebouwtje dat later in de plaats voor die primitieve blokkerk kwam, de „First Reformed Church".

En er voor trof mij iets al bijzonder. 't Waren van die allereerste oude helden dat er daar de beeltenissen hingen, vergeelde portretten soms al. Tegen planken waren ze er opgezet, 'n stille hulde aan hen. Op 'n afzonderlijk bord waren er gezichten uit Nederland en 'n portret van de Koningin en den Prins en ook natuurlijk één van „Teddy" (President Roosevelt). Zoowat 'n honderd waren er bij elkaar daar gebracht. Groote belangstelling vond natuurlijk die aardige origineele collectie en ze gaf duizendvoudig stof tot mijmeringen over het voorheen.

Ja, ze kenden al die stadsgezichten nog wel, daar had je Goes en daar kijk, Rotterdam en daar Axel en daar – „hadde nog die ouwe meulen waar ik jare hè 'ewerk". Ze mochten zich zoo verkneuteren aan al die ouwe „printjes". Honderden stonden er voor en je hoorde bijna geen enkel woord Engelsch. In alle dialecten van 't oude vaderland werd er nog steeds gepraat (door de ouderen wel te verstaan). De jongeren verstaan het nog wel, maar spreken wil niet meer vlotten. Zeker, er zijn er nog veel van die oudjes, die de landstaal hier nog steeds niet spreken, waarbij alles nog zoo echt op z'n Hollandsch gaat. En ze houden nog zooveel van 't oude Nederland maar toch; – „jong je ben hier zoo deksels vrie en zoo allegaar geliek".

Lange banen rood-wit-blauw hingen af van 't monument der „old settlers" op den anderen hoek van 't plein, 't monument voor, maar ook de grafsteen van die pioniers die vielen in dien allervroegsten tijd. „Here rest our early dead from 1847 to 1852".

Meer gasten kwamen al maar aan, „Old Folks" van 1847, 1848 en 1849. Krasse gebruinde kerels soms nog, met vriendelijke open gezichten, dik sneeuwwit haar en 't typisch Hollandsche schippersbaardje. En van de vrouwtje waren er niet weinig nog met 't kornetje en de lange zwarte „sjaal".

Alle die moesten hun naam, adres en geboorteplaats teekenen en ook datum van aankomst in Amerika. Dan kreeg elk 't oranje lint met beeltenis van Van Raalte en Van der Meulen op de borst. En op 't lint in gulden letters: 1847-1907. Oude nederzetters – 60-jarig feest. Augustus 21. Zeeland, Mich. – „Eeregast".

O, allerhartelijkst werden die menschen ontvangen en geen zorg kon genoeg er aan hen besteed. Al voller werd de groote tribune, al maar meer met 't lint „Eeregast". Met een opgewekte Yankee-marsch is de muziek nu aangekomen.

't Was tien uur. Jacob den Herder, die in 1847 met Van de Luyster naar Amerika overkwam, opende als president van den dag de feestelijkheid en na hem ging Dr. Wm. Moerdijk voor in 't gebed.

Zal ik nu gaan vertellen wat toen en toen en toen gebeurde? 't Zou zoo'n opsommen worden; beter dus iets van den totalen dag verteld.

Verscheidenen wel bevoegde sprekers dan voerden op dit feest het woord. De meesten van hen in 't Hollandsch, en enkele maar in de Engelsche taal. Ernstig door sommigen, geestig weer door anderen, werd over die ouwe tijden gepraat. Vergelijkingen tusschen toen en nu gaven reden tot weemoedig nadenken ja, maar ook tot alle vreugd. Ver avond was 't en 't maantje gluurde al lang door 't ahorngroen, voor 't rijke program was afgedaan.

Maar zou ik dan niet vertellen nog van het gezellig maal daar op die lommerrijke markt aan vijf honderd „Old Folks", ons Persmenschen en 'n enkelen genoodigde door jonge meisjes van Zeeland voortgezet, en zou 't niet vreeselijk ondankbaar wezen niet te gewagen van die alles-overtreffende gastvrijheid waarmee we daar overal in Zeeland werden ontvangen?

Tusschen de acht- en negenduizend menschen waren dien dag 't stedeke tot gast. En is 't niet bijzonder aardig dat onder hen Mrs. Edward Nedervelt van Grand Haven was, het eerste blanke kind dat in 't toen matig dorpje Zeeland werd geboren? En dat Johan Huyser en zijn vrouw, de beide eenige overlevenden in Zeeland nog die als man en vrouw 't eerst in 1847 meê overkwamen, op 88- en 89-jarigen leeftijd, dit twaalfde lustrum meevierden?

In het drukst van het feest was er de behoefte gevoeld, de Koningin van hun oude vaderland te groeten en 't volgende ging langs de kabel onder zee:

„Queen Wilhelmina", Hague, Netherlands

8 - 21 - 7

Cordial greeting from Hollanders celebrating sixtieth Anniversary of settlement here.

Den Herder, Pres.

en 't antwoord liet zich niet wachten:

Dobbin, Duetschland

Den Herder - Zeeland - Amerika

8 - 22 - 7

Her Majesty Queen of Netherlands appreciating homage from Hollanders orders me to thank for cablegram and wishes settlement prosperity.

Von Mühlen,
Aide de Camp.

Maar meer nog!

Toen George Birkhoff Jr., Nederlandsch Consul Generaal te Chicago, dezen zomer in Nederland was, genoot ZEd. de eer een ruim uur met H. M. Wilhelmina over deze Hollandsche nederzettingen in West Michigan te spreken. Tot in alle bijzonderheden wilde H.M. er over ingelicht zijn en toonde Haar grootste belangstelling en bij het afscheid gaf H.M. de volgende mondelinge boodschap mede:

„Harer Majesteits beste wenschen voor hun voortdurend geluk en welstand en dat het Haar altijd een genoegen zal wezen te vernemen, dat zij de beste Hollandsche tradities hoog houden in het nieuwe Vaderland."

Door drukke zaken verhinderd kon de Consul Generaal helaas op 't feest niet komen; maar in 'n uitvoerigen brief gaf hij gevolg aan Harer Majesteit's dringend verlangen.

„De Vader der Pelgrim-Vaderen". Albertus C. van Raalte.... Wat ware er buiten hem van Hollandsche kolonisatie in West Michigan gekomen! Wat, van dat handje-vol „Dutchmen", in 1846 op trek voor vrijheid naar groot, wild Amerika? Wat, van den reuzenstrijd die hun wachtte in dat vreemde, bange land?

„Wat?... Wat?... wanneer die edele Pelgrim-Vader, die krachtige pionier-leider die geweldige geest, daar niet meêgetrokken ware. Albertus C. van Raalte... Vader, stichter der Hollandsche nederzettingen in den Michigan-Staat van Noord-Amerika.

Den 17den van de Octobermaand in 1811 was hij te Wanneperveen, provincie Overijsel, geboren. Een der zeventien kinderen uit het huwelijk van Albertus van Raalte, een leeraar in de Nederlandsche Staatskerk, en Christine Catarine Harking, een Friezin van afkomst. Van zijn kinderdagen is weinig bekend, slechts dit schreef hij eens later er over neer:

„Bij een terugblik op mijzelven moet ik belijden dat mijn jeugdig leven zeer doelloos was en hoofdzakelijk eenige richting ontving van de achting, welke ik mijn vader toedroeg, en van de begeerte om hem tot vreugde te zijn."

In Leiden zou hij studeeren en hij was er, gedurende zijn propae-deutisch werk, als meest ieder ander student, lid van de „Kroeg" en een vroolijke Hollandsche jongen.

Toch, 1832, het moordend cholera-jaar in Nederland, moest 'n onuit-wischbaren indruk op hem achterlaten. De jonge Van Raalte werd bekeerd.

„Geen wereldsche ambitie", – zoo schreef Van Raalte – „maar de bediening des Evangelies, welke mij vroeger voor mijn persoon altoos het minst passende toescheen, werd van toen af mijn biddend streven; want ik had den schat der verzoening gevonden. Ik begeerde niets dan mijn leven in de prediking te slijten. Kerkvorm en Kerkregeering waren bij mij vrij doode denkbeelden."

Van z'n oude vrienden zag hij weinig meer; hij had ze opgegeven, om bij een anderen kring zich aan te sluiten. Viel hem dit offer al zwaar, weinig te benijden daarbij ook was de toestand, dien hij zich nu aan de academie geschapen had. Gebrandmerkt als 'n domper, 'n dweeper, 'n da Costiaan, was hij, met die enkele anderen, van omgang met zijn medestudenten verstooten.

Miskenning en heimelijke vervolging bleven bovendien niet gespaard aan dat groepje waarvan men met 'n lachend schoudergehaal niet anders sprak dan van de „nachtkijkersclub".

Zoo gingen de dagen van voorbereidende studie voorbij; het candidaats-examen werd afgelegd en Van Raalte zocht toelating tot de bediening des woords in de kerk der vaderen.

Doch anders wilden het de synodale heeren. Reeds was het land in gisting en waren de processen tegen de „afscheiding" in vollen gang. Met ernst zou men daarom die „muiterij" in de kerk bestrijden.

Van Raalte's proponents-examen beloofde geen succes. En 't bleek ook al zoo; tot twee maal werd hij afgewezen.

Ten volle overtuigd, „dat het kerkbestuur toen, in beginsel, strekking en werking anti-Gereformeerd was, strijdende tegen de eer van den Koning der Kerk en schendende de rechten der gemeente", wierp hij zich daarop in den strijd voor vrijheid en sloot zich aan bij de gejaagde, verachte Afgescheidenen. Waar hij z'n hoorders maar vinden mocht, in schuren of stallen, in kelders of op zolders, bij nacht en bij ontij, daar predikte de jeugdige Van Raalte en dra zou zijn naam bekend en geacht worden onder de schare der vervolgden. Formeele aansluiting bij hen was nu slechts een kwestie van korten tijd.

Toch, Van Raalte bleef het openhartig zeggen dat deze losscheuring van de Kerk der Vaderen hem een groote bron van smarte was. „Ik voor mij", – zo schreef hij – „haatte het, niet langer de preekstoelen van mijn vader te kunnen betreden, een smaad te worden voor mijne nog levende moeder en voor mijn geslacht; het was mij de pijnlijkste opoffering de zoo vurig begeerde prediking op te moeten geven, waarvan mij de Neder-landsche kerktyrannie wederrechtelijk beroofde."

Van Raalte lokte den strijd niet uit en zou waarschijnlijk, indien toe-gelaten, geen moedwillig rustverstoorder in de Kerk zijn geworden. Hij werd tot afscheiding „gedwongen" en de regeering „dwong" hem tot afzonderlijke organisatie en het aanvaarden van een nieuwen naam. Maar inderdaad gaf zijn hart noch recht op titel, noch dat op de goederen der oude Gereformeerde Kerk ooit op.

De kandidaat Van Raalte, nu beroepen als leeraar der gecombineerde gemeenten Genemuiden en Mastenbroek (Overijsel), werd in 'n algemeene vergadering op 2 Maart 1836 plechtig geordend tot de bediening des Woords. En op diezelfde vergadering trad hij ook in het huwelijk. Christina Johanna de Moen werd zijn levensgezellinne. Van nu af aan was hij vereenzelvigd met de reformatorische beweging in de Kerk van Nederland. Hoewel hij stond te Mastenbroek, was toch geheel Overijsel zijn veld van arbeid. Maar hoe waren de omstandigheden waaronder die arbeid verricht zou worden?

Opgehitst door de Haagsche Synode, was de Regeering, zich bedienend van 'n verouderd Napoleontisch dwangplakkaat, haar vervolgingen tegen de Afgescheidenen begonnen. En nauw was de jeugdige leeraar met zijn jonge vrouw in Mastenbroek verschenen, of een troep dragonders werd er ingekwartierd.

Een twaalftal manschappen vergezelden Van Raalte overal, zoodat prediking in aanvang totaal onmogelijk was. Later, toen ze voor enkele dagen naar elders vertrokken, kon hij zijn arbeid beginnen. Niet lang, want als gevolg kwam terstond 'n nieuwe inkwartiering en vier van de ruwste soldaten werden zijn opgedrongen logeergasten.

Weer stond het werk stil. En daarbij had zijn jeugdige vrouw voortdurend te lijden van de baldadigheden en ruwheid dier zoogenoemde rustbewaarders.

Reizen door de provincie was nu Van Raalte's taktiek, en ongelooflijk vlug was hij daarbij in zijn bewegingen, zoodat hij schijnbaar overal te gelijk aanwezig was.

Werd daardoor de gemeente wel uitgebreid, de fusie der Regering met die van het gepeupel kwam tot een gevaarlijke hoogte.

't Was op een Zondag, – 13 Nov. 1836, dat Van Raalte te Ommen preekte. Dien geheelen dag was er gedreigd en geschoold voor het huis waarin de gelovigen bijéén waren, doch eerst moest het donker wezen voor het gemeen zich voor de woning posteerde en de vergaderden en hun prediker met moord dreigde.

Door een achterdeur kon men nog bijtijds vluchten, vóór de bende tot baldadigheden oversloeg en de woningen der „nieuwlichters" met keien en vuil begon te bestoken.

's Maandags was Van Raalte al weer te Heemse, waar hij twee malen predikte, hier zou hem 't bericht bereiken van een aanslag tegen zijn leven. Maar hij was zijn vervolgers veel te vlug, want 's avonds leidde hij alweer een dienst te Ane. Dinsdagsavonds weer in Gramsbergen; dan weer was hij den volgende dag in Dedemsvaart waar hij in een stal de zijnen ontmoette.

Over Ommen zou 't dan weer op huis aan gaan. Doch zoo goed als zijn vrienden, voor wien hij weer zou preeken, was ook de vijand van zijn komst onderricht.

Alarm werd geslagen, de bende liep te wapen en het vergaderhuis der „gescheidenen" werd omsingeld. Deuren en ramen waren in een oogwenk verbrijzeld en met stokken en bijlen en messen drong men binnen. Van Raalte zag zijn dood nabij.

Maar plots scheen de aanvoerder der bende wel beducht voor de gevolgen van het oproer, althans op het laatste oogenblik werd hij de beschermer van Van Raalte, en het gelukte hem de bende te verwijderen.

De prediker ging onverwijld naar Den Ham, waar hij den dienst leidde en het avondmaal bediende. Toch ook hier stelde zich de burgemeester aan de spits van een bende. De gemeente werd uiteengejaagd en Van Raalte gevangen genomen.

Onder gewapend escorte werd de gevangene door den burgemeester van Den Ham naar de gevangenis in Ommen gebracht. De woede van 't volk daar kende geen grens meer, toen zij den gehaten prediker wéér in hun dorp zagen en tot twee malen toe werden pogingen gedaan om Van Raalte te lijf te gaan. Gewond en afgemat bereikte hij eindelijk de gevangenis, waar hij, met een verloopen boef in een smerig hok werd gesloten.

Als een gemeene schurk moest hij, omgeven van gewapende mannen, den volgende dag te voet den zeven uren langen weg afleggen naar Deventer, waar hij terstond weer werd gevangen gezet.

Eindelijk voor den Officier van Justitie gebracht, werd Van Raalte... oogenblikkelijk vrijgesproken en uit de gevangenis ontslagen. Enkele dagen later en hij was weer in Ommen aan 't werk. Zelfs levensgevaar deed Van Raalte er niet voor terugdeinzen.

Meer nog, – op diezelfde plaats waar men herhaaldelijk getracht had hem van het leven te berooven, op diezelfde plaats waar het volk onder gejoel en gevloek den „nieuwlichter" langs de straten naar de gevangenis had gesleurd, daar koos Van Raalte zich straks een woonplaats.

Ongeloofelijk schier schijnen de verhalen der vervolgingen, toentertijd den andersdenkenden in de verschillende provinciën aangedaan. Het leven dier oorspronkelijke leiders, 't was die eerste jaren van hun op-treden een gestadig martelaarschap.

Hendrik de Cock werd bij het verlaten van een vergadering te Uithuizen door het gepeupel in een scherpe doornhaag geworpen en mishandeld.

Van Velzen werd te Tjalleberd, in Friesland, tot drie malen toe op één dag, met de gemeente, verdreven en dien nacht verloor hij in een volksoploop bijkans het leven. Bovendien werd hij voor het dien dag gebeurde beboet voor honderd gulden.

Bij Brummelkamp te Hattem werden tien soldaten tegelijk ingekwartierd, terwijl men van zijn woning „een wachthuis" maakte.

Te Almkerk en Emmikhoven sloegen de militairen er bij het uiteenjagen van een vergadering van meer dan 19 personen met het scherp der sabels op en verwondden sommigen ernstig.

Volgens het oude politiereglement uit den „Code Napoléon" mocht geen vergadering van meer dan negentien personen zonder toestemming van plaatselijke autoriteiten gehouden worden.

Zoo werd Van Raalte door het gerechtshof te Zwolle veroordeeld tot een gevangenisstraf van drie maanden, omdat hij bij gelegenheid van het uiteendrijven eener vergadering, den burgemeester der plaats, die leider was der vervolgers, had durven vermanen tot bekeering. Van zijn vonnis in appèl gekomen, werd hij door de hoogere rechtbank vrijgesproken.

Zwaar was de arbeid van Van Raalte. Zelf overal beleedigd en getrapt, was nog de troost der gevangenen en verdrukten zijn taak.

Hoe was de indruk van dat al op hem? Hier schrijft hij 't: „Van achteren een blik op het gebeurde werpende, verblijdde ik mij de stem van het geweten gevolgd te hebben ofschoon zulks mij veel kostte; aan de andere zijde smart het mij nog altijd, daarom in mijn eigen vaderland door Neêrland's regeering en burgers, opgestookt door de Hervormde Synode en plaatselijke regeeringen, beboet met straf en inkwartiering gekweld, in gevangenissen geworpen, gedurende jaren gescholden, met slijk en steenen geworpen en, als uitvaagsel, in persoon en huis gejaagd en geplaagd te zijn.

„En zulks dermate, dat eenmaal met Ds. Brummelkamp zijnde, wij met een bedrukt en benauwd hart, in goeden ernst, elkander afvroegen: wat dunkt u, zou God ons nog eens een dag doen beleven dat wij eens vrij, ongemoeid en zonder schrik ons op de openbare straten kunnen vertoonen? Na onder andere natiën ingelijfd te zijn, heb ik vaak als Nederlander gewenscht, dat die vlek van de Nederlandsche natie, door herstelling van het ongelijk, zooveel mogelijk mocht afgewischt worden."

Een grote tien jaar aaneen had nu Van Raalte gezwoegd, geleden en geworsteld; doch, de uitkomsten bevredigden hem niet. Daarbij, de algemeene al evenmin als de bijzondere omstandigheden waren in de laatste tijden in Nederland verbeterd, zoodat begrijpelijk is hoe de emigratiekoorts, die in die dagen Duitschland sterk aantastte, aldra ook in 't bloed van vele Hollanders kwam. Ieder sprak van den overvloed en de schatten uit de nieuwe wereld. Men wond elkander op, en al spoedig begonnen er te vertrekken. Wie had toen kunnen denken, dat die kleine trek naar een toekomst wees, waarin steeds nieuwe aankomelingen, volgens betrouwbare gegevens ruim een half millioen Nederlanders Amerika tot hun nieuw vaderland zouden maken.

Ds Brummelkamp geeft ons een kort verhaal van de wijze waarop zij Amerika „ontdekten". Een schoolmeester uit den achterhoek passeerde Arnhem, op zijn weg naar de Nieuwe Wereld, en kwam afscheid nemen. In die dagen scheen Amerika buiten de wereld en de reis er heen vergde 'n vaarwel, dat veel had van een sterfbed. Landverhuizers waren toen nog zedelijke bannelingen, menschen meest die, in een kwaden reuk, maar liever werden afgescheept. Toen Brummelkamp zijn verwondering over des schoolmeesters plan toonde, liet deze hem brieven lezen, van vroegere landverhuizers ontvangen. Hij stond verbaasd en ontroerd, en liet Van Raalte roepen. Beiden hadden zij de briefschrijvers gekend als doodarme tobbers, en deze regelen spraken van een welvaart, zooals zich die in het vaderland niet meer denken liet; zij waren als verstomd.

„Daar ging", – vervolgt Brummelkamp – „een licht voor ons op; God opende ons oog en wij zagen dat een groot deel der ‚malaise', waarin wij ons bevonden, te zoeken was in de bouwers van Babels toren. Als die torenbouwers verdrongen wij malkander hier."

En Van Raalte? In hem ook was wat wakker geworden. Dag en nacht hield ze hem bezig, „de gedachte aan landverhuizing". Niet nog voor zichzelf, maar voor de honderden en duizenden van verarmde land- en geloofsgenooten.

Overal vond de vraag thans bespreking. Het geheele land door werden „meetings" gehouden en Ds. Scholte en Ds. Heldring van Hemmen, interesseerden zich bijzonder voor de zaak.

Nu echter de questie: waarheen? Daar was het onbekende Amerika; wie waagde zich er aan? Java dan was toch beter oord!

En op een monster-meeting te Utrecht, werden de heeren Scholte en Heldring afgevaardigd om met den minister van koloniën te onderhandelen over de kolonisatie der hooglanden van Java, op conditie van vrijheid van godsdienstoefening en tegemoetkoming der kolonisten. Maar al terstond werd alle hoop voor Java vernield, daar Z.Exc. de eilanden Ceram en Ubi noemde. Zoo dan besloot Ds. Scholte zelf mede naar Amerika te trekken.

Bitter was deze teleurstelling voor Van Raalte en dit blijkt ons duidelijk in een toen uitgegeven brochure, waarin hij o.a. schreef: „Maar op Java, waar de lucht gezonder is dan elders, de winden uitnemend waaien tot verkoeling, alle planten welig groeien, de bosschen wemelen van herten, runderen en wilde zwijnen, zoodat men al zijne krachten, die hier verspild worden in de verstikkende zorgen van het aardsche en in de arme vraag: ‚wat zullen wij eten en drinken’, Gode kan wijden; ons in de gelegenheid gesteld te zien om met eene volkplanting van Christenen ons daar neder te zetten; in de gelegenheid om met heel deze kolonie, met vrouwen en kinderen, als zendelingen daar werkzaam te zijn; daar te werken als een Williams onder de Zuidzeebewoners en er een centraalpunt van uitgang te vestigen tot verspreiding van het Evangelie; die gedachte ontvlamt ons het hart; ons gebed klom dikwerf om de vervulling er van, als het dierbaarste onzer wenschen, ten hemel en zou ons de verhuizing naar de op zich zelven zoo begeerlijke binnenlanden van Amerika bijna doen vergeten.”

Van Raalte mag zich de Javaansche toestanden te rooskleurig voorgesteld hebben, als Nederlander had hij de koloniën lief en 't lag dus in zijn wensch, den stroom der emigratie daarheen te leiden.

Maar ééns dan ook voor Amerika beslist hebbende, zette hij zich krachtig achter emigratie uitsluitend daar henen.

Was het wel zoo erg wijs van het Ministerie, de Javaansche hooglanden voor een machtige, zuiver Nederlandsche landverhuizing gesloten te houden?

De zomer van 1846 werd Van Raalte ziek. Een boosaardige typhus sloopte het lichaam en dagen aaneen scheen zijn werk hier op aarde afgedaan. Doch 't was anders beschikt; de zorgelijke teekenen minderden, de koortsen namen af en beterschap zou heel langzaam volgen. Toen kwam Brummelkamp op zekeren dag bij hem. Van Raalte kon nog niet meer dan even fluisteren, maar met alle krachtsinspanning verhaalde hij toch dat hij besloten had om, als God hem weêr geheel herstelde, mee te verhuizen naar Amerika.

Er was zooveel omgegaan in hem onder alle krankheid. Wat zou er van zijn menschen, zijn emigranten, onbekend met de taal des lands, Godvreezende lieden, zonder leeraar, zonder onderwijzer komen? Waar zouden ze aanlanden? Ziet, de beantwoording dier enkele, zichzelf gestelde vragen had hem tot zijn vast besluit geleid, om mede met hen te „trekken”.

En toen dan maar even zijn krachten wat opgekomen waren, begon hij zijn toebereidselen voor den grooten tocht te maken. Zoo verliet

Van Raalte met zijn vrouw en hun halfjarige zuigeling op 24 Sept. 1846 per Rijnboot de stad Arnhem om zich in Rotterdam met de anderen aan boord van een Amerikaanschen tweemaster, de „Southerner", voor het groote nieuwe land in te schepen.

Ruim zeven weken later kwamen zij te New-York. Het voornemen van Van Raalte, al in Nederland gevormd, was om in de vlakten en bosschen van Wisconsin Hollandsche nederzettingen te stichten. Men zou een streek lands aankoopen, in welks midden een tamelijk groote omtrek bestemd bleef voor kom der gemeente, waarin dan kerk en school zouden komen en alles wat tot gemeenschappelijk middelpunt zou moeten dienen; zoo zouden dan overal nederzettingen van verscheidene dorpen en pachthoeven verrijzen....

Chapter XIX

DUTCH EMIGRATION TO IOWA

64. H. BARENDREGT'S LETTER FROM ST. LOUIS, IOWA, DECEMBER 14, 1846

[On Chirstmas Day 1846, after much discussion and gathering of information, was formed at Utrecht the *Nederlandsche Vereeniging ter Verhuizing naar de Vereenigde Staten van Noord Amerika*, the rules of which were published in Scholte's *De Reformatie*, 3de Serie, III (1846). On October 2 an advance group of eight families, a total of thirty persons, sailed from Hellevoetsluis to seek settlement in the Midwest of the United States and report to their friends in de *Vereeniging*. Among these was Hendrik Barendregt and family who arrived in St. Louis *via* New Orleans and the Mississipi and subsequently settled in Pella. His letter of December 14, 1846, which figured importantly in the history of Dutch immigration, was published by Scholte in *De Reformatie*, 3de serie, III. For a translation of most of this letter, see J. van der Zee's *The Hollanders of Iowa* (Iowa City, 1912), pp. 339-348.]

St Louis, Missouri

14 December, 1846

Zeer geachte Leeraar en Broeder in den Heere!

Thans mag ik het voorregt van den Heere genieten tot het schrijven aan U eerw. mij eenigszins te rigten. Zeer gaarne had ik zulks van New Orleans gedaan, doch de verschrikkelijke drukte met zoeken naar het door U opgegeven kantoor, hetwelk te dier plaatse niet meer te vinden was, alsmede het zoeken naar eene stoomboot, die ons verder de Mississippi opvoer, een en ander heeft mij verhinderd.

Voordat ik iets van de reis meld, zij de Heere geloofd en gedankt, die ons bij den dag af heeft getoond met ons te zijn en zoo liefderijk geleid, gered, en kracht geschonken, zelfs meer dan wij konden verwachten. Vooral bleek dit in mijn persoon: alle passagiers zijn min of meer zee-ziek geweest; ik was eene uitzondering. Wanneer men de menschen in brakende toestand zag, was ik, waar ik mij ook begaf, onder of boven, frisch en gezond. Zoo ziet men, dat de rede beschaamd wordt, en de profetie des ongeloofs geheel wordt te leur gesteld; want zelfs deskundigen hadden voorspeld, dat ik de zee niet zou overkomen; thans zijn wij allen te St Louis, en zoo wel die niet als die wel tot mijn gezin behooren, zijn in redelijk goeden welstand. Wij hopen dat ook dit het deel zij van U Eerw. en die ten Uwent zijn.

Vooreerst kortelijk iets van de reis:

Vrijdag, den 2de October, verlieten wij Rotterdam, en den 4den zeilden wij van Hellevoetsluis. De wind was ons zeer gunstig; den 5den kwamen wij in het Kanaal. Hier kregen wij al spoedig den wind sterk tegen, zoo dat de zee hevige baren opgaf, hetgeen spoedig groote ongesteldheid onder de passagiers tengevolge had. Kasten en kisten vlogen door elkaar. Dit duurde 3 dagen en nachten, zoodat ons schip buiten het vaarwater geraakte en de kapitein in den nacht zich genoodzaakt vond het nood- licht op te halen; waarop de lootsbooten van Engeland tot ons kwamen, die in het eerst niet gemakkelijk op zij konden komen; doch tegen den morgen gelukte het ons eenen loots aan boord te krijgen, die ons dadelijk achter de stad Deal bragt, alwaar vele schepen ten anker lagen. Hier gaf de Heere verademing; evenwel de wind bleef sterk aanhouden, zoodat de kapitein spoedig tot het besluit kwam niet door het kanaal, maar de Noordzee op te zeilen achter Schotland om, hetwelk naar het zeggen van den stuurman ongeveer met eene goede gelegenheid 8 dagen zeilen om was. Hier werd het zeer koud, vooral nabij de bergen van Schotland, die wij in de verte zagen. Hier hebben wij nog eenen bangen nacht door- gestaan. U Eerw. weet, wij hadden de plaats bij het groote luik; nu gebeurde het, wanneer ik voor mijn bed zat, alwaar mijne vrouw reeds oplag, dat er eene golf over het schip sloeg in het luik, zoodat ik geheel onder stroomde hetwelk zoo lang duurde, dat ik dacht te bezwijken. Ons bed vloeide ook geheel onder, zoodat mijne vrouw geheel door nat was. Echter de Heere was ons goed. Hij baande door de woeste baren en breede stroomen ons een pad. Spoedig het bed omgekeerd en zooveel mogelijk droog goed aangetrokken, kwamen wij den nacht door. Den volgenden dag, zijnde Zaterdag, den 17de, was het redelijk goed weer; de zon scheen een weinig, zoodat ons beddegoed een weinig droog werd; de wind echter bleef nog even sterk en ons tegen, zoodat wij aanhoudend moesten laveeren, evenwel niet met dat gevaar als in het Kanaal. Den 28 kregen wij den wind van achteren, Noorden en Noord-Oost. Alle bange strijd hield op, en wij zeilden met een goeden wind den ruimen plas over; de eene voorspoed volgde op den anderen. Zelfs toen wij den 14de Novem- ber in de Golf van Mexico kwamen, veranderde de wind zoodanig, dat wij ook hier voor den wind zeilden, zoodat wij den 18 de oevers van de nieuwe wereld konden bezigtigen. Dit deed zich op in een vlak land. Verder voeren wij met de stoomboot voor ons, die, hoe ook de wind waait, de schepen uit zee haalt, de Mississippi op, en kwamen den 19 's morgens te 7 ure te New Orleans aan. Merkelijk had de Heere ons bijgestaan. Niettegenstaande wij eenen grooten omweg gemaakt hebben,

hebben wij in 45 dagen de reis van Holland naar Amerika en wel naar New Orleans afgelegd. Een oude vrouw en 4 kinderen zijn op de zee overleden, waarvan 2 op het schip geboren waren. Drie duitsche vrouwen hebben gebaard, allen in goeden welstand, zonder de minste hulp van eenige vroedvrouw of dergelijke. Om niet te lang te zijn, zal ik van 't geen wij op de Mississippi gezien hebben niet te veel melden, echter iets van Orleans; dit is eene zeer groote en uitgebreide stad in haar aanleg; alles schijnt nog maar in zijn begin, honderden huizen ziet men in de geboorte staan; alles is hier woelend, buitengewoon woelend wegens de wagens en karren, die men in beweging ziet. Zes honderd zeeschepen liggen 3 aan 3 aan de wal en eene menigte stoombooten meestal zeer groot in haar soort, doch van eene geheel andere inrigting als in Holland. Men zegt, dat er 1,300 op de Mississippi waren, en ik kan het best gelooven, wanneer ik alle beweging aanschouw. Zeilschepen ziet men hier niet; zij kunnen ook niet gebruikt worden, dewijl de rivier ontzettend krom loopt en dus de wind nooit zoo kan waaien, dat de schepen naar boven zouden kunnen zeilen; de stroom is altijd afloopend, en de kanten zijn vol houtgewas, zoodat er aan trekken door paarden of menschen niet te denken valt. Ook is alles zoo ver uit elkander, dat 10 à 12 uren hier in geen aanmerking komen. Van New Orleans naar St Louis is 12 à 13 honderd Engelsche mijlen. Schipderij gelijk in Holland komt dus niet te pas.

Toen wij des morgens te New Orleans zijn aangekomen, hebben wij dienzelfden dag nog eene stoomboot aangenomen, die ons de rivier op bragt. De vrachtprijs bestond in 2½ dollar de persoon, en onder 9 jaar half geld, daarbij had ieder persoon 100 lb gewigt vrij, overigens moest men van ieder 100 lb ¼ dollar betalen. Wij betaalden eenig handgeld, toen wij accordeerden. Ter onderrigting dient dit navolgende: Voor dat men te New Orleans komt, krijgt men gewoonlijk een ambtenaar aan boord; deze schrijft een ieder met zijne familie, die tot *een* behooren op, alsmede het getal kisten en schietgeweren. Ik raad alles goed op te geven, bij voorbeeld, geene kisten of eenig geweer te verzwijgen, de kosten zijn hetzelfde, of men 6 of 12 kisten enz. opgeeft. Zij willen alleen maar weten wat ieder heeft. Men krijgt twee papieren, deze moet men hoe eer hoe beter in het tolhuis (zoo noemt men dat bureau) laten afteekenen. Die ambtenaar heeft het regt om van elke twee papieren 50 Amerikaansche centen te nemen; ook kan en mag hij dezelve voor niet geven; het kan dus beproefd worden of men dezelve iets minder kan krijgen; met armen gebruikt men nog al eens ontferming. Bij de afteekening betaalt men nog 20 centen van elke twee papieren. Ik schrijf dit omdat sommigen veronderstellen dat dit alles onnoodig en afzetterij is, en dat is in den grond zoo niet; want de officier, die bij het uitlossen van de goederen tegenwoordig is, laat niets passeren, wanneer men die papieren niet heeft. Ook moet men een contract schrijven, en door den kapitein laten onderteekenen, waarin staat uitgedrukt het betaalde handgeld wegens de veraccordeerde vracht van de stoomboot. De stoombooten liggen allen aan wal met een bord omhoog, waarop staat uitgedrukt de dag van afvaart en de plaats waar naar toe. Men loopt er op en men vindt gewoonlijk den kapitein aan boord, waarmede men accordeeren moet; met een kantoor kan men dus niets beginnen. Er loopen makelaars genoeg, die u in alles behulpzaam zullen zijn; deze heeft men echter niet noodig, wanneer men iemand bij zich heeft die Engelsch spreekt; indien er onder het gezelschap niemand gevonden wordt, die deze taal magtig is, gelijk dit bij ons het geval was, dan is het best van hen eenig gebruik te maken, doch altijd met voorzichtigheid, want er zijn afzetters onder. Wij hadden het geluk een redelijk goed man te treffen.

Dit is nog eene kwade zaak, dat men onderweg overal zoekt te korten op het goud geld en ook op de 5 frankstukken, en alhier te St Louis doet een gouden cent behoorlijk 4 dollars; van de 5 frankstukken heb ik nog geene ondervinding.

Ook in dezen is het goed: „Kent den Heere in all uwe wegen." De ontmoeting, die wij hier omtrent gehad hebben is groot. Verbeeldt u, de stoomboot, waarop wij eerst met den makelaar geweest zijn, en die 3 dollars vroeg van ieder persoon, is eenigen tijd voor ons afgevaren en wij voeren haar den 3den dag voorbij, dewijl zij, ten gevolge van zware mist, door eene andere was ingevaren, en haar ketel gesprongen was, zoodat zij gezonken lag, waardoor 45 passagiers het leven hadden verloren. Wij hebben de scheepslieden met nog eenige anderen van het wrak gehaald en aan de eerstkomende stad aan wal gezet. Dat wij deze stoomboot niet gekozen hadden, was aan onze wijsheid niet toe te schrijven, want het geld was niet veel uit den haak; bovendien scheen het eene beste boot, daar die, welke wij hadden, veel ouder en zwakker was; ook ondervonden wij dat het eene zeer trage was; kortom, dat wij de verongelukte niet gekozen hebben, was alleen beleid van den Heere; Hij zij geloofd en gedankt. Wij hebben de reis in 9 dagen afgelegd van New Orleans naar St Louis. Langs deze rivier ziet men van begin tot eind altijd houtgewas. Nimmer had ik kunnen denken dat er zoo veel hout, dat tot nog toe geheel ten onnutte schijnt te staan, in de wereld was; en nu kan ik zeer goed gelooven, dat ik maar een begin van Amerika gezien heb, zoo hier en daar ziet men een begin of aanleg van eene stad.

In het eerst vindt men suikergewas, verder katoen, en al verder ziet men tusschen het houtgewas eenige hoeken maïs; ook drijft de revier geheel vol hout, dat gestadig uit de kanten uitschiet.

Alhier te St Louis is veel bedrijvigheid; 1300 nieuwe gebouwen zijn er onder handen, 500 zijn gedurende de voorloopen zomer afgewerkt, en alles schijnt nog maar een begin te hebben. Men zegt, dat de stad 3 uur lang is, dit komt mij wat lang voor; doch ik heb geen grond om het tegen te spreken. Twee van onze broeders hebben getracht dezelve te gaan bezien van het eene eind tot het andere; maar dewijl het zoo lang duurde, zijn zij het moede geworden en terug gekomen. De stoombooten, die hier afvaren en aankomen, zijn ook zeer talrijk, en alles wat hier en ook te New Orleans door de stad vervoerd wordt, geschiedt altijd met paarden, muilezels of ossen, waarvan men er soms 12, doch gewoonlijk 8 voor een wagen ziet staan. De boeren komen dagelijks met hunne waren naar de stad, dewijl het alle dag markt is, 10 à 12 schoon gemaakte varkens op een wagen. De beesten of liever het rundvleesch ligt gewoonlijk in 4 stukken op de wagens of karren. Alles komt naar de markt; groenten, appelen, aardappelen, hout, visch, alles in soorten; doch niets van dat alles behoort onder het goedkoope, dan alleen brood, meel of bloem, vleesch en spek; dit alleen is onder de goedkoope artikelen in Amerika te rekenen. Zelfs hoeveel hout men ook ziet, wanneer iemand het koopen moet, eer het dan op het vuur ligt, kost het zeer veel geld.

Alhier is het juist met onze aankomst geheel winter geworden. Alles is onder gesneeuwd, en daarbij is het nu vriezende, doch niet sterk. De reis naar Iowa of Wisconsin kan door ons niet voortgezet worden, dewijl de rivier te laag is, zoodat de stoombooten niet goed varen kunnen. Ook achten wij dezelve niet noodzakelijk, dewijl wij hier vele Winterwijksche broeders ontmoeten, en waarvan twee kort voor onze aankomst in Iowa geweest zijn. Bovendien zijn hier Duitsche broeders, Methodisten, die met alle zaken bekend zijn, althans..., die ons veel vriendschap en behulpzaamheid betoond hebben en ook op zich namen de vragen te beantwoorden die UEw mij ter onderzoeking en beantwoording van hier had opgedragen.

Zie hier ingesloten een, brief van hemzelven in het duitsch geschreven. Voor zoo ver hij den zelven mij heeft voorgelezen, kan ik best oordeelen de echte waarheid te zijn. Ter opheldering dient dit navolgende:

Art. 1. Het land langs de rivieren is overal in handen van de speculanten, van welke het nog wel te verkrijgen is, doch met verhooging van prijs.

3. Het vee is niet zoo duur. Voor 10 dollar koopt men eene beste koe met een kalf. Ook hebben Jan Schaap en ik een paard gezien, dat er goed en vlug uitzag, waarvoor niet meer dan 15 dollars werd geboden.

5. De metselsteenen zijn groot van stuk, omtrent als de roode moppen, doch zij zijn niet hard gebakken, dus van geene beste qualiteit. De kalk is vrij goed, 20 cents per bushel; komt overeen met 50 cents per Nederlandsch mud of 25 lb.

19. Is aan te merken, dat ik zelf het vleesch gekocht heb, goed vet voor 2 Amerikaansche centen en het spek voor $2\frac{1}{2}$ cent het pond. Wat de wigt betreft; ik geloof dat het pond hier kleiner is dan de 5 ons in Nederland.

23. De vederen zijn zeer goed voor $\frac{1}{4}$ dollar het pond.

Wanneer men volhardt bij het besluit om te coloniseeren in Noord-Amerika, dan dient ook dit nog ter inlichting.

1e Ieder landkooper, die het land voor eigen rekening begeert te bouwen, moet vooral rekenen, indien hij oordeelt hulp noodig te hebben, om zijn volk uit Holland mede te brengen.

2e De kosten van leeftogt zijn in het eerst, wanneer men nog geen vruchten trekt, gering; brood en vleesch benevens spek zijn hoofdzaken, en dat zijn hier de goedkoope artikelen; voor kleederen, huishuur en brandhout behoeft geen zorg.

3e Voor degenen, die ervaren zijn in boter en kaas maken, is het zeker goed; want deze komen niet dan slecht aan de markt.

4e De gereedschappen, hiertoe is goed zoo veel mogelijk mede te brengen, vooral wat men in kisten pakken kan; op het schip behoeft men er niets meer voor te betalen, en de stoomboot vracht is maar $\frac{1}{4}$ dollar per 100 lb; alles is hier verkrijgbaar, doch meestal duur. Hetzelfde raad ik aan van alle gereedschappen, bij voorb. van landbouw en voor allerlei ambachtslieden; doch ik zou niet volstrekt raden iets nieuws te koopen in Holland, om herwaarts mede te brengen, dan is het verschil niet groot genoeg, waarbij nog komt dat er in alle gereedschappen veel onderscheid is, en ieder moet zich voorstellen geen Hollander te kunnen blijven, wanneer hij in Amerika komt wonen; aard en manier moet gevolgd worden. Mijne bedoeling derhalve is, dat iemand het gereedschap, dat hij heeft, voor geen appel of peer uit de hand gooije, vooral niet wanneer het nog goed is; lorren mede te brengen is altijd groote gekheid. Ook moet ik hierbij voegen, dat ieder zoo veel mogelijk zijn best aardenwerk, dat niet van de geringste soort is, mede brenge; wanneer het goed tusschen de kleederen in kisten wordt gepakt, die goed tot aan het deksel vol zijn, dan kan men het best heel hier brengen; ons goed is althans vrij goed heel gebleven, niettegenstaande de kisten soms gerold worden als een vat of ton. Ieder kan dus goed begrijpen, dat de kisten vooral goed sterk moeten zijn; want vele kisten heb ik aan stukken zien breken, en dan ziet men veel ellende aan het goed; ook moeten de kisten niet te groot zijn, want dan worden zij al harder behandeld.

Verder wil ik iets melden aangaande de levensmiddelen en gereedschappen op de reis. 160 lb moet men hebben voor ieder persoon.

Dit verdeelt men in:

10 lb spek, redelijk dik om pannekoeken te bakken;
10 lb ham, om op brood te eten, enz.;
10 lb vleesch
20 lb rijst – deze is hier omtrent van denzelfden prijs;
20 lb bloem of meel – dit moet men niet overhouden;
15 lb aardappelen – dat is een half mud;
20 lb blauwe erwten – best van soort; kan men deze overhouden, dan zijn ze goed voor zaad, dewijl ik dezelve hier nog niet goed gezien heb en daarenboven duur;
20 lb kapucijner erwten, dito;
30 lb beste kropbrood aan stukken gesneden en goed gedroogd; ik bedoel 30 lb gedroogd zijnde;
5 lb gewone beschuit of bestellen

160 lb

Voorts is het goed en nuttig een pot hoofdkaas, benevens boter, kaas, suiker, klompjes, pruimen en al wat men zonder koken eten kan, zoete koek, verschillende dranken, wijn, brandewijn, rhijnsche wijn, jenever, azijn, zout, mosterd, peper, koffij, thee, alsmede eenige huismiddelen voor ongesteldheid, mede te nemen; want de Amerikanen hebben geen doctor aan boord, ieder zorgt dus voor zich zelven.

De gereedschappen bestaan in: theeketel of ijzeren kookketel, blikken schotel, blikken borden, waarop ieder zijn eten kan hebben, dewijl men zeldzaam geregeld bij elkander kan zitten, blikken waterkannen, of vaatjes enz. Wanneer men voor zich zelven gaan moet, dan raad ik ieder te groot en ook daar komt ligtelijk verschil onder. Verder moet ik melden, dat de cargadoors zeer onderscheidenlijk handelen; zij schijnen met niet meer dan 6 of 8 man zamen te doen, anders wordt het gezelschap zoo veel af te nemen als zij kunnen. Bij ons waren er die 30-35 à 36 gulden betaalden, en wij moesten fl 45 betalen. Ook waren er op ons schip, wien door... was aangeboden voor 35 gulden een goed schip te bezorgen, indien hunne familie daarvan in het voorjaar gebruik wilde maken.

Uw Liefhebbende en aandenkende broeder in den

Heere Jezus Christus,

Hendrik Barendregt

N.B. Groet vooral broeder Betten.

Van den brief door Brummelkamp en Van Raalte geschreven tot onder-steuning wegens behoeftigen is hier nog niets bekend. Wij weten ook nog niets van Van Raalte en degenen die met hem gevaren zijn.

Ons verlangen, is dat U Eerw. spoedig terug zult schrijven.

Wat ik een ieder raden moet, over New York of New Orleans, weet ik niet regt; dit weet ik, als men na de maand Februarij van Holland afvaart, is het te heet over New Orleans; dan raad ik over New York; men getroostte zich aan de meerdere kosten en moeiten, die de landreis oplevert; doch wanneer men voor of in Februarij vertrekken kan, dan over New Orleans, dit wint veel kosten en moeiten. Ook maakt het een groot onderscheid, waar men zich denkt te vestigen. Is het Iowa, dan wordt de reis over New York al slimmer; dewijl men altijd eerst naar Milwaukee moet, en dan van daar terug naar Iowa, hetwelk over New Orleans niet het geval is; dan kan men goed per stoomboot in Iowa komen. In alle gevallen is het voor degenen, die onbepaald naar hier komen willen, het best naar St Louis, terwijl men hier naar alle kanten goed weg kan. Aangaande het klimaat, ik verneem, dat het hier in den zomer voor ons ook veel te heet is; want het gebeurt, dat men in den zomer alhier voor een' daglooner, die hout hakt, of het hout uit de schepen lost 3 dollars looft per dag, en nu vindt zoo iemand $\frac{1}{2}$ tot $\frac{3}{4}$ dollar. In Iowa hoor ik, is het geheel noordelijk op dus ook veel kouder. Aller-hande vruchten worden hier geteeld: Maïs, tarwe, rogge, haver, boonen, enz. Wat het koolzaad aangaat, dit wordt weinig gewonnen; dewijl het vet hier goedkoop is, heeft men niet veel behoefte aan olie. De prijzen der granen zijn ook in hunne soorten niet hoog, er is wel opgaaf van te doen, maar dan zouden wij ons ook moeten inlaten met vele dingen, die daarmede in verband staan: b.v. de opbrengst van het land, den arbeid, de kosten van bouwen, zaaijen, enz.; dit zal wel met elkander overeenkomen. Doch ik ben met alles niet genoeg bekend om er iets van te melden en het is volstrekt noodig geheel of niets; want schrijf ik b.v. den prijs, dan is men in Holland terstond gereed om op Hollandsche wijze aan het balanceeren en aan het rekenen te gaan, hoewel er volstrekt niets aan te doen is, als men niet goed in het hart van Noord Amerika zit. Ondervinding zal hier de beste leermeesteres zijn.

Wat de godsdienst betreft: men vindt hier waarlijk bekeerde menschen onder de duitschers en ook onder de engelschen, zelfs hier vele zwarte Christenen. Van de duitschers hebben wij veel vriendschap; doch in alles hebben wij geen harmonie. De rustdag wordt redelijk in acht genomen. Men vindt geene grove buitensporigheden, gelijk in Rotterdam of in de hollandsche steden. Wat de scholen aangaat, gij weet die zijn hier vrij; gewoonlijk is er bij iedere kerk eene school. Ook hoor ik, dat er nog vrije scholen zijn; ik ben daarmede nog niet genoeg bekend om er een goed verslag van te geven. Zondagsscholen worden hier onderscheidene gevonden, waar men voor niet onderwijs bekomt; deze zijn ook goed voor ons, om wat van de engelsche taal te leeren. Die goed engelsch kan, bezit eenen rijkdom, wanneer hij uit Holland naar hier overkomt, ik kan dus een ieder niet genoeg aanraden om toch de Engelsche taal te leeren.

Verder heb ik geen bijzonderheden die ik noodzakelijk oordeel te moeten schrijven. Mijn verzoek is, dat U Eerw. zoo goed zult zijn, om dezen zooveel mogelijk ruchtbaar te maken, althans te zorgen dat broeder van H... te R... er spoedig mede bekend wordt. Zeg hem, dat hij als bakker in St Louis beter heer zou kunnen zijn dan in Rotterdam burger. Ook K..., die mij onderscheidene vragen heeft gedaan, die hierin zijn opgelost; ook te Heerjansdam, enz.

De Hoog heeft naar de Hitsert geschreven, doch niet uitvoerig; hij verwijst hen ook naar den brief aan U Eerw. Zorg vooral, dat mijn vader met deze eenigszins bekend wordt. Ik denk binnen 14 dagen aan mijne familie te schrijven. Zoo ik dan nog iets opmerkelijks had, zal ik zorgen dat U Eerw. dit te weten komt.

Groet alle broeders en zusters, die den Heere in onverderfelijkheid liefhebben, van ons allen. Wij groeten vooral U Eerw. en die met en bij U zijn, en hopen te mogen blijven bidden voor U en uwe betrekkingen, ook tevens voor de overkomst herwaarts; bidt gij ook voor ons.

De Heere zij uw en ons deel tot in eeuwigheid. Amen.

[No person like Gerrit van Schelven in Holland collected the memoirs of settlers in Pella. It has been possible to find only one such sketch worthy of a place in this collection. Adam P. Hasselman and wife sailed in the *Maasstroom* in April 1847 settled on a farm near Pella. This sketch written by his son-in-law G. van Horsen was published in *Pella's Weekblad*, May 26, 1922.]

In den loop van het eerste deel der negentiende eeuw werden de zoon van den schoolmeester te Nederhemert, Nederland, en de dochter van den schoolmeester te Noordeloos, Nederland, in de huwelijk vereenigd, Adam P. Hasselman en Alida Ch. Gordesse Timmermans. Deze Adam Hasselman ging in 1847 al gedurig eens naar Ds. Scholte, die toen de emigratie naar Amerika op touw had gezet, en in overleg met vele besliste christenen de voorbereidende maatregelen vaststelde, die genomen zouden worden om de overtocht te ondernemen, en zoo mogelijk, met Gods hulp in het nieuwe werelddeel een toevluchtsoord te zoeken, waar men God ongestoord naar den inspraak van geweten kon dienen.

Hasselman had eene levende begeerte om den oceaan over te steken, maar moeder, de vrouw, had daar geen oog op. Veel werd natuurlijk over de zaak gesproken, en toen ten laatste Mrs Hasselman telkens voor den geest kwam, dat God ook op de wateren zijne beschermende hand over zijne kinderen hield, en haar de woorden van de psalmist telkens in de gedachten kwamen: „U zullen, also op Mozes beên, wanneer uw pad loopt door de zee, geen golven overstromen" ,toen kon zij met volle vrijmoedigheid hare toestemming geven tot de groote reis, die in die dagen heel iets anders was, dan tegenwoordig, nu niet alleen de middelen van vervoer beter zijn maar ook zooveel vlugger gaat.

Dat de bezwaren, die Mrs Hasselmann had, geene denkbeeldige bezwaren waren, kan men geredelijk toestemmen, als men bedenkt, dat het gezin acht kinderen telde, die allen nog jeugdig waren. En dan de reis naar een onbekende, zeer dun bevolkte wereld waar een vreemde taal gesproken werd, en alles anders was, dan in het vaderland.

De reis werd aangevangen, en in het begin van April van 1847 zeilde het schip *Maasstroom* van uit de Rotterdamsche haven, en kwam te Baltimore aan, na een reis van 52 dagen. Onderweg stierf een der kinderen wier stoffelijk overschot ten jongsten dage ook weer zal verschijnen wanneer de boeken worden geopend.

Met zeven kinderen kwam het gezin na eerst geruimen tijd te St Louis, Missouri, vertoeft te hebben, te Pella aan, wat vanzelf niets anders was dan een plaats in de wildernis.

Mrs G. van Horsen, wier eigen naam Marie Hasselman is, nu eene oude weduwe van 84 jaren, die ons dit heeft medegedeeld, was toen een meisje van negen jaren en vijf maanden.

Vader Hasselman had genoeg middelen om zich een stuk land aan te schaffen van 40 acres. Bovendien bleef er genoeg in kas om voor een tijdlang in de nooden van het gezin te voorzien.

Gemakkelijk was het niet om levensmiddelen te verkrijgen. Tarwe kon men wel bekomen, maar er waren geene molens in de buurt.

Om die tarwe tot meel gemalen te krijgen moest een reis gemaakt worden van 70 à 80 mijlen. Dan ging de reis door kreken en over bergen, langs meestal ongebaande wegen. Soms bleef de wagen een week uit. Dat de spanning waarin de achtergeblevenen groot was, laat zich gemakkelijk denken.

Mr Ten Hagen had een team paarden en ging gewoonlijk heen om de tarwe te laten malen. Dat ging altijd naar nauwkeurige berekening. De bestellingen werden gedaan naar de grootte van elk huisgezin. Vele malen kwam het uit zooals men had gehoopt. Doordat allen gaarne hun aandeel ontvingen, kon Ten Hagen niet genoeg meenemen voor al de hongerige magen, die er behoefte aan hadden.

Als er geen meel genoeg was, viel het de kinderen te beurt, dat zij de koffiemolen ter hand konden nemen en corn moesten malen, waar dan brood van werd gebakken. En dat cornbrood met stroop was een heele lekkernij. Eens, toen een der broertjes werd uitgezonden om stroop te halen, verloor hij zijn tiencent stukje, en moest het brood naar binnen zonder stroop.

Toen zij hier ongeveer een jaar waren geweest, kwam er op zekere dag iemand van Oskaloosa, Parker bij naam, die een fabriek had, waar wandmolens werden vervaardigd. Hij vroeg Mrs Hasselman of zij niet een der kinderen kon afstaan om zijne vrouw behulpzaam te zijn in haar huishouding. Dat leek moeder Hasselman niet al te best toe; heel naar Oskaloosa, en bij een vreemde wiens taal men niet verstond! En bovendien, een zijn er kinderen aan een onbekende mee te geven! Maar, na eenige besprekingen waren de zwarigheden opgelost, vooral omdat Marie, toen ruim tien jaar oud, er wel op af durfde, en hier een schoone gelegenheid zag om Engelsch te leeren. Want men had van den beginne af dadelijk gevoeld, dat kennis van die taal volstrekt noodzakelijk was. Eens gebeurde het, dat iemand een paard verkocht aan een Amerikaan, en in ruil voor dat paard twee koeien zou ontvangen en het overige in „cash". De man was tevreden met den gedanen ruil en vertelde zijne vrouw hoe de zaken geregeld zouden worden. Wat in de wereld zou

men met zoveel „kaas" doen? Bij nadere beschouwing kwam de man
ook tot overtuiging, dat die kaas dan wel moest bederven, en ging
daarom naar de andere partij en zei hem dat zij onmogelijk zooveel
„kaas" (cash) ‚konden nemen. Toen evenwel de opheldering gegeven
werd, dat die cash geen kaas was, maar geld, kwam alles terecht en lachtte
men er samen eens hartelijk om.

Die schoone gelegenheid om de taal des lands te leeren duurde evenwel
niet bijzonder lang, want ofschoon er werk genoeg te doen was met op
de baby te passen en allerlei huiswerk te verrichten, en de dag dus niet
lang viel, kwam de nacht met die lange uren, die wakend werden doorgebracht; dan kwamen de huiselijke tafereelen voor den geest, dan dacht
de kleine meid aan vader en moeder en de broertjes en zusjes, en dan
werd het haar te benauwd om het hart. Gedurende haar verblijf van
een week bij dien fabrikant groeide het heimwee zoo sterk, dat zij
besloot om de eerste en beste gelegenheid waar te nemen om naar huis
te gaan. En die kwam spoediger dan wel haast gedacht. Den volgenden
Zondag ging de fabrikant met een lading wandmolens naar Des Moines.
Zij vergezelde hem tot aan Pella. O, wat een verlichting, nu weer bij
moeder! En toen die vreemde op den terugtocht weer aankwam om
haar mede te nemen, had zij den moed niet mee te gaan.

Het noordwestelijk deel van Pella, waar nu het Oakwood kerkhof is,
had toen den naam van „strooien stad", omdat de hutten, die in glooiing
van den heuvel waren gemaakt, met loof en takken en stroo waren overdekt. Daar werd kerk gehouden in de open lucht.

Daar kwam men saam om God te dienen. Eens op een Zondag toen
men na den dienst op pad naar huis was, kwam er een troep Indianen
voorbij. Gekleed in buffalo huiden, die over de schouder hingen en het
lichaam voor een groot deel onbedekt lieten, gezeten op kleine paardjes,
waar aan den eenen kant gebraden konijnen bengelden en aan den
anderen kant een papoose schommelde, om het evenwicht te bewaren,
maakten die vooral de vrouwen en kinderen ontsteld, met hunne
onbewegelijke bruine gelaatstrekken en diepe zwarte glazige oogen. En
tot overmaat van schrik kwam er een der Indianen naar hen toe en vroeg
om iets te eten, zooals gewoonlijk, want ze zijn echte bedelaars. Zien
ze iets van hunne gading, daar moeten ze daar hun deel van hebben, en
wordt het niet goedschiks gegeven, dan kan men er veilig op rekenen,
dat men het evenwel toch kwijt raakt, want tegen dieverij zien ze heel
niet op.

Op een andere keer waren de Indianen bij bakker Pos aan geweest en
hadden daar van dezen een zak koekjes gekregen. Die koekjes schenen

de roodhuiden of niet te bevallen of ze vertrouwden ze mogelijk niet, want de kinderen vonden ze een oogenblik later langs het pad weggeworpen.

Indianen komen nog af en toe hier in de buurt doortrekken. En menigmaal vallen sommige dingen bij vergissing in hunne handen. Zien zij iemand op de plaats, wiens oog zij niet kunnen ontgaan, dan komen zij meestal met smeekend gebaar en lijmerige stem, strekkend de hand met lamme beweging uit en vragen dan om „iets te eten".

In den loop des tijds had vader Hasselman een huis gebouwd dat de „ark" werd genoemd. Daar zijn heel wat bezoeken afgelegd door de ouden van dagen. Ieder was er welkom. Ook Mr Overkamp had een huis gebouwd, waar schrijver dezes goede gelegenheid heeft mee bekend te worden, omdat hij er nu woont, op den zuid-oost hoek van Washington en West First Street. Dat huis heeft een geschiedenis, gelijk zoo menig ander plaats te Pella. Daar werden de bidstonden gehouden onder leiding van Ds Scholte, daar rees op stem en snaren tot roem van Gods goedheid, het gejuich zijner kinderen. In dat huis van Mr Overkamp hoorde vader Hasselman Ds Scholte voor het eerst preeken in Amerika. Daar vonden ook velen een toevluchtsoord in den storm van 1848, toen het huis van Roovaart werd vernield en de „ark" zoo lek werd, dat ook de bewoners daarvan een beter heenkomen begeerden.

Die tijden zijn lang voorbij, maar in hare verbeelding hoort Mrs G. van Horsen de wolven nog rond het planken huis huilen en ziet zij ook de menigvuldige slangen kruipen; en 's avonds kan zij de lucht nog rood zien van de prairiebranden. Wolven zijn nu groote zeldzaamheden en wil iemand de prairie zien dan moet men verder op naar het westen.

Chapter XX

SETTLEMENTS IN SOUTH HOLLAND, ROSELAND, AND FULTON, ILLINOIS, 1847-1860

66. JOHN DE YOUNG'S HISTORY OF ROSELAND

[The author, son of *Meester* Pieter de Jong, a noteworthy figure in the early history of the Roseland community, in 1908 wrote this sketch based upon his intimate acquaintance with Roseland's history. This text was prepared from the manuscript preserved in the Netherlands Museum.]

Het was in 't jaar 1849 in de maand April dat tien huisgezinnen uit de Provincie Noord Holland na rijp beraad de reis aanvaardden om te verhuizen naar de Vereenigde Staten van Noord Amerika.

De namen der hoofden van deze tien huisgezinnen waren als volgt: Jacob de Jong, Pieter de Jong, Klaas Dalenberg, Cornelis Kuiper, Gerrit Eenigenburg, Hark Eenigenburg, Pieter Oudendijk, Johannes Ambuul, Jan Jonker en Jan Bras. Er waren twee oude vaders, Cornelis Dalenberg en Cornelis Hoogendonk, vader en schoonvader van Klaas Dalenberg. Deze beide oude mannen stierven op de reis aan de cholera, en de oceaan werd hun graf. Ook waren er noch twee jongelingen, Pieter Dalenberg en Jan Ton. Tot dit gezelschap werd nog toegevoegd het huisgezin van Leendert van der Sijde eer ze Rotterdam verlieten.

Het was op Zaterdag dat de goederen geladen werden in een schuit liggende in het Noord Hollandsche Kanaal om hen naar Rotterdam te brengen. Den dag hierop volgende zijnde Zondag ging het meerendeel van dit volkje de godsdienstoefening noch bijwonen in het Godshuis te Krabbendam, en des avonds gingen ze allen aan boord der schuit om den volgenden morgen (zijnde Maandag) den reis te beginnen, om hun Vaderland waarin zij geboren waren vaarwel te zeggen voor een ander en vreemd land.

Op deze reize van het Sluis naar Rotterdam door het kanaal en de revieren viel niets bijzonders voor, en kwam men goed en wel aan. Hier lagen we eenige dagen stil eer we verder konden gaan, en een van de kinderen van Klaas Dalenberg stierf aldaar en werd daar begraven. Wij verlieten Rotterdam per stoomboot naar Le Havre, Frankrijk. Dit gedeelte der reize was noch al stormachtig, en meest allen werden zeeziek en hadden eer we Havre bereikten ledige en schoone magen. Hier ter stede vertoefden we eenige dagen eer we aan boord konden gaan van het drie masterschip genaamd *Massachusetts* geeigend te Boston.

De reize op dit schip over den oceaan zal nooit uit het geheugen gewischt worden dergenen die oud genoeg waren om het te herrinneren; de hoofden der huisgezinnen van toen zijn niet meer. We waren noch niet lang op den oceaan of de cholera brak uit onder ons volk, en als ons geheugen ons niet vergist, stierven er negentien aan deze pestziekte, en hun graf werd de oceaan. De zeereis duurde twee en veertig dagen, zeer zware stormen hadden we niet; een enkele golfslag kwam er noch wel eens op dek, doch we meenden er was geen gevaar van vergaan. De zware verliezen aan dooden bragt van zelven rouwe te weeg en was zeer beproevend voor velen doch ons volkje had geleerd tot Hem te gaan die ons troosten kan en wil in zulke omstandigheden, zij gingen tot Hem ook toen ter tijd en vonden troost en sterkte bij de Heere onder de zware beproevingen en den laatsten Zondag hielden ze noch godsdienstoefening boven op het dek aan boord van het schip, lazen een preek, baden te zamen, en zongen ze ook noch psalmen tot Gods eer. We herinneren ons noch goed dat eenige Duitschers hiermede spotten, doch onze kapitein (een Amerikaan) had eerbied voor dit godsdienstig gezelschap, hij ontblootte het hoofd en verbood de Duitschers het spotten.

Na eene zeereis van twee en veertig dagen kwamen we eindelijk te New York aan wal en dan daar werd de reis voortgezet, eerst per stoomboot langs de Hudson rivier van New York City naar Albany, New York, en van daar per kanaalboot naar Buffalo, New York langs de Erie Kanaal. Dit was een reisje dat acht dagen duurde, en van daar ging het per stoomboot naar Chicago, Illinois. Hier werden we opgewacht door een oude kennis met name Klaas Pool die in het najaar van 1847 naar America verhuist was met een Klaas Paarlenberg, beiden van Noord Holland. Hier vonden we huisvesting in een huis aan Randolph Straat.

Nu was men in America! en moest er geraadpleegd worden wat te doen. Men kwam spoedig overeen om naar het land te gaan zien, en zoo gingen vier der hoofden met Klaas Pool te voet de country in, naar South Holland (toen Lage Prairie). Mr. Pool kende een weinig Engelsch spreken en verstaan, en door de voorzienigheid Gods kwamen wij in aanraking met een Amerikaan met name Oosterhout van Hollandsche afkomst die ook noch een weinig Hollandsch kon spreken en verstaan en ons volkje toen veel hielp in hunne zaken van land koopen, enz. Er werd rond gezien en land gekocht waar Roseland nu is, toen ter tijd Hooge Prairie genoemd. Zij kochten 160 acres land aan wat men noemde de „ridge" of „hooge road", en een weinig later noch tachtig. Dit strekte zich uit van wat nu is 106th Street tot 115th Street.

Het was toen ter tijd wat anders dan het nu is in het jaar 1908. Van Twaalfde Straat dat toen het uiterste was van de stad Chicago, tot wat nu is 115th Straat waren drie woonhuizen. Het laatste was [aan] wat nu is 111th Straat [en] bewoond door een Americaan met name Mr. Lob die zijn land en ook zijn huis verkocht aan deze eerste Hollanders voor den prijs van vijf dollars per acre. Hij vertrok spoedig naar elders. Het gras was toen ter tijd van de ridge tot Lake Calumet zoo lang, dat men het vee niet konde zien als ze daarin graasden; ten westen was het niet zoo lang en van beter qualiteit.

Daar deze eerste nederzetters gewoon waren den Zondag godsdienstig door te brengen gingen zij in den beginne naar de Lage Prairie (nu South Holland genoemd) ter kerke met den ossenwagen. Zij hadden daar toen al reeds een kerkje, en was er ook een predikant met name Ds. Willem Coenraad Wust. Hier kwamen, als we ons niet vergissen, de eerste settlers in 1847.

Daar deze twee nederzettingen 6 à 7 mijlen van elkaar verwijderd waren, vond men het niet wel doenlijk dit vol te houden elken Zondag daar heen te rijden. Zoo besloot men om des Zondags in de huizen te vergaderen, zoo spoedig als er lokalen opgerigt waren, waarin men zulks konde doen, en dit werd gedaan tot het volgende voorjaar toen ze met elkander een klein kerkje oprigten. Dit koste niet veel geld daar de lumber toen ter tijd goedkoop was en men sloeg de handen tezamen om het te verrigten. Het gebouw was klein doch voldeed aan den behoeften des tijds en men zong er psalmen tot Gods eer, en de zielen werden gevoed met het Brood des Levens.

Het duurde niet vele jaren of het kerkje werd te klein en vervangen door een grooter en wat beter, en later weder grooter en wat beter, en nu het groote gebouw aan [de] corner of 107th Street de gebouwen vergroot en verbeterd doch op dezelfde plaats gebleven.

In den beginnen moest men zich noch al wat behelpen, de geriefelijkheden des levens waren niet wat zij nu zijn. Met ossenwagen moest men het timmerhout halen uit de stad, doch dat ging toen wel; men zag toen tegen geen klein beetje op, en die wat handig waren met timmermans gereedschap te hanteeren bouwden hunnen eigene huizen. Er kwame noch een huisgezin uit Sheboygan, Wisconsin, met name Abraham de Koker die timmerman was en terstond als zoodanig gehuurd werd. En eer de winter inzette waren allen redelijk goed gehuisvest. Het waren geen paleizen, en met de koudste dagen konde men wel digt bij de kagchel zitten zonder over de warmte te klagen.

Het volk ging spoedig wat melk vee koopen en zoo hadden ze spoedig melk, boter, en kaas voor eigen gebruik; en wat men meer had konde men gereedelijk in de stad verkoopen. De arbeiders die men had medegenomen hadden overvloed van werk van den beginne. Het volgende voorjaar kocht men meer melk vee, zoodat men toen genoeg had om in de dagelijksche behoeften te voorzien. De inkomsten liepen wel niet in de duizenden, doch men had genoeg dagelijks brood, en dit was heel wat waard voor eerst beginnenden in dien tijd.

Zoo toen als nu de orde van den dag was trouwen, geboren worden, en sterven. In volgorde de eerste was een doode, een dochtertje van Pieter de Jong omstreeks twee jaren oud. Een begraafplaats moest men kiezen om de doode aldaar te begraven. Een geboorte volgde in het huisgezin van Jacob de Jong, een zoon werd geboren en genaamd Joris, deze beide gevallen gebeurden voor den winter, meenen we. Daarna volgde een huwelijk. Klaas Dalenberg die zijne echtgenoote in den oceaan had moeten begraven, trad nu in het huwelijk met Cornelia Gouwens.

De eerste storekeeper op kleine schaal was Cornelis Kuiper. Na eenigen tijd werd hij vervangen door Joris van der Sijde, die dit verscheidene jaren heeft volgehouden, en zoo ging het volkje leven heen in dit hun nieuw aangenomen vaderland.

Spoorwegen waren er toen ter tijd noch niet die het Westen met het Oosten vereenigden. Alleen een korte baan was er van Chicago naar Galena, Illinois. De eerste spoorweg uit het Oosten was in het najaar van 1850 genoemd de Michigan Southern en Northern Indiana, in het voorjaar van 1851 de Michigan Central, en ook in datzelfde jaar de Illinois Central.

Er kwamen van tijd tot tijd ook nieuwe emigranten aan; onder de eerste waren Pieter Prins en huisgezin, Benjamin Prins, Jan Verhoef, Teunis Maat, Pieter Madderom, Klaas Madderom, Cornelius Madderom, en later ook noch A. Verkley; en zoo noch al meer van tijd tot tijd,

De genoemde Ds. Wust vertrok al spoedig van de Lage Prairie, en nu werden we later bediend door leeraars uit Michigan en Wisconsin, met name Dr. A. C. van Raalte, Ds. Seine Bolks, Ds. Cornelius van der Meulen, Ds. Maarten A. Ypma en Ds. H. G. Klein [Klijn] van Milwaukee, Wisconsin.

De eerste gemeente begon met 13 ledematen, breide zich uit van tijd tot tijd, totdat de eerste gemeente nu ruim 800 ledematen telt, met noch vijf andere Gereformeerde gemeenten rond om zich henen. Jacob zeide: „Met mijnen staf ben ik over deze Jordaan gegaan en nu ben ik tot twee heiren geworden". Hier zouden we kunnen zeggen zes heiren, de eene gemeente tot zes geworden.

De eerste ouderling der eerste gemeente was Jacob de Jong, die als zoodanig de gemeente gediend heeft tot aan zijnen dood. De eerste diaken was Pieter de Jong die later verkozen werd tot het ambt van ouderling en ook als zoodanig de gemeente gediend heeft tot zijnen dood.

De hoofden der huisgezinnen die hier kwamen met hunne kinderen, hebben allen het tijdelijk met het eeuwige verwisseld en zijn niet meer, en de kinderen, die met hen hier kwamen begint men nu onder de ouden van dagen te tellen – tenminste schrijver dezes wordt menigmaal door de kleine kinderen begroet met „hallo grandpa!"

Van hunne kinderen die met hen hier kwamen zijn noch in leven Joris van der Sijde, de oudste van die allen en zijne zuster de Weduwe Jan Ton. Van Jacob de Jong zijn noch in leven vijf; van Pieter de Jong zes; van Klaas Dalenberg, een; van Hark Eenigenberg, een; en van Jan Jonker, een. De kleinkinderen zouden een heele schare tellen.

De eerste leeraar die beroepen werden door de gecombineerde gemeenten Hooge Prairie en Lage Prairie was Ds. Maarten Ypma, die de gemeenten verscheidene jaren bediend heeft [van 1855 tot 1861], daarna Ds. Seine Bolks [van 1862 tot 1865]. Na diens werk gingen de twee gemeenten ieder hun eigen leeraar roepen en als zoodanig werd door de Hooge Prairie beroepen en later verwelkomt Ds. Pieter Lepeltak [die de gemeente diende van 1865 tot 1869].

Op verzoek hebben wij deze schets geschreven, en hopen dat het moge dienen om de eerste settlers van de vergetelheid te ontrukken.

Minnesota

Grand Meadow, 1908. John P. de Young

Het boven geschreven stuk is van den wijlen oudsten zoon van „Meester" Pieter de Jong, een der eerste nederzetters. Hij was dus wel bekend met de feiten. De ondergetekende, kleinzoon van „Meester" de Jong, kan over die vroegere dagen niet spreken, maar alleen over hedendaagsche toestanden. Wat is het resultaat dier nederzetting? Hoe verschilt ze van die in Michigan?

In Michigan zat men tusschen den boom-stompen; in Illinois op het beste grond der Vereenigde Staaten. Een predikant is sterk in zijn kansel, maar als het op kolonie-stichten uitgaat volgt men beter een dozijn flinke boeren, vooral als er een godzalige schoolmeester meegaat. Gevolg is dat de kolonie in Illinois lang niet de ontberingen en moeiten te doorstaan had welke men ondervond in Michigan. De kinders en kleinkinders gevoelen zich heden gezegend door het beleid dier eerste nederzetters: wat niet elders het geval is, ze zitten er goed bij, hebben goede woningen, breede akkers, welgebouwde kerken, en studeeren aan de beste scholen en universiteiten ter lande.

Maar wat is het resultaat van den komst dier eerste Hollanders op het volk hier in het algemeen? Dit dunkt mij dat men meer spreekt van „Wicked Chicago"; maar wanneer men bedoelt het zuidelijk gedeelte van Chicago waar deze godzalige mannen en vrouwen zich vroeger vestigden, dan moet men voorzichtiger spreken.

Het zuidelijk gedeelte van Chicago, Roseland en omgeving is „churchly Chicago", met veertig kerken meestal in bloeienden toestand. Hier vindt men niet de kleine kerkjes die zoo verontmoedigend zijn en door hunne flauwheid zoo vele jongelingen en meisjes de wereld inzenden, maar kerken waar de diensten Zondags door groote blijde menigten bijgewoond worden. Het is niet te veel gezegd dat in de oude Eerste Gereformeerde Gemeente van Roseland bijna 4,000 geregeld ter kerke komen elke Zondag. Minstens vijftien jongelingen zijn van deze plaats uitgegaan als leeraars in Christus wijngaard.

Een gedeelte van een groote wereld-stad waar men vlijtigheid en goede zeden op aller hand bemerkt en Zondags een dichte schare stroomende naar Gods huis, met vroolijkheid God dienende, wie zal zeggen, dat dit niet het aller schoonst gevolg is van het vlijtig, moedig, vroom leven die eerste Nederlanders. God geve ons dankbaarheid voor hun exampel.

Pieter C. de Jong.

67. HARRY EENIGENBURG'S
ROSELAND AND SOUTH HOLLAND

[The author, when over ninety years of age, shortly after the opening of World War II penned this account of life in the Dutch settlements at Roseland and South Holland. It was prepared from the manuscript preserved in the Netherlands Museum.]

This history has been carefully compiled by the auther who was born and reared in the wild backwoods of the Lower Calumet Region, in my estimation the most beautiful panorama nature has provided in the Middle West. This area was frequently referred to as the "Garden of Eden" because of its abundance of wild animals and birds. The rivers and creeks, the sand dunes, the big trees, the canebrake marshes provided for the settlers a choice home, for everything they needed nature had provided in great abundance.

The first pioneer Dutch settlers arrived in 1847, from the Province of South Holland, the Netherlands, led by Dominie Willem Coenraad Wust. This settlement was called Low Prairie (Lage Prairie among the Dutch settlers), later South Holland. Two years later, in 1849, fifteen families from the Province of North Holland established themselves at the High Prairie (Hooge Prairie among the Dutch settlers), later Roseland. The streunous sacrifices our parents had to make will never be fully understood by thier children and their grandchildren: crossing the ocean in a sailboat; a voyage of two dreary months; the loss through death of nearly all their beloved children; their burial in the cruel sea; and after these trying experiences, the hardships incidental to pioneer life.

On or about June 16, 1849, the little company of immigrants from the Province of North Holland arrived in the then still small city of Chicago. They were met by a Hollander, one Klaas Pool who knew of their coming and directed them to a large frame building which had been rented for them as a temporary shelter. The families moved into it with their baggage. They did all their cooking, washing, and mending in common.

Klaas Pool told them that Dutch immigrants from the Province of South Holland mentioned above had settled in a place about twenty miles south of Chicago.

A delegation of four men was sent out afoot to visit them. After several days they returned with the welcome news that they had found the South Hollanders living just south of the Little Calumet at a place called Low Prairie. They had stopped at the halfway house to make some inquires of a Mr. Lob living near what is now 111th Street and Michigan Avenue. He spoke Low German so the immigrants could understand him, and through his help they bought some land in section 37 between the present 103rd and 111th Street. Mr. Lob also offered them shelter, a hay barn, while they built their shanties. So on July 4, 1849, the last of the fifteen families arrived in Roseland, or High Prairie, to start a Dutch colony. They had been sixty days on board ship during which voyage they lost seventeen members by death from the Asiatic cholera. All were buried at sea. My parents, Mr. and Mrs. Gerrit Eenigenburg, were among the passengers.

The immigrant Hollanders who founded this Colony were mostly young people; the men did not average over 33 years and the women not over 28. Twelve families had a total of thirty-four children ranging from one month to about twelve years of age. One man was a widower and three young men were unmarried. In all there were sixty-four souls including the children; four adults and thirteen children died on board ship and were buried in the sea.

The reason why these people wanted to go to America was simply this: They were mostly all farmers making a scanty living from small patches of ground. Many of them indeed owned their homes and land but saw no prospect of increasing their little farms; with families of from two to eight children what would their future be in Holland? They received glowing reports from the Province of South Holland about a colony of Hollanders who had emigrated two years previously to America, so they also decided to organize a colony. They were mostly all bound to each other by marriage or otherwise. As America seemed to be the land of promise they prayerfully held meetings in their little homes to make the necessary plans for their voyage. A number of men were appointed a committee to investigate and get all particulars: the cost of the voyage, all necessary expenses entailed with the trip; and the length of time required to make the trip. After all information was gathered more meetings were held. It was then decided that their property should be sold for cash; and when the required amount for the voyage and incidental expenses was set aside, the balance of their money was exchanged into twenty dollar gold pieces. These gold pieces were placed single file tightly against each other in canvas belts and sewed fast, to be worn on their persons right under their arms and fastened with large hooks and eyes. They wore these belts during the entire journey, a period of over sixty days. This precaution was taken to prevent robbery. Sufficient money for the trip was carried in their purses. One man in the group had $ 800, a few had $ 600 each. My father and some others had $ 500 each but others had less. The group had approximately a total of $ 6,000 after they landed in America.

The immigrants with bag and baggage boarded a Frisian barge for Rotterdam where they took a steamboat for Le Havre. During their stay of four days in Le Havre a baby was born to a member of the group. The entire colony then boarded an American sailing vessel named the *Massachusetts* from Boston. Board was not included in the fare, so they had to buy provisions for the entire trip. They also took with them a large barrel of wine. The boat crew, all rough and vulgar Frenchmen, utterly disregarded the immigrants and soon emptied the barrel. Pieter de Jong, a school teacher, had provided himself with a dictionary in the Holland and English languages, which was of great assistance to the group.

After the third day out on the ocean Asiatic cholera appeared among the passengers. This disease was the most dreaded, filthy, and destructive sickness they ever had to deal with while on the ocean. The contagion passed through the entire group in a few days and nearly everybody came down with it. Fathers and mothers, many of them sick themselves, tried to wait on their crying, dying children who begged for thelp while raving and choking in the greatest of agony. Many of them were doomed to die regardless of age; even four of the parents died.

These immigrant families were as follows: Meester Pieter de Jong, leader of the group, Jacob de Jong, Cornelius Kuyper, John Yonker, Johannes Ambuul, Jan Bras, Pieter Dalenberg, Klaas Dalenberg, Hark Eenigenburg, Gerrit Eenigenburg, Leendert van der Sijde, Jan Ton, Peter Oudendijke and Mrs. Klaas Dalenberg and her child. Cornelius Kuyper lost four children, Jacob de Jong, three, Gerrit Eenigenburg, three and Johannes Ambuul, two.

Besides our group there was still another party of Hollanders on board headed for another location who suffered an even greater loss of life. Thirty-eight of them died and so, adding the seventeen of our group, there were 55 deaths on this voyage. Whenever the ship's doctor pronounced a patient dead, the men would at once remove the body, wrap it in canvas, and slide it down the chute into the ocean for the sharks to devour. Mothers wept and wailed futilely; they were told "hands off, the dead belong to you no more!" One broken-hearted mother wailed "I wish we had stayed in Holland, for then we would still have our dear children." Yes, they all wished that. How they were ever going to forget seemed impossible. The fathers bore up well and tried to comfort their broken-hearted wives with the prospect of a brighter future before them, but this was all so far away an dseemed so uncertain.

Finally they reached America after 48 days on the ocean, and after a speedy inspection they were placed on board a steamboat which carried them up the Hudson River to Troy where they took passage on an Erie Canal boat to Buffalo whence they proceeded to Chicago, through the Great Lakes on the steamboat *Keystone State*. The entire journey from the Netherlands to Chicago consumed sixty days. During the three years following eleven more families from the Old Country joined them: they were Teunis Maat, Pieter Prins, Benjamin Prins, Klaas Madderom, Pieter Madderom, Barend van Mijnen, Maarten van der Star, Jan Verhoef, Jan Snip, Harm Tien, and Cornelius Roggeveen. Hence most of the original pioneer families arrived during the first four years of the settlement; after they had established themselves their sisters, brothers, and other relatives and also friends kept coming over, especially during the next two decades.

The newly arrived immigrants soon organized a place for worship. In 1850 they built their first church. In 1856 they erected a larger church. In 1867 they built a still larger church with steeple, bell, and balcony, thinking that this structure would serve them for all time to come. These three churches were built of wood. In 1887 they were compelled to build again, but this time it was of brick, stone, and steel, a commodious structure with a seating capacity of about 1200, which from the very first was not any too large. The pastors that served them are as follows: Maarten Anne Ypma, Seine Bolks, Pieter Lepeltak, H. R. Koopman, Cornelius Kriekard, and Balster van Ess, who was pastor at the time the last church was built, and after him came Willem Moerdyk, Henry Hospers, Martin Flipse, John F. Heemstra, Henry Harmeling, and John L. Klaaren, who presides at the present time.

It is noteworthy that succeeding generations had the honour and pleasure in 1939 of celebrating the ninetieth anniversary of this congregation started by our Godfearing parents in 1849 in spite of all the tribulation and sadness they experienced as pioneer settlers in this region. The splendid booklet containing a complete history recounting many events that took place during a period of ninety years is a masterpiece that will be cherished by the following generations.

This church is called First Reformed Church of Roseland. A group of 60 members left this congregation in 1877 to start a first Christian Reformed Church on the northeast corner of 111th Street and State Street. Rev. Geert Broene accepted their call. This church also has prospered, for in 1890 they were compelled to enlarge the building. In 1893 a group of 69 families left this congregation and built a church at 10643 Perry Avenue, the Second Christian Reformed Church of Chicago. In 1907 the Third Christian Reformed Church was built at 10942 Perry Avenue, and in 1919 the Fourth Christian Reformed Church at 130 West 104th Street. All these congregations were descendants of the 111th and State Street church which moved to 234 West 109th Street, a better location. All these changes were made on account of lack of adequate room and better suitable accomodation for people living at a distance. This denomination, always recognized by Christian people as thoroughly sound in doctrine, at all times stands on the firing line for Christ.

The pastors that have served this congregation are as follows: Geert Broene, Henry van der Werp, John Robbert, Bernard H. Einink,

John Walkotten, and Frank Doesema who presides at the present time.

Congregations formerly associated with the First Reformed Church of 107th Street were the First Reformed of Gano at 117th Street and Perry Avenue; the Emanuel Reformed at 10236 State Street; and the Mt. Greenwood Reformed Church and the Italian Mission at 116th and State Street.

I wish to call your attention to the members who left the mother church in 1890 and organized the Bethany Reformed Church, an English speaking congregation, and erected their first church building in 1891 at 52 West 111th Street. There were 26 charter members. In 1899 they enlarged their church, and in 1908 they built their parsonage. In 1925 they erected their present church building at the corner of 111th Place and Perry Avenue. The pastors that served them were Gerrit J. Hekhuis, John Steunenberg, John Lamar, John R. Mulder, and Harry J. Hager, their present pastor.

This church building, constructed of brick, stone, and steel, is in the Gothic style, 72 by 115 in size, with two Gothic towers. The main auditorium has 1,140 seats, the basement 600, and in addition there are a kitchen and classrooms. The Sunday School building, an annex 42 by 72 and three stories high, seats about 1,200. The membership of this church is approximately 155, made up of many different nationalities, and so is really cosmopolitan. Its consistory had about 36 members, the teaching force numbers about 100, and the Sunday School has an enrollment of about 800 pupils. The church also supports several missionaries, most of them in foreign lands. This church building is a monument among churches in the Calumet region. The total cost of the structure, including furniture and a Hinner organ, was $ 225,000 in addition to the ground. This building, filled to capacity on the Lord's Day, is used every day of the week by its different organizations and choirs.

When the pioneers arrived from Europe they bought the land along what is now Michigan Avenue at $ 5 per acre. My father wanted a stock farm, so in 1853 he moved to Oakglen about 15 miles south of Roseland near Lansing, and bought 160 acres at 93 cents an acre. Father was the second settler in that district.

The country was primitive and wild. One-third of the land was heavy timber and the remainder prairie and swamp. There were no railroads or wagon roads, only a trail running east and west which they called the Joliet and Michigan City Trail or Stage Road.

The Dutch settlers who had come to South Holland in 1847, led by dominie Willem Coenraad Wust from Giesendam in the Netherlands, immediately organized a meeting place. This was the first church in the entire Calumet region; and as the farmers moved south along the Michigan City trail, some of them had to travel six and eight miles to worship. My father and several other families had settled along the Ridge Road. They found it too far to go to South Holland, so about 1860 my father was asked to attend the Dutch Reformed Classis held in Milwaukee, Wisconsin. They appointed father elder and instructed him to buy a few acres of land for a church and burying ground and to build a church for the Ridge Road people. Father built a church about 24 by 40 feet in size, all complete with pews and pulpit and in addition a horse stable, at a total cost of $ 400. For fourteen years father conducted all the meetings until the congregation became too large for the small church, and as it was not centrally located, father bought five acres on the Ridge across the state line in Indiana where in 1874 they built new church at a cost of $ 2,200. This church was then organized and dedicated as the First Christian Reformed Church, and has swarmed several times. One swarm went to Highland, Indiana, and another went out as an English speaking church and established itself in Lansing. Father conducted the meetings until about 1880, when they got their first pastor, Henry Mollema. At that time had a total enrollment of about 80 members, including the children. Their next pastor was Hermanus Temple, then Peter van Vliet, William Borgman, J. H. Mokma, Daniel Zwier, Jan Karel van Baalen, and Johan Monsma, their present pastor. It has always been an effective religious institution doing much for the advancement of God's kingdom.

The first Reformed Church of Lansing was built by my father in 1860. When the congregation seceded and joined the First Christian Reformed Church, they naturally abandoned that property. Only one family remained true, but as new families moved into the neighborhood soon a large congregation came into existence. The church was enlarged, although it is not nearly big enough for its present attendance. We number 225 families, 478 members, or including communicants and baptized members, a total of 935. Our Sunday school enrollment, 450 with 33 teachers. Morning services in the Holland language. All others in the English language. All under the supervision of our beloved pastor, Gerrit J. Rozeboom.

Their first pastor, who came in 1883, was John Lubach. Next followed John W. Dunnewold, Johan Luxen, Peter Swart, Harm Douwstra, Dirk J. de Bey, William Duiker, Peter Braak, Anthony Karreman, and Gerrit J. Rozeboom who presides at the present time. On August 21, 1936, this church celebrated its 75th anniversary by publishing a splendid booklet with a complete record of its history. This church has also been the parent of other churches, an English speaking church a half mile west of the mother church on Ridge Road. A number of families from the Lansing church helped to build up the Reformed Church at Ross, Indiana.

The settlement of Hollanders at Low Prairie (South Holland) flourished from the very beginning. They could secure as much excellent farming land as they desired, and at a low price. Besides, they had the advantage of a beautiful river of clear water running through the entire length of their settlement. For many years the people of Low Prairie had an abundant supply of excellent farm land sufficient for all newcomers and also to satisfy the needs of the coming generation. These people always remained a purely Dutch community and were not invaded by other nationalities. So they built up a large and vigorous Dutch settlement. The first settlers were ambitious, honest, hard working, people, independent, and self-supporting. Not a cheat or a thief was to be found among them. They were kind hearted, friendly, and neighborly. The Roseland pioneers were of the same type, and so was my father. Many a time Dominie Zwemer, came from South Holland on Sunday evening to preach the gospel in our little Lansing church. And what a treat that was for us! We always packed the little church to the door.

The pioneers of Low Prairie were deeply religious, ever adhering firmly to the Gospel. They established a vigorous church which throve from the beginning. Their first pastor, as we have noted, was W. C. Wust. Next followed Maarten Anne Ypma, Seine Bolks, H. R. Koopman, Adriaan Zwemer, Ale Buursma, John Kremer, Willem Moerdyk, Jacob van Houte, Jan Broek, Henry Harmeling, Anthony van Duine, Henry Schuurman, J. W. Muilenberg, and John S. ter Louw, the present pastor. This, the first congregation organized in the entire Calumet Region to be founded by our pioneer Dutch settlers, has ever been a keystone of the Christian religion in our community. This congregation has swarmed a number of times; there are four other Dutch speaking congregations who originally were affiliated with the mother church. Out of a total pupulation of 1,800 the mother church has a membership of more than 600 besides a large Sunday school with many teachers. This church is known as the First Reformed Church of South Holland, Illinois.

Summing up all the Christian institutions, we have in the Calumet region south of 95th Street, all descendants of our Godfearing parents of 1847 and 1849 and subsequent arrivals from the Netherlands, we find twenty-four Reformed and Christian Reformed Churches and several Christian Schools.

My mother who acted as the historian of the group of fifteen families who arrived here in 1849 was a very devout Christian woman. She saw no need of neglecting the children because we lived in the backwoods. She made a determined effort to give them a thorough Christian training. She would gather them together at home or at church, teaching them as best she could. My Christian training has been a light upon my path all through life.

Our parents were never satisfied unless every member of their family was converted. They labored hard to that and end saw good results. We had many families in our neighborhood that had no religion and who called themselves neutral. Their children followed in their footsteps and died without Christ. One old lady of 77 lay on her deathbed begging for prayer but no one prayed. She had always been neutral and shunned God and now she was afraid to die. She was a member of a large family but they all went the same way. Christian training is a God-send and must never be neglected by Christian parents. The present wordly environment is filled with evil and draws young people in the wrong direction. When I review my journey of over 80 years I can truthfully say that I have seen thousands of people living and dying without Christ simply because they were neutral and would not listen to reason nor to God. This indeed is a sad world. God speaks to each one of us. He provides us with a Saviour, telling us to accept Him. He saves us, quides us, and protects us. But, no, Satan has framed up many *isms*, which compromise with sin and are more attractive to the carnal mind of blind sinners who gladly follow him and so are lost.

God has no neutral Chirstians. One is either for Christ or against Christ. I have always been in business since I was a young boy and mixed with all kinds of people. Nearly everybody had some religion made to suit their case, but they never read the Bible as they, did not think it necessary, and so they went marching on to doom. Our Christian people have a great responsibility to warn others and lead them to Christ but this is a task sorely negelected by many. Poor souls are lost who could be saved if Christian people would but do their duty. Only the followers of Christ see the great danger to unconverted souls marching on to doom. God surely wants us to do our duty and bring them to the cross of Christ. Yes, there are many Pauls preaching and broadcasting the Gospel to day but the people are nearly all smart alecs and will not listen to the Gospel. What they want is fun and pleasure, worldly excitement that destroys the soul and leads them to doom.

Now that I am in my ninth decade and practically a pioneer I will give some account of early Roseland history – what transpired in the early horse-and-buggy-days and what life on the farm was like. My father moved into his 160 acre farm in the fall of 1853 and built his little 16 by 24 foot house one story high with a small attic for the childrens' bedroom, right in the big woods on the edge of the marsh, 15 miles southeast of Roseland on the old stage road – the only trail they had at that time, for there were no railroads or wagon roads. Our nearest neighbor was a man who lived alone a half mile away. Three miles to the east was the Stalbum road house, the Homewood road house five miles west, both on the Michigan City stage road. Stage coaches drove through our community every day each drawn by four horses with a lot of baggage piled on top of the coaches, going from Coast to Coast on schedule time. Farmers cut lanes through the forest to their farms. Wild deer roamed in droves. The woods teemed with wild animals and birds. The river and creeks were full of clear water which often overflowed their banks. I have seen many a flood in the early days. As farmers moved into the neighborhood they started to drain that country. In 1862 they dug the big ditch at Wicker Park through the big sand ridge to the little Calumet River. In 1863 they extended the Harts ditch to the big ditch and in 1864 dug the Burns Ditch running to Deep River. In 1868 they removed the Mill Dam in the Grand Calumet River at Blue Island and connected the river with the Illinois and Michigan canal which lowered the water about 10 feet in all of our streams. By that time all the big trees and sand ridges had been sold to the railroad companies for ties, fuel, or the construction of roadbeds. The railroad companies started big gravel pits, one at Oak Glen, one at Lansing, one at Munster, and one at Highland. The pits were worked up to about 1890, and that is the reason why the beauty of the old stage road is gone. It really was the most beautiful country of the Middle West with all its streams, high sand ridges, big trees, meadow, and marshes. The years 1870 and 1871 were the dryest on record, scarcely any rain in two years. Then we got all the big fires. On October 8, 1871, the marsh was on fire, the city of Chicago on October 9; and the Indiana and Michigan pineries burned out at the same time. And so were destroyed about fifty million of our beautiful wild passenger pigeons which were became extinct about by 1874, at least in our neighborhood.

By 1870 we had about 30 prosperous farmers in the neighborhood. This was before the machine age. They sowed their grain by hand, cut it with cradles, threshed it with flails, and cleaned it with fanning mills. About

1870 they secured their first threshing machine run by a ten-horse power. They thought their troubles were solved for good. Next they got the Kirby Self Rake Reaper and other machinery. Farmers' families stayed at home until they got married. Parents gave their children some live stock, but no wages. Everybody seemed satisfied and made a good living. Our country was well supplied with all kinds of wild fruit and there was plenty of good hunting and fishing. There were no shops or factories, so the farm was the only place for them to stay. Almost every young man owned a horse and buggy or a team of horses by the time he married. Fathers outfitted them with everything they needed in getting started. I say from my experience that that was a Golden Age. There was real satisfaction in living. Just compare that with living today. Since I was fourteen years old I followed the building trade among the farmers, and later in the cities. Some of the buildings I erected are more than sixty years old, are still standing, and in use.

I have lived through the above-mentioned pioneer days, have seen all the new inventions such as telegraph, locomotive, harvesting selfbinder, moving picture, telephone, bicycle, automobile, airplane, potato digger, cornhusker, haybailer, grain thrasher, linotype, printing, and a thousand others. We see something new every day and without any surprise. In the early days when our women folk went out in public they dressed in their hoopskirts, bustles, and waterfall hairdress and looked like a stack of hay and enjoyed it. To day when they go on dress parade they don't wear enough clothes to flag a handcar, and seem to enjoy it very much. Our mothers of old would not tolerate such. They would rather be oldfashioned. When sixteen of our young men went to the Civil War in 1862, they all came back in 1864 none the worse for their hard experiences and got a good pension ever since. But to day the men are not supposed to come back for a pension but are all blown to pieces by Hitler's Blitzkrieg which eventually will get the old monster himself. Everything is changing except the Word of God which is forever true and changes not.

68. GERRIT VAN OOSTENBRUGGE'S
SETTLEMENT OF SOUTH HOLLAND

[Van Oostenbrugge lived many years in South Holland and was thoroughly acquainted with the history of that settlement. This account was prepared for the Semi-Centennial celebrations in Holland in August 1897. The text which follows was prepared from the original manuscript preserved in the Netherlands Museum.]

The request to furnish a historical sketch of Lage Prairie [or Low Prairie, subsequently South Holland], Illinois, a settlement of Hollanders, at first raised some doubts in my mind which caused me to hesitate. But finally I decided to comply, to the best of my knowledge and ability. I pray it will be understood that when the names of the first settlers are given, only the heads of families are meant.

Lage Prairie, the name by which this place was known some thirty years ago, was a strip of land about four miles long and three miles wide situated in the center of Thornton Township, Cook County, Illinois.

If I am well informed Lage Prairie derived its name from the nature of the surface of the land, which, it was thought, was lower than hat of our neighbor's settlment at Hooge Prairie [High Prairie, later Roseland]. This was an error, for Lage Prairie is actually several feet higher, when measured by the level of nearby Lake Michigan. It is easy to understand why people thought Lage Prairie was lower than Hooge Prairie, for the region was quite unimproved, with no ditches or drains and devoid of hillocks. From east to west Calumet River ran through the center of the settlement at which point it angled northward and westward. Two sloughs branched from this river at the center of the settlement, one running westward, the other southward and westward. At present these sloughs are without water but 40 years ago were filled to the depth of from four to ten feet, and teemed with fish.

The soil of "de Lage Prairie", as the first Hollanders called this area, was composed of sand, some clay, and a good deal of black soil. On the banks of the Calumet River there was a considerable amount of timber, some scrub trees and many shrubs. Great numbers of wild ducks and geese visited these waters and woods, especially in spring and autumn. Rabbits were plentiful, also prairie chickens. During winter wild deer roamed in the country.

Sweet indeed are the memories of those days in the hearts of the first settlers and their children. They were a religious people, few of them had any wealth, most of them belonged to the working class. Their aim was to improve their financial situation and secure freedom of religion.

Their journey to America was made under trying circumstances. The thought of leaving their homeland where their forefathers had lived, fought, and died, bidding farewell to friends and relatives, and never to return naturally saddened them. To cross the Atlantic in a sailing vessel was no light matter as compared with the voyages of the present day. Food was not very good – sea biscuit, hard and dry, meat and pork, salted down in tuns, and for most people too salty to eat, and water stored in large tanks which were opened according to a fixed rule. Such sailing craft carrying immigrants usually were crowded and uncomfortable. Sleeping bunks were arranged in rows and two above each other. It was not unusual to see children thrown from one bed to another by the rolling motion of the ship. Passengers became seasick from which as a rule they recovered speedily. Contagious disease such as smallpox frequently broke out, and the victims were consigned to a watery grave. Contrary winds delayed many a ship so that the voyage lasted six weeks or more.

Their difficulties were by no means over after they had landed. Other trials now had to be met. Not understanding the language of the country, they could not be understood. The journey overland proved difficult because railroads were few and accomodations for travellers generally absent. Much of this journey was by boat over lakes and rivers in vessels of various capacities, often of doubtful quality, and frequently commanded by untrustworthy people who sometimes dumped the immigrants ashore leaving them without protection for weeks. Two members of the families of our settlers died and sad it was for brothers, sisters, parents, relatives, and friends to bury them with their own hands.

Although our first settlers had prepared themselves to make their living in various trades, they turned to farming which promised the greatest success. Unimproved land of the best quality ranged from seventy-five cents to five dollars per acre. Some of the immigrants bought as much as 300 or 400 acres. The first settlers in the summer of 1847 were Cornelius Arensen [or Arentse], Jan Killewinger, Huip Schuurwater, Antonie Rombout, Hendrik de Jong, the widow Klaas Paarlberg, Klaas Pool, and, if I am well informed, Jacob Duim. They at once proceeded to erect cheap dwellings contructed of timbers from the neighboring woods and of lumber brought by oxen from Chicago. Such houses measured about 20 by 12 or 14 feet, 14 feet high, and some were even smaller. The immigrants built sheds on the sides of these houses, about 10 or 12 feet wide, usually as long as the house and provided with a roof, an extension of the roof which covered the house. These pioneer dwellings as a rule had two or three rooms.

The Hollanders turned to farming for a living. They succeeded in plowing the tough prairie sod and raised corn, potatoes, wheat, rye, oats, and buckwheat. Later when they became vegetable gardeners they added cabbage, carrots, and onions. In addition to agriculture they began to raise cattle which were permitted to roam freely over the unoccupied country around Lage Prairie. From these lands the settlers gathered quantities of hay for winter feeding. The cow barns were crude log structures from 10 to 16 feet long, the sidds about 6 feet, and the gable roof, supported by upright posts, was made of rafters covered with long hay. The sides of the barns were covered in the same manner. Barns built of lumber were exceptional. Sheds also were erected, adjoining the barns to protect the cattle from the blizzards of winter. Thus our immigrants provided themselves with the food they needed and also with the oxen which did most of the plowing and other heavy work.

Such were the simple beginnings of their life in the pioneer community. There was neither postoffice, store, school, or church. But in spite of such privations, they managed to hold religious services in their homes.

Some new families arrived in the following year, in 1848: Roel van Vuren, Willem Gouwens, Jacob de Vries, Cornelius Schaai, Dominie W.C. Wust, and Teunis and Hendrik Benschop. Hencefooth religious services were attended regularly, at least for a year or more until Dominie Wust left for the Netherlands in 1850. On August 11, 1848, the pioneers laid the first timbers of a new church building on a parcel of land donated for that purpose by Hendrik de Jong. This 20 by 36 foot structure was divided in two by a partition so that one part might serve as a dwelling house first occupied by Dominie Wust and subsequently used as a school-room. But the religious life of the community was troubled owing to the attempt of Jacob Duim to assume leadership.

Meanwhile the settlers of Lage Prairie cooperated with their neigh-boring Hollanders who had settled at Hooge Prairie [or Roseland]. In 1849 there were new arrivals: Tys Gouwens, Baart Baartman, and Willem K. Roodhuizen. Willem Anker, and Pieter Zwijnenberg came in the following year. There were few newcomers during the next three years. In 1854 Jan de Ridder and Arie van der Aa came, and also Jakob O. van Zanten who, however, did not come directly from the Old County but from Grand Haven, Michigan, where he had settled in 1847.

Meanwhile church life progressed, for the Board of the Reformed Church in America on October 16, 1853, sent Dominie Maarten Ypma, then minister at Graafschap, Michigan, who with the aid of Jakob O. van Zanten brought together the scattered families to form a Reformed church. Twelve families constituted the new organization. In 1854 a new school-house was erected, which served its purpose for about 30 years, in 1893 superseded by a more commodious structure 56 by 70 feet, built in the center of the village. This building has two storys and four rooms. Three teachers are needed to take care of all the pupils.

Until 1855 the settlers found it difficult to maintain their church organ-ization. On Christmas Day, 1854, a meeting was held by the congregation, led by Dominie A. C. van Raalte. The congregation had agreed with the Hollanders at Hooge Prairie to pool their religious activities and be served by one minister. A call was issued to Dominie Maarten Anne Ypma who began his duties early in 1855. Two previous efforts to secure a pastor had failed, the calls addressed to Dominie W. Gardenier at Kalamazoo, Michigan, and Dominie Seine Bolks at Overisel, Michigan, having been rejected.

Not many immigrants came from the Old Country in 1855; all I can recall were Jan Vinke and Arie van Drunen. But in the following year a considerable number of families arrived: Hendrik Swets, Wouter Swets, Bastiaan van Drunen, Rokus van Drunen, Johannes van Drunen, Pieter van Drunen, Antoon [Toon] van Drunen, Cornelius van Drunen, Johannes Ravesloot, Willem Ravesloot, D. Schaap, Mrs. L. van der Aa, Hendrik van der Wolf, Balt van Baarens, and Arie Pals, besides a few young men without families such as Wouter de Graaf, Johannes Schimmel, and perhaps a few others.

And so "de Lage Prairie" grew steadily and prosperity was evident. There was the church and the school, and a store where the most urgent necessaries could be obtained. Before this store was opened the settlers were compelled to go five miles for supplies. For all but the most necessary articles they had to go to Chicago, 20 miles distant.

During this time also the railroads constructed their tracks through Lage Prairie, a sure index of rising land values and of general prosperity. The Illinois Central in 1853 built its line along the western limits of the settlement. At that time the company operated one train daily between Chicago and Kankakee. In 1866 the Panhandle Railroad cut along the northeast border of Lage Prairie. About three years later, in 1871, was completed the Chicago and Eastern Illinois Railroad whose track passed through the center of the settlement from north to south. This road opened a station on 159th Street in the middle of Lage Prairie named South Holland.

There were other evidences of material progress. Roads were constructed and ditches opened which improved the value of the land. Not all the Dutch settlers were farmers, for there were carpenters, masons, and common laborers. In 1869 Pieter de Jong, son of Hendrik de Jong, then a young man, petitioned to open a postoffice, which was granted. At this time the people agreed that the name Lage Prairie should be changed to South Holland and this became the official name of the new postoffice. Further evidence of growth is provided by the fact that the Chicago and Eastern Illinois Railroad, in answer to a petition by the settlers in South Holland, opened a new passenger station and a freight depot. In the spring of that year a mail train began its daily stops delivering mail for the South Holland postoffice. Next, in 1880, the Chicago and Grand Trunk Railroad laid its roadbed across the southern part of the settlement, from northwest to southeast. A lumber yard was opened in South Holland near the Chicago and Eastern Illinois Railroad. Meanwhile more stores opened. Some of the settlers built better and more commodious houses. Obviously the financial condition of the Dutch community had progressed far from the simple beginnings of 1847. Finally, in the spring of 1894 a part of the settlement was incorporated as a village, its first president being Jan Schelling [or Schilling, the English version].

From the beginning religious life and church services had been simple. The platform on which the minister stood when preaching was 2½ feet high, 5 feet wide, and 5 feet deep. The pulpit was paneled; the two rows of benches separated by an aisle were made of common boards. Evening services were conducted by candle light. The structure was heated by a stove in the rear. The congregation had bought a plain wood building to be used as a parsonage and moved it with oxen for a distance of three miles. I well recall how one of the oxen fell and broke a leg.

New settlers continued to arrive in Lage Prairie. In 1857 Hendrik Wierema came from Grand Haven, Michigan, also Willem Blink, in 1858. Jan de Jong and Mrs. Niklaas Veldt, both immigrants, arrived in 1859 and 1860 respectively.

The Civil War which broke out in 1861 affected the settlement. Two of our young men were called to the colors, Teunis Benschop and Machiel [Giel] van der Aa. In 1861 Dominie Ypma was called to Alto, Wisconsin. Then came Dominie Seine Bolks, in 1862, the year when our congregation discontinued its joint services with the church of Hooge Prairie. Henceforth each church went its way managing its own affairs. Such was the growth of the Lage Prairie church that in 1863 the congregation was compelled to erect a larger building which, measuring 34 by 56 feet, was finished in that same year. A steeple 70 feet high towered above the church Dominie Bolks accepted a call from Zeeland, Michigan, in 1865. He was succeeded by Dominie Hendrik R. Koopman who in the following year came with a considerable number of immigrants from the Old Country. Among them were Piet Kaze, Hendrik Vos, J. Bos, and a few others.

Difficulties in the church led, in 1865, to the withdrawal of a group who in that same year organized themselves as the True Christian Reformed Church and built a church which they used until 1873. Such was the growth of this congregation that after securing as their pastor Dominie Ede Luurs Meinders they found it necessary to erect another place of worship which they finished before the close of the year. They prospered until 1885 when a part of the members left to form the Holland Christian Reformed Church which at once built a 30 by 50 foot church. This structure served their needs until 1896 when a larger house of worship, 52 by 70 feet, and an adjoining chapel 32 by 34 feet were built. A new site was chosen, an acre of land which was donated by Mrs. Willem Ravestein. The parsonage was moved from the old church site. These buildings added greatly to the appearance of the village of South Holland. In 1889 the Dominie Roelof T. Kuiper arrived and after his death in 1894, Dominie J. C. Groeneveld served from 1895 until 1903.

The Reformed congregation also prospered during these years. Dominie Keppman left Low Prairie in 1867, and was succeeded by Adriaan Zwemer who came from Vriesland, Michigan. After serving from 1868 to 1870 he moved to Milwaukee. Ale Buursma succeeded him in 1872 and served until 1879. In 1872 a gallery was built in the church, necessitated by the growing numbers, and in 1875 an organ was installed, which appealed especially to the young people of the congregation. Other ministers who followed were: John Kremer, from 1879 to 1883; Willem Moerdyk, from 1884 to 1886; Jacob van Houte, from 1886 to 1892; and John Broek, from 1893.

The steady increase in membership compelled the congregation to build a new church in 1890. Its centralportion measured 56 by 80 feet. Its size was considerably increased by a large wing on east side. Two towers, one 100 feet high, the other less were erected on the corners. Above the doors in front was a large circular window of stained glass 14 feet in diameter and two other windows similar to this one were put into the building. All other windows were made of colored glass. The foundation on which the structure rested was of stone, about three feet above the ground. Hendrik Wierema laid the cornerstone of the church. In 1896 the church was repaired at a cost of $ 1,600. This handsome structure added to the beauty of our village. In 1890, the membership was as follows: of the Reformed Church, 154 families; of the Holland Christian Reformed, about 108 families.

The year 1871 will long be remembered, for there was an epidemic among horses. So many of them died that the settlers had to use oxen. It was not unusual on account of this epidemic to see in Chicago oxen hauling truck wagons. In the fall, on October 8, occurred the Great

Fire which destroyed millions of dollars in property. I well remember the glow of the fire reflected in the evening clouds.

Great changes have taken place in our methods of farming. During the earlier days of the settlement there was little machinery and work had to be done by hand. The settlers relied upon hay to feed their cattle. Some of the men cut as much as 50 tons of it with an ordinary scythe, which was no slight task. Today a man takes his seat on a mower and with ease cuts all the grass he needs. Grain during the earliest years, had to be cut and bound by hand but at present this laborious taks is preformed by selfbinding harvesters drawen by three or four horses. Corn was plantd with a hoe, but soon this work was done with a hand planter, and finally came the horse drawn planter. Today the planting and digging of potatoes are accomplished with machinery. Corn cutting, formerly done by hand, is now done with machines. Produce raised by our earliest settlers was brought by oxen to market in Chicago. Roads were poor. But at the present time when markets are nearer, roads better, and loads drawn by horses the problem of marketing has been greatly simplified.

The community prospered as may be seen from the prices paid for real property in the early days and at later times. In the beginning, as we have stated, the price of land ran from seventy-five cents to $ 5 an acre. In 1860 the average price was about $ 30. Twenty years later this had risen to $ 50. But by 1890 purchasers were paying as much as $ 300 or even $ 500 per acre. Since then prices have declined somewhat. Times have been difficult, the laboring people finding it difficult to get ahead.

But against all these advantages there was one evil that detracted from our village. A large two story building erected in 1891 was occupied by a saloon. This place proved attractive to some of our young people. The saloon is a means of destruction of body and soul and cannot be regarded as a positive asset of the community. I disapprove of the habit of young people spending their time in saloons for amusement or to satisfy their appetites. I pity the young lad who takes this step, for he is not aware of the dangers awaiting him. Would that this could be impressed, upon the minds of all and that they would shun such habits.

69. GEORGE DE BEY'S HISTORY OF DUTCH SETTLEMENT AT FULTON, ILLINOIS

[This sketch of the Dutch settlement at Fulton, Illinois, which began its existence in 1860 was prepared for the Semi-Centennial celebrations at Holland in August 1897. Never printed, it has remained in manuscript form among Gerrit Van Schelven's papers at present reposing in the Netherlands Museum and is here published for the first time.

A dealer in wagons, buggies, and farm implements, De Bey was in a position to become well acquainted with the history of the settlement.]

De geschiedenis van een land wordt gekenmerkt door schoone geestelijke tradities door mannen voortgebragt, door groote daden in het licht gesteld, door natuurlijke ligging tentoongesteld, en gedeeltelijk door materieële bouwstoffen tot werkelijkheid gebragt. Griekenland muntte uit door groote wijsgeeren; Rome in bekwame volksleiders; Duitsland in diepzinnige theologen. Maar Amerika bekleedt de hoogste plaats van eer in dat zij voortbragt niet alleen wijsgeeren, volksleiders, en theologen, maar in, dat zij een vredelievend recht-handhavend volk uitmaakt – een land waar ieder de gelegenheid heeft, ja verpligt wordt om onderwezen te worden. De oude mogendheden mogen praalen met hunne kasteelen en afgoden tempels en zich beroemen op hunne schoone natuur tooneelen. Doch ook in dezen behoeft Amerika niet onder te doen. Prijkt zij niet van kerken en scholen, hoogere en lagere plaatsen van op- voeding die open staan voor iedereen? Handel en nijverheid is er bloeiend – en de bronnen van welvaart zijn nog maar in het begin van haar ont- wikkeling! – en ook daarbij dezen is er natuurschoon, verwisselend, opbeurend!

Van zulk een gelukkige natie dan maken ook de Hollanders in de ver- schillende oorden van dit groote land verspreid een deel uit. Ook wij in Fulton, Illinois, stellen prijs op ons Amerikaansch burgerschap. De Hollanders, misschien meer dan iemand anders zijn ten allen tijde gereed te bekennen dat de geschiedenis der menschheid in den loop der eeuwen is in overeenstemming met het plan Gods en vertrouwt daarom ook dat deze glorieuze herinneringsdagen Zijne goedkeuring wegdrage omdat zij getuigt van Gods trouw en schrijft aan Hem al de eer toe. God heeft niet alleen alles geschapen tot Zijn eer en verheerlijking maar Hij onder- houdt en verzorgt dezelve nog steeds met dat doel Gods daden te ver- melden, stelt ons in staat de noodige kennis te bekomen om Hem beter te dienen. Het doel van dit feest moet dan ook hiertoe strekken. Tot dat einde dan werden pogingen aangewend om van alle oorden dezer natie de geschiedenissen der verschillende nederzettingen te verzamelen. De heeren leden der commitee houden zich verzekerd te hebben de dankbetuiging van de inwoners der stad Fulton en omstreken voor de aan hen bewezen eer in het uitnoodiging om aan dit halve Eeuw Feest deel te nemen.

Om tot de zaak te komen willen we U in kort in kennis stellen met het omgevend land, de eerste nederzetting in Fulton, de komst der Hollan- ders, de stichting eener gemeente, en Fulton's tegenwoordige toestand.

Slechts enkele jaren meer dan een halve eeuw geleden kwamen de eerste blanken in het land dat de Indianen hun paradijs noemden, ofschoon de geschiedenis deze streek aanmeldt als de groote wildernis, 't land der prairies, land der roodhuiden, of het woudig west. De Winnebago, Sac, en Fox Indianen woonden hier ter tijde en beschouwden Rock River Valley waarvan Whiteside County een groot deel uitmaakte als hun paradijs. Verscheiden onderhandelingen of treaties werden gemaakt; de eerste in 't jaar 1804. De groote Black Hawk oorlog werd veroorzaakt door een poging der Indianen Whiteside County weer in bezit te nemen.

Doch de zaken hebben een wending genomen; de wildernis is veranderd in een vrugtbaar land, de paden der jagers en listige roodhuiden zijn vervangen door spoorwegen en andere wegen, armoedige hutten en kleine tuintjes zijn vervangen door genoegelijke huizen en breede akkers. Kerken, scholen, fabrieken van verschillenden aard worden hier gevonden waar vroeger alles woest was.

Het zuidoostelijk gedeelte der county is vlak; het westelijke meer heuvelachtig; in het midden is het rollend. Revieren en beeken in menigte stroomen door de dalen en ontlasten zich in den boesem der groote vader der wateren, de Mississippi. Verschillende soorten van grond worden hier gevonden doch principaal een zwarte loom, en dichter bij de revier meer zandig. Het is zeer vruchtbaar en geschikt voor allerhande produkten eigen aan en land liggende in 41 graden noord latitude.

Fulton ligt aan de snel vlietende stroom der Mississippi. Een van haar eerste nederzetters was John Baker, in 1835. Hij spande zijn tent en bouwde een huis binnen wat thans de stad Fulton is. Hij werd spoedig gevolgd door andere familien; dezen adverteerden hun geluk, en de schoonheid der plaats aan hun oostelijke vrienden, en zoo zag bijna iedere morgenzon nieuwe kolonisten aankomen in zwaar geladen wagens getrokken door muilezels. Spoedig was er eene kolonie gevormd. De eerste clame op land in Whiteside County was in 1834 reeds gemaakt, en den 16den Januari 1836 werden door een acte der wetgevende kamer van den staat Illinois de grenzen onzer county bepaald en de naam Whiteside, ter eere van een der generaals in de Black Hawk oorlog vastgesteld. Fulton Township werd den 6den April 1852 georganizeerd – 41 stemmen werden uitgebragt.

De eerste nederzetters zochten eigendommen kort bij de rivier waar het gedeelteijlk omzoomd was met bosch, niet denkende, dat de groote prairies ooit voor iets behalve voor weiland dienst zouden doen. Thans bevinden er zich op die uitgestrekte prairies welvarende boerderijen en schoone velden, hetwelk iemand met Ten Kate doet uitroepen: „Schoon is d'aarde; goed is 't leven."

De stad Fulton is gelegen aan wat men noemt het smalle [the Narrows] des Mississippi, 136 mijlen ten westen van Chicago, staande gedeeltelijk op de rotsen. In het noorden der stad vertoont zich aan den aanschouwer voorwaar een grootsch en indrukwekkend gezicht. Het zuidelijk gedeelte ligt op meer effen grond. Op de hoogten vertonen zich van 6 tot 14 mijlen wat men noemt de bluffs met hunne groene heuvels en wouden afgewisseld door steile rotsklippen, die in vroegere eeuwen de oostelijke zijden van de rivier uitmaakten. Ten westen ziet gij de breede wateren zich een kronkelend pad banen rondom de eilanden en uitstekende punten. Aan de west zijde der rivier aanschouwt de bezichtiger klippen en heuvelen met de steden Clinton en Lyons, beiden gelegen in den staat Iowa.

Fulton heeft al de aangelegenheden tot het maken van een groote stad. Zij heeft het gebruik van de groote stoomschepen als vervoermiddels op de Mississippi, verbindende St. Paul en Minneapolis ten noorden en St. Louis en Nieuw Orleans ten zuiden. Verder heeft zij verbinding met Chicago, Milwaukee en andere plaatsen in het oosten en met Kansas City, Council Bluffs, en San Francisco in het westen daar de groote spoorwegen, zooals de Chicago and Northwestern, de Chicago, Milwaukee, and St Paul, en de Chicago, Burlington and Quiney van onze stad een voornaam centrum gemaakt hebben.

Aan de vroege ontwikkeling van Fulton hebben ook onze Hollanders deel gehad, ofschoon zij beslist niet de eerste nederzetters waren. Wel 20 jaar nadat de origineele Amerikaansche pioniers zich hier vestigden kwamen eerst onze Nederlanders: G. Nanninga en F. Dijkema in 1860; Jan Munneke en A. van Dellen in 1861; F. Sterenberg en nog eenigen meer in 1863. Nog maar weinige huisgezinnen in getal slooten zij zich eerst aan bij de Presbyteriaansche [Engelsche] gemeente voor een tijd van drie jaren. In 1862 werd het eerste kind van Hollandsche ouders hier gedoopt, een zoon van Jan Munneke; Ds. H. G. Klijn las het doopsformulier. In 1866 werd de gereformeerde gemeente gesticht door Ds Klijn en ouderling Vastenhout van Chicago. F. Sterenberg en G. Nanninga werden gekozen tot ouderlingen en Jacob Tillema tot diaken.

Met heldenmoed vervuld en ijverig in 's Heeren dienst ondernam de kleine kudde het oprichten van een huis des gebeds. Dit werd ingewijd den 15 December 1867. In Augustus 1869 werd Ds. H. Woltman als hun eerste leeraar bevestigd. Onder tegenheden en moeiten hebben zij geworsteld, ook tijdens den burgeroorlog. Eens in 1863 toen een van ons volk dienen moest tengevolge van eene looting bragt men, met elkander door liefde gedrongen, gelden op voor een plaatsvervanger. Om niet in vergetelijkheid te worden gebragt dient hier te worden vermeld dat de eerste nederzetters van Muskegon, Michigan, naar Fulton zijn vertrokken. In Muskegon hadden zij eerst mede geholpen tot het beginnen van godsdienst en het bouwen der Eerste Gereformeerde gemeente. Het vuur huns ijvers hadden zij mede gebracht om ook hier in Fulton als pioniers in ons gereformeerde godsdienst op te treden.

Door ziekte en zwakheid heeft Ds. H. Woltman de gemeente weinig kunnen dienen. Den 30sten April 1870 werd hij der gemeente door den dood ontrukt. Hoewel deerlijk beproefd, werden zij niet ontmoedigd maar beriepen spoedig Ds. John van der Meulen die nu nog in leven is en in het midden dezer feestvierende menigte zich vertoont. De gemeente groeide gestadig onder Ds. van der Meulen. Na vijf jarigen arbeid vertrok hij, en in zijn plaats werd Ds. Willem Hazenburg den 22sten Augustus 1875 in hun midden als leeraar bevestigd. Na bijna twee jarigen arbeid, op den 18den Februari 1877 vertrok ook dezen dienstknecht. Op 30 Juni 1878 werd Ds. Lawrence Dijkstra onder hen bevestigd. Hij vertrok in Februari, 1882, naar Cleveland, Ohio, waarna ds Harmen van der Ploeg de gemeente bijna vijf jaren met zegen en vooruitgang heeft gediend. Hij vertrok naar Vriesland, Michigan, den 16 Maart 1887. Thans telde de gemeente ongeveer 200 huisgezinnen. Ook is het schoone en doelmatig kerkgebouw 50 × 90 onder zijnen arbeid opgericht en waarin thans een schoon pijporgel het gezang verhoogt. Nog zij hier opgemerkt dat deze gemeente in al die jaren van worsteling in het begin slechts 2 jaren onderstand gehad heeft, van de Board of Domestic Missions of the Reformed Church in Amerika, tot ondersteuning van hun leeraar. Te dezen tijde is ook door omstandigheden uit den boesem dezer gemeente een Christelijke Gereformeerde Kerk ontstaan, die thans 70 huisgezinnen telt. Na het vertrek van den onvergetelijken Ds. Harmen van der Ploeg werd in 1888 Ds. Jan Willem te Winkel beroepen die de gemeente zeven jaren met vrugt en zegen gediend heeft.

Aangezien de Hollanders zich verspreiden over het westelijke gedeelte der county, tot meer dan 20 mijlen in omtrek begon men ruim vijf jaren geleden, in 1892, acht mijlen ten zuidoosten van Fulton eerst een Sunday School, daarna ook andere godsdienst oefeningen waaruit in 1896 een gemeente is ontstaan in de stad Morrison, de county seat van Whiteside County, 12 mijlen oost van Fulton, met 38 huisgezinnen, en onder goede vooruitzichten en daar de landerijen rondom deze plaats van de beste gehalte zijn kan dit eerlang ook een bloeiende gemeente worden.

Thans wordt de gemeente te Fulton bediend door Ds. Willem J. Duiker. Door de groote opkomsten tot den geregelde godsdiensten blijft de ijver de eerste grondleggers steeds in de gemeente voortleven en groeide haar ledental steeds aan. Tegenwoordig tellen de Hollanders in en nabij Fulton ongeveer 350 huisgezinnen met een zielental van meer dan 2000.

Het kleine mosterdzaad is tot eed grote boom geworden De welvarenheid van velen bewijst dat met noesten vlijt de Hollanders niet achter aan behoeven te staan. Als een volk worden zij onder de Amerikanen steeds bemind.

Zoo zij dan ook deze kleine schets van Fulton en de Hollanders die daar wonen de vergeteldheid ontrukt. Moge deze geschiedenis door het herinneringsfeest van Hollands Semi-Centennial van 1897 bewaard worden voor de geslachten die nog zullen komen.

Chapter XXI

THE COMMUNITY OF ALTO, WISCONSIN, 1846–1897

70. HENRY HARMELING'S
SKETCH OF THE REFORMED CHURCH AT ALTO

[The author served the Alto congregation from 1894 to 1900. His *Een Historisch overzicht der Gereformeerde Gemeente te Alto Wisconsin* appeared in *De Hope*, December 28, 1898.]

Het is met eene hartelijke dankbaarheid aan den Heere, het Hoofd Zijner Kerk, dat wij de geschiedenis van de Gereformeerde gemeente te Alto, Wisconsin, mogen nagaan. En daar de geschiedenis der eerste neder-zettingen en die der gemeente alhier zeer nauw met elkaar verbonden staan, zoo zal deze omschrijving mogelijk een dienst doen niet alleen aan de belanghebbenden der gemeente, maar ook aan allen, die de planting der Hollanders in het Westen liefhebben . . . .

Het begin der Hollandsche nederzetting in het Westen dateert terug tot 1845 toen de eerste Hollander Albertus Meenk, te Alto arriveerde. Het volgend jaar zag men onderscheidene huisgezinnen alhier gevestigd, met name: ter Beest, Loomans, Rensink, van den Bosch, Slyster, Rikkers, Nieuwenhuis, Hoftiezer, en Boland. En in 1847 vermeerde dit getal nederzetters gestadiglijk, zoodat men, onder anderen, ook had de fa-miliën: Bruins, Boom, Veenhuis, de Groot, Veernhout, van Eck, en Walhuizen.

Er werd eene behoefte gevoeld om geregelde godsdienstige bijeen-komsten te hebben. Deze bijeenkomsten werden ten huize van David A. van Eck gehouden die voor dat doel het gebruik zijner woning aanbood en gewillig afstond. Maar er moest leiding aan zulke godsdienstige ver-gaderingen gegeven worden. Het was echter het geluk der nederzetters om de stichtelijke leiding van de broeders G. J. ter Beest, M. Duven, en Cornelius Veernhout te mogen genieten, die in deze vergadering beurte-lings voorgingen.

Of de woning van David A. van Eck te klein werd om de aangroeiende bijeenkomsten te bevatten, en of er eene andere oorzaak aanleiding toe gaf dat de nederzetters al spoedig in den nazomer van 1847 een eerst kerk-gebouw van loggen hebben opgericht, blijft, onbeantwoord. De grootte van deze blok kerk was 20 × 28 voeten. Dit gebouw werd gebouwd op de boerderij van David A. van Eck, een halve mijl west van de tegenwoor-dige standplaats der kerk.

Alhoewel er nog geen gemeente was georganiseerd, zoo werd er toch door de nederzetters een eenparig beroep [dus genoemd] uitgebracht, want de nood breekt wet. Dit beroep werd gedaan en opgezonden aan Ds. Gerrit Baai, in het Loo, Nederland. De dominé in het Loo gaf een gunstig antwoord op deze roeping, en arriveerde met zijn huisgezin in het voorjaar van 1848 in hun midden, en zette zich metterwoon in het afdak der blok kerk neder, want het kerkgebouw diende voor des leeraars woonhuis niet alleen, maar ook werd er dagelijks school in gehouden.

Ter bezoldiging van de diensten die Ds. G. Baai aan de eerste neder-zetters bewees, ontving hij aardappelen, tarwe en van andere opbrengsten des akkers. Ook werd des leeraars traktement aangevuld door wat er in kwam in een blikken bus door F. Beeuwkes gemaakt en aan den ingang van het kerkgebouw geplaatst. Daarom had ds G. Baai ook op deze bus de tekstwoorden van Galaten 6 : 6 tot opscherping van het geweten zijner lui, geschreven. Het waren wel deze woorden: ,,En die onderwezen wordt in het Woord, deele mede van alle goederen dengenen, die hem onderwijst."

Het was echter zeer treurig dat Ds. G. Baai's verblijf onder deze eerste nederzetters zoo spoedig eindigde, daar de Heere Zijnen getrouwen dienstknecht door den dood van zijn post afloste en opriep tot bezitting van het loon des rechtvaardigen. Hij stierf den 7den November 1849.

Gedurende anderhalf jaar had hij zegenend werkzaam geweest onder de nederzetters, in weerwil van veel moeite en wederwaardigheden en diepe armoede. En, worde het gemeld ter eere van onze Binnenlandsche Zendings Board, dat Dr. Wyckoff, toen ter tijde Secretaris van genoemde Board, Ds. Baai en gezin eens een bezoek bracht, en hen bij die gelegenheid geldelijke ondersteuning verleende. De Evangelie bediening van Ds. Baai in Amerika was zeer kort, nochthans in die korten tijd hadden er vele bekeeringen plaats gehad. Veel goed zaad zaaide hij, en de Heere deed den leeraar hier en daar beginselen leggen, die de zware beproevingen der nederzetters gedurende de volgende vijf jaren konden overleven. Wel is waar Ds. Baai werd in Amerika nooit over eene gemeente als leeraar bevestigd, maar de Heere bevestigde zijn werk . . . .

Het was in 1850 dat het volk alhier verblijd en vereerd werd met een bezoek van dr van Raalte. Bij die gelegenheid werden er kinderen ge-doopt, en het is overgeleverd dat de thans zich noemende Mrs. John Giesbers, de eerste ,,baby" was die in de nederzetting gedoopt werd.

Het gevoelen des volks te Alto was sympathiseerend met de Reformed Church in Amerika. Ds. P. Zonne van Sheboygan County kwam op ver-zoek en poogde herhaaldelijk het volk van dit gevoelen te ontdoen . . . .

Het begin der Gereformeerde gemeente van Alto, Wisconsin, gaat terug tot 1855. In dat jaar is de gemeente in 't leven geroepen door Ds. Bolks, destijds leeraar der Gereformeerde gemeente te Milwaukee, Wisconsin, die daartoe als commissie, van Classiswege, werd aangesteld. De kerkeraad, die toen verkozen werd, bestond uit F. Beeuwkes, en C. Landaal als ouderlingen; en M. Duven en G. Duitman als diakenen.

De pas georganiseerde gemeente verlangde in eigendom te hebben het naast en om de blok kerk liggende land, doch het schijnt dat David A. van Eck, om wat redenen dan ook, niet gewillig was om die vijf akkers te verkoopen. Dit was de aanleidende oorzaak dat er regeling moest worden gemaakt om de standplaats van het kerkgebouw te veranderen. In September 1856 slaagde de gemeente om de standplaats, alwaar thans het nieuwe kerkgebouw op staat – dat op 30 November 1898 ingewijd is – te verkrijgen, bevattende vijf akkers. Deze akkers waren eene gifte van eenige broeders der nieuwe gestichte gemeente. Ten spoedigste werd er een begin gemaakt met het oprichten van een „frame" kerkgebouw 30 × 50 voet, dat in Mei 1857 voltooid was.

Op den 17den Juli 1857 verwelkomde de gemeente Ds. H. Stobbelaar uit Nederland, die zich toen als leeraar onder hen vestigde. Daar natuurlijk de pas gekomene leeraar en gezin behoefte haddan aan een woonhuis, zoo werd er in voorzien door het oprichten van een pastorie 16 × 26 voet.

Ds. H. Stobbelaar heeft met zegen mogen arbeiden gedurende eene bediening van drie jaar en twee maanden. Het getal leden aangenomen, en de som der gemeentelijke bijdragen kan in dit verhaal niet worden gemeld, daar men in de notulen destijds van zulke zaken geen notitie nam. Ds. Stobbelaar was een leeraar die de harten van zijne gemeenteleden meer tot zich won door middel van de scherpe en strenge prediking der volle Waarheid dan door sociaal verkeer onder hen. Op den 6den September 1860 vertrok hij naar Zeeland, Michigan, zijn nieuw arbeidsveld.

Een jaar was de gemeente vacant en toen vestigde zich Ds. M. A. Ypma van de Lage Prairie, Illinois, te Alto. Ook zijne bediening was gelijk die van Ds. G. Baai betrekkelijk kort, daar het den Heere behaagde hem door den dood weg te nemen op den 1sten Mei, 1863. Als kenner aan medicijnen heeft Ds. Ypma veel lijden verzacht, en veler gezondheid bevorderd.

Tusschen het overlijden van Ds. M. A. Ypma en de komst van Ds. R. Pieters, werd de gemeente tot aller voldoening bearbeid door Ds. J. H. Karsten, die pas tot de heilige bediening was geordend, en onder aanstelling der Board van Buitenlandsche Zending gereed stond om, indien een open veld kon verkregen worden, als zendeling naar Afrika te gaan. Toen het jaar van Ds. Karstens gemeentelijke werkzaamheden ten einde was, aanvaarde Ds. R. Pieters van Drenthe, Michigan als herder en leeraar der gemeente Alto. Bij afwachting van zijne komst werden beide het kerkgebouw en de pastorie door den verfkwast opgeknapt. Kort na de intree van den leeraar werden er paardenstallen gebouwd, en het volgend jaar eene gemeentelijke school opgericht. Terwijl Ds. R. Pieters de Nationale District School voorstond en als een zegen der natie beschouwde, was het toch zijne uitgesproken overtuiging, dat de lagere school dan eerst volledig en voldoende is, voor kinderen van het belijdend Christendom, wanneer zij onder den invloed van Christelijke beginselen staan. . . .

Al spoedig nadat Ds. R. Pieters naar Holland, Michigan, vertrok, is de gemeente geslaagd Rev. J. H. Karsten als leeraar te verkrijgen, die dus in 1869 zijne lange gezegende bediening gedurende eene reeks van dertien en half jaar, aanving. Hoopvol was de toekomst! De verwachtingen der gemeente werden verwezenlijkt.

Het was in het najaar van 1876 en in 't begin van 1877 dat de Heere speciale stroomen Zijns Geestes op den akker – de gemeente – uitgoot. Veel zaad dat lang verborgen was blijven liggen, ontkiemde. Er was wasdom in het genade leven. Vruchten – gewonnen zielen voor Koning Jezus – werden geplukt. Zielen, waarvan het meerendeel de plaats in de strijdende met de overwinnende Kerk hebben verwisseld, alwaar het volmaakte wordt genooten. Wat anders is het hoogste doel van arbeid in de Gemeente Gods dan zielen te winnen voor den Meester?

In Rev. J. H. Karsten bezat het volk een getrouw getuige van Ds. Heeren waarheid, en genoot hem als eenen zorgdragenden herder. Zijn opvolger tot dit veld was Rev. James F. Zwemer, van Spring Lake, Michigan. De gemeente was blij om in bezit van zulk eenen waardigen opvolger te komen. In afwachting van zijn komst, werden in het kerkgebouw de gangen, enz. met tapijt verzien en het houdwerk geverfd. Nadat hij zijn dienstwerk aanvaarde, werden nieuwe lampen en een „chapel organ" aangekocht.

Onder de leiding van Rev. Zwemer als Superintendent, nam de Alto Sabbatsschool een aanvang, en het bestuur er van werd aan den Kerkenraad opgedragen.

Rev. Zwemer genoot hier, zoo wel als elders, zegen in zijn arbeids veld, en de vervullingen van des Heeren beloften aan Zijn volk werden met vreugde gesmaakt.

Achtereenvolgens stierven er vele pioneers, onder het getal ook Albertus Meenk, de eerste nederzetter.

In hetzelfde jaar, 1886, dat Rev. Zwemer Alto verliet, werd Rev. J. W. te Winkel over deze gemeente bevestigd. De opkomsten tot de eerediensten waren zeer bemoedigend. De zitbanken ondergingen eenige noodige veranderingen. Gedurende zijne werkzaamheden te Alto, werd er onder de Hollandsche huisgezinnen te Waupun, Wisconsin, door hem zendings-arbeid begonnen, dat gezegentlijk voortging tot het organiseeren van eene Gereformeerde gemeente . . . .

Na eene afwezigheid van zeven jaren werd de gemeente en haren vorigen leeraar, Rev. J. H. Karsten, weer samen gebracht. Zij betoonde bij zijne komst door daden hare blijdschap in de hereeniging, welk wederkeerig was.

De hervatting van zijn dienstwerk alhier kenmerkt zich in den aankoop van zitbanken voor het gebouw, dat tijdens Ds. Pieters bediening werd gebruikt voor eene kerkelijke school, maar nu diende voor teacher's meetings, bidvergaderingen en kerkeraads zittingen en tevens catechisatie. Gedurende deze bediening werd een groot doelmatig pijporgel uit de tweede hand van de St. James Episcopaalsche gemeente te Milwaukee gekocht, en naast den kansel geplaatst. En in den toren kwam een bel. Beide bel en pijporgel, hetwelk nu nieuw versierd is door eenen bekwamen schilder, doen dienst in het onlangs ingewijd kerkgebouw.

Al voor jaren waren er enkele Hollandsche gezinnen woonachtig te Randolph Centre, twintig mijlen van Alto verwijderd, die nochthans hun kerkelijk tehuis bij de gemeente Alto hadden. Maar in 1890 nam hun getal sterkte door emigratie zoo zeer toe, dat Rev. Karsten en zijn kerkeraad plannen beraamden in hunne godsdienstige behoeften te voorzien. Wat deze plannen waren, kunnen wij door gebrek aan plaatsruimte, hier niet melden.

De leeraar, die voor de laatste vier en een half jaar te Alto heeft mogen arbeiden, is Rev. Henry Harmeling, de schrijver van deze korte geschiedenis. Toen hij zijn dienstwerk hier begon, telden de huisgezinnen, volgens Classis statistiek van 1894, honderd en vijftien. De laatste opgave meldde het getal als honderd acht en vijftig. Deze toeneming in ledental en de groote opkomsten tot de openbare godsdiensten, mag op gewezen worden als eene der oorzaken, waarom het door de gemeente noodig werd geoordeeld een nieuw kerkgebouw te zetten. Dat de gemeentelijke bezittingen in de verloopene vier jaren vermeerderd en verbeterd zijn, zien wij uit de opsomming der volgende feiten: Eene nieuwe pastorie, naar den hedendaagschen stijl van bouw, doelmatig en prachtig ingericht, ruim $ 2,000 kostende.

Een nieuw kerkgebouw dat circa acht duizend dollars heeft gekost. De stijl en bouworde van 't nieuwe gebouw is een wijziging van de „English-Gothic style." Het gebouw bevat een groot „octagonaal auditorium" met twee toegangen. De zitbanken in het schip der kerk zijn in „circular" vorm, met het preekgestoelte in het midden van het „radius." De vloer is hellend. Dus wordt er van de zitbanken een goed uitzicht naar den preekstoel gegeven. Achter de preekstoel is een „choir loft", waar ook het pijporgel staat. De voornaamste van de twee toegangen der kerk is ruim, en heeft genoegzame plaats als „wardrobe" voor „overcoats and wraps." Met het auditorium is verbonden door middel van „Wilson's Patent Rolling partitions," een Zondagsschoollokaal, zitplaats hebbende voor 150. Boven dit lokaal is een galerij ook met dezelfde patent ophaal-deuren verbonden met het auditorium. En in het achterste gedeelte van 't gebouw is eene consistorie- en catechiseerkamer met een toegang tot den kansel. Het gebouw wordt verwarmd door middel van een groot „brick cased" fornuis. De verlichting geschied door middel van een „acytelene gas plant" in het basement . . . .

Dat in de laatste vier jaren de gemeentelijke bezittingen vermeerd en verbeterd zijn, zien wij uit de opsomming der volgende feiten: Eene nieuwe pastorie, prachtig en zeer doelmatig ingericht, kostende ruim $ 2,000; een kerkgebouw dat iets over de $ 8,000 kost en ingericht naar aller smaak. Het architectuur is het werk van de heeren van Rijn en de Gelleke van Milwaukee, Wisconsin.

Maar deze financieele vooruitgang zou op het geestelijk terrein der gemeente ontmoedigend zijn, zoo men er niet naast kon zetten eene ootmoedige berekening van den geestelijken toestand der gemeente. Tijdens de bediening van den tegenwoordigen leeraar zijn er twee en negentig leden aangenomen. Gode zij de eer en dank toegebracht.

Chapter XXII

EMIGRANT JOURNEYS TO WISCONSIN

71. JACOB QUINTUS' A BACKWARD GLANCE

[Quintus emigrated to America from Zeeland in 1946. For a short time he lived in Buffalo, but soon moved to Sheboygan, Wisconsin, where he founded the first Dutch newspaper in this country, *De Sheboygan Nieuwsbode*. This autobiographical sketch entitled *Een Terugblik over Vijftig Jaren*, written in 1897, was printed in *De Grondwet*, November 21, 1911. Quintus died in Grand Rapids, Michigan, in 1902.]

Op den 16den October 1849 is het eerste nummer in 't licht verschenen der eerste Hollandsche courant in deze Vereenigde Staten van Noord Amerika, en ik heb de eer van dat blad – *De Sheboygan Nieuwsbode* genaamd – de redacteur en uitgever geweest te zijn, te Sheboygan, in den staat Wisconsin.

Eenige dagen na die verschijning ontving ik van eenen hooggeachten vriend, die ik te Albany, New York, gedurende mijn eenjarig verblijf aldaar had leeren kennen, en die tot de afstammelingen der eerste Hollandsche nederzetters der stad New York, of liever gezegd, Nieuw Amsterdam, behoorde, en op zijne manier ouderwetsch Hollandsch sprak, eenen brief, in welken hij mij de indrukken mededeelde, die de landverhuizing uit Nederland naar deze gewesten van over vijftig jaren op hem maakten en tot welke landverhuizers van dien tijd velen uwer, of uwe ouders, met mij behooren. Deze indrukken en opmerkingen – nu eene halve eeuw oud – weder te geven en in herinnering te brengen is het doel van deze beknopte voordracht.

In 't voorbijgaan zij hier echter gezegd, dat ik nog niet juist vijftig jaren in Amerika ben, want op den 4den Augustus 1847 in een zeilschip van Rotterdam afgevaren, lagen wij in den morgen van den 7den Augustus op 't strand aan de Fransche kust voor de stad Calais vergezeld van onze hier tegenwoordige eerzame, vrienden ouderling Frans van Driele, diaken Johan A. S. Verdier, mijn neef Professor Marten Luther d'Ooge, van de Michigan Universiteit, en anderen, en zij kunnen getuigen hoe ik daar uit de Fransche taal driemaal heb gepredikt in het Hollandsch, ten aanhooren der vergaderde gemeente en onzer mede schipbreukelingen.

Neerland's geliefden dichter zingt in een zijner meesterstukken: Tafereel van de Overwintering van de Hollanders op Nova Zembla, in de jaren 1596 en 1597:

Maar, eerst den dag gevierd en God den Heer geloofd!
Zij slaan den Bijbel op, ontblooten allen 't hoofd;
Een hunner, beurt om beurt, met eerbied opgerezen,
Staat uit Gods Heilig Woord een roerend stuk te lezen;
Of aller ziel en zang smelt luidkeels zich ineen,
En Nova Zembla hoort de Psalmen van Datheen.

En het is de vraag, mijne toehoorders, of zij zongen met meer geest-
drift en een inniger gevoel van dankbaarheid aan God, dan wij als geredde
emigranten uit volle borst en ruim een honderd keelen Hollandsche
psalmen zongen in die Fransche Wesleyaansche kerk te Calais, op dien
voor ons gedenkwaardigen Zondagmorgen, 8 Augustus 1947.

Den 18den Augustus voeren wij van Calais naar Havre, en den 25sten
Augustus met een ander zeilschip van daar naar New York waar wij den
28sten September aan wal stapten. Doch ik mag niet verder hierover
spreken.

Wat waren de aanleidende oorzaken eener hernieuwde verhuizing uit
Nederland? Eene scheuring of afscheiding had plaats van de heerschende
Kerk, hetzij met eene gelijke partij of om goede en voldoende redenen,
hetwelk nu niet te beoordeelen valt. Het gouvernement ging onbezon-
nen te werk, hetwelk ieder gouvernement, zelfs ons eigen, bij geval doen
zou, en hadden zij niet gedwaald, misschien had de landverhuizing waarvan hier sprake is geen plaats gegrepen.

Zich aan de heerschende Kerk houdende, nadat verscheidene andere
plannen waren ontworpen en verijdeld, en om de scheuring tegen te
gaan, werd eene oude wet van Napoleon in wezen geroepen, makende
het verzamelen van meer dan een zeer klein getal personen, twintig —
tot einden niet in de wet vermeld, eene samenrotting, en onderworpen
aan het gezag der politie. Onder deze ongerijmdheid van het despotisme
werden de godsdienstige bijeenkomsten der afgescheidenen verhinderd,
verontrust, en tegen gegaan. Gelijk het immer in de geschiedenis der
wereld was en altijd zal zijn, blaasde deze vervolging de smeulende kolen
in vlam, en de Hollanders, die zooals zij dachten, om eene gewetenszaak
leden, besloten een land te gaan zoeken, waar plaats en gezag genoeg was
voor het geloof.

In 't eerst, schreef mijn vriend, kwamen er enkelen over, en deze waren
arme en nederige menschen. Zij hadden dezelfde beweegreden die hen
aanzette, welke die vermaarde mannen in het jaar 1620 naar Plymouth
voerde. In New York aankomende, vonden zij tot hunne verwondering,
vrienden die namen droegen gelijk de hunne, onder welke vele eene taal
spraken, slechts zoo veel van hunne spraak verschillende, als de oude

van de nieuwe. En nu was de wezenlijke voortgang en het spoor tot de landverhuizing daar. De brieven naar huis gewaagden van een voorspoedig land en een welkom, van beloonden arbeid, van goedkoop voedsel, van vrienden die met hen konden spreken en door hen verstaan worden, van consistories en domines, van Hollandsche namen en eene Hollandsche kerk.

Toen nam de verhuizing toe, niet alleen van de Afgescheidenen, maar ook van de oude Kerk, van elke gezindte en van alle ambten. En van jaar tot jaar zond Nederland naar ons land, deszelfs gouvernement er in berustende, doch niet goedkeurende, hare zonen en dochteren; dus, na eenen geregelden Rip van Winkle slaap van twee eeuwen, het voorbeeld volgende van de passagiers der *Halve Maan.*

Aardig en in 't oogloopend waren inderdaad de kleeding en versierselen der landverhuizers. In vele dingen geleken zij de volmaakste verwezenlijking van al de vertelsels der oude tijden, welke sommigen onzer hebben mogen hooren. Zij brachten meubels, kleeding, en sieraden mede, zoo als nog te zien zijn in oude huizen in Albany en Ulster en in sommige huizen dicht bij New York. Zij spraken dezelfde taal welke wij in onze kindsche dagen hebben gehoord uit den mond van oude menschen, die niets anders wilden zijn dan Dutch. Het kopje en schoteltje in miniatuur, de voetstoof, de Bijbel, deze waren door ons weggeborgen als heilige overblijfselen uit het verledene; al deze dingen hadden zij in bezit. De kleederen die zij droegen, waren dezelfde als wij konden zien op oude familie portretten, wier kleur en verguld van ouderdom verschoten waren. Onze oude vrienden konden gemeenzaam met hen spreken en het eenige verschil dat zij in ons gesprek in hunne taal vonden, was, dat wij woorden gebruikten, die bij hen dood en versleten waren. Onze Hollandsche taal had stil gestaan sedert de 17de eeuw; de hunne was gefatsoeneerd, verdraaid, en veranderd door den scepter en het voorbeeld der Franschen, door gemeenschap met Engeland, en door het verkeer met naburige plaatsen.

Dit groote aantal Hollanders verhuisde westwaarts, na een verblijf van eenige maanden in de steden, naar de kolonien welke zij hebben gevestigd in Michigan, Wisconsin, en Iowa. Die welke nu komen, gaan gewoonlijk door. Weinige blijven in de steden. Zij zijn, als een algemeen onderscheidingsteeken voorbeeldig matig en eerlijk. Tot dusver heb ik, ofschoon veel met hen omgegaan hebbende, nog niemand gevonden of hij kon lezen en schrijven, en de meesten hunner bezitten eenen Bijbel. Dat zwakheden en dwalingen, ondankbaarheid, ontevredenheid, en hardnekkigheid van natuur ook onder hen wonen, ontken ik niet, doch

ik bedoel den aard over 't algemeen, en deze is, van eene bijzondere gehoorzaamheid aan wet en orde in den volsten zin des woords. Zulk eenen
goeden naam hadden de Hollanders in Amerika vijftig jaren geleden.
Hebben zij dien opgehouden?

72. JAN W. BOSMAN'S MY EXPERIENCES

[Bosman, a tailer, left Gelderland in 1856, settling first in Milwaukee, next in Grand
Rapids, and finally in Holland where he died. Published in *De Grondwet*, Februari 13, 1912,
this sketch bore the title "*Ervaringen van Jan W. Bosman*"]

Afkomstig uit den Achterhoek van Gelderland, buurschap Kleinbredenbroek, gemeente Gendringen, was ik de tweede zoon van vader's
tweede huwelijk. Uit dat huwelijk werden geboren vijf jongens en één
meisje. Mijn moeder was zwak, en met een vijftal jongens, daar was heel
wat mede te doen. De boksen en buizen, gemaakt van pield of Engelsch
leer, zooals het genoemd werd, waren spoedig versleten. Zoo was het
moeder's wensch dat een harer jongens kleermaker werd. Ik liet me dat
welgevallen, en toen ik na twaalf jaren niet meer naar school ging, kwam
ik bij mijn eersten baas, in het laatst van het jaar 1842. In het jaar 1843
stierf mijn goede moeder.

Ik bleef bij het vak. Het was wel wat moeilijk, want het was een veracht
vak. Allerhande mooie namen werden hen gegeven:

Snieder, snieder, jik jak;
Steelt de boer de lappen af.

De gewoonte was dat de snieders met hun pers-ijzer bij boer en burger
aan huis gingen werken. Nu was dat zoo kwaad niet, want ons voorrecht
was dan ook om bij welgestelde boeren of burgers, bij mijnheer en
mevrouw, aan een extra tafel te mogen zitten, en van het beste te nuttigen.

De gewoonte was, om des morgens tusschen zes en zeven bij de boer
te zijn. Des middags had men een uur schofttijd, en dan tot 's avonds
zeven of acht, ja, soms tot negen uur toe liet men ons maar werken; en
als men dan gegeten had, dan werd de deur opengedaan en de snieder
er uit en de hond er in gelaten, om zijn maal te krijgen. Het loon voor
de baas was dertig Hollandsche centen per dag, en voor de knechts drie,
vier of vijf stuivers.

Nadat ik aldus bij drie bazen kleermakers gewerkt had, achtte ik mij
bekwaam om zelf baas te gaan spelen, met hetwelk ik goed succes had.

Nadat ik drie à vier jaren alzoo gewerkt had, begon ik te denken om
mijn lot te verbeteren, en dacht, het is niet goed dat de mensch alleen zij.
Maar dat ging niet zoo gemakkelijk in dien tijd bij ons. Er waren geen

huizen te bekomen, en om te bouwen daar was ik te arm voor; dat kon niet. Maar de Heere bestuurt alle dingen. Bij zekere gelegenheid was ik bij mijn halfzuster. Zij zeide haar man was in het dorp Varseveld geweest, en had gehoord, dat daar een man was overleden, nalatende een jeugdige weduwe, geen kinderen en een eigen woning. Ik luisterde goed, en spoedig daarna liet ik mij bij die weduwe zien. Die mijn vrouw gekend hebben, weten dat ze veel beter bespraakt was dan ik, en zoo was het akkoord spoedig gesloten. Mijn vrouw's naam was Hendrika Wilmina Schuurman, en den 20sten Juni, 1853, werd ons huwelijk ingezegend.

Toen wij anderhalf jaar getrouwd waren, vertrok mijn vrouw's broer naar Amerika. Hij was ook arm, zoo als wij allen waren. Hij leende geld van den boer waar hij het laatst voor werkte, en vertrok, hoewel ik en de geheele familie het hem afraadde.

Binnen het jaar stuurde hij het geleende geld terug, en zeide, dat hij nog eenige dollars over had. Ik begon toen te zien dat Amerika zoo geen kwaad land was, zoo als sommigen in dien tijd wel meenden, en ik zeide tegen mijn vrouw, wij moeten ook maar naar Amerika gaan. Dat beviel eerst maar slecht, en buurman Heusinkveld moest komen om mij toch te waarschuwen en het mij uit het hoofd te praten.

Het duurde echter maar kort of mijn vrouw was gewillig om te gaan. Wij gingen naar den notaris, ons huis werd geadverteerd en verkocht, en den 25sten April, 1856, gingen wij met een schip, de *Revenue* genaamd, van Rotterdam op reis naar Amerika. Het was een Amerikaansch schip, niet groot en ook niet bestemd voor het vervoer van menschen; maar er waren in der haast wat ruwe hokken in opgeslagen, waar men in kon liggen.

Den 25sten April, des avonds, gingen wij aan boord. Het was haast niet geschikt voor menschen; er was zulk een sterke reuk in het tusschendek, dat mijn vrouw in het eerst dacht, het er niet in te kunnen uithouden. Het was verre van een gemakkelijke reis, met twee kinderen; de oudste 22 maanden en de jongste 4 maanden oud. Doch de Heere God zorgde. Er was een jonge deern uit Winterswijk, Henrika Sikkink, die geen familie had en zoo de reis met ons mede deed. Die was door den makelaar, van wien wij onze biljetten gekocht hadden, bij ons aanbevolen om mede voor haar te zorgen, en o, wonder, wat hebben wij een hulp van dat meisje genoten.

Op 26 April, des morgens, toen wij uit onze kooi kwamen, waren wij al eenige roeden van het strand verwijderd, zoodat wij er niet meer af konden. Ons schip wer voortgetrokken, ja, ik weet niet meer hoe, maar wij voeren zachtjes voort.

Te Hellevoetsluis bleven wij een korten tijd voor anker liggen, en enkelen begaven zich toen met een roeiboot naar land, ten einde een flesch foezel, of jenever, of zoo iets, aan te koopen.

Nadat het anker geligt en wij ons op het ruime sop bevonden, ging het eerst goed vooruit. De kapitein, stuurlui en matrozen waren allen Engelschen. De scheepstimmerman was een Duitscher, daar konden wij mee praten, en hij zeide, als het zoo vooruit blijft gaan, zijn wij in twee weken in New-York.

Wij waren met ruim honderd passagiers in het tusschendek, en in de kajuit was Ds. P. J. Oggel, met twee broers en ééne zuster. Hij is later professor aan Hope College geweest. Zijn eerste gemeente was Grand Haven, waar hij toen een roeping van had.

Zoo als ik zeide, ging het eerst voorspoedig, maar later kwamen stormen en tegenwinden; menigmaal werd ons scheepje door de golven overdekt. Dat er dan geschrei en gekerm gehoord werd, begrijpt men gereedelijk.

Eens op een Zondag was er een zeer sterke wind en erg ruwe zee. In het midden van het schip raakte een zeil los; het was het eenigste dat toen in gebruik was; de anderen waren opgerold. Het raakte los aan een kant, en het fladderde en trok ons zeilschip zoo sterk op zij, dat wij dachten dat het zou omslaan. Wij dachten dat is het laatste. Mijn vrouw in haar verlegenheid greep de kinderen en kleedde ze, trok hen de beste schoentjes aan, net of ze met de kinderen uit moest gaan. Wellicht op het gebed van den een of andere vrome, redde de Heere God en deed de storm bedaren. Alhoewel wij Ds. Oggel aan boord hadden, zoo hebben wij toch geen godsdienst aan boord gehad, behalve eens; bij de begrafenis van een kind deed de dominee de dienst. Hij was zwak en veel zeeziek.

Ons eten was maar mager; des middags was het 't beste; anders werd ons harde scheepsbeschuit toegediend, zoo hard dat wij heet water moesten bedelen om het te kunnen weeken en te kunnen gebruiken, want water was er niet te overvloedig aan boord. Zoo voeren wij voort tot wij nabij New York zijnde een loods aan boord kregen, die ons met 's Heeren hulp in de haven van New York bracht.

Toen waren wij blijde en opgeruimd en wij beloofden onszelven, zoodra wij aan land waren een goed maal eten. In de haven zijnde werden wij en onze kisten overgeladen op een platboot, en toen werd die aan wal gezet en konden wij Castle Garden binnen gaan. Ons werden onderscheidene vragen gedaan; hoe oud, waar vandaan, hoeveel geld wij bij ons hadden, enz.

Een treffend voorval gebeurde hier. Een oud man bij ons aan boord, en ook bij ons van daan, was op zee door het slechte eten verzwakt. Met twee man werd hij ondersteund om van de platboot in Castle Garden te komen en daar stierf hij.

Wij en eenige anderen gingen in de stad; de meesten bleven in Castle Garden. Met behulp van Ds. Oggel vonden wij een Duitsch hotel. Daar kregen wij wat wij ons voorgesteld hadden – een goed maal eten. Den anderen dag werden wij met een stoomboot een eind weggesleept en toen op den trein gedaan. Het was een Hollander, die ons terecht hielp en ons waarschuwde om hoofd en handen binnen te houden, omdat wij anders gevaar liepen ons zeer te doen. Het was alles behalve een gemakkelijke wagon, maar wij reden toch, wel zeer langzaam, maar toch vooruit.

Op Zaterdagnacht kwamen wij te Cleveland, en daar moesten wij stil liggen over Zondag – een goede gewoonte, die nu reeds lang is afgeschaft. Wij vonden daar Hollandsche vrienden, die wij ook in Nederland gekend hadden. Die deden hun best om ons daar te houden. Wij luisterden hier in het eerst wel naar, omreden ons oudste kind erg ziek was. Maar wij hadden ons reisbiljet betaald tot Milwaukee, Wis., en zoo zetten wij Maandagmorgen onze reis voort.

De steden die wij aandeden waren Toledo en Detroit, en zoo sukkelden wij voort tot Chicago. Wij hadden onze reis betaald om met het spoor te reizen, omdat wij dachten, toen wij eerst weer aan land waren, dat wij vooreerst genoeg hadden van het water. Maar, te Chicago deden ze ons in een boot, bij de paarden. De boot vertrok 's avonds en des morgens waren wij te Milwaukee.

Het was reeds bij de weinige Hollanders bekend, dat er emigranten kwamen, en wij vonden op de pier enkele Hollanders, en met behulp van die vrienden, werden onze kisten op een wagen geladen, die ons naar „den Hollandschen berg" bracht. Mijn vrouw en ik, ieder met een kind op den arm, volgden den wagen. Dat wij moei en afgemat waren, kunnen allen wel begrijpen, want het was in Juni en het weer was warm. Er was een man, met name Scheevel, die bood ons aan om ons goed in zijn afdak of houthok te doen, en om dan naar een woning uit te zien. En zoo gedaan. In het houthok sliepen wij een nacht en vonden toen kamers bij Mrs. Doornink, die later te Grand Rapids gewoond hebben en daar overleden zijn.

Eerst was ik een paar weken ziek. Ik had kou opgedaan en moest een dokter hebben. Derk Doornink stond ons goed bij met raad en daad.

Eerst beproefde ik werk te vinden met kleermaken, maar dat wilde maar slecht vlotten. Toen zeiden eenige vrienden, ik moest mijn vak maar laten varen; zij wilden mij helpen. Goed gemeend. Zij werkten waar brandhout met een machine gezaagd en dan gespleten moest worden. Ik zou met hen gaan omdat ook te doen $ 1 daags was het loon, en ik, of wij, dachten, $ 1, dat is 2 gulden en 50 cents Hollandsch, dus in korten tijd rijk.

Ik ging er met de vrienden op af. Maar ik was altijd kleermaker geweest en had nooit een bijl gehanteerd; 't gevolg was, dat de baas, die 's middags eens kwam kijken, mij 50 cents gaf en verklaarde mij niet te kunnen gebruiken. Dat was een teleurstelling. Maar de Heere God wist beter wat goed voor ons was. Die vrienden hadden de gewoonte om wat sterker stof te gebruiken dan water, en had ik bij hen gebleven, zou dat wellicht slechte gevolgen kunnen hebben.

Aldus weggestuurd slenterde ik door de stad, en trof een kleerwinkel aan en bleef daar een poosje staan te kijken. Slechts kort stond ik daar, of een Israëliet stapt op mij toe, met de vraag: „Of ich kleiden wolte kauffen?" Ik antwoordde: „Nein, ich wolte arbeid haben." „Sind sie ein snijder?" vroeg hij hierop, waarop ik „ja" antwoordde. En, daar kreeg ik werk, en heb sedert altijd werk in overvloed gehad. Het loon was wel niet zoo als nu, maar wij waren tevreden.

Na vier maanden in Milwaukee gewerkte te hebben, kwam Hendrik Doornink uit Grand Rapids te Milwaukee, en die zoch een kleermakers-knecht. Hij beloofde mij $ 4 in de week van midden October tot Mei. Wij namen dat aan, en kwamen 18 October 1856, te Grand Rapids aan. De tijden waren toen slecht, het was juist in de geldcrisis, en zoo heb ik meer dan drie jaren voor $ 4 in de week moeten werken. Maar wij hadden het goed; de Heere God zorgde zoodat ons niets ontbrak.

Ik moet een weinig terug en weer naar Milwaukee. Wij waren gewoon ook in Nederland om trouw ter kerk te gaan, maar naar de Nederlandsch Hervormde. Daar werd ons zoo niet aangezegd, wat de mensch is van natuur, en wat er met de mensch moet gebeuren zal hij getroost kunnen leven en zalig sterven. En het was onder de prediking van Rev. Bolks dat mijn oogen open gingen en ik te zien kreeg, dat de mensch bij brood alleen niet kan leven, maar bij alle woord dat uit den mond des Heeren is uitgegaan. Het tijdelijke hadden wij gezocht, en de Heere God heeft ons uit genade in hope het eeuwige geschonken.

TRANSLATION

I was born in the Achterhoek of Gelderland, at Kleinbredenbroek in the commune of Gendringen. I was the second son of my father's second marriage.

Of that marriage were born five boys and one girl. My mother did not enjoy good health, and to take care of five boys was a hard task for her. They quickly wore out their trousers and stockings which were made of English leather. Hence mother's wish that one of her boys should become a tailor. I agreed to this and when twelve years old and I no longer went to school I began to work for my first master, in the latter part of 1842. My good mother died in 1843.

I continued my work as a tailor. This was not exactly easy, for the tailor's profession was a despised one. All manner of cutting things were said about tailors:

> *Tailor, oh tailor! snip, snip:*
> *Stealing the farmer's cloths!*

It was customary for tailors to work with their pressing irons and other tools at the homes of farmers and burghers. This was not a bad idea, for it was a privilege for us to sit at an extra table in the homes of well-to-do farmers or burghers, or for my lord or my lady, and enjoy the best.

Usually we arrived at the farmer's house ready for work at 6 or 7 in the morning. At 12 we had an hour's free period. After that they let us work until 7 or 8 in the evening, sometimes as late as 9 o'clock. Then after we had had our dinner the door was opened, the tailor departed and the family's dog was let in for his meal. Wages of the master were 30 Dutch cents per day; apprentices earned 3, 4, or 5 cents a day.

After I had worked in this way for three masters, I thought I was ready to play the part of a master, in which I was quite successful.

After working 3 or 4 years in this manner I began to think how I could improve my lot. I began to think that it was not well for man to be alone. But this was not a matter easily arranged among us at that time. No house could be had, and I was too poor to build one; this was out of the question. But the Lord directs all things. On a certain occasion I was at my half-sister's. She told me that her husband had been in the village of Varseveld and had heard that a certain man had died leaving a youthful widow, with no children, and having a house of her own. I listened carefully, and before long I called upon the widow. Those who have known my wife can attest that she was more ready with words than I was, and so we came to a speedy decision. My wife's name was Hendrika Wilmina Schuurman. Our marriage was blessed on June 20, 1853.

After we had been married for a year and a half my wife's brother emigrated to America. He, too, was poor, like all the rest of us. He borrowed money from the farmer for whom he worked last, and departed in spite of the fact that I and all his relatives advised him not to leave.

Before the end of one year he returned all the money he had borrowed and wrote that he still had some dollars left. Then I began to see that America was not so bad a country as some at that time thought, and I said to my wife: "We, too, must go to America."

She did not approve of this idea. And our neighbour Heusinkveld was asked by her, to caution me and talk me out of my plans.

It was not long, however, until my wife, too, was willing to go to America. We went to a notary, our house was advertised and sold, and on April 25, 1856, we left on our journey to America, in the *Revenue*, sailing from Rotterdam. This was a small American ship, not equipped to transport human beings. But they hastily erected some rude shelters, in which we were to sleep.

We went on board on April 25, in the evening. Our quarters were hardly fit for passengers. Such was the stench below deck, that my wife's first thought was that she could not stand it. This was no easy voyage with two children, the oldest 22 months, the youngest 4 months. But the Lord provided. A young orphaned girl from Winterswijk, Henrika Sikkink, accompanied us. She had been recommended to us by the agent who had sold us our tickets. That girl helped us very much.

On April 26, in the morning, when we came out of our cabin, we had moved some distance from the dock, so that it would have been impossible for us to go ashore. Our ship was slowly drawn forward; how this was done I do not recall.

We lay at anchor for a short time at Hellevoetsluis. Some of the passengers went ashore in a rowboat in order to buy a bottle of gin or something like it.

After the anchor was drawn up and we put out to sea, we made good progress. The captain, steersmen, and sailors were English. The ship's carpenter was a German. We were able to talk with him, and he declared that if progress continued at this rate we would be in New York within two weeks.

There were fully 100 passengers between decks. Dominie Pieter J. Oggel with two brothers and one sister had secured passage in the cabin. Later the dominie became a professor at Hope College. His first charge was the church in Grand Haven to which at that moment he had been called.

As I remarked above, all went prosperously at first, but later we had storms and contrary winds. Our small vessel frequently was engulfed by the sea. On such occasions one heard groans and anguished cries as one can readily understand.

One Sunday we had strong winds and a rough sea. A sail in the middle of the ship became loose. It was the only sail in use at that moment, the others being furled. Torn loose on one end, its fluttering drew the ship over on one side. We thought the ship would capsize and that this was our last. My wife, not knowing what else to do seized our children and clothed them, put on their best shoes, just as if she was to go for a walk with the children. Most likely, in answer to the prayer of one or other pious passenger, the Lord God spared us and caused the storm to abate. Although Dominie Oggel was aboard with us we had no regular religious services on our ship, except once at the bural of a child when the dominie led the service. The dominie was weak physically and suffered much from seasickness.

Our food was of meager quality. Dinner was best, at other times we were served hard ship biscuit. This was so hard that we had to ration hot water with which to soak it so that we could eat it, for water was not plentiful on board our ship. In this way we sailed until we were near New York when a pilot came aboard who with the Lord's help guided our ship into the harbor.

Then we were glad and filled with joy; we promised ourselves a good meal as soon as we set foot on land. Our boxes and trunks were trans-ferred to a flatboat. When these boxes were put on shore we were per-mitted to enter Castle Garden. We were asked various questions: How old we were; our place of origin; how much money we carried; and about other matters.

A touching incident happened here. An aged man, from our part of Gelderland, who traveled with us and had lost much strength because of the poor food was brought from the flatboat into Castle Garden sup-ported by two men. He died at Castle Garden.

Accompanied by several other traveling companions, we went into the city, but most of the passengers stayed in Castle Garden. With Dominie Oggels's help we found a German hotel. There we obtained what we had promised ourselves – a good meal. The next day we were drawn a distance by a steamship after which we were put on a train. Some Hollander who advised us in all these things warned us to keep our heads and hands inside the car, in order to prevent accidents. Our car was not a comfortable one; but we were satisfied, for we were on our way albeit slowly.

On Saturday night we arrived in Cleveland, where we had to stop for Sunday – an excellent custom now a long time ago discontinued. There we found Dutch friends whom we had known back in the Netherlands. They did their best to keep us in Cleveland. At first we listened to their suggestions, because our oldest child was sick. But we had paid for our ticket to Milwaukee, Wisconsin, and accordingly on Monday morning resumed our journey.

We stopped at a number of cities – Toledo and Detroit – and slowly traveled on to Chicago. We had paid our fare to travel by rail because we had enough of travel by water. But in Chicago they put us in a boat among the horses. The boat sailed in the evening and the following morning we arrived in Milwaukee.

It was known among the small number of Hollanders in Milwaukee that some Dutch immigrants were coming. Some Hollanders were standing on the pier. Our boxes were loaded on a wagon and, advised and helped by friends, we were brought to "de Hollandsche Berg" (Dutch Hill). My wife and myself, each carrying an infant in our arms, followed the wagon. That we arrived tired and exhausted everybody will understand, for it was June, and the weather was hot. A man named Scheevel offered to place our baggage in his shed and to help us find a place to live. The first night we slept in his woodshed. Then we found rooms at Mrs. Doornink's, mother of Hendrik and Derk Doornink, who later lived in Grand Rapids and died there. The first few weeks I was ill, for I had contracted a cold and had to have a doctor. Derk Doornink helped us much, not only with good advice, but also in practical ways.

At first I tried to find work as a tailor, but with little success. Some friends suggested that I abandon my craft and they would help me. This advice was well intended. They were employed at a place where firewood was being sawn by a machine, after which it had to be split. I was to accompany them to my new job. I was to earn $ 1 a day. We had the idea that $ 1 a day amounted to 2.50 guilders Dutch, which rate of pay soon would make us well-to-do.

But I had always been a tailor and had never wielded an axe. The result was that the boss, who at noon came to take a look at our work, gave me 50 cents and told me he could not use me. That was a disappointment. But the Lord God knew better what was good for us. Those friends were in the habit of consuming drink stronger that water, and had I continued with them, I probably would have suffered evil consequence.

Thus discharged, I sauntered through the city, saw a clothing store and stopped to look at it. I had not been looking very long before an

Israelite approached and asked [in German] whether I wanted to buy clothes? I replied: "Nein, ich wolte Arbeid haben". "Sind Sie ein Schneider?" he asked, to which I responded: "Ja." Then and there I had work, and ever since that time I had work aplenty. Wages were not as good as at present, but we were content with what we earned.

After I had worked four months in Milwaukee Hendrik Doornink came from Grand Rapids. He was looking for a tailor's apprentice. He promised to pay me $ 4 per week from the middle of October to May. We accepted his offer, and came to Grand Rapids on October 18, 1856. Times were difficult, for that was a time of money crisis; and I had to work more than three years for $ 4 a week. But we got along well, for the Lord God cared for us so that we lacked nothing.

I must retrace my steps back to Milwaukee. We were in the habit,while in the Netherlands, to attend the Netherlands Reformed Church faithfully. But in that church we were not told what kind of being man was and what must happen to him if he is to live in peace and die in the way of salvation. Hearing the sermons of Dominie Seine Bolks, my eyes were opened and I came to see that man cannot live by bread alone but by the teaching which issued from the mouth of the Lord. We sought for that which was temporal; the Lord God out of His Grace granted us the eternal.

73. JOHANNES REMEEUS'

JOURNEY OF AN EMIGRANT FAMILY, 1854

[Remeeus, born in 1815, with wife and five children emigrated from Middelburg on May 30, 1854, arrived in Boston on July 22, and settled in Milwaukee during August. On his journey Remeeus kept a diary which, translated by Herman Bottema of Milwaukee, was first published in *Wisconsin Magazine of History*, XXX (1946).]

A short description of our journey from Middelburg, Province of Zeeland,kingdom of the Netherlands, to Milwaukee, state of Wisconsin, United States of America, in the year 1854. Members of our family were as follows: father, Johannes Remeeus, 39; mother, Jacoba Helena Remeeus [nee Burck], 39; and five children: Anna Caterina, 17; Helena Johanna, 11; Caterine Jacoba, 5; Dina Antonia [Dientje], 3; and Jan Frederick, 6 months. In memory of our children.

On the evening of May 30, 1854 we left Middelburg for Vlissingen [Flushing] after bidding farewell to our dear and kind friends we cannot easily forget. The reason we left in the evening was because the steamer for Antwerp sailed early the following morning. We slept that night on board the steamer. Next morning at 4 o'clock the boat left for Antwerp where we arrived the same morning at 10 o'clock.

Upon our arrival a servant was already waiting for us. He took us to the office of the steamship company. We soon found, however, that they did not have very much respect for emigrants. They imposed upon us by charging an extra 7 florins for the passage; and there was no redress although Mr. Straus and I in April had made a verbal agreement as to the price. You can imagine that this was a great hardship for me as my purse was but a slender one; indeed, later when travelling through America we were in actual need of money. Meanwhile our baggage was transferred from the steamer's hold, piled up on the dock along with the baggage belonging to other passengers, to be stowed away in the ship which was to bring us to the Promised Land.

In the afternoon we went to the hotel which was maintained exclusively for emigrants. There were in Antwerp 2,700 emigrants, mostly Germans, waiting for ships to take them to America. For four weeks the winds had been blowing out of the wrong quarter; hence no ships had entered the harbors of Holland, Belgium, or Germany.

After we had enjoyed some food every man had to help bring the trunks, boxes, and other baggage on board. We were given permission to furnish our sleeping quarters as suitably as we wished. The women in company of Messrs Westveen and Snoep, and Vermeulen from Middelburg, the agent of the line, went to see the sights of the town. I was kept busy all afternoon fixing up my berth. I used a coarse wallpaper for this purpose. I also put up curtains around the bed and did everything I could to make our quarters pleasing and comfortable for my family. The captain and helmsmen observed me while thus engaged and smiled kindly, thereby showing that they were pleased with what I was doing.

When I had finished this task I went to the hotel to get mother and the children. This was the first night we slept in the ship that was to take us to America. It was the bark *Fedes Koo* from Portland, Maine, commanded by Captain H. Higgins.

The next morning, June 1, we were busy bringing aboard provisions for our long voyage. Later, when this labor was finished, our names were called from a list and two men distributed the food according to the size of each family. Provisions consisted of green peas, navy beans, rice, flour, ham, salt, and a small quantity of coffee and sugar. Everything was measured or weighed and had to be signed for. We were to receive potatoes and ship biscuit each week. We also were given enough bread to last about five days.

In the afternoon we had to appear with our families before an officer who examined our papers. When he found they were in order we were given our ship's papers.

Next we went to see something of Antwerp. In the evening we returned to our ship. Our thoughts often took a serious turn as the reader may surmise. The children readily fell asleep; but with mother and me it was different. The following morning, June 2, we went to the hotel for breakfast. In the afternoon we were required to be on board because we as well as the other passengers were going to have assigned our places on board the ship. The Hollanders were placed on one side; the Germans on the other. The total number of passengers was 130.

In the evening we again ate at the hotel after which we went aboard. On the morning of June 3 an officer, really [in Dutch, waterschout], police, and doctors came on board. We all were ordered to go on deck, nobody being permitted to remain below. Lanterns were lighted and the officers examined the entire ship below. They counted carefully to make sure there were no stowaways. The doctors examined each one of us and as they finished ordered us to go down to our cabins. They were strict on two points: that no person having a contagious disease should sail and that there should not be too many passengers on the ship. It was the practice of companies in those days to overcrowd their ships, something the Belgian police were ordered to prevent - hence their strict surveillance.

One family consisting of a father, mother, and four children who came from the country around the city of Goes on the island of Zuid-Beveland were brought to a hospital. They suffered from some form of rash, a malady doctors considered dangerous to the health of passengers. Of course it was unfortunate for them to be left behind but these precautions show how well the authorities guarded the health of emigrant passengers. Finally, with the aid of the tug "De Klok", our ship moved down the River Schelde and at 6 o'clock we dropped anchor at Terneuzen.

During the afternoon the captain and helmsman quarreled with the ship's carpenter, the cause of which we did not learn because we could not understand their language. But when the ship dropped anchor the carpenter left with his chest of tools. And so the ship lost the services of an invaluable helper.

The wind was blowing from the right direction and everything seemed ready for sailing. The captain sent for the Belgian pilot who asked the passengers if anyone understood the trade of ship carpenter. No, there was none. Soon he returned and asked if there was a house carpenter among us and, if so, would he be willing to help, should his services be needed. A German and I said we were willing, and the pilot thanked us. The German, however, asked the pilot who acted as interpreter, how much he would be paid for his work. The captain did not like the idea of paying for such work, according to the pilot, and the German was told his services would not be required.

I made no stipulation in regard to pay but told the pilot I had never sailed on any boat and so was not used to going up the mast and rigging. Nevertheless, I declared I was willing to help whenever the captain should need me. The first helmsman, who was taken charge of the carpenter work, approached me, gave me his hand, and in broken Dutch declared my offer to help was deeply appreciated. Indeed, as it turned out, I never was sorry for giving my services, for during the entire voyage we were treated politely and kindly, which gained for us no little jealousy from our fellow passengers.

Before darkness set in the helmsman and I were busy fastening the boxes, Now for the first time I learned how to drive American nails without previously having to drill holes as was necessary with the nails we used in Holland.

On June 4 at 6 o'clock in the morning we hove anchor and soon left Terneuzen, sailing before a strong east-northeast wind. Soon Flushing and Westkapelle were out of sight and we entered the North Sea. The rocking of the boat which now began made the healthy and happy passengers seasick.

We all – Hollanders, Germans, men, women, and schildren – celebrated Pentecost in proper fashion. Only a few did not take part. But there was something else to attract attention. At 6 o'clock in the evening we were in the English Channel; the sand dunes of Holland had long been out of sight and we beheld the chalk cliffs of England. Having escaped seasickness so far, I tried to write a few letters to be carried to port by the pilot. But suddenly I became sick from the rocking of the ship. From time to time I went on deck but I did not like the idea of leaving mother and children alone down below. Once when I appeared on deck the helmsman came to me, took me by the arm, and put me between two kettles, near the bowsprit. He advised me to draw deep breaths of fresh air, which agreed with me. Other passengers followed this advice with excellent results.

Soon I was able to work and all day I kept myself busy. Before evening we passed Dover Castle, the Isle of Wight, and the lighthouse of Dungeness. Here we saw a brig which had been on our starboard all day, also a bark and two-masted ships.

On the morning of June 5 we sailed out of the English Channel and as far as our eyes could see westward we beheld nothing but water. Now we were on the Atlantic Ocean. We sighted a steamboat bound for Falmouth. We now got used to the rolling and pitching of the ship and the people began to feel better. We had better appetites and each of us in turn began to cook something to eat. We still had a favoring wind.

On June 6 fair weather and a stiff breeze. Our Caterina was the first child to appear on deck. She found a piece of rope and started jumping rope as she used to do in the streets back home. She could not understand why the captain forbade her to do this. Soon more children came on deck. Toward evening the farmers from Goes fried ham and pancakes.

On the morning of June 7 we communicated with a schooner en route to Lisbon. This ship came so close to us that we could plainly hear its crew talking and everything on deck was clearly visible. We lowered a boat and when our captain returned he brought a box of lemons and a box of dried prunes.

Until now we had fair weather. But toward evening we met contrary winds. It began to blow very hard and we saw immense shoals of fish which, according to the sailors, signified an approaching storm.

June 8. Nothing worthy of note. We passed a bark, a schooner, and a brig.

June 9. Ditto. This day a baby was born to German parents. As soon as this became known the captain and the helmsman made the necessary arrangements to help them and assigned special quarters to them. Considering the limitations of our space, the room soon was made as comfortable as possible; but it was not, of course, a proper room in which a Dutch mother usually delivers her baby. The child was born without the aid of a doctor. Our Dutch women on board were surprised at the manner the baby was taken care of. In Holland such things received far more elaborate attention. All this gave our Dutch women a great deal to talk about.

June 10. During the day calm weather but toward evening the wind started to blow.

June 11. Today the hardest wind we had as yet experienced. Many were sick and mother who had been feeling so much better for the past few days was compelled to go to bed. The ship rolled violently

We now learned what a terrific force water exerts when stirred by a gale. The ship seemed not to respond to her sails but only to the white-capped waves. Our boxes and trunks broke loose out of their crates and were thrown from one side of the vessel to the other. One must witness the havoc such a storm causes on board a vessel to believe it. Kettles, bottles, nightchambers, and everything not nailed down rolled from port to starboard. The wind varied – now it died down a little but soon returned with unabated fury. There was much rain until June 15.

Meantime the Hollanders quarreled with the Germans over the time they could cook their food. But these differences did not amount to much. As soon as the helmsman heard of it, he ordered that each of the two groups should be first on alternate days and anyone who ignored this rule should help clean up the deck. This worked splendidly, for the ship below was spic-and-span during the rest of the voyage.

We saw only one bark that day, a lot of fish, and sea swallows. Our first helmsman, who was an expert harpooner, tried to catch some of the fish. He was nearly successful on two occasions. He struck the fish with the harpoon, but in trying to haul them on board they slipped off against the side of the vessel, which we regretted very much.

June 16. Fair weather, sea calm. At 6 in the morning a three-masted ship coming from North America hove in sight. Late that evening we witnessed an example of effective discipline on board a ship. Our first helmsman, a man of strong character capable of maintaining order, had become well acquainted with the passengers. There was an unmarried German couple on board. The man was a Mr. Smid [really, Schmidt], the girl was known as Dora. The helmsman had teased them a great deal but the couple seemed to think the officers would not molest them. Some of the passengers were suspicious of their conduct and informed the helmsman. This evening the helmsman hung up his lantern in the accustomed place and decided to investigate. Ordering one of the sailors to stand guard, he investigated the sleeping quarters and found the reports were true. With some difficulty the woman was removed from her berth. Mr. Smid was placed in the coalbin in the bow of the ship while Dora was locked up somewhere in the stern where she remained for the night.

June 17. Very agreeable weather. Unfortunately mother could not come on deck because our little Frederick, who was too young to take any food except his mother's milk, suffered greatly. The poor child cried all day and night.

At 10 o'clock Smid and Dora, the two lovers, were led out of their confinement and brought before the captain. A sailor acted as interpreter. The captain lectured them severly and ordered them to lead a more moral life. Thereupon the couple, being ashamed, were given their freedom, but for several days remained between decks.

In the afternoon the helmsman caught a large fish, a so-called "sea hog," which provided us with some entertainment. After it was killed, being butchered like a pig, it was cut up and prepared for food. Some of its red meat was salted. The fish fought so vigorously that in being hoisted aboard its tail struck a privy standing in the bow, hurling it overboard. I was ordered to make a new one, which kept me occupied for some time.

June 18. In the morning agreeable weather, but a contrary wind. Every passenger received a portion of the fish we caught yesterday. We cut it into slices and pounded it much as one prepares beefsteak. We fried the meat with some ham and the whole including fried potatoes proved very delicious.

Toward evening one of the sailors was placed in confinement. He had been talking with one of the passengers, which was against the rules of the ship. When the officers took him to task for it he became saucy and insulting.

June 19. This is the first beautiful Sunday since we set sail. In the afternoon the Hollanders asked permission to conduct a religious meeting. Mother Westveer prayed and, moved by our situation, we sang many a beautiful psalm. Toward evening the weather turned cold and raw but during the night the wind died down somewhat.

June 20 and 21. Quiet weather. Snoep and I were on deck as late as 12 o'clock and we witnessed a fire at sea. It seemed as if our ship was sailing through a mass of fire [St. Elmo's fire]. A beautiful and imposing phenomenon which well might move the hardest among us and fill us with respect for Him who said, "Mine is the sea".

June 22. Stormy in the morning; and there was some seasickness. During the day the sea became somewhat calmer but the ship rolled violently nevertheless. We saw a brig and a bark. Our Dientje drank some hot coffee and scalded her mouth.

June 23. Fair weather, the ship was steady. In the evening the Germans fittingly celebrated St. John's Day, which also was the twenty-fifth birthday of one of their group. This man was escorted to the aft deck where his sister presented him with a bottle of Rhenish wine of which they had a plentiful supply. In the neck of the bottle was placed a palm branch to which were tied a piece of sausage, a lemon, some dried prunes, etc. After having given him our congratulations, we all drank his health with many bottles of beer which the captain had in store. We also proposed a toast to the captain, the officers of the ship, and in fact everybody and everything. That evening we learned how the Germans surpassed all other peoples at singing.

June 24. Nothing noteworthy during this day. Toward evening we saw flying fish and again witnessed St. Elmo's fire.

June 26. Fair, cool weather; but the wind continued from the west and the ship made little progress. Toward evening another ship passed to our starboard. She was a frigate.

June 27. Fair weather, the first really pleasant warm day. The passengers played all kinds of games and the children amused themselves. Mother came on deck but could not stand it very long. I repaired the chicken coop and the hog's pen.

June 28. Again fair weather, but the ship made only slow progress. The Germans celebrated St. Peter's Day. They sang and drank some wine while one of their group played a violin. We heard the blowing of a big fish after it was dark but to our regret could not see it.

June 29. Beautiful weather in the morning. In the afternoon the wind began to blow, increasing in intensity toward evening so that we became anxious. The hatches were closed and secured, the sails hauled down. The bark rose on the white-capped waves and dropped down in the hollows. Everything was thrown about helter-skelter and we could not sleep. A bad night for mother and our poor little boy.

June 30. The sea calmer today. The captain called our attention to a big yellow sea turtle, but Snoeps and I, in spite of all our efforts, were not able to catch it. In the afternoon a sail approached from the east and came so close to starboard that the officers spoke with ours by means of a speaking tube. This was the packetship *Robert Wiltrop* from Liverpool, bound for Baltimore. She had fifty passengers on board.

July 1. Early this morning the captain called our attention to a big shark swimming alongside our ship. In the afternoon the wind started to blow and again we had a stormy night.

July 2. Nothing new; a ship in the distance.

July 3. Good weather in the forenoon. In the distance a ship, perhaps the same we saw yesterday. This day the two black pigs which remained were butchered by one of the Germans. Scalding water was used to clean them whereupon they were hung up on the deck. Again a ship in   sight.

July 4. Declaration of Independence, which is celebrated by every American. So did we. Early in the morning flags were run up, and at 8 the crew fired salutes. One man who had been a dealer in fireworks got permission to open a box of guns. Everybody who had a liking for shooting could do so as much of it as he wished. At 10 one of the pigs was distributed among the passengers. Saw many fish, also a ship. We had a fresh breeze; the evening was fair but cold. At the request of Mr. Westveer the captain gave the Hollanders permission to sing psalms.

The captain sang the last psalm with us. We were approaching the [Newfoundland] Banks.

July 5. Weather very cold. Captain and helmsman with instruments making observations from the rigging. At dawn the helmsman awoke Snoep and me to show us an iceberg we had expressed a desire to see. We could see it plainly without the aid of instruments. The day was cold, but the men remained on deck all day in order to see the icebergs that lay on both sides of our ship. One of the icebergs had the form of a village church. The officers estimated the last one we passed was about 160 feet high. We were struck with awe beholding these vast masses of ice gleaming in the sunlight and silently floating by. I shuddered when I thought of the great danger those icebergs were to the ships that crossed their path. We saw many large fish spouting water and believed they were whales. The air was cold, but we had a beautiful night. The officers placed a lantern at the bow and kept watch.

July 6. A happy day for all of us. Early in the morning we sailed through a fleet of more than a hundred vessels catching cod and soon left them behind. Later in the day the weather became foggy and rainy. Towards evening the wind shifted to the east. But soon the weather cleared and we enjoyed a beautiful sunset. The moon also was beautiful and so calm was the sea that we could not persuade ourselves to go to our berths. Late in the night we passed a fishing vessel at a stone's throw.

July 9 en 8. Nothing new. Wind steady but from the west and southwest. The delicacies we had been eating from the beginning of the voyage were nearly gone. Also sugar and vinegar were nearly exhausted. Potatoes became worse each day and drinking water was becoming brackish. Everybody was tired of peas and beans.

July 10. Nothing interesting. We now were drifting along the Grand Banks. All the passengers were on deck. Some were sewing, some darning or knitting, some reading, writing, or playing, some cooking meals, and some so wearied from the voyage that they did not know what to do. Mother and little Frederick also were on deck.

July 11. Much rain. A schooner came in sight.

July 12. The helmsman harpooned a big fish. As before, the meat was divided among all us of, which we appreciated. In the evening we saw a big fish spouting water.

July 13. The wind remained contrary. In the morning it was wet and dreary, but in the afternoon clear and bright. The passengers were eagerly expecting the sight of land. In the evening a fishing boat at port, a bark at starboard. The evening was beautiful. I believe no writer or painter has ever made an adequate portrayal of a calm night at sea.

July 16 and 17. A mist covered the sea, but the sun shone brightly above. We could scarcely see three ship lenghts ahead. A quarrel broke out between the Germans and the cook who complained that they had lit a fire after 6 in the evening.

July 18. The sea was quiet, and in the evening a clear sky. Again we saw sharks near the ship. When the moon rose, we noted clouds to the south – visibly portending a thunderstorm. Again we saw St. Elmo's fire. We sailed by a ship, more closely than ever before.

July 19. Weather calm. The ship, moving against a strong current, seemed to go backward. Big and small ships appeared all day long. In the evening a large English steamer passed by.

July 20. A stiff breeze from the east. We were pleased, and many passengers declared they would gladly be seasick for a day or two if only the ship would progress.

July 21. Beautiful sunrise. Also many ships, and at 8 p.m. a light in the distance, a lighthouse as it actually proved to be after an hour's sailing.

July 22. Warm weather, and suffocating below deck. Little or no breeze. We were excited and could scarely sleep. At about 11 o'clock a.m. we dropped anchor. Opposite, in Boston Bay, an island with the quarantine station on it. Here we were to remain all day until given orders. All useless objects were discarded. The helmsman even threw overboard some of the wooden shoes and caps belonging to the girls from Goes and Zierikzee. We were ordered to clean up everything and scrub the deck below and make ourselves presentable. Next morning we put on our best clothes. The health officers came aboard early and examined everyone. They complimented the captain and officers on the cleanliness of ship and passengers and took the captain with them to the island. After an hour our captain returned. Loud hurrahs went up from all of us; hats and handkerchiefs were waved and he literally was carried from the boat into the cabin, visibly pleased with the ovation. Soon a tug appeared to bring our ship into the bay on which the city of Boston is built. There were many steamers and sailing ships around us. There also were pleasure boats, nicely gilded and painted. We noted some steep cliffs on which were erected lighthouses. At 1 o'clock we arrived in Boston. As it was Saturday and no trains were running in New England on Sunday, we were given permission to stay on board till Monday morning.

More than once I had told the officers of our ship of my disappointment in not being landed in New York because our tickets read from that place. We had been on board only a short time when we learned that our ship's destination was Boston. I told them that I feared I would miss my connections entirely because I carried from the commissioner of emigration at New York a letter of recommendation to help us on our journey as quickly and as cheaply as possible and protect us against swindlers. The helmsman promised me he would see the captain about this point and he faithfully kept his promise. When we were drawing near Boston the captain called me to his cabin. It was difficult for us to understand each other, but he informed me that he would gladly map out for us our trip inland. He advised that we should not listen to anybody – English, Germans, Irish, or Hollanders – no matter how elegantly they might be dressed or how refined their manners. I informed my fellow passengers about his suggestions and nearly all of us accepted them. Our bark was towed to the dock and several people tried to board it but failed. Nevertheless they repeated the attempt. The captain accordingly went ashore to bring a police officer to stand guard and all those who had no business on board ship were turned back.

In the afternoon the captain brought on board a man representing the railroads. The heads of families and the single men, called into the cabin one by one, paid for their tickets, including fare for boat and railroad. Children under ten paid half fare. Our tickets and those of our friends who like us were destined for Milwaukee were issued by the Boston Railway. I was the first to get tickets and Snoep also got his very soon. Being free now to go ashore we bought some fresh milk and bread. We had never gotten used to the black coffee we drank on our voyage. The weather was very hot and so we each bought a straw hat. We suffered a good deal from the heat in spite of the fact we had taken off some of our clothes.

I now wrote a letter to Mr. Van den Broecke at Rochester informing him that his parents had arrived with us at Boston and not at New York as had been planned originally. As I wanted him to have this information as soon as possible I made it a short letter and without delay dropped it into a letter box.

Early Sunday morning Snoep and I went ashore to see as many of the sights of Boston as the heat would permit. Boston is one of the oldest and wealthiest commercial centers in the United States, built in a half circle along the bay, like an amphitheater. Streets were laid out on the tops of high rocks; and there were gushing fountains, beautiful parks, and elegant houses, some built with red pressed bricks, others constructed with rough hewn stone or with hard blue colored stone. There also were thousands of houses built of wood but these were none the less attractive on that account. They indeed were master creations of domestic architecture.

That evening we made ready to leave Boston on the first immigrant train and packed up our belongings.

Monday morning at 6 we left the ship which had been our home for the past fifty days. We did so with a feeling of regret in spite of the fact that the ship when we first embarked at Antwerp had given us a poor and miserable impression. But we were looking forward to our journey to our destination and left without hard feelings. Early that morning a baby was born on board. The father, Hendrik Moorman, came from Kattendijke on the island of Zuid-Beveland and his destination, like ours, was Milwaukee. But their family was well cared for until they could resume their journey.

One of the officers accompanied us to the station and acted as our interpreter. They weighed our baggage and we were assessed $ 18 more then we had expected, which so depleted our purse that we felt downhearted. I cannot decide whether we were cheated; a few said we were not but others insisted we had been swindled. But I paid for our excess baggage for the entire journey to Milwaukee and was given a receipt. At 12 o'clock we left Boston.

Springfield was the first place at which we stopped. Here we had a sad accident. A child belonging to one of the Germans who had crossed the ocean with us was thrown out of the car when the train suddenly began to move. The child fell under the wheels and both arms were cut off. The sorrowing parents had to take their child to the hospital.

At 4 o'clock a.m. we arrived at Worcester, a good-sized factory town with some foundries. Although free to leave our coaches because our train was not to leave until 12 o'clock, we stayed on the train. We were much annoyed during the night by strange Irish people, a low class who had attained to only a slight degree of civilization. The train crew had hitched about eight coaches on to the rear of our train, all crowded with immigrants. I noticed that the cars carrying our baggage ever since we left Boston no longer formed a part of our train. I had taken precaution, however, to take down the number of the car and note its color.

Riding through the state of Massachusetts we beheld wonders of nature impossible to describe adequately, at least for one who had never traveled farther from Zeeland than Gelderland and had never seen anything but level country. Here we saw gigantic rocks out of which roadbeds had been hewn, something that must have cost an enormous amount of labor and money. We passed through tunnels cut out of solid rock, so long that they required more than a quarter of an hour for our train to pass through. While passing through such tunnels we rode in darkness seeing nothing but the sparks of the locomotive. We also passed by bridges high up between mountains while below in the streams water rushed on its way with thundering noise.

Early in the morning of July 25 we arrived in the state of New York. The scenery had changed – how beautiful nature now was! This state has made much progress, for on every hand were cities and villages, on mountain sides as well as in the valleys, many of which had their own railroad stations at some of which our train stopped in order to take on water. At 12 o'clock we reached Albany and had to leave the train. Here we crossed the famous Hudson River on ferries, which continually crossed from bank to bank, thus taking the place of bridges.

Each ferry boat was divided into three compartments – one on each side for ladies and gentlemen and provided with comfortable seats and covered with a roof; and the center, a large space sufficiently wide to carry vehicles of every description. During the morning I had gotten a cinder in my eye while our train was passing through a tunnel. This gave me so much trouble that as soon as possible we went to a doctor who quickly relieved me of my pain. But it cost me $ 1 which shows that American doctors want sufficient remuneration for their services.

The first hotel or boarding place at which we stopped in America was in Albany. Its proprietor was a German. We considered ourselves fortunate because we arrived at this hotel before the others who traveled on the same train as we did. Three Dutch families from Walcheren were staying here. The other Hollanders and their families found quarters elsewhere. We were well pleased with the meals served at the hotel. Mother and our dear little sick child, after the long voyage and the journey on land during which they experienced many hardships, craved a good night's rest. But how we were disappointed! During the evening the boardinghouse was filled with guests and the heat was unendurable. The guests were constantly going up and down the steps and trying to open our bedroom door. We were afraid they might do us some harm and so we slept little.

Many Hollanders who lived in Albany visited us that same evening and also the following morning. They gave us some good advice about our railroad trip. A former Amsterdammer said, "Don't be afraid on account of your baggage. If it has been put on the car in Boston it will arrive in good order at Buffalo. But as soon as you reach Buffalo you will have to look after it in order to have it shipped across the Great Lakes."

We also received the bad news that cholera was raging in the Western states and that the epidemic was claiming many victims. This information deeply affected us but you can imagine how at this moment of depression I was pleased when a well-dressed man came rushing into our boarding place at about 10 in the morning asking in one of the dialects of Zeeland, "Is Remeeus here?" I replied, "Here I am!" It proved to be Van den Broecke from Rochester. "Where are my father and mother?" he asked. They had gone for a short walk. On the streets their odd costumes had attracted the attention of children. Thus surrounded, Van den Broecke discovered them and, deeply moved, he forced himself through the crowd and embraced his parents. Such a welcome! In Van den Broecke we had a trustworthy guide for the journey as far as Rochester. And as agent and advisor for our group I was thankful for his help.

Our bill at the hotel was $ 6, a large sum for a poor immigrant. I exclaimed, "What, $ 6 ?" For I knew that 6 Dutch *rijksdaalders* [15 guilders] were equivalent to $ 6.

After we had looked up a few other acquaintances of former days we boarded the immigrant train that was to take us to Rochester. We left at 12 o'clock and passed through towns and villages many of which seemed prosperous. It was startling how after having heard so many strange place names which we could not pronounce we noticed some familiar ones like Harlem and Amsterdam. During the evening we passed through Syracuse, a thriving city boasting several thousand inhabitants.

The following morning, July 27, we arrived at Rochester. We wanted to spend a day here in order to visit some old acquaintances from our home town, Middelburg. But the train stopped here only for a half hour. Rochester is a very large city, having more foundries than are to be found in all Holland and enjoying an immense commerce in flour. Some of the mills in Rochester have steam engines but most of them utilize water power.

From our car windows we beheld the Genesee River which at this point had a drop of ninety feet. But more interesting was the Erie Canal with its great locks regulating the water. It looked as if the canal carried its water over the city. Through it hundreds of barges drawn by horses moved from Albany to Buffalo.

Soon we resumed our route to Buffalo. The heat was unbearable. We passed Batavia and arrived at Buffalo at about 2 o'clock p.m. Here we had to leave our train, but we could not proceed at once to our destination because our baggage had not yet arrived. On account of the high prices charged in boardinghouses our fellow travelers – farmers from Zierikzee and Goes - decided to leave one member of each of their families in Buffalo to look after their baggage, and cross Lake Erie that same night.

We still had to travel nearly a thousand miles and I did not have enough money left to pay for a single night's lodging for my family. In those days there were no immigrant stations to help people like us. With a dejected feeling Westveer, Snoep, and I went to buy bread and butter. Westveer wanted to see a certain Mr. Huissoon, for he carried a letter of recommendation addressed to him. I had to deliver a letter to a Mr. De Graaf from his family in Holland. After a long search, finally at half past four, I knocked at his door, and I was received most cordially. They lodged my wife and children. During the evening a few other Hollanders called. Snoep and I spent that night at the home of Mr. Post, formerly a baker in Middelburg. They were very friendly and gave us every encouragement.

Buffalo is a large and beautiful city. We saw so many strange things there that it would be difficult to relate even a small number of them. But the pavement of the streets in American cities, young as compared is with those in Europe, left much to be desired.

On July 28 at 12 o'clock we met the train which carried our baggage. Nothing was missing but the boxes had been damaged very much owing to rough handling in spite of the fact that I myself had taken special pains to make them extra strong. Snoep and I drove extra nails here and there to strengthen the boxes. In later years I often wondered how in this crowd of people we ever managed to accomplish what we wanted. Here were Americans, Irish, Norwegians, Swedes, Dutch, and Germans, and everybody in that heterogeneous crowd tried to get his belongings transferred to the steamboat that was to carry us across Lake Erie.

It was 6 that evening when we got our baggage on board. We were sweating, covered with dust, and very tired. Snoep and I went to get my wife and children, boarded the steamer, and at 9 o'clock left for Detroit. This was a large steamer luxuriously furnished and provided with the best of accommodations. But alas! we poor immigrants had to sit with our baggage. There were more than 2,000 passengers on board and each of us had scarcely five square feet on which to sleep, and with that we had to be satisfied during the whole night. But, and this was worse, a fearful storm came up. There was much thunder and lightning and the water was as rough as one ever sees on the Atlantic. But during this dismal night we experienced the Lord's saving hand. In the afternoon of July 29 we arrived at Detroit, a large and well-known city situated on Lake Erie opposite Canada. I cannot write anything about the city itself, for the dock at which we arrived was situated near the railway station and in being transferred to our train we accordingly could not see much. On account of the storm was late in docking. The train was ready waiting for us, and we were hurried as fast as the horses could carry us. How thankful we were that God's kindness had provided us with good food sufficient to last until we reached Milwaukee. The passengers, overwhelmed by fear and seasickness, had not touched their supper and for a few Dutch dimes we were permitted to take as much of the food as we wanted.

Again we were on a train and the farther we traveled westward the poorer the equipment of the immigrant trains. Our cars were no better than freight cars and we sat on benches which gave us great discomfort. During the past eight days we had slept but one night. Traveling became almost unbearable because of the jarring of the train which sped rapidly in order to arrive at its destination on scheduled time. A number of our fellow passengers were mine workers who had just returned from California.

We had a burning thirst and only at the stations, whenever the train stopped, could we get water. As the train did not wait for us while we filled our jugs we always had to hurry. Considering all we had to go through it is a wonder that courage never left us. We made a short stop at Kalamazoo, 140 miles from Detroit. There a few Hollanders left us, some to stay in Kalamazoo, others to find employment in the vicinity.

Toward evening a six-year-old child belonging to Norwegian parents fell from one of the cars, landed under the wheels, and was instantly killed. The little corpse was taken from the train at the next station. It must have been a sad experience for the poor parents thus to lose one of its members and to be unable to attend the funeral.

The train passed through some rocky country. Suddenly it slowed down and we thought we were approaching some station. But there was a cry of "Fire! Fire!" which filled us with consternation. One of the baggage cars was on fire, but it soon was under control. A Swede had stored a large quantity of matches in a box which, when ignited, threatenend to set the whole car afire. But, praise the Lord, little harm was done; we were only terribly frightened.

Sunday morning, July 30, was beautiful. Our route lay through enchanting regions, extensive forests, magnificent views which we had from the hilltops, and extensive valleys – all wonderful and beautiful. Surely any person with plenty of money would be happy to travel for days through such beautiful and ever changing scenery. But traveling as we did on an immigrant train – accompanied by small children some of whom were sick, unable to obtain any but the commonest necessities, and above all sweltering in unbearable heat – was a sore trial, enough to make us downhearted. But it was through God's kindness that we were safe and able to see and enjoy as much as we did.

Late in the afternoon we arrived in Chicago. Our train went over a long trestle erected on piles. This bridge crossed some arm or inlet of Lake Michigan. Chicago, although a youthful city, already boasted a population of many thousands.

Cholera was raging in Illinois and Wisconsin and it was with great fear that we entered Chicago. It was quite dark when I found a place for my wife and children. I had only one dollar in my pocket. Snoep and I decided to walk around the city and rest here and there on some bench. At the station we had been told that our baggage would arrive on Monday morning. We feared that something might be missing, for it was no uncommon occurrence among immigrants that some box containing their most valuable articles would never arrive.

The next morning we heard the sad news that Mr. Goudzwaart, one of our fellow Hollanders, a tried and true friend who had come from Dreischor on the island of Schouwen, had been stricken with cholera and that he had died before he could reach the hospital. We liked him because he was alert and clever. For his aged father and mother and for his poor young widow and three children we had the deepest sympathy. Just think of it: to be within only one day's travel of one's destination and then to die!

I found that all our baggage shipped from Buffalo was in good order. One of the sons of our friend Post, the baker at Buffalo whom we mentioned above, had strongly advised me to note the exact weight of our boxes and so I keep a list of them. Our baggage was placed on handcars and brought to the steamer that was to bring us to Milwaukee. I made sure that the ship was safe, for one could never be too careful about such a matter. My fellow passengers from Antwerp agreed that I had the right system in marking our boxes with a red sign and printing on them our address in black letters. Thus I was able to recognize my property instantly.

Now I went to get mother and the children. They had suffered so many hardships and privations that they had lost weight and become weaker and weaker. They spent the night in a boarding house on some chairs placed near a table. They had nothing to eat. Yet when I came to get them this boarding house manager demanded $ 3. I told him I had only $ 2 but he didn't believe me. He seized me by my vest, ripped it

open to see if I had any money hidden in an inside pocket. So shocked
was I that to this very day I do not know how I got out on the street.
Not until I and my family had gone several blocks did I breathe freely.
Finally we were on our boat. They collected our tickets and then threw
them away. There were few passengers, and not many of them immigrants. The day was sunny and beautiful. We were so tired that we fell
asleep and consequently saw little of Lake Michigan. The Great Lakes
are bodies of fresh water. But ships sailing on them frequently encounter
dangerous storms – as serious as those on the ocean – and thousands
of immigrants have found untimely graves in the waves of these lakes.

At four o'clock p.m. on July 31 we arrived at Milwaukee. Our boat
landed alongside a very large pier – the landing place for all steamers.
Our boxes were unloaded and now we stood beside them on the pier
not knowing where to go. Soon a neatly-dressed man approached us
and told us in Dutch that he was running a boarding house. I explained
to him my financial condition and added that we had intented to join
Dominie Klijn but that when in Buffalo we had been told he had left
Wisconsin for Michigan. My own relatives, as I related to him, lived
eighteen miles from Milwaukee, and I mentioned the names of my
brother-in-law and Mr. P. Lankester. But as soon as he learned I had
no money and was willing to offer my baggage as security until I could
write to my brother-in-law, this Dutchman hastened away. For a
moment I lost courage, for this unsympathetic treatment dismayed
me. What would become of us in this land of strangers?

The heat was unbearable especially after the cool breeze we had enjoyed
on the steamer. We had a burning thirst which we tried to quench with
a bit of ice. At this moment a boy came to us, spoke in one of the dialects
of Zeeland, and asked if we had found a boardinghouse. When we said
"No," he offered to guide us to his house which was not far from the
pier. I did not say a word to him about my financial condition, but
placed our boxes in a separate pile, and followed him. His parents, who
had come from Zierikzee, lived with several other families in a large
house on which appeared the word "museum". These people were
making a living from fishing. I asked the boy's mother if we could stay
until our relatives were informed of our arrival. She agreed and at once
began to cook and bake for us.

Soon the man of the house came home. I related to him that my brother
in-law was a next door neighbor of P. Lankester. He at once ordered
an express man to bring our baggage to his house. He accompanied the
express man and paid all expenses. He also advised me not to eat any

vegetables and several other things on account of the cholera. During the night I took dangerously ill. I vomited and had a bad case of diarrhea. So weak was I that on the next day I could scarcely walk. I wrote a letter to my sister and another to Mr. Boda.

Most of the Hollanders in Milwaukee had no work because business was at a standstill. All who could afford it had gone to the country to escape the cholera epidemic. This of course depressed us as you can imagine. On Wednesday morning, August 2, Snoep went with our host to catch fish. In the afternoon of that day our brother-in-law, Sleijster, arrived from Franklin Prairie in a wagon that belonged to Mr. Lankester. Sleijster paid our host who had so kindly cared for us. We left our baggage with him and set out for Franklin Prairie where we arrived in the evening after traveling through forests and over many a hill. I need hardly tell you that we received a warm welcome. Mother had suffered so much on our long and arduous journey that her sister and family scarcely recognized her. Our youngest child, Jan Frederick, was in precarious health and we feared he would not be able to live much longer. Our sister and her family did not know that we had buried our Mietzie shortly before leaving Holland.

At eleven o'clock the following morning I began working at a carpenter's bench in Mr. Lankester's barn. I also had to help in the field. But this kind of work did not suit me. Finally I went to Milwaukee to look for work and to find a house for my family. Often I walked the many miles back and forth between Franklin Prairie and Milwaukee. Occasionally I was fortunate to get a ride on a hay wagon or some other wagon drawn by oxen. Because I was in a strange country I found it difficult to get ahead. I did not know anybody in Milwaukee and could speak neither English nor German. You can imagine how I felt in the evening when coming home after I had searched for work all day in vain. At last I found a house for my wife and children, a deserted parsonage. My sister had washed our clothing and on Tuesday, August 22, we left Franklin Prairie and came to Milwaukee. On August 28 I began to work for an English-speaking man, earning $ 1.25½ a day. Soon I became a citizen of Milwaukee, a youthful and beautiful city, ideally situated for commerce.

Chapter XXIII

FOUR SKETCHES OF DUTCH SETTLEMENT
IN WISCONSIN, 1846 - 1897.

74. HENRY HARMELING'S HISTORY OF AMSTERDAM
AND CEDAR GROVE

[The author, minister in the Reformed Church, was born in Oostburg in 1864, and served several Reformed pulpits in Wisconsin until his death in 1946. This article by him appeared in *The Sheboygan Press*, August 12, 1947.]

Already fatigued, owing to a jolty ride inland in the stage coach, and in trudging alongside of the heavily laden ox cart, holding their wilderness possessions, they reached the present side of Cedar Grove and camped for the night.

Joe Palmer had loaned his ox team and cart to them for their trek inland and he later became their neighbor on the Green Bay road. Father had pitched a tent that was to serve as their temporary dwelling, while building the log cabin home. Although dog-tired, he had insisted that they find a suitable spot for building on that very evening of their journey

At twilight, as the sun was setting in picturesque splendor over the Onion River, then a large stream, they chose their future cabin site. The exact location was to be on the right bank of the Onion River skirting the bend of that river's majestic channel. Its current at that point carried a large volume of water. However, it was not at all treacherous, for I recall that as a young lad I visited Aunt Hattie and her son Henry, and I myself, when the season was at all favorable, would take a dip in the Onion River at this very point.

On that memorable first night in the woods, Gerhard Johann [my father] and the hired man, Frank Ferick, slept out in the open under a canopy of stars while the Te Kolste family [Aunt Hattie] rested in the tent. They used the boughs of overhanging cedars for pallets to sleep on. All had a good night's rest – notwithstanding the occasional yelp of wolves, which infested the forests of those early days, and the terrifying and fearsome hoot of screech owls.

Early daybreak found them awake and ready to clear a space in the forest. After a frugal meal and thanksgiving prayers for their safe arrival here in their New World home, they set out with axes and saws to the task of chopping down these immense cedar trees. The sturdy, thickly-grown trees were all around them. Father's first choice was the linden tree, commonly called the basswood tree. It was the most suitable wood for use in building the log cabin. Basswood was soft wood and required less strength and effort to cut these mighty trees of the forest. The wood choppers felled these lindens first of all, and cut them in the proper lengths for uprights and posts for the body framework of their log house. They split logs in two by driving wedges of hickory wood into the crevices. This father did with the aid of a mallet. These half logs showed an interior smoothness and whiteness that had a straight grained sleekness. These half "boles", when properly spaced, tier upon tier to form the inner wall of the cabin room, greamed milky white and made a fresh and clean looking interior. The surface was smooth and had a fine appearance. When built, the looks of her new cabin home gave Aunt Hattie real pleasure, for she now had an abundance of smoothspaced walls on which she could hang the portraits of her dearly loved parents. She also purchased chromos, in the general store and trading post in Sheboygan, and bedecked the walls with "Washington crossing the Delaware" and other patriotic themes.

Gerhard Johann, having previously made a few trips to Ton Dertien [Town Thirteen] to visit the Te Kolstes in their log cabin home, had carefully noted the construction of that cabin. This leaves no doubt in my mind that the home of Aunt Hattie, his sister, was built according to the specifications of the Te Kolstes' log cabin. However, there was one marked difference. The Te Kolste's cabin roof was made of hemlock bark, while the cabin roof that father made had squares of birch bark overlapping each other with the white side to the weather. Each square was firmly nailed in place. When completed, the white roof and the grey contrasting log sides of this cabin were a pleasing combination. These colors were harmonious to the eye. A bright new cabin heightened the great beauty of the wildwood landscape of this beautiful Onion River country in Sheboygan County.

It is safe to say that with the united labor of the three men the log cabin, with a lean-to for a kitchen, was brought to completion in a few weeks' time. It was a happy change from the temporary shelter of the tent to the brand new cabin. The result of their pain and effort was startlingly beautiful.

The month of June arrived, after the completion of the log cabin, and it was time for the planting of ninety day corn. It was flint corn and the term was used because this corn would be ripe for use within ninety days from planting time. The Early Rose potato was also planted in June and buckwheat gave its best yield when planted in that month.

The swamp land near the river was chosen, for heavy, damp soil is best for a good crop of buckwheat. The planting and sowing of crops demanded haste on the part of the three men. They chopped down trees in the great forest around them and cleared enough land to make an acreage suitable for raising crops.

The stand of trees in the Wisconsin forests was made up of many and various types of wood. There was the sugar maple, the large oak, the ash, the beach, the linden, the rockelm on high ground, and the swampelm, on moist, swampy ground. There were also trees like the hickory ironwood, birch, butternut, and juniper.

I was brought up in these forests of Wisconsin where I could study the lore of woodcraft in my native state. At eighty-one years the memory of this large number of forest trees comes vividly back to my mind. I could distinguish them by their leaves and their branches, by the color and the texture of their bark, and I also learned to know them apart by the shape of their seeds and the fruit, or nuts, that they bore. Like many another Wisconsin boy, I used to gather for winter use bushels of butter and hickory nuts. Beechnuts were gathered into small bags and roasted on the hearth during the bitter cold winters of those early days. They were delicious when roasted in butter and proved to be a great delicacy.

To return to our three woodmen in the primeval forests of Wisconsin. Because of their limited time they worked exceedingly long hours. Branches of trees were trimmed away and hauled to great brush piles. After trimming, the trunks were cut into four-foot lengths. These lengths were called cord wood. This cord wood was carefully piled in heights of four feet by eight feet. They were exactly four feet in width. These neat piles of wood stood waiting for the heavy snow of winter when wood could be loaded by the men and taken to the market in Sheboygan or Amsterdam.

These eager workmen labored from rise to set of sun to clear this most valuable farm land. Cord wood at that time was also in great demand in the city of Milwaukee. However, the Milwaukee wood market was forty miles or more from these woodmen in Ton Dertien but they were enterprising and yolked the oxen to the clumsy oxcart to transport all of the enormous amount of cut cord wood to the best market there was to be had for it.

Down the Green Bay road they traveled, in weekly hauls to Milwaukee. When roads were impassable, after the heavily packed snow melted, Gerhard Johann often made this trip on foot. He trudged along the early blazed trail along the Lake. He carried a large firkin of butter on his shoulder, roped to it, and tied about his waist. Today this would amaze the onlooker, for it would seem to be giant's task but hardy men of the early days were used to herculean tasks and mastered them. There was no word like failure in their vocabulary. On his return trip father carried back a fifty pound sack of flour, for flour and meal was then ground at the mill in that city.

Travellers on the hardy route along the Lake saw the brilliant, sparkling water and the smooth beach, and had an easier tramp than through the wood. All pioneers were accustomed to travel these long distances on foot.

In 1848 there was a young trader in cord wood who founded the town of Amsterdam on Lake Michigan at a point near Te Kolste clearing. Cord wood was then shipped by sailing vessel from the Dutch town to Milwaukee.

Henry Walvoord was this ambitious trader. He was successful in selling lots to his fellow countrymen – the Hollanders in Ton Dertien. The lots had been painstakingly named and plotted and each lot was on the lake front.

He was a merchant of no mean ability. His trading post was eagerly sought by the Dutch immigrants because Walvoord spoke their language, was highly respected, and was an honest man. His trading post carried on a lively trade in cord wood. A century has passed since Henry Walvoord had his little hamlet registered in the Sheboygan County annals – but any present day historian may read with interest the terms under which the village was incorporated and the map on which are the original markings and names of streets given by the long forgotten founder, who was a most unfortunate merchant

Henry Walvoord was drowned off his own pier at the village of Amsterdam. He had employed a government dredge at Sheboygan harbor to sail eleven miles south to Amsterdam village and dredge a new harbor there. That would permit the deepwater sailing vessel, a two masted schooner from the Milwaukee port, to ply its trade in lumber and cord wood between the two ports. The pier at Walvoord's new trading post was piled high with cord wood awaiting the completion of the eight foot depth in dredging the new harbor.

When the first trip was made and Walvoord was seated at his dinner table he sighted this sailing vessel tacking toward the new port. In great haste he left his family and rushed down to his new pier. He attempted to climb over some of the cord wood and lumber, stacked and ready for shipment on this very schooner, when he missed his footing and fell headling into the icy waters of Lake Michigan. He undoubtedly

had been knocked unconscious in his plunge over the ledge, for he was
an expert swimmer, but his body was recovered only after the greatest
difficulty. Logs had rolled over the pier's side and had pinned his body
underneath the debris.

Adolph Stokdyk, a grandson of one of the early Amsterdam settlers,
related the story to me while I was summering at the lake on the former
site of Walvoord's village. Inspecting the site of this long-forgotten
settlement, I found the early red schoolhouse where schoolmaster
Behrens had held forth, and one remaining pile out in Lake Michigan, that
had originally been the end pile in Walvoord's strongly built pier. This pile
showed very few marks or signs of erosion, and it stands as firmly implanted
to-day as it did 100 years ago when it was a bulwark of the early pier.

Cord wood was the means of exchange and barter in the Amsterdam
trading post and it induced the Hollanders to clear their land and place
their cord wood with Henry Walvoord. His pier was consequently
piled high with wood. They received their much needed supplies in
return. With stout yokes of oxen the settlers hauled load after load to
the Amsterdam pier.

This colony of immigrants was strongly united – one in faith, one in
common cause, and one in heart and feeling. No bond could draw
them closer than human companionship in this wilderness of trees.

The trade in cord wood and lumber business was followed mostly
during winter months when sled-runners on the ox carts could glide
smoothly over the snow.

In summer the wood-choppers were busy with their numerous farm
duties. Then, too, roads were impassable during a greater part of the
late spring and summer months, but in mid winter the snow lay packed
on the primitive paths or ox cart roads and runners of sleds could then
glide easily over the drifts. When Henry Walvoord drowned his one man
enterprise collapsed and the trading post ceased to exist. The village,
in course of time disintregated and when the West Shore Railroad
was constructed from Milwaukee to Sheboygan its roadbed was laid
a full mile or more from the shores of the Lake. The depot was built
at a point designated as Cedar Grove on the railroad time table. Trade
soon centered around the new transportation.

If at that time editors of the Sheboygan County papers had taken the
trouble to have a wood-cut made of the most remarkable sight ever to
take place within its boundaries we would have had an authentic picture
of Hollanders moving their entire village of Amsterdam to the clearing
in the woods called Cedar Grove.

A cavalcade of ox-teams started from the about-to-be-abandoned town of Amsterdam, with the trading posthouses and the log chuch edifice loaded on sled runners in a snow storm that sent flurries of snow-flakes over the strange scene. This parade of twenty-two ox-teams drawing their ponderous loads of heavy log buildings up the grade to the new village site was indeed a spectacle.

The oxen were of various colors. Some were roan, black, bay, white, and spotted, while others were a solid black. Their horns were curved and of various lengths. It was a mark of affluence to have the oxen's horns tipped with brass knobs and it showed an owner's desire for adornment of his highly prized cattle under the yoke. No pioneer could have made any progress without his much needed oxteam. Oxen were grouped together in four, six, and ten team units, according to their respective loads. The large trading post building headed the procession, followed by the church on log supports over the sledrunners. Then the houses followed until all the hamlet of Amsterdam had disappeared over the hill.

The method of moving had been thus arranged. Buildings were hoisted onto tamarack boughs by raising each structure to the necessary height and then placing the temporary supports underneath them. The placing of thick, barkstripped tamarack logs, as runners, was carefully done. Once under the projecting timbers, they elevated the logstructure that was then lowered upon these stout sledrunners and hitched by means of a great logging chain to a team of oxen, which were to drau that building to its new site. Snow blanketed the primitive loggingroad and made it easier for the oxen to pull the sleepers over the upgrade route.

All the settlers turned out to give a helping hand. Indians from that neighborhood had driven up on ponies also to help and the festivity of the picture can easily be imagined. The highly colored blankets of the Indians were a symbol of hope as this caravan of stalwart men who rode oxen and buildings on runners jogged along to their new destinations Cedar Grove. All branches overhanging the road space were carried away and cleared before the buildings were drawn over the snow covered road. Heavy work was made light, many hands helping. When all the town had been moved the bleak Michigan shores were left just as Wal-voord found them before he started the Dutch *dorpje*, or town. With Robert Burns the Scottish poet I am tempted to remark, "The best laid schemes of mice and men, gang oft astray." For plans of men and mice often go the wrong way. This is perfectly applicable to the bygone day of Amsterdam on Lake Michigan. It became a vivid memory of the long ago.

The oxteam which father furnished for the task were bright and nimble. They knew the old road well, for it was down this land that they had hauled many a load of cord wood to the Walvoord pier when the early village flourished in the lumber business. Father received a dollar twenty-five cents for each cord of wood presented at the dock or wharf. Oftimes he took the equivalent of the price in trade for sugar, coffee, pepper, and spices which Henry Walvoord kept in stock at his trading post.

Henry Frerick, the hired help, cut unusually large amounts of wood and together with father disposed of it almost as soon as it was cut. They also cut a sizeable amount for the owner of the clearing, William te Kolste, who was stricken with tuberculosis. In the spring of 1850 he died of that much dreaded disease, and his widow, Aunt Hattie, had father, her brother, take over the supervision of their farm clearing. Dick Frerick and father were soon rewarded for their strenuous labor by having a very goodsized clearing of tall trees on both sides of the boundary line fences. As much of this land as they could possibly use was given to the planting and sowing of wheat, oats, and corn. An equal distribution of crops was made to Aunt Hattie so that at harvest time she realized exactly as much as father did.

The two men continued to cut wood until a proper snowfall made the rutted road fit for travel. Ox carts were placed on sled runners and the crude sleds were loaded with cord wood. This cut timber was laboriously moved to market at the lake. If the road was at times icy the oxen were shod by the old settlers' blacksmith. A different process had to be used in shoeing the ox' cloven hoof. A cloven hoof called for two pieces of iron shoe. The early blacksmith used a heavy sail canvas and stout pulleys. He used strong ropes in placing the canvas underneath the ox and securely fastened these ropes by the aid of the pulleys to great stakes driven into the ground. Thus, the ropes holding the canvas were strung through the rafter pulleys and wound around the ground stakes with a double tackle.

The ox was consequently raised to have its feet lifted off of the ground, free to be shod with tiny shoes. Shoes were properly fitted and the rims were then nailed to the horny part of the hoof. Since two iron pieces had to be used [because of the cloven hoof] they were shaped exactly alike and they bore caulks on the under surface of the iron piece. The payment for having a team of oxen shod was part time service to the blacksmith who also farmed a clearing.

In this way he got his cleared land planted and shared in the crops of the settlement. Toil from early morn until deep twilight hindered the workman from continuing, and made the settlement prosper, Splendid farms supplanted the stump laden clearings farmed by heroic effort on the part of the noble pioneers of that dense woodland of yester year.

They were closely united, one and all, by a sense of nationality, by a common cause of survival in a hostile, savage, primitive, world, and by a universal worship of God, in praise and thanksgiving for delivering them out of the tyranny of the Old World church, into the glorious freedom of America's religious worship. These were the stout hearted Hollanders of early Cedar Grove.

75. PIETER DAANE'S

SKETCH OF CEDAR GROVE AND OOSTBURG

[This series of articles in *The Sheboygan Herald* from January 16 to 19, March 1892 presents a view of the Dutch settlement in Sheboygan County. Daane lived many years at Oostburg. He spent most of his life in Oostburg and was acquainted with every phase of the history of the Dutch communities of Sheboygan County, Wisconsin.]

The town of Holland is located in the south east corner of Sheboygan County and embraces town thirteen, range twenty-two and the fraction of range twenty-three; is composed of forty-two full and six fractional sections, is six and one half miles long on the south line and eight and one half miles on the north line, and six miles wide north and south; borders on lake Michigan on the east and Ozaukee County on the south. The soil is clay except in the eastern portions near the lake where it is sandy. It is very productive and kept under a very high state of cultivation, being divided into many small farms. The land is principally owned by Hollanders, except the extreme southwest part by Germans and northwest by Americans and Irish many of the early American settlers having sold out to Hollanders. Up to January 1841 no white settler had settled within the limits of the town of Holland. This region was one unbroken forest, the Indians being the only residents. They had undisputed possession of the rich hunting ground containing such game as bear, wolves and deer in great abundance.

The first house in the town as a frame building, built by David Giddings in the summer of 1841, on section 25 where Cedar Grove now is built. An accident occurred at the raising of this house, owing to the want of sufficient help; the principal help was brought from Sheboygan Falls [then named Rochester] 12 miles distant. A part of the frame fell and struck B. H. Gibbs, a son of J. D. Gibbs then living at Gibbsville; he was struck on the back and nearly killed. When the house was completed a Mr. Elsworth and family moved into it, they being the first white family living in the town of Holland. The first birth in the town was in this family. a daughter born in 1842.

The first Holland family in the town and also in the county was that of John Zeefeld who built a shanty on the northwest quarter of section thirty-six in 1845.

In 1845 the following American families were living in the town: John Johnson, James Wood, a Shaw, Burnett, Eany, Own, and Willcox.

In 1846 the following Holland families settled in the town: G. H. te Kolste, Aplonia van den Driest with het two sons Daniel and William, Jan Caljow, and Hendrik Vryheid.

The first death that occurred among the Hollanders, and I think the first town, was Johny Daane, brother of the writer, a bright lad of eight years, a grandchild of Aplonia van den Dreist who came to Wisconsin with his grandmother, one year in advance of his parents. He died in the winter of 1846 on the northwest quarter of section 19, range 23, near where the present burying ground now is located on the Sauk Trail road. His remains were taken to Sheboygan Falls and buried.

The first school house was built in 1846 on section 25; it was a log building. In the same year a great many families settled in the town, and also in the year 1847 many Holland families settled in the town, among others the Rev. Pieter Zonne who settled on section 24 and who held services in the Holland language. The first postoffice was established in the town on January 27, 1849, and named Cedar Grove; it was so named for the reason that there was a cedar swamp within a few rods east from the post office. Sweezy Burr was appointed postmaster.

The town was organized in the spring of 1849, the first election being held at the post office, at which election 65 votes were cast. Edwin Palmer was elected chairman; William Mitchell and Pieter Soufrouw, supervisors; Joseph Palmer, town clerk; David Cook, assessor; John Pool, treasurer; and William Mitchell, superintendent of schools.

The early settlers cleared off ground, cut logs into proper lengths, and hauled them with a yoke of oxen to the spot designed for the house. Then they had a bee with what neighbors they could get together to help them "log up" or raise their house or shanty, as they were called. The house consisted of four sides "logged up" to a proper height, always taking care to have the back part about $1\frac{1}{2}$ feet lower than the front, so as to give sufficient slope to the roof. The roof consisted of bass wood troughs, or trees split in two and hollowed out so as to allow the rain to run out; these were laid on the top of the shanty, side by side, the hollow side up, and over the opening one was laid with the hollow down to shed the rain. So the roof was made. In the front an opening was cut for a door, and next to the door a place was cut for an 8 by 10 six light window. Very many had nothing but a ground floor; stools sawed from logs were the only seats, a chest answered for a table. Such were the houses of the early settlers. One of the greatest necessities of the early settlers was a yoke of oxen. Those were considered very fortunate who could also buy a cow. A yoke of oxen then cost from $ 90 to $ 100, and a cow from $ 10 to $ 18. They were turned into the forest for pasturage, taking care, however, to secure a good bell on the neck of the leader; some of these bells could occasionally be heard a distance of two miles in still weather. It was the task of one member of the family to go out each day about the middle of the afternoon to hunt the cattle and drive them home if he was fortunate enough to find them, and corral them for the night. In the winter the cattle subsisted on straw and browsing from the trees that were cut down in the clearing. In the spring the cattle were often very weak and on being turned out, frequently got mired in the swampy places where the first green sprouts of grass were found. Very many cattle perished in this way. The wild leeks were among the first greens in the spring, and many a time the butter and milk could not be used on account of the taste of the leeks.

Fortunately the outlay for farming tools in those days was not large. A drag constructed from a small ironwood tree of about 6 inches in diameter, joined together at once end in the shape of a V, with a cross-piece in the middle, furnished with $1\frac{1}{4}$ inch iron teeth and a heavy log chain were all the tools needed until the land became so weedy that it required "rooting up", for such was the plowing. The tool used for a plow was made similar to a corn shovel plow, only much stronger and heavier. The same was used to dig here and there between the roots; a flail was used instead of a threshing machine.

In 1846 the Smith family settled on the lake shore near the mouth of Bark Creek where they were engaged in fishing and hunting. Fishing then was carried on with seines from 80 to 100 rods long brought out from 3/4 of a mile to one mile in the lake, and hauled in shore with a windlass. The lake then was full of fish, mostly large white fish, very few trout being caught. Many a time they caught more fish in one haul they could take care of during the day. Fish stories then, as now, were sometimes very much exaggerated as it was reported that as many as one hundred barrels were caught in one haul; but the writer has helped to drag in the seine when it became necessary to let many of the fish escape before it could be hauled on the sand.

In the summer of 1847 four Hollanders under the leadership of the Rev. Pieter Zonne, came for the purpose of locating in the town of Holland, expecting to move their families later. An accident occurred when they landed on a dark and stormy night on Kirkland's north pier in Sheboygan. One of the men, a Mr. Venendaal, in the darkness stepped off the pier and was drowned. His body washed ashore the next day and was buried in Sheboygan . . . .

Some amusing incidents occurred among the Holland settlers who had never been on a farm before they came to make their home in the wilderness. One man who had but shortly arrived on a certain occasion went to hunt his cow in the woods and found his cow but got last himzelf. Having a rope with him he tied his cow to a tree and went to find his way out of the woods. Upon returning to get the cow he found the cow had tugged so hard at the rope that he could not untie the knot. Having no knife with which to cut the rope, he resolved to shoot it, but instead shot and killed his cow. . . .

The original inhabitants, the Indians, at one time had a large camp at the mouth of Bark Creek, where traces are yet to be found in the shape of arrow heads and pieces of earthen pottery that become visible by the blowing away of the sand.

The ancient mount builders have also left a trace of their work. On section 8, range 23, on the bluff of the lake shore was originally a large and well preserved mound, but since the land has been cleared and cultivated it has become nearly obliterated, leaving but a small trace of it visible now. So the traces of a once great race are fast disappearing and their most sacred places are quickly disappearing under the ax and ploughshare of the whites.

It was never known that the Indians troubled the white settlers in any way except by asking for something to eat. Neither have we ever heard of wild beasts or wild cats ever attacking the settlers, but it frequently happened that bears stole pigs out of the pens and made off with them.

A little incident occurred to the writer when about 14 years old. While hunting cows in the woods he discovered a large wolf only a short distance away. It was but a moment before he had climbed into a small tree to be out of harm's way. But as soon as the wolf found someone was near he made off. After the wolf had gone, upon the writer going to the place, he found that he had killed a hog and was devouring it when discovered.

Intense excitement was caused when the new reached here of the burning of the *Phoenix*, which occurred on November 21, 1847 whereby 210 people lost their lives, either by burning or drowing. The boat was filled mostly with Holland emigrants hoping to find homes in the west. The majority of them were bound for the town of Holland and had nearly reached their destination being but a few miles from the landing when the said catastrophe occurred which deprived them of fathers, mothers, brothers, sisters, and many dear relatives, besides all their earthly possessions. They were penniless in a strange land. Truly this was a deplorable state. But people in Sheboygan did all they could to assist the survivors in every way, for they were in need of everything. Of one family, one of the lucky ones, consisting of a father, mother, and seven children, only two were lost, while of other families only one was saved . . . .

In the fall of 1847, Pieter de Witte with his family, and Mrs. Susannah Eernisse, whose husband had preceded her, landed on the south pier in Sheboygan. The children of Mr. De Witte had been sick with the small pox before leaving Rochester, New York, and the marks were still plainly visible when they landed. It was reported in the city that a family had landed who had the small pox. A constable was sent to conduct them into the woods where they camped south of the river. My father hired a team but was obliged to drive it himself, for he could not get a driver; he drove them to the town of Holland.

A general election was held on the sixth of November 1849 for the election of state and county officers; a vote was also taken on an amendment to the constitution, as follows: number of votes poled for equal suffrage to colored persons; yes, thirteen; no, twenty.

For 1850 the following town officers were elected: Sweezy Burr, chairman, Pieter Suffrou and Hendrik J. Traas, supervisors; J. J. van Keulen, town clerk; William Higby, Jr, superintendent of schools; Hendrik J. Boland, assessor; Pieter Suffrou, Hendrik J. Traas, and Jan J. van Keulen, justices of the peace; H. K. Hekkert, H. J. Lemkuil, and J. B. de Graav, constables; C. Blom, sealer of weights and measures. . . .

For 1851 the following officers were elected: Edward Palmer, chairman, Charles Green and Isaac Clairbaut, supervisors; Pieter Suffrou, town clerk; Joseph Palmer, superintendent of schools; C. Snoeyenbos, John de Lyzer, and David Cook, assessors; John Pool, treasurer, J. L. Wheeler and David Graham, justices of the peace, Pieter Daane Sr., Matthias Sneider, and G. S. Arnold, constables. Some of the officers not being qualified, at a meeting of the supervisors the following appointments were made to fill vacancies: Matthias Sprangers, supervisor; William Lawson, George Nims, and P. Daane, constables.

For 1852 the following town officers were elected: Edward Palmer, chairman; C. Snoeyenbos and H. Zirbes, supervisors; J. R. Muller, clerk; H. J. Boland, treasurer; J. Palmer, superintendent; J. de Lyzer, H. J. Boland, and G. H. te Kolste, assessors; H. Leuf and J. R. Muller, justices; Mathias Heynen, Pieter Zeeveld, and Joe Palmer, constables. It has the appearance from the records that the people then, were not so anxious to hold office as they are in these days, for at a meeting of the supervisors held on the 6th day of May, the following appointments were made to fill vacancies: G. J. Walvoord, supervisor; William Mitchel assessor; H. J. Arnold, constable.

For 1853 the following officers were elected: Edward Palmer, chairman; P. Zeeveld and M. Schneider, supervisors; Anesus J. Hillebrands, clerk; William Mitchell, superintendent; Anesus J. Hillebrands and C. Bright, justices; A. Eernisse, treasurer; G. H. te Kolste, C. Soule, and William Mitchell, assessors; E. B. Wood, Pieter Zeeveld, and D. Harrington, constables.

For 1854 the following officers were elected: Edward Palmer, chairman; M. Schneider and Pieter Zeeveld, supervisors: W. F. Mitchell, superintendent; J. Kiezel and E. B. Wood, justices: Anesus J. Hillebrands, clerk; G. te Kolste, R. Kurvink, and R. van Camp, assessors; H. J. Boland, treasurer; T. McConkey, J. Shaver, and H. J. Ketman, constables. The following appointments were made to fill vacancies: A. Van de Wall, constable; and D. Harrington, assessor.

For 1855 the following officers were elected: Wm. Mitchell, chairman; P. Zeeveld and N. Kleutsch, supervisors, there being a tie vote on superintendent, A. van de Wal was appointed; A. J. Hillebrands and C. Bright, justices; A. J. Hillebrands, town clerk; G. H. te Kolste, J. Bright, and Jos. Palmer, assessors; H. J. Boland, treasurer; H. J. Ketman, J. York, and J. Shaver, constables; C. Goit, sealer of weights and measures. Fifty dollars was raised for town espenses, fifty dollars for support of poor, two hundred and fifty for town schools, and five hundred for road tax; the clerk and superintendent having resigned, the supervisors appointed William Higby, clerk, and A. van de Wal, superintendent. A Petition was made to the town board to call a special meeting to raise funds for town expenses which meeting was held on the 30th day of May when the following resolutions were passed: To raise one hundred dollards to pay the debt of the town, to raise fifty dollars to defray the expenses of the town, and resolved to raise nothing for town clerk's salary.

In 1856 two hundred and one votes were cast at the annual town meeting, and the following officers were elected: David Cook, chairman; I. H. Wonser and Matthias Schneider, supervisors; Anesus J. Hillebrands, clerk; A. van de Wal, treasurer; J. J. van Keulen, superintendent; J. Bright and J. R. Muller, justices; G. H. te Kolste, Nicholas Kleutsch, and Peter Daane, Jr., assessors; H. E. Wood, C. Goit, and E. F. Brethouwer, constables; R. Kurvink, sealer of weights and measures. Two hundred dollars were raised to build a town hall on the site bought for the town.

For 1857 the following officers were elected: W. F. Mitchell, chairman; C. van Tilburg and M. Schneider, supervisors; Anesus J. Hillebrands, clerk; J. J. van Keulen, superintendent; A. van de Wall, treasurer; E. B. Wood and C. Bright, justices; G. H. te Kolste, N. Kaufman, and I. H. Wonser, assessors; J. Shaver, J. de Lyzer and E. S. Burr, constables; R. Kurvink, sealer of weights and measures; S. Burr, E. B. Wood and J. Palmer, auditors. . . .

For 1858 the following officers were elected: W. F. Mitchell, chairman; C. van Tilburg, N. Kaufman, supervisors; C. Goit, superintendent; C. G. van Altena, treasurer; A. van de Wall and S. H. Salverda, justices; P. Daane Jr, Henry More, Sr, and N. Kleutsch, assessors; E. S. Burr, J. York and J. de Die, constables; R. Kurvink, sealer of weights and measures. At a meeting of the supervisors the following appointments were made to fill vacancies, J. Shaver, Jr., constable; and P. J. Ketman, assessor, also appointed to fill vacancy , John Feltes, supervisor.

For 1859 the following officers were elected: W. F. Mitchell, chairman; C. Snoeyenbos and J. Feltes, supervisors; J. J. van Keulen, clerk; E. W. Chase, superintendent; N. Kleutsch, treasurer; C. Bright and J. J. Keulen, justices; G. H. te Kolste, assessor; P. van Ouwerkerk, John Shaver Jr., and J. Reimich, constables; E. J. Brethouwer, sealer of weights and measures.

For 1860 the following officers were elected: W. F. Mitchell, chairman; C. Snoeyenbos and J. Feltes, supervisors; A. Stokdijk, clerk; Pieter Daane Jr. treasurer; G. H. te Kolste, assessor; Andrew Palmer, superintendent; E. W. Chase and C. French, justices for two years, and A. van de Wall for one year; J. Shaver, J. Eernisse, and J. Reimich, constables; C. Soul, sealer of weights and measures.

For 1861 the following officers were elected: C. van Tilburg, chairman; C. Snoeyenbos and M. Schneider, supervisors; A. Stokdyk, town clerk; William Higby, superintendent; A. Lubbers, treasurer; G. H. te Kolste, assessor; C. Bright and A. van de Wall, justices of the peace; J. Reimich, Willem Heyink and J. Brummels, constables; C. Soul, sealer of weights and measures.

For 1862 the whole number of votes cast at said town meeting was 268, and the following officers were elected: Pieter Daane, chairman; Matthias Schneider and J. J. Brill, supervisors; A. Stokdyk, town clerk; August Perring, treasurer; P. Huisheer, assessor; J. Kiesel and J. Reimchr justices; J. Brummels, P. van Ouwerkerk, and G. W. Heyink, constables; M. Brasser, sealer of weights and measures.

One hundred dollars was raised for support of poor, five hundred for public schools, two hundred for incidental expenses. A petition was made to the town clerk, on the 26th day of August 1862 calling a special town meeting for the purpose of raising fifty dollars for every able bodied volunteer who enlisted in the army of the United States in the year 1862 for said town. Said meeting was held on the 11th day of September and resulted as follows: one hundred and four votes were given in favor, and one hundred and nineteen against.

For 1863 the following officers were elected: Jacob de Smidt, chairman; Willem Berenscot and J. A. Ramaker, supervisors; A. Stokdijk, town clerk; Pieter Huisheer, assessor; Pieter Zeeveld, treasurer; C. Bright and J. de Smith, justices of the peace; C. de Smidt, J. Brummels and William Jackson, constables; R. Kurvink sealer of weights and measures

Here we drop the curtain for a short time on the town administration and take up the part that the boys of the town of Holland took in the war of the rebellion. The blood of their forefathers coursed yet through the veins of their offspring when they fought against oppression and tyrany; their sons who have made this their adopted country, reponded nobly to the call when the country was in danger, they stood shoulder to shoulder with the American born citizen in defense of their common country.

Very great was the excitement at the breaking out of the war of the rebellion when the news flashed over the wires of the firing of the first gun on Fort Sumpter, on that memorable morning of the 12th day of April 1861 and three days later on the 15th of the same month, when Abraham Lincoln made his first call for seventy-five thousand men, then it was that the people begain to realize that a great war was pending. William J. Turner was the first volunteer from the town of Holland; he enlisted on the 21st day of April 1861. The following is a list of the names of the men who served in the war of the rebellion, from the town of Holland, with the date of enlistment, company, and branch of service the served in:

W. J. Turner, corporal, April 21, 1861; Daniel Harkins, May 27, 1861; Nelson Jackson, corporal, Oct. 17, 1861; John Shaver, Dec. 1, 1864. All the above in Co. C. 4th Cavalry.

James E. Smith, Dec. 16, 1963, Co. H. 4th Cavalry.

Timothy Thomas, Febr. 29, 1864, 4th Battery.

Peter Daane Sr. Nov. 17, 1863; Chas. W. Wright Oct. 15, 1863 13th Battery, Light Artillery.

Charles A. Davis, Sept. 1, 1864; Adam Gartner, Sept. 1, 1864, Co. K. 1st Regiment Heavy Artillery.

George Hermon, Dec. 1, 1862, Co. E; Lucius E. Knowles, Aug. 17, 1861, Co. G; Samuel McConkey and Wesley York, Nov. 24, 1863, Co. H.; Daniel de Groot, Mathew de Master, Cornelius de Smidt, Abraham du Pons, Pieter Huibregtse, Derk Kapers, Jacob Kommers, Sergeant Cornelius Wagner, Lamert Wissink, Benjamin Ballard and Theodore Ott, enlisted Sept. 16, 1861, in Co. H, 1st Infantery.

Allen Cook, Sept. 28, Co. 1; Henry J. Mentink, Sept. 22, John Oonk, corporal, Oct. 3, 1861, and John Brazier, Nov. 24 1863, in Co. I, 1st Infantry.

William Coats, Nov. 7, 1863, Jacob N. de Grave and Josiah Marsielje, Nov. 24, 1863, in Co. K. 1st Infantry.

Jack Weskano and Charles H. Wescot, May 7, 1861, Co. I. 3rd Infantry.

Thomas McGee, John Schneider, August Schwant, and John te Kippe, Oct. 21, 1864, Co. D. 6th Infantry.

John Fontein, Dec. 7, 1864 Co. H; Isaac Eernisse and Cornelius Kool, Oct. 21, 1864; Abraham Lemahieu, Jan. 31, 1865; John G. Oonk, William Orlebeke, Gerrit te Lindert, Dirk W. te Ronde, John van der Jagt, Arend J. Vrugink and William Beernink, enlisted Oct. 21, 1864, Co. 1, 6th Infantry.

Christiaan Voskuil, Gerrit Jan Wieskamp, Arnoldus Zerink, John J. Scholten, and Arnout Wolfer, Oct. 21, 1864, Co. I, 6th Infantry.

Hendrik Jan Lensink, Jan. 31, 1865, Co. I. 7th Infantry.

Alvin K. Allen, Sept. 2, 1861; John Allen, Sept. 12, 1861, Co. I, 8th Infantry.

John W. Fokin and Jacob Roelse, Sept. 12, 1861; Peter Verhaage, Sept. 22, 1861, and John Weiland, Feb. 24, 1864, Co. A. 9th Infantry.

Christian te Paske, Oct. 21, 1864; Lindert van der Jagt, Jacob Zeeveld and Gerrit Gossink, Dec. 1, 1864, Co. D. 13th Infantry.

John Abbink, Oct. 21, 1864; John Brummels, Oct. 1, 1864; Marinus Flipse and Henry Vryheid, Dec. 1, 1864; Henry J. Prinsen, Dec. 2, 1864, Co. G. 14th Infantry.

Roswell H. Tripp, 1st Lieut, July 26, 1862; Richard M. Gifford, July 21, 1862, Co. B. 27th Infantry.

Harvey L. Wright, Febr. 20 1864; Mortem Ketman, Jan. 16, 1865, Co. E. 27th Infantry.

Pieter Daane, 1st Lieut, August 21, 1862; William Mitchell, 1st lieut, August 21, 1862; William Mitchell, 1st Lieut, Sept. 8, 1862; Adrian Daane, sergeant, Grades Leinen and Isaac Kommers, Aug. 21. 1862, Co. F. 27th Infantry.

Abraham Eernisse, sergeant, Abraham Eernisse, Peter J. Eernisse, Jacobus Eernisse, Mathew Eernisse, corporal, Johannis Eernisse, Samuel Eernisse, corporal, Abraham J. Kommers, Abraham Kommers, Andrew Jackson, Jan Liefbroer, Allonzo Loomis, Alexander Mc Mullen, Bern H. Obrink, Segwick W. Pettis, Arend J. Prange, Jan H. Rouwerdink, John Soul, Daniel Tellier, Gerrit J. te Camp, Gerrit J. te Slaa, Antonie Termaat, Jan H. Termaat, Antonie Voskuil, James Ward, Gerrit H. Winkelhorst, and Krijn Wolfert, Aug. 21, 1862, Co. F. 27th Infantry; Stewart E. Wierman, Mar. 21, 1864, Abraham van Akkeren, Nov. 22, 1862, Co. I, 27th Infantry; Peter van der Jagt, Nov. 29, 1862, Co. I, 27th Infantry; George Mabie and Henry ter Haar, Dec. 10, 1863, Co. H. 31st Infantry; Henry Kruenen, Abraham Loomis, Peter Liefbroer, Dirk Nederhand, sergeant, John B. Vonhof, Huibregt Risseeuw, Iman Serier, Gerrit van Lier, Peter van Owerkerk, sergeant Nov. 15, 1862. Co. D. 34th Infantry.

Patrick Ferry, David Patterson, Nov. 10, 1862, Co. U. 34th Infantry. Martin Brasser, Baarend G. Brethouwer, Dominick Dunn, Abraham Lammers, Nov. 10, 1862, Co. G. 34th Infantry.

John Fontaine, Nov. 15, 1862, Co. G. 34th Infantry.

Henry Rhodes, Oct. 21, 1864, Co. F. 37th Infantry.

Norman Shaver. Oct. 31, 1864, Co. F. 37th Infantry.

Nicolas Rottier, Oct. 21, 1864, Co. G. 37th Infantry.

James A. Bronson Nov. 18, 1864, Co. I. 37th Infantry.

Henry Schons. Nov. 21, 1863, Co. I. 27th Infantry.

John Dunck, Oct. 21, 1864, Co. G. 37th Infantry.

Charles B. French, Albert Kamstra, Jefferson C. Lombard, Alvinzo Lombard, Martin van der Weege, Izak Marsilye, Febr. 3, 1865, Co. F. 47th Infantry.

James Dunn, Oct. 1, 1864, Co. D. 22nd Infantry.

The following is a list of names of men whom I did not know, who were credited to the town, therefore supposed to have been some of those that were bought to fill the quota of the town: Lamert te Kolste,

Jan. 12, 1865, Co. K. 14th Reg. Infantry;Melvin I. Arnan, Feb. 24, 1864, Co. K. 14th Reg. Infantry; Frederik Fasset, Feb. 20, 1864, Co. F. 14th Reg. Infantry; James H. Cramer, Feb. 22, 1864, Co. F. 14th Reg. Infantry; Alexander Adams, Oct. 4, 1864, Co. F. 14th Reg. Infantry; Gerrit Inhoff, Jan. 6, 1865 Co. I. 22nd Reg. Infantry; Richard S. Allbe, Mar. 26, 1864, Co. I. 22nd Reg. Infantry; George Kendrick, Mar. 22, 1865, Hancock's Corp; William Clow, Mar. 22, 1865 Hancock's Corps; Jack Pender, Feb. 23, 1865, Colored Troops; James Nelson, Nov. 30, 1864, Colored Troops.

Making in all 142 men enlisted and drafted, and 11 bought, a grand total of 153 able bodied men; a very heavy drain upon the town, when we take into consideration that the vote of the town in April, 1862, numbered only 268 when very few had enlisted. We also find that 13 men that enlisted in the first Infantry were credited to Sheboygan Falls, if they had been properly credited to the town, there would have been no necessity of raising the eight thousand dollars above referred to. . . .

George Hermon, at Chickamauga, Ga.; Theodore Ott, taken prisoner at Chickamauga, Ga., and reported dead; Henry J. Mentink, at Chickamauga, Ga.; John Schneider, of wounds at Hatchers Run, Va.; Charles H. Wescot, of wounds at Antietam; Arnoldus Zwerink, Gravelly Run, Va.; John Liefbroer, Pine Bluff, Ark. The above is a list of those killed in action or died of wounds.

List of those who died of disease while in the service: Derk Kappers, at Madison, Wis.; Alvin K. Allen, at Youngs Point, Va.; John Allen, at Farmington, Miss.; Gerrit Gossink, on Hospital boat, Henry Vryheid, at Baton Rouge, La.; Harvey L. Wright, at Madison, Wis.; Jacob Eernesse, at Helena, Ark.; Abram J. Kommers, at St. Louis, Mo.; Andrew Jackson, at Memphis, Tenn.; Allonzo Loomis, at Helena, Ark.; Gerrit te Camp, at Memphis, Tenn.; Gerrit J. te Slaa, on Hospital boat; Antonie ter Maat, at Columbus, Ky.; John H. ter Maat, at Memphis; Tenn., Antonie Voskuil, at Helena, Ark.; Gerrit H. Winkelhorst, at Little Rock, Ark.; Abram Lammers, at Columbus, Ky.; Barend Brethouwer, at Columbia, Ky.; Marten Brasser, at Columbus, Ky.; Henry Schons, at Philadelphia, Pa.

There was a most remarkable event in those days, when it is taken in consideration that so few Indians were then remaining in the bounds of the state. . . . I have sometimes thought that probably the great broom tailed comet that swept through the western heavens one or two years before might have something to do with it, for many people consider such events as a foreboding of great evil; that, combined with the war of the rebellion that had just commenced, in my opinion had much to do to make the people easily excited and was undoubtely in some measure the cause of the wide spread scare, not alone in the state of Wisconsin, but over the greater part of Illinois. It was in the early part of September, 1862, about 10 o'clock in the day, that large groups of men gathered together in the principal streets of Sheboygan looking northward from whence one courier after another came bringing the dreadful news that the Indians were advancing, slaughtering all that they fell in with. Manitowoc was in ashes, Centerville was attacked; such was the news they brought. Many of the men who had just enlisted in the 27th Wisconsin, were among the group. After a hasty consultation the first move was on the hardware stores in the city to obtain all the available weapons; some proposed to take the old cannon that was used to celebrate the 4th of July and march out and meet the enemy and turn their flank if possible. Intense was the excitement in the country where the news rapidly spread, where one after another came riding on horseback in full gallop, yelling as they came, "flee for your lives, the Indians are coming", not one of whom had seen a Indian that day; the people fled from their homes, crowded together in houses that were selected as places of refuge. The men gathered together in groups with what weapons were available, some with shotguns, some armed with hay and manure forks, others with old scythes wherewith they hoped to check the advancing foe. When night came large companies of men were posted on the principal roads in the town of Holland, watching for the enemy; couriers on horseback were sent out as a patrol during the night to act as advance pickets to give timely warning of the advance of the enemy; two others and myself were selected for the advance pickets; with an old sword dating from the time of Napoleon, buckled on my waist, and a shotgun on our shoulders we set out on our dangerous task. In reality it was dangerous, not from the supposed enemy, but from our own friends, for how easily could they have mistaken us for the Indians in the dark! Very many were less courageous and loaded their families with their valuables on wagons and fled to Milwaukee; others beyond Milwaukee, fled to Chicago; threshers left their machines, grain standing in sacks and fences open so that cattle and horses ran at large over the farms; some hid for the night in corn fields, so the night was passed in suspense by many, all this growing out of a drunken spree of a few Indians, wherein one Indian was killed as we afterward learned. The next day the great scare wore gradually away and the great Indian war, as some termed it, was over....

76. JOHN H. KARSTEN'S A HALF CENTURY OF DUTCH SETTLEMENT IN WISCONSIN 1847-1897

[The Rev. John H. Karsten served Reformed congregations at Oostburg and Alto in Wisconsin. This sketch was prepared to be read at the Semi-Centennial celebrations in August 1897. The author fails to note the Dutch Catholic settlements in the Fox River Valley, numerically larger than all other Dutch settlements in Wisconsin combined. This sketch has lain unpublished among the manuscript materials kept by the Netherlands Museum.]

When for various reasons fifty years ago the question of seeking new homes beyond the seas began to be agitated among Netherlanders in the Old Country, Wisconsin was considered a desirable state for settlement. In printed pamphlets and private letters her advantages were set forth at length. Her geographical position in the Middle West, her salubrious climate subject to neither extremes of heat and cold; the fertility of her soil; her many beautiful lakes and rivers invited occupation by the sturdy Hollander.

Within her borders were to be found all necessary conditions to make a people strong and prosperous. Preference for any kind of agricultural pursuit could be satisfied. The small fruit farmer could find a soil adapted to his purpose; the large farmer ample opportunity to raise the coarser grains.

Numerous beautiful and rich prairies, interspersed between the heavily timbered regions, offered homes to those who dreaded the laborious task of clearing forest land; to them such prairies offered a welcome home. The field laborer, the man of wealth, the artisan and man of industrial enterprise or commercial interests, all could here find a chance to found comfortable homes and lay foundations for wealth.

The extensive lake coasts of Wisconsin, with harbors adapted to commercial intercourse with distant points would prevent isolation, and in time transform this region into a powerful commonwealth, a member of the family composing this union. And so history has proved it was to be.

Why, then, was Wisconsin, thus possessing the climate, soil, and geographical location which met so ideally the needs of Hollanders not chosen as the main place of settlement? As far as we know, the decision to locate in Pella, Iowa, and Holland, Michigan, was not reached until after the leaders had crossed the ocean. After long, deliberate consideration and much prayer Dominie Albertus Christiaan van Raalte selected the site of Holland for his colony, and Dominie Hendrik Pieter Scholte that of Pella, Iowa. With the reasons for their decision this paper is not concerned.

Those acquainted with the history of immigration know that men like Van Raalte and Scholte served as stars to guide the people who were to follow. Further, it is certain that religious views had something to do with determining their choice. Through such influences Wisconsin fell out of sight as an object of colonization. But this was only temporary, for its very location compelled occupation.

How, then, was Dutch immigration directed to Wisconsin? Simply by the efforts and example of private parties. It was distinguished by the fact that it did not have the leadership of men of superior knowledge or of any far seeing policy. There were Hollanders in Wisconsin before Hollanders settled in Michigan. The beginning of this immigration antedates the arrival in Michigan by more than a year. In the summer of 1845 a few Hollanders from the province of Zeeland arrived in Milwaukee. Their names were rcorded as the pioneers of a great movement. They were: Jakobus Tak, Jan Pleite, Jakobus Ameele, Andries du Mez, and Hendrik Bruggink, the last two being from the province of Gelderland. On November 15 of that same year arrived the Siefeld family of which a member – Pieter Siefeld still is living in Cedar Grove, Sheboygan County, Wisconsin.

The Hollanders did not settle in Wisconsin in the same manner as in Michigan or Iowa. The pioneers had no leaders. Individualism characterized the movement. There were no concerted plans of organized efforts. Places for settlement were not selected with any definite object in view-industrial, educational, or religious. Many places were settled by the merest chance. For example, a young man, Albert Meenk had become acquainted with an American friend back East who subsequently moved West. Desiring to see him again, he followed him to Alto in Fond du Lac County. This proved to be the beginning of the Dutch settlement of Alto. Another Hollander from Milwaukee went to the Land Office in Sheboygan Falls, in search of good farming lands. Finding the soil in Sheboygan County excellent for agriculture, he remained there.

How different the history of Dutch immigration would have been if with proper forethought and wise leadership Hollanders had concentrated in Milwaukee, Sheboygan, and other places along the shore of Lake Michigan! They soon would have become successful in commerce which stimulates rapid development, especially in social standing, in power and influence. But the vast majority of the Dutch immigrants, being farmers, wanted farms. They established themselves on fertile soil; we know of one case where poor soil was the cause of comparative failure.

Settling in the country instead of in places along the Lake Michigan shore or on navigable rivers, the Hollanders were exposed to the dangers of disintegration and absorption. Internal dissensions threatened to ruin the common interest. A self-assertive individualism in the midst of a group isolated in a strange land tended to foster extreme conservatism which might destroy the group within a generation or two. Equally great were the dangers of being absorbed into the social and political life of the country without retaining the ancient virtues which the immigrants believed were good. Demagogues might estimate the value of individuals only according to the number of their votes. From these evils they were protected in their common religious life and their interest in higher education. The unity of their churches for them was an object of the gravest concern. The question of religion was one of the chief causes of their emigration from the Netherlands. Churches were formed and organized into Classes. Higher education was provided for by the establishment of the Pioneer School in 1851 at Holland, Michigan. Three topics in their religious life worked for unity-higher education, domestic missions, and foreign missions. Individual absorption into the broad stream of America was prevented by common colonization. This strengthened the Dutch settlements and enriched American life. We believe that the history of the past fifty years has vindicated this policy of founding colonies rather than to permit immigrants to scatter. Today we rejoice in the power and influence of our Dutch immigrants. The founding of our academies and of Hope College have proved a blessing; such institutions were possible only when the Dutch immigrants established themselves in colonies.

The Dutch immigrants who came to Wisconsin in a small but steady stream numbered between 15,000 and 20,000. They were poor people, ignorant of the language, customs, and business methods of the land of their adoption. The causes of their success were several. One was the spirit of unselfishness that moved them. Unselfishness never ruined a settlement; nowhere was there a Dutch community that ended disastrously like Port Sheldon in Michigan. Further, a noble aim was cherished among the emigrants that left the Netherlands. They wished to live godly lives, which object was bound to be successful. Also, thrift, economy and an indomitable spirit of perserverance made pioneer life under adverse and discouraging circumstances a success. And the consecration of material things to the mental and spiritual interests of the people led to rich rewards. We hear even today the thundering voice of our great leader, the Rev. A. C. Van Raalte, ringing in our ears when in impassioned language he set forth to his listeners the meaning of life, the worth of the human soul, the value of wealth in the service of man. His soul glowed with the thought that Christ was for man, and man for Christ. And he and his associates have not labored in vain. Their spirit is marching on. They still are with us. They have left the impress of their thinking upon our generation and on others to follow. As a result we have material prosperity, excellent social standing, flourishing churches, and good institutions of higher learning. Last but not least the great course of success is: *Immanuel* – God with us. If ever there was a movement inspired in divine wisdom and love, protected by the Almighty, it was the planting of this people in the wilds of America. It is God's work, and it is marvelous in our eyes. Let us praise Him today, from Whom all blessings flow.

A number of Hollanders occupied places of eminence and influence in the state. This was to be expected, for the Dutch immigrant possessed a perservering spirit, but is modest withal. His worth is to be discovered, for he does not push himself forward. He often shines in retirement. Trustworthiness of character makes him eligible for public office. The following have held positions of public trust:

Gijsbert van Steenwyk, Bank Controller, 1860-2;
State Senator, 1879-'80.

Peter Daane Sr.,	Member of the Assembly 1873
Henry Walvoord,	„ „ „ „ 1885
Roelof Sleyster,	„ „ „ „ 1870
Frederick J. Zetteler Sr,	„ „ „ „ 1864-'75
Peter Fagg	„ „ „ „ 1875-'76
John H. W. Wigman,	District Attorney, Outagamie County, 1864-'70; Mayor of Green Bay, 1882; and District Attorney for the Eastern District of Wisconsin, under President Cleveland, 1891-'93.
Martin Gerrits,	Supt. of Schools Outagamie County, 1862-'64.
C. A. Hamer,	Clerk of the Circuit Court, Outagamie County, 1856-'64; Register of Deeds, 1866-'70.
Bernard Beerondben,	Register of Deeds, Brown County, 1874-'90.

Henry Watemolen,	Clerk Circuit Court, Brown County, 1886-'90.
John B. A. Massé,	Clerk Circuit Court, Brown County, 1856-'74.
Charles A. Masse,	County Judge, Door County, 1890-1901.
John H. Corscot,	Mayor of Madison, Wisconsin, 1893-'95.

In 1847 a few Dutch families under the leadership of Jan Kotvis and P. Lankester settled at Franklin Prairie, Milwaukee County, about fourteen miles southwest from the city of Milwaukee. This is a beautiful spot well adapted to farming. It is a small prairie of rich soil; its nearness to Milwaukee always insures good markets. This land is equally well adapted to stock raising and the growing of all kinds of grains and fruits. Hardly a place could have been selected which promised greater success. It is one of the garden spots of the State.

These settlers came from the province of Zeeland in the Netherlands. Many of them, especially the leaders mentioned above, suffered from religious persecution, they came across the ocean seeking religious freedom in this country. Although they were men of some means and did not need to emigrate, they came to found comfortable homes for themselves and their children. Kotvis and Lankester, men of considerable ability, possessed profound religious convictions. Being earnest men, they influenced people to think and live correctly. Imbued with the moral and religious purpose of the immigration as preached by its first promoters in the Old Country, they were zealous supporters of higher education; sound in their faith as well as their views of church history. They believed these immigrants of the Reformed faith should join the Reformed Church in America. As soon as the number of families made it possible, they effected a church organization. Both men were elected elders and, excepting preaching of the Gospel and administration of the sacraments, discharged all the duties that devolved upon ministers. After a few years Lankester moved to Wilwaukee and later to Grand Rapids, Michigan, where he died in a ripe old age, beloved and mourned by children and many friends. Kotvis remained in Franklin Prairie and labored on like a father of the community, exercising patriarchal care over the people until he died in 1895.

But in spite of every economic and other advantage, Franklin Prairie never became a thriving Dutch settlement. The population soon began to decrease and is sill decreasing so that at the present moment not more

than twenty families remain. The settlement thus appears to be threatened
with early distinction. One reason for this decline is the lack of consistent
preaching of the Gospel. Without this advantage the Dutch settler was
not likely to be drawn to any settlement. Dutch communities are built
up around churches, which results in the development of a vigorous
religious and church life. Nevertheless the church of Franklin Prairie
has carried on a moribund existence without a pastor for almost fifty
years.

The city of Milwaukee naturally attracted the attention of Dutch
immigrants, being situated ideally for commerce on the western shore of
Lake Michigan, eighty four miles north of Chicago, and possessing a
splendid harbor. As stated above, a few Hollanders had arrived in the
summer of 1845. Others followed them, especially after 1850. The first
comers were from the provinces of Zeeland and Gelderland. Those who
followed them naturally came from the same communities in the
Netherlands; and hence the Hollanders of Milwaukee, as well as the
Hollanders in the colonies which may be regarded as offshoots of the
settlement activity that centered at Milwaukee, for the most part were
Zeelanders of Gelderlanders. Attachment to local peculiarities in thought
and speech and the desire for help and advice in a strange land encouraged
them to settle among friends, thus perpetuating the provincial peculiarities
in thought, manners and language we find in the Netherlands.

Prominent among those who came to Milwaukee between 1850 and
1860 were S. ter Horst, Dirk J. Doornink, A. J. te Brake, Jan le Grand,
E. Janssen, H. J. Mentinck, Jakobus Guequierre, F. T. Zetteler, and the
Christiaanson, Jan L. Rademaker, Geerlings, Houtkamp, Davelaars,
and other families.

In 1849 the first Dutch settlers organized a Reformed church which
soon became a large congregation, now situated on the corner of Tenth
and Harmon streets. Later, owing to differences of opinion, some of its
members broke away and founded the Dutch Presbyterian church on
Walnut Street. A second Dutch Presbyterian church, also on Walnut
Street was founded.

The Dutch element in Milwaukee is represented in nearly every branch
of the city and county government, and also in business and professional
life. From them have come aldermen, doctors, lawyers, druggist, bankers,
architects, merchants, contractors, and other business men. Every branch
of trade is represented: there are bricklayers, carpenters, painters, brass
finishers, plumbers. These Hollanders are rapidly being Americanized.
The number of Milwaukee Hollanders born in the Netherlands is

conservatively estimated as 600 out of a total of about 3,000 Holland Americans of whom about 1,400 are qualified voters.

Early in the 1850's a few Dutch families settled at Bethlehem about eight miles north of Milwaukee, in what was generally called Town Eight. This settlement, it appears, never flourished. An influx of Germans throttled its development. The church organized by them in 1850 soon became extinct, and all but two or three families of the Hollanders who settled there moved away.

As early as 1846 a number of Hollanders settled in Sheboygan County. Among the pioneers were Gerrit te Kolste, Evert Haartman, J. B. Meerdink, Pieter Ziefeld, Pieter Daane, Claerbout, and a few others. Soon after their settlement Dominie Pieter Zonne settled in Cedar Grove. Gradually as the influx of Hollanders continued the settlements of Cedar Grove, Oostburg, Gibbsville, and Hingham came into existence. In time Hollanders also established themselves in Sheboygan and Sheboygan Falls where, however, they always remained a small minority.

This colony, situated between forty and fifty miles north from Milwaukee flourished from the beginning. The soil was excellent for farming, consisting of heavy, fertile clay. The Township of Holland is with few exceptions entirely settled by Hollanders. Wilson and Lima are only partially occupied by them. In general, their thrift and industry have enabled them to establish comfortable homes, and in some cases acquire an accumulation of some wealth. Ecclesiastically, they belong to different denominations; there are six Reformed churches, two Christian Reformed, and two Presbyterian.

With the history of the colonization of Sheboygan County is connected one of the saddest of events, the loss through fire of the propeller *Phoenix* just after midnight of November 21, 1847, within only three or four miles off shore and only six miles north from the harbor of Sheboygan toward which the vessel was proceeding. The passengers, almost entirely composed of Gelderlanders who had just come from the Netherlands and intended to make their homes in Wisconsin, had on the evening before united in worship singing Psalm CXXXI, 4:

> *Dat Israel op den Heer vertrouw'*
> *Zijn hoop op Gods ontferming bouw'*
> *En stil berust' in Zijn beleid*
> *Van nu tot in all' eeuwigheid.*

When the War of the Rebellion broke out in 1861 the Hollanders of Sheboygan County proved worthy descendants of their fathers who

resisted Spanish tyranny for eighty long years. Eighty-six men from
Township Holland alone offered their lives for the Republic. They
enlisted in the several branches of the military services in the following
regiments:

  1 in Light Artillery,
 13 in 1st Regiment, Infantry (Chickamauga, Chaplin Hills, Kentucky,
    Kenesaw Mountain)
 15 in 6th Infantry (Antietam, South Mountain, Wilderness,
    Gettysburg),
  3 in 9th Infantry (Jenkins Ferry, Newtonia)
  4 in 13th Infantry (no prominent engagement)
  5 in 14th Infantry (Shiloh, Corinth, Spanish Fort)
 26 in 27th Infantry (Prairie d'Ane, Jenkins Ferry, Spanish Fort,
    Vicksburg)
 12 in 34th Infantry (not engaged in battle)
  1 in 31st Infantry (not engaged in battle)
  2 in 37th Infantry (Petersburg)
  3 in 47th Infantry (not engaged in battle)
  1 in 14th Infantry (not engaged in battle)

Among the officers were the following Hollanders: 1st Regiment,
Infantry: Matthew de Master and John Oonk, corporals; Jacob Kommers, sergeant; Pieter Daane Sr. of Oostburg, first lieutenant; 27th
Infantry, Adriaan Daane of Alto, sergeant, Abraham Eernisse of Gibbsville, sergeant; and Matthew and Samuel Eernisse, corporals. In the
34th Infantry: Dirk Nederhand and Per van Ouwerkerk, sergeants.

The city of Sheboygan with a population of 2,000 situated on Lake
Michigan and having a fine harbor and good railroad connections at
first attracted a few Hollanders. But only in recent years have their
numbers increased to a considerable extent so that a Reformed church
was organized by the Classis of Wisconsin. This congregation possesses
a neat and commodious church and a comfortable parsonage. There also
is a small Christian Reformed congregation. In Sheboygan Falls, six
miles west of Sheboygan and five north of Gibbsville, a small community
of Hollanders has lived ever since about 1856. Some of them make their
living by farming, others work at some trade, and some are in business.
They belong to the Reformed Church but have never had a pastor of
their own until 1892. Their number, about thirty or forty families, remains the same from year to year. These people are moderately well-
to-do.

Alto, situated in a township of the same name in the southwest corner of Fond du Lac County, six miles west of Waupun, 68 from Milwaukee on the Chicago, Milwaukee and St. Paul Railroad, was settled in 1846, by Hollanders, mostly from the Province of Gelderland. The very first Dutch pioneers of Alto were Albert Meenk and Nelson Hallerdyk, who arrived in 1845. The country around Alto consists mostly of openings in the forest in the eastern part of the settlement, but the western part is a fertile prairie producing large yields. Without much acquaintance with the soil of the State, the Dutch pioneers as if by accident stumbled upon this beautiful corner. At first Alto was peculiarly isolated before the railroad came. But their church relations saved the settlers from a strangling isolation. They early formed a congregation of the Reformed Church in America under the leadership of Dominie Gerrit Baay from Apeldoorn in the province of Gelderland in the Netherlands. His little log house served him and his family as dwelling and the Dutch community as house of worship and as a school. It was in that log house that the religious life of the settlement received its first direction. First influences never die. Alto still feels the effects of that godly and devoted man who only too soon was removed from earth to heaven. He labored only a year and a half among his followers at Alto. We believe that this firm stand for education and vital godliness saved this community from a strangulating materialism.

The Reformed congregation has always been the largest church organization, although in the course of time a Dutch Presbyterian and a Christian Reformed church have come into existence. A Congregational church, begun many years ago, never flourished and has passed out of existence. An independent Christian school, supported by private subscription and established years ago stimulated an appreciation for education. This school no longer is in existence.

These Hollanders are prosperous, inclined to be generous. The entire township of Alto is with few exceptions settled by Hollanders. A number of Dutch families have established themselves in the townships of Waupun and of Metomen. Public religious services are all conducted in the Dutch tongue although the people are quite generally Americanized in everything but the use of English. The younger generation, however, uses English in daily life.

From the beginning of Dutch immigration to Fond du Lac County a few Hollanders have lived in Waupun, a city at present having about 3,000 inhabitants. But only in recent years have there been a sufficient number to organize a congregation separate from that of Alto. There

now are between fifty and sixty families, all belonging to the Reformed
Church. These people follow various trades: harness making, black-
smithing, umbrella manufacturing, tinsmithing, and the like. Among
these also are merchants, storekeepers, coal and lumber dealers, and
professional men. The English language is used in some of the religious
services. This community is growing slowly, recruited from farmers
who upon retiring go to live in Waupun, and from others who prefer
to work in factories.

About thirty five years ago a group of Hollanders established themselves
at Randolph Center in Columbia County, about twenty miles southwest
of Alto. This is a beautiful farming country consisting of openings and
high rolling prairie. A Friesian family by the name of Tillema came here
from Town Eight near Milwaukee. Others followed them, for the most
part relatives and of course all Friesians. Teunis, a son of the old Tillema
family, still lives here. A man of strong religious faith, earnest purpose,
believing in acquiring wealth solely for the sake of God and the good of
man, he has all his life been a strong factor in building this farming
community. Though few in number and isolated from other Dutch
groups, they had a strong faith in the future of their little colony, at the
present consisting in about thirty families. For the most part these
people are not rich but they are earnest and perservering.

There is another settlement of Friesians at New Amsterdam, about
fourteen miles north of La Crosse on the Black River near its confluence
with the Mississippi. Oepke Bonnema, a wealthy farmer at Harlingen in
the province of Friesland in 1853 sold his estates, having decided to
emigrate to the United States. A man of sympathetic nature, pitying his
poor neighbors, he decided to alleviate their sufferings and pay their
transportation expenses if they would accompany him. On February 26,
1853, they embarked at Harlingen and went by steamer, the *City of
Norwich* to Lowestoft, England. Separation from relatives and friends
was heartrending. Speeding before a strong northeast wind, they soon
lost sight of the crowds waving a last farewell. Soon the snow-covered
coast of Friesland sank from sight.

Their ocean voyage proved eventful, for a violent storm overtook them.
Shipwrecked on the coast of the Great Bahama Island, they were forsaken
by their captain and their crew. But they received help on May 5, the
day of Our Lord's Ascension, and were taken off their sinking ship. On
that day they invoked His wisdom, his invisible power and majesty.
They were filled with grateful feelings when in the early morning of that
day they descried land, and a little later a ship, the schooner *Creole*,

commanded by Captain Robert Sands, a Negro from the Bahama Islands. After remaining on the Bahamas for a short time the group embarked for Nassau and thence proceeded to New Orleans and by boat up · the Mississippi to La Crosse where they arrived on July 1, and on the 15th of that month at New Amsterdam, 92 persons in all. The colony at present numbers between 400 and 500.

The reason why Bonnema settled on this spot was the great abundance of timber and the opportunity of opening a profitable sawmill. Large rafts of logs were sent down the Black River from the north. When the lumbering business ceased, the settlers fell back upon farming. But the sandy soil was poorly adapted to this purpose, and so the settlement failed to grow. The bottom lands along the river indeed are quite productive, but the high bluffs which wall in the settlement are very poor land. But there are other reasons perhaps for the partial failure of New Amsterdam – reasons which relate to the moral condition of the settlers. But of these we need not speak here. It was many years before they had regular services on the Lord's Day. At present, however, and for some time they have enjoyed the ministrations of a resident pastor.

About ten years ago a number of Hollanders settled at Baldwin in St. Croix County. The greater part came from Sheboygan County; others came from Fond du Lac County. This place accordingly was not settled by immigrants directly from The Netherlands. Almost all of them are prosperous farmers. Ecclesiastically they belong to the Presbyterian and Christian Reformed Churches. In all, the settlement numbers between 40 and 50 families.

77. HERMAN BOTTEMA'S IN AMERICA'S FRIESLAND

[Bottema, born in Gorredijk, long a resident of Milwaukee, published the following report of what he saw and heard on a visit to Friesland, Wisconsin, in 1928. This account appeared in *Leeuwarder Courant*, August 8 and 9, 1928.]

In het Amerikaansche Friesland

„Uitstappen Friesland!" riep de conducteur. Ik was dus in Friesland, 80 mijl van Milwaukee gelegen. Dit is een zeer mooi oord. En de meerderheid van de bevolking is uit Friesland afkomstig en wel uit de nabijheid van Dokkum.

Maar hier niet alleen; in de onmiddellijke nabijheid liggen East Friesland en Randolph waar eveneens de Friesche bevolking wel vertegenwoordigd is. Getuige: 93 huisgezinnen in Friesland zijn lid van de Gereformeerde kerk; in Randolph 70 gezinnen en in East Friesland zijn er 76, die lidmaat zijn van de Christelijk Gereformeerde kerk. Naar schatting is ongeveer de helft van de inwoners of iets meer direct uit Friesland hier gekomen en hun aantal is vermeerderd door hun kinderen en kleinkinderen, die hier geboren zijn.

Als men, nadat men 42 jaren in de stad gewoond heeft en daar nooit een enkel woord Friesch hoorde, tenminste niet op straat, dan hier in Friesland zelfs de kleine kleuters, Friesch hoort spreken, dan is dat wel verrassend. De oude nederzetters spreken nog echt Friesch, zonder, zooals dat bij vele personen van andere naties het geval is, er vele Engelsche woorden doorheen te mengen. Het dorpje Friesland is ongeveer zestig jaar of even ouder.

Later kwam de spoorweg hier door en dit gaf een geduchten stoot aan groei en bloei van deze omgeving.

Het is de North Western Railway die hier doorloopt. De meeste Friezen hier zijn boeren en velen hebben naar het schijnt hun schaapjes op het droge. Deze wonen nu rustig en tevreden in dit dorpje Friesland. Sommigen waren boerenarbeider in Friesland en na hard en zwaar werk hier en spaarzaam, en mogelijk gelukkig ook te zijn geweest, hebben ze thans een onbezorgden ouden dag.

De eerste persoon, die ik hier toesprak, toen ik uit den trein kwam, was toevallig geen Fries, maar een zekere Gerrit J. Vredeveld, afkomstig uit Dalfsen, Overijssel, die hier post-directeur is. Hij spreekt de Friesche taal in de puntjes en is thans 16 jaar in Amerika. Benevens zijn ambt als post-directeur, dat natuurlijk in zoo'n klein plaatsje geen groot tractement opbrengt, heeft hij een winkel van room-ijs, sigaren, enz.

De tweede persoon, die ik ontmoette, was een jongen van elf jaar. Ik sprak hem in de Friesche taal aan en tot mijn verbazing antwoordde hij mij, „Ja, myn heit en mem binne in Fryslan geboaren, en ik kin ek Frysk sprekke." Nu, dat gaat goed, dacht ik. Naar het schijnt kan iemand, die noch Hollandsch, noch Engelsch, noch Duitsch spreekt, met de taal, in Friesland gesproken, goed terecht. En na hier een paar dagen te hebben vertoefd, is mij dat ook gebleken.

Men moet 's morgens in het postkantoor zijn, waar de menschen hun post afhalen, wil men eenige uren in een gezelligen kout met zijn oude landslieden vertoeven. De luitjes komen daar bijeen om met elkaar het nieuws van den dag en vele andere zaken te bespreken. Zeer gezellig inderdaad.

De derde, of beter gezegd de derden, met wie ik hier sprak, was Mr. Jan Wiersma, vrouw, zoon en schoondochter. Ik had dorst gekregen en klopte aan. „Kom yn", zei iemand uit de keuken. Ze zaten juist het avondeten te nuttigen en ik werd „eingeladen", zooals de Duitscher zegt, om „maar aan te schikken."

Deze Mr. Jan Wiersma en vrouw komen van Morra, Oostdongeradeel, en zijn reeds twee en dertig jaar hier in Friesland. Het bevalt hun hier zeer goed, beter dan in Friesland, waar het werken bij den boer daar hen nooit had kunnen brengen tot dien materieelen welstand, waarin ze zich hier verheugen. Onder den maaltijd kwam Mr. Sjoerd Kramer, timmerman, afkomstig uit de stad Leeuwarden, binnenstappen. Deze is vroeger aan den ambachtsschool te Leeuwarden geweest. Men vertelde mij, dat een zekere Harm de Fries, afkomstig uit Nijkerk, Oostdongeradeel, verleden jaar treurig om het leven is gekomen door van een stal te vallen.

In het postkantoor ben ik bekend geworden met de meeste Friezen en daar hoorde ik vele namen, die ons vroeger zoo bekend waren op de Gorredijk.

Daar is bijvoorbeeld Yense Tamminga, van Hiaure bij Dokkum. Hij is hier reeds zeven en dertig jaar en rentenier. Mr. Bote Kok, vijf en dertig jaar in Amerika, komt uit Brandgum, gelegen tusschen Holwerd en Dokkum. Hij sprak nog over de toestanden in de venen in Beets en omstreken en de onlusten, die daaruit voortvloeiden – de concentratie van soldaten te Gorredijk b.v., daar hij toen ook onder de wapens was en dit alles heeft meegemaakt. Hij had Domela Nieuwenhuis nog hooren spreken te Tijnje.

Poppe van der Velde is afkomstig uit Ee, anderhalf uur van Dokkum, tusschen Metslawier en Engwierum. Hij was verver in Friesland en heeft hier een groot magazijn. Mr. van der Velde is achttien jaar in Amerika en heeft juist voor den oorlog weer eens een bezoek aan Friesland gebracht. Hij is een buitengewoon beleefd en gedienstig man, die me hier goed bijgestaan heeft. Men moet weten, dat hier geen enkel hotel is en daar het al laat in den avond werd en hij zelf het huis vol bezoek had, heeft hij mij door zijn invloed en goed woord onderdak bezorgd bij een buur van hem – Mr. Jan Posthuma. Hij was pas 8 jaar oud toen hij hier met zijne ouders landde. Die kwamen hier in Friesland van Ooster-Nijkerk. Maar Jan ging, naar hij mij vertelde, het laatst school te Metslawier.

Dan is daar Lolke Gaastra, hier hoefsmid, die uit Workum afkomstig is en thans 16 jaar in Friesland woonachtig.

Harm Kloostra, van Niawier, is ook reeds vijf en twintig jaar in Amerika. Mrs Kloostra is afkomstig uit Nes, Westdongeradeel (Niawier: Oostdongeradeel). Ze rentenieren en waren eenige jaren geleden op bezoek bij hun dochter in Californie. Ook Jan Braaksma is hier aan het rentenieren, zijn geboorteplaats is Morra. Hij is hier twintig jaar.

Tjerk Westra, zes en dertig jaar in Amerika, arbeider in Friesland, werd hier boer, gevolg: schaapjes op het droge – rentenier. Hij zeide tegen me, dat Friesland in de laatste tien jaren zeer uitgebreid is.

Mr. Pieter D. Westra was boerenknecht in Friesland, geboortig te Hattum, noordelijk van Dokkum. Hij is nu reeds veertig jaar in Friesland en zijn zoon bewerkt de boerderij.

Mr. Andries de Jong komt van Lioessens, twee uren oost van Dokkum; hij is hier vijf jaar en is henne boer.

Mr. Gerrit Levy, woonde vroeger te Morra, is hier ook al zes en dertig jaar en rentenier.

Nonne de Jong, vader van Andries de Jong, komt uit Liossens, werkte daar bij den boer en is hier nu vijf en twintig jaar.

Mr. Sietse Visser stamt uit Paessens, gemeente Oostdongeradeel, is hier 25 jaar en veehandelaar.

Daar valt ons in het oog het uithangbord van Fillema; ook een groot magazijn, zijn vader kwam hier in Amerika reeds vijf en zeventig jaar geleden, maar woonde vroeger in Town Eight.

Mr. Gilbert Vredeveld is de barbier hier in Friesland. Een uiterst vriendelijk man. Ja, het komt mij voor, dat alle menschen hier vriendelijk zijn.

Maar zoo zouden wij kunnen voortgaan en eenige kolommen met namen van Friezen vullen. Doch ik vergat nog; Onne Sjoerdsma, voorheen van Ternaard, te noemen. Ik ontmoette hem vanmiddag. Hij was in zijn auto op weg naar zijn boerderij. Hij is hier een en twintig jaar en woont in Oost Friesland. En dan is er nog Jenske Tamminga, die hier een roomijs-salon en kruidenierszaak heeft.

Men ziet hier verschillende uithangborden met echt Friesche namen als N. Alsum, Jan Kloostra, enz. En industrie is er ook, maar natuurlijk niet half genoeg. Het ware beter als hier in dit opzicht wat meer leven en beweging was. Wel is hier de „Friesland Canning Co". Ik ontmoette daar Ely Cupery, kassier van de maatschappij, die, in Hiaure geboren, hier in 1881 aankwam. Deze fabriek werkt slechts 4 of 5 weken in het jaar. De productie van erwten beloopt zoo ongeveer 2,000,000 blikken per seizoen. Deze erwten groeien in den onmiddellijken omtrek en worden hier in blikken of bussen door geheel Amerika verzonden. Daar werken vele Friezen en jongedochters van Friesche afkomst. Ook zijn hier twee kaasfabrieken.

Mij beviel ten zeerste de gemoedelijkheid van de menschen hier. En in het postkantoor kan men schertsen met de oude nederzetters van Friesland, onder wie menigeen al aardig bedaagd is.

Zooals reeds gezegd, zijn 93 huisgezinnen van Friesland in Wisconsin lidmaat van de Gereformeerde kerk. Ik geloof niet, dat er een enkel gezin van Friesche afkomst is, dat niet tot de kerk behoort. De predikant, de heer Kleerekooper, bewoont het mooiste huis van de stad. Ik heb hem persoonlijk niet gezien of gesproken, maar men vertelde mij, dat hij van joodsche afkomst was. Hieruit blijkt de bloei van de Nederlandsche Gereformeerde kerk in deze streek. De eerbied voor de geestelijkheid is hier ongeveer dezelfde als b.v. op de Gorredijk zoo'n kleine eeuw terug. En dit is eigenlijk wel merkwaardig, gezien de geweldige verandering op bijna elk ander gebied. Hier is in dit opzicht een totale stilstand te constateeren.

Het verwonderde ons echter niet het minst, dat hier en elders de geestesgesteldheid geen verandering heeft ondergaan. De kinderen groeien op in dezelfde atmosfeer, waarin hun ouders en voorouders geleefd hebben en zijn, geestelijk gesproken, van hetzelfde model als hun voorvaders.

Het is duidelijk genoeg, dat de bewoners van het Iberische schiereiland in 1558 in Nederland een geduchten vijand ontmoetten. Diezelfde oppositie is onder onze landslui nog waar te nemen. Spreek maar eens met hen en tracht eens wat anders te beweren dan zij gewoon zijn te hooren. Men weet wat de gevolgen zijn.

Zedelijk staan de menschen hoog. Ze zijn goedhartig en steeds bereid voor een vreemdeling, zooals ik, het uiterste te doen. Natuurlijk is de lieve jeugd, ten minste de jongens, overal gelijk – altijd bedacht op, „ondeugende streken". Toen ik mijn eersten brief reeds in het couvert had hoorde ik de brandklok kleppen. „Brand!" hoorde ik roepen. Maar toen wij buiten kwamen vernamen we dat er nergens brand te ontdekken was – een paar belhamels hadden eenige forsche rukken aan het touw gedaan waaraan de klepel van de brandklok bevestigd is.

Het moet hier in Friesland wel een gezond oord zijn. Een Mr. Ketels stierf hier 14 jaar geleden in den ouderdom van 94 jaar. Deze kwam ongeveer in het jaar 1840 in Amerika. Hij was afkomstig uit de provincie Zeeland. Eigenlijk was het nog een oude bekende van me, daar wij het eerst in Milwaukee in het jaar 1888 bij hem gewoond hebben. Toen Ketels in zijn jonge jaren hier aankwam, liep hij van het toenmalige Chicago naar Milwaukee. Een kuiertje van ongeveer drie dagen! (Afstand: 90 Engelsche mijlen).

Friesland had drie en twintig jaar geleden slechts een winkel, maar, zooals gezegd, toen men het spoor er langs legde, is deze streek zeer vooruitgegaan en gegroeid.

Er zijn nu vier groote winkels waar men alles koopen kan. Natuurlijk is er gebrek aan werk voor 'n grootere bevolking. Een of twee fabrieken, waar men geregeld het jaar door zou kunnen werken, zou zoo'n oord

oord zeer in bloei doen toenemen. Maar die zijn er nu eenmaal niet.

Men heeft hier ook een houtstek, waar timmerhout verkocht wordt. Er is ook een school. De kinderen hebben hier in de zomermaanden maar eventjes drie maanden vacantie. In vroeger dagen moet het schoolgaan wel gebrekkig zijn geweest. Ten minste men vertelde mij zoo het een en ander hieromtrent. Er wordt hier wel gesproken in de Nederlandsche taal, doch er is geen school voor de jeugd om zich ook maar eenigszins in de taal van het oude land te kunnen bekwamen. En ik ben van meening, dat het nooit kwaad zou kunnen als den kinderen Nederlandsch werd geleerd. Want zooiets is altijd licht mee te nemen en komt mogelijk hier of daar wel eens te pas. En bovendien is de Nederlandsche taal rijk aan woorden, waarvan velen bijvoorbeeld ook in de Noorsche taal voorkomen. En in het Engelsch ook. Ik denk ook wel eens aan mijzelf en de groote meerderheid van de Friezen, die eveneens niet in staat zijn hun moedertaal te schrijven. Met hoeveel meer kracht en energie, hoeveel duidelijker en helderder had ik dit op papier kunnen zetten, als ik mij van de Friesche taal had kunnen bedienen. Het is alsof de taal, in een zeker oord gesproken, veel beter en zuiverder de indrukken weergeeft, die men daar opdoet, dan eenige andere taal. Daar zijn gezegden en uitdrukkingen gebezigd, terwijl ik in Friesland was, die ik, als dertienjarige jongen uit Friesland in Nederland gekomen zijnde, niet getrouw in het Nederlandsch zou kunnen weergeven. Daar is dus kracht en helderheid verloren in den zinsbouw en bijgevolg in iemands schrijven.

Met leedwezen heb ik het Amerikaansche Friesland weer verlaten en afscheid van de goede menschen daar genomen die, hoe korten tijd dan ook, ware en warme vrienden voor mij zijn geweest. En mijn bezoek aan hen zal mij nog lang, mogelijk levenslang, in het geheugen blijven.

Ik ben over South Beaverdam en Beaverdam gereisd. Bevers waren hier vroeger in grooten getale, vandaar de naam. En nu landde ik gisteren hier in Watertown, evenals Beaverdam een mooi stadje van ongeveer 8,000 zielen. Hier, evenals in geheel dezen staat, is de Duitsche bevolking sterk vertegenwoordigd.

De hotels waren hier tamelijk bezet toen ik aankwam, maar ik bespeurde aldra een uithangbord „kamers te huur". Een bejaarde vrouw kwam aan de deur en vroeg of ik een Zimmer haben wollte. Ik antwoordde met „ja", of beter gezegd „Yes". „Sprechen Sie Deutsch?" vroeg zij. Ik zei tegen haar, dat iemand, die meer dan veertig jaar in Milwaukee is geweest, *nolens volens* wel de Duitsche taal moest leeren spreken. Dus wel een bewijs, dat hier een massa Duitschers zijn.

Chapter XXIV

DUTCH CATHOLIC SETTLEMENT IN WISCONSIN

78. JOHN VERBOORT'S
VOYAGE OF THE LIBERA AND FOUNDING OF HOLLANDTOWN

[This is the fullest account of the voyage in 1848 of a group of Hollanders from Volkel who settled in the forest at what was to become known as Hollandtown. This article is in the form of a letter written in 1897 by John Verboort in Washington County, Oregon, and published in *De Gids*, December 20, 1897, a small magazine published at De Pere, Wisconsin.]

Verboort, Washington County, Oregon

November 23, 1897

Geachte vriend John Smith:

Uwe geachte letteren, van 17 dezer, heden ontvangen. Met genoegen zal ik zooveel mogelijk aan uw verzoek voldoen en mijne beste pogingen aanwenden om u een relaas te geven van onze reis naar Amerika onze aankomst, enz. Hoewel ik mij alles nog duidelijk kan voorstellen, zal er toch nog al veel in het vergeetboek geraakt zijn. Kunt gij echter van andere personen betere of meer volmaakte inlichtingen verkrijgen, dan kunt gij mij genoegen doen mijne mededeeling te verbeteren.

Het was op 9 Maart 1948 dat wij Volkel (gemeente Uden) verlieten om de reis naar Amerika te ondernemen. Tot Vechel werden onze koffers en overige reisbenoodigdheden met de kar, ik vermeen gratis, vervoerd door een vriend Hendrik Rombouts genaamd. Van Vechel reisden wij met de treckschuit naar 's Bosch, waar dezelfde schuit door eene stoomboot op sleeptouw werd genomen tot Rotterdam waar wij den 10den Maart op het schip *Libera*, een kleinen driemaster, werden ingescheept.

Wij waren met dertien families, alle Hollanders, in ons gezelschap met Pater Godhart als liedsman. De kapitein van het schip en de matrozen waren ook Hollanders. Het juiste getal landverhuizers aan boord van het schip *Libera* heb ik vergeten, maar het was omstreeks 80 personen. De volgende zijn de namen van de hoofden des families: Jan Klaassens, van Grave; Martinus Verkuilen, van Uden; Hein Groens, van Volkel; Niklaas Dennissen, van Volkel; Antoon Verkampen, van Volkel; Antoon Verwijst, van Uden (een lid dezer familie is nu Franciscaner pater te Ashland, Wisconsin); Mr. Denkboom, van Amsterdam; Albert van den Berg, van Cuyk; Ebben, van Mill; Johannes Tillemans met zijne aanstaande vrouw, van Boekel; Jan Verboort, van Volkel; en nog twee jonge mannen die bij de familie van Verkampen gerekend werden.

Wij vertoefden nog eenige dagen te Rotterdam, aan boord, van het schip *Libera*, om nog wat eetwaren en andere benoodigdheden te koopen; want in dien tijd moest een ieder voor zijne eigene provisie zorgen; en de kapitein nam niemand aan boord, die niet zooveel daarvan had als de scheepsorder voorschreef; alles werd juist gewogen, een nummer op elk zijn zak of pak geschreven en dan door den kapitein opgesloten en bewaard, om nader volgens scheepsorder aan ieder zooveel per dag te worden uitgedeeld. Men kon dus niet zooveel eten van zijn eigen provisie als men verkoos, maar slechts zooveel als de scheepswet toeliet en als de kapitein veroorloofde. Het drinkwater werd ook elken dag toegemeten en de maat was klein. De passagiers hadden echter niet voor water te zorgen; dit was door de rederij te Rotterdam aan boord genomen.

Toen alles in gereedheid was, vertrok de *Libera* van Rotterdam; eerst door eene stoomboot gesleept en verder door het Kanaal naar Helle-voetsluis met paarden getrokken. Er waren bijna tegelijkertijd nog twee andere schepen met landverhuizers voor Amerika, te Rotterdam, reis-vaardig; maar van deze weet ik weinig en zal daarom er maar niets van vertellen. Ons schip was de eerste van de drie dat uitvoer en was ook de eerste aan land.

In het Engelsch Kanaal kregen wij den eersten storm, zoodat de kapi-tein voorzichtigheidshalve in eene Engelsche haven binnenliep en daar drie dagen verbleef. Ik denk de haven heette Isle of Wight. Later hadden wij nog groote stormen te doorstaan waarvan de felste zoo ik mij goed herinner, op Paasch-Zondag begon en drie dagen duurde en zoo geweldig woedde dat de luiken van het schip overal werden dicht gemaakt en er voor de passagiers maar eene kleine ruimte werd gelaten om uit en in te gaan, als de noodzakelijkheid dit vereischte. De masten werden van alle zeilen ontdaan, doch ongelukken waren er niet voorgekomen. Juist voor den storm konden wij om ons heen ongeveer vijftig schepen tellen, maar zoodra de storm begon te woeden was er geen enkel schip meer te zien. Verder was er niets bijzonders op zee voorgevallen; de reis was langzaam, maar voor dien tijd de omstandigheden in aanmerking nemende, nog al verdragelijk.

Na eene zeereis van twee en vijftig dagen kwamen wij op Vrijdag, 5den Mei, te Bosten behouden aan wal. Den volgenden dag vertrokken wij per spoor in „boxcars" naar Buffalo. Drie van de dertien families waren te Boston achtergebleven: Denkboom, die niet van plan was om verder te gaan, en Antoon Verkampen en Antoon Verwijst, dien daartoe de middelen ontbraken. Dennissen bleef te Buffalo, omdat zijne vrouw ziek was, die aldaar overleed. Dan reisden wij van Buffalo naar Mackinaw, waar wij drie dagen bleven voor al eer wij met een zeilschip naar Green Bay konden vertrekken. Klaasens bleef te Green Bay en van daar gingen wij op een schouw of schuit met platten bodem, voortbewogen door zes mannen met polsstokken, hetgeen twee volle dagen geduurd heeft. Van Kaukauna bracht men ons met twee wagens, elk met zes ossen bespannen, naar Little Chute, waar wij op 22 Mei aankwamen en waar wij eenige dagen verbleven, om uit te rusten en verdere plannen voor de toekomst te beramen.

Gedurende die dagen dat wij te Little Chute vertoefden was er iemand van ons die het tegenwoordige Hollandtown op het spoor gekregen had; ik meen het was Pater Godhart en men maakte dan ook werk, om verder te onderzoeken of de plaats voor ons geschikt was. Met Pater Godhart aan het hoofd gingen Verkuilen, Van den Berg, Ebben en Verboort daarheen, ook gingen nog mede de oude Driek van der Hey met zijne talrijke familie waarvan er drie gehuwd waren, namelijk, Cornelius van der Hey, Johannes Arts en Hendrikus Hoevenaars, deze twee laatsten waren met dochters van Driek van der Hey getrouwd. Laatstgenoemde en familie waren met een ander schip overgekomen en hadden zich later bij ons aangesloten. Dit zijn de families, die zich het eerst te Hollandtown hebben nedergezet en Driek van der Hey kan als een der eerste nederzetters van dit nu belangrijke dorp beschouwd worden. Venken en Vleugels waren de eerste opvolgers, maar behooren niet tot de eerste nederzetters. Hollandtown is in den vollen zin des woords, de eerste plaats, voor zoover als mij bekend, die door Hollanders in 1848, is gevestigd. Toen wij aankwamen waren weliswaar Little Chute, Freedom en Bay Settlement reeds begonnen, maar niet uitsluitend door Hollanders.

In de eerste dagen van Juni 1848 werd Hollandtown door bovengenoemde personen in het midden van 't bosch aangelegd. Eene „shanty" ongeveer drie mijlen van ons verwijderd, was onze meest naburige plaats, anders was er geen hutje noch huis binnen vijf mijlen afstand. In de eerste jaren was er aan alles gebrek, behalve aan brandhout; armoede was troef, zoowel bij hen, die nog wat geld hadden als bij hen die het geen hadden, vooral omdat alles zoo ver van de hand was, om het noodige te gaan koopen voor hen die zoo gelukkig waren nog eenige centen te bezitten. Doch bij alle ontberingen was het volk doorgaans moedig en opgeruimd. Het geheugt mij niet, dat er in die dagen ooit twist of tweedracht van eenige beteekenis plaats had. Den eersten zomer had niemand een huis, maar allen woonden in tenten, uit takken gemaakt, en die wel eene beschutting waren tegen de heete zonnestralen, maar niet tegen den regen. Ook had niemand een kachel, behalve misschien Pater Godhart, allen moesten zich behelpen met ketel of pan, die zij van Holland hadden medegebracht, om het weinige, dat zij hadden te koken en te bakken over een vuur in vrije lucht of onder de asch. Het brood bakken werd meest gedaan onder de asch of onder heete steenen en de uitslag daarvan was dikwijls beneden het middelmatige, omdat de kennis en wetenschap er toe geheel en al ontbrak. Als eene vrouw nu en dan eens zoo gelukkig was, dat het brood zoo goed was uitgevallen, dat de deeg niet geheel of gedeeltelijk tegen den boom bleef plakken als men het daar tegenwierp, dan ging zij daarmede de buurt af, om hare kunst als een wonder des tijds te laten zien en hare bakkerskunst te hooren loven en prijzen, zij moest dan aan iedereen vertellen hoe zij het had aangelegd.

Hiermede zal ik maar eindigen. Albert en zijne vrouw zijn den 24sten dezer hier bij ons welbehouden aangekomen, reis was gunstig afgeloopen, hij en wij allen groeten u vriendschappelijk en wenschen u en de uwen alle geluk en zegen.

Steets tot uwen dienst bereid verblijf ik,

De uwe,
John Verboort.

[Translation]

Verboort, Washington County,
Oregon, November 23, 1897.

Dear friend John Smith:

Your honored letter, written the 17th instant, was received today. With pleasure I shall, in so as I shall be able to comply with your request, furnish you an account of our journey to America, our arrival in this country, etc. Although I recall those events clearly, much escapes my memory. Should you, however, be able to obtain a better or fuller account from other persons you will please me by improving my statements.

We left Volkel (commune of Uden) on March 9, 1848, to undertake our journey to America. Our trunks and other baggage were brought to Vechel by wagon gratis, I believe, by a friend named Hendrik Rombouts. From Vechel we traveled by canal boat to 's-Hertogenbosch from which place our boat was pulled to Rotterdam where on March 10 we boarded a small three master, the *Libera*.

We were thirteen families, all Hollanders. Father Godhart was our leader. The captain and sailors of our ship also were Hollanders. I have forgotten the exact number of emigrants on board the *Libera*, but it was about 80 persons. The following are the names of the heads of these families: Jan Klaasens, from Grave; Martinus Verkuilen, from Uden; Hein Groens, from Volkel; Niklaas Dennison, from Volkel; Antoon Verkampen, from Volkel; Antoon Verwijst, from Uden (a member of this family at present is a Franciscan father at Ashland, Wisconsin); Mr. Denkboom, from Amsterdam; Albert van den Berg, from Cuyk; Ebben, from Mill; Johannes Tillemans and fiancee, from Boekel; Jan Verboort, from Volkel; and two youths reckoned as belonging to the Verkampen family.

We spent several days at Rotterdam, on board the *Libera* in order to purchase food and other necessaries, for in those days each passenger had to buy his own provisions, and the captain was not allowed to accept any passenger who had not complied with prescribed regulations. Everything was carefully weighed, a number was put on each passenger's bag or package which the captain put under lock so that later, according to the ship's rules a fixed daily portion could be doled out. Passengers were not premitted to use as much of their provisions as they wished but only as much as the captain allowed, in accordance with the rules. A small amount of drinkwater was portioned out each day. The passengers, however, did not have to provide their own drinkwater; this the shipping company brought on board at Rotterdam.

When everything was in readiness, the *Libera* left Rotterdam. At first our boat was drawn [by another boat], later it was pulled by horses to Hellevoetsluis. There were at the moment of our departure from Rotterdam two other ships with emigrants ready to leave for America. About these ships I know little, so I shall say nothing about them. Our's was the first of the three to depart, it also was the first to arrive at its destination.

We encountered our first storm in the English Channel. The captain, as a measure of precaution, took refuge for three days in an English harbor. I believe it was the Isle of Wight. Later we had other serious storms, the worst being, if I recall accurately, on Easter Sunday [April 11]. It lasted three days and blew so violently that the hatches were closed and only a small space was allowed the passengers to go on deck when necessary. Sails were furled, but accidents could not be prevented. Just before the storm struck we could count about fifty ships around us. But as soon as the storm began to blow not a single ship could be seen any more. Except for this storm nothing noteworthy happened on our voyage which was tedious but, considering the time and circumstances, tolerable.

After a voyage of 52 days we arrived safely at the dock in Boston on Friday, May 5. The next day we left by train, in boxcars, for Buffalo. Three of the thirteen families stayed in Boston: Denkboom, who did not want to travel further, Antoon Verkampen, and Antoon Verwijst who did not have the money to travel farther. Dennissen stayed in Buffalo because his wife was sick and died. We sailed from Buffalo to Mackinaw Island where we stayed three days until we could get a sailing ship for Green Bay. From there we proceeded up the Fox River by scouw or flatboat propelled by six men who used poles. This took two entire days. From Kaukama we were brought in two wagons, drawn by six oxen, to Little Chute where we arrived on 22 May. There we rested and laid plans for the future.

While staying at Little Chute someone of our group heard about the area where the present Hollandtown is situated. I believe this was Father Godhart. We decided to investigate the place and learn if it suited us. Led by Father Godhart, Verkuilen, Van den Berg, Ebben, and Verboort went to see it. The aged Driek van der Hey and his large family of whom three were married – Cornelius van der Hey, Johannes Arts, and Hendrikus Hoevenaars – accompanied them. The last two persons named were married to Driek's daughters. They had made the journey to America in another ship and had joined us later. These were the first families to settle at Hollandtown. Driek van der Hey may be regarded as being one of the first settlers of this important community. Venkens and Vleugels followed, but they did not belong to the first settlers. Hollandtown is, in the full sense of the word, the first place where, so far as I know only Hollanders settled in 1848. When we arrived in this area, it is true, Little Chute, Freedom and Bay Settlement had already been founded, but not exclusively by Hollanders.

The above named persons founded Hollandtown in the midst of the woods during the opening days of June. A shanty three miles distant was our nearest house. There was no other such building within a radius of five miles. During the first years we lacked everything except firewood. Poverty was our normal lot, not only among those of us who had no money, but also among those who had a little. These latter, like the others lived, too far from stores to be able to buy anything. But in spite of all hardships our people were happy. I do not recall there ever were quarrels or dissensions of any importance. During the first summer none of us had houses, but we lived in tents made of branches which protected us against the heat of the sun, but could not keep out the rain. No one had a stove except perhaps Father Godhart. We had to get along as well as we could with some pan or kettle we had brought with us from the Netherlands. In such things we had to prepare our scanty food over open fires or under ashes. Bread was baked in ashes or among hot stones. It usually was poor in quality, for we lacked all skill and knowledge to prepare food in this way. Whenever any of the women was so successful in baking bread that the dough would not entirely stick to a tree when thrown against it she would be praised by her neighbors and would have to show then how she accomplished this feat.

With this I shall close. On the 24th Albert and his wife arrived, and in good health. Their journey ended well, and we greet you friendly and wish you and yours all good fortune and blessing.

Ever at your service,

I remain, yours,

John Verboort

79. ARNOLD VERSTEGEN'S LETTERS FROM LITTLE CHUTE, WISCONSIN

[Verstegen with wife, Anna Biemens and four children from Noord-Brabant arrived in Little Chute in 1850. The following letters to his father-in-law Delis Biemens of Erp in Noord-Brabant portray something of conditions in the country near Little Chute. These letters were edited and translated by the Rev Matthias van der Elsen O. Praem, and published in *The Annals of St. Joseph*, LV (1943) and LVI (1944).]

Little Chute, Wisconsin, August 12, 1850

Dear Father:

I should have written long ago, but my brother has kept me busy planting, seeding, and working at the house which he is building, and besides, I did not feel like writing. I was very much disappointed at first; the country appeared too wild – woods, woods, nothing but woods, and only a small clearing here and there with a ramshackle building upon it. And worst of all, the crops looked bad, because it had not rained all spring. I thought at first that I could never like a country like this. I felt as though I wanted to go back home right away. My brother, however, laughed at me, and said that he had experienced the same feeling when he arrived; I should have a little patience, and I would soon get over my gloomy spell. He was right; everything is changed now. There has been a good rain, the crops are much improved, the country looks more friendly, and I am in the mood to write a long letter!

You know that we left Rotterdam on the 25th of March [1850]. We sailed along, making good progress with favorable winds, until we reached the banks of Newfoundland; there we encountered a mild storm and adverse winds, and our ship, which was an old one, was leaking so badly that we had to pump day and night. We finally arrived at New York on May 2. By steamer we went to Albany, and by train on to Buffalo. From there to Green Bay there were two routes: the one by boat through the Great Lakes, and the other for some distance overland and then by boat through Lake Michigan. Most of our party took the former route, which is the longer; with Father Van den Heuvel I chose the shorter way. At Milwaukee, Father Van den Heuvel went to see the Bishop, while I went on to Green Bay alone with my family.

When we finally reached Green Bay, I left Anna and the children at the dock, comfortably seated on a bench, and went up town to inquire which was the best way to go to Little Chute. It so happened that on that same day brother John was in Green Bay on business; and although he did not expect us for at least two weeks, when from a distance he saw a strange lady, dressed in Holland fashion, he was anxious to find out who she was, and walked up to meet her. You can imagine how they both were surprised, and how happy a meeting it was. Our anxieties and cares of the last several weeks were now at an end; we now had a leader for the rest of the journey, and that was a short one. The next day, June 9, we arrived at Little Chute, where Father Van den Heuvel had arrived the previous day.

I had expected that our coming to Little Chute would be an event of some importance, and that the Hollanders at least would be anxious to see us and to bid us welcome. Here again I was disappointed. The people were all excited about the expected visit of the Most Reverend Henni, Bishop of Milwaukee, and had no time to bother about anything else. The church was being decorated, the women were housecleaning and getting their best clothes ready; they were baking and cooking as if the Bishop was surely going to eat dinner in every house.

Father Van den Heuvel and H. Bongers had been sent to Green Bay to escort his Lordship to the town, and when the great day arrived, soon after sunrise people began to congregate at the church, coming from every direction, and some from a great distance. At 7 o'clock the crowd became restless and brother John was dispatched on horseback to determine the cause for the delay. At 7 : 30 he came back, galloping at full speed and shouting, "I've seen them! They are coming!" A procession was formed; the priests and altar boys leading with the cross, and when we met the Bishop's carriage we all knelt down and received his blessing. Then the procession returned to the church, little girls strewing flowers from the little baskets onto the road, and the church bell ringing. It was like Our Lord coming to Jerusalem on Palm Sunday.

After a short visit at the church and in the priests' house, the Bishop offered Mass, assisted by four priests; the Rev. Fathers Van den Broek, Van den Heuvel, Ferenacci (an Italian), and Bullock (an American). After Mass the Sacrament of Confirmation was administered, and the Bishop gave a fatherly talk, which made a deep impression upon the children and the grown up people as well. It was a great day for Nepomuc of "Little Chute".

Meanwhile our companions, from whom we had become separated in Buffalo, had not yet arrived, and we were beginning to feel uneasy about them; our apprehension grew especially when news reached us that a boat on the Lakes had a disasterous fire and had sunk with all on board. Our fears were dispelled, however, when they arrived on June 27. We all went to Confession and Holy Communion, and Father Van den Broek offered a Mass of Thanksgiving.

Father Van den Broek has willed all his possessions to the church at Little Chute; it is his earnest wisht that the church of which he is the first pastor shall always have a resident priest. He is in good health now, but in the event that something unforseen should happen, Father Van den Heuvel will be his admimstrator – until the Bishop appoints a new successor. He wants to build a larger church, twice the size of the present one, and asks us all to do our share. At first he had it in mind to build of stone, but finding the cost prohibitive, he has now decided to build of wood.

I have bought forty acres of land, at ten dollars an acre; it is close to the river and joins the ground where the locks of the canal are going to be located. It is all woodland, but consists of good clay soil, and should make an excellent farm; that however, will take a few years of hard work.

For the present we are staying with brother John, and are working together. John, who can talk with the Frenchmen and the Germans, as well as with the Hollanders, thought he could make use of his linguistic talents, and has gone into the store business. Our stock is rather small now, but our ambition is to have a general store some day. We are now settled down; we like the country and the people, we are glad to be here, and we feel right at home. Anna was sensible from the beginning, and I am ashamed of myself, to have acted like such a baby!

Our little boy got sick in New York. On the journey we made him as comfortable as could be done under the circumstances, but he seemed to be getting weaker right along. We hoped that as soon as we had settled here, there would be a change for the better. Father Van den Broek came to see him every day, and did everything he could to save the life of the child, but he said that there was little hope. He died on the 8th of July and was buried on the next day; eight small boys carried him to his little grave.

There, father, you have all the news. We wish you and all of our friends good health and God's blessing.

Your devoted son and daughter,
Arnoldus Verstegen and Anna Maria Verstegen

B.

Little Chute, Wisconsin, December 26, 1851

Dear Parents-in-law:

We received your letter dated February 19th, but since the questions did not press for an immediate answer, we waited until we were settled in our new house, and can give you a description of the same. It isn't a rich man's castle, but has all the room and convenience we want, and that ought to satisfy anybody. The ground plan is 32 by 24 feet; the downstairs is 8 feet to the ceiling, the upper story $7\frac{1}{2}$ feet. Both gable ends go straight up to the peak of the roof. Besides two small attic windows there are thirteen windows with twelve glass panes in each, size 12 by 10 inches, so you see that all the rooms are well lighted. To air the rooms the windows can be raised and they stay up without a prop put under them. A cord, a trolley, and a weight are doing the trick, and everything is so well concealed, that those who see the window stand up all by itself, and don't know the secret, are puzzled. It is a new American invention. The roof is covered with small boards, which they call shingles. We cut logs in lengths of about 16 inches, split them into slices about half an inch thick, shave them so they taper to one end, and nail them op the roof. Exposed to the weather they turn to a grayish color, and in the course of time it looks like a genuine slate roof. Not many houses in Little Chute compare to ours; I wish you could come over and see it.

You like to know the progress we have made on our farm. This year we had 13 acres under cultivation, and everything we planted did fairly well; the potatoes here have the same disease or blight as in Holland, but not quite so bad. The coming winter we will start clearing another five acre plot of land. It isn't heavily timbered but covered with small oaks, hazelnut, and wild apple trees and all kinds of brush wood; nearly everything can be cut out with a root axe.

Next we will build an American fence around it, to keep cattle and pigs from rooting it up; because every farmer lets his animals roam where they please, and feed themselves on whatever they can find. The American fence is a peculiar structure. We take good sized tree trunks, about 15 feet long – those that are too thick are split in four parts – we lay them down on the ground in a zigzag line, crossing them at the ends, and keep on piling them up until they reach the required height. It is a good fence and even the pigs cannot squeeze themselves through. The top and branches and the brush wood will be piled up in the field and burned.

I know what is now on your mind, father. You would like to know what is the idea of wasting food fire wood. You will be shocked when I tell you that here in Little Chute since the first settlers came, hundreds of acres of dense primeval forests have been literally destroyed. Except for a few timbers used to build a log house, the rest went up in smoke, because there was no sawmill and no market for the lumber, and the land was needed for grain fields and pastures. Compare this with conditions in Holland. Around their fields you farmers plant hedges, to serve double purpose of fence and fire wood. Every few years the hedges are thinned out; the sticks are cut up and tied in bundles to supply the family with fire wood. The poor people of the town are allowed to search for dead branches in the hedges, and that is their scanty source of fuel.

Even now wood here has little value; it is being used as material for paving roads, instead of brick of stone. The highway which runs between our house and barn is being paved with planks over a distance of nine miles. We farmers think that the first heavy rain will scatter the planks all over the land, but we must wait and see first; the Americans like to experiment, and often their seemingly foolish exploits are surprisingly successful.

Take for instance the electric telegraph. A telegraph line is under construction, coming from Milwaukee and heading for Green Bay, and passing a few rods from my house. First they put up poles about 200 feet apart; then an iron wire is stretched from pole to pole, suspended on something that looks to me like a door knob, and high enough so that a load of hay can pass under it. The construction boss claims that by means of electricity short messages can be sent over the wire, and are received the same instant they are being dispatched, no matter what distance.

You asked me if the kermess is celebrated in American, and if we have any parties or amusements. In winter the young people, and especially the French, have parties and dance to the music of the violin. In summer everyone is too busy, and meeting at the church on Sundays and exchanging the news of the week is about our only pastime.

The only kermess celebrated all over America is the Fourth of July. This country was once a colony of England, but on the 4th of July 1776 some patriotic citizens boldly signed a declaration of independence, telling the world that this country was free and had a right to govern itself. England, hating to lose the revenue of a rich colony, used all her might to suppress the revolution. It was like Goliath fighting David, but David won, and England had to recognize the independence of the United States. The Fourth of July is therefore rightly called the birthday of the nation, and is celebrated in the cities with parades and speeches and fireworks. Here in Little Chute there are not enough to have a parade, or if we had one, there would be nobody left to see us march. The best we can do is to set fire in the evening to a big brush pile and light up the sky, and show the people in Appleton that we are just as patriotic as they are.

Father Van den Broek is dead. On All Saints day, when he was singing the High Mass, he was struck with paralysis, and a week later funeral services were held with great solemnity. People came from everywhere to pay their last respects to the man who had brought them to this country, and who as a kind father took an interest in everybody's welfare. Father Van den Broek left all his property for the upkeep of the church of Little Chute, of which he was the founder. If I am well informed, he named the Crozier Fathers in his last will, and if they establish a community here, there will always be one or more priests, and our church will be as well served as yours in Erp or Uden. Even now there is catechism instruction every Saturday; the French children come in the morning, and the Holland and German children at two o'clock in the afternoon. Adriana and Anna Maria know many answers of the catechism, and can say their prayers well.

You asked me about our livestock; we have two horses, two cows, one calf, ten pigs, and eleven chickens. We butchered two oxen weighing a little over 700 pounds each; they had worked hard plowing in the spring, and that accounts for their light weight.

Arnoldus Dirks lives a half mile from here, and his family is doing well. My wife, father, and brother John send you their best wishes for a happy and prosperous New Year.   Yours respectfully,

Arnold Verstegen

C.

Little Chute, Wisconsin, June 16, 1852

Dear Parents:

Your letter of April 24, received here May 23, afforded us great pleasure. Not getting an answer sooner, we were afraid that perhaps our letter might have been lost. You tell us that Mother has been sick, but is now improving; we wish her a speedy and complete recovery.

While I was reading the rest of your letter, tears came to my eyes. You suggest that we take our inheritance at this time; and I read between the lines that you are under the impression that we are living here in great poverty and are too proud to ask for help. We are happy to hear that we still have a place in your heart, although undeserving of it, since we came to America against your advice. But Father, we are not poor, we are rich! We have more and better food than we ever had in Holland; we live in a warm house and have good clothes; we have Mass in our church each Sunday; and the children go to school and catechism. The little patch of land which we have cleared is sufficient to supply all of our wants. No, Father, don't give your money away; rather keep control of what is yours as long as you live, and may that be for many more years.

If, however, you have some money lying idle in the house, and wish to invest it, that is a different proposition. I need a few more horses and cows, and have no money on hand to buy them. My credit is good, and I can borrow the money here, but not for less than 12%; some moneylenders charge as high as 30%, although the legal limit is 12%. Two hundred dollars is all that I need, and I will promplty pay you 6%; in this way we both will make a profit.

The best way to send money is to buy a money order from a bank in Rotterdam which has connections with a New York bank. They will give you three draughts if you ask for them; mail them to me, one at a time, about a month apart; one out of three will always reach its destination. Store-keepers in Appleton are glad to give me cash for them. Instead of going to Rotterdam in person, you could ask Doctor Van Loo in Veghel to arrange that matter for you; his first wife was a sister-in-law of Mr. J. Wap; the banker in Rotterdam.

It has been two years now since we arrived here, and we are becoming accustomed to the country and its people; so I shall give you my impressions. The country is still in the making, and much of the improvement is of a makeshift character. The land, after clearing, is left full of tree stumps, which will be removed as soon as the roots have decayed enough so that they can be pulled out. But in the meantime we must plow between them the best way we can, and everything grows without fertilizer. The buildings are mostly constructed of logs; there is no beauty about them, but they are warm and serviceable. The roads are rough, and during a wet spell heavily loaded wagons have to keep off, lest they sink into the mud up to the hub.

This is a free country where only a few necessary and useful laws are made. Ordinances and restrictions which would benefit only a few, and would be a burden to the people generally, are wisely avoided. And with few laws and few officers to enforce them, the people have respect for the law and like to see it enforced; as a whole the people cooperate with the officers, so that transgressions are few.

There are policemen in the cities, but we never see one; still we don't have to lock the house or the stable or keep a vicious watchdog to frighten burglars away. You can leave a spade or any implement or tool in the field after using it, and it will still be there whenever you go back to use it again.

Is there a kommies (revenue collector) in Little Chute? Of course you think that no town should be without one, to watch everyone's every move, to prevent illegal butchering, brewing, or baking, etc. No ,we have no kommies, and that is another reason why I like this country!

There is no compulsory military service here. Every state in Europe maintains a large standing army because each country is afraid of its neighbor. The United States has no dangerous neighbors, and the quarrelsome nations of Europe are too far away to cause any serious concern. We have only a small army of volunteers, and no compulsory service.

There are no game laws; you can go fishing or hunting whenever you please. There is plenty of game, big and small, in the woods; the rivers are full of fish.

Do we pay taxes? Certainly we pay taxes, and enjoy doing it! I am paying taxes on 160 acres of land, and I am highly assessed because my land is of the best; yet I am only paying twelve dollars a year, and that includes schooltax. My brother John has been elected taxcollector, the highest paid office in town; he receives 5% of all the money taken in, and it will bring him the neat sum of $ 80 a year, but he must go from house to house to collect it.

Now, Father, you will understand why we love our new country, and you will not be surprised when I say that we have made up our minds to make it our home for the rest of our days, bringing up our children to become American citizens. But to come over to Holland for a visit and spend a winter with you is what we are wishing and praying for. However it will take at least two more years of hard work before the conditon of our farm will allow us that luxury.

Now for a bit of local news. The Fox River, a river as big as the Meuse, is shallow and fast-flowing, because Lake Winnebago, its origin, is seventy-five feet higher than the Green Bay, into which it empties, and the distance is only forty miles. A plan has been adopted whereby the river can be made navigable. Dams are being built at several points to retard the flow and raise the water to a higher level, and locks will be installed at each dam to help the boats form one level to another. One of the locks will come right opposite my land. Water transportaion will be a great boom to towns along the river. At this moment the work has stopped on account of a dispute between the contractor, Mr. Martin, and the Governor of the State. They say that will come to a lawsuit, and that may be some time before the work will be resumed.

Another public work, now in progress, is the paving of our main road with planks. They want to straighten out the road, and run it through my land, which will necessitate the moving of my house. There is also a dispute here between a certain road boss and one Mr. Verstegen, governor of this manor! They have not come to terms yet about the cost of moving the house, and the price of the land. In the meantime they have skipped my land and are already two miles beyond it, grading the road and making a bedding for the planks. The planks have been laid for a distance of five miles, up to the house of Brother John, and that part of the road is open for traffic.

The price of produce is as follows: wheat, per bushel, 75 ¢; rye, 60¢; buckwheat, 60¢; oats, 30¢; beans, $ 1.60; peas, $ 1—. Flour is $ 4— a barrel (200 punds); salt pork, per pound, 10¢; butter, 14¢; coffee (not roasted), 14¢; rice, 8¢; and eggs, 12¢ per dozen.

Father is still with us. Adriana and Anna Marie are going to school to learn English, and are beginning to read and speak it quite well. J. van Lisshout says that he will pay his share and that you can go ahead.

With best wishes, respectfully, Your children,

Arnoldus Verstegen

Anna Maria Verstegen (Biemans)

D.

Little Chute, Wisconsin, August 30, 1857.

Dear Parents:

Arnold Hurkmans, a friend and neighbor of ours, will be leaving in a few days on a visit to Holland. We would like to go with him in person, but that being impossible, he will bring you our portraits. They have been made by a new process, not painted by the slow brush of an artist, but by a clever device which does the work quick and neat, although the pictures are small. It must be a new American invention, because I never heard of it in Holland. There is a man here in Appleton who knows all about it and gets many customers because he is doing wonderful work. A few weeks ago I went there with Ma and the two youngest children, the ones who were born in America, Anna Maria and Egidius. The machine that performs the mysterious work is simple enough – just a square box that has a big glass eye in front. I was told to sit down a few feet away from the machine and hold the little girl on my knees. Next he told me to look pleasant and to try not to move. Then he removed a cover and let the magic eye look at us for a few seconds, and that is all there was to it. Ma and the baby were next. A few days later we got the pictures and they were just wonderful. When I look at mine, I seem to be looking at myself in the looking glass. It is too bad that the children's faces didn't turn out so well; they are a little foggy.

Are we not living in a wonderful world? One marvelous invention looms up after another. It took us two months and a half to come to this country, and that is only seven years ago, and now your letters reach us within a month.

The wild land we undertook to tame a few years ago has seen a great change. We have almost forty acres under cultivation, a nice herd of cattle, and can take life a little easier this year than any previous year. But Hurkmans will tell you all about that. He knows us and our circumstances. Just ask him, and he will tell you everything. In Holland they think that visitors coming from America are fond of telling tall stories, that they like to make things look twice as big as they really are. However, Hurkmans is not that kind of a man; everything he says can be taken at its full value.

Hoping to receive an answer with Hurkmans, I am your obedient son,

Arnold Verstegen

P.S. We recommend Hurkmans to your kind hospitality.

E.

Little Chute, Wisconsin, October 28, 1858

Dear Parents:

We received your letter of October, 20 of last year, but did not answer because Arnold Hurkmans was on his way to Holland with a letter from us and would bring all the news personally. In the meantine there has been an increase in the family. On the 15th of September a baby boy arrived. His name is Hermanus. That brings the total again up to five, three girls and two boys. The baby is doing fine, but the mother suffers from cramps in the legs, although she is otherwise in good health.

Hurkmans tells us that you liked the pictures but that you would sooner have seen us in person. It has always been our plan to come to see you as soon as the condition of our farm would allow us, but we overlooked one thing and that is the children. For no money in the world would Anna leave them to the care of strangers. A few years from now it will be different; Adriana, who is a willing and handy worker and already does much of the housework will then be able to take the place of her mother, and then you can expect us. We left Holland, not because we disliked the country, but to give our children better opportunities. Here I will be able to put each one of them on a farm, something I never would have expected to do in Holland. But if it is God's will, we hope to see Holland once more, and walk the streets of Erp and Boekel and Uden, and meet our old friends and have a happy family reunion.

Hurkmans tells us that he spent many hours with you, and that you were delighted to hear of the progress we have made on our farm. He told us, too, how he had to draw maps of Little Chute and point out the location of our house, and the house of John, and of the church. I am sure you now have a pretty good picture in your mind of the entire town.

Late in the summer an unusual sight was noticed in the sky; it was a star with a tail. As weeks passed by, the tail grew longer and the head grew brighter, and it seemed to come nearer the earth. In the month of October it began to look so threatening that people began to fear that something was amiss, and that the end of the world was coming. One Sunday our priest talked about it in church and said that it was a comet and that similar stars had been seen in the past; that it was a friendly wanderer of the universe, not intent upon any mischief, and that it would disappear noiselessly, just as it had arrived. The papers tell us that it was seen all over the world; you must have seen it in Holland too.

Father has been very sick this summer and hasn't been in the church for three months; he was annointed, and for a few days his condition was such that any moment he was expected to pass away. To the surprise of every one, he recovered, and is going to church again, although he is not quite as strong as he used to be. Next summer he will again be seen working in the garden and doing odd jobs around the house and taking the children for a walk.

Now a little about the weather. There was so much rain this spring that the work in the field was much delayed. The horses would sink in the mud as deep as the land had been plowed before. It was July before all the seeding was done. Then a dry hot spell came, once the thermometer registered 105 degress; and the latter part of the summer was wet again. Wheat is only 85 cents a bushel, so that farmers in some states, considering the low price and the poor quality of grain, have set fire to the crops, not thinking it worth while to harvest them. I myself have two acres of wheat still standing in the field; it has plenty of straw but little grain, and even that is infested with smut.

The money you have sent I have put on interest. Home breeding has taken care of the increase of my stock, so that I need not buy any more. When I see a good piece of property I will buy it.

I was told two years ago that Cornelius Elsen was married. Is it true that Uncle Cornelis of Boekel is also married? Give my best regards to all relatives and friends.

Yours truly,

A. Verstegen

F.

Little Chute, Wisconsin, January, 2, 1860

Dear Parents, Brothers, and Sisters-in-law,

Anna has been telling me right along that the new year was coming fast, and that it was time to look for pen and ink and send our New Year's greetings to Holland; and I kept on saying that there was no hurry, for no other reason that I know if, except that I dislike the mention of pen and ink; that puts the blame on me for their coming so late.

Accept our sincere wishes for a happy New Year. So far God has been kind to you and given you a good share of the blessings of this life, and we pray that you may enjoy the same happiness for many more years.

Your welcome letter of January 8, 1859, found us all in good health, except that Anna is till suffering from cramps in the legs; it is four years now since she began to complain, and now it is so bad that she has difficulty in walking, otherwise she is in good health.

Wheat, rye, and oats were fairly good last year, but most of the winter wheat had to be seeded over in the spring. Early in the month of July a severe frost did much damange to turkish wheat, buckwheat, and potatoes, and another killing frost the last days of August aggravated the damage done earlier in the season. That is the climate of Wisconsin – impetuous extreme cold and long winters, and short, hot summers; everything must grow in four months time; and it is surprising what a wealth of grain and fruits can grow in so short a period. Buckwheat seeded the latter part of June is ready to be cut during the week of the Boekel kermess. All in all we did fairly well this year.

The prices of produce are as follows: wheat $ 1; oats 30 cents; potatoes, 50 cents per bushel; flour $ 5 the barrel; butter, one shilling per pound. I have two fine work horses for sale and three milk cows; that would leave me seven horses and as many cows; but although grain brings a good price, livestock is cheap and I don't like to sell at the prevailing price. I think I have told you everything worth while mentioning, and we remain as ever, with respect and love, your son and daughter.

Arnold Verstegen
Anna Marie Biemans

G.

Little Chute, Wisconsin, August 20, 1860.

Your letter of May thirtieth brought us the sad news that father is dead. It was a shock to all of us, not only because it came so unexpected but also because we realize that all of us now suffer a great loss. Father was always so sympathetic and so anxious about our welfare, although we had left home like wayard children. He would write such beautiful and encouraging letters, and was much interested in everything we were doing here, and was always looking forward to the day that we would come over for a visit. And that happy day never dawned for him; God willed it otherwise. We surely are remembering him in our prayers; I have a Mass offered for the repose of his soul on the 23rd of every month for one year. It will not be said this week because there is no priest here now, but we are expecting one next Sunday.

You say mother would like us to come over now, and not to wait any longer, because she feels that her days too are numbered, and fears that we shall find an empty house, if we keep on postponing our long promised visit. We have talked the matter over and discussed it from every angle. Anna cannot come for a new baby girl arrived the latter part of July (we named her Ardina) and besides she dreads a long journey because of the conditon of her legs. She urges me to go alone and not wait for her any longer. Adriana is now a big and strong girl, a willing and handy house maid, well able to take care of the house and of the children; and brother John can alwyas be depended upon, if help or advice of any kind is needed.

It has been agreed upon that I go alone, and I intend to leave here about All Saints day; in case something should happen to upset our plans, I will let you know. Don't send any money – we can arrange that matter upon my arrival.

The harvest this year is abundant; the wheat crop is heavy and is already in the barn; oats and other cereals too look promising. This summer we had many thunderstorms, and rain at the right time, and that, combined with warm weather, always means a heavy crop. It would also mean long sessions on the threshing floor in the barn next winter, but I have solved that problem by the purchase of a threshing machine. You wonder how a machine can be made to swing a flail, and therefore I will explain to you how it works.

First there is the power plant which stands outside and looks like the coffee grinder which Anna brought from Holland; only a hundred times magnified. A team of horses, hitched to a long pole, goes around it in a wide circle, turning a big wheel. By means of a long shaft the power is transmitted to a second machine, which stands in the barn, and does the actual work, and which for size and outward appearance resembles the fanning mill which I had in Holland. The main feature of it is a big open mouth full of teeth. Some of the teeth are set in the roof of the mouth and are stationary; others are planted in the tongue, which in this case is a fast revolving drum. Sheaves of grain are fed into the mouth and the monster swallows them greedily, crunching them between its teeth. The chaff must still be winnowed out in the old way but the threshing is done, and no flails are used.

Threshing was always a tedious occupation on the farm; to stand there day after day swinging a flail, with the regularity of the pendulum of a clock, was monotonous drudgery; and now an American invention comes to the rescue. I paid close to a $ 100 for the macine and consider it the best investment I ever made. With the help of a few assistants I can thresh a hundred bushel of grain with it in a day. It is rumored here that soon there will be a machine that will cut hay and grain, and when it comes I will not be last one to discard the scythe and the sickle.

Some of my neighbors say that they don't like the deafening noise of the machine and that the rhythmic beat of four or six flails, handled by an expert crew, is more musical and soothing to the nerves. Their objections don't seem to be very serious though, for I hear that some of them have already taken steps to install the unmusical machines in their own barns.

But why am I taking up so much time writing all this? If it is God's will, I will spend the coming winter months with you in Erp, and we will have plenty of time to discuss these and other matters.

Anna is very sorry that she cannot be with you at this time, Mother, and prays that God may give you strength to carry your heavy burden of sorrow. With greetings to all and hoping to find you all in good health, I am your son and brother,

Arnold Verstegen

H.

Little Chute, Wisconsin, May 6, 1861

Dear Mother, Brothers, and Sisters:

You have been waiting a long time to hear from me, wondering if I would find my way back home again, and here I am to tell you that I found it and without much trouble. As you know I left Erp on Wednesday March 13 and went only as far as Veghel that day; the next day to Den Bosch, and Friday to Rotterdam. A boat took us across the English Channel and landed us in Hull on Sunday. On Monday we left for Goole where we boarded a fast train which speeded us all the way across England, from East to West, until we reached the seaport of Liverpool. On Wednesday in a small boat we were taken to the big ocean liner, which was waiting outside of the harbor. The sea was rough and we were shaken up pretty badly, and I was glad when I set foot again on more solid ground, that is, on the deck of the big ship. After sailing for a day and a half we arrived on Friday, March 22, at daybreak, in Queenstown, Ireland, where we stopped for half a day and took 200 more passengers on board, which brought the total to 400.

From Queenstown we crossed the Atlantic to New York in a straight line; a steamer pays no attention to where the wind blows from, and depends wholly on its faithful giant engine which keeps on going day and night and never seems to get tired. Twelve days later, on Wednesday after Easter, April 3rd, we arrived in New York. Here I spent at couple of days sightseeing, and again I stopped over at Buffalo for two days to seen an American on some business, and on Saturday, April 13th, I was back home in Little Chute.

I was happy to be again surrounded by my family after an absence of almost half a year. We had much to tell each other; Anna was much interested to know how her mother was feeling, how her brothers and sisters were getting along, how the home town looked; the children were never tired of hearing me tell about the big buildings and busy streets and beautiful stores of New York. The news of my return soon spread all over the neighborhood, and my house has been stampeded ever since by Hollanders and Frenchmen alike. The latter just drop in to shake hands and tell me that they are glad to see me back home again. The Hollanders, however, are not so easy to get rid of. In Holland I visited their home towns and their relatives and they have a hundred questions to ask, and people begin to ask me where I caught a cold. In the house and in the stable everything is in good shape, and the cattle were well taken care of during my long absence – which goes to show that no matter how important a person thinks himself to be, he is after all only a figurehead.

There was much talk on the boat about a civil war threatening the United States. In New York papers were bought eagerly everybody wanted to know the latest developments and on the train, war was the only topic of conversation. The cause of it all is the Negro question. In the Southern states slavery is a legal institution; slaves are bought and sold and forced to do hard work for no pay, just as we do with horses. The North condemns slavery as an unjust and barbarous institution, and for many years the question has caused friction between the North and South. Of late years the South is showing impatience and threatens to withdraw from the Union and set up a government of its own. And that is what has actually happened now. Abraham Lincoln was elected president last November, and because his announced policies did not suit the South, several southern states held a convention, declared themselves free, and a man by the name of Jefferson Davis was chosen president of the new republic. So you see the mess we are in now. President Lincoln has pledged himself to keep the union intact, and if it cannot be done in a conciliatory manner, war is sure to follow.

One of the passengers on the train had this to say on the situation, "I worked one summer as foreman on a plantation in Louisiana." He said, "The boss would come very day to see the niggers work, and his attendant would carry a chair for him so he could sit down in the shade whenever he felt tired. The attendant had to stand by and fan the boss and chase the flies away. When they moved to a new location and had to cross a mud puddle, the boss would climb on the nigger's back to be ferried across, so as not to dirty his shoes. Now that man was not old or sick but the average type of Southerner. And that is the kind of soldier our tough boys of the North will meet in the battlefield. I predict a speedy and easy victory for our side, and I know what I am talking about."

Nowadays we hear that hostilities have begun and that the South has fired the first shot and taken possession of Fort Sumter; on April 14th, the day after I came home. Both sides are preparing for war on a big scale. President Lincoln calls for 75,000 volunteers and many respond, attracted to the high wages, eight dollars a month and 16 acres of land when the war will be over. Prices are going up on account of the war; wheat is now $ 1.10 a bushel. We hope the prophecy of the man on the train will come true.

There was much snow last winter, too much rain this spring. From all indications the crops will be bad and wheat will suffer much from smut, as often happens after too much rain.

Anna sends her love and best wishes to you, mother, and to her brothers and sisters.

Yours truly,
Arnold Verstegen

I.

Little Chute, Wisconsin, June 1, 1862

Dear Mother, Brothers, and Sisters:

We must bring you again some very sad news; Adriana our eldest daughter is dead. You know her well; the nice little girl who was of school age before we left Holland, and came often to see you and you liked her sweet disposition. Here too she went to school a couple of years and learned so well that she could talk and read English as if she had been American born. When she grew up she was a favorite with everybody because she had such winning ways, not proud or selfish, but satisfied with the humblest place, just like her mother.

Now she was a grown up lady, a stout and healthy looking woman. She started young to help her mother with the housework, and the last couple of years she did practically all the work alone, until she got married two weeks before lent, February 16th. We could hardly afford to lose her much needed help, but her companion, Arnold Hurkmans, was a nice young man and they seemed well matched; and it would have been unwise to interfere with plans concerning her own future happiness. On the wedding day there was much feasting and rejoicing and well wishing, in which nearly the whole of Little Chute took part.

Two weeks after he wedding Adriana took sick; on Ash Wednesday the doctor was called and he found it to be a serious case, an infection of the liver. She grew steadily worse and wasted away so fast and so completely that he friends who came to see her towards the last said that she did not look any more like the Adriana they had known so well. As soon as she realized that her condition was hopeless she became reconciled to God's will, and suffered patiently asking only for our prayers. She died peacefully on Saturday, May the 24th.

Eighteen hours after Adriana had breathed her last, her mother gave birth to another girl. Mother had looked forward to that event, expecting to have Adriana at her bedside; Adriana was always happy when she could wait on her frail mother. Her ways were so gentle, and as by instinct, she would always do and say the right thing; her presence alone gave her mother a feeling of security and comfort.

And now preparations were being made for her funeral, which was to be held the next day. We felt great anxiety for mother; but her trust in God, and her calmness and patience in the most trying situations did not desert her this time; she is doing well now. The baby was baptized on the day of her sister's funeral, May the 26th, and named Adriana, to honor the memory of our first Adriana, hoping that she will grow up to be as fine and viruous a woman as her predecessor was. Of the four children which we brought from Holland, Johanna is the only one left; she is now 13 years old. On our farm we have done well since we came here, but misfortunes in our family have been too many and too severe. But it is God's will, and we must carry our Cross no matter how heavy it is.

The war between the North and South is still going on with great fury; the papers bring news every day of new battles being fought, more soldiers being killed, more property being destroyed; and we don't seem to be making any headway. The end is not yet in sight. Only volunteers are being asked for, to raise an army of over 600,000 men.

With best wishes for you all, and asking you o remember Adriana in; your prayers, I remain with love and respect.

Arnold Verstegen

J.

Little Chute, June 19, 1862

Dear Mother, Brithers, and Sisters:

Only two weeks ago I wrote you about the death of Adriana, and the arrival of a new baby fgirl. Now I am writing again to let you know that mother has stood the ordeal well and that the baby too is doing fine. However, we still miss Adriana and I don't think we will ever forget her; but it is God's will and we must carry our cross with patience.

Now I want to tell you about the great works which are here in progress. The railroad is coming to Little Chute. Already for some time trains have been running as far as Fond du Lac and Oshkosh and now the line is being extended through Appleton and Little Chute to Fort Howard and Green Bay. At first the road had been surveyed through my land, but now it will run between my two properties, and will pass within 500 paces from my house and 300 paces from my land. A big crew of men is working with shovels and pickaxes and scrapers drawn by horses, making a perfectly level roadbed. It is surprising that in these times of uncertainty, funds can be found to finance so big an undertaking, and that with so many young men joining the army enough labor is available. But the work is progressing nicely and we expect trains to be running soon. This will be a great boon for our part of the country; it will mean markets for our produce and mechandise for our stores; factories may locate here and Little Chute may become a big city. When we want to go to Appleton on business of for pleasure, the train will bring us there in less time than it takes now to hitch up a team of horses.

It is also rumored (and rumors of this kind are usually based on good authority) that the canal will be widened to one and a half its present size, to accomodate the big lake steamers, which cannot now pass through the locks. That also will give employment to many workmen so that there will be jobs for everybody for a long time.

The other items that will interest you is that we are building a mill. Of course you think of a windmill, which is a common sight all over Holland; you can look at one in Erp without leaving your house. That kind of a mill is not known in America, although Little Chute came once very near having one. When I first came here the notion came to my mind to build one. We farmers had to sell our wheat cheap and buy flour at a high price. A windmill would have solved the problem nicely, just as it does in Holland. I spoke to my neighbors about it and they all encouraged me; the sight of it alone, they said, would be worth a great deal and would cure the homesickness of newcomers. Brother John, however, ridiculed the idea and wouldn't listen to my arguments. "Don't you remember," he said, "that our miller in Erp often was sittting in the doorway of the mill scratching his head, watching the weather, when stacks of grain were piling up waiting to go through the grindstones, and that the wings of the mill with all sails spread stood motionless, as if paralyzed, because there wasn't the slightest breeze to turn them around? Why don't you put a water wheel here in the river? The river never stops flowing; and the water that goes over the dam here in Little Chute has more power than all the windmills in the whole of North Brabant combined." From then on we started figuring and planning and negotiating, with the result that today the foundations for a mill to be driven by water power are finished. We cut through five feet of limestone on the bank of the river, to make room for the installation of up-to-date machinery; enough stone has been excavated to build the foundation walls, the lumber for the superstructure is on hand, and it won't be long before we will be ready for business. We call it the Zeeland Mill, after our home town. Little Chute has now a railroad, a canal, and a factory. Watch her grow from now on.

The newspapers every day are filled with accounts from the battlefront. If I wanted to repeat all that, I would run out of paper before I had half done; I am sure that your papers carry the news too. Everybody here would have it over with.

The crops are generally good; the winter wheat is excellent. Best regards from Anna, and greetings to all relatives and friends.

Yours very truly,

Arnold Verstegen

K.

Little Chute, Wisconsin, November 17, 1870

Dear Brothers and Sisters-in-Law:

For a long time I have been anxiously waiting for an answer to my last letter. I began to think that you were all displeased with my second marriage, and that my letters were no longer welcome and I should not bother you any more. Now Martin Dirks comes and brings me your best regards, and tells me that you have been waiting for a letter from me for ever so long. Evidently the letter I wrote last year got lost, and all my suspicions have been unfounded. On my part I can assure you that you are still as close to my heart as ever, and that Anna will be rememberd as long as we live.

It is true I am married again; shortly before I left Holland I was married in secret. I know how people like to talk; and I didn't want to see them point the finger at me, and to hear them whisper behind my back, and leave Erp with unpleasant memories of my visit. I should have let you in on the secret, however, but I didn't have the courage, not knowing how you would take it.

What some have criticized me for has been done with the best intentions. I was left with five children, the oldest one fourteen, the youngest a year and a half old. Someone was needed to take care of them and to manage the household. Of course a stepmother cannot have the same affection for children that are not her own, that a real mother has, but in my case I thought it was the best solution. And that my wife is of a poor family should not make her less eligible; she has fine qualities of mind and character, and that is in my estimation worth more than money; she has proved to be a real mother for her adopted children. When we arrived in Little Chute we received a hearty welcome and congratulations from the priest as well as from our old friends. Three children have been born since; one of them died.

I have lived in this country now twenty years, and the progress that I have seen in that short space of time is like a dream. Our Little Chute was then a hamlet with one store, where only the most necessary household articles could be obtained. The news from the outside world was weeks old before it would reach us. Traveling any distance was slow and hazardous. Now passengers arrive here in the afternoon, who in the morning were still in Chicago. Daily papers gather news by telegraph from distant parts of the country, and it reaches the readers when it is still fresh. The hamlets of the fifties have become cities with factories and fine churches and schools, and beautiful stores and office buildings. When I first came here I felt as if I was fated to lead the life of a hermit the rest of my living days, and now I am surrounded with more luxuries than I have ever seen.

The Catholic Church too has made great progress. When the Most Rev. Henni came to Milwaukee as the first bishop of Wisconsin, and that was in 1843, only seven years before I came, he had only four priests to administer the spiritual needs of a small number of Catholics scattered all over Wisconsin and the northern part of Michigan. Now this large territory has been divided into four dioceses: Milwaukee, La Crosse,

Green Bay, and Sault Ste. Marie. The diocese of Green Bay alone has forty priests in charge of flourishing congregations and needs more priests. Father Daems, a Crozier Father from Uden, the Vicar General of the diocese and a good friend of mine, often speaks of the scarcity of priests, and says that ten or twelve priests could be placed immediately in charge of congregations with more than a thousand souls. If you know of any priests or theologians willing to come to this country tell them to write to me, and I will forward the letter to Father Daems. If they need money to continue their studies or to make the journey, let me know about it and the matter will be taken care of.

The Little Chute congregation too has prospered and increased in numbers. For a year now we are using our new church – a brick building 110 feet long, 50 feet wide and the walls 35 feet high; masons are still working on the tower.

Last summer my brother John died, who was a great friend of our family and to whom we are indebted for much of what we have done. If John had not been here first, we probably would never have come here either. When we arrived here first he took the whole family in his house and helped us in every way. His wife received the bulk of his estate, and in his last will he bequeathed his share of the mill too me. Shortly before he died he had given $ 200 and another $ 150 for the purchase of a new church bell, and it was tolled the first time at his funeral.

I am now the sole owner of the mill, which represents an investment of $ 16,000. I bought last year a 33 acre piece of land for $ 1,000, and have now 180 acres in all. Land opposite my house has been sold for $ 100 an acre.

I had he portrait of Adriana reproduced to give one to each of my children. If you are still in possession of the portrait of Anna, will you please send it to me, and I will have it also enlarged and reproduced for the children, and have an extra copy for you.

My nephew, Johannes Verstegen, is pastor of the church of Freedom, where he is well liked and doing good work; my daughter Johanna Catherine is keeping house for him. My wife and the children send you their best regards. Yours with love and respect,   Arnold Verstegen

L.

Little Chute, October 20, 1871

Dear Brothers and Sisters-in-law:

I suppose the newspapers in Holland have told you all about the terrible forest fires which have raged in Wisconsin, and you have thought of us wondering if we were still alive. I hasten therefore to let you know that we are all well, but we have heard and seen enought of a terrible catastrophe. In the first week of October the air was so saturated with smoke that it pained the eyes, and at night a reddish glow hung in the sky and struck fear in the heart of everyone. It looked as if the world all around us was on fire, and that it was closing in on us leaving no escape. All we could do was pray and hope that God in his mercy would spare us. There is much land cleared around Little Chute and the remaining woods stand like islands in a sea, so that the fire could not leap across the intervening space, or was at least much retarded. A heavy rain coming at the opportune time quenched the fire before it had reached us, and that saved Little Chute.

For you in Holland it is difficult to form an idea of the woods in America. The only forests you have are patches of stunted pine trees, planted in a soil too poor to be used for anything else. Here the forests cover hundreds of square miles of rich soil and the climate is favorable, so that trees of many varieties grow to immense size. From the time of Adam they never felt the woodman's ax; when they die of old age, and the decayed roots can no longer support them, they crash to the ground and become the food for a new generation which grows upon them.

Now it happened that we had a long dry spell this summer so that the dead trunks and branches scattered in great profusion throughout the woods became very inflammable, and when once they caught fire by some accident, it spread very rapidly, and fanned by a strong wind it leaped to the tops of the trees devouring everything in its path. Thousands of acres of beautiful forests become a sea of fire and are now a scene of desolation. It had taken nature to build a beautiful paradise and now through the carelessness of perhaps one human being it has become a black and charred waste.

As I said our many clearings saved us, but about 60 miles north of here where the woods were more contiguous, the town of Peshtigo with a population of 1,200 inhabitants has been completely wiped out, except that one boarding house remains standing. On October the eigth, at ten o'clock in the evening, a fiery cloud rolled over the town like a hurricane, setting every building on fire almost at once, and in four hours time, there was nothing left but smouldering ruins. 300 people died in the flames and many more have died since of wounds. Those who managed to reach the river saved themselves by standing in the water up to their necks and ducking under water every so often to keep their hair from burning. Burning logs were floating on the surface and added to the danger. I talked to some of those who had that harrowing experience. Johannes van Rysen of Uden is said to be one of the victims. We must be thankful to God for our personal good fortune, and as the recent conflagration has removed a great fire hazard, a similar catastrophe will never happen again.

On the same day, October the 8th, the big city of Chicago of 250,000 people had also a disastrous fire. It had no connection with the forest fires of Wisconsin; that it occured at the same time was just a coincidence. I happened to be in Appleton the next day, Monday, where telegraphic accounts came in of the disaster all day long. In the evening it was reported that 2,000 acres covered with residential and busniess houses had been laid waste by the fire, and that many lives were lost. Chicago is a big and beautiful city and has many large buildings; some are said to have cost a million dollars, and their contents were worth an equal sum. Their fireproof construction did not save them, because the heat was so intense that the iron pillars which supported them melted as if they had been wax candles; at least that is the story.

The dry season that started the fires has also damaged the crops; the wheat is poor and the other crops are only fair. Hay was good, but many haystacks have burned. As to my occupation I spend most of my time in the mill supervising the work. I have worked hard enough in my younger days and I think I am entitled to take it a little easier now. My oldest son, Egidius, is also working in the mill and learning the trade.

Please let me hear from you soon and forget it that my wife's relations are poor. For my children it is better to have a kindly stepmother than a rich and hard one, but let us not metion that subject anymore. Kind regards and best wishes to all brothers and sisters-in-law, and to all relatives and friends, with love and respect.　　　　　A. Verstegen

PS. I had this letter ready for the mail but now I have a chance to send it with Janus van den Boom, who will deliver it in person, and tell you all about the big fire and everything else. My brother's wife and I are not on friendly terms just now. It has been caused by the last will and testament of my brother, who bequeathed his share in the mill to me and my descendants.　　　　　　　　　　　　　　　A. Verstegen

80. C. A. VERWYST'S REMINISCENSES OF A PIONEER MISSIONARY

[Chrysostom Adrian Verwyst, born in Uden in 1841, emigrated to Wisconsin settling in Hollandtown, first known as Franciscus Bosch. His *Reminiscences* published in the *Publications of the State Historical Society of Wisconsin Proceedings*, 1916, possesses much information on Dutch Catholic settlement in Hollandtown and Little Chute.]

I was born November 23, 1841, in the land of windmills, dikes, and wooden shoes, in Uden, a town of North Brabant, Holland. My parents migrated to the United States in 1848, and of my life in Holland I remember almost nothing.

The occasion of our removal to the United States was as follows: Rev. Theodore van den Broek, a Dominican priest, had come from Holland to this country in 1832 and had resided for a time in a house of his order, St. Rose, near Springfield, Washington County, Kentucky. In 1834 he removed to Green Bay where a brother Dominican, Father Samuel C. Mazzuchelli, had been working among the whites and the Indians. Thereafter the two Fathers labored along the shores of Green Bay, sometimes separately, sometimes together. Father van den Broek was stationed at Little Chute and along the upper Fox River until his death at Little Chute in 1851. In 1847 he returned to Holland on some family mission, and his description of the cheap and good lands to be had in Wisconsin induced many of the people of North Brabant, among them my father, to migrate thither. Accompanied by Father van den Broek and by Father Godhard, a Fanciscan, they set sail in three ships, two of which landed at New York and the third at Boston.

On the latter ship my father had embarked. We were fifty-five days on the ocean but the voyage was a prosperous one and none of the passengers died at sea. On reaching America Father van den Broek returned to the scene of his labors at Little Chute, while Father Godhard went with a number of his countrymen to Hollandtown, Brown County. This settlement was originally called Franciscus Bosch in honor of the patron saint of the church. On the arrival of our ship at Boston most of our fellow passengers went immediately to the West, but our family and another by the name of Verkampen were obliged, through lack of means to travel farther, to stay in Boston. It was in the month of May and we therefore made our living at first by going into the woods, to Dorchester and other places near Roxbury, and picking blueberries, blackberries, and huckleberries, and cutting water cress.

Soon after our arrival a laughable adventure happened to our neighbor, Verkampen. Rooms had been engaged for the two families together, the Verkampens occupying those in front of the building and our family those in the rear. One night the owner came with a German boy who acted as interpreter and told Verkampen we would have to vacate the premises immediately. When Verkampen at length comprehended the demand thus made upon him he seized an ax and made for the proprietor with the intention of scaring him away. The latter promptly beat a hasty retreat, but shortly afterwards Verkampen was arrested and lodged in jail. His poor wife was disconsolate. "Scarcely in America and my man in jail," she lamented. Verkampen, however, urged her not to feel worried He was getting plenty to eat, more than he had ever enjoyed in Holland, and was living, he wrote, "like a prince in a palace".

A few days after his arrest many of the townsmen celebrated the Fourth of July by inbibing too freely of liquor, and as a result were landed in jail. Verkampen, who had a bottomless stomach, ate not only his own rations but also those of the drunken fellows incarcerated with him. For the first time in all his life, probably, he enjoyed a full meal. A day or two after the Fourth the prisoners were brought to trial. Verkampen, who was defended by a German lawyer, was dismissed since it was shown that the owner of the building had no right to attempt to eject us in the middle of the night and that Verkampen had intended only to scare him away and not to kill him.

We soon removed to East Boston where my Father and my oldest brother engaged in the copper trade. About the year 1850 we moved to Roxbury where they obtained employment in a rope factory. I have omitted to mention, I find, that prior to 1850 Father and my two brothers, Martin and John, went to Vermont to work on a railroad, and there John died. Thereupon my Father and my brother Martin returned to Boston or East Boston. We two boys-both of us still alive (1916) – attended the German Catholic school in Boston.

Finally, in the early spring of 1855, our family migrated to Wisconsin. We left Boston in pleasant spring weather but when the train reached Rutland, Vermont, the same evening it was snowing and when we arrived at Albany it was raining. In the depot at Albany there was posted in a conspicuous place a large placard warning travelers against "thieves, pickpockets, and confidence men". The notice appeared somewhat strange to us but to our cost we found out that it was not uncalled for. Father engaged a man to convey our baggage to another depot, paying him in advance. When we arrived at the depot he refused to surrender our belongings unless we again paid him. In vain father protested. Finally, he appealed to a policeman, and that worthy representative of law and order declared that father had no right to prepay the baggage man; so he was compeled to pay the bill a second time.

From Albany we went by way of Niagara Falls, where we passed over into Canada, to Detroit. The train moved very slowly, and it took us many days – how many I do not now remember – to reach Chicago. That city left a decidedly dismal impression on my boyish mind. It certainly did not look neat and clean like Boston. From Chicago we took a steamboat which brought us to Sheboygan, Wisconsin. Here mother and we two boys tarried for over a week while father and my oldest brother started out in quest of land. Finally, they returned and we hired a conveyance to bring us and our baggage to Fond du Lac. On the way a man ran against our wagon; the two drivers became very angry, each blaming the other for the collision, and nearly came to blows. We dined at Green Bush and arrived late that evening at Fond du Lac. The next morning we took a small steamer on Lake Winnebago which brought us to Menasha. From there we took a wagon and through mud, stones, and deep holes on the road we finally came to Hollandtown in Brown County.

Father bought sixty acres of land from a man named Stephen Fink, and we started to erect a cabin of unhewn logs, the neighbors helping at the raising. The house had no floor but there was a wretched wooden chimney which at times smoked fearfully. In cold weather the occupants would be too warm in front while their backs were almost freezing. Luckily for us we carried a floor about with us in the shape of wooden shoes made of poplar. My brother Cornelius and myself worked hard all winter with father cutting down hardwood and other trees and chopping them into logs about sixteen feet long. We tacked a piece of old cloth to our wooden shoes and tied strings together around our legs below the knees to prevent the snow from falling into our shoes. In this way we kept our feet dry and warm, better in fact, than we could have done with leather boots.

In the spring father would split fence rails, at which work we boys faithfully assisted him. After the clearing had been fenced, having neither horses nor oxen to plow the ground, we made potato hills and planted corn and potatoes, doing the work with heavy grub hoes. There was a clearing of about seven acres when we bought the land of which one-half was meadowland. We had to work like beavers all the year round and our only leisure was on Sunday afternoons, when we were allowed to visit the neighbor boys. At the end of four years of such toil we had thirty acres cleared, on which we raised wheat, rye, barley, potatoes, beans, and other vegetables.

In Hollandtown, where a stately brick church now stands, prior to 1855 a small church had been built. A priest used to visit our settlement about once a month, the good man being obliged to walk all the way from Little Chute, a distance of about fifteen miles, over most horrible roads. Every Sunday we had religious services. As the church had neither steeple nor bell the blowing of a horn announced the time for religious services. An old man named Van der Hey used to give out the prayers and read a short sermon. The men and boys sat on one side of the church and the women and girls on the other. The women used to wear those queer Holland-fashioned dresses and some had gold earrings. Nearly all of them came to church in their wooden shoes. A man named Verhulst was doorkeeper and woe to the luckless canine that happened to get into the church. Verhulst would grab him in his giant hands and drag him out of the church, the poor dog howling loudly. Once outdoors Verhulst would swing the dog in a circle and hit him against the church, the animal meanwhile howling for mercy. When finally released the unfortunate dog would take care to avoid the vicinity of the church in future. Of course such proceedings did not serve to increase the gravity and attentive devotion of the youngsters.

Whenever the Father came from Little Chute there was always a great rush to get to him first to make one's confession. I think if any or our non-Catholic people had been present on such an occasion and had seen how we fairly raced to get to the priest first, they would have concluded that confession after all is not so difficult an ordeal as some of those outside the church have imagined it to be.

I will now give the names of some of the people I recall who were at Hollandtown and its vicinity in the period from 1855 to 1860: Van den Berg, Verkuilen, Kobussen, Verhulst, Van den Loop, Ballard, Beach, Fink, Eittings, Verkamp, Van der Jagt, Loftus, Curtin, Malloy, Glachine, Sievers, Kersten, Rolf, Kordsmeider, De Bruin, School, Hoevenaar, Tillemans, Van Aerts, Hintermeister; besides these there were many others whose names I can not now remember.

My countrymen used to have an occasional jollification. There was, for instance, the carnival entertainment just before Lenten fast. After mass was over they would betake themselves to the home of Mr. Van den Berg. The house was a large building for those primitive days, and there they would dance – the younger generation, of course – all day till sundown, when all would go home. Night dancing was never carried on, and I believe the present generation religiously follows this custom of their grandparents; that is, they dance only during the day, and every decent woman and girl is supposed to be at home before dark.

Our people also had a guild, that is, a certain kind of society at the head of which were a king and a queen for the year. On an appointed day all the members would meet at the chosen rendezvous to shoot down the wooden bird, made of very tough material, placed at the top of a high pole like a flagstaff. Sometimes it took much shooting to bring down the last piece of the wooden bird, whereupon the lucky marksman would be proclaimed king, with the privilege of choosing a queen and getting a large silver heart made which he was to wear during the year as a token of his royal dignity. Of course innocent day-dancing and other jollification were indulged in by the younger generation on this great day.

Occasionally we heard of a fight, or of some poor fellow becoming tipsy, but nothing more serious than that occured. There was a universal good will among all and toward all. Our neighbors lived the simple life of hardworking, religious, God-fearing people. From time to time they gathered on Sunday afternoon at the house of some neighbor, where the men played cards and took an occasional drink from a jug of liquor; the women, meantime, sipped their tea or coffee and chatted over household affairs and current news; while the boys found amusement in innocent games. Such entertainments fostered friendly neighborly feelings and promoted good will in the community. Indeed, in the four years I spent on the farm from 1855-60 I do not recall a single instance of a man or woman being arrested for disorderly conduct.

At house raisings and marriage feasts there would be some liquor consumed and all kinds of fun indulged in, but all with a neighborly feeling and not for the mere indulgence of drinking. When I recall my boyhood days in Wisconsin sixty or more years ago, I feel a certain regret that they are gone, never to return. It seems to me that people are now becoming too civilized, and their life is too artificial and filled with too much sham.

In those days bears, deer, racoons, and wild pigeons abounded. In some years pigeons could be seen on the ground and in the air by millions, but alas! man's greed has exterminated the wild pigeons. Year by year they become scarcer until now I believe there is not a single one in the whole length and breadth of the United States. We have exterminated the buffalo, and we are as fast exterminating the deer, elk, whitefish, and lake trout. The white man's philosophy seems to be summed up in Mark Twain's observation when told that we should provide for posterity: "Provide for posterity! Do something for posterity! *What has posterity done for us?*" In those days bears were plentiful and occasionally they paid unwelcome visits to the farmers' cornfields and pigpens. They were fond of pork and would often catch a squealing pig and make away with him to the woods to enjoy a hearty meal. One day – it was on a Sunday and people had all gone to church – a big bear invaded the precincts of Mrs. Van der Heide of Hollandtown. Hearing the squeals of one of her pigs, Mrs. Van der Heide rushed out of the house and saw a bear trying to carry one of them away. The animal was attempting to pull the struggling porker over a rail fence. In this he failed, however, for Mrs. Van der Heide, forgetting all fear, grabbed the hind feet of the pig and pulled with might and main while the bear, growling fiercely on the other side of the fence, did likewise. It was a pitched battle between the undaunted woman and the bear for the ownersship of the pig, but at length the woman won. She told her little boy to take a stick and hit the bear on his hind legs. The bear growled firecely but had to give up. Mrs. Van der Heide saved her pig, but the animal had to be butchered as it was so badly lacerated by the teeth of the bear. Everyone wondered at the courage of the woman and that the bear did not attack her. Let her name be immortalized in the annals of Wisconsin!

Occasionally an Indian would pay us a visit, although I never saw one in the village itself. The neighbors advised us not to give them anything when they came to beg for something to eat, for if we once gave them food they would come again and again. I considered their well-meant advice heartless. Mother, too, pitied the poor people when they would come asking for something to eat. I remember perfectly one occasion when she gave a hungry Indian a whole loaf of bread. He asked for a knife and cut off a slice two or more inches thick to eat immediately.

One time the Father in Little Chute had several guests at table, among them an Indian. When the meat was passed to the latter he emptied the whole dish into his bag thinking that it now belonged to him. The other guests were not particularly pleased with the procedure, but the thing was done, and they had to make out their dinner as best they could.

Another time mother had made some homemade beer which consisted of hops, water, and molasses boiled in the wash boiler. This time the brew proved to be a failure. We had some neighbors as guests on Sunday afternoon, and some of this homemade product was served them, but very little of it was drunk for it was fearfully bitter. An Indian happened to come along, and mother offered him some of it, but after taking some of it in his mouth he spat it out. Mother afterwards threw away the remainder of the beer. Next day I was working, planting or hoeing potatoes near a creek that ran through our land. Suddenly I heard mother screaming at the top of her voice. I ran up to the house to see what was the matter. On reaching it I found four Indians on horseback who said they had come to drink the beer of which their comrade – the Indian of yesterday – had told them .We explained to them that we had thrown it all away because it was not good. Father, who was working nearby for a neighbor, hearing mother's loud call came running with a pitchfork intent on defending his wife and children, but luckily he was not needed, the Indians laughed good-naturedly at the poor man's simplicity in thinking to fight four Indians with a pitchfork.

A neighbor of ours, a distant relative, Martin School by name, lived some three miles away in a deep valley, or rather ravine through which a creek ran. One night he heard some noise near the creek and thinking it was a deer coming to drink he tried to shoot it. His gun, which was one of the old-fashioned kind, failed to go off, and so he went back in the dark to his house to fix it. In a moment in rushed an Indian in a terrible rage, exclaiming: "You want to shoot Indian! shoot Indian!" The poor man tried to make the Indian understand that he was very near-sighted and that he had thought it was a deer drinking at the creek. Gradually the Indian comprehended his explanation, which was given more by signs and motions than by words. The red man's anger gradually died away but he insisted on having a dance then and there. Probably he had imbided too much fire water somewhere. So School had to do the singing and clapping with his hands to keep time, while the Indian danced around on the floor until finally he became tired and departed.

On one occasion in the wintertime my oldest brother, Martin, who used to work every winter in the pineries near Green Bay to help support the family, was walking along when he came upon a drunken Indian. The latter insisted on dancing with him immediately. Martin had never danced in all his life and, in fact, knew no more about dancing than the man in the moon, but dance he must, for the Indian demanded it and to refuse might cost him his life. So the two jumped around in the snow on the road, yelling as loudly as they could to keep time and moving about like two inmates of a lunatic asylum. My brother began to get tired of this strenuous exercise, but he dared not stop for fear of the Indian's gun. At length the Indian suddenly started off and Martin gladly took the opposite route.

The roads in those primitive days were generally poor, often in miserable condition. The only good one I knew of was the Military Road from Fond du Lac to Green Bay. It was a plank road from the county line between Calumet and Brown counties to Green Bay, a distance of about twenty-four miles. The south end of the road – not planked through Calumet County to Fond du Lac – was fairly good, considering the general condition of Wisconsin roads in those days, but it was very poor when compared with the public roads of the present time. Two or three times in my boyhood days I went to Green Bay on this plank road; the first time with my father about the year 1857. My brother had earned a little over $ 200 in the pinery north of Green Bay, but instead of the cash had received only a note, or check, for his pay. He had left the check with Timothy Howe in Green Bay for collection. I went along with father to act as interpreter on this occasion; but we made a long journey of some fifty miles going and returning for nothing. Ever since then I have felt rather unkindly towards lawyers. The second occasion was about a year later when I went to call Martin van den Broek, then working in Green Bay, to the funeral of his father. The latter had died from the effects of partaking too freely of icecold water while assisting in haymaking at Ballard's farm. On this occasion I walked continuously for twenty-four hours, going to Green Bay in the daytime and returning to Hollandtown the ensuing night, a total distance of about fifty miles.

The most wretched road I remember was the one from Hollandtown to Kaukauna, or Kaukaulo, as it was then called. This road followed no particular town or section line but zigzagged through the woods. There were innumerable mudholes, each one apparently worse than the rest, and no attempt had been made to improve the road. It struck the river bottom not far from Beaulieu's Mill and then continued up the river to the dam, above which people would cross the river to the village of Kaukaulo. This consisted of some half a dozen houses in addition to a store kept by Hunt. On the south side of the river there were in 1855 only two settlers; one was Beaulieu, an Indian, or half-breed, who had a small farm and a grist-mill; the other was one Sanders, a Dutchman, who had a large farm across the river from Hunt's store.

One time a Dutchman named Jan den Dickken (John the Thick, John the Fat) wanted to buy some pork at Hunt's store. Someone had told him he should ask for pig's pork. When he told Hunt what he wanted, the latter did not understand him. Finally, thinking that John wanted to buy a pitchfork, he brought some samples of the latter article for him to choose from. "No, No! Pick pork!" replied John the Fat. Luckily a pig chanced to run by the door, whereupon John pointed at it, at the same time making a motion with his knife as if he wanted to cut off a piece. Thus assisted Hunt at length comprehended the fat Dutchman's request.

In those days it was sometimes difficult to obtain provisions. For some time our nearest store was Hunt's at Kaukauna, eight or nine miles away. After some years Bertus van den Berg opened a store at Hollandtown, and then we were no longer compelled to travel through mud and slush to Kaukauna to procure the necessaries and conveniences of life. Before our arrival at Hollandtown things had been still worse. Some of the settlers actually had to carry sacks of flour on their backs all the way from Green Bay to Hollandtown, a distance of about twenty-four miles. I remember vividly an incident of my own boyhood days. Father and I carried a sack of grain, either wheat or rye, I have forgotten which, on our backs to Beaulieu's gristmill about a mile or so below the dam opposite Hunt's store. It was a trip of some sixteen miles going and coming, over horrible roads. We were compelled to make this trip three times before we got our grain ground.

After a time things grew more conveninent. In the winter time farmers near Fond du Lac used to take loads of flour to Green Bay, a distance of about sixty-five miles. Of course they would gladly sell their whole load somewhere on the way if they could find a buyer. John Kobussen, our rich neighbor, occasionally bought one or more loads of flour and then disposed of it to his neighbors....

Road making was carried on in those days in rather primitive fashion. The citizens would vote a certain amount of road tax at the regular town meeting, or election day. The farmers elected a "pathmaster" who had charge of the roads in a certain district. When the time came to work on them, he would send notice to all the tax payers within his district to come on a certain day to the place appointed to work on the road. The farmers would meet, perhaps at nine o'clock in the morning, with axes, shovels, and grub hoes and begin to build a corduroy bridge over some creek, throwing over the logs a few shovelsful of dirt; or, if there was a mudhole to be filled up, they would cut some green brush, throw it into the hole, and scatter over it a few shovels of earth and lo! the road was fixed. More than once I have worked on the road and though but a boy of fifteen to seventeen years I believe I did more work than the average farmer when working out his road tax.

I traveled very little during my boyhood. I went a few times to Green Bay, Appleton, and Little Chute. As to De Pere I have no distinct recollection, although of course I must have passed through it on my way to Green Bay. In those days we called the place "Rapides des Peres", which was afterwards abbreviated to De Pere. The ancient name, a French appellation, was derived from the fact that from 1672 to about the year 1720 the Jesuit Fathers had a house of their order and a church there....

I made several trips to Appleton. One of them, I remember, I went with a neighbor of ours to get a load of grain ground. Both Green Bay and Appleton seem to me to have been then about the size of Bayfield at the present time. Little Chute was a rural hamlet with from twelve to fifteen houses, a store belonging to John Verstegen, and a long, low, frame church on the bluff facing Fox River. The majority of the farmers in that vicinity were Hollanders who had come to America in 1848 and the following years.

Farming in those days on land full of stumps and roots was conducted in very primitive fashion. When a man had succeeded in cutting down the trees and chopping them into logs of fourteen to sixteen feet in length, he had to pile them up. This was a laborious task, especially if he had no oxen or horses. I remember how, when I was a lad of about thirteen, we had to work with might and main to roll up the heavy logs into piles to burn. Father was a small man, below medium size, but Mother was a large and strong woman and we boys had to work like little men. When the difficult task of burning the logs and brush had been accomplished, we cultivated the land thus wrested from the primitive forest.

For the first two years we had no oxen and so were compelled to plow with heavy grub hoes. Oftentimes our wrists would ache from digging and working in the hard, rooty ground. We could hoe a great number of hills in which to plant potatoes and corn. When the plants appeared above ground it was necessary to hoe them again to kill the weeds and get the crop to grow. Of course we had to dig the potatoes with our heavy grub hoes and stow them away in some kind of root house or cellar. It was hard, slavish work throughout the entire year. There were no mowing machines, and I remember seeing father cut our grain with a sickle, such as was used 4,000 years ago. The first improvement on the sickle was the cradle, with which a good cradler might but five acres in a day, provided he had strong arms and an iron will. Haymaking was carried on much as it had been in Old Testament times. Heat, fatigues, and sweat were expended lavishly in procuring food for the stock.

In spite of the want of modern machinery, however, the farms grew in size and value year by year. First, five to ten acres of stumpy and rooty land, a small log house with wooden chimney and floor made of hewn logs or rough boards, a small stable for the cattle, a pigpen, and a hen-house – such were the rude beginnings of farm life in those days. However things began gradually to change for the better. Frame house and barn took the place of the old log buildings; horses replaced the slow, patient oxen; the roads became more fit for travel; board fences replaced those made of rails; thus primitive Wisconsin developed into one of the most prosperous states of the Union. This transformation was largely wrought by the strong arm and tireless industry of the now-sometimes-despised foreigner. The German, Dutch, and Irish immigrants dug our canals, built our railroads, cleared our forests, and made a paradise of what was but a few years before a dreary wilderness, the habitation of uncivilized Indians and of wild animals.

In the summer of 1859 I determined to train for the priesthood and began to study Latin, Greek, and French under the instruction of our first pastor in Hollandtown, Reverend Father Spierings. He was a countryman of mine and was also a dear friend whom I shall never forget. After the death of my father Reverend Spierings sent me to the Seminary of St. Francis near Milwaukee to continue my studies. A neighbor took me as far as Brothertown and from there I walked all the way to Fond du Lac, arriving late in the evening or rather in the night. It ever there was a tired boy, I was the one, for I had walked twenty-five or thirty miles carrying a heavy grip. Next day I took the train to Milwaukee and walked out to the Seminary, a distance of about five or six miles. A Jew, a countryman, accosted me on the sidewalk and, overflowing with suavity, smiles, and friendliness, invited me to enter his store and urged me to buy a watch, but his officiousness and excessive suavity made me distrust him. I began to surmise that he must be a Jew, a race of which I had heard so much at home, and I told him I did not need a watch just then, nor anything else. He then pressed me to buy at least a pair of suspenders, but without avail, and I finally got away from my importunate Jewish countryman.

My seminary days were passed during the stormy period of our Civil War, 1861-65. I was drafted for service but I attempted to be released on the plea of being a subject of the king of Holland. To establish this fact I obtained from our Dutch consul in Milwaukee a document about two feet square, the cost of which was $ 3. Armed with it and with $ 300 in my pocket, partly procured at home and partly through the efforts of kind friends, especially Father Gernbauer, I presented myself at the provost marshal's office in Milwaukee. That officer questioned me as to my parents and I told him that father had taken out his first citizenship papers in Boston; and that subsequently he had voted in Wisconsin, as other aliens had done. I was thereupon most solemnly declared to be a citizen of the United States, having been a minor when I came into the country in 1848 and my father having voted; accordingly I was told to step into a side room to be examined. I was as sound as a dollar and knew that I would not have any chance to escape military duty on the score of physical ailments or defects. So I told the marshal I would pay the commutation fee of $ 300, in order to be absolved from military duty. I was then taken by a soldier to an adjoining building where I paid my money and received a receipt exempting me from militray duty for three years. This document is still preserved in the courthouse in Superior.

I walked back to the Seminary in a very pensive mood. About three or four months later came the spring election, and as I had paid $ 300 for my American citizenship I thought I would go to the polls to vote. The voting lords recognized that I was a stranger and some one challenged my right to vote, requiring me to swear to my citizenship. I told them how I had been drafted and been declared a citizen liable to military duty, and that I had paid $ 300 commutation money to exempt me from military service. Notwithstanding this the election board declared I was no citizen and, therefore, had no right to vote. I was so deeply disgusted at this manifest humbug and conceived so great a dislike for Uncle Sam that I did not take out my citizenship papers until about fifteen years later.

During my vacation time in the summer of 1862 I was working at a neighbor's place helping to thresh grain. I believe it was the first time I ever saw grain threshed with a machine instead of with the flail as had always been done in my boyhood. While thus engaged there suddenly came to us the startling report: "The Indians are coming! they are killing the whites!" The threshing ceased instantly and every man hastened home to get his gun to go to fight the Indians. I, too, hurried home. Father was dead, and mother and brother Cornelius were the only remaining members of the family. The latter was confined to the house on account of a sore foot. Not having bullets or lead, I pounded some pewter spoons into bullets and started for Hollandtown with loaded gun. There all was in an uproar. People had abandoned their farms in terror and dismay, some to hide in the woods, others to seek refuge in the village. Reverend Van Luytelaar was then the pastor of the Hollandtown congregation. His house was full of women with crying babies, many of whom were laid crosswise on his bed. All kinds of wild reports were in circulation; some said that the Indians had been driven into a swamp and surrounded; others had still wilder tales to relate.

I think it was in the afternoon when we first heard of the Indians coming and killing the white people. It was decided that after dark some men should be posted on the outskirts of the town as sentinels to watch and report any Indians that might be coming; others, myself amongst the rest, were to go to the intersection of the Military and Kaukaulo roads and watch there. It was a bright, moonlight night when my worthy neighbor, Ballard, carrying two guns, and I wended our way homeward, for we were hungry, not having eaten anything since noon. "Look out, general," the fat Yankee would say to me, when I would walk carelessly along, "look out, general, walk as much as possible in the shade, not in the moonlight. The Indians may see and shoot you." At length we posted ourselves behind a fence near the road. Woe to the poor Indian, if he had come along that way! He would have been shot down without mercy or inquiry. Luckily no redskins showed themselves, and we finally got up and went home.

After eating supper I went alone to the crossing mentioned above. There was a small clearing near by in which I noticed a fire burning. Probably the people had been burning brush and chips on the land that afternoon and had fled into the woods or to town when news of the Indian foray came. Seeing nothing suspicious I walked a few rods from the road into the woods, stood my gun up against a tree, and lay down and slept soundly until morning, for I was tired out by the day's work and my trip to the village and return. I learned afterwards that some men, who had been working on the Fox River Canal near Little Chute and whose folks lived in or near Hollandtown, had been on their way to this village that night. When they reached the intersection of the Military and Kaukaulo roads they saw the fire and all at once some pigs began to squeal. "Oh! the Indians are there! See the fire! Hear the pigs! They are killing everything!" And my brave countrymen ran at top speed back to Little Chute to tell the terrified people there the fearful news about the Indians' doings. Of course they had not seen a single Indian, but terror made them imagine all kinds of wild sights. The next day the Indian scare which, I subsequently learned, extended all over Wisconsin was over, and many a ludicrous story was told about what had been done during the universal fright.

This scare on the part of the people of Wisconsin, especially of those dwelling in the northern part of the State, was not without some reason, for at that very time Hole-in-the-Day had planned to attack Crow Wing, Minnesota, and kill the whites there and in that vicinity. The project was frustrated by the efforts of a venerable Catholic priest of seventy-seven years, Reverend Father Pierz (Pirec was his Slavonian name) who inuduced Hole-in-the-Day to give up his cruel design....

Chapter *XXV*

NETHERLANDERS IN MINNESOTA

81. ANNA BROWN'S LIFE STORY OF JOHN TUININGA

[Anna Brown was the daughter of Jan Tuininga who with his farther, also a Jan Tuininga, in 1853 emigrated from Pietersbierum in Friesland ad, after suffering shipwreck in the Bahamas, settled in New Amsterdam near La Crosse, later moving to Houston County, Minnesota. Copy of this sketch written in 1934 was provided for inclusion here by Sjoerd Chalsma (Tjalsma) of La Crosse.]

In Pietersbierum, Holland, lived Jan Tuininga and his wife Trintzy and their five children, Jan, Tsjoukje, Albertza, Anna, and Gerrit.

Jan, the second child, was my father and about whom this story is written. As a child he and his sisters had pleasant times with their playmates, a dog and their petted, tame rabbits. In Holland dogs were used extensively for draught animals. Father trained his dog to pull a small cart; often he and his sisters, Shoukia [as we called her] and Albertza would visit their grandmother Mrs. Anna Adam Tuininga who lived in the same village. She usually bought them a sweet cake in the near-by bake shop. How many times I have heard papa mention the goodness of that cake! The two younger children were not yet old enough to leave their mother.

In winter they had pleasure in skating on the canals that threaded their way through so much of the country of Holland. They also attended school. It was the custom of the children to kick off their little wooden shoes at the schoolhouse door – a Dutch idea of thrift and cleanliness which prevented mud being tracked in. Even though the children wore heavy woolen socks the stone floors were too cold for them. So each child was provided with a little fire box made from hard wood with a perforated top. One side was left open and in it was placed a bowl of hot coals. On top of these boxes they rested their feet. So all the time during their study hours their little toes were toasted to a turn.

On Sunday grandfather and his family attended church. They were quite poor and grandfather was discontented because of the low wages he received. Still their lives were serene and the children healthy.

In 1853 when father was fourteen grandfather joined a colony which Oepke Bonnema was organizing to emigrate to the United States.

During their passage to this country they were badly shipwrecked and papa was one of the crew that was appointed to service pumping the water out of the sinking ship. The vessel drifted south for several days. Then yellow fever broke out and my grandparents' two youngest children, Anna and Gerrit, died and were buried at sea. Through all my grandmother's grief and weakness she held tight in her hand a bag containing articles she valued. To begin with, there was her head dress which consisted of a lace cap with a gold chain over the brow to hold the lace in place and ending at each temple with loops of lace held in place by engraved gold knobs which completed the decoration. Almost the last advice grandmother had received from her mother was this, "No matter how poor you may become, Treen, never give up your head-dress, for without that you will lose caste and your social standing." So grandmother was very careful. Then, too, in this bag were silver spoons, laces, some trinkets and keepsakes, and, most precious of all, the clothing of her dead children.

When all on board were nearly dead from disease, thirst and starvation a small sloop manned by Bahama negroes found and rescued them. In the confusion of leaving the sinking ship to board the small sloop a sailor snatched away grandmother's bag. Her weak cries were unheard, and she was too near dead to protest. Grandmother never saw her treasures again.

The negroes took the colony to a sandy shore on a barren island and left them there. And not understanding the language they spoke, the poor people were completely mystified and lost courage. A friend of grandfather's was so cast down that he took an eating fork made from pewter, and sticking it into the sand, said, "There, I'll never need that again. All is over and we are left here to die." But grandfather replied, "Not so, I still think there is hope and as an emblem of my faith I'll take this fork", and he picked it up. Granfather ate with that fork during the rest of his life until there was hardly a tine left on the fork.

Soon a larger boat came and took them all to the island of Nassau, where they were tenderly cared for and nursed back to health. The United States Government arranged for their passage to New Orleans and on up the Mississippi River to their final destination. The colony finally settled fifteen miles up the Mississippi River from La Crosse, Wisconsin, at that time just a trading post in the low flat lands. They named the place New Amsterdam. But grandfather had grown weary of the bickerings, quarrelings, and petty jealousies rife in the colony, and would have no further association with them. Choosing for his home a place on the Minnesota side of the river in Houston County, in La Crescent Township, he claimed 160 acres of land with rolling hills, heavily wooded bluffs of hard timber and swampy meadow with a large creek running at its edge. The creek was from twenty to thirty feet wide in places and deep enough to swim in. Not many years after settling, papa and his father enlarged their claim by buying 200 additional acres. They remained on these lands as long as they lived.

When grandfather announced to his family that he proposed to build their home near a large oak tree, papa stared at this father in silence. So, this was the end! For during the hardship of the long, tedious journey he had been very brave and never lost courage, for were they not going to the land of promise? But was this what it amounted to? A wilderness of strange looking trees? [There are no trees in Holland except those that have been planted]. It was too much. He went on the other side of the large oak, sat down, drew up his knees and cried, and who could blame the poor fellow?

In due time they had erected sturdy log buildings, a house, a barn and some smaller buildings; and in the new clearings were planted fields. And papa was the owner of a pair of oxen in which he took great pride. He trained them, also bought brass knobs for their horns. These, he slipped down over the horns until they wedged tight, then he sawed off the tip of the horn even with the knob. He always kept these knobs brightly polished. Papa could make his own ox yokes, which in those days was considered quite a feat. Also he was regarded as the best ox driver and trainer in the neighborhood.

In these early times peculiar value was placed on things and objects. As papa's sisters were lonely for domestic pets, grandfather traded a load of hay for a cat. Soon there were many more little cats and the girls treasured these as precious pets.

Into this vicinity came a German colony settling on scattered claims, which delighted grandfather and his family, for they understood and could speak German. There were small social gatherings whicht he neighbors attended, coming for miles with their slow ox teams. At these meetings they would always sing hymns, read a chapter in the Bibel, and someone would offer a prayer.

The Indians at that time were not yet subdued. A drunken Indian was a bad actor. This was another serious matter with which they had to contend. So grandfather procured a muzzle loading gun, quite a weapon of combat they thought it. Papa also used this gun for hunting small game. Otherwise, it stood ever loaded for their protection.

By this time they owned a small band of sheep and were particular in the breeding of their animals. One of their rams took first prize at the county fair. In the side of one of the high bluffs was a cave, and into this cave, one day grandfather went searching for a lost sheep. He kept going further back until he saw two glaring eyes which were not the eyes of his lost lamb. It probably was the wolf who had killed it. Grandfather left the cave and took large rocks and closed and sealed the opening so securely, it remains closed to this day. They also owned thirty or forty head of cattle, and as there were thieving neighbors, papa and his father branded JT on all their calves. At one time their farm tools disappeared mysteriously. Once papa retrieved a stolen crowbar by tracing the three cornered punch holes left in the earth, as the iron bar was too havey for the thief to carry. After that they bought an iron stamping tool with "J. Tuininga" in raised letters at the end of the punch, so that their name could be stamped on everything they owned.

The membership of the German circle had now grown so large that they were able to build a church under the jurisdiction of the German Methodist organization, erecting a sturdy little building with two rows of benches, the men sitting decorously on one side and the women on the other. The minister was a circuit rider who made fortnightly visits. As the church was built near the Tuininga farm it was the custom of my grandparents to entertain their pastor over night. The family greatly enjoyed these visits for they could hear all the news from the other churches and talk about the future of their own. And grandma would bustle about to prepare a good supper.

Living in the community with her family and a member of the German church was a buxom German girl, Emma Tyson, a sweetheart of papa's. They were engaged to be married when a bitter misunderstanding came between them. The members of the church gossiped freely about the lovers' quarrel; evidently their trouble couldn't be straightened out, for papa asked for the return of the engagement ring, which was granted. Emma eventually married an enterprising man, a Mr. Berry, and they left the valley. I think, however, they always loved each other for papa named his first daughter "Emma". In the church on the day of papa's funeral I saw a well dressed lady weeping beside my father's coffin and I asked mama who it was. She answered rather dryly, "That's Emma Tyson, Mrs. Berry."

Papa's sisters, Tsjoukje and Albertza, were married to thrifty Dutch farmers and lived on neighboring farms. If their brother Jan's heart ached, he never told anyone.

There was much work to be done on the farm, the rotation of crops and the marketing of produce was a serious problem. Their market place was La Crosse, Wisconsin, the farmers depending on an old steamboat to ferry them across the river. Papa and his father were careful to prevent the soil in the fields from deteriorating, and they fertilized after each harvesting. Also they were particular about cutting down the trees. They lost some, however, for on the other side of the bluff beyond their watchful eyes many a cord of wood was taken by poachers.

About this time a Masonic Lodge was organized in the village of La Crescent, papa and his father becoming charter members.

For social life there were the neigbhborhood parties. Old friends have told me they never considered their party had really begun until John Tuininga had arrived, as they could always depend on him to liven things up.

Grandfather had an intriguing friend who inveigled him into borrowing money to gamble in the stock markets. Grandfather lost every cent he had borrowed. This was real woe and the family grieved greatly over the burden of debt which they had to repay.

On the top of one of the bluffs on the Tuininga land was a limestone quarry. From this stone the Toledo Woolen Mill was built about a quarter mile up the creek. The English settlers, who owned the mill built their homes nearby. These hills were so steep that no team or wagon was ever able to get up their sides, so the rock used for the mill had to be rolled down the mountain side.

Papa was thirty five years old now and grandfather often admonished his son in good Dutch, saying, "Jan, if you never marry, the name will surely die out." He knew of no other family who bore this name, and his only brother, who still lived in Holland, had a family of daughters. So naturally he was anxious.

Occasionally, on Sunday afternoons, in the little German church, were held English services and papa always attended. Also to these meetings came a quiet dark-eyed English girl, Elizabeth Thompson, a comely young woman with a pouty mouth. She seemed quite religious and papa was rather attracted. Their courtship was brief and their wedding day unromantic. Mama felt quite humiliated because she had married a Dutchman. Their union was not very happy, although they had eight children, John the 3rd, Emma, Anna, Charles, William, Albert, Arthur, and Grace. Mama always held an arrogant and unsocial attitude towards papa's relatives. Mama's pleasure was in taking every opportunity to go home where her parents lived in the English settlement. There mama would visit in content with her relatives and English friends.

Papa also seemed to want the companionship of his parents and was beginning to spend more of his leisure in their home which was only a few rods from his own. With them it was very agreeable to converse in their familiar tongue about the farm, their debts, his sisters' families, the church, etc. Here he could peacefully smoke his pipe, as mama discouraged smoking in her house. And grandma, at half ten every morning, served a coffee lunch to papa, his father, and the hired man.

Near my grandparents' house papa had his carpenter shop where he occupied himself on rainy days and during the cold winter months, in repairing farm machinery, making mama a cupboard or a new firebox for his mother. Also he would build necessary farm implements such as a stone-boat, a wheelbarrow, etc. Often in the shop his father and mother would visit him for they loved to watch their son busy at his bench and enjoy a *praatje*, a term in Dutch for idle chatter.

Frequently on Sundays, after church service papa's sisters and their families would spend the rest of the day with their parents; and often their friends would come from New Amsterdam to visit them. There would be coffee lunches at these times and much *praatje*. Papa enjoyed these affairs greatly but mama held aloof. Though in true politeness grandma's guests always came over and made a social call on Jan's wife.

So time moved slowly on, mama producing her offspring in due regularity, and we were all dutifully taken into the little church and baptized. Papa and his father continued with their farming and were faithful in their attendance at the meetings of the Masonic Lodge. But mama strenuously charged papa with paying out money for something from which she was sure he would never derive any benefit. At first these accusations were not heeded, but so persistent was the complaint that papa finally yielded and did not meet with his brother Masons any more nor did he keep up the payments of his lodge dues, an act which he seemed always to have regretted.

Never having robust health since his unfortunate experience on shipboard and being ill twice from pneumonia, papa's health began to fall when he was fifty years of age. He found he could not lead the work in the fields any more. Many times he would come in taken with a chill and have to remain in bed until he recuperated. These attacks became more frequent. Also his sorrows increased, for his sister Albertza had died, and Tsjoukje and her husband, whom papa loved as a brother, had moved with their family to Wisconsin. His beloved mother was now a paralytic and his father old and irritable. He felt lonely. Then there was anxiety over his son's discontent, and reluctance about remaining on the farm.

The everlasting restlessness of youth! Patiently he listened to mama's constant suggestions that if he would only brace up and stop thinking about himself, he would feel a whole lot better. Life seemed so dreary. Too ill to work and not sick enough to die, he became greatly discouraged and would wander away by himself and sit alone for hours cutting designs from a bit of wood, only to toss them away when finished. I have often wondered what his thoughts were then.

In 1897 in his sixtieth year on a hot June night Jan Tuininga the 2nd died of paralysis of the throat and other complications. There was a large funeral, for papa had many friends. On that day grandmother asked grandfather to raise her up in bed so she might watch the funeral procession disappear over the hill. Tears rolled down her cheeks and she cried in anguish, "Jan my son, come back to me." A few years later papa's aged parents also died, grandma going first.

Today the valley is changed. Its beauty and glory have disappeared and the country looks ravaged. The people who used to live there are gone. Not a tree seems to have been spared from the woodman's ax. The goodness in the virgin soil seems to have been exhausted. The mill-wheel is silent and the old woolen mill burned long ago; the small English settlement deserted and the houses falling apart in decay. The little church has been pulled down; it was sold for the lumber that was in it. Those good Germans had built well. The old Tuininga farm looks bleak and desolate. Some stranger has gone over it and cut down about every available tree on the high mountainous bluffs. The creek is drying up and willows like weeds grow everywhere. Farm buildings are in ruins, hardly an original building left except the rambling old farmhouse mama insisted on having built.

About half a mile from the old farm is a cemetery on a sloping hill at the foot of a high bluff, and there sleep our Dutch ancestors. John Tuininga the 1st, and his wife Trintzy Dehon Tuininga. Close by is the grave of their son John Tuininga the 2nd. Near him are buried his two little children, sister Grace and Baby Brother Willie. Close to the graves of my grandparents is buried their daughter Albertza Tuininga van Loon and near her are the graves of some of her children. The last information I had was that the grave monuments were still resting firmly on their foundations.

In allegiance to the English speaking country in which grandfather and his family had become American citizens the following names were adopted: John for Jan, Kathrine for Trinty, Susan for Tsjoukje, Betsy for Albertza. But in their own family circle they addressed each other by their Dutch names.

I have truthfully and most sincerely written this story as well as I can remember from what was told me by grandma Tuininga, aunt Susan (Tsjoukje) and by my parents, also from events I can remember myself.

82. HERMAN BORGERS' HOLLANDERS IN MINNESOTA

[Born in the Netherlands in 1843 the auther, a minister in the Reformed Church and graduate of Hope College and Western Theological Seminary, served the Reformed congregation at Greenleafton from 1886 to 1893. This sketch, prepared for the Semi-Centennial celebrations at Holland in August 1897 was provided by the Netherlands Museum which owns the original manuscript.]

While a few isolated Hollanders and Holland families are scattered throughout the State of Minnesota and especially in St. Paul and Minneapolis, distinct settlements are to be found in Fillmore County; Kandiyohi, Chippewa, and Renville counties; Pipestone, Nobles, and Rock counties, and in Pine County.

I. Fillmore County. Of all the Dutch settlements in the state of Minnesota, Greenleafton in Fillmore County is the oldest. During the spring of 1856 a group of Hollanders left Alto, Wisconsin, in search of cheap lands and a favorable location for a new colony. This group was composed of Derk Alink, his wife, and children, who traveled in two wagons each drawn by a yoke of oxen; Willem Boland and his wife in a wagon also drawn by a yoke of oxen; and Arend J. Nagel, a muledriver who drove one of Alink's wagons. From Alto they slowly traveled southwards through Wisconsin, northern Iowa, and southern Minnesota, through areas where there were cultivated as well as uncultivated lands, through timber and prairie. Having no specific spot in mind, but being bent on exploring the country, they traveled in a roundabout way westward along a route so circuitous that today they would not be able to find it again. Finally, on May 19, weary of travel, they halted in Fillmore County on the spot which now is Alink's farm, unyoked their weary oxen, and said, "Here shall be our dwelling place."

During the autumn of that same year other Hollanders joined them: Berend Nagel and his wife, their sons Derk and Gerrit and daughter Diana. Meanwhile Alink erected his house – the first in the new Dutch colony. Boland and his wife spent the summer in their canvas-covered wagon. They built a log house of one room, as had done the Nagel family. These houses were little better than mere huts and scarcely kept out the

Minnesota storms. But the newcomers rejoiced that they had accomplished so much. Other people had settled at some distance away, but
had little to do with these strangers. To the west stretched a vast prairie
dotted with forests. Hardly a road was to be found anywhere.

But in spite of the hardships incidental to their pioneer life, this little
Dutch community grew steadily. In 1856 arrived Willem Boland's
mother, his brother Hendrik and wife, and Jan, an unmarried brother.
During the following year came Willem Vriege and his daughter who
became the wife of Arend Nagel. These people possessed the courage
necessary to cope with frontier conditons, make the sacrifices required
to conquer the primitive character of life far removed from civilization.
Their markets at Prairie La Crosse and other places along the Mississippi
River were as much as 70 miles distant. Lumber and other building
materials had to be brought in from those places. Wheat and corn had
to be transported in oxdrawn wagons. Primitive log houses and dugouts
had to serve as homes – some of them may be seen even at this date. The
prairie had to be broken, for not a furrow had ever been turned here;
stores where they might procure necessaries did not exist. Such were the
privations and hardships of their life; they were enough to put Dutch
persistency to a severe test.

The first winters proved especially severe, chiefly because the settlers
were not prepared to face the rigors of a new environment. This is
illustrated by the tale about Arend Nagel, who with two others undertook
to bring supplies from Preston, a town twelve miles distant. So difficult
was the journey through the ice encrusted snow and so sore became the
feet of their oxen that the travelers were forced to abandon their bags of
flour in a grove and later even to part company with their bobsleigh.
One night the snow fell so deep that the settlers had great difficulty
getting out of their primitive abodes. In those days there were no articles
specially adapted to winter wear, such as rubber shoes and rubber coats.
Ordinary leather shoes had to serve during the winter.

Some time elapsed before the colonists could provide for their religious
needs satisfactorily. Their first meetings were held in a school house.
Soon the German Evangelicals came to preach and some of our
Hollanders alternated their services occasionally. The Reformed Church
was not officially organized until 1869, but a nucleus of the church had
existed ever since 1856, which managed to maintain some services. In
August 1869 Dominie Pieter Lepeltak came, who served as pastor until
April 1877. This was the formative period of their church. A Miss.
Anna Greenleaf, a member of one of the eastern churches of our denomi-

nation, furnished all the money necessary for the erection and furnishing of the present church structure. In honor of her generosity this settlement was named Greenleafton. Other pastors followed: Dominie Harmen van der Ploeg, 1879-'82; Dominie Jacob B. de Jonge 1883-'85; Dominie Hermanus Borgers, 1886-'93; and Dominie Albert Oosterhoff, from 1895. During Borger's pastorate the church was renovated and greatly improved at an expense of about $ 600, and now is a substantial structure. A new barn has been built recently and plans for a new parsonage are actively being considered. This church at the present time has a membership of 60 families, in all 132 souls.

There also is a Dutch Presbyterian church, organized in 1876, with a membership of 20 families. Its pastors in the order of their service were the Rev. J. W. P. Roth Sr., J. W. P. Roth Jr., Sysko Redeus, G. I. Bloemendaal, and the present incumbent, K. Tietema. The organization and subsequent history of this church did nog spring from a legitimate need of the community but had its origin in dissatisfaction and dissension. At no time did this church have any but a tentative existence, although under the present incumbent there are signs of improvement. Only 50 members are enrolled, 15 of whom do not attend because of distance. The Reformed Church, on the other hand, has had a more successful existence; yet had the Hollanders as a settlement been united religiously and ecclesiastically they might have accomplished much more. At least there might have been one other prosperous Dutch church five miles to the west, where, in the German Evangelical church above mentioned, the Hollanders at present constitute a majority.

The settlement of Greenleafton at present forms a Holland community about 4 by 12 miles, numbers about 320 souls, and is situated south of the Chicago, Milwaukee, and Saint Paul Railroad, all parts of the colony being between 12 to 20 miles south of Preston. Years ago these distances were felt to be disadvantageous, but now no more. Our settlement is a quiet rural section. God had abundanly blessed our people. The soil is incomparably rich; during all these years crops generally have been abundant and there has never been a failure. Today there is little room for expansion and all growth can come only through the reduction of the size of the farms which, it must be granted, really are too large. The price of land in Greenleafton generally is at least as high or higher than anywhere else in Fillmore County. Three of the first settlers still are living: Arend J. Nagel, Willem Boland, and Derk Alink. On May 19, 1896, there was a quiet and pleasant commemoration of the 40th anniversary of settlement on the Alink farm, with fitting thanks for divine blessing and guidance.

II. Kandiyohi, Chippewa, and Renville counties. There is a settlement of Hollanders at Renville and vicinity dating from the spring of 1886. It had its origin in the real-estate activities of the Chicago firm of Prins and Koch, which in the autumn of 1884 had bought for the purpose of a Dutch settlement about 34,000 acres of prairie land from the St. Paul and Duluth Railroad. In the spring of 1885 they began to advertise in papers in The Netherlands and in Dutch papers in this country. At the same time they placed their local agent, a Mr. Pieter Haan, in charge of their interests at Olivia, situated in Renville County. Soon many Hollanders from different states came to investigate the company's lands. Almost every visitor was well pleased with the prospects for farming and many bought land with the intention of settling there in the spring of 1886. Among the first to come were: Derk Bunkersberg and Willem van Arum with their families, from Amsterdam in The Netherlands; Gerrit Knot and family from Maywood near Chicago; Simon Dykema and family from Chicago; Derk Ritzema and family from Grand Rapids, Michigan. Hilke Fischer, John Flynn, and Corolas van der Einde with their families from Michigan; Jan van Akkeren and family from Oostburg Wisconsin; Albert K. Kleinhuizen from Roseland, Illinois; Dutmur Zuidema and Bouke Terpstra and families from Indiana; Ewe Bolt and Albeertis Huizinga and families from Iowa; and a number of others from New York, Ohio, the Dakotas, and other states.

These pioneers were earnest, energetic souls. With a determined will and fixed purpose they came, with God's help, to build homes for themselves and their families, to induce the wild, naked prairie to bring forth its hidden treasures in response to diligent and intelligent farming. Not a house or tree was to be seen for miles, nor were there any landmarks to set off the land they had bought. Hard work it was to break the thick, tough hide of this prairie sod. Digging wells, building homes, and erecting shelters for their cattle meant much labor. But they accomplished all these things and laid a firm foundation for the future. Soon the fertile soil brought forth an abundance of crops, stimulating the hope of ultimate success and encouraging those whose hearts had faltered.

Soon these Hollanders thought of organizing a church. In response to a request from them to the classis of Iowa of the Reformed Church in America, two ministers came in May 1887 and organized a Reformed congregation. Soon after this ministers of the Christian Reformed Church also came to organize a church of their own. In 1887 they built a church in Prinsburg, four miles west from Roseland, at a cost of $ 500, an equal sum having been contributed by the firm of Prins and Koch.

This company had made similar promises to the Reformed people, but no Reformed church was erected until 1892, a delay detrimental to the growth of that church because many were weaned away from the Reformed Church when there was no church they could attend regularly. At the present time [1897] the membership of the Reformed Church living at Prinsburg is about 30 families, at Roseland about 40. Some of the Reformed people, however, joined the Christian Reformed Church whose center, as we have observed, is Prinsburg. This congregation, whose present pastor is Dominie J. H. Schultz, has a membership of about 60 families with about 300 attending services, while the Reformed Church has about 200. The total area of the settlement is about 20 square miles.

In adjoining Chippewa County to the west there is a settlement of Hollanders at Clara City 12 miles west from Roseland. Here, however, they do not constitute a compact Dutch population as at Prinsburg and Roseland. They form only about half of the population. Recently [in 1896] a Reformed church was organized, but was joined with the Roseland congregation and now is served by energetic Dominie Cornelius Kriekaard. Apart from these two purely Holland churches there are two other congregations, each possessing its own church. These are East Friesians, who use the Dutch tongue in their services. The first of these is Bunde near Clara City; the second Emden, located in Renville County, six miles north and one mile west of Renville, thus adjoining the Dutch settlement of Prinsburg and Roseland to the north. Both these churches belong to the Christian Reformed Church and are in a flourishing condition, under the united charge of Dominie Potgieter.

Not all the Hollanders living in this region, however, belong to these churches. At Clara City there is a German Presbyterian, a German Lutheran, and a Roman Catholic church, and each of these has some Dutch members and some Dutch-speaking East Friesians. At Raymond, a village generally regarded as belonging to the Dutch colony, eight miles northeast from Clara City on the Great Western Railroad, there is a Methodist Episcopal church to which a few Hollanders belong. At Renville also some Hollanders have joined the Methodist Episcopal church. The other Hollanders living there attend the churches at Emden, Prinsburg, or Roseland, while a few have abandoned churchgoing altogether.

At the close of one brief decade of development, this settlement of Dutch-speaking people numbers about 1,500, to whom ought to be added 1,000 East Friesians, who together own no less than 360 farmsteads. During this period these people have helped to built two villages, Prinsburg and Roseland, totalling about 1,000 souls and situated on the Minnesota and Western Railroad. These villages provide all necessaries and even luxuries for the colony. Most of the business in both places is in the hands of Hollanders. These people provided for their religious needs and also developed their educational opportunities. They have erected 20 schools for their children, and, in addition high schools in the villages. They have built more than 20 expensive bridges over creeks and rivers, and opened 200 miles of good roads. The desert blossoms like a rose, the wild grasses and heavy sod have vanished – made room for beautiful gardens and golden grain where but a few years ago the buffalo, fox, wild cat, skunk, and other animals roamed freely. The psalm of praise:

> *Hoe lieflijk, hoe vol heilgenot,*
> *O Heer der legerscharen God,*
> *Zijn mij Uw huis en tempelzangen!*
> Psalm 84, 1.

has supplanted the call of wild beasts. All this has been effected with Dutch arms and Dutch hearts, through the blessing of the Most High.

Truly our people – Dutch as well as East Friesians – have prospered. The soil is rich, the rewards of labor are rich indeed. Few misfortunes have come to this colony, the climate is healthful, there have been no serious epidemics, and there has never been a crop failure. The settlement is expanding rapidly, and land has doubled in value in the one decade since the first settlers made their homes here. The original purchase price was $ 8 per acre; but there are many who would not sell it at $ 25. Not a few who came with nothing in their hands now own farms free of all encumberance. Had they remained in the Old Country they perhaps would have to end their days in some charitable institution. And still there is room for hundreds of Dutch families. Mr. Pieter Haan, who sold land to Hollanders 10 or 12 years ago, is ready to provide all comers with whatever they need.

III. Pipestone, Nobles, and Rock counties. The earliest settlement of Hollanders in Pipestone County was established at the village of Holland in 1887. The first settlers were D. van Beck, H. Beyers, G. van den Berg, E. Lokhorst, and E. van Essen and their families, all from Alto, Wisconsin; D. Mouw from Sioux City, Iowa; and J. H. Ubrechsen from Oostburg, Wisconsin. Other Hollanders followed, chiefly from Sioux County, Iowa, a colony only about 70 miles to the south.

These settlers at once thought of their religious needs, and so on May 22, 1888, the Classis of Iowa of the Reformed Church organized the congregation of Churchville, the center of the Dutch colony situated 7½ miles north and 3½ east from Pipestone and 5 miles north from the village of Holland. The church and parsonage were erected partly by funds provided by the church. The congregation, which at present has a membership of 28 souls, has been served by Dominie Gerrit Dangremond and also at times by Jan Willem Kots, at that time a theological student at the Western Theological Seminary in Holland, Michigan, but later a dominie.

The soil of this county is excellent for farming, resembling that of Sioux County, Iowa. The farmers prospered, and never suffered reverses except in 1893 and 1894, when the very general drought ruined all crops so that scarcely nothing was raised. Today this land is worth from $ 15 to $ 25 an acre. This prosperity is reflected in the character of the villages where the farmers transact their business. The village of Holland has two stores, a blacksmith shop, two grain elevators, two churches – one Lutheran and one Presbyterian. Here two Hollanders are engaged in business. Pipestone, a larger and more thriving place situated on several railroads, furnishes a good market. The people of this vicinity are eager for more Dutch settlers, and there is plenty of room for them. Surely, God who has so richly blessed the first settlers of this region also will reward newcomers.

Nobles County, southeast of Pipestone County, also offered excellent opportunities for settlers, and Hollanders first settled at Leota in 1890. This region had been occupied by several other nationalities for 16 or 17 years. But in 1890 a considerable amount of railroad land was offered for sale and farmers from Sioux County investigated the prairie land and bought a good deal of it at $ 10 per acre. Some of the Hollanders bought this land for speculation and rented it to other Hollanders. But many Hollanders at once took possession of their properties, the first settlers being M. Kalemeyn, G. Hofkamp, Jan Kreun, E. de Graaf, Derk de Graaf, Wolter Sterrenberg, T. Sterrenberg, H. van der Meer, Ab. Eernisse, Willem Olivier [also spelled Oliver], D. Prins, and Abel J. Smol, all of these heads of families.

Leota, 65 miles from Orange City, Iowa, has a general store and a blacksmith shop; 40 people live within a quarter mile from the village. Edgerton, in the southeastern corner of Pipestone County, generally is a better market for the farmers. Here, too, Dutch farmers settled, especially as new settlers constantly arrived, mostly from the Netherlands.

In Rock County, west of Nobles County and south of Pipestone County there are a few Dutch settlers, but I have been unable to get any information from them.

The Reformed Church has a congregation in this region, at Bethel near Leota. Founded in 1891 by the Classis of Iowa, it at first had only 13 members. Its church structure, which cost $ 1,500, towards which the Christian Endeavor Society contributed $ 800, was ready for occupancy in the fall of 1892. Several futile attempts were made to secure a pastor until Dominie Hendrik J. Pietenpol arrived in July 1895. As there was no parsonage, the dominie and his wife lived with one of the farmers until December 23 of that year, when they moved into the present commodious parsonage built at an expense of $ 1,500. Today the stables of the congregation provide room for 26 teams, but this is not enough in view of the growing church. In all, 50 families now belong to this church, 62 members being in full communion.

For several years all these settlers worshiped together; but in February 1895 came a split. The Christian Reformed Church was formed, and henceforth there were two rival congregations. The Christian Reformed group numbers about a dozen families, hold their services in schoolhouse, and have no pastor as yet.

If good soil, favorable climate, excellent markets, and religious facilities possess any advantages, this colony promises to become a growing Dutch settlement. The newcomers usually are poor and for the most part come from Sioux County, Iowa. But they are likely to prosper, and advanced education may even attract them, for there are high schools in the neighboring villages, and at Orange City there is the Western Classical Academy. The Lord God has manifold blessings for all who come to Leota and vicinity.

IV. Pine County. Most recent of Dutch settlements in Minnesota are Friesland and Groningen, two communities about five miles apart situated in the middle of Pine County, 80 miles from St Paul and 70 from Duluth. These places may be regarded as one settlement which owes its inception to the desire of Mr. Theodore T. Koch, General Land Agent for the St Paul and Duluth Railroad Company, to attract settlers for the lands owned by the railroad. From February 1 to September 1, 1895, he sold about 25,000 acres to Hollanders at from $ 3 to $ 6 per acre; they at once began to take possession.

The soil of this burned-over pine country is a mixture of gray, yellow, and brown clay with some black soil in the lower parts. Although not quite so rich as the lands occupied by Hollanders in other parts of

Minnesota, the proverbial economy and industry of the Dutch colonist will convert these acres into good farming lands. The soil is excellent for grass, clover, potatoes, fruit, vegetables, beets, and for all kinds of fodder for hogs, cattle, and horses.

Because of the cheapness of this land, abundance of timber, and the liberal terms on which it was sold, the Hollanders came in such numbers that in 1897 there were as many as 75 families of them and in addition 50 unmarried men. Among the first arrivals were Martin Eikman from West Duluth; G. Zwakman and Jan Kooistra from Minneapolis; K. Fyema from Dresbach, Minnesota; G. Hanenburg from La Crescent, Minnesota; and J. Smit, from Harrison, South Dakota. Others came from Iowa, Michigan, Wisconsin, the Dakotas, Illinois, New Jersey, Nebraska, and Indiana.

Friesland and Groningen each have elementary schools; those who desire advanced education can go to the high schools in Sandstone or Hinckley, each of which is about five miles distant. Mr. Koch at his own expense built a church for the free use of the settlers. These have formed two congregations; a Christian Reformed Church, organized in April 1896; and a Reformed Church organized on October 21, of the same year. Each congregation has a membership of 30 families or more.

Besides the advantages already mentioned, this region has many lakes, rivers, and creeks. It offers peculiar opportunities for poor people as well as for those who possess some money. There still are avaiblable 150,000 acres to Hollanders at the most advantageous terms. The future of this colony seems secure and promises, with God's blessing, to become a prosperous Holland settlement.

Chapter XXVI

BEGINNINGS OF DUTCH SETTLEMENT
IN SIOUX COUNTY, IOWA

83. A. J. BETTEN'S HISTORY OF SIOUX COUNTY

[Betten established himself in Orange City in 1871 and took an active part in the development of the new community. This account tracing some of the history of the Dutch settlement until 1897 was taken from *De Volksvriend*, September 19, 1895.]

Een Correspondent schreef mij eens: „In den herfst van het jaar 1856 verkeerde ik in uwe county. Destijds was het land nog een gedeelte van Woodbury County. Het eerste werk aldaar werd verricht door mijn persoon, Mr. Mills, en een gebochelden viervoeter. Wij deden er niets dan gras maaien en hooisteken. Wij hebben er nooit over beslist, wie van ons drieën de grootste ezel was."

Volgens statistieke opgaven waren er in het jaar 1860 in Sioux County tien inwoners, namelijk negen manspersonen en eene vrouw. In het jaar 1865 was het getal vermeerderd tot twintig en in 1869 telde de bevolking ruim honderd zielen. Uit de geschiedenis van die eerste jaren is ons weinig bekend; alleen dat de z.g. administratie, niet weinige schuld-brieven uitgaf, die de later inkomende bevolking mocht betalen.

Maar ge verlangt een en andere mededeeling uit de geschiedenis der pioneers in de eerste jaren van de kolonisatie alhier. In een beknopt artikel kan aan dit onderwerp geen volledig recht gedaan worden. Mijns bedunkens ware die taak beter toevertrouwd geweest aan een van de eerste baanbrekers die met de moeder van de Kolonie (Mrs. Vennema) van het begin aan mede getuige is geweest van al hetgeen den home-steaders hier is wedervaren. Men moet ook voor den aandacht houden, dat het hier in die eerste jaren wel eens duchtig kon stormen; zoodat uit de oude doos, gedurende die sneeuw-blizzards, wel een en ander, dat thans wetenswaardig zou geacht worden, zal zijn te loor geraakt.

Schrijver dezes vestigde zich hier in het jaar 1871. Er waren toen in deze kolonie alreeds 70 à 80 huisgezinnen woonachtig. Menigeen dezer woonde in een vrij goed planken huis. De anderen in een zoden hut, of een z.g. dugout. Een klein gedeelte des lands was al ontgonnen. Men had reeds een weinig koren en aardappelen verbouwd.

In 1870 had Tjeerd Heemstra, ten gerieve van de pioneers, een klein-handel begonnen. In October werd hij verkozen als lid van de county board of supervisors. Den ın Januari 1871, werd hij door die Board tot voorzitter verkozen.

In Augustus 1870 was een der eerste pioneers voor wien het eerste planken huis hier gebouwd werd, Jelle Pelmulder, reeds aangesteld tot griffier van de rechtbank. Dit ambt bleef hij, bij volksverkiezing, bekleeden tot 1887. Hij was in deze kolonie ook de eerste schoolmeester. Van den ın December 1870 tot den ın Maart 1871 was hij in het schoolhuis op sectie 10, Townstreep 95, Range 44, de onderwijzer der jeugd.

In 1870 waren er drie overledenen te betreuren. De eerste was een bejaarde vrouw, de weduwe Rijsdam. Op de homestead der familie werd haar een rustplaats gegeven.

In het huisgezin van Chris Nieuwendorp was er, het eerst, blijdschap over een nieuwen werelburger. Het was een jongsken; men noemde zijn naam Hendrik.

De eerste bijeenkomst tot openbare godsdienstoefening werd gehouden ten huize van Sipma, section 14, Townstreep 95, range 44.

De plaats waar Orange City zou verrijzen was door een landmeter van Sioux City uitgelegd.

In het jaar 1870 was aldaar een woonhuis en een schoollokaal gebouwd. De bevolking bestond in een drietal, namelijk een timmerman (A. J. Lenderink) met vrouw en zoon. Laatstgenoemde is thans onze county auditeur.

De eerste winter was, uitgezonderd de laatste week in December, niet streng koud geweest.

De eerste kolonisten hebben, bij onze komst alhier, reeds meer dan een jaar van zorgvolle ondervinding doorleefd.

Naar het ons voorkomt, zijn eenige der nederzetters niet onbemiddeld. Doch bij menigeen schijnt de rijkdom hoofdzakelijk te bestaan in den weelderigen bodem, en het kapitaal, in de hoop op een goeden oogst.

Henry Hospers, de leider en voorname raadsman in zake de kolonizatie, woont nog te Pella. Hij zond in het voorjaar van 1871 herwaarts een aannemer D. Gleysteen (thans een welgezeten burger van Alton) en laat aan de noordzijde van het stadsplein een winkelgebouw oprichten. Toen het gebouw bijna gereed was, werd het op zekeren Zondag door een geweldig gedreven stormwind van de fondamentstenen geworpen. Het werd door den bouwmeester weer op de plaats gesteld en daarna spoedig voltooid.

Op dienzelfden Zondag is ten zuiden van de stad op de homestead van Rijsdam een stal en een span ossen verbrand.

Binnen korten tijd was in het opgerichte gebouw een winkel affaire in vollen gang. De eerste lading goederen, die ontvangen werd, bestond voornamelijk in eetwaren: grutte, gerst, rijst, erwten, meel, visch, koffie, suiker, stroop, enz. De zaakgelastigde, die waarschijnlijk niet over een te groot kapitaal had te beschikken, of wellicht niet volkomen op de hoogte van zaken was, om te weten, wat er in zulk een nieuwe nederzetting wordt vereischt, gaf geen krediet. Boter en eieren werden in ruil genomen voor goederen. Overigens was er bij velen nog geen ruilmiddel te over.

De eigenaar van de affaire komt kort na dat de winkel begonnen is van Pella om zich hier permament te vestigen. Toen hij de eerste maal den winkel binnen kwam zei een tot schrijver dezes: „Daar heb je den vader van de Kolonie, nu zal het wel goed gaan." Het duurde ook niet lang of hij vond er een nieuw ruilmiddel op uit. Aan papier en inkt had hij geen gebrek. Hij vulde de leemte aan, door van tijd tot tijd z.g. store orders in circulatie te brengen, die in Orange City even gangbaar waren als eenig ander soort „fractional currency". De vader van de Kolonie neemt voor deze orders meesttijds zijn betaling in het doen scheuren van prairieland. Voorts moet hij het maar zien te „fiksen" hoe aan zijn geld te komen.

De nederzetting breidt zich uit. De bevolking blijft gestadig aan vermeerderen.

In Orange City worden gedurende den zomer 'n achttal huizen gebouwd. De plaats is in korten tijd voorzien van een hotel, een smidse, schoenmaker, en barbier. Wil men van slager of banketbakker gediend worden, men begeve zich dan slechts even buiten de stadsgrenzen. Ieder landbouwer voorziet zijn plantsoen met van een tot vijf akkers boomen. Dit dient mettertijd als beschutting tegen den barren noordwestewind en vrijwaart van de betaling van een deel der belasting. Op de homesteads beginnen meer gebouwen te verrijzen. Het reeds te voren ontgonnen land blijkt vruchtbaar te zijn.

In de Junimaand, op zekeren Zondag, predikt Ds. Egbert Winter van Pella hier in het schoolhuis. Gedurende den middaggodsdienst breekt een hevige storm los. Het land wordt verrijkt met een milden regen.

Den 12den Juli 1871 wordt de Eerste Gereformeerde gemeente van Orange City georganizeerd.

In dit jaar werd ook de Hollandsche Christelijke Gereformeerde gemeente georganizeerd, met een dertiental huisgezinnen.

Den 13den Juli 1871 verschijnt te Calliope (de hoofdstad der county) het eerste nommer van de *Sioux County Herald*.

De najaarsverkiezing is op handen. De kolonisten zijn in goede verstandhouding met de pioneers van de naburige nederzettingen der county. De 29n September wordt er conventie gehouden. De candidaten worden benoemd. Den tweeden Dinsdag in October is het stemdag. Den 16n dezer maand houdt de Board of Supervisors zitting en verklaart de volgende personen als tot de respectieve ambten verkozen:

Henry Hospers, lid v. d. board of supervisors,

A. J. Betten Jr., auditor,

J. W. Greattrax, treasurer,

T. J. Dunham, sheriff,

H. Jones, surveyor,

John Newell, superintendent of schools,

J. O. Beals, coroner.

Een strenge winter valt in. De homesteaders, die van nu af in den winter verre reizen moeten maken om brandstof, zijn dikwerf in de zoo verblindende sneeuw-blizzards en strenge koude niet buiten gevaar.

In December gaan de griffier van de rechtbank en de nieuwgekozen auditor te voet naar de hoofdstad. Het is een meerendeels onbegane weg met een diepe sneeuwlaag bedekt. 't Is slechts vijfentwintig mijl. Ze tuimelen wel eens tot onder de armen in het donzig sneeuwbed, doch dan is er meteen gelegenheid om uit te rusten en daar liggende rookt de griffier flink uit zijn groote Hollandsche pijp. Bij sterrelicht komen ze ter bestemder plaats aan. Na kort verblijf keeren ze huiswaarts.

Den eersten Januari 1872 gaan al de nieuwgekozen beambten met nog eenige vrienden weer naar de hoofdstad. Het is weer niet weinig koud. De board houdt zitting. Hospers wordt, na afgelegden ambtseed, zitting verleend als een lid van de board. (Hij bleef dit ambt bekleeden tot den 16den November 1887. Toen legde hij die betrekking neer, omreden hij verkozen was tot voksvertegenwoordiger). De andere verkozen beambten genoten niet het voorrecht hun ambt te aanvaarden. Twee leden der board weigerden hun goedkeuring te geven aan den aangeboden borgstelling. Den 9den Januari was er weer zitting der board, met hetzelfde resultaat. De nieuwe countyvader mocht al met vaderlijke ernst tegen deze handelwijze protest indienen, doch hij had slechts eene stem en de tegenpartij twee. Den 10n ging Klaas Jongewaard met een der prospectieve beambten per slede op weg naar Orange City. Ze geraakten spoedig zonder spoor en dwaalden tot middernacht rond. Mettertijd komen ze op 't veld bij een hooimijt; ze schuilen daar en rusten een weinig. Na nog geruimen tijd onderzoek in die omgeving wordt de reis voortgezet en ze arriveeren nog onbevroren bij het huis van den voerman. De board was verdaagd tot den 21n der maand. Men ging om de zitting bij te wonen. Een rechtsgeleerde was medegegaan om de zaak te bepleiten. Den 22n kwam een groot getal der kolonisten om bij de meeting tegenwoordig te zijn. Toen men tot geen resultaat kon komen ging Mr. Hospers huiswaarts. Het volk beschouwde dat de afkeuring der bonds gezocht was, en geschiedde omreden er iets ten ongunste was met de in functie zijnde beambten. Later is het gebleken, dat die beschouwing niet ongegrond was. Er werd nog eens tezamen geraadpleegd. Na eenparig besluit werden alle boeken en toebehooren der county genomen, opgeladen en per slede naar Orange City gebracht. Het was laat eer men vertrok. Het was buitengewoon streng koud en menigeen had bij aankomst hier wel wat vreemd gevoel in den neus of stijve ooren. Sommigen waren zoo verkleumd dat ze bij het wat ruim warme vuur bedwelmden. Doch door koffie en lunch kwamen dezulken weer spoedig in normalen toestand. Na eenigen tijd kwam de zaak in rechten. Er ontstond ook nieuwe wetgeving, waardoor men zich op hooger recht kon beroepen. Er werd appèl genomen. Mettertijd werden de nieuwgekozen beambten in hun ambt geïnstalleerd.

Den 13den Januari zal wel bij velen in 't geheugen zijn, als de dag waar- op een hevige sneeuwstorm over ons losbrak en tot aan den derden dag voortwoedde. Gedurende deze blizzard werd in de nederige hut van den stadssmid een zoon geboren, die deze en de latere stormen tot heden toe heeft doorleefd.

In een dergelijken sneeuwstorm in dezen winter geraakte de griffier van de rechtbank, op weg naar huis, bijna van koers. Hij keerde terug en kwam met een ijs- en sneeuwbedekt gezicht nog intijds in de stad terecht. In dien storm ging een weduwe in de stad buitenshuis en verdwaalde. Na een angstig zoeken werd ze nog intijds bij de toen in aanbouw zijnde pastorie gevonden en gered. Meer dergelijke gevallen konden medegedeeld worden, doch ze zijn van gelijken aard. Niettegenstaande deze gevaren zijn de kolonisten, door al die gevreesde en zoo gevaarlijke stormen heen, merkelijk bewaard gebleven. In die eerste jaren is niet een hunner er door omgekomen.

In het voorjaar vestigt zich hier weer een vrij groot aantal huisgezinnen.

In dit jaar werd de Sioux City en St. Paul spoorweg gebouwd. Dat spaart menige verre reis, en de gelegenheid tot vervoer van graan en bouwmateriaal, brandstof, enz., wordt daardoor niet weinig verbeterd.

Nummer 53, jaargang 1, van de *Sioux County Herald* wordt te Orange City uitgegeven en begint wat Hollandsch te praten.

De akker van den landman blijkt vruchtbaar te zijn. Zijn werk wordt dit jaar met een goeden oogst beloond.

De uitslag der verkiezing is weer naar wensch der kolonisten.

Den 16n October wordt voor de eerste maal de zitting van het circuit court gehouden in Orange City, met Hon. Addison Oliver als rechter.

Den 11n November vergadert de Board of Supervisors en verklaart bij resolutie, volgens uitslag der verkiezing, Orange City als hoofdstad van Sioux County. Na eenige dagen worden de boeken en toebehooren der county naar Orange City overgeplaatst.

Tot nu toe is er gestadige vooruitgang. De pioneer heeft wel nog zeer beperkte middelen, maar met zuinigheid en vlijt blijkt hier een goed vooruitzicht te zijn. Er zijn nog veel ontberingen die men zich moet getroosten, doch, in het algemeen gesproken, heeft men nog een bijzonder voorrecht, namelijk: den vrede dien men geniet. Zooals van het begin af aan is er nog het gemeenzame verkeer, de band der eenheid en het waken voor elkanders belangen. Tot in de nederigste hut is gulhartigheid en gast-vrijheid bijna altijd aan de orde. Geschillen van ernstigen aard komen nog zelden voor, en waar ze ontstaan worden ze in de meeste gevallen in der minne geschikt. De een staat den ander bij met raad en daad. Rechtspleidooien vallen zelden voor.

Van het begin af was bij het meerendeel des volks de godsdienst in eer. Het Boek der Boeken werd geacht als de onmisbare levensgids. Opvoe-ding en godsdienst hadden eene plaats in huis en hart. Wie zal deze voor-rechten niet waardeeren?

De godsdienstoefeningen werden eerst gehouden in private woningen; ze werden geleid door den een of anderen broeder, tenzij een leeraar van elders tegenwoordig was. Later kwam men bijeen in het stads schoolhuis.

Den 12n Juli 1871 werd de eerste Gereformeerde gemeente georgani-zeerd. Mettertijd werd door deze een leeraar beroepen, namelijk Ds. Seine Bolks, die de roeping aannam en zich hier in het jaar 1872 vestigde. Hij bediende de gemeente tot Juli 1878.

In het jaar 1872 ontstond er eene bijzondere godsdienstige opwekking die een geruimen tijd voortduurde. Door velen werd het goede deel gekozen en niet weinigen werden tot de gemeente toegedaan. De ge-meente was met een veertig tal leden gesticht en bij het einde van het jaar 1872 was het ledental vermeerderd tot ruim driehonderd. Alzoo werd een duurzaam goed ontvangen en genoten. Veler harten werden gesterkt door genade, alvorens de tijd van druk en meerdere beproeving aanbrak.

Bij het einde van dit jaar telt de bevolking dezer kolonie ruim vijftien honderd zielen.

Den 6n Januari 1873 vergadert de Board of Supervisors voor de eerste maal te Orange City. Henry Hospers wordt verkozen tot voorzitter van de board.

Den 13n Januari wordt voor de eerste maal de zitting van het district court gehouden te Orange City. De county wordt bedreigd met een vonnis van $ 10,000 voor frauduleuze schuldbrieven. Het wordt bestreden en afgeweerd.

In den voorzomer schijnt het vooruitzicht van den landman weer gunstig te zijn. Tot aan Juni groeien de vruchten welig. Doch in deze maand daalt er een gevleugeld leger opeters op den akker neder. Het zijn sprinkhanen. Deze schijnen in hun vraatzucht al het graan te zullen verderven. De mensch vermag niets tegen dit heir. Het waren toen dagen van bedruktheid en weemoed des harten. Doch het waren ook dagen des gebeds. Niet lang daarna werd de plaag opgeheven. Er was vrij wat vernield. Maar er bleef nog veel over om den Gever alles goeds voor te danken.

Den 19n Mei 1874 wordt er gestemd over de vraag of er jaarlijks al of niet tien mill belasting zal geheven worden totdat de county schulden zullen betaald zijn. Het wordt afgestemd met 194 tegen 117.

De eerste Gereformeerde gemeente wordt een som gelds toegezegd, genoegzaam om een kerkgebouw op te richten. Tot den bouw werd besloten. Otto Rouwenhorst aannemer. De materialen worden door het volk, zonder betaling voor 't vervoer van East Orange, te Orange City op het bouwterrein gebracht.

Den 2n Juni 1874 wordt er een nieuw county court-huis aanbesteed. Het wordt op het stadsplein gebouwd. Gerrit Dorsman is de aannemer.

De sprinkhanen trekken in tallooze menigte over ons heen. Nu en dan dalen ze in hoopen neer en doen hier en daar min of meer schade.

Den 20n Juni verschijnt het eerste nommer van *De Volksvriend*.

Den derden Zondag in de Julimaand dalen de sprinkhanen in massa neder en bedekken het gezicht des lands. Donderdag daaraanvolgende gaan ze met een groot gedruisch omhoog en verdwijnen nog veel haastiger dan ze gekomen zijn. Er is niet weinig vernield. Er blijft evenwel weer veel over. Voor menigeen is door deze ramp een drukkende tij daangebroken. De schade is zeer ongelijk. Bij dezen veel, bij genen minder.

Den 25n September valt er in de West Branch buurt een andere treurmare voor. Twee der kolonisten (Kleuvers en Wesselink) waren om brandhout uitgegaan. Ze gaan over de Rock River op een gevaarlijke plaats en verdrinken.

In Februari 1875 werd er hier aangevraagde hulp verleend aan noodlijdenden, woonachtig in een naburigen staat.

Er is sprake om een sectie land te koopen; het te laten bewerken, en de opbrengst er van mettertijd te besteden voor onderwijs aan een op te richten Academie. Sommigen meenen dat men het maar eens moet afzien of er nog weer van die gevleugelde opeters komen.

Er wordt van tijd tot tijd gesproken over het bouwen van een wind-molen. In Maart 1875 wordt dienaangaande vergadering gehouden in het court-huis. Er werd acht honderd dollars tot dat doel ingeschreven. De korenmolen werd gebouwd ten zuidoosten van de stad.

De akker des landmans draagt rijke vrucht. Door overvloed van regen en stormachtig weder wordt er veel graan benadeeld. In het najaar is door regens veel schade toegebracht aan de graanstekken. Sommigen meenen dat het muizengeslacht op het land ruim talrijk wordt.

In het begin van October wordt de eerste Sioux County tentoon-stelling gehouden.

In het laatst dezer maand heeft het eerste examen plaats aan de genees-kundige school. Er geschiedt dit najaar veel schade door prairie-branden.

6 Januari 1876 wordt door de Board van Supervisors $ 2,000 premie uitgeloofd voor ontdekking van steenkool in deze county. Later werd drie duizend uitgeloofd. De premie is nog door niemand opgeëischt.

In deze maand wordt een landbouwersvereeniging georganizeerd. Ze vergaderen Zaterdagsmiddags en debatteeren over onderscheiden onder-werpen: b.v., „De elevator een vloek voor den landbouwer"; „De tarwebouw het grootste voordeel voor den landbouwer"; „De predik-stoel oefent meer invloed uit dan de drukpers". Gedurende de winter-maanden vermaken vele jongelieden zich op de country spelling school. Er wordt een jongelingsvereeniging opgericht met bejaarde mannen aan 't hoofd. In de Meimaand wordt er een vrije christelijke gemeente georganizeerd.

De veldgewassen staan goed. Den 13n Juni is er gerucht in omloop dat er eenige honderde roodhuiden in aantocht zijn. Dit baart onrust. Ze verschijnen niet. De wapenen worden weggeborgen.

Twee weken later verschijnen er sprinkhanen in menigte en blijven omstreeks tien dagen. De schade is zeer ongelijk, op sommige plaatsen is er veel vernield, in andere buurten minder. Er blijft veel graan over. Doch vooral voor dengene dien het telkens treft, is het een oorzaak van druk en niet weinig ontmoedigend.

Uit het noorden van de county verhuist een deel des volks naar elders. Onder onze nederzetters zijn er ook eenigen die weg willen; doch al het mogelijke wordt gedaan om elkanders moed in te spreken. Slechts enkelen gaan weg.

Jan Krediet, die intusschen eene vrij groote rol speelde, wordt ook lastig.

De board of supervisors heeft besloten een gevangenhuis te bouwen. Den 6n September 1876 werd het uitbesteed aan John Sembke.

Het bouwen van een armenhuis wordt uitbesteed aan W. S. Okey. De schuur op de poorfarm wordt uitbesteed aan A. J. Lenderink. F. E. Hewitt is de eerste armen vader. Uit deze Kolonie werd slechts een arme verpleegd.

De county wordt bedreigd met een rechtspleidooi over circa $ 37,000 frauduleuze schuldbrieven. Op last van de board gaat H. Hospers naar Dubuque, Iowa, en slaagt om de geheele som voor ruim $ 700 te vereffenen. Deze zaak was al meermalen in rechten geweest en had de county reeds veel geld en moeite gekost.

In Mei 1877 worden er twee gereformeerde gemeenten gesticht; een te Alton en een te Sioux Center.

De sprinkhanen van het vorige jaar lieten eieren na, vooral in de zoden van het nieuw gescheurde land. In de Juni maand komen de jonge sprinkhanen te voorschijn en doen veel schade. Allerlei middelen worden aangewend om ze te vernielen of te verdrijven. Er is echter meer raad dan baat. In de volgende maand trekken de sprinkhanen uit het noorden voorbij en nemen hun gezelschap van hier mede. Niettegenstaande den opeter is er nog veel te oogsten.

Den 15 November 1877 werd men te dezer stede omstreeks half twaalf des voormiddags aardschokken gewaar.

In het jaar 1878 heeft de landman een zwaar gewas. Er geschiedt zeer veel schade door overvloed van regen. Menigeen is genoodzaakt zijn graan met de grass mower te maaien, het bij elkaar te harken om als hooi te stekken. Door buitengewone hitte en zware regenstormen was een gedeelte van het graan tegen den grond geraakt en kon het niet gebonden worden. In de September maand komen er sprinkhanen. Deze doen niet veel schade. Zij laten niet weinig eieren na.

In de October maand, schade door prairiebrand.

Er is sterfte onder het vee. Oorzaak is, naar men meent, smut in het koren.

De brass band, die hier is georganiseerd, ontvangt nieuwe instrumenten.

In het voorjaar van 1879 is er klacht over droogte.

In de Meimaand wordt het Sioux County Bijbelgenootschap georganizeerd.

De jonge sprinkhanen komen te voorschijn en doen veel schade. Allerlei middel wordt aangewend ze te vernielen. Het is een verdrietig en moeitevol werk, waarin men maar ten deele kan slagen.

Op den laatsten Zondag in Juni wordt Ds. Ale Buursma beroepen leeraar bij de 1e Gereformeerde gemeente, door Ds. Johannes Willem Warnshuis bevestigd. Er was een talrijke schare tegenwoordig.

In het laatst van Juni en ook in de Juli maand zware stormen en on-weersbuien, waardoor veel schade en onheil wordt teweeggebracht. Het kleine graan wordt nog voortdurend door den vernielenden opeter geteisterd. Van tarwe en haver blijft niet veel over. In het laatst van Juli trekken de sprinkhanen weg.

De farmers houden vergadering met doel om middelen te beramen tegen het verspreiden van de kwade droes onder de paarden.

In Augustus een storm die als een orkaan woedt. Door wind en hagel geschiedt er schade over de West Branch en aan de Rock rivier. Bij het dorschen valt het graan en vlas zeer tegen. Het koren is bij velen een goed gewas.

Gedurende dit laatste jaar dat de plaag dit oord bezocht, is er veel over de sprinkhanen geschreven. De beschouwingen daarover liepen nogal uiteen. De een had het naar het oordeel van sommigen te licht, de ander te donker geschilderd. Dat zij zoo. Temidden der tegenheden en moeite-volle jaren, is nog de hand des vlijtigen gezegend geweest. De band der eenheid, de hulpvaardigheid om elkanders lasten te dragen is een groote zegen geweest. Wij spreken in den algemeenen zin, niet alsof er geen uitzondering ware.

Wij roemen ook niet in menschen. Want wat heeft de mensch dat hij niet uit Hooger hand heeft ontvangen. Laat ons den Heere loven voor Zijne goedertierenheden. De uitbreiding van deze nederzetting is, niet-tegenstaande den tegenspoed, langzaam doch gestadig voortgegaan, zoodat de bevolking van deze Kolonie bij het einde van het jaar 1879 omstreeks drie duizend zielen telt.

84. HENRY HOSPERS' MIGRATION TO SIOUX COUNTY

[Following is an account written by Henry Hospers of the initial steps toward founding the Dutch settlement of Sioux County. From the moment of its inception, Hospers until his death in 1902 was intimately associated with the history of Sioux County. This account is taken from the Twenty-fifth Anniversary number of *De Volksvriend*, September 19, 1895.]

Plannen tot verhuizing werden gemaakt ten gevolge van de sterk toenemende bevolking en den steeds stijgende prijs van landerijen in de Hollandsche Kolonie Pella, zoodat mingegoeden bezwaarlijk een eigen stuk land konden bekomen. Zij, die in 1847 met een huisgezin van kleine kinderen zich in Pella vestigden, zagen deze opgroeien en sommigen tot huwbare jaren komen. Steeds meer en meer werd de behoefte gevoeld en de begeerte ernstiger om elders in het Westen eene geschikte plaats voor eene Hollandsche nederzetting te vinden.

In 1860 moest schrijver dezes eenige weken in St. Joseph, Missouri, doorbrengen. Hij zag daar hoe dagelijks groote getallen wagens met huisgezinnen, vee en landbouwersgereedschappen de Missouri rivier overtogen om in oostelijk Nebraska homes te zoeken; hij vernam hoe allen, die den moed hadden, om zich op de prairien te vestigen, vonden wat zij zoo zeer begeerden.

In Pella teruggekomen zijnde sprak hij met enkelen over de indrukken, die hij omtrent landverhuizing naar het westen ontvangen had. Met de heeren A. C. Kuyper, destijds ouderling bij de 1e Gereformeerde gemeente te Pella, W. van Asch, W. Sleyster, en G. P. H. Zahn, allen nu overleden, werd menige conferentie gehouden over de mogelijkheid om met eenige Hollandsche huisgezinnen naar die streken te emigreeren. Zelfs werden plannen beraamd om, voor het doel om landerijen te koopen, fondsen te verkrijgen, doch deze pogingen werden met teleurstelling bekroond, en de losweg gemaakte plannen vielen in duigen.

Niettemin werd de behoefte naar emigratie dringender gevoeld en de begeerte naar verhuizing sterker. Vooral in 1867 en 1868 was het de heer Jelle Pelmulder, die het kolonisatieplan met ijver en ernst onderhanden nam, de aandacht op westelijk of noordwestelijk Iowa vestigde, correspondentie met landkantoren aanknoopte, vele informatiën inwon, en met Friesche doortastendheid de emigratiebal een frisschen stoot gaf, en, inderdaad genoemd mag worden de eerste ontwerper van het plan om in noordwestelijk Iowa eene Hollandsche Kolonie te vestigen.

Van tijd tot tijd werden in 1868 in Pella vergaderingen gehouden om de kolonisatieplannen te bespreken. Deze vergaderingen werden druk bezocht, en het bleek, dat er algemeene belangstelling in de zaak aan den dag werd gelegd. Er werd eene geregelde organizatie daargesteld, en eene commissie benoemd, bestaande uit vier vertrouwde en praktikale farmers, t.w. Jelle Pelmulder, Huibert Muilenberg, Sjoerd A. Sipma, Hendrik J. van der Waa, om het noordwestelijk gedeelte van Iowa te gaan bezien, en te onderzoeken of aldaar eene geschikte plaats voor eene Hollandsche Kolonie gevonden kon worden.

Deze commissie vertrok in een huifwagen met twee muilezels bespannen, en richtte haar schreden naar het toen nog onbekende noordwesten. Na drie of vier weken keerden zij terug. Onmiddellijk werd eene vergadering zamen geroepen, waarop met gespannen aandacht en groote belangstelling het rapport dier commissie werd aangehoord. De commissie rapporteerde rijke en zeer geschikte landerijen gevonden te hebben, en was zeer ingenomen, voornamelijk met eene streek nabij Cherokee in Iowa.

Op deze vergadering werden meer beslissende stappen genomen; eene lijst werd gemaakt van personen, die wenschten te verhuizen en land te nemen, en het bleek, dat de begeerte om eene nieuwe kolonie te vestigen werkelijk aanwezig en het getal deelnemers grooter was, dan men verwacht had. Als ik mij wel herinner namen een zestigtal hoofden van huisgezinnen deel. Nu werd besloten om eene tweede commissie uit te zenden, gemachtigd om eene bepaalde keuze te doen, en landerijen onder de bestaande preëmptie- en homestead-wetten in beslag te nemen. Deze commissie bestond uit de heeren Leendert van der Meer, Dirk van den Bosch, Hendrik J. van der Waa en Henry Hospers. De laatstgenoemde zou per spoor naar het landkantoor te Sioux City gaan, om aldaar kaarten te nemen en verder de noodige informatiën in te winnen, terwijl de drie eerstgenoemden, met dezelfde trouwe muilezel-team over land naar Sioux City zouden reizen, om aldaar Henry Hospers te ontmoeten, en dan gezamenlijk met eenen landmeter het noordwesten van Iowa te exploreeren.

Toen de vier personen te Sioux City bij elkander kwamen, had men bevonden, dat in de streek rondom Cherokee reeds veel land was opgenomen geworden; en daar men wenschte eene plaats in te nemen voor Hollanders alleen, en die gelegenheid genoeg bevatte om eene groote Hollandsche Kolonie te vestigen, besloot men niet naar Cherokee te gaan, maar liever Sioux of Lyon counties alwaar nog overvloed van gouvernements- en spoorweglanden te verkrijgen waren, in oogenschouw te nemen.

In Sioux City werd provisie ingeslagen voor een verblijf van waarschijnlijk drie weken op de prairiën, en vertrok de commissie naar Junction City, nu Le Mars, en verder noordwaarts langs de kabbelende Floyd rivier tot aan de zuidelijke lijn van Sioux County. Wegen, woningen of boomen werden niet aangetroffen; het was niets dan zachtgolvende, prachtige, rijke vette prairiegronden. Zonder eenige twijfel was het de eenstemmige keuze der commissie; HIER IS DE PLAATS!

Met de kaart in de hand, en het landmeterskompas tot gids, werden een paar townships doorkruist, de gouvernements sectiehoeken gezocht en gevonden, en een dertigtal sectiën in beslag genomen, voor diegenen onzer landgenooten, welke zich als kolonisten hadden aangegeven.

Zelfs werd de plaats voor de uit te leggen stad gekozen. De commissie keerde na een aangename doch vermoeiende werkzaamheid per as naar Pella terug, terwijl Henry Hospers op het landkantoor vertoefde om de naar de wet vereischte papieren en beëedigde verklaringen te deponeeren en de landerijen in naam der verschillende homesteaders te verzekeren.

Van de keuze dezer nieuwe Kolonie werd door middel der Hollandsche nieuwsbladen publicitiet gegeven, en weldra namen Hollanders, uit Wisconsin vooral, en uit andere Staten dezer Unie deel.

In het najaar van 1869 vertrokken een 60-tal mannen naar de nieuwe nog onbewoonde kolonie, om van hun 160 akkers bezit te nemen, en zulke werkzaamheden daar op te verrichten om aan de vereischten van de wet te voldoen.

Door de wetgevende vergadering van Iowa daartoe aangesteld bezocht Henry Hospers, in den winter van 1869-70, Nederland, om als Commissioner of Emigration den staat Iowa en voral de nieuwe Kolonie voor te stellen, hetwelk met goed succes bekroond werd.

In 1870 arriveerden de volgende huisgezinnen in de nieuwe kolonie: Jelle Pelmulder, Hendrik J. van der Waa, Leendert van der Meer, Dirk van den Bosch, W. de Haan, Dirk van der Meer, Arie Noteboom, C. Nieuwendorp, L. van Pelt, D. van Pelt, D. van Zanten, W. van der Zalm, G. de Zeeuw, C. Lakeman, Joh. Klein, A. van Marel, Arie van der Meide, Wed. Beukelman, H. Luymers, M. Verheul, B. van Zijl, W. van Rooijen, I. van Iperen, J. Windhorst, A. Schippers, A. Jansma, J. Muilenburg, P. de Jong, Cornelis Jongewaard, H. Boersma, L. Boersma, K. Wierenga, J. Sipma, J. Logterman, J. Groen, A. Lenderink, Hymen den Hartog, J. Sinnema, S. Pool, Ulbe Wynia, J. van Wijk, P. Dieleman, J. Brinks, Arie de Raad, T. Heemstra, J. Fennema, D. de Ruysch, Adr. van den Berge, J. van der Meer, W. Rijsdam, G. Rijsdam, A. Werkhoven, O. de Jong, G. van der Steeg, H. Pas, T. Brouwer, Rijn Talsma, G. Beijer, J. Gorter, K. de Jong, Iepe van der Ploeg, P. van Horsen en A. Versteeg. Heb ik per abuis iemens naam vergeten, dan vraag ik verschooning.

Het land werd gebroken, eenvoudige woningen, meest hutten van zoden, gebouwd, een goed frame schoolhuis opgericht, en in het stedeke Orange City een winkel geopend. Het volk was blijde, dankbaar en tevreden.

85. HENDRIK JAN VAN DER WAA'S
BEGINNINGS OF THE COLONY

[Written by one of the leaders of the migration to Sioux County from Pella, the following by Hendrik Jan van der Waa presents a vivid account of the earliest beginnings of the settlement in the spring of 1870. This account was prepared by Van der Waa for the *Standard Historical Atlas of Sioux County Iowa* published at Chicago, 1908.]

After renting land for two years and giving a third of the crop for rent I made up my mind in that way I could not get a place of my own, for the land around Pella was high. My wife and I made up our minds to have a sale and move to Northwestern Iowa and take a homestead. I had written to Mr. Harlan, a land agent at Storm Lake, regarding homesteads there; his answer was, there were, and for all my friends. I then went to the printing office of Henry Hospers to have my sale bills printed. He asked me what I intended to do; I told him I intended to move to Storm Lake and take a homestead. He asked me if I knew if there was government land enough for a colony; I told him as far as I knew there was; he said he would write immediately to the agent, and he would receive a reply before my sale, and if he received a favorable answer we might call a meeting and try to organize a colony there. In about a week he received a favorable answer and called me to his office and read the letter to me. Then and there we decided to call a meeting to be held at his office in three weeks for the purpose of starting a colony. During the meantime we had ample time to talk about the subject which was well discussed. Hospers had the meeting well advertised and wrote about the necessity of seeking a place where we could go in a body. At the appointed time the people came from far and near; there was so much interest shown at the first meeting that the office was well filled, there being hardly standing room; the meeting was called to order and the object of the meeting stated. Hospers was chosen chairman; then the subject was thoroughly discussed and the necessity of a colony where parents with their children could spread out and get land for them. On motion it was decided to send a committee to Northwestern Iowa and look up a suitable place where we could get land in a body; and especially examine soil and subsoil. The committee chosen were Hendrik Muilenburg, Sjoerd A. Sipma, Jelle Pelmulder, and Hendrik J. van der Waa. Necessary funds were raised to bear the expense of the trip and the writer offered to take his team and wagon without charge. We went to work at once getting the necessary articles ready for the trip; the wagon had to be fixed; bow and cover put on; mess chest and tent were secured; the mess chest had to be well filled for we expected to be gone four weeks. The morning before starting I traded off my team of horses for a span of young mules; I thought they would be better although they had never had a harness on. For a time it seemed that we would not get them harnessed; they would kick the harness off as fast as we could put it on; this delayed us two hours before we had them hitched to the wagon, so when we got started we left Pella in quick time and kept it up for several miles. The harness was not taken off the mules until on our return trip, when they were well broken and gentle.

The spring was very wet; rivers and creeks were full to their banks and had to be forded, for most of them had no bridges or they were washed away by the high water. We drove out to Jelle Pelmulder's, eight miles north of Pella, and stayed there the first night. The next morning we started early for Newton, and from there we went to Fort Dodge where we stopped a day or two to look at the country; but it did not suit the committee. From there we went to Storm Lake; we had no roads or bridges all the way; we went by the compass and Railroad stakes; a river had to be forded with steep banks on either side, three of our party got out to shove the team in while I drove; when the mules came near the water they would stop and the men back of the wagon shoved them in, and then they jumped in the back end of the wagon; when the mules swam to the other side they could not pull the wagon up the steep bank; after getting the mules across, we hitched a chain to the tongue, dug trenches for the wheels and finally got the wagon out. We arrived in Storm Lake Saturday night and decided to stop there over Sunday. We stayed with a Methodist preacher who had been sent there to do missionary work among the early settlers; his home was a small sod house in the northwest part of the town. Monday morning we went on our journey, following the old government road from Storm Lake to Cherokee; there were no settlers living along the road; the bridge across the little Sioux River had been washed away by high water. There was some kind of a ferry and they took us across for $ 5; as we did not like to swim our team we paid the price and took the ferry. There were a few houses there and an old stockade and some barracks where soldiers had been stationed; we bought some provisions and went on. We passed through some fine country; here we stopped for one half day to examine the soil and subsoil and also the water and drainage of the land. The committee thought if we could get a township or two here in a body, it would be a suitable place to locate a colony. We were very careful in looking over the land between Fort Dodge and Storm Lake; so when we arrived at the land office in Sioux City and found what land was government land and in a body, we knew what we would choose from. It was Saturday evening when we came through Melbourne, a small settlement and a German church; we camped near the town on the Floyd River, and Sunday morning the minister's wife came to us, and seeing that we were going to rest on the Sabbath day, brought us some religious tracts, and invited us to attend the services and hear her husband preach, so we all went to church; he preached in the German language; we, being Hollanders, could not understand it at all, but enough to know that we had heard a good sermon.

Monday we arrived in Sioux City, just two weeks from the time we left Pella. The next morning we went to the land office. The doors were open at nine o'clock, but before that time there was such a mob in front of the door trying to get in as soon as the door opened; some of them after the same quarter section, and fights were frequent and races run to see who could get there first. At noon we got to speak to one of the land officers; we told him what our business was and made arrangements to meet him in the office after supper. He let us in at the back door and we got all the information we wanted and told him we would report favorably on the land from ten to fifteen miles west from Cherokee on both sides of the Railroad survey. In the land office we found that in Cherokee, Sioux, Lyon, and Obrien counties, that land could be got in a body for a large colony.

After a thorought investigation, we returned to Pella to report, arriving there just four weeks from the time we had started. A meeting was called at the office of Henry Hospers, and when the committee reported great interest was shown and the excitement was great. At that time government land could be bought for $ 2.50 per acre every alternate section, the other section belonging to the railroad company and could be bought when the company built their road. A motion was made and carried that all who were willing could go and homestead 80 acres, or preempt 160 acres. It was also then and there agreed to buy a half section for a town sight, and several men wanted to buy land for themselves, so a few thousand dollars was deposited for that purpose and 120 names were given for homesteads, who were willing to go; then a committee was appointed to buy a town site, and also buy land for those to purchase. The names of the committee chosen were Hospers, Van der Meer, Van den Bosch, and Van der Waa. It was decided that Hospers should go by rail, and the others by wagon, and the same mule team was taken on the second trip. It was also decided that the homesteads should be drawn by the committee, and the head of every family should have his relatives on the same adjoining section. After arriving at the land office in Sioux City, what a disappointment it was for us to find that the land for miles west of Cherokee had been taken by speculators, and they were there to sell to us at a great profit; we also found that the government had taken their land out of the market, so no land could be bought for those who wanted to buy, and the town site fell through. So the next thing to do was to take a surveyor with us, and go and look at land in Sioux County. When we came to where Le Mars now is we found one building in which Blodget and Flint had a store; from there to where Seney is now located along the

Floyd River there were a few settlers, the Reeves and Mr. Dayton. Soon after leaving Dayton's we struck Sioux County, and began the survey and throwing up high knolls so that we could find our way back; those knolls served us as land marks the next time, and also the next spring when we moved our families. After two days we got back to Sioux City, being satisfied that where Orange City, Sioux Center, and Alton now stand would be the place for the colony; most all the homesteads were taken in Holland and adjoining townships. The next day the committee secured the office room of Mr. L. Wynn [our surveyor] and proceeded to select the homesteads. The committee seated themselves around the table, the number of the section was put on a slip of paper and placed in a box, then the names of those who wanted a homestead were written on a separate slip and put in another box; one of the committee would draw the number of some section, and then a name would be drawn out of the other box, one would call off the number of the section while the other would read the name in this wise: section 30 was drawn and J. Smith's name was taken out, so Smith's homestead was in the northeast $\frac{1}{4}$ of section 30 and he was allowed to name his relatives or friends to take for themselves land in the same section, and sometimes the question is asked, how is it that you have taken homesteads and have your relatives around you? We also named the township Holland. Having done all we could at this time, we started for home. After arriving in Pella, we called a meeting and reported what had been done, so the Holland colony would be located in Sioux County, Holland Township, but today the settlement covers at least two thirds of Sioux County. The next meeting was called for the purpose of having our homesteads, or preemptions surveyed, and some breaking done in order to hold the same, and comply with the law; about eighteen or twenty teams went with from four to six men to each team and Mr. Wynn, our first surveyor. This time surveying and breaking took from one to two weeks.

Early in the spring of 1870, the first train of five families started for Sioux County, Van der Waa taking the lead as he and his team had traveled the road three times; G. van de Steeg Sr., H. J. Luymers, A. van der Meide, and the Beukelman Bros. Old lady Beukelman and her daughter were the only women that came along, and were the first women of the colony to settle in Sioux County; Charles Draayom married the daughter. The second train was from Sand Ridge; their leader was Pelmulder, one of the committee; this train consisted of several families, I think all were Frieslanders.

The third train started from Amsterdam, three miles south of Pella, leaders Van der Meer and Van den Bos. There were from twenty to twenty-five teams and from two to four yoke of oxen to each wagon. Other trains followed during the spring and summer, all from Pella and vicinity. I also recollect two families coming all the way from Chicago; we met them on the road with their teams tired out but they were helped along by our party; their names were W. de Vos and Simon de Bruin.

86. ARIE VAN DER MEIDE'S
REMINISCENCES OF EARLY DAYS IN SIOUX COUNTY

[These *Reminiscences* taken from the *Standard Historical Atlas of Sioux County Iowa* (Chicago, 1908) present much detail about the history of the first arrival from Pella of Hollanders to settle in Sioux County.]

Having read the foregoing article written by Hendrik Jan van der Waa, I do not think it out of place to add a few incidents to it since we were with him on this trip to Sioux County in 1870, he being considered our leader, as he had been over the road before.

At the start of our trip he showed poor generalship, as it was only the second day, I think, that he led us onto the bridge in Polk County that proves my assertion as to his generalship. Five teams were in our party: Hendrik Jan van der Waa, Gerrit van de Steeg, Sr., who died some time ago, and his three sons – John van de Steeg who is now a merchant in Orange City, G. L. van de Steeg, postmaster at present in Orange City, and Gerrit van de Steeg, who was recently killed in a railroad accident in Minnesota, H. J. Luymers and his three sons – Robert, Johannes, and Teunis; Robert and Johannes having died some time ago and Teunis at present janitor in our Sioux County courthouse, Arie Beukelman and his mother and only sister, all of whom have passed away from this earth, and the writer, making the fifth team. As stated before, we were led on the bridge following Van der Waa as closely as we could. Crossing it in a zig zag way, four teams managed to get it in safety. The fifth team belonging to Beukelman, his mother, and sister, they not being accustomed to driving horses, having been in this country but a little over a year, did not fare so well. He had three horses with him, two hitched to his wagon and one led on behind, and between them they had only one eye they could see with. The result was that he did not keep the same track the other had done but intended to drive straight across the bridge, and the flooring being loose, having worked to the north by traveling over it, tipped and the whole outfit came down twelve feet in the creek, horses and all, where there was about two feet of water. It did not take us very long to hitch our teams and go to their rescue, expecting to find some of them dead under the heavy load they had, but we were happily surprised when we got to them to find that the old lady and her daughter had fallen outside of the wagon and Beukelman was held on the wagon box with his legs, receiving only slight bruises, and the others not as much as a scratch. The only death loss was the chickens that were drowned before we got to them. This was in the forenoon of the second day of our trip, so we stopped for the day to make repairs to the wagon and to dry the goods which they had with them by spreading the same out on quilts and blankets on the grass, and the old lady was kept busy drying the few greenbacks she had with her. By the following morning, all was repaired again so that we could go on with our journey, and by so doing Polk County was saved several thousand dollars for damages.

After the accident we must say that we never had a better leader and general than Van der Waa. From then on we moved along slowly as the roads were bad and there was a great deal of swampy country to pass through and we did not venture on any more bridges without examining them before we undertook to cross them, so that we were sure they were safe. We preferred to get stalled rather than to have a fall. It took us nineteen days to make the trip of about two hundred and fifty miles, and hard work at that, as I well remember that there was one day when we only made three miles, and working from daylight to sundown, by loading and unloading our loads, and in crossing sloughs and swamps. But is did not affect us as it did the Israelites of old, as we did not murmur or care to go back home. We had faith in what our leader said: "There is no fairer country or better land under the sun than Sioux County," and correct he was, having finally arrived in Sioux County it proved to us that his statement was true.

The first night when we reached Sioux County, we camped on what is now called "The Orange City Slough", three-fourths of a mile north of Orange City. The next morning we started out to look up our lands, going as we thought, with our map in our hands, northward and north-west, following as near as we could the section lines. After having traveled all day and when the sun was fast sinking away in the west, we started for camp, thinking we had seen most of our claims and being well satisfied with the same. Having gone but a short distance towards our camp as we thought, we noticed someone with some horses to the west of us who were grazing along a slough. Of course we wished to know who else was in Sioux County except our party, and going to where he was we found it to be one of our own party whom we had left with our horses and wagon, and we were not a little surprised to find out that we had been going southeast and south all day instead of north and northwest. If it had not been for meeting him we do not know where we would have landed; probably we would still be going south and would never have reached our camp. After having been here a few days, a good many more colonists arrived and we all got busy breaking prairie and raising a crop the following year. The winter was mild and there was no snow so that in the early spring we commenced our work by putting in our grain and we raised a very good crop. By fall we had to have sheds, cribs, etc., so most of us went to Rock River to get some wood, there being some timber along said river. Of course it all belonged to the government or Uncle Sam, as we supposed, but there were a few settlers on the Rock by this time who thought and claimed different and claimed to be the owners of some of the lands. The result was that some of our people were driven away with pitch forks and others were cut down with axes and laid up for several weeks but no one was fatally hurt. The hauling of timber continued just the same. The meanest thing that was done by these people claiming the land was this: they would take fire wood from some of the piles that were prepared by the settlers, make a hole in it with an auger, place a certain quantity of powder in it, and plug the hole with a wooden plug and then place it back again in the pile so that it could not be detected, in order to be exploded in the cook stove, which happened serveral times.

During this winter, the courthouse war started which lasted for almost thirty years, off and on. The county seat was at Calliope at the time we came here, and at our first election, Tjeerd Heemstra was elected as member of the Board of Supervisors from our district and served one year. Henry Hospers was elected the second year to fill his place and J. W. Greatrax as treasurer, and A. J. Betten, Jr. as auditor. On January 1, 1872, Henry Hospers took the oath of office and was seated with the Board of Supervisors, but when it came to approving the bonds of Mr. Greatrax and Mr. Betten, the board refused to approve the same, Hospers voting to accept and the other to reject, claiming that the bonds were illegal, not duly signed, amount not sufficient, and various other reasons, all in order to keep them out of office. They undoubtedly saw that it was the beginning of the end of their career as office holders of Sioux County which had been very profitable to them as the county had a good many bonds outstanding and nothing to show for them. Meeting after meeting was held by the board but all to no avail; they would not approve the bonds. So the word was sent to the settlers in the east and northeast of the county that something had to be done to bring them to time. The board having adjourned to meet again January 22, 1872, some twenty odd teams gathered early on that day at Orange City and decided to go to Calliope and attend the meeting of the Honorable board and beg of them the acceptance of the bonds and place our people in office whom we had legally elected to the same. As the train of teams came in sight of the courthouse at Calliope where the board was in session, the chairman seeing the string of teams heading for their place, at once adjourned the meeting and prepared to take flight for the Dakotas, but he had no sooner hitched his horses when they were again unhitched by the settlers and placed back in the barn and he was left in his sled and told that he had no business in the Dakotas but that he was to attend the meeting, approve the bonds, and place our men in office, but he still refused. The late Judge Pendleton of Sioux City was there by request of the people to plead their cause which he kept up all day, aided by Henry Hospers, while the visitors kept themselves busy by taking care of their teams and frying bacon and ham of which there was a good quantity found in a barrel in the courthouse, evidently belonging to the county, at least no evidence to the contrary as it was taken by the visitors. We have heard it said that it was the best ham that was ever had and especially since the weather was very cold, being several degrees below zero.

The board refusing to do anything in regard to the bonds, the judge threw up his hands and said "Boys, it is all up," whereupon the visitors at once hitched their teams and took action by loading all the books of the different officers on sleds and preparing to start for home. But there was the large safe in the treasurer's office which has been overlooked for a while and the question was raised what should be done with this. "Go it must," was the reply. But having no tools or tackle, how to get it out of the building and on to a sled was a question which was soon answered. A sled was backed up against a corner of the building where the safe stood, the wall of the building was cut away with an ax, and in less time than it takes to write this, the safe was put on the sled, the horses hitched, and off we started for Orange City, with the wind and snow blowing at the rate of sixty miles an hour. They arrived at Orange City at about midnight with all their belongings with the exception of the safe which got stalled on the west branch of the Floyd where it was left until the following morning and brought to Orange City by Hymen den Hartog when great was the rejoicing and a thousand guns were fired in honor of the occasion. This only lasted for a few days when the sheriff, Thomas Dunham, came with the necessary documents and several yoke of cattle and took it all back to Calliope again, the board having agreed to approve the bonds and settle the matter.

During the summer a petition was circulated for the removal of the county seat in a legal manner to Orange City, which was signed by every inhabitant except those on the west side, and the question was brought before the people at the election and carried, so the county seat was legally moved to Orange City where it has remained ever since although it has been contested time and again by other towns asking for the removal to their place. Also the question of issuing bonds for a new building having been defeated several times until the question was raised again and the people were asked to vote bonds for $ 60,000, Orange City putting up a bonus of Fifteen Thousand Dollars. The bonds carried and the building was erected at the cost of $ 100,000.

The next incident that befell the pioneers was the grass-hopper siege, which is probably still remembered by a good many of the old settlers. It was on a Sunday forenoon, we being in the old schoolhouse where services were being held, it looked as though snow was falling outside, but when we came out we found it to be nothing but grass-hoppers. They came so thick and heavy that by Monday morning all our crops were stripped and gone. They remained with us for only a few days and moved on northward, coming back in the fall of the year, depositing their eggs and going on south. The following spring when warm weather set in, the grass-hoppers were hatched by the millions and destroyed the crops. The same thing was repeated for two years. The people did all they could to destroy the hoppers by building large pans or scrapers of sheet iron, sixteen feet long, three feet wide, and a back of two feet high, placing some tar and coal oil in the same and hitching a span of horses to each end would scrape the fields and catch bushels of grass-hoppers, but it did not seem to have any effect on the amount and on their appetite for destroying crops. We have heard it said that they were so thick and so hungry that they ate a pitchfork handle in one night although I have not seen it. It is true that a person could stand and count the 'hoppers on one side of a cornstalk and could count three hundred and eighty-seven on one stalk. The result of the grass-hoppers was that a good many of our settlers left us, some of them selling their lands, others leaving it unsold. In one instance a man got so disgusted that he sold his eighty acres for $ 225 throwing in a span of mules, wagon, and cow, worth at least $ 200. But those who withstood the siege and remained on their farms have never since regretted it as we have raised crops enough to keep us and to spare, ever since.

People often talk about blizzards. No one who has not actually seen and been in one knows what they are. The sky would be as clear as could be and you could see a cloud coming from the west and north-west, and in less than an hour a blinding snow storm would be on you so that you could not see six feet ahead of you. It happened at one time that five teams were on their way from Le Mars when a snow storm struck them eight miles south of Orange City at one o'clock at noon, which lasted for three days. Those five teams made the trip to Orange City having to depend upon the horses alone, the leaders being a span that had traveled the road often. The others were tied one behind the other, the drivers walking along the side, when the horses led up against the one store that was then in Orange City. Two of the teams got left behind but made their escape by stopping at A. van Wechel's who happened to have a sign right on the road and the horses turned in towards their barn. There was a barn in town which could comfortably hold ten head of horses; that night twentyfour were packed in it. The owner of the barn, an old lady, Mother Mouw as she was called, attempted to go from her house to the barn, a distance of about sixty feet, with a lamp, to see that the horses were well provided for. She lost her way and strayed from the place. As soon as it was found out that the old lady was lost, some ten or fifteen men turned out and started on a hunt, yelling at the top of their voices in order to keep within hailing distance. This lasted fully an hour when the old lady was found not over seventy-five feet from her residence with her lamp in her hand. Her fingers, ears, and toes were frozen and she would not have lived another hour if she had not been found. Others did not fare so well; in the north part of the county several were frozen to death by being lost. Some who were lost would travel all night in a circle until daylight when they could then see their house or barn, they having strayed away only to feed cattle or do some errand around the house. Such were the experiences with blizzards in those days.

Chapter XXVII

DUTCH COMMUNITIES IN SIOUX COUNTY

87. ARIE VAN DER MEIDE'S ORANGE CITY, IOWA

[Published in *De Volksvriend*, September 19, 1895, Van der Meide's account of the earliest history of Orange City fills an important lacuna in this collection of sources.]

De nederzetting eenmaal gevestigd zijnde, moest er eene stad zijn. Daartoe was geld noodig. Eene organisatie werd gevormd met Jelle Pelmulder aan 't hoofd; aandeelen werden verkocht en personen gemachtigd om het land te koopen, en deze kochten van Izaak van der Meer de tegenwoordige standplaats. Hier werden straten uitgelegd en alleys en de naam gegeven van Orange City. Dit was in 1870. A. Lenderink was de eerste die een woning bouwde in de stad en die ook aannemer werd van 't eerste schoolgebouw, aanbesteed door Buncombe township voor $ 2,400 in warrants [waard 40 cents op den dollar].

1871. De burgers [drie] van de stad moesten 2 mijl gaan om hun winkelwaren, bij Tjeerd Heemstra op de farm. In dit jaar werd door Henry Hospers een store gebouwd en met goederen gevuld, met A. J. Betten Jr. als klerk. Deze verkocht de waren voor geld en goede woorden; voor goede woorden het meest, is wel eens gezegd. Dat jaar vestigde zich hier smid Van Olst, die een gebouw opzette, voor woning en smidse te gelijk, van zoden en met een planken dak, en dra klonken heel gezellig de slagen van zijn hamer op het aanbeeld, en de affaire van den ouden smid is nog heden aanwezig en in welvarenden staat. Ook Joost Vos bouwde schoenwinkel en woonhuis aaneen, en bracht er tevens een barbiers-affaire in, waar de burgers des Zaterdags werden opgeknapt. „Moeder Mouw" zooals zij hier bekend stond, liet een hotel bouwen. In het najaar werd een begin gemaakt met een pastorie voor de Gereformeerde gemeente [alhier gesticht] en 't volgende jaar voltooid. De bevolking telde nu 24.

In 1871 bouwden Henry Hospers, Tjeerd J. Heemstra en nog anderen huizen. De eerste bouwde het eerste kantoor, waarin een bankierszaak gedreven werd, de Orange City Bank. Dr. E. O. Plumb vestigde zich hier als dokter, J. J. Bell als advokaat, G. Rozeboom als tweede smid en G. Dingemans als tweede hotel keeper. Nu was de bevolking gestegen tot bijna 50.

In 1873 zagen wij andere gebouwen verrijzen; als daar zijn: de store van W. Sleyster en C. Hospers, Pierce & Lewis' landkantoor, A. J. Betten's store, die dit jaar ook gebruikt werd voor county kantoren, daar de county seat hierheen verplaatst was van Calliope, A. K. Webbs' law office, P. Ellerbroek's drugstore, Mrs. W. Pas' woonhuis, Dr. Plumbs' en andere woonhuizen, waaronder Dr. de Lespinasse, die zich hier gevestigd had en wiens zoon, nu dokter, toen de photograaf was. Bevolking 151. Ook werd toen een moderne kerk gebouwd. Wegens gebrek aan sympathie werd die spoedig veranderd in een woonhuis, dat later een prooi der vlammen werd. Nu ondernam W. B. Raymond de uitgave eener courant, de *Sioux County Herald*, waarna dra een tweede, de *Homesteader*. Deze laatste is overgegaan in *De Volksvriend*.

De groei der plaats was vertraagd door de aanwezigheid der sprinkhanen. Later, toen die bezoeking voorbij was, ging het met den vooruitgang sneller. In 1875 werd de eerste kerk gebouwd door O. Rouwenhorst.

Eerste Gereformeerde gemeente. [Het volgende is inhoud van wat op ons verzoek Ouderling H. A. de Haan aan ons indiende]. Georganizeerd in het begin van 1871, door Ds. N. D. Williamson en Ouderling N. Gesman, met 45 huisgezinnen. Tot ouderlingen gekozen: Tjeerd Heemstra, G. van de Steeg, en M. Verheul; Diakenen: Sjoerd Sipma, Jelle Pelmulder en W. van Rooyen. Tot leeraar werd eenparig beroepen Ds. Seine Bolks van Zeeland, Michigan. Ofschoon men te nauwernood het durfde verwachten, nam ZEw de roeping aan en kwam tot ons over in April 1872. En ZEw was in zijn werk als leeraar, dokter en raadsman niet ongezegend. De plaats van samenkomst was het eerste schoolhuis.

Wegens ongesteldheid werd Ds. Bolks in 1878 emeritus en beriep de gemeente Ds. Ale Buursma, die in Mei 1879 tot ons kwam en de gem. bediende tot Juli 1889.

Uit deze gemeente zijn binnen weinige jaren na de vestiging der Nederzetting voortgesproten de gemeenten Alton, Newkirk, Sioux Center, de Amerikaansche, Maurice, Hull, Middleburg, Boyden, Hospers, en Rock Valley, 10 in getal, die alle haar eigen leeraar en pastorie hebben.

Na het vertrek van Ds. Buursma werd de gemeente bediend door Ds. Harmen van der Ploeg, van Juli 1890 tot 1893 toen ZEw door den dood werd weggenomen.

In November 1893, aanvaardde Ds. Matthew Kolijn zijn werk alhier en is thans nog met vrucht als zoodanig bezig.

Zoo is deze kleine plant van 45 huisgezinnen met bijvoeging van later komenden een boom geworden, die onder Gods zegen zijn takken heeft verspreid over de geheele county. Voorwaar, "dit is van den Heere geschied en het is wonderlijk in onze oogen."

Het aantal huisgezinnen van deze gemeente, die alle tot de Gereformeerde kerk behooren in Sioux County, bedraagt 1028: avondmaalgangers, 1774; en gedoopte leden, 3423.

Van Ds. Evert Breen hebben wij de volgende mededeeling ontvangen aangaande de Hollandsche Christelijke Gereformeerde gemeente.

Hollandsche Christelijke Gereformeerde gemeente. Met 12 huisgezinnen, vijftig zielental, werd deze gemeente in 1871 georganizeerd.

Haar eerste leeraar, Rev. John Stadt, aanvaarde den arbeid in 1877, December 2, en diende haar tot 1884, Juli 7, toen zij 45 huisgezinnen telde, met een zielental van 200.

Rev. John Gulker, de tweede leeraar begon den dienst October 5, 1884, met 55 huisgezinnen, 245 zielental. Onder diens arbeid nam de gemeente zeer toe en toen hij haar November 5, 1890, verliet, was de gemeente gegroeid tot eene grootte van 90 huisgezinnen, 500 zielental.

Zijn opvolger, Rev. E. van den Berge, was in haar midden werkzaam van àf April 5, 1891, tot October 29, 1893. Hij mocht zien, dat de gemeente, onder zijnen arbeid, van 100 huisgezinnen, tot 147 werd vermeerderd. Het zielental klom van 528 tot 775.

Rev. Evert Breen, de tegenwoordige leeraar, volgde hem December 24, 1893, op, en mag zich in den bloei der gemeente verheugen. Zij heeft thans de grootte bereikt van 194 huisgezinnen, met een zielental van 987. Zij geniet bestendigen groei en bloei. De Heere deed haar wel en met het oog op Hem wil zij met vertrouwen de toekomst verder ingaan.

Belangende de Amerikaansche Gereformeerde gemeente bericht ouderling M. Rhynsburger het volgende: de Amerikaansche Gereformeerde Gemeente werd georganizeerd April 17, 1885. De behoefte aan eene Engelsch sprekende gemeente was gevoeld en duidelijk aangewezen. Onder de bevolking van Orange City bevonden zich een niet onbeduidend getal Engelsche huisgezinnen, behalve verscheidene Hollandsche familien die Engelsch begeerden, vooral met het oog op hun kinderen. De Rev. John A. de Spelder was hier in bijzonder belangstellend, en werkte dan ook, dat door de classis Iowa eene commissie aangesteld werd om eene gemeente te organizeeren, hetwelk op bovengenoemden datum geschiedde. De nieuwe gemeente koos, onder leiding van Rev. Ale Buursma, als kerkeraad: Jacob J. van Zanten, ouderling, J. M. Oggel, diaken. De eerste vergadering van den kerkeraad werd gehouden in de court room Mei 15, 1885, maakte regeling tot het houden van godsdienst, en verkreeg voor dat doel het gebruik van de courtroom voor Zondagsschool en morgendienst en de Eerste kerk voor 's avonds.

Op een gemeentevergadering, gehouden Mei 22, werd Prof. John A. de Spelder, met algemene stemmen verzocht de nieuwe gemeente te bedienen, hetwelk door hem werd aangenomen. October 4, 1885, verkreeg de gemeente het gebruik van een lokaal in de tegenwoordige City Hall, en het volgende jaar de bovenverdieping. In Juli 1887 werd Rev. John A. de Spelder beroepen als leeraar. Deze roeping werd aangenomen. Zijne bediening alhier duurde tot Maart 1894 toen hij eene roeping in een ander veld had aangenomen. De gemeente groeide en kwam in bezit van haar eigen kerkgebouw Januari 25, 1889. De gemeente is georganiseerd met 23 leden; het tegenwoordig getal is 97. Rev. Albert A. Zabriskie is haar predikant. En hier de draad weer opgevat.

In dat zelfde jaar werd het tegenwoordige schoone courthouse opgericht en eenige woningen. P. Pfanstiehl heeft hier een echt Hollandsche windmolen gebouwd. Deze heeft, wegens verren afstand naar andere molens, veel goed gedaan. Hymen den Hartog nam hem later over en herschiep hem in een stoom "roller mill", die dezen zomer is afgebrand, zeer tot schade van den eigenaar. Dirk van den Bosch en B. van der Aarde hadden den eersten ijzerwinkel; deze werd later overgenomen door den tegenwoordigen eigenaar A. Bolks. We kregen nu gaandeweg betere gebouwen.

Jacob Versteeg en N. Snoek richtten eene steenbakkerij op; brandstof en dagloon bleken echter te hoog. In 1893 ondernamen B. van der Aarde en anderen deze zaak, en op heden is zij in goede werking onder den naam van de Orange City Brick Yard Company. Tot de factories van het verledene behoort de kaasfabriek van M. P. van Oosterhout en C. Slotemaker, wegens ongenoegzame deelneming.

In 1881 werd een tweede bank geopend: de Bank of Northwestern Iowa, door de firma Pitts en Kessey, in een houten gebouw dat later afbrandde, met vier andere gebouwen. Onder deze het woonhuis van A. Lenderink. Daarna lieten Pitts en Kessey een steenen gebouw zetten voor hunne bankierszaak en is de naam veranderd in Northwestern State Bank of Iowa nog steeds aanwezig.

In 1882 kwam ook hier de skating rink koorts en werd een gebouw gezet van 40 × 100 voet, 2 verdiepingen hoog. Dit gebouw werd later verkocht aan de Board van de Northwest Classical Academy en deze heeft het weder van de hand gedaan en nu is het de City Hall.

In datzelfde jaar werd de Chicago and Northwestern spoorweg hier door gelegd.

Daar de verhuizing nu toenam werden nog 160 akkers land gekocht en in lots uitgelegd, en vele huizen gebouwd. In 1883 werd Orange City als eene stad geïncorporeerd. De commissioners door den Rechter daartoe aangesteld waren Jelle Pelmulder, W. Sleyster, John Kolvoord, W. H. Casady, en schrijver dezes.

Sedert dien zijn er verscheidene van baksteen gebouwde winkels gezet, waarin keur van allerlei goederen, zooals men dikwijls niet vindt in steden tweemaal zoo oud als Orange City. Onder andere werd hier ook een electric light plant opgericht door eenigen onzer burgers, zoodat vele burgers electric light in woning en winkel hebben. Ook zijn er de straten met verlicht. Deze instelling heeft $ 14,000 gekost. Een jaar geleden werd een telefoon company opgericht, zoodat Orange City nu verbinding heeft per telefoon met meest alle plaatsen in de county en elders.

88. T. WAYENBERG'S SIOUX CENTER

[This brief sketch of the history of Sioux Center and environs appeared in *De Volksvriend*, September 19, 1895.]

In verband met het feit der geschiedenis van Sioux County, aangaande haar verleden van 25 jaren en waarvan feest staat gevierd te worden ter herdenking hoe wij als Hollanders eerst in klein getal hier op deze uitgestrekte prairies zijn gevestigd, was het onder de leidende voorzienigheid Gods, dat onder Zijne bewerking de bevolking van Pella, Iowa, de noodzakelijkheid inzag om eene nieuwe settling te bewerken. Het gevolg was, dat de aandacht op Sioux County werd gevestigd door hen, die als een commissie van onderzoek werden aangesteld, waar de vestiging zou plaats hebben. Aan het hoofd dier commissie stond de heer Henry Hospers, ook thans nog in ons midden. En deze heeft, hoe groot ook soms de moeielijkheden waren welke aan zulk een onderneming verbonden zijn, trouwelijk geholpen in vele zorgvolle tijden die zijn doorgeworsteld, en die tot op dit oogenblik nog steeds werkzaam is om de belangen dezer nederzetting te behartigen.

Zoo is dan middelijk onder deze goede en wijze leiding het geschiedt dat in het voorjaar van 1870 de eerste nederzetters in een klein getal zich in Sioux County gevestigd hebben, hetwelk nu tot een groote menigte is aangegroeid, en waar velen van elders zijn toegevloeid.

Her zijnde werd het spoedig gevoeld, in navolging van onze Hollandsche vaders, dat stoffelijke dingen niet genoeg zijn voor den redelijken mensch en dat er dus behoefte was aan Godsdienst en onderwijs voor de jeugd.

Dat dan had ten gevolge dat spoedig een gemeente werd gevestigd en vervolgens een schoolgebouw opgericht, dat tevens ook des Zondags als kerk werd gebruikt en waar de settlers van alle zijden samen kwamen.

Deze begonnen al zeer tè vermenigvuldigen en zoo werd er behoefte gevoeld aan een geestelijken leider, zoodat er een samenroeping van het volk plaats had en het besluit genomen werd om een leeraar te roepen. Dit had ten gevolge, dat de keus viel op den nu zalig ontslapen Eerw. heer Seine Bolks, die dan ook met algemeene stemmen beroepen werd. En deze roeping werd door ZEw opgevolgd, hoe ook tegen de verwachting van sommigen. En het is van achter gebleken, hoe hij was de rechte man op de rechte plaats; bijzonder in de drukkende tijden die het volk hier te doorworstelen kreeg, om een woord van opbeuring en bemoediging ter rechter tijd te spreken en gebruik wist te maken om door den druk der omstandigheden bijna tot moedeloosheid was verzonken, weder op te beuren en om bij vernieuwing in de kracht en de mogendheid des Heeren den strijd des levens met moed voort te zetten. En zoo zien wij dan heden wat in dit korte tijdsbestek van een kwart eeuw uit een klein begin tot stand kan komen onder den zegen des Heeren en een getrouwe leiding dergenen die door God geroepen zijn en zich door Hem willen laten gebruiken.

Het was in het jaar 1872, dat Ds. Seine Bolks zijn arbeid begon in Orange City, in een kleine zwakke gemeente, welke toen bestond uit menschen alom verspreid over de prairies van Sioux County; behalve nog eenige personen behoorende tot de Hollandsche Christelijke Gereformeerde kerk, die later ook tot een gemeente zijn georganizeerd. Uit dit zoo kleine begin zien wij thans (in 1895) in deze omgeving elf gereformeerde gemeenten geboren, die wij als wettige dochters en kleindochters hebben te erkennen, en waarvan wij ons, de tweede in ouderdom, mogen noemen bij den naam van Sioux Center.

Wij hier in Sioux Center mogen er ons eigenlijk niet op beroemen tot de allereerste settlers van Sioux County te behooren. Het was op den 17n Juni van het jaar 1871 dat wij den eersten blik hier wierpen en ons met drie families op deze uitgestrekte vlakte aan de westzijde van den kleinen stroom, de Branch genaamd, nederzetten. Wij zouden maar moeielijk de plaats onzer bestemming hebben gevonden, hadden we Willem van der Zalm niet ontmoet. Door zijn hulp dan daar aangekomen, spanden wij onze paarden af, die wellicht, hadden zij kunnen spreken, gezegd zouden hebben: wij zijn blijde hier te zijn. Doch dit was met mij zoo niet. Daar op die eenzame vlakte, niet wetende of verder west nog menschen woonden, en ten oosten door een stroom gescheiden waar geen enkele brug

over was, gevoelde ik mij als van de gemeenschap met menschen afgescheiden. Daar kwam nog bij dat de eerste ontmoeting op mij land was
met twee prairie wolven: geluk dat zij zoowel als ik bang waren, en
zoodoende raakten wij niet in strijd. Doch dit alles had ten gevolge dat
ik tot mijne vrouw zeide, dat, al was het goud hier met den schoffel op
te scheppen, toch kon ik hier niet blijven. Echter ik kon ook maar zoo
niet weggaan. En gelukkig ook; want het duurde niet lang of er kwamen
meer settlers bij, en dat deed de hoop herleven dat wij nog meer met
anderen in gemeenschap zouden leven.

En wat gebeurde? De settling nam zoo spoedig toe, dat het volgend
jaar een school werd gebouwd waar onze kinderen onderwijs ontvingen
en wij des Zondags in vergaderden om godsdienst te houden en waar de
oude heer Seine Bolks veelmalen ons met veel zegen heeft toegesproken.
Dit leidde er dan ook toe, dat ZEw ons bearbeidde om tot een gemeente
te worden gevormd, zoodat dan ook spoedig daartoe werd overgegaan;
en de organizatie plaats had den 17n Mei 1874, met een ledental van 24
personen. Niet dat er niet meer leden waren bij dien tijd, maar, zooals
't vaak gaat in zulke omstandigheden: Veel hoofden, veel zinnen. Er
kwam namelijk verschil over de plaats waar de kerk zou worden gebouwd;
en zoo onttrokken zich in de eerste plaats verscheidenen, hetwelk
Ds. Bolks veel arbeid heeft gekost om die breuk te genezen; doch door
zijn arbeid om 's Heeren zegen is dat naar wensch gelukt. En zoo werd
de eerste kerk hier gebouwd; een gebouw van 16 × 24 voet, dat later
viermaal is vergroot.

En nu begon van tijd tot tijd er meer behoefte te worden gevoeld aan
een eigen leeraar. Alhoewel de oude leeraar Bolks ons trouw bearbeidde,
zagen wij toch de noodzakelijkheid in van een eigen geestelijken leider,
zoodat wij besloten een pastorie te bouwen. Daartoe werden wij aangemoedigd door den Dr. Jacob West, secretaris van het Board of
Domestic Missions (van de Reformed Church in America), die ons veld
in oogenschouw had genomen. Zoo werd Januari 12, 1880, daarmede
een aanvang gemaakt; en na goede vordering met dit werk, werd op
Maart 30, 1880, de gemeente saamgeroepen onder leiding van Ds. Ale
Buursma, die destijds leeraar te Orange City was, en werd een beroep
uitgebracht op Ds. Johannes Willem Warnshuis. Daar ZEw bedankte
werd onder dezelfde leiding Ds. James de Pree beroepen; dit werd door
ZEw opgevolgd, en hij is sinds dien met zegen onder ons werkzaam
geweest. Hij kwam Juni 17, 1880.

Van toen aan was het dat de gemeente zich zoo snel uitbreidde, dat,
hoe wij ook trachtten voor elk eene plaats te bezorgen, ons gebouwtje

was niet toereikend. Zoo werd Maart 14, 1884, besloten om een nieuwe kerk te bouwen, waarin een 600 menschen plaats konden vinden, en dit werd nog datzelfde jaar tot stand gebracht. Toen dachten wij ruimte te hebben voor alle tijden; doch hierin zijn wij teleurgesteld, schoon niet op onaangenaame wijze. Daarom waren wij in 1893 genoodzaakt eene gallerij te bouwen, die aan een hondertal gelegenheid geeft om plaats te vinden.

In verband met de uitbreiding alhier zij gemeld, dat onlangs, den 18n Juli, 1895, een gedeelte van onze gemeente een eigen kudde is geworden met 26 leden in volle gemeenschap. Zij is gelegen zeven mijl ten noord-westen en heet de Carmel Church. Dus zien wij hoe uit een zeer klein zaad een groote plant kan te voorschijn komen. Nevens de Gereformeerde gemeente bestaat hier een Hollandsche Christelijke Gereformeerde en een Presbyteriaansche; de laatste bestaat voor het meerendeel uit Duitschers en Amerikanen.

Wat de town betreft, deze heeft 650 inwoners. Haar stichting is in hoofd-zaak toe te schrijven aan het leggen van een spoorweg door onze streek, den Great Northern Railroad in 1890. Thans hebben wij zestien handels-plaatsen, waaronder twee bankiershuizen, twee lumberyards en vier elevators. Ook is er een publieke school met vier onderwijzers. Dus is Sioux Center, ofschoon er in den beginne niet veel van gedacht werd, een der drukste plaatsjes in de county, en is nog steeds groeiend. Bij het einde van dit schrijven komt mij in de gedachten wat men leest in Deuteronomium 6, 2 en 3.

89. JAMES DE PREE'S REMINISCENCES OF EARLY SETTLEMENT AT SIOUX CENTER

[The Rev. James De Pree, minister in the Reformed Church, served the congregation of Sioux Center from 1880, became the son-in-law of the Rev. Seine Bolks, and identified himself with the settlement of Sioux Center. This article describing early conditions in Sioux Center is taken from the *Standard Historical Atlas of Sioux County, Iowa* (Chicago, 1908).]

To dwell on reminiscences of former day life and experiences is something we all love to do; the veteran soldier loves to recall, and relate the many thrilling adventures of battles in which he took part, and the striking incidents of camp life. The old time sailor can interest and amuse a whole company with an account of his many remarkable experiences on the deep. The traveler, or explorer delights to rehearse what he met with in his journey through several parts of the world. The student also has no greater delight than in amusing you, and relating in detail the adventures of school life. And so, early colonists also take a special delight in dwelling upon the various difficulties and privations connected with pioneer life, as well as upon the many pleasant experiences that are met with.

The early settlement by the Hollanders of Sioux County in general, and of West Branch township in particular, was of such a nature, and attended with such striking incidents also, that one will find it a no less pleasant task to dwell awhile upon the reminiscensces of those primitive days. The writer, having been requested to compile some of those reminiscences of those primitive days for this atlas, realizes that a more competent person might have been chosen for this purpose, as he is not one of the earliest settlers and did not arrive upon the scene until many of the most remarkable difficulties and struggles connected with the settlement of this particular colony had become a thing of the past, relies wholly upon accounts received from others, given indeed when they were still fresh in the memories of those who related them; but at best, they must be regarded chiefly as second hand statements. If therefore, some incorrect statements should be made or some incidents should be related somewhat varying from the actual occurrences, or lacking in all the particulars, it will please be kindly pardoned.

We may divide the reminiscences of these day into different classes; for instance, mention can be made of some that have a more direct bearing upon the religious life of the early settlers, and of others in connection with their temporal circumstances; some may be given that are of a sad and pathetic nature, while others have a tendency to amuse and create merriment. To begin with such incidents as were more particularly in connection with the religious advantages of those early colonists, we know of nothing that was more frequently referred to, and rehearsed with the most intense delight, and is even to this day often mentioned with feelings of deepest appreciation, than the fortnightly midweek preaching services, rendered in schoolhouses by the faithful and zealous pastor of the Orange City church, Rev. Seine Bolks. No matter how cold or stormy it might be, or how rough or muddy the roads, or how deep the water in the sloughs, he was always at his post; his prompt presence and his earnest efforts for the spiritual welfare of the people could always be depended upon. His words of wise council, of kind admonition, and of encouragement and good cheer in the days of severe struggle and afflictions are ever remembered with gratitude and sincere regard; in many, many instances he was used as an instrument in God's hand not merely for encouraging and helping on these pioneers with sound words of comfort and advice in their struggles for temporal existence, but especially also to bring sinners to a sense of their lost condition, and from that to a saving knowledge of Christ; and also to strengthen the faith of God's people, and aid them in their spiritual struggles and development.

To mention another incident in this particular line, we might refer to the lack of sufficient accommodation and room that had to be contended with, as long as the services were held in the building that was first erected to serve as a house of worship. Its length, and breadth, and height were in accordance with the financial capacity of their purses, and in a very short time its seating capacity was taken in, and with the weakest effort the voice of the speaker could fill the whole space. No up-to-date architect had been consulted in its construction, nor an accomplished carpenter engaged in its erection; the seats too were not of the cushioned and easy backed kind, nor symmetrically arranged, and the aisle at the center could only be passed throught in something like a serpentine motion, on account of the different length of seats. None of these were fastened to the floor and they were not immovable or firm, and the writer can call to mind one instance, when he had his catechumens gathered in the seats, by some quick turn of one of the pupils in the front seat, it fell backward with all its occupants, and it overturned the next one, and that again the third one, until all my pupils were on the floor. It goes without saying, that this occurrence for awhile did not tend to make the minds of the children more receptive for the instruction of the hour. At the regular Sabbath services, in the summer time, the people, to make up for lack of accommodations would bring the spring seats of their lumber wagons, which were the only means of conveyance to church at that time, and place them on available floor space inside the building, or, they wheeled their wagons near the open windows outside, increasing the seating capacity of the church, and be as attentive listeners to, and as quiet partakers in the solemn worship as the occasion allowed. This method was all right and satisfactory while the balmy days of summer lasted; but when autumn came, and the cold, raw winds drove the pew holders on the outside of the building to seek shelter within its walls, the strength of the seats, and the capacity of the building were taxed to the utmost. Every Sabbath afternoon, after the writer and his family, who always brought their chairs with them, had been crowded into the church, every inch of floor space and even of the speaker's platform was taken in. Every Monday morning, hammer and nails were brought to use in repairing seats that had given way under the loads and pressure of the previous day.

Having recalled some of the incidents of the early church life, we will next take a look at, and into the homes that afforded shelter and comfort to the pioneers of the seventies; they were of course far inferior to the large and commodious dwellings of the present day, but happiness and contentment reigned within them to no smaller degree. Nearly all of the first settlers dwelt in dugouts for some time; these were very ingeniously built into the east or south side, mostly on a slope, to secure protection from the northwest blasts. One might be walking down a slope, and very unexpectedly, without having seen it from a distance, land right down on one of these abodes for the pioneers. Or they made mud huts, constructed of the sods of the broken prarie, forming of them thick, substantial walls, to close out both the icy cold breezes of winter, and the burning heat of summer; generally these sod houses had one opening for a window, and one for a door; one man told the writer of having constructed such a sod house after an outlay of only $ 1.28 for the door and window. In most cases these homes consisted of but one apartment, that serving as parlor, living room, dining-room, bedroom, kitchen, cellar, and all. The more elaborate ones had one room partitioned off by a sod wall, which did service as a bedroom, where berths were arranged against the wall, sometimes two or three, above another, according to the number of occupants that had to be accommodated. The furniture of these homes was also very simple and limited, as a drygoods box placed in the center of the room was often used as a wardrobe, a cupboard and a dining-table; the walls were so dug out that a seat all the way around, about the height of an ordinary chair was left, this obviating the necessity of buying chairs. The fuel of these days consisted of slough grass, very ingeniously and tightly twisted, in order to last longer in the fire.

The stables and sheltering places for cattle were no more adequate or pretentious than the dwelling places for man, and one can hardly understand how in but a little more than a quarter of a century such immense changes could have come about, both as to the fine, handsome homes than can now everywhere be found, and as to the huge barns and extensive stables with all the modern equipments, that have taken the place of mere hovels of former years.

The most exciting and thrilling stories can be related concerning combats with prairie wolves, and fierce prairie fires that would sweep across the country and lick up everything in their path; and of fearful blizzards that in these days would break very suddenly upon the early settlers in winter time. Many narrow escapes from death could be placed on record, and many happy reunions after hours and even days of anxiety on account of husbands or sons that on their way were overtaken by such violent storms, when they were brought back in safety to the dear ones at home. In winter time a line was generally streched from the door of the dwelling place to the door of the stable, to prevent any one going from one to the other from loosing his way in these blinding snowstorms; or the good housewife would stand in the door of the house, while her husband or son went to feed the catlle, and call out loudly from time to time so as to let him know the direction he must take through the storm to find his home, just as the fog whistle on the pier guides the vessel to the harbor in a heavy mist. While these fierce snowstorms have been the occasion of loss of cattle in a number of instances, the writer has no remembrance of any human life that was lost thereby in this community, and we may well note the protecting hand of Providence.

One of the sad reminiscensce of these days is the drowning of two men, Gerrit Vleuvers and D. J. Wesselink in the Rock River. As was very often done by the early settlers, these men had gone to the Rock River to hew some trees from its banks, to be used either for fuel, or for some building purpose; in crossing the stream, they must have been caught on some whirlpools that abound in some parts of this river, and lost their lives. The former left a wife and three daughters almost grown up, to mourn his untimely death; the latter a wife and several small children to battle alone now with the great proposition of pioneer life.

The saddest and most pathetic reminiscence is the death of a little girl by prairie fire, which occurred on a spot very near to where now the residence of John Mouw is located in the town of Sioux Center. It was the daughter of Mr. and Mrs. Jacob Koster (Mrs. Koster is still one of Sioux Center's inhabitants) who lived but a few rods east from the spot, on the other side of the road. When the heartrending cries of the child were heard, and the parents flew to its rescue, the flames had already done their horrible work, and the child died shortly afterwards. This child was the first to be interred in what afterwards became the cemetery of Sioux Center. Often have we heard the mother relate with aching heart and streaming eyes the terrible pangs of this awful tragedy, the saddest of all the early accidents in this settlement. We have however, also been permitted to note in this very instance the all sufficiency of God's sustaining grace; not only for herself did the mother taste of this, but she was after this sad experience enabled to convey consolation and encouragement to others also in times of sorrow and bereavement. The writer and his wife can speak of this by experience; when, arriving here perhaps about two years after this sad incident, we were led through a way of mourning and grief, her frequent visits with us, and her words of solid truth and comfort were a balm to our aching hearts, and they will ever be remembered with profound appreciation and gratitude. And now it cannot be amiss further to name one or two instances that will give evidence of the genuine good-will and kindly feeling that was generally experienced by the early colonists toward one another, and the disposition to bear each other's burdens. When any one was in distress, or in need of aid, all hands were joined together; and while most of them were about equally penniless, and unable to open their empty purses in rendering assistance, they all found some way of serving one another. They helped build each other's houses and stalls; they watered each other's cattle; they took charge of each other's children; they dug each other's graves, and assisted in every kind of work and way, so that no one need to run into debt for these common necessities of life. In that way the hearts were brought into close union with each other, and general peace and harmony prevailed in these days of common privation. To relate one instance; Mr. H. J. Teesselink's house was, one cold wintry night, destroyed by fire, and the occupants barely escaped with their lives; soon all opened their scant purses, and extended willing hands to obtain the necessary material for a new dwelling, and everyone applied saw and hammer, and built the same in a remarkably short time. Another instance was when a man with very limited means expressed a desire to start a general store over the Branch, thus bringing articles of merchandise nearer to the people having settled here, all hands helped again to procure the material, erect the building, and haul the stock; and so he was aided in the enterprise, and the people were accommodated. That building, by the way, being the first dwelling to be raised on what was later platted into the town of Sioux Center, had but two apartments, and an attic; for a long time it served as a residnece, store, hotel and postoffice.

Grasshopper Times. We have not yet mentioned the grasshoppers, which for some years were sent annually by a wise Providence to prove the people, and to reap for them their richly promising fields of grain, and to disappoint all their expectations and plans for paying off incurred debts for necessary implements they had purchased, or for improving their homes and their stables. It is safe to say that even under these circumstances there was more real contentment and gratitude in the hearts, and more heartfelt appreciation of the corn bread meal, than is now manifested with all the abundance and luxury that is possessed. The grasshoppers were indeed a scourge, a means of robbing the pioneers of a vast amount of the transitory and perishable things of this world; but

they have also been used by Providence to create in many hearts a thirst
after and an earnest seeking for the meat which perisheth not. Many of the
pioneers here date the time of their new birth to these years of affliction
and sore bereavements.

Allow me now in conclusion to name a few items which will give
evidence of the extreme privations to which the settlers were subjected
on the one hand, but which also very amusingly show on the other hand
how cheerfully they adapted themselves to their circumstances. In one
instance we know of a family who, as has already been stated, had mud
seats for the children fixed against the wall in their hut, and the parents
had appropriated for their own use as seats the luxury of two huge
pumpkins raised in their field. On one occasion the family received a
friendly visit from two elders of the Orange City church to look after
their spiritual needs; the father and mother now denied themselves the
use of the pumpkins, and offered them to their visitors with the same
cheerfulness and grace wherewith the luxurious easy chairs are now called
to service for visiting friends. This man now is a retired farmer, has a
comfortable home in the town of Sioux Center, and owns several quarter
sections of Sioux County land.

Another family had for the second time been robbed of their sodhouse
by fire and had succeeded in procuring now a small frame building,
consisting of one room and an attic, the attic was to serve as a sleeping
room for the half dozen boys, of whom some were fast approaching
manhood, now there was an opening in the ceiling to the attic, but there
was no stairway or ladder to climb up to it, as much on account of lack
of space for it in the room, as on account of saving additional expense.
The mother, a very tall, strong woman, weighing about two hundred and
sixty pounds, was prepared for the emergency, and she would serve as the
stairway; every evening at bedtime she arose and bent forward, and
allowed her boys one by one to climb on her back, and from it to raise
themselves through the opening in the low ceiling to the attic, and retire
for the night.

One more instance in which the writer himself had a part. It was in the
memorable winter of 1880-81, when the first real blizzard of the season
came on the 15th day of October, and after that storm and severe cold
weather, and an abundance of snow remained until the middle of April.
It was our first winter in these parts, and while we had brought all our
furniture from Michigan and the house that had been erected as a manse
was one of the best then to be found in the whole country; and while we
had stoves to heat that home, and the parishioners had bountifully

supplied us with all that we could wish for the table, we could not have suffered very much, if only coal could have been obtained. But that was out of the question, sometimes for weeks in succession, because of the distance to the nearest railroad station, and especially because even these distant trains were handicapped by the snowdrifts, and unable to bring the coal. We had managed to feel contented and happy,   notwithstanding the great sacrifice of home comforts we had made, as well as of the splendid school privileges for the children we had left behind. But for one week a feeling of dissatisfaction, and of longing for the fleshpots of Egypt took possession of our heart, and we took pity on ourselves. It so happened that the writer with his family, and one of the elders and his lady were invited to spend the day with one of our parishioners, a large family, with but very limited means. Upon arriving there, we found but three chairs in the house, not enough even to accommodate the adults of the invited guests; but contentment and happiness shone from the faces, and were echoed in every word that our entertainers spoke the whole day. It was ten and there that the writer became ashamed and penitent for his feeling of dissatisfaction, and resolved that, if these people could be so grateful and full of happiness and true joy under such circumstances, I indeed had no reason whatever to complain, but only cause for gratitude and full resignation....

90. JAMES DE PREE'S
WEST BRANCH TOWNSHIP AND SIOUX CENTER

[In this sketch the Rev. James De Pree describes the life and achievements of the Hollanders who settled in West Branch Township shortly after 1870. Like the preceding, this sketch by the same author was taken from the *Standard Historical Atlas of Sioux County Iowa* (Chicago, 1908).]

West Branch Township, which presumably derives its name from the fact that the west branch of the Floyd River flows through it from about the Northeast corner to the Southwest, cutting it into nearly two triangles, is bounded as follows: on the North by Welcome, on the East by Holland, on the South by Sherman, and on the West by Center Township. The above named stream provides an abundant water supply, and as the land gently slopes and undulates towards the river from both sides, it also provides ample drainage, so that nearly every acre of its 35 sections is very valuable for agricultural purposes.

   Less than half a century ago it was the roaming place and home of the buffalo, elk, prairie, wolf, etc., while now hardly one square foot of unbroken prarie can be found within its borders. Its entire space has been turned into beautiful and most productive farms, with luxurious homes, extensive and commodious barns and stables, well filled granaries protected and nestled behind artificial groves. Thousands of cattle are grazing in the meadows, and annually tens of thousands of fat porkers are shipped from its borders to the world's markets; all this tells the tale of abundance and wealth the township affords, and of the industry and thrift of its inhabitants.

Soon after the Hollanders came to Sioux County in 1870, this township was also taken possession of, and after but a few years it had been almost entirely "taken by the Dutch". According to the records the first ones to take a claim were John and Henry Hospers, who both received a patent on the same date, December 1, 1871. Somewhat more than two years later the first patent west of the West Branch River was obtained by Jacob Westra, the northwest ¼ of section 4. This very parcel was, fifteen years later, sold to the Great Northern Land Co. and with the tract just opposite in section 5, bought by the same company from Mrs. De Mots, became the site for the now thriving and steadily growing village of Sioux Center. This is the only town in the township, and, as its name indicates, is located very near the geographical center of Sioux County.

In the spring of 1881 the writer himself assisted the survey, or in laying out the north half of the northwest ¼ of the northwest ¼ of section 9, twenty acres owned by the First Reformed Church organization, into four blocks of five lots each. The plat was filed for record May 30th, 1881. Upon the northwest block of the plat, the First Reformed Church still has its beautiful church edifice and commodious parsonage. This became the nucleus for a little town, some business enterprises were started here, and for a time it seemed that its location was established. But when, in 1890, the Great Northern Railroad Co. platted its property about three-quarters of a mile north from this plat, into village blocks and lots, and built its road, and located its depot there, all the business was soon removed to that site. When, however, later on the village was incorporated, what is generally called "the old town", was included in the corporation and the name Sioux Center retained for the whole; and now one continuous line of homes on three adjoining streets has already connected the two sites and formed them into one.

The population of the town is rapidly approaching the 1,000 mark. It has three good sized churches, all of brick; two school houses, one bank, one hotel, and several fine brick business blocks, two lumber yards and two elevators. To give some idea of the prosperity of the place, and the surrounding community, as also of the religous status of the same, we may state that within the last five years as much as $ 50,000 has been collected or pledged for the erection of the three handsome church structures that have been reared in that time; all this was done without any aid from outside.

Among some of the homesteaders who took claims in West Branch Township, and who are still living in and around Sioux Center, or who remained there until their departure from this life, may be given the following names: T. Wayenberg, H. Mouw, H. J. Wissink, G. H. Rensink, H. W. Rensink, G. van Beek, P. Schut, D. J. Wesselink, D. W. Doorink, Aart Franken, J. Franken, J. Vermeer, E. den Herder, J. van den Berg, J. van Grevenhof, E. Mouw, Gerben de Vries, section 20; Sander Schut, section 2; H. W. Beernink, section 8; John Pekeler, section 8; G. Zeutenhorst, section 6; Gysbert de Zeeuw, section 26; G. W. Wesselink, section 10; B. W. Jansen, section 10; Gerrit Niekamp, section 18; G. Kempers, section 3; E. van de Brake, section 20; J. W. te Grotenhuis, section 6; J. R. van der Schaaf, section 26; Hein Kosters, section 8; Hendrikus Kosters, section 8; Frederick Kuhl, section 10; Jacob Oolman, G. van de Brake, section 20; J. D. Wandscheer and Fred Franke, section 30. They bravely bore the brunt of the struggle and privations which are always incident upon pioneer life; courageously and hopefully continued to till these fertile fields, even when for several successive years, their efforts were thwarted by the grasshopper scourge, which devastated thousands upon thousands of richly promising acres of grain. To their industry and perseverance, confidently relying upon God's kind providence in leading them to these regions, and above all, to the Lord's goodness and mercy, who granted unto them this measure of perseverence and industry, and heard their prayers, and in His own good time bestowed upon them His richest blessings, is due the fact that these once bleak praries have been converted into a veritable garden spot, and from the abode and haunts of wild animals into the heritage of thrifty and prosperous tillers of the soil.

This sketch could hardly be considered complete unless mention was also made of the religious, or ecclesiastical advantages that were sought and obtained. While it is certain that the object of all who settled here was to improve their temporal condition, we may be assured, however, that they by no means intended to sacrifice their own, or their offsprings' spiritual welfare. The fact in all the different localities and towns that have sprung up in this colony, churches were organized and commodious church edifices were built is evidence of the deeply religious tendencies of the people, and this is equally true of those that took possession of West Branch Township and of those who inhabited the town of Sioux Center. For three or four years their church home was at Orange City, and they were very regular in their attendance upon the Sabbath services there, though most of them lacked facilities to ride, and had, therefore, to walk eight or ten, or even twelve miles, and then we do not speak yet of the absence of bridges in these primitive days, and of the necessity of wading through sloughs and even the West Branch River. In order, also, to meet the spiritual needs of all, the pastor of the Orange City Church, the venerable Rev. Seine Bolks, with his characteristic zeal and strong desire for the spiritual interests of all the colonists, came every other week, on some week day, and preached in school houses in two or three different localities. The Lord was pleased to greatly bless these ministrations and even now these early settlers can never forget the pastoral love and care that was bestowed upon them by this servant of God. In May 1877 the first church organization was established under the care of the Reformed Church in America, with twenty-five charter members, and soon a small building was erected upon almost the same site where the present First Reformed Church edifice stands, and from that time regular Sabbath services were held there. In March 1880 a call was extended to Rev. James de Pree, and in July he began his labors as pastor here, the church at that time consisting of thirty-one families and sixty members. He still continues to be the pastor of this church, having for more than a quarter of a century enjoyed the good will of the people, and the favor of Him who sent him there. About two years ago the church commemorated the twenty-fifth anniversary of this pastorate here with appropriate festivities.

For several years the church enjoyed a phenomenal increase, as the country was rapidly taken in. In 1884 a large new church was built, a frame building which after but a few years could hardly accommodate the ever increasing numbers that were gathered in. A gallery was then built, which increased the seating capacity to seven hundred, but that too was soon filled. In the year 1895, however, several families living from five to ten miles northwest of Sioux Center were organized into a church at what subsequently was named Carmel, this giving more room again, and the following year when the Christian Reformed organization received a regular pastor, another drain occured, several families wishing to be transferred to it. Then again in 1900 a number of the church families were transferred to what became the Second Reformed Church of Sioux Center. Since then it has never been necessary to say "the place where we dwell with Thee is too straight for us." Yet the church has always held its own, and still ranks second among the churches of the classis of Iowa.

The great calamity of the church came in June 1902 when the church building was blown down by a hurricane, completely destroying its sixteen-hundred dollar pipe organ, and two of the four stables, and half of another which were built for sheltering the teams during the hours of service on the Sabbath. For just about one year the people were without any church home and deprived of many of the regular privileges of church life, although they were fraternally permitted to make use of the Christian Reformed Church for some of the Sabbath services. But even that calamity seemed but a blessing in disguise, as just one year later they were enabled to dedicate to the Lord's service a very substantial, commodious brick edifice, which in strength and beauty and convenience, far surpasses the one that was destroyed and exceeds any other house of worship in the county at the present time.

91. D. GLEYSTEEN'S REMINISCENCES

[These *Reminiscences*, prepared for the *Standard Historical Atlas of Sioux County Iowa* (Chicago, 1908) faithfully portray some of the circumstances attending Dutch settlement at Alton and adjoining parts.]

I do not remember my grandmother kissing me goodbye nor hearing her remark that I would never reach Sioux County alive. I was an infant in arms weak and ready to die. But it was the old story. In a few years as a healthy robust lad I accompanied my mother back to Pella to attend the funeral of my grandmother.

We came to Sioux County in March 1871. The rivers were swollen and both we and our furniture were hauled from Le Mars to the Old Homestead by wagon. As we approached the farm the bridge over the Floyd which was a temporary structure broke and my father tumbled into the water. All the money he had was in his vest pocket and this was lost in his endeavor to save himself and the furniture. Of our early experience on the farm I remember but little. We had no well and our stock was watered in the river from which we also got all our drinking and washing water. One day my sisters and brothers took me along in a clothes basket and set me upon a narrow plank bridge while they filled the barrels. My movements dislodged the basket which fell into the water and I floated down the stream to where John Schuller was fishing. Thinking me another Moses he acted the part of Pharaoh's daughter and fished me out. After a couple of years on the farm we moved to town – then called East Orange. It consisted of our house, the depot and depot cottage, Kilburg's store and De Kraay's hotel and all the rest was prairie. These buildings except the depot, are still standing. My sisters and I and a few other children spent our time in snaring gophers and hunting flowers. There were no dandelions in Sioux County in those days but plenty of roses, sweet williams, violets, wind flowers, prairie lillies, and bluebells. These last three have almost disappeared. Once in a while a band of Indians would come and then we scampered to our mothers or as we grew older we would let them shoot at pennies with their arrows-letting them have those they hit. In the early days there was neither church nor school house in the town and school was taught in a room above Kilburg's saloon – now Mike Allen's restaurant. The people went to church in Orange City. It was in Orange City too that our holidays were spent-Christmas and Fourth of July. The celebrations generally consisted of a service in the church, after which the children were given a bag of nuts and candy. For many years there was neither minister nor doctor nor lawyer in the community. Rev. Seine Bolks combined these three professions in one person and when cases were mild or in emergencies he was a never failing help. For many years before Alton had a church – and occasionally for many years after – the old gentleman would come and preach for us. I can see him yet, the venerable patriarch, as he stood in the pulpit, tall and erect and all dressed in black, his long hair and beard a snowy white. When he began to speak his face would flush and he always reminded me of a picture I once saw of Moses transfigured on the mountain. And how he preached – without notes and without time – hammering the bible until the leaves flew out over the audience – thundering away until the sun went down. But all was rapt attention and no one ever attempted to leave. To my youthful mind it was mostly a jargon of words in which hell and sin and eternal fire stood out prominent. He was not a leader like Van Raalte nor a scholar like Scholte of the parent colony but the old Dominie did what he could and will be remembered kindly by a generation of men now fast disappearing. When there were cases of serious sickness a doctor was summoned from Le Mars. Often too we depended upon home remedies. I remember when some six of our family had the whooping cough. An old lady visited my mother and advised her to take a horse radish and hollow it out and fill that with sugar water. After standing twenty-four hours we were to take a tablespoon full. My mother never succeeded in giving us more than that first dose.

For a few years things went fairly well and then came the grasshoppers. To one who did not experience that scourge a description must always remain inadequate. My first personal experience with this pest was when one day near noon I lay down in the garden and fell asleep behind the vines. I was awakened by a voice calling me to dinner, but it was with difficulty that I arose. The grasshoppers had settled on my body three or four layers thick. After dinner there was not a vestige of green left in the garden. For a number of years in succession they came and destroyed nearly everything. Many of the settlers left and those who remained did so because they could not get away. Many experiments were tried. Rollers were made to crush them and tar boxes to ensnare them, but to no avail. They finally disappeared and the people of Sioux County again came to their own. Even when the grasshoppers left, conditions did not immediately improve. The farmers were hopelessly in debt and the business men carried thousands of dollars on their books on which they could not realize. Money was borrowed from the banks at Le Mars at twenty-four per cent interest, paid in advance, and then on the best security. A half section farm today will carry a greater loan at five per cent than could be carried then on a whole township at the interest mentioned above. This generation of farmers will never know what their fathers owed to those few sturdy business men whose labors and honesty kept the community from starvation and upheld the credit of the county. It is needless to say that mail order houses did not exploit the farmers of that day.

This was the home of the prairie chicken and I remember how we hunted the eggs and watched the chickens as they flew against the telegraph wires and broke their necks. When we first came here we did not have to leave our yard to shoot all the chickens we needed for the table. As the land was taken up the hatching ground disappeared and the chickens and snipe were doomed. There was also some deer in the country when we came. Once four large stags were caught in a snow drift and clubbed to death by the farmers. One afternoon as we children were playing in the school yard a fawn flew past us pursued by some dogs and two hunters. We all joined in the chase. The animal was brought to bay on my father's farm and shot by Henry Goebel. That night the whole town ate venison. Wolves were quite common and though I never heard of any damage done by them they were soon exterminated.

Early in the seventies the Sioux City and St. Paul Railroad was opened and East Orange became the distributing point for the east end of the county. Orange City and all the farmers had to get their flour and groceries and lumber and coal here and here they marketed all their grain and farm products. There were no elevators and the grain was unloaded into a hopper holding some 250 pounds – this being weighed and carried into the car. To load a car meant hard work and lame backs. Flour was generally hauled from Le Mars though there was an old fashioned Dutch windmill at Orange City where wheat was ground. This quaint structure stood just east of what are now the Academy grounds. If I am not mistaken the materials were brought from the Netherlands. Nearly every schoolboy has seen a picture of the famous windmill at Potsdam where the German Emperor has his winter residence. Well, the old Orange City Grist and Flour mill was externally, at least, the exact counterpart of that famous structure. It was afterwards dismantled but deserved a better fate. It should have been preserved as the one landmark typically national of the early settlers and a park laid out around it where Old Settler's picnics and other commemorative celebrations could have been held. When in 1881 the Northwestern road was build it was our – the small boy's – regret that the raisins and prunes and cookies and candies shipped to Orange City no longer came here for it had long been our privilege to help ourselves to stuff going to Orange City so long as we did not take anything belonging to our home people. Before 1881 our railroad service was poor enough in summer and irregular in winter. I remember how there was only one train a day and it remained long enough so the crew could get out and play base ball with the town people. In winter there would often be no train service for a week or longer. I remember the winter of 1881 when it began to snow on the fifteenth of October and the snow banks were piled so high that instead of making paths, I made two tunnels, one to the barn and the other to my brother-in-law's house. There was a snow bank extending from the Dutch Church across the railroad track. One night when there had been no train for several days the town people were awakened by a whistle and as many people as could went down the line to near Seney where a freight was trying to plough through the snowdrifts. The following day I watched them for several hours as they worked in the cut just north of the river. It took more than twenty-four hours to go from Seney to Hospers – a distance of twenty miles. Fuel was scarce that winter and many people burned corn and even hay. One day when a train was temporarily stalled in the yards here the farmers came in and unloaded a car of coal destined for some other town. They had it weighed and paid for it, but no doubt some other village along the line wondered what had become of its fuel. I was about eight years old before hard coal was brought into this part of the country. Before that time soft coal and corn and cobs and hay had been our fuel. To the present generation it may seem strange that the people burned hay and may well wonder how a stove fire could be kept burning with such light combustible stuff. Long slough grass was taken, which by means of a hook and wheel, was twisted into bundles the size of stove wood and I have seen some that were almost as solid.

Early in 1881 the people desired to incorporate the village and change its name to something simpler than East Orange. Alexander Beach headed the petition asking it to be changed to Wilfred, the name of his son, the first child born in the town. John Meyer had another petition asking that the name be changed to Delft. A meeting was finally held in the postoffice when Dr. Owens looking over a postal guide, remarked that there was no Alton in Iowa. This name was agreed to by both factions and the newly incorporated town was so called.

In the fall of 1882 some Dutch ministers and a few business men came together and founded the Northwestern Academy. As originally planned it was to be built on some site midway between Orange City and Alton. The following year Henry Hospers donated a piece of ground on the outskirts of Orange City and that has remained the location of the academy to the present day save a temporary removal to the Orange City skating rink. Alton's delegation to the academy that first year consisted of five boys – Sjoerd Menning, Gerrit Ruisch, Thomas Kooreman, William Warnshuis, and the writer. Of these but one finished the course. We walked up every morning and back every noon. Our number during those four years gradually became less – so that for more than a year in wet weather and dry, hot and cold – often ploughing through snow up to my waist I walked the weary way alone – developing a pair of calves out of all proportion to my intellect. In 1887 I left Sioux County to go off to college – the first Alton boy to seek a higher education away from home. Since then many boys and girls from Alton and the surrounding country have gone to the academy and then off to different schools. And the academy, too, has prospered both in number of students and financially until now it is, perhaps, the most cherished heritage of the Hollanders of Sioux County.

Fourteen years later I returned to Alton. What a change! The entire county was under cultivation. Land values had risen from ten to seventy-five dollars an acre. Beautiful homes and churches had been built in the village and spacious barns and substantial houses on the farms. Groves of trees had sprung up where in the early days there was one vast stretch of prairie. There had been a change as by the touch of Aladdin's lamp – transforming the whole into the Garden of the Lord.

Often as I ride through the country and behold this fertile valley of the
Floyd, whose hillsides are covered with grain and in whose bottoms
thousands of cattle browse, my memory reverts to when I was a boy and
again I play out on the open prairie and hunt the wild bird nests or pick
the modest bluebells or carry the lunch to haymakers and it is only by an
effort that I realize that these changes have come about during the short
span of my life – for I am still a young man, being several years younger
than my father was when he – a young man – came as one of the first
pioneers to this part of Sioux County.

92. JOE REXWINKEL'S NASSAU TOWNSHIP, SIOUX COUNTY

[The author portrays pioneer days in Nassau Township where Hollanders settled during the
spring and summer of 1870. The poem inserted by him in his account is from the hand of
C. Pelmulder, son of Jelle Pelmulder pioneer of Pella and Sioux County who died in 1910.
This article was published in the *Standard Historical Atlas of Sioux County Iowa* (Chicago, 1908).]

Nassau Township was organized in the year 1870. At that time it comprised what are now Nassau, East Orange, and Sherman townships. In
the year 1876 Sherman Township, by petition signed by residents of
said township, was given an organization of her own, and some time
later East Orange organized as a separate township.

Nassau is located in the southern tier of townships with Holland on the
north, Plymouth County on the south, East Orange on the east, and
Sherman on the west. It is a rich and beautiful township with gently
rolling praries, not steep so as to cause farming difficult, nor flat, but
every foot of land good for cultivation, and it is all well drained with
sloughs and creeks which yield a heavy crop of grass. The Floyd River
courses its way through the township, entering near the northeast corner
on section 2 and flowing in a southwesterly direction leaving the township
on section 33.

The first election held in the township was on the 11th day of October
1870 in the house of Tjeerd Heemstra on section 4, with Tjeerd Heemstra,
P. van Horsen and J. van Wyk as judges, and A. M. van den Berg and
F. Heemstra as clerks. The following officers were elected: Justice of the
Peace, T. Heemstra and John van Syk; Township Trustees, A. M. van
den Berg, John van Wyk and P. Dieleman; Clerk ,F. Heemstra; Assessor,
T. Heemstra; Constables, W. Rysdam, Arie de Raad; Road Supervisors,
P. van Horsen and G. Rysdam.

The names of the voters at this election [17 in number] were as follows:
T. Heemstra, W. Rysdam, G. Rysdam, A. M. van den Berg, P. van

Horsen, John van Wyk, Arie de Raad, P. Dieleman, M. Dieleman, Jacob Sinnema, Theo. Gehlen, Nicholas Frantzen, Peter Frantzen, M. Biever, A. Henrich, Benhard Henrich, F. Heemstra. Eleven of the above named were Hollanders and six Germans; to the best of our knowledge, three of these are still living. W. Rysdam and M. Dieleman retired and are now living in Orange City, and P. Frantzen, one of our prosperous farmers, iss till living on his own farm on section 23.

In the fall of 1873 the writer who was then but eleven years of age, came to Nassau Township with his parents, from Fond du Lac County, Wisconsin, and has lived here ever since that time, his occupation being a tiller of the soil. At that time our neighbors were more distant than now, they were doubly precious; will mention but one of them, Mr. A. van Wechel, on section 7, who, because of his hospitality, his house was dedicated as the Elk Horn tavern. Those living in the northern part of the county, had their important place of business [if not their markets], at Le Mars, and as it was a distance of from twenty-five to thirty miles, made Elk Horn tavern their stopping place. Mr. Van Wechel was a prosperous farmer, is now retired and living in Orange City.

Experiences of the early settlers were varied, although they had one thing in common, they were all poor, poor in money when we came and poorer still when the grasshoppers came; for a few years it surely was a trying time, especially the years 1874 to 1878.

A great many of the early settlers had to depend almost entirely on corn stalks for fuel in winter, some would chop the stalks in pieces, others would use them whole; it kept one of the family busy keeping a fire.

The winter of 1876 was another trying time, as the wheat crop was a total failure; our neighbor Joe Kleinhesselink, who had a large field planted to wheat told father that he would not get his harvester out that year. It was the following winter that we had johnny cake for breakfast, and johnny cake at school for dinner, and potatoes and corn meal mush for supper, but I will say that we all thrived and were healthy. Sunday we had wheat bread which was considered quite a treat.

Well do I remember the first summer we were here [1874] how on a Sunday noon the grasshoppers came from the north, clouds of them just about harvest time, and lit on our fields; the ground was covered with them. Joe Kleinhesselink, on section 9, had a field containing about five acres of sod corn; it was very good in the morning, looked tall and green; in the afternoon it was all stripped, just the bare stalks left, the smaller fields were mostly ruined, while the larger fields held out better. We were very fortunate. They stayed only a few days, and left us a small share of the crop.

THE CHARGE OF THE GRASSHOPPER BRIGADE

What see I yonder rise,
There in the northern skies,
    Like a tall oak?
Say, are they clouds of blue,
That to the south pursue,
    Or, is it smoke?

See, see how it doth fly,
Soon 'twill o'erspread the sky
    Like a dark pall.
That's no smoke, nor clouds,
But grasshoppers in crowds;
    Down, down they fall.

Numerous like the dust,
Come the hoppers or locust;
    They fill the air.
The corn that looks so green
Will soon no more be seen,
    All will be bare.

Then will the harvest field,
Naught to the farmer yield,
    If they abide.
But on the coming day,
They very likely may
    Float with the tide.

A visit brief they made,
With us three days they stayed,
    Then went away.
Onward their course they bent,
Straight to the south they went,
    On the third day.

Great was the damage done,
But helped by the shining sun,
And a few rains,
Plenty of corn and wheat,
For man and beast to eat,
There still remains.

If they do not appear,
Upon another year,
Our crops to spoil,
Then will the people see
What splendid crops that we
Raise on our soil.

For 'tis not alone for health,
But 'tis the place for wealth —
In the far west.
Of all the countries wide,
Around on every side,
It is the best.

The following spring when the grains were up, the little grasshopper came up also, and although he was small he left his marks. Most of the eggs were laid in hard ground or breaking. I well remember, father had a field of oats and there was a piece of breaking alongside of it; when the little hoppers could hop, they aimed for the oat field; it was a sight to watch them, they traveled slow but sure. To prevent their going from one field to another ,some would plow deep furrows, hoping they would not be able to cross; other would take boards covered with tar and in that way would catch them; the settlers tried various means, but with no marked success. Some farmers became discouraged and sold their lands for whatever they could get and went back east; they realized but very little for their farms. One man near Orange City sold his homestead of eighty acres and a yoke of oxen for $ 300; the same land sells in 1907 at from $ 100 to $ 145 per acre. These were very strenuous times for the pioneers.

Nassau is now one of the best townships in Sioux County, as everyone will concede who takes a drive over our well graded roads, to see the beautiful farm houses and large barns, the rich fields and pastures, well stocked with horses, cattle and hogs.

The township has two railroads, the Chicago, St. Paul, Minneapolis and Omaha, which was built in the years 1872-73 through the Floyd valley. On that road is the town of Alton, which, previous to 1880 was called East Orange. In the southern part of the township on the same road is a siding or place called Carnes, with two elevators, stock yards, lumber yard, one store and a Post Office. The Chicago and Northwestern runs through the north part of the township from east to west. The north half of the northeast quarter of section 5, Nassau Township, is incorporated in the town plat of Orange City; on this tract of land the electric light plant is located, also the grain and stock market. With the above three named towns, the farmers only have a short haul to the different markets and places of business.

Chapter XXVIII

SETTLEMENTS IN NORTHERN MICHIGAN

93. JAN VOGEL'S MEMOIR

[Jan Vogel, died in Muskegon September 25, 1907, was intimately acquainted with the Dutch communities of Michigan, particularly Vogel Center which place was named after him. His *memoir*, originally written in Dutch, was translated by Benjamin G. Oosterbaan and published in *Michigan History* XXX (1946).]

Frans Vogel, my father, was born August 15, 1804, in the province of South Holland, in The Netherlands. My mother was Derkje Beesemer, also born in The Netherlands; but I never knew her, for she died when I was only two years old. My father married Geertruide van Weenen in 1843, that being his second marriage.

I was born at Giessen Nieuwkerk in the province of South Holland, on September 8, 1839. From my sixth to my eight year I attended school at Giessen-Oudekerk. My parents moved to Noordeloos, a town situated nearby in the same province, where I continued my schooling until my twelfth birthday. During these years we experienced severe poverty because of the sickness of my father as well as the generally difficult times.

When I was twelve I began to help my father support the family. After about six months I secured a position in a carpenter's shop as an apprentice. This step was undertaken with the aid and encouragement of my father who wanted me to learn the useful trade of carpentering. The shopkeeper's name was Hermanus Diepenhorst who, like our family, lived at Noordeloos. The contract made with him provided for an apprenticeship of three years. It was agreed that my parents were to provide my food and clothing during the first year, that I was to earn my board during the second year, and that during the third year I was to receive such compensation as my ability warranted.

After two and a half years, when Diepenhorst emigrated with his family to Holland, Michigan, this contract came to an end. I was eager to accompany them and with Diepenhorst's help tried to persuade my parents to let me go. My father's mind had long been favorably inclined toward America but owing to poverty never was able to emigrate. The fact that I was his only living son filled him with apprehension. Yet after long consideration he decided to part with me, hoping that at some future time I might be able to help him go to America. He had the fullest confidence in Diepenhorst's promise to look after my welfare. Diepenhorst paid my traveling expenses, and we left Noordeloos on August 6, 1854. My father, mother, and sisters accompanied me to Gorinchem where we took passage to Rotterdam and proceeded by sail to New York, by way of Hull and Liverpool. We lost some time while in England, and as our ship was a sailing vessel we did not arrive at New York until about September 20. About eight days later we reached Holland, Michigan. My fifteenth birthday took place during the voyage, on September 8.

After making a brief investigation of the dense forest, we settled six miles north of Holland at Noordeloos. We attacked the forest courageously but after a while our zeal vanished, and we moved to Grand Haven where we hoped to earn good wages at carpentering. But the financial reverses of the year 1856 so reduced the value of paper money that my savings amounted to nothing. Nevertheless, Diepenhorst had hired me for the past two years at a monthly rate so that my November 1, I was able to pay everything I owed him on account of my traveling expenses from the Old Country. As I was unable to agree with him further about wages, I went to Zeeland, Michigan, where I spent the ensuing winter, remaining there till the spring of 1857. While living with a man named K. Schoenmaker that winter I had the most important experience of my life. This adventure during my eighteenth year will outlast the annals of time, being destined for eternity. I had come to see that man's ultimate object is his Maker, that he must glorify God in every relation of life. I acquired a firm trust that God had made a covenant with me in accordance with the second chapter of Hosea.

On the first of April I left for Grand Rapids where I intended to continue my carpentering and in the meantime improve my knowledge of English. While in Grand Rapids I received my religious education at the *afgescheiden* [Seceded] *Kerk*, later Christian Reformed Church. Soon I found employment at a shop and was paid regularly by the month. In the fall I accompanied my boss to Jamestown, Ottawa County, where I remained until the following spring, 1858.

Thereafter I worked as a carpenter for Jan Rabbers at Groningen. In this family I enjoyed the privileges of a parental home. This hospitality continued into the following year, 1859, during which time I earned a dollar a day. But Jan Rabbers fell ill during 1860 and died on August 12, being assured of a glorious reward in the hereafter. Next to my parents I was most attached to him.

The summer of 1860 was marked with a passionate struggle between the Republican and Democratic parties. In the November elections Abraham Lincoln was chosen president. In December began the great rebellion, breaking out first in South Carolina. The perfidious Democratic government in power did nothing to arrest this rebellion. Only when the just and strong administration of Abraham Lincoln began in March was any attempt made to check the uprising. I remained at my carpenter's work in spite of the fact there was much excitement throughout the entire country due to the increasing proportions of the southern rebellion. In September 1861 Lincoln issued a patriotic call for 300,000 volunteers and at the same time asked everybody to work loyally for the preservation of the Union. With almost unbelievable dispatch did volunteers answer his call. On September 18, I and 25 other Hollanders volunteered our services, enlisting in Company D, 2d Regiment, Michigan cavalry. Twenty-four hundred strong, we set ou for St. Louis, Missouri. Thousands of loyal citizens escorted us to the depot. Many a hearty and touching parting took place – and for many, the last. Upon our arrival at Detroit we were served a bountiful meal prepared for us in the Detroit and Michigan depot. We continued our journey by way of the Michigan Central Railroad to Chicago, from Chicago by way of the Alton and St. Louis Railway to Alton, Illinois, and from Alton by boat down the Mississippi River to St. Louis. Everywhere we received a hearty reception. But as we reached the southern part of Illinois, this friendliness cooled noticeably. At St. Louis we met many colored slaves and also their inwardly blacker so-called owners – men who had soiled their bloody hands mistreating human creatures. Now these selfsame men, in an attempt to perpetuate their abominable system, were adding to their guilt by raising their soiled hands against a lawful government.

All our time at Camp Benton near St. Louis was occupied in military training. Weapons were furnished us – Colt revolvers, six shooters, and side arms, also Colt 5 revolving carbines. In February 1862 there were about 40,000 well drilled and well equipped men in camp under General Henry W. Halleck. On the 22nd the War Department ordered these tropps to proceed by boat down the Mississippi, the object being to reopen navigation on the river to New Orleans and cut the forces of the rebellious South in two. But many long and bloody battles had to be fought before this object could be realized.

On February 23 landed at Commerce, Missouri, and from there as mounted forces proceeded toward Fort New Madrid where we had our first real encounter with rebel forces. After a short battle we were ordered to make camp, and there we remained until the early part of March. While in that place we daily heard the heavy bombardment of Island Number Ten, and from time to time we were attacked by the rebels who still held Fort New Madrid. On March 13 we took part in a general battle under General John Pope, which during the following night resulted in a retreat by the rebel forces. Pursuing them we crossed the Mississippi River into Tennessee and at Tiptonville captured 2,400 of the rebel forces.

Early in April we moved down the Mississippi by boat toward Memphis, but owing to our inability to land and to our lack of provisions by the time we arrived at Pittsburg Landing on the Tennessee River, we were forced to turn back. After the Battle of Shiloh we took part in the siege of Corinth, Mississippi, and in several other battles. In the latter part of May the 2nd Iowa and the 4th Kansas Cavalry joined us. We rode around the rebel army to Booneville, thirty miles south of Corinth. In an expedition which lasted four days we destroyed railroads, burned bridges, and found Corinth abandoned. We spent most of this summer in different places in Mississippi and along the Mobile and Ohio Railroad. I took part in a battle at Blackhead on June 4, when I received a slight wound below the knees.

In September 1862 our detachment proceeded by rail through western Tennessee to Paducah, Kentucky, where we embarked for Louisville, proceeding by ship on the Ohio River because the rebels were assembled in great numbers throughout Kentucky, and we encountered one of their forces at Elizabethtown. On October 8, we had a heavy engagement with the enemy near Perryville and in what is known as the Battle of Champlain Hills after which the enemy withdrew to Tennessee. Early in December we and two other cavalry regiments, the 2nd Iowa and 9th Pennsylvania, moved from Nicolasville, Kentucky, to West Virginia and into eastern Tennessee, in order to destroy the Knoxville and Richmond Railroad. While at Murfreesboro in Tennessee our troops commanded by General William S. Rosecrans fought the rebels in the Battle of Stone River. Colonel Samuel P. Carter also was without command. We had several other engagements, and on December 31, 1802, and on January 1, 1863, took many prisoners. We also burned bridges, set fire to supply depots, and captured trains loaded with provisions. This raid lasted 26 days of which 18 were spent within enemy lines. We narrowly escaped over the Cumberland Mountains by way of Frank's Gap.

Toward the close of January 1863 we were ordered to Louisville whence we proceeded by rail to Nashville, and from there as mounted forces to

Murfreesboro where we stayed until March. Then we moved to Franklin, Tennessee, the enemy facing our forces during all of this time. We engaged in many skirmishes, including those at Spring Hill and Columbia. In July we advanced with the entire army corps known as the Army of the Cumberland and moved through the center of Tennessee, the object being to capture Chattanooga. On July 27, we fought a desperate battle at Shelbyville, captured the place, and took many prisoners. Thence we proceeded to Pollahoma and Winchester in spite of heavy rains which forced us to find shelter in the corn and cotton fields. During these nights we slept in mud and water covered fields. Finally we arrived at Bridgeport, Alabama, on the Tennessee River. At this place our cavalry forced a crossing. Our sharpshooters and artillery held back the enemy on the opposite bank while we swam for a half mile across the river. A pontoon bridge was constructed which enabled a large part of our army to cross. Next we moved upon Rome, Georgia, where we found the enemy under General James Longstreet strongly entrenched and ready for battle. Our rations at this time for the most part consisted of large sweet potatoes. Two Hollanders were taken prisoner; one of them, Albert de Groot of Vriesland, Michigan, died in Andersonville prison.

We were forced to draw back and after strenuous marches day and night, during the forenoon of September 19, arrived at the battle-field of Chickamauga where the struggle continued with fury during the following day. We were stationed on the right wing and lost many of our men. Our own right together with other cavalry forces had much difficulty when toward evening they tried to stem the retreating army and their wagon trains. The night fortunately was dark, which made their task much easier. The next forenoon we arrived at Chattanooga. The rebels next took up positions on Lookout Mountain and Missionary Ridge. Hardly had we crossed the river when the rebel cavalry under General Joseph Wheeler appeared, attacking our rear and completely destroying our wagon trains. Our army and all our cavalry pursued them and captured a few prisoners. After one of the battles I and 19 others under a flag of truce went within the enemy's lines remaining there for an hour and a half, talking and eating. Next day we again pursued them and took a few prisoners and continued following them until we approached Florence, Alabama, when we returned in the direction of McMinnville, Tennessee, and from that place by way of Kingston went to Knoxville, Tennessee, the eastern part of which was occupied by General James Longstreet. We fought many other battles in that vicinity during the fall and winter also farther east in Tennessee, among them Strawberry Plains, Mossy Creek, Sevierville, New Market, and some others.

On March 29, 1864, I re-enlisted with many others for another period of three years, or for the duration of the war. I was granted a 30 day furlough, and immediately left to visit my friends in Michigan. At the expiration of my furlough I reported for duty at Jackson, Michigan, and was ordered to Nashville. Arrived there, I was sent to Franklin where the rebel cavalry was opposing us. Our cavalry was ordered to pursue them to Huntsville, Alabama, following the course of the Tennessee River in order to intercept, if possible, the rebel army under General John B. Hood while General William T. Sherman was continuing his March to the Sea.

On October 7, 1864 I received a gunshot wound in my forehead, three inches above my right eye. I fell from my horse but was assisted to safety. My wound, cleansed and treated by a skillful regimental surgeon, healed so rapidly that in the following month I was able to report for duty in my regiment. At that time we were daily forced to retreat before the rebel army under General John B. Hood. There were many cavalry clashes until on November 30, 1864, a general engagement began in which at about 3 p.m. a musket ball passed through my left leg four inches above the ankle. Together with my good Dutch friend Martin de Groot who was slightly wounded, I rode 14 miles on horseback that same evening and lodged for the night at the home of a rich planter, quite against his wishes; but with weapons in our hands we made him see that in this case might was right. We ordered his colored slaves to bring food for us. The following morning we proceeded toward Nashville, four miles distant but experienced great difficulty in riding because of our wounds. At Nashville we surrendered our horses and were consigned to a hospital in which hundreds of soldiers were resting, who had been wounded in engagements around Franklin. The city of Nashville at this moment was surrounded by a rebel army while our forces stationed within were endeavoring to hold it.

When it became necesary to find room for more seriously wounded who were constantly being brought in, we were transferred to Louisville. After a stay of two weeks in that place it again became necessary to make room for newcomers injured in the three day battle before Nashville. I was placed on a boat destined for Keokuk, Iowa; but arriving at Cairo, Illinois, my wound assumed a most serious aspect, as gangrene was developing. I was transferred to Post Hospital, losing during the transfer all my battle mementos – a hat, socks, boots, all marked with bullet holes.

My would did not heal, in fact became worse so that it seemed that amputation might become necessary. But the splendid care I received contributed decisively to my recovery so that toward the close of March I was transferred to Detroit. I was obliged, however, to use crutches during the summer. On August 1, 1865, after the war had come to an end I received my discharge while in Harper Hospital in Detroit. Immediately after the Battle of Perryville in 1862 I had been made a corporal, and shortly thereafter was promoted to the rank of sergeant. For two weeks I remained with friends at Zeeland and vicinity, and on August 25 left for New York. I wanted to see my parents, sisters, and other relatives in The Netherlands. I arrived in Rotterdam on September 8, 1865, that day being my birthday. The next day I reached my parents' home at Noordeloos and learned that one of my brothers-in-law had passed away two days before.

I remained with my parents until the close of September and left for Hull, England, where, it had been agreed, I was to meet my parents and sister who intended to emigrate to America. We sailed from Liverpool and after a voyage of 17 days reached New York, and finally, travelling directly to Michigan, arrived at Noordeloos. I had paid all the transportation expenses of my parents, my sister, and my brother-in-law Arie Hoekwater. I at once purchased five acres of land near Noordeloos, acquired a half share in a small steam sawmill, and built a home.

My financial condition during these years, until January 1, 1866, was as follows:

September, 1854, my immigration debt	$ 56
May 1, 1855, my immigration debt	$ 56
May 1, 1856, my immigration debt	$ 36
December 1, 1856, indebtedness due me	$ 8
[This amount was never paid me]	
April 1, 1857, to Grand Rapids with cash	$ 2
September 18, 1861, when I enlisted I had about	$ 600
August 15, 1865, after discharge from service	$ 1500
October 15, 1865, after trip to the Netherlands	$ 900
April 1, 1866, after purchase of land, buying mill, and building mill, in debt	$ 200

With my own hands I constructed a grist mill in the sawmill and operated it in that same year. On February 9, 1867, the mill burned down, which left me owning only the house and parcel of land. Besides I had a debt of $ 200. On June 23 I was married and continued working as a carpenter, which trade I had once more taken up after the mill burned. But I felt I was rich although not in money or other possessions.

By this time Ottawa County was thickly settled by Hollanders, and there was much demand for farming land. Many of our people began to discuss the advisability of opening up new settlements, mention being made especially of good government lands north of Big Rapids, Michigan. There was much discussion on the subject; meetings were held, and it was decided that as I possessed more knowledge of forests and had had more experience in seeing lands, I should inspect the area proposed for settlement. Three other persons were chosen to accompany me, to serve as companions and help me in passing judgment upon the quality of the land to be visited. Early in October 1867 we started in a wagon for Big Rapids and Hersey. From Hersey we went on foot northeast on the Middle Branch and Clam rivers, investigating government land along the Clam River, which to our party appeared excellent for farming. After two weeks we returned and made our report. This task being finished, I went to Grand Haven, walking all the way, proceeded by boat to Manistee, walked from Manistee to Traverse City where on November 7, 1867, together with three other persons – the first white pepole to do so – we took up homesteads in Missaukee County. Next we traveled afoot from Grand Traverse to Missaukee County, 60 miles distant, through a dense forest without a road to follow. From there we went on foot back to Noordeloos, there being no railroad or other means of transportation in that section of the country at that time.

On October 6, 1868, with my wife and one child Derkje, my wife's brother Jakob and his sister Eiftje, Hendrik Zagers and his wife, Hendrik Westerveld, and Jan Abbing, I left for Missaukee County, using wagons as conveyance. It was not until April 18, 1869, that my family arrived at our destination after traveling twelve days in an old wagon drawn by a yoke of oxen. We arrived with two borrowed wheels, the old wagon having broken down several times during the journey. We camped along the road as we proceeded northward. We had purchased $ 30 worth of provisions in Big Rapids. When we arrived at our homestead, the south-east quarter of Section 20, Township 21 north, Range 6 West, Missaukee County, we built log shanties on our homestead property, planted some potatoes and corn, and were happy. On Sundays we met and read sermons and passages from the Bible and sang psalms. During the following fall my wife's parents and my own parents followed us and so our settlement grew. Repeatedly ,along with others, I had to travel through the woods for 60 miles to Traverse City in order to take up more land. Soon I became interested in pine lands, and frequently camped in the woods. I hired a man to cut down my forest, clear the land during the summer, and put in crops during the fall.

In 1874 I drafted a petition to organize the township of Clam Union, which proved successful, at the same time that Reeder and Riverside townships also were organized. In the spring of 1872 I was elected supervisor, justice of the peace, and highway commissioner of Clam Union Township. I also served as judge of probate in Missaukee County for a period of nine years. I was supervisor in Clam Township for nine years.

During the summer of 1872 I assessed two townships in 40 acre parcels, placing a valuation thereon for purposes of taxation according to the estimated value of the land and the pine timber on it. During the fall of that same year I assumed a lumber position, estimating two million feet of logs, but as I realized only 1,800,000 feet I made no profit. The following winter I did not follow lumbering. I rented my farm and worked on it only when my official duties permitted. During the fall of 1874 I purchased some more government and state land. The next winter I cut the pine timber standing on this new property and realized a profit. This enabled me during the following summer to open a general store with a small amount of stock. As I now owned a frame dwelling, I opened the store in our old log house. During the next winter I again engaged in lumbering, buying pine logs and selling them in Muskegon. Each winter I handled from two to five million feet of logs. During the summer of 1876 I served for two months on the jury in the United States Court at Grand Rapids. I also contracted to have a larger frame house built than the one in which we were living, steadily kept adding to my stock, and bought up produce which I resold to lumber camps.

In 1872 we organized a church community and opened a school. Both church and school were built on property I freely gave for that purpose. In 1877 I opened a store in Lake City, the county seat of Missaukee County. Soon after I sold a half interest in this store to Arlington C. Lewis, after which we worked as partners for three years. During 1878 the government authorized a post office in our settlement which now was officially called Vogel Center. The post office was officially conducted in my store. I also sold general merchandise on commission at Falmouth, five miles from Vogel Center. My agent was Dr. L. Moorhouse, but the contract I made with him came to an end after being in effect one year. I also rented and operated a saw mill at Falmouth at this time. From then, and until August 1881, my principal business was lumbering and conducting a general store. But I had also acquired a good farm consisting of about a hundred acres of cleared land. In addition I owned 45 acres of stump land sown with grass, a stock of cattle, horses, etc. During the spring of 1881 I put 5,000,000 feet of pine logs into the river, a venture in which I lost $ 3,000. This disaster was due to difficulties in floating the logs out of the West Branch of the Clam into the Muskegon River. Greatly discouraged, I gave up the lumbering business.

Northern Michigan being too far north for profitable farming, I eventually changed my residence. Early in August I left on a trip through the West and purchased 320 acres of land in Lancaster County, Nebraska, at a price of $ 8 per acre and also secured two lots in the city of Lincoln, the state capitol. I rented my store at Vogel Center, sold my horses, fourteen in all, disposed of my other stock and all chattels, rented my farm and moved to Muskegon on October 10, 1881. There I had been given a position with the firm of Torrent and Ducey at a salary of $ 1,200 a year to act as their agent in purchasing pine logs and to serve as superintendent and pay-master for the transportation of logs to their mills. During the fall of 1881 I spent five weeks in the northern part of New York where, in behalf of my employers, in Franklin County on the St. Regis River, I purchased 53,000 acres of forest for $ 130,000. When this was accomplished I returned in order to resume my duties on the Muskegon River.

On June 17, 1882, I left Muskegon for the Upper Peninsula of Michigan to purchase pine lands, and arrived at Marquette. After investigating the possibilities of lumbering in the woods nearby I returned to Muskegon where I arrived on July 13, finding my entire family afflicted with measles. My beloved child Maggie was very sick, and to out great sorrow passed away on the morning of the 16th and was buried on the 18th. Meanwhile our new house, situated at the corner of Terrace and Catawha streets, was being completed, and we moved into it on the 18th. The two lots cost $ 600, and the house and fence $ 1,900. A few days later I again left for the Lake Superior country where I stayed until September 2, purchasing for the firm of Torrent and Ducey approximately 195 million feet of standing pine for $ 110,000, part of this being government land. During the following fall I continued to buy and supervise the operations of my firm on the Muskegon River.

Gradually I sold my farm of 165 acres at Vogel Center. I was sole owner of part of this farm, in part of the rest I had a third, in the remainder only a half. I had purchased 80 acres of land from my father, Frans Vogel, when he came too old to work his farm, on the agreement that I was to furnish a home for my parents as long as they lived. Accordingly, in the spring of 1883 I built a new house for them on my farm at Vogel Center at a cost of $ 250.

On July 27, 1883, I sold my homestead farm of 160 acres to Dominie Jan Schepers at a price of $ 4,200, reserving one acre on which I had built a house for my parents, and also the land I previously had given for the church and the school. During all of that year I continued to work for Torrent and Ducey at a salary of $ 1,200, purchasing pine lands and looking after their logging operations on Muskegon River.

94. CORNELIUS STEKETEE'S
HOLLANDERS IN MUSKEGON 1850-1897

[The writer of this sketch preserved in a manuscript kept in the Netherlands Museum and first published in *Michigan History*, XXXI(1947), was born in Borsselen, the son of Jan Steketee who with his family left Zeeland in 1847 and settled in Zeeland, Michigan, during the summer of that year. Cornelius Steketee, born in 1831, took up residence in Muskegon in 1864 and died in 1899.]

The request for a paper dealing with the pioneer Hollanders of Muskegon and the progress they have made allowed me so little time that I can scarcely do justice to the subject, and so I pray that any shortcomings and omissions be kindly overlooked. I have, however, secured the names of as many of the prioneers as possible.

Until 1859 Muskegon County constituted a part of Ottawa County. In that year the state legislature organized Muskegon County, designated their village of Muskegon as its county seat. The first Hollanders there – in 1850, so far as I can ascertain – were two young ladies who worked in boarding houses. One of them married Mr. Isaac Lloyd who died some years ago. In 1850 Leonard d'Ooge served as mail carrier, making the journey on horseback all the way from Grand Rapids to Muskegon.

I am unable to learn of any other Hollanders who settled in Muskegon until the year 1856, except a man named Meyer who soon moved away. John Beukema, a Groninger, settled here in 1856. He was the father of one of the city's mail carriers. Other Hollanders who came here at that time were Izaac Brandt and his brother, Cornelius Wagenaar [or Wagener] Sr. and family, Jan Bronson, Arends Dobbema, Cornelius Hoeksema, Maarten Penny, A. Slaghuis, Egbert N. van Balen [also spelled Baalen], Pieter Hofman, Aart van Arendonk, Cornelius Achterom, and some others. This was the advance guard of a steady stream of Dutch immigrants to Muskegon, so numerous that at the present time they constitute a quarter or more of our population of between 22,000 and 28,00. During the earlier days there were six sawmills in Muskegon, and employment was easy to secure. There was no railroad leading to Muskegon, and as the roads to Grand Haven and Grand Rapids were newly made and impassable, travel was mostly on foot. But as the population grew and industry became more important, boats began to operate and stage lines were established so that travel became easier. The stage lines to Grand Haven and Grand Rapids were succeeded by railroads. At present Muskegon has three railroads.

Opportunity to work attracted the industrious Dutch immigrant. Nearly all of the first comers were poor laboring men who depended on their daily labor for a living. They saved some of their earnings which enabled them to send for relatives and friends in the Old Country. Three-fourths of our Dutch citizens, it is estimated, originally came from the province of Groningen. A devout Christian people, the first arrivals never forgot to worship God. They met in the house of Cornelius Wagenaar Sr., who with A. Slaghuis and Egbert N. van Balen, read sermons and gave edifying discourses.

At first from seven to ten families attended such meetings. But they were dissatisfied with this inadequate church life, and so took steps to organize a conrgegation. This was accomplished in June 1859 when at a preliminary meeting, Dominie Pieter J. Oggel, in behalf of the Reformed Church, presided. Thus was inaugurated the first Holland Reformed Church of Muskegon. Klaas Zuidema en Jan de Haas were chosen elders, Izaac Brandt and G. Nanninga, deacons. In August 1863 a call was issued to Dominie W. A. Houbolt of Albany, New York, who accepted and arrived in May 1864. Soon a small church structure was erected on Spring Street on the spot occupied by the present church of the same congregation.

Other congregations gradually came into existence. The First Christian Reformed congregation was founded in 1867, Dominie Leendert Rietdijk serving as its pastor from 1870 till 1872. A second congregation was organized in 1887 of which Dominie Andreas Keizer served as pastor from 1888 till 1891. The rapid growth of the Christian Reformed group necessitated the organization of a third congregation, which was effected in 1889, Dominie Pieter Kosten serving as pastor from 1889 till 1892. Meanwhile the membership of the Reformed church grew more slowly so that a new congregation, the Second Reformed, was not organized until 1891 when Dominie Gerrit H. Hospers came as its first pastor.

Each of these five congregations possesses a commodious church building and also an excellent parsonage.

Muskegon was a kind of mecca for poor people seeking labor, which they readily found in the sawmills. Thus Willem Moerdijk during his vacations while a student at Hope College, as well as other students, came to Muskegon to earn some money with which to prosecute their studies. Everybody who wanted work got it and at good wages. The sawmills increased in number until there were as many as thirty-four or thirty-six. Some of the Hollanders organized as crews to load boats with lumber at a fixed rate per hour and per boat. Such workers earned as much as $ 5 or $ 6 per day, but this kind of work was not very steady. It happened frequently that there were no vessels in the harbor for them to load and so they would be idle. During these earlier days lumber was carried to Chicago in sailing ships. Later barges took their place whereupon fewer of the Hollanders found employment in loading lumber and their wages also went down. As the number of laborers increased, work became more and more difficult to procure, and wages steadily tended to be reduced. The laborers, not being accustomed to work with machinery because most of them had come from farms in the Old Country, frequently met with accidents. Some were killed, some suffered fractures of arms or legs, others lost fingers, etc.

One horrible accident occured a few years ago. Someone had invented the refuse burner and one of these devices was erected near one of the mills. Pieces of bark, sawdust, and other waste were brought to it from all parts of the mill by an endless belt. So hot was the fire in the burner that it burned everything no matter how wet or green it might be. The son of Albert Doornbos fell into this fire and was burned alive in a few minutes. The father met with a second misfortune when, a year or two later, his wife died, being struck by lightning.

The Hollanders who settled in Muskegon were hardworking, industrious, and economical. Through faithful work and careful saving, they soon had some dollars laid up for a rainy day. Soon many a Hollander who formerly seemed fit only to labor in sawmills opened grocery stores, boot and shoe stores, meat markets, and other businesses. One firm deserves special mention. Johannes and Adriaan Mulder, now dead, erected a large brick block on the corner of Pine and Myrtle streets. They came from the Old County without any money, worked in a lathmill and after a while opened a grocery store. A big fire swept away their wooden buildings along with those of many other people. But in a few days after this misfortune they took heart and began to erect the splendid brick structure just mentioned. John A. Tinholt now occupies one of the stores, dealing in drugs; the Van der Made sisters, Effie, Mattie, and Orpha, assist their father, William van der Made, in a millinery enterprise; and Charles Brower, a son-in-law of Johannes Mulder and dealer in insurance, occupies a room in the building. Another block, on the corner of Spring and Myrtle streets, built by Gerrit Wagener [Wagner], a son of Cornelius Wagenaar Sr., is used as a grocery by Martin Knoeihuizen.

To give the names of all the Hollanders engaged in some business would, however, require too much space and time. As near as I can ascertain, the Hollanders at the present moment are operating at least twenty-four grocery stores, some of which are doing an extensive business; eight or ten meat markets; two drugstores; one dry goods store; and two or three handle dry goods along with groceries. I myself had a large boot and shoe shop, but there also were two or three smaller boot and shoe businesses in Muskegon. Two or three Hollanders are in the hardware business. The firms of John Boersema and Company and Karel and Dekker Company occupy their own buildings, which are constructed of brick. Two large furniture stores are operated by Hollanders, one by John D. van der Werp, another by Nicholas G. van der Linde. A third and smaller is owned by George D. van der Werp. Three of four of our Dutch countrymen are in the flour and feed business, two having gristmills, two are conducting ladies' furnishing goods establishments, Henry D. Baker [formerly spelled Bakker] has a large bookstore and owns the brick block in which his business is housed, and Arend and Andrew Cloetingk have a bookbindery. William J. Steketee is half owner of one of our daily papers in connection with which he operates a book and job printing and bookbinding establishment. Several Hollanders have barbershops; three are in the undertaking business; Henry E. Langeland owns a planing mill and box factory, does an extensive business; and many of our people earn their livelihood in his mill. John Lankheet operates a large bakery in a splendid brick block which he owns. Two or three others are engaged in the same business but on a smaller scale. At present there are four physicians among our Dutch people; John van der Laan, Henry S. Baron, Rynsberg, and Jacob Oosting.

That the Hollanders in Muskegon have enjoyed the respect of their neighbors who are not of Dutch descent is shown by the fact that the latter have helped to elect many of them to public office. Martin Waalkes served three years as mayor, was county treasurer for two years, and also was deputy county treasurer. Others to hold office were: John Hulst, city recorder; Alice Brandt, assistent city recorder, for several years; Benjamin H. Telman [Tellman], city weighmaster; Henry J. van Zalingen, county treasurer; Egbert N. van Balen, John de Haas, Izaac Brandt, John H. Banninga, Johannes Mulder, and Cornelius Steketee, directors of the poor. The following holding office at the present moment among the Dutch are: Dr. John van der Laan, member of the board of education; Leonard Eyke, city treasurer; John D. van der Werp and Cornelius Karel, superviors; William Bierema, alderman; John van der Werp, judge of probate; and Nicholas G. van der Linde, coroner. Peter Mulder and Charles J. Beukema have responsible positions in the post office.

In June 1874 Muskegon was visited by a disastrous fire, but the part of the city occupied by the Hollanders escaped destruction. Nevertheless, a number of our people lost thier homes and businesses. A second extensive fire occurred in 1891 when a large number lost their homes and stores. Among the buildings destroyed was the First Christian Reformed Church on Terrace Street, but it was speedily replaced by a brick church and parsonage.

Our Dutch people, coming as they did in most cases from the farm lands of the Old Country, were not satisfied with life in the ity. Many a Hollander moved out of town, bought some land, and began to raise vegetables for city consumption. Chief among these was Julien Bierema, who inaugurated celery farming in the environs of Muskegon. Beginning on a small scale, he proved that this was a profitable enterprise, and gradually extended his business. Others followed his example and at present about fifteen Hollanders are engaged in this lucrative activity. Not only is celery raising profitable for the farmers but it provides steady labor for a large number of our people. The enterprising Hollander can prove to our American brethren that low land is good for something provided it is properly managed. Formerly these lands were regarded as good for nothing and could be purchased for a song. But all this has changed. Today Muskegon celery enjoys a good market in Chicago and other cities, and this season [1897] many carloads are being shipped as far as New York.

During the early days of Muskegon's existence, when Hollanders first began to settle here, the city was an excellent market for butter, eggs, and all sorts of provisions. Several Hollanders who lived in Grand Haven and Holland and owned sailing vessels made regular trips to Muskegon. But their profitable business was cut short when the railroads came to Muskegon and the surrounding country became settled by farmers.

In education our people have always shown keen interest. They send their children to the public schools. If they want them to learn the Dutch language, parents send them to the Christian schools.

North Muskegon also attracted Dutch settlers. At present three Hollanders are engaged in business in this suburb of Muskegon: John Dyk, dealer in flour and feed; and James E. Balkema and John Balkema, dealers in general merchandise. These men are doing a profitable business and own their own store buildings. John Balkema is the present mayor of North Muskegon.

95. JOSIAS MEULENDYKE'S
DUTCH SETTLEMENT NORTH OF MUSKEGON 1867-1897

[Meulendyke, born in Rochester, New York, in 1849, was ordained to the ministry in the Reformed Church and served as pastor in a number of the congregations north of Muskegon and Grands Rapids. His account, written in 1897 and preserved in manuscript kept in the Netherlands Museum, was first published in *Michigan History*, XXXI (1947).]

The writer of the following sketch disclaims any special qualification for the work allotted to him. Although as classical home missionary in Michigan closely identified with the localities in northern Michigan for a year or two, he has in no sense been a pioneer. Hence he must depend upon the observation and experience of others quite as much as upon his own. He wishes to acknowledge his indebtedness to the following individuals: Domine Jan Hoekje, of Fremont, Michigan; Mr. Hendrik de Bree, of Vogel Center; Dominie Herman van der Ploeg, of New Era; Jan Scholten, of Lucas; and Dominie Willem Pool, of Atwood.

It is a curious fact in the history here under review that when, thirty or twenty years ago, new schemes of colonization were agitated among our Holland people of Michigan, the remote south and far west of the United States found greater favor than the near north. This appears particularly striking when we reflect that the Dutch colonies in southern Michigan had passed the experimental stage of their existence, and pioneer life in the north, though in many ways similar, could hardly prove to be as difficult as it had been in the south. But the lonely woods and virgin soil of northern Michigan were bound to attract the attention of the Hollanders living in the Dutch colonies of Michigan. And so today the Dutch settler in the north asserts his kinship with the Dutch colonists to the south. But the mention of kinship suggests a striking difference. The colonies of Hollanders in Ottawa and adjacent counties grew up under special circumstances. Some were planted close together and so in the course of a few years formed compact settlements. On the other hand, some of the larger settlements are offshoots of earlier Dutch colonies. The settlements of northern Michigan, however, sprang up independently of each other, ans so no two of the colonies mentioned in this article bear the relation of mother and daughter. Except as they resemble each other somewhat, because of common social, geographic, and economic factors, no two are sisters of each other. In point of territorial separation also they are remotely related.

The honor of priority in the forming of these new Dutch settlements belongs to Fremont, formerly known as Fremont Center, situated in Newaygo County on the Chicago and West Michigan Railroad.

The first Hollander to settle in those parts was Frank Boone, formerly a resident of Muskegon. Making his way through the woods, he arrived at his destination in August 1867. At that time, what now is the flourishing town of Fremont had scarcely attained the minor dignity of a hamlet. Three weeks later he was followed by Cornelius Addison, a Zeelander it is believed, and J. Wieringa, also from Muskegon. People of other nationalities had already settled in this region, and so the Hollanders who now arrived profited from their example and made this colonization a success.

At this time the lumber industry of Muskegon was in a flourishing condition, giving employment to a large number of Hollanders. Many of these longed to exchange their lot for the more independent one of the farmer. As there was a considerable amount of land around Fremont obtainable at reasonable prices, it was natural that those Hollanders who had already settled there should inform their friends and relatives in Muskegon about opportunities at Fremont. So it came to pass that soon after the three men just mentioned had established themselves others bought land and moved to Fremont. Among them the first were Abel Kuizinga, Aart van Arendonk, Cornelius Achterom, and Klaas Zuidema, all of whom were Groningers. In course of time, as the settlement attracted the attention of people living in older Dutch communities, many others arrived and cast their lot with the pioneers of Newaygo County. Their ranks were further swelled by immigrants who came directly from the Old Country. And so within a few years Fremont increased in population and material prosperity.

True to their traditions, these Hollanders did not delay to provide for themselves public worship in their own tongue and after their own desires. In the first meeting called for this purpose on March 3, 1869, a congregation was formed. Dominie W. A. Houbolt, pastor of the First

Reformed Church of Muskegon, directed the services. Their faith in the future of their settlement and their desire to lead Christian lives is revealed by the fact that in that very meeting it was decided to petition the Classis of Michigan of the Reformed Church to effect an organization in the near future. This was achieved on June 14, 1869, when seven adults and seventeen communicants agreed to this step. Dominie Mannes Kiekintveld was the first pastor. But ecclesiastical strife and denominational rivalry made themselves felt here as elsewhere. A Christian Reformed congregation was formed in 1882 of which Jacob Noordewier served as the first pastor. A second church of the same denomination had been formed some six miles southwest of Fremont.

Although all improved land, which sells at about $ 40 per acre or less in the vicinity of Fremont, is in the hands of farmers, land held by people not of Dutch origin is constantly being offered for sale and bought by Hollanders. As the Hollanders already have a share in the business enterprises, it is clear that the Holland settlement at Fremont has not yet reached its limits. The Dutch population at Fremont now numbers from 250 to 300 families.

Next in order of settlement is Vogel Center. This flourishing community is situated in Missaukee County about one hundred miles nearly due north of Grand Rapids. The nearest railroad station is McBain on the Toledo, Ann Arbor, and Northern Railroad, eight miles due west. In 1868 a number of individuals in the mother colony who desired more room for themselves were attracted to desirable lands in northern Michigan available as homesteads. In that year Jan Vogel, Hendrik Westvelt, and Jan Zager set out to view this country. Soon they were followed by Vogel's brother-in-law, Gerrit Herweijer, Jan Abbing, and Fred Banis, an unmarried man who ultimately went blind and returned to the Old Country. Satisfied with what they had observed, they secured claims in this land of promise. On their return they interested others and so in the spring of 1869 the axes of Dutch pioneers resounded in the lonely woods of Missaukee County. Without any railroad connection with Holland or Grand Rapids, travel to Missaukee County was possible only in ox wagons along primitive roads cut through trackless forests.

The giants of the forests had to be converted into logs before shelters could be built. Clearings had to be made with great labor before a scanty harvest could be coaxed from the soil. For supplies, Grand Rapids was the Egypt most accessible whence anxious Jacobs could secure supplies for their families. The settlers at Vogel Center experienced frontier hardship like those of the colonists of Ottawa County.

Many a homemaker, fearing the privations of the forests and the heavy labor necessary to clear the land, was frightened away from Michigan. But these very forests have proved the salvation of many an enterprise. Where the soil is slow to yield grass and grain, trees abundantly make up for this deficiency. The ax in winter brought better results than the plow in summer. And the lumber camps, which always hovered in the forests along the edge of new settlements in northern Michigan, afforded better markets for farm produce than the cities and villages of communities that had passed out of the pioneer stage.

These considerations also apply to the pioneers of Vogel Center. Although at first dependent for supplies upon Grand Rapids, they were not dependent upon that city for markets. The rivers that carried their logs to distant sawmills in Muskegon frequently were a source of greater return than the railroads. The farther these settlers were removed from railroads the better prices they received for their produce. And so the colony prospered, for new settlers kept coming and the Dutch settlement expanded on every side.

Thus Falmouth, four and a half miles northwest of Vogel Center and on Clam River, a branch of the Muskegon, came into existence. It has a general store, sawmill, and church. Moddersville, a place five and a half miles northeast of Vogel Center, was founded by Wynand Modders. He emigrated from the Old Country in 1872 that his two oldest sons might avoid military service. A butcher by trade, he lived in Harlingen in Friesland. For five years he ran a grocery in Grand Rapids and in 1877 settled on a homestead of pine and hardwood timberland. Their first home was a log shanty fourteen by twenty-two feet which could scarcely accomodate their large family, originally of seventeen children, some of whom, however, no longer were with their parents. Modders became the community's first postmaster in 1890. In these newly founded settlements life is more primitive than in Vogel Center. The Americans usually vie with the Hollanders in securing possession of such good land as might be found in the community. Between Falmouth and Moddersville lies East Falmouth [later Prosper], center of a growing farming community on good farming land, where a church building and parsonage lend some dignity to the country.

The first church, of the Christian Reformed denomination, at Vogel Center was formed in 1872. In 1877 the Christian Reformed people built a church which still serves as their place of worship. In 1870 Dominie Mannes Kiekintveld of the Reformed Church had preached at Vogel Center and administered baptism but his labors were without results for the Reformed Church. But finally, in 1890, a Reformed congregation was organized, followed in 1891 by two others, one at Falmouth and another at Moddersville. At present these three churches are served by the same pastor, who resides at Falmouth where a parsonge has been built for him.

About two hundred families constitute the population of Vogel Center. The unimproved land of that community, though extensive, is worthless for farming; and as only few of the farms admit of division, it would appear that Vogel Center will soon reach the limits of its population, though not of its wealth.

New Era, a Dutch settlement in Oceana County near the shore of Lake Michigan about thirty miles northwest of Muskegon on the Chicago and West Michigan Railroad, was founded in 1878. With but one exception, all its first settlers came from Montague, a lumber town a few miles to the south, where they were employed as mill hands. The only exception is Meus Hulsebos, whose record as a pioneer deserves special notice. He began his frontier life near Zeeland in Ottawa County. Later he joined Dominie Albertus C. van Raalte, Mrs. Sprik, and others in the Virginia enterprise and settled at Chule in that state. Failing where so few succeeded, he returned with the scant remains of his investment and settled in New Era, where he is living at the present time. The names of the other first settlers are Hendrik Westveld, Berend van den Berg, Otto Bolt, Herman van der Ven, and Frank Veltman.

At first the land, much of which was of a good quality, was cheap. There was a ready market for logs, kiln wood, and bark so that the colony grew rapidly, encouraged by some emigration from the Old Country. At the present moment this community comprises eighty-five families. Further, New Era is situated in the fruit belt of Michigan, and the Hollanders were not slow to take advantage of this activity, which they saw would ultimately prevail. Many Hollanders own large peach orchards. Improved land at present is worth from $ 25 to $ 40 per acre.

As soon as the first log houses were built, religious services were held in the Dutch language. Hulsebos was the leader of these people, a pioneer exhorter common enough among our pioneer Hollanders. Later, when the question of church affiliation came up, the majority were inclined to join the Christian Reformed Church, and an organization was effected in 1884. Later, in 1894, because of differences in this congregation, a Reformed church was organized.

Lucas, situated in the southwest corner of Missaukee County and extending into Wexford County to the west, was founded in 1882, fourteen years after Vogel Center. It lies six miles southeast of Cadillac, a handsome city with which it is connected by the Toledo, Ann Arbor, and Northern Railroad.

First to establish temselves in this locality were Harm Lucas and his sons Abraham, Dick, Simon, Henry, and Thomas; Hendrik Koel; Jan Loeks; Ralph van Wieren; Jan Slaar; Hendrik Klomparens; Jan Harm Pel; Jan Bode; and Horace Doll. Harm Lucas and his group all came from Graafschap, being driven by the desire for more room and for cheap land. They were followed soon after by Jan H. Eppink from Allegan, Jan Scholten from Overisel, Josua Elenbaas from Beaverdam, and Pieter van den Bosch from Zeeland.

Nearness to Cadillac proved advantageous from the start of the settlement, especially when the railroad was extended through the settlement. This quickened the hopes of the settlers, roused their energies; and soon the whistle of a sawmill and the sound of a shingle mill rose in the silent forest. Dwellings were erected near the railroad station, and the local merchant began to compete with this neighbors in Cadillac. But progress has been unsteady, and Lucas never became more than a hamlet. On the other hand, the farmer who at times worked in the woods improved his condition. Accordingly, land which originally sold at $ 7 an acre improved until at the present time it sells at about $ 20. The total number of Dutch families in Lucas is between 150 and 200. The oldest church organization is Christian Reformed, but a Reformed Church was organized in 1890.

Finally the last Dutch settlement in northern Michigan that remains to be noticed is Atwood in Antrim County about two hundred miles north of Grand Rapids, a few miles west from Central Lake, and a station on the Chicago and West Michigan Railroad. This, the northernmost Dutch settlement east of the Mississippi, was begun in 1882 and 1883. Some of the Hollanders living near Jamestown in Ottawa County were attracted to this land of promise. The first to move to Antrim County were Maarten van der Schouw, Jan Smallegang, Jellies Elzinga, Jacob Klooster, Melle Klooster, Jan Boss, Matthias Struik, Hendrik Wassenaar, and Egbert van der Streek.

As in the case of Fremont, the Hollanders were not the first pioneers in these parts, for other people had preceded them in settling this region. Nevertheless plenty pioneer experiences were in store for them. In Antrim situated far to the north, the winters were long and severe, summers short and cool. But the new settlement offered opportunities, especially in raising apples. Further, the air is bracing and malaria is absent. The Hollanders, now approximately fifty families, accordingly prospered;

improved land is now valued from $ 30 to $ 40 per acre. Religious services were first held in 1886, and a Reformed Church was oragnized three years later.

96. BENJAMIN TELMAN'S
HOLLANDERS IN MUSKEGON POLITICS, 1872-1914

[Telman served as city recorder and treasurer of Muskegon and was thoroughly conversant with Muskegon politics and especially with the part Hollanders had in it. This sketch was taken from *Muskegon Chronicle*, April 9, 1914.]

The pleasing duty has been assigned to me to give a little history on Holland politics in Muskegon County.

Three men of the Dutch race have been elected mayor of Muskegon and altogether served the city for nine out of the forty-four years since Muskegon was incorporated. So practically one-fifth of the period during which Muskegon has been a city, Holland mayors have filled the office. It speaks well for the Holland mayors that each of them served more than one term. Martin Waalkes, who was elected in 1888, officiated for three terms. Leonard Eyke was elected twice and Harry Rietdyk broke the record of service in the city by winning in four successive contests. Charles van der Linde was defeated in the race for the office of mayor in 1898 by Ansel F. Temple, and you all remember the "Dutch race" between Rietdyk and Mr. Langeland.

Up to 1872, the Hollanders of Muskegon do not seem to have had any ambition along political lines although they were quite numerous and many had become naturalized. Egbert van Balen, well known to the older members of this society, was the pioneer candidate of our race in Muskegon. Van Balen was an old resident and I think followed the occupation of tallyman. It was in 1872 that he was elected director of the poor, a position he filled for several terms. Isaac Brandt was the next Hollander who was entrusted with a local office, having been elected director of the poor in 1874. Brandt filled this place for several terms. He was one of the early Dutch settlers and was popular with all nationalities. John de Haas, one of the few survivors of the genuine pioneer element of the city and for close to half a century engaged in business, was made poor director in 1878. He also served for several years. John Banninga, now deceased, was elected to this office during the palmy days of the Workingman's Party in 1883. Since the time that poor directors have been appointed instead of elected, several Hollanders have had charge of the city's poor. Among them have been John Boersema, Cornelius Steketee, Johannes Mulder, and the present incumbent, Benjamin Pekelder.

One of the live wires of the early Dutch colony was John Bronson. He was an agressive politician, active in the ranks of the Democratic party for many years. Bronson was one of the first flour and feed merchants of the city. At one time his store was in a warehouse near where the People's Milling Company's plant is located and afterwards on Western Avenue where the Goldberg grocery is now located. Bronson was the first of a long line of Holland-American aldermen and he was elected forty years ago this spring. He was elected from the first ward, which then included all of the city east of Pine Street. In 1878 Bola Borgman, who a few years before purchased the Sissing grocery at the corner of Myrtle and Spring streets, was elected one of the aldermen from the first ward. Borgman held this office off and on for several years and during his lifetime was an influential man in politics. He was also supervisor from the second ward in 1890.

In those days it was a great personal triumph for a Dutchman to win a seat in the city council, but the Hollanders were modest in urging their personal claims and it was not until 1883 that the next of our nationality won a seat in the city's parliament, when Martin Waalkes began his political career. Afterwards he was county treasurer as well as mayor. In 1912-13 his son, Bert Waalkes, was alderman from the sixth ward, covering much of the territory of the old third ward, which his father once represented. Many important public improvements were carried out during the years Waalkes was mayor and alderman. When he was alderman, the council definitely abandoned sawdust and plank as paving materials and really began the attempt permanently to improve the thoroughfares of the city. Waalkes is known as the father of the Lake Michigan Waterworks system, which began during his incumbency as mayor. In 1888 Willem S. Bos was elected alderman from the second Ward and Peter Hoeksema from the third ward. Hoeksema was a cigarmaker and a son of a pioneer Hollander, Ky Hoeksema, who died not long ago. Two years later, two more Hollanders broke into the city council. They were Peter Battema, elected from the second, and Cornelius de Young from the fourth ward. De Young later moved to Allegan County, where he is conducting a large grocery store. Charles van der Linde for the first time appeared as alderman from the eighth ward in 1891. He has since been elected to represent this ward several times. My father, Henry B. Telman, was elected alderman from the second ward in 1893. He had previously been elected supervisor from the second ward in 1891.

The same year Paul Tanis acquired the habit of running for supervisor and getting elected; this feat he performs every few years so as to keep in practice. G. H. Banning was elected alderman from the sixth ward in 1894, but Siebolt Temple and Rentje Hyma found 1984 a bad year to run, both suffering defeat. However, 1901 was a year in which the people showed partiality to Holland supervisors and Temple was elected, as also were Benjamin Pekelder and John D. van der Werp, who represented the second and fifth wards respectively for the two following years on the county board. Several years before this, in 1885, John D. van der Werp served his apprenticeship as supervisor. Mr. Van Balen was his colleague from the fifth ward. At the next election, Henry D. Baker [Bakker] was elected supervisor of the same ward. The same year J. D. van der Werp became county coroner for the first time. Henry Langeland escaped the honor of representing the fifth ward as supervisor by a narrow margin in 1893. Arend Cloetingh, a prioneer bookbinder, was active in politics for a long time and was elected supervisor of the third ward in 1894. The same year Julle Bierma, afterwards county road commissioner, captured the affections of the second ward and became one of its aldermen; while Harry Klont won the aldermanship contest in the third ward. Gerrit Bomers proved his ability as political sprinter in 1902 by a successful race for alderman of the second ward on the Democratic ticket; a feat which Chris Nife had previously accomplished.

In 1902 Harry Rietdyk began to prove his ability to win votes. That year he was elected alderman from the fifth ward and two years afterward he was elected by an increased majority. In the fall of 1902, Rietdyk made a notable run for county treasurer. Before he was elected mayor, in 1903, Leonard Eyke had served several terms as city treasurer. He made his first race for city mayor in 1888 but lost by a norraw margin of seventy-four votes. In 1891 he was elected, defeating his countryman, John D. van der Werp. John Torrent, defeated him for mayor the following year. In 1895, 1897, 1899, and 1901 Van der Werp was elected treasurer. Peter Zuidema made an effort to win the treasurership in 1903, and Rinder Cooper [Kuiper] was successful in 1913.

Benjamin G. Oosterbaan began dispensing justice and awarding fines and incidentally supplying our friend Beukema with material for romances and history in 1903. Twice since then he was re-elected, once defeating our assistant prosecutor, Christian A. Broek.

Getting elected alderman or supervisor has become quite a popular diversion among Holland-Americans during recent years. Before he became absorbed in the livestock industry or in the art of raising crowing and clucking machines, Joseph Bouwsma served as alderman of the second ward. Walter van Dam, the present popular night sergeant at police head-quarters, also was alderman for a term. Previous to his emigration to Muskegon Township, Robert Douma represented the third ward, now the stronghold of Alderman Peter Kemp. Henry J. Katz was alderman from the sixth ward until Bert Waalkes interfered, Mitchell Brown of the second and Edward M. Langeland of the fifth ward make, with Alderman Kemp, a trio of Holland-American city fathers at present. Nicholas G. van der Linde served as alderman of the fifth ward before Langeland. He has also been a coroner.

Among recent supervisors have been Gerrit Cooper of the sixth ward; Ralph Buitendorp and the present supervisor of the second ward, Edward Kolkema; John Damminga of the sixth ward; Harm Wagner of the third ward; and Fred Winter of the fifth ward; Tiede Clock was once supervisor of the second ward and also served as county coroner.

Your humble servant had a Holland-American predecessor as recorder in the person of John Hulst, now of Grand Rapids. Hulst was elected in 1884 and served one term. Our esteemed ex-president, John A. Tinholt, was defeated for the recorder's post by postmaster Schnorbach in 1894. Peter Zuidema was a candidate in 1906. I was elected in 1908. This year I had the honor of having two Hollanders as opponents, Menno de Witt and John W. Schuitema.

Henry van Zalingen was elected county treasurer in 1890.

In Muskegon Heights, Alexander van Zanten has served several years as recorder, and in the county, John van der Werp was twice elected judge of probate. Van der Werp was also state senator. Peter Wenting is the present representative of the county in the state legislature. I notice that a Holland-American, William Bos, has just been elected supervisor of Muskegon Township, and another, Nicholas van der Velde, won the race for the supervisor's office in Sullivan.

Dr. John van der Laan and John van der Werp are members of the school board.

Judging from the manner in which some of the younger generation of Knickerbockers are getting to the front in the House of Representatives and other forums it will not be many years before the descendants of the Dutch immigrant workingman who made the sawmill owners of Muskegon rich and famous will be shooting for bigger political game than is found around the courthouse, city hall, or even at Lansing, the state capital.

[The writer of this sketch who lived all her life in the Atwood Dutch community penned this contribution in 1941 shortly before her death. It was first published in *Michigan History*, XXXI(1947).]

The sound of wagon wheels grinding steadily over dusty trails, bumping over corduroy roads, splashing into mudholes became quite common in this part of Northern Michigan in the early 1880's. The occupants of such a wagon might have been a young man and woman seated upon two or three boxes containing all their wordly goods. A few hours before they very likely had arrived by train at Traverse City or Mancelona. Weary and worn by the many days' journey from the Netherlands and a several days' train trip from New York City, how good it would have seemed to have rested for a day or two! Why had they come? Money was scarce and land here was very cheap. Should they stay down in the Dutch settlements farther south, the only work for many of them might be that of hired help to other farmers. On the other hand, perhaps some relative or friend had come up to this territory before them and had written in glowing terms of the country, the springs, and the lakes.

In most cases, however, months of hard labor passed before the dreams of a home were realized. The log cabin of the friend or relative became their home, while laboriously a small piece of land was cleared. Wood was worthless – $ 3 a thousand – and cases are cited of offers made to neighboring lumber companies in which they might have the lumber free of charge, cut from the land the companies would clear; and such offers were refused. Not knowing what else to do, the pioneers piled the logs and brush high and burned them.

By the year 1886 several clearings had been made and new families were moving in quite regularly. They felt one handicap greatly, the distance to church. Many families walked the four or five miles to the church in Atwood, for on Sunday, if at all possible, they must be in the House of the Lord. Feeling the need of weekday services, in which they might present to Him their prayers and petitions, a new type of meeting was begun, upon which we may surely believe God looked with gladness of heart. Many of the settlers of the community, Dutch and English alike, gathered at the little schoolhouse on the corner every Thursday evening and despite handicaps of language and difference of denomination, together brought their prayers and petitions before the throne of Grace. This is the way an attendant, who lives in Kalamazoo, describes it: We had good times in those olden days when that good man of God,

Martin van der Schouw, led in prayer – meetings to the glory of God. After reading and explaining a portion of Scripture he led us in prayer. Then everybody who wanted to pray or testify could do so. The audience in the old schoolhouse consisted of Reformed, Christian Reformed, Methodists, Presbyterians, etc., but they were united around the Cross of Calvary. The road to the meeting place was not so smooth as it is these days. We drove in ox wagons, came over drifting logs, through marsh and swamp. It happened some nights that there were more mosquitoes in the schoolhouse than people, but I for one must confess, that afterwards we could say, "It was good for us to be there, for the Lord was in our midst."

As the Dutch settlers arrived in the community, the talk of organizing a church became common. More children were coming, and the walk was almost too much for them. How wonderful it would be to have a church in the community which would make possible regular Sunday services for all the members of the family. Finally, in 1889 the request for organization was made and heard by the Grand River Classis and on September 10, a committee composed of Rev. Egbert Winter and Rev. Henry P. de Pree were sent. Eight families joined together as a nucleus of the church on that memorable night – the families of Jakob Klooster, Herman Potter, Melle Klooster, Henry Wassenaar, Corneil Sprick, Gerrit Dykstra, John Adema, John Bos, Jakob Klooster, and Henry Klooster joined on confession of faith. Two elders and two deacons were elected, and it was decided that the church should be called the Atwood Reformed Church.

They had no pastor to guide them or to preach to them but they were united in spirit so that the church progressed under its consistory. Communion services were held once or twice a year, when an ordained minister could visit the church. One can imagine how they looked forward to partaking of the Lord's Supper.

In May 1893 the services of elder William Wormser were accepted by the church. In that year the present church property was purchased and a fence was placed around it. It was rented to Mr. Groenink for hay for $ 8.25. There was a discussion concerning buying the Presbyterian church at Atwood, tearing it down, and rebuilding it, but it was found that this was impossible. In 1894 it was decided to build a church in the following year. Each member was requested to pledge what he could in lumber or money. The Board of Domestic Missions of the Reformed Church in America aided financially so that in the fall of 1895 Gerrit Vyn was given the task of building the church for $ 375. A good foundation was necessary; Henry Wassenaar and Mr. Groenink were appointed to provide it.

After the building was completed, a stove was to have been placed in the auditorium. Two visitors from the Woman's Board of Domestic Missions offered to furnish the sum needed for a furnace. Each family was asked to furnish a cord of wood if possible.

In November 1896 Mr. Wormser moved to South Barnard and on February 10, 1897, Rev. Willem Pool of Grand Rapids was called. He became the first ordained pastor to serve the church. The house on the Moore property was rented for two years.

On the twenty-fourth of June 1897 several women of the congregation met and, under the direction of the pastor, organized a ladies' missionary society. The members of the first society were: Mrs. Willem Pool, Mrs. Alle Brower, Mrs. Henry van der Jacht, Mrs. Melle Klooster, Mrs. John Adema, Mrs. John Bos, Mrs. Albert van der Jacht, Mrs. Henry Wassenaar, Mrs. Bouke de Young, Mrs. Harm Potter, Mrs. Corneil Sprick.

By 1893 the church had grown to forty families, with sixty-two partaking of Communion, and 146 baptized non-communicants. Seventy persons were enrolled in the Sunday School. In 1898 the parsonage property was purchased by the church and in 1900 the horse barns were built at the rear of the church. In July 1902 the Rev. Willem Pool left for Kalamazoo, having served the church faithfully for five years.

A senior from the Western Theological Seminary in Holland, Michigan, Bernard J. van Heuvelen, worked in the church during that summer, and in the fall of 1902, was called to serve as pastor. In the next year, through the aid of the Board of Domestic Missions, an organ was procured for the church. So happy were the members with this acquisition that a dedication service was held. Besides the address of the pastor, the Ladies Aid Members sang, "Er Ruist Langs de Wolken een Liefelijke Naam." They sang without the accompaniment of the organ, as was their custom, but one of the members recalls that the singers did stay in tune, so the new organ was doubly appreciated. Two young ladies, relatives of the pastor, sang a duet in the English language, to which the listeners were entirely unaccustomed. The beauty and the message of "The Bird with the Broken Wing" is still remembered.

Soon after this the young people felt that the church should have a bell and they collected enough money to purchase the bell that still calls us to worship.

During the ministry of the Rev. Van Heuvelen, a group of ten families moved to Lynden, Washington, and another group of eleven families were organized as a separate church at South Barnard. Thus in the spring of 1908, the church could report only thirty-six families, where previously there had been fifty-five families. At the time this seemed a serious reverse to the growth of the church, but those who remained united their efforts in regaining spiritual ground. In the fall of 1908 the Rev. Van Heuvelen left to make his pastorate at Rotterdam, Kansas.

In July 1909 the church asked Elder B. Burgraff to take over leadership of the organization. He served the church ably until 1912 when Rev. C. W. Deelsnyder was called.

In 1914 the Rev. Arie van den Heuvel became pastor of the church and served until December 14, 1916. Upon his departure he requested that Mr. Nicholas de Young serve as superintendent of the Sunday school, which position Mr. De Young served faithfully for over twenty years.

In 1916 it was decided to have English services once each month. The envelope system was also adopted at this time that those who desired might give systematically to the work of the Kingdom.

On April 23, 1917, Rev. John Wybenga came as pastor. Under his pastorate the choir had its beginning, with Mrs. James van den Berg, Mrs. H. van der Ark, Mrs. Nicholas de Young, Miss. Rose Klooster, Mr. Richard de Young, Mr. Nicholas de Young, Mr. P. Goonan, Mr. Alex Klooster, and Mrs. Gerrit Klooster were some of its members.

In September 1920 Rev. Wybenga left for Clifton, New Jersey, and in October 1921 the Rev. Paul Schroeder came to take his place. On July 20, 1923, the church became part of the Muskegon Classis, which resulted from the divison of the Grand River Classis.

In 1924 the young people decided that it was time to have a piano. There was, however, no fund from which to draw and no wealthy person to give them the desired instrument. They gave an ice-cream social and a play entitled, "Brown Eyed Betty". Finally they were able to purchase the piano. It was placed in the church in December 1924.

The Rev. Mr. Schroeder accepted a call to Vesper, Wisconsin, in October 1925. During the following summer the church was supplied by two different pastors, the Rev. John Rikkers and Mr. Brouwer. In September 1926 the old parsonage was sold and the new parsonage was, during the following winter and spring, provided. The Rev. and Mrs. Gerrit J. Rozeboom who came to the church in the summer of 1927, were the first occupants of the new manse. Their stay until the summer of 1929 was marked by great spiritual advancement. Under the leadership of Mrs. Rozeboom, a League for Service was organized for the younger ladies of the church. During these years our choir was accorded a marked honor by winning first prize in the upper Michigan choir contest held in Gaylord.

In July 1930 Mr. Peter G. Koopman, a recent graduate of the seminary, was called to the church and became its pastor. Under his guidance a new basement was built under the church, which has become a very important factor in the life of the church. In 1930 it was decided to use the English language at the services. At this time the League for Service and the Ladies Missionary Society united to form one strong working organization of the church.

In the fall of 1936 the Koopmans left for Redlands, California, and in July 1937 Rev. Chester Meengs and his wife came to serve the church. Under the providence of God the work is till progressing. We praise Him Who has given us great blessings during the past fifty years, and petition before His throne of Grace that He continue to use us, pastor and congregation, in the work of His Kingdom, that He we may hear from His lips those coveted words, "Well done".

Chapter XXIX

SCATTERED DUTCH SETTLEMENTS
– EAST AND WEST

98. JOHN HOFFMAN'S SAYVILLE, LONG ISLAND

[Hoffman was born in Holland, Michigan, in 1849 and served as pastor to the Reformed Dutch community at Sayville on Long Island from 1893 to 1899. The manuscript of his sketch, prepared for the Semi-Centennial celebrations at Holland Michigan in August 1897 and never published, was preserved in the Netherlands Museum.]

In giving you, on the occasion of this Semi-Centennial Celebration of the Holland Immigration in the United States, a historical sketch of Sayville, the chief interest of course centres in the settlement of the Hollanders there. For a clear understanding of our subject I deem it necessary to touch briefly upon the place and its environment.

Sayville is situated, as you are aware, on Long Island which is a part of New York State. The first settlement on the island was made in 1625, under Dutch protection, by some French Protestants, who founded an asylum here to worship God according to the dictates of their conscience. The first settler was George Jansen de Rapalje, and his daughter Sarah was the first white child to be born on Long Island. In 1636 several Hollanders settled at its western end near New York while the larger part, especially its eastern section, was populated by New Englanders and for the most by people from Connecticut. Its length from the East River to Montauk Point is 125 miles, and its average breadth 14 miles, with an area of 1682 square miles. By reason of its length the Hollanders called it "Lange Eiland", which the English in 1693 changed by law to "Island of Nassau". This name, however, never came into popular use, so that it is still known by its original appelation. It is noted for its picturesque coast indented by numerous bays and inlets as also for its splendid villages and watering places. On the south coast are many villages and watering places, together with several lighthouses, and it has some 30 lifesaving stations.

Sayville is situated 50 miles East from New York City, in the town of Islip, Suffolk County. Islip derives its name from a small town in England. It was settled back in 1666 when a patent was granted to the inhabitants of Satuaket by Governor Nicholle, which grant was reaffirmed by Governor Donnegan in 1686, reserving to the crown all lands not

purchased by them from the Indians. Sayville is near the Great South
Bay, with a frontage of one and a half miles, and about five miles from
the Atlantic Ocian. Between the bay and the ocean stretches a narrow
strip of land, 30 miles long. Fire Island – so named, it is said, because
formerly nightly fires at times were kindled by pirates on its beach for
the purpose of wrecking ships in order to plunder them.

Seaville, or *village by the sea*, was the original name intended for this
beautiful village. The citizens, at a meeting in 1836, concluded it was
time to ask Uncle Sam to give the hamlet a name and a post office; but
by some mistake the clerk at Washington who copied the petition wrote
"Sayville", and so it has remained to this day. Its first settlers were
Willet Green and John Edwards. The names of Green and Edwards are
still common in and around Sayville. In 1847, two years before any
Hollander arrived here, the first church, the Methodist Episcopal, was
built; in 1849 the Congregational; in 1866 the Episcopal; and in 1896
the Catholic. The original Methodist and Congregational structures have
since been succeeded by attractive, handsome, and substantial edifices.
While on the subject of churches, I can state that before any church was
erected in Sayville, there existed and still exists – though no longer in use
– a church, two miles West from Sayville, at what is now Oakdale. It is
the St. John's Episcopal Church built several years before the war of the
Revolution. A few weeks ago a prominent wedding was solemnized in
that church. The population of Sayville and its surrounding regions,
though mainly composed of Americans, also had a goodly sprinkling
of Hollanders, Germans, Irish, and Bohemians.

Our chief industry, like that of other Long Island towns, is shell fishing
– oysters in winter and clams in summer. The land around Sayville is,
on the whole, poor, sandy soil, not suitable for farming unless heavily
manured. It is, besides, too dear for agricultural purposes, as most of it
is in the hands of the rich, like the van der Bilts, Cuttings, and others
belonging to the South Side Club, who are loath to part with it. These
lands are covered with either primeval or second growth forests, abounding in smaller kinds of game. But deer also roam through these woods to
the no small detriment of the farmers on the outskirts. Large droves are
frequently seen in the evening on the ublic road two miles west from
Sayville. According to the game laws of the State of New York deer are
allowed to be hunted each Wednesday during every week in November.

Speaking of the shellfish industry. I mention the fact that in the first
part of the present century our oysters – known then and now us "Blue
Points" – were famous for their size and flavor; and on account of their

scarcity sold in New York for $ 5 a hundred, while a common laborer could get but 60 or 75 cents a day and a good mechanic only $ 1. In 1848 the oyster industry began to flourish and has since been developed more extensively. The Long Island Railroad was extended through Sayville in 1867. In educational matters we are in no ways behind other towns of its size. We have as fine a High School as is met with in any country place, employing ten or eleven first class teachers who are all able to prepare their pupils for college.

The first Hollanders in Sayville were Cornelius De Waal and Cornelius Hage who came here in 1849. Hage turned his attention to farming, but De Waal bought a boat in which he conveyed oysters and clams to market in New York. De Waal's brother Jacob who arrived with him in America at the same time went on with his family to Ravenna, Michigan, settling on a farm, having D'Ooge and Hodenpyl as neighbors; but in 1852 removed to Sayville. His son Gabriel is still living here with his family. Mrs. Jacob de Waal resided a number of years in Grand Rapids, Michigan, being married to Jacob de Haas, her second husband.

Prior to these arrivals a couple of Holland families – Verney and Hiddink – were living at Lake Land, a few miles outside Sayville. Verney brought his wagon and plow and other farming implements with him from across the ocean, thinking these tools were not to be had in America. After the beginnings of a settlement had been made, Hollanders immigrated hither, the greater part of them from the province of Zeeland, where having made their living by shell, they speedily recognized their opportunities in Sayville.

Although not kindly received by the native population who did not favor foreigners and viewed them as intruders, the Hollanders struggled on quietly and patiently, persevering in what they had undertaken. Having put their hand to the plow they never looked back. They did not try to get to the top of the ladder at once, but began to climb from the lowest rung. They bought old boats from the Americans, worth from $ 100 to $ 150, and with those went about their business. Gradually they succeeded, for at present they are the owners not only of splendid boats, valued at from $ 700 to $ 1,000, but also control the shell-fishing business in and around Sayville. The first extensive oyster shipper among them was Dirk van Wyen, now deceased.

Every spring, at an enormous outlay of money, the Hollanders plant thousands of bushels of oysters in the Bay, and take them up during the autumn and winter months. The Blue Point oysters, besides being much sought after wherever konwn, are shipped not only to all points of our own country, but also to Europe, the greater part being taken by England. Our wide awake oyster planters and shippers are Jacob Ockers, the Westerheke Brothers, the Van der Borgh Brothers, John van Wyen, Wolfert van Popering, and William Rudolph.

Lest I should leave a mistaken impression, I wish to remark here that far the majority of the Hollanders live in West Sayville instead of Sayville. We have a post office of our own and two churches – one Reformed and one Christian Reformed. The two places are separated by a narrow stretch of marshy woodland through which flows a limpid crystal brook whose outlet is in the Bay. The population of the two villages is between 2000 and 2500. According to the census of 1875 there were 328 Hollanders including their children. We may estimate that at present there are between 500 and 600 of them.

Having thus far treated the material interests of Sayville, especially as regards the Hollanders, my sketch would be imcomplete if I failed to notice its religious aspects. From the beginning of their settling here, the Hollanders held religous services on the Lord's day. They would meet in someone's house and one of their number would read a sermon. The first preacher they had, before there was any church organization, was John Koppejan of Oostburg, Wisconsin, who had been an elder in the Old Country among the *Afgescheidenen,* or Seceders, from the State Church. In Wisconsin he had started an independent church and was ordained by one of his elders.

As nearly all the Hollanders who had settled in Sayville had been brought up in the Reformed State Church in the Netherlands, they naturally were attracted to the Reformed Church in America, both having the same creed and polity. Here they found the daughter of the mother they had left behind. Seeing that they could not do effective work unless organized into a church, steps were taken to that end in view. The organization of the Reformed Church here, accordingly, took place on December 19, 1866, with thirty one members, the first ruling elders being John Westerlake, Sr. and John Hiddink, and the first deacons, Marinus Boot and John Otto. Dominie Louis Jongeneel from South Africa, who had already labored among them for sometime, was called as their pastor in December of that year. The installation services were held in the old school house of Sayville on April 3, 1867. Active measures now were taken to secure a church in which to worship; a building committee was appointed and the work vigorously pushed so that by their own exertions and by some outside help the present church edifice was dedicated on the

17th of November, 1867, Dominie Jongeneel labored here for nearly five years, until the summer of 1878.

The following year Dominie Gerrit van Emmerick, a lay preacher from Amsterdam, the Netherlands, then in New York City, was called, ordained, and installed as pastor of this church. His pastoral services continued from June 1872 till the summer of 1886 – a period of 14 years. He was followed by Jean S. Crousaz, another lay candidate. He was licensed to preach by the North Classis of Long Island and ordained and installed in the pastorate in the latter part of 1887, and served the church for about two years. The church was then without a pastor until October, 1889, when Dr. J. C. Calkoen from South Africa ministered to its needs for nearly six months. In January, 1893, the writer of this sketch, then stationed at Clymer, New York, was invited to take charge of the pulpit and began his ministry in May of that year.

If the Dutch motto *Eendracht maakt macht* had been observed – that is if the Hollanders had been united from the beginning – we might have had a single strong church in West Sayville. But wherever Hollanders have settled in America, they have been religiously divided and so it was here. From the first some were unwilling to cast their lot with the Reformed Church. They stood aloof and, at the time when Dominie Willem Coenraad Wust of Lodi, New Jersey, made such a stir in the church because the word "Dutch" was dropped from its name, seceded, calling themselves "Dutch Reformed" and became Wust's followers. His followers and other elements later were organized into a Christian Reformed Church which was established more than twenty years ago. The first and only minister they have had was Dominie John de Vries who left them two years ago. At the time when a call was presented to him, he was a candidate for the ministry from the Theological School at Grand Rapids, Michigan. In this his first congregation he labored for nearly four years.

Thus I have briefly given you an outline of the history of Sayville and of the settling of the Hollanders there. They immigrated to the New World not for the sake of enjoying liberty of conscience, as so many of their countrymen did, but for the purpose of bettering their worldly fortunes. They had no leaders, as did the Hollanders who went West, such as Dominie H. P. Scholte, Dr. A. C. van Raalte, Dominie Seine Bolks, Dominie C. van der Meulen, Dominie Maarten Anne Ypma, and others. With their limited education these Dutch settlers did the best they could; and it is surprising that they steered their craft well in a land so strange to them in speech and manners. But in all this we note a higher guiding hand that had a hidden destiny in store for them to fulfill for themselves and their posterity on these American shores.

In conclusion I would say that although these Hollanders came without money or means they never suffered the hardships and privations incident to so many of the new Dutch settlements in the West. They always were able to earn some money, and by industry and economy make a decent living. Able bodied men at present make from $ 1.50 to $ 2 a day. Providence has blessed them and smiled upon them so they need not lack the necessaries of life. May they and all the Hollanders who came as strangers to a strange land prove grateful to Him who led them to a land of plenty blessed with the fullest political and religious liberty. May their descendants always acknowledge Him as the One who caused them to be born citizens of this great Republic. We may well be proud of the fact that American citizenship is ours, whether by adoption or by birth. Notwithstanding the privileges we are enjoying there is danger that posterity may forget God and His mercies; for the tendency of our times is materialistic. It requires special grace from on high not to be swallowed up by wordly mindedness, by pleasures and amusements so detrimental to the stability of the commonwealth, the higher interests of God's kingdom, and the soul's eternal welfare. Cherishing a truly religious spirit, observing strictly the moral law, and copying the example of Jesus Christ will be our only safeguard. So let it be.

99. PIETER ZUIDEMA'S SETTLEMENT IN VIRGINIA

[In 1869 at Amelia Court House and Mattoax, Virginia, a group of Hollanders founded a settlement which was destined to fail. Pieter Zuidema, one of the children among the immigrants, was born at Blija and came to Virginia in 1869. The following account is based upon his childhood memories and subsequent conversations and was prepared for the Netherlands Museum in 1940, at the suggestion of Mr. Willard Wichers.]

Complying with your request, I am writing this synopsis of the Holland settlement in Amelia County, Virginia. This settlement came into existence in the following manner and to the best of my memory.

In March 1869 some agent in the Netherlands received a letter from Dominie A. C. van Raalte, who was staying at Amelia Court House in Virginia, telling of the wonderful opportunities in that place for the establishment of a Holland colony. Dominie Van Raalte stated that he had spent some time in the South during the war between the States and that he was deeply impressed by the mild and even climate, the beauty of the land, the fertility of the soil, and its cheap price which ran from five to ten dollars per acre. Van Raalte, however, stressed the fact that as all the slaves had been freed, labor was cheap. For that reason he advised that any Hollanders who contemplated coming to Virginia should have enough money to buy some land and, in addition, sufficient funds to support them for at least one year. He also urged that they should not purchase more land than they could pay for. Those who came with little or no money should rent land on shares or obtain work in the cities, either Richmond or Norfolk.

Whether Dominie Van Raalte had visited Virginia as an army chaplain or to visit his son Benjamin who was a soldier in the army I do not know. But in the spring of 1869 about fifty families left the Netherlands for the New World, as they called America. I, the writer of this sketch, at that time was a boy of eight and sailed with my father and mother, two sisters, and two brothers. Together with about 28 or 30 families we got off the train at Mattoax. The rest of the immigrating families proceeded to Amelia Court House ten miles further, a place situated on the Richmond and Danville Railroad as it was known at that time. Upon our arrival we discovered that some Hollanders already had settled at Mattoax; they had prepared a good dinner for us and welcomed us heartily. There also were some Hollanders at Amelia Court House. They, it appeared, had come with Dominie Van Raalte from Holland, Michigan. Among these were a Mr. Jan Brinks and family. It was on May 9 that the settlers arrived at their destinations. During the autumn some more people came from Michigan, and all were enthused with the prospect of a prosperous settlement. True to the customs of Hollanders, they followed the example of the ancient patriarch Abraham. The first thing they thought of was to erect a church in which they could worship the God of their fathers according to the dictates of their own conscience and sing the good old psalms in the customary manner.

So in the spring of 1870 Dominie Seine Bolks, then stationed in Zeeland, Michigan, visited us and with Dominie Van Raalte organized a church at Amelia and another at Mattoax. I do know much about the church at Amelia, but at Mattoax the following officers were elected and installed: Hendrik de Vries, Melis Hulsebos, Jan Geerlings, Meindert Zuidema [my father] as elders, and Gradus van der Riet, Klaas Bultje, Teunis de Vries, and Pieter van Dyke as deacons. Besides these men and their families there were the families of Hendrik Maarten, C. Blink, Gerrit Koster, M. Pluimer, Mr. Nijkamp, J. Donkers, A. T. Leistra, Bakker van der Riet, Mr. Bordewyk, Hendrik Koert, Mr. Wieringa, and

Bernardus Briefsma. There were some others, but I cannot recall their names. Soon after effecting the organization of the church and election of officers they began to build their house of worship. The first structure was made of hewn logs – not fancy but sufficiently large and warm. It also served as a schoolhouse.

At first it appeared all was going well. But, alas, some became dissatisfied. They had not understood Dominie Van Raalte's advice or else had not heeded it. Many of the immigrants had come without money, and being unskilled laborers either could not find any work or at least work that would pay sufficiently for them to live decently. So quite a number left during the summer and autumn of 1870. Some returned to the Old Country, others moved to Chicago, New Jersey, Iowa, Michigan, and other places. Before leaving, some of these people vented their wrath on Dominie Van Raalte and, blaming him for their mistakes, even threatened bodily harm. What was especially unfortunate was the great shortage of crops due to the fact that 1870 was the driest year that had been experienced for a long time in Virginia.

The Dutch settlers at Amelia Court House were not as numerous as at Mattoax. Among them I recall the families of the following: Jan Brinks, G. Oldgers, Mr. S. Haver, Oege Spoelstra, J. Veltman, and a Mr. Leis. Jan Brinks, the wealthiest and most prominent of them, and G. Oldgers were chosen to serve as elders. Who the deacons were I do not recall. The Hollanders at Amelia never built a church, but held meetings on Sundays in the homes of the members of the group. I recall that on one Suday my father and I – when I was nine years old – attended a meeting in the home of Jan Brinks. On that occasion I saw Dominie Van Raalte, a fine looking and mild mannered gentlemen who appeared to be in his late fifties. At that time there also was at Amelia a Mr. Gilmore – who, I believe, was a son-in-law of Dominie Van Raalte and also a preacher, for I always heard him spoken of as "Dominie Gilmore". If I am not mistaken he was to be the Principal of the Amelia Institute. I remember the building well. This old structure, called the "Amelia Collge", had been used as a school before the Civil War. I recall only one young man who enrolled in the new seminary. This was young John Brinks who later went to Holland, Michigan, to complete his studies for the ministry. But the college did not prosper and soon the building was converted into a hotel. The settlers of Amelia also were disappointed and stirred up so much ado that Dominie Van Raalte feared mob violence and went back to Holland, Michigan. This took place sometime in 1871. A few years later we heard of his death and no doubt felt sad and downcast, if not disgusted with the whole scheme on which the dominie had pinned such great hopes. I believe that Dominie Gilmore also went with him, or went somewhere else – I am not sure, and can give no further information about the church of Amelia.

As stated before, a large number of the Hollanders at Mattoax, disheartened by failures and disappointment, moved away. But enough remained to keep up the church work. We obtained a minister from Holland, Michigan. He was an unmarried man by the name of Johannes Huizinga who preached for us on Sundays and taught school during the week. He was an ideal man for these tasks because most of his pupils were Dutch and could not speak English. He helped us learn the meaning of words sooner than it would have been possible without such help. Everything now seemed promising. But again serious mistakes were made in the purchasing of land. The Hollanders were urged to buy an excessive amount of land by a man whose name I prefer not to give and who posed as a "Hollandsche Land Agent" [I want it understood that this was not Mr. Brinks who also was a land agent]. These misguided people bought four or five times as much land as they could pay for, being led to believe that this land would soon prove unobtainable because of soaring prices. One man, for example, bought 1,200 acres at $25 an acre, paid $10,000 and contracted to pay the remainder in three equal annual installments at eight per cent interest. To make these payments naturally proved as impossible as to fly to the moon on a wheelbarrow. In this way the most venturesome farmers lost all they owned.

Meanwhile Dominie Huizinga went on a visit to Michigan and after an absence of one month returned with a bride, a lady by the name of Miss. Boonstra from Zeeland, Michigan. During 1876 or 1877, as I believe, some of the Hollanders moved to Nebraska. After they had been there a year or two they invited our dominie to join them, which he accepted. From that time we had no pastor but nevertheless we continued to hold services in the Dutch language, the elders reading the sermons of C. H. Spurgeon. We were too few in number to maintain a minister. We younger folk had learned enough English to understand sermons in that language and after carrying on our church activities half in English and half in Dutch we were visited by a Presbyterian minister from Amelia. Understanding our situation, he suggested that we join the East Hanover Presbytery and make over our own church property accordingly. This would assure us the regular services a of minister. At a special meeting of the Hollanders who still remained, the presiding elders, M. Zuidema and G. van der Riet, this suggestion was unanimously approved. So we

joined the Presbyterian Church and henceforth were served by a certain
Mr. Denny. Soon thereafter we were able to erect an attractive and commodious church building because many of the American people became
members and we were in a much better financial condition than before.
This church is now known as the Memorial Presbyterian Branch Church
of Amelia.

100. A. M. DONNER'S THE HOLLANDERS IN ALBANY, NEW YORK

[Donner lived in Arnhem, a deacon in the congregation served by Van Raalte. He played an
active part in the plans for emigration made during the spring and summer of 1846, but did
not come to America until 1857. He never came to Holland, Michigan, it appears. The
following account prepared by him in 1897 for the Semicentennial celebrations is preserved
in manuscript in the Netherlands Museum.]

Aan het Committee tot Viering van het 50-jarig bestaan der Hollandsche-
Emigratie in de Vereenigde Staten van Noord Amerika.

Door Uw geacht committee verzocht zijnde, om het een en ander mede
te deelen omtrent de wording en vooruitgang van de Hollandsche
Gemeente te Albany, New York, zal ik trachten aan uw geëerd verzoek
te voldoen, alhoewel mijn hand en gedachten niet zoo vast meer zijn,
wijl ik bijna eene 80-jarige ouderdom bereikt heb.

Ik kan echter niet nalaten iets mede te deelen omtrent de reden waarom
wij onze ouders, broeders, zusters en vrienden en ook Vaderland hebben
verlaten. Enkelen leven nog die ons kunnen mededelen dat Ds. Hendrik
J. de Cock uit Groningen zich niet aan de regelmenten der Haagsche
Synode kon onderwerpen, die in strijd waren met Gods woord. Daarom
werd hij gecensureerd, maar hij kende den lastbrief van zijnen grooten
Zender, „Predikt het Evangelie" en daar hij geene kerk had, verzamelde
zich het volk dat hem lief had in schuren of kamers waaruit zij menigmaal
door den arm van het gerecht werden uit elkander gedreven, werden
beboet of in de gevangenis geworpen. Dit bleef voortduren tot het
jaar 1839. Maar Ds. De Cock bleef niet alleen want zes of zeven mannen
in gehoorzaamheid des geloofs en door zijn voorbeeld aangespoord
voegden zich bij hem en verspreiden zich door het geheele land en ver-
kondigden „Jezus, geen anderen naam onder den Hemel gegeven om
zalig te worden" en „Jezus, koning zijner kerke" en geene Haagsche
synode.

Ik zal U dat ongelijke worstelpark niet verder beschrijven, alleen nog
dat er o! zoovelen van alles waren beroofd en had God de Almagtige het

niet verhoed gebrek hadden moeten lijden. Van hoeveel uitredding en liefde de goede hands Gods voor hen was geweest in die dagen, kan betuigd worden als zij zongen:

De Heer is ons tot hulp en sterkte
Hij is mijn lied en psalmgezang.

Gemeenschap der heiligen was hen dierbaar en verkwikkend. In 1839 verkregen zij vrijheid, maar was er geene vervolging meer door den regterlijken arm van onze medeburgers echter niet minder; die gehate Afgescheidenen was het hard voor om werk te krijgen. Er werd veel gebeden maar tevens ook veel gezongen; de psalmen waren dierbaar in die dagen:

O God toen Gij met Majesteit
Uw Israel hebt uitgeleid....

of

Uw God, O Israel, heeft de kracht
Door zijn bevel U toegebracht....

Daarbij hadden wij het voorregt Ds. Antony Brummelkamp en Ds. Albertus van Raalte bij ons in Arnhem te hebben, mannen zooals door Jethro aan Mozes werden aanbevolen, „kloeke godvruchtige mannen, mannen die de gierigheid haatten" en met zulke mannen vooraan gaat men door dik en dun mede.

Van Raalte was een geboren „Leider en Pionier". Wat Tollens van Barends zingt mag ook van Van Raalte gezegd worden, „Hij rustig in gevaar, wat stormen omheen gieren. Jong in ijver, oud in kennis, vast van ziel." en ik voeg erbij:

„*Christen* in zijn hart, staat zeilree op de kiel."

Maar ik moet nog melden wat eigenlijk de stoot gaf aan de landverhuizing. Het waren geene zeven magere jaren, maar elf jaren van verdrukking en miskenning. Velen hadden alles opgeteerd. Ook Ds. van Raalte en echtgenoote, beiden uit de deftige familiën, hadden alles er bij opgeofferd.

De Heere hoorde evenwel onze gebeden en zond zijnen slaande engel. Eene ziekte ontstond in de aardappelen en dat in eene der eerste levensbehoeften en voor velen hunne dagelijksche spijze. Waar men in 1845 een mud voor 1 gulden kon koopen moest men in 1846-'47 10 gulden betalen. De rogge was in 1845 ƒ 3.50 waard, en in 1846-'47 moest men daarvoor 17 à 18 gulden betalen; en nu werd de slaande engel een zegende engel voor duizenden. Ik word weder jong als ik aan dien tijd van uittreding denk, want

Een net belemmerde onze schreden....

of

Door 's Hoogsten arm 't geweld onttogen,
Zal ik genoopt tot dankbaarheid....

Door Gods genade mag ik nu de harp van de willigen nemen en zingen:

Wat zal ik met Gods gunsten overlaan,
Dien trouwen Heer voor Zijn gena vergelden?

Maar nu moet ik van dien zegenden engel schrijven. Daar kwam berigt uit Amerika: „Vrijheid van Conscientie en brood om te eten." Aan mijn huis werd in 1846 het eerste eene vergadering belegd waarbij Ds. Van Raalte en Ds. Antonie Brummelkamp tegenwoordig waren, en daarop werd besloten om de twee gebroeders Arnold met hunne familiën over te zenden. Nog datzelfde jaar vertrok Ds. Van Raalte met de eerste pioniers naar Amerika. Omstandigheden verhinderden mij evenwel om mijnen wensch om met hem mede te gaan, ten uitvoer te brengen. Ik kan zoodoende niet veel van de eerste landverhuizers hier ter stede aangekomen mededeelen, want ik kwam eerst den 3den Julij 1857 te New York aan. Wij namen tickets naar Chicago voor vijf huisgezinnen ten getale van vijf en dertig personen. Wij vertrokken per boot naar Albany waarop wij als haringen op elkaar gepakt werden. Door die benauwde reis werd mijne vrouw nog erger ziek dan op het schip. Ik vond in Albany mijn vriend Arnold, die ons met groote vriendelijkheid in hun huis opnamen en ten gevolge van de ongesteldheid van mijn vrouw haar voor 10 dagen herbergde. Voor mijzelve en verdere familie huurde ik een woning. Door de paniek die toen in 1857 uitbrak werden wij verhinderd om onze reis naar Chicago voort te zetten en, daar het hier toen ter tijde beter was dan in het Westen, bleef ik hier en na 40 jaren zit ik nog in Albany met 7 gehuwde kinderen en 24 kleinkinderen.

Maar nu moet ik evenwel van de wording en voortgang der Hollandsche Gemeente te Albany schrijven.

Van 1847 tot 1857 moet ik navertellen wat mij is medegedeeld. Ds. A. B. Veenhuizen kwam hier in 1847. In het begin van 1848 is hij naar Rochester vertrokken. In 1851 kwam Ds. Fris en is geen jaar hier geweest. In 1853 of 1854 kwam Ds. Jacobus de Rooy, benoemde of koos ouderlingen en diakenen. Het duurde geen jaar of hij ging weder heen. De Hollandsche bevolking hier ter stede bestond wat godsdienst aanbetreft uit lieden met eene verscheidenheid van gevoelens en een ieder deed zoo te zeggen wat regt was in zijne eigen oogen; vandaar dan ook de mislukking van het stichten eener gemeente.

Toen ik hier in 1857 aankwam vond ik dan ook geene geregelde gemeente. Daar waren eenige huisgezinnen waarmede ik hartelijk vereenigd was: namelijk Mr. en Mrs. Van Nouhuijs, Mr. F. Mol, die gehuwd was met eene dochter van Mr. Van Nouhuijs, Mr. en Mrs. D. Knox, Mr. Jacobus van den Bergh en echtgenoote, Mr. G. Rotman die gehuwd was met een dochter van Mr. Van den Bergh, Mr. Nicholas van den Berge en echtgenoote, Mr. Hendrick Geurtze en familie en nog eenige andere familiën waaronder ook onze tegenwoordige ouderling Jan Bakker en echtgenoote. Met deze en meer andere huisgezinnen kwamen wij Zondags bijeen, in de lecture room van de Eerste Gereformeerde gemeente alhier. De godsdienstoefeningen werden waargenomen door het lezen van preeken en door onderlinge gebeden. Mr. Jan Bakker die kortelings te voren hier weder uit Rochester terug keerde bevool ons aan om Ds. Willem Coenraad Wust uit Rochester hier eens te laten prediken. Toen hij hier kwam raadde hij de vrienden aan eene gemeente te stichten. Ds. Jan Willem Dunnewold bezocht ons ook in 1857 en drong er op aan dat wij ons als eene gemeente zouden openbaren. Datzelfde najaar werden wij op de zitting der klassis als gemeente erkend, en werd onze gemeente georganizeerd door Ds. Isaac N. Wyckoff en Ds. W. C. Wust. Als ouderlingen werden verkozen broeders F. Mol en A. M. Donner, en als diakenen broeders H. J. Geurtze en D. Knox.

Ik kan echter niet nalaten een en andere te melden van al het goede dat Ds. Wyckoff voor de Hollanders en voor onze gemeente heeft gedaan. Hij was als een moeder voor de arme Hollanders die hier aankwamen; hij ging met hen persoonlijk naar de fabriek of winkel en vond hij geen werk voor hen dan voorzag hij voor hunnen behoeften uit zijn eigen middelen.

In 1860 kwam onze eerste predikant, Ds. W. A. Houbolt, dien wij beroepen hadden, tot ons over. Wij gaven hem $ 600 tractement, waarvan de Board of Domestic Missions ons $ 300 toekende. Uit dit bedrag moest hij nog zijn huur betalen voor zijne woning. Tot 1862 heeft hij ons bediend. In 1864 kwam Ds. Pierre B. Bähler van Hellendoorn, Nederland, op zijne doorreis naar het Westen, hier aan. Hij nam het beroep dat wij hem gaven aan en bleef bij ons tot 1866 toen hij een beroep naar Rochester aannam. Toen beriepen wij Ds. Houbolt voor de tweede maal in 1866, hetwelk hij aannam, maar bleef evenwel slechts een jaar hier. Van 1867 tot 1872 was de gemeente vacant en werden de godsdienstoefeningen geleid door ouderling broeder F. Mol die preeken voorlas en anderzins de gemeente stichtte. Hij was een begaafd lezer, daarbij was hij de man des gebeds.

In 1872 nam Ds. Adriaan Zwemer het op hem uitgebracht beroep aan. Die stille, evenwel rustelooze man, die zijn doel niet uit het oog verliest, mogt het met groote volharding gelukken om ons een kergebouw te verschaffen. Tot hiertoe hadden onze godsdienstoefeningen nog plaats in de lecture room van de 1ste Gereformeerde Kerk, maar in 1873 zagen wij ons kerkgebouw met pastorie er onder voltooid ten koste van ruim $ 8,000 waarvan de gemeente ruim $ 1,500 betaalde en door de andere Gereformeerde kerken ons circa $ 3,000 gedoneerd. Het overige bleef als een hypotheek op het kergkebouw staan. In 1875 vertrok Ds. Zwemer.

In Maart 1877 kwam Ds. Cornelius Kriekaard die tot April 1879 bij ons bleef. In Augustus 1879 kwam Ds. Hendrik K. Boer bij ons in de gemeente en is tot het najaar van 1885 met zegen werkzaam geweest. Hij had een klein salaris, en toch werd door zijn toedoen nog $ 1,200 op de hypotheek die nog op het kerkgebouw rustte afbetaald. In December 1887, kwam Ds. Lawrence Dijkstra en is 23 maanden bij ons gebleven. Daar de bestaande pastorie door sommigen beschouwd werd als vochtig, werd onder leiding van Ds. Dijkstra eene nieuwe pastorie nevens het kerkgebouw opgetrokken welke ongeveer $ 2,500 kostte.

In Julij 1890 kwam Ds. Willem J. Duiker en bleef bij ons tot Maart, 1892. De gemeente deed toen weder $ 1,000 op de hypotheek af waaraan Ds. Duiker het zijne heeft toegebracht.

In den zomer van 1893 kwam Ds. Martin Flipse hier van de theologische school te New Brunswick. Hij nam het beroep aan op voorwaarde dat hij 's avonds in de Engelsche taal zoude spreken. Hoe moeilijk dit ook was voor de ouden, moesten zij evenwel bukken. Nu, het was meer dan tijd. Velen der jonge menschen der gemeente gingen naar de Engelsche kerken, maar nu kwamen zij 's avonds en bragten nog anderen mede. De avond godsdienstoefeningen werden goed bijgewoond. Vóór de geregelde oefening wordt eene prayer meeting gehouden door de Young People's Association, welke tot veel zegen verstrekt heeft. Er bleef nog een hypotheek van circa $ 1,100 op het kerkgebouw dat tevens ook reparatie noodig had. Op Dankgevings dag van het jaar 1895 werd door toedoen van Ds. Flipse die hypotheek op ons kerkgebouw afbetaald en was er tevens nog geld genoeg voorhanden om het gebouw in- en uitwendig te verfraaijen. Tot ons groot leedwezen bleef Ds. Flipse niet lang bij ons maar vertrok reeds in het voorjaar van 1896 naar Passaic, New Jersey, waar hij beroepen was.

In Januari 1897 kwam onze tegenwoordige predikant, Ds. Johannes van Westenberg hier van Brighton, New York; hij werkt met lust en liefde in de gemeente en nu hopen en bidden wij dat hij minstens vijf jaren in ons midden mag werkzaam zijn, voornamelijk dat onze kinderen een goed catechetisch onderwijs ontvangen, want daar blijft gewoonlijk veel te wenschen aan over. Ik heb jonge predikanten hooren zeggen, dat hun makkelijker was een preek op te stellen dan één uur met de kinderen te spreken, om te kunnen afdalen tot het verstand der jeugd, en nu, heeft een jonge leeraar in die twee jaren wat geleerd, maar *wat* de jeugd?

Ook behoef ik niet te zeggen dat de achting der gemeente minder wordt voor hunner leeraars. Zijn wij verblijd met onze dierbare gereformeerde leer, vele onzer kennen haar niet. Ik hoop dat èn school èn klassis de zaak zal ter harte nemen.

Ik kan echter niet eindigen zonder te melden dat de vrouwen en jonge dochters der gemeente veel hebben bijgedragen ter afbetaling van de hypotheek op het kerkgebouw. Zingt de dichter:

De buit van 't verwonnen land
Viel zelfs de vrouwen in de hand
Schoon niet mee uitgetogen.

Maar ik kan met dankzegging melden zij zijn vooraan in de spitze geweest. Nu waar de vrouw of moeder of dochter de dienende liefde is, daar is de uitslag niet onzeker. Zij werkt meer met het hart en dat moet toch de stoot geven. Zij kan twijfelmoedig worden, soms met een traan in 't oog, maar niet mismoedig, want zij grijpt Gods belofte aan, „Ik ben uw God en uws zaads God," en de Heilige Geest fluistert haar in 't hart: „De poorten der hel zullen mijne gemeente niet overweldigen."

Gelukkige gemeente die zulke moeders in hun midden hebben.

Wat den tegenwoordigen toestand der Hollandsche gemeente alhier betreft, kan het volgende daaromtrent medegedeeld worden.

Zoals hier te voren gemeld is, is zij in het bezit eener fraaije kerk en pastorie die, Gode zij dank, geheel van schuld bevrijd zijn.

Ofschoon wij tot op het jaar 1894 nog jaarlijks van de Board der Inwendige zending eene jaarlijksche toelage ontvangen hebben wij toen ter tijd daarvoor evenwel bedankt, wijl de inkomsten der gemeente toen zulks niet meer noodzakelijk maakten.

Het aantal familiën of huisgezinnen bedraagt nu 73 met een ledental in volle gemeenschap van 142. De cathechisatie voor de jeugd wordt door circa 40 bijgewoond; de Bijbelklas voor de meer volwassenen door ongeveer hetzelfde aantal.

Voor de liefdadige bijdragen is verleden jaar ongeveer $ 250 bijeengebragt, en voor de gemeentelijke bijdragen ongeveer $ 1,100. De Zondagsschool, de Vrouwen Zendings Vereeniging, de Young People's

Association, en de Junior Association verkeeren in eene bloeijende toestand, en dragen veel bij tot de vooruitgang en bloei der gemeente.

Moge de Heere verder de pogingen die aangewend worden om Zijne gemeente alhier verder uit te breiden met Zijnen zegen achtervolgen en Hem de eere toegebragt worden dat Hij ons tot hiertoe geholpen heeft, niettegenstaande vele moeiten en wederwaardigheden.

101. HOLLANDERS IN CLEVELAND AND DETROIT

[As at Albany and Buffalo and Rochester, Dutch immigrants halted their journey at Cleveland and Detroit, some of whom never reaching the settlements at Holland, Roseland, Pella, or Milwaukee and Sheboygan. In 1847 some Hollanders settled in Cleveland, most of whom appear to have been Catholics. A few established themselves in Detroit. Their fewness demonstrates the strong spirit of kinship which existed among the Dutch immigrants of 1847 and after, for being Seceders, they hurried westward to Holland and other settlements where they hoped to find their friends and relatives. This anonymous account in manuscript is preserved in the Netherlands Museum.]

Toen in 1847 de eerste Hollanders in Cleveland aankwamen, was de stad die thans ongeveer 300,000 inwoners telt en die het vorige jaar haar honderdjarig bestaan vierde, vergelijkender wijze gesproken niet meer dan een groot dorp; en indien de groei der Hollanders geëvenredigd ware geweest aan den groei der stad hun invloed zou ongetwijfeld veel grooter zijn geweest dan nu.

De eerst aankomenden in het voorjaar van 1847 waren Jacobus Boot, C. van Laazen, Cornelius Dekker, en diens schoonvader Hazebroek, die spoedig na zijne aankomst stierf. Dekker, de schoonzoon, werd krankzinnig, en is, na 46 jaar in het krankzinnigen gesticht opgesloten te hebben, aldaar overleden. Hij was reeds begraven voor de familie iets van zijne ziekte of dood af wist.

Bovengenoemde personen waren met hunne huisgezinnen in den herfst van 1846 te Rochester, New York, gearriveerd en brachten aldaar den winter onder groote moeielijkheden door. Later in 1847 kwamen onder meer anderen aan, de families Ochsnaar, Rozen, Zoeter, Johannes Gilde, Hofstede, en Geesen. De meesten kwamen uit Zeeland, enkele uit Gelderland.

Van de familie Boot is thans nog in leven eene dochter die toen ze met hare ouders aankwam slechts vijf jaar oud was. Zij is op een na de jongste van de oud settlers, eene dochter van Van Laazen nog in leven was bij hare aankomst slechts één jaar oud.

Hendrik Ochsnaar, met vrouw en zeven kinderen, maakte de zeereis in 42 dagen en de landreis van Baltimore naar Cleveland in 19 dagen.

Van de 7 kinderen zijn nog 5 in leven, die tezamen den hoogen ouderdom van 380 jaren bereikt hebben. In 1848 en 1849 kwamen nog enkele huisgezinnen meer onder anderen de families Dekker, Keek, en De Mooy. Maar het aantal Hollanders was langen tijd zeer gering. Er waren er die kwamen en gingen, maar slechts enkele families vestigden zich voor goed.

De meesten kwamen na den burgeroorlog en voor een aanzienlijk deel uit de provincie Gelderland, en het geheele getal Hollanders wordt thans berekend op ongeveer 5,000. De meesten zijn daglooners en werken in fabrieken, enkelen zooals de Ochsnaars en Dekker hebben fortuin gemaakt maar de meerderheid heeft met harden arbeid in het zweet huns aanschijns hun brood te eten.

Op kerkelijk godsdienstig gebied is gelijk elders onder de Hollanders veel verscheidenheid. Er zijn er Gereformeerden, Roomschen, Joden, Darbysten, en Irvingianen. De Roomsche heeft het leeuwen aandeel. De Gereformeerden ontbrak het in den beginne aan leiding. Zij hadden geen predikant voor 1864. Omtrent dien tijd werd de 1ste Gereformeerde gemeente gesticht onder de leiding van Ds. Jan W. Dunnewold daartoe afgevaardigd door de Classis van Geneva. Er zijn thans vier gemeenten; twee van de Gereformeerde Kerk in Amerika en twee van de Hollandsche Christelijke Gereformeerde Kerk. Indien de Gereformeerden één waren gebleven zouden twee kerken genoeg zijn geweest, eene aan de Oost- en de andere aan de West zijde. Maar het verschil op kerkelijk gebied heeft hen zoo verbrokkeld dat men thans heeft vier kerken die wegens geringe stoffelijke middelen een kwijnend leven leiden. Zij tellen tezamen nog geen twee honderd huisgezinnen.

De anderen zijn meerendeels zeer gehecht aan de Hollandsche taal en zeden. Bij de jongeren komt dit natuurlijk wegens hunne geboorte en opvoeding in dit land minder sterk uit. Terwijl door huwelijken met andere nationaliteiten de belangstelling in wat specifiek Hollandsch is al meer en meer afneemt. Over 't geheel genomen heeft de naam Hollander een goeden klank. Zij zijn bekend als eerlijk, vlijtig, en getrouw. Zelden komt een Hollander met de politie in aanraking. En de kosten voor politie en gevangeniswezen zouden tot een minimum worden gereduceerd indien alle anderen zoo goed hunne verplichting als burgers naleefden.

Detroit. Ofschoon de vader der Hollandsche nederzetting in Michigan, Dr. A. C. van Raalte zich gedurende den winter van 1846-'47 in Detroit ophield en er een zeer gunstig onthaal vond, verliepen er eenige jaren voor men van eene eigenlijke gezegde nederzetting van Hollanders in Detroit kan spreken. Die nu en dan aankwamen waren komende en gaande en kozen meestal elders hun verblijf of verdwenen als men zegt met de noorder zon. Van de anderen, die zich hier meer bepaald hebben gevestigd zou men kunnen noemen de families Huizer en Laurence. Huizer kwam uit de provincie Zuid Holland met veertien kinderen, zeven zoons en zeven dochters. De moeder stierf reeds enkele maanden na aankomst der familie. De vader stierf in 1872. De jongste zoon is thans nog predikant bij de Presbyteriaansche gemeente te Brighton, Michigan. Van de dochters is er een getrouwd met Peter Smith, die met zijne ouders van Zwolle over gekomen, eerst een tijd lang in Holland woonde, maar zich later hier vestigde en zich een vrij aanzienlijk vermogen verwierf.

De familie Laurence kwam hier kort voor den burger oorlog. Vader en moeder met zes kinderen, vier dochters en twee zoons. De vader is reeds verscheidene jaren geleden gestorven. De moeder en de kinderen zijn nog alleen in leven. Deze familie heeft zoo veel fortuin gemaakt dat zij wat het stoffelijke aangaat onbekommerd kunnen leven. De oudste zoon Leonard Lawrence heeft zich door zijn huwelijk en door bedrijf een vrij aanzienlijk vermogen verworven en is, vooral op godsdienstig kerkelijk gebied als ouderling bij eene Presbyteriaansche gemeente een man van invloed en beteekenis.

Verder zou men kunnen noemen de families Oostdijk, Van Vliet, Van Koeveren, en Willebrandts. Laatst genoemde kwam hier in 1860 en is ook bij de Hollanders in Ottawa County en Grand Rapids bekend. De Willebrandts, ofschoon behoorende tot eene Amerikaansche kerk, zijn zeer gunstig bekend onder de Hollanders wegens hunne hulpvaardigheid en opoffering als er nood is onder hunne vroegere landgenooten.

Maar de meesten der ouden bekommeren zich weinig of niet meer over hunne Hollandsche afkomst en komen zelden met hunne vroegere landgenooten in aanraking.

Maar eerst sinds 1880 heeft men met eenigszins meer recht kunnen spreken van eene Hollandsche nederzetting in Detroit. Het was omtrent dien tijd dat eenige huisgezinnen over kwamen uit de provinciën Zuid Holland en Friesland die van tijd tot tijd gevolgd zijn door vrienden en betrekkingen uit het oude vaderland.

Onder de tegenwoordige Hollanders van beteekenis mogen in de eerste plaats genoemd worden de gebroeders Friezema. In 1880 kwamen ze als kinderen met hunne ouders over uit Friesland en vestigden zich eerst in Paterson, New Jersey. Een der broeders, het tegenwoordige hoofd der firma, werkte gedurende drie jaren als letter zetter op eene Hollandsche drukkerij. In 1884 kwamen ze naar Detroit en begonnen hier in 1887 een drukkerij op eigen hand. Men had geen geld en leende om te beginnen $ 250. Met onvoldoende middelen maar met een vasten wil om te slagen werkte men en, „Luctor en Emergo", al worstelende kwam men op. In 1893 werkte men nog slechts met vier personen, maar ondanks de harde tijden breidde men zijne zaken uit. Nieuwe en betere machinerie werd aangeschaft. Meer handen werden in dienst genomen en thans werkt men geregeld met 20 personen en betaalt wekelijks aan werkloon ongeveer $ 200 en de geheele plant vertegenwoordigt eene waarde van $ 10,000. Deze firma bewijst dat men ook zelfs nog in den laatsten tijd met geringe middelen, onder den zegen van God en met eigen krachtsinspanning in korten tijd het tot betrekkelijken welvaart kan brengen.

Over 't algemeen hebben de Hollanders in Detroit noch den tijd noch de gelegenheid gehad om fortuin te maken. Zij behoren tot de nijvere arbeidende klasse en zijn bekend als eerlijk, vlijtig, en zuinig.

Van het kerkelijk en godsdienstig leven der eerste Hollanders alhier valt wegens hun kleine aantal weinig te zeggen. Toch verloochenden zij in dit opzicht hun karakter als Hollanders niet. In den beginne vergaderde men des Zondags in een of ander privaat gebouw en stichtte elkander door het lezen van een preek. Er was geene georganizeerde gemeente. Maar in 1869 stichtte men eene Presbyteriaansche gemeente, die echter het volgende jaar, onder goedkeuring der Presbyterie tot de Classis Grand River der Gereformeerde kerk in Amerika overging. Men beriep met de hulp van de Board of Domestic Missions een predikant en eene dame gaf $ 1,000 voor den bouw van een kerkje dat in 1875 werd opgericht. De gemeente was echter zeer klein en leidde een sukkelend leven, zoodat het bijna niet was op te houden. In de laatste jaren nam echter het getal van lieverlede toe, zoodat de gemeente thans vijftig huisgezinnen telt. Wegens de uitbreiding der gemeente werd in 1895 besloten tot het bouwen eener nieuwe kerk. En de gemeente is thans in het bezit van een nieuw doelmatig kerkgebouw, dat beantwoordt aan de eischen des tijds en de Hollandsche naam eere aan doet.

Of de tegenwoordige gemeente, klein als zij nog altijd is, eene nucleus zal worden voor eene vermeerderde Hollandsche bevolking, zal de tijd leeren. Het geheele getal Hollanders bedraagt zeker niet meer dan 500. Waarom zijn er in Detroit slechts 500 terwijl er in Cleveland 5,000 zijn? Zeker is het dat Detroit de beste gelegenheden aanbiedt voor den werkman die met zijne eigen handen op eene eerlijke wijze zijn brood wenscht te verdienen.

[In 1892 a settlement of Hollanders at Alamosa in Colorado was attempted, with disastrous consequences. This real estate venture managed by incompetent directors brought much hardship upon a group of immigrants who soon scattered to various Dutch and other settlements. The author of this sketch which appeared in *Tekenen der Tijden*, November 9, 1922, witnessed the disaster.]

Het zal Zondag, 12 November 1922 dertig jaar geleden zijn dat eene Hollandsche kolonie van twee honderd zielen uit Amsterdam vertrok met bestemming naar de San Luis vallei, Colorado, Noord Amerika.

Het was den 12den November 1892 op eenen Zaterdag, des middags te twaalf uur, dat het stoomschip *Dubbeldam* van de Holland Amerika lijn van Amsterdam vertrok met eene kolonie van ruim twee honderd Nederlanders, uit alle oorden van Nederland afkomstig.

Er waren Gelderschen zooals A. Heersink en huisgezin van Varseveld, A. J. van Lummel en gezin, J. Bleijenberg van Ede, en meer anderen, wier namen ons op dit oogenblik niet voor den geest staan. Uit Overijssel, zooals H. en J. van Dalen, A. Bruintjes, H. Boxum, en anderen van Ambt Vollenhove. Uit Friesland, Andries Hof en gezin, de onderwijzer F. Zijlstra en gezin, en zijn broeder. Uit Amsterdam: L. Verburg en gezin. Uit het noordelijke gedeelte van Noord Holland, C. Sluys en gezin. Uit de Haarlemmermeer, Uitenboomgaard en anderen. Uit een andere Noord-Hollandsche plaats, J. Zwier en gezin. Verscheidene gezinnen uit het Protestantsche deel van Noord Brabant, zooals het gezin van J. van der Beek van Almkerk, van Vos, en anderen. Eenige gezinnen uit Zeeland, zooals het gezin van J. de Kruyter, van Goes; van L. van der Linde, van 's Heer Hendrikskinderen; van C. Kloosterman, van Rilland; Moerman, van Ierseke. De bejaarde Jacobus Oranje; zijn zoon Johannes Oranje en kinderen en zijn jongste dochter Neeltje; S. Hartog en gezin. [Mrs. S. Hartog was ook een dochter van den bejaarden Jacobus Oranje en is eenige maanden geleden te Edgerton, Minnesota, overleden]. Ook eenige personen uit Walcheren en 'n gezin uit Oud Vosmeer, eiland Tholen. Deze lijst is lang niet volledig. Onder dit schrijven komen ons nog voor den geest D. Sjaardema en gezin, W. Verhoef, T. Teunissen en W. Hols.

De eerste vier dagen hadden wij gunstig weder, of schoon reeds in het Engelsch Kanaal velen aan zeeziekte leden. Doch den 5den dag, toen wij in den vollen oceaan waren, stak er een geweldigen storm uit het Westen op, tengevolge waarvan het stoomschip weinig vorderingen maakte. Deze storm duurde drie à vier dagen, ook des nachts en was zoo geweldig, dat enkele passagiers en leden der bemanning verwondingen bekwamen.

Een der passagiers, Mrs. De Kruyter, werd van de eene zijde van het schip naar de andere zijde tegen een stoel geworpen, zoodat de dokter de hoofdwonde moest dichtnaaien.

Borden, koppen, en andere tafelgerei werd menigmaal verguisd. Eens sloeg een hooge golf over het schip, zoodat een kleine jongen van de eene zijde der boot naar de andere spoelde en zeker in den oceaan terecht gekomen zoude zijn, ware hij niet voor de verschansing blijven liggen.

Wat worstelde de *Dubbeldam* door dien woedenden Atlantischen oceaan! We stonden menigmaal die worsteling gade te slaan, terwijl de boeg zich verhief en in het volgende oogenblik weer een plons naar beneden maakte. Alles om ons heen schuimde, ziedde en kookte als een reusachtige pot met woedende baren, die in de grimmigheid hunner kracht tegen de zijden van de *Dubbeldam* aan beukten en raasden dat hooren en zien verging. De machinerie zwoegde met alle kracht. Dikke zwarte rookwolken stegen uit den schoorsteen als uit een krater op en bewees wel dat alle handen benedendeks hun best deden, om voort te komen. Het touwwerk kletterde tegen de masten. Af en toe hoorden wij de zee vogels, die ons schip volgden, een angstig gekrijsch voortbrengen alsof ook zij door de woede van den storm bevreesd instinktmatig beschutting zochten.

De zeelieden, in oliejassen, zuidwester en hooge laarzen gekleed, deden zwijgend hunnen plicht.

Boven het loeien van den wind en het bruisen der wateren hoorden wij telkens het verdoovend geraas van de schroef, wanneer zij boven water kwam.

Toen wij de banken van Newfoundland naderden, verminderde de storm! Welke eene verandering wanneer er stilte na de storm komt!

Gedurende den storm waren de dekken en de eet- en spreekkamers haast verlaten geweest, doch nu was ieder verblijd en opgeruimd en men zag de kolonisten overal in groepen zitten.

Wij ontmoetten verscheidene schepen met welke wij seinen wisselden. In die dagen was er nog geen draadlooze telegraphie, zoodat alle berichten werden overgeseind, overdag met vlaggen en des nachts met lichten.

In dien tijd waren de zeilschepen nog lang niet zeldzaam. Op eenen Zondagmiddag zeilde een prachtig fregatschip met volle zeilen ons op korten afstand voorbij. Zoo sierlijk en majestueus een opgetuigd zeilschip de zeeën doorklieft, is niet te beschrijven. Den 25sten November 1892 op eenen Zaterdagmiddag arriveerden wij te New York. De reis had juist veertien dagen geduurd.

De spoorreis van Hoboken naar de San Luis vallei, Colorado, duurde vier dagen en drie nachten. Met een specialen trein bestaande uit een aantal wagons voor de meer dan twee honderd reizigers en eenige wagons voor de baggage vertrokken wij van Hoboken over den Pennsylvanië spoorweg. Aan de stations der groote steden trok onze trein met de Nederlandsche kolonie natuurlijk zeer de aandacht. Want het gebeurt niet iederen dag, dat zulk een tamelijk groot getal landverhuizers, die allen naar eenen plaats gaan, passeeren.

Te St Louis hielden wij eenige uren stil. Daar was een maaltijd gereed gemaakt in de zalen van het station. Daar moesten wij ook van trein verwisselen en gingen des avonds van daar verder met den Missouri Pacific Spoorweg.

De reis in Kansas, door de onafzienbare prairies was zeer eentonig. Woensdagmorgen kwamen wij in den staat Colorado. De gesteldheid van den bodem veranderde zichtbaar, naarmate wij dichter bij het Rotsgebergte kwamen. De bodem werd al ruwer en ruwer. De rotsbergen al hooger en hooger, totdat wij al in de verte de hooge rotsbergen zagen. Ongeveer met den middag bereikten wij Pueblo, alwaar wij een paar uur vertoefden.

Vandaar reisden wij over den Denver en Rio Grande spoorweg door de wereldberoemde Royal Gorge naar de San Luis Vallei. Onderweg werd de oude moeder van D. Ballast uit Leeuwarden zeer ziek. In het midden van het hooge gebergte, te Salida, werd een geneesheer gehaald, doch de reis moest doorgezet worden. Deze oude vrouw heeft nog eenige dagen in de emigranten huizen, dicht bij Alamosa, geleefd en is toen gestorven. Zij was de eerste die uit de kolonie aan het kille graf in de San Luis Vallei werd toevertrouwd. Zij had de lange en moeilijke reis op haar ouden dag gedaan, om in het vreemde en toen o zoo onherbergzame oord te sterven en begraven te worden.

Woensdagavond kwamen wij te Alamosa aan. Eenige mijlen vandaar, in eene woeste, naakte streek, waren in der haast twee groote planken gebouwen opgetrokken. Daar werden de kolonisten des anderen dag onder dak gebracht. De huisgezinnen zaten daar als haringen in een ton op elkaar gepakt. Er was slechts eene zeer onvoldoende regeling getroffen, om in de dagelijksche behoeften van dit groot aantal menschen te voorzien, zoo dat er soms aan het noodige gebrek was.

Bovendien waren de menschen teleurgesteld, omdat de schoone voorspiegelingen, die de emigratiemaatschappij had verbreid, niet waren uitgekomen.

Keelziekte en roodvonk vertoonden zich in de gebouwen en in korten tijd waren elf kinderen uit verschillende gezinnen gestorven. Ook stierf in een ander huis de oudste dochter van Mr. J. de Kruyter.

Over de bedriegelijke voorspiegelingen waarmede de kolonisten waren gelokt, zullen wij nu niet uitweiden Deze hebben wij toen ter tijd scherp genoeg – volgens sommigen *te* scherp – aan de kaak gesteld De nederzetting bleek eene mislukking en de kolonisten zijn – op enkele gezinnen na – uit Colorado vertrokken naar onderscheidene staten van dit uitgestrekte land.

103. L. BOEVE'S SETTLEMENT IN PHILLIPS COUNTY, KANSAS

[The Phillips County Dutch colony was begun in 1877 by settlers from Nebraska. L. Boeve's account portrays the manner of settlement on prairies and describes some of the practical difficulties confronting settlers. Boeve lived many years in Luctor, as the center of the Dutch community was known. He wrote this sketch in 1896 preserved in the Netherlands Museum and here printed for the first time.]

The colony of which we are requested to write a brief history is located at Luctor in Phillips County, a little west of the north central part of the State of Kansas.

The Dutch pioneers who established themselves in this place were B. Kappers, A. Kip, G. Kolste, and B. Roland who were accompanied by their families. These people emigrated from Holland, Nebraska, in the year 1877. Although this was not a committee delegated to determine a place for colonial settlement as was the case with Pella and Orange City, places settled under the leadership of men like the Henry P. Scholte and Henry Hospers, it may nevertheless be stated that this group of men truly were the founders of Luctor, a colony which now numbers a score of years.

Setting out from Holland, Nebraska, early in the spring of 1877, the settlers arrived in Phillips County, after a journey of several days. They were early enough to seed a small plot of ground, but prepared to return in the following year when they intended to acquire more of the fertile prairie land.

As the soil of Phillips County proved very productive, the list of colonists soon increased. Among the people who settled here beside the first comers were H. Kroese, G. ter Maat, J. Renerdink, and H. Brethouwer. Others, and in larger numbers, came in each succeeding year. Neither love of adventure nor desire for gain was the essential purpose of their immigration; they had come simply to establish homes.

The earliest settlers of Phillips County were confronted with severe trials and privations. Like most pioneers, they paid dearly for the land they obtained and for all supposed advantages of a frontier community. They were isolated, so to speak, from the rest of the world – to shift for themselves as best they could. Money usually was scarce, and so they were forced to seek a chance to labor in the adjoining state of Colorado. Each year they trekked to that state to provide themselves and their families with necessaries while their loved ones in the meanwhile remained on their homesteads. As the climate was not severe in winter, they erected rude sod houses and so solved the problem of shelter cheaply. Many of these houses are occupied even at the present time; and whenever the lack of money today prevents the erection of more imposing buildings this material still is used to make comfortable, if rude, dwellings.

By 1878 the number of families had so increased that the colony wanted to have a place of worship. First, they built a church of sod, two miles west from the present site of Luctor in which they met regularly on the Sabbath day. Mr. H. Kroese usually conducted the services. Weak as this organization was and humble its character, its founders look back upon first days with gratitude and satisfaction, and the memory of many happy days spent amidst those simple beginnings.

Finally, on August 14, 1884, a committee of the Classis of Wisconsin consisting of Dominie Harmen van der Ploeg, Dominie Johannes Huizinga, and Elder Quirinus Huyzer organized the Reformed Church of Philadelphia, or as it is known at present, Luctor. Fifteen members were received by certificate and two upon confession. H. Kroese and L. ter Maat were chosen elders, and A. Nyland and J. Ledeboer deacons. J. Renerdink and A. van der Velde each donated five acres of ground for the support of a church. The colonists erected a small frame shanty to serve until they were able to build a permanent and more convenient structure. They also erected, in 1886, a modest parsonage, and with the help of the Board of Domestic Missions made plans to call a pastor. In August of that same year – 1886 – Dominie Dirck Scholten was installed and served the congregation for five years – until 1891, when he accepted a call to Muscatine, Iowa. He was succeeded by Dominie Johannes Smidt who came from Pella, Iowa, and was installed in 1892, but remained only nine months. Next Dominie Jacob van der Meulen of Dispatch, Kansas, was called; he assumed his pastorate in May 1893 and remained until November 1896 when he accepted an invitation by the church in Graafschap, Michigan. Dominie Arthur van Arendonk came next, was installed on July 4, 1897, and at present serves the congregation which numbers about seventy families.

Meanwhile, the Christian Reformed Church was organized in 1885. The six families which formed this congregation erected a small church a half mile north of Luctor in which the Elder J. J. Dragt held services regularly. In 1892 they extended a call to Dominie Evert Bos of Holland, Michigan, whose installation took place in 1892. During the following year the congregation grew perceptably when a considerable number of newcomers arrived, mostly from the province of Groningen in the Netherlands. It was necessary to provide a new building; and a handsome and commodious church was completed in that same year. Dominie Bos continued his pastoral labors until 1896 when he left on a call to Dispatch, Kansas. This Christian Reformed congregation at the present moment numbers about 45 families.

The Chicago, Burlington, and Quincy Railroad extended its lines into the northern part of Phillips County in 1885 and located its depot at Long Island six miles north of Luctor, in the Prairie Dog River valley. In consequence Long Island became a thriving little town having two flour mills. Two years later the Chicago, Rock Island, and Pacific Railroad, in extending its road to Denver, Colorado, traversed our county through the heart of the Dutch settlement, – establishing a station at Prairie Valley on the banks of Deer Creek, four miles from Luctor. This place also has become a prosperous town.

The first place of business, a general merchandise store, established in 1884, was founded at Luctor with a branch at Prairie View by Mr. A. van Diest who began dealing in farm implements and buying broomcorn, a crop the farmers of this section found profitable.

The land of Phillips County occupied by the Dutch settlers is a rolling prairie intersected by running streams with native timber growing on its banks. Our chief pursuit was agriculture and the raising of cattle. The level parts of our county are well adapted to the raising of corn and wheat, while the rougher areas are reserved for grazing.

Although this country has its disadvantages as is the case with every frontier community, particularly the drought, our settlers have prospered, most of them living upon farms wholly or practically clear of debt. Evidence of such prosperity are many improved farms stocked with swine and herds of cattle.

Our settlers for the most part are immigrants from Nebraska, Minnesota, Wisconsin, and Michigan, but a few have come directly from The Netherlands. This settlement, which began twenty years ago with the arrival of four families now numbers 140 families. The area of this colony extends about 20 miles from east to west, about 12 from north to south. There still is room for Hollanders who want to build their homes besides their brethren in this remote settlement.

Chapter XXX

FOUNDING OF DUTCH COMMUNITIES
IN THE DAKOTAS

104. FRANK LE COCQ'S DOUGLAS COUNTY,
SOUTH DAKOTA

[Frank le Cocq, Sr. was born in Amsterdam in 1824, emigrated to Pella, moved to Sioux County in 1872, and in 1883 established himself at Harrison, South Dakota, where he died in May 1907. Few persons could have written more authoritatively on the early settlement of Douglas County. This account, prepared for the Semi-Centennial celebrations in August 1897, was never published. Its text was taken from the author's manuscript preserved in the Netherlands Museum.]

Zoowat tien jaren na de vestiging der Hollandsche Kolonie in Sioux County, Iowa, onder leiding van den Heer Henry Hospers [nu senator van Iowa] werd de behoefte alweer gevoeld om een nieuwe plaats voor ons Hollandsch volk te zoeken. De uitgestrekte landerijen in Sioux County's Kolonie waren te dien tijde door het instromen der emigranten uit andere oorden zoo wel als uit het oude vaderland zoo in waarde verhoogd dat het voor de huisgezinnen die zonder middelen daar gekomen zijnde onmogelijk was om voor hunne kinderen land te krijgen daar de prijs van land toen reeds van 10 tot 25 dollars per akker bedroeg en steeds om hoog ging. Door eenige ondernemende mannen werd de noodzakelijkheid ingezien om in deze behoefte te voorzien en een nog geheel nieuwe landstreek op te zoeken waar het land nog als „homesteads" van ons gouvernement kon worden verkregen.

Dientengevolge werd er eene vergadering gehouden te Orange City in October 1881 ten doel hebbende om te gaan onderzoeken naar een geschikte plaats voor eene nieuwe Kolonie. Op deze eerste vergadering waren een paar mannen tegenwoordig die het jaar te voren in Dakota geweest waren ten einde eene groote verkoping van Indiaansche ponies bij te wonen die door het gouvernement van het beruchte Indiaansche opperhoofd Sitting Bull waren afgenomen. Deze mannen hadden bij die gelegenheid gezien dat er zeer schoone, zacht golvende, en zeer uitgestrekte grasvelden in Dakota lagen.

De commissie op die vergadering verkozen bestond uit Leendert van der Meer, Dirk van den Bos, en Frank le Cocq, Jr. Op den 1sten November 1881 trokken deze mannen zoo goed mogelijk uitgerust de Big Sioux Rivier over, die de grenslijn vormt tusschen Iowa en Dakota, en vervolgens door Turner, Bon Homme, Douglas, en Charles Mix counties en keerde zoowat November terug en brachten rapport in van hunne reis, enz. Op deze vergadering werd voorlopig besloten om in Douglas County de nieuwe Kolonie te stichten. Nu gingen half January 1882 per as met de voornoemde commissie, Leendert van der Meer, Dirk van den Bos, en Frank le Cocq, Jr., de volgende personen mee, namelijk Jacob Muilenburg, T. T. Joustra, en Arie Beukelman om zelfs te gaan zien als gids vergezeld door den ouden landmeter van Bon Homme County, Mr. Harrington.

Van Orange City ging het west op naar het dorpje Calliope, de Big Sioux Rivier over en Dakota in, naar de toenmalige hoofdstad Yankton waar het gouvernements land kantoor was. De commissie was voorzien van goede brieven van aanbeveling van Mr. George Carpenter toen gouverneur van Iowa en de Honorable Henry Hospers aan Mr. G. H. Weston toen registrar van het land kantoor en aan Mr. L. Wyna. Laatstgenoemde kende de geschiedenis der zoo welgeslaagde volksplanting in Sioux County. Deze mannen hebben veel gedaan voor de Hollanders van Douglas County de goede zaak der Kolonizatie te doen slagen.

Nu begon eindelijk de moeielijke reis. Alles moest natuurlijk met paarden en wagens west op naar een stadje aan de Missouri Rivier in Charles Mix County; geheele dagen gereden over de prairie vlakte van zons op tot den ondergang, zonder weg, huis, of eenig teeken van aanwezigheid van menschen – en dat in het midden van den winter. Dat er op die lange en moeielijke tocht nog al wat ondervonden werd is ligt te verstaan. Men moest natuurlijk op zulk eene onafzienbare vlakte juist zoo als de schepen op de zee op het compas reizen. Na een reis van 5 dagen kwam men aan de Missouri rivier.

Van den mond der Pease Kreek in Charles Mix County naar Douglas County was te dier tijd en voornamelijk in den winter een gevaarlijke tocht. De commissie en andere [twee rijtuigen] ondernamen dien den 3den Februarij 1882. Door Van den Bos werden bij het krieken van de dageraad allen uit den slaap gewekt want men moest heel vroeg weg wilde men des avonds voor donker op de bestemde plaats in Douglas County komen. Met zons opgang zaten alle reeds op hun plaats in de rijtuigen, en nu ging het oostwaarts naar Brownsdale, een klein huisje met een planken shanty 10 bij 12 voet dat het courthuis verbeelden moest van Douglas County.

De dag was zeer schoon en geen sneeuw op den grond, den geheelen voormiddag goed doorgereden, maar aan hunne krachten en vooral dat der paarden kwam een einde en daarom een weinig adem geschept. De paarden wat laten eten in het buffel gras, van het meegenomen proviand door een met algemeene stemmen verkozen kok uit hun midden wat klaar gemaakt tot versterking der krachten, een vuurtje van Missouri river hout, water uit een nabij gelegen lake gehaald, coffy gezet, ham gebraden, God gebeden en gedankt, en midden op deze groote vlakte gegeten.

Maar toen men nu de reis weder aanvaarden zou, „ziet", merkt er eene op, „wat komt daar aan?" Op die aanwijzing werd nu aller aandacht gevestigd en jawel de reuk van de gebraden ham had hun verraden want een uitgehongerde troep wolven kwamen op hun aanzetten. En of het nu kwam dat er een van onze reizigers als sommige vermaarde dieren-temmers een betooverende kracht op die hongerige bende uitoefende, of uit andere oorzaken genoeg, zij bleven gelukkig op eenige afstand en vergenoegden zich dit maal met de geur van de ham ofschoon ze toch op slechts geringen afstand den geheelen dag verder de reizigers ver-volgden, en om hunne woede niet op te wekken door er onder te schieten liet men hen maar stil loopen zoo lang zij op behoorlijken afstand bleven. Gelukkig kwam ons gezelschap juist voor dat het donker werd in 't ge-zicht van Brownsdale en voor den donker nog binnenshuis en de paarden op stal.

Op een andere keer gebeurde het op eene dezer tochten dat men door mistig weer en in vallende sneeuwstorm verdwaalde en in een Indiaansche hut vernachten moest waar het zeer koud in was zoodat men haast niet onbevroren kon blijven.

Op een ander dezer tochten werden onze baanbrekers door een woedende troep van wel twintig Indianen achtervolgd omdat er op de plaats waar zij hadden uitgekampt prairie brand ontstaan was in hun reservation door het uitkloppen der pijp waardoor het drooge gras, het eenige levensmiddel hunner ponies, verteerd werd. De Indianen omringden „our boys" en zouden hen alle gevangen genomen hebben en bij de Indian agent te Greenwood verklaagd wegens stichten van prairie brand als niet op dat zelfde oogenblik een man van Brownsdale verschenen was die goed Indiaansch sprak als tolk diende en de Indianen wist tevreden te stellen zoodat de vriendschap niet verbroken werd en ook naderhand geen vijandige houding meer bestond want men begreep dat het een ongeschikt en geen moedwil geweest was.

Nu konden onze moedige pioneers weer ongehinderd en met blijdschap en dankbaarheid aan God voor de goede uitkomst hunne reis vervolgen. Maar toen deed zich weer eene andere groote moeijelijkheid op, namelijk: naar nauwkeurige verkenning van de mijlen, die men had afgelegd, merkten zij dat men het spoor of liever de rechte richting kwijt waren en dat na lang gereden te hebben menschen en paarden zeer vermoeid waren. Toen vond men in het bosch aan de Missouri rivier een klein blokhuisje. Men vond het geraden, daar het alreeds 10 uur in den avond was, om daar maar te vernachten en het daglicht af te wachten. Na een supper van spek, koffij, en brood gegeten te hebben wierp men zich op de buffel vellen en jassen neer op de vloer der hut en rustte tot den morgen. Des morgens weer vroeg op weg.

Eindelijk na vele honderden van mijlen te hebben rondgereden werd er besloten dat westelijk Douglas County de meest geschikte plaats was voor een Hollandsche nederzetting. Zoodra dit besluit genomen was werd de terug reis naar Orange City aanvaard en de 15den Februarij 1882 kwamen allen behouden en wel te Orange City aan. Na een volledig verslag gegeven te hebben van de ervaringen werd er besloten zoo spoedig mogelijk eene genoegzame hoeveelheid land te verzekeren. Daartoe moesten allen die deel namen aan de nieuwe Kolonie naar Calliope [nu Hawarden] en de Sioux Rivier over om daar [in Dakota], ingezworen te worden bij het nemen van goevernements land.

Op den 6den April 1882 vertrokken de eerste kolonisten van Hull in Sioux County naar Plankinton in Dakota. Van daar moest het per as verder. Gelukkig voor onze landgenooten waren in Plankinton het vorige jaar reeds stores, lumberyards, etc., geopend door oostelijke kapitalisten, zoodat men alle benoodigdheden kon koopen. Spoedig de vracht karren ontladen, de paarden voor de wagen, lumber en proviand gekocht, en daar ging het zuiden op naar die „Nieuwe Kolonie" waar nog niets aanwezig was dan een pleisterlat met een oester kan er op als het middel punt aangewezen.

Men kan wel denken dat deze reis voor onze koene pioniers een onvergetelijke was te meer nog doordat er in de nawinter en vooral in Maart veel sneeuw en regen gevallen was waardoor de landen zeer week waren en vele lage plaatsen zeer te gevaarlijk met een zwaar beladen wagen te passeeren waren. Ook kon men geen rechte lijn houden; en moest er menig omwegje gemaakt worden waardoor de afstand die slechts 25 mijlen bedroeg aanmerkelijk verlengd werd zoodat men met het invallen van den avond nog niet op de plaats der bestemming zijnde besluiten moest om op de prairie te vernachten en men den volgenden dag doodelijk vermoeid tegen middag aankwam op de plaats, n.l. het stokje met den oester kan er op.

Maar van uitrusten kon nog niets komen. Daar moest een huis komen, dus aan 't werk. De planken van de wagen; spijkers, hamers, en zagen voor den dag, eer nog den zelfden nacht rusten zij heerlijk in de nieuwe woning – een shanty van 12 bij 14 alwaar men verblijf hield tot dat door F. le Cocq, Jr. de landen gemeten konden worden en aan de verschillende „homesteaders" aangewezen zoodat er vervolgens door ieder „homesteader" een hut gebouwd en een begin met ploegen gemaakt kon worden, volgens den eisch der wet. Het eerste bestendige werkhuis werd gebouwd door A. J. Brink, schoonzoon van Leendert van der Meer, lid van het committee die zelfs benevens Dirk van den Bos de eerste settlers van Plankinton vergezeld hadden.

Na deze eerste nederzetters nam de bevolking zoo sterk toe dat reeds in het voorjaar van 1883 al het goevernements land genomen was.

Voor wij echter verder gaan verdienen eenige gewichtige zaken vermelding. In 1881 was er in Douglas County door een troep schurken een county bestuur gevormd en de county georganizeerd, een hut van 10 × 12 voor courthouse gebouwd, een stuk land uitgelegd als hoofdstad der county dat Brownsdale genoemd werd in „honor" van een der schurken; en die heeren waren al druk aan 't uitgeven van county warrants en andere schuld warrants en schuldbrieven der county.

Het spreekt vanzelf dat toen onze koene mannen in den winter van 1882 op hunne reis boven vermeld veel onderzoek gedaan hadden te Brownsdale alles hen van de schoonste zijde werd voorgespiegeld door die schurken. Maar men kwam toch tot de overtuiging dat het een bedriegelijke boel zou worden en leiden tot ontzettende financieele druk en wellicht tot een totale vernietiging en mislukking der Hollandsche Kolonie. De bespreking en behandeling dezer gewichtige zaak drongen de commissie tot handelen en zoo mogelijk middelen te beramen die frauduleuze organisatie te vernietigen. Om dit doel te bereiken werd er een smeekschrift gericht naar de Goeverneur van Dakota die aanstonds zelf in de county kwam om de zaak te onderzoeken. Op het gerucht hiervan namen de schurken te Brownsdale de vlucht en namen bijna alle boeken van waarde met zich. De county werd opnieuw georganiseerd en de Brownsdale organisatie vernietigd, maar dit heeft jaren in de courts en veel tijd en geld gekost.

In het najaar van 1882 werd er ten tijde der algemeene verkiezingen een ticket voor county beambten opgesteld waarop onze Hollanders goed vertegenwoordigd waren; en de uitslag was dan ook zoover gunstig dat er een geheel ander en vertrouwbaar bestuur aan het roer kwam in de county. Bij die verkiezing werd Frank le Cocq, Jr. door de Hollanders als lid van de county board verkozen. Ook werd bij deze verkiezing een ander punt in de county gekozen als hoofdplaats [county seat], n.l. Grand View, bijna het midden punt der county.

Tot dusver was nu alles in orde. Maar nu kwam er voor de Hollandsche Kolonie weer een nieuwe beproeving. Door de uitslag der verkiezing waren eenige invloedrijke menschen verbitterd op de Hollanders. Daar het land zoo spoedig opgenomen was wist men te Washington op het landkantoor het vermoeden te planten dat alle Hollanders land speculanten waren; en daar de toen Commissioner of the General Land Office, een zekere [William A. J.] Sparks, spoedig over te halen was, daar hij alle baanbrekers in het Westen als land dieven beschouwde, werden al de homestead en pre-emties der Hollanders verbeurd verklaard.

Dit was natuurlijk een ramp die alles dreigde te vernietigen, maar de mannen der commissie gaven den moed niet op. Er werd een der bekwaamste advocaten te Sioux City aangesteld om voor de Hollanders te Washington op te treden. Rekesten werden opgesteld door invloedrijke vrienden waarin alles werd blootgelegd en vele brieven werden gericht aan Mr [Frederick Theo.] Frelinghuysen die toen ter tijd Secretaris van Binnenlandsche Zaken was. Deze persoon heeft veel voor de Hollandsche nederzetting gedaan. Hij was ouderling in een onzer Gereformeerde kerken in New York. Door zijn invloed werden de Hollanders weder in hun recht op het land hersteld, doch dit proces duurde wel twee jaar en heeft de commissie veel tijd, moeite, en geld gekost. Eindelijk echter werd aan onze commissie een stuk gezonden van het lands kantoor te Washington hetwelk de Hollanders in hun recht op het genomen land herstelde. Door de commissie werd dit aan alle belanghebbenden bekend gemaakt. Dat er blijdschap en dankbaarheid was in de gehele nederzetting behoeft geen betoog. Vooral aan hen die mede gewerkt hadden de landzaken te Washington in orde te brengen door het schrijven van brieven, enz., verdienen in het bijzonder de vrienden te Orange City alle lof, onder anderen den Honorable Henry Hospers, Frank le Cocq, Sr., nu inwoner van Douglas County en president van de Bank of Harrison, en meer andere personen, die zich gene moeite of tijd spaarden om de belangen van de nieuwe nederzetting te bevorderen.

Maar nu kwam dan ook duidelijk de ergste zaak eerst aan het licht n.l. door het reeds genoemde zet schurken was reeds in Januarij 1882 een schuld op de county gemaakt door het uitgeven van county warrants van omstreeks $ 50,000, die voordat die invloedrijke geheimzinnige bende en haar aanhang van buiten verbroken kon worden, tot wel $ 100,000 aan valsche warrants en bonds waren aangegroeid. Dat was al weer een ding dat tot ondergang der Kolonie kon zijn, maar het volk van Douglas County, krachtig bijgestaan door onze Hollanders, ondersteunde de board van county commissioners op zoodanige wijze dat men in

staat was goede advokaten te nemen die de daden door die vrijbuiters
gepleegd tot den wortel onderzochten en eindelijk na tien jaren lang in
de verschillende courts der staat aanhangig geweest te zijn werden al de
zoogenoemden „bogus" warrants waardeloos verklaard en vernietigd en
dus de nu wettige county organisatie van al die schuld ontheven. Gedurende al die jaren hadden de Hollanders gezorgd dat Frank le Cocq, Jr.
als chairman van de county board in functie bleef. Door de lieden van de
board werd hij benoemd met de advokaten in het bestrijden dezer bogus
warrants handelend op te treden.

Nu moeten wij echter weer eens terug naar de eerste jaren onzer nederzetting. Op godsdienstig gebied gevoelde de Hollandsche bevolking
maar al te zeer dat zij verstoken waren van de prediking van het evangelie. Wel werd er geregeld des Zondags godsdienstoefening gehouden
door Leendert van der Meer, ouderling bij de gemeente te Orange City,
en ook wel door ouderling L. Mais van de Christelijke Gereformeerde
Gemeente, in het office van Frank le Cocq, Jr. Ook werden zij zoo nu
en dan eens verblijd door de komst van een leeraar welke dan een of twee
Zondagen bleef en het brood des levens brak. Veel hebben de Hollanders
te dien tijd genoten van Ds. Steven J. Harmeling van Marion Junction
die, zelfs verhinderd veel te komen, zorgde dat er andere leeraars kwamen
en het nog kleine hoopje volk uit 't verre westen niet vergeten werd.
Ook houde de eerste settlers in aangename herinnering het bezoek in
't najaar van 1882 van Ds. A. G. Ziegeler, thans leeraar der gemeente te
Harrison, die een paar weken bij hen bleef en hen het Woord des Levens
verkondigde.

Maar men wilde organizeeren en een leeraar hebben. In het voorjaar
van 1883 werd door eene gifte van de nu overleden Dr. Jacob West, secretaris van de Board van Binnenlandsche Zending onzer Kerk, bedragende
honderd dollars, eene loods opgeslagen van 45 voet lang en 24 breed,
hetwelk ook tevens gebruikt werd als school gebouw en waar Sophia le
Cocq, nu Mrs. Markus, de eerste onderwijzer der jeugd was. Doch daar
de bevolking steeds aangroeide werd de noodzakelijkheid meer en meer
gevoeld om eene gemeente te organizeeren en na algemeen bijval werd
onder de naam van the „First Reformed Church of Douglas County"
de eerste Gereformeerde Gemeente van Dakota gesticht. Bij die gelegenheid waren tegenwoordig Ds. James de Pree van Sioux Center, Ds.
Ale Buursma van Orange City, Ds. Johannes Warnshuis van Alton, en
diens broer Hendrik Warnshuis predikant te Centerville. Ook werd er
besloten over te gaan tot het beroepen van een herder en leeraar. De
keuze viel op candidaat Abraham Stegeman van Holland, Michigan, die

·dan ook de beroepsbrief ontving en tot groote blijdschap der Hollandsche bevolking besloot tot hun over te komen en tot groote zegen der gemeente ruim acht jaren onder hun heeft gearbeid. Tot ouderlingen der gemeente werden verkozen Frank le Cocq, Sr., Leendert van der Meer, en A. Kuiper; en tot diakenen Cornelius Beukelman, P. Eernisse, en Jacob Muilenberg.

Nadat de kerkeraad der nieuwe gemeente bericht had ontvangen van hunne beroepen leeraar wanner hij te Plankinton, 25 mijlen van ons verwijderd, zou aankomen werd er een ouderling uitgezonden om hem af te halen en met de buggy te Harrison brengen daar hij bij deze ouderling voorlopig ook zou inwonen. Maar te Plankinton aangekomen kon onze ouderling de dominee maar niet vinden. Aan het station was hij niet. Niemand kende onze Abraham Stegeman, candidaat leeraar. Overal in de verschillende hotels gevraagd en gezocht, maar hoewel onze oude man als met arends oogen naar zijn man zocht hij kon, zoo min als Saul zijns vaders ezels, onze nog onbekende vriend niet vinden en ging vermoeid en teleurgesteld in de barroom van een der hotels op een stoel zitten peinzende wat hij doen zou, weg rijden dat deed hij niet, vinden moest en zou hij hem al zoude het de geheele week duren. Maar ziet terwijl onze oude vriend daar zoo zat te peinzen trok dit de aandacht van een jong mensch netjes doch eenvoudig gekleed met een vast beraden en uitvorschenden blik. Deze naderde den ouden man en vroeg in 't Engelsch, „Mijnheer, kent U of hebt U hier ook iemand ontmoet wier naam zoo-en-zoo is?" „Wel, mijnheer, die persoon ben ik, en ik ben hier om iemand te ontmoeten van Holland, Michigan, wiens naam Abraham Stegeman is." „En die persoon ben ik," was het antwoord. „Wel, wel," was de blijde uitroep van onzen vriend, „dan hebben wij na lang zoeken toch elkander gevonden." Na een hartelijken handdruk werd er besloten om maar dadelijk op reis te gaan naar Harrison waar ze beiden opgeruimd en wel na een uur of drie gereden te hebben aankwamen. Spoedig na de aankomst werd op eene te Harrison gehouden klassis onze jonge vriend geëxamineerd en als leeraar der gemeente geordend en bevestigd.

Veel zouden wij hier bij kunnen voegen van de eerste jaren der kerkelijke geschiedenis, dat van veel belang zou zijn, maar het bestek moet kort blijven; alleen dit, de gemeente te Harrison had voorspoed en werd kennelijk gezegend. Reeds in 1884 verheugde zij zich in eene flinke kerk en pastorie die door hulp van de board gebouwd werden en tezamen ongeveer $ 5,000 gekost hebben en was het ledental der gemeente te dier tijd reeds tot over de honderd huisgezinnen vermeerderd.

Ook de Christelijke Gereformeerde Kerk had vele leden die behoefte gevoelden aan organizatie. Reeds in 't najaar van 1883 werd er te New Holland, 4 mijlen west van Harrison een gemeente gevormd en in 't volgende jaar werd er kerk en pastorie gebouwd en Ds. Tamme M. van den Bosch van Overisel, Michigan, beroepen als herder en leeraar die een jaar daar met vrucht gearbeid heeft. Terzelfder tijd werd er ook te Harrison een gemeente georganizeerd die door de finantieele hulp van ouderling Roelof H. Brinks spoedig in het bezit van eene zeer nette kerk en pastorie was en die na eenige mislukte pogingen zich verheugde in een eigen herder in de persoon van Ds. Van den Bosch van New Holland.

In 1885 was de Hollandsche bevolking in de Kolonie reeds tot 3,000 zielen gestegen, en zou spoedig een der meest uitgebreide nederzettingen van Hollanders geworden zijn; maar de slechte tijden, de misgewassen, en de drooge jaren hebben de uitbreiding der Kolonie zeer belemmerd en is de oorzaak geweest dat vele der eerste kolonisten in 1891 en 1892 de kolonie verlieten. Doch bij de verandering der tijden en de goede oogsten gedurende de laatste jaren begint er weer volk in te komen en breidt zich de kolonie weer sterk uit.

Ziedaar! dit zijn slechts eenige der ervaringen en omstandigheden der eerste jaren onzer nederzetting en volksplanting in Douglas County, alles kort maar nauwkeurig beschreven. Mocht het op de halve eeuw feesten van onze vaders en stamgenoten in het oosten iets bijdragen ter verhoging van hunne en onze vreugde over de vele zegeningen Gods ons Hollandsch volk in de verschillende oorden en onder zware beproevingen geschonken in dit goede land, zoo is mijn moeite ruimschoots betaald.

[Translation]

Ten years after the Dutch settlers under the leadership of Mr. Henry Hospers [at present state senator in Iowa] had founded their Kolonie in Sioux County, need was felt for another settlement. Hollanders from states other than Iowa and immigrants from the Netherlands had taken up all vacant lands in Sioux County. The price of farmlands had risen from $ 10 to $ 25 per acre. Poor families could not acquire land for their children. Several enterprising persons realized the necessity of finding an area where it would be possible to secure homestead land from our national government.

A meeting was held in Orange City in October 1881, the aim of which was to look for a proper location of a new Kolonie. At this meeting two men were present who had paid a recent visit to Dakota on the occasion of a sale of Indian ponies the government had seized from the well-known chief Sitting Bull. These men reported that they had seen beautiful, undulating, and extensive prairies in Dakota.

A committee was named to investigate this region. Its members were Leendert van der Meer, Dirk van den Bos, and Frank le Cocq, Jr. As well equipped as was possbile, these men crossed the Big Sioux River which forms the boundary between Iowa and Dakota. They traveled through Turner, Bon Homme, Douglas, and Charles Mix counties. On their return, about the close of November, they reported what they had seen. Another meeting was held and decision was made provisionally to found a Kolonie in Douglas County. About the middle of January 1882 the above named committee accompanied by Jacob Muilenberg, T. T. Joustra, and Arie Beukelman and guided by a Mr. Harrington, former surveyor in Bon Homme County, set out to observe the country more thoroughly.

Leaving Orange City, they proceeded to Calliope, crossed the Big Sioux River into Dakota, and reached Yankton, the seat of a government land office. The committee was provided with letters of introduction from Mr. Cyrus C. Carpenter, then governor of Iowa, and the Hon. Henry Hospers to Mr. G. H. Weston, registrar at the land office, and to Mr. L. Wyna, a person well acquainted with the history of the Sioux County settlement. These men subsequently rendered many a service to the Hollanders of Douglas County and are to be given much credit for the success of the new Kolonie.

Beyond this point their journey became difficult. Everything they needed had to be carried on horses or in wagons. They traveled toward some small place on the Missouri River and in Charles Mix County. They moved westward over the boundless prairie, by compass, like ships on the ocean. This was a difficult journey, in the depth of winter and accompanied with difficulties. Finally, after five days, they arrived at the Missouri River.

From the mouth of Pease Creek in Charles Mix County to Douglas County was a dangerous trip in winter and especially in those days. The committee accompanied by Muilenberg, Joustra, and Beukelman, riding in two wagons, undertook this journey on February 3, 1882. At the crack of dawn Van den Bos roused his companions, for it was necessary to start early if in one day they wanted to reach destination.

When the sun rose, they were on their way eastward to Brownsdale, a place consisting of a small house and a 10 by 20 foot board shanty which served as the county courthouse of Douglas County.

It was a fair day and there was no snow on the ground. After riding all morning at a good rate they stopped at noon to have a moment's rest. They let the horses feed on buffalo grass. Their cook, chosen by his companions, prepared some food. A fire was made from Missouri River wood, water taken from a lake nearby, coffee prepared, ham fried. And so with prayer and thanks to God they had their meal on that vast open prairie.

Just as the men were about to resume their journey one of them, looking into the distance, exclaimed, "See what's coming yonder!" A starving pack of wolves, attracted by the smell of frying ham, was approaching. But whether because some one of our group exerted the magical influence of a wild animal trainer or for some other reason, the animals kept their distance. The Hollanders, in order not to rouse their fury, made no attempt to shoot them. Fortunately, just before nightfall the travelers arrived at Brownsdale. There they stabled their horses and secured lodging.

On another occasion when they were lost in foggy weather and a snowstorm, they spent a night in an Indian hut so cold that they nearly froze to death.

On still another of their expeditions our pioneer investigators were pursued by a band of about 20 Indians who were angered by the fact that when our men had camped out on their reservation they had thoughtlessly emptied their pipes and started a fire which burned the dried grass, the only food for the Indians' ponies. The Indians surrounded them and would have seized them and accused them before their agent at Greenwood, but someone from Brownsdale who spoke the Indians' language well appeared on the scene. Acting as interpreter, he satisfied the Indians that the fire was an unfortunate accident and that it had not been started purposely. He was able to persuade the Indians not to break the peace and to abstain from all hostility.

Happy and thankful, our hardy pioneers resumed their journey. But another difficulty presented itself. Although they kept careful account of the miles they had traveled, they noted that they had lost their course. They had traveled a great distance and their horses were weary. They spied a small loghouse in the woods along the Missouri River. It was 10 o'clock and they decided to spend their night in this house. After a supper of pork, coffee, and bread, they spread their coats and buffalo hides on the floor and awaited dawn. Early in the morning they continued their journey.

After travelling many hundreds of miles they decided that the western parts of Douglas County offered the most suitable prospect for a Holland Kolonie. They at once set out for Orange City where on February 15, 1882, they gave a full report of their experiences. It was at once decided to establish claims to a sufficient quantity of land. All who wanted to participate in the new Kolonie had to go to Calliope [at present Hawarden] and cross the Sioux River into Dakota where they offered their oaths when they took out their claims.

The first settlers departed Hull in Sioux County on April 6, 1882, and traveled by train to Plankinton in Dakota. Fortunately, some business men from the East had opened stores, lumber yards, and other businesses where the settlers could buy all needed supplies. They quickly unloaded the freight cars, hitched their horses to the wagons, purchased lumber and provisions, and set out southward to the "New Kolonie", the central point of which the investigating committee had marked by a plaster lath on which they had placed an oyster can.

One can well imagine that to these pioneers this was a never-to-be-forgotten journey. Much snow and rain had fallen and the prairie was so water soaked that in many places it was dangerous for a heavily laden wagon to attempt to cross. To avoid treacherous low spots they followed a circuitous route so that the distance, 25 miles in a straight line, was greatly increased. Exhausted, they had to spend the night out on the open prairie. Not until next day at about noon did they arrive at their destination, the plaster lath with the oyster can on it.

The new arrivals at once went to work building a shelter for common use. The wagons were unloaded and nails, hammers, and saws came into play. Before nightfall they were resting in the shanty, a structure 12 by 14 feet. Here they were to stay until Frank le Cocq, Jr. had surveyed the land so that the homesteaders could move onto their claims, build huts, and begin plowing as the law prescribed. The first settler to build such a hut was A. J. Brink, brother-in-law of Leendert van der Meer who besides Dirk van den Bos, both members of the committee of investigation, had accompanied the settlers. Other settlers followed so that by the spring of 1883 all available government land had been taken up.

Before proceeding with our account we must notice a matter of great concern for the new settlers. A group of scoundrels had organized a county government in 1881, built a county courthouse – a hut 10 by 12 feet in size, and laid out a town named Brownsdale, so named "in honor" of one of the rascals. These men were active in issuing county warrants and other obligations which had to be paid by the county.

Naturally when in the winter of 1882 our men had investigated the situation at Brownsdale the scoundrels had represented everything as being in order. But it was not long until they learned about the true nature of affairs. They realized that these obligations weighed heavily upon the county and might entail the total ruin of the Dutch Kolonie. The committee decided to have an end put to this fraudulent organization. An appeal was sent to the governor of Dakota Territory, who at once came in person in order to investigate. The Brownsdale rascals, hearing of the governor's arrival, took to flight, carrying with them nearly all the county's valuable papers. Douglas County was reorganized anew and the Brownsdale organization was declared null and void. These steps required years of litigation in the courts and cost much money.

At the time of the general elections, in the fall of 1882, a county ticket was drawn up on which our Hollanders were well represented. A reliable and very different set of officials was chosen, who assumed the direction of county matters. Frank le Cocq, Jr. was elected, largely by the Dutch vote, a member of the county Board of Supervisors. At this election, also, a new county seat was chosen, namely Grand View, situated nearly in the center of the county.

Until now success had crowned their efforts. But new trials lay ahead for the Dutch Kolonie. Several influential persons were bitter toward the Hollanders because of the outcome of the election. As the land had been rapidly taken up, these people knew how to plant the idea that the Hollanders were merely land speculators and to win for their schemes certain persons in Washington [D.C.]. One of these persons who supported the plotters was William A. J. Sparks, Commissioner of the General Land Office, who believed that pioneer settlers were thieves. Through Sparks' instrumentality all homestead and preemption claims of the Hollanders were voided.

Naturally this disaster threatened to ruin the settlement, but the men of the committee did not lose all courage. They engaged the services of one of the most competent attorneys of Sioux City to defend the Hollanders in their claims made in Washington. Petitions were addressed to influential friends in which full statement was made of the case. Many letters were written to Frederick Theo. Frelinghuysen, at that time Secretary of State. This person rendered great service for the Holland settlement. He was an elder in one of our Reformed churches in New York. Through his influence the Hollanders were restored in their rights and their land was returned. This involved a legal process which lasted more than two years and involved the committee in the loss of much time and money. Finally the committee received a document from the Land Office in Washington which restored the Dutch claimants in all their rights. When informed of the recovery of their just titles, the entire settlement was thankful. Many had contributed to the happy conclusion of the question of land titles by writing letters and taking other steps deserving praise. Among them were the Honorable Henry Hospers and Frank le Cocq, Sr., then citizen of Douglas County and later president of the Bank of Harrison, besides other persons.

An even more serious threat appeared. The scoundrels entrenched in the county government at Brownsdale had, by January 1882, issued warrants in the sum of $ 50,000. Before they could be legally stopped this sum had grown to more than $ 100,000. This indebtedness might have ruined the Kolonie, but the population, supported by the Hollanders and the Board of County Commissioners, succeeded in averting disaster. Capable attorneys were appointed who investigated the crooked activities of the men at Brownsdale. They were able to void all the warrants. Frank le Cocq, Jr , during all this time chairman of the Board of Supervisers, was prominently associated with these attorneys.

But to return to the first years of our settlement. The Hollanders missed the preaching of the Gospel. Services were conducted regularly by Leendert van der Meer, an elder in the Reformed congregation in Orange City. Similar services were held by Elder L. Mais in the office of Frank le Cocq, Jr., for the Christian Reformed group. Occasionally some minister spent a Sunday or two among the settlers, and broke for them the Bread of Life. They were grateful to Dominie Steven J. Harmeling of Marion Junction. Although unable to visit them frequently, he saw to it that other ministers visited them; and so the little group of Hollanders in farthest West was not entirely forgotten. These people also gratefully remember Dominie A. G. Ziegler, who visited them in the fall of 1882 and who at present is pastor of the congregation at Harrison.

The people wanted to have a permanent church organization with a resident pastor. A gift of $ 100 made by the late Dr. Jacob West, Secretary of the Board of Domestic Missions [of the Reformed Church], enabled them to erect a shed 24 by 45 feet. This building was used also as a school where Sophia le Cocq, now Mrs. Markus, served as the first teacher. But as the Dutch population continued to grow the first Reformed Church in Douglas County was formed. Present on that occasion were the dominies James de Pree of Sioux Center, Ale Buursma of Orange City,

Johannes Warnshuis of Alton, and Hendrik Warnshuis [Presbyterian]
pastor at Centerville, [Dakota]. An invitation was issued to Abraham
Stegeman of Holland, Michigan, to assume the pastorate, which he
accepted. As elders were chosen Frank le Cocq, Sr., Leendert van der
Meer, and A. Kuiper and as deacons, Cornelius Beukelman, P. Eernisse,
and J. Muilenberg.

The consistory, learning when their newly called pastor would arrive
at Plankinton, distant 25 miles, sent one of its elders with whom their
minister was to stay temporarily. But the elder, arrived in Plankinton,
could not find him at the station. No one knew our Abraham Stegeman.
Our elder looked everywhere in the hotels of the place. Although he
looked with eagle eye he could not find the new pastor any more than
Saul could find his father's asses [see 1 Samuel, 9, 3-4]. Weary and disappointed he sat down in the hotel's bar, debating what to do. He decided
not to return, for find him he would even though it would take a whole
week. While thus engaged in his thoughts, a plainly but neatly dressed
young man with a meditative and enquiring expression noted the elder.
Approaching, he asked him in English, "Do you know anyone here
named Mr. ——— or have you seen such a person?" "Well, sir," was
the answer," I am that person, and I am to meet somenone here by the
name of Abraham Stegeman." "I am that person." "Well, well," was the
elder's glad response, "we have finally found each other." They departed
at once for Harrison which they reached after driving more than three
hours. Soon after his arrival the youthful candidate for the ministry was
examined by the consistory and duly ordained and installed.

We could tell many more things about our religious life during our
early years, but space does not permit. The congregation of Harrison,
abundantly blessed, prospered. By 1884 it had a splendid church building
and parsonage. The total cost of these buildings, partly defrayed by the
Board of Domestic Missions, was about $ 5,000. The membership of the
congregation by that date had increased to more than 100 families.

The Christian Reformed group, organized in the fall of 1883, in the
following year erected a new church building and parsonage at New Holland, four miles west of Harrison. Dominie Tamme van den Bosch of
Overisel, Michigan, served them for a year. At this time another Christian
Reformed congregation was organized at Harrison. This group, with
the financial assistance of Roelof H. Brinks, soon was in possession of a
neat church and parsonage. After several unsuccessful attempts to
acquire a pastor, they invited Van den Bosch from New Holland, who
accepted.

In 1885 the total Dutch population of the Kolonie had risen to 3,000. This new settlement would have become one of the largest Dutch communities had it not been for hard times, crop failures, and prolonged drought. These misfortunes caused many of the first settlers to abandon the Kolonie in 1891 and 1892. But times have changed. Good harvests during recent years have induced people to move in and the Kolonie is again expanding.

These are but a few of the experiences of our pioneers, told briefly and accurately, during the first years of the settlement in Douglas County. May the semi-centennial celebrations of our fathers and our fellow Hollanders in eastern states multiply our happiness in the abundant blessings God has given our Dutch people in various places and under grave trials, in this good country of ours. If this wish is fulfilled I shall deem my efforts amply repaid.

105. CHRISTINA PLEMP'S MEMOIRES

[Mrs. Christina Plemp, daughter of Frank le Cocq, Sr., spent her early years in the settlement at Harrison, South Dakota. The following account of the traials of the first Dutch settlers was especially prepared for inclusion in this collection.]

Prosperity had come to the pioneer Hollanders who had settled in Sioux County, Iowa, since 1871. Hard times were past, the ravages of grasshoppers forgotten. Land prices were high when the welcome news came that the government had opened a tract of land for settlement in South Dakota. Homesteads, preëmptions, tree claims could be filed. Free land – but how free it ultimately was to prove time only could tell. Leendert van der Meer, Dirk van den Bos, and Frank le Cocq, Jr., my brother, went to investigate and came back with glowing accounts. Southeastern Dakota was a rolling prairie, rich with tall buffalo grass so nutritious that cattle could fatten on it. The country was dotted with small lakes teeming with water fowl.

My brother opened a temporary office in mother's dismantled sitting room in Orange City. Here the promoters held their meetings. Daily landseekers came to Orange City to learn about filing claims and get information about transportation and other matters. Young men wishing to start out for themselves, to whom the prospect of free land was most alluring, came eagerly. Also farmers who had been renting land had visions of independence and plenty when they learned how easily 160 acres could be obtained in Dakota. Brother Frank was tired from solving the many perplexing problems of those who proposed to migrate. One man rich in ten children but poor in money came for advice. "What is

the best way to go?" "By train." "But I have no money!" "Then go
overland!" "But it is raining torrents," he wailed. Frank sighed, "I can't
stop that."

Many Hollanders from Sioux County, despite the torrential rains in
those days, of the exodus, traveled westward in prairie schooners. Others
went by rail to Plankinton, 25 miles from the plotted town site of
Harrison. The town consisted simply of a small land office, Pieter Eernisse's general store, a blacksmith's shop, and a small house serving as a
boarding house, built by Cornelius van den Bos. A mile to the south
Leendert van der Meer had built a neat house for himself near a small
body of water named Lake Pleasant.

Land we filed on in Yankton, claims were staked out; some of the
newcomers erected soddies, but others financially able built shanties
from lumber. Occupation of claims was immediately imperative, for
unscrupulous claim jumpers were ever on the watch, and many a claim
had to be defended with a shotgun. There was an abundance of grass for
stock, also tall slough grass to cut and twist for fuel. Buffalo chips,
scattered about in great quantities, were gathered in piles by the children,
later to be hauled home and burned along with the tightly twisted hay.
A sheet metal box shaped like a drum and placed upon the cook stove
retained for some time the heat of the burning hay and buffalo chips.

Like Phoenix from its ashes, so the pioneering spirit rose in the mind
of my father, Frank le Cocq, Sr. He also went to Dakota, saw its promising prairies, and yielded to the alluring prospect of founding a new settlement. Over the protests and tears of Mary, his wife, he built a home just
across a picturesque small body of water close to the hamlet which my
brother decided to call Harrison in honor of the president with whom he
recently had had an interview. The next spring we set out on the journey,
to our still unfinished home, being driven by buggy to Pattersonville, at
present Hull, Iowa. Next we proceeded by train to Plankinton, and from
there, the last part of the journey 25 miles over Stony Ridge south again
by buggy to the hamlet of Harrison. The low hanging clouds which
threatened rain chilled mother's heart as she looked over the lonesome,
treeless plain she was to call her home, and with yearning she thought of
the comfortable home she had left behind in Sioux County.

The downpour that had threatened all day mercifully waited until we
had squeezed into the small boarding house and had supper of hot
biscuits and steaming tea. We slept on quilts spread upon the floor, but
soon in water when the rain came down in torrents being driven by a
furious east wind which poured a stream of water through doors and

windows. The next day we moved into our unfinished house. But alas! during the next few months from behind the rough laths emerged hundreds, yes myriads of bedbugs. In spite of the vigilant efforts of mother and my two older sisters, Cornelia and Sophia, to exterminate them they so increased that our house inside was plastered and painted with them. And again the next spring it rained unceasingly.

One day we saw a new settler, Pieter Meyer, with his family drive into the settlement. A quarter of a mile from our house he erected a flimsy shelter, in the downpour. Toward dusk while we were shut in by the violent rain, father said "I think I will walk over, I feel that family needs help." "In all this rain?" asked mother surprised. Father was glad, for what a sight greeted him! A woman sat on the bed with five children around her, and water ankle deep on the floor. On a box in a corner lay the body of a little child. It had just died, and the mother burst into tears when she saw father. My father turned to the grief stricken husband and said, "Hitch up your team and bring your family to my house." Cold, wet, bewildered, and hungry, the little band arrived; but washed, warmed, and fed, they soon fell asleep in our front room on beds of shavings, covered with blankets. But the poor mother could not rest. "Our darling little sister, Joey," she leamented, "is all alone there in that cold house." "I'll go back to her" soothed the silent suffering man, and she was comforted when she saw her other children sleeping quietly. Next morning a small grave was dug and funeral services were held – the first burial in the new settlement.

The first Sunday church services in Harrison were conducted in our unfinished upstairs. Dominie K. B. Weiland, who had come in behalf of the Reformed Church in America to investigate the possibility of a new congregation, presided. Soon thereafter a long building or rough boards was constructed. In it we celebrated our first Fourth of July. In it also father conducted a catechetical class. Later this building was used as the church barn.

One morning disturbing rumors of an Indian uprising came to our village. The Indians had had ghost and war dances; their spirits were inflamed, and they were ready to attack the whites. Shanties and haystacks of settlers near the reservation were burned. Families from near the line of the Indian reservation fled to town, confirming the report. "What shall we do? Where can we find refuge?" asked our terrified mother. "Plankinton is so far away, how can we possibly get there ahead of those fiends on their fast ponies?" Our hired man, Sim Dykshoorn, brought the big lumber wagon before the door. We loaded on it the supplies we would need should flight become necessary. Our two big horses, Baby and Charley, stood in the barn, ready to be hitched to the wagon. We sat up that night, listening and waiting for the sounds we feared to hear. Suddenly an ominous shout paled mother's face. "Here they come!" But the heavy gutteral sounds came from Sim, who had fallen asleep while listening and waiting and was snoring peacefully. In the morning reassuring news came that the soldiers from Fort Randall had driven the Indians back to their reservation. Calm was restored.

The Board of Domestic Missions of the Reformed Church in America with headquarters in New York took notice of the religious needs of the new settlement and sent Dominie Ale Buursma of Orange City, Dominie James de Pree of Sioux Center, and one or two other ministers to investigate the situation, who in due course organized a congregation. Dominie Buursma advised the newly elected elders to invite a recently ordained and highly recommended young minister from Holland, Michigan. The call was accepted, and when the tall, bronzed, stalwart, earnest young man came we at once knew we had no mistake, and everyone loved him, for he had a kindly look and humorous glance in his eye, and a heart filled with love for the wide horizons and rolling prairies of the West.

Landseekers poured in. That fall the big prairie fire threatened to wipe out our village. It was a beautiful Sunday morning when a cloud of thick smoke was noticed in the northwest. All the men, including the dominie, went to meet it in wagons loaded with gunny sacks and barrels of water; but the fire outran them and came straight for the town. However, no damage was done beyond cracking window panes and burning the haystacks. The men came back with blackened faces, minus eyebrows, eyelashes, beards, and moustaches. One young man had just succeeded in raising a small mustache and, as his wife told us when we were all seated around the table after the excitement, eating sandwiches and drinking coffee, had that very same morning been preening before the mirror declaring that "the new moustache made him a handsome fellow."

When our congregation learned that Dominie Abraham Stegeman's fiancée, Bertha ten Eyck, in the East was waiting to come out West, we voted to build a parsonage and construction began at once. The farmers volunteered to haul the lumber, sand, lime, and cement. By the first of October the house was shingled and the siding had been put on, and so even if early snow came the inside could be finished with ease. But when the sharp October winds whistled over the treeless prairie the school-house, which had been finished during the summer, proved too cold for the children. The dominie was asked to relinquish the house which during the following winter served as a school and church. He agreed at once in spite of the fact that the young fiancée in the East would have to wait. But not for long, for mother offered the dominie the use of our large front room which was separate from the rest of our house. Miss Ten Eyck was willing to accept this room as her home and so before the year 1882 came to a close our colony was enriched with a minister's youthful wife. Meanwhile school was held in the parsonage and my sister, Sophy (Sophia) le Cocq, was our first teacher.

New buildings gave evidence that Harrison was prosperous. A new schoolhouse was erected, and in the only room that was finished seven grades were taught, by Oscar Pickens, a young man from the east. Later on, in the summer of 1883, the Board of Domestic Missions of the Reformed Church in America loaned money to build a church. The Christian Reformed congregation likewise received help from their synod and so two fine church buildings were erected almost at the same time. The parsonages also were finished and the hamlet grew into a village. Neat barns were built and fences appeared. The soil was fertile. Flint corn and vegetables were raised very successfully on the newly turned sod, for the rain was abundant. Potatoes grew large and flat, but the best crop during the first years was flax which could be sown as late as June 20, and brought $ 1.20 a bushel.

The first winters in the new country, treeless and windswept, were severe. Our well was quite far from the house, so Sim, the hired man, filled a barrel at the well and hauled it home on a stone boat. After it stood out in the open for a few hours it was frozen solid, and so he rolled it into the kitchen.

Soon the village could boast of a weekly newspaper, *The Globe*, of which George Culver was the editor. Not long after, John Hospers, son of Henry Hospers of Orange City, began publishing *De Bode*, a weekly in the Dutch language. Later Hospers moved to Springfield, South Dakota, where he continued to publish the paper. Everything was booming, everyone was happy-until the epidemic came. Dr. Gregory, the recently arrived physician, diagnosed it as cholera infantum, and, although he worked night and day to save precious lives, many new little graves had to be dug in the recently plotted cemetery, and a pall like a dark cloud hung over our pleasant village. There was fear and deep sadness in many a family.

In November 1883 our dominie received a letter from New York stating that the new settlement on the prairie of South Dakota had aroused much interest among the Reformed people in New York City. With the consent of teachers, parents, and pupils, the leaders of two large Sunday Schools had decided to abandon the usual Christmas custom of giving presents to each other and send gifts for the struggling new Sunday School on the South Dakota prairie. A week or two later the boxes and barrels arrived, filled with many pretty things testifying to the love that loyal hearts in a great city bore us. There were dolls, many of them accompanied with trunks of doll's clothes. There were beautiful toys and also clothing, some new, some worn a little. Also mittens, gloves, and warm stockings. And there was a box of small candles with holders and some ornaments. Dominie said "We must have a tree." He sent for a suitable Christmas tree, but it never arrived.

It was the day before Christmas: every family from far and near came eagerly and expectantly to fill the church; but there was no Christmas tree. Then one of the boys brought in a small cottonwood tree. Where he found it no one knew, but in the absence of a better, it took the place of a real tree. "If only we had some green tissue paper," said some one. Yes, there was some and soon all hands were busily at work winding and twisting the paper on the tree's branches, creating an imitation Christmas tree. Next they made popcorn and strung it in snowlike streamers along the branches. Glittering toys filled the empty gaps; it was a warisome task but one of love, for on Christmas Eve the new church building was filled with happy parents and their children, and so the workers felt amply repaid. Little girls into whose arms a doll was laid sat stunned with delight; boys shivered at the sight of big, colored balls, barns full of animals, and huge tops. This seemed like heaven to these prairie children whose lives were drab and plain. There was a package of candy and peanuts and a popcorn ball for each child. The adults got hot chocolate and sandwiches, and all went home utterly and completely satisfied, their faces shining with happiness. Many of them looked up to the glittering stars thanking the Giver of all good things and the loving hearts in far away New York who had so kindly provided for this wonderful, never-to-be-forgotten evening.

New settlers came to make their homes in the colony. The first pioneers for the most part came from Sioux County, Iowa. Others came from Michigan, and a smaller number from the Dutch colony that had just failed in Virginia. In addition, some immigrants arrived from the Netherlands. A new general store was opened, next a drugstore, a hotel, a livery stable, and a larger blacksmith's shop. The village of Harrison fairly rang with activity. Cattlemen bought sections of land on which to graze their herds. They shipped their fattened stock to Sioux City, Iowa.

Everything was booming, everybody was rejoicing, for the Chicago, Milwaukee, St. Paul and Pacific Railroad sent surveyors to survey a prospective right of way through Harrison, in fact right in front of our church. Everybody was sure our village would be chosen for a station. Thereafter, every spring rumors of the coming railroad gladdened our hopeful hearts. Some even saw, as in a vision, the engine rolling along Stony Ridge, miles away, the smoke belching from the funnel leaving a dark cloud behind. It was a mirage these people had seen, something that happened occasionally in the morning. For example, the hills along the Missouri River, more than 30 miles distant would become plainly visible, but, as the sun rose higher and higher, they seemed to break apart and melt away. Years came and went, but the railroad remained no more than a cherished hope. Finally, a railroad was built through the country, but alas! the site for the station was Armour, 16 miles from Harrison. This was a keen disappointment, for my father had hoped that Harrison would become the central point of a happy and prosperous Dutch settlement. Grand View, a small village a few miles east from Harrison was moved to Armour and stood deserted. Only the church, store, and a few other buildings remained, for the most part to be demolished later in a cyclone.

In Harrison as everywhere else politics made bitter enemies. Feeling between Republicans and Democrats ran high. In those days men took their voting seriously. Arguments often ended in fights. They were real patriots in those days, although in overalls and coarse shirts, statesmen at heart. They followed the events of the day with the keenest interest and discussed them without end. There were not pacifists then, no youth movements, no citizens who uttered the degrading words "We won't fight for any cause!" The Washington and Lincoln ideal of citizenship predominated. The citizens were willing to fight for home and liberty, for law and justice. The two bitterest opponents were Frank le Cocq, Jr. and Peter Hospers, farmer-schoolmaster, pals from the old swimming hole back in boyhood days in Iowa. As Frank was victorious he was hoisted on the shoulders of his supporters and amid cheers brought to the hall. But the defeated party shouted "Dutch Cattle" and "Foul Play!" The winning side held a parade with torches and banners. Frank le Cocq, Sr., something of an artist, painted a cow on a banner with the words "The Dutch Cattle Won" underneath.

The cycle of drought years, from which the new settlement had been spared thus far, arrived. Rains were plentiful again in spring, and the grain and corn fields looked promising. But the month of June passed, without any rain. Severe heat followed the prolonged drought. Hot winds devastated and dwindled the produce to half a crop. The Dutch settlers took the loss in patience; next year would be better, so they plowed and sowed again. But the next year and the next were even worse. Corn that stood up straight and fresh in the morning would be torn and shredded toward evening, the tattered leaves rattling in the hot wind. The window-panes in the houses felt hot to the touch. The vegetables in the garden fairly seemed to cook. Dust storms added to the discomfort. Dry electrical storms were so fierce it seemed as if the very heavens exploded. Balls of blue flame were seen rolling across the yard, and the kitchen stove crackled. The little lakes that had beautified the country had long since dried, their bottoms baked and curled up in hard dry crusts. The wells that had been dug were dry. The shade trees gave up life. The poplars died. The long suffering cottonwood trees that had so bravely withstood the drought and still merrily twinkled their leaves were attacked by another enemy, the cottonwood bug, a small yellow striped pest which accomplished what heat and drought had failed to do. The little groves, our only comfort, were dying. In those dry years rain seemed impossible. Many times the east wind would work up a beautiful bank of clouds in the northwest. It would surely rain now. For did not that east wind spell rain? The parched corn seemed to look up hopefully at the promising sky, the heads of grain shriveling in the burning heat gently stirred in expectation. But then the treacherous wind would creep up silently behind those thick banks of dark clouds and with terrific force drive them onward past longing, waiting fields, leaving nothing but blighted hopes. A few big drops would fall making a hissing sound in the hot dust and that was all. Behind the rain clouds appeared the dust clouds. Sometimes we had a fine shower and we hoped this would last three or four days or a week. But in vain, for the shower always stopped.

The persevering Hollander, however, did not give up. Every spring he sowed and planted with renewed hope. "This year," he thought, "will be a good year." But each fall saw him facing the winter with less. Some of the deeply discouraged got out the old covered wagon that originally had brought them with high hopes to this promising land which now had betrayed their trust. Taking with them only their most necessary be-longings, they left their baked acres, their machinery, and their scanty furniture to creditors, men who had loaned them money and who too seemed to have been betrayed. The pioneer was finished; he was going back to his original home in Iowa or some other state. For the last time he looked at the place of his family's vain hopes, its hard toil, its bitter disappointments. Passing one of those deserted homes one would wish to stop as at a shrine. The groves and orchards stood stark and dead. The pitiful attempts of some woman's hand to beautify a primitive pioneer home now were only some parched, rattling vines clinging to a porch or wall. Desolate barns that had sheltered shivering stock now stood cold and empty. Still there were the ghosts of childbearing women, ever hopeful of a better tomorrow. When in this age of automobiles, electrical conveniences, steam heated and airconditioned homes, we hear complaints ,when we see the expensive clothes, and the luxurious lives of our people, our thoughts go back to those other women, isolated sometimes for weeks on snow-bound farms, uncomplainingly taking up their daily tasks, caring for their children, nursing new arrivals brought into the world without medical care, helping with the chores, and working in barn and field to save hired help. Strange it was there were so few complaints, so little murmuring of discontent. With little money mothers contrived to keep the children warm and well fed. Many farmers kept sheep. The sheared wool was dyed, spun, carded, and knitted into stockings and socks. Mittens and gloves were cut out of canvas grain sacks. From the same material they made low shoes to be worn in the house. Some of the women became real experts in such makeshifts. Youth had few pleasures in those days. Sleighing and bobsledding gave the greatest delight. Tucked under arm buffalo robes which in those days were very common they rode through the country, the frosty, night air ringing with their favorite sleighing songs.

Those that stayed on went forward undefeated. "Go on, go on!" was the slogan. And to their everlasting credit it must be recorded that every father believed the support of wife and children was his first responsibility even on the meagerest rations. Government aid was not asked nor expected. The sturdy Hollander thought it was not the duty of county, state, or national government to support him during these trials incidental to pioneer life in Dakota. But the mother colony in Sioux County, Iowa, generously sent seed, clothes, food, and other necessaries.

In these terrible days when all hope thus seemed lost, Dominie Stegeman received a call to a pastorate in his home state of Michigan. His wife, homesick and weary from the trials of pioneer life in Dakota, was jubilant at the thought of conforts, shade and fruit trees, rain, and abundance in everything. It was a sore temptation for the dominie whose salary, cut down to pitiful proportions, could not be paid by the penniless farmers. But to the joy and surprise of all, the dominie in simple

words announced to the congregation when it met for worship on the
following Sunday, "I have declined the call to Michigan." To his wife
in tears of disappointment he said, simply "How could I leave these
people in sore distress?" Self sacrificing Abraham Stegeman, your name
will long be remembered with love and gratitude!

Water was precious. "Conserve water" was the general admonishment.
We saved the water in which we washed vegetables. With it we scrubbed
our floors. Old Albert van der Ploeg owned a well which became a gold
mine for him, and he kept it under lock and key. With an old horse, a
stone boat, and a barrel he hauled water to the housewives for their
weekly washing. He charged twenty-five cents for each barrelful brought
to the door. The barrel was covered with a square piece of canvas, held
down by an iron hoop so none of the precious contents could splash out.
The big, white cow belonging to Frank Le Cocq, Sr. had often from behind the wire fence in her pasture longingly watched this cool-looking
barrel when it passed by. One day the thisty creature found a way to
follow the tempting water. Silently she watched from a distance until
Mrs. Peter Eernisse when engaged in washing left the barrel unguarded.
On coming back to it she beheld the huge cow greedily drinking the
water in audible gulps. Mrs. Eernisse hit her with a broom, whereupon
the startled creature overturned the barrel and so spilled all its contents.
This was a real calamity both for Mrs. Eernisse and the cow, and her
washing could not be finished until Albert could bring out another barrel
for her.

And so the drought continued; the earth seemed like iron, the sky like
brass. One hot unbearable morning, the Reformed dominie Tamme van
den Bosch, came to see father. "Mr. le Cocq, wij moeten vasten!" (We
must fast!) And fast we did, but of the result I am not sure.

Finally, in August 1886, came the day when the cattle plaintively
lowed for water, but there was none to give them. Dominie Frederick
James Zwemer drove from Charles Mix County (the county south of
Douglas County in which Harrison is situated) to talk it over with
father. "Mr. le Cocq, don't you realize something must be done?" he
asked. "Yes," replied father, "but what?" "Men," he said, "where is
your faith? Let's have a prayer meeting!" The dominie took a big cotton
umbrella with him to the meeting. He was amply rewarded for his firm
faith, for the petitions addressed to the Creator were answered. Before
the meeting was finished it began to pour, and we ran home in the
streaming rain, dripping wet. The dominie, laughed under his umbrella.
"What did I tell you?" he said. "My clothes are dry." The lightning

flashed, the thunder rolled; but the low distressed moan of the cattle had ceased.

The investors, men who had bought large tracts of land and those who had made loans to the farmers, took over many of the drought-burnt farms. They decided to drill artesian wells. The soil was fertile they reasoned, and all that was needed to make it productive was a constant supply of water. The work started in spite of the fact that many were dubious. When the first well came in with a loud rumble and the water spouted up into the air like a geyser in Yellowstone Park, there was great celebration and new hopes were born. The well flowed day and night and soon a small lake was formed. Many such wells, it was reasoned, would create small lakes, and the country again would look as it did when first settled. The lakes would fill the air with moisture and the rains would come back; and so more wells were drilled. But after a few years the wells went dry. Tubular wells now took their place and windmills were installed to pump the water. Although breeze seldom was lacking to keep the mills spinning, not enough water could be supplied in this manner. And so the failure of the artesian wells proved to be another blow. The ditches dug for purposes of irrigation were useless, but again the dauntless spirit of those first settlers remained unbroken. Doggedly they persevered. One farmer after planting his corn, in dry humor said to his wife, "zie zoo, ik heb mijn corn te droogen gelegd." ("see, I've put away my corn for drying!").

The 12th of January 1888 still is remembered as the day of the fearful hurricane blizzard when in the midst of an arctic cold and in a blinding snowstorm the settlers heard the crack of thunder. It was a beautiful dawn on that terrible day. Snow melted in the sun. Farmers turned out their cattle. But by eleven o'clock it suddenly grew cold, and there was a strange light in the sky. Weatherwise stockmen took warning and hurried to get their cattle home. In one hour a blizzard of unsurpassed violence was raging. School children and their teachers were compelled to stay in the schoolhouses all night. One young teacher in charge of 19 pupils feared that the insubstantial frame structure of the building could hardly withstand the fierce blasts of the storm. She was afraid that it would not survive till morning. There was a batchelor living a half mile to the west. She debated – could she and her charges make it? She looked out upon the fierce white swirling snow that was obliterating every familiar path and landmark. Dared she take the risk? Or should she stay? Even as she hesitated she felt the building lurch, heard it creak as if about blow away. She determined to make the attempt, no matter how dangerous. She gathered her pupils, and with all the ropes, lines, and straps they could find, tied them together, fastened one end to her waist, and ordered the children to hang on for dear life. Boldly she stepped out into the raging blizzard unmindful of the fact this step might mean certain death. But instead of falling, she kept looking upward, and brought her small charges to safety. The parents, knowing that the rickety building could scarcely withstand such violent blasts, did not sleep that night. When morning came and the storm passed, they went out to discover what they feared – only some boards with rusted nails in them sticking out of the snow bank where the school had stood. In dispair they looked around at the curious hummocks of snow. Would they discover the frozen forms of their children and the teacher? What a joy it was to find them all safe– through the brave courage of a young girl.

Dominie Zwemer, by some nicknamed "Gods jachthond" (God's sleuth), classical missionary in Dakota and still a young man, on that fatal day found himself far out on the wide prairie with his "gospel car," as he called his dilapidated buggy, and his wiry Indian ponies. Suddenly the storm burst upon him. The cold seemed unendurable, the icy swirl as if filled with points sharp as a needle's cut his breath and bewildered him. What could this mean? Never had he seen so savage a blizzard. At once he lost all sense of direction, all he knew was that he was several miles from the nearest farmstead. He began to feel the un-mistakable sensation of freezing coming upon him – what should he do? He recalled what some person had told him about the remarkable sense of direction possessed by horses. So he gave them free rein and trusted his life to the small faithful animals. So thick was the swirl of icy snow, so fierce the windy blasts, that at times he could not even see their little bodies. But the sturdy ponies trudged ahead in spite of the ice that filled their eyes and noses. Suddenly they stopped. Holding on to his ponies the dominie stepped out of his buggy on his stiff numb legs. Feeling around he found the wall of a building. It was a schoolhouse. Taking his life savers with him inside, he spent that fearful night with teacher, pupils, and his smart ponies. Many a person spent that night in a barn, not daring to take the few familiar steps to his house. Many suffered from severe frost bite. Amputations of hands or feet were not uncommon. One man, a Mr. Rhodes, went out to look for his stock, but did not return. In the spring his body was found not far from his house, where it had lain all winter under a huge snowbank. One young man, Jake van Gorkom, had bought some stock with money he had earned as a teacher. Caught in the storm, he could not get home and lost sight of his cattle.

He rode over miles of territory, but his inquiries were in vain; no one had seen them. In spring, when riding the range, he came upon a dugout. Dismounting, he pushed the door open and there beheld his stock, dead. Evidently they had gone into this shelter to escape the biting cold of the blizzard. The door closed, probably because of crowding; they were trapped without a person knowing of their plight and so they all perished.

But the cycle of dry years passed. Bountiful rains came in the spring and produced a marvelous growth of grass. The farmer who had never given up hope again sowed and planted. Good rains came in June and July – always regarded as the danger months – and produced what farmers termed a "half crop". The next year was better, and the third brought full crops. Once more stock fattened on the grazing land. There was more corn, and more hogs went to market. Surreys with fringed tops and two-seated buggies now replaced the lumber wagon in which the pioneer at first drove to town or to church. Young swains, sporting shining top buggies and sleek horses, escorted young ladies to Fourth of July celebrations and to picnics. Better homes were built and bigger farms appeared on every hand.

The government gave the Indians permission to haul stovewood from the flats along the Missouri River and sell it in Harrison. Almost every day during summer till late in fall they came with their loads of wood, their wigwams, squaws, papooses, and numerous brown-haired boys and girls. When stopping, papa would sit down in the shade of the wagon. Mama unhitched the ponies, watered them, and staked them out. She then set op the tent, hauled water, built the fire, prepared the meal, and then served her lord and master. After he had finished, she and her children ate, then the thin ever-hungry dogs got the leavings. His nap finished, papa hitched up and took his load to town to sell, and then came the real fun for the squaws. They would go into the stores, papooses strapped to their backs in a basket which left nothing of the babies visible but their sweet round faces and big black eyes. The mothers set them down on the porch, then went into the store to buy the gayest calicoes. The shopkeeper made a point of having a plentiful supply of reds, greens, and yellows. Meanwhile the men would be on their backs, and the boys riding the ponies bareback and without bridles in wild grace across the prairie. Sometimes it took days to dispose of their loads during which the air was filled with the smoke of their campfires, the tepees gleaming in the red glow of their evening fires. As wood now was readily obtainable, our Dutch settlers no longer were forced to rely on twisted hay and buffalo chips; life was becoming easier and more pleasant.

The Indians were friendly. A loaf of bread or a few biscuits made them happy. They were fond of dog meat and gratefully received the gift of an unwanted or stray dog. Sitting Bull, the chief of these Indians, was a prisoner and the tribesmen wanted him released. One day at dinner time two Indians (one of them was named Black Hawk) came to our house. Father, always friendly to the red man, invited them to dinner. They ate everything offered them except sugar. One of the Indians sniffed at it and with a suspicious grunt warned his companion not to take it. After the meal they presented father with a paper which they asked him to read. It was a petition to the governor for the release of Sitting Bull. They asked father to sign it, but when he refused the old fire of hatred for the white man shone in their eyes.

With the coming of the rainy years the tide turned and nowcomers flocked in. A second general store was opened by Isaac de Haan. Other new businesses were established: a drugstore by Heyme Vis; a black-smith shop by Leen (Leendert) Markus; a bank by Frank le Cocq, Sr. and son; a hardware store by Kees ten Beste; and a millinery and dress-making ship by Cornelia le Cocq, my sister. As there was an abundance of feed, the women raised flocks of chickens. During the difficult years they never had thought to spend any money on themselves, but the butter and egg money filled their pockets. They spent it eagerly for hats and dresses the feminine heart longs to have. Some new houses were built, some of them equipped with modern conveniences.

But another dream, cherished ever since the railroad came to Armour, faded. Our people hoped ardently for an extention of the line, but it never came. The railroad built its tracks northward to Corsica, a new town, and many of the villagers of Harrison moved to that place. The new, large department store built by Leen Markus and Heyme Vis, however, stayed in Harrison. So the years went by. Some were good, others poor. Today, many comfortable homes grace these plains, some of them equipped with light plants and running water. In spite of their many hardships and long suffering our courageous farmers were well rewarded. Stout hearts filled with despair never quite gave up hope. The merchants of Harrison also had carried a heavy load during those dry years because our people could not pay their debts. But the people had faith in each other and in the country. There was honesty and willingness to stand by. The wholesale houses of Sioux City and Minneapolis extended credit and so helped carry our people through the hard times.

106. STEPHEN J. HARMELINGS'
BEGINNINGS OF DAKOTA SETTLEMENT

[Harmeling, born March 8, 1851, in Gibbsville, Wisconsin, became a minister in the Reformed Church of America, served the Reformed congregation at Marion, South Dakota, from 1883 to 1901, knew at first hand the earliest history of Dutch settlement in South Dakota. This text was taken from a copy, preserved in the Netherlands Museum, of an original now lost.]

Mr. John Binnekant of Holland, Michigan, has declared "The emigration of the Hollanders from the Old Country in 1847 to the United States, was very similar to that of the Puritans in the sixteenth century." It was for the purpose of finding religious liberty in the New World. But the immigration of Hollanders from the states into the territory of the Dakotas in the early 1880's was altogether for another object. It was to secure farming land, to get rich quickly.

In 1879 the great railroad systems began to push their lines westward into the Great Western Desert, as that region was named in our early geographies. It was discovered that this region was no desert at all, but a fertile rolling prairie on which millions of bison grazed thoughout the year. The railroads commenced systematic advertisement. Towns sprang up like Jonah's gourd, as fast as the railroads were built. Land agents were ready in each town to bring the land seeker out West and locate him on a claim. There was an abundance of water, which produced a a phenominal growth of grass. In 1885, the governor of Dakota Territory, Gilbert A. Pierce, authorized Mr. O. B. Holt to compile a book on the Dakotas, entitled *Behold, I Show You a Delightsome Land*. Pamphlets with pictures of waving grain and selfbinding reapers – all on a large scale telling what was being done in agriculture – were scattered broadcast throughout the states. The migration that had begun as early as 1880 was wonderful. There never had been anything like it in the history of the Union; and it can never be repeated again, for in those years nearly all the land east of the Missouri River was taken up by settlers. Every person who had attained his majority and every head of a family was intitled to three rights: a homesread entry, a preemption, and a tree claim – which gave him 480 acres of the best and richest land in the Union.

This was a great opportunity for widows and girls who possessed energy and a sense of business. Those who had a mother-in-law or a father-in-law or had an aged parent were permitted to double the size of their holdings and thus acquire 960 acres of this rich "delightsome land". Wealth and independence were in sight for all, and so very easy to obtain. There were no trees to cut down. The fields were ready for the plow. With the help of the patient reaper, 15 to 20 bushels of wheat could be realized, a moderate yield, although the advertising pamphlets declared the yield would be from 30 to 20. Wheat at that time was worth a dollar per bushel. Flax was worth $ 1.50, and the freshly turned virgin sod would yield from 8 to 12 bushels.

This was the poor man's land, his fairy dream. Some people who had a good living in the states, seeing this opportunity for gaining great wealth, sold out and bought large tracts of land in the territory of the Dakotas.

Money flowed into the country like a stream, and there was great demand for it. A preemption could be proved after six months' residence on it whereupon a loan could be secured. As high as 60% interest was paid regularly on chattle security. The farmer needed it to purchase teams and machinery, and why not? These fertile acres surely would pay such loans in a few years. Such were the prospects in the years 1881, 1882, 1883, and 1884; such the belief that the fertility of this virgin soil and the high prices of farm products would bring fulfillment of the immigrants highest hopes.

During these years, according to the estimate of Frank Le Cocq, Jr. of Harrison, South Dakota, 5,000 Hollanders settled in the Dakotas. They came with few exceptions from the older Dutch Colonies in Michigan, Wisconsin, Minnesota, and Iowa. It has been stated repeatedly that the enterprising and energetic moved westward. But it should not be left unmentioned that some of the indolent who could not succeed in the states came to try their fortunes in the territory of the Dakotas, and succeeded no better.

There are Hollanders in every county of South Dakota [organized as a state in 1889] but while some are scattered over the entire state, most of them have settled in groups or colonies. School and church have always been dear to the hearts of Hollanders and in founding their communities in the Dakotas they knew that these sacred privileges would be guaranteed to them. This is at least one redeeming feature of the present mad rush for earthly possessions. Four colonies were established in South Dakota during the early 1880's – one in Douglas County, one in Bon Homme County, one in Charles Mix County, and one in Campbell County. Only one colony was founded at this time in North Dakota [organized as a state in 1889]. This was in Emmons County and really was an extension of Dutch settlement in Campbell County in South Dakota. But I know of no better way of telling the story of these settlements than by letting the early settlers themselves speak for the colonies they represent.

HISTORY OF SETTLEMENTS IN CAMPBELL COUNTY

[The author of this sketch in 1885 moved from Greenleafton, Minnesota, to Campbell County in South Dakota, a new settlement of farmers drawn from other Dutch communities. This account written for the Semi-Centennial celebrations at Holland in 1897 was never published. The text was prepared from a manuscript kept in the Netherlands Museum.]

It is now twelve years since I came here. We set our faces westward – were to control large tracts of land. Nine tenths of the people wanted land – lots of it and with the idea of building up a colony and getting rich in a short time.

Twelve years ago the attention of people was attracted by articles in *De Volksvriend* by Pieter Ellerbroek that the East was no good. Turn your eyes to Dakota and the country of the West, was his advice. Letters flocked in and in great number. But it was surprising none came from children between the ages of sixteen and twenty-one. All were over 21 years, all could became possessors of 80 acres of land. Our good natured land agents such as P. Bakker, J. van Putten and later on Charles Bowet, G. Haak, and H. van Beek, bled the poor settlers in good shape and no wonder – the picture stretched out before us promised happy homes in a few years so that we did not mind $ 10 for showing us a claim or $ 25 for taking us to the land office. We were poor then, but would be rich in a few years when land would be worth $ 25 per acre. A vast majority of these settlers stopped their wagons on what they called their pre-emptions, put up their houses out of "Dakota brick", better known as sod .

They started to dig wells and to turn over the promising soil, and now something else had to be done. In order to get more settlers the matter of a school and church must be considered, for if you meet a Hollander from the East and speak about a new colony the first question will be, "Is there a school?" The second, "Is there a church?" These were two necessary matters, but the question was how to get them. The school state tax provides for, but the Dakota law requires, a certain number of pupils and a certain amount of taxable property. The land belonged to Uncle Sam and was not taxable. Reserved property was all that was taxable. Bank accounts were unknown. So some of our poor victims when the occasion came around listed ten cows when they would have been correct if the cipher had been left off. Horses, the same way, and our sharpers made them believe it was all right for them to have a certain amount of taxable property to get the first school. But the settlers were surprised when the tax gatherers came around and demanded the taxes on the property listed. Then, of course, they wanted their taxes rebated, but that was too late. They got the schools all right.

A church had to be organized. The Seceders were on deck at an early date, but they went back discouraged. A church had to be organized. John W. Warnshuis and Ale Buursma were called on and they came ninety miles on wheels, organized a church, charter of which was filed – the first church in Emmons County of any denomination. But a year later Rev. Ale Stegeman and Rev. Frederick J. Zwemer came to visit the colony. To their surprise they found a church had been organized, elders and deacons chosen, articles of incorporation filed, but no members. Even elders and deacons were no members of the Reformed Church. So they decided with other new settlers that had come in, to do the work over again which had been done before and annul the former organization. Then we were ready and everyone was in the harness. Everything went smoothly: Sunday School, Bible class, and singing class were started and the colony prospered.

But our promising soil that had been turned over did not yield as abundantly as we expected on account of hail and drouth. The first winter was a mild one. Farmers were busy hauling hay made the previous summer, also wood out of the gulches. The second summer promised fair. Lots of settlers came in from the states, preemptions were proved up and homesteads filed, and large tracts of the carpeted prairie were overturned. The railroad extended thirty-five miles from Ipswich to Bowdle, encouraging the settlers; horses were bought at high prices, a good team being worth $ 300 to $ 350, a yoke of oxen $ 150, a good milk cow $ 40. Eggs cost from twelve to twenty five cents a dozen, butter about as much per pound. Pork brought from ten to fifteen cents per pound and was in demand at that price. Oats and corn were worth from forty to sixty cents per bushel. Wheat sold at ninety cents a bushel, flax was worth $ 1.30. Who would dare say this was not a glorious country for a farmer? Our crop was fair that season (1886). People were in the firm belief that there would not be snow in Dakota. Sleighs, they thought, were of no use. But again we were surprised when on the 22d October in the morning a howling blizzard was raging and lasted for three days and so severe you could not see a rod away. That snow remained till about April 12th next. We used to say "it storms six days in the week and we break a sabbath to get hay for the cattle from the stacks." During all this time there was only one case of death and no sickness; and as there was no doctor within 40 miles, the Lord was kind to us.

Came the following spring; the settlers were poor, but of course soon would be rich. They had only a little ground under cultivation the year previous. Seed grain and horse feed were scarce articles. Lucky the man that had oxen which could subsist on prairie grass and also work. Money was a scarce article, but the Chicago, Milwaukee, and St. Paul Railroad stated we would have seed grain free of charge. So one of our settlers, John Pekelder went to Sioux County, Iowa, also horse feed for the settlers. Most of the money was donated by eastern friends. But when the seed grain came it was found to be foul with mustard and cockle. Many of us did not know how noxious mustard was but we soon found out. The Northern Pacific Railroad also gave the people seed grain which was to be returned in the fall of 1887 with ten percent interest. So we were helped out again once more.

After the organization of the church the eastern churches sent us a little money to erect a church. And now came the difficulty- where should it stand? The eastern part of the colony known as the valley wanted the church built in their section. Those living in the western part insisted they should have the church; and there was strife, till finally it was settled to build the church about midway between the two points on G. Haak's place. The West had lost the battle, but G. Haak was surprised to learn that a certain bachelor had got the best of him and filed on the claim. But the losing party ordered the lumber which consisted of cottonwood, sawed on the Missouri River fourteen miles away and brought to the place. To our surprice none of those who took part in this dispute were on hand. Soon we learned that the valley was dissatisfied, for Haak intended to have the church on his claim and not on the claim of the bachelor. There the lumber lay for some time until Rev. James F. Zwemer came to visit the colony and decided this matter. He said enough money could be had to build two churches. The colony, he argued, was too large for one church; there should be two churches for worship – one not more than a half mile from H. van Beek's store and the other not more than a half mile from Pekelder's store. The merchants were satisfied and G. Haak and the rest fell in line. The building of the church in the west went on at the place now known as Westfield and was completed in the fall of 1890. The other church at Hull was not built immediately. The lumber, in part at least, was used for dwelling houses and the settlers at Hull began to be dissatisfied and wanted a church for themselves. So some eight or ten families were set apart and a church was built with the aid of eastern churches. The Seceders also organized and built a church. We then had three churches and were well equipped with churches but no minister. The Seceder church was built in 1891 and the other, the Haak church in 1892, both at Hull.

Recapitulating: the first organization, by Rev. Warnshius took place in 1885. The second organization, or reorganization by Rev. Abram Stegeman and Frederick J. Zwemer came in 1886. Until this time the colony had formed one church. In 1887 the Westfield church was built and the Seceder organized at Hull. In 1888 the James F. Zwemer or Haak church was organized.

The crop of 1887 was a good yield. The winter of 1887 and 1888 was a very severe one. The crop of 1888 was a total failure so that people had neither seed or feed for stock and the colonists were compelled to apply for aid to their friends in the East who generously helped them. The crop of 1889 was a partial failure, still most of the people had enough for seed and bread. Some living in the eastern part of the colony had to be helped. In the year 1890 the crops again were a partical failure.

In the fall of 1890 the settlers had an Indian scare. Sitting Bull claimed to have met a spirit in the Bad Lands that told him the white man would be swept away in the next summer when the grass grew, that there was a wave of mud coming over these plains which would bury all the whites and all the bad Indians. Those who wished to be saved must carry and eagle's feather and the pony one wished to save must have an eagle feather in the tail, that the white man's stock would turn into bisons and the sheep into deer and antelope. Over this prophecy the Indians were much delighted and had war dances.

Some of the tenderfeet began to be afraid, but the brave mossbacks were not in the least afraid. Suddenly an Indian came to the little village of La Grace wishing to buy at a low figure some cartridges from a lady clerking in the store, but was refused. He protested, saying "You may just as well let me have them now, for we will have them all anyway bye and bye." This excited the clerk and the alarm went forth "The Indians are coming!" The alarm went over the plains as fast as lightfooted horses could carry it, and the farther it went the greater the scare. It came to the people living along the Missouri River while they were fast asleep. Twenty miles away people were fleeing for their lives, but there was not an Indian in sight. A hundred families were loaded on their wagons. They started for the town of Eureka. It was a horrible night. People going to or coming from Eureka met with all kinds of excitement. G. W. Renskers with J. Pool and H. de Boer who were on their way to Eureka stopped at Mr. Scholten's. While eating supper Mr. Scholten same in and said "There are unfortunate reports going about Indians." Oh! said

Renskers, the boys in blue will take care of them. A few minutes later a messenger came along on a panting steed and shouted "Six hundred Indians have crossed below La Grace!" A family came up fleeing from the Indians announcing "Fort Yates is taken!" Then said Renskers to his comrades "I am going home." He would have to face the Indians on a trip of twenty-two miles. His comrads said "We are with you!" Unloading their wagons, they turned their horses westward to reach their families if possible. They encountered fleeing families all of whom repeated the same advice "Turn around, boys, the Indians are upon us!" They even asserted they could hear the Indians shooting, and part of the company became discouraged. One of the group heatedly ordered him "either shut up or get out of the wagon! I am going forward even if it takes my life!" Thus encouraged they went on. They met one of their neighbors who informed them his brother-in law had been in La Grace that very same day. They decided to call on him to learn what he had to say. They arrived at his house six miles further, rapped at his door. They asked him what he had heard or seen. He stated he had left La Grace at five o'clock in the afternoon and that the place was quiet as usual. He had seen no Indians, only one squaw, a good looking one too! Nor had he heard anything about the excitement. And so it was apparent the Indian attach was an idle rumor. Resuming their journey into the settlement, they saw lights in nearly all the houses. Pool and Renskers who had pushed ahead went home and to bed. The Hollanders of Emmons County, greatly excited, quieted down, although some of them were badly scared.

The following morning H. van Beek and G. W. Renskers set out for Fort Yates to find out if indeed everything was quiet. After traveling eighteen miles they met an old timer and said to him "Jack, we came to bury you!" "Wait till I am dead," he replied. "We thought the Indians had scalped you long ago," was our explanation. We told him of the excitement in the settlement. He laughed heartily saying, "You ought to have been here twelve years ago. Then you would not be scared now!" We went on and arrived at Winona. There the old mossbacks laughed at us for being scared. They told us there was nothing to this wild rumor. Then we went on across the river to Fort Yates where we found the Indian Agent, also the Indian trader and the colonel of the army who told us there was no basis for the fright. "The Sioux Indians are peaceful," they said, "and, besides, it would be but a small matter to reduce them the order." The men went back home. The missionary Frederick James Zwemer, at that time in Spring Lake, Michigan, heard about the report, hurried to the settlement, encouraged the frightened people to return to their homes. This was a great comfort to those who believe in the guidance and protection of the Almighty.

During the winter of 1890 all who could leave their homes found work across the river teaming for the government. Others who could not leave their families were employed with their teams at Eureka and westward to Fort Yates. So what we first thought would be destruction turned out to be a blessing, for the increase in the number of soldiers required a greater amount of supplies and demanded the labor of many workmen and the people had a chance to earn some money.

The winter of 1890 and 1891 was a very mild one. The crop was fair in 1891, but some of the people lost theirs by hail. The winter of 1891 and 1892 was mild, there being scarcely any snow. The spring opened fair and a favorable summer followed. But in the fall when threshing commenced the prairie was set afire by an engine, which swept over a large tract of country, and two persons lost their lives. The following day, while a shower passed along the south side of the colony, lightening set the prairie afire in five different places. The east wind fanned the blaze of a width of twelve miles. Suddenly at ten o'clock at night it shifted to the south and, accompanied by an electric storm, drove the blaze northward with great rapidity carrying with it destruction of grain, buildings, stock, and machinery. It seemed as if the air was filled with flame. Grain and stacks were set afire three forths of a mile in advance of the oncoming blaze.

This disaster affected all the settlers more or less. A few were made destitute, barely escaping with their lives. Some lost part of their grain and hay. Heaviest loss was in grain and horses. During the following severe winter a lot of the stock that had escaped the fire perished for wont of feed . People in need again were helped by those who had been assisted by eastern friends and by their more fortunate neighbors. Only one Hollander was hurt during this fire, but no lives were lost. Five dwelling houses were burned.

In the summer of 1893 crops were fair, but prices so very low that after counting the expense of hauling forty miles to market the settler realized little or nothing. The winter of 1893 and 1894 was a severe one. The summer of 1894 was fair. A dash of hail struck a few of the settlers. Crops were fair but prices low. Horses declined in value. The country was overstocked with bronchos from Oregon and Washington so that there was no money in horses. Stock began to rise in value, however, and the settlers turned their attention to stock and hogs. Flint or squaw corn had been raised in small patches and with good results, yielding from twenty to forty bushels per acre. It was found that dent corn would not ripen in this part of Dakota. From Eureka they began to ship hogs to eastern markets. The winter of 1894 and 1895 was open, no snow falling, so the stock could live, even thrive on the open prairie.

Probably it would be well to say a word about the native grasses we found in Emmons and Campbell counties. Grass does not mature here as in eastern parts of the country. It does not ripen and die. The heat and drought dries the grass on the ground so that it retains its strength like hay. This is particularly true of buffalo and "bunch grass". At any time in fall, winter, or spring cattle and horses and sheep will thrive on the prairie if the ground is not covered with snow. In open winters thousands of cattle live on the all the time and without shelter. It seems nature provides range cattle and horses with an extra coat of hair to resist the cold while the same cattle and horses kept in the stable do not develop this extra coat.

The winter of 1894 and 1895 also was open, and all stock did well. The crop of 1895 was average. Prices were still lower and hogs and cattle brought low prices. The winter of 1895 and 1896 again was open, with only a little snow falling in the month of March. Cattle fared well, and rose in price although grain was very sheap. The summer of 1896 was fair and crops were medium. Corn was splendid, flax poor. Prices for stock were better, but there was no market for horses. Hogs were cheap.

The winter of 1896 and 1897 set in unusually early, commencing on the 23d of October and continuing until about the 12th of April. There was a very heavy fall of snow, the grazing grounds were covered with snow, and stock had to be fed. So scarce was feed in the spring of 1897 that the old straw of 1895 brought a price. Among the Hollanders little stock perished for want of feed. Among the ranchmen losses were heavy. One of the sheep men, a Hollander lost fifty head. But the Hollanders learned the raising of stock, sheep, and hogs; and selling milk to creameries was more profitable than producing small grain. Had the Hollanders when they first settled here known what this country could produce most advantageously they might have been better off. This country is best adapted to raising stock. A sucking calf is brought a marketable condition as a steer for about six dollars. Farmers now prefer mixed farming, raising stock, sheep, and hogs. Those who have devoted their efforts to raising small grains have lost.

Westfield, or Hope church, combined with Campbell or the Van Raalte church in calling Rev. Jacob van der Meulen who served as pastor during

1889 and 1890. The Van Raalte church at first was much opposed to
this plan, but Hope church had a two-thirds majority of the votes. It was
agreed the parsonage should built at Hope church which, with the help
of the Board of Domestic Missions, should bear all expenses. Van der
Meulen came to us with surprising speed. He promptly accepted the call,
packed his things, and came West, Some of us, with teams and wagons,
there being no buggy in the entire settlement, went to meet him at Eureka
forty-five miles distant. Those personally acquainted with the dominie
shook hands and the rest were left to introduce themselves as best they
could.

From the depot the dominie and his family were brought to the section
house. It is not to be wondered that the dominie's wife looked sober when
she found the best the landlady could do for them was to offer one room
for the entire family. Nevertheless the dominie grinned and bore it. During the afternoon of that day his goods were taken out of the cars and
loaded in wagons. The following morning the Van der Meulen family,
which is quite numerous, was loaded on a heavy lumber wagon well fitted
out with spring seats, and started for Westfield. At about midway, in
Campbell County, they halted at K. Scholten's for dinner and in the
afternoon arrived in Westfield. Their furniture and other articles followed
closely. But there was no parsonage to put them in. So what could we do
but put them in the church where the family was to live, while the parsonage was building. Meanwhile we had services in H. van Beek's store.
This went very well for a few days, but presently the dominie's wife began
to complain. We well were aware there were fleas in the country and
good jumpers too. The dominie's wife, by examining them closely, found
they had wings, thought the little pests were a great annoyance. And the
old dominie, though a splendid preacher, had no practice catching fleas,
nor had any other members of his family any skill in this art. Nevertheless
the dominie did a good work here. He established a Young Peoples
Society which was kept up long after he had left. But the endurance
required of him because of the long distance between the two churches
and because of the trying climate was more than the dominie could stand.
Besides, there was the complaint of his family about the sticky mud,
lack of trees, no side walks, scarcity of fresh beef and besides there was no
milkman! The dominie got a cow, but every member of the family was
too nervous to milk her. It was not strange that when the dominie received a call from Baldwin, Wisconsin, he considered it an answer to his
prayer. By this time the two churches, Van Raalte and Hope, had erected
a comfortable parsonage, a large stable. But this proved of no avail, and

after a stay of fourteen months the dominie and his family left us, just before the Indian scare. Before Van der Meulen's charge the Rev. Frederick J. Zwemer looked after our religious interests, and he resumed his labors as classical missionary after Van de Meulen's departure.

As we stated before, Haak and some seven other families asked to be dismissed as a congregation. They did not belong to the combination with Thule and Hope. They were under the care of the missionary pastor Rev. Frederick J. Zwemer. He rustled up some money among eastern friends to build for them a church. When the outside shell was completed they held services in it for one year. But it seemed not to have God's approval, for a small cyclone came cantering along and without doing any other damage literally tore the church into fragments and scattered it for miles over the prairie. The fragments were gathered together and sold to different parties, the money being pocketed by G. Haak. He then saw a chance to become an elder in the Seceder church, and induced his whole party with the exception of a couple families to join that church. Thus ended the story of the Haak church.

It is a trying life the settlers in Emmons County experienced. They met with much misfortune, many discouragements. Their first object, to make a speedy success, could not be attained. Some moved away. Still we hear that many of them wish they were back in Dakota. But what would have been the aspect of things if these people had become rich quickly as had hoped? In all probability the Lord would have forgotten them. With the old King they would have said, "Is not this the great Babylon which I have built?" Still we must say the Lord has been with us in all our trials and in all our temptations. Never a family has gone to bed hungry. There has always been plenty to eat. Our clothing was poor and old fashioned. Girls and boys many a time obtained clothing given the church and Sunday school. Even the babies were not forgotten.

During the winter after the great prairie fire boxes and barrels of clothing were sent by eastern churches in such quantity that the poor people exclaimed they had enough and to spare. These kind acts shown by eastern churches are warm in the hearts of the settlers. Today the colony is well able to take care of itself. Some still are embarassed, others have money in the bank.

DUTCH SETTLEMENT IN CAMPBELL COUNTY

[The following account entitled *De Hollandsche Nederzetting in Campbell County, South Dakota*, was written in July, 1897, for the Semi-Centennial celebrations held in Holland, Michigan by J. van Erve, one of the first setllers at Thule in Campbell County. The following text was taken from the original hitherto unpublished manuscript preserved in the Netherlands Museum.]

Pieter Ellerbroek, een winkelier uit Douglas County (South Dakota), in het begin van het jaar 1885 wekte onder de overbevolking van Iowa en in Michigan veel lieden op om in de schoone vallei van Campbell County (althans volgens zijn zeggen) ons geluk te beproeven. Zoo als gewoonlijk alle landspekulanten doen spiegelde hij ons het schoonste voor: 480 ackers prachtig land voor weinig geld te verkrijgen, een tree kleam preemtion en een homestead. Nu aan die lokstem gaven veelen gehoor, voornamelijk hen die geen eigen farm hetzij in Michigan, Iowa, of in andere staten bezaten.

Hiermede wil ik slechts te kennen geven dat de meeste nederzetters vrij arm waren. Ellerbroek, na wij naderhand gehoord hebben, was het alleen te doen om door de profijten welke hij van de settlers trok zijn winkel van de schulden die er op rusten te ontlasten. Wat er van waar is kunnen wij met geen zekerheid mededeelen, maar wel nadat hij de groot-ste winst genoten had liet hij de onervaren settlers aan hun lot over en is sedert hier niet meer gezien. Allen hadden wij in hem een groot vertrou-wen, en had hij als Mr. Henry Hospers, ons met raad en daad blijven ondersteunen wij gelooven dat hij dan goede zaken zoude gedaan hebben.

Dit was toch niettemin de oorzaak dat er enkele uit Iowa doch de meesten uit Michigan zich hier in het voorjaar van 1885 nabij de oever der Missouri rivier zich vestigden. Onder hen bevond zich ook mijn gezin uit Iowa en wel uit Sioux County met eenen G. van Surksum, doch die na eenige weken hier geweest te zijn na Emmons County [North Dakota] vertrokken is. Dit waren de eerste gezinnen die zich hier vestigden, doch spoedig kwamen er anderen opdagen en wel onze tegen-woordige vrienden uit Michigan. Wel waren er niet velen, maar de meesten hadden eene onderneemende geest die wij ook wel noodig hadden want het was geen ligte zaak om in de wildernis 70 tot 100 mijlen verwijdert van het station de prairie in te trekken langs meestal ongebaande wegen.

Met het moeven [verhuizen] ging het soms wonderlijk toe. Nu en dan 's nachts op de prairie vertoeven, dan soms een verlaten zoden huis was ons nacht plaats broederlijk gedeelt met onze paarden. Soms ging een trip welke van 4 tot 6 dagen duurde met vele merkwaardigheden gepaard, soms droevig, en dan weder vermakelijk. Op een mijner reizen kwam

ik bij een farmer om over nacht te blijven, maar vond niemand te huis.
Ik kon niet verder wegens de duisternis, dus ik deed of ik zelvers huis
heer was. Ik bezorgde mijn paarden en ging daarna in huis om mijn
eigen avond eten klaar te maken. Alles zocht ik op, koffij, suiker, brood,
en boter. Nadat ik dit genuttigd had begaf ik mij te bed uit voorzorg de
meesten mijner kleederen aanhoudende om, mocht de eigenaar onver-
hoede binnen komen, ik spoedig gereed zou zijn. Met het krieken van
den dag weder mijn morgen eten zelf gemaakt en genuttigd, ging ik
mijn reis verder vervolgen. Naderhand weder eens bij hem stoppende
vraagde ik hem of er voorheen niet een tramp (landlooper) wonderlijk
in zijn huis had huisgehouden en maakte ik hem bekend dat ik die vreemde snuiter geweest was en vraagde hem wat hij er voor eischte. „Niets,"
gaf hij ten antwoord. „Gij hebt het veel te goed afgebragt, ik ben bijna
niet gewaar geworden dat een vreemden zich eigenaar van mijn goed
had gemaakt."

Doch als men wat troebel had zooals het breken van de wagen of
andersins, zat men soms geweldig in het nauw. Het was in het eerst dan
ook geweldig eenzaam, en voornamelijk de eerste winter welke bar was.
Mijne vrouw had gedurende 7 maanden geene hare kennis gezien. Men
zou menschenschuw worden. Mijn jongste zoon, toen omstreeks 5
jaren, als hij iemand zag naderen kwam met verbaasdheid in huis en
riep „Moeder, doe de deur digt, daar komt een mensch aan." Doch
de eenzaamheid is vervlogen. De railroad heeft doorgebouwd,
eerst tot Bowdle en daarna een zijtak tot Eureka, nu omstreeks 20
mijlen van mij verwijderd. Eureka is naar ik denk de grootste marktplaats van Dakota, ten minste wat er per as wordt henengebragt. Sommige farmers komen over de 80 mijlen ver. In Europa zegt men, „alle
wegen leiden na Rome"; hier is het alle wegen leiden naar Eureka.

Bij de ongebaande wegen en de weinige bevolking alhier was het niet
te verwonderen dat men voornamelijk in het schemeravonduur aan het
dwalen raakte. Een buurman van mij welke met oudejaarsavond bij een
andere vriend was geweest ging des avonds om 10 uur met een lantaarn
gewapend na zijn huis terug, een distantie van 1 halve mijl. Doch wat
wil het geval? De olie in zijn lantaarn bevroor en een Egyptische duisternis overviel hem met het gevolg dat na den geheele nacht gewandelt
te hebben hij des morgens ten 9 uur weder zijn huis bereikte. Ook mijn
persoon kan van zulke omzwervingen gewaar maken. Menigen nacht
heb ik op de prairie doorgebragt luidkeelsch psalmen aanheffende om te
tijd te verkorten. Was 't in de zomer dan was het niet zoo onaangenaam,
maar in de winter wanneer de sneeuwstorm loeide, dacht ik als de dief

die gehangen moest worden, „Ik wou dat ik bij moeder 't huis was!"

In de eerste winter nadat ik een visite had wezen maken bij mijn gewezen buurman G. van Surksum een distancie van 20 mijlen had mij ongeveer 4 dagen genomen. Het was ook sneeuwstorm op sneeuwstorm. Ik moet dan ook bekennen dat de Heer mij genadiglijk bewaard heeft. Mijn buurman J. de Vries zeide dikwijls, „van de Erve blijft nog eens op de prairie," doch uitgezonderd de top mijner neus is niet een mijner ledematen bevroren. Ook niet een onzer Hollandsche buren heeft zijn leven op de prairie door bevriezen verloren, maar wel eenige Russen en Engelsmannen.

Met het begin onzer nederzetting ging het met de godsdienst wat ongeregeld toe. Door onbekendheid met elkander hielden wij op 2 à 3 plaatsen des Zondags onze godsdienstoefeningen. Soms waren wij wel eens in de war met de Zondag zooals bijvoorbeeld onze vriend P. Droog die na Zondags gewerkt te hebben, in zijn zondagssche kleeren met den Bijbel onder zijn armen bij K. Scholten aankwam en maar moeijelijk te overtuigen was dat het Maandag was.

Doch hierin kwam spoedig verandering. Door vermeerdering der settlers werd de behoefte gevoeld een eigen kerkgebouw te hebben overmits het huis van broeder Vork te klein werd om onze godsdienstoefening te houden, en werd er besloten om er maar dadelijk toe over te gaan. In de zomer van 1886 togen op een schoonen dag bijna alle nederzetters, oud en jong, met zwaarden en stokken uit: ik bedoel spaden, breakploeg, wagens meestal met ossen bespannen, en timmergereedschap na de plaats bestemd om de kerk te doen verrijzen, en in een dag was bijna het kerkgebouw gerezen, een gebouw niet ten volle zoo prachtig als Salomons tempel, maar ook niet een van ons kondet zeggen met David, „Zie, wij wonen in een cederen huis; en de arke Gods [staat in] het midden der gordijnen." De kerk was groot 16 bij 32 zoo ik meen, inzijde, en uitzijde 21 bij 37, dus de wanden waren uit geen keurige beurs gebouwd, trouwens zoden waren er plentie, en de roef [dak] van de tabernakel met 3 overdekkingen planken, tearpapier, en zoden. Zonder overdreven te zijn toen het klaar was droeg het ieders tevredenheid weg, wel is waar als het regende moest men onze stoelen wel eens verzetten om van de regen in de drop te komen doch de lofzangen ter eere van God klonken er niet te minder om. Deze kerk is ingewijd den 10 October 1886 en ontving den naam van A. C. van Raalte. Mede werd de gemeente op dien dag georganizeerd met 14 volle leden en 9 doopleden door de Rev. Frederik J. Zwemer en Ds. Abraham Stegeman.

Na ruim 5 jaar dienst gedaan te hebben hebben mij een schoon houten kerk gebouwd meestendeels door vrijwillige giften van onze nederzetters. Deze kerk, groot 28 bij 36, heeft prachtige zitplaatsen, geschonken uit het Oosten. Deze kerk is ingewijd door Frederik J. Zwemer bij gelegenheid zijner huwelijksreisje, op 20 Augustus 1893. In al de twaalf jaren van onze vestiging alhier hebben wij slechts ander half jaar met de gemeente van Westfield [Emmons County] vereenigd een eigen leeraar gehad, Jacob van der Meulen, doch onze godsdienst oefeningen worden noch al trouw bezocht voornaamelijk als een vliegende draak in de gedaante van een predikant of een student ons gedurende zijn vakantion ons voorgaat. Jammer dat de gemeente in plaats van grooter kleiner wordt zoodat het uitzicht om weder een eigen leeraar te hebben steeds kleiner wordt. Een kudde zonder herder is bedroevend. Wat onze finantieelen toestand betreft, wat zal ik zeggen? Klagen past ons niet; wel is waar in onze eerste jaren hadden wij het over het algemeen wel niet breed, doch God had de harte van onze oostersche vrienden geopend en ruime giften zijn ons toegevloeid zoodat ik vrijmoedig durf zeggen: Niet eener onzer Hollanders heeft gebrek geleden. Waarom dan zoo vele vertrokken? Wat zal ik zeggen? Hadden wij een Van Raalte of Bolks tot onze voorgangers gehad ik geloof niet dat de gemeente kleiner geworden zou zijn, neen in tegendeel het zou vermeerdert zijn. Want de meesten van hen die hier gekomen zijn zijn met een aardig stuivertje vertrokken en zoo we vernemen zouden zij als de Israelieten van ouds weder gaarne na de vleespotten van Egypte, ik bedoel Campbell County, terugkeeren. In de laatste twee jaren is de schulden last van deze gemeente grootendeels geslonken en met het vooruitzigt van een prachtigen oogst is onze nederzetting weder vol moed. Wij hebben hier twee flinke storen, Albert van Dijk en de gebroeders Tinholt, die beide naar wij vernemen goede zaken doen. Ook is hier verleden jaar een creamerie [melkfabriek] gebouwd die uitstekend bevalt.

In een nieuwe colonie vallen soms wederwaardigheden voor die de vergetenheid dienen ontrukt te worden. Zoude ik die alle opnemen die hier gebeurd zijn ik denk dit zou wel een boekdeel vullen. Ik wil slechts mededeelen die hier in deze omgeving geschied is, namelijk de Indianen vlugt.

In den avond van den 20 November 1890 ging het berigt rond, „De Indianen zijn de rivier [genaamd Missouri] overgetogen en zijn reeds aan het uitmoorden!" Gelijk een bliksem straal doorkleeft het wereldrond en een pijl zweeft door de lugt zoo snel verspreide zich het gerugt door de colonie. Alles werd in gereedheid gebracht om te vlugten. Het

was ter tijde toen Sitting Bull met zijn volgelingen oproerig was tegen
Onkel Sam en waarvoor hij dit met zijn leven heeft geboet. De schrik
sloeg om aller harten. De vrouw van Arie Schaap welke juist de vorige
avond haren eersteling een zoon had ter wereld gebragt, werd met bed
en al op de buckie [buggy] geheven en zoo vervoerd. Naderhand toen
het kind gedoopt werd ontving het op aanraden van Frederik J. Zwemer,
onze classicale zendeling, den naam van Cornelius met den toenaam
Gersom hetwelk in het hollandsch „vlugteling" moest beteekenen. Nu
kan ik wel in Exodus 2, 22, lezen dat Gersom vreemdeling beteekend,
doch welligt zooals in meerdere gevallen heeft een woord meer dan eene
beteekenis. Hoe dit zij, die hier meer van wil weten verwijs ik ter in-
ligting tot bovengenoemde Rev. Frederik J. Zwemer, Pella, Iowa. S. E.
Pas liet in der haast zijn geldbeurs op de commode liggen en vergat
dezelve in zijn zak te steken. A. O. van Dijk had 2 varkens voor de
Indianen in gereedheid gebragt hangenden schoon op den ladder
meenende zeker te toonen dat de Hollanders ook wel slagten konden.
Mrs H. C. Zuidman kwam met de familie Kuipers bij Tinholt aan in der
haast zich vergetende behoorlijk aan te kleeden. „Ach," kermde zij,
„ik ben om dezen tijd welligt al weduw vrouw; mijn man is na de rivier
om hout, en de Indianen zullen hem wel geschalpt" [geschalpeert]
hebben! Jan Schaap liep dwars door een weijervensch [wire fence]. Zoo
zeer was de schrik om zijn hart geslagen dat Van Dijk zijn varkens ten
prooi liet van de Indianen. Jan Slotman was zelfzuchtiger, riep nadat
allen op den wagen zaten, „Vrouw, war is Popje? De Indianen zullen van
mijn huishondje geen soep kooken! Kom hier, Popje, mee op de wagen!"
Daar ik het verst van het westen verwijderd was werd ik het laatst
van alle gewaar van het ontrustbarend berigt. Des avonds om tien uren
in onze eerste sluimering werden wij gewekt door de families Schaap en
De Haan die met gepakt en geladen wagens voor de deur stonden. Ons
veerenbed zoo nadat wij het verlaten hadden werd op een van hun wagens
geladen ter ligplaats van den kranken jongeling Rudolf de Haan die het
stooten op den wagen niet kon uitstaan. Nu was in mijn huis alles in
rep en roer, de beesten op de prairie gebragt, onze voorraad goederen
zooveel mogelijk geladen, en de rest na ons beste weten verstopt te
hebben, gingen wij ook op de vlugt na Eureka.

Het was een prachtigen nacht, de maan scheen helder en de sterren
flonkerden aan den hemel, doch zagen wij wat rood aan den hemel dan
was ons zeggen, „Daar zijn de Indianen al aan 't branden." In Eureka
bij onze aankomst was alles in verwarring, de wagens ramelden, de
paarden hinnekten, de koeijen loeiden, en de telegraaf werkte onop-

houdelijk, meestal kwade gerugten overbrengende zoals „Mandan [North Dakota] is genomen en de Indianen hebben de inwoners gedood." Meer dergelijke gerugten verspreiden zich door de stad. Een speciale car werd besteld uit Aberdeen om de vlugtelingen en wel de vrouwen en kinderen naar het oosten te vervoeren. Het was een verwarring, bijna zou ik zeggen als bij de Babylonische spraakverwarring.

Dit alles kwam grootendeelsch daar vandaan, zoo als wij naderhand vernamen, doordat de telegrafist onder de invloed van sterke drank was. Ook onze Russische naburen waren niet minder door de schrik bevangen. Ook zij toogen op de vlugt met overhasting na dat sommigen hunner het spek en flour [tarwe bloem] in den wel [put] geworpen hadden om bij hunne terugkomst alles bedorven te vinden. Een paard dat achter de wagen gebonden was werd door het geladen geweer, dat op de wagen lei en door ongeluk afging, doodgeschoten. Een man met een groot gezin op de wagen zittende werd door zijn vrouw opmerkzaam gemaakt dat een hunner kinderen verloren was, doch hij antwoorde, „Laat liggen, vrouw, het is beter een te verliezen dan alle dood; wij hebben er toch genoeg over" [volgens grapmakers]!

Na een op twee dagen afwezig geweest te zijn keerden wij allen weder huiswaarts en vonden alles zoo als wij het verlaten hadden. De Indianen hadden niet van Van Dijk's gesnoept. Pas vond zijn geld op de eigen plaats, en bij de anderen was niets ontvreemd. Hiermede wil ik eindigen want als ik op mijn praatstoel zit zou ik niet gemakkelijk kunnen uitscheiden.

[Translation]

During the early part of 1885 Pieter Ellerbroek, a storekeeper in Douglas County, induced many persons in Iowa and Michigan who wanted farms to try their fortune [as he put it] in the fair valley of the Missouri River in Campbell County. In common with land speculators he held before us an alluring prospect: 480 acres of the best land to be had for little money – a tree claim preëmtion and a homestead Many a person listened to these representations, especially farmless persons in Michigan or Iowa or in other states.

I want to make it clear that most of our settlers were poor. According to later information Ellerbroek's desire was to make some money so that he could pay a heavy debt on his store. Whether this is true or not we cannot state. But it is certain that as soon as he had drawn most of his gains from his transactions here he abandned the inexperienced settlers and was not again seen in these parts. We all had great confidence in

him. Had he, like Mr. Henry Hospers, continued to help and advise us
we believe he would have profited handsomely.

Such, then, were the circumstances under which some farmers from
Iowa and many more from Michigan came here in the spring of 1885 to
settle near the banks of the Missouri River. Among the settlers from
Sioux County in Iowa was my family and that of G. van Surksum which,
however, after staying several weeks moved to Emmons County in
North Dakota. We were the first families to settle here. But soon others
came from Michigan who still are our neighbors. The settlers were not
numerous, but they were enterprising. We had great need of such spirit,
for it was no slight venture to move to our properties 70 to 100 miles
distant from the railway station to which we had come by train. For
this distance into the prairie wilderness had to be covered without the
benefit of roads. Such journeys were made amid unusual hardships.
Sometimes the settler camped on the prairie, sometimes he spent the
night in an abandoned sodhouse which he shared with his horses. Such
a trip required from four to six days and had its unusual incidents. On one
of my trips I stopped at a farmer's sodhouse in the hope of spending the
night, but I found no one at home. I could not proceed on account of
the darkness. I acted as if I was master of the house. After tending
to my horses I went into the house in order to prepare my supper. I
found coffee, sugar, bread, and butter. Next I went to bed but kept on
most of my clothes, should the owner of the house suddenly return.
When day dawned I prepared my breakfast and went on my way. Later,
stopping at this place, I asked the owner if some tramp had made use of
his house during his absence. I told him I was the person, and asked how
much I owned him. "Nothing," he replied. "You took good care of
my property. I scarcely noticed that some stranger had made
use of it."

The slightest accident to our wagon or some other mishap might spell
the greatest difficulty. And, besides, the prairie was very lonesome,
especially during our first winter, for the weather was most cold. For
seven months my wife did not see anybody she knew. We seemed to
become fearful of strangers. My youngest son, then about five, was
greatly disturbed when he saw a stranger approaching the house and
called to his mother, "Shut that door, there is a man coming to the house."
But today that lonesomeness has vanished. The railroad has extended its
lines, first to Bowdle and thereafter to Eureka which brought the railroad to within twenty miles from my place. Eureka is, I believe, the
largest market place in Dakota for goods transported by wagon. Some

farmers come a distance of 80 miles to attend this market. In Europe we say, "All roads lead to Rome", but here all roads lead to Eureka.

It was no wonder that people became lost on the trackless and un-inhabited prairie, especially at dusk. One of my neighbors spent New Year's Eve with a friend. At ten o'clock he left for his home, a half mile distant. The kerosene in his lantern froze, and an Egyptian darkness fell upon him. After wandering about on the prairie all night he reached his home at nine o'clock the following morning. I too was lost several times. Many a night I spent on the prairie loudly singing psalms in order to pass away the time. Such experiences during the summer were not unpleasant. But during winter when snowstorms roared over this prairie it was quite a different matter. I felt like the thief who was about to be hanged, "I wish I was home with mother!"

During my first winter in this place I paid my neighbor, G. van Surk-sum, a visit, a distance of twenty miles on which I spent four days. Snowstorm followed snowstorm. I must confess that at such times the Lord was gracious. My neighbor J. de Vries frequently said, "Some day Van Erve will perish out on the prairie." But aside from the tip of my nose I never suffered from frost bites. Not one of our Dutch neighbors lost his life on the prairie. Some Russians and Americans, however, were frozen to death.

Our religious life was more or less irregular during the first years of our settlement. We were not well acquainted with each other and we had Sunday services at two or three different places. Sometimes we lost track of the days of the week. So, for example, our friend P. Droog who after having worked on Sunday, on the next day dressed himself for church and, with his Bible under his arm, arrived at K. Scholten's house where they convinced him with difficulty that it really was Monday.

But such conditions changed quickly. As the number of settlers in-creased a need was felt for a church building. The house of brother Vork, which we used at first, proved too small. We decided to build a new church without delay. One beautiful day in the summer of 1886 nearly the entire settlement, old as well as young, set out with swords and pikes. By this I mean shovels, a plow to break the prairie sod, wagons drawn by oxen, and carpenter's equipment. In one day we erected a church struc-ture. It was not quite so magnificent as Solomon's temple. Nor could any of us say with David, "Behold we live in a house of cedar; and the ark of God stands in the midst of the curtains." The dimensions of the church were 16 by 32 feet inside, and 21 by 37 feet outside. We had no critical tastes to consider in erecting the church. There were plenty of sods for building the walls; the roof of the tabernacle was covered with a triple layer of boards on which were placed tarpaper and sods. We do not exaggerate in saying that when finished everybody was pleased. True, when it rained we had to move our chairs to get out of the rain into the drip. But the praises to the honor of God were not dampened by such rains. This church was dedicated on October 10, 1886, and was given the name A. C. van Raalte. On that day also was organized the congregation composed of 14 communicants and nine baptized members, the Rev. Frederick J. Zwemer and Rev. Abraham Stegeman officiating.

After having been served for five years by this structure, we built another. The splendid new church, built of wood, was financed by voluntary offerings. Its dimensions were 28 by 36 feet; its beautiful pews were contributed by the eastern churches of the denomination. This church was dedicated by Frederick J. Zwemer on August 20, 1893, at the occasion of his marriage trip. During the entire twelve year period of our settlement we shared the services of a minister with the church at Westfield in Emmons County. This was Jacob van der Meulen. But our religious services are pretty faithfully attended, especially when some flying dragon in the shape of a minister or some student during his vacation leads us. Unfortunately, however, the congregation does not grow so that the prospect of acquiring a minister steadily decreases. A flock without a shepherd is something unfortunate. What shall I say about our financial condition? It is not befitting for us to complain. It is true that during our first years in this settlement we were not well off. But God opened the hearts of our friends in the East. They sent us many gifts. I can truthfully state that none of our Hollanders has suffered want. But why have so many moved away? Had we had a Van Raalte or a Bolks to lead us I believe our congregation would not have grown smaller. For most of those who came here have left carrying with them a handsome profit. We hear that they would like to return to Campbell County, just as the Israelites of old wanted to return to the fleshpots of Egypt. The indebtedness of our congregation has greatly decreased during the past two years. The prospect of a good harvest has filled our settlers with courage. We have two excellent stores – one owned by Albert van Dijk, the other by Tinholt Brothers, who are doing a good business. A creamery erected last year contributes much to the community's well being.

In a new settlement like this there are extraordinary occurrences which deserve to be recorded. Were I to recount them all I believe they would fill an entire volume. But I choose to relate only one that happened here – the Indian stampede.

In the evening of November 20, 1890, rumor went forth, "The Indians have crossed the Missouri and have begun to massacre the people!" This report spread through the settlement swift as the flash of lightning, fast as the flight of an arrow. Everybody got ready to flee. That was when Sitting Bull and his followers were in rebellion against Uncle Sam. Everybody was in terror. Mrs. Arie Schaap who the night before had presented her first-born, a son, to the world was put on a buggy, with bed and all, and so driven away. Later, when the infant was baptized, Frederick J. Zwemer, our classical missionary, suggested it be called Cornelius and be given a second name Gersom which seemed to be equivalent to the Dutch wordt for "fugitive," that is *vluchteling*. I note, however, that in Exodus 2, 22, Gersom means "stranger" [that is *vreemdeling*]. But it is possible that this name may have more than one meaning, as in the case with other words. If anyone wants more information on this point I refer him to the above mentioned Rev. Frederick J. Zwemer, Pella, Iowa. In his eagerness to escape the Indians S. E. Pas forgot to put his purse in his pocket and left it lying on the commode. A. O. van Dijk had killed and dressed two hogs. They were hanging from a ladder – obviously he had intended to show the Indians that the Hollanders knew how to kill and dress pigs! The terrified man abandoned his pigs to the Indians. Mrs. H. C. Zuidman, accompanied by the Kuipers family, arrived in breathless haste at the Tinholt's. In her great fright she had forgotten to put on all her clothes. "Alas," she moaned, "I now am a widow. The Indians surely will have scalped my husband, for he went to the river to get some wood!" Panic stricken Jan Schaap ran right through a wire fence. Jan Slotman was more collected. When all his family had climbed onto the wagon in order to flee he missed his puppy. "Wife," he called, "where is Popje? I will not let the Indians make soup of my dog!" As my farm was situated farthest east in the settlement and farthest from these scenes of terror I was the last to hear of the frightening news. At ten o'clock in the evening, just as we were in our first sleep, the Schaap and De Haan families woke us. They had come in their wagons piled high with household and other articles. We hastily got up. Our feather bed was placed on top of one of their wagons. On it was placed the ailing Rudolf de Haan who could not stand the shaking of the wagon. Our house was in wild confusion, the cattle were turned out onto the prairie, our furniture was hurriedly loaded on a wagon, and what we could not carry with us in our flight we hid as well as we could. And then we fled to Eureka. It was a beautiful night. The moon shone clear in the sky, and the stars gleamed brightly.

But when we noted a glow in the sky, we said, "That's from the Indians' fires!" Arrived in Eureka we found nothing but confusion. Wagons rumbled, horses whinnied, cattle lowed, and the telegraph office was busy sending and receiving messages. Most of the news received inspired fright. It was reported that Mandan in North Dakota had been seized, that the Indians were killing the inhabitants. Other reports spread through the town. A special railroad coach was ordered from Aberdeen to take the fugitives, especially the women and children, to places further east. Great was the confusion, I should say it was as great as the confusion of tongues at the tower of Babel.

This turmoil, we later found out, was caused by a telegrapher under the influence of liquor. Our Russian neighbors also had succumbed to fright and like ourselves had sought safety in flight. Some of them hid pork and flour in wells, but on their return found everything had spoiled. The only casualty was a horse which, tied behind a wagon, was accidentally shot by a gun lying in the wagon. A mother of a large family, sitting on a loaded wagon about to rush away, noted that one of her children was missing. Her husband, however, urged haste, saying, "Let us not stop for the child. It is better that one is lost than that all of us die! We have enough children in any case!" [At least such were his words according to jokers.]

After an absence of two days we all went back to our homes. There we found everything precisely as when we had left. The Indians never cut a slice from Van Dijk's butchered pigs. Pas found his money where he had left it – on the commode in his house. No one had lost anything. With this I will close, for when I begin to talk it is not easy for me to stop.

Chapter XXXI

FOUR IMMIGRANT BIOGRAPHIES

109. JACOB VAN DER MEULEN'S LIFE OF HIS FATHER

[The writer (d. 1901) was born in Middelharnis in the Netherlands in 1834, the son of Cornelius van der Meulen (1800-1876). This sketch, written at Graafschap in 1896 for the Semi-Centennial celebrations, was published in *De Grondwet*, September 5, 1911].

Cornelius van der Meulen werd geboren te Middelharnis, provincie Zuid-Holland, Nederland, op den 15den December 1800. Zijne ouders behoorden tot den burgerstand. Hij verloor zijne moeder toen hij vier jaar oud was. Zijn vader, een verstandig man, was verknocht aan de Gereformeerde leer. Niettegenstaande mijn vader in de Gereformeerde leer gekweekt was, koos hij, onder den invloed zijner leeraars, de meer vrijzinnige richting, en sloog eindelijk tot het ongeloof over.

In 1827 trad hij in het huwelijk met Elizabeth G. van der Roovaart. Hij had slechts de gewone schoolopvoeding gehad, maar las veel en beoefende bij zichzelven de wiskunde, met het doel om aannemer te kunnen zijn van dijkwerken.

De dood van zijne twee eenige kinderen, die hem op een dag ontvielen, bracht hem tot bekeering. De omkeering was zeer beslist. Bij mijne moeder waren altijd godsdienstige indrukken geweest, maar die waren na haar huwelijk afgenomen, en kwamen nu meer beslist te voorschijn. Hij sloot zich aan bij de vromen en zijn huis werd een herberg voor de kinderen Gods.

Toen de Afscheiding van de Hervormde Kerk doorbrak, was hij de eerste in zijn dorp, die zich bij die beweging aansloot. Enkelen meer deden hetzelfde, en van de gemeente alzoo ontstaan, werd hij ouderling en leider in hunnen openbaren godsdienst. Overgehaald zijnde om het oefenen te beproeven was het gevolg, dat de gemeente hem als leeraar beriep. Na beraad van verscheidenen maanden nam hij dat beroep aan en begaf zich met zijn gezin naar Utrecht om opleiding te ontvangen onder Ds. Hendrik Pieter Scholte, den godsdienstigen leider der Afgescheidenen in de streek waar mijn vader woonde. Van het onderwijs geven kwam niet veel; mijn vader moest iedere Zondag prediken en na ongeveer een jaar in de studie doorgebracht te hebben, werd hij als leeraar geordend in het jaar 1839. Voor eenige maanden deelde ook de gemeente te Rotterdam in zijne diensten. Die gemeente nam zoo snel toe dat zijn gevolg eene grootere vergaderplaats moest huren, en begon met het bouwen van een kerk.

Zoo spoedig als eene pastorie gereed was, ging mijn vader wonen te Middelharnis. Echter, zijn voornaam arbeidsveld in de Nederlanden zou blijken de provincie Zeeland te zijn. Hij werd beroepen als leeraar door de twaalf Afgescheidene gemeenten aldaar. Hij ging wonen te Goes en had iedere Zondag in een andere gemeente te prediken tot hij de twaalf gemeenten rond geweest was. De moeiten, verbonden aan dit werk, waren velen, er was vooruitzicht van veel tegenstand en vele ontberingen. Niettegenstaande al dit, met het oog op de groote behoeften, nam hij het beroep aan.

Den 13den Juli 1841 begon hij zijn werk in Zeeland. Hij predikte in schuren, woonhuizen, op velden, en waar immer de gelegenheid zich aanbood. Het volk kwam van wijd en zijd om hem te hooren, en een goed getal werd tot God bekeerd. Eene predikatie werd gezegend tot de bekeering van meer dan honderd menschen.

Te dier tijde bestond er eene wet oorspronkelijk bedoeld voor politieke vergaderingen, maar die toegepast werd op vergaderingen der Afgescheidenen. Die wet liet niet toe een te zamen vergadering van meer den negentien personen. Eene schending van die wet werd gestraft met eene zware geldboete. Die boete werd bereidwillig betaald door die gemeenten, die prediking ontvingen.

Van eene prediking zal ik korte melding maken. Die werd gedaan in het land van Axel, Terneuzen, en Zaamslag. Mijn vader stond op een wagen geplaatst voor dat doel op een dorschvloer. De schuur was propvol. Na het voorgebed traden twee gewapende gerechtsdienaars op den wagen toe en zeiden, ,,In de naam van den koning komen wij u aanzeggen, dat gij niet voor deze vergadering moet prediken, en bevelen u allen van hier te gaan en deze plaats te verlaten.''

Het antwoord was, ,,Gij hebt uwe boodschap gebracht in den naam des konings, maar nu moet ik u aanzeggen in den naam van den Koning der koningen, dat ik belast ben met de roeping om hier dezen dag het Evangelie te brengen aan het volk, dat hier vergaderd is.'' Na een kort stilzwijgen, zeide hij verder, ,,Gij hebt gezondigd, maar deze, die u gezonden hebben, hebben grootere zonde.'' De predikaties, gedurende den tijd der vervolging gedaan, werden buitengewoon gezegend in de bekeering van menschen en den groei der Afgescheidene gemeenten. Nieuwe gemeenten kwamen er bij, kerken werden gebouwd, en meerdere leeraars kwamen mijn vader helpen in zijn herderlijk werk.

Er was eene beweging in welke hij schoorvoetend deel nam en die hij naderhand geloofde verkeerd in zijn toedracht geweest te zijn. Aanvraag werd gedaan aan de regeering om "erkenning", de voorwaarde waarop vrijheid toegestaan werd was het afleggen van den naam Gereformeerd en het afstand doen van alle aanspraak op de goederen en eigendommen der Hervormde Kerk. De naam aangenomen was Christelijke Afgescheidene Kerk. Sommigen weigerden om zulk eene aanvraag te doen en noemden zich „Gereformeerden onder het Kruis". Tot op dien tijd waren zij die zich afscheidden altijd zorgvuldig geweest te verklaren dat zij zich afscheidden van het Hervormde Kerkbestuur, dus niet van het kerkelijk lichaam. Zij zagen het toenmalig kerkbestuur aan als eene tyrannie, welke te weerstaan Christelijke roeping was.

Maatschappelijke uitsluiting en vervolging werden tegen het nieuwe genootschap gebezigd, nadat erkenning verkregen was van de landsregeering. Scheldnamen werden hen gegeven en nageroepen op de straat; die in zaken waren, verloren hunne klandizie; daglooners werden afgedankt; de kinderen der Afgescheidenen werden op de publieke scholen door de andere kinderen dagelijks uitgescholden en zelfs lichamelijk mishandeld. Zelfs werd er nu en dan een onderwijzer gevonden, die zijn haat aan die onnoozle kinderen moest afkoelen. Het gevolg van dit alles was de landverhuizersbeweging van 1846 en 1847. Godsdienst was de drijfkracht van de beweging, waarvan deze Hollandsche nederzetting het resultaat is.

Een groot getal Zeelanders besloten hun vaderland te verlaten. Zij brachten een beroep uit op mijn vader om hen als hun leeraar te vergezellen; zij betaalden de reiskosten van hem en zijn gezin.

Het gezelschap verliet Nederland in drie schepen, twee gingen af van Antwerpen, en een waarop mijn vader was, voer af van Rotterdam. Eene onophoudelijke reeks van tegenheden was het deel dezer reizigers, reeds eer zij Nederlands kust verlaten konden. Te New York aangekomen, vernamen zij dat de twee voor hen aangekomene gezelschappen van Zeeuwen, naar Michigan gegaan waren.

De tegenheden hielden niet op met de zeereis. Met bedriegers in aanraking gekomen zijnde en mijn vader zich op zijne rechten beroepende, zou men hem in Troy, New York, in het water geworpen hebben, zoo hij niet ontzet ware geworden.

Wij zullen niet in alle de ondervindingen der baanbrekers treden, alleen melden wij dat ons gezin twee nachten onder den blooten hemel moest vertoeven, een nacht en een deel van een dag blootgesteld aan een stortregen, met zwaar onweder vergezeld, en eenige weken onder een niet meer dan in naam dak. Zulk een blokhuis als hier op de College Campus, tijdens de Semi-Centennial feestvieringen ten toon gesteld is geworden, zou door ons als weelde beschouwd zijn geworden, zoo wij in zulk een huis intrek hadden kunnen nemen.

Wij zullen maar niet over het hongerlijden spreken, noch het schrale ongeschikte voedsel voor mijn vader, die veel van de verandering van het klimaat te lijden had. Gedurende eene geheele winter kregen wij als een groote gunst, tot tweemaal toe een pond boter voor mijn toen zwakken vader, en met het voorjaar van 1848 nu en dan een ei. Spoedig kwam het tot cornbrood en cornkoffie van cornmeel, geborgd te Grand Rapids. Maar wij zullen het hier maar kort mee maken.

Mijn vader arbeidde op het dorp Zeeland tot 1859, toen hij een beroep aannam naar Chicago, Illinois. Het vooruitzicht van eene gemeente op te bouwen in die wereldstad lokte hem aan. Toen hij zijne intree-predikatie deed, waren er slechts weinigen om hem te hooren. Het kerkgebouw was klein en onooglijk; het stond in Foster Street, het middenpunt in ligging van de toenmalige Hollandsche kerkgangers. Mijn vader, verwonderd over het klein getal hoorders - daar er toch vele landgenooten moesten wonen in zulk eene groote stad - vernam dat er verscheidene Hollanders woonden in een afgelegen deel der stad, den naam onder de Hollanders dragende van „Groninger Hoek", maar dat deze menschen geheel onverschillig waren omtrent de godsdienst en dat er niets met hen op dat gebied aan te vangen was.

Mijn vader besloot die menschen op te zoeken en uit de noodigen zijne prediking bij te wonen. Het antwoord was afwijzend: „de kerk was te verweg," enz. Hij stelde hun toen voor in hunne eigene buurt in een hunner woningen te prediken. Hij ging daar iedere week heen; de eene week predikte hij des avonds en de andere catechiseerde hij de volwassenen. Spoedig volgden bekeeringen en velen voegden zich bij de gemeente. Er was behoefte aan een ander kerkgebouw op eene plaats te bouwen meer in het midden der Hollandsche bevolking. Eindelijk kwam het nieuwe kerkgebouw te staan op de oude standplaats.

Mijn vader beschouwde deze uitkomst als zoo schadelijk voor de evangeliseering der Hollandsche bevolking en zoo belemmerend voor den groei der gemeente, dat dit eene voorname rede was voor het aannemen van het beroep op hem uitgebracht door de Tweede Gereformeerde gemeente te Grand Rapids. De behoeften van die gemeente waren zeer groot; zij was lijdend aan inwendige verdeeldheid. De toestanden eischten veel christelijke voorzichtigheid en standvastigheid. De verhuizing naar Grand Rapids had plaats in Mei 1861. Ds. van Raalte bevestigde hem als leeraar in zijne laatste standplaats.

Het was voor mijn vader een vreugdevolle dat toen hij op den 28sten Juli van dit jaar zijn oudsten zoon bevestigde als leeraar te Cedar Grove, Sheboygan County, Wisconsin. Hij had eene gelofte gedaan na den dood zijner twee kinderen in Rotterdam, dat zoo God hem een ander kind gaf en dat een zoon zou zijn, hij die aan den evangeliedienst zou toeweiden. In 1862 bevestigde hij zijn anderen zoon als leeraar te Milwaukee. Hij maakte groote opofferingen opdat zijne zonen zouden verkrijgen, die volle opleiding voor den evangeliedienst, die hij had moeten missen, en die hij geloofde groote waarde te hebben. Ds. van Raalte vond in hem een beslisten steun in zijne pogingen om hooger onderwijs te verkrijgen. Hij was van eersten af aan lid van den Council van Hope College en woonde, zoolang zijne lichaamskrachten het toelieten, de vergaderingen van dat lichaam bij. Ook arbeidde hij en droeg bij, ook met legaat, voor het Ebenezer-fonds.

De zegen, die op zijn arbeid rustte in Grand Rapids, is wel bekend. Gedurende zijn dienst kwam het groote kerkgebouw, aan Bostwick Street, en de twee dochter-gemeentens, de Derde en Vierde Gereformeerde, tot stand. Toen hij zijne gemeente aan zijn opvolger overdroeg, telde die 376 huisgezinnen en 481 avondmaalgangers.

Toen zijne lichaamskrachten hem beslist begonnen te begeven, verkreeg hij op zijn dringend verzoek het emeritaat van de Classis Grand River. De herdersstaf werd overgedragen aan Ds. Nicholas H. Dosker in 1873. De loslating had plaats op voorwaarden zeer ter ere voor het christelijk karakter des kerkenraads en der gemeente, en die getuigden van de hoogachting en liefde hem toegedragen.

Waar wij afscheid nemen van zijne herderlijke bediening, dienen wij te melden de verliezen die hem door den dood in Amerika troffen. Op den 8sten Maart, 1849, stierf zijne dochter Anna, oud acht jaren. In Februari, 1857, verloor hij voor de tweede maal in zijn leven twee kinderen op eenen dag: Sara van der Meulen, oud bijkans twaalf jaar, en Anna, oud vier jaar.

Op den 7den Februari 1869 stierf zijne vrouw, de gezellin van zijn leven, en zijne waardige hulpgenoote. Zij stierf plotseling in het kerkgebouw onder het gehoor van eene predikatie gedaan door Ds. Willem Moerdijk, toen theologisch student te Holland, Michigan. Haar lichaam, ter ruste gelegd te Zeeland, werd ten grave gevolgd door eene zeer groote schare. Zijne dochter, Mrs. Elizabeth G. Oggel, stierf op den 7den Mei 1870.

Wij dienden nog verder te melden als onder de meer belangrijke gebeurtenissen van zijn leven, zijne tegenwoordigheid als afgevaardigde van de Algemeene Synode der Reformed Church op de Synode der Christelijke Gereformeerde kerken te Middelburg, gezeten in het jaar 1869, waar hij getuige was van de heeling der kerkelijke breuk en aanneming van den naam Christelijk Gereformeerd.

Op den 21sten Februari 1870 trad hij voor de tweede maal in het huwelijk met de weduwe Frouwke Idema, die hem liefderijk en zorgvuldig verpleegde in de laatste maanden van toenemende zwakheid en eindigende in den dood.

Na zijn verkrijgen van het emeritaat liet zijn geest hem geene werkeloosheid toe. Hij bleef den leeraar in zijne veelvuldige werkzaamheden helpen door het leiden van biduren, begrafenissen, en nu en dan eene predikatie doende in zijne vorige en omliggende gemeenten.

De zwaakheden van zijn ouderdom lieten zich meer gelden. Hij zag zijn einde met gelatenheid te gemoet, gereed om heen te gaan en met Christus te zijn. Hij zeide kort voor zijn dood, „Ik ben blij dat ik geleefd heb, en nu ben ik blij dat ik ga sterven." Hij verliet ons den 23sten Augustus 1876. Hij had zelve alle schikkingen gemaakt omtrent zijne begrafenis. Te Grand Rapids deed Ds. Nicholas H. Dosker de lijkrede naar aanleiding van de woorden, „Lazarus onze vriend slaapt." De kerkenraad der gemeente, de Jongelings-Vereeniging en velen van Grand Rapids volgden het stoffelijk overschot naar Zeeland, waar het gelegd werd bij de zijde van zijne eerste vrouw.

Aldaar werden toespraken gehouden in het kerkgebouw door Albert C. Kuiper, Willem P. de Jong, Adriaan Zwemer, Dirk Broek, James de Pree, en Henry Uiterwijk. Het slotgebed werd gedaan door Prof. Charles Scott, Ds. Willem Moerdijk deed eene toespraak by het graf, en Ds. Engelbert C. Oggel sprak den zegen uit. Eene zeer groote schare drukte door tegenwoordigheid de achting en de liefde uit, die het volk voor hem had.

[Translation]

Cornelius van der Meulen was born at Middelharnis in the province of South Holland, the Netherlands, on December 15, 1800. His parents belonged to the burgher class. His mother died when he was four years old. His father, an intelligent man, was devoted to Reformed teaching. But although my father was brought up in Reformed doctrine, he choose, under the influence of his teachers, a more liberal attitude, and finally gave up his faith altogether.

In 1827 he married Elizebeth G. van der Roovaart. Although he had only an ordinary school education, he read extensively and developed a knowledge of geometry, intending to make use of this knowledge when and if he should become contractor in the construction of dykes.

The death of his two only children, both on the same day, led him to conversion. This wrought a decisive change in his life. My mother always had had religious impressions. These, however, declined after her marriage. But now they once more became prominent. Father then united with pious friends and his house became a home for the children of God.

When the secession from the Reformed Church took place, he was the first in his village to join the movement. A number of others also seceded, and of the congregation thus formed he became elder and assumed direction of public worship. Induced to try preaching resulted in an invitation by his congregation to serve as their minister. After considering this invitation many months he accepted it and, accompanied by his family, went to Utrecht in order to be prepared for his calling under the tuition of Hendrik Pieter Scholte, the religious leader of the Afgescheidenen [Seceders] in the area where my father was living. Instruction was slight and irregular, for my father had to preach each Sunday. After about a year's study he was ordained, in the year 1839. For several months he served the congregation at Rotterdam. That church grew so rapidly that they had to hire a larger meeting place, and so they began to build their own church building.

As soon as a parsonage was ready, father moved to Middelharnis. But his significant field of labor was the province of Zeeland. He was invited to become the pastor of the twelve Seceder [Afgescheiden] congregations there. He took up his residence in Goes. Every Sunday he preached in these churches in turn until he had preached in each of the twelve congregations. Many were the difficulties connected with this work and there was prospect of much opposition and much privation. But in spite of all these difficulties, seeing the greater needs of the people, he accepted their invitation.

He began his pastoral labors in Zeeland on July 13, 1841. He preached in barns, houses, fields, in fact in any place where opportunity presented itself. People came from far and wide to hear him and a goodly number were turned to God. One sermon alone was blessed by the conversion of more than 100 people.

At that time there was a law originally intended to control political meetings but was applied to the services of the Seceders [Afgescheidenen] That law forbade the meeting of more than 19 persons. Violation was punished by a heavy fine. Such fines, however, were willingly paid by the congregations who sponsored preaching.

I shall describe one such service. A meeting was held in the land of Axel, Ter Neuzen, and Zaamslag. My father stood on a wagon which had been put on the barn floor for that purpose. The barn was filled to the limit. As soon as the introductory prayer was finished two armed officers approached the wagon and said: "In the name of the king we come to tell you that you may not preach before this group; we order you all to leave this place."

Father's answer was: "You have indeed brought the message in the name of the king. But now I must say to you in the name of the King of kings that I am charged to proclaim the Gospel to the people gathered here." After a brief pause, father continued: "You have sinned, but those who sent you have sinned more grievously." Preaching during that time of public prosecution was unusually blessed both in the conversion of people and in the grown of the Seceded [Afgescheiden] congregations. New congregations came into existence, churches were built, and other ministers came to help father in his pastoral labor.

There was a movement which father joined cautiously. Later he judged his conduct to have been wrong. Application was made to the government for official recognition of the new congragations. Liberty was accorded on the condition only if they gave up the name Reformed and renounced any claim upon the properties of the Reformed Church. The name the new congregations adopted was the Christian Seceded [Afgescheiden] Church. Some of the congregations refused to take this step; they called themselves "Reformed under the Cross". Until that time the congregations had always made it a point that they simple had seceded from the ecclesiastical governing body of the Reformed Church, not from the Reformed Church. They regarded the then existing church government as a tyranny and thought it was a Christian duty to oppose it.

Social discrimination and even persecution were directed against the new organization after it had acquired recognition from the government.

Insulting names were given them, and hurled at them in the streets. Those in business lost their customers. Wage earners were dismissed. Children of parents who were Seceders [Afgescheidenen] constantly were given ugly epithets by their comrades in the public schools, and even were physically mistreated. There were teachers who visited their hatred upon the harmless children. A consequence of this state of affairs was the movement during 1846 and 1847, in favor of emigration. Religion was the driving force of this movement which resulted in the founding of this place [Zeeland, Michigan].

A large number of Zeelanders decided to leave their fatherland. They invited my father to accompany them as their pastor, and paid his travel expenses and those of his family.

The group left the Netherlands in three ships, two from Antwerp, and one, on which my father sailed, from Rotterdam. An endless series of adverse incidents was the lot of these travelers, even before they left the Dutch coast. Arrived at New York, they learned that the two shiploads of Zeelanders from Antwerp had arrived and had gone on to Michigan.

Although the voyage was over, their trials continued. They had contact with cheats. My father, when he stood on his rights at Troy, New York, would have been thrown into the water had he not been rescued.

We shall not describe all the experiences of our pioneers. Only, we shall mention the fact that our family had to spend two nights under the open sky, were exposed to a pelting rain for one night and part of the following day and to a violent thunder storm, and living for several weeks under a roof which was a roof in name only.

Nor shall we talk about hunger, nor about the inadequate and unfit food which father had to endure while suffering from the change of climate. During one whole winter we had only one pound of butter for father who then was weak, and in the spring of 1848 an occasional egg. Soon we had to get along with coffee and bread made from corn which was bought on credit in Grand Rapids. But we shall not extend our comments on this subject farther.

My father labored in the village of Zeeland until 1859 when he accepted an invitation to go to Chicago, Illinois. The prospect of building a congregation in that great city lured him. The church structure was small and unsightly; it stood on Foster Street, at a central point for the Dutch churchgoers of that time. My father was surprised that so few came to hear him, for there indeed were many Netherlanders in that great city who, generally referred to as "Hollanders of the Groninger Section", were quite indifferent in the matter of religion. It was said that these people would have nothing to do with it.

Father decided to call on these people and invite them to his services. Their answer was evasive: the church was too far distant, etc. He thereupon suggested that he preach in their neighborhood in one of their homes. He went to this place every week, one week conducting evening service, the following giving catechetical instruction to the grownup folk. Soon there were conversions, and many joined the congregation. There was need of another church building at a point more central to the Dutch population. Finally, a new church was erected on the site of the old.

Father thought that this was unfortunate from the standpoint of evangelization among the Dutch population, throttling the growth of the congregation. This was one of the reasons why he accepted a call from the second Reformed congregation in Grand Papids. The needs of that group were very great, for the people were divided. This situation demanded Christian caution and firmess. Father moved to Grand Rapids in May 1861. Dominie Van Raalte installed him as minister in this his last ministerial charge.

For father it was a happy day when on July 28 of that same year he installed his oldest son as pastor at Cedar Grove, Sheboygan County, Wisconsin. He had made a promise, after the death of his two children in Rotterdam that, should God grant him another child and that it should be a son he would consecrate him to the service of the Gospel. In 1862 he installed his second son as pastor in Milwaukee. He made great sacrifices that his sons should have that complete training for the ministry which he himself had not had and which be believed very important. Dr. A. C. van Raalte found in him a firm support in his efforts to establish higher education. He was from the beginning a member of the Council of Hope College. So long as his physical strenght lasted he always attended the meetings of that body. He also worked hard for the establishment of the Ebenezer Fund, contributed money and made bequests to the same.

Well known is the blessing that rested on his labors in Grand Rapids. The large church edifice on Bostwick Street was erected during his pastorate. During this time also the Third and Fourth Reformed congregations were organized. When he passed his charge on to his successor, his congregation numbered 376 families, 481 communicants.

When father's physical strenght definitely began to decline, the Classis Grand River at his request gave him an emeritus status. His pastoral work was taken over in 1873 by Dominie Nicholas H. Dosker. His labors were concluded on conditions very much to the credit of the Christian character of the consistory of the congregation. They gave evidence of respect and affection.

Having traced the history of his pastoral services we should say something about his children who died here in America. His oldest daughter Anna died on March 8, 1849, at the age of eight. In February 1857 for the second time in his life, he lost two of his children in one day: Sara, hardly eight, and Anna, four.

His wife and worthy helper passed away on February 7, 1869. She died suddenly in church while Dominie Willem Moerdijk, then student in theology at Holland, Michigan, was preaching a sermon. Her body, carried to its final resting place was followed by a great number of people. His daughter Mrs. Elizabeth G. Oggel died on May 7, 1870.

We should mention also, as being one of the most important events of his life, the fact that he was delegate of the General Synod of the Reformed Church to the Synod of the Christian Reformed Churches, held in 1869 at Middelburg. There he witnessed the healing of an ecclesiastical schism and the general adoption of the title "Christian Reformed".

For the second time in his life, on February 21, 1870, he was married, this time to the widow Frouwke Idema, who watched over him and cared for him affectionately during the final days of his increasing illness.

After he was given his emeritus status he did not lapse into idleness. He remained very much the minister, helping the pastor in his many duties by leading at prayers and funerals, and occasionally preaching to his former congregations and also to others nearby.

The feebleness of old age became more evident, but he viewed his approaching end with resignation, being ready to depart and to be with Christ. Shortly before his death he said: "I am glad that I have lived and now am glad to die." He departed from us on August 23, 1876. He had made all preparation for his own funeral. Dominie Nicholas Dosker, at Grand Rapids, gave the funeral sermon based on the words "Lazarus our friend sleeps". The consistory of the congregation, the Young People's Society, and many persons from Grand Rapids followed his remains as they were carried to Zeeland where they were laid away beside those of his first wife.

Addresses were made in the church in Zeeland by Albert C. Kuiper, Willem P. de Jong, Adriaan Zwemer, Dirk Broek, James de Pree, and Henry Uiterwijk. The concluding prayer was offered by Professor Charles Scott. The Reverend Willem Moerdijk said a few words at the graveside and the Reverend Engelbert C. Oggel offered a prayer. The large group of people attending the funeral expressed their respect and affection for him, which the people also generally had for him.

110. JAMES DE PREE'S REVEREND SEINE BOLKS

[Son-in-law of Bolks, and a minister in the Reformed Church, the writer was exceptionally qualified to pen this pioneer minister's life. James de Pree was born in Axel, the Netherlands, in 1845 and was ordained in 1870. From 1880 he was minister at Sioux Center, Sioux County, Iowa. During this charge he was associated with Seine Bolks who had identified himself intimately with the Dutch settlement in Sioux County. Written for the Semi-Centennial celebrations of 1897, this sketch was printed in *De Grondwet*, September 19, 1911.]

Seine Bolks werd geboren den 30sten April 1814 te Den Ham, in de provincie Overijsel, Nederland. Zijne ouders behoorden niet tot de grooten der aarde, maar wel tot het volk dat God vreest. Al zeer vroeg verloor hij zijn vader, zoodat hij zich van hem niets kon herinneren. Toch deed het zijne ziel altijd goed dat hij de vromen vaak van de oprechte godsvrucht van zijn vader had hooren getuigen. In zijne vroege jeugd scheen het voor een tijd alsof hij met het gezelschap der ijdele jongelieden zou worden meegevoerd om met de wereld hen te dienen; zijn opgeruimd gul, en vriendelijk karakter maakte hem de vriend van elk. Maar God had wat anders met hem voor, en tegenover al den sterken invloed der zonde bleef de kweeking van de godvreezende moeder niet ongezegend.

Toen Seine Bolks tot omstreeks 16 jarigen leeftijd gekomen was, brak de Heere door en maakte woning in zijn hart; hij kwam tot het volle besluit om met de zonde te breken en zich aan den dienst des Heeren te wijden. Hoewel hij weinig of niets van eene schoolkweeking genoten had, wat hij van God begiftigd met schoone gaven, en die zette hij nu al zeer spoedig voor den Heere op winst. Als jongeling hoedde hij de schapen; wanneer hij des daags daarmee in het veld was, was een Bijbeltje, hem door zijn moeder gegeven, zijn gestadige metgezel, en deed hij daarin veel biddend onderzoek. Zoo ontving hij al vroeg veel kennis in Gods Woord, en de ernst en vurige ijver van zijn hart deden hem weldra een werkend aandeel nemen in de godsdienstige vergaderingen.

Op 20 jarigen leeftijd was hij reeds gedurig werkzaam als oefenaar en dat met vrucht en tot genoegen van velen. Door de vromen werd het ras opgemerkt dat de Heere hem bijzondere gaven gegeven had – gaven van ernst, vuur, vrijmoedigheid, belangstelling, en van een helder inzicht in de waarheid. En daar de behoefte aan getrouwe uitleggers van het Evangelie destijds zeer groot was, kwam er van uit de gemeente waaraan hij behoorde een voorstel om hem tot de Evangelie bediening te laten opleiden. Het was de gemeente Hellendoorn die het voorstel deed en die het ook blijmoedig op zich nam om hem te Ommen, onder het opzicht van Ds. Van Raalte, te laten studeeren. Nadat hij 15 maanden studie genoten had was de behoefte zoo groot en het verlangen der gemeente die hem onderhield zoo sterk, dat zij meende niet langer meer te moeten wachten. Hoewel hij zelf gaarne langer zou gestudeerd hebben liet hij zich evenwel door de drang der omstandigheden bewegen en werd hij tot den dienst des Evangelies geordend.

Reeds voor dezen, 11 July 1838 was hij gehuwd met Geertje Brouwer, eene eenvoudige maar godvreezende jonge dochter; en de oudste zoon was ook al geboren eer vader zich naar de studie begaf. Elk die moeder Bolks gekend heeft zal het ons toestemmen dat zij waarlijk eene gave van God voor vader was; juist geschikt om hem tot steun, hulp, en bemoediging in het werk des Heeren te dienen, en inzonderheid in de verschillende omstandigheden en betrekkingen waarin de Heere hem wilde gebruiken. In geen betrekking was hij haar meer dierbaar en diende zij hem liever dan als dienstknecht des Heeren. Ware het om de geheele week te dienen als leidsman en raadsman in de wouden van Overisel ten tijde van de eerste settling aldaar; of ware het om ten tijde der in Chicago heerschende cholera den landgenooten aldaar tot verstrooster en helper te dienen; of ware het om somwijlen weken en zelfs maanden uit te gaan in het belang van den dierbaren kweekhof te dezer plaatse [Sioux County, Iowa], – altijd stond zij hem gewillig af om 's Heeren wil.

In Nederland heeft vader Bolks als herder geen andere gemeente bediend dan Hellendoorn. Vanwege de groote schaarschheid van trouwe Evangelie predikers, en vanwege de menigvuldigheid der plaatsen die naar de zuivere leer der waarheid dorstten ging hij, even als de andere broeders, in de week veel rond en deelde overal het Brood des levens uit. Zoo werd hij alom bekend in het oude vaderland. De Heere gaf kennelijk zijnen zegen op die onvermoeide pogingen, en in vele harten viel het dierbare zaad van waarachtig geloof en leven. Het waren dagen van bittere tegenstand en vervolging van de zijde des vijands, maar tevens dagen van onvergetelijk zalig genot en leven voor Gods kinderen. Geen geweldige brandbrieven of dreigementen van vurige tegenstanders, of spottenden hoon van ongeloovigen, schrikten af.

Eenmaal zou vader prediken in eene plaats waar men hem en de omstandigheden van zijne ouders kende. Een onverschillig man, die zijn vader had gekend als eigenaar van ganzen, zeide, ,,Ik wil ook eens hooren wat die ganzeboer te zeggen heeft." En voor dat de predikatie ten einde was greep God hem in het hart. Ook werd gebrek aan geschikte preekplaatsen niet gebruikt als eene reden om het werk te laten varen. Men vergaderde in den grooten tempel Gods, onder het geboomte, in woningen, op dorschvloeren, ja, zelfs in schaapskooien om het Woord des levens te hooren.

Bij eene gelegenheid was hij verzocht in eene naburige plaats te prediken. Kort voor de bepaalde tijd werd het jongste kind plotseling ziek, en stierf. Er was echter geen gelegenheid geweest om het volk er kennis van te geven, en hij wist dus dat zij zouden samenkomen en hem wachten. Nadat het kind gestorven was haastte hij zich daarom nog derwaarts en stelde hen niet teleur.

In het jaar 1846, toen vanwege de zware lasten die hem drukten de gedachten van velen in het ouderland naar Amerika getrokken werden, besloot ook vader Bolks en velen van de gemeente die hij bediende, met hem al zeer spoedig zich derwaarts te begeven. Met het oog op de langdurige reis en op de te vestigen nieuwe Kolonie in een vreemd klimaat en onbewoonde streken oefende hij zich nu voor eenigen tijd in de geneeskunde. Dit kwam hem al aanstonds op het schip, en later in de nederzetting te Overisel, Michigan, alsmede in de nieuwe kolonie in Sioux County, Iowa, zeer te stade.

Met 23 huisgezinnen verlieten zij den 3den September 1847 hun geboorteland en kwamen na eene zeer voorspoedige reis den 10 Oct. te New York aan. Vandaar ging men naar Albany met het doel om daar te overwinteren omdat het strenge seizoen te nabij was om verder te trekken. Te Albany echter werd de raad gegeven om naar Syracuse, New York, te gaan alwaar de gelegenheid voor woning en werk gunstiger was. Daar vertoefde men tot de volgende lente.

Na veel onderzoek en rijp beraad werd toen goed gevonden om naar Michigan te trekken waar Ds. Van Raalte zich reeds gevestigd had. Daar gekomen, vond men overvloedige gelegenheid om voor een geringen prijs zich een eigen stuk lands te verkrijgen, al was het alles bosch grond. Hoewel Ds. Bolks te Graafschap begeerd werd, viel toch de keuze van land op eene streek negen mijlen zuidoost van Holland. Men ging aanstonds aan het werk om zich hier te vestigen. Eerst gaf men den naam der gemeente, Hellendoorn, later, Overisel.

Deze vestiging ging met de gewone moeilijkheden en ontberingen gepaard; door middel echter van den wijzen raad en trouwe medearbeid en inzonderheid van de ernstige voorbede en vertroostende prediking van Ds. Bolks bleef het volk moedig en volhardend. Hij diende het volk in verschillende capaciteiten van predikant, geneesheer, landmeter, architect, en wat niet al. In alle deze kwam de verscheidenheid van gaven uit welke God hem had geschonken. Elk die tot hem kwam om raad, zij het ook in betrekking tot tijdelijke aangelegenheden, vond in hem een bereidwilligen en verstandigen raadgever. Zijn salaris ontving hij in werk; elk man gaf hem een dag werk in twee weken.

Spoedig na de komst der eerste settlers werd een gebouw van loggen opgetrokken om als kerkgebouw te dienen, juist op de lijn van Overisel en Fillmore townships. Dit gebouw werd echter al zeer spoedig gebruikt om de nu ras aankomende landverhuizers te herbergen. En daar de standplaats niet zeer wenschelijk werd beschouwd, besloot men een gebouw op te richten een weinig oost van waar de tegenwoordige kerk staat. Dit gebouw, hoewel niet sierlijk noch smaakvol, diende als heiligdom voor de gemeente tot het jaar 1866. Ruim vier jaren heeft hij de gemeente te Overisel gediend. De warme liefde en achting welke men hem daar steeds toedroeg en de teederheid waarmede zijne nagedachtenis daar nog in eere gehouden wordt geven getuigenis van den rijken zegen Gods hier over zijnen arbeid geschonken.

Het was gedurende het jaar 1853, dat hij zich gedrongen zag zijne bediening in Overisel neer te leggen, en voor eenige maanden woonde hij in Holland. Als wij ons niet vergissen, dan was het omstreeks dezen tijd dat te Chicago de cholera hevig heerschte. Ook onder onze landgenooten aldaar werden slachtoffers geeischt. Een dringend verzoek kwam tot hem om, daar de Hollanders aldaar geen voorganger hadden en zij in die dagen van donkerheid en nood behoefte aan de vertroostingen des Evangelies gevoelden, derwaarts te komen. Aanstonds gaf hij gehoor aan deze roepstem, en met veel vrucht en tot vertroosting en heil voor velen mocht hij daar eenige weken werkzaam zijn.

Nadat hij Overisel had verlaten was de eerste roeping die hij ontving van de gemeente Grand Haven, die nog maar pas gesticht was. Hij nam dat beroep aan [in 1853] en de Heere zegende zijn arbeid. Zonder kerkgebouw zijnde, hielp hij het volk de lumber uit de rivier opzamelen, en zoo slaagden zij er in materialen te verkrijgen voor het eerste nederige kerkgebouw.

Terwijl zij te Grand Haven woonden, den 26sten September 1954 trof aan vader en moeder Bolks een slag zoo hartverscheurend dat die voor een oogenblik dreigde hem voor altoos ongeschikt te maken voor zijn werk. Moeder's moeder, te Overisel wonende en reeds tot hoogen ouderdom geklommen, was krank. Zij begaven zich per voertuig derwaarts om haar te bezoeken. Des morgens verlieten zij hunne woning, de drie oudste kinderen welke nu nog in leven zijn te huis latende, en de drie jongste met zich nemende – een dochtertje van ruim zes jaren, een zoontje van vier jaren, en een zuigeling van ruim zes maanden. Op de brug over de rivier te Port Sheldon rijdende, begon het paard te steigeren. Zoodra vader dit bemerkte sprong hij er ijlings af om het verschrikte dier te leiden; maar eer hij er bij kon komen, vielen buggy en paard achterover in de rivier, en natuurlijk moeder met de drie kinderen mede. In radeloosheid sprong vader hen achterna en, met behulp van toesnellende vrienden, mocht het hem gelukken moeder te redden. Toen men echter de kinderen op de brug had waren de levensgeesten te ver heen dan dat die opgewekt konden worden. Met gebrokene harten moesten zij nu met de lijken van hunne drie lievelingen huiswaarts keeren.

Van Grand Haven werd vader beroepen naar Milwaukee, omstreeks het jaar 1855. Daar ook deze gemeente in hare kindsheid was, moest zij door hem gekweekt en opgebeurd worden. Voor een zevental

jaren is hij daar met veel zegen werkzaam geweest; en terwijl hij Milwaukee bediende als herder en leeraar, werden door hem de omliggende
plaatsen Alto, Franklin Prairie, Town Eight, en die in Sheboygan County
ook geregeld bezocht en bearbeidt.

Vandaar werd hij beroepen naar Chicago [in 1861], waar hij slechts
anderhalf jaar heeft verkeerd. Hoewel niet geheel zonder vrucht, beschouwde vader zijn werk hier toch als het minst gezegende van zijne
bediening. Eene roeping werd nu op hem uitgebracht van de gecombineerde gemeenten Lage Prairie en Hooge Prairie zooals zij toen genoemd
werden, of South Holland en Roseland zooals nu de namen zijn. Toen
lagen die gemeenten verscheidene mijlen buiten Chicago, nu worden die
streken als binnen de corporatie van die groote wereldstad gerekend. In
de overtuiging dat de Heere hem daarheen riep, nam hij de roeping aan
en bediende die gemeenten met veel zegen tot in Mei van het jaar 1865.

In 1865 begeerde de gemeente Zeeland hem, waar hij ook zeven jaar
lang gezegend werkzaam is geweest. Ook op stoffelijk gebied mocht hij
daar Gods zegen op zijnen arbeid genieten; in zijnen tijd verwisselde de
gemeente de oude blokke kerk voor het ruime godshuis dat nu nog door
haar gebruikt wordt; ook werd onder zijne leiding, door de aankoop
van een pijporgel, de gemeente Zeeland de eerste van de Hollandsche
gemeenten in dit land, die het orgelspel bij de godsdienst invoerde.

Toen de Classis van Illinois in het jaar 1871 eene gemeente van onze
Kerk organiseerde te Orange City, in Sioux County, Iowa, alwaar onder de
leiding van Henry Hospers van Pella eene nieuwe Kolonie was aanvaardt,
werd de aandacht op Ds. Bolks gevestigd, als de geschikte persoon om
als geestelijke voorganger deze Kolonie te helpen welslagen. In het najaar
van 1871 werd de eerste correspondentie hierover ontvangen en niet
lang daarna een beroep op vader uitgebracht.

In April 1872 verlieten zij de gemeente die hen lief had, en die het werk
van den trouwen Godsgezant hoogschatte – zij verlieten een grooten
familiekring die hen gaarne in de nabijheid zou gehouden hebben.

En ook hier, in zijn laatste werkkring, gebruikte de Heere hem, en
liet hij zich gaarne gebruiken in welken weg of tot welke taak God hem
riep. In lichaamsnooden en zieleangsten; met het Woord Gods en met
stoffelijke hulp; bij dag en nacht; in koude en hitte; in regen en zonne-
schijn; met de koets of met de lumberwagen langs gebaande en ongebaande wegen; in sneeuwstormen en onder heirlegers van sprinkhanen; altijd en overal en onder alle omstandigheden waar hij iets voor
den Heere of tot heil van het volk kon doen behoefde men hem nimmer
voor de tweede maal te vragen.

In ongelooflijk korten tijd ontwikkelde deze Kolonie. Toch zag men zich teleurgesteld in de verwachtingen van in enkele jaren rijk te worden, welke door een paar van de eerste oogsten waren opgewekt. De Heere wilde Zijn volk naar rijkere schatten doen uitzien; wilde hen leeren boven alles te waardeeren en zoeken, voor zichzelven en voor het nageslacht, de schatten welke geen sprinkhaan of kever kan verwoesten. Jaren achtereen werden hunne rijkbeladene velden door het ongedierte vernield, en er kwamen armoede en bezwaren van ernstige aard waar men niet op had gerekend. In die dagen van de geweldig verwoestende sprinkhanen plaag gebruikte de Heere Zijn gezant om het zwaar beproefde volk te onderwijzen, bemoedigen, troosten, en helpen. Eenmaal, toen de velden schoon en veelbelovend stonden, zag men de sprinkhanen aankomen, juist toen op den Sabbat de voormiddagdienst geeindigd was; met o! zulke bezwaarde gemoederen kwam men van wijd en zuid naar de namiddagdienst. Zich weer bij vernieuwing beroofd ziende van den schoonen oogst, die men als loon van 's landman's zweet had verwacht, gevoelden zij des te meer behoefte aan de verkwikkingen en vervullingen van het Evangelie. Vader zelf ging ook met een bezwaard hart naar de kerk; maar God gordde Zijnen dienaar aan met moed en kracht toen hij voor het volk moest optreden; en zoo versterkend was het Woord van God voor het volk, dat, al was alles alweer haast vernield toen zij uit de kerk kwamen, zij zich rijk en blij gevoelden in den Heere en Zijn heil.

In het begin werd te Orange City het schoolgebouw gebruikt om de openbare dienst op den Sabbat; toen dat te klein werd, bouwde men een lokaal van ruwhout er achteraan. Dit diende tot dat met behulp van de Board van Binnenlandsche Zending in 1874 een ruim kerkgebouw werd opgericht. En toen de Kolonie zoo ver uitbreidde, dat allen niet meer naar Orange City konden komen, ging vader in de week op drie á vier verschillende plaatsen, beurtelings in schoolhuizen der afgelegene buurten, prediken. Zeer waarschijnlijk zijn die tochten het middel geweest, dat hij zich de bange kwaal op den hals gehaald heeft welke hem de laatste 16 jaaren van zijn leven zooveel benauwdheid heeft veroorzaakt. In het vroege voorjaar van 1878 werd hij door eene ernstige longziekte aangetast; hoewel hij daarvan herstelde, duurde het niet land of de eerste teekenen van de bange asthma-kwaal begonnen zich te openbaren, en namen ras een zeer kwaadaardig karakter aan. Zoo sterk nam het toe, en zoo aanhoudend kleefde het hem aan, dat hij een jaar later op 65 jarigen leeftijd zich genoodzaakt zag het werk neer te leggen.

Reeds twee andere gemeenten waren er bij dien tijd van de moedergemeente afgeleid: eene te Alton, zuidoost; en de andere te Sioux Center, noordwest van Orange City. Nadat vader zijn werk te Orange City had neergelegd, werd Ds. Ale Buursma spoedig zijn opvolger aldaar.

Waar vader ook bijzonder belang in stelde, en voor de alhier gevestigde Kolonie groote behoefte in zag, was de oprichting van eenen kweekhof, waar jeugdigen onder het opzicht en bestuur van de Kerk eene degelijke Christelijke kweeking zouden kunnen ontvangen. Van den aanvang zijner komst in Sioux County had hij daarom het oog daar al heen gericht, en zoodra er tijd en gelegenheid voor was, werden pogingen voor dat doel aangewend. En toen in 1882 het daartoe kwam en de Northwestern Classical Academy werd gesticht, heeft hij tot aan zijnen dood toe dezelve met raad en daad gesteund.

Het laatste werk dat hij in het openbaar verricht heeft, en waar zijn hart door verkwikt werd, was het helpen bevestigen van een zijner vroegere catechisanten in de gemeente Zeeland, Michigan, Ds. Mattheus Kolyn, over de hem steeds dierbare gemeente van Orange City, Iowa. Dit had plaats ruim een half jaar voor zijn dood. Het was de laatste maal dat hij van den kansel sprak; ruim een half jaar later werd hij in de eeuwige rust geroepen. Den 11den July 1888 vierde men in zijne woning te Orange City, op eenvoudige wijze, de gouden bruiloft in de tegenwoordigheid van de in leven zijnde kinderen en kindskinderen, een getal uitmakende van 26; ook waren er vele belangstellende en heilwenschende vrienden. Twee maanden later, den 10den September nam de Heere moeder tot Zich, en nu begon vader ook meer los van het leven te worden. In de vroegen morgen van den 16den Juni 1894 nam de Heere hem op in de rust, die voor Gods volk is weggelegd. Zoo eindigde een leven dat nimmer aanspraak maakte op bijzondere grootheid of waardigheid, maar dat in eenvoudigheid en oprechten ernst gewijd was an 's Heeren dienst.

Hoewel Ds. Bolks een van de eersten was, die in Nederland met de Afscheiding was meegegaan, en hij daar in de vervolgingen en heete tegenstand heeft gedeeld, nam hij zonder aarzeling een werkzaam aandeel in het tot stand brengen van de vereeniging der Hollandsche gemeenten dezer Nederzetting met de Gereformeerde Kerk in Amerika. Overtuigd dat men in den boezem dier Kerk, zonder eenige knelling of dwang des gewetens en met besef van de ware gemeenschap der heiligen, God naar Zijn Woord en Instellingen vrij en blij kon dienen, bleef zijne liefde voor die Kerk onverbroken en sterk tot aan het einde van zijn leven. Geen zaak, die hem meer smartte, dan de verwijdering en verdeeldheid die er onder het volk was gekomen; zijn hart bloedde bij de gedachte aan de groote klove die er veroorzaakt was; en dat onder een volk, die wat afkomst, taal, en inzonderheid liefde voor de waarheid en den dienst van God betreft, een kond en moest zijn. Toen hij gestorven was, was de laatste van de leiders dezer Nederzetting heengegaan. . . .

[Translation]

Seine Bolks was born at Den Ham in the province of Overijsel, the Netherlands, on April 30, 1814. His parents did not belong to the great of this world, but they did belong to the folk who fear God. While a child he lost his father and in later years had no memory of him. But he was always happy to hear people testify of his father's piety. During his youth it appeared he would waste his time in the company of vain companions. His cheerful, generous, and friendly character made him a friend of everybody. But God had serious intentions with him. In spite of all sinful distractions the teaching of his pious mother continued to inspire him.

When Seine Bolks became sixteen the Lord established His dwelling in his heart and he resolved to break with sin and devote himself to the Lord. He had practically no schooling. But God had endowed him with striking gifts which He placed at his service. As a youth tending sheep on the heath he carried a Bible his mother had given him. This he subjected to prayerful study. So at an early age he acquired considerable acquaintance with God's Word. Soon an earnest and fiery zeal led him to take part in religious gatherings.

In his twentieth year Bolks was active as an exhorter, with much effectiveness and to the edification of many. Pious folk noted that the Lord had given him special graces, gifts of earnestness, zeal, frankness, sympathy, and a clear insight into the truth. It was suggested by members of the congregation of Hellendoorn to which he belonged that as there was a scarcity of reliable exponders of the Gospel, he ought to prepare himself for the ministry. This group was happy to support him while studying with Dominie A. C. van Raalte at Ommen. But such was the need for ministers and such the desire of the congregation which supported him that after fifteen months of study, it was thought he should wait no longer. Bolks gladly would have spent more time in study, but he allowed himself to be moved by their desires and accordingly was ordained.

Some time prior to this, on July 11, 1838, he was married to Geertje Brouwer, a modest and pious young woman. The couple's eldest son was born before Bolks undertook to study for the ministry. Everybody who has known mother Bolks will grant that she truly was a gift from God, being exactly the person to help and encourage her husband in his service of the Lord, especially under the circumstances in which the Lord wanted to use him. She was deeply devoted to him. She encouraged him whether it was while he spent every week day in the woods at Overisel during the beginning of the settlement there encouraging and advising his followers, or while he comforted his fellow countrymen in Chicago during a cholera epidemic, or while he was away from home for weeks or months at a time looking after the spiritual interests of the Dutch settlement in Sioux County.

In the Netherlands Bolks served only one congregation – that of Hellendoorn. Because of the scarcity of faithful preachers of the Gospel and on account of the numerous groups who desired to hear the truth and listen to the exposition of true doctrine he traveled about seeking to serve them with the Bread of life. In this way he became well known in the old Fatherland. The Lord blessed his tireless efforts to plant the seed, which brought forth the fruit of true faith. Those were days of bitter opposition and persecution. But they also were the never-to-be-forgotten days of holy comfort for God's children. Never was he frightened by denunciatory letters or by the insults of unbelievers.

On one occasion father was to preach in a place where people knew about him and his parents. A devil-may-care man who had known Bolks' father as a keeper of geese said, "I'd like to hear what that goose-farmer has to tell us." Before the sermon was finished God touched this man's heart. Bolks' discourses were eagerly listened to. Meetings were held in all kinds of places – in God's out-of-doors, under trees, in dwellings, on threshing floors, yes, even in sheep pens, to hear the Word of Life.

On one occasion Bolks was invited to preach before some people. But his youngest child suddenly fell sick and died. There was no time to notify the people who would gather to hear him. But as soon as his child was dead Bolks hurried to preach to them.

In 1846, because of the difficulties that oppressed him and because of the thought that many had left the fatherland to emigrate to America, Bolks also decided to leave, taking with him a large part of his congregation. In order to serve them on their journey and found a new settlement in a new climate and in uninhabited areas, he studied medicine. This proved useful while on board ship, in the settlement at Overisel, Michigan, and in Sioux County, Iowa.

Bolks and his company of 23 persons set out on September 3, 1847, and after a prosperous voyage arrived in New York on October 10. From there they set out for Albany where they intended to pass the winter.

But they were advised to move on to Syracuse, New York, where there was opportunity for work and it was possible to find shelter. There they stayed until the next spring.

After much enquiry they decided to go to Michigan where Dominie Van Raalte had settled. Arrived there, they secured land at a low cost, although of course wooded. Dominie Bolks was invited to go to Graafschap, but the choice of his followers fell upon a region nine miles southeast of Holland on which they settled. At first they called their settlement Hellendoorn, but later this was changed to Overisel.

The new settlement, like others, had its difficulties. But determination and good counsel and Bolk's comforting preaching inspired the settlers to perservere. The dominie served his people as minister, physician, surveyor, architect, and in other capacities as God had given them to him. Instead of a salary each man in the settlement gave him a day's work once every two weeks.

Soon after their arrival the first settlers built a log structure to serve as a church, on the line between Overisel and Fillmore townships. But this building also was used to house newcomers until they could be established on their own land. The people thought the church was not conveniently situated. They decided to build a new one (a little east of the present structure) which, though not striking in appearance, served as the congregation's meeting place until 1866.

In 1853 Bolks gave up his ministerial duties in Overisel, and retired to Holland. It was about the time when the Chicago cholera raged, unless we are mistaken. Many of our Dutch countrymen fell victims to this sickness. A pressing invitation came to Bolks to serve the Hollanders in Chicago, for they had no pastor. This call he accepted and he worked among them for several weeks.

Bolks' first call after he left Overisel came in 1853, from the newly founded congregation in Grand Haven, which he accepted. His charges, being without a church building, collected lumber from the river. With his own hands Bolks helped them gather their building materials, for their first simple church.

On September 26, 1854, a dreadful accident befell Bolks and his wife, which for a moment threatened to incapacitate him completely. Mrs. Bolks' mother living in Overisel was ill, and Bolks, Mrs. Bolks, and their three youngest children, a girl of six, a boy of four, and a baby of six months set out to see her, leaving their three oldest children in Grand Haven. Riding over the bridge at Port Sheldon, their horse reared and threatened to pass out of control. To quiet him Bolks jumped out of the buggy in order to lead the horse safely across the bridge. But the horse and the buggy carrying Mrs. Bolks and the children fell backward into the river. Bolks jumped into the water and was able, with the help of people who came running up, to save Mrs. Bolks. But the children, when taken from the water to the bridge, were dead. With grieving spirits the father and mother returned to Grand Haven carrying the dead bodies of their children.

Bolks' next call came from Milwaukee, about 1855. This congregation too was in its infancy and needed his fostering care. For seven years he labored for its advancement. During this charge he visited nearby congregations at Alto, Franklin Prairie, and Town Eight [Bethlehem], regularly, and also those in Sheboygan County.

From Milwaukee Bolks was called to Chicago where he labored with some success. But he ever afterwards regarded this the least successful of his charges. Next he went to the combined congregations of Lage Prairie [Low Priarie] and Hooge Prairie [High Prairie], as they were known at that time. Today these places, called South Holland and Roseland, are reckoned as lying within the limits of a great world city. Convinced that the Lord was guiding him he served these charges until May 1865.

Next he went to Zeeland where he served for seven years. During these years the congregation abandoned their old log church and built a larger one, which today is still used as their meeting place. During his pastorate the congregation bought a pipe organ. The Zeeland congregation was the first Dutch immigrant congregation in this country to use an organ in its services.

In 1871 Classis Illinois organized a congregation of our church at Sioux City in Sioux County, Iowa. This new colony had been founded by Henry Hospers of Pella. Bolks was thought of as the proper person to guide the settlers to success. An exchange of letters, in the fall of 1871, was followed by an invitation to assume the pastor's functions in the new settlement. In April 1872 Bolks and his family left Zeeland and moved to Sioux County. This was to be his last scene of activity. He served his people in all ways – in physical and spiritual needs, day and night, in cold weather and in hot, in rain or sunshine; he visited them with buggy and with lumber wagon over all sorts of roads, and was not deterred by snowstorm or by multitudes of grasshoppers, in fact he was ready at all times to render some service for the good of the people.

The new Kolonie developed with astonishing rapidity. Nevertheless people were disappointed, for they did not become rich in a few years. Their hopes for riches had been roused by the first few bountiful harvests. The Lord wanted to test the people, teach them that there are treasures which neither beetle nor grasshopper can ever destroy. Year after year the grasshoppers ruined the promising crops. Poverty and despair were everywhere. The Lord sent his servant to comfort and encourage the people. On one Sunday when the crops were especially promising the people saw the devastating hosts of grasshoppers approaching, just as the morning service was finished. With heavy hearts the people who had lost their crops returned to the afternoon service. Robbed of the fruit of their labor they had greater need of the Gospel than ever. Father went to church with a heavy heart, but the Lord strengthened him so that he could encourage the people.

In the beginning the people held services in the schoolhouse in Orange City. This building soon proved too small for this purpose and, using rough boards, they built a large addition to its rear. This structure satisfied the peoples' needs until 1874 when the Board of Domestic Missions built a new church for them. When the Dutch community became numerous and lived too far distant from Orange City to attend services there, father visited outlying places three or four times a week preaching in schoolhouses. These activities no doubt brought on serious throat trouble which rendered the last sixteen years of his life miserable. Early in 1878 he suffered from a lung infection but as soon as this passed he contracted asthma which became so severe that in his sixty-fifth year he was forced to give up his labors.

By this date two new congregations had been formed out of the mother church in Orange City. One of these was Alton, situated a distance to the southeast; the other was Sioux Center, northwest of Orange City. Dominie Ale Buursma succeeded father in Orange City.

Father took a keen interest in the founding of a school in which boys could acquire a Christian education. This school, under church auspices, came into existence in 1882 and was called the Northwestern Classical Academy. To the end of his life he took an active interest in it.

His last public appearance was the installation of Dominie Matthew Kolyn, one of his catechumens in Zeeland, Michigan, as pastor of the Orange City church. This took place about a half year before father's death. On July 11, 1888, he celebrated in his house in Orange City, his golden wedding anniversary, in the presence of his children and his children's children, twenty-six in all. Many were the callers to pay their respects. Two months later mother Bolks died, after which father took less and less interest in things. Finally, in the early morning of June 16, 1894, the Lord called him to the rest which is the portion reserved for His people. Thus ended a life that never had any pretensions of greatness or of wisdom. He lived simply and earnestly, dedicated to God's service.

Dominie Bolks was one of the first of the ministers who in the great Secession [of 1834] left the state church and shared in the persecutions and the opposition which followed. He took an active part in uniting the Dutch settlements with the Reformed Church of America. He was convinced that in that church he could freely unite with his brethren of the faith in the worship of God according to His Word and His ordonnances. The schisms which came later pained him, for he believed the Dutch immigrants should have continued to live in unity. At the time of his death he was the last of the leaders of this Kolonie....

III. JOHN H. KARSTEN'S LIFE SKETCH OF THE REV. MARTEN ANNE YPMA

[This life history of the pioneer dominie Marten Anne Ypma (1810-63) was prepared by the Rev. John H. Karsten, born in Heerenveen in 1833, who emigrated to Michigan, settled in Vriesland, and was ordained to the ministry in the Reformed Church in 1863. Prepared for the Semi-Centennial celebrations in Holland in August 1897, it appeared in *De Grondwet*, March 14, 1911.]

Martin Anne Ypma was born in the city of Minnertsga, province of Vriesland, Netherlands, August 26, 1810. In his youth he received an education such as the public schools of the country afforded at that time. From what he proved himself afterwards to be, it is evident that he was a child of good mental ability.

The history of the child does not begin with his birth. Its genesis lies back of it. The study of the human race leads more and more to the conviction that the child inherits more from his parents than mere flesh and blood. Mental traits and characteristics, which go to make up the man in his essential being, can be traced from parents to children.

We are sorry we cannot trace the lineage of the subject of this sketch. We know nothing of his parents, of their circumstances in life, their social standing, their religious convictions. We may well assume, however, that the well known self-asserting character of the Vrieslander, which he possessed, came to him from his ancestors. He did not belong to the wealthy class, which is evident from the fact that after his schooldays were over he was engaged in buying and selling produce on a small scale. How long he continued in this business we know not.

When war broke out between Holland and Belgium, in 1830, he gave his services to his country, and served with distinction in a regiment of cavalry, then called the "kurassiers", who were provided with helmet and brass shield, weapons of defence abolished in 1841.

In his younger days he became a follower of Christ. Of the time and manner and history of his conversion we are ignorant. He was an ardent lover of souls, and soon the desire to save others by the preaching of the Gospel of Peace manifested itself. The desire became an irresistible conviction. His native abilities and sincere Christian love warranted the choice. To prepare himself for the work of the gospel ministry he first received private instruction from a minister by the name of Vos, at Marum, Vriesland. From there he went to Kampen, and studied two years under Professor Antonie Brummelkamp and Professor Hendrik de Cock. After graduation he was ordained and installed in the church of Hallum, Vriesland, which he served two years, the only charge he had in the Netherlands.

When in 1846-'47 the movement to emigrate to America began he was soon ready with others to follow the divine call. With several families of his church – which formed the nucleus of a church in the New World – he left his native land. They sailed on the English bark, the *Vesta*, and arrived in New York on May 31, 1847. The following day, June 1, being Sunday, and also the day of Pentecost, he preached on board the ship, his first sermon in this country. With great animation and thankful hearts they sang in their native tongue:

> *God baande door de woeste baren*
> *En brede stroomen ons een pad.* Psalm 66, 3.

From New York they went by boat to Troy, and thence by canalboat to Buffalo. From Buffalo by steamer to Chicago and thence to Black Lake, Michigan, and in the month of August 1847 they arrived in what is now known as Vriesland, Michigan, ten miles east from Holland, and settled there. Here they experienced all the trials of pioneer life in what was then a perfect wilderness.

Reverend Ypma was a man well equipped by nature and experience to pass successfully through the hardships of such a life. He could suffer with the suffering. Not possessed of large means he willingly labored six days of the week for the support of himself and family. To travel on foot to Grand Rapids and back to preach there on a Sunday was a labor willingly rendered. And when upon his return home he could exhibit four dollars as his fee, what gladness there was on account of this unheard of sum – in those days.

After serving the church of Vriesland four years he labored successively in the churches of Graafschap, Michigan; the combined churches of South Holland and Roseland, Illinois, and the church of Alto, Wisconsin, where he died May 1, 1863, leaving a wife and four children, of whom some are still living. His remains lie buried in Vriesland, Michigan, the place of his first settlement. His widow afterwards married Mr. L. van der Beld, of South Holland, Illinois. She died September 15, 1865, and was buried beside her first husband in Vriesland, Michigan.

The departed, as stated above, possessed qualities which made him a helpful factor in promoting the interests of the people in those trying years of pioneer life. His cheerful and buoyant spirit was often medicine to desponding souls. He lived very near to the people, and was in all things one with them. His practicability proved him a successful leader in securing desired results. The early immigration of our Holland people was peculiarly blessed with leading men who were of the people and for the people. The ministry of those days honored their profession by proving themselves worthy followers of the lowly Nazarene, who came not to be ministered unto, but to minister.

Reverend Ypma was also a man of great conversational powers. Hour after hour, often until long after midnight, he could entertain his friends with relating his experiences without wearying them. He was a man sound in the faith. He had clear and well defined convictions in regard to the aim and purposes of the immigration, and the stand the immigrant churches should take in the New World. His vision may not have been as broad and far reaching as that for instance, of Van Raalte, but it was equally true, and in the same direction.

He had early to contend with a local sickly religious sentiment, and with an extreme conservatism, which always seeks its strength in isolation rather than in amalgamation. The history of that section of the Holland Colony in Michigan might have been very different from what it is, but for the firm stand taken by our esteemed pastor and brother in those early days. He was a firm believer in the indications of Providence that the Reformed people from the Netherlands should find a home in the Reformed Church of America. He was an ardent friend and supporter of higher education, and as far as we know the ministry of those years was a unit on that all important subject.

Ypma's preaching was thoroughly Biblical. He magnified Christ, and although often opposed in this he took a firm stand. He could not be swayed from preaching the Gospel as Christ has given it to us. He was clear in his conception of objective truth. He believed in man's inability to save himself, but also in his responsibility for the rejection of the Gospel. For this he was sometimes accused of Arminianism. Once he was told: "If you will preach as we would have it, we will pay you more salary." To which he made answer: "If you withhold my bread, God will prevent my hunger." His loyalty to Christ and to the truth and to the best and highest social and religious interests of the people of his day, is unquestioned, and has been a cause of much good.

Our brother was an ardent lover of his adopted Fatherland, and his patriotism took a high flight. His soul burned with patriotic zeal when Southern traitors drew the sword to ruin this fair land of ours. His inflaming speeches sent many a young man to the front. Some blamed him that he, a minister of the Gospel of peace, should incite young men to thus risk their lives for home and native land. He rose above that paltry sentiment, believing that self-sacrificing patriotism is of heavenly birth to save the cause of man, which is the cause of God.

We think of Maarten Anne Ypma as a gift of God to the people in those early days, to help them on in their hard struggles for a livelihood; to aid them to right views of truth and life; to help them to appreciate their privileges, and to recognize their duties. To the extent of his abilities and qualifications he must be regarded as one of its factors in securing the desired results of the immigration.

Perhaps of all the ministers of those primitive days he is the least known. If what we have written in this brief paper shall bring him into proper recognition for what he has been and done, our object in writing it has been secured and our labor doubley repaid.

This Semi-Centennial celebration is not so much for the purpose of glorifying the men and the agencies that brought about the happy result of the immigration which we behold this day, but rather to fix their place in history, to know and to restate the principles by which they were guided, and ascertain the object for which they lived. It was theirs to lay foundations; it is ours to continue the building. The walls are not yet ready for the copestone. The building is only in process of completion. We are simply an army of workmen to add a few stones in our day. Let us continue the work in the same faith and spirit in which it was begun, knowing that like principles will produce like results, whatever the changed environment may be.

112. CORNELIUS VAN LOO'S JANNES VAN DE LUYSTER

[This article, the chief source of information about Jannes van de Luyster, was published in *Historical Souvenir of the Celebration of the Sixtieth Anniversary*.... *Held in Zeeland, Michigan August* 21, 1907 (Zeeland 1908) and reprinted in *De Grondwet*, January 6, 1914. Its original title was *De Stichter van Zeeland, Jannes van de Luyster*.]

Reeds voor 1845 bezocht zekere Vroegop New York, Pennsylvania, Ohio, Indiana, en andere Staten en publiceerde zijne reisbeschrijving, welke grooten aftrek had en Amerika overal ter sprake bracht. In het jaar 1843 [lees 1846], reeds, werd er eene vereeniging opgericht te Arnhem, Provincie Gelderland, om behoeftige gezinnen te helpen naar Amerika, en vertrokken er velen uit Gelderland, Holland, en Overijssel.

Antonie de Bree met zijn gezin verliet vroeg in 1846 zijn woonplaats Oudelande, provincie Zeeland, en zette zich in Oakland County, Michigan, neder. Hij kan gezegd worden de eerste landverhuizer te zijn geweest in dien grooten trek, die in 1846 begon, en in de volgende jaren zulke groote afmetingen kreeg. Hij was geen kolonist. Hij verliet Oakland County in 't voorjaar van 1850 en zette zich neder te Greenville, Montcalm County, waar twee zijner nog levende kinderen met zijn verder nageslacht nog wonen en geheel door de Amerikanen zijn opgeslorpt. In 't zelfde voorjaar gingen ook A. Hartgerink en J. Arnold, daartoe door hunne kerk en vrienden uitgezonden, op eene onderzoekingsreis en zonden den uitslag in een vrij uitvoerig pamflet naar Nederland.

Dit stuwde de landverhuizingsbal, die onder de krachtige bemoeiing van Ds. H. P. Scholte en Ds. A. C. van Raalte, aan 't rollen was, door dorp, stad en provincie en geheel Nederland. Scholte vertrok in 't voorjaar van 1847, en stichtte Pella, Iowa. Van Raalte besliste voor westelijk Michigan en werd alzoo de stichter van Holland en omgeving, wat men vroeger de Kolonie noemde. Dit is alles breedvoerig door anderen beschreven, en wij behoeven er hier niet over uit te wijden. In verband met het 60-jarig feest dat te Zeeland werd gevierd, willen wij iets mededeelen omtrent de stichting en den stichter van de thans zoo bloeiende plaats.

Zoo als hieronder verder blijken zal, besliste Jannes van de Luyster, op 1 Januari 1847 om alles te verkoopen en koers te zetten naar Amerika. Drie vergaderingen werden er vroeg in 1847 in de stad Goes gehouden van verhuizingsgezinden, en men besloot naar Amerika te gaan. Deze menschen, hongerende naar brood en de vrije uitoefening der godsdienst, meenden dan ook niet in het wilde en als op zichzelf staande personen of huisgezinnen te mogen gaan, maar organiseerden zich tot eene gemeente en verkozen Jannes van de Luyster en Johannes Hoogesteger als ouderlingen, en Jan Steketee en Adriaan Glerum als diakenen. Dit gedaan zijnde, meende een der aanwezigen, een eenvoudig man, dat men niet zonder leeraar moest optrekken. Dit vond bijval, en men ging over tot een beroep. Dit viel op Ds. Cornelius van der Meulen, leeraar te Goes, en vroeger te Middelharnis, die het aannam. Dus reisden zij en vestigden zich alhier als eene georganiseerde gemeente.

Den 10den April 1847 zou men van Antwerpen vertrekken, hetwelk geschiedde, met twee schepen. Aan 't hoofd op het eene schip, stond Jannes van de Luyster; op het tweede Jan Steketee; terwijl het derde onder leiding van Johannes Kaboord, met 157 personen, insluitende Ds. van der Meulen en gezin, van uit Rotterdam vertrok.

Van de Luyster arriveerde het eerst te New York, na eene reis van 45 dagen. Hij besliste, volgens vooraf gemaakte overeenkomst, waar men zich zou nederzetten. Hij koos Van Raalte's Kolonie, en dus zette hij koers naar Black Lake, Michigan, en werd later gevolgd door de anderen.

In Michigan aangekomen zijnde, kocht hij van het gouvernement sectie 17 en 19 en 400 acres in sectie 9, township 5 noord, range 14 west, in het tegenwoordige township Zeeland, te zamen 1,680 acres. In dit township was Jan Hulst de eerste die er land kocht en zich aldaar nederzette. Hij had zijne woonplaats in Nederland verlaten 2 Maart 1847, verliet Hellevoetsluis op 19 Maart, en arriveerde te Baltimore, Maryland, op April 27. Van daar deed hij met zijn gezin de reis overland, gedeeltelijk per ossenwagen [deze zes weken durende], en kwam den 8sten Juni 1847 op de oost helft van de zuidwest kwart van sectie 28 aan. Hij werd een week daarna gevolgd door Hilbert Mast en later door Jan en Hendrik Mast.

Van de Luyster verbleef eenigen tijd aan Black Lake tot zijn huis gereed was. Dit begon hij te bouwen op 21 Juli 1847 terwijl Jacobus de Hond en Jan Steketee alreede in de nabijheid woonden. Op een Zaterdagmiddag van Zeeland de terugreis naar Black Lake aanvaardende verdwaalde van de Luyster in het bosch, waaruit hij des Zondags elf ure eerst weer aankwam ten huize van Jan Steketee, toen deze aan de schaduwzijde van zijn blokhuis zat, na de voormiddagpredikatie te hebben gelezen. Baasje werd verzorgd van voedsel en droogge kleederen en op het rechte pad gebracht.

Jannes van de Luyster werd geboren te Cadzand, provincie Zeeland, den 12den Maart 1789, en stierf te Zeeland, Michigan, den 13den Maart 1862. Zijne vrouw was Diena Naeije, geboren op 20 April 1796 en overleden op 10 Januari 1874 nalatende 7 kinderen, als volgt: twee zoons,

Willem en Jan, en vijf dochters, Jannetje, weduwe Jan den Herder; Dina, huisvrouw van Hendrik de Kruif; Elizabeth, huisvrouw van Cornelis de Putter; Janna, huisvrouw van Willem Benjaminse; Maartje, huisvrouw van Willem Leenhouts. Er is een groot getal klein en achterkleinkinderen, verspreid door westelijk Michigan en het westen.

Na zijn huwelijk was hij eerst landbouwer in Cadzand, daartoe land hurende. Doch reeds in 1817 kocht hij eene hofstede onder Borsele, eiland Zuid-Beveland [Goesche Land], groot 137 gemeten, 6931/4 roeden, voor de som van 34,585.59 guldens; de brief van eigendom berust nog in handen van Henry de Kruif, een der kleinzoons. Dertig jaren lang bewoonde hij deze hofstede, tot dat hij in 1847 dezelve verkocht voor 66,000 guldens, en naar Amerika vertrok.

Hoe hij daartoe kwam? Eerst wegens den druk op godsdienstig gebied, en dan den druk der tijden voor arbeider, ambachtsman, en landbouwer. Doch laat ons uit zijn eigenhandig geschrift in zijn dagboek, ook noch bij genoemde De Kruif berustende, zien wat hij zelf daaromtrent heeft te zeggen. Hij was reeds in de eerste dagen der Afscheiding ouderling te Borsele en zijne aanteekeningen als lid des kerkeraads beginnen 21 October 1837. Voor dien tijd moet hij ook ouderling in de Hervormde of Staats Kerk geweest zijn, al van al 1818, daar hij 44 jaren ouderling is geweest en in 1862 stierf. Hij schrijft in zijn dagboek onder meer belangrijks, als volgt:

Den 21 Juni 1840. C. van der Meulen, Domine te Middelharnis bij mij, Jannes van de Luyster, in de schuur op Zondag gepredikt met mooi weer en wel 1,000 menschen. Alles in stilheid en tot stigting afgeloopen. Zelfs de vele vreemde paarden by malkander op de weide in grooten vrede. En de Heere heeft getuigenis gegeven van het woord der waarheid aan vele conscientien der menschen en vooral aan zijne kinderen.

's Morgens gepredikt Openbaring 11 : 5; 's middags, den 24sten Zondag, 's avonds, 1 Johannes 3, 1; voor den armen gegeven 68 gulden.

Evenwel door Dirk Wisse, smitsbaas en burgemeester, proces verbaal geteekend. Den 20 Julij met mijn Broeder diacon Jan Steketee voor de rechtbank geweest in Goes, en van den domenee, mij en Jan Steketee, ieder door het ministerie 100 Gulden boete geeischt, zonder behoorlijk de misdaad te bewijzen. De uitspraak van het vonnis uitgesteld tot den 15 Augustus.

Den 4 September 1840 betaald voor boete aan den
ontvanger, De Kanter, te Goes, Gulden 306.29½
Voor quitantie op Zegel 21

Samen 306.50½

Den 3 September onfangen van Jan Steketee, voor hem
en zijn vader Cornelius Steketee en zijn broer Cornelius
Steketee, Jr., Gulden 127.00
maar
van Jannes Karelse terug getrokken 12.50
Den [ ] September, ontvangen
van Jan Smallegange, Gulden 25.00
Den 16 September ontvangen
van Leendert Smallegange 26.00
Den 11 November van Jannes
Karelse 25.00
Voor mij J. van de Luyster 116.00

Gulden 306.00

Zulke geschiedenissen werden menigvuldig doorleefd, en soms liep het met boete niet af, maar werden er gevangen gezet waaronder ook de leeraars. Den menschen werd het werk ontnomen en werden zij verguisd, bespot, en gescholden. Ook na de vergunning van vrije uitoefening der godsdienst door de regeering werd het leven moeielijk gemaakt voor velen. Ook was het zeer armoedig in het land gesteld, waarom dan ook velen uitzagen naar Amerika.

Hoe van de Luyster er toe kwam om het vaderland te verlaten, moge uit 's man's dagboek blijken:

De Heere spreekt in zijn woord, Psalm 77, 15, eerste deel: Gij zijt die God die wonderen doet. Dat woord wonderlijk aan my Jannes van de Luyster, ouderling van de afgescheidene Gemeente te Borsele, Provincie Zeeland, Eiland Goes [Zuid-Beveland] in Europa, en aan mijne vrouw, Diena Naeije, en onze zeven kinderen en zes kindskinderen [bevestigd].

Willem van de Luyster, onze oudste zoon, is geboren op de Hoofdplaat in het land van Kadzand, ook Provincie Zeeland, de overige 6 kinders geboren te Borsele.

Door een bijzondere voorzienige regeeringe Gods zijn wij met ons eene kind Willem verhuist van de Hoofdplaat naar de gemeente Borsele, Eiland Goes, den 19 Maart tot 27 [Maart 1817] toen wij met onze goederen over de Schelde waren.

En daar dertig jaar op een schoon bebouwde hofstede van 137 gemeten gewoond en den Heere in voorspoed en tegenspoed ontmoet, evenwel in veel eere en staat geweest in de gemeente, ja in heel dat land.

Maar nadat Nederlands volk algemeen, en de overheid bijzonder, des Heeren wetten en inzettingen verlaten hebben, zoo zond hij de oordeelen van een drukkinge des lands en eene drukkende duurte van alle levensmiddelen, zoo dat niemand in den burgerstand met vrouw en kinderen meer bestaan kon; zoo dat er velen tot den Heere uit ellende beginnen te roepen en de Heere begint het geroep te hooren tot verlossing. Ik heb die wondere wegen Gods in het openbaren van die weg naar Noord Amerika opgemerkt.

En daar er in 1843 en 1844 al velen uit Gelderland en Holland en Overijssel begonnen optetrekken, heb ik die gelukkig geschat die uit de ellende verlost waren.

Daaronder heb ik biddende verkeert om den Heere raad te vragen voor mij en mijne kinderen of de Heere ons mogt genadig zijn. Niet dat wij er aanspraak op hebben van wegen onze zonden, daar ik vrijwillig voor mij en vrouw en kinderen belijdenis van mocht doen. En zoo heeft het den Heere, wiens ik ben en naar de begeerte mijns harten, met veel zwakheid en droefheid des harten diene, behaagd, mijn hart overtebuigen in den morgen van den 1sten Januari 1847 toen ik des Heeren aangezicht zogt om hen dankbaar te erkennen voor al zijne weldaden in het afgelopene jaar weer bewezen aan ons en het onze. En ook in die zaak van Amerika gaf de Heere mij een gezicht van zijne oordeelen die reeds drukten en nog dreigden, en bepaalde mij bij de woorden van Paulus tot de Joden: "nademaal gij het evangelie verwerpt, zoo keeren wij ons tot de Heidenen." Hetwelk dadelijk bevestigd is; zoo dat de Heere zijn zegen en Geest van de Joden weg nam en de Heidenen namen het woord aan en zoo was de val der Joden de zaligheid der Heidenen.

Alzoo ook in Nederland, ja in Europa, daar het Evangelie zoo vele eeuwen geschenen heeft maar nu ook van de massa verworpen, die tot een zorgeloos en goddeloos leven zijn overgevallen. Alleen is er een klein overblijfsel naar de verkiezing der genade dat nog bij de zuivere waarheid naar Gods woord blijft.

Zoo werd dan mijn hart overgebogen als dat van mijne vrouw die mede genade in des Heeren oogen gevonden heeft voor de eeuwigheid, als ook de harten onzer vier, nog in huis zijnde kinderen van alles losgemaakt om de verlossing aan te nemen en om den weg die de Heere voor ons opend alles te verlaten en naar Noord Amerika op te trekken. De Heere heeft daarenboven onze oudste zoon Willem met zijne dierbare vrouw, Maatje Daane, die beide den Heere vreezen, overgebogen om mee te trekken. Als ook onze tweede zoon, Jan, die op studie was voor domine in Arnhem, Gelderland, omdat twee zijner leermeesters, Ds. van Raalte en de Heer A. B. Veenhuizen die onderwijs gaf in de talen, beide naar Amerika vertrokken en Ds. Anthony Brummelkamp dus alleen geen genoegzaam onderwijs meer kon geven en dit dus ook voor hem den weg baande om mee te gaan. Daarenboven is onze oudste dochter Jannetje, die gehuwd is met Jan den Herder, ook wonderlijk losgemaakt, en heeft hare goederen verkogt om met ons te trekken met vier kinderen, twee van haar man die weduwnaar was, en twee van hen beide. Dus met onze zeven kinderen en kindskinderen.

De volgende personen met hunne vrouwen en kinderen zijn ook meegetrokken: Gillis Dok, zijne huisvrouw Jannetje Bogaard, en 6 kinderen: Johannes Jonkheer en vrouw Diena Leenhouts, onze nicht, kind myner vrouws zuster, met 6 kinderen; Christiaan den Herder en vrouw, Cornelia de Jonge, met 4 kinderen; Jacob Steketee en vrouw, Cornelia Rottier; Cornelis Boonman en vrouw Adriana Geluk, met een kind; Marinus Verburg en vrouw Jannetje Mulder, met 2 kinderen; de Weduwe van de Laare, met 8 kinderen; Marinus van Dyke en vrouw Maria, [   ] en 3 kinderen; Jan Rademaker, jongman; Adriaan de Puit en vrouw Willemijntje de Jonge en 4 kinderen; Cornelis de Jonge en zijn vrouw, onafgescheiden, Peternella Steketee, met 3 kinderen; Jan Steketee en vrouw Maria Franje, met 9 kinderen; deze al te zamen van de gemeente Borsele met Johannes Albrechtse mijn opperknecht, zeven en zeventig zielen. Daar beneven in vereeniging uit Kadzand, Axel, en het Goesche land nog twee honderd drie en twintig, te zamen 300, bestemd per schip van Antwerpen, den 10 April 1847. En ook Ds. Cornelius van der Meulen met een gezelschap van honderd zeven en vijftig zielen. Alzoo eene wonderlijke Gods regering dat na dezen zal verstaan worden door onze kinderen.

Maar na de beproeving, eer wij weg waren en daardoor tot den Heere vlugtende heeft de Heere kennelijk geopenbaard ons niet te zullen verlaten. Hij heeft ons in des vijands hand niet overgegeven, maar tot hiertoe geholpen.

De beproeving hierboven bedoeld is dat de regeering verbood dat de

300, met Van de Luyster gaande, allen op een schip zouden ingescheept worden. Steketee voer dus met een gedeelte op het bestemde schip af, terwijl van de Luyster met de overigen tien dagen moesten wachten op een tweede schip. Hoewel hij dus later afvoer bereikte hij echter eerst New York, naardien hij slechts 45 dagen op zee was, terwijl Steketee er 63 op doorbracht. Kaboord en Ds. van der Meulen voeren af van Rotterdam en dobberden 54 dagen op de wateren.

Dus ziet men de redenen waarom, als ook den geest waarin, men het vaderland verliet en zich hier in de bosschen nederzette.

Van de Luyster was de maatschappelijke vader, zoo als van der Meulen de godsdienstige vader was. Deze twee mannen waren de ziel der Zeeuwsche landverhuizing en der wording van Zeeland, in Michigan. Een boekdeel kon geschreven worden omtrent de geschiedenis der eerste 15 jaren, tot aan den dood van Van de Luyster, toonende wat hij deed en was voor dit volk.

Zoo als hierboven reeds gezien is, bracht hij voor eigen rekening 77 personen hier. Dezen waren allen mingegoeden en sommigen dood arm. Een dezer arme huisgezinnen moest hij zelfs nog verzorgen van kleederen tot de reis. De rekening van dit huisgezin geeft hij in zijn rekenboek dus aan. [Ik verzwijg de namen].

Vijf personen, voor de reis
naar Noord Amerika . . . . $ 184.06
Van 30 Junij tot Aug. 28, 1847,
voor onderhoud van spijs, enz. 9.10
Een rekening van geleend geld
in Nederland en van lijnwaad
en katoen en schoenen tot de reis 52.89
               Zamen . . . . $ 246.05

De man [   ] overleed den 8 Julij; den 5den Augustus de weduwe verlost van een dochtertje, doch dit 15 Augustus overleden. Een zoon overleden 10 Augustus; een dochter Augustus 18; de weduwe overleden 28 December, allen in 1847. Dus is M [   ] alleen overgelaten en daarbij nog kreupel. De Heere zij hem genadig voor de tijd en de eeuwigheid. En alzoo zou de vijfde portie voor hem bedragen negen en veertig dollars en 21 cent; de interest is zes percent 's jaar, van wegen een wees te zijn; den 1 April 1853 tot den 1 April 1858, 4 jaar interest, $ 10.08; op rekening in stoor tot 27 October 1857 $ 4.89, restant $ 5.19.

Wat er verder van deze rekening is weten wij niet; zeer waarschijnlijk is zij kwijtgescholden, met die der vier dooden, alsmede die van anderen die gestorven zijn en niet hadden kunnen betalen voor hun dood. Sommigen van die hij overbracht hielp hij aan land, anderen met geld om aan den gang te komen. Als men zijn rekenboek naziet moet men verwondert zijn hoevelen hij heeft geholpen. Jammer is het dat sommigen vergaten terug te betalen.

Hoewel hij in 1861, als lid des kerkeraads protesteerde tegen de prediking van wijlen Ds. Hermanus Stobbelaar en het zelf ter klassikale vergadering bracht, scheidde hij toch nimmer af, hoewel drie zijner kinderen der Kerk vaarwel zeiden. Midden in die troebel stierf hij, en ging dus uit de strijdende in de triumfeerende Kerk over. Hij was een man van ernstig karakter die meer over eigen hart klaagde dan anderen critiseerde. Hij was wel wat eenzijdig, zou men tegenwoordig zeggen, in zijn zienswijze en opvatting der belijdenisschriften, waarom hij dan ook bij het aannemen van twee lidmaten in zijn vragen door den leeraar werd gestuit met den uitroep, „Houdt op! Broeder, houdt op! Gij wordt Labadistisch." De strekking der prediking die hij toen tegenstond is thans vrij algemeen geworden.

Zijn verlaten van het land zijner geboorte, zich losscheurende uit een ruim boerenbestaan; zijne opofferingen van tijd, gemak, en geld, om armen uit den nood te verlossen; zijn geduldig worstelen in de eerste jaren hier waarin hij anderen zag vooruitgaan, terwijl eigen fortuin inkromp – dit alles bewees ondernemingsgeest, volharding, en zelfopofferende liefde. Hij verrichte een groot, een grootsch werk, duizenden ten zegen, en zijne nagedachtenis is velen zoet. Blijve die in eere tot in geslachten. Hij rust, gelijk zijn medestrijder Ds. Van der Meulen, midden onder die ouden die met hem de worsteling in de wouden begonnen, maar de volle overwinning nooit aanschouwden. Straks verrijzen ze weer om dan het oog te openen voor een schooner wereld dan zij immer hier konden aanschouwen.

Van de Luyster was wars van een portret van zich te laten nemen, en daarom is er ook geen in wezen. Gaarne hadden wij dit naders opdat men 's mans beeltenis hier mocht kunnen weergeven.

Behalve van de Luyster, brachten ook Jan Wabeke, Jan Smallegange, en nog anderen, verscheidene huisgezinnen met zich uit Nederland, en verlostten dus menig arme uit den nood. Smallegange bracht er minstens tien, en kwam in Mei 1849 te Zeeland aan. Niet lang mocht hij hier vertoeven maar stierf vroegtijdig op de terugreis van Chicago en werd te Singapore in de zandduinen begraven. Niemand weet zijn graf dan Hij, die alleen ook dat van Moses wist. Het schuimend nat van het schoone

Michigan meer breekt er soms overheen, en het geklots der golven zingt zijn voortdurend refrein. En zoo is menigeen der eerste pioniers begraven in het bosch of aan den weg, sommigen zonder kist, als een soldaat op het slagveld. En waarom zou dat niet? Waren het dan geen dappere strijders, worstelaars ter zee en te lande, met taal en gewoonte, met bosch en moeras, met klimaat en ongekende ziekten, met armoede en ontbering?

En als dat alles overwonnen was wat tal onzer dierbare ouden waren er gevallen die de lauweren en vruchten der overwinning nimmer plukten! Overal rusten zij, in bijna elken Staat onzer Unie, in verlaten kerkhoven en in vergeten graven. Maar, wat nood? 't Zal zoo zijn, even als Ds. Van der Meulen zeide bij het graf waarin hij te midden van een hevigen sneeuwstorm, twee zijner kinderen te gelijk begroef. De doodgraver wilde het graf nog al wat ophoopen, doch de oude dominee voegde hem toe: „Laat maar begaan, Wissekerke, God zal ze wel vinden."

Overal liggen zij, het gansche pad langs, van Nederland tot hiertoe – in de zee, langs het Erie kanaal, op Blackwell's Eiland, in bosch en veld.

> *'t Is wel; ja, 't is wel!*
> *Amerika! welk dichtren lied*
> *Verheft tot hooger galm zich niet!*
> *Waar gij 't geklank der snaar laat hooren.*
> *God sprak, toen in Columbus's ziel*
> *Het grootsch bevruchtend denkbeeld viel;*
> *Een wereld stond daar jong geboren.*

Zo zong Neerland's dichter Bernard ter Haar, en wij mogen zijne woorden, met verandering van den bezongen naam, wel overnemen en zeggen:

> *God sprak toen in Van Raalte's ziel*
> *Het grootsche bevruchtend denkbeeld viel,*
> *Een' nederzetting werd geboren.*

[Translation]

Before the year 1845 a certain Vroegop visited New York, Pennsylvania, Ohio, Indiana, and other states and published his travel experiences, which attracted wide attention and were extensively discussed. [It has proved impossible to verify this statement]. As early as 1843 [really 1846] a society was formed at Arnhem, province of Gelderland, to help needy families to emigrate to America, and a large number of emigrants departed from Gelderland, Holland [Noord-Holland and Zuid-Holland], and Overijsel.

In the early part of 1846 Antonie de Bree and his family departed from Oudelande, province of Zeeland, and settled in Oakland County, Michigan. He may be regarded as the first of the immigrants in that emigration which began in 1846 and attained large proportions during the following years. He was not a pioneer settler. In the spring of 1850 he moved from Oakland County and established himself at Greenville in Montcalm County where his two surviving children and other descendents are still living, completely absorbed by Americans. During the same spring [really 1846] Alexander Hartgerink and J. Arnold departed being sent by their church and friends on a journey of inspection and sent back to the Netherlands a report in the form of an extensive pamphlet.

This caused the people in village, town, and province, and in all the Netherlands to discuss the idea of emigration which already had been strongly encouraged by Dominie Hendrik P. Scholte and Dominie Albertus C. van Raalte. Scholte departed for America in the spring of 1847, and founded Pella, Iowa. Van Raalte decided to settle in Western Michigan and so became the founder of Holland and the surrounding settlement – what formerly was know as the "Kolonie". All this has been fully described by others, and so it is not necessary for us to discuss this matter further. In connection with the Sixtieth Anniversary celebrated at Zeeland we want to contribute something about the founder and the founding of that now flourishing place.

As we shall relate more fully below, Jannes van de Luyster decided on January 1, 1847, to sell his property and set his course for America. People interested in emigration, early in 1847, held three meetings in the city of Goes, and it was decided to emigrate to America. These people, hungering for bread and yearning for the free exercise of their faith, thought they should not settle in America without plan or simply as individuals or as families, but form an organized community and so chose Jannes van de Luyster and Johannes Hoogesteger as elders and Jan Steketee and Adriaan Glerum as deacon. This accomplished, one of those present, an unpretentious man, expressed his opinion that the group should not depart without a pastor. This suggestion met with the approval of all, and they proceeded to call a pastor. Choice fell upon Cornelius van der Meulen, minister in Goes, formerly pastor at Middelharnis, who accepted their call. Thus organized as a parish these people departed on their journey and established themselves in this place.

They decided to depart on April 10, 1847, in three ships, a plan which was carried out. In charge of one of the ships was Jannes van de Luyster; of the second, Jan Steketee; of the third Johannes Kaboord, forming a total of 157 persons, not including Dominie van der Meulen and family.

Van de Luyster was the first to arrive in New York, after a voyage of 45 days. He decided, in accordance with previous agreement, where they were to settle. He chose Van Raalte's Kolonie, set his course for Black Lake, Michigan, later followed by the rest of the group.

Arrived in Michigan, Van de Luyster bought from the government sections 17 and 19, and 400 acres in section 9, township 5 north, range 14 west, in the present township of Zeeland, a total of 1,680 acres. Jan Hulst was the first to purchase land in this township and settle on it. He had left his home in the Netherlands on March 2, 1847, sailed from Hellevoetsluis on March 19, and arrived at Baltimore, Maryland, on April 27. From there he and his family journeyed overland partly in an ox wagon, a journey of six weeks, and on June 8, 1847, arrived at the east half of the southwest quarter of section 28. He was followed one week later by Hilbert Mast, and later also by Jan and Hendrik Mast.

Van de Luyster stayed a brief time at Black Lake, until he had finished his house. He began to build it on July 21, 1847, by which time Jacobus de Hond and Jan Steketee were already living nearby. On one Saturday noon Van de Luyster, returning from a trip from Zeeland to Black Lake, lost his way in the woods. On the next day, Sunday, at eleven o'clock he came upon the house of Jan Steketee, who at that moment was sitting on the shady side of his loghouse, after he had read a sermon. Van de Luyster after being provided with food and dry clothing was put on the right path.

Jannes van de Luyster was born at Cadzand, province of Zeeland, on March 12, 1789, and died at Zeeland, Michigan, on March 13, 1862. His wife was Diena Naeije, born on April 20, 1796, died January 10, 1874, leaving 7 children as follows: two sons, Willem and Jan; and five daughters, Jannetje, widow of Jan den Herder; Dina, wife of Hendrik de Kruif; Elizabeth, wife of Cornelius de Putter; Janna, wife of Willem Benjaminse; and Maartje, wife of Willem Leenhouts. There is a large number of grand children and great-grandchildren, scattered throughout western Michigan and in the West.

After his marriage Van de Luyster at first was a farmer at Cadzand, working land he had rented. But in 1817 he bought a farm near Borsele on the island of Zuid-Beveland [Land of Goes], an area of 137 measures, 693 1/4 rods, for a sum of 34,585.59 florins. The deed to this property at present is the property of Henry de Kruif, one of Van der Luyster's grandsons. For thirty years Van der Luyster lived on this farm, until in 1847 when he sold it for 66,000 florins, and moved to America.

How did he come to make this decision? First, there were difficulties in connection with religion. Second, times were difficult for laborers, craftsmen, and farmers. But let us hear what with his own hand he wrote in his diary, likewise the property of Henry de Kruif. During the earlier years of the Secession, beginning October 21, 1837, Van de Luyster was elder at Borsele. Before that date he must have served as elder in the state church as early as 1818, for it is known that at his death in 1862 he had functioned in that capacity for 44 years. In his diary he recorded, besides other interesting facts, the following:

> June 21, 1840. C. van der Meulen, dominie at Middelharnis, preached in my barn on Sunday. The weather was fair and there were at least 1,000 people. Everything was quiet and edifying. Even the strange horses were peacefully together in the large pasture. And the Lord gave witness of His word of truth delivered to the consciences of many people, and especially to His children.
>
> In the morning preached on Revelation 11 : 5; in the afternoon, on the 24th Sunday of the Catechism]; evening, 1 John 3,1; and collected for the poor 68 florins.
>
> Nevertheless articles of arrest were drawn up by Dirk Wisse, master smith and burgomaster. On July 21, I and my brother deacon Jan Steketee appeared before the judge in Goes. Dominie, I, and Jan Steketee each were fined 100 florins, without our guilt having been proved. Final sentence postponed until August 15.

On September 1840 paid as fine to the receiver
De Kanter at Goes, ... florins   306.29½
Charge for stamp   21

                        Total florins   306.50½

On September 3 received from Jan Steketee, for him,
his father, Cornelius Steketee, and his brother,
Cornelius Steketee Jr. . . . . florins   127.00
But for Jannes Karelse 12.50
On September [   ], received from Jan Smallegange . .   25.00
On September 16 received from Leendert Smallegange .   26.00
On November 11 from Jannes Karelse 25.00
For me, J. van de Luyster 116.00

                           Florins   306.00

There were many episodes like this. Sometimes severer penalties were imposed, and people were put in prison, sometimes even ministers were fined and imprisoned. People were also deprived of work and they were despised, mocked, and cursed. Even after the government granted free exercise of religion, life was made difficult for many. Furthermore, there was much poverty in the country, which was the reason why many were turning toward America.

How Van de Luyster came to the decision to abandon his fatherland appears from the following passage in his diary:

> The Lord speaks in His Word, Psalm 77, 55, first part "Thou art the God that doeth wonders." That word was marvelously confirmed to me Jannes van de Luyster, elder of the seceded church at Borsele, province of Zeeland, Island of Goes [Zuid-Beveland] in Europe, and to my wife Diena Naeije, and to our seven children and six grand-children.

> Willem van de Luyster, our oldest son, was born at Hoofdplaat in the land of Cadzand, also in the province of Zeeland. Our other children were born at Borsele.

> Through the special providence of God, we and our child William moved from Hoofdplaat to the parish of Borsele, Island of Goes, on March 19, to [March] 27, [1817], when we with our things crossed the Schelde, and [we lived] thirty years on a beautiful and well cultivated farm of 137 measures and met the Lord in prosperity as well as in misfortune, and we also occupied a position of respect in our parish, also throughout the country.

> But after the people of the Netherlands, and expecially their Government, deserted the Lord's laws and commandments he sent His judgements, difficulties in the life of the country and an oppresively high price of life's necessaries so that no one of the burgher class, married and having children, could support himself. The result was that many from the depths of misery began to call to the Lord to hear them and deliver them. I myself have noticed these wonderful ways of God's hand in opening the way to North America.

> And as many from Gelderland, Noord-Holland, and Zuid-Holland have begun to emigrate during 1843 and 1844 I have thought that these people were fortunate who thus were freed from these trials. Burdened by these matters I turned prayerfully to the Lord to ask His advice for me and my children, if He would be gracious to us. And so the Lord, whose I am and whom I serve according to the desire of my heart, but with much weakness and sorrow of soul, was

pleased to incline my heart on the morning of January 1, 1847, when I sought the face of the Lord to offer Him thanks for all kindness shown by Him to us and to ours during the past year. And also in the matter of America the Lord gave me a view of His judgement: which oppressed us and still threatened us, and called to my mind the words of Paul to the Jews: Inasmuch as you have rejected the Gospel we turn to the heathen. This was immediately confirmed, in such manner that the Lord withdrew His blessing and His spirit from the Jews and the heathen acceepted His word, and thus the fall of the Jews became the salvation of the heathen. And so likewise in the Netherlands, yea also in Europe, where the Gospel has shone so many centuries but now also has been rejected by most of the population who have gone over to a careless and godless life. Only a small remainder, following their election through grace, still remain faithful to the truth taught in God's Word.

So then was my heart inclined as was also that of my wife who like myself found favor in the Lord's eyes for eternity, and also the hearts of our four children still living with us, to accept this deliverance and follow the way which the Lord is opening, and abandon everything and leave for North America. Also, the Lord inclined our eldest son Willem and his beloved wife Maatje Daane, both of whom have the fear the Lord, to depart with us. Likewise our second son, Jan, who was studying for the ministry in Arnhem, Gelderland, inasmuch as two of his teachers, Dominie A. C. van Raalte and Mr. A. B. Veenhuizen, who gave instruction in languages, both had left for America so that Dominie Anthony Brummelkamp could not give sufficient instruction; and this prepared the way for him to depart with us. Further, our oldest daughter Jannetje who was married to Jan den Herder also was freed and marvelously, and sold her property in order to go with us with four childern, two of her husband's who had been widower and two of herself and her husband. Hence we left with seven children and grandchildren.

The following persons with their wives and children also came with us: Gillis Dok, his wife Jannetje Bogaard, and 6 children; Johannes Jonkheer and wife Diena Leenhouts, our niece, a child of my wife's sister, with 6 children; Christiaan den Herder and his wife, Cornelia de Jonge, with 4 children; Jacob Steketee and wife, Cornelia Rottier; Cornelis Boonman and wife; Adriana Geluk, with one child; Marinus Verburg and wife Jannetje Mulder, with two children; the widow Van de Laare, with 8 children; Marinus van

Dijke and wife Maria [   ] and 3 children; Jan Rademaker, unmarried; Adriaan de Puit and wife; Willemijntje de Jonge and 4 children; Cornelius de Jonge and wife [not Seceders]; Peternella Steketee and 3 children; Jan Steketee and wife, Maria Franje, and 9 children.

All these together from the commune of Borsele, and also Johannes Albrechtse, my chief hired man, 77 souls.

In addition to these there were others to the number of 223 [making a total of 300] from Cadzand, Axel, and Goes who were to leave by ship from Antwerp, on April 10, 1847. Also Dominie Cornelius van der Meulen with a company of 157 souls. Thus a marvelous evidence of God's governance which in the future will so be understood by our children. But after our trials before we departed, and for that reason had fled to the Lord, he clearly indicated He would not abandon us. He did not deliver us into the hand of the enemy, but instead has until now helped us.

The trials referred to above were the novel requirements of the government which forbade that the 300 going with Van der Luyster should sail in one ship. Accordingly Steketee sailed with a part of these people in the designated ship, while Van der Luyster and the rest had to wait ten days for a second ship. Although he sailed later he was the first to arrive in New York, after sailing 45 days while Steketee spent 63.

Kaboord and Ds. Van der Meulen sailed from Rotterdam, their voyage lasted 54 days.

Thus are revealed the reasons on account of which we left our fatherland and settled here in the woods.

Van der Luyster was the community's father, much as Van der Meulen was its religious father. These two men were the soul of Zeeland emigration and also of the founding of Zeeland, Michigan. A whole volume could be written on the history of the community during its first 15 years, until the death of Van der Luyster, to explain what sort of a man he was and what he meant for his people.

As recounted above, he brought with him to this place at his own expense 77 persons. These all were people of small means and some of them were desperately poor. He had to provide one of these families with clothing in order they could leave with him on their journey. His account dealing with that family is recorded as follows [I shall not mention any names]:

Five persons, for the journey to North America   . . . . $ 184.06
From 30 June to August 28,1847, for food and
    other necessaries 9.10
Payment of a sum of borrowed money in the
    Netherlands, of linen and cotton and shoes needed
    for the journey 52.89

Summa . . . . $ 246.05

The husband[   ] died July 8; on August 5 his widow gave birth
to a daughter who died on August 20. A son died on August 10, a
daughter on August 18. The widow died on December 28, all in
1847. So M [   ] alone has survived, and he is a cripple. May
God be gracious to him not only in time but in eternity. So the
fifth part owed by him is $ 49.21. Interest is at 6% per year, being
a orphan. Total interest for four years, from April 1, 1853, to April 1,
1858, is $ 10.08. Account at the store, to October 1857, $ 4.59,
restant $ 5.19.

Nothing further is recorded about the history of this account. Most
likely it was cancelled as was also the case with the others who died and
were unable to repay before their death. He gave land to some of
those he brought over, to others he loaned money that they might get a
start. Looking through his account book one marvels that he helped so
many poor people. Unfortunately, some of these people forgot to pay
their debts to him.

  Although, as member of the consistory, he protested against the
preaching of the late Dominie Hermannus Stobbelaar, and himself
presented a complaint before the Classis, he never separated from the
[Reformed] Church, although three of his children did say farewell to it.
In the midest of that church trouble Van der Luyster died, and so passed
out of the church militant into the church triumphant. An earnest
character, he complained more about his own shortcomings than he
criticized others. It must be granted that he was somewhat one-sided, as
one would call it today, in his way of viewing matters and in his understanding of the Confession of Faith. That is the explanation why on one
occasion when two members were being added to the church, and were
being questioned, the minister said to him sharply, "Stop, brother, stop!
You are becoming Labadist." The character of preaching which he
opposed has today become quite general.

Leaving the land of his birth, taking himself away from a comfortable farmer's existence, his sacrifice of time, comfort, and money to help the poor, his patient struggles during the first years [in the Kolonie] in which he saw others become prosperous while his own fortune diminished indicate a man of enterprise, perseverance, and self-sacrificing love. He accomplish a vast and great work, was a blessing for thousands. His memory is a sweet thing to many. May it remain in honor for generations. Like his fellow laborer Dominie Van der Meulen, he is resting amid the old ones who began with him their struggle in the forest but who never witnessed the complete victory in that struggle. Soon they will rise again; then their eyes will behold a world fairer than they have ever been able to witness here.

Van de Luyster was reluctant to have a portrait made of himself, and that is the reason there is none in existence.

Besides Van der Luyster, Jan Wabeke and Jan Smallegange and some others also brought many a family from the Netherlands, thus rescuing many a poor person from dire need. Smallegange brought at lest ten such families with him, and arrived in Zeeland during May 1849. It was not his lot to tarry here many years, for he died soon after his arrival, on his return from a trip to Chicago, and was buried at Singapore, in the sand dunes. No person knows his grave, but He, who knows Moses' grave, knows also where Smallegange lies buried. The waves of fair Lake Michigan sometimes break over his resting place and the murmer of its waters sing a requiem in memory of him. And so also many another of our first pioneer settlers has been buried in forgotten spots in the woods or along the roads, some of them without coffins, like soldiers on the field of battle. And why should they not be so buried? Were they not courageous fighters, warriors on sea and on land, contending with a strange language and with strange customs, with hardships of woods and swamps, with adversities of climate and strange illnesses, with proverty and self-denial?

Although our beloved old folk overcame these trials and tribulations, how many of them never plucked the fruit and laurels of their victory! Today they rest in widely scattered places, in nearly every state of our Union, in deserted cemeteries, in forgotten graves. But why grieve? It will be as Dominie Van der Meulen spoke when at the grave in which, in a blinding snowstorm, in one ceremony he buried two of his own children. The grave digger wanted to heap up the earth. But the aged dominie stopped him, exclaiming, "It is enough, Wissekerke, God will know His own!"

Scattered they lie in many places, along the entire route from the Netherlands to this place – in the sea, along Erie Canal, on Blackwell's Island, in wood and in field.

> *'T is well, yea, 't is well!*
> *America! what poet's song*
> *Does not inspire fairer echo*
> *When thy strings are sounded!*
>
> *God then spoke in Columbus' soul*
> *Then was conceived a mighty thought –*
> *A new world then was born!*

Thus sang Holland's poet Bernard ter Haar. We may copy his words, change the name to which they are addressed, and say:

> *God then spoke in Van Raalte's soul*
> *Then was conceived a mighty thought –*
> *A new settlement was born!*

Chapter XXXII

TWO IMMIGRANT PIONEER AUTOBIOGRAPHIES

113. JAMES MOERDYKE'S AUTOBIOGRAPHY

[This sketch tells the story of a Dutch family before emigrating from Zeeland and after settling in America. It portrays some of the features of the Dutch immigrant's life and thought as found in Michigan's Dutch Kolonie during the first generation after the founding of Zeeland. Its author, James Moerdyke Sr., was born in 1816, died in Zeeland, Michigan, May 22, 1884. He was the father of Pieter and Willem Moerdyke, both ministers in the Reformed Church. The text, taken from a manuscript preserved in the Netherlands Museum, is an English translation of a Dutch original now lost, prepared by the author's son William. It has been amended and abbreviated for the sake of clarity.]

At the urgent request of my children I undertake to record my life's history. I was born January 21, 1816, in the Netherlands, in Biervliet, Fourth District of the Province of Zeeland, on the estate then belonging to my mother's father, Jacobus Faro. This farm is situated on the highway between Biervliet and Yzendijke, and bears the name of Oranje Polder; the street being called the Oudelande.

My father's name was Willem Moerdyke and mother's Cathelyntje Faro. I never knew father's parents. I was named after mother's father, was always with him, during his latest years slept with him.

Jacobus Faro, my maternal grandfather, was an intelligent man and a conscientious Christian. During Napoleon's reign in the Netherlands grandfather Faro was burgomaster of our city. He spoke French readily. He died when I was six years old, and I clearly recall the sad event. Conscious to the last, he lay upon his deathbed giving advice and preaching God's truth, and died at the age of seventy-five, leaving children, to wit: my mother, and Magdalena, Maria, Sarah, and a son Johannes. Maria and Johannes died early. Maria was the wife of a Mr. Risseeuw of Schoondijke, at which place she died and was buried. Johannes never married. Magdalena was the wife of Pieter Meulendijke; these were the grandparents of the seven children of cousin John de Pree. Sarah was the wife of Dingenis de Die of Biervliet who never had children. Uncle Pieter Meulendijke and wife had two children, Jacobus and Magdalena, the last being the mother of the children of cousin Jan de Pree.

Grandfather Faro was a wealthy man; after his decease his estate was divided among my mother, Sarah and Magdalena. Hence father had to sell the farm. It is a pity that none of the three heirs became the owners; all passed into the hands of strangers; and saddest of all is the fact that a Catholic from Ghent in Belgium purchased the property. His children own it to this day.

Father then rented a place on contract for twenty-one years. Mother's sister Aunt Sarah was not then married, but lived with us. She was afflicted with epilepsy. A couple of years after father's death she became the wife of Dingenis de Die, a farmer. He married her for her money, for he was deeply in debt, and father had warned her against this step, but in vain. Their married life was all right; he was a good man, but she lost all her money, and after her husband's death was dependent. Because of her affliction she received by the will of grandfather 7,500 florins more than mother and Aunt Magdalena. Grandfather desired her to remain single, but she did not heed his counsel.

Of my father's family I know little, only that his mother, by an earlier marriage was the wife of a Mr. Versluis. I knew two of the children of that marriage: Adriaan and Gilles Versluis. Gillis lived in Ter Goes at Colynsplaats, where some of his children now reside. Adriaan lived on a farm near Biervliet, now the property of Abraham Cornelis whose wife was a daughter of Adriaan Versluis. Several children of Uncle Adriaan live in Biervliet, and one daughter lives near us, hard by Holland, Michigan, the wife of a Mr. Boinga.

My father was a poor young man when he married, but his wife's money by the blessing of God made him what he was. Before his marriage he had been in French military service under Napoleon, but because he had an ailment in one of his legs he was sent home. Said ailment was feigned – to escape hated service in the army of the French ruler and usurper. Father knew how to conduct his business, and also held government offices, especially the superintendance of polders and waterworks. For several years he was Justice in Biervliet. He served as elder in the church, and was, until his death in 1849, a trustee. He was 66 years of age at the time of his death, being born in 1783.

Of my sixth and seventh years I recall nothing. When seven I was sent to school at Yzendijke. Father regarded Marinus Quintus, the schoolmaster, superior to the teacher in the Biervliet school, which must have been true, for many children within the Biervliet school district attended at Yzendyke, as for example, the Marsiljes, of whom three live here. One, Hubrecht, died last year near Holland; Mrs. A. de Kubber, and her sister, widow Van de Kreeke, are the two others. These schoolmates lived a fifteen minutes walk from Biervliet. I went to school with the children of Uncle Pieter Meulendijke, Jacobus and Magdalena. Every morning they waited for me at the end of the meadow at the highway and returned with me in the evening.

Father and mother had taught me at home so that when I first attended school I knew the letters of the alphabet and could spell a little. I advanced rapidly and after a few weeks could read. I attended there seven years, after which I was so far advanced that the teacher, though excellent in all branches he understood, could not lead me to any higher grade. I ranked first in my studies and won several prizes. Every Friday the Bible was read by the pupils, and biblical instruction, also singing, was given. A Mr. Quintus understood music and taught it well. When fourteen father wanted me to choose some occupation. I was a carefree boy. Father proposed that I attend the University of Leiden or Utrecht to prepare for the ministry, but I had no desire to become a minister. Neither did I care to go any farther with my studies, for I was tired of school life. "Well," said father, "then you'll have to be a laborer or hired man." Later, when I was converted, I deeply regretted my refusal to prepare for the ministry.

But, to go back somewhat, when I was twelve my mother died on December 10, 1827, after childbirth. The babe, a daughter, died soon after. This loss was a severe blow to father and to us. There were then five of whom I was the oldest. The burial of mother was the last permitted in the old cemetery by the church. A new cemetery had been opened by the city government and the date fixed when burials in the old had to cease. Father obtained the favor of burying the babe by mother's grave, though it was after the aforesaid date. It was father's good fortune to have in this time of affliction two good maids – Flora Walhoud, first maid, and Sarah Jansen, the second, who took care of the children. Being twelve years old I could help myself, but Magdalena was only two and Johannes five. Peternella, my only full sister who is still living, the wife of William de Visser of Kalamazoo, was nine or ten. She attended school with us.

Brother Johannes was married twice; he died eighteen years ago in Ghent, leaving seven children one of whom, a daughter, came to America last winter, and is now with us in Zeeland, Michigan. Three of those seven children are still in Ghent.

My father was a widower for a year and a half, and then married Janneke, daughter of Cornelia van der Hooft. She was, I think, about twenty-two years old. Four of the ten children of this union survive: Cornelis and Anna [in Kalamazoo], Janneke and William [in Biervliet].

Janneke married a man of means, the son of Abraham Cornelis of Biervliet. William and family reside in Biervliet, making a living as farm help.

Our stepmother was good to us. She was gentle and quiet, a good
farmer's wife, and we children never received any punishment from her.
If we deserved any, she reported it to father. We could not have had a
better mother. I corresponded with her after we came to America. May
the Lord reward her, is my prayer! In regard to religion she, like the
people of Biervliet, was not much enlightened. No wonder, for the
doctrine of salvation was not heard. The church was in a corrupt state.

When called to choose my occupation, I decided, though quite averse
to it, to try farming. I was appointed fourth servant. I learned to manage
horses and ploughing, yet I disliked the work. Neither was I strong
enough for it, and as this labor was too heavy, it wasted my strength and I
often was ailing. Still I kept on, for I saw no other opening. I had for
some time asked father's permission to learn a trade, but in vain. The
time for his consent had not yet arrived.

In 1830 we had another calamity. War broke between Holland and
Belgium. These were dreadful days because we lived near the boundary.
In the fall of 1830 came De Potter, chief of the Revolution, to Biervliet
with soldiers and brought the Belgian flag, placing it in the tower of our
church. He went to the city hall, took the arms stored there and the
funds out of the treasury. We were helpless. This proved a serious time
for our District; many living near the boundary were plundered. After a
while a large army arrived, which our government placed in towns along
the border. They were quartered with the farmers. Father had ten soldiers
and some officers, of high and low rank, who remained with us from the
spring of 1831 until August 2, 1832, when the Ten Days Campaign began,
and the Belgians were driven out. There was little fighting after that,
for through the mediation of England and France a treaty was concluded,
after conferences till 1838, when Leopold I was placed upon the throne
of Belguim.

In the spring of 1831 father occupied a difficult position, for we had
some land lying opposite the Belgium guard. It was called Het Verlaat.
In March we had to sow beans there, but how to get to the land was a
question. Father was courageous, never frightened; he decided to go for
permission from the commandant. He was obliged also to obtain a
permit from the General of the Dutch Army, and a written passport to
get through the Dutch guards. This he secured and went with a spade
upon his shoulder and a flask of gin in his pocket to the Belgians. The
sentinel called "halt!" and asked what he wanted. The entire guard came

to the scene with their officer. Father related his errand and passed his flask around; he got their consent, so the next day we were busy on those acres. Every month there was a change of guard and father had to ask permission anew. He obtained it, but had to furnish a great deal of gin. This lasted till August 1832, when the Belgians were driven back to their country. They fought longest to take Antwerp, and if the French had not assisted them they would never have captured it.

At this time it was hard to get laborers, because men over twenty-five were in army service. In 1831 and 1832 our harvesting was done by men, women and children. There were no harvesting machines at that time, for grain was cut with sickles. When the danger was passed, many came home in 1833, discharged by the government.

Among the Zeeland Home Guards [schutters] was cousin Jan de Pree from Axel, Fifth District of Zeeland. He had been in the standing army, in a regiment of infantry. He was fairly well educated and a good writer, a carpenter by trade, and had risen to the rank of sub-officer in the commissary department caring for the feeding of men and horses. He had to buy provisions, keep books and hence had a good position. His regiment was encamped at the socalled Kapitalen Dam, on the river Scheldt. Two or three warships were always in readiness at this point during the war, for the Belgians were only twenty minutes from the Witte Huis within the Netherlands border.

While Jan de Pree was there, he formed the acquaintance of Magdalena, daughter of Uncle Pieter Meulendijke, who died in 1831 or 1832. This acquaintance ripened into engagement: but as De Pree was in the royal service and his time had not expired, he resolved to buy a substitute for the balance of his service, in which he succeeded, for the sum of 300 guilders. De Pree, honorably discharged, prepared for his marriage in the spring of 1833. His bride owned a small farm opposite our's which was leased to Pieter Larooi, the husband of my stepmother's sister. Later Larooi came to America, but his wife died on the voyage, leaving three children. He settled on a farm some six miles from Kalamazoo, near Cooper. He later married the widow of Grootemaat, mother of Jan and Johannes Grootemaat and of Mrs. Frank Lucas.

When Jan de Pree married and his farm was leased, he settled at Axel, his birthplace, where his parents resided. He bought a home and a carpenter shop, and dwelt there until he emigrated to the United States. His wife was my cousin Leentje, or Magdalena. When in 1833 I wanted to learn the carpenter's trade to which my father had long objected preferring to make a farmer of me, I asked my father's consent one day in harvesting season, in the presence of our chief farm servant. The servant advised my father to consent, as he never could make a farmer out of me. This friend was Peter de Jonge, who pleaded still further with my father, and successfully.

Father said he would write to cousin De Pree and ask if he would take me as apprentice. The reply was, "We shall be glad to have him come." So in the fall I took the boat to Axel, arriving in the evening. Father had come with me so as to make a contract with cousin De Pree. The first year I was to work for my board. In the second year I received sixteen stuivers per day, but had to pay for my board. The third year I received the highest wages then paid to carpenter's apprentices, which was one florin per day. This shows that I advanced nicely.

In the year 1834 began the schism in the Reformed Church, and cousin De Pree and wife seceded with his family. His father lived in Zaamslag and came almost every day to Axel, generally getting into the city at four o'clock in the morning, to stay with us or with Mr. J. Oggel. The latter's wife was his daughter. Pieter de Pree, brother of John, a blacksmith, owned a fine place in the Lange Straat, had plenty work, but later also emigrated to America with his family. He and his wife were buried in Zeeland. Three of their children live here – the wife of P. Benjamins, John the expressman, and Dirk de Pree, the tailor. A brother died here, viz. Dirk, and also a sister, wife of J. Busquet. All these just mentioned, and others in Axel, separated from the State Church because of its heresies.

My cousin, wife of Jan de Pree of Axel, was converted by the pure teachings of the Gospel. I cannot describe the change this produced in her character. She had been a vain, worldly woman, but was completely changed. She became sobermined, sedate, and ready to exhort everyone and lived earnestly for the Lord. Quite often she admonished me, spoke of God's service and exerted great influence on me.

There was at Axel a small congregation of Seceders, having no minister. Mr. Moerhof from Middelburg, garderner, came to Axel and found employment as expert garderner. He was a pious Christian, with great spiritual gifts and knowledge of the Word of God and Christian life. He became the leader of the Seceders, preached, and edified the people. Now and then an ordained minister came to administer the sacraments. The Seceders at that time were persecuted by the government which forbade assemblies of more than 19 persons, so that they often had to pay fines. This Secession spread throughout the Kingdom; the first to withdraw from the Reformed Church being Hendrik de Cock and Hendrik P. Scholte. Persecution of these Godfearing people was dishonoring to God in such a land as the Netherlands. Everywhere innocent people paid fines and were cast into prison; yet the Lord cut that period short. When William the Second ascended the throne in 1840 presecution ceased. He said if there is no other work for the soldiers than the persecution of these people he would rather send them home; he would not permit compulsion. The effect was visible; churches sprang up everywhere; congregations grew and flourished and the Lord added daily to the saved.

Naturally I did not join these people, for I was too worldly, and yet this movement influenced my later life.

In the spring of 1834 I had to submit to the draft for the militia. I stood a poor chance, for there were only 19 young men from whom five were to be drawn. I drew within two of the highest number. The two highest were well qualified for service, and some would probably be rejected as unfit. One had cut off the forefinger of his right hand to escape service. This was proved and he was sent to serve among soldiers as unwilling as himself and at hard labor. He died after a few months. If this man had been rejected, I would have had to serve, being next man liable. I had also asked exemption on account of deafness, for I became deaf through scarlet fever when two years old. I was hard of hearing. I was twice examined by physicians in Middelburg, who judged I should serve; they could not exempt me. Those doctors had evidently expected father to bribe them, but he refused. He was right, for had I been called to serve, they could not have used me as a soldier. However, I remained free and had no further trouble.

I lived with Jan de Pree from 1833 until the winter of 1838. I longed to return to my home, the more since I had decided to set up a carpenter's shop in Biervliet. In the spring of 1839 I was in the employ of Isaac Kools, but only a few months, for he failed and spent a few weeks in jail at Middelburg for debt. I hired out to Jacob Hijnberg and worked as carpenter for him till the spring of 1841, when I resolved to try for myself. I hired a barn on the corner of the market near the parsonage, named the Green Market, and boarded with Hubregt Haefnagel who kept a hotel and whose wife was a sister of my step-mother. Payments were slow and bad, so that at the end of the first year I had quite an account against my patrons, but I did not give up courage. In the winter of 1841 or 1842 I began courtship with Maria Faas, daughter of Peter Faas and Janna Du Mez, and we decided to marry in May. On May, 5 1842, we were joined in marriage at the City Hall before the burgomaster Matthew Verplanke and secretary Dr. Van Altena, who became burgomaster and later lived and died in Milwaukee. The first year of our wedded life we lived at the home of my wife's parents, but in the spring of 1843, we and brother-in-law De Visser together bought a home. De Visser had married my sister Peternella about three months before; both now residing in Kalamazoo. The house we bought belonged to Daniel Baart, grandfather of Sr. Baart of Zeeland, Michigan, but at the time of our purchase it was the property of the so-called "rich Thomas", member of a Catholic family. The house had a large yard and a fine orchard in the rear, with quite a variety of fruit trees. We moved in the spring of 1843.

On the 27th of January our oldest son William was born at the home of my wife's parents. Father Faas kept a hotel, also was a roof thatcher, and kept a grocery in which my wife was the clerk until we moved to America when one of her sisters took her place. She had three sisters and a brother. The eldest is the wife of Abram Willems, who keeps a market in Biervliet, and is also a thatcher; Anna living in Biervliet is the wife of Dingenis Versluis, who continued the hotel business after her partner's death; and the son Pieter who remained single and died young; fifth was a daughter Lijntje, who became the wife of Arenhoud [Arnold] Vergouwe; they lived at Sluiskil in the land of Axel. He was a blacksmith and also had a grocery. He later came with his family to Kalamazoo where he and his children now reside, his wife having died two years ago. He manages a prosperous grocery in Kalamazoo.

In 1843 I had work enough to keep two other carpenters in my employment; and later I kept one, but collections were slow and poor. My wife tried a small grocery business but everything was disappointing, so that we lost every year.

In 1845, January 29, another son was born and named Pieter after my wife's father and on May 8th 1847 a daughter Janna [Jane] was born and named after her maternal grandmother. The family increased but not our business.

In 1845 or 1846 I went with my brother Johannes to Hulst on an errand for father. As Hulst was only six miles from Axel I had taken this trip to make a brief visit to cousin Jan de Pree and his wife. The route was by boat to Ter Neuzen, where we landed at noon. There we called on Dirk de Pree and his excellent family, a Christian wife, where I was always welcome. Cousins De Pree were surprised to see us, and Lena [Leentje or Magdalena] said, "That's fine, cousin, you came just in time, for Dominie Van der Meulen is here and will preach this evening and you'll go with us, won't you?" I answered, "Of course I will."

She hastened to prepare refreshments for us. The church was crowded, but the father of Dominie Pieter J. Oggel and Dominie Chris Oggel, and of Dr. H. P. Oggel, who knew that I was hard of hearing, gave me a seat near the pulpit. The sermon was based on Luke 12, 22-31. I paid little attention to the exposition of this passage, but when he began to apply the truth and grew earnest in exhortation and warning, my attention was arrested. That 31st verse – "Seek ye first the Kingdom of God and His righteousness and all other things shall be added unto you" gripped me. I had never sought that Kingdom. I went home smitten in conscience and found no more rest. I could no longer serve the world. I endured prayerful anxieties, yet did not understand the way of salvation through Christ. The faithful and kind exhortations received during my residence with cousin De Pree and wife were now painfully recollected, to accuse me of my sins and unbelief. On returning to Biervliet, where only "peace, peace" was preached [and false security], I got no further than my conviction of sin. At the home of De Pree that evening we discussed the sermon, and I was again invited to seek the Lord but dared not utter a word.

The next day brother John and I went to Hulst and in the evening returned to the De Pree's, spent the night with them, and the next day got home. It was the first time I had met Dominie Van der Meulen. From that day I loved him and desired to hear him oftener but had no opportunity until in 1849 when I arrived in Zeeland, Michigan.

We struggled along in business bearing heavy burdens of interest, debt, and high taxes, [over 100 florins annually]; there was little work, for there were many carpenters in town, and hence we got along with difficulty, and I began to think of emigration. Families from our city had gone to the new world and sent tidings of prosperity enjoyed there. In 1847 we heard that a large company was going from Ter Goes under the leadership of Cornelius van der Meulen to the United States, and we also heard of parties going with Albertus C. van Raalte and Hendrik P. Scholte. The Seceders [the bulk of those emigrating people were Seceders] were still oppressed, excluded from State Church subsidy and support, grossly maligned, shunned in business. They sought religious freedom and a chance for themselves and their children and to enjoy a measure of freedom. I would gladly have gone at that time but could not.

In January 1847 we received the sad news our cousin Mrs. Jan de Pree had died, after the birth of Adriana who is still living. This was a calamity for De Pree with his seven children, who now live in Zeeland. Though the relatives were invited to the funeral, only myself and another cousin of the deceased, Pieter Meulendyke attended. The funeral sermon was by Dominie A. G. de Waal then living as emeritus in Enschede. After cousin Lena's death, I was appointed guardian of the children, as being the nearest relative. Father was second guardian.

Emigration to America increased and I could think of little else, and talked it over with father, explaining to him our circumstances. But he would not listen to anything about America. When in 1847 I spoke of the departure of so many people, he remarked, "They are Seceders of little consequence, and create opposition to the government." I replied, "Father, do you know what you are saying? These people are not creating disturbance in the church, but are convinced that the Reformed Church has departed from the faith of the fathers, and now they are persecuted. Their refusal to submit to the government is confined to the matter of religion. They recognize only Jesus Christ as Head of the Church and not an earthly King. In other relations they are the best of subjects and none love the House of Orange more than they. All they ask is they be protected in religious and church life. Persecution and wrongs compel them to seek refuge in America." My father was incensed.

I was intensely wrought up in mind about America, and the spiritual superiority of those emigrant bands. I prayed I might follow them soon. God's presence seemed very real to me. When at home I concealed my emotions from my wife who was opposed to leaving for America. But shortly after New Year 1848 I received a letter from cousin Jan de Pree requesting me to sign an enclosed document, a petition for license to sell his goods and property, since he too had resolved to emigrate, and invited me and my family to go with him. I had to call on burgomaster Van Altena, to sign and seal this document as witness. He knew I was anxious to go to America, and said "Now you can go free of cost, for unless you as guardian sign this, Jan de Pree cannot dispose of his property. He can go to America, but must leave at least all that belongs to his children. You can offer to sign on condition that he let you and family accompany him at his expense." I replied, that I would never emigrate if I had to get to America that way, for I believed God would punish such crooked methods. He then signed officially, and when I related this to my wife, she agreed with my refusal. I asked if she could not agree to emigrate even though she could not persuade her parents to consent.

I forwarded that document to De Pree, and added that I would like to go with him, but two things stood in the way: first that my wife would not consent, and second that I thought I had no money for the voyage. A week later came his answer, that if my wife could be persuaded, he would provide the funds. I had expected such a reply, for I knew how he esteemed me. I discussed the question at home, representing to my wife our prospect of poverty, and said more that I can report here, for I was sleepless and unable to do my work. After a couple of days of thought, she replied, "If you can persuade Willem de Visser and his wife to go, I will yield." With brother-in-law De Visser I had no difficulty, for he was as ready as I to become an American, but it was not easy to persuade Mrs. De Visser, my sister. Meanwhile my father changed his mind about America, for he now regarded the Seceders as God's people. Since the De Vissers also were in difficult circumstances he advised my sister to emigrate, for he believed we would succeed in America better than in Biervliet. Father had read a great deal about America. Consequently he gave his consent and De Pree informed us we must get ready to depart about the middle of June 1849.

We sold all we could at a private sale, and later held an auction. A quantity of lumber I left for father to dispose of gradually. Notary Benteyn sent notice to my creditors to call at a certain day for their payment, for I was too busy to see them personally.

De Pree sent word we must be at Rotterdam on the 22nd of June. On the 20th we bade farewell to family and friends. In the afternoon we went to father's home on the farm. He brought us to the Kappetalen Dam. Skipper W. P. de Jonge of Biervliet fixed our time of sailing – when the tide favored, which was late that day. Uncle Abraham Faas accompanied us; mother Faas came with us but father Faas was too sad to accompany us, and with my wife's sisters took leave of us in the city. Mother Faas bade us goodbye in the evening, which was sorely trying to my wife. At 10 P.M. we had to separate and the parting was painful, especially for my sister. Our step-mother wept even more than father, who, like myself controlled his feelings. One of the farm servants drove the team and Abram and Jacobus Faro, [who later lived near Kalamazoo, in Plainfield] and John Verplanke, our stepmother's cousin accompanied us to the boat. It was about a mile and a half ride. The captain sent a row-boat to bring us aboard, me, wife and three children, De Visser, wife and three children, Gerard Boeije and wife and son. Boeije had for 16 years been in the employ of my father.

At about two or three A.M. anchor was weighed and the ship started on its way. The weather was fine, the wind favorable; and we reached Rotterdam before dark, June 21. We enjoyed the trip and the scenery. De Pree had arrived a couple of hours earlier by boat from Ter Neuzen. Dominie Hendrik Geert Klijn, who was going with us, arrived from Middelburg, and Adriaan Zwemer was aboard. Another ship came from Breskens with J. Kotvis, Matthew and Abraham Naaije and the old man

Ver Lee, and their families. In this way we met at Rotterdam, but learned next day our ship for New York was not yet ready. It was being loaded with freight and gin from Schiedam, so we had to wait about four days. I visited the city every day and we spent a Sunday there.

Whilst still on our boat we came near having a fatality. Our children, Willem, six years, and Pieter, four years, were playing on deck with Lyntje [Helen] and Willem de Visser, their cousins. After playing tag around the mast, Pieter, resting on the gunwale, grew dizzy and fell into the Maas. The captain's son heard him just as he rose to the surface. Had he drifted under the next boat, he would have been lost, but the Lord had a different destiny for him.

After four or five days we got on board our ocean ship [the *Leyala* of Baltimore], on June 29 or 30. A steam tug towed us too fast and we collided with the bridge. Willem and I escaped injury by taking refuge in the cabin. Next day Dominie Klijn preached in the church at Helle-voetsluis. On Monday we left the harbor, and had to wait at anchor for favoring tide and wind till July 6 or 7, after which we got into the English Channel and enjoyed the beautiful sight of the English coast and the chalk cliffs as white as snow. We spent three days in the channel because the wind was contrary, and reached the Atlantic.

Sailing was retarded by contrary winds and two days of severe storm. Some children died and were buried at sea. Two German young men had trouble; one stole the other's money and was punished by the captain, who made him occupy a conspicuous place for one hour, with a placard on his chest saying, "Thief". On August 13 the evening was fine and groups were chatting on deck, when the captain in good Dutch asked if we had not yet seen land. "No," was our reply, "Well," said he, "if all goes well you'll see it in the morning early." He had been unwilling before to speak the Holland language to us. Next morning at three o'clock the sailors shouted "Land!" but we saw only the light of Staten Island and after daylight the Island itself. Soon the pilot came aboard and a powerful tug towed us into the harbor.

We were astonished at the sight. We thought the long journey was over but did not know the worst was yet to come. After a sea voyage of thirty eight days we landed on American soil, in the country which for three years I had longed to see. My desire was realized on August 14 in the middle of the afternoon. De Visser and I and several more immediately went to a bakery for bread and coffee. Our little Jane was hungry. We returned to the ship and had a good supper. Jane ate almost a whole loaf and was cured of her gloom and hunger. We slept aboard that night and rested well; our anxiety was over. Next day our goods were brought out of the hold and weighed, examined in the custom house, duty paid, and taken to the steamer on the Hudson River for Albany. Toward evening of August 15, the boat departed; we saw nothing on the trip, as it was night. We could not sleep, for the steamer was so crowded we had no place to sleep. For the children we improvised a bed on the floor. We had been warned against thieves looking for a chance to rob immigrants. We arrived at Albany early the 16th of August.

Fortunately it was fair weather to be outdoors while waiting for the weighing and transfer of our freight to the Erie Canal boat. Three canal boats were loaded with the passengers and freight of our company. At noon the women on the dock prepared a dinner of potatoes and fish with gravy which we relished, having had no potatoes since we left our native land. In the evening we started on the trip to Buffalo. Having laid the children to rest on bedding spread on the floor, and being about a couple of miles out from Albany, the crew came and ordered us out of the boat. Not understanding English, we were frightened and thought the boat was sinking. Our children cried from fright. But we soon saw that the boat was to be weighed. After ten minutes we returned to our place on the boat. To our disgust we discovered that we had stood on the bank of the canal in indescribable filth in the darkness of the night, which fouled everything on our return. This was a consternation; the women wept, and we did our utmost to get our bedding into some condition to be used. Rough and cruel treatment by the crew was the cause of it. It could easily have been prevented by some decent regard for our comfort. Then we moved on and nothing special occurred until we were between Utica and Rochester, when there was cholera aboard. Probably cholera morbus, from eating green apples in orchards near the canal. A young lad from Axel was taken, and died in a couple of hours, and was hastily buried near the canal, in a rough coffin. All were shocked and sought the best possible composure under the circumstances. I believed we were led by the Lord and so kept calm trusting His protection.

After a voyage of nine days we arrived in Buffalo. There Mrs. Joseph Rijgen was taken with cholera and removed to the hospital; she recovered and followed later on. How glad to be on land again! We were cramped for room and sat on freight during the heat of midsummer. The other two boats had not kept up with ours, so we stopped two days in a hotel kept by some Germans and were well treated. Next day, Saturday, the other boats arrived and we had to wait till Monday to proceed. While waiting, the widow Hercules, who had come from Axel with Jan de Pree, and was the stepmother of Mrs. Pieter de Pree came down with cholera and died in a hospital in Buffalo, and on Monday, when boarding the steamer on Lake Erie a child of J. Kotvis died.

After four days and nights on the Lakes we got into Milwaukee Friday at 11 P.M. The aged Ver Lee was taken sick, and four of us carried him on a stretcher to the home of the Pieter Leenhouts who had lived there a year. The sufferer lived only two hours more. The city was very small then; all was quiet at the harbor, and we prepared to rest as best we could on shore between our freight. But Mr. Idema whose wife later married Dominie C. van der Meulen came and he asked if we were Hollanders. After giving full information, he said it would be imprudent to stay on the dock, and that for a shilling each could lodge at his house, and we could use his kitchen to cook for ourselves. We accepted his kind offer and reached his house after a very long walk, at midnight. Being hungry and tired we made coffee and got bread at a bakery for the company.

After a good breakfast we returned to the pier where we had left four men to guard our goods. About a dozen draymen wanted to cart our goods, but we understood nothing and said nothing. Cousin De Pree and others arrived with the information that we and our goods had to be moved to another pier, where the steamboat lay, that was to carry us to Grand Haven, Michigan. The draymen asked a dollar a load for transfer, which we refused to pay. Later they charged $ 1.25 a load. We had bought tickets in New York, thinking these would carry us to our destination, with no charge for transfer of goods. We submitted and helped unload and transfer to the steamboat.

After dinner on August 31, I had an attack of cholera morbus. I was very weak, and from fear of being kept there, I got aboard, and a Holland sailor allowed me to sit near the boiler of the steamer, for I was chilly. De Pree prepared a hot drink of cinnamon and sugar which I drank. When we reached Grand Haven I was well. Some of us who were taken ill in Milwaukee were left at Mr. Idema's, and some children died; one of Jacob Boeije and the still surviving wife of Mr. De Spelder of Holland, Michigan. Idema cared for their burial and was paid for this by Jan de Pree.

At Grand Haven the captain, with the Dutch sailor as interpreter, came to collect the tickets. He told us they were not good on this trip; that we had been defrauded by a New York agent, and must pay again. The amount was $ 90. Being a good man, the captain took pity on this swindled party and took a note for the amount signed by four or the responsible men of our company, which had to be paid him, unless we could recover the $ 90 from the New York agent.

On shore we met quite a number of Hollanders residing there, among them F. Reigard and another from Biervliet. Our goods were left in the warehouse. It was Saturday, September 1, Reigard took us to his home and on the next day Dominie Klijn preached for us and the other Hollanders. Mrs. Abraham Naaije and her maid, present wife of F. Bakker of Holland, were attacked by cholera and had to stay in Grand Haven but soon recovered. J. Boeije again lost children there; Mrs. De Spelder, a widow, lost the last of three. Boeije lost five of seven children, later his wife in Zeeland.

On Monday morning we resumed our journey by a river steamboat up the Grand River to Grandville, where we arrived in the evening and remained untill Tuesday, September 4, when ox-teams and wagons brought us to Zeeland. We traveled all the way from Biervliet to within 15 miles of our destination by water. Grandville was then an insignificant settlement with a few scattered houses. Dominie H. G. Klijn had left Grand Haven with people who had come to take him to Graafschap. On Tuesday 4 or 5 oxwagons were loaded. Our wives and children found seats among our goods.

A more miserable journey I have never taken, for the road was through forest and we rode over stumps and trees and log bridges and through water, so that it was hard to keep our seats and not tumble off the cart. When halfway to Zeeland we met Dominie C. van der Meulen with a two-wheel oxcart. He was on his way to Grand Rapids to purchase provisions. He said to C. Nies, his ox-driver, "We will return to Zeeland and load as many of the people on our cart as we can." After traveling a couple of miles the cart broke down, and the minister ordered the cart placed at the side of the road and the driver to go to Zeeland with the oxen. He invited De Visser, who was ailing, to mount his horse, and Dominie and De Pree went ahead on foot to Zeeland to prepare lodging and food. We moved slowly for oxen are careful. With horses accidents would have been unavoidable. Between Grandville and Zeeland we came to a tavern where liquor was sold and some of our company drank a little too much. Among these was Matthew Naaije, brother-in-law of Jannes van de Luyster; he was excited and asked me to drink. I took a little, for we were getting discouraged by the long journey, our disappointments and hardships, and finally in landing here in this wilderness. We began to wonder how we could make our living here. It was a fearful sight of endless dense forests and giant trees. But, resigned, we rode on. At last we

came to the farm of Willem van de Luyster; he and others met us with
lanterns and led us to safety. At 11 P.M. September 4, 1849, we reached
Zeeland, our destination in the New World. We had been looking for
houses and church spires, but saw only trees.

We were taken to a log house on the site of the Christian Reformed
Church parsonage, on the street running north and south and between
the now Main Street and Park opposite the First Reformed Church.
Our nearest neighbor was Jan de Peyster, who now resides in Holland.
At request of Dominie Van der Meulen, he provided light and refreshments. We ate a little, and laid ourselves to rest on our beds spread upon
the floor. We arose early next morning, curious to see the town, and
were amazed at the sight of nothing but trees and stumps, and asked
how we were to earn a living here.

Again we resigned ourselves to the situation, and unpacked our goods.
I made a rough bedstead and we got things in the best order we could,
for chairs, table and cook stove we did not have, and had to get our meals
at De Peyster's. His wife was kind to us. I made a couple of benches for
seats and our chests served for a table. That day Jan de Pree called to see
us and furnished us some money to live on, for we had no more money.

Dominie Van der Meulen also called to comfort and cheer us and said,
"When you get settled, you must come and build my barn, and A.
Doornheim will help you." For this barn the logs were brought by
oxen from the woods to the site, and there we had to shape them.

Getting back to work ended our discouragement. Cousin De Pree
supplied a stove and De Visser got another house, so that we lived alone
and had room enough. It began to get cold, but there was plenty of fuel
to be had for the chopping. After two or three weeks of labor I had a
fever. We had a sort of doctor here whose prescriptions proved helpful.
I returned, though weak, to my work and when the barn was finished,
we built a house for J. Busquet. Next we built Jan de Pree's house on his
farm, and I worked at this all the mild winter of 1849-50, until late in the
spring. Building houses was slow work, as the carpenter had to make
everything by hand. All material was in the rough, and the frame was of
hewn timber. There was a small sawmill at Groningen run by Jan
Rabbers, but he could not keep up with the demand for lumber – hence
we had to prepare all material out of logs. There was plenty of work for
the three of us – De Visser, myself and Doornheim.

One noonday when passing the home of Van der Meulen we met a
Grand Rapids man who had brought a lot of fat hogs to the town for sale.
We, and many others looked on, and we would gladly have bought one,

but had no money, earning only seventy-five cents per day, or $ 4.50 per week, and I paid De Pree fifty cents weekly on my debt to him. I owed him $ 150. Our minister saw us standing, came out and said, "Moerdyke and De Visser, you must buy one, for it may be your last chance this winter." We replied that we had no money. "Well," said he, "pick out one and I will pay." We did so, but said, "When will you be repaid by us?" "Oh, that will come out all right," was his answer. We did repay, whether in cash or labor I've forgotten. We were thankful and the pastor found a large place in my heart. I always deeply respected him; he assisted us and all whom he could.

When we had finished De Pree's house, Mr. Rokus, father of Mrs. Joshua Elenbaas, hired us to build a house and we were busy till fall. Then, on the advice of cousin De Pree, we built our own house, in which many years later, cousin and Mrs. Jan de Pree lived and died. We moved into our new home and were soon without work, for immigration had ceased for the moment and hence there was no demand for building. Besides, not a few people had gone to neighboring places to find employment.

In September 1850 De Visser and I walked fifty miles to Kalamazoo and got work from a Mr. Knerr, at one dollar a day, half in cash and half in store-pay. This was common at that time. I boarded with A. van Ess, but, as Van Ess and wife could not accept my store orders for my board, I paid out nearly all my cash and knew not what to do with those orders. I could not carry groceries to Zeeland and to hire a wagon to carry them would cost more than the goods were worth. I grew discouraged and wrote my wife that if the family were only in Kalamazoo we could live nicely. This seemed impracticable, however, because we were too poor to move. At last I decided to go home, whatever the consequences might be. I returned afoot to Zeeland carrying as many groceries as I could. My wife and the boys, William and Peter, were digging potatoes. No one was home. It was early in the morning and I was tired and hungry. I found and ate a piece of bread and lay down to rest, expecting them home soon. But after a short rest I went to find them. Jane then about three years leaped into my arms for joy.

I got some work but we planned to move to Kalamazoo if possible. I had told friends about our intentions and offered our stove, which had cost $ 16 and been used only a year, as payment to anyone who would take us and our goods to Kalamazoo. Joshua Elenbaas appeared with the offer, but wanted to wait till snow fell. He wanted me to make a sleigh for him. We agreed, and I worked on to earn our living and pay our debts. I transferred our house to cousin De Pree for what it had cost and we were ready to move. The week before Christmas 1850 we prepared for the journey. I had built the sleigh box so that it could hold three boxes and besides leave room for my wife and children. On Thursday before Christmas we left Zeeland.

Accompanying us in a second sleigh were A. Glerum and his family. Both drivers of oxen survive – Anthony Elenbaas, brother of Joshua, and Matthew [Teeuwtje] Naaije who later married the widow Westrate. We got an early start, but had gone only three miles, when we got stuck in a spring. The road was not yet cleared; no one had made any track through the snow, and we could not get the sled out of the hole without unloading. We proceeded without delay, but got about six miles the first day and stayed at the farmhouse of Mr. Isaac Fairbanks, who treated us very kindly. On Friday we started early and moved along all day without trouble. It was so dark that we had to go ahead of the oxen to find the road until we got out of the pine forest. We inquired at a farmhouse whether we could stay there for the night. This family treated us excellently. On Saturday morning early we started, found the road better and we got along faster and in the evening arrived three miles beyond Allegan, where a Holland family kept a boarding house, and we spent the night. Because next day was Sunday, we rested. Glerum that Sunday read the Scripture and a sermon for us and we had worship. On Monday we started quite early so as to reach Kalamazoo late that evening. There were few Hollanders in Kalamazoo then, most of them unknown to us, and besides we did not know where they lived. But Willem Kakebeeke had learned we were on our way and stood waiting on the road by which we had to enter town. He told us that he had hired a house for each of the families.

We were taken to a shanty belonging to Harm Wiersma. He had hired out on a farm and left his furniture in the house, which was lucky for us. There was a cook stove. The friendly old gentleman Molag, whose wife had died, lived in another part of the shanty. He supplied wood and started the fire for us. It was very cold that evening. Our driver found a place for his oxen and slept on the floor of the house. We slept for the first time on an American bedstead, the whole family of five occupying one bed. Molag got around early to furnish us wood and other necessities, and Kakebeeke called, and I asked where to go to buy a cord of wood. Molag advised me to go to Paulus den Bleyker, who had just bought the farm of ex-governor Ransom and was clearing the marsh at the south end of town. They told me he would trust me for wood.

As I was going to see Den Bleyker, I met Mr. Lankheet and J. Niesen, elders of the Reformed Church. They told me they were on the way to visit us, so I returned with them. They asked if they could assist us. I thanked them for their offer and said we could manage. They assured us of readiness to help, if we needed, and that we must not hesitate to come for aid. And then, having heard that I could sing, they wanted to know if I would become the *voorzinger* in the church. I replied that I hesitated to lead in church, for I feared lack of courage would get me off tune. But the following Sunday I filled that place, and got along all right at first, and soon grew used to it, so that I led the congregation for several years until the schoolmaster Monning began teaching the Holland school here. We had not, in Zeeland or Kalamazoo, joined the church, though we brought with us our certificates of dismissal from Biervliet; for in Zeeland we learned church letters from the Reformed Church in the Netherlands were not accepted. But later we were led by the divine spirit to a different conviction. We resided three years there before we were received upon a confession of faith. We were received into the church in 1853 or 1854, when Dominie Ypma came from Vriesland, to supply the pulpit for us.

J. de Peyster, our neighbor in Zeeland, had gone with De Visser and me to Kalamazoo when we left our families in Zeeland. He sent for his family, and worked for a Mr. Hopkins. I inquired if I also could find employment there. He asked Hopkins, who replied that he had little work in winter, but De Peyster pleaded. Then Hopkins wanted to see me, and I called with De Peyster. We met Hopkins at the corner of Main and Burdick Streets. By the light of a street lamp Hopkins looked me over from head to foot and asked what I wanted to earn. I told him I would work a week and he could pay what he considered right. I was to begin in the shop next day and he would keep me as long as he had work for me. I rejoiced and was overcome with emotion as I went home, seeing the hand of God in thus opening the way for us.

Next day I went to work, taking the tools I had brought with me from the Netherlands, at which a couple of Americans laughed considerably, especially at my jointer [plane] which was about four feet long. I did not know why they laughed, but afterwards I dropped that tool. Hopkins assigned me to a bench, and came to me with a sample drawer. He had to make 150 such for the drug store of A. D. Archanbal. This was to be exact and nice work, and he through De Peyster as interpreter, for I did not understand a word, asked if I could make them. I answered that I could, that he must see the first one I made and then judge the work. When I had finished one, he was perfectly pleased and when the week ended I received as my wages a dollar a day, but all in store orders which paid for the necessaries of life. We lived well but had no money.

After six weeks Hopkins told me there was no more work for me but said, "Come with me and I'll get you a place." He introduced me to Frank Denison who was then building the Burdick House and who had a store, and asked him to hire me. In reply to his questions Hopkins stated I had been in his employ six weeks and had given satisfaction. So I was employed at a dollar per day payable in orders on his store. As I needed some cash for house rent, I asked for a little cash, but Denison said, "Come and live above my store [adjoining the Burdick House on Main Street]; then you'll not have to pay rent." I told him I was willing, but we had no stove. He told me he sold stoves, and though I could not pay for one he said, "Oh, that's nothing. Go and get your wife and pick out a suitable stove and then move upstairs." Next day I was at work, and was astonished at God's goodness toward us, for I recognized His mercy in all of this good fortune.

Our greatest difficulty was the lack of money. We could not pay for milk and could make no contribution for the church. John Santvoord with whom we had become acquainted when on the canal boat and who had stopped a while in Rochester had come to Kalamazoo the day of our arrival now came to us. He had taken a job of sawing wood at the depot for the Michigan Central Railroad Co. He asked me if I had found work, and I told him I had, but could not get any cash. He wanted to know if I could file saws. Of course, I said I could. "Well then, I'll bring mine and if it is well sharpened, I shall see that you have the filing of all the woodsawers." So I made an apparatus which I set upon the table and after supper filed saws, sometimes five or six in an evening, and the boys, Willem and Pieter, had to hold the candle for me. In this way I obtained some cash. One evening I filed a large log-saw, and made such a noise, that my neighbor went to deacon A. Geerlings and said, "I come here for a little while, for my neighbor Moerdyke plays on the fiddle every evening, which annoys me." At first Geerlings took the story literally.

After living six weeks upstairs we had to move, for Denison's new store in the Burdick House building was completed. We then occupied a house belonging to a Mr. Trowbridge for seventy-five cents per week, but I think we never paid as much as two dollars to him, for Mrs. Trowbridge wanted my wife's help for an hour a day. She declined to receive rent and also gave us a great many things besides. Trowbridge lived on the southwest corner opposite the Park in the center of Kalamazoo and our house was just back of his. In the spring of 1851 I tried to persuade Denison to pay me a little cash every week. He said, "Jacob, I have no money." I could not reduce my remaining debt of $ 100 to cousin De Pree. This debt worried me greatly. I had an offer to work for the railroad at seven shillings in cash per day, which I accepted and told Denison. He said, "Oh Jacob, you must not do that; it is much too hard work for you." I replied that I must have money. He stated again that he had none to give, so I left his employment and for six weeks worked for the Michigan Central Railroad during which we lived in a hastily-built shanty on railroad property at Lawton, then called Paw Paw Station about twelve miles west of Kalamazoo.

I received word from Denison to come back and he offered me four dollars per week in cash, the balance in store orders, which I accepted, and we returned to Mr. Trowbridge's house, where we had lived before. Mr. and Mrs. van Ess afore mentioned also lived at Paw Paw Station, next door to us. Later we moved into an old house owned by Kakebeeke, on Walnut Street. I got on nicely with Denison who made prompt payments. But in the fall of 1851 again there was no work, but I believed that there would be relief from some source. About October Albert Kappinga hired me to finish his house. He said, "When done you can work for Albert Siersema and Sakke Dogger about four weeks and they will pay seven shillings cash per day". So I took the work, though Denison wished to keep me.

I worked for those people until February 1852 and in the following spring I was employed by Kraus and Denison, who as contractors were building the new Congregational Church still standing opposite the Park where later the fine church edifice was erected. More of our countrymen came to Kalamazoo, who employed me to build their houses. Den Bleyker plotted his farm in lots, and I worked for him, so that we got ahead somewhat. We had also bought a lot on Walnut Street near the foot of Prospect Hill, and built a small house. By 1852 I had paid all my debt to Jan de Pree. Now I felt at home in America, and was glad I had emigrated. I had plenty of work, sometimes more than I could do, and was employed more than half the time by Den Bleyker. The times also improved, so that laborers and mechanics were paid in cash. Store pay was a thing of the past, and wages were higher. I earned $ 1.50 and later as much as $ 2.

But in 1857 I made a mistake. I sold our home and bought 20 acres, 1½ miles west of Zeeland, and would try farming. In the Netherlands I had refused to be a farmer; now I wanted to try it. Fortunately my eyes were opened to my folly, and soon after settling on our farm, J. Beekman came with an offer to buy. I sold my farm to him, making $ 75 on my sale. We settled on the farm near harvest time. Willem and I came all the way from Kalamazoo on foot, leading a heifer we had raised. The family followed with our loaded wagon. As winter was drawing near we decided to live in Zeeland, hired a house from Dirk Oggel. While I was working for the widow Van den Berge, Karl Mechels asked me to buy his house, for he wanted to return to Keokuk, Iowa. This house stood next to the Reformed Church, on the west side, where Jacob den Herder now resides. It was partly a log, partly a frame house, with good barn and fine orchard. I stated our intention to buy nothing, for we were going back to Kalamazoo in the spring of 1858 .He offered the property at $ 300. I suggested $ 200. That same evening he accepted my offer.

Robbertus de Bruin, school teacher of the village, father of the late Dominie Pieter de Bruin, and a notary, drew up the papers. Mechels soon left, but a few weeks later I received through his wife's uncle, Hubertus Keppel, the news that he regretted selling and would gladly take the place again for $ 200. I sold it to him, for we could not stay in Zeeland, as work was scarce, wages low and there was but little money. In the spring of 1858, therefore, we left for Kalamazoo and were moved by Keppel with his horses and wagon.

We hired a house from Mr. Hoedemaker, about a block southeast of corner of North and West Streets, about two blocks north of the Michigan Central Railway. Rev. Hendrik Geert Klijn had just become pastor in Kalamazoo and called on us the first day we arrived. Not busy then, I strolled around and called on G. Heilman, who spoke of a house for sale nearby at a low price. I looked it over and bought it that day for $ 200, which was for the building alone, the lot being mortgaged to Den Bleyker. When it came to the legal transfer, the owner backed out, stating that his wife thought the price was too cheap. He said she wanted to get a new dress out of the deal. When asked how much more he wanted, he referred me to his wife, who asked an advance of $ 20 which in those days would dress a queen. The man had purchased the lot for $ 300 and paid one-eighth and I had seven years time for the balance, with interest at seven per cent. I granted the lady's request, and required of her a written statement that I had made an agreement with her, and then went to her husband, paid him $ 20, and took his receipt. All went well and we had a home where we lived for many years, until we moved to Zeeland in 1879. This home was on South Burdick Street, right opposite the east end of Burr Oak Street. I owe much, next to God, to Den Bleyker, and loved the man, who could not dispense with me, as he said. When I began to work in the shop of Kellogg and Holtenhouse, Den Bleyker often came for my services, and I helped him. His wife was friendly and called me every forenoon I was working on their place on Burdick Street to have a glass of wine and some cake.

I labored on till 1864, when our sons were at Hope College felt sorry I had such hard work especially in winter. I worked in the country for Den Bleyker and others, which meant long days and much hardship. My sons advised me to work in a shop and find ease and comfort. I was building a barn for Den Bleyker 5 miles south of Kalamazoo. To get to my work I had to be in his yard very early to hitch up my horse, and in the evening I did not get home before seven. So when the barn was built I obtained a place in Kellogg and Holtenhouse's shop, and worked there seven years, when the shop including my tools was destroyed by fire, and I lost $ 60. Meanwhile I was in the shop of Dewing and Son about three months. I returned to the shop of Kellogg and Holtenhouse for a year, when Fred Bush bought it, and ran it for different purposes, so that the carpenters were out of a job.

James van Brooke, my son-in-law, obtained work in Mendon south of Kalamazoo, where I also went to work later on. James and his family resided at Mendon for a year and I worked with him nearly all that year. James found work in Dewing and Son's Shop at Kalamazoo, then manufacturing blinds, in which he is foreman at present. A couple of months later I began to work there and stayed until 1879.

In the winter of 1878-89 Berend J. Veneklaasen and wife of Zeeland visited us. They came to see Ralph, their son, who had been with us some three winters while attending business school. Not long after he married our daughter Nellie. James our youngest son, was then a clerk in L. Clark's Dry Goods Store. James showed Veneklaasen through the store, and Veneklasen remarked, "James, we need such a store in Zeeland; you are the right man to start it and you will prosper." James favored this idea and proposed mortgaging our home. I argued we had no capital. At last I yielded. From Den Bleyker we borrowed $ 700 on our property and in April 1879 moved to Zeeland, but could not occupy the store before May. We paid $ 100 rent and did very well the first year. Next year the owner of the store building, J. den Herder, wanted us to make him a partner as a condition of renewing the lease. We refused, and he demanded $ 150 for another year. Before the year ended we resolved to build a store, bought a lot from Keppel, borrowed from Mr. Larabee of Boston [representing the house James chiefly dealt with] and, because our building was not ready, we got an extension of our lease for half a year, but Den Herder demanded $ 100 for that half year.

In 1886, May 3, James suddenly died after a brief illness, leaving his wife and two children, the oldest two years, the youngest only a few months. James was twenty-seven the day before his death. He was an earnest Christian and died in the enjoyment of a blessed hope. This loss was a shock and great sorrow to us all.

We now are spending our last years in Zeeland enjoying life. Mary [Mrs. William de Pree] and Nellie [Mrs. R. Veneklaasen] do all in their power to make our life pleasant. Here ends my history, but I must yet record a severe loss. On August 29, 1886 our eldest daughter Jane, wife of James van Brooke died after an illness of three days, leaving her husband, a son John and a daughter Mamie. She had for years led a consecrated Christian life.

I omitted a story of my father's death. While our ship lay at Hellevoetsluis till July 7, 1849, father died, and we did not learn of his departure till January 1850. Only ten days after our farewells he passed away. It may have been best for us that we did not know, for had we heard, we might never have reached the United States.

I visited Europe in 1886, and was given some information by Rev. De Waal, then eighty and blind, residing at Middleburg. He was the pastor of our family and relatives in Biervliet in 1849, and related to me the following, "Your grandfather, William Moerdyke was a bosom friend. He was an able, intelligent and noble man. He had a great soul. He was always in his place at church. The Sunday after your family left Biervliet he sat in his usual place with bowed head in sadness. From the church he went home and to his bed, and on Thursday died of a broken heart, sorrowing over the loss of his son, your father and of his family." De Waal was delighted to meet me, and pleased that I made a special trip from Flushing to make his acquaintance and convey the greetings of my parents. Father had requested that I find him if possible.

I am now seventy-two years of age. The Lord has cared for us and will continue His loving care.

When we settled in Kalamazoo in 1850 our church had no minister but enjoyed monthly supplies of the pulpit by Van Raalte, Van der Meulen, Ypma and Bolks. There was a great revival in 1853 or 1854. Van der Meulen preached almost every evening, and we had prayer meetings. At this time I became a believer unto salvation. Later we benefited greatly by the labors of our pastors, Wynand Gardenier and H. G. Klijn. Now I recall father's offer to educate me for the ministry and wish

I had become a minister, for my love and zeal for Christ and His cause were great. I prayed that the Lord too would use my sons for His work and incline them to the ministry. During the pastorate of Klijn, there was a revival and many were brought to Christ and confessed their faith, among whom my sons. There were numerous prayer meetings.

When news of my sons' decision reached the Colony, the Rev. Pieter J. Oggel came to Kalamazoo, invited the boys to the parsonage and asked if they would like to attend the Academy at Holland. They expressed their willingness. Oggel asked if I was willing to send my sons to school. I answered, "Yes, but then I am left alone to earn the family support, for William and Peter had been great helpers, earning money in various ways. I would be unable to support them at their studies." Oggel replied that he would confer with the Board at Holland and let us know what could be done. A reply came at about the opening of the fall term, September 1859. Then we received work form Rev. A. C. van Raalte to send the boys, stating that Board would provide for their support. We resolved to send William alone, but Peter was so disappointed that we decided to send both. So they entered on a ten years course of study, graduating and beginning their ministry in June 1869. I rejoiced in this, for my prayer was heard, and am thankful two of my children are preachers of the glorious Gospel.

I am yet well and strong, enjoy life, and purpose by the grace of God to serve Him to the end of my life. I conclude with the words of Psalm 17 [versified in the Psalter of the Reformed Church, and a favorite verse of mine]. "As for me, I shall behold Thy face in righteousness; I shall be satisfied when I awake with Thy likeness."

114. ADRIAAN ZWEMER'S LIFE AND
EMIGRATION TO AMERICA

[Born in Oostkapelle in Zeeland in 1823, Adriaan Zwemer (d. 1898) experienced the hardships caused by the Secession from the Reformed Church in 1834, emigrated with his family to America in 1849, spent a brief time in Rochester, New York, then moved to Michigan where he and his family were influential in the early history of the Michigan Kolonie. The following account is taken from *Genealogy and History of the Zwemer-Boon Family Recorded for his Children* by *Adrian Zwemer* (Harrisburg, Pa., 1932). An important part of this article written in Dutch originally appeared in *De Grondwet*, June 10, 1913, under the title *De Reis naar America*.]

Everything was ready for our departure from Middelburg and the last stragglers stepped on board just as the boat put off. Soon we were out of the city along the canal and in the three-mile harbor. Then we rounded the island and the mouths of the Schelde, the Maas, and the Rhine. We arrived at Rotterdam where our goods and all passengers were transferred to the ocean ship *Leyla*.

On the way from Middelburg to Rotterdam I wrote a poem entitled "Farewell". It is found on page 179 of my book *Hartestemming en Leering*. When we arrived on board they were still busy carpentering, preparing the rude bedsteads for the steerage passengers. Soon we were ready to place our baggage and spread our blankets. We were allowed to eat and sleep on board, but you can imagine that the carpenters preferred to have us, especially the invalid wife of the clergyman, out of the way. The reason was that by some strange misunderstanding or miscalculation, we had arrived ten days before the sailing date! This gave us opportunity to see Rotterdam, and to attend church on Sunday. Most of us considered it a privilege to have so long a time at Rotterdam. We were weary with the burden of departure; the constant visits of friends and relatives and especially the prolonged visits of those who only came to ask questions and pressed on us their advice robbed us of every bit of liberty because they felt that they owed us a farewell visit, so that they might relate to one and all their experiences with those who were leaving the country.

The ten days in Rotterdam were a Passover visit, before the wilderness of the sea. The minister's wife went out with mother every day to old acquaintances and I went with [Hendrik Geert] Klyn for longer walks around about the city. Klyn's brother from The Hague paid him a visit at one of the hotels. He was a man-of-the-world with no religious convictions. I remember his words now: "Brother, I have come to say good-bye to you as man to man, and I do not want to hear anything about our never seeing each other again, and no religious talk; I have just come to shake hands and be off." He ordered wine, cake, and tobacco and prepared his pipe alone; spoke of the storms ahead of us, told us to have brave hearts and hoped that the dry climate of America might benefit his brother's invalid wife. "But," said he, "there are so many women who are invalids." Looking at his watch he said "It's time for me to go, brother – good-bye, Hendrik, – good-bye all of you." And so the two brothers parted. On the fifth or sixth of July 1849 everything was ready and we went on board. Everything, included our personal baggage in boxes and bundles and also enough food and clothing for sixty days, if need be. A committee had been appointed and their restrictions regarding food supply were strictly followed. A sort of cabin and kitchen had been arranged on the poop deck where the immigrants cooked their food and every day they received an allowance of firewood; water was handed out to each passenger by measure. By patiently waiting and standing in line, everybody received his or her share, and the work in the kitchen went forward, but the water supply was very meager, and everyone carefully husbanded their store. There were one hundred and twenty-eight Hollanders in our party, all from the province of Zeeland, and fifty Germans. Two of the sailors were Hollanders and the captain was said to have understood Dutch. One of the cabin passengers had lived in America and spoke Dutch, German, and English. Just as we were leaving the harbor, Mr. Lankester climbed on the roof of the poop deck in order to see how the ship left its moorings. A steam tug was to tow us through the river to the outer harbor and there we remained from Sunday at three o'clock until Monday two o'clock at anchor. Everyone was on deck watching the loosening of the cables and the gradual departure of the ship. Suddenly a cry was raised by those on the steam tug and the sailors on our ship. The reason was that one of the cables was crossing the roof of the poop deck where Lankester stood. Many cried, "jump off, jump off", but before he understood what they desired him to do, the cable caught him and threw him on the deck eight feet below, on his back. He was unconscious from the shock and was carried below, but by the care of the ship's doctor was able to be on deck again in a few days. The wife of Dominie Klyn suffered from nervous breakdown even before we started on the journey. The ship's doctor thought that she was too weak to cross the Atlantic and she spent thirty-eight days, the entire journey, in her berth. Mother took care of her day and night and I was, as it were, the personal servant of Klyn, as well as guardian of his two lively boys. The first four weeks of the journey we had a calm sea and scarcely any suffering from seasickness. Trouble, however, arose among the German passengers at the other end of the ship. There were loud words followed by blows. When the captain heard of the difficulty he sent the helmsman and one of the cabin passengers who could speak their language together with some of the sailors, to make an investigation. The cause of the trouble was that thirty German dollars had been stolen, and one man was accused of the theft. He said, "I have taken nothing," and refused to have his baggage opened for a search. The helmsman, however, bade the sailors bring his chest out of the hold. The man refused to give up the key until they brought an axe. When the chest was opened they found the money at the very bottom wrapped in some socks. The whole amount was discovered. The man said it was his own money and wept, but the captain placed him in confinement for the rest of the voyage. He then confessed his theft. They bound his hands and feet and placed him on a large barrel and above him put the placard "Thief". In this way the man became ashamed and afterwards received his liberty.

During these four weeks of calm weather the sails hung idle for many hours, but we slowly made progress. On Saturday, the 28th of July, there were indications not only of gathering clouds and wind, but the activity of the sailors proved they expected bad weather. When we asked whether storm was brooding, the only answer we received was "a little". Mother was preparing some rice cakes for the invalid, when suddenly a wave dashed over the ship, put out the fire, and carried away the open hearth. Shortly after, all passengers were ordered below. The scattering of the firebrands over the deck almost caused an alarm of fire. The ship continued to toss from side to side on the waves. Altho we were below deck the water leaked in profusely. There was no danger but it was disagreeable. When night came we were forbidden to light the four or five lanterns which were under the poop deck. This was to prevent the danger of fire. Most of the emigrants spent the night in prayer. When morning came the only light we had was through one of the port-holes near the gangway. So much water leaked in through the port holes that on the lee side of the ship in the hold the water stood as high as the lower bunks. Some said the ship was sinking.

The following day Braam and I crawled up the gangway to see what was the significance of a peculiar noise we heard, like a child crying. It turned out that it was the captain's dog which was thrown from side to sight by the violent movement of the ship. The sailors had now tied him fast and he was thoroughly unhappy. We went down the gangway and found, when we came below, that some of the barrels and boxes which had been fastened to spars, had become loose and were rolling and moving about striking the bedposts of the berth. With some difficulty things were fastened again. It was a terrible day, but the following night, toward morning, the wind grew less and some of us found sleep. Even the invalid wife of Mr. Klyn seemed to have suffered no more than the other passengers. Monday morning at eight o'clock we saw light, and breathed air again, for they opened the hold. The helmsman proclaimed that the storm was over; but the sea was still rough. Meanwhile the the sailors were bailing between decks and fastening the luggage. By noon floors of our cabins were dry enough so we could walk on them. A few hours later the captain himself came to inquire after our welfare and that afternoon the male passengers were allowed to come up on deck. The following day there was beautiful sunshine and the wind became favorable.

Because of the theft which had taken place, there was much suspicion and much unrest among the passengers. Our company resolved to ask permission to appoint a watch at night and request that some of the young men should in turn be on guard and that one light be allowed us for the guard. The captain agreed and Klyn and I were appointed the organizing committee and since I had been a soldier, it was proposed that I should be captain of the guard. Sixteen young men were selected and registered by name and number and appointed to the various night watches. Without any difficulty for us, this arrangement gave a sense of security to the women and children and was continued throughout the voyage. The guard was stationed near the gangway between the cabins of the Hollanders and the Germans.

It was easy for us to put up a guard against thieves but not against death. Seven little children of the Dutch emigrants died during the voyage and were buried at sea. Sickness, death, and burial of dear children, these are always the bitterest domestic trials; but burial at sea means increase of sorrow and the cry of mothers when their treasures were consigned to the deep was sometimes too pitiful. Most of the children were between one and three years of age, but one was seven. The funerals were conducted in silence and the usual work on board the ship ceased. The body, properly weighted, lay on a board plank which rested on the bulwarks of the ship, and was held in balance by the sailors. After a short service the plank was lifted and the body slipped into the sea. Besides those already mentioned of our company, there was Elder Lankaster, and a school teacher named [James] Huyssoon, who was married shortly before we set out from Rotterdam. Most of the emigrants were from the province of Zeeland and represented the families of Kotvis, De Pree, Moerdyk, Klyn, and others. Concerning this company the Reverend J. van der Meulen wrote many years later in *De Hope* – "No other ship of emigrants sailed which had so many future ministers of the Gospel as this ship, the *Leyla*." One of them was already in the ministry and seven of those who crossed over served the Gospel later on.

On the thirty-seventh day of the long voyage toward evening a sailor cried from the top mast, "land, land!" Everyone looked out, but we could not see it. However, we lay down to sleep in hope that the voyage would soon be over and the following morning we were sailing along the coasts of Long Island. At ten o'clock the invalid wife of the Dominie was placed in an easy chair, through the kindness of the captain, and carried on deck. Our eyes were refreshed to see a beautiful coast with trees and grass and beautiful homes. It seemed almost that we were on the borders of Paradise. On the suggestion of the doctor, the invalid and mother, who was caring for her, remained on deck for the rest of the voyage. This was also to avoid quarantime, so that she herself might give evidence that she was able to land and was not seriously ill. All other passengers were examined and a bill of health given to our ship. We entered the great seaport of America and landed at the Battery. One of the passengers was required to answer the question whether we carried weapons or dutiable goods. As far as I can remember, all of us could answer in the negative and none of our baggage was examined. It was a strange sensation to leave the ship after thirty-eight days and actually be on *terra firma*. Our boxes and baggage were brought on shore, and there we stood, a group of emigrants surrounded by a miscellaneous collection of personal possessions, resembling a company of Franciscan monks. Pilgrims and strangers, we scarcely knew what to do, but kept saying to each other, "this is a great country; now we are in America."

Dominie Klyn, Mr. Lankester, and Mr. Kotvis had the address of a Mr. D'Ooge who had opened an office to help emigrants on their way. A servant of D'Ooge's came to the ship to welcome us even before we had landed. A carriage was hired in which Klyn, the *juffrouw* [colloquial Dutch for the wife of a pastor], mother and Kotvis and Lankester were taken to D'Ooge's home.

I was left on board ship to guard our goods; these were being unloaded and I had to look after them so that they would not be confused with those of the Germans. Their goods were destined for Pennsylvania, ours for Michigan. The unloading and the placing went forward in so orderly a fashion that there seemed no need of my keeping watch.

In Rotterdam I had bought a little English hymn book at the old book market. I had started reading these hymns in order to learn the language. As far as I could make out they were more evangelical and expressive of devotion than the evangelical hymns were in use at that time in the churches of the Netherlands. However, my feelings in the matter were doubtless based more on preference than on knowledge.

While I was sitting on a chest reading this book a woman glanced over my shoulder and doubtless thought the book was a Catholic litany. From her rapid and earnest conversation I gathered that she was praising the book and the reader. I asked her as well as I could if she knew and loved the Lord Jesus. Vigorously she threw open her cloak and showed me a fairly large crucifix hanging on a chain. I had seen these crosses worn in Maastricht at least a thousand times. Now I recognized the church to which the woman belonged as well as her religion. I told her that we must have Christ in our hearts and not only on the outside. At that she smote her breast with satisfaction. Again I said that our heart must be made new – that Christ must be in our heart, not only on the outside. The woman now understood to what church I belonged, for her only answer was "Protestant", and she turned away from me as quickly as if I had chased her away. This was my first sermon in America.

The committee aforementioned had made an arrangement that we be carried with our baggage to Albany on a river boat and from there to Buffalo on a canal boat, for seven or eight dollars per adult. [This amount is my guess; it was not recorded.] Moreover D'Ooge's clerk, Mr. Hofma, who had formerly served as a member of Klyn's consistory in Netherlands, would travel with us as adviser and interpreter. That afternoon I also went to D'Ooge's home. There, for the first time, I saw a large map of the United States with all the states, rivers and places marked on it, – among them the forests in western Michigan where our former pastor Dominie van der Meulen lived with his people and other Hollanders. Indeed it made us feel proud to become citizens of such a land!

On the map they pointed out the way that we must travel, up the Hudson River by steamboat, along the canal to Buffalo, and then the journey through the Lakes to Detroit or Milwaukee. The fare for this long journey seemed so little that we all rejoiced. On the way across, the more I had thought of the coming journey over land and the possible mishaps, the more I had valued the few dollars left us as our little capital with which to make a beginning in a strange land. The contract was closed and the sum paid by the representatives, Lankester and Kotvis. Concerning the unloading which I had been left to look after, D'Ooge said we did not have to trouble ourselves as the men could do that better than we could. This was indeed so.

It was now time for the boat so we rode to the dock. Our fellow passengers were already there waiting for the arrival of Lankester and Kotvis. We got on the boat, Hofma with us. A large open space on an almost entirely enclosed deck was assigned us. They gave us to understand that we must spend the night there. Hofma disappeared from sight and we could find him nowhere. We all ate supper; there was bread, cheese, and smoked-beef enough for all, and I managed to buy a cup of tea for the juffrouw with the help of a kitchen boy, after much asking, running about and waiting. In a place which we thought most suitable Braam and I made a sort of bedstead out of chests, and a bed out of coats and shawls. The juffrouw was helped to bed by mother and other women but she could not lie down. The excitement of the day made her ready to collapse.

Once again some one called a doctor. He asked us if we hadn't money enough to secure a bed for the sick woman. That was not lacking, so a double berth was engaged and paid for. Now we all thought that the dominie would go to bed with the juffrouw. I went along with the dominie to do the interpreting and mother went along to help the juffrouw. A young man showed us the salon and a lady opened the door and motioned us to go in. The dominie wanted to go along into the stateroom but was refused admission and no explanation of the matter could be secured. The juffrouw did not dare to sleep alone and was trembling with weakness. "For two persons," said the maidservant who was helping the juffrouw on one side while mother was on the other, – and the door was locked. We, dominie and I, remained standing in front of the door thinking that mother would come out and the dominie could go in. But soon we were called away and shown to our former place. So mother spent her first night in America in a very fine room. The dominie was displeased. At that time the sleeping quarters of men and women were apart whether or not they were married.

Each sought and found, somewhere, a place to lie down. I was tired and slept restfully between two oak-chests, my first night in America; and though the dominie was somewhat displeased, I rejoiced that mother could sleep in such fine state.

The next morning the men and young people awakened early, at break of day. They went out on deck while the mothers dressed the children. Out on deck we marveled at the beautiful country. We came from a fruitful land yet it is flat as a sheet of water. Except for the sand dunes at the seaside most of us had never seen a hill. Was this the land where we were to live? For the first few weeks the emigrant is only a stranger and a sojourner; it takes some time to feel at home in a strange land. How much farther must we journey? When would we reach Albany? These questions could be answered only by our guide, Hofma. Kotvis sent me to find him but he was nowhere to be found.

When we had almost reached Albany Hofma came to ask politely how Klyn had slept and why he had not gone to the salon for men. Kotvis administered a polite and friendly reproof and asked the reason why he had disappeared just when we so needed his services. The reason he gave was so mysterious that no one understood him and brother Hofma seemed confused.

At the appointed time we reached Albany. Chests and barrels and trunks were set out on the wharf. Everyone looked after his own belongings. Kotvis ordered a couple of young men to set his things apart and so did the others. Soon a number of workmen approached who piled up all the baggage without any regard for name or order, but mixed them all together on a large platform scale in order to weigh them. Hofma was sought and called but not found. I had to ask the reason for the weighing of our goods; it was already paid for, but if we must pay more [which we had never dreamed of] why could not the baggage of each family be weighed separately? I could hardly make them understand this although they seemed to grasp my meaning. The officials, however, had no care for family divisions but concerned themselves only with the sum to be collected for the whole lot.

Four or five of us rushed angrily back to the boat to find Hofma. He was running around and excused himself by reason of his being interested in the activities on the river. He had not thought that the weighing was to be done so soon. The canal boat would not leave before evening. In spite of these excuses we made him come along with us to the scales. There he became interpreter for the officials and told us how much must be paid for the whole amount which could easily be arranged between us. Kotvis said that this charge was not in the agreement with D'Ooge. Hofma answered that that was a misunderstanding; for the small sum paid D'Ooge no one could expect to travel with his goods for a distance of 300 miles. This was undoubtedly true, but the arrangements at the office had been such that the committee had understood that everything was paid for as far as Buffalo.

Some angry words were spoken at this turn of affairs. Hofma looked at his watch. We heard the steam whistle on the boat bound for New York. "I must go," exclaimed Hofma. "God be with you, my dear brother Klyn," and so he left us.

I was sent after him to ask when he would come back to interpret for us and to lead us farther. His answer was "Brother, I knew that you had misunderstood that the fare was the full sum for the trip to Buffalo; no one could travel so far for such a small sum; but I'm not going along to Buffalo. You misunderstood that too, although I had no right to say it; I am only a servant of D'Ooge's and now I must go back immediately to New York. I must go. Farewell, brother!" With these words he stepped on the boat. Klyn stood looking after his friend in astonishment; the day before he had greeted him on the street with kisses and with tears.

In the afternoon we were taken over to the canal boat. The baggage and chests were stowed away in the hold; the men sat on top, the women sought a place below between the baggage. Again we made a sort of bedstead for the juffrouw, between the chests. There she spent the night groaning, all the way to Troy, and then declared that she couldn't live any longer if she had to travel further in that fashion.

Meanwhile Lankester had decided to travel by train as far as Buffalo. He tried to persuade Klyn to do the same but though the dominie generally had an inclination to help his feeble wife he didn't feel that he could stand the extra expense of taking us both along as the canal fare was already paid. If we had traveled with Lankester to Buffalo, as mother, and I really wished to do, we should not have seen Rochester, and our history would possibly have taken another turn.

Klyn had the next best sleeping place that night. About twenty-five persons were aboard the canal boat. The old people and the children first found a place below; the little ones crept between the chests and the older ones lay on top. There were thirteen adults left standing on the deck, when all the places were taken. We were still at Albany when it grew dark. Before the boat left shore the captain motioned to us to lie down. There were two groups; seven young men and six young women, among them, mother. The captain himself secured two sailcloths and spread them over us. We all slept well.

The following morning we reached Troy, seven miles from Albany. The boat lay at dock so there seemed no need for haste. Mr. De Naaye also was on board. He had heard the juffrouw groaning and said, "This won't do! If no other arrangement can be made I will go back to Albany and take the train as Lankester did yesterday. By now he must be in Buffalo." Klyn could not be persuaded to adopt this plan. I had to go to the captain to tell him about the weak state of the juffrouw and to ask his advice. The friendly man said that his boat was not made for passengers, only for freight, but that perhaps we could hire a cabin suited for eight or ten persons at a moderate price. However, we had to make haste. The captain himself went to see about it. A bargain was made and we were transferred to a boat which came alongside.

There was a double cabin on the upper deck. On both sides were two double beds one above the other – eight beds in all – just as many as there were in the party. An armchair was brought in for the juffrouw; the rest of us had camp stools, while the two boys sat on little boxes. We were a party of eight; De Naaye and his wife, the dominie and the juffrouw, and their two sons, besides mother and myself.

The juffrouw grew stronger from sheer happiness. The following day when the boat stopped at a village the dominie noticed a bakery; after being assured that the boat would remain for a half hour I went out to buy some fresh bread and cakes. The dominie gave me a ten guilder gold piece; the captain changed it for four dollars, and from this fund I had to buy daily whatever mother thought suitable for the juffrouw, if it was approved by her.

This journey through the beautiful Mohawk valley, during which the juffrouw often sat out on the deck in her armchair, gave us fresh hope and promoted the health of this really tender and godly woman. From a tree along the way I cut off a branch with twigs which I made into a frame for a fan. Mother covered it with cloth and the present was accepted as if it were a princely gift.

Thus we traveled by canal boat to Buffalo; from that point our journey would lie by way of the Lakes to Michigan. Letters written by earlier emigrants to that locality, some of which had been read in church, gave us the impression that the western part of Michigan was like another Canaan: a land full of pious people and so far in the western part of the world that evil had not yet penetrated there; while Graafschap, where Klyn had been called and where the dominie knew several good people, was to be the end of our journey and the hope of our longing hearts. Yet God had destined another dwelling place for us. We did not know it. At present we were journeying to Rochester. Five years later we reached the colony and twenty-seven years later we went to Graafschap.

We stopped at Rochester just after noon. Several men were standing about watching the unhitching of the tired horses. Our dock was in front of a canal-hotel and the town lay before us. Klyn said: "In this town lives Mr. Wykhuisen, but where can we find him?" A man who was standing at the side of the canal said, "I can tell you that. Are you Dominie Klyn? Wykhuisen said that Klyn was going west with some of his church people and that they would have to travel this way." At that the dominie made himself known to the man and he showed us the neighborhood in which Wykhuisen's house was located.

When we learned that the boat would stay at dock for a short hour more, we went to visit Wykhuisen. His only word of advice was that we should not go west but remain in Rochester. We could go there later if we so desired.

Some obscure influence made us decide, in that short time, to change our plans for the future. Our aim had been this: shut off from the restless world, in the woods of Michigan to help in the upbuilding of a colony where the kingdom of God was valued above the affairs of the world, and where there was a livelihood to be won by honest labor. That was the expressed aim of the first leaders of the emigration; that was the original plan, and now we were to live in a city!

We hastened back to the boat to take leave of the very much astonished juffrouw and to tell the captain of our plan and to ask him if the two chests with our goods could not be sent back from Buffalo to Rochester. With only a little bundle in our hands we stepped off the boat. The boat receded toward the west and we turned back to the home of Wykhuisen scarcely knowing *why* and, still less, *to what end* we had so suddenly changed our original plan. God alone knew both.

If I remember correctly it was the 18th day of August 1849 when we went to the home of Wykhuisen. That was the beginning of our residence in America. We had landed in New York about a week earlier. We remained with the Wykhuisens until Monday, the 24th day of September. The day before that we were married "in church" by Rev. A. B. Veenhuizen; this church was a hired room on Hen Street, a by-street of State-Street, and was often used for public meetings. It seated an audience of about two hundred or more. On Sundays it was rented for the purpose of Dutch services by Veenhuizen. That was why the building was named "Our Church" by the Hollanders.

For many days after our decision to stay in Rochester we were not at peace with ourselves. We had abandoned a plan which had slowly come to a head through many months of prayerful preparation, and, as we believed, with God's approval and the knowledge of the whole company of travelers, so that when Klyn would reach the rest of the company at Buffalo it would be considered a break in the family, as we were numbered with them. Then how could we explain to our families in the Netherlands that we had followed Providence and not our own whim? We both felt this way, yet dared not tell each other our misgivings. Moreover we were at the home of acquaintances but we did not feel at home with them. That was the reason for our haste to be married and our desire for a home of our own. Yet it was only a beginning of a home, for our means for this venture were very slim.

There was one more trial in store. In the Netherlands I had ordered our village carpenter to make two chests, one for each of us. All our clothes, books, and papers, besides a good bed and bedding together with a few little household articles, were packed in them. Now these chests were on their way with the others from Albany to Buffalo, without further address. We dared not tell each other how we feared they had been lost. The captain of the boat on which we had taken passage had indeed promised to look after them, but rash prophets in Rochester said, "They will go to Michigan and the people there are far too poor to send them back." If ever we prayed in earnest for worldly goods, it was then.

We had thought that our journey from the Netherlands would lead to the Colony [Kolonie] in America, a name which, in the Netherlands at that time, was in the same class as the honored Brotherhood of the Moravians. The leaders of our company of emigrants, such as Kotvis and others, had no other conception and spoke of nothing else. In an earnest discussion on the way over, about the aim of "The Emigration Movement under the Afgescheiden Church" [in truth they had opened the door of emigration for the Hollanders and ten thousand had gone in] Kotvis said: "The time has come when the faithful of God's people must dwell in the waste places of the earth"; and at still another time; "If any desire to amass worldly goods or strive for pleasure, God will bring to naught all the plans of men."

In Rochester we were not in a Brotherhood; the great majority of the people were not acquainted with prayer-life. The church people were mostly members from the State Church and the barren church corner of Zeeuwsch Vlaanderen, so many did not know the teachings of the Gospel. We felt as if we were outside of our sphere, in the church as well as in the home of Wykhuisen.

After three weeks' waiting, we learned that God had given us back the two chests, our entire worldly store [for we thought we saw God's hand in it], and that is why we have kept these chests so many years. When the goods were again in our hands we said that it was time for us to be married although we were advised against it as we had anticipated. People said, "How can you keep house without household goods?" and "For three months in winter there is no work obtainable except some wood to be cut and split."

These reasons had made us hesitate before but now led to a legitimate though unusual procedure. Friday, the 14th day of September, the consistory of the church was to meet. Our certificates had not arrived although Klyn had promised to send them. I went to the consistory meeting and told them how our plans had been changed, that we were yet strangers here, and asked if they would think us rash and improvident if we would marry at this time.

Veenhuizen asked one of the elders present to answer my question. This brother said, "We learned the conditions of your change of plan some time ago, and know what is your purpose. Now it's best for you that the dominie announce your intended marriage day after tomorrow, and the following Sunday he can marry you."

And that is what happened. On the 23rd day of September 1849 we were united in marriage. The following Monday we went to our own hired dwelling, an upstairs backroom in the home of Mr. Eichhorn, a tailor, on Goodman Street. There we unpacked our two chests and were more thankful over the returned property than we had ever been before. We had to pay five dollars for storage and transportation.

Now we began to keep house. We set up one of the chests which was to serve as a clothespress in a convenient corner of the little room, four feet from the wall. Between the chest and the wall our bed was spread on the floor. Our books were sorted and arranged in four low piles, and on these the other chest was set to serve as a table. The following day we bought a small new stove, some kitchen utensils, three chairs, a wash-tub, and a lamp, and with the cups, plates, and dishes brought from Netherlands we could keep house nicely.

Mother knew how to do that very economically. We had work and wages the whole winter long. We bought what need required and still had something to put away for future use, for there might be a time in midwinter when there would be no work, as the prophets of doom had warned us. Mother had her heart set on a house clock. The 4th of March we bought one for four dollars. This was considered an unwarranted extravagance by our thrifty neighbors. Almost all the Hollanders had clocks of this kind but they cost only two dollars, and since ours was a little more fancy it was considered a mark of pride by the neighbors. I do not write this for public perusal. The criticism hurt us more than you can now understand.

Yet mother came to feel at home in Rochester, and why not? There she became the mother of the first four of our dear children, and that makes any place a home for a mother. I began to feel at home, too, in city and later in church work, but never without blaming myself for changing our plans, although I still believed they met God's approval.

I did tailor's work until early in the spring of 1851; then I began to work for a Dutch painter, and later for Mr. Lesley who had me work with his English paper hanger as his assistant. Very soon I became efficient enough to do it alone, and after that paper hanging and inside work became my sole occupation, for I always disliked climbing up on high ladders. The last two years that I worked for Mr. Lesley he did not have a foreman. In the winter of 1853-54 his foreman had been the means of his losing a profitable job at the round house, repair place of the railway company.

During the owner's absence from the office in his shop he always left someone to take orders for work. This job was given to me. I always had the keys of the shop with me. I had to open the shop in the morning and close it in the evening. Most of the time my work was in the shop where there was nothing locked from me, except my employer's small office.

The church at Rochester belonged to the Presbyterian denomination. Her history had led to this. Just as in Albany, the emigrants of 1846-48 had remained here instead of moving farther west. Some years earlier, emigrants from Zeeuwsch Vlaanderen had settled in western New York state and had become prosperous. These were the first of the Holland folk who went now to one, then to another eastern state until they had reached quite a considerable number. Dominie Cheesman of the Presbyterian Church in Rochester could speak Dutch and he began work among the Hollanders. Accordingly they were organized into a church belonging to the Presbyterian fellowship in Rochester. The exact date is not known to me. This dominie cared for the little flock and advised them to speedily call a minister. Their first minister was Veenhuizen who had been in that position for about a year or longer when we arrived.

After a couple of months' residence in Rochester our letters of church membership arrived and these we laid before the consistory. Our two oldest children are Presbyterians by birth and baptism.

Early in the spring of 1851 Veenhuizen moved to Pultneyville. In 1851 a division occurred over the unconstitutional expulsion of a quarrelsome elder which led to trouble. Some assented to the action; others deemed the way in which he had been expelled had not been according to church regulations. These last named were dropped from membership without any trial. Rev. A. K. Kasse informed this group of the existence of the Reformed Church in the East and in the state of New York and they decided to apply for admission to the Classis of Geneva. The classis sent us Mr. Whitbeck who could speak Dutch, together with Kasse of Williamsburg who, with the Hollanders then resident there, belonged to this classis.

Dominie Whitbeck asked particularly about the doctrine of the state church of Holland, and wished to have one of us write an exposition of the doctrine of Election. Mr. de Jong and Mr. Van Doren insisted that I should write it. I told Whitbeck that we, who did not belong to the State Church of Netherlands, heartily believed and acknowledged the doctrine just as it was found in the Formula of the Confession, and that we could not express it in better language than that form which was in the aforementioned confession.

He kept insisting however, until finally I wrote it all out, under his eyes. It was read aloud and recognized by Kasse, by De Jong, and by Van Doren as the expression of our belief concerning this doctrine. Whitbeck translated my writing into English and read it for us in order to find out if that were exactly the meaning. A month later Dominie Whitbeck came to visit us again and we were organized into a church.

In the fall of 1852, after Veenhuizen had left, the consistory of the Presbyterian Dutch Church came to make a proposition to join us. In January of 1853, after some objection from those who had no desire for the meddling of the ministers of the western colony with our church affairs, I was permitted at last to ask Dominie van der Meulen of Zeeland, Michigan, to come to visit us in order to lead the Holland people in Rochester in this aforementioned union.

He came, preached for three Sundays, and wisely and dutifully corrected, admonished and encouraged us. He did not aim to make a new organization but to mend the breaks and strengthen the walls. The grateful church gave Van der Meulen a new suit of clothes and a collection, which was not counted, but was a considerable sum. To the church at Zeeland was sent, from private contributions, a silverplated communion set in recognition of the service to which they had lent their minister. The suit of clothes was also bought from private contributions, and his traveling expenses were paid besides.

By this time Rochester had quite a large congregation belonging to the Eastern branch of the Dutch Reformed Church. I had previously been made an elder and remained so, just as all others kept their places in the consistory. I was asked to give notification of these affairs in a letter to the Presbytery of Rochester.

Van der Meulen had said at the time of the organization that "Zwemer must teach the catechism class for adults." I taught all the catechism classes as long as we lived there. I also conducted burial services, and was almost always one of the two delegates to the Classis of Geneva, so becoming familiar with the affairs of the Dutch Reformed Church and with the ministers of our Holland Church and its consistory.

In June of 1854 Van Raalte and Van der Meulen reached Rochester on their way home from General Synod. Van der Meulen went on, but Van Raalte remained for a few days. He was lodged at Elder De Jong's home. One day he came to our house and said that I should write to the Rev. George J. van Nest, our Stated Clerk. To the question why I should write his answer was, "About your going to New Brunswick to study for the ministry." He asked me further what I thought about the plan. A long conversation followed and, after prayer, he departed.

A week later Van Nest came to our home and advised me to go as a delegate of our church to a special gathering of the classis of Buffalo which was to be held in the middle of July. At that time he hoped to obtain a quorum of Dutch-speaking ministers and elders in order to receive Dominie [Willem Coenraad] Wust from the "Church under the Cross" in the Netherlands, and if everything were satisfactory to install him. The Classis could then examine me at the same time, in accordance with the rules of the Synod, for the purpose of recommending me for aid in my studies. He thought that the Classis could easily find the means for this.

Wust was received as a minister from the "Church under the Cross" in the Netherlands. The Classis voted unanimously for my recommendation.

Thus matters stood until the fall Session when there was much discussion about means, but no other decision made than that they should inquire from the churches whether they were willing to aid me with $ 300 a year during my period of study. The following spring the matter would be concluded. Van Nest wrote me: "Be sure to come; your presence will help matters for us, for there may be some difficulty."

I was appointed delegate together with Elder de Jong. He told me on the day before the meeting that he was not going. I started out alone. When I reached his house he called me in; he was going along after all; he had still to dress. For that reason we were late and had to wait for the afternoon train. We could still make connection with the boat and be at Watkins overnight. From there an early morning train ride of 16 miles would take us to Ithaca where the Classis was meeting. A heavy thunderstorm and driving rain held us up on the way and we had to wait over in a hotel for a couple of hours.

It was twelve o'clock when we reached the church. The president, seeing us come in, said, "Here are our Dutch brethren; we will now have recess until two o'clock." A motion was made to read the minutes and adjourn the classis. In the afternoon the classis named a committee, with Rev. Van Nest as chairman, to acquaint me with the decision of the morning. This was that the classis cherished all good hopes and wishes for me, yet they had never done this before and could not consent to lay a burden of about $ 300 on the churches. Van Nest was very much disappointed over this decision of the classis and had fought it but could not win his way. If he had been able to do so the decision would have been more favorable. The president asked how I felt about this decision; my answer was: "I have prayed, but never sought to go into the ministry in any other way than through the door which God would open to me." The president gave his approval of this answer and with good wishes and friendly words he declared. "This affair has now been disposed of."

The disappointment was keen. All the Hollanders in Rochester knew of the matter and considered my going to study as a certainty. Mother felt very badly about it; talkative people came to gossip with her, and this almost caused her alienation from the city and from the house, our house, where she had felt so much at home. All that I could say was, "Wait on God." On the dunes of Walcheren's shores had been my place of withdrawal and wrestling in prayer. That I might be led into the ministry, in the footsteps of Van der Meulen, was the constant burden of that prayer.

While I was still living with my brother I held a weekly catechism class with his children. The struggle in my heart over this matter was very pressing at the time. One day when I had asked Borstius' question "How old was Jesus when he began to preach?" the answer came: "thirty years." Then it seemed as if a voice in my heart said, "And you must wait as long."

On my way home after the class that first Friday evening after my return my thoughts were led in this direction: "Tomorrow is your thirtieth birthday and you have begun to preach." Some time later I told this to Mother and her sensible answer was, "We can't count on wandering thoughts." Yet it left some impression on her. In the Netherlands, she had known, before I did, about the Classis of Zeeland recommending me for study. She had told me of the plan at the time as a reason for staying in the Netherlands, and now I told her of my first class. For that reason my thirtieth birthday made a great impression on her although she appeared not to make much of it. I continued holding the catechism classes and serving as elder in Rochester until we moved to Holland, Michigan. Dominie Van Vleck was superintendent of the Sunday School there and he gave me one of the student classes to teach.

The next fall our church was not represented at Classis. The reason I do not recall, but I am sure it was not on account of the Classis' refusal to support me. Some weeks later a special meeting of Classis was called to install a minister. Van Nest wrote me: "Do not fail to go to this meeting of Classis as a delegate. I've received a letter from Van Raalte saying that they wish you as a student in the Holland Academy in Michigan; but you must have a recommendation from this classis, supported by the Board of Education."

So I attended Classis. I had no part in the service of installation but after the sermon and before the benediction Van Nest, as stated clerk of the classis, announced that as there was still a bit of business to be transacted he would present the matter now. He knew that after the benediction the people would want to welcome their minister and this would hinder the work of the classis. The matter yet to be treated was very fitting to this occasion because a brother was about to take the first step leading to the ministry. The brother was asked to rise and to bring his circumstances to the attention of the classis.

At that time I always spoke English in my daily work, so it was more familiar to me then than now, and I had no fear on that score; but I did wonder what to say about the matter before such a large church ful of people. I stood up and, after a short introduction, proceeded as follows: Speaking on this occasion and about my own affairs was somewhat of an undertaking for me. Yet it was not too difficult, for I had nothing to say beyond the expression of the desire of my heart, and my part in trying to obtain this desire. In a few words I told how, formerly, in the Netherlands, a door had been half opened for me to go in, that here again there had been indications that had reawakened in me this desire, but that both in the land of my birth and here in America lack of means had closed the door. Perhaps this hope could be realized by the recommendation of classis.

Van Nest said, in addition, that the desire for the ministry had indeed come from the heart, but the request for help had come from others. He read a few lines from Van Raalte's letter and then made the proposition that Mr. Z. be recommended to the Holland Academy for study leading to the ministry, which recommendation from the classis should be approved by the Board of Education.

The Classis of Geneva voted a unanimous "Yes". Several members of the church had voted with them. The newly installed minister noticed this and said, "As the minister of this church and also as a member of the classis I ask for the approval of my church as well in regard to this brother." The church again rang with "Yes." Then the people welcomed their pastor and led him to the parsonage. I went to my lodging to rest and to sleep. The next day I journeyed home. Now I had the recommendation of the classis.

I went back to my daily work in the shop; the Board had yet to give me permission to be received in Holland, Michigan. So again we were bothered by questioners whom we could not answer. I wrote to Van Raalte about the action of Classis, but the recommendation would be of no use as long as the Board did not lend its promise of support. Of that there was no sign nor notice. "Patience maketh perfect," says James.

Early in November 1855 the General Synod met at New York to decide: "Whether the Classis of North Carolina, with nine churches, all of them slave-holding, could remain in the fellowship of our church in that condition." Van Nest and Dominie See of Buffalo were going to attend. Van Nest wrote me: "Get ready to go to New Brunswick and back. The professors there are ready to see you, and if everything is favorable will give you a recommendation to the Board of Education. Should this be obtained you must go as soon as possible with your family to Holland, Michigan, and once there Van Raalte will tell you what to do further. Take the 9 o'clock morning train [I've forgotten the date] to New York City; you will find Mr. See of Buffalo on board, and I will board the train at Geneva. Then we can talk matters over together."

These plans all worked out as suggested. From New York City I traveled on to New Brunswick, and was announced to one of the professors by a janitor. Dominie [Samuel A.]van Vranken and three other Professors spoke to me and asked the reason for my having waited so long with my studies. The reason lay in the act of Providence which had not opened the way earlier. Their decision was to recommend me for help although they did not know whether the Board could do this for the school in Michigan.

Van Vranken asked me to stay for dinner and to talk Dutch with him. This dinner and conversation made me feel like Paul: "I took courage." They gave me a recommendation to Dr. [Mancius S.] Hutton, Secretary of the Board of Education.

Late in the evening I reached New York. I knew the address of the church where the Synod was meeting and asked the way from a policeman. I found the church on 23rd Street and went in. The church was more than full; how could I find Van Nest? He promised to take me with him to his lodging. I climbed to the gallery and as quietly as possible walked to the end above the pulpit. From that point I looked over pew after pew, and found Van Nest in the thirteenth pew from the back. Quietly I went downstairs and in a pause between the speakers I took my place beside him.

That night I stayed with him in his lodgings. The following morning Van Nest went with me to Hutton, and the help of the Board was promised to the amount of $150. The decision of the professors at New Brunswick was that I should study for four years at Holland, Michigan, and then, with a dispensation from the Synod, study theology for three years at New Brunswick.

Then I went home. There I found a letter from Van Raalte saying that I must make haste to come. When I told Mother about the recommendation from the Board she said, "Now God has opened the way and we must make haste to go."

And we did make haste. We sold what we thought was not necessary and packed the rest. Our journey was prosperous, although Mother had not been well for some time. Some weeks later when we had to go to Dr. March for advice he said that mother had become anaemic, and talkative women told us that the doctor meant that she had consumption. Sometimes mother would say, "I'll never hear you preach." My over-whelmed heart often spoke more to me than my lips. Yet we could not but believe: "God has spoken in His holiness and He will not forget His promises." We reached Holland late in the evening. The driver who took us from Allegan to Holland did not know where Van Raalte's home was so we had him take us to the only hotel in the town where we might spend the night.

I went directly to look up Van Raalte who gave me a letter of intro-duction to Labots, who was working in [Alderd] Plugger's store. When I reached the store Deacon Te Roller was also there and we were taken to the home of Mr. Kroes. They were holding an evening meeting there and were about to close with prayer. Brother Kroes asked me to do this, with the remark that we should be feeling grateful for our safe arrival after the fatiguing journey. This I did and speedily we were shown a place of rest.

As there was no house in all of Holland for rent at that time we were cared for at the home of Mr. Kroes for three weeks. The friendship and conversation of the kind, openhearted elder then enjoyed, is gratefully recognized and has never been forgotten. After three weeks we were lodged in a house of Mr. Jonker which was situated in the depression north of Van Raalte's dwelling, on the way to Zeeland.

The very first Monday after our arrival I started school. A Latin grammar was my first book and "Parts of Speech with Accidents of the Noun" was my first lesson. There was nothing new for me in this, other than the nomenclature in the English language. Later lessons in Latin and Greek were more difficult; and though the English and Dutch language study were less strange yet they were difficult enough, too. In my younger school-days a lesson was never too hard for me, but now I had grown older and studying was more difficult. In this respect as well, I was as one born out of due season.

Our income was very small, about $ 4.50 a week. Mother was often ill and our family was growing. We lived through trying days in those years of study. Mother's faith and courage were always stronger than mine....

Near this house of Jonker's were ten acres of land. They had not been cultivated for a few years; they were wild as a sandy moor, and barren as only sandy soil can be, yet I wanted to plant it early in the spring. Dominie [John] van Vleck was not in favor of this plan but Van Raalte agreed to it. Neighbors in the vicinity ploughed and harrowed the land, in order to help me. Van Raalte, Elder Broek and my neighbor Van Putten must be thanked for this. A good piece of the land I myself planted with potatoes and corn. Van Putten sowed several acres in oats, of which he promised to purchase the produce. He advised me to sow a piece of land of about an acre and a half in buckwheat for my own use. Student Broek [now Rev. Dirk Broek] helped me prepare the land for the buckwheat. Buckwheat seed must be sowed with an open hand, otherwise the seed falls in streaks. The good student Broek was very willing to help me, but though he was a farmer's son and I was not familiar with farm work it was noticeable that I was more handy than he was. So I myself did the planting in the late spring.

At first everything grew well enough, but a cold, dry spring dried up the oats and it was choked with weeds. The seed corn had been bought in a store and did not come up and the second planting grew to a height of two feet and then disappeared in the weeds. Of the potatoes I obtained about twenty bushels of small, second-rate kind. The last sowing of buckwheat grew very fast in the late summer season which was warm and damp. At the time of blossoming it was luxuriant. People on the way to church would look over the field and say that this would make a good crop for the poor student. In August came heavy frosts, and the blooming plants blackened and were laid low.

Our hearts were troubled and we asked, "Why does all this happen?" Van der Meulen said, "A student must not, and can not do farming. He must get his support in some other way."

In Rochester we had never been dependent on any one but ourselves; moreover we had our own house and garden and could do something for the poor besides. Truly in our case, too, "Straight was the gate and narrow was the way" for us to enter the ministry.

Late in the fall of 1856 we could rent a house from Mr. Nagelkerk. We lived there through the bitter winter that followed. Mother remained sickly. In January 1857 the cold was especially bitter and mother was very ill. Day by day I had to go out into the nearest woods to get the firewood with my ax. I found blocks of dead wood from trees that had fallen, as heavy as I could carry on my back, and these I took home and chopped into small pieces.

On a certain Saturday I thought I had enough on hand to last until Monday. That Sunday was unusually cold and although I stoked the fire carefully, by nine o'clock in the evening the last stick of firewood had been burnt up. It was bed-time, however; a howling storm had set in. At midnight mother's neuralgia in her head had become so painful that light and fire had to be made. I lighted the lamp; the thermometer registered four degrees below zero in the room. I went out to fetch some wood; mother thought there was some in the back shed, but I knew better. I took the ax and went out to where the Park now is. I knew that there lay one or more condemned fence poles but I didn't know exactly where they were. The snow lay a foot deep and all about was the howling storm.

I trailed the sharp end of the ax along the ground and ploughed through the snow. God knew how I felt and what my heart was saying. I had hardly gone twenty steps backwards and forwards when the ax stuck fast. A block of wood lay half buried in the ground and frozen fast. I struck at it, hacked it and pounded it with the ax now on one end, then on the other. It seemed to move; I bent down, seized it and it came loose. I threw the pole over my shoulder and thought of the words: "He shall give His angels charge over thee." And so I carried the load of wood home through the blinding snow-storm.

Then I took out the lantern, split the wood, chopped some kindling, made a fire and went in to mother. She was sleeping, after the medicine we had given her which she used in a severe attack of the pain. Not until afterwards did she know anything of that night's adventure.

In February 1857 Mr. Nagelkerk informed me we had to leave the house in May because he himself wanted to move in at that time. Nowhere was there a house to let. I had a plan in mind which would need the help of Van Raalte. I talked it over with him and he said he would help me carry out the plan. It was this: From Van Raalte I would buy a lot south of the city which was still partly wooded. I would pay for it at interest during the first five years after purchase but if I could not meet the payments the land would again be his. I would buy shingles and lumber from [Alderd Plugger] on these same terms and then I myself would build our house.

Van Raalte agreed to this plan, but said that Plugger had need of money just then and so all his lumber would have to be paid for with cash. He referred me to Mr. Trimpe and since I was not acquainted with that wood-dealer Dominie van Raalte told me that I could say that he had sent me.

I had made a plan of a house 18 feet by 24 feet, with a lean-to at the back, and had reckoned out the amount of lumber needed. The prosperous lumberman laughed and asked if I must study as long as the house would last. He agreed to the terms on condition that he should be the first buyer if I should sell. He sold me doors and windows on the same terms with interest at five percent on the loaned capital and materials.

It was Easter vacation so Van Vleck gave me two weeks additional. Between classes and by moonlight and in snowstorm I dug a cellar almost five feet deep and a foot wider than the house was to be. When Caucus Day came all the voters had to go past our lot on the way to the schoolhouse. It was bitterly cold and was snowing a little. Trimpe came along with others and said, "Student, this is no kind of weather for such work. You're sweating and if you get cold you'll become sick and then you won't be able to do anything."

Van Raalte gave me permission to take trees out of his woods for any purpose that they might serve. I hired a man for three days to cut down small trees, split them lengthwise and help set up the cellar. Later, carpenter Van Beek helped me with the roof; hanging doors and fitting of windows was done by student Pieters who was a carpenter, and sometimes the students lent a helping hand. When I was building the cellar Trimpe came past and said with a laugh, "Student, you haven't counted on spikes and locks. They will cost you a good deal." I had no idea where I should get them. "What will you do, then?" he asked. I thought that perhaps he would help me. But God made other provision.

Now came an interruption to my building. Dominie van Vleck asked me and student Brandt to come to his house. He had received a letter from the secretary of the Governor and wished to have the Proclamation of the Governor translated into the Dutch language for the many Hollanders in the state. He asked Van Vleck to have this done by capable students of the Holland group; the work would be paid for. Van Vleck thought that we two were most in need of earning a bit.

Mother and I were almost sorry over the interruption to the building. The next morning Van Vleck brought over the English copy. It was not as long as we had expected for a state paper. In the afternoon Brandt and I sat down to work. Each translated a half and then criticized and improved each other's work where it was necessary. After one more reading and rehearsing it was ready for the copying by eleven o'clock. After a cup of tea Brandt went home. Van Vleck sent it up. I had made the copy for the printer, for though Brandt wrote a free hand it was somewhat straggling and often unintelligible, and it would be a strange language for the typesetter and the printer.

I went back busily to my building. The secretary asked what were the charges. Van Vleck replied that no price had been set; two poor students had done the work and he knew that the translation was a good one. Whatever the secretary thought right to pay would be satisfactory. A few days later we each received fifteen dollars. I looked upon this man as if he were God's paymaster, and mother thought it was as if the fifteen dollars had fallen directly out of God's hand.

At last the house was far enough built to be habitable. It was very plain, – upright boards on the outside of the frame, and for the first summer these were the only covering. But there was no mortgage on it; no other note than the estimate for the lumber which exacted six percent interest.

We moved in with happy hearts without knowing for how long a stay. Already more than two years had been spent at the Holland Academy, but how little more knowledge and how much more care had been our lot since we had left our home in Rochester! Blindly we went forward. Vacation came. Our practise in New Testament Greek continued on Friday afternoons because Van Vleck was also spending his vacation in Holland in connection with the building of the Holland Academy [now Van Vleck Hall].

Van Vleck had given me the contract for painting the Academy. The outside of the whole building was to have three coats of paint of which the last two were to be sanded. We had to do good work, no matter how long it took. Scaffolds and ladders of the carpenters were still on the grounds.

Van Vleck was to provide the brushes and the pay was to be a dollar a day. I figured out that it would take about thirty days. That would mean that much more income. [This paint was still in good condition in 1890, thirty-two years later.]

About the middle of May Van Raalte called me to his home. When I arrived I found C. van der Meulen and Pieter G. Oggel already there. Van der Meulen was asked to give the professors' opinion of me. I couldn't help believing they would say it was a waste of time for me to study any longer, and I had nothing to reply so far as the studies were concerned. Yet, considering the way in which God had so far led me this would have been a strange and shocking action. Their plan was to ask a dispensation for my further study from General Synod which would meet next June, but because it related to me especially I had to give my consent. For a few minutes I begged to be allowed to finish my studies in the next three or four years, for now I had hoped I would fare better in the future. But their advice prevailed and I agreed to their plan and returned to my work.

The upright boards which formed the exterior of our house shrank so from the summer heat that in the evenings the swarms of mosquitoes came in through the cracks until we could not sleep at night. As the cellar was roomy, dry and cool we decided to sleep there. On a Tuesday morning, as I was taking the bedding down cellar, Van Vleck came in. When I told him my purpose in carrying down the bedding and our reason for sleeping in the cellar he almost wanted to forbid it; he was sure that it would make Mrs. Zwemer ill. He went down cellar. There were two little windows opposite each other to let in the light. He felt to see how dry the sand floor was, and then said, "well, go on with your plan. I hope there will soon come an end to your struggles."

He had come to bring this message: I must not go on painting the Academy that week, a thing I had already decided upon. The third coat had still to go on and I wanted the first two coats to be not only dry but hard before I put on the third. The work he now had for me was this: I must write two sermons and let him read them. He was sure they would be good, but those were his orders. The following Sunday I must preach twice at Vriesland. I could go along with student Karsten on Saturday and he would take me to the home of one of the elders.

The two sermons were written, and read by Mrs. van Vleck. [She could read Dutch better than the Professor.] After the reading she pronounced them good. For each sermon I had made a short outline, just as I always did later, – a single sheet of paper written on both sides. What I wrote thus in my younger years, I could always remember by heart.

I had to preach in the old log-school; it was more than crowded. My heart was also almost too full to speak. First I had them sing Psalm 52,7, then I followed the accustomed order of service and could speak without difficulty. That evening I returned home with two or three dollars in my pocket. [At that time this was of much more commercial value than now.] It was the last Sunday in June, 1857.

On Friday, July 10, Elder Zylstra brought me a call from Vriesland church. The salary was to be $ 400 plus free living, free fire-wood and the use of ten acres of land. "You did very well, and must come to preach for us again, and often," said Zylstra. My answer was that my studies took all my time and I did not have the right to make the promise unless the professor gave his consent. He said, "That's true, but circumstances can change. Here, read this letter." And he gave it to me. I read it and did not know what to say. He said, "Let the juffrouw read it, too." Mother said, "I'm no juffrouw!" but she read the letter in amazement.

"What do you think of the call?" asked Zylstra, and then went right on. "Now don't say 'No,' but pray over it together and then talk with Van Raalte. Send your answer to Yntema's address or else come to see us again." When Zylstra had gone mother and I prayed together with grateful hearts, much wondering, and peculiar feelings. I went to see Van Vleck who said, "I have a message from Van Raalte that a few weeks ago he had word that the Synod has granted you the dispensation, and given one to G. J. Nykerk and one to J. van de Luyster as well. You now have the right to accept the call if it seems good to you. In such a case the professors at New Brunswick always say: "A first call must not be lightly refused but rather looked upon as a sign from God."

When I talked to Van Raalte he said: "You can promise to accept the call under the provision that Classis must first approve your examination. See here! Make the promise but ask the consistory to let you study one year longer, and meanwhile provide you some support for that year. It will do both you and the church good."

I accepted this suggestion joyfully and so did the church at Vriesland. The greatest poverty of our student years was at an end and during the next year we received an income of $ 8 a week from the church. The last two years at Rochester I had earned $ 9 a week, but without fire-wood and free lodging. There's and end to every beginning; so, too, came an end to this agreeable year, so full of hope. Yet there are always trials awaiting us even when we live at the doors of Paradise.

The following winter Mary came down, and the other children, with an attack of whooping-cough, and in January and February there seemed no hope of her recovery. Dominie and Mrs. van Vleck came often to see her. She looked like a skeleton, she was so thin. Yet she recovered and became well and strong.

The spring of 1858 arrived. I had to prepare myself for the examinations. Van der Meulen would give us the text for our trial sermon; that was the old method of examination. Dominie [G. J.] Nykerk was given a text about Sanctification; mine was about Justification, namely Romans 5,1. These sermons had to be preached before the regular examinations began.

Van Vleck had me read John 15, 1-8 in the Greek. I should have prepared myself for that. It was the first examination that had ever been held by the Holland Classis in America. The church at Zeeland was crowded. So when Pieter J. Oggel said that I must now read out the same words that the Apostle had used in writing, several climbed up on the benches to hear it. After the reading in the Greek I had to translate it word for word, thus, "I am the true vine, and my Father is the husbandman," etc.; the people looked at one another in amazement.

Oggel conducted the examination in theology, C. van der Meulen that in church history, and Van Raalte in pastoral care. We both took the oath against simony. This last has not been customary since.

Nykerk, J. van de Luyster, and I had studied a year of theology with Van Vleck. This was our method: At the beginning of the week of study, Friday evening, I was given the "Thesis of Dr. Van Vranken" as Van Vleck himself had written it in his student years in English. This I translated into Dutch. This copy was handed to Nykerk and by him to Van de Luyster so they could study it and write it over if they wished, and then it was returned to Van Vleck. He followed this plan so that he could have a copy of all these theses in the Holland language. For that reason he furnished me with paper, all of a kind. We had to learn these theses almost by heart and then he had a sort of catechetical class every Friday evening. The examination was approved by the Classis and the time for Nykerk's and my installation appointed.

On the 16th day of April 1858 the new church at Vriesland was crowded. Van der Meulen took for his text John 10, 3a: "To him the porter openeth." The installation blessing was pronounced with the big Bible held over my head by two of the elders.

My inaugural text was 2 Cor. 5,20: "And now are we ambassadors of Christ." I spoke on the influence that had led me to the ministry and the authority of the ministry. I have never felt uneasy over that sermon, but always over that text. It was too free and bold. This, then, was my first sermon as pastor and preacher, and the sermon was spoiled by a faulty text.

We bought some more household goods for the new parsonage, because there was a large living-room and then, so many more rooms, as the children said. The parsonage was newly built, still unpainted and unpapered. The children thought it a palace; we thought of it as a gift. Besides there were a large garden, a big pasture, prospects of having a cow, a barn full of hay in which to play, and chickens to keep which would lay many eggs. Oh, how happy the children were in Vriesland and with Vriesland! Then in 1860 we bought a stiff, old horse for forty dollars, a wagon and later a sleigh and then the joys of a country pastorate were complete.

Vriesland also brought its trials. In the spring of 1860 our first Nellie became ill with chronic rheumatism. Her sufferings were great but her patience was still greater, and her faith unusually firm and strong. Early in her illness she said that she would not get better but would die and go to the Lord Jesus. The previous winter she had read and reread Guthrie's *Examples of Early Conversion in Children*. She also read John Bunyan's *Pilgrim's Progress*. Often we had to persuade her to go out doors to play, and sometimes we were disquieted by her answer, "I would rather read than play." We do not know whether or not she was already indisposed and troubled with pain. Early one morning she began to complain about the pain in her arms, her legs and her back. This attack of pain lasted about half an hour. The following and the third day it came again, each time a little later.

Dr. W. van den Berg was called in. He thought at once that she was in a serious condition. Later the attacks came at shorter intervals, even to the last day when they came every hour. Cupping, rubbing, hot baths as well as medicine were applied but she only grew worse. She was unusually patient. Many came to see her between the attacks of pain. Her knowledge of the Scriptures and the expression of her faith and hope were beyond her years. Van Raalte, who had gone in to see her, said, "Thank God for such a child and such suffering. It's a testing of God's gold."

Nellie soon entered the rest she had hoped for, – to be with Jesus. This saying was for her far more than hackneyed words. The date of her death is not recorded: possibly the 15th of September 1860. She was the second child to be taken from us. In February 1855 the first sacrifice was demanded, our Frederick James. We were still feeling the loss keenly when we moved to Michigan. In that November we were leaving one behind on "Mount Hope", the name of the cemetery in Rochester.

The third death in the family was that of Anna Levina, "born to die," said the doctor. She was thirteen days old. Our fourth loss was that of Hendrik, our last born. He died when almost a year old, after a life of suffering, at Milwaukee, April 8, 1872.

After ten years of service in Vriesland [eleven years after my first sermon in June 1857] came a call from South Holland, Illinois, which we accepted. When we moved the oldest of our children was almost eighteen years old, and since that time you yourselves are acquainted with the history of our family. Accordingly your historian will now cease his tale.

Mother traveled with me, as did Sara with Abraham, as we journeyed through the length and breadth of the land, from Albany in the East to

Middleburg in western Iowa. The farthest journey, into western Iowa, we made with aching hearts. Mother was no longer with us. I think that she still knows our happenings. But we do not speak of what has not been revealed. Yet even if the events of our lives here on earth are not known to those above, yet the beloved name of "Mother" remains always in my thoughts, and my heart says like David, "She will not return to me, but I shall go to her."

APPENDIX

THE DISAPPOINTED IMMIGRANT

[This humorous song, *De Teleurgestelde Landverhuizer* [The disappointed immigrant], was especially prepared for the 1897 semicentennial celebration in Holland and was sung by Van Lente's Choir. The Dutch text, which appears in Lucas's Foreword, provides deep insights into the immigrant mentality. The song was published in the article of F. M. Knobel, "Holland City en de Hollandsche Amerikaan," *Vragen Van Den Dag,* XXI (1906): 556-67. Henrietta Ten Harmsel, professor emeritus of English at Calvin College, superbly translated the song and rendered it into English rhyme for this reprint edition.]

With courage glowing at its best
They traveled to the distant West.
They'd surely get their money's worth:
There gold was shoveled from the earth.
But, ah, their hopes were far too great:
No wheat! Corn bread was what they ate!

"At any time," each told his wife,
"The pigs stand ready for the knife.
Pears hang on trees from North to South,
Spiced, fried, and ready for your mouth!"
But, ah, their hopes were far too great:
Corn mush, corn bread was all they ate!

Tell me, could things get worse than that?
They smeared their pans with candle fat.
And each spoiled sweet tooth who had come
Soon had to live like a poor bum.
Instead of luscious, fluffy bread,
What they ate now all weighed like lead.

Nowhere, nowhere is life so fine:
The brooks themselves all flow with wine!
But no! Spoiled Dutchmen had to try
For Java coffee, home-brewed rye;
So weak, it hardly made them tight."
At least, no drunkards walked at night.

But finally, to God be praise,

Their hardships changed to better days.
The wilderness has given way
To the fine land they see today.
Although their hopes were first too high,
They now eat not just bread, but pie!

Just fifty years, and now this feast!
They've gathered here from West and East.
Content with all that God has given,
They raise a song of thanks to heaven.
All sing: Our God is great and good!
For poverty we now have food.

Vol. 1, chapter 8, no. 33, pp. 311-14

ORIGINS OF NORTH HOLLAND, NOORDELOOS, AND BEAVERDAM [SOETERMEER] 1848-1849

33. PIETER G. VAN TONGEREN'S "NORTH HOLLAND"

[A son of Jan van Tongeren, one of the first settlers of North Holland in 1849, Pieter spent most of his years in that place and so speaks with authority. His sketch, published in *De Grondwet,* July 25, 1911, was translated by the late E. R. Post and Dr. George Harper, professor emeritus of English, Calvin College.]

In 1848 Rev. A. C. van Raalte said to my father, Jan van Tongeren: "About 5 or 6 miles northeast of the city of Holland there must be some very good land, according to what the Indians have told me." In the spring of 1849 my father settled on the place where later the sawmill of Eildert Nienhuis was located, 2½ miles north of Holland. In the fall of that year Van Dijk, Van Tongeren, and I were walking in a northeasterly direction along an Indian trail, picking cranberries. When we were near the town line between Holland and Olive, Van Dijk and Van Tongeren stopped to rest. I, a lad of ten, went on a little further and came to a nice woods where there were no hemlocks. I returned and told the others what I had found, whereupon my father said to Van Dijk: "Then that is the land about which Rev. van Raalte told us." They stood up and went to investigate, and sure enough, it was true. This later became what is called North Holland. We were then about a ½ mile west of where the Reformed Church is now.

Soon it was generally known that there was such good land there, as is evident from the fact that people began to build log cabins that same year. The first log cabin was that of Jan Kramer, a brother of Lambert Kramer, well known in Noordeloos. The second one built was my father's, Jan van Tongeren's, on the spot where the home of Minnie P. Stegenga is now located, across from the church in the town of Olive.

The first winter our main food was venison, for deer were plentiful. That meat solved our problem, for we had no money, no cattle, nor hogs, and if we had owned them there would have been no hay or fodder for them. I will never forget the deer hunting of the early years. North Holland had the first hunters — Steven Coleman, farmer Veldheer, Otto G. van Dijk, B. W. Kooijers, and others. The number of deer that they killed runs into hundreds. I myself have shot thirty. As far as I know no lives were lost, which is not the case now in the northern woods.

On January 2, 1850, we moved into our house. It was about 10×20 feet but large enough for six people — father, mother, and son, besides three boarders: H. Brouwer, Wiger van der Kolk, and Geert Raak. The sow had to have a place too, so it was a real Noah's Ark. Sometimes the house also had to serve as a church, for divine worship was not forgotten. Simple though it was, I remember one time when the elder was not present and my father was not feeling well. I, a boy of 11 or 12 years of age, had to read a sermon. In those days no one who was not sick stayed at home. This must be said in favor of the early settlers.

Were there any roads? Well, no, not really: Everything had to be carried through the woods and swamps and over fallen trees. Our first stove was brought in on a small sled, as well as other furniture later. But gradually there were changes. A road was built and more families moved in. Hein van der Haar drove in now and then from the city of Holland with his rust-colored oxen. The third house was that of Gerrit van Dijke, on the place where Jan Meijer lives now.

In the summer of 1850 more families came, so that by the end of the year the following lived there: Jan van Tongeren, Jan Kramer, Jan G. van Dijk, P. J. Kuiper, Brouwer, Jan Spijkerman, Jan Veldheer, and Jan van der Kolk. Soon after that the following families also arrived: Jan Slag, Jan C. Smit, Evert Luidens, Van den Berg, Kerst Weener, Ten Have, P. M. Stegenga, and others, so that after 5 years there were quite a few residents.

As I said, the first public worship was in the home of Van Tongeren; later at the homes of K. Weener, Otto G. van Dijke, and Jacob van Dijk, and still later in the school. The first sermon was delivered by Rev. A. C. van Raalte. His text was Matthew 6:10: "Thy Kingdom come." I still remember these words: "Friends, you have begun a new settlement here. I wish for the Lord's sake that you would not dare to cut down a single tree before having asked God for the coming of his Kingdom."

The first communion was served at the home of K. Weener, with Rev. Ypma officiating. The church was organized, Jan C. Smit told me, at the home of Van Dijk. As far as I can determine, no minutes were kept, but as I recall, it must have been in 1851, surely not later. The first elder was Alexander Hartgerink, and the first deacon Jan van Tongeren; they were both installed by Rev. C. van der Meulen.

The first child born in North Holland was Gerrit Jan Spijkerman, on April 23, 1851. The first adult who died there was Jan van der Kolk, in May, 1855. The body was taken to Holland on a wagon drawn by oxen for burial. The first couple married were Jan ten Have and Trijntje van Dijk, on July 26, 1854, by Rev. Ypma. Mrs. ten Have is still living. The first public school was built in 1856; the first teacher was Herman Grebel. In the highest class were Katherina van Dijk, Ale P. Stegenga, and Peter G. van Tongeren; they are all still living.

Just a few details about the community. In 1855 a man by the name of Jacob Duim came. He claimed to be a minister or teacher and in sole possession of the truth. "The people," so he said one time, "are in the wilderness and for that reason the children cannot be baptized. Even though the preachers are Baal-ministers and not leaders, but deceivers, I still see a beam of light in Switzerland, etc." The result was that the majority of the people followed him, the congregation was split, and some went to Noordeloos. The children were not baptized, so that when Rev. E. C. Oggel came to North Holland in 1866, there were 75 unbaptized children. This lasted for about five years, after which the congregation was reorganized, as it were, and Duim's following was reduced to five or six families. At the time of his death in 1879, only two families remained loyal to him.

The first church building was erected in 1862 and the second, still standing, in 1867. The dedication took place on February 5, 1868. The first pastor, Rev. Engelbert C. Oggel, was installed on October 14, 1866, by Rev. C. van der Meulen and Engelbert's brother, Prof. Pieter J. Oggel. He served the congregation for 3½ years. The first wedding at which he officiated was that of myself and Jentje Brouwer, on February 28, 1867.

The second minister, Rev. Balster van Ess, came in February, 1867. In 1876 and 1877 the congregation experienced a great revival. Many came to profess their faith in Christ. In 1877 a Sunday school was organized. After serving the congregation for more than 14 years, this pastor accepted a call to Roseland, Illinois, where he died. In 1856 a choral society was organized. Among the members were Jan ten Have (leader), Jan Spijkerman, Albert van Dijk, Kerst Weener, Otto van Dijk, and P. G. van Tongeren. We can also report that J. Brouwer started a lye plant; Veldheer, Oostenrijk, and Heiboer, a sawmill; and H. Pelgrim a cheese factory, but these have all disappeared.

The following North Holland residents volunteered for service during the Civil War, 1861-65: Wouter Weener, who lost his life at Stone River, Broer van Dijk, Jan Hofman, Bartel van der Zwaag, Arend Brouwer, Willem Frik, Derk P. Stegenga, Jan Dunnink, Willem de Fouw, and Peter G. van Tongeren. To the best of my knowledge, of all those who settled in North Holland in 1850, there are eight still living.

Vol. 1, chapter 8, no. 34, pp. 314-17

34. ANTHONY ROSBACH'S
"SETTLEMENT IN NOORDELOOS, MICHIGAN"

[This account, written by Anthony Rosbach under the title *De Nederzetting in Noordeloos Michigan,* was published in *De Grondwet,* February 21, 1911. Although the community began its existence as early as 1848, it was not until 1856, upon the arrival of Dominie Koene van den Bosch from Noordeloos in the Netherlands, that it received the name of Noordeloos. The account was translated by the late E. R. Post and Dr. George Harper, professor emeritus of English, Calvin College.]

To experience history or to write about it are two different matters, not always equally easy. It is usually the task of descendants to describe the history of the fathers. Although this results in a more impersonal and more accurate description, there is not that uniqueness which is inherent in personal experiences. Still, we descendants of the pioneers have heartaches when we think of the struggles of our fathers as they made their way in a strange country, through the wilderness, amid difficulties and trials, surrounded by wild people and animals, to transform the centuries-old forest into fruitful fields.

As we write the history of the settlement of Noordeloos, we prefer not to mention those matters which are less pleasant; we only want to record for memory's sake what can serve to honor the Hollanders in America.

The foundations of Noordeloos were laid in 1848. It was in the course of that year that a party of young people from the province of Groningen left the old fatherland. Upon their arrival they came to stay with friends in the old village of Groningen in "the Van Raalte Colony." From here they explored the northeast to look for land. They had been born and reared in Groningerland — the land of rich clay soil. When they climbed the clay hill that marks the southern boundary of Noordeloos, they cried out: "We must have land here." So they settled there.

The party consisted of P. A. van Dyk and his wife, M. Hulsebos and his wife, J. de Slachter and P. Bos. They built a house of logs in the northeastern corner of Section 15, Holland township. They were joined by Alexander Hartgerink, who was in possession of a quarter-section of government land granted to him for his military service in the Mexican War. We note that although a Netherlander by birth, he had taken part in the war against Mexico. This land, in the northwest quarter of Section 11, became, roughly, the midpoint of Noordeloos.

Soon more colonists came. Among others, the following arrived with their families: T. Bos, C. Weninger, Liesveld Blankezee, G. J. Renskers, and W. van den Berge; in 1852, A. van den Bosch; in 1853, B. W. Kooijers and P. van den Bosch; in 1854, H. Willink; in 1855, H. Diepenhorst and P. Verduin. They built log houses farther north and east. At an earlier date several of them had settled elsewhere in America before coming here; others soon left.

As in other places, these settlers, too, faced many trials, but with God's gracious hand over them they never lacked food. Store goods had to be brought from Holland and Zeeland by foot or oxen-drawn wagon. It was not until 1865 that the first store was opened by Adrian Wagenaar. The forests consisted mostly of beech, maple, and ash. A great deal of valuable wood was burned in the early days because people did not know what else to do with it. Later, Jan Vogel built a sawmill by the creek between the properties of Van den Bosch and Diepenhorst.

Although Noordeloos made its social contribution to the progress of this colony, it is in religion that the little place played its most significant role in the history of the settlement. The earliest arrivals were God-fearing folk who sought not only a temporal livelihood but also greater religious freedom in this new world. They joined the congregation of Zeeland and attended worship services as often as a 3- to 4-mile trip through the woods allowed. But finding the distance to be too great, they soon prepared to organize their own congregation. When Diepenhorst and Verduin came in 1855, they, with A. van den Bosch, undertook the task. The organization of the congregation was under the leadership of Rev. C. van der Meulen from Zeeland. When the question arose as to what to call the congregation, it was decided to adopt the name of Noordeloos because they planned to call as their pastor K. van den Bosch from Noordeloos, Province of South Holland, in the Netherlands. A log church was built on a few acres of land donated by C. Wentger. This would later become the site for the home of G. A. A. Rosbach.

In 1856 Rev. van den Bosch was called. He accepted, and soon the congregation enjoyed having its own pastor. When he was installed by Rev. C. van der Meulen, the church was too small to accommodate the crowd, so the service was conducted under the trees of the woods, with a farmer's wagon serving as the pulpit. It was a ceremonious occasion. The silence of the woods, formerly broken only by the cries of wild animals or the shouts of Indians, echoed with the Psalms of David. In the afternoon Rev. van den Bosch preached his inaugural sermon in the church. He was an energetic minister and worked among the people with great blessing.

Accompanying the minister were the P. Heyboer family, the Vogel family, and others who contributed much to the development of the settlement. P. Heyboer spent some time in teaching the children the Dutch language, so that the education of the youth was also provided for.

It would be fine if the history of the settlement could be ended at this point, but something of grave importance to the Colony occurred and should not be left untold. Soon after Rev. van den Bosch arrived, he became dissatisfied with the Dutch Reformed Church with which the Hollanders had affiliated. His concern was that, as he saw it, the church had deserted Reformed principles. Many here and in other places shared his concerns and sought relief in secession.

On March 14, 1857, Rev. van den Bosch submitted his act of secession to the consistory of Zeeland. Sixteen members left with him and were organized as the first congregation of the Seceders, the Christian Reformed Church in North America. They built a little church on the southeast corner of Section 2 near the home of Rev. van den Bosch. Later it was moved a half mile to the west near Diepenhorst. This congregation increased in membership steadily, and as it grew, the congregation that remained became smaller. After a few years it ceased to exist. Such is, in brief, the history of the settlement in Noordeloos.

Much has been experienced in the years of its existence. Many tears, both of joy and of sadness, have been shed, and here also many prayers have ascended to the throne of grace.

Vol. 1, chapter 8, no. 35, pp. 317-19

35. P. HUYSER'S "FROM SOETERMEER TO SOETERMEER"

[Four brothers of the Huyser family, of whom this author was one, emigrated from Soetermeer near The Hague to Michigan and settled in the woods northeast of Zeeland. This place briefly was known as Soetermeer, but was soon, however, called Beaverdam. This sketch, which first appeared in *De Grondwet*, May 28, 1912, was translated by the late E. R. Post and Dr. George Harper, professor emeritus of English, Calvin College.]

The undersigned, P. Huyser, Sr., who lived in Soetermeer, South Holland, to the age of 25 years, decided in August, 1847, to go to America, and left on the three-mast sailing vessel, *Sabina,* from Rotterdam to Hellevoetsluis, where we had to stay for 4 weeks because of contrary winds. On a Sunday afternoon we were towed to sea by a steamboat and the next morning we were in the English Channel.

After a very pleasant voyage of 21 days, we came in sight of New York at 9 o'clock on a Sunday morning, and our Dutch party (consisting of my two married brothers Quirinus and Johannes, J. G. van Hees and family, R. M. de Bruin, De Ruitenberge, A. van den Berg and his wife, and Van Wingeren) sang Psalm 66:3 [sic]: "God prepared for us a way," etc.

After the anchor had been dropped, we went ashore and visited Rev. de Wit[t]. On Monday evening we traveled on by steamer to Albany, and from there by canalboat to Buffalo, where my two brothers and I stayed for the winter. In the spring of 1848 when my brother Cornelius came from the Netherlands, we traveled on to Michigan. We went by boat to Chicago, where I met Mr. Robbertus M. de Bruin, who was prepared to move to the Colony with the storekeeper, Aldred Plugger.

We left that same day and arrived the following morning at 9 o'clock at the mouth of the Kalamazoo River. We brought our baggage on a flatboat that came out from the Colony; and then the fun began with four inexperienced boatmen — two pulling on a long rope and two at the rear. We were stuck on the sand several times, and then we had to jump overboard and stand in the water up to our waists and lift the boat over the sand bank and push it ahead. After three hours of hard work we reached our destination, the mouth of Black Lake, and then Jacobus Vink hitched a horse to our boat and in that way brought us to the so-called city. We placed our baggage under large hemlock trees, and making our way over fallen trees, we came to a small hotel operated by Jan Binnekant, on the site of the present Holland City Bank. At what is now Eighth

Street there were only small and large stumps, here and there a small wooden or log cabin. Except for that, there was only the forest. Then we went to the father of the Colony, the highly esteemed Rev. A. C. van Raalte, whom we met in his garden.

Later we went to the village of Zeeland, always through woods; we were scared when we thought we saw a bear, but it was only a porcupine. When we came to the small water house, where the baggage sent to Zeeland was picked up, we had to be very careful as we crept over a tree not to fall into the river. When people came this way with an oxen-drawn wagon, the oxen had to swim across the river. After having struggled through the woods for 3 miles, protected by the good hand of the Lord, we arrived in Zeeland, where we at once went to the esteemed Rev. C. van der Meulen, who had just come into the woods to show newcomers land northeast of Zeeland. The following day he took us there also, and allotted 40 acres to each one of us. All we could see was all kinds of trees, 60, 80, and 100 feet tall.

My first job was to cut down trees to make room for a log cabin. Since I expected two married brothers (who soon arrived), we divided that cabin into two sections, into which they moved immediately. But I had given each one 10 acres, where they soon built a shanty in which they lived.

The writer of this account now owned 40 acres of land and a log cabin with two apartments, but I had no one to help me. So I felt the need of asking the Lord to make provision in this need also, and in His mercy he heard my prayer, so that I married Trjntje Kok on April 20, 1851. We at once went to our humble property where we have now lived without interruption for 58 years.

We have had to cope with great trials, but on each Lord's Day we were again comforted and encouraged by the services led by Rev. van der Meulen. For there was much with which we had to contend, not only the heavy and large trees but also with the wild animals, because the deer cropped the buckwheat at night and the raccoons and porcupines devoured the corn. When the corn began to develop, they broke down the stalks and ate the ears. One time I had sown an acre of summer wheat; when it was ready to be mowed I could find only the stalks and the ears scattered among the large stumps that stood all around. But the Lord had helped us through all of these and other problems, so that we may well ask: "What shall I render unto the Lord for all the benefits he has shown to me?" [Psalm 116:12]. And finally, as Jacob could declare: "With my staff I crossed over Jordan" etc. [Genesis 32:10] so I am able to say: "I crossed the ocean on a ship, and now I have become two bands," as we now have married children, grandchildren and great-grandchildren, a total of 73 souls.

Vol. 1, chapter 9, no. 36, pp. 320-25

36. P. SCHUT'S "ACCOUNT OF MY JOURNEYS"

[The author, about whom nothing is known, lived in Overisel, Michigan, and in 1891 he wrote these *Reisverhalen*, published in the *Jaarboekje voor de Hollandsche Christelijke Gereformeerde Kerken Noord Amerika voor het jaar 1891* (1890). The Reverend Henry De Mots translated this account.]

I shall write what I have been told just as I remember having heard it, so that I can make real the first days and struggles of the old colonists. I hope that some of the humor will cause your lips to curl in laughter. I also hope that the old people will remember some of these things and laugh at them — surely they will not have forgotten how to laugh.

I. From Holland to Grand Haven

It happened in 1847. Many families lived in the city of Holland, underneath the branches of trees. Eighteen family households were fortunate to get shelter in a large shed of logs, about 20 × 30 feet in size. Everything was evolving. Many pious people had made the trip to America with Rev. van Raalte. The leader of the colonists knew this, but he also knew that the most precious coin is the first to be counterfeited, and that among the upright people there might be bad ones that creep in as well. In order to prevent the worst, he had appointed a dozen constables, among whom was H.G.M., my informant. It will soon become clear that this act was not superfluous.

People were still living in the just-mentioned log shed among crates and parcels, when a complaint was made to Van Raalte about a theft. Van Raalte, who held every post simultaneously, went to search for the goods, followed by two constables, and yes, they found the stolen goods at the bottom of a crate that belonged to two married people. They were the thieves. They now had to go to Grand Haven, because that is where the jail and the judge were. How to get there? There was no easy answer. Roads were nonexistent. Lake shipping was in poor condition. They had no horse, no wagon, not even an ox. They did not have an ordinary boat, just a flat-bottomed rig, two-inch boards nailed together, roughly constructed and of dubious strength. With this they would sail on the Lake to Grand Haven.

Soon they brought the thieves with their baggage into the boat; H.G.M. and J.R. had to go along. A certain E. also wanted to go to Grand Haven, and he came on board. Van Raalte was the leading spirit. Without him nobody would have the courage to sail on the Lake. He did not seem to have any fear, and he knew how to encourage the group with his very presence. Two men took the oars. The dominie was the man at the helm. They left Black Lake and sailed on the big Lake Michigan.

At first, things were pleasant. In order to shorten the time a bit, one of the men asked a question: "Dominie, how is it really, does the sun turn or does the earth turn?" The dominie did not answer. "Maybe Dominie did not hear; ask him again," said the rower to his comrade. Once again the same question was posed. Finally the dominie said: "I believe that there are a lot of people in heaven who believed that the earth turns; and I also believe that there are many people in heaven who believed that the suns turns." Nothing more. They still did not know anything and they felt a little bit self-conscious about the meaningless question and the very characteristic answer.

Finally, the two rowers decided to look behind them. They were going awfully far from the shore and the western sky did not look good. J.R., who incited rather than acted openly, said to his shipmate: "Tell the dominie that he should not move so far away from shore." The dominie ignored this, and kept on going further from shore. The sky became more menacing. Once more he said: "Dominie, you should not move so far into the lake, just look to the west." This still did not help.

"You know what," said J.R. to H.G.M., "if we keep on rowing, the dominie will steer us into the deep water to perish there. We should tell him that if he does not want to steer towards the shore, we will no longer do the rowing." And this is what they did. To no avail the dominie told them: "If we come closer to shore, we will get into the breakers and our boat will fall apart."

He had to give in because the men could not be persuaded. Then straight to shore and into the breakers and, as Rev. van Raalte had predicted, the boat was knocked into pieces. All of them reached the shore safely, dripping wet because of the high waves, except for the Rev. van Raalte. Quick as he was and always calculating, he jumped off the boat between the waves and managed to stay dry. He laughed at his courageous crew. They did not like it too well, but it was their fault. As well as they could, they hoisted the baggage on their backs and with both thieves they searched for the path and started on the road to Grand Haven.

It did not take long for the company to reach the river. They had to wade through it. The thieves refused and they were carried across. When the dominie saw this he said: "Fellows, you are wet anyway; just carry me across as well." The two rowers were on the other side of the river. The one whispered to the other: "You had better go and get the dominie, and remember how he laughed at us a while ago. When you are in midstream, just trip and you know the rest." M.

went to get the dominie, while J.R. guarded the thieves. Like a real coolie M. carried the dominie on his shoulders. "Hold me tight!" said the dominie. "Yes," was the answer, "You have to hold on to me." Well, in the middle of the river the pack animal started to stumble and dove headfirst into the water. After some gasping and puffing the dominie said: "I figured this would happen!" Nothing more.

They now neared Port Sheldon and stayed there overnight. The following morning Dominie van Raalte wanted to travel by boat to Grand Haven, for they were still 12 miles away from this city. He borrowed a boat, a thick pole, and a bed sheet, and transformed the rowboat into a small sailboat. The company, however, was still badly shook up on account of the shipwreck of the day before, and they did not want to go along. H.G.M. was the only one who could muster enough courage also to step into the boat, thinking: "If you dare do this, then I will do it too."

The little boat slid away, a good breeze swelling the sail. After a beautiful trip of two hours they arrived in Grand Haven. The rest of the company arrived there too after a few hours, dead tired, and again they had to acknowledge that the Reverend laughed at them because of their cowardly behavior.

I have not been told how they returned. It was said that the thieves, even before they were brought before the judge, cursed Dominie van Raalte in an atrocious way, which he endured with much patience. The thieves were banned from the Colony and, on the promise that they would never again set foot in Holland, they were set free. What may have appealed most is the calm courage, the unyielding willpower, and the practical sense of him who was rightly called the Father of the Colony.

II. From Overisel to Saugatuck and Back

It must have been during the winter of 1849 and 1850. The snow was deep, the roads still nonexistent, when five men decided to make a trip to Saugatuck. They did this on behalf of their families and neighbors, or rather, they felt forced to go there. The women had no needles and thread, no ribbon or string left. Coffee, tea, and sugar were already long-forgotten articles, or may not even have been experienced yet. The need became quite urgent, because they could not fix a shirt or sew a button or a loop. The mothers had been thrifty during the last few days and they had made excellent butter. Beforehand it was decided to meet at the log cabin of Rev. Seine Bolks, who lived just south of the village.

And so it happened. First they prayed together. At that time people prayed more than now. Rev. Bolks said: "Fellows, I will stay up this evening, until you return, and I will have the coffee ready." With courage, and happy about this generous kindness, the five men got on their way, and each one had his basket with butter on his arm. They took a southwest direction. There are no fences along the road, at least not for the first four miles. Is this possible now? — one misses the luxury of going alongside the fences on the beaten roads.

First they headed for Mr. Schoner's [Anton Schorno], an old settler, a German, and from there to the "townline." How much the road was curved and bent I do not know, but the five miles was very much extended, because they could not follow the "Indian Trail" or the "footpath of the wood cutters." And whenever they had neither to follow, they had to find their own way around the pits and pools.

Further towards Saugatuck there is a beaten road, of sorts; but our group was tired before they even reached that road. In the evening, when people were starting to light their lamps, they arrived in Saugatuck. They put the butter on the counter and with a little knife cut the pieces in half, because it should not contain one single little hair. The mothers had been very careful. The butter passed the test, and then the question: how much money? No, in those days people did not think this way and did not expect to receive money. Everything was bartered. Barter was the only basis for trade. The storekeeper, who was in charge of everything, gave only what he wanted. Everyone now received just enough needles, pins, thread, ribbon, buttons, etc., as were necessary, and for this they walked 14 miles through deep snow and along unbeaten roads!

As quickly as possible they ate the small piece of cornbread and started on the way back. It was not advisable to go in the evening the way they had come in the morning. They did not know it well enough and the last 4 or 5 miles was totally untrodden. It was not without danger that one went into the forest. To get lost and then stay in the snow overnight after such a tiring trip could prove to be fatal. For this reason the group decided to go via Graafschap. Although this was 4 miles further and thus would make the trip a total of 18 miles, the benefit was that they were in better-known territory and would pass once in a while the huts of the first settlers. In case of emergency one might be able to find shelter there.

They started on the way back. They were strong men — in those days they had to be very strong. I have always believed that the Lord, in whose strength the voyage across the waters had been accomplished, gave special physical strength and moral courage for these initial struggles. The group had passed Graafschap already. It was late, but now every step brought them closer to home and the thought of the happy reunion gave new courage. To make the wife happy with such a treasure, which can only be appreciated in such a time, was a pleasant thought.

It was about nine o'clock. One of the group was so exhausted that only with the greatest difficulty could he go any further. They dragged themselves as far as Mr. Hellenthal's house and decided to knock on the door to see if he might have something for them to eat. After they knocked, the door of the hospitable hut was opened and Hellenthal observed our group before him, shone upon by the weak light of the oil lamp. They told him that they would like to rest a bit and have something to eat, if he had something in the house, that is. But Hellenthal did not have an abundance either; he asked, "Wife, do you have anything in the house?" The woman had nothing other than some dry cornbread, which was intended for the following day. But in those days people were willing to share with each other.

Coffee made of roasted rye was quickly made, and soon after the most cordial meal and drink they talked already about leaving. The group would have liked to stay overnight, but one of them had left his wife in such circumstances that he really had to leave, even if the others would stay. The others would not allow that, and so after thanksgiving and prayer and wishing God's care on each other, the group stepped outside again — Hellenthal lended them his lantern, so they could better find the path with the light. Alas! This luxury was only short-lived. Still 2½ miles away from Overisel, the lantern went out. If anywhere, this was where they most needed light on their way. After a mile of trudging in the dark on a beaten path, they found the road cleared for half a mile, but the trees were across the path. Mr. F., one of the group, had taken part with laying out this section of the road, so he would go ahead a piece to explore the terrain, because he knew better where the holes were. He would call: "Fellows, this way!" and then they would go in his direction. But they were so tired and stiff that instead of climbing over the trees, they would let themselves fall down. They would sit on the tree, first pulling up the one leg and then the other over it. But it was in the direction of home, and once they had this behind them, it was only one more mile to the point of departure, the log cabin of Rev. Bolks.

This misery was also overcome. It was midnight already, but Rev. Bolks and his wife were still waiting for them. According to their promise, the coffee was ready. They stayed there a while yet and then the group dispersed; each one returned to his waiting wife and children in their simple cabins. You can imagine that reunion — I will not describe it. It is understandable that the older people were attached to each other with strong bonds. With tears in their eyes and with thanks to the Lord, they acknowledged God's help in keeping a stand during these scary times. We question if the younger generation will be able to appreciate the struggles of the older ones, as well as the blessings of God that were granted to their parents. We doubt it, and for that reason we urge them to remember.

I would also like to express my wish that the older settlers who live here and elsewhere will carefully write down their various exploits. From this we can learn about the help of the Lord and we can appreciate the persevering courage of the older people. And this might help the younger generation to better appreciate the privileges of the present.

Vol. 1, chapter 12, no. 54, pp. 429-35

54. GEERT S. DE WITT'S "EXPERIENCES"

[Geert S. de Witt arrived in the Michigan settlement from Eenrum, Province of Groningen, in June 1848, at length establishing himself on a homestead in Fillmore Township in Allegan County. His reminiscences, entitled *Ervaringen,* appeared in *De Grondwet,* June 25, 1912. The late E. R. Post and Dr. George Harper, professor emeritus of English, Calvin College, translated this interesting account, which ends abruptly because, according to Gerrit van Schelven, illness and death made it impossible for De Witt to continue. He died December 13, 1911.]

The writer was born on April 10, 1830, at Eenrum, Province of Groningen, Netherlands. We left for America on March 20, 1848, when I was seventeen years old. We traveled on a sailboat from Zoutkamp to Amsterdam, and from there to Hellevoetsluis. There we had to wait for a few days for the ship to be prepared to continue the voyage and to arrange everything for the meals, for everyone had to provide his own food. Everything was weighed to make sure everybody had brought enough. We received our drinking water from the ship's officers, which was rationed out to us daily, depending on the individual and number of people. That was not done very efficiently; each had to await his turn, and at such times people occasionally became impatient. We had to bury two or three people who died at sea; I cannot recall their names.

After being tossed about for 41 days on the ocean, we arrived in New York. From there we traveled on a steamboat to Albany and from there by canalboat to Buffalo. Then we went on to Chicago on a steamboat. At Chicago we were transferred to a sailing vessel to travel on to Holland, Michigan, but because the wind and waves were too unfavorable we were taken to Grand Haven, and the following day back to Black Lake. Here we were transferred to a flatboat with our baggage the next day, and we had to pull that flatboat over the sand that blocked the entrance to Black Lake. Finally we were in the harbor and the boat was afloat again, and we went on across Black Lake toward Holland, and, as we thought, to the city of Holland. But instead of a city we found an impenetrable forest. Only 8th and River Streets had been cleared so that a team of oxen could pass through.

We asked where the city was and we were told we were in the middle of it. Then we turned right around and went back to the shore of Black Lake, and remained there that day and spent the next night under a few boards, which we propped up against each other. It was now around June 20; I do not remember the exact date, after a trip of about three months. I was then cared for by Pieter Naber; I was 18 years old.

The next morning we traveled on a wagon drawn by oxen through the woods to a place now called East Holland. A few families lived there, namely Simon Sluiter, Willem Mulder, and Mr. Holman, by whom we were welcomed and given shelter. Holman later moved to Kalamazoo. Another family by the name of Molog was also living there; they had arrived there in 1847 and were busy building a log cabin. It took an entire day to get through the woods with the oxen to reach East Holland.

After having looked around for a couple of days at the land in the vicinity, the older members of our group went on foot to Grand Rapids to buy the land there if the deal appealed to them. Johannes Naber, Pieter Naber, Egbert Pilon, and Jan Kramer did buy land. It was located in Section 35, Holland township, Ottawa County.

But we young folk walked to Kalamazoo. Our party consisted of Jacob Sluiter, Albert Kapinga and his betrothed wife Afkie, and another girl, Cornelia (a sister of J. Naber's wife), Cornelius Noorhuis, Jan de Fuiter, and myself. The first day we walked as far as Allegan and spent the night there at the home of the widow Kok. The next day we had the opportunity to ride to Cooper, located six miles north of Kalamazoo. There C. Noorhuis, Cornelia, and I were hired by farmers in the vicinity. The others went on to Kalamazoo, found employment there, and remained for a month.

Shortly thereafter Jacob Sluiter and I began working on the farm of Governor Epaphraditus Ransom near Kalamazoo, where celery was raised, and at that time (a couple of years later) the farm was sold to Den Bleyker, a wealthy farmer from Texel, Netherlands. In the fall I worked for the Michigan Central Railroad for 75 cents a day and 25 cents for board. But in the winter, when everything was covered with snow, work on the railroad ceased, and then the future was dark for me, being entirely alone and without a family. But the Lord provided and granted relief.

I heard that there was a farmer who was in need of a hired man. He lived 15 miles from Kalamazoo, and I did not know the way nor the farmer's name. But I started out, walked south, and asked now and then where I could find the South Prairie, not knowing the area to which I was to go. The place where the village of Schoolcraft is located is called Round Prairie, in the southern part of Kalamazoo County; it was really supposed to be in Schoolcraft. Walking on, I did succeed in reaching the village at three o'clock in the afternoon. Arriving there I asked for directions to reach a farmer who had fifteen horses and was looking for a hired man. I was told that he must be Andrew Y. Moore, whose sons were attending school there. So I went to the school and asked for the sons of Mr. A. Y. Moore. They directed me to a house a half mile east of Schoolcraft. I was welcomed when I arrived and remained there until the following fall.

Mr. A. Y. Moore was the father of Colonel Moore of the 25th Michigan Infantry Regiment, well known by our Dutch young men. That is where I first saw a large machine drawn by sixteen horses. This machine cut wheat and put it into bags. Later the machine was sent to California because it did not pay to use such a large machine here. This was the first time that I became aware of the fact that the Lord was also present there, and also directed my ways and would not leave me.

More Hollanders arrived in the summer to find employment there; on Sundays they met in a barn and called upon the name of the Lord. My bedroom was in the barn so it was a place for prayer and meditation, and that was a blessing for me, something I appreciate more now than I did then.

My next place was a mile to the east, working for a farmer by the name of Darnel Bruss, a good man who practiced his religion with his family and was the superintendent of the Sunday school in the Presbyterian Church. So in this way four and a half years passed by as I lived in the country as a stranger. By then I had a team of horses and worked for myself on the farm of a widow, a sister of my former boss, Mr. D. Brigs.

Every year I visited the Colony at least once to see my friends. The first time I took a team of oxen for P. Naber, and the next year a team for Johannes Naber. On another occasion I brought a horse which I traded for 40 acres of land in Fillmore Township, which later became my home.

There was no money to be had in those days, so I had none to buy my oxen. Everything was done on credit in the faith that there would be better times. And we were not put to shame, in spite of the fact that all transactions were carried on without written proofs of indebtedness and without interest.

Since, as I have stated, I worked for myself, I had to board with others, and now and then I had to locate new boarding places, which I did not like to do. Therefore, I began to look for a wife, and that winter I went to Kalamazoo to look for a job as a teamster. Upon arrival I began to board with Albert Kapinga and his wife. There I became acquainted with Maria Meijaard. On April 10, 1853 (my twenty-third birthday; she was twenty years old), we were married in the church by Rev. Cornelius van der Meulen.

Then we went to live on a farm owned by a lawyer 14 miles east by southeast from Kalamazoo in Climax Township. There I lost all faith in lawyers. He wanted to do his part, but not according to our contract. We were there two years. In the fall of 1856 we loaded our furniture on a wagon and moved to the Colony to seek our fortune there. What it means to make a beginning in a dense forest is well known to all those who have struggled through the experience — hard work and poverty.

But I had lived among Americans for seven years, had learned the language fairly well, and how the work should be carried on, and that came in handy. But there was also another side, so that I had to say with Asaph: "My feet were almost gone, my steps had well-nigh slipped" [Psalm 73:2]. For, especially during the past two years, I was in bad company. Because I had left the farm I had to begin something else. Then I became acquainted with a certain Mr. Kamfiel and agreed with him to buy a piece of land that had not been cultivated and to plow it. For this purpose we used four teams of oxen with my two horses in the lead. But Kamfiel was a wicked man who did not fear God, and when one reads the first Psalm, it is clear how dangerous it is to associate with such people. It was for that reason that we decided to go back to the Colony.

But I must tell you incidentally how we were treated by the Yankees. Once I had planned to take a load of flour to the Colony. Five miles north of Allegan my sleigh with its load got stuck in the woods where no road had been cut through. Confused by the deep snow, I could not determine just what the trouble was. Naturally, I wanted to go on if possible. Therefore, I tried hard to get the horses to move, with the result that they broke the shaft and I was stuck as badly as ever. Of necessity I had to go for help to the nearest house that could be reached. Fortunately the man was at home, and he went back with me at once, and helped me free the sleigh and repair the shaft. But by that time it was evening and I could not reach Hamilton that day. The good man took me to his home, served me a meal, and allowed me to spend the night with his family at his house. He had only one stable, and that was for his oxen, but he decided to turn his oxen loose and gave their place to my horses. The next day I paid him and went on.

When I reached Holland with my load of flour, I could find no buyers. If I had brought corn meal, they told me, I would have found many buyers, but for flour there was no market in Holland. After a long delay I finally sold the flour to Mr. Schaddelee, Sr. for $3.25 per barrel, and I had paid $3.00 per barrel in Galesburg, fifteen miles from Kalamazoo. My profit on that load of flour amounted to $2.55 and for that I had to make a trip of 65 miles. But to get back to our trip back to the Colony, we reached our destination in early December, 1856: namely, Fillmore, Allegan County, Michigan.

We planned to go to Albert Kapinga's but it became too dark. So we spent the night near our land with Jannes van den Beldt, who was our neighbor for years. The next day we found a small house nearby that belonged to Isaac Fairbanks and had been built by the Indians, and we lived there that winter because winter overtook us while we were building a log cabin.

In the spring we built a shanty and began the difficult task of clearing the land in a virgin forest. We cut down the trees and as far as possible had them fall into piles, and we planted corn and potatoes between them. That was done quite easily, but the problem we had was to cover them because there were so few leaves or anything else available. But the Lord blessed our efforts with a good crop of potatoes. The corn did not do as well. To plant the corn we made a hole in the ground and we placed the seed between roots and stumps. In such a situation cultivation is out of the question.

There was some improvement the next year, and because we owned our own oxen we soon had some land cleared. The third year everything was a failure. I then had a couple of acres of wheat, which came up well, but in June we had heavy frost one night that killed all the wheat, so we mowed it to use as hay. Potatoes and corn rotted in the ground. And since the buckwheat was also frozen, we harvested only a few turnips. As a result, our daily food that winter consisted of almost nothing but johnnycake and turnips. We had to butcher the hogs because of lack of food for them, and got rid of them. But the Lord sent us relief again. We still had oak trees, and assisted by Egbert Bol, we made staves and in that way provided for two families.

During that time a Methodist minister came now and then to preach in the schoolhouse (Mr. Clapper also came occasionally to conduct revival meetings). And, as we had not yet made confession of faith, and also felt that there were many children of God among the Methodists, we and many of the Dutch people frequently went to the schoolhouse to listen to the sermons.

Not long after that, Rev. van Raalte came to visit us, and when he left he promised to return soon. And he did come back for a visit in the company of two elders, and after some conversation and after asking a few questions, they decided to accept us as members and to baptize our children, which took place in the schoolhouse (then known as the district Van Broek. Now we were members of the congregation of Holland, now known as the Ninth Street congregation. Later the church at Fillmore was built on the county line; it is known to this day as the Ebenezer Church.

But we now return to life on the land and its difficulties. During one of the early years, when there had been a crop failure, six of us (accompanied by a woman who served as cook) went to Laketown to earn some money cutting cordwood for H. Walsh, who had a general store in Holland. We built a shanty there and lived in it from Monday to Saturday. My wife had to be by herself with four children during that time to take care of the livestock. In this way we managed to get through the winter. In the spring before ships began to arrive, the need was still more pressing. But the Lord has always provided.

From year to year we increased the clearing in size. But it took several years before we could raise enough to take care of ourselves and our livestock. For that reason, when spring arrived and the snow was gone, we were obliged to send our animals into the woods to fend for themselves. Then, for example, when you needed the oxen, you would have to go and find them. One time shortly after noon, I went into the woods for that purpose, but could not find the oxen. Toward evening it began to rain and it became dark, so I could not find my way and had to spend the night in the woods (where at that time there were many wolves). Since everything was wet I could not start a fire. I spent the entire night standing behind a tree, begging the Lord to protect me.

When daylight returned, I could find my way again, and in the morning I got out of the woods a half mile south of Jan Kleinheksel's place. When I had left the woods, and had begun to walk toward home, to my joy I found my oxen grazing along the trail.

Vol. 1, chapter 15, no. 59, pp. 481-88

59. VAN RAALTE'S "COMMEMORATION ADDRESS, 1872"

[This translation of Van Raalte's *Toespraak* (Address) is from Henry Lucas, *Ebenezer 1847-1947* (New York, 1947), 21-28. Van Raalte delivered the address in the woods one mile east of Holland on September 17, 1872, at ceremonies commemorating the twenty-fifth year of the founding of Holland. This *Toespraak*, which is the first history of the settlement, was printed in *De Hope* of September 1, 1872, and reprinted in the September 1, 1897, issue of the same paper.]

With mingled emotion, thanks and joy, the events associated with our arrival as strangers in a strange land today rise before our minds. Out of the depths of affliction our prayer rose to God, and His hand brought us to this land. We have struggled through the difficulties of a quarter of a century; and viewing the consequences of our steps and their fruits we want to confess with thanks and jubilation: "The Lord has wrought great things for us because of which we are happy." And to our successors to whom we entrust our inheritance we wish to say, "Forget not, it is God who pointed it out to us!"

Permit me to relate something of the history of our immigration which has molded your destiny. For about thirty-five [*sic*] years we in the land of our birth had carried on a heavy struggle for religious freedom. After years of hateful persecutions which violated our civil rights, we finally acquired an equally hateful and unjust freedom.

During these difficulties we became acquainted with the impoverished condition of many of our people. After fruitless efforts to help them materially, finally, in 1845 [*sic*] an organization was created in Arnhem to assist needy families to America, being impelled thereto by the good reports we received about that land. At the same time, in a meeting of certain so-called Hague Gentlemen [*Haagsche Heeren*], this emigration project was treated with contempt. So strong were the ties of love that bound us to the Netherlands that I promised Dominie [Otto G.] Heldring under certain conditions to lead the emigration to the uplands of Java; but the government of the Netherlands did not dare to permit liberty to flourish on Java.

Our purpose to emigrate was denounced as impious and faithless to Church and Fatherland and aroused opposition and bitter comment. Nevertheless a thirst, a hope, even a fiery desire rose in the breasts of many to seek a more spacious and freer field for themselves and their progeny. Like the breath of God it moved over the entire country. The desire to emigrate ripened simultaneously in Zeeland under Dominie [Cornelius] van der Meulen, in Utrecht under Dominie [Hendrik P.] Scholte, in Friesland under Dominie [Maarten A.] Ypma, in Overijssel under Dominie [Seine] Bolks. The pamphlet Dominie [Anthony] Brummelkamp and I published in defense of our undertaking under the title *Emigration, Or Why We Advocate Emigration to North America and Not to Java* hastened the movement. In my own heart I was able to bring myself to drink this cup — in the conviction that this step was equivalent to breaking ice in order to open a broad and deep stream of emigration. I had the conviction and burning desire that these people, reared in a struggle for freedom, faithful to its calling and to God, would prove much more useful, influential, and fortunate in the new world than in the old where we could enjoy peace and civil rights only by permission and where so many had to look forward with uneasiness and worry for bread for themselves and their families and for room in which to work. At the same time I believed that the establishment of Christian colonies was the same as to labor in behalf of the Gospel.

In September 1846 the ships that sailed from Holland to America were filled with emigrants. To encourage me in that heartbreaking moment my beloved brother Dominie Brummelkamp wrote me: "Thousands of God's children in the Netherlands with their prayers accompany you on the ocean." A mighty emotion rose in the hearts of our people. Thousands prepared to follow us in the next year.

The conviction that when God calls us to some task He also offers His helping arm supported me during the storms on the sea and also in the face of my helplessness and my lack of knowledge. In December at the entrance to the harbor of New York we offered our psalms of thankfulness for our safe arrival. In New York we were encouraged by the friendly interest of Dr. [Thomas] de Witt and Elder [James] Forrester. We have not forgotten the difficulties we experienced upon our arrival as immigrants nor God's friendly and paternal solicitude in offering us the loving help of many people, as, for example, Dr. [Isaac] Wyckoff. To us they truly were as angels of God.

Winter weather and the lack of railway communications forced me to leave my family in Detroit. There Rev. [George] Duffield, Rev. West, and Mr. [Theodore] Romeyn also showed their sincerest interest. Through our association with the aged Christian gentleman, Mr. [Robert] Stuart, a Presbyterian elder and supervisor of the Illinois Canal, we gained much information about the country that would be useful in my work.

The kind of life I saw in American pioneer homes, the credit which poor folk acquired by husbanding their earnings, their joyful labor to improve their condition in life and not merely to gain their daily bread, their civilized manner of life, their obvious educational development and their love for school and Sabbath, influenced me strongly. On the other hand, the decay of pioneer settlements which, I heard, frequently happened impressed upon me the necessity of securing good market prices, means of transportation, and employment for our poor. Our workmen were my first care and also a source of strength. Some acquaintance with the Grand and Kalamazoo Rivers and the splendid future they offered as well as an inexhaustible opportunity for working men led me to choose a spot for settlement on Lake Michigan between these two rivers, provided a personal investigation should show that we had not been misled by maps or by Land Office representations.

Judge [John R.] Kellogg of Allegan, my never-to-be-forgotten friend, offered me the service of a horse, and accompanied by a few of his friends, all of whom have passed beyond, conducted me to the house of a minister, the Rev. [George N.] Smith, the missionary among the Ottawa Indians who lodged me and extended to me many services in examining the region. Because of his influence, the Indians served me faithfully, gave me information, and even were pleased to let me stand behind them on their snowshoes so that raising my feet with theirs I was freed from the wearisome sinking in the snow, which thus made my travels much easier. But these wanderings proved too much for my strength so that on one occasion when we were lost, Rev. Smith, at my request, left me in the snow. The bark of the dogs brought him back to the right place, but it was with much labor that he was able to assist me to his house where, in that unforgettable night, I rejoiced being especially in God's care, although I could sleep but little on account of my excessive exertions.

Although the Americans recommended the localities along rivers, and for the most part thought it too great a hazard to settle here, although the Hollanders avoided the forests — and it occasioned a great struggle to subject my family and myself to the difficulties of such pioneer living — nevertheless, the combination of so many advantages, although at first they could be only slowly developed, left me no doubt as to my duty. I knew that the rich forest soil was better fitted for dairying and the raising of winter wheat; that because of manufacturing and navigation, far higher market prices could be obtained here than in any place in the West; and that the country near the shore of Lake Michigan, protected by the water from severe frosts, was a region peculiarly adapted to the raising of fruit. I could find no other place for our group where along inhabited rivers, lined with manufactories and mills, tens of thousands of our people could find work without danger of being scattered and at the same time be certain of an opportunity continually to obtain new land without any interference. I chose this region therefore on account of its great variety, being assured that if immigration from the Netherlands should develop into a powerful movement we ought to remain together for mutual support and ought to have this variety for labor and for capital, especially with a view to the future.

In my mind I saw not only homes for a stream of working men but I also saw the ships of Hollanders, their flourishing fisheries, a fair harbor which inevitably would develop by the side of such activities, and also areas devoted to the production of fruit. And especially I beheld the richest of rural villages for which even at that moment I thanked God. I was hopeful that our people also would manage mills and factories. The object of my settling between these two rivers was to secure the advantage of both streams, for we could not get along without the nearby settled areas, and at the same time to secure a center of unifying religious life and labor for the advancement of God's Kingdom.

More than we expected have we received! The Lord has granted more than we ever imagined or even prayed for! Is there anyone who can visit our villages and townships, covered with the richest farmsteads, and not be astonished? It is impossible to estimate the value of our ships, fisheries, mills, factories, and fruit farms. These sources of wealth have scarcely begun to flow; others remain to be opened as, for example, our stone quarries and iron mines, all of them advantageously situated because we possess shipping lines and railway communications. In truth God has wrought great things for us!

In addition, our hearts' desire for the realization of a unifying religious life and labors for the Kingdom has been given us. In Michigan alone our churches already number 26. Already 33 ministers and 15 school teachers have gone forth from our midst. Illinois, Iowa, and Wisconsin, as well as Michigan, and yes, even the churches in the eastern parts of the country have received blessings from these contributions. To them we have to thank our colonies in Minnesota, Nebraska, and Kansas. Because of them our people in Virginia are enjoying the benefits of preaching and the school recently established but already influential. Even may we rejoice that India also possesses our beloved brother [Enne J.] Heeren. And finally, we have been granted the privilege of educating Japanese in our midst; we hope that the three entrusted to our care may return to their people under God's guidance and prove a rich blessing.

God indeed established in our midst a unifying life and work. May His name be praised for this and also because He moved our hearts to give for this work a thank-offering now already amounting to $20,000. May we view this as a gift and increasingly regard it as a treasure, a privilege and calling, as a crown, strength, and pleasure.

So far we have related to you some of the reasons for our settling in this place; but let us now turn our attention to the history of our settlement. In the closing days [really, second week] of February 1847 we brought our small group — B[ernardus] Grootenhuis and family, [Jan] Laarman and family, E[gbert] Frederiks, [Willem] Notting, [Evert] Sagers, [Frans] Smit, [Hermanus] Lankheet, etc., from Detroit and St. Clair and sent the tidings of our plans to our people scattered throughout the land. We proceeded to Kalamazoo where we enjoyed many tokens of friendship, especially from the Rev. [Ova P.] Hoyt. We traveled by way of Allegan to the site chosen for our homes. I left my family in the care of Mr. John R. Kellogg and his wife from whom our people have received much help.

We took up our quarters in the church belonging to the Indians, which stood beside the Rev. Smith's house. Our first work was to open a road for oxen along the farms later owned by Hellenthal, Kamper, [H.] van Duren, and [Wouter] van der Haar. In these labors we were assisted by [Edward J.] Harrington, a trustworthy and capable American. But our task became too arduous when we reached Cedar Swamp on the present Zeeland Road, and we were forced to open a path along the higher land on Van der Haar's farm and my own house to the landing place. The first log houses — no better than ox sheds — were erected on the spot now occupied by Van der Haar's barn. These log houses served as dwellings in which we held our public meetings. The first meeting of this kind, which I shall never forget, was opened with prayer; it gave me an emphatic impression of our labors and our future. Then was built the log house occupied by Van Lente. At the same time Grootenhuis and Laarman began their labors and also the erection of my house. None of these houses are now in existence except the one I live in at present.

Quite seasonably to strengthen our courage and our hands in March arrived from St. Louis the groups of [Teunis] Keppel, [Hein] van der Haar, and [Jan] Binnekant, men well known for their skill at work. From Albany came the family of [Jan] Kolvoort and others. In anticipation of the arrival of friends, the groups sought out locations suitable for farming communities or for villages. In this manner searching for land north of an ice-covered river in the company of [Hendrik] Plaggemars, [Jan] Stegeman, [Hendrik] Oldemeyer, and [Egbert] Dunnewind once exposed us to great danger of death. A heavy, warm rain broke up the ice and cut us off from all help. We would have succumbed from cold and want; for the weather changed, and by night our clothes were frozen. But behold, just above the spot where [Gerrit Jan] Boone's mill now stands, the Indians had felled a long slender tree which was held in place by trees and supported by cakes of ice, thus making a bridge for us which indicated the only means to save us from certain death. For me it was a bridge, but some of our group cried and wept with fear when I began to cross over. Contrary to every expectation, we all escaped death. I enjoyed a happy and thankful night which was too cold to enable me to keep myself warm in my unfinished house.

Early in the spring arrived [Jan] Rabbers and his following, and many of us know how helpfully he labored in Groningen. At about the same time came the Frisians under the leadership of Dominie Ypma, who showed that they knew how to pick good land. Drenthe and Graafschap occupied a prominent place in the first year of the settlement. Toward the close of May I brought my own family through the trackless woods to my own log house. To this day I thank God that my now-departed wife without hesitation, and with the singing of psalms, oc-·cupied our unfinished house.

The organization of the Zeelanders was under the leadership of Dominie van der Meulen and Elder [Jannes] van de Luyster. It had been well planned, was provided with some funds, and had betimes sent word that sheds were to be erected for them. The three shiploads of immigrants established the strong and extensive settlement of Zeeland Village, which definitely was destined to make a compact and extensive colony of our settlements. The places chosen by the settlers automatically received the names of the provinces from which the groups had come. In the second year Dominie Bolks and his friends from Overijssel, after spending about a year at Syracuse [New York], established themselves southeast of us, in our Overisel. Township 5, consisting of Ranges 14, 15, and 16 of Ottawa County, was formed at my request and given the name of Holland, from which Zeeland later was organized as a separate township. Our landing place at the head of Black Lake was generally known as the *Lake.*

This place consisted in the sheds built for Zeelanders, a few log houses, and a place to store things. But some of the people were already talking of going to "de stad." Because of the absence of bridges, the roads were only temporary, and all labor expended upon them ultimately proved a loss, except on the main roads. Importation of necessaries by land was most difficult. Our provisions had to come along the coast in flatboats from the mouths of the Grand and Kalamazoo Rivers, which because of the sandbar in our harbor occasioned much labor and loss. It is no wonder that immigrants who had been informed by letter, when they arrived in the city of Holland, were bewildered and asked where they might find the city of Holland or its storekeepers, bakers, etc., and that they were greatly disappointed to learn everything as it had been represented existed only in the future.

Many were the difficulties of those days; but the singing of psalms which rose from under the branches and in the log houses presented something inexplicable to the superficial observer. With many there was an abiding hope in God and a consciousness of noble purpose. The sweet enjoyment of complete freedom, and living without terror or fear of violating a man-made command and without the fear of insults from people, was also deeply appreciated and as thankfully enjoyed. Around my house, using logs for seats, we enjoyed our first place of worship in the open air. There also we held our general public meetings in which we registered our common interests by majority vote. Not until the latter part of the year did we learn from Mr. H[enry] D. Post how to manage our government in accordance with the custom of the country, and then we chose our officers.

Our trials rose to the highest point during the latter part of that first summer when the entire settlement became a sickbed, and, although physicians had been called in at the common expense, many succumbed, especially through lack of suitable houses and properly prepared and adequate food. This heart-breaking and discouraging situation produced a sharp conflict between painful necessity and human sentiment. Never had I been so near collapse as when in those crowded log houses in which each family had to manage to live in a few square feet of space, I saw how all sorts of family activities — housekeeping, being sick, dying, and the care of the dead — had to be discharged. Small wonder that in that hour of trial there appeared traces of despair and indifference. But God granted a change! The sufferers recovered, the autumn was most beautiful, and the winter that followed was unusually mild so that everybody could continue building and while at work even enjoy his meals under the open sky. Most of our settlers went to work on their land; those who were sick and in need of care remained at the landing place by the lake.

Our church was built outside the so-called town in order to better serve our farmers. At the corner of the churchyard stood our never-to-be-forgotten church, which also served as a schoolhouse. Not until 1856 was this structure abandoned for the first church in Holland when the growing numbers had made it impracticable for the people of the town to go to church through the long swamp road.

Our colonization efforts were based upon religious principles; they drew their strength from God. So long as they remain permeated with this spirit, they will succeed. The sweet comfort inspired by independence and unlimited freedom we drank in deep drafts which gave our hearts joy and strength. Joy in the Sabbath, the power of the truth that strengthens the heart, prayer, and the comforts of living and working together in our many nearby communities have supported, encouraged, and helped our people to succeed in their heavy and difficult task. Many were God's evidences of help in material things; every village and every family has its own special history in this respect. The speakers who follow undoubtedly will recount some of this history.

After a struggle of twenty-five years, in spite of sin, misery, and severe discipline, we can nevertheless enjoy a beautiful festival. Because God has built, we live in the happy conviction that He has done well with us and granted our hearts' desires. We desire to praise Him as the One who answers prayers. We want to honor His name as being our gracious supporter, our almighty Helper, our God who forgives manifoldly.

In those hearts wherein the praise of God is born, there, my beloved friends, will it live beyond the grave and beyond death. Then will we be able not only to derive joy from our history but also to demonstrate it in a more perfect way.

Beloved, to you who follow us in our field of labor, we are ready with a sense of happiness to bequeath this inheritance. But do not forget that we have received it from God. We received it as God's nursery for eternity and as a work for God's Kingdom; we received it prayerfully out of God's hand and with this inheritance we desire to attain God's end.

This inheritance will bloom under your hand provided God, His day, His Christ, His Kingdom, and His work remain the beloved aim of your lives. Sin, the corroding canker of nations, is the consuming rust of your joy and strength. Neglect of prayer means neglect of God and, finally, unbelief. We confidently expect better things, O youth, than the laying waste of our inheritance. May it shine in your hands like God's city on earth! And may God grant you in 1897 a very happy semicentennial celebration of our settlement that will be dedicated to Him and praise His name. May this inheritance be to you in all eternity the beloved spot in which you yourselves have learned to know God, where you have found your God. So be it!

Vol. 2, chapter 17, no. 62, pp. 7-13

62. "A CONTEMPORARY ACCOUNT OF THE HOLLAND FIRE"

[The following account of the burning of Holland on October 9, 1871, was published in a joint issue of *De Grondwet, De Wachter,* and *De Hollander* on October 12, 1871. The Reverend Henry De Mots translated the report.]

Holland was, and is no more. Holland's catastrophe. Days of anguish, need, and suffering! We are confronted with one of the most sad and difficult tasks which has ever been laid upon us. Our minds refuse to ponder and our hands are reluctant to write down the dreadful series of disasters which have befallen us. We are not able to share all the particulars with you and so we must considerably limit ourselves. Through the kindness of the publishers of *De Hope* we are able to share this account with you in this brief paper, and we express our appreciation to the above-mentioned paper for this kind service.

The Almighty has spoken and the effect of that voice is powerful. It can be said that our beloved city of Holland no longer exists. The entire business district lies in ruins. Entire streets have disappeared; every businessman has lost everything, and between 200 and 300 houses have been destroyed by fire. The most beautiful part of our city has become an unsightly level plain full of smoking and smoldering ruins.

Throughout the past week large forest fires raged in our vicinity, particularly in the direction of Graafschap. Several areas of the city were dangerously threatened, and during the night leading from Wednesday to Thursday of last week successful efforts were made to spare the Hope printing establishment, and the home of Dr. Crispell and the College buildings. Since that time the fire continued to advance, destroying barns and houses here and there. However, there did not appear to be any danger for us. On Sunday afternoon, however, it began to become very stormy south of the city, and before the afternoon services were ended the alarm was sounded. Even so, the danger which threatened appeared to be directed toward the surrounding areas rather than the city itself. If the wind had continued to blow from that same direction, then Holland would still be here. However, between 11 and 1 o'clock the wind turned to the west and increased in intensity so that in violence it resembled a hurricane. The so-called creek, a low spot, which was filled with trees which had been cut down, trees which were dead and partially decayed, and all kinds of brush, soon became a sea of flames. The wind drove the rain of sparks toward the tannery of Sprietsma and Elferdink and a moment later to the large wharf of Cappon and Bertsch, which immediately was ignited, together with 2000 to 3000 cords of bark. From there the fire leaped over toward 8th Street, beyond River Street and several side streets, sweeping away everything, depending on the direction of the wind. A bit to the south the flames attacked the 3rd Reformed Church and also the New Methodist Church and then moved on to destroy other parts of the city. The flames spread with unbelievable rapidity, and in less than an hour the larger and more beautiful parts of Holland had been reduced to ashes. We can say that the entire business district had been destroyed by the fire, and seven-eighths of the city had been laid waste. It is impossible to calculate the loss, but it is somewhere between $800,000 and one million dollars. Between 150 and 200 families are homeless, having lost everything, their clothes, their furniture; in a word, they have lost everything and they are called upon to eat the bread of compassion. Generous means of support have arrived from surrounding areas, especially from Grand Haven and Grand Rapids, and we are greatly indebted to the citizens of these communities for their generosity. We have also been informed that in Grand Rapids, Kalamazoo, and even Detroit money is being collected and clothing is also being collected for our entirely bereft citizens.

That night from Sunday to Monday, that night when Holland was destroyed, will never be forgotten. That was a night of deadly anxiety and unspeakable suffering. As far as we know there was no loss of life to mourn because of the fire except Sara Ooms, and the widow of Jacob Tolk, who were among the missing and whose bones were found.

Holland was, and is — and we can say this from many points of view — no more. The city as city is gone and only a few houses on the outskirts remain. The entire industrial fabric and business have been swept away, and everything must be rebuilt from the ground up. The scene is eerie and heartbreaking. Where the city once stood there is a level plain covered with smoldering heaps of ruins and rubbish and people digging through the ruins in the hope of finding something and looking for something that had been hidden in their houses. This prosperous place has been made poor in a moment. They are helpless and are bereft of all income, and are dependent on the surrounding areas for the necessities of life. The circumstances are crushing, and it is impossible to appreciate or comprehend the loss of those directly involved. The labor of 25 years has been swept away. And what makes the circumstances even much more fearful is the well-founded fear that the fire insurance companies will go bankrupt, based on the experience of the great world city, Chicago, when it was destroyed, root and branch. And now, will our citizens in Holland be called upon to face the future and begin anew without even this security, although small, and thus be totally poor, helpless, naked, and bereft of everything?

In this dark night a few faint flickers of light, however, have remained. The citizens have not given up or lost their courage. Already here and there we see men who are busy with timber and boards erecting small pilot projects. Our friend J. van Landegend, who has been burned out for the second time, E. van der Veen, and many others are busy at work. At a gathering of the community, which was held on Tuesday at noon, it was universally agreed and witnessed that with resolve they would begin anew. A committee was appointed to receive and to distribute gifts.

It should be noted that in other places of our settlement houses, barns, and enclosures, etc. had been destroyed by fire. In Graafschap and Noordeloos many houses and barns were destroyed. In Collendoorn the church and parsonage were burned down. Between Groningen and Zeeland the fire raged furiously, and the town of Zeeland was dangerously threatened for some time. Among the public buildings that were destroyed that Sunday night into Monday morning were 3rd Reformed Church and parsonage, 2nd Reformed (American) Church, the New Methodist Church, and the Protestant Episcopal Church.

First Reformed Church, surrounded by a sea of fire, and now surrounded by heaps of rubbish and ruins, has been spared in a singular way for a second time. The Union School and the Hope printing office and the College buildings remain standing. The parsonage of 3rd Reformed Church was spared, as was the Townhouse. The True Reformed Church and parsonage remained standing. Among the factories which were spared were Pluggers saw- and flour-mill and Heald's plow factory and ironworks. Also, the depots of both railroads escaped the fire.

Eighth Street, or Main Street, was swept clean by the fire, on the south side from the place where E. Harold's dwelling stood all the way to the home of Mr. G. Wakker. On this side of the street the homes of the following were destroyed: E. Herald, I. Cappon, J. Parks, F. Kieft, W. Blom, Widow Klijn, Widow Tolk, E. van der Veen, H. Wiersema, A. Verplanke, H. Meengs's 2 buildings, Beukema's saloon, *Gazeteer* printing, City Hotel, E. van der Veen's ironmonger's shop, J. Duursema's store, P. Sakker's furniture store, Sprietsma's shoe store, D. Bertsch's store, Nibbelink's meat market, Koningsberg's saloon and boardinghouse, Mrs. Wheeler's milliner's shop, De Weerd's meat market and dwelling, P. van Landegend's cigar store, the post office, Van der Haar's meat market, N. Zalsman's store, Joslin and Breyman's jewelry store, E. Herold's shoe and boot store, Pessink's City Bakery, J. Albers' dwelling, Albers' jewelry store, Van Landegend's hardware store, Doornink and Steketee's store, P. Boot's dwelling, J. Doesburg's pharmacy, the homes of A. Vennema and W. Brouwer, K. Schaddelee's office, and two houses belonging to Mr. E. J. Harrington.

On the north side of 8th Street everything was swept clean by the fire from the place where the beautiful dwelling of Mr. P. van den Bosch once stood to the home of Mr. G. van Schelven, which remained standing. On this side of the street the following establishments were burned down: the home of P. van den Bosch, H. Koning's dwelling and store, E. Winter's smithy, E. van Zee's home, J. Roost, a rented house, J. Binnekant's Pioneer bakery and bookstore, *Hollander* printing, G. H. van Winkel (?), M. D. Howard's dwelling, H. D. Post's pharmacy, store, and dwelling, H. Bennett's restaurant, C. Hofman's dwelling, J. W. Bosman's clothing store, Kroon and Everhard's ironworks store, Widow J. Vervennes's saddlers shop, Kanters and Co.'s store, Bosch and Co.'s store, City Bank, De Jong, Van Schelven and Oggel's store, an old building belonging to J. Koning, J. O. Bakker's shoe and boot store, Cloetingh's bookstore, H. Walsh pharmacy and dwelling, Labarden and Son's furniture store, U. de Vries saddle maker, milliners shop of the Van den Berge sisters, A. Geerlings's dwelling, and H. Vaupell's saddle shop and dwelling.

River Street is burned out on the west side of the homes of H. Uiterwijk and M. Russel. The houses between here and the corner of River and 10th Street remained standing, from the corner of River and 10th Street to the dwelling of Kraai, not far from the Grand Haven bridge. On this side the following establishments were burned down: a rental house belonging to P. Pfanstiehl, Mr. J. Roost's store and living quarters, Koffers and Gringhuis's store, Dr. Nichol's dental office, the new shoe and boots store of W. Elverding and Co., the dwelling of P. Pfanstiehl, the barn of the City Hotel, M. D. Howard's office, De Kraker's meat market, Werkman, Geerlings and Co.'s store, a rental house of D. T. Werkman, M. P. Visser's new store, *American Exchange* and barn, Holland Brewery, H. Gezon's house, the dwelling of E. Nienhuis, 3 or 4 small houses belonging to an unknown person, and E. Kraai's home.

On the east side of the street the following structures were destroyed by the fire: the old factory building of Verbeek and Company, H. W. Verbeek and Co.'s furniture store, W. van Putten's pharmacy, the store of D. te Roller the tailor, *De Grondwet* printing establishment. H. Meengs's store, G. Lauder's portrait gallery, Aling's store, the establishment of Flieman the smith and maker of wagons, Wilson's barber shop, Butkan's boardinghouse, another, of T. Sullivan, Storing's saloon and boardinghouse, City Mills, an old blacksmith shop, American Hotel, the dwelling of R. P. Ferris, the home of R. van Kampen, and the homes of Arnold and M. Clark.

On Lake Street the following structures were burned down: O. I. Pfanstiehl's shingle, stove, and bolt factory, E. J. Harrington's forwarding office and dock, part of the side-track of the Michigan Lake Shore railroad, and the sawmill of R. P. Ferris. Also destroyed by fire were the tug boats *Day Spring* and the old *Mayflower,* which were docked at the wharf at the time. In addition 3 or 4 scows were destroyed.

As we come to Fish Street we see that on the west side the rentals of K. van Haaften have been destroyed. On the east side the rental house of B. van Rij suffered a similar fate as did that of A. Geerlings and the dwelling of Teunis Keppel.

When we turn to Market Street we discover the following losses: the rental house of the widow Nies, the livery stable of H. Boone, the homes of L. D. Visser and J. Paulus, and the house and barn of D. de Vries.

As we turn our attention to the west side we observe the following losses: the dwelling of P. Nagelkerk, the rental house owned by H. Keppel, which was a small house, Helling and Busch's sewing machine store, Bostwick's portrait gallery and dwelling place, the old store of Mrs. H. C. Knol, the home of K. Mulder, the barn and rental home of Widow H. G. Knol, the house and barn of P. Kleis, and the home of Mrs. Jacobs.

On the west side of Pine Street the following losses were sustained: the homes of H. J. Peckler, Mrs. Minderhout, Rev. W. H. Bronson, and M. van de Vrede were destroyed. And on Maple Street the tannery of Sprietsma and Company was destroyed.

As we move along to 1st Street we see that the following losses have been sustained: the steam-driven sawmill of W. K. Fleitstra and the home of J. de Feyter. On neighboring 2nd Street the homes of P. de Kraker, G. Dalman's small house, and one belonging to E. Sawyer. Moving on to 3rd Street we see that the homes of H. Beukema and G. Raak and also the two houses of C. Blom Sr. and J. Louwis have been leveled.

As we continue to survey the damage we come to 4th Street and see that C. de Wit, G. Gringhuis, P. Pfanstiehl, J. de Spelder, Widow Winters, and Burke have lost their homes. On 5th Street the home of Van Symonds and the new brick house of P. Winter, and also the homes of W. Finch and J. Fliemen have become the victims of the fire.

As we move along we come to 6th Street and on the north side of the street the following losses have been sustained: the home and soap works of M. Mehr, the home of P. Gunst, the Wesleyan Church, and the dwellings of P. Pfanstiehl and J. Verschure. On the south side of this street the dwellings of M. de Feyter, Bouman, A. Meerman, and the Widow Mulder, 2 houses belonging to the Widow H. G. Knol, G. Bos, W. J. Scott, and A. Verschuur were leveled.

On neighboring 7th Street, on the north side of the street, the following people sustained losses: the homes of L. van Dis, Heetebrij, L. ter Brink, J. M. Reidsema, G. Ijskes, Mrs. Vinke, P. Bouman, P. van der Stel, A. Rot, Kamferbeek, B. Volmari, the Widow H. G. Knol, H. de Vries, and the brick home of T. A. Berkompas, the home and the machine shop of G. H. Brooks, and the house of J. Trimpe. On the south side of 7th Street a barn owned by T. Keppel,

2 houses owned by J. Smit, Rev. C. van der Veen, J. de Peyster, W. Joslin, P. Geense, P. van Geenen, J. Labots, P. J. Kamperman, Widow Kooijers and the new house of D. J. Werkman, all were consumed by the fire.

As we continue our survey of the ruins we come to 9th Street and view the desolation on the north side of the street and take note of the following losses: Cappon and Bertsch's big steam tannery, the homes of I. Kramer, G. Boot, and 2 rentals of F. van der Veen, 1 rental house of H. Wiersema, buildings belonging to S. Reidsema, M. van Regenmorter, J. Verplanke, J. van de Roovaard, J. Kramer, J. Nibbelink, W. C. Nibbelink, W. Verbeek, A. Meerman, rentals of H. Boone and R. Takken, A. Westveer, J. Albertis's rental house and livery stable, homes of P. de Vries, P. de Koning, R. Oostema, and K. van Haafte.

On the south side of 9th Street the places destroyed were the homes of S. Schmidt, J. R. Kleyn, C. Dok, E. Everhard, J. D. Everhard, H. Vergter, D. Verschuur, A. Woltman, R. Schilleman, Prof. C. Scott, the rental building of Verbeek and Co., G. van Putten, D. te Roller, J. Schoon, C. Vorst (2 small rentals), G. Steketee, and H. W. Verbeek. This street was swept clean by the fire on the north side from Cappon's Tannery to the corner of 9th and Cedar Street. And on the south side from J. R. Kleyn up to the J. W. Bosman house, which was near 1st Reformed Church.

When we turn our attention to 10th Street we note that the fire destroyed the following on the north side of the street: rentals owned by Hermanus Boone and Mrs. C. B. Baily, the home of M. Mulder, the old and the new Methodist and Episcopal Churches, the dwellings of Mrs. Broadmore, P. de Vries, H. Barendregt, the large and new plow factory of H. W. Verbeek and Co., the barn of G. van Putten, the Grace Episcopal Church, and the home of J. Duursema. The fire destroyed the following on the south side of 10th street: the homes of J. Elverdink, S. Davis, W. H. Deming, and Hope (2nd Reformed) Church.

On 12th Street the homes of J. Boersema, F. van Rij, and Westerhof, located on the north side of the street, were destroyed. On the south side of the street, C. de Jong's large and beautiful brick home and 3rd Reformed Church and parsonage were consumed by the flames.

This is an accurate account of the structures which were destroyed by the fire. The churches which were destroyed are 2nd and 3rd Reformed, Methodist Episcopal, and Wesleyan Methodist. Only 1st Reformed and the True Holland Reformed Churches were left standing. From here you can see the old geographical locations of the city, and these are 1st Reformed Church, the True Holland Reformed Church, Union School, the College buildings, *Hope* printing, and both depots.

Vol. 2, chapter 17, no. 63, pp. 14-31

63. THEODORE DE VEER'S "OUR HOLLANDERS IN MICHIGAN"

[The author, a Dutch journalist, visited Zeeland on the occasion of its sixtieth anniversary celebrations. His spirited article appeared in *Eigenhaard,* 1907. The report was translated by the late E. R. Post and Dr. George Harper, professor emeritus of English, Calvin College.]

In the western part of Michigan, some twenty miles southwest of Grand Rapids, lies a small, tidy town of real old-country name. It was baptized with the name of Zeeland. It is a sunny, prosperous little place with luxurious farmland, in a land with yellow waving acres and extensive grassy meadows and flowering gardens and orchards. It numbers about two thousand fine, energetic people, sterling workers, who were born primarily of Dutch stock.

Everything there points to prosperity and consistent forward motion. There are sawmills where furniture and furnishings for the home are built. There is also a clock factory, the biggest in the world no less, as well as two steam mills for grain, a factory where wagons are made, and a factory for doors and windows. There are also banks and large shops, and each resident has a separate house or dwelling with a small garden surrounding it. And beyond the main street there are lanes, cool under the wide shadows of the trees. In that industrious and gallant Zeeland, in that little town composed of Zeeuwen, a glorious celebration was held recently in honor of her brave "Old Folks." The "Old Folks Day" had special character and significance — the sixtieth anniversary of the *kolonie* was being celebrated. It was a fitting and emotional demonstration in honor of the courageous men and women who had the daring to settle in that dark and unknown land.

On the 21st of August, 1907, a feast was held for the brave and sturdy pioneers of 1847, 1848, and 1849, those pilgrim fathers of West Michigan — ten years after neighboring Holland celebrated a half-century of existence. Little Zeeland surpassed the celebration of the emigration to the great and open West. With gratitude they paid homage to those heroes who struggled and even lost their lives in the gigantic wilderness. They struggled with unknown disease and also with the pangs of hunger. Does the "old country" know about the courage and the perseverance described above?

Sixty years have passed since that noble pioneer, Dr. A. C. van Raalte, came to this "land of liberty." How dark and sad and somber the times were in the old fatherland. It was in reaction to the French occupation, a reaction which also made a big impact upon the church.

The freedom to worship God in keeping with one's own thinking was a right that was not acknowledged. After the church reorganization of 1816 by King Willem I, State and Church were one. Slavish submission to the Synodical authority was demanded. No departure from that church and no difference in religious conviction were tolerated by the state. How could tension not develop in all this haste? The agitation had grown stronger and stronger. Hundreds upon hundreds desired to break with the Hervormde Church. It was a church revolution.

At the same time, yet independently, two ministers, Hendrik de Cock in Ulrum and H. P. Scholte in Doeveren, raised the question of separation for the first time. This they did as defenders of Reformed doctrine. A suspension of these two, quite naturally, became a possibility. People simply were not free in their worship of God. However, it was this spark that ignited the wider fire of the revolution. Everywhere throughout the land Separatists began to appear. People began to hold services in barns and out in the open fields; that was in 1834. However, an old police regulation found in the Napoleonic Code had not lost its power. No meeting of more than nineteen persons could be held without the permission of the local authorities. And so it was that permission was denied for the Separatists to gather for religious worship.

It is not difficult for us to imagine the result. The services were held and fines imposed. However, the authorities soon moved beyond imposing fines. Soldiers were billeted in homes; gatherings were rudely disrupted by armed guards, and some Separatists were imprisoned; property was confiscated; and some were treated very rudely. Mobs turned on those despised members of that sect of Separatists — they had to be punished. And there were many instances of arson. Matters became worse; even in the schools the stupid persecution continued. And why? Simply because in their religious convictions these people differed with the rest of the nation. Thus in that enlightened nineteenth century, in a Christian land, Christians were persecuted. The lines were drawn so narrowly that followers of the Reformed faith found life to be almost impossible. And protest was not possible because of the power behind the police regulation.

The times also became more oppressive from a social point of view. A disease in the potato crop threatened to destroy the food supply, and a general malaise darkened the horizon as the Separatists looked to the future. Even so, the strugglers remained standing, among them the noble pioneer, the great leader and the father of the present-day settlement in West Michigan, the minister Dr. A. C. van Raalte.

However, it became evident that something had to be done. And so it was that in the winter of 1845-46, the leading men, H. P. Scholte first of all, came to Amsterdam to discuss the question of emigration. A committee was appointed from among them to negotiate with the government the matter of colonization to the island of Java. However, so many obstacles were placed in their path that their eyes were turned elsewhere. For many, the Cape of Good Hope appeared to be a safe place and thought was given to this possibility, until America was accepted as the land for the future.

In the spring of 1846, before any system of emigration had been arranged, A. Hartgerink and J. Arnold, equipped by their friends and their church, were sent to that big North America to investigate and then to bring back a report to the brethren. That extensive report about their journey and their experiences in the new world, a voluminous document for which eleven *gulden* postage was paid, was read in the Netherlands with satisfaction.

During the same summer of 1846, Rev. Thomas de Witt was sent by the General Synod of the Reformed Dutch Church in America from New York on an official mission to the old fatherland. What influence did his visit have on the decision to emigrate? It isn't difficult to understand. In his report to the General Synod in 1847 he says, "When in Holland I received information of a rising spirit of emigration to America and especially among the seceders from the established church. Soon two important colonies from this class will be founded in the West."

There was a great deal of discussion about emigration; very frequently conversation involved "the West" and mention was made about such places as Texas, Michigan, Wisconsin, and Iowa as preferable locations. And so it was that on September 14, 1846, a two-masted American ship, the *Southerner* from Boston, left Rotterdam, under the command of Captain Crosby, for the trip across the wide Atlantic, bringing Dr. A. C. van Raalte and the first emigrants to the great America. Here before me on my writing desk is the list of almost all those courageous pilgrims. It caused them a great deal of mental anguish and suffering to leave the land of their birthplace. It offended them deeply to experience this religious intolerance. And yet banishment with freedom was to be preferred to remaining in their fatherland without it. And those reviled Separatists about whom I write with the deepest respect, those brave men and women who awaited in the wild Indian Territory a gigantic task, laid there the beautiful foundation for the present blossoming Dutch settlements — the pride of Michigan. Netherlands, those were your daughters and your sons. You may not simply be proud of them, you *must* be proud.

What was demanded of Dr. van Raalte and those with him? It would lead me too far afield to answer that question. My only purpose is to give a brief account of how and why the emigration of 1847, 1848, and 1849 took place, and the great *Zeeuwen Trek* and the "Old Folks Day" in Zeeland are related to this. It's sufficient at this point to relate that after much difficulty and struggle, the mighty pioneer and his men settled down on February 12, 1847, in the untouched woods of West Michigan on the shores of Black Lake.

Meanwhile, in the province of Zeeland, the separation was spreading more and more. In Goes the movement was in full swing when the first news of Van Raalte in West Michigan was received. Some two hundred people who had been persecuted came together there to discuss the news, and plans were made for the trek to North America. The meeting was organized into a congregation of the *Afgescheiden* church.

It was decided that they would emigrate en masse and that a minister would accompany the congregation on the long and difficult journey. A call was therefore extended to Rev. Cornelius van der Meulen, the leader of a struggling congregation in Goes. Van der Meulen accepted the call and stood ready to go. Three ships full of emigrants soon went to sea. A ship under the leadership of Jannes van de Luyster and another ship under the leadership of Jan Steketee left from Rotterdam, and a third ship led by Rev. Cornelius van der Meulen set sail from Antwerp.

It was very painful to say farewell to the fatherland, and it was with great hurt in their hearts that they left the Zeeuwsche coasts. Many were from Borselen [Borssele] on South Beveland, and when on that Saturday noon the ship of Van de Luyster came into view with its full sails, thirty or more who were left behind stood on the dike. They waved their farewells to those who had been their neighbors in the town, and far across the water they raised their voices, "We are also coming." That was their last message.

The long, long trip by sail had begun. It would be a journey taking months on the turbulent water. Each person made himself as comfortable as conditions allowed. With respect to food, they had to provide for their own needs. At the stern of the ship there were a couple of kitchen ranges on which the women, provided they were not sick, could cook pots of food. There was ample water on board, but toward the end of the journey it was no longer fresh. And hundreds of other inconveniences were part of the long journey.

Steketee's trip was the longest; his ship was on the ocean for 63 days. Jannes van de Luyster made the trip in 54 days, and C. van der Meulen made the trip in 45 days. Thus they all arrived at different times at the mouth of the Hudson River in the summer of 1847.

In any event, with the exception of the Pilgrim Fathers, we have here a religious group for the first time setting foot in the new world as an organized church. They sailed up the Hudson River to Albany. Here the emigrants were placed on a canalboat which was drawn by two horses; they were thus drawn for two weeks down the Erie Canal until they came to Buffalo. Not only did they experience inconveniences, but also twice there was fire on board. At Buffalo they once more boarded sailboats and went to Chicago by way of the Great Lakes, and then once more on other boats over Lake Michigan to Black Lake and their new home. The trip from New York to Black Lake, a small lake off Lake Michigan, required a full month.

In the meanwhile Dr. van Raalte received word in June of 1847 that a large Zeeuwen emigration had arrived in Albany and had decided after long and earnest discussion to settle in Michigan. Several block houses were immediately constructed near Black Lake in order to accommodate the 400 weary travelers so that all might have a roof over their heads. These travelers arrived in July and found a secure place with Dr. A. C. van Raalte and his sturdy pioneers. They were poor, these people who settled here. This was true of most of them. A malaise and persecution had robbed them of almost everything.

Even so, there was one among them for whom it had not been necessary to leave the fatherland because of poverty. That person was Jannes van de Luyster. He was a well-off landowner. He sold his land for 60,000 *guilders* in order to join the emigrants, but he also took with him 17 families consisting of 70 persons for whom he paid the passage and bought clothing and food. After a highly necessary period of rest, exploration was undertaken for the purpose of finding a suitable place to settle. It was finally decided to settle eastward from where Dr. van Raalte had settled, which he had "baptized" Holland. Through the leadership of Jannes van de Luyster, the present area of Zeeland was chosen.

To this community, now known as Zeeland, the first white settler, a certain Jan Hulst, came on June 8, 1847. This Jan Hulst had left his home in the Netherlands on March 2, 1847, and on March 19 had sailed out of the harbor of Hellevoetsluis and had arrived in Baltimore on April 27. From there, for a period of six weeks he had traveled through well nigh impenetrable forests. So the Zeeuwen found there the wilderness and the Indians. Here they would live from now on in a thick wilderness, without anything, without roads, not knowing the language of the land in which they lived, and also strangers to the difficult work required to cut down the forests. They were poor and hungry, and slept under the open sky. They drank water from the pools, and sickness such as cholera, typhus, and smallpox broke out among them. Malaria weakened their bodies, which had been undermined by eating unhealthy food and living in inadequate housing. That suffering, that lack of necessities, that struggle we cannot fully imagine.

Many gave up the struggle and moved to cities like Grand Rapids and Kalamazoo. However, the majority were stayers. With their aged minister, Cornelius van der Meulen, as their leader, they fought with an indomitable will against the woods, against the treacherous swamps, against an unfamiliar climate. Poor as they all were, each with a family to support, Van der Meulen was for them their minister, physician, and judge, all at the same time. And when the colonists came out of the woods on Sunday morning, exhausted, overworked, and discouraged, he knew how to lift them up with rare, well-spoken words and with enormous power so that in the evening they would return to their log houses refreshed in spirit to continue the struggle in the forest and to continue the struggle of cutting out a home in the woods.

These people with little or no knowledge were called upon to reclaim acres for cultivation from primeval forests. Many didn't even know how to put an axe on a handle and in chopping down a tree they did just like the rats and worked on all sides so that they never knew in advance which direction the tree would fall. As a bit of evidence as to how very little these people, while still in the fatherland, anticipated what awaited them here, some of the families had taken heavy sauerkraut stones with them, which they actually imagined could be put to good use. Also, some Frisians brought useless utensils with them, even ship hooks.

Also, the building of roads and the building of bridges over small streams and swamps were very hard work in those early days, and with their limited experience this labor devoured more than half the time of those early settlers. The work proceeded very slowly. Felled trees had to be burned, but then the stump with the roots remained, and that presented another job. Gradually, potatoes and corn were cultivated, and here and there one would have cows.

The Indians, primarily the Ottawas, were fortunately kindly disposed toward the Dutchmen and conducted themselves peacefully and orderly. As far as wild beasts were concerned, there were a few bears, wolves, foxes, and wildcats, but these disappeared quite soon after the trees were cut down.

However, there was no possibility of earning any money. There was no income. Transporting anything was done on the backs of people. There were many women who carried their corn two or three miles in order to have it ground. Others made their own meal by using their coffee mills. It was only later that they could make use of oxcarts. For the present everything went by way of the primitive Indian trails.

Would you like to hear how these pilgrims sometimes arrived? This is the tale that one of the older pilgrims will still tell you. "My father and mother left the Netherlands on March 22, 1849. From New York they sailed up the Hudson River to Albany, then by way of a canalboat they traveled to Buffalo. From there they traveled by way of the lakes to Milwaukee, and then across Lake Michigan to Grand Haven, then by river boat to Grandville, and then by way of an oxcart to Zeeland. It was on May 25 that we arrived there. My younger sister, who was born on the boat in Buffalo, was eleven days old at the time. I was about ten years old, and my brother was twelve years old. We had to travel on foot for 18 miles through the woods. Naturally, Father walked, and Mother also had to walk that distance while her eleven-day-old little child lay in the lap of an elderly woman who rode in the oxcart."

Out of such valuable, powerful wood these rejected people were made. A sort of post office, which they called Black River, had been established, and here mail was delivered once every week. In 1849 the town of Zeeland was mapped out by Jannes van de Luyster, and in 1850 Zeeland became its own township, where on July 14, 1851, the first town meeting was held.

It was always a matter of drudgery and toil, but there was progress. Opposite the simple little church on the marketplace a small schoolhouse was built. The number of small houses increased and the settlers became increasingly adjusted to the climate. Gradually things improved; the little town increased in size and became more important. Industry sprang up, and the village didn't remain a village — the village became a town and the town became a city. That took place in the winter of the previous year. And now, there is no town of her size in Michigan which surpasses the "city of Zeeland" in industrial importance. Everything is thriving. May it long remain that way! For this, people have labored; for this people have fought. It has been a beautiful fight, great, immense, titanic!

Now those sixty years, so filled with events, have been recalled briefly. I cannot remember that I ever took part in a nicer and more pleasant festival of this nature in all my life than this "Old Folks Day" as celebrated by the Zeelanders. Early in the morning I came from the city of Holland by way of the interurban train. The streets were adorned with flags, as were the shops and the dwellings of this brave town. Bunting was everywhere, and the flags of the new fatherland and those of the old motherland — the latter certainly not yet forgotten. Where the Stars and Stripes were fluttering in the breeze, the bright colors of the Netherlands flag also floated in the wind. Here and there one could also see a pennant adorned with an *oranje* [the coat of arms] of the great William the Silent flapping in the wind. In the display windows were prints of Zeeuwsche clothing, and also dolls that had been dressed in Zeeuwsch costumes. And the U. S. Post Office adorned itself for this festive occasion with a banner in white with large letters: "Post Office."

It was the "orange sun" that gave promise of a beautiful day, and a festive atmosphere was increasing everywhere. Everywhere there were the pleasant, festive faces, the festive decor, and the festive laughter. People had come from far away, even from other states, those Holland-Americans, in order to be part of this day. But the old marketplace was the focal point where true joy would be evidenced. A colorful banner joyfully called out the word *welcome* to all. In the cool shadow of the maple trees there was a rostrum, and also long tables where soon a banquet was to be served to those advanced in age. There was also the simple white wooden church, First Reformed Church, built to replace the primitive log church. And for me there was something quite special that touched me. It was the pictures of those oldest heroes, now yellow with age. They were placed or hung on boards, and people paid their respect to them. On a separate board there were pictures from the Netherlands and a portrait of the Queen and the Prince, and quite naturally a picture of "Teddy" (President Roosevelt). About a hundred pictures were brought together. There was great interest in this original collection, which gave a thousandfold cause for musing about the past.

Yes, they recognized those pictures of the cities where they once lived. There was Goes; and look, there was Rotterdam, and there Axel. They rubbed their hands with joy and chuckled as they viewed these old prints. Hundreds stood in front of these prints, and one rarely heard a word of English. There was conversation in the dialects of the old fatherland (understood by all the older people). The younger people still understand the language, but don't speak it fluently anymore. To be sure there are many of the older folks who still do not speak the language of the land, and then all the conversation is carried on in real Dutch fashion. They still maintain and hold fast to much that is part of the old Netherlands; however, one of them says, "I am so confoundedly free and so very fortunate!"

Long banners of red and white were hung from the monument for the "old settlers"; on another corner of the public square there was also a monument, a gravestone in memory of the pioneers "who died in the early days of the settlement." Here rest our early dead from 1847 to 1852.

More guests came: "old folks" from 1847, 1848, and 1849. There were strong, tanned men with open, friendly faces and men with thick, snow-white beards, and also typical Dutch boatmen's little beards. There were also many women with white lace cornets and long black shawls. They all were requested to give their names, their addresses, and their places of birth, and the dates of their arrivals in America. At this time each was given an orange ribbon with a picture of Van Raalte and Van der Meulen printed on it. This was to be worn on the chest. On the ribbon these words were also inscribed in golden letters — "1847-1907, Old Settlers 60th Anniversary Festival, August 21, Zeeland, Michigan, Guest of Honor." Then the music began with a spirited Yankee march. At ten o'clock, Jacob den Herder, who in 1847 came to America with Van de Luyster, as president of the day opened the festivities, and at that time Dr. William Moerdijk led the gathering in an opening prayer.

Now, should I begin to tell you what happened then? That would become a matter of enumeration; it is better that I tell you something about the totality of the day. Several very competent speakers gave addresses during the day. Most of them spoke in Dutch, while a few spoke in English. Some of them spoke earnestly and others in spirited fashion as they recalled the old or former times.

Comparison between then and now gave cause for sad recollection, but also for joy. It was evening and the moon was shining through the green leaves of the maple trees before the program reached its conclusion.

And surely I must tell you about the dinner that was served in the market-place beneath the shady trees. This dinner was served to five hundred Old Folks and people from the press and several invited guests. It was served by the young girls of Zeeland. Wouldn't it be extremely ungrateful if I didn't make mention of the surpassing hospitality with which we were received? Between eight and nine thousand people were guests of the little city that day. And isn't it particularly pleasant that among these people was Mrs. Edward Nedervelt of Grand Haven, who was the first white child born in the little town of Zeeland? Also, that Johan Huyser and his wife, the only survivors in Zeeland who emigrated in 1847, at the ages of 88 and 89, were able to join in this festival?

Amidst all the business of the festival the need was felt to greet the Queen of the old fatherland, and the following greeting was sent to her by way of the cable under the ocean:

Queen Wilhelmina, Hague, Netherlands
8-21-7

Cordial greeting from Hollanders celebrating Sixtieth Anniversary of settlement here.

Den Herder, President

We didn't have to wait long for a response:

Dobbin, [on board the] *Deutschland*
Den Herder — Zeeland — America
8-22-7

Her Majesty Queen of Netherlands appreciating homage from Hollanders orders me to thank for cablegram and wishes settlement prosperity.

Von Mühlen,
Aide de Camp

But there is still more!

When George Birkhoff Jr., the Netherlands Consul-General in Chicago, visited The Netherlands this past summer, his Honor had the distinction to spend a full hour with Her Majesty Queen Wilhelmina discussing the Dutch settlements in West Michigan. Her Majesty was eager to hear about all the details and to be fully enlightened. Upon his departure she gave this verbal message:

"Her Majesty sends her best wishes for the continued good fortune and well-being of the settlement, and it gives her great satisfaction to observe that the best traditions of the Netherlands people are held high in the New Fatherland."

Because of pressing business the consul-general, unfortunately, was not able to come to the festival, but in a copious letter he gave an account of Her Majesty's deep desires.

The Father of the Pilgrim Fathers — Albertus C. van Raalte. Without him what would have happened to that colony in West Michigan? Yes, what would have become of that handful of Dutchmen in 1846 on their journey to freedom in that big, wild America? Yes, what would have happened in that gigantic struggle that awaited them in that big and fearful land? If that noble Pilgrim Father, that mighty pioneer leader, that mighty spirit, Albertus C. van Raalte — father and founder of the Holland settlement in the state of Michigan in North America — had not accompanied them?

Van Raalte was born in the month of October in 1811 in Wanneperveen in the province of Overijssel. He was one of seventeen children born to Albertus van Raalte, a minister in the State Church of the Netherlands, and Christine Caterine Harking, of Frisian ancestry. Little is known of his childhood days, except what he wrote sometime later: "As I look back on my younger years I must confess that it was without much direction, except that I was kindly disposed to my father, and my life received its only direction from my desire to be a source of joy to him."

He studied in Leiden and during the preparatory phase of his studies he was, like most every other student, a client of the pub, a merry young Dutch lad. However, the murderous cholera epidemic in the Netherlands in 1832 made an indelible impression on him, and the young Van Raalte was converted. "No worldly ambition," so wrote Van Raalte, "but the proclamation of the Gospel, which earlier had appealed the least to my person, now became my prayerful endeavor; because I had found the great treasure of salvation. I desired nothing other than to spend my life in preaching. Church liturgy and Church order were for me dead ideas for the most part." He saw very little of his old friends. He had parted company with them and had joined himself to a new circle of friends. This sacrifice was difficult for him, and the situation that he had created for himself at the academy was not to be envied. He was branded as being stuffy and fanatical and a follower of Da Costa, together with a few others, and he was rejected by his fellow students. He and his friends were not spared the pain of being ignored and ridiculed. With amusement and laughter they were spoken of

as the *nachtkijkersclub* [night peepers club]. Van Raalte's entrance examination
results did not appear to be very promising, and it turned out that way. Twice
he was rejected and turned away.

Fully convinced that his consistory was anti-Reformed in principle, direction, and action, and contending against the honor of the King of the Church
and violating the rights of the congregation, Van Raalte threw himself into the
battle for freedom and joined the hunted and despised Separatists. Van Raalte
preached the word wherever he could find listeners. It mattered not whether it
was in granaries or barns, in cellars or in attics, at night or other unseasonable
hours, the youthful Van Raalte would preach. Soon his name became known
among those being persecuted. Joining formally was now only a matter of time.

Even so, Van Raalte continued to affirm that separation from the Church
of his father was a source of great sorrow for him. "It grieved me greatly," he
wrote, "no longer to enter the pulpit of my father, and to become a source of
revilement for my still living mother and my generation. It was my most painful
sacrifice to surrender my very deep desire to preach the word. Of this I was
robbed by the tyrannical power of the Netherlands Church authorities."

Van Raalte was not eager for a battle, and evidently, if it were possible and
he were permitted, would not have willfully become a disturber of the peace of
the Church. He was "coerced" into separation, and the authorities forced him
to establish a separate organization and to assume a new name. But in his heart
he never surrendered either the right to the title or what was right in the Reformed
Church.

The candidate Van Raalte, now called as the pastor of the combined
congregation of Genemuiden and Mastenbroek (Overijssel), was ordained to the
office of Minister of the Word in a solemn ceremony on March 2, 1836. He was
also united in marriage, in this same gathering, to Christina Johanna de Moen,
who became his life's companion. From this point in his life he was identified
with the Reformation movement in the Church of the Netherlands. He was
stationed at Mastenbroek; however, all of Overijssel was his field of labor. The
question was — under what circumstances was this work to be carried out?

Under the instigation of the Synod of Den Haag, the government, using
an old Napoleonic coercive ruling, undertook its persecution of the Separatists.
Scarcely had the young minister and his wife made their appearance in Mastenbroek but a band of soldiers were quartered there. A group of twelve men
accompanied Van Raalte wherever he went, so that preaching at the beginning
was totally impossible. Later, when for a few days they were sent elsewhere, he
was able to begin his work, but this didn't last long because forthwith a new
band quartered themselves there and four of the rudest soldiers imposed themselves on them as their house guests. Once again the work came to a halt. In

addition, his youthful wife constantly suffered because of the wantonness and the rudeness of the so-called keepers of the peace. Traveling through the province was the tactic that Van Raalte now employed. He was unbelievably nimble in his travels, so that it seemed that he was present everywhere at the same time. Even though the congregation became more extensive through his work, the fusion of the government and the rabble brought the matter to a dangerous pitch.

On Sunday, November 13, 1836, Van Raalte preached at Ommen. Throughout the day there were threatening voices in front of the house where the believers were gathered together. However, the mob waited until it was dark before they came and protested in front of the house and threatened Van Raalte with murder. It was possible to flee by way of a back door before the mob turned to violence and began to batter the homes of the "newly enlightened" with stones and filth.

On Monday Van Raalte had already moved on to Heemse, where he preached twice. Here the report of a planned attempt on his life reached him. But he was too nimble for his persecutors and that very evening he led a worship service at Ane. On Tuesday evening he was back at Gramsbergen; the following evening he was in Dedemsvaart, where he met with his followers in a barn.

It was his plan to return to his home by way of Ommen. However, not only were his friends for whom he was to preach informed of his plans, but also his enemies. An alarm was sounded and a mob was called to arms; the place where the Separatists were gathered for worship was surrounded. Doors and windows were shattered in an instant and the mob forced their way in, carrying sticks and axes and knives. Van Raalte felt that his death was at hand. Suddenly, however, the leader of the mob appeared to become apprehensive about the results of this uproar, and at the last moment, as the protector of Van Raalte, he persuaded the mob to leave.

Without delay Van Raalte went to Den Ham, where he led the worship service and officiated at the celebration of the Lord's Supper. Here the burgomaster placed himself at the head of a mob, the congregation was driven from the place of worship, and Van Raalte was taken prisoner. Under armed escort the prisoner was taken by the mayor of Den Ham to the prison in Ommen. The rage of the people knew no limits when they saw the hated preacher back in their town. Twice attempts were made to do Van Raalte bodily harm. Wounded and exhausted, he finally reached the prison, where he was locked up in a dirty cell with a seedy convict. The following day, surrounded by armed men, he was forced to walk for seven long hours to Deventer where, as a common criminal, he was again imprisoned. Finally he appeared before the Officer of Justice, and he was temporarily acquitted and released from prison. Several days later Van

Raalte was back at work in Ommen. Even the fact that his life was in danger did not cause him to shrink from his work.

Moreover, in the same place where repeated attempts had been made to kill him, in the very place where the people had dragged him to prison accompanied by shouting and profanity, and referring to him as the "enlightened one," there Van Raalte chose to settle and make his home. This persecution, as related in the various reports, seems almost unbelievable. It took place in the various provinces. Life for the original leaders was a constant martyr's life those first years.

Hendrik de Cock, upon leaving a meeting in Uithuizen, was mistreated by the people and thrown into a thorn hedge. Van Velzen and his congregation, in Tjalleberd in Friesland, were driven apart three times in one day, and that night he almost lost his life. In addition to this he was fined one hundred *gulden* because of the happenings of the day. Brummelkamp, in Hatten, had to submit to ten soldiers being quartered in his house and to accept the fact that his home was designated as a sentry house.

At Almkerk and Emmikhoven the military disrupted gatherings of more than 19 people, using sharp sabers and wounding some seriously. According to the police regulation in the Napoleonic Code, no gathering of more than nineteen could take place without the permission of the local authorities. Under these circumstances the court in Zwolle sentenced Van Raalte to three months in prison because, at the occasion of one of the gatherings, when they were scattered by the mob under the leadership of the mayor, Van Raalte had dared to admonish him to be converted. Upon appeal to a higher court, Van Raalte was released and the sentence was rendered null and void. The task and responsibility weighed heavily on Van Raalte. Personally he was accused everywhere and even trampled, and yet it was incumbent on him to comfort those who were oppressed or imprisoned.

What was the impression of all of this on him? He writes the following: "As I cast a glance into the past and review what happened, I am happy that I followed the voice of my conscience, even although it cost me a great deal. On the other hand, it grieves me considerably that in my own fatherland now stirred up by the Hervormde Synod and the Netherlands government and citizens, I was fined, tormented by having soldiers quartered in our home, thrown into prison, and throughout the years had filth and stones thrown at me as though I were the scum of society, and thus abused as a person. In my own home, I was tormented and driven. One time, when I was with Rev. Brummelkamp, with depressed and anxious hearts, in great sincerity we raised the question with each other — What do you think? Will God still grant us a day that we will be able to freely walk the streets, without trouble and fear? Now, after having been incorporated into another nation, I have often wished, as a Netherlander, that this blot on our Netherlands nation could be washed away by way of restoration of that which is owed."

For a period of ten years Van Raalte had toiled, suffered, and struggled. However, the results had not satisfied him. Even although the special circumstances in the Netherlands had improved in the last years, it is quite understandable that the emigration fever present in Germany also entered the blood of the Hollanders. Everybody spoke of the abundant treasures that were to be found in the new world. People encouraged each other, and very soon people began to leave. Who could have imagined at that time that this small beginning pointed to a future in which, according to reliable statistics, in excess of a half million would leave the Netherlands and make America their new fatherland.

The Reverend Brummelkamp gives us a brief account of the manner in which they "discovered" America. A teacher from one of the more remote provinces passed through Arnhem on his way to the New World. He had come to say good-bye. In those days America seemed to be "outside" the world, and a trip to America had much in common with a farewell at a deathbed. Emigrants in those days, considered to be moral exiles with a bad smell, were better shipped out. When Brummelkamp expressed surprise upon hearing of the teacher's intention, the teacher allowed him to read letters that he had received from previous emigrants. He was amazed and disturbed and called upon Van Raalte. Both had known the two writers of the letters as extremely poor drudges, yet these letters spoke about a prosperity beyond imagination in the Dutch fatherland; they were speechless. "A ray of hope shined for us," said Brummelkamp. "God opened our eyes and we saw that a great deal of the malaise in which we found ourselves was to be found in the builders of Babel. Even like those tower builders, we were crowding out each other."

And what about Van Raalte? In him something was aroused also. Day and night he kept himself busy with the thought of emigration. This thought involved not first of all himself, but the hundreds and thousands of impoverished fellow citizens and fellow believers. Everywhere this became a matter of discussion, and Rev. Scholte and Rev. Heldring from Hemmen became particularly interested in the matter. Now the question arose as meetings were held — where to? There was the unknown America, but who would dare to venture to go there? Java appeared to be a better place.

At a large meeting in Utrecht, Scholte and Heldring were delegated to negotiate with the minister of colonies concerning the prospect of colonization in the highlands of Java, on condition that the liberty to exercise religious worship services and the gathering together of the colonists for that purpose be permitted. But all hope of going to Java was denied by his Excellency, and the islands of

Ceram and Ubi were suggested. At this point Scholte decided to emigrate to America.

Van Raalte was bitterly disappointed, which became evident in a brochure in which he wrote the following: "But on Java, where the air is more healthful than elsewhere, where the breezes blow and cool the atmosphere, where plants grow luxuriantly, where the forests swarm with deer, stags, and wild swine, so that all our energy which is used up here in the stifling exercise and cares of matters that are earthly and in the poor question: What shall we eat and what shall we drink, can all be directed or dedicated to God? To us is given the opportunity to establish a planting of Christians there; and furthermore ours would be the opportunity as a colony, with our wives and children, to be involved as missionaries. We could work there as Williams worked among the inhabitants of the Zuider Zee and establish a central point from which to spread the Gospel. This thought kindled my heart; my prayer often arose that this might be realized. This is one of the dearest desires of my heart, and this thought, to emigrate there, is so strong that the desirable midlands of America are almost forgotten because of it."

Van Raalte may well have imagined the condition in Java as too rosy, but as a Netherlander he loved the colonies and thus it was his desire to direct the stream of emigrants in that direction. However, once having decided for America, he gave his energies mightily and explosively in that direction. The question which arises is whether or not it was wise on the part of the Ministry to close the Javanese highlands to pure Netherlandic emigration.

In the summer of 1846, Van Raalte became ill. A severe typhus invaded his body, and for many days it seemed as though his work on earth was finished. However, it was to be otherwise. The signs that gave such cause for concern lessened; the fever declined, and recovery, although slow, took place. One day Brummelkamp came to visit him, and although Van Raalte could only whisper, he summoned all of his energy and told him that if the Lord would completely restore him, he would emigrate to America.

Much had transpired in Van Raalte during his illness. Questions had arisen in his mind: What would happen to these people, his emigrants, who were not familiar with the language of the land? What would become of these God-fearing people without a minister, and without a teacher? Where would they land? You see, the answer to these questions led him to the firm conclusion to accompany them on their trek.

As soon as his strength began to return, he made preparations for the great expedition that must be undertaken. And so it was that on September 24, 1846, Van Raalte, together with his wife and their half-year-old infant, left the city of Arnhem on a Rhine boat in order to join themselves with others at Rotterdam in boarding the two-masted ship the *Southerner* for the great new land. Seven weeks later they arrived at New York. The intention of Van Raalte, already decided in the Netherlands, was to establish a Dutch settlement in the plains and forests of Wisconsin. It was also his intention to purchase land in which a reasonably large area would be reserved for the future congregation, where a church and a school would be built which would serve as a community center. So it was that different towns and farms would arise.

Vol. 2, chapter 19, no. 64, pp. 32-40

64. H. BARENDREGT'S
"LETTER FROM ST. LOUIS, MISSOURI, DECEMBER 14, 1846"

[The translation of this letter, except for the first three paragraphs and the two concluding paragraphs (in the original Dutch text), is from Jacob Van der Zee, *The Hollanders of Iowa* (Iowa City: University of Iowa Press, 1912), 339-348. The postscript in the Van der Zee English text is slightly revised to conform to the original Dutch text in Lucas. Zwanet C. Janssens, Archivist at Heritage Hall, Calvin College Library, translated the five paragraphs not included in Van der Zee.]

Today it is my privilege by God's grace to write to you. I planned to do this from New Orleans, but the tremendous effort to find the office which you indicated, which was not found at that address, together with the search for a steamboat that was to take us up the Mississippi, prevented me from writing.

Before I tell you about the journey, God be praised and thanked for leading us lovingly day by day. He saved and strengthened us, even above our expectations. This was especially true for me: all the other passengers were seasick, more or less; I was the exception. Wherever I went on deck or below, there were ill people, while I was fresh and healthy. This shows that reason is put to shame and the prophecy of unbelief disappointed; for even the well informed had predicted that I would not be able to cross the sea. At present we are in St. Louis, and my family members and all the others are in reasonably good health. We hope that this is true of you and your family.

First, briefly something about the journey:

On Friday, the 2nd of October, we left Rotterdam, and on the 4th of October we sailed from Hellevoetsluis. The wind was favorable; on the 5th we sailed into the Channel. Here we experienced a head wind with heavy seas, which caused severe sickness among the passengers. Chests and crates flew all over. This lasted for 3 days and nights. Our ship was driven to the coast, and during the night the captain thought it necessary to hoist the distress signal, whereupon the pilot boats from England came to us. At first it was very difficult to come alongside, but by morning we succeeded in getting a pilot on board who immediately brought us into shelter in the city called Deal, where many ships were anchored.

Here the Lord gave us relief; however, the wind remained strong and soon the captain came to the decision not to proceed through the Channel but to sail across the North Sea and around Scotland, which according to the first mate would take 8 days longer if all went well. It became very cold, especially near the mountains of Scotland, which we saw in the distance. Here we experienced another frightful night. You remember that we had a place near a large hatch. Now it happened as I was sitting in front of the bed in which my wife was already resting, that a wave rolled over the ship and into the hatch so that I was completely under water; this lasted so long that I thought I would perish. Our bed was totally flooded and my wife thoroughly wet. But the Lord was with us. He cleared a path for us through the wild waves and broad streams. We quickly turned the bed over, put on some dry clothes, and passed the night. The following day, Saturday the 17th, the weather was reasonably good; the sun shone sometimes so that our bedding dried partially. However, we still had a strong headwind, so we had to tack often but with less danger than we experienced in the Channel. On the 28th the wind turned north and northeast. All worries ceased, and we sailed with a good wind across the great sea while we experienced one good day after another.

As we entered the Gulf of Mexico on the 14th of November, the wind changed so that we sailed before it, and on the 18th we could see the low shores of the New World. We were pulled along farther by a steam tug which tows vessels up the Mississippi, no matter how the wind blows, and at 7:00 a.m. we arrived at New Orleans. The Lord had surely helped us. Although we came by a roundabout way, we completed the voyage from Holland to New Orleans in 45 days. We had 5 deaths and 3 births — all Germans.

To be brief I shall not write too much of what we saw upon the Mississippi, only something of New Orleans: this is a very large and extensive city; everything seems to be but just begun, and one sees hundreds of houses rising up everywhere; all is bustle, unusually so on account of the rattle and rumble of wagons and carts. Six hundred ocean ships lie alongside the wharves 3 by 3, also a large number of steamboats, mostly very big for their kind but of construction entirely different from that of boats in Holland. They say that 1,300 of these are engaged upon the Mississippi, and I can easily believe it judging from all the hustle and hurry. Sailing vessels one does not see; they cannot be used since the river channel is very crooked and the wind can never blow in such a way as to allow ships to make headway. The stream flows constantly and the riverbanks are covered with trees so that neither horses nor human beings can draw a ship. Then, too, distances are so long that ten or twelve hours is a mere trifle. From New Orleans to St. Louis is 1200 or 1300 English miles. Shipping as in Holland is therefore impracticable.

Arriving at New Orleans in the morning, that same day we took a steamboat to carry us up the river. The fare was $2.50 or one half for children under 9 years of age, while each person had 100 pounds of baggage free, and for additional freight one had to pay 25 cents per 100 pounds. We paid some money down before starting.

The following will serve as a bit of information: before a ship arrives at

New Orleans, a customs officer comes on board. He makes out a list of the families and the number of people composing them as well as the number of trunks and firearms. I advise everyone to answer his questions accurately and not to conceal anything, as the expense is the same whether one has 6 or 12 trunks. He only wishes to know what every immigrant has. One receives two blank papers — these one must get filled out in the tollhouse, as the office is called; the sooner the better. The officer has the right to demand 50 American cents for the two papers; but he may also give them free of cost and so one can try to get them for less money — the poor elicit pity now and then. At the time of signing one pays 20 cents more for the two papers. I write this because some imagine that all this is unnecessary graft, but this is really not so, for the officer who superintends the inspection of one's property lets nothing pass for which one does not have papers. One must also make out a paper and have it signed by the captain, wherein is receipted the amount of money paid down for freight upon the steamboat.

The river steamboats all lie at the wharves, with signboards which bear the date of departure and the destination. One goes aboard and usually finds the captain, with whom one makes the contract. . . . Everywhere there are interpreters who desire to be of service to you at all times; these are unnecessary if you have with you a person who speaks English; if among your company no one can be found who has a command of this language, as was the case with us, it is best to employ them, but always with caution, because some of them are grafters. We were fortunate to get a reasonably good man.

This too is a serious matter: everywhere along our route people tried to reduce the value of our gold money and also the 5-franc pieces. Here a gold piece is worth about 4 dollars; as to the 5-franc pieces I have had no experience.

This also is good advice: "Know the Lord in all thy ways." The application which we have made of this is broad. Think of this: the steamboat which we visited first with our interpreter and which asked a 3-dollar fare departed a short while before we did, and when we overtook her 3 days later, we learned that she had collided with another boat in the midst of a thick fog, had burst a boiler and had sunk, and the 45 passengers lost their lives! We saved the crew and a few others from the wreck and put them ashore at the first town. That we did not take passage on the steamboat is not to be ascribed to our wisdom, because the fare demanded was not at all extortionate; besides, she appeared to be a good boat, while ours was much older and weaker; we also learned that she was very slow; in short, that we did not choose the unfortunate boat was the Lord's work: let Him be thanked and praised.

We finished the trip from New Orleans to St. Louis in 9 days. Along this river from beginning to end are wooded banks. Never would I have imagined that there was still so much apparently quite useless timber in the world; and now I can very readily believe that I have seen but a small portion of America, as here and there one perceives the beginning or laying out of a city. At first one sees sugar cane, further on cotton, and then, through openings in the timber, fields of maize; furthermore, the river is filled with floating logs which are everywhere sent adrift along the banks.

Here at St. Louis there is much industry; 1300 new buildings are being constructed, 500 were completed this past summer, and everything seems to be just begun. They say that the city is 3 hours long; this strikes me as rather exaggerated, but I have no good reason to doubt it. Two of our brethren tried to see the city from one end to the other; but it took so long that they got tired and turned back.

The incoming and outgoing steamboats are also very numerous here. Everything is conveyed across the city here and at New Orleans by means of horses, mules, or oxen, of which one sometimes sees as many as 12 but usually 8 drawing a wagon. Cattle are butchered, quartered, and piled on carts.

Everything comes to market: vegetables, apples, potatoes, mutton, and fish of all sorts; but nothing can be called cheap, except bread, meal or flour, meat, and pork: these alone are to be classed among cheap articles in America. And although there is so much timber, if one has to buy firewood, he has to pay a big price.

Here winter set in just as we arrived. Everything is snowed under, and just now it is freezing besides, but not severely. The journey to Iowa or Wisconsin we cannot continue because the river is too low for steamboat travel. But this we don't consider necessary since we have met with several brothers from Winterswijk, of whom two had just been to Iowa shortly before our arrival. Besides, there are German brethren here, Methodists, who are acquainted with all conditions, have shown us much friendliness and willingness to help, and have undertaken to answer the questions which you gave me to prompt my investigations.

Enclosed is a letter by one of them in the German language. As much of it as he read to me, I can best guarantee to be the exact truth. The following will serve to explain matters:

1. Land along the rivers is everywhere in the hands of speculators, from whom it is still to be obtained at an increased price.
2. Stock is not so expensive. For 10 dollars one can buy a good cow with calf. Also, Jan Schaap and I saw a horse which looked sound and fast, for which not more than 15 dollars was offered.
3. Bricks are large, almost like the red bricks of Holland, but they are not

baked hard, hence not of the best quality. Lime is fairly good: 20 cents per bushel, which is equivalent to 50 cents for 25 lbs. in the Netherlands.

4. I myself have bought good fat meat for 2 cents and pork for 2¼ cents per pound. As to the weight, I believe the pound here is less than the pound of 5 ounces in Holland.

5. Feathers are very good at a ¼ dollar per pound.

If you abide by your decision to settle in North America, then the following will also serve to inform you:

1st: Every land buyer who wants to cultivate land of his own must above all manage to bring his laborers with him from Holland, if he thinks he will need help.

2nd: The cost of living will be moderate before one gets a crop; bread and meat and pork are necessities and they are cheap here; for clothing, house rent, and firewood one need have no anxiety.

3rd: For those who are good makers of butter and cheese, prospects are certainly fine, because these products are bad in the market here. As to dairy appliances it will be well to take along as many as possible, especially what can be packed into boxes. On shipboard one needs pay no more for them and steamboat freight is only a ¼ dollar per 100 lbs. Everything is obtainable here, but generally expensive. I give the same advice as to all tools and implements, for example, those needed for agriculture and all sorts of trades; yet I should certainly not advise you to buy anything new in Holland to take with you, since the difference in price is not large enough. Besides, there is much difference in tools, and not everyone must expect to be able to remain a Hollander if he comes to live in America; ways and manners should be followed here. My meaning is that he who has tools should not throw them away for a trifle, especially not if they are still good; but to take trash along to America is always nonsense.

I may also add that everyone should take his best tableware if it is not too easily broken; if it is well packed between clothing in boxes full to the cover, one can easily keep it whole; our things thus far are pretty well preserved despite the fact that our boxes are sometimes rolled along like barrels. Thus anyone can well understand that boxes should be particularly strong; for I have seen many smashed and then much hard treatment of the contents; also, the boxes must not be too big, for in that event they are handled more harshly still.

Further I shall give some advice relative to foodstuff and household articles. There should be 160 pounds for each person, distributed as follows:

10 pounds of bacon, reasonably thick, for making pancakes;
10 pounds of ham to eat with bread, etc.;
10 pounds of meat;
20 pounds of rice, which costs nearly the same here;
20 pounds of flour, which should all be used up;
15 pounds of potatoes;
20 pounds of green peas, of the best quality; if one can save these, they can be used as seed, as I have seen only poor ones here and expensive ones at that;
20 pounds of capuchin peas;
30 pounds of the best bread cut into slices and well dried;
 5 pounds of ordinary rusks.

160 lbs.

Furthermore, it is well and useful to bring a quantity of headcheese, besides butter, cheese, loaf-sugar, prunes, and everything one can eat without cooking, sweet cake, various drinks, wine, brandy, Rhine wine, gin, vinegar, salt, mustard, pepper, coffee, tea, as well as some household remedies for illness, for the Americans have no doctor on board, and so everyone takes care of himself.

The household utensils consist of a teakettle, a copper or iron cooking-pot, a tin pan, tin plates from which to eat, since passengers can seldom sit together regularly, tin water cans or kegs, etc. If a person must go singly, I advise him to cooperate with six or eight others, or else the company will be too large, and differences of opinion are likely to arise.

Further, I must say that the carriers here treat people variously; they appear to deduct as much as possible. Among us there were some who paid from 30 to 35 florins [$12 to $14], and we had to pay 45 florins. There were also some on board our ship who were offered transportation on a good ship at 35 florins if their families wanted to take advantage of the offer in the spring.

Your respectful and affectionate brother in the Lord Jesus Christ,

Hendrik Barendregt

N.B. Be sure to greet brother Betten.

Of the letter written by Brummelkamp and Van Raalte to procure financial aid for the worthy poor, we here are not informed. Nor do we know anything of Van Raalte and those who sailed with him.

Our desire is that you will write back soon.

I do not exactly know whether to advise people to come by way of New York or New Orleans; but this I know, that if one sails from Holland after the month of February, the journey by way of New Orleans is too hot; in that case I prefer New York; one should take into consideration the increased expense and trouble involved in taking a land journey; but if one can depart before or during the month of February, come to New Orleans, because that means a saving of trouble and expense.

It also makes a great deal of difference where one expects to settle. If Iowa is the place, the journey by way of New York is more difficult, as one must in all events go to Milwaukee first and from there back to Iowa, which is not necessary if one comes by way of New Orleans; for then one can easily get to Iowa by steamboat. In all cases it is best for those who undoubtedly intend to settle in this region to come to St. Louis, whence it is so easy to depart in all directions.

As to the climate, I understand it is much too warm for us here in the summer; for it happens that a laborer who chops wood or unloads wood from ships is offered 3 dollars a day in summer, and now can get only a ½ to a ¾ dollar. Iowa, I hear, is a good ways north and therefore much colder.

All sorts of products are raised here: maize, wheat, rye, oats, beans, etc. As for cabbage seed, it is hardly to be found; since lard is cheap here, there is not much need of cabbage-seed oil. The prices of grain are not high — there is reason for this, but then we should have to enter into a discussion of several matters, viz., the yield of the land, labor, cost of planting, sowing, etc. But I am not well enough acquainted with the facts to speak about the matter, and there is little or no need to do so; if for example I give a price, a person in Holland will prepare at once to make comparisons and figure according to Dutch standards. . . . Experience will be the best teacher here.

As for the worship of God, one finds really God-fearing people among the Germans and also among the English; indeed, there are many Christian negroes here. We find the Germans very friendly; but we do not harmonize in everything. The Sabbath is reasonably respected. One finds no shocking immorality here, as in Rotterdam or other cities of Holland.

As for the schools, you know they are free here; usually there is a school with every church. I am not yet well enough informed so as to give a good account of the school system. Sunday schools are numerous here, and one can get free instruction: these are also good to enable us to learn a little of the English language. He who knows English well possesses riches, if he comes here from Holland. I cannot therefore urge everyone enough by all means to learn the English language.

I have nothing special which I consider necessary to add. My request is that you be so good as to publish this letter so far as you are able, likewise to see to it that brother van H——— of Rotterdam be informed at an early date. Tell him that as a baker he could more easily be lord in St. Louis than citizen in Rotterdam. Also K———, who put to me many questions which are answered herein; also to Heerjansdam [city in province of South Holland], etc.

De Hoog has written to De Hitsert but did not give details. He refused to list them also in the letter written to you. See to it especially that my father hears something about this letter. Within the next two weeks I will write to my family. If I have additional news I will ask that you be informed. Greet all the brothers and sisters who love the Lord from all of us. We send especially greetings to you, Reverend, and those who are with you, and we hope to be able to pray for you and your family also for your journey. Pray also for us.

The Lord be your portion and ours through all eternity. Amen.

Vol. 2, chapter 19, no. 65, pp. 41-44

65. G. VAN HORSEN'S "GLIMPSES OF EARLY LIFE IN PELLA"

[No person like Gerrit van Schelven in Holland collected the memoirs of settlers in Pella. It has been possible to find only one such sketch worthy of a place in this collection. Adam P. Hasselman and wife sailed in the *Maasstroom* in April 1847 and settled on a farm near Pella. This sketch, written by his son-in-law, G. van Horsen, was published in the *Pella Weekblad,* May 26, 1922. The Reverend Henry P. Baak and Dr. George Harper, professor emeritus of English, Calvin College, translated the sketch.]

In the course of the first part of the nineteenth century the son of the schoolmaster at Nederhemert, Netherlands, and the daughter of the schoolmaster at Noordeloos, Netherlands, were joined together in marriage. They were Adam P. Hasselman and Alida Ch. Gordesse Timmermans. In 1847 this Adam Hasselman went constantly to Dominie Scholte, who then set up the emigration to America, and in consultation with many ardent Christians, laid plans and decided who would be taken and who was prepared to undertake the passage. So with God's help they would seek a refuge in the new world, where men could serve God according to one's conscience without being disturbed.

Hasselman had a keen desire to cross the ocean, but my mother, his wife, had no eye for it. Naturally they talked much about the matter, and then at last Mrs. Hasselman came before the Spirit again and again, and understood that God also holds His protecting Hand over His children on the water. For her the words of the psalmist came constantly to mind: "You shall be, also as Moses was, whenever your path goes through the sea the waves will not go over you." Then she with full confidence gave her consent to the big trip, which in those days was something very different from now; not only is the means of transportation better but it also goes so much faster.

That the burdens which Mrs. Hasselman had were no imaginary burdens one can readily admit. Also, one must bear in mind that the family numbered eight children, who were all still young. And then the trip was to a very sparsely populated world where a strange language was being spoken, and everything was different than in the fatherland.

The journey was begun and in the beginning of April 1847 the ship *Maasstroom* sailed out of the Rotterdam harbor and came to Baltimore, a journey of 52 days. On the way, one of the children died, and the mortal remains of the youngest days will appear when the books are opened. The family with seven children came first to St. Louis, Missouri, having spent considerable time there, and then went on to Pella, which in itself was nothing more than a place in the wilderness. Mrs. G. van Horsen, a widow of 84 years whose maiden name is Marie Hasselman, communicated this to us when she was a little girl of nine years and five months.

Father Hasselman had sufficient means to procure for himself a piece of land of 40 acres. In addition, there remained enough in the money chest to provide for the needs of the family for awhile. It was not easy to obtain food. A person could readily obtain wheat, but there were no mills in the area. To get the wheat ground into meal, a trip of 70 to 80 miles had to be made through creeks and over hills along unbeaten roads. Sometimes the wagon remained out for a week. You can easily imagine that the strain on those who remained behind was great.

Mr. Ten Hagen had a team of horses and ordinarily went there to get the wheat ground. That always went according to exact measure. The orders were filled according to the size of each family. Many mills came from this, just as people had hoped. Because all gladly received their share, Ten Hagen could not take along enough for the hungry stomachs who needed it. If there was not enough flour, it fell to the children to take the coffee mill in hand and grind corn from which bread was baked. That cornbread with syrup was a great delicacy. Once when one of the brothers was sent out to fetch syrup, he lost his ten cent piece and had to eat the bread without syrup.

When they were here about a year, on a certain day someone came from Oskaloosa, Parker by name, who had a factory where wall mills were manufactured. He asked if Mrs. Hasselman could part with one of her children to be a help to his wife in her housekeeping. That didn't look too good to Mother Hasselman — way to Oskaloosa and with someone whose language one could not understand! And besides, to send one of her children along with a stranger! But after talking it over, the problem was worked out, especially because Marie, then around ten years old, really dared to go because she saw this as a good opportunity to learn English. From the beginning people felt directly that knowledge of the language was absolutely necessary.

Once it happened that someone agreed to sell a horse to an American, and in exchange for the horse would receive two cows with the remainder in "cash." The man was satisfied with the exchange and told his wife that the business would be done in an orderly fashion; but what in the world would a person do with so much "cheese"? After further reflection the man also came to the conviction that the cash must be bad, and therefore he went to the other party and told him that it would be impossible to take so much "cash" (cheese). However, when the explanation was given that cash was not cheese but money, everything came out right and the men had a hearty laugh over it.

Marie's fine opportunity to learn the language of this land did not last particularly long. The day went quickly because there was enough work to do taking care of the baby and doing all kinds of housework. But when night came with its long hours that were spent lying awake thinking about home, then the little girl thought of father and mother and brothers and sisters, and it lay heavy on her heart. During her weeklong stay at the manufacturer, the homesickness grew so strong that she decided to take the first opportunity to go home. That came sooner than she had thought. The following Sunday the manufacturer went to Des Moines with a load of wall mills. She accompanied him as far as Pella. Oh, what a relief to be with mother again! And when the stranger came again on his way back to take her back again, she did not have the courage to go back with him.

The northwestern part of Pella, where the Oakwood cemetery is now, then had the name of "straw town," because the cabins that were made on the slope of the hill were covered with leaves, twigs, and straw. There church was held in the open air and people came together to serve God. Once on a Sunday when people were on their way home from the service, a party of Indians came by. Dressed in buffalo skins that hung over the shoulder and body, letting a great deal go uncovered, and sitting on small horses from which on one side swung roasted rabbits and on the other a papoose to keep the balance, they appeared with their stretched faces and deep, black, glassy eyes to be especially frightening to the women and children. To make matters worse, one of the Indians usually came to them and asked for something to eat, because they are real beggars. Seeing that they each do their own thing, they then have to share it, which isn't done willingly. When people count on being safe, they still lose because Indians do not shrink from thievery.

At another time the Indians came to baker Pos and received from him a sack of cookies. The cookies appeared not to satisfy the redskins, or it is possible they did not trust them because the children found them a short time later thrown away along the path. Indians still come traversing off and on through the neighborhood. And often some things fall by mistake into their hands. When they see someone on the place whose eye they cannot escape, then they come mostly with beseeching gestures and begging voice extending the hand with awkward movement and asking for "something to eat."

In the course of time Father Hasselman built a house that was named the "ark." The elderly came for many visits and everyone was welcomed there. Mr. Overkamp also built a house there, where the writer had a good opportunity to become acquainted, because he now lives at the southeast corner of Washington and West First Streets. That house has a history just like so many other places in Pella. Prayer meetings were held there under the leadership of Dominie Scholte, and there the shouts of joy of God's children rose up in voice and stringed instruments to the glory of His goodness. In that house father heard Dr. Scholte do his first preaching in America. There many also found a refuge in the storm of 1848 when the house of Roovaart was wrecked and the "ark" leaked, which caused the inhabitants to wish for a better escape.

These times are long gone by, but in her imagination Mrs. G. van Horsen still hears the wolves howling around the wooden house and sees the frequent snakes creeping by. In the evening she can still see the red sky of the prairie fires. Wolves are now a rarity, and if someone wants to see the prairie they will have to go further west.

Vol. 2, chapter 20, no. 66, pp. 45-50

66. JOHN DE YOUNG'S "HISTORY OF ROSELAND, ILLINOIS"

[The author, son of *Meester* Pieter de Jong, a noteworthy figure in the early history of the Roseland community, in 1908 wrote this sketch based upon his intimate acquaintance with Roseland's history. John de Young, son of Pieter C. de Jong, added the postscript. This text, prepared from the manuscript preserved in the Joint Archives of Holland, Hope College Library, was translated by the Reverend Henry De Mots.]

It was in the year 1849, in the month of April, that ten families, after mature consideration, undertook the journey from the Province of North Holland to the United States of North America. The names of the heads of the households were as follows: Jacob de Jong, Pieter de Jong, Klaas Dalenberg, Cornelis Kuiper, Gerrit Eenigenburg, Hark Eenigenburg, Pieter Oudendijk, Johannes Ambuul, Jan Jonker, and Jan Bras. There were also two old fathers, Cornelis Dalenberg and Cornelis Hoogendonk, father and father-in-law of Klaas Dalenberg. Both of these elderly men died en route of cholera and were buried at sea. In addition to the above there were also two young men, Pieter Dalenberg and Jan Ton. Before they left Rotterdam the family of Leendert van der Sijde was also added to this company.

On a Saturday the goods were loaded on a barge (which was moored in the North Holland Canal) for the purpose of being transported to Rotterdam. Because the following day was Sunday, most of the people comprising this company attended the worship services in the Church at Krabbendam, and that evening they all boarded the barge to begin their journey the following day (Monday). So they said "farewell" to the land in which they were born, and moved on to a strange land.

On the trip from the Sluis to Rotterdam, through the channel and by way of the rivers, nothing untoward took place and we arrived as scheduled. Here we were delayed for a few days before we could proceed to move on. While we were thus delayed one of the children of Klaas Dalenberg died and was buried there. We left Rotterdam by steamboat and went to Le Havre, France. This part of our journey was very stormy and almost everybody became seasick, so that before we reached Le Havre we had empty and clean stomachs. Here we stayed for several days before we could go on board a three-masted ship, named the *Massachusetts* and registered in Boston.

The journey on that ship will never be erased from the memory of those who were old enough at the time to remember; but the heads of the households of that time have passed on. Soon after we were on the ocean an epidemic of cholera broke out among our people. If my memory serves me correctly, nineteen died because of this epidemic; the ocean became their grave. The journey across the ocean lasted forty-two days. We did not encounter severe storms at sea, even though an occasional wave would sweep over the deck. We never felt in great danger of perishing. The severe losses through death naturally brought great sorrow, which was a severe trial for many, but our people had learned to go to Him who is able and willing to comfort in such circumstances. They went to Him and found comfort and strength in the Lord in these very severe afflictions. The last Sunday worship services were held on deck; they read a sermon, prayed together, and sang psalms to the praise of God. We recall very vividly how there were some Germans on board who mocked us, but the captain of the ship, an American, had respect for this religious fellowship and removed his cap and forbade the Germans to continue their mocking.

After a journey of forty-two days at sea, we finally arrived at New York. From there the journey was continued, first by steamboat on the Hudson River from New York to Albany, and from Albany to Buffalo by canalboat on the Erie Canal. This trip lasted eight days. From there we went by steamboat to Chicago, Illinois. Here we were met, as expected, by an old acquaintance, Klaas Pool, who had emigrated to America in 1847, together with Klaas Paarleberg, both of whom were from North Holland. Here we found lodging in a house on Randolph Street.

Now we were in America, and we consulted with each other as to our next move. We soon decided that we agreed with each other that we should go out and take a look at the country. And so we set out; four heads of households went to South Holland (Low Prairie at the time) on foot with Klaas Pool. Mr. Pool could speak and understand a lot of English, and through the providence of God we encountered an American of Dutch descent, named Oosterhout, who was also able to speak and understand a bit of Dutch; he was able to be of help to our people in the business of buying land, etc. We surveyed the possibilities, and land was purchased where today Roseland is located, which at that time was known as High Prairie. We purchased 160 acres adjoining what was known as the "ridge" or "the high road," and shortly afterwards purchased another eighty acres. This acreage stretched out from what is now 106th Street to 115th Street.

At that time matters were quite different than they are now in the year 1908. From Twelfth Street, which was the outer limit of Chicago at that time, to what is now 115th Street, there were only three homes. The last one of these three homes, which was located on what is now 111th Street, was occupied by an American named Mr. Lob. He sold his house and his land to the first Hollanders for the price of five dollars per acre. He soon moved elsewhere. The grass from the ridge to Lake Calumet was so long at that time that it was impossible to see the cattle when they grazed there. The grass farther west, which was not as long, was of better quality.

Inasmuch as these early settlers were accustomed to spend their Sundays in a godly manner, they traveled to Low Prairie (now South Holland), at first by oxcart, in order to attend the religious services there. At South Holland they had built a small church; the minister there was Rev. Willem Coenraad Wust. The settlers arrived here first in 1847, if I am not mistaken.

However, inasmuch as these settlements were separated from each other by a distance of 6 or 7 miles, it was not convenient to continue the practice of riding by oxcart every Sunday. So it was decided to come together for worship in their homes. It was also decided as soon as possible to construct a place of worship; this was done the following spring of the year when together they built a small church building. This did not cost a great deal of money because lumber was cheap, and all joined hands in order to accomplish the work and reach their goal. The building was small, but it was sufficient for the needs of the time; they sang psalms to the glory of God and souls were fed with the Bread of Life.

Before many years passed, the little church building became too small and was replaced by one better and bigger; later this was replaced by another still bigger and somewhat better. The large structure which stands on the corner of 107th Street is bigger and better yet; it stands on the same location.

In the beginning it was necessary to adjust oneself to circumstances. The comforts of life were not what we see today. It was necessary to transport the lumber from the city by way of oxcarts; however, that presented no problem at that time — they courageously faced their problems. Those who were handy with carpenter's tools built their own houses. A family headed by Abraham de Koker, a carpenter, came from Sheboygan, Wisconsin, and was immediately hired. Before winter set in most of the families were reasonably well housed. The houses were no palaces, yet on the coldest winter days one could sit close to the stove without complaining about the heat.

Very soon the people began to buy dairy cattle, and thus before long they had milk, butter, and cheese for their own use. If they had more than they needed there was a good market for that in the town. The laboring men whom they had taken with them from the Netherlands had from the very beginning ample work. The following spring they bought more dairy cattle so that they now had enough to supply their daily needs. The receipts surely did not run into the thousands, but the people were supplied with their daily bread, and this was worth a great deal for these early beginners at this time.

Even now, the sequence of events consisted in being born, being married, and dying. As events developed, the first that occurred was a death, the little daughter of Mr. and Mrs. Pieter de Jong, who passed away at the age of about two years. And so it was necessary to choose a burial place for the child. A birth followed in the family of Jacob de Jong, a son, named Joris. Both of these events took place, we believe, before winter came. Soon a marriage took place: Klaas Dalenberg, who had been called upon to bury his wife at sea, became united in marriage to Cornelia Gouwens.

The first storekeeper, on a very modest scale, was Cornelis Kuiper. After some time he was replaced by Joris van der Sijde, who continued to maintain his business for several years. For this community of people, life moved on in their newly accepted fatherland. At that time there were no railroads connecting East and West. The only rail that had been laid connected Chicago and Galena, Illinois. The first railroad from the east, laid in the fall of 1850, was named the Michigan Southern and Northern Indiana. In the spring of 1851 the Michigan Central was laid, and the Illinois Central was constructed that same year.

From time to time new emigrants would arrive. Among the first were Pieter Prins and family, Benjamin Prins, Jan Verhoef, Teunis Maat, Pieter Madderom, Klaas Madderom, and Cornelius Madderom, later A. Verkley, and others from time to time.

The above-mentioned Rev. Wust soon left Low Prairie, and now we were served by ministers who came to us from Michigan and Wisconsin. Among those who came to serve us were Dr. A. C. van Raalte, Rev. Seine Bolks, Rev. Cornelius van der Meulen, Rev. Martin A. Ypma, and Rev. H. G. Klein (Klijn) from Milwaukee, Wisconsin. The first congregation began with 13 members, and increased from time to time until the first church numbered 800 members, with five other Reformed congregations nestled around her. Jacob said, "With my staff I crossed over this Jordan, and now I have become two groups" [Gen. 32:10]. Here we could say six groups because the one congregation had become six. The first elder of the first church was Jacob de Jong, who served this congregation in that capacity until his death. The first deacon was Pieter de Jong, who was later elected to the office of elder, and served the congregation in that capacity until the day of his death.

The heads of households who came here with their children have all passed on, exchanging the temporal for the eternal. The children who came with them at the time are now being numbered among the senior citizens; they have become the elderly. This is underscored by the fact that the writer of these lines is often greeted by little children with a cheery, "Hello, Grandpa!" Among the children who came over with their parents, the following are still living: Joris van der Sijde, who is the oldest of all, and his sister, the widow of Jan Ton. Five children of Jacob de Jong are still living, as are six children of Pieter de Jong; one child of Klaas Dalenberg is still with us; similarly one child of Hark Eenigenburg and one child of Jan Jonker. The grandchildren would constitute a multitude.

The first minister called by the combined congregations of High Prairie and Low Prairie was Rev. Martin Ypma, who served the congregation for a number of years (1855-1861). He was followed by Rev. Seine Bolks (1862-1865). After this date the two congregations each called their own pastor. Under this arrangement High Prairie called and later welcomed Rev. Pieter Lepeltak, who served the congregation from 1865 to 1869.

I have written this sketch at the request of some of you in the hope that it might rescue the memory of those early settlers from the morass of forgetfulness.

John P. de Young, Grand Meadow, Minnesota, 1908

[Postscript]

The above piece is from the late oldest son of Mr. Pieter de Jong, one of the first settlers. So, he surely was well acquainted with the facts. The undersigned is a grandson of Mr. de Jong and is not competent to speak about those early days, only about things as they are today. What is the consequence of this settlement? How does it differ from Michigan?

In Michigan men lived between tree stumps; in Illinois we lived on the best ground in the United States. A minister is strong in his pulpit, but when it comes to the matter of founding a settlement, it is better to begin with a dozen stalwart farmers, especially if they are accompanied by a godly schoolteacher. The result was that the settlement in Illinois did not suffer the hardships and difficulties that were experienced by the settlers in Michigan. The children and the grandchildren today feel themselves richly blessed because of the prudence of those first settlers. In contrast to others, we are comfortably situated, have good houses, broad and wide-open acres, and well-constructed churches, and are able to study at the best schools and universities in the land.

But what, generally speaking, is the legacy of those first Hollanders? It seems to me that they speak a great deal about "Wicked Chicago." However, when reference is made to the south side of Chicago, where these God-fearing men and women settled in earlier years, then one must express himself a bit more carefully.

The south side of Chicago, Roseland and surroundings, is "Churchly Chicago" with forty churches, most of them in very flourishing condition. Here we do not find those disheartening little churches, which because of their insipidity allow young men and girls to drift into the world. Here we find churches where great multitudes meet together on Sunday, and do so with great joy. It is no exaggeration when I say that 4,000 attend the worship services every Sunday in First Reformed Church of Roseland. Also, it should be noted that at least fifteen young men have gone out from this church to serve as ministers in Christ's vineyard.

Here we find a part of a big world-class city where hard work and good morals can be observed on all sides, and then on Sunday we see a great multitude streaming to God's house, to serve Him with joy. Who can but observe that this is the beautiful result of the industrious, courageous, and godly life of those first settlers. We give thanks to God for their example.

Pieter C. de Jong

Vol. 2, chapter 20, no. 69, pp. 67-72

69. GEORGE DE BEY'S
"HISTORY OF THE DUTCH SETTLEMENT AT FULTON, ILLINOIS"

[This sketch of the Dutch settlement at Fulton, Illinois, which began its existence in 1860, was prepared for the semicentennial celebrations at Holland in 1897. De Bey, who dealt in wagons, buggies, and farm implements, was in a position to become well acquainted with the history of the settlement. His manuscript, now in the Gerrit Van Schelven Papers, Joint Archives of Holland, Hope College Library, was translated by the Reverend Henry De Mots.]

The history of a land is manifested by beautiful spiritual traditions that are generated by men through great deeds brought to light, through the exhibition of natural situations, and partially through the development of natural resources. The wealth of Greece was her philosophers; the wealth of Rome was her political leaders; the wealth of Germany was her penetrating theologians. But America holds the highest place of honor in that she not only produces philosophers, political leaders, and theologians, but she also is composed of a liberty-loving people who vindicate the rights of others — a land where each person has a right, yes, even the duty, to receive an education. The old powers may flaunt their castles and the temples of their false gods and their natural wonders; however, even in these America need not feel inferior. She can pride herself on her churches and schools — lower and higher places of education which are open for everybody. Commerce and industry flourish, and sources of well-being are only now beginning to develop! And besides this, there is great natural beauty of great variety that inspires and uplifts a person.

In this fortunate nation, the Hollanders spread throughout the various parts of this great land also make up part of the population. We who live in Fulton, Illinois, also prize our American citizenship. The Hollanders, perhaps more than anybody else, are ready to confess or acknowledge that the history of mankind throughout the ages is in keeping with the plan of God, and therefore they believe that these glorious days of remembrance carry with them His approval because they are a testimony of God's faithfulness, and they ascribe all praise to Him. God not only created all things for His praise and glory, but also He upholds and cares for and provides so that we in turn should proclaim His deeds. This makes it necessary that we learn to know Him better so that we are better able to serve Him. The purpose of this celebration must therefore be directed to that end and for that purpose. In order to reach that goal, efforts have been made to collect the histories of the various settlements scattered throughout the nation and to bring them together. The members of the committee have been assured by the citizens of Fulton and surroundings that they will honor the invitation extended to them to participate in this half-century feast. For this we express our appreciation.

In order to come to the matter that I want to present, I want to inform you briefly about the surrounding land, the first settlement in Fulton, the arrival of the Hollanders, the organizing of a congregation, and Fulton's present state of affairs. Somewhat more than a half-century ago, the first whites came to this land that the Indians called their paradise, despite the fact that this area actually was a great wilderness, a land of prairies, a land inhabited by Indians, and a wooded west. The Winnebego, Sac, and Fox Indians lived here at that time, and considered Fox Valley, comprised to a large extent of Whiteside County, as their paradise. Several business deals or treaties were made, the first in the year 1804. The great Black Hawk War was occasioned by an attempt by the Indians to reclaim Whiteside County for themselves. However, matters had taken a turn; the wilderness was changed into a fruitful land, the paths of the hunters and crafty redskins replaced by railroads and other roads; poorly constructed huts and gardens were replaced by comfortable houses and expansive acres. Churches, schools, and factories of several kinds are now to be found where everything was once wild and undeveloped.

The southeastern part of the county is flat; the western part is more hilly; the middle part is more rolling. Rivers and streams in great number flow through the valleys and empty themselves into the bosom of the great father of waters, the Mississippi. Differing kinds of soil are to be found here, but the soil is predominantly black loam. The closer one comes to the river the more sandy the soil becomes. The soil is very fertile and productive, bearing all kinds of crops. It lies at 41 degrees north latitude.

Fulton lies on the swiftly flowing Mississippi. One of the first settlers was John Baker, who came here in 1835. He pitched his tent and built his home inside what is now the city of Fulton. He was soon followed by other families, who publicized their good fortune and the beauty of this place to their friends living in the East. Because of this, at almost every rising sun new colonists could be seen coming with their heavily laden wagons pulled by mules. A small colony was speedily formed. The first claim on land had already been made in Whiteside County in 1834; on January 16, 1836, by an act of the legislature of the state of Illinois, the boundaries of the county were established and the county was given the name of Whiteside in honor of one of the generals in the Black Hawk War. Fulton township was organized with a vote of 41 on April 6, 1852.

The early settlers sought property close to the river, which was partially covered with brush, but did not consider the fact that the wide-open prairies would also be profitable. Thus we find that today there are very prosperous farming communities on the open prairies. These beautiful fields prompted someone to exclaim with Ten Kate, "Beautiful is the earth and life is good!"

The town of Fulton, located on what is referred to as the narrows of the Mississippi, 186 miles west of Chicago, stands partially on rocks. The north part of the town certainly gives the viewer an impressive sight. The south part of the town is built on more even ground. One can see the heights some six to fourteen miles in the distance. These are called bluffs, with their green tops, and they are interchanged with steep rocky cliffs that in earlier times and ages constituted the east side of the river. When one looks to the west, one sees the wide water of the river as it makes its winding path around islands and points that rise above the water. On the west side of the river the viewer can see the cliffs and hills and also the towns of Clinton and Lyons, both of which are located in the state of Iowa.

Fulton has all the business possibilities for becoming a large city. She has large steamships as the means of transportation on the Mississippi; these connect the town with St. Paul and Minneapolis to the north and St. Louis and New Orleans to the south. Further, she has connections with Chicago and Milwaukee and other places to the east and with Kansas City, Council Bluffs, and San Francisco by way of great railroads, such as the Chicago and Northwestern; the Chicago, Milwaukee, and St. Paul; and the Chicago, Burlington, and Quincy, which all make our city an important transportation center.

Our Hollanders also had a part in the early development of Fulton, even though they certainly were not the first settlers. Some 20 years after the original American pioneers settled here, the first Dutch settlers arrived in this area. Among them were G. Nanninga and F. Dijkema in 1860; Jan Munneke and A. van Dellen in 1861; F. Sterenberg and a few others in 1863. Because the families were few in number they at first joined the Presbyterian Church for a period of three years. In 1862 the first child born to these Dutch families, a son of Jan Munneke, was baptized in this church. Rev. H. G. Klijn read the baptismal formulary. In 1866 the first Reformed congregation was organized under the leadership of Rev. Klijn and Elder Vastenhout of Chicago. F. Sterenberg and G. Nanninga were chosen as elders, and Jacob Tillema was chosen as deacon.

With heroic courage and zealous in the service of the Lord, this small flock undertook the construction of a house of prayer, which was dedicated on December 15, 1867. In August of 1869 Rev. H. Woltman was installed as their first pastor. The flock struggled in the face of obstacles and difficulties, especially during the time of the Civil War. Once when in 1863 one of our number was called into service by way of the lot (the draft), motivated by love, we raised sufficient money among us to purchase a substitute. Lest we forget, this is the place to recall that early settlers from Muskegon, Michigan, had moved to Fulton.

In Muskegon these people had first assisted with the establishment of religious services and the organizing of First Reformed Church. They carried the fire of their enthusiasm with them when they came to Fulton, and they demonstrated this when as pioneers in our religious life they showed leadership.

Because of weakness and sickness Rev. H. Woltman was not able to be of much service to the congregation, and on April 30, 1870, he was taken away from us by death. However, even though severely tried, the people did not become discouraged and soon extended a call to Rev. John van der Meulen, who is still living and makes a periodic appearance in this festive multitude. After five years he left. The congregation had experienced steady growth during the ministry of Rev. van der Meulen. On August 22, 1875, Rev. Willem Hazenburg was installed as Fulton's minister. After two years of labor this servant also left (on February 18, 1877). On June 30, 1878, Rev. Lawrence Dykstra was installed as our minister. He left us in February of 1882, having accepted a call to Cleveland, Ohio. Rev. Harmen van der Ploeg was then installed as pastor and served the congregation for five years. The congregation was blessed by his ministry, and these years were a time of progress. On March 16, 1887, he accepted a call to Vriesland, Michigan. At this time the congregation numbered about 200 families. In addition, during the ministry of Rev. van der Ploeg the beautiful church building was constructed. This building is 50 × 90 feet, and in this sanctuary we have a beautiful pipe organ that elevates the quality of our singing. Also, it should be observed that in all the years of struggle as a congregation, support from the Board of Domestic Missions to supplement the salary of the minister was given and received for only 2 years, and that in the beginning. Also at this time, due to circumstances, a Christian Reformed Church came into being. The members of this church came out of the bosom of the Reformed Church. This church numbers 70 families at the present time. After the departure of the unforgettable Rev. Harmen van der Ploeg, the Rev. Jan Willem te Winkel was called; he served the church accompanied by fruit and blessing for seven years.

In view of the fact that the Hollanders were spreading out over the western part of the county, even to the distance of 20 miles, about five years ago, in 1892, a Sunday school was established eight miles southeast of Fulton. Soon other religious exercises were held there. In 1896 a congregation was organized in the city of Morrison, the county seat of Whiteside County; Morrison is situated 12 miles east of Fulton. This congregation numbered 38 families at its organization. The prospects here are good. The land around Morrison is of the best quality, and thus before long this newly organized church will become a prosperous congregation.

At the present time the congregation at Fulton is being served by Rev. Willem J. Duiker. Through the large attendance at the regularly held worship services, the zeal of the early settlers is maintained and the congregation continues to grow in membership. At the present time the Hollanders living in and near Fulton number approximately 350 families with a total of more than 2,000 souls. The little mustard seed has become a large tree. The prosperity of many signifies the fact that with hard work and industriousness the Hollanders need not stand behind. As a people we are admired by the Americans.

So may this brief sketch concerning Fulton and the Hollanders who lived there be used to rescue these memories from the pit of forgetfulness. May this account be securely kept by way of the Holland semicentennial celebration of 1897 for generations that are still to come.

Vol. 2, chapter 21, no. 70, pp. 73-78

70. HENRY HARMELING'S
"SKETCH OF THE REFORMED CHURCH AT ALTO, WISCONSIN"

[The author served the Alto congregation from 1894 to 1900. His *Een Historisch overzicht der Gereformeerde Gemeente te Alto Wisconsin,* appeared in *De Hope,* December 28, 1898. Ellie Dekker, a staff member in the A. C. Van Raalte Institute for Historical Studies at Hope College, translated the document.]

It is with a feeling of warm thankfulness to the Lord, the Head of His Church, that we are able to trace the history of the Reformed congregation in Alto. And since the history of the first settlers and that of the first congregation are closely tied to each other, this narrative will probably be of interest not only to the members of the congregation but also to those who care about the establishment of Holland colonies in the West.

The beginning of the Holland settlements in the West dates back to the year 1845 when the first Hollander, Albertus Meenk, arrived at Alto. The following year people saw various families settle themselves here, namely, Ter Beest, Loomans, Rensink, Van den Bosch, Slyster, Rikkers, Nieuwenhuis, Hoftiezer, and Boland. In 1847 this number of settlers steadily increased, so that, among others, the families of Bruins, Boom, Veenhuis, De Groot, Veernhout, Van Eck, and Walhuizen could be added to the settlement.

A need was felt to hold regular religious services. These meetings were held at the home of David A. van Eck, who had willingly offered his home to the congregation's service. But leadership had to be given in such religious meetings. It was very fortunate that the settlers were able to enjoy the sound leadership of the brothers G. J. ter Beest, M. Duven, and Cornelius Veernhout, who took turns leading the meetings.

It is not known whether the home of David A. van Eck was becoming too small to hold the growing meetings, or if another factor gave rise to the building of a new log church by the settlers in the fall of 1847. The block church of 20 × 28 feet was built on the farm of David A. van Eck, a half mile west of the present site of the church.

Although there wasn't an organized congregation yet, the settlers still issued a unanimous call for an appointment of a dominie, because urgent need breaks all convention. This desired appointment was written and sent to Rev. Gerrit Baai [Baay] in Het Loo, Netherlands. The dominie in Het Loo gave a favorable answer to this call and arrived with his family in the spring of 1848, and immediately they settled under the roof of the block church. The church building didn't just serve as the dominie's living quarters, but school was also held there daily. Payment for the services that Rev. Baai gave to the first settlers was partially given in staples such as potatoes, wheat, and other produce from the surrounding farmland. His salary was also supplemented by what was put in a tin can made by F. Beeuwkes and hung at the entrance of the church. That's why Rev. Baai also wrote on this can the words from the text in Galatians 6:6 to sharpen the conscience of his people. The words were these: "Those who are taught the word must share in all good things with their teacher."

It was very sad that Rev. G. Baai's stay among these first settlers ended so quickly when the Lord relieved His faithful servant by death and called him up to claim the reward of the righteous. He died on November 7, 1849. For a year and a half his work among the settlers was blessed in spite of the ups and downs of many daily struggles, much effort, and deep poverty. It should be mentioned that our Board of Domestic Missions, of which Dr. Wyckoff was then named secretary, visited Rev. Baai and his family and on this occasion rendered them financial support.

The evangelical service of Rev. Baai in America was very short, yet in that short time many conversions had taken place. He sowed many good seeds, and the Lord guided him to lay a foundation here and there that would survive the difficult trials of the settlers during the following five years. It is true that Rev. Baai was never officially instituted as a dominie over a congregation in America, but the Lord ordained his work.

It was in 1850 that the people here were gladdened and honored by a visit from Dr. van Raalte. On this occasion children were baptized, and it is recalled that Mrs. John Giesbers, as she is called now, was the first baby to be baptized in the settlement. The feelings of the people in Alto were sympathetic towards the Reformed Church in America. Rev. P. Zonne came to visit on request from Sheboygan County and made repeated attempts to sway the people away from this feeling.

The beginning of the Reformed congregation of Alto, Wisconsin, goes back to 1855. In that year the congregation was called to life by Rev. Bolks, who had been dominie of the Reformed congregation in Milwaukee, Wisconsin. The church consistory which was chosen then consisted of F. Beeuwkes and C. Landaal as elders and M. Duven and G. Duitman as deacons. The recently organized congregation wished to own the land that surrounded the church, yet it appears that David A. van Eck, for whatever reason, was not willing to sell those five acres. This was the primary reason that arrangements needed to be made to change the church's location. In September 1856 the congregation was able to buy the five acres on which the new church now stands, and the church was dedicated on November 30, 1898. These five acres were a gift from several brothers of the newly organized congregation. A "frame" church 30 × 50 feet was erected soon afterward and completed in May, 1857.

On July 17, 1857, the congregation welcomed Rev. H. Stobbelaar from the Netherlands, who was then established among them as dominie. Naturally the newly arrived dominie and his family needed a home to live in, and so the need was met by building a new parsonage, 16 × 26 feet. Rev. H. Stobbelaar's work was blessed during a service of three years and two months. The number of new members and the amount of congregational contributions cannot be recorded in this narrative because people didn't make a written note of these things during that time. Rev. Stobbelaar was a dominie who won the hearts of his congregation more with the sharp and stern preaching of the full Truth than with socializing among them. On September 6, 1860, he departed for his new field of work in Zeeland, Michigan.

For one year the pulpit was vacant, and then Rev. M. A. Ypma from Lage Prairie, Illinois, settled in Alto. His service, like that of Rev. Baai, was also relatively short, because it was the Lord's wish to take him away by death on May 1, 1863. As someone who had knowledge of medicine, Rev. Ypma softened much suffering and promoted many people's health.

Between Rev. M. A. Ypma's passing away and the arrival of Rev. R. Pieters, the congregation was served to everyone's satisfaction by Rev. J. H. Karsten. He had only recently been admitted into the holy profession and was ready to be sent as a missionary to Africa if a post could be obtained under appointment of the Board of Foreign Missions. When the year of Rev. Karsten's congregational work ended, Rev. R. Pieters from Drenthe, Michigan, accepted the position as pastor and minister. While they waited for his arrival, both the church and the parsonage were brightened with a new coat of paint. Shortly after the dominie arrived, new stables for the horses were built, and the following year a congregational school was established. Even though Rev. R. Pieters understood and viewed the National District School as a blessing to the nation, it was his outspoken conviction that the elementary school wasn't complete and comprehensive enough for confessing Christians unless they were under the influence of Christian beginnings.

Very soon after Rev. R. Pieters departed to Holland, Michigan, the congregation was successful in obtaining Rev. J. H. Karsten as dominie. He began a long and blessed service that lasted thirteen and a half years. The future was hopeful! The expectations of the congregation were realized.

It was in the fall of 1876 and the beginning of 1877 that the Lord poured special streams of his spirit over the fields of the congregation. Many seeds that had been hidden for a long time began to grow. There was a new harvest in the life of grace. Fruits — souls won for the Lord Jesus — were picked. The majority of those souls have exchanged their struggles on earth for the church triumphant, where all that is perfect is enjoyed. What else is the highest goal within the community of God's people than to win souls for the Lord?

In Rev. J. H. Karsten the people had a loyal witness of the Lord's truth, and they enjoyed him as a caring shepherd. His successor to this field was Rev. James F. Zwemer from Spring Lake, Michigan. The congregation was happy to have such a worthy successor. In expectation of his arrival, the halls and so on in the church were carpeted and the woodwork was painted. After he began his service new lamps and a chapel organ were bought. Under Rev. Zwemer's leadership as superintendent, the Alto Sunday school began and the church consistory was given the responsibility of its management. Here as well as elsewhere, Rev. Zwemer enjoyed blessings in his field of work and the fulfillment of the Lord's promises to his people were joyfully felt. Many pioneers passed away, however, one after the other, among them also the first settler, Albertus Meenk.

In the same year, 1886, that Rev. Zwemer left Alto, Rev. J. W. te Winkel was instituted over this congregation. The attendance at the public services was very encouraging. The pews underwent several necessary changes. During his labors in Alto he began missionary work among Dutch families in Waupun, Wisconsin, which resulted in the blessed organization of a new Reformed congregation.

After an absence of seven years the congregation was brought together again by their former dominie, Rev. J. H. Karsten. Rev. Karsten and the congregation were both glad to be reunited. The renewal of his service was noted here by the purchase of pews for the building which was used during Rev. Pieters' ministry as a church school but now served for teacher's meetings, prayer meetings, church consistory gatherings, and catechism. During Rev. Karsten's pastorate a large secondhand organ was bought from the St. James Episcopalian Church in Milwaukee and placed next to the pulpit, and a bell was placed in the steeple. Both the bell and the pipe organ, which were newly decorated by an able painter, are doing service in the recently dedicated church.

Already for many years there were several Dutch families residing at Randolph Center, twenty miles away from Alto, that considered the church in Alto as their own. But through immigration in 1890, their number grew so rapidly that Rev. Karsten and his church council outlined plans to accommodate their religious needs. What these plans were we cannot report here due to lack of space.

The dominie who has been allowed to work here in Alto for the last four and a half years is Rev. Henry Harmeling, the writer of this short history. When he began his service the families numbered, according to the classis statistics of 1894, 115. The last report announced the number as 158.

This increase in membership and the large attendance at the public services may be pointed to as reasons why the congregation was forced to build a new church. That the property of the church grew and was improved during the last four years can be seen from the following facts: a new parsonage costing $2,000 was built according to the modern style and practically and beautifully furnished, and a new church costing about $8,000 was built in a modified English Gothic style. The building contains a large octagonal auditorium with two entrances. The pews in the knave of the church are in a circular form with the pulpit platform in the middle of the radius. The floor is inclined so that a good view of the pulpit can be seen from the pews. Behind the pulpit is a choir loft where the pipe organ also stands. The main entrance is spacious and has adequate wardrobe space for overcoats and wraps.

This church is connected to the auditorium through "Wilson's Patent Rolling partitions," providing a Sunday school classroom that seats 150. Above this classroom is a gallery also connected to the auditorium by the same patent rolling doors. And at the back of the building is a consistory and catechism room with an entrance to the pulpit. The building is heated by a large brick-cased furnace. The lighting is provided through an "acetylene gas plant" in the basement. That in the last four years the congregational property has increased and improved we can thus see from the following facts: a new parsonage, practically and beautifully furnished, costing about $2,000, and a church that cost a little more than $8,000 and is furnished according to everyone's taste. The architecture is the work of the gentlemen Van Rijn and De Gelleke of Milwaukee, Wisconsin.

But this financial progress would be discouraging to the spiritual domain of the congregation if people could not give an encouraging spiritual testimony along with it. During the service of the present dominie, ninety-two members were added. God is given the honor and thanks.

Vol. 2, chapter 22, no. 71, pp. 79-82

71. JACOB QUINTUS'S "A BACKWARD GLANCE"

[Quintus emigrated to America from the province of Zeeland in 1846. For a short time he lived in Buffalo, but soon moved to Sheboygan, Wisconsin, where he founded the first Dutch newspaper in this country, *De Sheboygan Nieuwsbode*. This autobiographical sketch, entitled *Een terugblik over vijftig jaren*, written in 1897, was printed in *De Grondwet*, November 21, 1911. Quintus died in Grand Rapids, Michigan, in 1902. The Reverend Henry De Mots translated this account.]

The first edition of the first Dutch paper in America saw the light of day on October 16, 1849. The name of this paper, of which I had the honor of being the first editor and publisher, was *De Sheboygan Nieuwsbode*. It was published in Sheboygan, Wisconsin.

A few days after my newspaper appeared, I received a letter from a friend who lived in Albany, New York. I had gotten to know him during my one-year stay in Albany. He belongs to the descendants of the first Hollanders who had settled in the city of New York or, more correctly said, New Amsterdam. He, in his own way, spoke old-fashioned Dutch. He shared with me the impressions that emigrating from the Netherlands had made on him some fifty years ago. To this group of emigrants many of you, or your parents, belong. His request to me, by way of this letter, was that the impressions of that time, fifty years ago, might be recalled and printed in an abbreviated fashion.

In passing let me say that I have been in America for just short of fifty years. On August 4, 1847, I left Rotterdam in a sailboat, and on the morning of August 7 we were off the French coast near the city of Calais. We were accompanied by our presently esteemed friends Elder Frans van Driele, Deacon Johan A. S. Verdier, and my nephew Professor Marten Luther d'Ooge from the University of Michigan, and others. They can testify that I preached three times in the French language and in the Dutch. This was done to an audience of the assembled congregation and our fellow shipwrecked persons.

The Netherlands' well-beloved poet sings in one of his masterpieces: "Scene of the Hollanders Wintering on Nova Zembla in the years 1596 and 1597":

> "But, first the day is celebrated and God our Lord is praised!
> They open their Bibles and all uncover the head;
> Each of them, each in turn, arises reverently,
> Stands to read a moving part of God's Holy Word;
> Every soul and song blends full-throated into one,
> And Nova Zembla hears the Psalms of Datheen."

And the question, my listeners, is if they sang with more spirit and gusto with an inner feeling of thankfulness to God than we as saved emigrants with full breast and at least a hundred throats sang Dutch psalms in that French Wesleyan Church in Calais, on that memorable Sunday morning on August 8, 1847.

On the 18th of August we sailed from Calais to Le Havre, and on the 25th of August, aboard another sailboat, we left for New York, where we arrived on September 28. However, I should not speak of this any further.

What were the principal reasons for a renewed emigration from the Netherlands? A rupture or separation had taken place in the ruling church, whether for good and adequate reason is something we do not judge at this point. The government proceeded rashly, which every government, even our own, does from time to time. It is possible that if they had not moved erroneously, the emigration of which we speak would not have taken place.

In order to compel members to remain in the ruling church, after several plans had been considered and rejected, and in order to oppose the rupture, an old law of Napoleon was revived which designated the gathering of a very small number of people — twenty — for purposes not recorded in the law to be a seditious gathering and subject to the authority and power of the police. Because of this absurd and despotic ruling, the worship services of the Separatists were hindered, disturbed, and opposed. However, as always happens in the history of the world, this persecution fanned the smoldering coals into a flame, and the Hollanders, who assumed they were suffering for a matter of conscience, decided to seek a land where there would be a place and an authority broad enough for their faith.

At first, so wrote my friends, a few came over. These were poor and humble people. They were moved by the same motivation as the renowned men who sailed to Plymouth in 1620. When they arrived in New York, to their surprise, they found people who carried the same names as theirs, among whom many spoke the same language, differing in their speech only as the old differs from the new. And now the incentive and path for emigration was at hand. The letters to the homeland spoke of a prosperous land which welcomed them; of labor which was rewarded; of reasonable prices for food; of friends with whom they could speak and who could understand them. They also spoke of consistories and ministers, of Dutch names and a Dutch church.

At this time the emigration accelerated, not only among the Separatists but also from among the members of the old church, and from every persuasion and every employment. And every year the Netherlands sent more people to our land. The government acquiesced to but did not approve this emigration of her sons and daughters. Thus, after a Rip Van Winkle kind of slumber for two centuries, they followed the example of the *Halve Maan*.

The clothes and the adornments of these immigrants were eye-catching and pleasant. In many ways they resembled completely the people in the tales formerly told which some of us have heard. They brought furniture, clothing, and ornaments with them, some of which are still to be seen in the old houses in Albany and Ulster and in some houses near New York. They spoke the same language that we as children heard from the mouths of older people who didn't want to speak anything other than Dutch. The miniature cup and saucer, the foot warmer, the Bible, these had been stored away here as holy remnants of the past; all these things they had in their possession. The clothing which they wore was the same as that which we see on old family portraits, the colors and gilt-edged frames faded with the passage of time. Our old friends were able to quite easily converse with them. The one difference which was to be noted is that we used words that by then had become dead and worn out and no longer in use. Our Dutch language had stood still since the seventeenth century; theirs had been fashioned, twisted, and changed through the power and example of the French, and through association with the English, and commerce with neighboring places.

Most of the Hollanders moved westward, after a brief start in the cities. They moved to Michigan, Wisconsin, and Iowa, where they established settlements. Those who come now go directly through; very few remain in the cities. They are for the most part people who live exemplary, frugal, and honest lives. Thus far, even although I have associated with many, I have not found any who were unable to read and write, and most of them possess a Bible. I do not deny that weaknesses, ingratitude, dissatisfaction, stubbornness, and a tendency to go astray are to be found among them. However, I am speaking about them in general, and here I find very unusual compliance with law and good order, in the fullest sense of the word. Such a reputation the Hollanders in America had fifty years ago. Have they maintained this reputation?

Vol. 2, chapter 23, no. 77, pp. 139-144

77. HERMAN BOTTEMA'S "IN AMERICA'S FRIESLAND"

[Bottema, born in Gorredijk and long a resident of Milwaukee, published the following report of what he saw and heard on a visit to Friesland, Wisconsin, in 1928. The account appeared in *Leeuwarder Courant,* August 8 and 9, 1928. The Reverend Henry De Mots translated the report.]

"Step down, Friesland!" the conductor shouted. I was thus in Friesland, Wisconsin, situated 80 miles from Milwaukee. This is a very lovely region. Most of the people living here are from Friesland, Netherlands; they came here from the environs of Dokkum.

But not only here; in the immediate surroundings lie East Friesland and Randolph, and the Frisian people are well represented in these communities also. Note the following: 93 families in Friesland are members of the Reformed Church; in Randolph and in East Friesland 76 families are members of the Christian Reformed Church. It is estimated that approximately one half of the people living in this community, and possibly even more, have come directly from Friesland, and their number has increased by the birth of children and grandchildren.

When a person has lived in the city for 42 years and hasn't heard a single word of Frisian, at least not on the street, it is surprising to hear Frisian spoken, even by the toddlers. The old settlers speak real Frisian to this day, without, as is the case with many other nationalities, mixing in a number of English words. The little town of Friesland is sixty years old and perhaps even a bit older. Later the railroad came through here, and that gave a real impetus for growth and development. It is the North Western Railway which runs through the town.

Most of the Frisians are farmers, and many, so it seems, have their "sheep on dry ground." They now live peacefully and with satisfaction in the little town of Friesland. Some were hired hands on the farm at one time here in Friesland and now after hard and heavy work, and by living frugally, and possibly by means of some good fortune, they are able to live without anxiety or concern in their older years.

The first person with whom I spoke when I disembarked from the train was, as it happened, no Frisian, but a man who at one time had been a resident in Dalfsen, Overijssel. His name is Gerrit J. Vredeveld, and he is the local portmaster. He is able to speak the Frisian language well and has been in America for 16 years. Besides his job as portmaster, which doesn't pay a large salary in such a small place, he operates a store which sells ice cream, cigars, and so on.

The second person I met was a lad who was eleven years old. I addressed him in the Frisian language and to my amazement he responded in the Frisian language and said, "Yes, my father and my mother were born in Friesland and I also can speak the Frisian language." Now, I thought, that is good. It appears to me that a person who is unable to speak Dutch, nor English, nor German is able to manage quite well by using the Frisian language. And after having spent a few days here, that appeared to me to be true.

In the morning it is customary to go to the post office to fetch one's mail for the day. Here several hours are spent in sociable conversation with the elderly citizens of the community. Here the folks come together to discuss the news of the day and other matters of common interest. All this is very pleasant and sociable indeed.

The third, or rather the third party, with whom I spoke was Jan Wiersma, his wife, and his daughter-in-law and his son. I had become thirsty and I knocked at the door. "Come in," someone said. The person was in the kitchen. They had just seated themselves at the kitchen to enjoy their evening meal, and I was invited, as the German is wont to say, to "arrange myself at the table." Jan Wiersma and his wife come from Morra, Oostdongeradeel, and have lived in Friesland for some thirty-two years. They are very pleased to be living here; much better than in Friesland where working for the farmers would never bring them to the point of material well-being in which they could rejoice. During our mealtime Sjoerd Kramer, a carpenter, arrived and was invited in. He had come from the city of Leeuwarden, Netherlands. He had formerly been associated with a technical school in the city of Leeuwarden. I was told that a man named Harm de Fries met a tragic death last year when he fell from a barn. Mr. de Fries had lived at one time in Nijkerk, Oostdongeradeel.

At the post office I became acquainted with most of the Frisians and heard many of the names with which I was formerly familiar in Gorredijk. By way of example there is Yense Tamminga from Hiaure near Dokkum. He has lived here for thirty-seven years and is a landlord. Then there is Bote Kok, who comes from Brandgum, which is located between Holwerd and Dokkum. He has been in America for thirty years. He spoke about the conditions in the fens in Beets and the neighboring areas, and the riots which flowed from these conditions — the concentration of soldiers stationed at Gorredijk, and how he himself had been under arms and had experienced this unrest. He had also heard Domela Nieuwenhuis speak at Tijnje.

Poppe van der Velde hails from Ee, which is located an hour and a half from Dokkum, and lies between Metslawier and Engwierum. He was a painter in Friesland and has a large store here. Van der Velde has been in America for eighteen years and paid a visit to Friesland just before the war. He is an unusually courteous and obliging person and was of considerable help to me. You must remember that there was not even a single hotel in town and inasmuch as it was now late in the evening, and inasmuch as his own house was filled with visitors, he, through his influence and a kindly word, succeeded in providing lodging for me in the home of his neighbor, Jan Posthuma. Posthuma was 8 years old when he arrived here with his parents. They hailed from Oosternijkerk, in Friesland. But Jan informed me that he attended school in Metslawier. Then there is Lolke Gaastra, who is a farrier here. He hailed from Workum and had lived here in Friesland for 16 years.

Harm Kloostra hails from Niawier, and has been in America for twenty-five years. Mrs. Kloostra comes from Nes, Westdongeradeel (Niawier: Oostdongeradeel). They are landlords, and a few years ago they made a visit to their daughter in California. Jan Braaksma, who was born in Morra and who has been here for twenty years, is involved in the same enterprise.

Tjerk Westra, who had been a laborer in Friesland, has been here thirty years. He became a farmer here and then raised sheep on dry land and then became a landlord. He informed me that Friesland has spread out a great deal in the last ten years.

Pieter D. Westra was a hired man in Friesland. He was born in Hattum, which is north of Dokkum. He has lived in Friesland for forty years, and he and his son operate a farm. Andries de Jong hails from Lioessens, which is two hours east of Dokkum. He has been here five years and is a chicken farmer. Gerrit Levy formerly lived in Morra. He has been here thirty-six years and is a landowner. Nonne de Jong, father of Andries de Jong, hails from Lioessens, worked for a farmer, and has been here twenty-five years. Sietse Visser comes from Paessens, the congregation of Oostdongeradeel; he has been here twenty-five years and is a cattle dealer.

Then, as I walk along, I spy a signboard with the name Fillema on it; the signboard is attached to a large store. Fillema's father came to America seventy-five years ago, but formerly lived in Town Eight. Gilbert Vredeveld, the barber here in Friesland, is a very friendly man. Yes, it appears to me that all the people here are very friendly.

So I could continue and fill several columns with Frisian names. However, I forgot to mention Onne Sjoerdsma, who came from Ternaard. I met him this afternoon. He was in his automobile on his way to his farm. He has been here for twenty-five years and lives in East Friesland. And then I should also mention Jenske Tamminga, who operates an ice cream parlor and a grocery store.

One sees a variety of signboards with real Frisian names, such as N. Alsum, Jan Kloostra, etc. There is some industry, but naturally not half enough. It would be better if in this area there would be more life and movement. True, there is the Friesland Canning Company. There I met Ely Cupery, the cashier of the company, who was born in Hiaure and arrived here in 1881. This company operates only 4 or 5 weeks in a year. The production of peas totals about 2,000,000 tins per season. These peas are grown in the immediate vicinity and are distributed in tins throughout all America. Many Frisians and daughters of Frisians work for this company. There are also two cheese factories here.

I was impressed with the good-natured character of the people here. And at the post office one can banter with the old settlers of Friesland, many of whom are advanced in years.

As previously stated, 93 families are members of the Friesland, Wisconsin Reformed Church. I don't believe that there is a single family of Frisian ancestry which does not belong to the church. The minister, Rev. Kleerekooper, occupies the nicest house in the town. I did not meet him personally, but I was told that he is of Jewish ancestry. This gives evidence of the growth of the Reformed Church in this area. The respect for spirituality is about the same as it was in Gorredijk about a century ago. And that is noteworthy indeed when one considers the changes that have taken place in almost every other area of life. Here, in this aspect of life, a certain constancy is to be observed.

Here, and elsewhere, we were not very surprised to note that the spiritual has seen no change. The children grow up in the same atmosphere in which their parents and grandparents lived, spiritually speaking. They had the same models as their forefathers. It is obvious that the inhabitants of the Iberian Peninsula encountered a formidable foe in the Netherlands in 1558. The same opposition is still evident among our citizens. When you speak with them and attempt to maintain something contrary to this issue than they have always maintained, you can quite well imagine what the results will be.

Morally the people maintain a high level. They are good-hearted and are always ready to do their very best for a stranger such as I. Naturally the dear youth, especially the boys, are the same everywhere; — always planning some "mischievous conduct." When I had my first letter in my envelope I heard the firebell strike and I heard the cry, "Fire!" However, when we came out of doors no fire was to be seen anywhere. What had happened was that a couple of rascals had given a few strong tugs on the rope which is attached to the hammer which strikes the bell, and so the alarm rang.

Friesland, so it appears, must be a healthy place to live. A certain Mr. Ketels died here 14 years ago at the age of 94 years. Mr. Ketels came to America in approximately the year 1840. He came from the province of Zeeland. Actually he was an old acquaintance of mine, inasmuch as I had first met him in Milwaukee in 1888 and lived with him at that time. When Ketels arrived here in his younger years, he walked from what was then Chicago to Milwaukee. This was a stroll of 90 miles; a trip that took three days.

Friesland had only one store twenty-three years ago, but as I stated previously, when the railroad came through, the town grew and made progress. Now there are four large stores where one is able to purchase anything and everything. Naturally, there is lack of opportunity to work for a larger population. One or two factories where a person would be able to work the year round would certainly enable the town to grow and to blossom. However, these simply don't exist.

There is a lumberyard where wood for carpentry is sold. There is also a school. The school children have three months of vacation in the summer months. In earlier years the schooling must have been deficient. At least, I was told about this poor schooling now and again. The Dutch language was spoken in the school, but there was no school for the youth to learn even the minimum of the language of the "old country." I am of the opinion that it is always profitable to know the Dutch language, because there are often circumstances in which it is convenient to know it. Moreover, the Dutch language is rich in words, and many of these appear, for example, in the Norwegian language. This is also true of the English language. Sometimes I think of myself and the great majority of the Frisians who are not able to write in the mother language. I would have been able to write with much greater power and energy and with much greater clarity if I had been able to put my words on paper in the Frisian language. It seems as if the language which is spoken in a certain region enables a person to reproduce their impressions much better and with greater purity than is possible in any other language. There are sayings and expressions which were used when I was a thirteen-year-old boy in Friesland, which now, having left Friesland, I could never reproduce in Dutch. Thus, the power and the clarity in the construction of a sentence are lost.

With regret I took leave of the American Friesland, from the good people that I met and of whom I made mention. Although the time was short, they were true and warm friends to me. My visit with them shall remain in my memory for a long time, yes, perhaps as long as I live.

I also traveled to South Beaverdam and to Beaverdam. At an earlier date beavers were to be found here in great numbers; hence the name. Yesterday I arrived at Watertown, which like Beaverdam is a lovely town with a population of about 8,000. Here, as well as throughout the state, the German people are well represented.

The hotels here were quite well filled, but I noticed a signboard with these words, "room for rent." An elderly lady came to the door and in German asked me if I was interested in a room. I answered, "Ja" or, better said, "yes." She then asked me, "Sprechen Sie Deutsch?" (Do you speak German?). I answered her by saying that anyone who has lived in Milwaukee for forty years would certainly learn to speak the German language of necessity. This surely was evidence that we find a large number of Germans here.

Vol. 2, chapter 26, no. 83, pp. 204-213

83. A. J. BETTEN'S "HISTORY OF SIOUX COUNTY, IOWA"

[Betten established himself in Orange City in 1871 and took an active part in the development of the new community. This account, based on his diary, describes daily life in farming, politics, and religion until 1879. The account was first published in *De Volksvriend*, September 19, 1895. Cornelia Breugem Kennedy of Northwestern College, Orange City, translated the account for the Sioux County centennial celebrations in 1970 and published the English text in a special Tulip Festival edition of the *Sioux County Capital*, called *"De Volksvriend,"* May 1970, pp. 5, 6, 34.]

A reporter once wrote to me: "In the fall of 1856 I lived in your county. At that time the land was still a part of Woodbury County. The first work there was carried out by me, Mr. Mills, and a hunch-backed four-footer. We did not do anything but mow and stack hay. We have never decided who of us was the greatest ass."

According to statistics there were ten inhabitants in Sioux County in the year 1860: nine men and one woman. In the year 1865 this number increased to twenty, and in 1869 the population amounted to more than one hundred souls. From the history of these early years very little is known, except that the so-called administration issued quite a few debentures, which later settlers had to pay.

If you desire other information about the history of the pioneers in the first years of the colonization here, the limited length of this article can hardly do justice to this subject. It seems to me that this task could better be handled by one of the first pioneers who has been a witness, like the mother of the Colony (Mrs. Vennema), who from the beginning saw all that happened here to the homesteaders. We should also pay attention to the fact that in those first years it could storm quite a bit, and that many things happened in those blizzards that now are lost to memory.

The writer of this piece settled here in the year 1871. In this colony at the time there already lived 70 to 80 families. Many of those lived in fairly good frame houses. The others lived in sod huts, or so-called "dugouts." A small part of the land was already cleared. Wheat and potatoes had already been cultivated. In 1870, Mr. Tjeerd Heemstra, in order to accommodate the pioneers, had begun a retail store. In October he was elected to the board of supervisors, who on January 1, 1871, elected him as their chairman. In August of 1870 one of the first pioneers, Jelle Pelmulder, for whom the first frame house was built here, was appointed clerk of the court. He served in this office by election until 1887. He was also the first teacher in this colony. From December 1, 1870, until March

1, 1871, he was the teacher of youth in the schoolhouse in Section 10, Township 95, Range 44.

In 1870 three deceased were mourned. The first one was the aged woman, the widow Rijsdam. She was interred on the homestead of the family. In the family of Chris Nieuwendorp the first son was born; they called him Hendrik. The first public worship service was held at the home of Sjoerd Aukes Sipma, Section 14, Township 95, Range 44. The place which became Orange City was laid out by a surveyor from Sioux City.

In the year 1870 a house and school building had been built there. The population consisted of three people: a carpenter (A. J. Lenderink) and his wife and son. The last named is our current county auditor. The first winter, except for the last week in December, had not been particularly cold. The first colonists, when they arrived here, had already experienced a year of difficulty. As it seems to us, several of our settlers are fairly prosperous. But with many this wealth consists of the rich soil, with the capital being the hope of a good harvest.

Henry Hospers, the leader and principal advisor in matters of colonization, was still living in Pella. In the spring of 1871 he sent a builder here, D. Gleysteen, now a man of substance in Alton, who constructed a store on the north side of the town square. When the building was almost completed it was swept from its foundation by a violent storm on a certain Sunday. The builder put it back in its place and quickly completed it. That same Sunday, south of the town, a stable and a team of oxen were burned on the homestead of Rijsdam.

Within a short time the newly constructed store did a brisk business. The first load of goods that came in consisted of edibles: grits, barley, rice, peas, flour, fish, coffee, sugar, syrup, etc. The agent, who probably did not have a large amount of capital at his disposal, or who did not really know what was demanded in such a new colony, did not give credit. Butter and eggs were exchanged for goods. Besides, many barely had a medium of exchange.

The owner of the store came here from Pella shortly after the store had opened for business to settle here permanently. When he came into the store for the first time, someone said to this writer: "There is the father of the Colony; from now on everything will go well." It was not long before he found a new medium of exchange. He did not lack ink and paper. From time to time he filled the void by bringing into circulation the so-called "store orders," which were just as saleable in Orange City as any other kind of "fractional currency." The father of the Colony generally took the plowing of prairie land for these orders as his payment. So he had to arrange how to get his money.

The settlement expanded and the population steadily increased. In Orange City that summer about eight houses were built. In a short time the place was provided with a hotel, a smithy, a shoemaker, and a barber. If one wanted a butcher or baker, then one could be served a short distance out of town. Every farmer provided his yard with from one to five acres of trees. This was at that time a shelter against the fierce northwest wind and assured an exemption from payment of part of the [property] tax. On homesteads more and more buildings were erected. The already cleared land appeared to be fruitful.

On a certain Sunday in June, the Rev. Egbert Winter from Pella preached here in the schoolhouse. During the afternoon service a violent storm broke loose. The land was enriched by a mild rain. On July 12, 1871, the First Reformed Church of Orange City was organized. In the same year the Holland Christian Reformed Church was organized with about thirteen families.

In Calliope, the county seat, the first issue of the *Sioux County Herald* was published. The fall elections were at hand: the colonists were in close agreement with the pioneers of the neighboring settlements of the county. On September 29 a convention was held and candidates were nominated. The second Tuesday in October was election day. The 16th day of this month the Board of Supervisors met and declared the following persons elected to the respective offices:

Henry Hospers, member of the board of supervisors;
A. J. Betten, Jr., auditor;
J. W. Greattrax, treasurer;
T. J. Dunham, sheriff;
H. Jones, surveyor;
John Newell, superintendent of schools;
J. O. Beals, coroner.

A severe winter set in. The homesteaders, who had to make long trips to get fuel, were often in danger in the blinding blizzards and severe cold. In December the county clerk and the newly elected auditor went by foot to the county seat. It was a generally impassable road, covered with a deep layer of snow. It was only twenty-five miles. Now and then they tumbled up to their arms in the soft snow bed, yet then there was the opportunity to rest a bit, and the clerk at those moments smoked his big Dutch pipe. By starlight they arrived at their destination and after a short stay returned home again.

On the first of January 1872 the newly elected officers with some of their friends again went to the county seat to attend a board meeting. The weather was quite cold. Hospers was allowed a seat as a member of the board after the swearing of the oath. He kept his office until November 16, 1887, when he resigned because he was elected a state representative. The other elected officers did not enjoy the privilege of accepting their offices, because two members of the board refused to give their approval to the surety bonds they offered. On

January 9 there was another meeting with the same result. The new "county father" tried to protest this treatment, but he had only one voice and the opposition had two.

On January 10 Klaas Jongewaard, with one of the prospective officers, went by sleigh to Orange City. They lost their way quickly and wandered around until midnight. Then they saw a haystack in the field where they took shelter and rested a bit. After having searched the surroundings, they continued the journey and arrived — still unfrozen — at the house of a wagoner. The board had been adjourned until the 21st of the month. Many people wanted to attend this meeting, and a lawyer went along to plead the case. On January 22 a great number of colonists also came to be present at the meeting. When no conclusion could be reached, Hospers returned home. The people thought that the disapproval of the bonds was because of something unfavorable about the functioning officers, but later it was shown that this suspicion was not grounded. People met again. After a unanimous decision, all books and appurtenances of the County were taken, loaded, and brought to Orange City. It was late when they left. It was unusually cold, and many had strange feelings in the nose or stiff ears. Some were so cold that they fainted when they warmed themselves too closely at the big fire. But with coffee and lunch the people revived again quickly. After some time the matter was set straight. A new law was passed by which people could appeal to a higher court, and they did appeal. After a while the newly elected officers were installed in their new offices.

January 13 is remembered by many as the day in which a heavy snowstorm broke loose that continued for three days. During this blizzard, in the humble cottage of the blacksmith, a son was born who survived that storm and subsequent storms up to this day. In a similar snowstorm, the county clerk almost got lost on his way home. He returned and arrived back in town with an ice- and snow-covered face. In that storm a widow in town went out and got lost. After an anxious search she was found in time near the manse, then being built. More such events could be recited, but they are all similar. Notwithstanding these dangers, the colonists have been kept remarkably safe in all these feared and dangerous storms. In the first years not one of them perished because of them.

In the spring a large number of families settled here. In this year the Sioux City and St. Paul Railroad was built. This saved many a long trip and vastly improved the opportunity for the transport of grain and building materials, fuel, etc. Number 50, volume 1, of the *Sioux County Herald* was published in Orange City and began to include a little Dutch.

The fields of the farmer appeared to be fruitful. His work was rewarded with a good crop. The result of the election again was according to the wishes of the colonists. On October 16 a meeting of the circuit court was held in Orange City for the first time, with the Hon. Addison Oliver as Judge. On November 11 the board of supervisors met and declared by resolution, according to the results of the election, that Orange City was the seat of Sioux County. After several days the books and appurtenances of the county were taken to Orange City.

Up to now there was steady progress. The pioneer still has limited means, but with thrift and industry there seem to be good prospects. There are still many privations which people face, but generally speaking, they have a particular privilege: the peace that they enjoy. As it was from the beginning, there is much visiting, a bond of unity, and the guarding of each other's interests. Even in the most humble cottage, generosity and hospitality are always shown. Conflicts of a serious nature hardly ever arise anymore, and if they do arise, they are settled amicably most of the time. Each is ready with word and deed for the other. Lawsuits seldom occur.

From the beginning on, religion was very important for most of the people. The Book of books was considered to be an indispensable guide for life. Education and religion had a place in house and heart. Who cannot but appreciate these privileges? Worship services were first held in private homes; they were led by laymen unless a preacher was present from somewhere else. Later they met in the town schoolhouse. On July 12, 1871, the first Reformed congregation was organized. In due time this congregation called a preacher, namely the Rev. Seine Bolks, who accepted the call and moved here in the year 1872. He served the congregation until July, 1878. In the year 1872 a particular religious revival began that lasted for a considerable time. Many chose "the good part" and were added to the congregation. The congregation had been organized by about forty members, and at the end of 1872 membership had climbed to more than three hundred. Thus an imperishable good was received and enjoyed. Many hearts were strengthened by grace before the time of stress and trials began. At the end of that year the population of this colony amounted to almost fifteen hundred souls.

On January 6, 1873, the Board of Supervisors met in Orange City for the first time, and Henry Hospers was elected president. On January 13 the district court met for the first time in Orange City. The county was threatened with a suit for $10,000 for fraudulent debentures. It was contested and the loss averted.

In the spring the prospect of the farmer seemed to be favorable again. Until June the fruits grew luxuriantly. But in this month a winged army of eaters descended on the fields. They were grasshoppers. In their voracity they seemed to eat all the corn — man was helpless against this army. These were days of depression and sadness. But they were also days of prayer. Not long after this the plague was lifted. Very much was destroyed, but enough was left to thank the Giver for all good things.

On May 19, 1874, there was an election about the question as to whether or not there would be a yearly tax of ten mills to pay off the county debts. It was defeated by 194 to 117.

The First Reformed Church was given a sum which was large enough to begin the erection of a church building. They decided to build, with Otto Rouwenhorst as the builder. The materials were taken to Orange City from East Orange by the people; the transportation was therefore free of charge.

On June 2, 1874, a bidding was made for a new county courthouse to be contracted. It was constructed on the town square by builder Gerrit Dorsman.

On June 20 the first number of *De Volksvriend* came into print.

That summer the grasshoppers flew over us in numerous swarms. Now and then they descended in heaps and did intermittent damage. On the third Sunday in July, the grasshoppers descended en masse and covered the face of the land. By Thursday they ascended with much noise and disappeared even more quickly than they came. Quite a lot was destroyed, and for many, this catastrophe meant a time of despair. Although there was much left, the damage was very uneven; for some it meant much damage, for others little.

Another sad occurrence happened in the West Branch area on September 25. Two of the colonists (Kleuvers and Wesselink) had gone out for firewood. They crossed the Rock River in a dangerous spot and were drowned.

On October 13 the Herd law was accepted by popular vote. In February 1875 aid was given to the distressed in a neighboring state at their request. There was also talk of buying a section of land, to make it productive, and to use the yield for the establishment of an Academy in time. Some felt that we should wait to see whether more of those winged eaters would come. From time to time there was talk about the building of a windmill as well. A meeting about this was held in the courthouse in March 1875. Eight hundred dollars was inscribed for this purpose. The cornmill was built southeast of town.

The field of the farmer bore rich fruits, but because of an abundance of rain and stormy weather, much corn was damaged. In the fall much damage was done to the plants by rain. Some seemed to think that the increase in mice in the fields was alarming.

In the beginning of October the first Sioux County Fair was held. During the last part of the month the first exam in medical school was given. Much damage occurred this fall in the form of prairie fires.

On January 6, 1876, a premium of $2,000 was offered by the Board of Supervisors for the discovery of coal in this county. Later this was increased to $3,000. The premium has not been claimed by anyone.

In this month an agricultural society was organized. They meet on Saturday afternoon and debate various subjects, e.g., "The elevator, a curse for the farmer"; "The wheat crop, the greatest advantage for the farmer"; "The pulpit exerts more influence than the printing press." During the winter months many youngsters amused themselves in the country spelling school. A young men's society was organized with older men leading. In the month of May a free Christian congregation was organized.

The crops promised much. On June 13 a rumor was circulated that the redskins were coming. This caused much anxiety. But they did not appear and the weapons were put away again.

Two weeks later the grasshoppers appeared en masse and stayed about ten days. The damage was uneven; in some places much was damaged and in other areas hardly anything. Much corn was left. But for those who have been repeatedly hit this was a cause of pressure and discouragement. From the north part of the county some of the people departed for elsewhere. Among our settlers there were a few who wanted to leave, yet everything possible was done to encourage them to stay. Only a few left.

"John Credit" played a large role meanwhile, and was becoming troublesome. The board of supervisors decided to build a prison, which was contracted by John Sembke on September 6, 1876.

The building of a poorhouse was contracted by W. S. Okey.

The barn on the seed farm was contracted by A. J. Lenderink.

F. E. Hewitt was the first workhouse master. In this Colony only one pauper was under their care.

The county was threatened with a lawsuit of about $37,000 for fraudulent debentures. The board delegated H. Hospers to go to Dubuque, and he was able to settle the sum for a little more than $700. This matter had been repeatedly brought to court and had already cost the county much money and effort.

In May of 1877 two Reformed churches were organized: one in Alton and one in Sioux Center.

The grasshoppers of the previous year laid their eggs here, especially in the sod of the newly plowed field. In the month of June the young grasshoppers appeared and did much damage. Various means were tried to destroy or drive them away, but there was much advice and little cure. The next month the grasshoppers from the north flew over and took with them the group from here. In spite of the eaters there was much left to harvest.

On November 15, 1877, around 11:30 a.m. earth tremors were felt.

In the year of 1878 the farmers had a bad crop. Much damage was caused by an abundance of rain. Many were forced to mow the corn with the grass mower, to rake it together, and to bundle it together like haystacks. Because of the extraordinary heat and heavy rainstorms, part of the grain had been driven to the ground and could not be bound. During the month of September the grasshoppers arrived. They did little damage but left quite a few eggs.

In the month of October much damage was done due to prairie fires. There was death among the cattle. The cause was likely smut in the corn. The brass band that had been organized here received new instruments. In the spring of 1879 there were complaints about the drought.

In the month of May the Sioux County Bible Society was organized.

The young grasshoppers appeared and did much damage. All sorts of methods were used to destroy them. It is a disheartening and difficult work, in which one is only partly successful.

On the last Sunday in June, the Rev. Ale Buursma, who had been called by the First Reformed Church, was installed by the Rev. Johannes Willem Warnshuis, with many attending.

During the last part of June and the early part of July, heavy storms and thunder caused much damage and calamity. The small grain was continually ravaged by the destructive eaters, and not much was left of wheat and oats. During the last part of July the grasshoppers moved away. The farmers met with the purpose of trying to find means to fight the spreading of glanders among horses.

In August a storm arose which raged like a hurricane. Wind and hail caused much damage over the West Branch and on the Rock River. The harvest of corn and flax was a disappointment, but corn was a good crop for many. During the last year that the plague visited this locality, much has been written about the grasshoppers. The observations varied a great deal. Some had painted it too light, while others had painted it too dark. Let it be. Despite the difficult and sorrowful years, the hand of the industrious has always been blessed. The tie of unity, the willingness to carry one another's burdens, has been a great blessing. We are speaking in general, because there were exceptions.

We do not boast about the people, because what does a person have that he has not gotten first from a Higher Hand? Let us praise the Lord for his goodness. The expansion of this settlement, despite adversity, continued slowly yet steadily, so that the population of this Colony amounted to about three thousand souls at the end of the year 1879.

Vol. 2, chapter 26, no. 84, pp. 213-216

84. HENRY HOSPERS' "MIGRATION TO SIOUX COUNTY, IOWA"

[Hospers was intimately associated with the affairs of Sioux County from his arrival in 1870 until his death in 1902. This account is from the twenty-fifth anniversary number of *De Volksvriend,* September 19, 1895. Cornelia Breugem Kennedy of Northwestern College, Orange City, translated the account for the Sioux County centennial celebrations in 1970 and published the English text in a special Tulip Festival edition of the *Sioux County Capital,* called *"De Volksvriend,"* May 1970, pp. 5, 34.]

Plans for a move were made as a result of the rapidly increasing population and the ever-rising cost of farmland in the Dutch colony of Pella, so the less fortunate had a hard time obtaining their own pieces of land. Those who had settled with a family of small children in Pella saw these children grow up and come to a marriageable age. More and more the need was felt and the desire became urgent to find a suitable place for a Dutch settlement somewhere in the west.

In 1860 the writer of this piece had to spend a few weeks in St. Joseph, Missouri. He saw there how a great number of wagons with families, cattle, and farm tools crossed the Missouri River daily to look for "homes" in Nebraska. He heard that all who had the courage to settle on the prairies found what they had desired so much.

Having come back to Pella he talked with a few people about the impressions that he had gained about the migration to the west. Many conferences were held about the possibilities of moving to these parts with a few Dutch families. Involved were the Messrs. A. C. Kuyper, former elder of the First Reformed congregation of Pella; W. van Asch, W. Sleyster, and G. P. H. Zahn, all since deceased. Plans were even made to obtain funds to buy farms, yet these attempts were doomed to failure and the loosely made plans fell through. Nevertheless, the need for emigration was felt more urgently and the craving for a move became stronger.

Especially in 1867 and 1868, it was Mr. Jelle Pelmulder who treated the colonization plan with zeal and seriousness and drew the attention to western or northwestern Iowa. He corresponded with land offices, gained much information, and with Frisian determination kicked the emigration ball with fresh energy. He indeed may be called the first draftsman of the plan to settle a Dutch Colony in northwestern Iowa.

In Pella meetings were held from time to time in 1868 to discuss colonization plans. These meetings were well attended, and it appeared that a general interest in the matter had been created. A regular organization and a committee was formed, consisting of four trusted and practical farmers: Jelle Pelmulder, Huibert Muilenburg, Sjoerd A. Sipma, and Hendrik J. van der Waa, who were delegated to visit the northwestern part of Iowa and to investigate whether or not it would be a suitable place for a Dutch Colony.

This committee departed in a covered wagon drawn by two mules for the then still unknown Northwest. They returned after three or four weeks. A meeting was called immediately and the report of the committee was heard with rapt attention and great interest. The committee reported to have found rich and very suitable farmland; they were especially impressed with an area near Cherokee in Iowa.

At this meeting many decisive steps were taken: a list of names was made of persons who wished to move and take land, and it was apparent that the desire for the settlement of a new colony was greater than initially expected. If I remember well, sixty heads of family took part. It was decided to send a second committee, authorized to make a particular choice and to occupy lands under the present preemption and homestead laws. This committee consisted of Messrs. Leendert van der Meer, Dirk van den Bos, Hendrik J. van der Waa, and Henry Hospers. The last mentioned would go to the land office in Sioux City by train to take cards there and to gain the necessary information, while the first three mentioned would travel to Sioux City with the same faithful mule team, meet Henry Hospers there, and then explore northwestern Iowa with a surveyor.

When these four persons met each other in Sioux City, they found that in the area around Cherokee too much land had already been taken. Since they wished to occupy a place for Dutchmen only that was large enough to settle a large Colony, it was decided not to visit Cherokee, but instead to go view Sioux or Lyon counties where an abundance of government and railroad lands were still obtainable.

In Sioux City supplies were bought to last them for a stay of about three weeks on the prairies, and the committee departed for Junction City (now Le Mars) and further north along the babbling Floyd River to the southern border of Sioux County. They did not come across roads, houses, or trees; there was nothing else but gently rolling, beautiful, rich, and fertile prairie soil. Without any doubt the unanimous choice of the committee was: THIS IS THE PLACE!

With the map in hand and the surveyor's compass as a guide, a few townships were crossed. They looked for and found the government section-corners, and they reserved about thirty sections for those fellow countrymen who had signed up for this colonization. Even the place for the future town was chosen. The committee returned to Pella after agreeable yet tiring activities, while Henry Hospers stayed at the land office to file the legal papers and sworn statements and to secure the lands in the name of several homesteaders.

Publicity of the choice of this new Colony was given by means of Dutch newspapers, and very soon Dutchmen, especially from Wisconsin but also from other states, were taking part. In the fall of 1869 about 60 men left for the new colony to take possession of their 160 acres in order to satisfy the demands of the law. Henry Hospers, appointed by the legislature as commissioner of emigration, visited the Netherlands in the winter of 1869-70 to represent the state of Iowa, and the new Colony in particular, and his mission was crowned with good success.

In 1870 the following families arrived in the new colony: Jelle Pelmulder, Hendrik J. van der Waa, Leendert van der Meer, Dirk van den Bosch, W. de Haan, Dirk van der Meer, A. Noteboom, C. Nieuwendorp, L. van Pelt, D. van Pelt, D. van Zanten, W. van der Zalm, G. de Zeeuw, C. Lakeman, Joh. Klein, A. van Marel, A. van der Meide, Widow Beukelman, H. Luymers, M. Verheul, B. van Zijl, W. van Rooyen, I. van Iperen, J. Windhorst, A. Schippers, A. Jansma, J. Muilenburg, P. de Jong, C. Jongewaard, H. Boersma, L. Boersma, K. Wierenga, J. Sipma, J. Logterman, J. Groen, A. Lenderink, Hymen den Hartog, J. Sinnema, S. Pool, Ulbe Wynia, J. van Wijk, P. Dieleman, J. Brinks, Arie de Raad, T. Heemstra, J. Fennema, D. de Ruysch, Adr. van den Berge, J. van der Meer, W. Rijsdam, G. Rijsdam, A. Werkhoven, O. de Jong, G. van der Steeg, H. Pas, T. Brouwer, Rijn Talsma, G. Beijer, J. Gorter, K. de Jong, Iepe van der Ploeg, P. van Horsen, and A. Versteeg. If I have forgotten any names inadvertently, I beg forgiveness.

The land was cleared, simple houses (generally sod huts) built, a good frame schoolhouse erected, and a store opened in the little town of Orange City. The people were glad, thankful, and satisfied.

Vol. 2, chapter 27, no. 87, pp. 227-231

87. ARIE VAN DER MEIDE'S "ORANGE CITY, IOWA"

[Published in *De Volksvriend,* September 19, 1895, Van der Meide's account of the earliest history of Orange City fills an important lacuna in this collection. Cornelia Breugem Kennedy of Northwestern College, Orange City, translated the account for the Sioux County centennial celebrations in 1970 and published the English text in a special Tulip Festival edition of the *Sioux County Capital,* called *"De Volksvriend,"* May 1970, pp. 13, 34.]

Once the settlement was established, a city had to be formed. Money for that purpose was needed. An organization was formed under the chairmanship of Jelle Pelmulder; shares were sold, and persons were authorized to buy land. They bought the land of Izaak van der Meer for the present location. Streets and alleys were laid out, and the town was named Orange City. This was in 1870. A. Lenderink was the first one to build a house in town, and he also became the builder of the first school building, contracted by Buncombe township for $2,400 in bonds (valued at 40 cents on the dollar).

In 1871 the townspeople (three in all) had to travel 2 miles to buy their wares at the farm of Tjeerd Heemstra. In this year a store was built by Henry Hospers which was supplied with goods, and A. J. Betten served as clerk. He sold the goods for money and good words — mostly good words, it is often said. That year the blacksmith Van Olst settled here and constructed a building that served as a house and smithy at the same time. It was built of sod and had a plank roof. Very soon the amiable sounds of the hammer on the anvil were heard; in fact, the old smith is still working and is quite prosperous. Additionally, Joost Vos built a shoe store and home under the same roof, and also installed in it a barber shop, where citizens can come on Saturday to be touched up. "Mother Mouw," as she was affectionately called, had a hotel built. In the fall a beginning was made for a parsonage for the newly organized Reformed Church and was completed by the next year. The population then numbered 24.

In 1871 Henry Hospers, Tjeerd J. Heemstra, and still others built houses. Hospers built the first office building, in which a bank was begun: the Orange City Bank. Dr. E. O. Plumb settled here as a medical doctor, J. J. Bell as a lawyer, G. Rozeboom as the second smith, and G. Dingeman as the second hotel keeper. The population had increased now to almost 50.

In 1873 we saw other buildings go up: the store of W. Sleyster & C. Hospers, Pierce & Lewis's land office, A. J. Betten's store, which was also used that year for county offices since the county seat had been changed from Calliope to Orange City, A. K. Webb's law office, P. Ellerbroek's drugstore, and the residences of Mrs. W. Pas, Dr. Plumb, and many others. It also included the house of Dr. de Lespinasse, who had settled here and whose son, who is a doctor now, was the photographer. A modern church building was built. Because of criticism it was speedily changed into a residence, which was consumed by fire shortly thereafter. W. B. Raymond began publishing the *Sioux County Herald*, which was soon followed by a second newspaper, the *Homesteader*. The last mentioned changed into *De Volksvriend*.

The growth of the town was retarded by the presence of grasshoppers. Later, when this trial had passed, progress went faster. In 1875 the first church was built by O. Rouwenhorst.

The following is information that the Elder H. A. de Haan wrote for us concerning First Reformed Church, after we had requested him to do so:

"It was organized in the beginning of 1871 by the Rev. N. D. Williamson and Elder N. Gesman, with 45 families. The following elders were elected: Tjeerd Heemstra, G. van de Steeg, and M. Verheul. Deacons: Sjoerd Sipma, Jelle Pelmulder, and W. van Rooyen. The Rev. Seine Bolks from Zeeland, Michigan, was called by unanimous choice. Although people hardly dared to hope that he would accept it, he did accept the call and came here in April of 1872. His work as teacher, doctor, and counselor did not remain unblessed. The meeting place was the first schoolhouse.

"Since his health was precarious, the Rev. Bolks became emeritus in 1878 and the congregation called the Rev. Ale Buursma, who came here in May of 1879 and served the congregation until July of 1889. From this congregation sprouted forth the following congregations within a few years after organizing: Alton, Newkirk, Sioux Center, the American Reformed Church, Maurice, Hull, Middleburg, Boyden, Hospers, and Rock Valley. These 10 churches all have their own ministers and manse.

"After the Rev. Buursma left, the congregation was served by the Rev. Harmen van der Ploeg from July 1890 until 1893, when he was taken from us by death. In November 1893 the Rev. Matthew Kolijn accepted his work here and is still fruitfully working. So this little church with a few families has grown to a large tree with the subsequent arrivals of other families, which has spread its branches with God's blessings over the whole country. Truly, 'this is from the Lord's hand, and is wonderful to behold." The number of families of this congregation, who all belong to the Reformed Church in Sioux County, amounts to 1,028; confessing members 1,774 and baptized members 3,423."

From the Rev. Evert Breen we received the following information concerning the Christian Reformed Church:

"This congregation was organized in 1871 with 12 families (fifty souls).

Her first minister, the Rev. John Stadt, began his labors on December 2, 1877, and served the congregation until July 7, 1884. At that time the congregation numbered 45 families (200 souls). The Rev. John Gulker, the second minister, began his service on October 5, 1884, with 55 families (245 souls). Under his labors the congregation increased rapidly, and when he left on November 5, 1890, the congregation had grown to the size of 90 families (500 souls). His successor, the Rev. E. van den Berge, ministered in the congregation from April 5, 1891, until October 29, 1883. Under his ministry the church grew from 100 families to 147 families. The number of souls climbed from 528 to 755. The Rev. Evert Breen, the present minister, succeeded him on December 24, 1893, and he is thankful for the steady growth of the congregation. At present she has 194 members (987 souls). The Lord has blessed her and with uplifted eyes she may look into the future with trust."

Elder M. Rhynsburger reports the following about the American Reformed Church:

"The American Reformed Church was organized on April 17, 1885. The need for an English-speaking congregation was felt and clearly read; a considerable number of English-speaking families were living among the population of Orange City. In addition, several Dutch families felt that with their children's future in mind they would prefer to speak English. The Rev. John A. de Spelder was especially interested in this, and he saw to it that the Iowa Classis appointed a committee to organize a congregation. This happened on the above-mentioned date.

"The new congregation, led by the Rev. Ale Buursma, elected the following consistory: Jacob J. van Zanten, elder; J. M. Oggel, deacon. The first meeting of the consistory was held in the courtroom on May 15, 1885. Arrangements were made for the holding of worship services, and they were able to obtain for that purpose the use of the courtroom for Sunday school and morning service, and the First Church at night.

"The congregational meeting, held on May 23, unanimously called Prof. John A. de Spelder to serve the new organization, and he accepted. On October 4, 1885, the congregation received permission to use a room in the present city hall, and the next the use of the second story. In July of 1887 the Rev. J. A. de Spelder was called to be their minister. He accepted the call. His ministry lasted until March of 1894, when he accepted a call in another field. The congregation grew and came into the possession of her own church building on January 25, 1889. The congregation was organized with 23 members; the present membership numbers 97. The Rev. A. A. Zabriskie is her minister."

And now we will pick up here again. In that same year the beautiful courthouse and some other residences were built. P. Pfanstiehl built a genuine

Dutch windmill here. It has done much good, since the other mills were too far away. Hymen den Hartog took it over later and converted it into a steam "roller mill," which burned down this summer, causing much damage to the owner. D. van den Bosch and B. van der Aarde had the first hardware store; it was taken over by the present owner, A. Bolks.

Better buildings were being constructed all the time. Jac. Versteeg and N. Snoek constructed a brick yard; fuel and labor were too high, however. In 1893 B. van der Aarde and others took over this enterprise, and at present it is doing well under the name of the Orange City Brick Yard Company. To the factories of the past belong the cheese factory of M. P. van Oosterhout and C. Slotemaker, which failed because of lack of support. In 1881 the firm of Pitts and Kessey opened a second bank: the Bank of Northwestern Iowa, in a building that burned down later along with four other buildings, and the name changed to the Northwestern State Bank of Iowa. It is still in business.

In 1882 the skating rink fever blew over here, too, and a building was constructed of 40 × 100 feet, 2 stories high. The building was sold later to the Board of the Northwest Classical Academy, they sold it again, and at present it is the city hall. In that same year the Chicago and Northwestern Railroad was laid through town. Since immigration continued, another 160 acres were bought and laid out into lots, and many houses were built.

In 1883 Orange City was incorporated as a town. The commissioners appointed by a judge were Jelle Pelmulder, W. Sleyster, John Kolvoord, W. H. Casady, and the writer of this account. Since that time brick stores have been erected, in which a choice of many kinds of goods is to be found, which is often not found in towns twice as old as Orange City. An electric light plant was also built by some of our citizens, so that many would be able to use electric lights in their homes and stores. Also the streets are lighted now by electricity. This innovation cost $14,000. A year ago a telephone company was built, so that Orange City has communication with most of the towns in the county and elsewhere as well.

Vol. 2, chapter 27, no. 88, pp. 231-234

88. T. WAYENBERG'S "SIOUX CENTER, IOWA"

[This brief sketch of Sioux Center and environs first appeared in *De Volksvriend*, September 19, 1895. Cornelia Breugem Kennedy of Northwestern College, Orange City, translated the account for the Sioux County centennial celebrations in 1970 and published the English text in a special Tulip Festival edition of the *Sioux County Capital*, called *"De Volksvriend,"* May 1970, pp. 23, 34].

In connection with the history of Sioux County during its past of 25 years, which we are going to celebrate, we remember how we as a small town of Dutchmen settled on these vast prairies. It was through God's providence that the population of Pella, Iowa, realized the necessity to prepare a new settlement. The result was that attention was focused on Sioux County by those who had been appointed as a committee to investigate where the settlement would be made. The chairman of this committee was Mr. Henry Hospers, who is still among us. He has faithfully helped us in the difficult time we went through. And he is still busy looking after the interests of this settlement.

So it happened that under his guidance the first small group of settlers came in Sioux County in the spring of 1870. This settlement expanded, and many people from elsewhere settled here. Being here, we soon felt, like our Dutch fathers, that material things were not sufficient, and that we needed religion and education for the youth. Because of this, a congregation was established and a school was built that was used as a church on Sunday and where settlers from all directions came together.

People began to multiply, and they felt the necessity for a religious leader. So the population came together and decided to call a minister. Thereupon it chose the Rev. Seine Bolks, who has now passed away. He was called unanimously. He accepted the call, though some people had not expected that he would. And he proved to be the right man for this position, especially in the oppressing times that the people here went through. He knew how to encourage and cheer up the people with the rich promises of the gospel, so that their faith was renewed and they could go on in the struggle of life. And so we see what can be achieved under the blessing of the Lord and under the faithful guidance of those who are called by God and let themselves be used by Him.

In 1872 the Rev. Bolks started his ministry in Orange City, a small, weak community which then consisted of people spread all over the prairie of Sioux County, except for some who belonged to the Holland Christian Reformed Church, which was later organized into a congregation. We can see now (1895) how from a small beginning in these surroundings eleven Reformed congregations were established, which we recognize and may call Sioux Center.

We here in Sioux Center may not really boast of belonging to the first group of settlers of Sioux County. On June 17, 1871, we came here and settled with three families on this vast plain west of the small stream, the Branch River. If we would not have met W. van der Zalm, we should hardly have found our place of destination. After we arrived there with his help, we put out the horses, which perhaps if they could speak would have said: "We are glad to be here." But this was not the case with me. On that lonely, desolate plain, not knowing if there were people living further to the west and separated in the east by a stream, I felt cut off from communication with people. Besides, my first encounter on my land was with two prairie wolves. Fortunately, they were afraid, just like me, and so we did not get into a fight. But all this caused me to tell my wife that I could not stay here, though the gold may be ever so abundant. However, I could not just leave. And this was fortunate, for it was not long before more settlers came and this revived my hope that we would live again in community with others.

And what happened? The settlement expanded so soon that the following year a school was built for our children. On Sundays we gathered there for a religious meeting and the old Mr. Bolks many times spoke the blessing to us. This led the Reverend to urge us to form a congregation, and soon we did so. The organization took place May 17, 1874, with 24 members. This was not because there were not enough members then, but as is often the case in such circumstances, "so many men, so many minds." There was a difference of opinion about where to locate the church and so several people withdrew, and the Rev. Bolks went through much trouble to prevent the break. But by his work and the Lord's blessing he achieved it. And the first church was built here: a building of 16 × 24 feet that was enlarged four times later.

And now people felt the need for a full-time pastor. Though the old Rev. Bolks served us faithfully, we yet saw the need for our own pastor, so we decided to build a parsonage. Dr. West, who had observed our area, encouraged us in this matter. Thus, on January 12, 1889, we started it, and after making good progress the congregation came together on March 30, 1880, under the leadership of the Rev. Ale Buursma, who was at that time the pastor at Orange City, and called the Rev. Johannes Willem Warnshuis. After he declined the call, the Rev. Jan de Pree was called. He accepted it and has worked here since. He came June 17, 1880.

Since that time the congregation grew so rapidly that there was not room enough in our small building, though we tried to give everyone a place. So on March 14, 1884, they decided to build a new church to provide space for 600 people, and it was built that very year. We then thought we had room enough for a long time, but we were disappointed, although not unpleasantly. Therefore we were compelled to build a gallery in 1893 providing places for 100 people.

In connection with the expansion we can mention that recently, on July 18, 1895, part of our congregation formed a separate group with 26 members in full membership. It is situated seven miles northwest of here and called the Carmel Church. So we see how from a very small seed a large plant can grow. Besides the Reformed congregation, a Holland Christian Reformed church and a Presbyterian congregation exist; the latter consists mainly of Germans and Americans.

So far as the town is concerned, it has 650 inhabitants. Its foundation is mainly due to the railroad through our area, the Great Northern Railroad, in 1890. Now we have sixteen businesses, including two banks, two lumberyards, and four elevators. There is also a public school with four teachers. Though one might not have thought much of it at first, Sioux Center is one of the busiest places in the county and it is still growing.

When finishing this writing, the thought comes to mind of Deuteronomy 6:2-3.

Vol. 2, chapter 29, no. 100, pp. 294-300

100. A. M. DONNER'S "THE HOLLANDERS IN ALBANY, NEW YORK"

[Donner lived in Arnhem and was a deacon in the congregation served by Van Raalte. He played an active part in the plans for emigration made during the spring and summer of 1846, but did not come to America until 1857. He never came to Holland, Michigan, it appears. The following account prepared by him in 1897 for the semicentennial celebrations is preserved in manuscript in the Joint Archives of Holland, Hope College Library. The Reverend Peter De Gelder and Dr. George Harper, professor emeritus of English, Calvin College, translated the account.]

To the Committee for the Celebration of the fiftieth anniversary of the Dutch Emigration in the United States of North America.

Since your esteemed committee has requested me to tell you a few things about the establishment and progress of the Dutch community in Albany, New York, I will try to comply with your honored request, although my hand and mind are not as reliable today as before, since I have just about reached the age of 80 years.

I cannot refrain from telling you a few things about the reasons why we left our parents, brothers, sisters, and friends, and also our native country. A few people are still alive who can tell us that Rev. Hendrik J. de Cock from Groningen could not submit himself to the rules of the Synod of The Hague, which were in variance with the Word of God. That is why he was censored, but he knew the mandate of his great Missionary, "Preach the Gospel," and since he did not have a church, the people who loved him gathered in barns and living rooms, from which they often were driven by the arm of the law, were fined, or cast into prison. This continued till the year 1839. But Rev. de Cock did not remain alone, because six or seven men, spurred on by his example and in obedience of faith, joined him and then scattered through the country and proclaimed "Jesus, no other name is given under the Heavens to be saved" and "Jesus, King of His church" and not of a Synod of The Hague.

I shall not further describe this unequal struggle, but only that many were robbed of everything, and if God the Almighty had not prevented it, they would have suffered poverty. How much deliverance and love they received from the hand of God in those days can be witnessed from their song:

> The Lord is our help and strength
> He is my song and psalter.

The community of saints was dear and comforting to them.

In 1839 they obtained their freedom, but although the arm of the law did not persecute them anymore, the persecution of their fellow citizens did not cease; those hated Seceders had a tough time getting jobs. Many prayers were offered, but also many songs were sung; the psalms were beloved in those days:

O God, when You with Majesty
Led Your Israel from. . . .

or

Your God, O Israel, has the Power
Granted to you by His command. . . .

We also had the privilege of having Rev. Antony Brummelkamp and Rev. Albertus van Raalte with us in Arnhem, men who, as Jethro recommended to Moses, were "brave devoted men; men who hated miserliness," and with such men in the lead, people will go through thick and thin with them.

Van Raalte was a born "Leader and Pioneer." Whatever Tollens sings about Barends can also be said about Van Raalte, "He is calm in danger, whatever storms howl around him. Young in diligence, old in knowledge, firm in spirit." And I add to this:

"*Christian* in his heart,
stands ready to sail."

But I have to inform you yet what really gave the push to the emigration. They were not the seven lean years, but it was eleven years of oppression and lack of appreciation. Many had used up everything. Rev. van Raalte and his wife, both from high-class families, had sacrificed everything.

The Lord heard our prayers and sent his striking angel. A sickness developed in the potatoes, and the potato was one of the most important necessities of life, and for many their daily food. While in the year 1845 you could buy a hectoliter for one guilder, in 1846-47 you had to pay 10 guilders. In 1845 rye was worth f3.50, and in 1846-47 one had to pay 17 to 18 guilders; and now the striking angel became a blessing angel for thousands of people. I feel young again when I think of that time of deliverance, because

A net hampered our steps. . . .

or

By the Supreme arm saved from violence,
I am inclined to thankfulness. . . .

By God's grace I can now take the harp from the willows and sing:

What shall I, showered with God's favors,
Repay our faithful God for his grace?

But now I have to write about that blessing angel. Word came from America: "Freedom of conscience and bread to eat." In 1846 the first meeting was held at my house, and Rev. van Raalte and Rev. Antonie Brummelkamp were present. It was decided to send the two Arnold brothers with their families across. That same year Rev. van Raalte left for America with the first pioneers. Circumstances prevented me from fulfilling my wish to go with them. Thus I cannot tell you much about the first emigrants who arrived here in Albany, because I only arrived in New York on the 3rd of July, 1857. We bought tickets to Chicago for five families, a total of thirty-five persons. We left by boat for Albany and we were packed like sardines on that boat! Because of that rather cramped and oppressive journey, my wife's illness became even worse. In Albany I found my friend Arnold, who took us into his home with great kindness, and because of my wife's illness he looked after her for ten days. I rented a house for myself and other family members. We were stopped by the panic of 1857 from continuing our travels to Chicago. At that time the situation in Albany was much better than in the west, so I decided to stay. And so after 40 years I am here in Albany with 7 children, all married, and 24 grandchildren.

But now I have to write about the origin and progress of the Dutch community in Albany. About the period between 1847 and 1857 I have to repeat what others told me. Rev. A. B. Veenhuizen came here in 1847. In the early part of 1848 he left for Rochester. In 1851 Rev. Fris came, but only stayed for part of a year. In 1853 or 1854 Rev. Jacobus de Rooy arrived; he appointed or chose elders and deacons. In less than a year he also left. The Dutch population in this city consisted, as far as religion is concerned, of folks with a diverse sentiment of feelings, and everyone did what was right in his own eyes; and this was the reason for the failure in founding a congregation.

When I arrived here in 1857, I did not find an orderly congregation. I had a cordial association with a few families: namely Mr. and Mrs. van Nouhuijs, Mr. F. Mol, who was married to a daughter of Mr. van Nouhuijs, Mr. and Mrs. D. Knox, Mr. Jacobus van den Bergh and spouse, Mr. G. Rotman, who was married to a daughter of Mr. van den Bergh, Mr. Nicholas van den Berge and spouse, Mr. Hendrick Geurtze and family, and some other families. Among them was also our present elder Jan Bakker and spouse. With these and some other families we met on Sundays in the lecture room of First Reformed Church. The worship services were performed by reading of sermons and by mutual prayers. Jan Bakker, who had recently returned from Rochester, advised us to ask Rev. Willem Coenraad Wust from Rochester to come and preach for us sometimes.

When he came, he advised the friends to found their own congregation. Rev. Jan Willem Dunnewold also visited us in 1857, and he too insisted that we should start our own congregation. In the autumn of that same year classis acknowledged us as a congregation, and our church [Holland Reformed Church, now Fifth Reformed] was organized by Rev. Isaac N. Wyckoff and Rev. W. C. Wust. Chosen as elders were brothers F. Mol and A. M. Donner, and as deacons brothers H. J. Geurtze and D. Knox.

However, I can't omit mention of the excellent work Rev. Wyckoff did for the Hollanders and for our congregation. He was like a mother to the poor Dutchmen who arrived here. He personally went with them to factory or store to find a job, and if he did not find a job for them he provided for them in their needs from his own means.

In 1860, after we had called him, our first preacher, Rev. W. A. Houbolt, arrived. We gave him a salary of $600, of which the Board of Domestic Missions provided $300. From that amount he had to pay rent for his house. He served us till 1862. In 1864 Rev. Pierre B. Bähler from Hellendoorn, Netherlands, stopped by on his travels towards the west. He accepted the call we offered him, and he stayed with us till 1866, when he accepted a call to Rochester. In 1866 we called Rev. Houbolt for the second time, which call he accepted, but he stayed with us for only one year. From 1867 to 1872 our pulpit was vacant and the church services were led by elder brother P. Mol, who read sermons and edified our congregation. He was a gifted reader and was also a man of prayer.

In 1872 Rev. Adriaan Zwemer accepted our call to him. This quiet though restless man, who never lost sight of his goal, managed with great perseverance to obtain a church building for us. Thus far we had our church services in the lecture room of First Reformed [Gereformeerde] Church, but in 1873 we saw our church building, with the parsonage under it, finished at the cost of well over $8,000, of which the congregation paid over $1,500, and other Reformed churches donated about $3,000. The rest remained as a mortgage on our church building. In 1875 Rev. Zwemer left.

In March of 1877 Rev. Cornelius Kriekaard arrived, and he stayed with us till April 1879. In August 1879 Rev. Hendrik K. Boer came to our congregation, and he worked among us with blessing till the fall of 1885. He received a small salary, and yet through his hard work we could pay off $1,200 on the mortgage that we still had on the church building. In December 1887 Rev. Lawrence Dykstra arrived, and he stayed with us for 23 months. Because some people considered the existing parsonage as too damp, a new parsonage next to the church building was built under the direction of Rev. Dykstra, which cost about $2,500.

Rev. Willem J. Duiker arrived in July 1890 and stayed with us till March

1892. The congregation again managed to deduct $1,000 from the mortgage, with the excellent help of Rev. Duiker.

During the summer of 1893 Rev. Martin Flipse arrived; he came from the New Brunswick Theological School. He accepted our call with the condition that during the evening service he could preach in English. Although it was very difficult for the older members, they reluctantly agreed. Well, it was about time! Many of the young people of the congregation attended English churches, but now they attended our evening services and also brought others along. The evening worship services were very well attended. Before the regular service the Young People's Society held a prayer meeting, which was a blessing to many. A mortgage of about $1,100 remained on the church building, which at this time needed repairs. Through Rev. Flipse's efforts, the mortgage on our church build-ing was paid off on Thanksgiving Day of the year 1895, and there was even extra money available to beautify the interior as well as the exterior of the church building. To our regret, Rev. Flipse did not stay with us for very long, but left in the spring of 1896 to Passaic, New Jersey, where he had been called.

Our present minister, Rev. Johannes van Westerburg, arrived here in January 1897, from Brighton, New York. He works with pleasure and love in the congregation, and we hope and pray that he will work among us for at least five years, mainly so that our children will receive good education in the cate-chism, since this usually leaves a lot to be desired. I have heard it said by young preachers that it was easier for them to write a sermon than to speak with the children for one hour, to get down to the intellectual level of the youth. In these two years the young teacher has learned a few things, but what about the young people? I don't have to say either that the esteem of the congregation grows less for their teachers. We are happy with the beloved Reformed teachings, but many of us don't know them. I hope that both the school and the classis will consider this.

I should not finish this writing without having made mention of the fact that the women and young daughters of the congregation have contributed a lot towards the redemption of the mortgage on the church building. The poet sings:

> *The spoils of the conquered land*
> *were received by the women*
> *even if they did not come out to battle.*

I can mention with thanks, however, that they were at the forefront. And whenever there is the serving love of the wife, the mother, or the daughter, the outcome is not uncertain. She works more with the heart, and that gives the push. She might become doubtful, sometimes with a tear in the eye, but not despondent, because she clings to God's promise: "I am your God and the God of your seed," and the Holy Spirit whispers in her heart: "The gates of hell will not overpower my congregation." Congregations who have such mothers in their midst are fortunate.

About the present situation of the Dutch congregation here, I can tell you the following: As we mentioned before, they have a beautiful church and parsonage, and with thanks to God, all is totally free of debt. Until the year 1894 we received an annual grant from the Board of Home Missions, but at that time we refused the grant, because due to the income of the congregation this was no longer necessary. The number of families or households totals 73 now, and 142 persons have full membership. Catechism classes for the young people are attended by about 40, with about the same number attending Bible class for the adults.

Last year our collections for charity amounted to about $250, and for the local expenses about $1,100. The Sunday school, Women's Mission Society, Young People's Society, and Junior Society are all flourishing and contribute greatly to the advancement and prosperity of the congregation.

May the Lord bless the attempts to expand His congregation here and may He be praised for having helped us with this, notwithstanding the hardships and ups and downs.

Vol. 2, chapter 29, no. 101, pp. 300-303

101. [JOHN KREMER], "HOLLANDERS IN CLEVELAND AND DETROIT"

[As at Albany, Buffalo, and Rochester, Dutch immigrants halted their journey at Cleveland and Detroit, some of them never reaching the settlements at Holland, Roseland, Pella, or Milwaukee and Sheboygan. In 1847 some Hollanders settled in Cleveland, most of whom appear to have been Catholics. A few established themselves in Detroit. Their small number demonstrates the strong spirit of kinship that existed among the Dutch immigrants of 1847 and after because, being Seceders, they hurried westward to Holland and other settlements where they hoped to find their friends and relatives. This unsigned manuscript, now in the Joint Archives of Holland, Hope College Library, was likely written by the Reverend John Kremer, pastor of First Reformed Church of Detroit from 1892 to 1902. The Reverend Peter De Gelder and Dr. George Harper, professor emeritus of English, Calvin College, translated the report.]

When in 1847 the first Hollanders arrived in Cleveland, the city, which now counts about 300,000 inhabitants and which last year celebrated its first centennial (its one hundredth year of existence), was comparatively speaking no more than a large village. And if the growth in the number of Hollanders had been proportional to the growth of the city, their influence would no doubt have been far greater than it is now.

The first to arrive in the spring of 1847 were Jacobus Boot, C. van Laazen, Cornelius Dekker, and his father-in-law Hazebroek, who died shortly after his arrival. Dekker, the son-in-law, became insane, and after having been locked up in the asylum for 46 years, he died there. He was already buried before the relatives knew anything about his illness or his death. The above-mentioned persons and their families had arrived in Rochester, New York, in the fall of 1846 and spent the winter there under great difficulties.

Later in 1847 several others arrived, among whom were the families Ochsnaar, Rozen, Zoeter, Johannes Gilde, Hofstede, and Geesen. Most of them came from Zeeland; a few came from Gelderland. One daughter is still alive of the Boot family; she was only five years old when she arrived with her parents. Except for one other person, she is the youngest of the old settlers. The youngest one who is still alive is a daughter of Van Laazen; she was only one year old when she arrived. Hendrik Ochsnaar, with wife and seven children, completed the sea voyage in 42 days, and the trip over land from Baltimore to Cleveland took 19 days. Of the 7 children there are 5 still alive, and together they have reached the advanced age of 380 years. A few more households arrived in 1848 and 1849; among them were the families of Dekker, Keek, and De Mooy.

For a long time the number of Hollanders remained very low. There were some who came and went, while only a few families settled permanently. Most of them came after the Civil War, to a considerable extent from the province of Gelderland. The total number of Hollanders is now figured to be about 5,000. Most of them are day laborers working in factories; a few, such as the Ochsnaars and Dekker, made their fortunes, but the majority had to earn their bread with hard work in the sweat of their brow.

Concerning church and religion there is much diversity among the Hollanders, just like everywhere. There are Reformed, Roman Catholics, Jews, Darbyites, and Irvingians. The Roman Catholics have the lion's share. The Reformed people lacked leadership in the beginning. They did not have a preacher until 1864. Around that time the first Reformed congregation was formed under the leadership of Rev. Jan W. Dunnewold, who had been delegated for that purpose by the classis of Geneva. Presently there are four congregations: two of the Reformed Church in America and two of the Dutch Christian Reformed Church. If the Reformed had remained one, two churches would have been sufficient: one on the east side and one on the west side. But the differences in church matters have dismembered them so much that they now have four churches, and due to scanty physical resources they all lead a languishing existence. Together they number not quite two hundred households.

The older people are mostly very attached to the Dutch language and customs. Among the young people this is less prominent, of course, due to their birth and education in this country. Furthermore, because of marriage with other nationalities, the interest in what is specifically Dutch is waning more and more. Overall, the Hollanders enjoy a good reputation (the name Hollander has a good ring). They are known as being honest, hard-working, and loyal. It is seldom that a Hollander gets into trouble with the police. And the cost of the police and prison system would be reduced to a minimum if all the others observed their citizens' obligations so well.

Detroit. Even though the father of the Dutch settlement in Michigan, Dr. A. C. van Raalte, remained in Detroit during the winter of 1846-47 and was very favorably received there, a few years went by before one could speak of an actual and real settlement of Hollanders in Detroit. The ones who arrived now and then came and went again and usually chose to live elsewhere or completely disappeared with, as they say, the Northern Sun. We could mention a few of the ones who settled here, such as the families Huizer and Laurence. Huizer came with fourteen children, seven sons and seven daughters, from the province of South Holland. The mother died a few months after the arrival of the family. The father died in 1872. The youngest son is presently a preacher of the Presbyterian congregation of Brighton, Michigan. One of the daughters is married to Peter Smith, who came from Zwolle with his parents. At first he lived in Holland, but later he settled here and earned a considerable fortune.

The family Laurence came here shortly before the Civil War, including father and mother with six children, four daughters and two sons. The father died several years ago. The mother and children are all still alive. This family has made such a large fortune that they can live without worries about material things. The eldest son, Leonard Laurence, has made quite a large fortune through marriage and business. He has become a man of influence and importance, especially in religious and church matters as an elder in a Presbyterian congregation.

Furthermore, one could mention the families Oostdijk, Van Vliet, Van Koeveren, and Willebrandts. The latter arrived here in 1860 and is also known by the Hollanders in Ottawa County and Grand Rapids. Although the Willebrandts belong to an American church, they are very favorably known among the Dutch because of their willingness to help and sacrifice if there is a need among their former countrymen. Most of the older ones, however, concern themselves very little or not at all with their Dutch heritage, and they hardly ever are in touch with their former countrymen.

Only since 1880 could one speak with a degree of justice about a Dutch settlement in Detroit. Around that time a few families arrived from the provinces of South Holland and Friesland, and from time to time they were followed by friends and acquaintances from the old fatherland.

Among the present Hollanders of importance, mention should be made in the first place of the Friezema brothers. In 1880 they arrived as children with their parents from Friesland, and at first they settled in Paterson, New Jersey. One of the brothers, the head of the firm at present, worked as a typesetter in a Dutch printing shop. They came to Detroit in 1884, and in 1887 they started their own printing business. They had no money and borrowed $250 to start. With insufficient resources but with a steadfast will to succeed, they worked and, "Luctor en Emergo," while struggling they succeeded. They worked with only four people in 1893, yet in spite of the difficult times they could expand the business. New and better equipment was purchased. More personnel were hired and at the present time they regularly work with 20 persons, with a weekly payroll of about $200; the entire plant is worth $10,000. This firm proves that even in the present times, with limited resources but with the blessing of God and hard work, one can attain a reasonable degree of prosperity in a short period of time. In general, the Dutch in Detroit have not had the time or the opportunity to make a fortune. They belong to the industrious working class and are known for being honest, industrious, and thrifty.

Because of their small numbers, little can be said about the church and religious life of the first Hollanders here. But they did not forsake their character as Hollanders. At first they met on Sundays in a private building and edified one another with the reading of a sermon. There was not an organized congregation. In 1869, however, they formed a Presbyterian congregation. The next year, with permission of the Presbyter, they joined Classis Grand River of the Reformed Church in America. With the assistance of the Board of Domestic Missions they called a preacher, and a lady donated $1,000 for the building of a small church, which was erected in 1875. The congregation was very small, however, and had an ailing existence that could hardly be sustained. During the last few years the numbers increased slowly, and at present the congregation counts fifty households. Due to growth of the congregation, they decided in 1895 to build a new church. And now the congregation owns a new and functional church building that satisfies the demands of the times and compliments the Dutch name.

Time will tell if the present congregation, small as it still is, will become the nucleus for a larger Dutch population. The total number of Hollanders is certainly not more than 500. Why are there only 500 in Detroit, while we have 5,000 in Cleveland? It is quite certain that Detroit offers the best opportunity for the workman who wishes to earn an honest living with his hands.

Vol. 2, chapter 29, no. 102, pp. 304-307

102. JAN VAN BOVEN'S "TRAGEDY IN COLORADO, 1892"

[In 1892 a settlement of Hollanders at Alamosa in Colorado was attempted, with disastrous consequences. This real estate venture managed by incompetent directors brought much hardship upon a group of immigrants who soon scattered to various Dutch and other settlements. The author of this sketch, which appeared in *Tekenen der Tijden,* November 9, 1922, witnessed the disaster. Dr. George Harper, professor emeritus of English, Calvin College, translated the account.]

On Sunday, November 12, 1922, it will be thirty years ago that a Dutch colony of two hundred souls left Amsterdam with the San Luis Valley, Colorado, North America, as their destination. It was on the 12th of November, 1892, on a Saturday at twelve o'clock noon, that the steamship *Dubbeldam,* of the Holland American Line, left Amsterdam with a large colony of two hundred Netherlanders from all over the Dutch provinces.

There were those from Gelderland, such as A. Heersink and family from Varseveld, A. J. van Lummel and family, J. Bleijenberg from Ede, and many others whose names, for the moment, do not come to mind. From Overijssel came H. and J. van Dalen, A. Bruintjes, H. Boxum, and others from Ambt Vollenhove. From Friesland, Andries Hof and family, the teacher F. Zijlstra and family, and his brother. From Amsterdam, L. Verburg and family. From the northern section of North Holland, C. Sluys and family. From the Haarlemmermeer, Uitenboomgaard and others. From another North Holland place, J. Zwier and family. Several families from the Protestant part of North Brabant, such as the family of J. Vander Beek from Almkerk, from Vos, and others.

Some families came from Zeeland, such as the family of J. de Kruyter of Goes, L. van der Linde from 's Heer Hendrikskinderen, C. Kloosterman from Rilland, Moerman from Ierseke, the elderly Jacobus Oranje and his son Johannes Oranje and children with their youngest daughter Neeltje, and S. Hartog and family. [Mrs. S. Hartog was also a daughter of the elderly Jacobus Oranje and passed away some months ago at Edgerton, Minnesota.] People from Walcheren and families from Oud Vosmeer on the Island of Tholen also came. The list is not near complete. As I write this there come to mind D. Sjaardema and family, W. Verhoef, T. Teunissen, and W. Hols.

For the first four days we had favorable weather, although already in the English Channel many were suffering from seasickness. But on the 5th day, when we were on the wide ocean, we were struck by a violent storm from the west. As a consequence, the steamship made very little progress. This storm lasted three or four days. At night it was so violent that some of the passengers and members of the crew suffered injuries. One of the passengers, Mrs. De Kruyter, was thrown from one side of the ship to the other side against a chair, so that the doctor had to sew shut a head wound. Plates, cups, and other tableware were often smashed. Once, a high wave passed over the ship so that a small boy was washed from one side of the boat to the other and truly would have gone into the ocean were it not for the rail that kept him lying there.

How the *Dubbeldam* struggled through the raging Atlantic Ocean! We often stood watching this struggle, while the prow lifted itself and in the next moment plunged to the depths. Everything around us was a seething and boiling foam like a gigantic pot in a furious turmoil, which in the fury of its strength beat and crashed against the sides of the *Dubbeldam* so that hearing and seeing were lost. The machinery strained with all its might. Thick clouds of smoke rolled out of the smokestack as out of a crater, proving that all the hands below deck were doing their best to proceed. The rigging clattered to and fro against the masts. We heard the sea birds that followed our ship producing a fearful screaming as if they too, being afraid, were seeking shelter from the fury of the storm. The seamen, dressed in oil skins, southwesters, and high boats, silently did their duty. Above the roaring of the wind and the foaming of the water we heard every moment the deafening noise of the propeller whenever it came above water.

When we neared the banks of Newfoundland, the storm decreased! What a change when there comes a quiet after the storm! During the storm the dining rooms and lounges were nearly abandoned, but now everyone was happy and cheerful and one saw the colonists sitting in groups all over.

We met several ships with whom we exchanged signals. In those days there was not yet a wireless telegraph, so that all information was transmitted during the day with flags and during the night with lights. In that time sailing ships were by no means rare. On a Sunday afternoon a beautiful frigate in full sails went by us at a short distance. Such a graceful and majestic rig of a sailing ship that ever plowed through the seas is beyond description. On the 25th of November, 1892, on Saturday at noon, we arrived in New York. The journey had lasted exactly fourteen days.

The train trip from Hoboken to the San Luis Valley, Colorado, lasted four days and three nights. With a special train consisting of a number of carriages for more than two hundred travelers and some carriages for the baggage, we departed from Hoboken on the Pennsylvania Railroad. At the stations in large towns our train with the Dutch settlers naturally drew a great deal of attention, because it doesn't happen every day that such a large number of immigrants pass through all going to one place.

At St. Louis we tarried for some hours and made a meal in the waiting room of the station. There we had to change trains, and in the evening we continued with the Missouri Pacific Railroad. The trip in Kansas through the immense prairies was very monotonous. Wednesday morning we entered the state of Colorado. The condition of the soil changed perceptibly as we came closer to the Rocky Mountains, becoming more and more rugged. The Rocky Mountains rose higher and higher until we saw the real, high Rocky Mountains in the distance. About noon we reached Pueblo, where we stayed a couple of hours.

From there we journeyed over the Denver and Rio Grande Railroad through the famous Royal Gorge to the San Luis Valley. On the way, the old mother of D. Ballast from Leeuwarden became very sick. In the middle of the high mountains at Salida, a doctor was fetched, although the journey had to continue. This old lady lived for a few days in the immigrant house near Alamosa and then she died. She was the first one from the colony who was committed to a cold grave in the San Luis Valley. She had done the long and tiresome trip in her old days, only to die and be buried in a strange and oh so inhospitable a place.

Wednesday evening we came to Alamosa. Some miles from there, in a desolate, bare region, two large board buildings were hastily raised up. There the settlers were brought like herring in a barrel packed on top of each other. There were very inadequate arrangements to provide for the daily needs of such a large number of people, so that sometimes there was a critical lack. Besides, the people were disappointed because the nice hopes that the Immigrant Society had propagated did not come true.

Throat disease and scarlet fever broke out in the buildings, and in a short time eleven children from various families died. The oldest daughter of Mr. J. de Kruyter also passed away in another house.

Over the fraudulent false hopes with which the colonists were enticed we will not now digress. These we have already dealt with at the time sharply enough, and for some too sharply. The settlement appeared to be a failure, and the colonists, except for a few families, departed from this tract of land in Colorado to different states.

INDEX

The original "index of names" is augmented with a subject index by Robert P. Swierenga, with the assistance of Jerome Kemp, who copied the original with an optical scanner. The twenty-two newly translated memoirs are also indexed. The American, rather than Dutch, system of prefix ordering and capitalization of family names is used; i.e., Van Raalte, Albertus Christiaan, rather than Raalte, Albertus Christiaan van. Variant spellings of proper names are retained, and entire families are grouped under the name of the father. Thr letter i designates volume one and the letter ii designates volume two.